So Fast, So Easy
PRESSURE COOKER
COOKBOOK

More Than **725** Fresh, Delicious Recipes
for Electric and Stovetop Pressure Cookers

Beth Hensperger

with Julie Kaufmann

STACKPOLE
BOOKS

In Memory of Isabel Fischer Kaufmann
February 11, 1920–October 8, 2012

Gracious, kind, and hospitable, a passionate cook
who believed in the power of good food to bring people together.

Copyright © 2015 by Beth Hensperger and Julie Kaufmann

Published by
STACKPOLE BOOKS
5067 Ritter Road
Mechanicsburg, PA 17055
www.stackpolebooks.com

Printed in the United States of America

10 9 8 7 6 5 4 3 2 1

First edition

Cover design by Wendy A. Reynolds
Cover photograph by Fred Thompson
Recipes shown: Char Siu Pork Ribs (page 286), Summer Potato Salad with Olive Oil and Green Onions (page 458), and Bok Choy with Ginger (page 481).

Library of Congress Cataloging-in-Publication Data

Hensperger, Beth, author.
  So fast, so easy pressure cooker cookbook : more than 500 fresh, delicious recipes ready in minutes / Beth Hensperger with Julie Kaufmann. — First edition.
    pages cm
  Includes index.
  ISBN 978-0-8117-1477-8
1. Pressure cooking. I. Kaufmann, Julie, author. II. Title.
  TX840.P7H36 2015
  641.5'87—dc23
                                    2015032261

Contents

Acknowledgments

Thank you for the culinary insights, generosity, and encouragement of the editors, designers, and recipe contributors used in the production of this book: fellow food writers and cookbook authors, home cooks, restaurateurs, cooking teachers, and virtual foodie friends. They are each acknowledged in their respective headnotes but we'd like to extend our thanks again here: Ac. Anaghananada, Annabelle Blake and MiniMo, Valerie Bushell, Mary and Carlo Cantori, Ying Compestine, Peggy Fallon, Ned Hearn, Carolyn Jung, the late Dolores Kostelni, Leslie Mansfield, Oscar Mariscal, Aunt Rose Newman, Trudy Paul, Diane Phillips, Rick Rodgers, Gilda Senter, Phoebe Spires, Laura Stec, Peggy Tank, Judith Thomas, and Victoria Wise.

Recipes were tested in a variety of stovetop brands and the Cuisinart and Instant Pot 6-quart electric pressure cookers.

The Ancient Cooking Pot

Fire above
and wood below
the image of the cooking pot.

Nothing transforms things so much
as the cooking pot.
It is the ultimate of human designs.

Mother of the arts
and father of technology,
it is the beginning of human endeavor.

Through its artful and proper use
all that we see and all that we hear
becomes clear.

It is the link we create with Nature.
It is the beginning of Human Creation.

The cooking pot of all things,
embodies and reminds us of this:
our own health and our own happiness we create
by accepting our nourishment
from the Universe.

Life is cooking in the cooking pot.

—Translated and adapted from the I Ching hexagram 50, Ting

Welcome to the Wonderful World of Pressure Cooking!

The stovetop pressure cooker is a unique piece of kitchen cooking equipment. It is designed to cook food in a very particular manner—with steam heat under pressure. It is a simple method of cooking and treats food in a way that maintains its integrity and freshness by not evaporating off the nutrients. The pressure cooker has long been an integral part of the home kitchen and it's very likely that your mother, grandmother, or even great-grandmother owned one.

Pressure cookers are experiencing a renaissance in popularity because it cooks so efficiently in regard to time and fuel. A pressure cooker requires very little energy to run and is considered an integral appliance in a green, environmentally sound kitchen. *Mother Earth News* uses the motto "Save Time, Save Money, Save Energy, and Eat Good Food." We feel this is a perfect description of preparing meals with the pressure cooker.

Macrobiotic vegetarians have been using the pressure cooker for decades. Want to make your own baby food? It takes just minutes in the pressure cooker. The pressure cooker is a perfect weekday appliance to make meals in minutes rather than hours. It consistently reduces cooking time for all dishes. It is the modern day *la cucina rapida*. One of our friends takes music lessons and then cooks dinner afterward for the teacher, the other students in the class, and invited guests. It takes MaryAnn just thirty minutes, from start to finish, to serve up delicious bowls of beef stew to all her guests.

Once you get familiar with using a pressure cooker properly, with a mind to its methods and safety rules, you will be amazed how often you will use it. With this cookbook as your guide, success in everyday good cooking is guaranteed.

Pressure cooking has been an integral part of European, Asian, Latin American, and East Indian food preparation for generations. Families with a mind to conserving energy and getting a meal on the table fast find the pressure cooker invaluable. Sherpa guides carry the small stovetop model on their treks in the Himalayas.

Available in a range of sizes, from $2^1/_2$ to 12 quarts, there is a size for every need. European models are measured in liters (5 to 7 liters, which translates to 6 and 8 quarts respectively). Skillet and smaller models are great for preparing baby food, risotto, small amounts of vegetables, chops, and one- or two-serving meals. Often the skillet model can be bought as part of a pair with a large-capacity deep pot with interchangeable lids. There is even a lightweight anodized aluminum model made specifically for use with a camp stove, perfect for backpacking.

A 6-quart-capacity pressure cooker is the general all-purpose size for a family and industry standard, serving 4 to 8, and can accommodate the widest range of recipes. Most recipes are gauged for a 6-quart cooker, which means you can easily use a 5- to 8-quart model for the recipes. The largest size, 10-quart, is suitable for pressure canning as well as everyday cooking and is a boon for family style cooking and stock making.

When buying a new pressure cooker, always read the list of safety precautions included in the accompanying owner's manual. Never use a pressure cooker for anything other than cooking food.

SHOULD I BE AFRAID TO USE A PRESSURE COOKER?

Absolutely not. Pressure cookers of decades long past, post–WWII, were poorly designed and used lower grade metals in their construction. These pots did rupture, as much from poor materials as from cooks who did not read their owner's manual. We don't recommend using pressure cookers of dubious origins and age, such as those bought at yard sales. Today's pressure cookers are safe, a joy to use, and, with proper care, can last a lifetime. They have been redesigned with multiple safety features, including a double-locking system that ensures that the lid of the cooker can only be opened when the pressure inside the pot completely comes back to normal; you cannot open the pot while there is pressure inside.

Another safety feature of the new generation of pressure cookers is the weight release valve, which automatically releases any excess vapor pressure. There is also a gasket release system; if the weight valve malfunctions, a portion of the gasket is pushed through an opening in the lid to release the excess vapor.

The newest evolution in pressure cookers, the countertop electric pressure cooker, is so safe that you can leave the pot unattended while it cooks.

Replace the gasket in your pressure cooker every year or so and you will have an optimum cooking experience.

ABOUT THE RECIPES

This book is not a diet book. It contains a wide range of homemade recipes, from classic comfort food to vegetarian recipes using fresh and wholesome foods. We like to juxtapose different styles and ingredients, so you will find modern, traditional, ethnic, and fusion dishes. We designed this cookbook for both the novice and seasoned home cook, with an eye to empowering you to cook with confidence. We want you to open this book, start reading, and know you can make something for dinner tonight using what's in your pantry and freezer.

Cooks (and gardeners) love to share recipes and techniques. We believe that every single person needs to know how to cook for themselves. It comes under the category of life skills these days. Eating well has always been important to us. And cooking has been a part of our daily lives for as long as we can remember. We are proponents of the use of healthy, natural foods, like fresh fruits, grains, and vegetables, and we believe one of the keys to good health and well-being is to eat a balanced diet and regular meals. When you can plan healthy meals, you will have more energy, as well as optimum control over your health through food.

You can make the favorite dishes that your mom taught you. You can learn new dishes with a mind to the global culinary flavor trends. You can experiment with herbs and other natural flavorings. You can make your own broths, which will have a depth of flavor that commercial canned brands just can't reproduce. If you are a vegan or vegetarian, the ability to make fresh cooked beans in 10 to 30 minutes (depending on the kind of bean) is a real nutritional and flavor boon. Worried about salt and preservatives? With pressure cooking the flavors in fresh foods remain vibrant, requiring little help from add-ins.

Welcome to our wonderful world of pressure cooking!

A SHORT HISTORY OF THE PRESSURE COOKER

The pressure cooker traces its roots in the Age of Discovery. Who could have known hundreds of years ago that it would evolve into the must-have cooking appliance of the fast-paced, health-oriented, and green-conscious twenty-first century?

The pressure cooker was invented in seventeenth-century France. Physicist and mathematician Denis Papin, who was experimenting with steam, found a way to use it to raise water's boiling point and cook food faster than over the traditional open fire. He called it a "steam digester"; it looked like a small boiler and the water for the steam was heated by its own furnace. Later versions looked more like contraptions out of *20,000 Leagues Under the Sea*—kind of like over-sized cast iron balls balanced on a tripod that could stand over an open fire. These early cookers were used in royal kitchens and deluxe hotels.

In 1795, the Napoleonic government offered a reward of 12,000 francs (a fortune in those days) for anyone who could develop a method of preserving food supplies for the French armed forces. Confectioner Nicolas Appert took on the challenge and developed a process for packing food in glass jars, sealing them with a cork, and cooking them in boiling water, a process patterned after wine bottling. In 1809, Napoleon Bonaparte awarded Appert the prize money; he used his payment to open The House of Appert, the world's first commercial cannery. At this point, canning was a French military secret, but not for long. By 1810, the British had developed a process for canning food in metal cans, and tinned food was used to feed the troops at the battle of Waterloo.

The first U.S. patents for the pressure cooker show up in 1902. Those cookers were gigantic and used for commercial canning. Pressure canners were important for food preservation since refrigeration didn't exist yet. Smaller aluminum cookers were developed for the home kitchen based on 50-gallon commercial models. In 1938, a saucepan-style aluminum pressure cooker for home use (called the Flex-Seal Speed Cooker) was debuted at a NYC trade show. At the 1939 World's Fair, National Presto Industries unveiled its Presto pressure cooker to huge success. By 1941, there were 11 companies in the U.S. manufacturing pressure cookers.

Production of pressure cookers was stopped during WWII as the metal was needed for the war effort. By the end of the war, there was huge pent-up demand. Unfortunately many of the pressure cookers made after the war were manufactured using a process called die-casting. Molten metal, usually aluminum, was poured into a mold to create the pot. These cookers were not well made and could explode, giving PCs their bad reputation and causing a steep fall-off in sales.

In the mid-'70s, pressure cookers took a key step forward in the U.S. with the introduction of cookers with contemporary styling and new safety features. An interlocking lid that prevented the cooker from being opened unless pressure was safely reduced and the addition of secondary failsafe overpressure features eased consumers' fears cookers malfunctioning. In this period the pressure cooker was rediscovered and enthusiastically adopted by the back-to-the-land lifestyle of the counterculture for canning and cooking.

Pressure cookers are now made using a stamped metal technique introduced in France during the 1950s. The jiggly weight top has been joined by a spring-valve pressure regulator as well as other safety features and scorch-resistant bottoms. Millions of cooks in Europe and Asia rely on pressure cookers. In France, the birthplace of the invention, almost every home has a *cocotte minute*, affectionately nicknamed *la cocotte*.

The electric pressure cooker had its first patent filed on January 9, 1991, by the Chinese scientist Yong-Guang Wang. Its design and electrical workings are based on those of the electric rice cooker (hence the resemblance of the machine housing), and they are manufactured in a range of pressures, depending on the manufacturer. The patent is currently owned by the #1 electric pressure cooker manufacturer, Medea. Instant Pot is made by Medea and was designed by a team of Canadians specifically for North American consumers. With its cutting-edge digital technology and a microprocessor that controls heat level, pressure, and cook time, the electric pressure cooker is the newest page in the history and evolution of the pressure cooker, known as the "third generation."

1

Pressure Cooker 101

The pressure cooker is a stainless steel or heavy-duty aluminum cook pot with a lid fitted with a rubber gasket that can be locked closed. The sealed pressure cooker, when placed over a heat source, builds up pressure as the liquid inside boils and converts to steam. As the pressure builds, the pot expands slightly, causing the rubber gasket to create an airtight seal, keeping any steam from escaping and allowing the pressure and heat to continue to build in the pot.

This method of cooking with moist heat within a pressurized environment has a lot of pluses. Nutrients are conserved because of the closed environment. Flavors are more concentrated for the same reason. The significantly reduced cook times make the pressure cooker a much more energy-efficient way to prepare food. Cooking under pressure requires less fat and salt compared to other cooking methods, making it a more health-conscious way to prepare food.

Long-cooking dishes like stews and braises, soups, and stocks, and ingredients like dried beans and lentils, grains, and firm vegetables like potatoes and winter squash work particularly well in the pressure cooker, yielding deliciously tender results. Artichokes and risotto come out perfect.

WHAT A PRESSURE COOKER DOES

- Steam
- Stew
- Braise
- Pot-roast
- Boil
- Poach

WHAT A PRESSURE COOKER DOES NOT

- Sauté (except as a preliminary step with the lid off)
- Roast
- Deep-fry
- Grill
- Broil
- Bake

THE IMPORTANCE OF PSI

The pressure in the pot is measured in PSI, or pounds per square inch. At a PSI of 13 to 15, the temperature in the pot will exceed the boiling point of water (212° F) and can go as high as 250° F. It is this super-heated, pressurized environment that allows the food inside to cook at an incredibly rapid rate, in half or even a third of the time compared to other methods. For a stovetop pressure cooker, HIGH pressure is 15 PSI, MEDIUM pressure is 9 PSI. For the Instant Pot electric pressure cooker, HIGH pressure is 10.2 to 11.6 PSI, and other models can max out at 8 PSI; LOW pressure for electrics is 5 to 7.2 PSI. Most all of the recipes in this book are cooked at HIGH pressure.

CHOOSING A PRESSURE COOKER

Whether you are buying a pressure cooker for the first time or replacing an older cooker, here are some tips on choosing a cooker that will work for you and your family.

Size

One of your first decisions will be how large a cooker you want, which will depend on how many people you cook for, what type of foods you prepare most, and if you want leftovers. The most popular stovetop pressure cooker sizes are 4-, 5-, 6-, 7-, and 8-quart liquid capacities. Electric pressure cookers are usually 6 or 8 quart. Here is a general rundown:

- **4- to 5-quart:** The size to prepare a whole meal for a one- or two-person household or to make one side dish for a family, such as potatoes. Any pressure cooker that holds less than 5 quarts will not be big enough to cook a meal for an average size family, or soups, dried beans, or large foods like a roast or turkey breast. This size is nice to have as a second auxiliary pressure cooker.
- **6-quart:** This is the most popular size for families of two to six or if you want leftovers. It can accommodate most foods and our pressure cooker recipes, and most books and recipes on the internet, are developed for a 6-quart pressure cooker. Pressure cooker accessories, like the trivet and steamer basket, are designed for this size cooker.
- **8-quart:** This size is perfect for families four to eight and if you regularly make stock in large quantity or cook whole roasts or chickens, turkey breasts, ribs, and/or brisket. If you are cooking for a small family, you still might prefer this size for leftovers.
- **12- to 16-quart and larger:** These are designed for pressure canning low-acid foods (like tuna or vegetables) or preparing food for a very large group.

Construction and Type of Cooktop You Have

Economy is a big decision here. Aluminum is lightweight and inexpensive. It is a great heat conductor. The drawback is that acid foods, like tomato sauce and vinegar, will pit the pot over time. Also, some cooks have issues about cooking in aluminum and aluminum cookware cannot be used on certain stovetops, like an induction stovetop. (For more information on pressure cookers and different types of cooktops, see pages 8–9.)

Stainless steel is slightly heavier in weight and thickness than aluminum, more expensive, and more durable. If you can afford it, go for 18/10 stainless steel with a three-ply layered bottom of aluminum or copper sandwiched in stainless steel; this will keep the heat even and improve the overall performance (i.e., no sticking or scorching as it comes up to pressure on high heat).

Indian-manufactured stovetop pressure cookers, made of aluminum or a lighter weight, thinner gauge stainless steel, are a good choice for shoppers on a budget.

Pressure Cook Rate (PSI)

Stovetop pressure cookers all can cook at HIGH pressure or 15 PSI (pounds of pressure per square inch) but some brands/models of electric pressure cookers cook at a lower PSI, so be sure to check. If you have a cooker that cooks at a pressure rate lower than 10 PSI, you will need to adjust the cook times in this cookbook, adding slightly more time unless the recipe indicates the dish should be cooked at pressure lower than HIGH, in which case the cook time would be the same.

Type of Pressure Cooker

Unlike in the early days of the pressure cooker, you have a number of different options when shopping for a pressure cooker.

Jiggle-Top Stovetop Pressure Cooker

This is the kind of pressure cooker many of us grew up with; it is also known as a "first generation" pressure cooker. They are usually manufactured from aluminum. It features a jiggle-top or weighted pressure regulator (and only one level of pressure, HIGH), and functions in much the same way as a piston in a steam engine. When the cooker comes up to pressure, the regulator will rock and emit steam and quite a lot of noise. This type of cooker is still being made by U.S. manufacturers Presto and Mirro, and for many cooks, it's the pressure cooker they prefer—Julie swears by her Presto jiggle-top pressure cooker.

Spring-Valve Stovetop Pressure Cooker

This type (also known as a "second generation" pressure cooker) operates with a spring-loaded valve (called the stationary pressure regulator) instead of the weighted-top/jiggle-top pressure regulator. Depending on the manufacturer, it may or may not emit steam while under pressure, except as part of a safety override feature. These cookers usually allow for two different pressure settings, which are indicated on the pressure regulator. They are manufactured from heavy-gauge stainless steel with a mixed-metal bottom for even heat conduction, which prevents scorching.

Electric (or Automatic) Pressure Cooker

The newest member ("third generation") of the pressure cooker family is the digital electric pressure cooker. It is a plug-in countertop appliance with a precision thermostat and an internal heating element with an automatic pressure controller that maintains the operating pressure. It also includes a spring-loaded rising indicator rod valve with two heat levels. The cutting edge digital technology and microprocessor controls varying heat levels, temperature, pressure, and cook time plus more safety features.

This machine is growing in popularity due to its convenience, ease of use, the excellent quality of the food it produces, and its more affordable price, under $100. Many users say this is the best type of pressure cooker to start with if you are a novice because you don't need to stand by the stove to adjust the burner to regulate pressure or watch the

OTHER CONSIDERATIONS WHEN CHOOSING A PRESSURE COOKER

- **Handles:** Models have either a long regular handle on one side and a smaller handle on the opposite side, or two small handles on opposite sides. You want a handle set-up that is comfortable for you to manipulate the pot when filled with food.
- **Warranty:** You want at least a 10-year warranty.
- **Instruction manual and recipe book:** Most quality pressure cookers come with an excellent reference booklet. Read it immediately to familiarize yourself with the features of your PC and keep it as a reference. There are some fantastic recipes in these booklets.
- **Storage space:** Consider how much room you have available in your cupboard to comfortably store a pressure cooker.

clock. The directions are so easy to follow that you can take it out of the box and start cooking right away.

When shopping for an electric pressure cooker, be sure to check on the maximum PSI it can achieve, as they can range from 9 to 15 PSI, depending on the brand and model; some models will allow you to cook at different pressure levels. You'll want to purchase one that can achieve 11.6 to 15 PSI at HIGH pressure for best results. Many have a nonstick coating on the cooking insert, but there are some brands that also offer as an accessory an interchangeable stainless steel pot, as the nonstick coating can be an issue for some cooks. All brands include a built-in timer; some include Function menus, with choices like Rice, Meat, etc., that you can select instead of entering a specific cook time. Some models include Browning, Simmering, and Sauté functions, and others are multi-function—anywhere from 3 to 6—and can be used as a rice cooker, slow cooker, yogurt maker, etc., in addition to its use as a pressure cooker.

Electric pressure cookers cook a bit slower than stovetop models as the heating element needs more time to heat up due to the insulation of the pot and depending on how much is in the pot; it usually takes about 15 minutes for it to reach HIGH pressure. This cooker does not do a good job of cooking foods with short cook times, so if you prepare a lot of vegetables and baby food, you'll want a stovetop model instead. Finally, do not set an electric pressure cooker on a counter under kitchen cabinets, as they can be damaged from the release of steam during cooking.

Microwave Pressure Cooker

Also part of the third generation of pressure cookers, the microwave pressure cooker is perfect for a small kitchen, a kitchen without a stove (like during renovations), dorm room, residency hotel room, or the just plain busy cook. It provides all the benefits of an electric or stovetop model, while having a much simpler design than many stovetop models. On the secured lid is a valve that allows excess pressure to escape slowly while cooking (called the Visual Pressure Indicator, or VPI) and a regulator to show if pressure is still built up inside the cooker. When transferring the cooker, always use oven mitts.

Microwave pressure cookers come in graduated sizes from 2/2½-quart to 4½-quart capacity, with a steamer plate/basket and plastic trivet included. Be sure to coordinate the size cooker you want to buy with the size of your microwave oven so that the cooker has plenty of clearance all the way around; it should not touch the walls of the microwave. They are made from BPA-free plastic and cook at 4 to 6 PSI; the combination of the way the microwave cooks food and cooking under pressure allows the microwave pressure cooker to achieve HIGH pressure with a lower PSI than the stovetop and electric models. The cooker does not work with any heat source other than the microwave. Check the wattage of your oven; as in standard microwave recipes, a higher or lower wattage will slightly affect cook times. Check your manufacturer's manual for timing based on the wattage of your microwave. Brands include NordicWare, SilverStone, and Tupperware.

Pressure Canner

The pressure canner (which is not the same as a water-bath canner) is a big kettle with handles on both sides designed specifically for home food preservation. The lids have a weighted gauge and/or a dial gauge. Precise dial gauges are very important at high altitudes. Sizes run from small batch 10- to 15½-quart pressure canners to large batch 23-quart; they are usually made from aluminum and come with a canning rack. The 23-quart holds 7 quart jars, 20 pint jars, or 24 half-pint jars, and is deep enough that the jars can be stacked. The new pressure canners have triple safety designs and are similar to the electric pressure cooker in their ease of use. A larger and heavier pressure canner is not recommended for use on smooth-top glass/ceramic cooktops, because the excess weight can cause it to crack.

There are two types of canning—boiling water bath and pressure canning. The type you use depends on the food being canned and whether it is considered low or high acid. Canning is not simply placing food in jars and processing it. Pressure canners are required for preserving low-acid foods such as pumpkin puree, garden vegetables, tuna or salmon, wild game, salsa, and sauerkraut. High-acid foods such as jam, tomatoes, fruit, and whole fruit (like peaches) can be done in a water bath canner. The extra-large pot of the pressure canner can also be used as a large-quantity pressure cooker.

Check dial gauges for accuracy before use each year and replace if they read high by more than 12-

pound pressure. Gauges may be checked at most county Cooperative Extension offices.

A 10-quart pressure canner (think 4 jars at a time) is the largest pot recommended for a smooth top range as well as gas and electric and can double as the family pressure cooker. Do not use smaller pressure cookers for canning.

Brand

If you are looking for the highest recommended brands, *Cook's Illustrated* magazine in 2013, as part of a product evaluation of pressure cookers, rated Fissler number one, Swiss-made Kuhn Rikon number two, and Spanish Fagor number three. B/R/K Germany was the winner of the Gourmet Gold and Kitchen Innovation awards at the Gourmet Housewares Show in 2007. Fagor and Presto are the most economical. The top selling brands for electric pressure cookers are Instant Pot (particularly the 6-quart, with its multiple features), Cuisinart, MaxiMatic 8-quart, Secura, and Fagor; other popular brands include Cook's Essentials and the Wolfgang Puck Automatic Rapid Pressure Cooker. Electric pressure cookers are in demand because you can leave them unattended as they cook and because of their ease of use. All stovetop pressure cookers come with a steamer basket, steamer rack, and trivet basket stand, which sits on the bottom of the pot, holding the steamer basket above the water so it will not touch the food. Different brands of electric pressure cookers offer a variety of pot inserts.

SPECIALTY PRESSURE COOKERS

Here are some of the new and exciting specialty pressure cookers available at this writing. If you are a pressure cooker advocate, you might want to own more than one or two cookers, depending on how much you use them and the types of foods you make.

- GSI Outdoors Halulite Pressure Cooker. This pressure cooker designed for use on a camp stove weighs in at a mere 2 pounds, perfect for backpacking. It is made from anodized aluminum and comes in 2.8- and 5.8-liter sizes.
- Nordic Ware 2.5-Quart Tender Cooker microwave pressure cooker. It looks like Sputnik and is made by the creators of the Bundt pan. Users give it high marks. Great for dorms with only a microwave. Recipe proportions will need to be scaled back appropriately since the cooker is so small.
- Hawkins Contura Pressure Cooker (2-liter), Futura by Hawkins Hard Anodized Pressure Cooker (available in 2- and 3-liter sizes, with a coating like Calphalon), and Prestige Deluxe Stainless Steel Mini Handi Pressure Cooker, in 2- or 3.3-liter sizes. These adorable small pressure cookers have all the safety feature bells and whistles of the bigger cookers. With rounded bodies, they are designed for greater capacity. The Indian-made Futura has a simpler, sleeker design and is very popular. These are the perfect size for making baby food.
- Instant Pot 6-in-1 Programmable Pressure Cooker. Made in Canada for the American market, Instant Pot boasts third generation technology, putting in one digital pot the functions of a pressure cooker, slow cooker, rice cooker, steamer, warmer, and the capacity to sauté and brown. The three-ply stainless steel inner pot is extremely durable, a plus for cooks who have concerns about using nonstick coatings. They are adding new models every year.
- Granite Ware Anodized Pressure Canner, Cooker & Steamer, 20-quart, F0730-2 is a heavy-duty hard-anodized aluminum cooker, the lightest weight on the market, with a stainless steel lid with multiple functions specifically for pressure cooking, pressure canning, and steaming. It has 3 adjustable pressures, 5 PSI, 10 PSI, and 15 PSI, to use for safe canning at different altitudes with different foods. A steamer insert converts the canner into a high-capacity pressure steamer to steam large amounts of tamales, crabs and lobster, or vegetables. It has the maximum capacity to hold 7 quart-size canning jars, 8 pint jars, or 24 1/2-pint jars and comes with the metal wire jar rack and steamer trivet.

Manufacturer/brand websites are an excellent source for researching different models and getting recipes designed specifically for those brands, though they can be adapted for any pressure cooker. Another site that is very helpful for research is bestpressurecookerreviews.com.

All brands carry 4- to 8-quart or -liter models, but a few, like Manttra and WMF Perfect Plus, have 2-liter models as well. Kuhn Rikon has a 2-liter braising pan with alternate glass lid for traditional cooking. It also fits the airtight lid and is used for risotto and small amounts of steaming. These smaller models are convenient for making baby food or cooking for one. Calphalon offers a 6-quart cooker with handles on both sides for easy lifting. Many manufacturers offer both stovetop and electric models, and aluminum or stainless steel construction for the stovetop models.

The pressure cooker market is global, a sort of culinary alliance of users. Cooks all over the world use pressure cookers with every manner of heat source. So you will find Magefesa from Spain marketed in Guatemala; Sitram Asia is marketing in China; Manttra from India in the U.K., U.S., and Europe; Italy has Lagostina and Aeternum; and the Swiss brand Kuhn Rikon is sold all over the world.

PRESSURE COOKER ACCESSORIES

Your new stovetop pressure cooker will come with a steamer basket, steamer rack, and trivet. If it is an electric model, it will include a stainless steel or nonstick cook pot insert. Other accessories can be bought separately if you need them. Always measure your pressure cooker when acquiring new accessories to be sure they will fit as you will need to have room around the mold or form to let the vapor circulate around it.

Must Haves

- A steamer basket or perforated steamer plate with a handle (necessary for steaming vegetables and fish). The alternate is a collapsible metal steamer insert that folds inward. We like the silicone version, since it will not scratch. Get the largest size that will fit in your pot so you will have the surface area available to pile in with vegetables or whatever you are cooking. Use the silicone steamer basket in the electric pressure cooker so as not to scratch the pot's nonstick lining.
- A metal trivet to raise up the steamer basket so it will not touch the water underneath. Even though it looks like a hanger, it is made from special food grade metal that will not rust in the presence of acidic or caustic foods such as tomato sauce, salt, and wine. Do not try to make your own.
- A heat diffuser, especially useful when making tomato sauce.
- A digital timer is absolutely essential since timing needs to be exact, not approximate. Electric pressure cookers have a built-in digital timer.
- Immersion blender for pureeing soups right in the pot.

Nice to Have

- A glass lid so you can see into the pot at it cooks. Check to see if the manufacturer of your pressure cooker offers this as an option.
- Springform metal pans, 4 to 7 inches in diameter (for steamed cakes and cheesecake).
- Individual heatproof molds, such as Pyrex custard cups (round and oval), Emile Henry and Apilco ceramic ramekins, $1^1/2$- and 2-quart soufflé dishes, disposable aluminum molds, small stainless steel mixing bowls, brioche tins (for puddings and flans).
- Classic tin-plated, decorative pudding steamer molds with clip on lids.

THE PARTS OF THE PRESSURE COOKER

Here is a quick guide to the key components.

Gasket

A rubber seal ring that fits inside the lid, this is the piece that makes the pressure cooker work, creating an airtight seal when the lid is locked on. It should be clean, dry, flexible (no cracks), and fit snugly. The lid will not close if the gasket is not in place. If you see steam escaping around the pan's lid, replace the gasket. If it is cracked, replace it. If the gasket is in place but the lid won't close, rub the gasket with cooking oil and try again; if it still won't close, it's time to replace it.

WHAT IS A HEAT DIFFUSER?

A heat diffuser (also called a flame tamer) is a flat piece of metal—usually copper or cast iron—or ceramic that you place between the stove burner and the pressure cooker. The plate will even out the heat distribution to the pot. It's a good idea to use a heat diffuser with a less expensive pressure cooker. Also, for electric coil, ceramic glass (smooth), and induction cooktops, which are slower to respond to temperature control changes than gas, a heat diffuser will help keep the bottom of the pot from getting too hot, which can cause burning or sticking. Also consider using a diffuser when preparing foods that tend to scorch, like tomato-based sauces, rice dishes, beans, and foods high in sugar like jams and chutneys. Two of our favorites are the 7-inch Ilsa Cast Iron Heat Diffuser and the Bella Copper Heat Diffuser.

Using a Heat Diffuser/Flame Tamer

1. Place the heat diffuser on a burner on your stove so that it is centered. If you are using one with a handle, position it so that the handle is not sticking straight out. Make sure the diffuser is mounted securely on top of the burner; you don't want your pressure cooker sliding off it and onto the floor.
2. Place the pressure cooker on the diffuser, making sure to center it evenly. Turn the burner on as directed in the recipe and bring the cooker up to pressure. The diffuser will heat up along with the cooker.
3. Leave the diffuser in place as you cook the dish.
4. At time, turn off the heat, lift the pressure cooker off the diffuser, and place it on an unheated burner to cool down. Allow the diffuser to cool down to room temperature.
   Heat diffusers can be washed but should not be subjected to extreme temperature changes, particularly ceramic diffusers, which can crack.

Lid

The pressure cooker lid is not like an ordinary pot lid; it is specially designed to create an airtight environment in the pot. Without that, the pot cannot build pressure and cook at the super speed it does. In some models with double handles, the airtight lock is created by first lining up the lid marker with the lid, then pushing and twisting the lid into place with the handles. Other models have a manual lock with a switch you slide into place. Still others have an indicator light window or lock button that tells you the lid is closed and locked. Check the manufacturer's manual for your specific model. If you have not properly locked the lid, you will not be able to close the pot. The pressure will not build up. Never open a lid with steam coming out. As a safety feature, second and third generation pots will not allow the lid to be opened while there is steam still in the pot.

Pressure Valve

Your model will either have a secure valve built into the lid or a freestanding plug (the jiggle top) that balances on top of the lid. A quality pressure cooker will have valves that are attached to the lid with easy-to-read gauge lines that indicate the amount of pressure. With freestanding valves, it's more difficult to determine when the appropriate level of pressure has been reached. Look for a model with a valve that can be removed and cleaned easily.

Pressure Release

Most new models have an easy method for releasing steam by quickly pushing a button or turning a valve. Each manufacturer will include directions in their booklet or read Release Methods (page 13).

COOKTOPS AND MANAGING PRESSURE LEVEL

When using a stovetop pressure cooker, the kind of cooktop you have matters. Pressure cookers require tight regulation of the pressure; they cook differently at no pressure, low pressure, and high pressure. You need to get the pressure to a specific level, and then to hold that pressure constant for the duration of the cooking period. Not all cooktops have the same response rate in regard to heating up and cooling down when a burner is turned on, turned down, or turned off. Please see our guidelines below for techniques you may need to employ with your particular cooktop for proper temperature management when using the pressure cooker.

Gas Range Cooktop

The stovetop pressure cooker recipes in books, manufacturers' pamphlets, and on the internet are written for a gas cooktop, which is considered the ideal: immediate on/off regulated heat source, temperature control, the average time to come to and come down to and from pressure. If the recipe does not specify a cook top, consider that recipe is timed and handled for the gas range (this would include a propane range as well). You can use both stainless steel and aluminum pressure cookers on a gas range.

Set the pressure cooker on the burner and turn the heat to high, then lower the flame to the lowest setting to maintain pressure during the cook time. When the pressure is established, start your digital timer as directed by the recipe. For a Natural Release, the pot doesn't need to be removed from the burner (even though in all our recipes we say to remove the pot from the heat after the specified cook time).

Electric Range Cooktop

You can use both stainless steel and aluminum pressure cookers on an electric cooktop. Electric coil burners do not respond quickly to changes in heat level; think slow to heat/slow to cool, so be certain you will be able to lift and move the filled cooker off the still-hot burner as soon as the cook time has finished. To start the process, place the pressure cooker on a burner set to high heat. At the same time, heat another burner to very low heat. When the cooker reaches pressure, turn off the burner and, holding the handles carefully, gently move the cooker to the low-heat burner and start your digital timer. **Do not turn the high-heat burner off and leave the cooker on it.** Many cooks with electric stoves use a flame tamer or heat diffuser to help control the heat of the coil element, especially with things like tomato sauce that can scorch. For a Natural Release, the pot will need to be transferred to a cold burner.

Halogen Cooktop

You can use both stainless steel and aluminum pressure cookers on this range. Also known as a ceramic cooktop, the halogen cooktop use rings of halogen bulbs to create radiant heat, which heats up the ceramic tile or glass top above it. They are also safe for use by children or the disabled since nothing will burn on it. Use the same instructions for manipulating the cooking process as for the electric coil cooktop with the difference that the halogen can heat up in seconds and turn off immediately, but the ceramic top retains heat just like an electric coil. When the pressure is established, move the cooker to a preheated low heat burner and start your digital timer.

Induction Cooktop

Induction cooking uses a copper coil to transmit a low-voltage, alternating electric current to the cooking vessel, which creates a magnetic field and generates heat. It looks like a regular range with four separate burner surfaces sealed beneath a glass-ceramic cooktop. It also comes as a hotplate with one burner. If you have an induction cooktop, be sure to check with the manufacturer of the pressure cooker you intend to buy to be sure it will work with an induction cooktop, as the base must contain iron—cast iron or high-iron stainless steel (not all types of stainless steel will work).

Induction cooktops are at least twice as fast as gas when bringing the pot up to pressure. When visualizing the time difference, think half the time plus some, like 4 minutes to come to pressure instead of 10 minutes. An induction cooktop concentrates heat in the base of the cook pot. They are also the coolest method of cooking, which means the liquid inside the pressure cooker will come to a boil, generate steam, and come to pressure before the pot is even hot. When the pressure is established, start your digital timer to time the cook time as per recipe instructions. Adjust cook times by adding 2 minutes. When turned off, the heat descends a bit faster than gas. If the recipe cools by the Natural Release method, add 5 minutes to the total cook time.

COOKWARE AND INDUCTION STOVETOPS

Materials Compatible with Induction

- Stainless steel with a magnetic base
- Enameled cast iron and regular cast iron
- Enameled steel
- Medium- to heavy-gauge stainless steel pressure cookers

Materials NOT Compatible with Induction

- Copper
- Tempered glass
- Aluminum
- Pottery/ceramic

USING A JIGGLE-TOP PRESSURE COOKER

1. Prior to using the cooker, look through the vent pipe to make sure it is clear and not blocked by a piece of food left over from your last recipe. Clean the pipe if necessary with a pipe cleaner.
2. Fill the pot as directed by the recipe.
3. Close and lock the lid. Place the weight (regulator) on the top of the pressure cooker lid when you close the lid or the minute the cooker emits a continuous jet of steam; check your owner's manual. If you place it later, the water might completely evaporate, resulting in the cooker as well as the gasket burning dry.

    On the Presto brand cookers, the weight will sit evenly on the lid but it will be loose. If you touch the plastic handle on top, it will jiggle; that's okay.
4. Place the pot on the burner and turn the heat to high. As the steam in the pot builds to full pressure, the round metal pressure relief valve will pop up and stay up, and the plastic overpressure plug will also rise and stay in place. The weight will begin to rock back and forth as the pressure builds. When the weight is rocking and steam is escaping with a hiss, full pressure has been reached. This is the moment to start the timer for whatever the recipe recommends.
5. Reduce the heat under the pot to maintain a gentle hiss of steam and a gentle but steady rocking motion of the regulator. Stay close and keep adjusting the heat under the burner as needed to keep the weight rocking gently and steadily throughout the cooking time.

IMPORTANT NOTE

With the old-style Presto cookers, the inner gasket (the sealing ring) and the plastic overpressure plug should be replaced periodically, especially if they are hard, sticky, cracked, or damaged in any other way. If you are adopting an old jiggle-top pressure cooker from a friend or relative or have bought one at a garage sale, it's best to play it safe and replace the parts, or better yet, we recommend that you buy a new model.

6. At the end of the cook time, you can release the pressure with the Natural Release or Quick Release method (use the cold-water method for the jiggle-top; see page 14), whichever is indicated in the recipe.
7. When the metal valve and plastic plug have dropped back flat against the lid, you may open the cooker. Remove the lid by sliding the top handle to the right and pulling off the lid away from you to avoid the steam.

USING A SPRING-TOP PRESSURE COOKER

1. Prior to using the cooker, pull up on the valve cap so that the pressure regulator is free to move up and down. Check to see that the lid gasket is tucked under the lid rim.
2. Fill the pot as directed by the recipe.
3. Close and lock the lid by turning it clockwise to line up the handle or grip on the lid with the handle or grip on the bottom pan. When the handles are lined up, the lid is locked.
4. Place the pot on the burner and turn the heat to high. As the steam in the pot builds to full pressure, the valve stem will move up. The first red line is low or medium pressure (8 PSI; many cooks use this pressure level to cook vegetables). The second red line indicates 15 PSI has been reached. Both red lines need to be visible for the entire cook time. Once the appropriate level of pressure has been reached, this is the moment to set the timer for whatever is indicated in the recipe.
5. Reduce the heat under the pot to the lowest level that still maintains a gentle hiss of steam. Stay close and keep adjusting the heat under the burner as needed to keep the second red line visible throughout the cooking time.
6. At the end of the cook time, you can release the pressure with the Natural Release or Quick Release method, whichever is indicated in the recipe. For Natural Release, lift the valve cap and rotate to Stage 1. For Quick Release, use a spoon and press on the valve stem to let the steam escape. Stand back, as this happens immediately.
7. When the metal valve stem has dropped back flat against the lid, you may open the cooker. Remove the lid by sliding the top handle to the right and pulling off the lid away from you to avoid the steam.

USING AN ELECTRIC PRESSURE COOKER

There are two different electric pressure cookers, both with sophisticated integrated energy-efficient heating elements located within an insulated housing. One is designed just for pressure cooking, the other is a multi-function cooker, with anywhere from 3 to 7 options that can include slow cooker, rice cooker, and/or yogurt maker as well as pressure cooker. Many models have delay timers and a built-in smart cooker with preset cooking programs, but most cooks like to set the timer themselves

1. Plug it in and fill the cooker pot insert with the ingredients. The LED display will light up. On some models, you will need to press for Pressure or Pressure Release. Be sure the function is selected for Pressure.
2. Close and lock the lid by turning it to the left until it clicks shut. Press the Start/Cancel button (or the Menu button), then the LOW or HIGH pressure option, then the Time button. Set the timer. Press Start/Cancel to begin the cooking. The cooker will automatically start. The pressure cooker will come up to pressure, level off, then the timer will Auto Start and begin the cook time countdown. There is about 30 seconds of escaping steam between boiling and the pressure seal popping up; other than that, the cooker is silent. The machine will automatically set and maintain the pressure designated for the time or food programmed.
3. When the cooking time is done, the cooker beeps, cuts the heat, and enters a Keep Warm function to start a Natural Release of pressure, which will take a bit longer than on stovetop. As with the stovetop models, pressure is released by one of three methods: Natural Release, Quick Release, or a combination of the two.

   To effect a Quick Release of pressure with an electric pressure cooker, first hit Start/Cancel. Then, depending on the model you have, there is a little protrusion on the side of the steam valve that you will gently and carefully lift or shift to pressure release. It is a small protrusion; use tongs or the tip of a spoon or knife to lift it. It's easy to do but pay attention; the steam that is released is insanely hot—keep your hands and face clear of it. Be extra careful when releasing steam in this way with foods that tend to foam when cooked (beans, lentils, grains) and liquids like stock. After the steam is released, unplug the cooker.
4. To turn off the machine completely, unplug it. When the red float on the lid goes down, the pressure is gone and the lid is safe to remove.

Electric pressure cookers collect an excess of condensation that can drip when you open the lid. You can purchase a collector cup that snaps onto the back of the lid that will catch the excess instead of it dripping onto your counter.

You can reset functions or cancel the timing at any time by pressing the Start/Cancel button.

Using the Preset Cooking Features in the Electric Pressure Cooker

Use the preset browning feature to sear meat before pressure cooking. Plug the cooker in to light up the LED display. Press Menu, then Brown, then Start. Add oil to the pot and let it heat up without the lid on. Brown the food as directed in the recipe. An added benefit of this is that hot food will take less time to come to pressure. Use the Sauté feature to precook vegetables, and the Simmer feature to preheat liquid before pressure cooking. When using these functions, when you are done, press Start/Cancel to end the cooking, then let the machine cool down a few minutes before locking the lid. Then you can set the timer and press Start to begin pressure cooking.

When the cooking time is done, the cooker will beep, then cut the heat. After the release is complete, if the liquid is too thin, transfer the protein and vegetables to a serving bowl with a slotted spoon, then select Brown and cook, uncovered, until the liquid is reduced to the desired consistency.

The Brown feature is not all that great on some models. You might find it easier to do your browning or sautéing in another pot, then transfer everything to the pressure cooker. At the end of cooking, transfer the contents to another pot to reduce the cooking liquid, if you desire.

USING A MICROWAVE PRESSURE COOKER

Here are the basic steps, but refer to the manufacturer's booklet for specific instructions.

1. Do not overfill the cooker. The food should never touch the mesh assembly for the steam release. Like traditional stovetop models, they should never be filled more than two thirds or they can explode and ruin your microwave (please see the fill chart on page 16, and underfill it slightly from what it indicated).

2. After filling the cooker, secure the lid. Make sure the lid is on tight and the latches are secured. Move the steam release valve to see if it feels gummy; if it does, clean it. If it does not, it is working correctly.

3. Place the pressure cooker in the microwave.

4. Program the microwave for your recipe's recommended cook time. There is no warm-up time, since the microwave is at maximum cooking heat immediately. Most recipes will cook for the same amount of time in a microwave pressure cooker as in a traditional stovetop version. Cook on HIGH power on your oven. To determine whether the pot has come up to full pressure, look for the pop-up red pressure indicator, which for most brands and models of microwave pressure cookers is located on the lid. It will raise up when the pot is at pressure; also steam will be released and there may be a hissing sound.

5. When the timing is completed and oven shuts off at the beep, let the pressure cooker sit in the microwave for several minutes. This lets the rest of the steam escape and allows the pressure to drop inside the cooker. At this point, you can either allow your cooker to continue to rest (Natural Release method) or remove it from the microwave and press the pressure indicator with the back of a spoon to release the pressure. When depressurized, the cooker will be quiet, with no steam escaping, and the pressure indicator will have dropped. With the Natural Release method, this can take 20 to 30 minutes and the food will continue to cook during this time, so don't rush the cooling process if Natural Release is called for—this can result in food that is not cooked properly. Always handle the cooker and remove from the oven with oven mitts.

6. Once the regulator drops showing that the pressure is gone, remove the lid. Always wait until the cooker is completely depressurized to open it or you may be at risk for steam burns. Open the lid away from your face for the same reason.

USING A PRESSURE CANNER

The following steps are the same for all pressure-canned foods. Refer to your manufacturer's guide for specifics for your canner. Do not use a regular size stovetop pressure cooker for pressure canning. Be sure to use recipes specifically developed for pressure canning (they will come with your pot) and follow the directions exactly for success; don't ad lib or adapt.

1. Prepare the jars. Most cooks prefer the wide-mouth canning jars. Use half pints for jams and chutneys; pint jars for marinated artichoke hearts, pickled vegetables, brandied cherries; quart size for marinara sauce, canned tomatoes, pickles, and fruit halves. Do not use leftover jars from commercial foods such as applesauce. You need heat-resistant jars specifically manufactured for home canning, such as from Ball Company. Heat 3 inches of water in the pressure canner with the lid ajar. Set the jars in the canner to sterilize with the lid loosely in place (no pressure needed here).

2. Prepare the food you intend to can.

3. Remove the hot jars one at a time from the canner pot with a jar lifter. Using a funnel where appropriate to keep the rims clean, fill the sterilized jars. Pack with your fingers if needed. Add the hot liquid or brine as specified in the recipe, leaving the directed amount of headspace. With a thin spatula, thin knife, or canning tool (known as a bubble freer), remove the bubbles. Add more liquid if needed and wipe the rim with a clean cloth. Place the lid on top and screw the band on the jar tight enough to be able to turn it another $^1/_4$ inch so that some air can escape to make the proper seal. Place the jar back in the canner before filling the next jar.

4. Place the last jar in the canner which still contains the water used to sterilize the jars; you should have about 3 inches of water, which is enough to create steam but only comes a short way up the jars. Lock the lid of the canner in place. Turn the burner to high. When steam escapes, reduce the heat to get a moderate steam flow. Let the steam vent for 10 minutes. Adjust the weights on the pressure regulator as specified in the recipe. Set the pressure regulator on the vent to plug it. When it starts to rock, adjust the heat to keep it steady. The safety valve will pop up when pressure is reached. DO NOT open the lid. Set the timer.

5. When the timer sounds, depressurize by turning off the heat. You can leave it on the burner. DO NOT open the lid. Wait until the safety valve drops to show that canner is no longer pressurized and is safe to open. Remove the regulator. No steam should escape. Open the canner by unlocking the handles and open the cover away from you to avoid the blast of steam.

6. Let the jars stand in the uncovered canner to cool for 10 to 15 minutes. Remove the jars with the jar lifter and set on a wire rack or folded dishcloth to cool on the countertop. Do not tighten the lids. Let cool 12 to 24 hours. When cool, test the seals by pressing on the lids with your finger. They should not be flexible, popping up and down, but indented. Refrigerate any unsealed jars to eat immediately. Store sealed jars in a cool cupboard.

NEVER LEAVE A STOVETOP OR MICROWAVE PRESSURE COOKER UNATTENDED!

Make sure you are in the same room and paying close attention once a stovetop or microwave pressure cooker (and a camping pressure cooker as well) is under pressure. You may need to make adjustments to the heat level to keep the pressure level from getting too high and cook times are often very short. The only pressure cooker you can leave to cook on its own, with no monitoring, is the electric cooker, as it has an automatic override system that will automatically shut it off and switch it to Keep Warm for a Natural Release.

HOW TO TELL YOUR PRESSURE COOKER IS UP TO FULL PRESSURE

This will depend on the type of pressure regulator you have and it can also vary from brand to brand, depending on the specific design and type of the cooker. Your first resource on this information should be your owner's manual. On average, with a stovetop model set on a burner at high heat, it will take about 10 minutes for the pressure to build up inside the pot. Once the appropriate level of pressure has been achieved as directed by your recipe, you will begin the timing for the recipe.

Here is how to tell when your pressure cooker is up to pressure and ready to start cooking:

- **Spring valve:** The spring-loaded valve will pop up with the pressure to give a visual aid as to when the pressure is established. The first ring is LOW pressure and the second ring is HIGH pressure. Start timing when the appropriate ring pops up. These models are considered the most accurate in gauging temperature.
- **Jiggle top:** The weighted valve will rhythmically rock when the steam starts to escape; this is when you start your timer. You should place the pressure regulator when you lock the lid or the minute the cooker emits a continuous jet of steam; see your owner's manual. If you place it later, the water might completely evaporate, resulting in the cooker as well as the gasket burning dry.
- **Whistling pressure:** This is characteristic of stovetop pressure cookers manufactured in India. When steam begins to escape, the 15 PSI stationary weighted valve is put on the lid. As the pressure builds, the steam lifts up the valve to release the pressure in a blast, making a hissing or whistling sound. The first whistle takes the longest to occur, about 7 minutes, and indicates the cooker is fully pressurized, after which the heat is reduced to lowest level possible to still maintain pressure. The hissing, or whistles, occur every 3 to 5 minutes allowing you to time the pot. It is an auditory cue rather than visual with a timer. The Natural Release method is used with these pressure cookers.
- **Electric pressure cooker:** The digital face will show a lighted P and/or Beep to indicate the contents have reached pressure.

TIMING IS EVERYTHING

Because of the super-hot, über-pressurized environment in the pressure cooker, minutes (make that seconds) matter. Use a digital timer with an alarm when you pressure cook. As soon as the cooker comes up to pressure, set the timer as directed in the recipe and keep close so you can hear it when it goes off, then immediately remove the pot from the heat or unplug it if you're using an electric pressure cooker.

- **Microwave pressure cooker:** Look for the red pressure regulator indicator, which for most brands and models of microwave pressure cookers is located on the lid. It will pop up when the pot is at pressure; also steam will be released and there may be a hissing sound.

RELEASING PRESSURE

After the cook time is completed, the pressure needs to be brought down in the pot before it can be opened. There are three methods for doing this, Quick Release, Natural Release, and a combination of both, and our recipes indicate which type should be used for the best results with that particular dish. *No matter what release method you use, always carefully remove the lid, tilting it away from you to avoid the super-hot steam.*

Natural Release Method

To use this method (which can be used with any kind of pressure cooker), remove the pot from the burner and let the pressure drop naturally as the pot sits and cools down; for an electric pressure cooker, simply unplug the machine. With this method, the food will continue to cook in the residual heat and in our recipes that is taken into account in the cook time. In most all of our recipes, we will tell you how long to let the cooker stand off the heat before opening.

HOW TO TELL WHEN THE PRESSURE HAS BEEN RELEASED ON STOVETOP COOKERS

For a jiggle-top, the regulator will stop releasing steam (and the hissing will stop). For a spring-valve pressure cooker, the pressure indicator pin will drop all the way down.

Use the Natural Release method for whole grains, cereals, beans, peas, lentils (so they don't split apart when pressure is released), stocks, applesauce, custards, rice puddings, and bread puddings. Natural release should also be used with hard vegetables such as artichokes, celery root, whole beets, and winter squash. A partial Natural Release (followed by a Quick Release for the remaining steam) is used for certain meat and poultry stews, pot roast, chilis, and soups.

Quick Release Method

This method is used to drop the pressure in the cooker as fast as possible to stop the cooking process.

For non-jiggle-top pressure cookers and electric pressure cookers, this is done by moving a lever or pushing a button on the lid, which will release all the steam. On some models (and for all electric pressure cookers), you will turn the pressure selector dial on the lid to the Release position and the steam will release. Check your owner's manual.

For jiggle-top pressure cookers, Quick Release can be accomplished using the cold-water release method. Carefully remove the pressure cooker from the burner, place it in the sink, and run cold tap water gently over the lid until the pressure indicator is lowered and the pressure is completely released. With the handle, tilt the pressure cooker so that when you run the water over the top of it, the water flows away from you; also be sure not to let the water make contact with the pressure regulator. Once the pressure has been released, place the cooker on a folded dish towel or a cold burner before opening. Be sure to open the lid away from you for safety. The jiggle-top is the only type of pot you can do a cold-water release with. For obvious reasons, do not attempt it with an electric pressure cooker.

For a Quick Release with an electric pressure cooker, see page 10.

Use the Quick Release method for seafood, meat and vegetable stews, lamb shanks, fruits, and vegetables, especially greens, potatoes, sweet potatoes, broccoli, cabbage, carrots, corn on the cob, green beans, turnips, rutabagas, and zucchini.

RULES OF THE POT

Please be sure to read this section before your first foray into cooking under pressure and use it as a reference guide thereafter. The pressure cooker is a wonderful tool in your kitchen arsenal but you need to use it properly for safe cooking.

Before You Begin to Cook

- Make sure your stove is compatible with your pressure cooker. Aluminum pressure cookers cannot be used with induction cooktops but stainless steel models with three-ply bottoms are fine.
- Read your owner's manual before using your pressure cooker. You need to understand the particulars of your specific model.
- Inspect the gasket. For older pots and pots that are used regularly, replace the gasket every year or when it becomes hard, cracked, or sticky-soft. When in doubt, replace the gasket. Keep an extra gasket in reserve so it's there when you need it.
- Check that the vent pipe is clear before every use. Hold the lid up to the light to check. If a jiggle-top is blocked, use a wooden toothpick or bamboo pick to clean it out. For the spring-valve model, press the rod to be sure it moves freely.

Cooking in the Pressure Cooker

- Do not use metal utensils with the cooker. Metal will scratch and if you hit the rim of the cooker with a metal utensil, you can dent it, which will affect the gasket's ability to seal the pot properly. Use heat-resistant rubber or silicone or wooden utensils.
- Do not add salt to the bottom of the pot as it will corrode the stainless steel. If using salt, sprinkle the salt on top of the liquid.
- Do not cook acid foods like tomatoes in an aluminum pot.
- When steaming, lightly oil the trivet and steamer basket or rack to prevent sticking or scorching.
- Do not place the pressure cooker on a burner larger than its bottom dimensions. You want the heat centered under the bottom.
- If using a gas range, do not let the flames get so high that they go up the side of the pot; otherwise you might melt the gasket.
- For added flavor, you can brown meat and poultry lightly before pressure cooking. Be careful not to overbrown, though, as flavors intensify when pressure cooking.
- Precooking vegetables, such as onions, before pressure cooking is not necessary to develop flavor. A quick turn in the pot before adding the other ingredients is all that is needed.
- Be careful with adding salt to the pot before pressure cooking as the flavor will concentrate under pressure. Always add salt at the end of cooking for beans and grains.
- For the same reason, be careful adding spices and dried herbs. If converting a conventional recipe to the pressure cooker, use half the amount you would normally use, then add more to taste after pressure cooking.
- The high heat of the pressure cooker destroys the flavor and texture of fresh herbs. Add fresh herbs at the end of cooking for the best flavor. Some cooks use both dried and fresh herbs together to accent the flavor.
- When cooking leafy greens, which in their raw state will fill the entire pot, use a saucepan lid from your regular cookware, one without a plastic knob, and place it on top of the greens to weight them down, then close and lock the lid. This will keep the greens from clogging the pressure valve as they cook.
- Beans and legumes need a tablespoon or two of oil drizzled over the top before locking the lid to keep them from foaming up as they cook, which can block the pressure release or steam vent.
- There are other foods that can foam in this way: cranberries, rhubarb, oatmeal, and pasta. To keep the pressure release/steam vent clear, when cooking these foods, don't fill the pressure cooker more than half full. And where appropriate add a tablespoon or two of oil, as for beans.

LIQUID IS THE KEY

No liquid in your pot, no steam. Adding sufficient liquid to cook the ingredients in the pot is the key to success and safety. You do not want your pressure cooker to boil dry while cooking under pressure. This can happen if the food has cooked too long at too high a pressure or if the gasket is leaking. And it can happen if you shortchange the amount of liquid asked for in a recipe.

The amount of liquid needed depends more on how long you are cooking rather than how much food is in the pot. Generally, use a minimum of 1 cup liquid for both stovetop and electric cookers. Figure that 1 to 1½ cups liquid are necessary for the first 15 minutes of cooking, then ¾ cup for every 15 minutes thereafter. This assures there is enough liquid to create the proper amount of steam for cooking. A minimum of ½ to 1½ cups of liquid is used for steaming vegetables (like corn or potatoes) and 2 cups for steaming puddings and cup custards. For braising and stewing, recipes will call for the solid ingredients to be partially or fully covered with a liquid.

Wet ingredients such as tomatoes and ingredients that give off liquid (like onions and celery) when heated count as liquid when combined with regular liquids like water, juice, broth, and spirits. If you end up with excess juices at the end of cooking, you can thicken them, if you like. But better safe than sorry.

DO NOT!

- Do not use just tomato sauce or pureed vegetables as the cooking liquid; there is not enough water in either one to generate steam and they will burn.
- Do not thicken liquids with flour, potato flakes, potato starch, or a vegetable puree before pressure cooking. This step will remove the precious liquid needed to generate steam and will affect the overall quality of your finished dish. Use thickeners after pressure cooking and simmer a few minutes with the lid off to thicken.
- Do not use high-alcohol liquor as the liquid in the pressure cooker because it can create vapor that can ignite. Add it at the end of cooking if you must. You can use wine, champagne, or beer, or a few tablespoons of liquor, as a liquid with no problem but bring them to a boil to evaporate a little of the alcohol before locking the lid.

- Don't try to cook dumplings in the pressure cooker. It just doesn't work. Make them after the stew is cooked and simmer them with the lid off.
- When using wine as an ingredient, such as 1 cup plus, it is important to note that it will not evaporate under pressure. Raw wine is not tasty (especially in stews and risottos), so add the wine to the pot before pressure and let it come to a boil before adding the rest of the ingredients and locking the lid.

Filling the Pressure Cooker

Fill the pressure cooker pot no more than one half to two-thirds full of ingredients. Foods expand under pressure and if the cooker is overfilled, you run the risk that the vent pipe can become clogged. Certain foods require different fill levels. UNDERFILL IF POSSIBLE. Follow this guide religiously:

- *Meats, one-pot meals, and vegetables:* No more than *two-thirds full.* When making stocks, the bones cannot extend above the two-thirds level (consider a super large pressure cooker if you make lots of stock from a turkey carcass or leg of lamb bone). This includes all the ingredients plus the liquid.
- *Pasta, soups, and stews:* No more than *one-half full,* including the liquid. These foods swell a lot as they cook.
- *Dried beans, lentils, rice, cereal grains and whole grains:* No more than *one-third full,* including the liquid. These foods expand the most and produce foam. If you prepare large quantities of these items regularly, consider getting a larger model, such as an 8-quart.

GUIDE TO FILLING YOUR PRESSURE COOKER

Contents	Fill Level
Cereals, grains, beans, lentils, rice	1/3 full including liquid
Soups and stews	1/2 full including liquid
Vegetables, solid meats, stocks, one-pot meals	2/3 full including liquid

Under Pressure

- Before closing the lid, wipe the rim of spills with a moist cloth.
- Make sure the lid is locked firmly and securely into place before heating to bring the food to pressure. Double check your manufacturer's booklet for directions specific to your model for locking the pot.
- After turning up the heat, it can take anywhere from 30 seconds to 20 minutes, with the average about 10 minutes, to bring the boiling liquid up to pressure depending on the type of food and amount of food in the cooker.
- Do not allow your pressure pot to overheat, as it can warp. Do not leave an empty pressure cooker on a hot element or allow it to boil dry.
- Never leave a stovetop pressure cooker unattended on the hot stove. An electric pressure cooker countertop appliance can be left unattended, but you should still be in the house.
- Always use a digital kitchen timer (every second counts), as exact timing is often necessary when cooking in a pressure cooker, especially for fish,

vegetables, and fruits. When the proper level of steam is reached, start the timer for the cook time. Be ready to set the timer, as a few seconds can make a difference when cooking some foods.

- When doubling or tripling a recipe, the cook time stays the same.
- Never open or try to open a pressure cooker when it is under pressure.
- Only hold a pressure cooker by its handles and use oven mitts for extra protection.

After Cooking

- Always lift up the pressure cooker to move it from the burner or coil, as sliding the cooker will scratch the cooktop.
- The difference between cooling the cooker immediately with the Quick Release and letting pressure drop on its own with the Natural Release is determined by the food being cooked. With the Natural Release, the food continues to cook in the residual heat.
- Pressure has reduced when the jiggle-top stops releasing steam (the hissing will stop). For a spring valve pressure cooker, the pressure indicator pin will drop all the way down.
- Be very careful when opening the lid after the pressure has been released. The steam is still scalding hot. Never put your face over the pot when opening it. Make sure the cooker is on a heatproof solid surface and open the lid away from your body. The food will also be very hot.

HOW TO READ OUR RECIPES

The pressure cooker does a host of jobs very well, but has its limitations. In this book, we focused on recipes that utilize the pot to its best advantage. This includes a wide range of traditional American dishes as well as recipes that vary in flavor from India-inspired to Mediterranean to East-West Fusion cuisine.

Our readers are not only good home cooks, but good eaters and good thinkers. We strive to make our recipes easy to follow but also want to give you that dash of motivation to get you out of your cooking rut. Before you know it, you will be serving and feasting on fabulous whole foods, planning your meals, and eating better than you have in a while. It's a step-by-step process for the first time or two, then you get more confident and can prep and cook faster.

Our recipes include a head note, yield, ingredients listed in the order used, directions, and a quick reference for size of pressure cooker needed, the cook time under pressure, and the level of pressure. Always read through a recipe before starting to prepare it.

Head note: A head note can include some history, cultural, linguistic, or geographic details; specific ingredient notes not included in the body of the recipe; our personal advice comments or kitchen story; source or inspiration of the recipe if relevant; mail order resources for special ingredients or equipment; and serving suggestions.

Yield: We always include a yield per recipe based on moderate portions. You will need to adjust the recipe for big or small eaters, fewer or more diners, and whether you want enough for leftovers. Many cooks prepare for more than one meal or for the freezer.

Ingredients: Ingredients are always listed in order of their use so you can go back and forth checking between the ingredients and directions while making the recipe. We strive to create recipes that use widely available ingredients. You can use the ingredient list as your checklist for available pantry items and as a shopping list.

USING OUR RECIPES WITH AN ELECTRIC PRESSURE COOKER

You will use the directions for the stove top recipe with the exception of setting the automatic timer by pressing a button that will designate the different functions. For a machine with 10 to 15 PSI, you can follow our directions exactly. For machines with 5 to 9 PSI, you will have to increase the time by 20 percent. For recipes with instructions for Quick Release, turn off the Keep Warm setting and unplug the machine when the cook time is completed.

USING OUR RECIPES WITH A MICROWAVE PRESSURE COOKER

Food will cook for the same amount of time in a microwave pressure cooker as in a traditional stovetop version, but with a big difference. The microwave pressure cooker is geared for preparing recipes for 1 to 2 people, so your recipes need to be adapted to these smaller proportions. In the case of the recipes in this book, as a general rule you will need to cut them back by 50 to 75 percent, depending on the yield of any particular recipe, to ensure that the pot is not overfilled (see the fill chart on page 16 and underfill it slightly from what is indicated; the cooker should never be more than two-thirds full). Use the recipes specifically developed for the microwave pressure cooker in the accompanying manufacturer's recipe booklet and use those as a template. The recipes in this book that can be used in the micro pressure cooker without adapting are the vegetables included in the pressure-steamed vegetables chart on page 466.

Directions: In each recipe we specify the size pressure cooker for that recipe. Recipes' cook times are calibrated to sea level.

We specify when to lock the lid of your pressure cooker. Bringing a pressure cooker up to HIGH pressure takes on the average about 10 minutes, but specifically depends upon what you're cooking and how much of it. Check your manual for specific instructions on how to recognize when pressure is established or see page 13. Once the pot is brought to pressure, the heat underneath the pot needs to be adjusted to the lowest level that will still maintain the level of pressure you need to cook, either MEDIUM or HIGH. How this is done depends on the type of cooktop you have (gas, electric, etc.); see page 8 for guidelines.

Once the pot is brought to pressure, timing begins. We strongly recommend that you use a digital timer with an alarm. The cook times we give you are exact, not approximations.

The method used to release the pressure from the pot (Natural or Quick Release will be specified; in some recipes either type of release is acceptable) is just as important as the cook time. See pages 13–14 for guidelines on both types of release.

HIGH ALTITUDE PRESSURE COOKING

The recipes in this book were developed and tested at sea level; the cook times must be adjusted if you live at an elevation higher than 2,500 feet.

As one increases in altitude, atmospheric pressure decreases, which causes liquid to come to a boil more slowly, resulting in longer cook times. The general rule is to increase the cook times by 5 percent for every 1,000 feet in elevation above 2,000 feet. This translates to adding 1 minute per 20 minutes of cook time designated in the recipe for every 1,000 feet above sea level. For example, if you are cooking a pot roast for 60 minutes at 4,000 feet, you will add 6 minutes to the total cook time. That same pot roast will cook 15 minutes longer, 75 minutes, at 7,000 feet. If you are cooking chicken stock for 40 minutes, at 7,000 feet you will add 10 minutes, for a cook time of 50 minutes. At 7,000 feet, a 7-minute risotto will now require $8\frac{3}{4}$ minutes. We recommend keeping a small digital calculator at hand in the kitchen for doing these calculations to avoid under- or overcooking.

ADJUSTING SEA LEVEL COOK TIMES FOR HIGHER ELEVATIONS

Altitude (feet)	Increase Cook Time (CT) Calculation
3,000	5% (1 minute per 20 minutes CT)
4,000	10% (2 minutes per 20 minutes CT)
5,000	15% (3 minutes per 20 minutes CT)
6,000	20% (4 minutes per 20 minutes CT)
7,000	25% (5 minutes per 20 minutes CT)
8,000	30% (6 minutes per 20 minutes CT)

The pressure canner uses a different method for high altitude canning guide due to the weight-gauged lid. Be sure to use recipes that have been scientifically tested, dated 1988 or later. Pressure canners come with excellent manufacturer's booklets that include guidelines for operating them at high elevations.

ADJUSTING SEA LEVEL COOK TIMES FOR PRESSURE CANNERS FOR HIGHER ELEVATIONS		
Altitude (feet)	*Weighted Gauge*	*Dial Gauge*
0–1,000	10	11
1,001–2,000	15	11
2,001–4,000	15	12
4,001–6,000	15	13
6,001–8,000	15	14
8,001–10,000	15	15

ADAPTING CONVENTIONAL AND SLOW COOKER RECIPES FOR THE PRESSURE COOKER

Once you get familiar with your pressure cooker, you will want to use it to make your favorite recipes. The four key elements to be considered are:

- amount of liquid
- timing
- the volume of food being cooked versus the size of the pressure cooker
- seasoning

Slow cooker recipes convert easily since both methods use pressurized steam to cook the food and basically most of the ingredients are loaded in the pot at once, so all you have to adapt is the cook time. Recipes that convert from slow cooker to pressure cooker perfectly are soups, stews, and braises. Look up a recipe in this book that is similar to the one you want to convert, and use it for a guide to timing and liquid proportions.

Amount of liquid. Your recipe must contain at least 1 cup cooking liquid in order to generate the amount of steam needed to get the pot up to pressure and to keep the contents from burning. Slow cooker recipes use about the same amount of liquid as a pressure cooker but the liquid in a conventional recipe may need to be adjusted downward since no evaporation takes place. What you put in before cooking and what you have after cooking will be the same. A pressure cooker without liquid will not create pressure.

Cook time. You have to adjust the cook time since the pressure cooker cooks two-thirds quicker than conventional recipes and in a fraction of the time compared to the slow cooker. For example, a conventional braise recipe that takes 3 hours stovetop or in the oven will take 1 hour. A conventional soup recipe that requires 60 minutes stovetop will take 20 minutes. Brown rice, which normally takes 40 to 50 minutes, will take 15 minutes. Basmati rice, which cooks in 20 minutes, will take 4 to 5 minutes in the pressure cooker. Tender vegetables like cauliflower and bell peppers take just 1 to 3 minutes under pressure. The longest cooking vegetables—hard squashes and roots like potatoes, turnips, and sweet potatoes—will take just 5 to 8 minutes at pressure, depending on whether they are cubed or sliced.

The biggest time saver is with dried beans. Generally presoaked beans such as black, pinto, or kidney cook in just 8 to 10 minutes at pressure; unsoaked, they will take 25 to 30 minutes at pressure, still a huge time saver. Soaked garbanzo beans, notoriously the longest bean to cook, take just 14 to 18 minutes at pressure. Always follow your pressure cooker manufacturer's directions for exact cooking times for particular foods or liquid requirements because the strength of pressure cookers may vary depending on the brand.

Here is an approximate guide for translating timing in recipes for the slow cooker or conventional cooking to the pressure cooker. You can also refer to a recipe similar to what you want to make as a reference.

- If a slow cooker recipe calls for a cook time of 4 to 6 hours on LOW and 3 to 4 hours on HIGH, that translates to 30 minutes stovetop or 10 to 12 minutes in the pressure cooker.
- If a slow cooker recipe calls for a cook time of 6 to 10 hours on LOW and 2 hours on HIGH, that translates to 45 minutes stovetop or 15 to 18 minutes in the pressure cooker.
- If a slow cooker recipe calls for a cook time of 8 to 18 hours on LOW and 4 to 6 hours on HIGH, that translates to 1 to 3 hours stovetop or 20 to 60 minutes in the pressure cooker.

Fill level. You must look at the total amount of food in the original recipe and make sure it will not fill the pressure cooker more than half to two-thirds (see the chart of page 16 for guidelines on fill levels). You might have to adjust the recipe proportions so it doesn't overfill your pressure cooker.

Seasoning. Flavors are intensified in the pressure cooker. The first time you prepare a recipe you've adapted for the pressure cooker, you might want to cut back on the seasonings and adjust them after cooking, if need be.

PRESSURE COOKER CLEANING AND STORAGE TIPS

The pressure cooker needs to be washed after every cooking session.

- As soon as the pot cools down, remove the gasket.
- Clean the vent after each use to remove any collected food residue.
- **Never** put the lid or gasket in the dishwasher.
- Hand wash the pot bottom and gasket in warm water after each use with mild dishwashing soap (never use an abrasive cleaner) and a nonabrasive sponge. You can soak the pot if need be. Towel dry.
- Do not immerse the lid in water or place in the dishwasher; wipe it clean using a nonabrasive sponge, mild dishwashing soap, and warm water. Towel dry.
- To remove starchy deposits on the pot left from cooking lentils and beans, take this tip from The

Happy Cook, Dolores Kostelni: Wet the surface down with hot water. Squirt some Original Scent Dawn dishwashing liquid on the spots. Wet a red Weiman cooktop scrubbing pad and rub away the spots.

- To remove burned-on foods from the pot, pour in 1 cup cold water, heat over medium heat, then scrape the food up with a plastic spatula. **Do not** use steel wool or Brillo pads.
- To polish a stainless steel pressure cooker, use Bar Keepers Friend.
- To store the pressure cooker, place the clean, dry gasket back on the lid or hang it until the pot's next use (follow the directions in your owner's manual). Store the lid upside down on the pot bottom, with a paper towel or clean dish towel in between to prevent scratching, or store the pot and lid separately and leave the pot open.
- Never store the pot with the lid locked in place.
- Store your pressure cooker in a cupboard so there is space around it.
- Replace pressure cooker parts regularly. In general, the sealing ring, overpressure plug, and rubber gasket from the air vent/cover lock should be replaced about every two years or sooner if the part is not functioning properly. Remember, pressure cooker parts are not interchangeable. Use only the parts made for your cooker. Refer to your manufacturer's instruction manual.

2

Liquid Gold: Homemade Stocks and Broths

One of the most wonderful foods a pressure cooker can make is homemade stocks, reducing hours of simmering to literally minutes of cook time. To make stock, you need to use at least a 6-quart pressure cooker. If you make stock often and want large amounts, use an 8- to 10-quart model.

Why make homemade stock? You have full control of the ingredients, the sodium content, and the flavors, from simple to complex. Also, properly prepared, meat stock is extremely nutritious, containing minerals dissolved from the bones, cartilage, marrow, and vegetables in a form that is easy to assimilate. Acidic wine or vinegar added during cooking helps to draw the mineral ions, particularly calcium, magnesium, and potassium, into the broth.

While stock and broth are basically the same when you are talking canned, with homemade there is a slight difference. Stocks are made from bony parts, meat scraps, vegetables, and some form of aromatic (like parsley and garlic) cooked until all their flavor is extracted. They are usually unsalted and contain lots of gelatin, released from the bones. Refrigerated, a meat or poultry stock will become a semi-solid, like Jell-O, because of that gelatin. That translates into incredible flavor and a rich silkiness on the tongue. Broth is lighter in taste and texture, requiring a shorter cook time. Technically speaking, a stock or broth listed in a recipe can be used interchangeably.

Whether you're making stock or broth, always remember to keep the total amount of solids and liquid below the two-thirds maximum-fill mark on your pressure cooker for efficient cooking. If you fill it more than that, there will not be enough room to create the cooking steam.

Cold water usually produces a stock with a clearer color and more intense flavor in standard recipes, but in the pressure cooker, you can use cold or hot water with equal success since the liquid comes to a boil so quickly.

What looks like a lot of stock in the pot when you start will be a bit less after you strain it. Use a small saucepan or large ladle to transfer the still-warm stock (ideally around 160° F) into a cheese-cloth-lined colander set in a larger bowl. You might need to use tongs or a slotted spoon to remove bones first. Do this over the sink, since there is the chance of splashing. After straining, let the stock cool to lukewarm, uncovered, then refrigerate until cold. Do not put hot stock directly into the refrigerator, as the heat from the liquid will raise the temperature inside the refrigerator to an unsafe level.

After a few hours of chilling, if this is a meat or poultry stock, the fat will coagulate on top and be easy to lift right off with a large spoon. Leave the fat on while you store the stock in the refrigerator (it provides an airtight seal), but remove it when freezing. Some people do not skim off all the fat; leaving a few tablespoons contributes to the overall flavor.

Always reboil stock in whatever recipe you add it to. Homemade stocks are a tasty powerhouse of minerals, just like a liquid vitamin pill. Add a bit of salt and pepper and you can savor a bowl of this on its own, poured over toasted country bread, with some tortellini or gnocchi, or with the addition of some noodles, pastina, orzo, or rice for a great lunch.

Everyday Vegetable Stock

Makes about 1$^1/_2$ quarts • Cooker: 5- to 8-quart • Time: 7 minutes at HIGH pressure

Vegetable stock can be made with almost any combination of vegetables. Many cooks keep their trimmings in a freezer bag and when they have enough, dump the entire bag into the pot and cover with water and add some herbs. It is okay to cook the stock with the trimmings still frozen. The general rule is that 5 cups of chopped vegetables simmered in 7 cups of water will yield one quart of stock. Stovetop that would take 1 hour, but in the pressure cooker it's a mere 7 minutes under pressure, then 15 minutes off heat to let the pressure release. Consider loading the pressure cooker while you are doing the dishes. By the time you are finished, your stock will be too. This stock doesn't call for salt, but you can add it if you like. Consider a nice sea salt or Himalayan salt.

2 medium carrots, or 1 carrot and 1 parsnip, cut
  into chunks
2 or 3 large mushrooms, chopped
1 leek (white and green parts), trimmed, cut in half
  lengthwise, rinsed well, and chopped, or 6 green
  onions, trimmed and chopped
1 medium white onion, quartered
4 ribs celery with leaves, cut into chunks
1 small head garlic, left unpeeled and cut in half
  horizontally
1 tablespoon reduced-sodium soy sauce
6 sprigs fresh flatleaf parsley
2 sprigs fresh thyme or savory
1 bay leaf
$^1/_2$ teaspoon black peppercorns
8 to 10 cups water, or as needed
Salt

1. In a 5- to 8-quart pressure cooker, combine the vegetables, garlic, soy sauce, herbs, and peppercorns. Add water to cover by 2 inches. The vegetables should be thick in the water but floating. If you do not have enough vegetables, the stock will be weak.

2. Close and lock the lid. Set the burner heat to high. When the cooker reaches HIGH pressure, reduce the burner heat as low as you can and still maintain HIGH pressure. Set a timer to cook for 7 minutes.

3. Remove the pot from the heat. Open the cooker with the Natural Release method; let stand for 15 minutes. Be careful of the steam as you remove the lid.

4. Set a large colander lined with a double layer of cheesecloth over a large bowl and pour the broth through to strain. Press the vegetables to extract all the liquid. Discard the solids. Salt to taste or leave unsalted. Cool completely.

5. The stock is ready for use and will keep in an airtight container in the refrigerator up to 4 days or the freezer 4 to 6 months.

White Wine Vegetable Stock: In Step 1, add $^1/_2$ cup light white wine, such as Pinot Grigio or Sauvignon Blanc, after adding the vegetables. Bring to a boil and reduce a bit before adding the water. Continue as directed.

Red Wine Vegetable Stock: Add 2 or 3 seeded plum tomatoes and use 2 portobello mushrooms. After adding all the vegetables, add $^1/_2$ cup dry red wine, such as Pinot Noir, Merlot, or Chianti. Bring to a boil and reduce a bit before adding the water. Continue as directed.

Brodo di Verdura (Vegetable Broth)

Makes about 2 quarts • Cooker: 6- to 8-quart • Time: 15 minutes at HIGH pressure

Vegetables that have strong flavors, like cabbage, turnips, brussels sprouts, green peppers, broccoli, and cauliflower, should be used with care—or not at all—when making vegetable stock; they will flavor your stock distinctly, even make it bitter. Save the rice and beans to add to your soup, not stock. The addition of potatoes will give a stock body because of their starch, but it will also cloud the stock, if that matters to you. Beets will instantly tint a stock a brilliant, earthy color. Good choices for vegetable stock are leeks (both the green and white parts), tomato ends, spinach and parsley stems, carrot peelings, and green bean strings. We like to use fresh vegetables; over-the-hill vegetables do not cook up into a nice tasting stock.

2 medium yellow or white onions, left unpeeled
    and cut in half
2 leeks (white and green parts), trimmed, cut in half
    lengthwise, rinsed well, and chopped
2 medium carrots, cut into chunks
1 medium zucchini, cut into chunks
3 ribs celery with leaves, cut into chunks
12 pea pods
3 cloves garlic, peeled and smashed
$^{1}/_{2}$ bunch fresh flatleaf parsley
$^{1}/_{4}$ bunch fresh cilantro with stems
2 sprigs fresh thyme or marjoram
1 bay leaf
2 teaspoons black peppercorns
8 to 10 cups water, or as needed
2 teaspoons sea salt

1. In a 6- to 8-quart pressure cooker, combine the vegetables, garlic, herbs, and peppercorns. Add the water to cover by 2 to 3 inches. The vegetables should be thick in the water but still float. If you do not have enough vegetables, the stock will be weak.
2. Close and lock the lid. Set the burner heat to high. When the cooker reaches HIGH pressure, reduce the burner heat as low as you can and still maintain HIGH pressure. Set a timer to cook for 15 minutes.
3. Remove the pot from the heat. Open the cooker with the Natural Release method; let stand for 15 minutes. Be careful of the steam as you remove the lid.
4. Set a large colander lined with a double layer of cheesecloth over a large bowl and pour the broth through to strain. Press the vegetables to extract all the liquid. Discard the solids. Add the salt, then taste to see if more is needed. Cool completely.
5. The stock is ready for use and will keep in an airtight container in the refrigerator up to 4 days or the freezer 4 to 6 months.

FLAVOR ADDITIONS FOR A DELUXE VEGETABLE BROTH

- 2 to 3 plum tomatoes, roughly chopped, will add color, flavor, and acidity to the broth; a nice addition for summer soups.
- 1 fennel bulb, diced, and its stalks and leaves, add bold anise flavor; use this broth in the preparation of seafood dishes.
- 4 to 6 ounces sliced fresh mushrooms or a few dried mushrooms (no need to rehydrate) will add a deep, woodsy flavor to the broth; fresh ones are tamer in flavor.

Asian Vegetable Stock

Makes about 2 quarts • Cooker: 5- to 8-quart • Time: 8 minutes at HIGH pressure

The addition of fresh-tasting cilantro, dried shiitake mushrooms, lemongrass stalk, and slices of spicy fresh ginger root make a stock that is still quite delicately flavored. If you have mirin on hand, add $1/4$ cup with the water if you like. Look for the mushrooms in the Asian food section of the supermarket or where other dried mushrooms are sold. When we strain the stock, we reserve the reconstituted mushrooms and slice them to add to a stir-fry or soup (they are delicious with bok choy, page 466).

2 medium yellow or white onions, quartered
1 bunch green onions, trimmed and cut into 2-inch
  lengths
3 medium carrots, cut into chunks
6 ribs celery with leaves, cut into chunks
2 baby bok choy, cut into chunks
$1/2$ bunch fresh cilantro
5 large dried shiitake or Chinese mushrooms
1 head garlic, unpeeled, cut in half horizontally
8 thin slices fresh ginger
2 stalks lemongrass (inner white parts only), each
  cut into 3 pieces
5 black peppercorns
1 tablespoon reduced-sodium soy sauce
1 (6-inch) piece kombu (optional)
8 to 9 cups water, or as needed

1. In a 5- to 8-quart pressure cooker, add the vegetables, cilantro, dried mushroom, garlic, ginger, lemongrass, peppercorns, and soy sauce. Add the water to cover by 2 inches. The vegetables should be thick in the water but floating. If you do not have enough vegetables, the stock will be weak.
2. Close and lock the lid. Set the burner heat to high. When the cooker reaches HIGH pressure, reduce the burner heat as low as you can and still maintain HIGH pressure. Set a timer to cook for 8 minutes.
3. Remove the pot from the heat. Open the cooker with the Natural Release method; let stand for 15 minutes. Be careful of the steam as you remove the lid.
4. Set a large colander lined with a double layer of cheesecloth over a large bowl and pour the broth through to strain. Press the vegetables to extract all the liquid. Discard the solids. Salt to taste or leave unsalted. Cool completely.
5. The stock is ready for use. It will keep in an airtight container in the refrigerator for up to 4 days or the freezer for 4 months.

FREEZING STOCK

Buy a variety of stackable 2- and 4-cup freezer containers. Be sure to leave 2 inches of headspace in the container for expansion when the stock freezes. Alternately, you can freeze the stock in quart or gallon ziptop freezer bags, laying the bags on a cookie sheet so that the stock freezes into a flat sheet and can be stacked for storage.

Vegetable Parmesan Broth

Makes about 2 quarts • Cooker: 6- to 8-quart • Time: 12 minutes at HIGH pressure

Have a lovely hunk of Parmigiano-Reggiano in the fridge to grate over your pasta? Well, the rind is edible as well and perfect for making this *brodo*. The rind will dissolve into the broth, giving it a spark of umami; it's a great substitute for chicken broth. Please remember that only authentic Parmigiano-Reggiano cheese can be used for making this, as the rinds of other cheeses may be inedible. You can also use this in vegetarian pasta sauces, soups, and risottos, as well as vegetable braises. You don't need salt because of the cheese. *Bueno gusto!* This recipe is adapted from one on parmesan.com.

3 tablespoons olive oil
1 large white onion, coarsely chopped
2 cloves garlic, peeled and crushed
1 medium fennel bulb, halved, cored and sliced,
    with stalks and fronds
3 ribs celery with leaves, chopped
1 plum tomato, chopped
$^1/_2$ bunch fresh flatleaf parsley
1 ($^1/_3$- to $^1/_2$-pound) Parmigiano-Reggiano rind
    (3- to 4-inch square piece), cut into pieces, or a
    selection of accumulated chunks
1 bay leaf
$^1/_2$ teaspoon dried Italian herb blend or 2 sprigs
    fresh basil
1 teaspoon black or white peppercorns
8 to 10 cups water, to cover

1. In a 6- to 8-quart pressure cooker, heat the oil over medium-high heat until very hot. Add the onion, garlic, fennel, and celery and cook, stirring a few times, until the vegetables begin to soften, about 3 minutes. Lay the tomato and parsley on top of the vegetables, then add the cheese pieces (so they don't stick to the bottom), bay leaf, herbs, and peppercorns. Carefully pour in the water to just cover.

2. Close and lock the lid. Set the burner heat to high. When the cooker reaches HIGH pressure, reduce the burner heat as low as you can and still maintain HIGH pressure. Set a timer to cook for 12 minutes.

3. Remove the cooker from the heat. Open the cooker with the Natural Release method; let stand for 15 minutes. Be careful of the steam as you remove the lid.

4. Set a large colander lined with a double layer of cheesecloth over a large bowl and pour the broth through to strain. Press the vegetables and rind to extract all the liquid. Discard the solids. Cool completely. Skim the surface of any fat with an oversized spoon.

5. The broth is ready for use. It will keep in an airtight container in the refrigerator for up to 4 days or the freezer up to 4 months.

Parmesan Stock

Makes about 1 quart • Cooker: 5- to 8-quart • Time: 10 minutes at HIGH pressure

This is a restaurant version of Parmesan vegetable stock using the cheese rind as the main flavoring agent with an onion. It is simple and it is delicious, savory without tasting of vegetables. Collect Parmesan rinds as you use blocks or wedges, or ask for them from your cheesemonger. Whole Foods actually sells cheese rinds by themselves if you don't have a collection of rinds in your refrigerator. Tightly wrap the heels and ends of the cheese in plastic wrap and store in a ziptop freezer bag. They should have roughly one inch of cheese left on the rind; more than that is fine, too. Don't worry about the printing on the rind. Freeze until you have about half a pound. Please remember that only authentic Parmigiano-Reggiano cheese can be used for making Parmesan broth, as other cheeses may be inedible due to having inedible substances added to their rinds.

2 tablespoons olive oil
1 large white onion, sliced
1 cup dry white wine
1 (^{1}/2-pound) Parmigiano-Reggiano rind (about 4-inch square piece), cut into pieces, or a selection of accumulated chunks
1 bay leaf
1 teaspoon black or white peppercorns
4 cups water, or as needed

1. In a 5- to 8-quart pressure cooker, heat the oil over medium-high heat until very hot. Add the onion, reduce the heat to low, place a round of parchment paper directly on top of the slices, and sweat them for 15 minutes. The onions will cook without browning. Discard the parchment and add the wine. Increase the heat to high and bring to a lively simmer. Add the cheese rinds, bay leaf, and peppercorns. Add enough water to cover and bring to a boil.

2. Close and lock the lid. Set the burner heat to high. When the cooker reaches HIGH pressure, reduce the burner heat as low as you can and still maintain HIGH pressure. Set a timer to cook for 10 minutes.

3. Remove the pot from the heat. Open the cooker with the Natural Release method; let stand for 15 minutes. Be careful of the steam as you remove the lid.

4. Set a large colander lined with a double layer of cheesecloth over a large bowl and pour the broth through to strain. Press the vegetables and rind to extract all the liquid. Discard the solids. Cool completely. Skim the surface of any fat with an oversized spoon.

5. The broth is ready for use. It will keep in an airtight container in the refrigerator for up to 4 days and the freezer up to 3 months.

Corncob Broth

Makes about 2 quarts • Cooker: 6- to 8-quart • Time: 20 minutes at HIGH pressure

This is a very old-fashioned vegetable broth harkening back to the days when nothing got thrown away, even corncobs. This recipe takes full advantage of sweet corn when it just comes into the market. It is made by cutting the kernels off the cob and scraping the starchy pulp, then chopping the bare cobs into 2-inch lengths and pressure-cooking them with water and a little salt. This recipe makes a light broth that has the powerful, enticing aroma you get when you open a freshly steamed tamale: true corn-ability. Use in risotto, stews, chowders, and soups like you would any vegetable broth.

10 small ears fresh sweet corn
1 large white onion, quartered
2 medium carrots, cut into chunks
3 ribs celery with leaves, cut into chunks
3 cloves garlic, smashed but unpeeled
1 bay leaf
$1/2$ bunch fresh flatleaf parsley
8 to 9 cups water, or as needed
Sea salt (optional)

1. Husk the corn and remove all the silks. Cut the kernels from 8 of the cobs, then hold each one over a bowl and scrape with the dull side of a knife to squeeze out all the milk. Set the kernels aside for another use, or place in a quart freezer plastic bag and freeze. Break the scraped cobs and the remaining 2 whole ears of corn in 2- to 4-inch hunks or thirds, to fit your pressure cooker.
2. In a 6- to 8-quart pressure cooker, combine the corncobs, onion, carrots, celery, garlic, bay leaf, and parsley; toss together. Add water to just cover. Do not fill over two-thirds full.
3. Close and lock the lid. Set the burner heat to high. When the cooker reaches HIGH pressure, reduce the burner heat as low as you can and still maintain HIGH pressure. Set a timer to cook for 20 minutes.
4. Remove the pot from the heat. Open the cooker with the Natural Release method; let stand for 15 minutes. Be careful of the steam as you remove the lid.
5. Set a large colander lined with a double layer of cheesecloth over a large bowl and pour the broth through to strain. Discard the corncobs and solids. Salt to taste or leave unsalted. Cool completely.
6. The broth is ready for use. It will keep in an airtight container in the refrigerator for up to 3 days or the freezer up to 4 months.

CUTTING FRESH CORN KERNELS FROM THE COB

To keep the kernels from flying all over the place, cut them with the cob laying down on the cutting board instead of holding it upright. Also, don't cut too deep, as you can take the back of your knife (never the blade!) and scrape all the juicy corn that you've left behind, leaving the tough outer shell of the kernels. There is also a great tool called a corn zipper that we like to use.

Hauser Detox Broth

Makes about 2 quarts • Cooker: 5- to 8-quart • Time: 8 minutes at HIGH pressure

Not too many cooks remember the name Gaylord Hauser, the Hollywood health guru of the 1930s and '40s. He was popular on the lecture and social circuits pre–WWII; his name is largely forgotten today. He opened a health clinic in Chicago, wrote cookbooks that focused on whole foods as natural remedies and vitamins, and glamorized health food as part of holistic living practices. Hauser had all of Hollywood's elite drinking vegetable cocktails instead of martinis with great gusto for a while. His Look Younger Live Longer movement urged people to avoid starch, gluten, sugar, and excessive consumption of meat. When enriched white breads were introduced in the 1950s, Hauser denounced them as "devitalized." His commercial company is still in business today, selling Spike® seasoned vegetable salt, Swiss Kriss® natural laxative tea, and a boxed version of his broth. His recipes, based on the mantra "Only living foods can make a living body," are remarkably simple. The clear vegetable-based Hauser Broth, also known as Potassium Broth, was part of all his diet plans and based on one created 500 years before Christ by the Greek physician Hippocrates. Here it is, updated for the pressure cooker, perfect for detox days. If you use the shred blade on your food processor, you'll have the ingredients in the pressure cooker in a flash. Don't skip the leeks, as they are essential.

3 large carrots, or 2 carrots and 1 parsnip, cut into
    chunks or coarsely grated
2 medium leeks (white and pale green parts),
    trimmed, cut in half lengthwise, rinsed well, and
    chopped
1 medium white onion, chopped
6 ribs celery with leaves, cut into chunks
2 handfuls baby spinach or chopped leaf spinach
1 clove garlic, peeled
3 tablespoons chopped fresh flatleaf parsley leaves
    plus some stems
1 bay leaf
1 teaspoon black peppercorns
8 to 10 cups water, or as needed
Spike seasoned vegetable salt

1. In a 5- to 8-quart pressure cooker, combine the vegetables, garlic, parsley, bay leaf, and peppercorns. Add the water to cover by 2 inches. The vegetables should be thick in the water but float. If you do not have enough vegetables, the broth will be weak.
2. Close and lock the lid. Set the burner heat to high. When the cooker reaches HIGH pressure, reduce the burner heat as low as you can and still maintain HIGH pressure. Set a timer to cook for 8 minutes.
3. Remove the pot from the heat. Open the cooker with the Natural Release method; let stand for 15 minutes. Be careful of the steam as you remove the lid.
4. Set a large colander lined with a double layer of cheesecloth over a large bowl and pour the broth through to strain. Press the vegetables to extract all the liquid. Discard the solids. Taste for seasoning and add Spike vegetable seasoning salt. Cool completely.
5. The broth is ready for use. It will keep in an airtight container in the refrigerator for up to 4 days or the freezer up to 4 months.

Hauser Vegetable Cocktail: To make a hot or cold vegetable cocktail from the broth, add 1 cup tomato juice and pinch of brown sugar or honey to every quart of broth and sprinkle with Spike vegetable salt.

White Wine Mushroom Stock

Makes 1^1/$_2$ quarts • Cooker: 6- to 8-quart • Time: 16 minutes at HIGH pressure

Ever-so-delicious mushroom vegetable stock is a must for mushroom barley soup and mushroom risotto, but is also a nice rich stock for meat stews. It is considered the vegetable alternative to beef stock. It is also a very easy basic stock and can be tossed together after dinner and be ready by the time you finish cleaning up the kitchen.

^{1}/$_4$ cup light olive oil
1^1/$_2$ pounds mixed fresh white and cremini
    mushrooms, finely chopped, including stems and
    trimmings (will be a heaping 8 cups)
1 large white onion, coarsely chopped
2 cloves garlic, peeled and smashed
1 rib celery with leaves, chopped
2 medium carrots, chopped
2 cups dry white wine or flat Prosecco
^{1}/$_4$ cup dried mushrooms, such as porcini or
    shiitake (^{1}/$_4$ ounce), rinsed well
1 bay leaf
3 sprigs fresh thyme, or ^{1}/$_2$ teaspoon dried herbes
    de Provence
10 black peppercorns
^{1}/$_4$ cup reduced-sodium soy sauce or tamari
5 to 6 cups water, or as needed

1. In a 6- to 8-quart pressure cooker, heat the oil over medium-high heat until very hot. Add the mushrooms and cook, stirring a few times, until they start to brown and release their liquid, about 6 minutes. Add the onion, garlic, celery, and carrots and cook, stirring a few times, until softened, about 5 minutes. It is okay if they brown on the edges. Add the wine and bring to a boil. Add the dried mushrooms, bay leaf, thyme, and peppercorns and enough of the water to cover everything.

2. Close and lock the lid. Set the burner heat to high. When the cooker reaches HIGH pressure, reduce the burner heat as low as you can and still maintain HIGH pressure. Set a timer to cook for 16 minutes.

3. Remove the pot from the heat. Open the cooker with the Natural Release method; let stand for 15 minutes. Be careful of the steam as you remove the lid.

4. Set a large colander lined with a double layer of cheesecloth over a large bowl and pour the broth through to strain. Strain a second time, if necessary, to remove all the mushroom bits. Press on the solids to get all the liquid. Discard the solids. Stir in the soy sauce. Cool to lukewarm.

5. The stock is ready for use. It will keep in an airtight container in the refrigerator for up to 4 days or the freezer up to 3 months.

Porcini-Marsala Stock

Makes 1¹/₂ quarts • Cooker: 6- to 7-quart • Time: 20 minutes at HIGH pressure

Here is a simplified version of mushroom stock. It is earthy, woodsy, and rich-flavored. You will strain out the mushrooms and use them in other recipes such as stews and soups. This is great for risotto.

1 full cup dried porcini mushrooms (1 ounce)
1 medium white onion, halved
¹/₂ cup dry Marsala
2 bay leaves
4 sprigs fresh flatleaf parsley
¹/₄ cup reduced-sodium soy sauce or tamari
10 black peppercorns
6 to 7 cups water, or as needed
1 teaspoon sea salt, or to taste

1. In a 6- to 7-quart pressure cooker, combine the mushrooms, onion, Marsala, bay leaves, parsley, soy sauce, peppercorns, and enough water to just cover the ingredients. Bring to a boil.
2. Close and lock the lid. Set the burner heat to high. When the cooker reaches HIGH pressure, reduce the burner heat as low as you can and still maintain HIGH pressure. Set a timer to cook for 20 minutes.
3. Remove the pot from the heat. Open the cooker with the Natural Release method; let stand for 15 minutes. Be careful of the steam as you remove the lid. Let cool completely in the pot, cover with plastic wrap, and refrigerate overnight to let the flavor further develop.
4. Set a large colander lined with a double layer of cheesecloth over a large bowl and pour the broth through to strain. The mushrooms will have settled to the bottom of the pot, so you can carefully pour the stock through the sieve, then spoon out the mushrooms to refrigerate and use in another dish within the next 2 days. Discard the other solids.
5. The stock is ready for use. It will keep in an airtight container in the refrigerator for up to 3 days or the freezer up to 3 months.

DRIED MUSHROOMS

Dried mushrooms have an intense, earthy flavor and texture that enhance stocks, soups, braises, and sautés. The drying process concentrates their flavor. They must be rehydrated before use to remove particles of grit, unless you use them powdered or in soups, stews, and stocks, in which case you can rinse the mushrooms, then toss them to reconstitute in the liquid of the dish. The soaking liquid is perfect for adding to dishes. It also makes a great vegetarian/vegan friendly substitute for chicken and beef stock in recipes.

Bags of dried mushrooms are usually found in the produce section of your supermarket, though shitakes and Chinese black mushrooms might end up in the Asian food aisle. Dried mushrooms store indefinitely.

The exact timing for soaking will depend on the thickness of the caps. You can use cold water, but if you do increase the soak time to 1 to 2 hours. Strain the liquid through a fine mesh strainer (like a tea strainer) to remove any grit or impurities before using.

Chicken Stock

Makes about 1¹/₂ quarts • Cooker: 6- to 8-quart • Time: 30 minutes at HIGH pressure

If you only make one type of homemade stock, this should be it. Clear, unsalted chicken stock with no herbs is a cornerstone of good cooking and is called for in many recipes in this book. There is no canned or packaged chicken broth that can compare to this flavorful, all natural stock. Many cooks use only accumulated scrap parts (kept in the freezer); we buy a big pack of chicken wings or ask our butcher for backs (the least fat) and/or use up raw parts stored in the freezer from cutting up whole chicken like backs and necks. You can also add legs or 1 to 2 pounds of chicken feet, which is an old-fashioned way to make stock; they are available fresh in Asian specialty markets.

2 to 2¹/₂ pounds chicken backs, necks, wings, or all
    chicken wings (don't ever include the liver)
1 large yellow or white onion, cut into quarters
1 small turnip, peeled and quartered
2 ribs celery with leaves, each cut into 4 chunks
7 to 8 cups water, or as needed
2 tablespoons cider vinegar
10 sprigs fresh flatleaf parsley
6 black peppercorns

1. In a 6- to 8-quart pressure cooker, combine the chicken parts, onion, turnip, and celery. Carefully pour in the water to just cover by 2 inches. All of the chicken needs to be covered. Add the vinegar, parsley, and peppercorns.
2. Close and lock the lid. Set the burner heat to high. When the cooker reaches HIGH pressure, reduce the burner heat as low as you can and still maintain HIGH pressure. Set a timer to cook for 30 minutes.
3. Remove the pot from the heat. Open the cooker with the Natural Release method; let stand for 25 minutes. Be careful of the steam as you remove the lid.
4. Set a large colander lined with a double layer of cheesecloth over a large bowl and pour the broth through to strain. Press the vegetables to extract all the liquid. Discard the solids. Cool to lukewarm. Skim the surface of fat with an oversized spoon. Cover with plastic wrap and refrigerate overnight.
5. The next day, remove the layer of congealed fat on the surface. The stock is ready for use and will keep in an airtight container in the refrigerator up to 4 days or the freezer up to 4 months.

Parmesan Chicken Stock: Add 1 (¹/₄- to ¹/₃-pound) Parmigiano-Reggiano rind (about 3-inch square), cut into pieces, or a combination of accumulated chunks in Step 1. Do not substitute other cheeses, as the rinds are inedible.

Rich Chicken Stock: Preheat the oven to 400° F. Place the chicken pieces in a roasting pan in a single layer. Arrange the onion, turnip, and celery over the top. Roast until golden, 30 to 40 minutes. Transfer everything, including any juices in the pan, to the pressure cooker and continue with Step 1.

Poached Whole Chicken Broth

Makes about 2 quarts • Cooker: 6- to 8-quart • Time: 40 minutes at HIGH pressure

This method gently cooks the chicken while making a lovely light broth at the same time. It's the perfect way to make chicken soup, or you can use the broth and cooked chicken meat separately, however you choose. Farm-raised, free-range chickens are the tastiest and create a wonderfully gelatinous broth. The bones add body; the meat adds the flavor.

1 (3¹/₂-pound) chicken
1 large yellow or white onion, cut into quarters
1 medium carrot, cut into chunks
1 medium tomato, halved
2 ribs celery with leaves, cut into chunks
¹/₂ cup dry white wine
8 cups water, or as needed
1 sprig fresh flatleaf parsley
1 sprig fresh thyme (optional)
¹/₂ teaspoon black or white peppercorns
About 1 tablespoon grated peeled fresh ginger
Sea salt

1. Rinse the chicken and remove the packet of inner parts; discard or save for another use. Remove the skin and cut off any extra fatty parts. Place the chicken breast side up in a 6- to 8-quart pressure cooker. Add the onion, carrot, tomato, and celery. Pour in the wine, then enough of the water to just come up to the breast; you want the breast above the liquid so that it can steam. Add the parsley, thyme, and ginger.
2. Close and lock the lid. Set the burner heat to high. When the cooker reaches HIGH pressure, reduce the burner heat as low as you can and still maintain HIGH pressure. Set a timer to cook for 40 minutes.
3. Remove the pot from the heat. Open the cooker with the Natural Release method; let stand for 20 minutes. Be careful of the steam as you remove the lid.
4. Transfer the chicken with a slotted spoon to a plate. Let cool, then remove the meat from the carcass. Discard the bones and gristle. Reserve the meat for soup, salad, curries, or another purpose (it will keep in the fridge for 2 days and the freezer up to 6 months). Set a large colander lined with a double layer of cheesecloth over a large bowl and pour the broth through to strain. Press the vegetables to extract all the liquid. Discard the solids. Cool the broth to lukewarm. Skim the surface of any fat with an oversized spoon. Season to taste with salt. Cover with plastic wrap and refrigerate overnight.
5. The next day, remove the layer of congealed fat on the surface. The stock is ready for use and will keep in an airtight container in the refrigerator 2 to 3 days or the freezer up to 6 months.

Mexican Chicken Broth: Add 3 quartered or chopped white or yellow onions and 4 chopped cloves garlic in Step 1 in place of the vegetables, wine, thyme, and ginger. Add 1 or 2 small jalapeño peppers, left whole. Use the peppercorns and substitute cilantro for the parsley. If you have some tomato trimmings or a corncob, you can toss them in. This is a very simple, gentle broth.

Asian Chicken Stock

Makes about 2¹/₂ quarts • Cooker: 6- to 8-quart • Time: 30 minutes at HIGH pressure

This is so delicious. Use it to drink hot with some miso stirred in, as a base for soups or jook, or in an Asian-style risotto. If you use drumsticks and thighs, you will have plenty of meat to make a pot pie, cold salad, or casserole for dinner. We always marvel at cooks who get the extra-rich-tasting broths. The secret? Stirring in some Better Than Bouillon stock concentrate at the end.

3 pounds chicken drumsticks, bone-in thighs, or wings, or combination

1 medium yellow or white onion, cut into wedges

10 cloves garlic, peeled and crushed

1 bunch green onions, trimmed and cut into 2-inch pieces

2 stalks lemongrass (inner white parts only), cut into 3 pieces each

12 coin-sized slices fresh ginger, peeled

10 cups water, or as needed

1 to 2 tablespoons organic chicken Better Than Bouillon

1. In a 6- to 8-quart pressure cooker, combine the chicken parts, onion, garlic, scallions, lemongrass, and ginger. Carefully pour in the water to just cover by 2 inches. The chicken needs to be entirely covered.

2. Close and lock the lid. Set the burner heat to high. When the cooker reaches HIGH pressure, reduce the burner heat as low as you can and still maintain HIGH pressure. Set a timer to cook for 30 minutes.

3. Remove the pot from the heat. Open the cooker with the Natural Release method; let stand for 15 minutes. Be careful of the steam as you remove the lid.

4. Set a large colander lined with a double layer of cheesecloth over a large bowl and pour the broth through to strain. Transfer the chicken pieces to a plate, let cool, and remove the meat from the bones (it will keep in the fridge for 2 days and the freezer up to 6 months). Discard the skin and bones. Press the vegetables to extract all the liquid, then discard the solids. Stir the Better Than Bouillon into the hot broth. Cool the broth to lukewarm. Skim the surface of fat with an oversized spoon. Cover with plastic wrap and refrigerate overnight.

5. The next day, remove the layer of congealed fat on the surface. The stock is ready for use and will keep in an airtight container in the refrigerator up to 4 days or the freezer up to 4 months.

Rotisserie Chicken Stock

Makes about 2 quarts • Cooker: 6- to 8-quart • Time: 30 minutes at HIGH pressure

Rotisserie chickens have boomed in popularity over the last decade. The convenience is undeniable—you can put a roast chicken dinner on the table in minutes, or pull off the meat to use in sandwiches or other dishes. After the meal, you are usually left with the carcass, which will have some meat on it, as well as a pile of skin and a good amount of juice. You can toss it out (oh no!), or better yet, toss it directly into the pressure cooker. The roasted flavor is desired in this stock. Cook on high pressure for half an hour while you do the dishes and you will have a rather cloudy, often slightly salty, stock. Refrigerate it and skim the fat. We would never serve this on its own, but as a base for soups, braises, or chili, it's an excellent alternative to canned. If you freeze it, be sure to label it clearly so you don't mistake it for your clear chicken stock.

1 (3-pound) roast chicken carcass, broken up to fit your pot
1 medium yellow or white onion, cut into quarters, or 2 leeks (white and green parts), trimmed, cut in half lengthwise, rinsed well, and coarsely chopped
3 ribs celery with leaves, cut into 4-inch chunks
2 medium carrots, cut into 2-inch chunks
1 medium parsnip, peeled and cut into 2-inch chunks
2 cloves garlic, peeled
8 cups water, or as needed
2 tablespoons cider vinegar
8 sprigs fresh flatleaf parsley or cilantro
2 sprigs fresh dill or thyme
6 black peppercorns

1. In a 6- to 8-quart pressure cooker, combine the chicken carcass, onion, celery, carrots, parsnip, and garlic. Carefully pour in the water to just cover by 2 inches. The chicken needs to be entirely covered. Add the vinegar, herbs, and peppercorns.
2. Close and lock the lid. Set the burner heat to high. When the cooker reaches HIGH pressure, reduce the burner heat as low as you can and still maintain HIGH pressure. Set a timer to cook for 30 minutes.
3. Remove the pot from the heat. Open the cooker with the Natural Release method; let stand for 15 minutes. Be careful of the steam as you remove the lid.
4. Set a large colander lined with a double layer of cheesecloth over a large bowl and pour the broth through to strain. Press the vegetables to extract all the liquid. Discard the solids. Cool completely. Skim the surface of fat with an oversized spoon. Cover with plastic wrap and refrigerate overnight.
5. The next day, remove the layer of congealed fat on the surface. The stock is ready for use and will keep in an airtight container in the refrigerator up to 4 days and the freezer up to 6 months.

Roast Duck Stock: Leftover carcass after a roast duck dinner? Substitute 2 duck carcasses for the chicken carcass in Step 1 and proceed with the recipe. Use parsley, not cilantro, especially the stems, as they have more flavor than the leaves.

Thanksgiving Turkey Stock

Makes about 2 quarts • Cooker: 6- to 8-quart • Time: 45 minutes at HIGH pressure

Next to chicken stock, turkey stock is most commonly made in the home kitchen. The broth is ever so delicious and homemade turkey soup is such a treat. When you break up the carcass, wear rubber gloves, as it can be slippery, or wrap the carcass in a damp kitchen towel and pound it with a meat mallet to break it into pieces that will fit in the cooker.

1 roast turkey carcass with some meat left on, including the wings
1 medium yellow or white onion, quartered
1 leek (white and green parts), trimmed, cut in half lengthwise, rinsed well, and chopped
1 medium carrot, cut into chunks
2 ribs celery with leaves, cut into chunks
8 to 10 cups water, or as needed
2 tablespoons cider vinegar
$^1/_2$ bunch fresh flatleaf parsley or cilantro
1 bay leaf
1 tablespoon black peppercorns
1 to 2 tablespoons organic chicken Better Than Bouillon (optional)
1 teaspoon sea salt

1. Remove the excess skin and fat from the turkey carcass but leave any browned, crispy pieces for additional flavor. To help fit the carcass into a pot, first cut it in half with a heavy knife or cleaver, breaking it across the backbone along the ribs. Break into 4 to 6 pieces, to fit the pot.

2. In a 6- to 8-quart pressure cooker, combine the turkey carcass, onion, leek, carrot, and celery. Carefully pour in the water and vinegar to just cover by 2 inches. Add the parsley, bay leaf, and peppercorns. Stir in the Better Than Bouillon.

3. Close and lock the lid. Set the burner heat to high. When the cooker reaches HIGH pressure, reduce the burner heat as low as you can and still maintain HIGH pressure. Set a timer to cook for 45 minutes.

4. Remove the pot from the heat. Open the cooker with the Natural Release method; let stand for 15 minutes. Be careful of the steam as you remove the lid.

5. Set a large colander lined with a double layer of cheesecloth over a large bowl and pour the broth through to strain. Press the vegetables to extract all the liquid. Pick any meat off the bones (save separately) and discard the bones and other solids (the nutrition will be cooked out of the vegetables). Cool completely. Skim the surface of fat with an oversized spoon. Stir in the salt. Cover with plastic wrap and refrigerate overnight.

6. The next day, remove the layer of congealed fat on the surface. The stock is ready for use and will keep in an airtight container in the refrigerator up to 3 days or the freezer up to 6 months.

Beth's Turkey Stock

Makes about 2 quarts • Cooker: 6- to 8-quart • Time: 30 minutes at HIGH pressure

We love turkey stock but don't always have that big ol' carcass to make it. So here is the turkey stock for the rest of the year.

2 turkey drumsticks
1 turkey thigh
2 or 3 turkey wings (whatever comes in the package)
2 large white onions, quartered
2 medium carrots, cut into chunks
4 ribs celery with leaves, cut into chunks
2 tablespoons cider vinegar
8 to 10 cups water, or as needed
$^1/_2$ bunch fresh flatleaf parsley or cilantro
2 bay leaves
1 tablespoon black peppercorns
1 teaspoon sea salt

1. Preheat the oven to 425° F. Place the turkey parts and onions in a roasting pan and roast until the skin browns, about 35 minutes. You can make stock with raw turkey, but this short roasting really enhances the flavor.

2. In a 6- to 8-quart pressure cooker, combine the turkey, onions, carrots, and celery. Carefully pour in the vinegar and water to just cover by 2 inches. Add the parsley, bay leaves, and peppercorns, and salt.

3. Close and lock the lid. Set the burner heat to high. When the cooker reaches HIGH pressure, reduce the burner heat as low as you can and still maintain HIGH pressure. Set a timer to cook for 30 minutes.

4. Remove the pot from the heat. Open the cooker with the Natural Release method; let stand for 15 minutes. Be careful of the steam as you remove the lid.

5. Set a large colander lined with a double layer of cheesecloth over a large bowl and pour the broth through to strain. Discard the solids (the nutrition will be cooked out of the vegetables). Cool completely. Skim the surface of fat with an oversized spoon. Cover with plastic wrap and refrigerate overnight.

6. The next day, remove the layer of congealed fat on the surface. The stock is ready for use and will keep in an airtight container in the refrigerator up to 3 days or the freezer up to 6 months.

Turkey Giblet Stock

Makes about 1 quart • Cooker: 5- to 7-quart • Time: 25 minutes at HIGH pressure

Remember on holidays when the big bird was in the oven, and on the stovetop a saucepan with water, giblets, and neck was simmering away? Well, here it is. Use it to make gravy or moisten the stuffing; it can also be used in soups and sauces.

Giblets and neck from 1 turkey, rinsed
1 small yellow or white onion, chopped
1 carrot, cut into chunks
1 rib celery with leaves, cut in half
4 cups water, or as needed
1 bay leaf
4 black peppercorns

1. In a 5- to 7-quart pressure cooker, combine the turkey parts, onion, carrot, and celery. Carefully pour in the water to just cover by 2 inches. The turkey needs to be entirely covered. Add the bay leaf and peppercorns.
2. Close and lock the lid. Set the burner heat to high. When the cooker reaches HIGH pressure, reduce the burner heat as low as you can and still maintain HIGH pressure. Set a timer to cook for 25 minutes.
3. Remove the pot from the heat. Open the cooker with the Natural Release method; let stand for 15 minutes. Be careful of the steam as you remove the lid.
4. Set a large colander lined with a double layer of cheesecloth over a large bowl and pour the broth through to strain. Press the vegetables to extract all the liquid. Discard the solids. You can remove the meat from the neck and chop it along with the giblets to add to the gravy or a soup. Cool completely. Skim the surface of fat with an oversized spoon. Usually giblet stock is used the same day it is made but you can store it if you like. Cover with plastic wrap and refrigerate overnight.
5. The next day, remove the layer of congealed fat on the surface. The stock is ready for use and will keep in an airtight container up to 2 days or in the freezer up to 3 months.

Chicken Giblet Stock: Use the giblets and necks from 2 chickens, rinsed, and proceed as directed in the recipe.

Fresh Fish Stock

Makes 1¹/₂ quarts • Cooker: 5- to 7-quart • Time: 10 minutes at HIGH pressure

This is an all-purpose fish stock, and it's very fast to make; only minutes of simmering are needed to get a nicely flavored stock. Be sure to only use the bones of mild white fish, not salmon or rockfish, or else the stock will be too strong. Most fishmongers will give you the bones for free. This recipe is adapted from one on the Magefesa pressure cooker website.

2 pounds meaty halibut, cod, or sea bass bones, and/or a fish head
1 large white onion, thinly sliced
1 large leek (white and light green parts), trimmed, cut in half lengthwise, rinsed well, and thinly sliced across
2 medium carrots, cut into chunks
4 sprigs fresh flatleaf parsley
5 black peppercorns
6 cups water, or as needed
1 tablespoon light olive oil

1. If using, rinse the fish head and remove the gills, if necessary, leaving the gill plates intact. Using a sharp knife, split the head in half lengthwise. Place the bones and head in a 5- to 7-quart pressure cooker. Add the onion, leek, carrots, parsley, and peppercorns. Add the water or as much as is needed so that the bones and head are completely submerged. Bring to a boil and skim off the foam with a large spoon. Drizzle with the oil.
2. Close and lock the lid. Set the burner heat to high. When the cooker reaches HIGH pressure, reduce the burner heat as low as you can and still maintain HIGH pressure. Set a timer to cook for 10 minutes.
3. Remove the pot from the heat. Open the cooker with the Natural Release method; let stand for 15 minutes. Be careful of the steam as you remove the lid.
4. Set a large colander lined with a double layer of cheesecloth over a large bowl and pour the broth through to strain. DO NOT press on the solids. Discard the solids. Cool completely. Cover with plastic wrap and refrigerate overnight.
5. The next day, skim any fat from the surface. The stock is ready for use and will keep in an airtight container in the refrigerator up to 2 days or the freezer up to 2 months.

Salmon Stock

Makes 1¹/₂ quarts • Cooker: 5- to 8-quart • Time: 10 minutes at HIGH pressure

The bones and head of salmon make a lovely stock, beautifully pale peach in color. Since salmon is an oily fish, it is not good to use in place of regular mild fish stock. Save this for special dishes where you want a more assertive flavor base. Use for poaching salmon fillets, as a base for a chowder, or in bouillabaisse. If you don't have friends who fish, ask your fishmonger to save you a salmon head that has the gills removed. Be careful about the cook time: Fish stocks cook very quickly and overcooking makes them bitter. Fish stock is best used the day it is made, or else frozen.

1 salmon head (2 to 2¹/₂ pounds) and bones
   (1 pound)
1 medium white or yellow onion, quartered
2 cloves garlic, peeled
1 medium carrot, cut into 2-inch chunks
1 bay leaf
2 sprigs fresh thyme
5 black peppercorns
1 cup light-flavored dry white wine (not an oaked
   Chardonnay, for instance)
5 cups water or vegetable broth, or as needed
1 tablespoon light olive oil

1. Rinse the salmon head and bones in cold water. Remove the gills from the head, if necessary, leaving the gill plates intact. Using a sharp knife, split the head in half lengthwise. Place the head and bones in a 5- to 8-quart pressure cooker. Add the onion, garlic, carrot, bay leaf, thyme, and peppercorns. Add the wine and enough water so that the bones and fish head are completely submerged. Bring to a boil and skim off the foam with a large spoon. Drizzle with the oil.

2. Close and lock the lid. Set the burner heat to high. When the cooker reaches HIGH pressure, reduce the burner heat as low as you can and still maintain HIGH pressure. Set a timer to cook for 10 minutes.

3. Remove the pot from the heat. Open the cooker with the Natural Release method; let stand for 15 minutes. Be careful of the steam as you remove the lid.

4. Set a large colander lined with a double layer of cheesecloth over a large bowl and pour the broth through to strain. DO NOT press on the solids. Discard the solids. Cool completely. Cover with plastic wrap and refrigerate overnight.

5. The next day, skim any fat from the surface. The stock is ready for use and will keep in an airtight container in the refrigerator up to 2 days or the freezer up to 2 months.

Shrimp Stock

Makes about 1 quart • Cooker: 6- to 8-quart • Time: 12 minutes at HIGH pressure

Shrimp shells have a ton of flavor and make a lovely all-purpose fish stock. You'll need a pound of shells to produce about a pint of stock, you're not going to have enough shells for stock every time you cook shrimp. What you're going to do is save the shells each time, putting them in a ziptop plastic bag and tossing them in the freezer. Over time, you'll accumulate enough shells to make a good amount of delicious stock. Use shrimp stock in risotto, seafood gumbo, chowder, paella, or any kind of fish soup, like *zuppa del pescatore,* cioppino, or bouillabaisse, for a delicious flavor boost. You can halve this recipe and make a pint of shrimp stock.

2 pounds shrimp shells and/or heads and tails
1 tablespoon light olive oil
1 cup coarsely chopped white onions
$^1/_2$ cup coarsely chopped celery
$^1/_2$ cup coarsely chopped carrots
$^1/_2$ bunch fresh flatleaf parsley
1 bay leaf
$^1/_2$ teaspoon black peppercorns
$^1/_2$ teaspoon dried thyme
$5^1/_2$ cups water, or as needed
1 teaspoon sea salt

1. Rinse the shrimp shells and heads in a large colander under cold running water.
2. In a 6- to 8-quart pressure cooker, heat the oil over medium-high heat until very hot. Add the onions, celery, and carrot and cook, stirring a few times, until softened, about 5 minutes. Stir in the shrimp shells. When the shells turn pink, after 30 to 60 seconds, add the parsley, bay leaf, salt, peppercorns, and thyme. Add just enough water so that everything is submerged. Bring to a boil and skim off the foam with a large spoon.
3. Close and lock the lid. Set the burner heat to high. When the cooker reaches HIGH pressure, reduce the burner heat as low as you can and still maintain HIGH pressure. Set a timer to cook for 12 minutes.
4. Remove the pot from the heat. Open the cooker with the Natural Release method; let stand for 15 minutes. Be careful of the steam as you remove the lid.
5. Set a large colander lined with a double layer of cheesecloth over a large bowl and pour the broth through to strain. Discard the solids. Stir in the salt. Cool completely.
6. Cover with plastic wrap and refrigerate overnight. The stock is ready for use and will keep in an airtight container in the refrigerator up to 3 days or the freezer up to 2 months.

Crab Shell Stock

Makes about 1 1/2 quarts • Cooker: 6- to 8-quart • Time: 12 minutes at HIGH pressure

Christmas Eve in California means a meal of cracked Dungeness crab since the winter holiday season is smack-dab in the middle of crab season. What to do with the pile of leftover shells? Crab stock (and you can add the leftover white wine from dinner too). It is ultra simple and a great addition to your stock repertoire for use in soups, chowders, and bisques, as a poaching liquid for fish, and on seafood risottos.

2 tablespoons light olive oil
3 pounds shells from cooked Dungeness crab (1 to 2 whole crabs)
2 leeks (white and light green parts), trimmed, cut in half lengthwise, rinsed well, and thinly sliced across
3 ribs celery with leaves, cut into pieces
1 cup chopped fennel bulb
1/2 cup coarsely chopped carrot
2 cups dry white wine
1/2 bunch fresh flatleaf parsley
2 long strips lemon zest
1 teaspoon black peppercorns
4 cups water, or as needed

1. In a 6- to 8-quart pressure cooker, heat the oil over medium-high heat until very hot. Add the shells and cook, stirring a few times, until nice and hot, about 5 minutes. Add the leeks, celery, fennel, and carrot and cook, stirring occasionally, until they are softened, about 5 minutes. Add the wine and bring to a boil. Add the parsley, lemon zest, peppercorns, and enough of the water so everything is just submerged. Bring to a boil and skim off the foam with a large spoon.

2. Close and lock the lid. Set the burner heat to high. When the cooker reaches HIGH pressure, reduce the burner heat as low as you can and still maintain HIGH pressure. Set a timer to cook for 12 minutes.

3. Remove the pot from the heat. Open the cooker with the Natural Release method; let stand for 15 minutes. Be careful of the steam as you remove the lid.

4. Set a large colander lined with a double layer of cheesecloth over a large bowl and pour the broth through to strain. Discard the solids. Cool to lukewarm.

5. Cover with plastic wrap and refrigerate overnight. The stock is ready for use and will keep in an airtight container in the refrigerator up to 3 days or the freezer up to 3 months.

Ham Stock

Makes about 2 quarts • Cooker: 6- to 8-quart • Time: 40 minutes at HIGH pressure

While ham stock is a lesser known brew than chicken or beef, Spanish or Latin cuisines utilize it in bean soups, pork stews, baked beans, and braised cabbage and greens of all types. Ham stock will become one of your culinary passions once you taste it. It is earthy, rich, and intensely flavored, its exact flavor depending on the type of ham and aromatics you use. Never add salt to a ham stock.

1 meaty ham bone from a leftover half ham, plus
    scraps left from trimming
2 medium white onions, cut into quarters
2 medium carrots, cut into chunks
2 ribs celery with leaves, cut into chunks
2 cloves garlic, peeled
6 sprigs fresh flatleaf parsley
1 bay leaf
1 teaspoon black peppercorns
8 to 10 cups water, or as needed
2 tablespoons cider vinegar

1. In a 6- to 8-quart pressure cooker, combine the ham bone, onions, carrots, and celery. Tuck in the garlic, parsley, and bay leaf, and add the peppercorns. Carefully pour in the water to just cover by 2 inches. Add the vinegar. Do not fill the pressure cooker pot more than two-thirds full. The bone might be sticking up out of the water; this is okay. Bring to a boil, then skim off the foam with a large spoon.

2. Close and lock the lid. Set the burner heat to high. When the cooker reaches HIGH pressure, reduce the burner heat as low as you can and still maintain HIGH pressure. Set a timer to cook for 40 minutes.

3. Remove the pot from the heat. Open the cooker with the Natural Release method; let stand for 20 minutes. Be careful of the steam as you remove the lid.

4. Set a large colander lined with a double layer of cheesecloth over a large bowl. Remove the bone and pour the broth through to strain. Press on the vegetables to extract all the liquid. Discard the solids. Pick any meat off the bone, shred into bite-size pieces, and reserve. Discard the bone. Cool the broth completely. Skim the surface of fat. Cover with plastic wrap and refrigerate overnight.

5. The next day, remove the layer of congealed fat on the surface. The stock is ready for use and will keep in an airtight container in the refrigerator up to 4 days or the freezer up to 6 months.

Beef Bone Stock (a.k.a. White Beef Stock)

Makes 2 quarts • Cooker: 6- to 8-quart • Time: 60 minutes at HIGH pressure

This is your basic brown stock. Just put everything in the pot and let it cook away. Try to use several types of bones (you can toss in some beef ribs as well), not more than half of them marrow bones. These can be hard to find in a supermarket meat department but you can get them from a butcher pretty cheaply. Lucky for us cooks, butcher shops are now coming back into vogue. The addition of vinegar helps to draw the minerals out of the bones. Some cooks use fish sauce, made from anchovies, which is considered a powerhouse of minerals on its own, instead of salt. You won't taste the anchovies—promise. Normally a bone stock would take three to four hours, the maximum time to get all the flavors out of the bones. In the pressure cooker you have deeply flavored stock in just one hour. Delicious, nourishing bone broth is quite the rage as a health drink but it has been for as long as it has been made.

2 to 3 pounds cross-cut meaty beef marrow bones (ask the butcher to cut into 2-inch pieces for you on the bandsaw), knuckle bones, and shin bones, cracked (a mixture is best)
1 large white or yellow onion, cut into 8 wedges, or 2 medium leeks (white and part of green), rinsed well, trimmed, and cut in half crosswise
1 large carrot, cut into 2-inch pieces
2 ribs celery with leaves, cut into 2-inch pieces
6 black peppercorns
1 sprig fresh thyme
4 sprigs fresh flatleaf parsley
8 cups water, or as needed
1 tablespoon cider vinegar
1 tablespoon sea salt or 2 tablespoons Asian fish sauce

1. In a 6- to 8-quart pressure cooker, combine the bones, onion, carrot, celery, peppercorns, and herbs. Add enough of the water to just cover all the ingredients. Add the vinegar. Bring to a boil and skim off the foam with a large spoon.

2. Close and lock the lid. Set the burner heat to high. When the cooker reaches HIGH pressure, reduce the burner heat as low as you can and still maintain HIGH pressure. Set a timer to cook for 60 minutes.

3. Remove the pot from the heat. Open the cooker with the Natural Release method; let stand for 25 minutes. Be careful of the steam as you remove the lid.

4. Set a large colander lined with a double layer of cheesecloth over a large bowl and pour the stock through to strain. Press on the solids to extract all the liquid. Discard the solids. Cool to lukewarm. Skim the surface of fat. Stir in the salt. Cover with plastic wrap and refrigerate overnight.

5. The next day, remove the layer of congealed fat on the surface. The stock is ready for use and will keep in an airtight container in the refrigerator up to 5 days or the freezer up to 3 months.

Brown Beef Broth

Makes 2 quarts • Cooker: 6- to 8-quart • Time: 60 minutes at HIGH pressure

When Beth went to visit at the home of the late food writer Marion Cunningham in the East Bay of San Francisco, Marion served a rich homemade beef broth and homemade bread and butter for lunch. It was a memorable lunch, even in its simplicity. Once you taste homemade beef stock, you will never buy another can of commercial beef broth again. Its deep color and flavor are created by roasting the bones and some of the vegetables before placing them in the pot. This is the stock you use as a base for a myriad of soups and stews and brown sauces. Or salt it to taste, add some rice or a little pasta like pastina or orzo, and a dash of Madeira for a prelude to dinner or as a restorative when you're feeling under the weather.

2 tablespoons tomato paste
2 to 2^1/$_2$ pounds cross-cut meaty beef marrow
    bones (ask the butcher to cut into 2-inch pieces
    for you on the bandsaw) or small oxtail pieces
1 large carrot, cut into 2-inch chunks
1 large white or yellow onion, cut into 8 wedges
1 to 1^1/$_2$ pounds meaty beef shanks, 1 inch thick
2 ribs celery with leaves, cut into 2-inch chunks
1 tablespoon black peppercorns
2 bay leaves
^{1}/$_4$ bunch fresh flatleaf parsley
1 cup red or white wine (optional)
8 cups water, or as needed

1. Preheat the oven to 425° F. Place the bones (not the shanks) in a large shallow roasting pan. Brush the tomato paste evenly over them. Add the carrot and onion to pan; lightly coat with olive oil cooking spray. Roast for 45 minutes.
2. In a 6- to 8-quart pressure cooker, combine the roasted bones and vegetables, shanks, celery, peppercorns, bay leaves, and parsley. Add the wine if using. Add enough of the water to just cover the ingredients. Bring to a boil and skim off the foam with a large spoon.
3. Close and lock the lid. Set the burner heat to high. When the cooker reaches HIGH pressure, reduce the burner heat as low as you can and still maintain HIGH pressure. Set a timer to cook for 60 minutes.
4. Remove the pot from the heat. Open the cooker with the Natural Release method; let stand for 20 minutes. Be careful of the steam as you remove the lid.
5. Set a large colander lined with a double layer of cheesecloth over a large bowl and pour the stock through to strain. Press on the solids to extract all the liquid. Discard the solids. Cool to lukewarm. Skim the surface of fat with an oversized spoon. Cover with plastic wrap and refrigerate overnight.
6. The next day, remove the layer of congealed fat on the surface. The stock is ready for use and will keep in an airtight container in the refrigerator up to 3 days or the freezer up to 6 months.

Brown Veal Stock: Substitute veal bones and shanks for the beef. Proceed with the recipe. This is a really yummy stock for soups and veal stews. And very French.

White Stock

Makes about 2 quarts • Cooker: 6- to 8-quart • Time: 45 minutes at HIGH pressure

This version of white stock, also known as *fond de veau* or foundation veal stock, is made with veal and chicken bones, making a much more light-colored and delicately flavored stock than one made with beef. It is the savory delight of the country kitchen (and restaurant kitchens in the know) and can be used in place of chicken stock. It makes a marvelous vegetable soup. We buy chicken breasts for dinner, debone them, and keep the raw bones in plastic freezer bags until we are ready to make the stock. This is a recipe adapted for the pressure cooker from the 1957 edition of *The Gourmet Cookbook,* compiled by the original publisher and creator of the magazine devoted to good eating, Earle R. MacAusland. You will need to ask a butcher for the veal knuckles.

1 medium yellow or white onion, cut into quarters
1 leek (white and green parts), trimmed, cut in half lengthwise, rinsed well, and chopped
1 medium carrot, cut into chunks
3 ribs celery with leaves, roughly chopped
3 tablespoons butter
2 veal knuckles
4 to 6 raw chicken half-breast bones (leftover from deboning)
4 sprigs fresh flatleaf parsley
6 black peppercorns
2 tablespoons cider vinegar
8 cups water, or as needed

1. In a 6- to 8-quart pressure cooker, combine the onion, leek, carrot, and celery. Add the butter and heat the pot to medium-high. Cook the vegetables, stirring a few times, until softened, about 5 minutes. Add the veal knuckles, chicken bones, parsley, peppercorns, and vinegar. Add enough of the water to cover the ingredients by 2 inches.

2. Close and lock the lid. Set the burner heat to high. When the cooker reaches HIGH pressure, reduce the burner heat as low as you can and still maintain HIGH pressure. Set a timer to cook for 45 minutes.

3. Remove the pot from the heat. Open the cooker with the Natural Release method; let stand for 15 minutes. Be careful of the steam as you remove the lid.

4. Set a large colander lined with a double layer of cheesecloth over a large bowl and pour the stock through to strain. Press on the vegetables to extract all the liquid. Discard the solids. Cool to lukewarm. Skim the surface of fat with an oversized spoon. Cover with plastic wrap and refrigerate overnight.

5. The next day, remove the layer of congealed fat on the surface. The stock is ready for use and will keep in an airtight container in the refrigerator up to 3 days or the freezer up to 3 months.

Pho with Beef

Serves 4 • Cooker: 6- to 8-quart • Time: 60 minutes at HIGH pressure

Pho is a wildly popular Vietnamese noodle soup and must be made with homemade stock or it will simply be a ghost of what it should taste like. The charring of the ginger and onion as well as the toasting of the spices are important, so don't leave those steps out. Usually the broth has to simmer for hours—in the pressure cooker, one hour does the trick.

Asian markets carry a commercial blend of the pho spices or you can mix your own. Black cardamom is not the same as white cardamom. The pods are dried whole over open flames and have a savory, smoky quality with a light camphorlike aroma. It is native to the Himalayas and used in the Indian garam masala spice blend, dal soups, and stews. Alternately, you can simplify the spices and use only star anise, cloves, and cinnamon. Star anise creates the aroma that says "pho."

The meat must be very thinly sliced. For best results, put the meat in the freezer 15 minutes prior to slicing. You can also ask the butcher to slice it; just be sure to use the meat the same day. Fresh rice noodles contain gluten, so if you are gluten free, use dried *banh pho* noodles instead, which are made of rice flour and tapioca starch.

Sriracha is a traditional accompaniment to pho. It's a sweet-hot sauce made from sun-ripened chili peppers, vinegar, garlic, sugar, and salt. You can substitute Tabasco sauce or another favorite hot sauce if you like.

This recipe is loosely adapted for the pressure cooker from one in *Into the Vietnamese Kitchen* (Ten Speed Press, 2006) by our friend Andrea Nguyen, our go-to book for Vietnamese soul food cooking. Andrea notes that Vietnamese cooks don't make pho in the pressure cooker—one couldn't buy a pressure cooker big enough, for one thing—but she cheerfully considered our ideas for a "shortcut" version. The traditional color for pho broth is taupe. Because we leave in the onion skins, ours is a bit darker. If you like it darker still, by all means add the Better than Bouillon, which will further deepen the flavor. We were delighted to find a meat case piled high with ready-to-go soup bones at our local Asian supermarket. If you wish to use the cooked chuck, brisket, or short ribs in the soup, as a Viet cook would, set a timer for 30 minutes, open the pressure cooker using the Quick Release method, and remove the meat with tongs to a bowl of cold water. Relock the pressure cooker, bring back up to HIGH pressure, and cook the broth another 30 minutes. Remove the meat from the water after 10 minutes (Andrea notes that the soak keeps the meat from turning dark) and refrigerate it until serving time. Slice it into thin slices across the grain and add it to the soup bowls with the noodles.

PHO

In this country and Vietnam, there are restaurants devoted to all manner of pho, including beef *(phở bò),* chicken *(phở gà),* and vegetarian *(phở chay),* a Buddhist variation with cubed tofu or tempeh. It is a relatively new soup, showing up in the 1920s in North Vietnam and as a street food in South Vietnam in the 1950s. Vietnam was a French colony until it declared its independence after World War II, and the word pho may derive from the French *pot-au-feu.* Pho came to America with the returning GIs and refugees after the Vietnam War in the 1970s. The fun of pho is customizing your bowl with the fresh herbs, bean sprouts, chiles, and sauces that come alongside your steaming bowl of broth, noodles, and the thinly sliced beef, chicken, or other protein. If you prefer your pho with chicken, use Poached Whole Chicken Broth (page 32) instead of the pho stock used here. Pho is pronounced as "fun" without the "n."

PHO STOCK:

3 pounds cross-cut meaty beef marrow bones (ask the butcher to cut into 2-inch pieces, knuckle bones, and shin bones, cracked (a mixture is best)

1 pound boneless chuck, brisket, or beef short ribs

1 package Vietnamese pho spices (or 2 cinnamon sticks, 2 teaspoons coriander seeds, 1 teaspoon fennel seeds, 3 star anise pods, 3 cloves, and 1 black cardamom pod) OR 3 star anise pods, 1 cinnamon stick, and 4 cloves

2 tablespoons olive oil

1 medium white onion, cut in half

1 (4- to 5-inch) knob fresh ginger, sliced

8 cups water

2^{1}/$_{2}$ tablespoons Asian fish sauce or soy sauce

1 teaspoon brown sugar

1 to 2 tablespoons organic beef Better Than Bouillon (optional) or salt to taste

PHO BOWLS:

12 ounces extra thin (^{1}/$_{16}$- to ^{1}/$_{4}$-inch-wide) fresh rice noodles (*bánh pho tuoi*; also labeled Pad Thai noodles), dried *bánh pho* rice sticks, linguine, or fettuccine

^{1}/$_{2}$ pound flank steak, London broil, or eye of round steak, sliced as thin as possible, across the grain

FOR SERVING:

2 limes, cut into wedges

Sprigs fresh cilantro, basil (preferably Thai basil), and mint

1 bunch green onions (white part and some of the green), thinly sliced

2 jalapeño peppers, thinly sliced

2 big handfuls mung bean sprouts

1 bunch watercress

Hoisin sauce

Sriracha hot chili sauce

1. Bring a large stockpot with water to a rolling boil over high heat. Add the beef bones and boil vigorously for 10 minutes.

2. In the meantime, heat a heavy skillet on medium-low heat. Add the pho spices and toast, stirring, until fragrant, about 2 minutes. Dump the spices into a 6- to 8-quart pressure cooker. Return the skillet to medium-high heat and add 1 to 2 tablespoons of oil. When the oil is hot, add the onion halves and ginger slices. Cook until the ginger is browned on both sides and the onion halves are browned and softened. Add the

ginger and the onion to the pressure cooker pot. Add the short ribs to the skillet and brown on all sides. Add to the pot.

3. When the bones have been boiled, drain, discarding the water, and rinse bones briefly to clean them. Add the bones to the pressure cooker. Fill with fresh water to just cover; add the fish sauce and sugar.

4. Close and lock the lid. Set the burner heat to high. When the cooker reaches HIGH pressure, reduce the burner heat as low as you can and still maintain HIGH pressure. Set a timer to cook for 60 minutes.

5. Remove the pot from the heat. Open the cooker with the Natural Release method; let stand for 20 minutes. Be careful of the steam as you remove the lid.

6. Set a large colander lined with a double layer of cheesecloth over a large bowl and pour the broth through to strain. Press on the solids to extract all the liquid. Discard the solids. Stir in the Better Than Bouillon, if using, for a richer beef flavor. Taste and season with salt or additional fish sauce, if needed. The pho broth is ready. If using right away, keep at a simmer or cool to lukewarm, cover, and refrigerate overnight or up to 5 days (or freeze up to 3 months).

7. When you are ready to eat, bring a pot of water to a boil. The fresh rice noodles come folded over in coils and can stick mercilessly. If yours are stuck together, place the block of noodles on a microwave-safe plate and microwave on HIGH for 90 seconds, then at 15-second intervals until you can separate the outer layer, then, after a few more bursts, easily separate the noodles. It will take about 2^{1}/$_{2}$ to 3 minutes. Cut in half if desired. Add the fresh noodles to the boiling water and boil just to soften to al dente—as few as 10 seconds or up to a minute. If using dried noodles, soak them in hot tap water for 10 to 20 minutes before a quick cook to al dente stage in the boiling water. Drain in a colander and rinse immediately with hot water.

8. Line up 4 large soup bowls. Arrange a plate with the lime wedges, fresh herbs, green onions, jalapeño chile slices, bean sprouts, and watercress on the table. Distribute the noodles and thin steak slices evenly among the bowls. Ladle the hot pho stock into each bowl. The hot stock will immediately cook the thin steak slices. Serve immediately with the hoisin sauce and Sriracha hot chili sauce.

3

The Soup Master

One of the tasks the pressure cooker excels at is making soup. In literally minutes, you have flavor that usually requires hours of gentle simmering to achieve.

Most cooks have one or two soups in their repertoire. We want to change that—we want you to make soup every week. So in this chapter you will find a wide selection—vegetable, bean, split pea, and lentil soups, hearty meat- and poultry-based soups, and even a few seafood chowders. Most call for inexpensive ingredients and allow you to use things already in your refrigerator and/or pantry.

If you want to take your soups from delicious to extraordinary, use homemade stock instead of store-bought broth. Most stocks take less than 30 minutes to make in the pressure cooker; let them cool, portion into containers, freeze, and they are at the ready whenever you feel like making soup. Check out the recipes on pages 21–47.

Serve soup steaming hot out of the pot. These recipes will offer you and yours comfort as well as sustenance. We hope you will cook these many times.

TIPS FOR THE BEST PRESSURE COOKER SOUPS

- Soups cook best if all the ingredients are cut to a uniform size so that they cook evenly.
- Add water or broth to at least cover the solid ingredients for the proper consistency. The vegetables in the soup will cook and add their liquid as well. Take into account how much you wish to serve; is this an appetizer, with about 1 cup soup needed per serving, or a family style main dish, which can be 2 cups or more per serving?

- **Do not fill the pot more than two-thirds full;** you need to leave room for the steam that will be created. This means all the ingredients, including the liquid. If you have added lots of leafy greens, which will cook down to a fraction of their size, place a metal pot lid with metal handle on top to weight down the greens to keep the two-thirds head space. You can always put the greens in first and pile the heavier vegetables, like onions and potatoes, on top to press them down.
- The temperature of the liquid when you lock the lid doesn't matter. If it's warm, the contents of the soup will come up to pressure faster.
- Use herbs and spices sparingly at the beginning of the cook time and always taste for the seasonings at the end of cooking. Pressure cookers tend to intensify the flavors of dried herbs and wash out those of fresh herbs.
- If you like, you can initially sweat some of the vegetables, such as onions and garlic, in butter or oil before locking the lid. It's a nice flavor addition, but totally optional.
- To puree soups, use a handheld immersion blender, taking care not to hit the side of the pot with it, or carefully transfer in batches to a food processor and pulse. Some soups are best put through a coarse metal sieve, like puree of artichoke or asparagus, since they have tough fibers.
- As easy as it is to prepare soups in the pressure cooker, it is important not to overcook them. If you do, the flavor of your ingredients could become a murky mess. Pay attention to the times recommended in the recipes.

Caldo Verde

Serves 4 • Cooker: 5- to 7-quart • Time: 6 minutes at HIGH pressure

Caldo verde means green soup in Portuguese and is considered Portugal's national dish, though the popularity of the soup extends far beyond its shores. It is a rustic and tasty combination of kale, potatoes, and onions. This is a vegetarian version, without the addition of the traditional linguica or chourico sausage. It contains beans instead, which is the style of this soup made in the Azores. Make sure you cut the kale into really thin slices. This tastes even better the next day.

2 tablespoons olive oil
1 large white onion, chopped
1 clove garlic, minced or pressed
1 bunch kale (about 1 pound), rinsed well, thick middle ribs removed, and leaves sliced into thin strips
$^1/_2$ cup chopped fresh flatleaf parsley
2 large russet potatoes, peeled and cut into 1-inch chunks (4 to 5 cups)
2 small turnips, peeled and cut into $^1/_2$-inch chunks (2 to 3 cups)
6 cups chicken or vegetable broth
$^1/_4$ to $^1/_2$ teaspoon ground white pepper, to taste
1 (15-ounce) can cannellini beans, drained and rinsed, or 1$^3/_4$ cups cooked beans
$^1/_2$ cup diced roasted red bell peppers
Salt

1. In a 5- to 7-quart pressure cooker, heat the oil over medium heat. Add the onion, reduce the heat to medium-low, and cook, stirring a few times, until softened, about 3 minutes. Stir in the garlic. Add the kale, parsley, potatoes, turnips, and broth in that order (you want the potato and turnip chunks to weigh down the kale. The broth should just cover the potatoes; it's okay if a few potato edges are exposed. Add water if necessary, but be careful—too much will make for watery soup. Make sure the pot is no more than two-thirds full. Add the pepper.

2. Close and lock the lid. Set the burner heat to high. When the cooker reaches HIGH pressure, reduce the burner heat as low as you can and still maintain HIGH pressure. Set a timer to cook for 6 minutes.

3. Remove the pot from the heat. Open the cooker with the Quick Release method. Be careful of the steam as you remove the lid.

4. Stir in the beans and red peppers. Cook, uncovered, for 10 minutes to heat the beans. Taste for salt. To thicken the soup, mash some of the beans and potatoes against the side of the pot with the back of a large spoon. Serve immediately with French bread and butter.

Saffron Vegetable Soup with Parmesan Garlic Toasts

Serves 6 to 8 • Cooker: 5- to 7-quart • Time: 10 minutes at HIGH pressure

Since the saffron crocus is grown in Sardinia, it's not surprising that Italians would add a dash of it to one of their vegetable soups, bless it with pesto, and end the whole symphony of flavors with garlic toasts.

PARMESAN GARLIC TOASTS:
1/2 French baguette, split horizontally in half
1/2 cup mayonnaise
1/2 cup sour cream or plain Greek yogurt
1 cup grated Parmesan cheese
2 cloves garlic, pressed
1 heaping tablespoon minced fresh flatleaf parsley

SOUP:
2 tablespoons olive oil
2 leeks (white parts only), trimmed, cut in half
    lengthwise, rinsed well, and thinly sliced across
2 (2-finger) pinches saffron threads or 1/8 teaspoon
    ground saffron
10 ounces fresh green beans, ends trimmed and cut
    into 1-inch pieces
3 large carrots, chopped
3 small zucchini, cut into 1/2-inch-thick rounds
2 Roma tomatoes, seeded and chopped
3 medium Yukon Gold potatoes, peeled and cut
    into 1-inch cubes
2 cloves garlic, minced
1/4 cup finely chopped fresh flatleaf parsley
4 cups vegetable broth
4 cups water
2 (15-ounce) cans cannellini beans, drained and
    rinsed, or 3 cups cooked beans
Sea salt and freshly ground black pepper
2 to 3 tablespoons basil pesto, to taste, homemade
    or store-bought

1. Preheat the oven to 425° F. Line a baking sheet with parchment paper. In a small bowl, mix the mayonnaise, sour cream, Parmesan, garlic, and parsley together. With a rubber spatula, spread the mixture over the cut sides of the bread. If you don't use all the spread, cover and refrigerate to use for a dip or topping. Place in the oven and bake, until the mixture is brown and bubbly, 10 to 15 minutes. Remove from the oven and cut into 1-inch slices or 2-inch chunks.

2. In a 5- to 7-quart pressure cooker, heat the oil over medium heat. Add the leeks and saffron, reduce the heat to medium-low, and cook, stirring a few times, until the leeks are aromatic and begin to soften, about 2 minutes. Add the green beans, carrots, zucchini, tomatoes, potatoes, garlic, and parsley. Cook, stirring occasionally, for 5 minutes to heat and soften. Add the broth and water.

3. Close and lock the lid. Set the burner heat to high. When the cooker reaches HIGH pressure, reduce the burner heat as low as you can and still maintain HIGH pressure. Set a timer to cook for 10 minutes.

4. Remove the pot from the heat. Open the cooker with the Quick Release method. Be careful of the steam as you remove the lid.

5. Stir in the cannellini beans and heat, uncovered, over medium heat for 5 to 7 minutes. Season with salt and pepper to taste. Rewarm the toasts in the oven for a few minutes if you like.

6. Serve the soup immediately in deep soup bowls with a teaspoon of pesto on top for diners to swirl in. Serve with 2 toasts per bowl.

SAFFRON

Saffron has a unique bitter, grassy taste and a strong, earthy fragrance like no other spice. It also stains whatever food it graces golden yellow, like the full sun it grows in. Saffron is the most expensive spice in the world and no wonder—saffron threads are the stigmas of a particular kind of crocus and they must be harvested by hand. By some estimations, it requires 70,000 flowers or over 200,000 stigmas to yield one pound of saffron. There is Iranian saffron, Kashmiri saffron, American saffron (grown in Lancaster County, Pennsylvania), Moroccan saffron, and Italian saffron, which is grown in Sardinia.

Winter Minestrone

Serves 6 • Cooker: 5- to 8-quart • Time: 10 minutes at HIGH pressure

This recipe is adapted from a favorite in the *Sunset Complete Vegetarian Cookbook* (Lane Publishing, 1983), a relic from the early vegetarian days, when a vegetarian main dish meant crepes, enchiladas, macaroni and cheese, or lasagna. It is a hearty, soul-satisfying soup with potatoes, pasta, beans, winter vegetables, and a hint of barley.

3 tablespoons olive oil
1 large white or yellow onion, finely chopped
2 ribs celery, finely chopped
2 cloves garlic, minced or pressed
1 1/2 teaspoons dried Italian herb blend
1/4 cup pearl barley, rinsed and drained
2 medium white or red waxy potatoes (about 12 ounces), left unpeeled and cut into bite-size pieces
2 medium carrots, diced
1 large turnip, peeled and diced
8 cups vegetable broth, homemade preferred
1/4 cup tomato paste
1 (15-ounce) can cannellini or red kidney beans, undrained, or 1 3/4 cups cooked beans
2/3 cup small soup pasta (shells, ditali, or orzo)
2 cups finely shredded green cabbage
Sea salt and freshly ground black pepper
1 1/2 cups shredded Monterey Jack cheese, for serving

1. In a 5- to 8-quart pressure cooker, heat the oil over medium-high heat. Add the onion, celery, garlic, and herb blend and cook, stirring often, until the onion is softened, about 3 minutes. Add the barley, potatoes, carrots, turnip, and broth. Place the tomato paste in a dollop right on top. Do not stir it in.

2. Close and lock the lid. Set the burner heat to high. When the cooker reaches HIGH pressure, reduce the burner heat as low as you can and still maintain HIGH pressure. Set a timer to cook for 10 minutes.

3. Remove the cooker from the heat. Open the cooker with the Quick Release method. Be careful of the steam as you remove the lid.

4. Stir in beans and their liquid and the pasta. Bring to a boil over high heat; reduce the heat to a low boil, cover partially (without pressure), and boil gently until the macaroni is tender to bite, 8 to 10 minutes. Add the cabbage and cook over low heat, uncovered, until the cabbage is tender-crisp, 4 to 5 minutes. Season with salt and pepper to taste. Serve nice and hot with the grated cheese on the side.

Mexican Salsa Minestrone

Serves 6 • Cooker: 5- to 8-quart • Time: 10 minutes at HIGH pressure

This version of minestrone is nothing but vegetables. Of course, you can add some beans if you like, but we feel it doesn't need it. Use a nice chunky salsa fresca, which will provide tomatoes, onions, and jalapeño or serrano chiles. Chayote is sweet-flavored and handled like summer squash. Rosmarina pasta derives its name from the fact that it resembles rosemary needles (*rosmarino* in Italian). It is most often used in soups to replace rice. If you can't find it, substitute orzo. You can toss the corn and peas in still frozen.

10 cups vegetable broth or chicken broth, homemade preferred
1 cup chunky tomato salsa, store-bought or homemade
$1/2$ large white or yellow onion, finely chopped
2 cloves garlic, minced
1 teaspoon dried oregano
1 teaspoon dried basil
2 white or red waxy potatoes, left unpeeled and cut into bite-size pieces
2 medium carrots, diced
1 cup diced zucchini
1 cup chopped fresh green beans
1 cup diced peeled chayote (1 medium chayote)
1 cup frozen white corn kernels
$1/2$ cup frozen petite peas
$1/2$ cup small soup pasta, such as rosmarina or orzo
Sea salt and freshly ground black pepper
$1/2$ cup chopped fresh cilantro

1. In a 5- to 8-quart pressure cooker, combine the broth, salsa, onion, garlic, herbs, potatoes, carrots, zucchini, green beans, chayote, corn, and peas.
2. Close and lock the lid. Set the burner heat to high. When the cooker reaches HIGH pressure, reduce the burner heat as low as you can and still maintain HIGH pressure. Set a timer to cook for 10 minutes.
3. Remove the pot from the heat. Open the cooker with the Quick Release method. Be careful of the steam as you remove the lid.
4. Stir in the pasta. Bring to a boil, uncovered, over high; reduce the heat to a low boil, cover partially (without pressure), and boil gently until the pasta is tender to bite, 6 to 8 minutes. Season with salt and pepper to taste. Stir in the cilantro. Serve nice and hot with warm fresh tortillas and butter on the side.

Tomato-Basil Tortellini Soup

Serves 6 • Cooker: 5- to 8-quart • Time: 5 minutes at HIGH pressure

Think that a can of tomato soup is the ultimate in fast food? Well, homemade tomato soup comes together quickly in the pressure cooker and is even more delicious when made with canned organic tomatoes like Muir Glen or your own. The Neiman Marcus café serves a fresh, simple tortellini soup that has shoppers coming back again and again to enjoy it. This version utilizes the superb fresh cheese tortellini you can buy in the cold case in the supermarket.

3 tablespoons olive oil
1 large white onion, chopped
2 cloves garlic, minced
1 medium carrot, coarsely chopped
6 cups reduced-sodium chicken broth or
    homemade chicken stock (page 31)
$^1/_8$ teaspoon red pepper flakes
1 (28-ounce) can tomato puree
1 (14.5-ounce) can diced tomatoes in juice,
    undrained
1 (9-ounce) package fresh cheese tortellini
1 cup minced fresh basil
Salt and freshly ground black pepper
$^3/_4$ to 1 cup shredded or grated Parmesan cheese,
    for serving
Extra virgin olive oil, for serving

1. In a 5- to 8-quart pressure cooker, heat the oil over medium-high heat. Add onion and cook, stirring often, until softened, about 5 minutes. Add the garlic and cook, stirring, until just fragrant, 30 to 60 seconds; do not brown or it will get bitter. Add the carrot, broth, and pepper flakes. Stir in the tomato puree, diced tomatoes with their juice, and tortellini.

2. Close and lock the lid. Set the burner heat to high. When the cooker reaches HIGH pressure, reduce the burner heat as low as you can and still maintain HIGH pressure. Set a timer to cook for 5 minutes.

3. Remove the pot from the heat. Open the cooker with the Natural Release method; let stand for 10 minutes. Be careful of the steam as you remove the lid.

4. Stir in the basil and let stand 2 minutes. Season with salt and pepper to taste. Serve nice and hot with the grated cheese on the side. Drizzle each bowl with some very green fruity olive oil.

Sopa de Tortilla with Calabaza

Serves 4 to 5 • Cooker: 5- to 7-quart • Time: 6 minutes at HIGH pressure

Throughout Mexico and Baja California every restaurant has a version of tortilla soup. It is usually quite thin, almost a consommé, with tortilla strips and shreds of chicken added. Here we load the pot with fresh vegetables and pumpkin puree (the calabaza) for a wonderful vegetarian version that can be a main course with salad. Feel free to add shredded leftover chicken or turkey along with the corn.

4 corn tortillas, cut into wide strips
Olive oil spray
2 tablespoons olive oil
1 large white onion, chopped
2 small zucchini, cut into bite-size pieces
1 red, green, or yellow bell pepper, seeded and
    diced
1 clove garlic, minced
$1/3$ cup fresh lime juice
1 (28-ounce) can diced tomatoes in juice,
    undrained
1 cup chunky salsa fresca of your choice
1 cup canned or fresh pumpkin puree
1 teaspoon ground cumin
1 teaspoon chili powder, Mexican red chile powder,
    or ancho chile powder
$3/4$ teaspoon dried oregano, preferably Mexican
$1/2$ teaspoon salt
A few grinds black pepper
6 cups water, chicken broth, or vegetable broth
$1 1/2$ cups frozen baby white corn kernels (no need
    to thaw)
$1/4$ cup chopped fresh cilantro

FOR SERVING:
Shredded Monterey Jack cheese
1 (8-ounce) container sour cream (thinned with a
    few tablespoons milk), crema Mexicana, or plain
    Greek yogurt
1 firm-ripe avocado, peeled, pitted, and sliced
$1/2$ cup fresh cilantro leaves, chopped
1 lime, cut into wedges

1. Preheat the oven to 400° F. Lightly spray both sides of each tortilla with the olive oil spray. With a knife, cut the tortillas into $2^{1}/_{2}$ x 1-inch strips. Spread the tortilla strips onto a parchment paper-lined baking sheet. Bake until crisp but not browned, turning once halfway through baking, 8 to 10 minutes.

2. In a 5- to 7-quart pressure cooker, heat the oil over medium heat. Add the onion, reduce the heat to medium-low, and cook, stirring a few times, until it begins to soften, about 2 minutes. Add the zucchini, bell pepper, and garlic. Add the lime juice and bring to a boil; let the liquid reduce by half. Add the tomatoes and their juice, the salsa, pumpkin, spices, oregano, salt, and pepper. Add the broth.

3. Close and lock the lid. Set the burner heat to high. When the cooker reaches HIGH pressure, reduce the burner heat as low as you can and still maintain HIGH pressure. Set a timer to cook for 6 minutes.

4. Remove the pot from the heat. Open the cooker with the Quick Release method. Be careful of the steam as you remove the lid.

5. Stir in the corn and cilantro. Simmer over medium heat, uncovered, 2 minutes to cook the corn. Taste for seasoning.

6. To serve, place tortilla chips on the bottom of each bowl and ladle over the soup. Sprinkle with grated cheese. Drizzle with a tablespoon of sour cream, and top with a few slices of avocado and some cilantro. Serve immediately with lime wedges on the side.

Carrot-Potato-Orange Soup with Fragrant Indian Spices

Serves 8 • Cooker: 6- to 8-quart • Time: 12 minutes at HIGH pressure

This recipe is simplicity itself and deliciously satisfying. If you can, buy bunches of carrots with their tops on; the carrots will be sweeter. If you want a garnish, top with chopped cilantro and plain Greek yogurt, but it is fine without.

$1/4$ cup olive oil or butter
1 large white onion, chopped
$1^1/2$ tablespoons brown sugar
1 tablespoon mild or hot curry powder
$1/2$ teaspoon ground coriander
$1/4$ teaspoon ground cardamom
2 large russet potatoes, peeled and cut into 1-inch cubes
2 pounds carrots (about 10 medium), thickly sliced
$1/2$ cup orange juice
6 cups vegetable broth, or as needed
1 tablespoon honey
Freshly grated nutmeg
Sea salt and freshly ground black pepper

1. In a 6- to 8-quart pressure cooker, heat the oil over medium heat. Add the onion, reduce the heat to medium-low, and cook, stirring a few times, until it begins to soften, about 3 minutes. Add the sugar and spices and cook, stirring, about 1 minute longer. Add the potatoes, carrots, orange juice, and broth. The broth should just barely cover the vegetables; it's okay if a few potato edges are exposed.

2. Close and lock the lid. Set the burner heat to high. When the cooker reaches HIGH pressure, reduce the burner heat as low as you can and still maintain HIGH pressure. Set a timer to cook for 12 minutes.

3. Remove the pot from the heat. Open the cooker with the Quick Release method. Be careful of the heat as you remove the lid.

4. Puree the soup in the pot using an immersion blender; the soup will be nice and thick. Stir in the honey and grate in a bit of nutmeg. Season to taste with salt and pepper. Keep warm over low heat without letting it come to a boil until serving. Ladle the hot soup into bowls and enjoy.

Carrot-Potato-Cilantro Soup: Add the roughly chopped leaves from 1 bunch fresh cilantro in Step 4 and heat a few minutes. Puree with the immersion blender.

Creamy Carrot-Potato-Orange Soup: Add 2 cups organic heavy cream, or 1 cup milk and 1 (8-ounce) container sour cream in Step 4, after pureeing the soup. Let it heat through without coming to a boil. You can add this to either version.

Mushroom Barley Soup

Serves 6 to 8 • Cooker: 5- to 8-quart • Time: 20 minutes at HIGH pressure

If you love mushrooms, this soup will be love at first bite. The broth is so rich that you won't notice it doesn't contain meat or dairy.

7 dried shiitake mushrooms
3 cups water
$^1/_4$ cup olive oil
1 large white onion, diced
2 medium shallots, chopped
2 cloves garlic, minced
2 medium carrots, diced
3 ribs celery, diced
2 ripe plum tomatoes, seeded and diced
6 to 8 ounces portobello mushrooms, stems discarded, caps sliced, then coarsely chopped
12 to 16 ounces white or cremini mushrooms, sliced
4 cups vegetable broth
$^3/_4$ cup pearl barley, rinsed and drained
2 sprigs fresh thyme
1 bay leaf
Sea salt and freshly ground black pepper
Juice of 1 lemon

PORTOBELLO PRIMER

Portobello mushrooms are native to the grasslands of Europe and North America. When immature, it is the cremini mushroom. When mature, it develops its characteristic open, flat cap with exposed gills. It has less moisture than the smaller cremini mushroom, so the texture is firm, so firm that many describe it as meaty, and it is used as a meat substitute in vegetarian recipes. Wonder where the name portobello came from? Use of the evocative name began in the 1980s as a marketing ploy to popularize the overgrown mushrooms, which previously couldn't be sold. Fun fact: The Pasteur Institute in France created the sterilized culture for growing commercial mushrooms in 1893.

1. Place the shiitake mushrooms in a small saucepan with the water. Bring to a boil, then remove from the heat and let soak for 20 minutes. Drain the mushrooms through a coffee filter set into a mesh strainer. Reserve the mushroom liquid. Remove and discard the stems and finely chop the mushrooms. Set aside.

2. In a 5- to 8-quart pressure cooker, heat the oil over medium-high heat. Add the onion and shallots and cook, stirring often, until the onion is soft, about 5 minutes. Add the garlic and cook, stirring, until just fragrant, 30 seconds; do not brown or it will get bitter. Add the carrots, celery, tomatoes, fresh and dried mushrooms, broth, and reserved mushroom liquid. Stir in the barley, thyme, and bay leaf.

3. Close and lock the lid. Set the burner heat to high. When the cooker reaches HIGH pressure, reduce the burner heat as low as you can and still maintain HIGH pressure. Set a timer to cook for 20 minutes.

4. Remove the pot from the heat. Open the cooker with the Natural Release method; let stand for 10 minutes. Be careful of the steam as you remove the lid. The barley should be tender and soup thickened. Discard the thyme and bay leaf.

5. Taste and season with salt and lots of pepper. Stir in the lemon juice. Serve hot. The soup will thicken as it cools.

Hungarian Mushroom Barley Soup: In place of the thyme and bay leaf, add 1 tablespoon dried dill and 1 tablespoon sweet Hungarian paprika. At serving, stir in 1 cup sour cream.

Roasted Butternut Squash Soup with Apples, Goat Cheese, and Fried Sage Leaves

Serves 4 to 6 • Cooker: 5- to 7-quart • Time: 6 minutes at HIGH pressure

No collection of soups is complete without one for butternut squash soup. Here the squash is roasted first to develop the flavor. It also makes the squash ever so much easier to handle. If you are stretched for time, you can substitute either the bagged precut pieces you find in the produce section, or two 1-pound packages frozen butternut squash. Then it is cooked with onions and apples. But the fun part is the condiment toppings, which are integral to the soup's flavor: balsamic syrup, tangy goat cheese, and fried sage leaves (a restaurant style touch).

1 (2^1/$_2$- to 3^1/$_2$-pound) butternut squash
1^1/$_4$ cups balsamic vinegar
6 tablespoons (^{3}/$_4$ stick) unsalted butter
1 medium white onion, chopped
3 ribs celery, chopped
1 large leek (white part only), trimmed, cut in half lengthwise, rinsed well, and chopped
1 large tart apple, peeled, cored, and chopped
2 medium shallots, chopped
2 cloves garlic, peeled and smashed
3 tablespoons minced peeled fresh ginger
2 teaspoons curry powder of choice
5 to 6 cups chicken or vegetable broth, as needed
Sea salt and ground white pepper
12 fresh sage leaves
6 ounces soft goat cheese, crumbled

1. Preheat the oven to 375° F. Line a baking sheet with aluminum foil or parchment paper. Cut the squash in half lengthwise; scoop out the seeds and discard. Set the squash halves, cut side down, on the pan and roast until tender, about 40 minutes. Remove from the oven and let cool. Scoop the flesh (about 2 cups worth) into a bowl with a spoon and set aside.
2. While the squash roasts, make the balsamic reduction. In a small saucepan, bring the vinegar to a boil over high heat. Once it boils, reduce the heat to medium-low, to just a simmer. Reduce the balsamic vinegar by at least 50 to 75 percent, until it is syrupy and slightly thickened, about 10 minutes; stir occasionally. Watch that it doesn't burn, and let the slow simmering take its time. Set aside to cool. Store in a covered con-

tainer in the refrigerator until needed if made ahead; it will keep for at least a month.

3. In a 5- to 7-quart pressure cooker, melt 4 tablespoons of the butter over medium heat. When it starts to foam, add the onion, celery, leek, apple, shallots, and garlic, reduce the heat to medium-low, and cook, stirring a few times, until the leeks are aromatic and begin to soften, 3 to 5 minutes. Add the ginger and curry powder and stir until fragrant, about 1 minute. Add the squash and stir in the broth.
4. Close and lock the lid. Set the burner heat to high. When the cooker reaches HIGH pressure, reduce the burner heat as low as you can and still maintain HIGH pressure. Set a timer to cook for 6 minutes.
5. Remove the pot from the heat. Open the cooker with the Quick Release method. Be careful of the steam as you remove the lid.
6. Puree the soup in the pot using an immersion blender. Taste for salt and pepper. Leave the soup on low while you fry the sage leaves.
7. Melt the remaining 2 tablespoons butter in a small skillet. Add the sage leaves and cook, swirling the pan, until the leaves are crispy and the butter has browned but not burned, about 2 minutes. Drain the leaves on a layer of paper towel until serving.
8. Divide the soup among 6 bowls. Drizzle with 2 to 3 teaspoons balsamic syrup in a swirl pattern, then garnish with a sprinkle of goat cheese and 2 sage leaves plopped right in the middle.

BALSAMIC VINEGAR REDUCTION

Don't spend extra money to buy a balsamic reduction—make it yourself! We keep less-expensive balsamics on hand just for reducing. When you reduce balsamic vinegar, you concentrate the flavor, yielding a delicious, aromatic syrup. It can be used in savory as well as sweet applications, like drizzling it over figs, cheesecake, cheese crostini, or sliced tomatoes.

Tomato-Fennel Soup

Serves 6 to 8 • Cooker: 5- to 7-quart • Time: 12 minutes at HIGH pressure

Beth's mother loves fennel bulb. She has decided that it is her favorite vegetable and adores the aroma. One day Beth's mother says she made this new soup, tomato and fennel, from a recipe in a magazine that said it was made by the singer Lady Gaga. "I like her," she says, "She's got a lot of get up and go." She shared the recipe with Beth and a few months later, Beth found the recipe in Art Smith's *Back to the Family* cookbook, from which this version is adapted. You will love this marvelous soup, with its elusive licorice flavor. Fresh basil is a must.

3 tablespoons olive oil
1 large white onion, chopped
2 ribs celery, chopped
1 clove garlic, minced
2 fennel bulbs, stalks removed, root end trimmed
    off, cored, and chopped
2 (28-ounce) cans whole plum tomatoes in juice,
    undrained
1 (4-inch-long) thick strip orange zest from an
    organic orange
6 cups chicken broth
$1/4$ cup chopped fresh basil or cilantro
Salt and freshly ground black pepper

1. In a 5- to 7-quart pressure cooker, heat the oil over medium heat. Add the onion, celery, garlic, and fennel, reduce the heat to medium-low, and cook, stirring a few times, until softened, about 3 minutes. Add the tomatoes with their juice, the strip of orange zest, and broth. The liquid should just cover the vegetables.
2. Close and lock the lid. Set the burner heat to high. When the cooker reaches HIGH pressure, reduce the burner heat as low as you can and still maintain HIGH pressure. Set a timer to cook for 12 minutes.
3. Remove the pot from the heat. Open the cooker with the Quick Release method. Be careful of the steam as you remove the lid. Discard the orange zest if you can find it (if not, don't worry about it).
4. Stir in the basil. Puree the soup in the pot with an immersion blender until smooth. Taste for salt and pepper and serve.

Creamy Tomato-Fennel Soup: Add $1^1/2$ cups organic heavy cream after pureeing and reheat slowly. This soup is fabulously elegant for a dinner party.

Tomato-Fennel-Red Pepper Soup: Add 1 (12-ounce) jar roasted bell peppers, drained, in Step 1 along with the tomatoes.

Vegetarian Borscht with Porcini

Serves 6 • Cooker: 5- to 7-quart • Time: 10 minutes at HIGH pressure

Earthy, fragrant borscht soup is usually made with beef. This meatless version topped with sour cream is a popular "dairy" dish in Jewish cuisine—meat and dairy products may not be mixed in kosher cooking. The sour cream is essential, adding richness as well as turning the soup a beautiful color. This oh-so-good soup is prepared in minutes; it turns a stunning ruby-red as soon as the water hits the beets and deepens in color as it cooks. The beets end up looking like jewels. It is as good hot as it is cold on a summer day. You definitely want the beet greens! You can use fresh dill or tarragon in place of the dried. This is homemade good, just like a loving *babushka* (Russian grandmother) would make it.

$^1/_2$ ounce ($^1/_2$ cup) dried porcini mushrooms
1 cup hot water
1 bunch red beets, greens trimmed off and beets peeled and cut into bite-size dice
1 large white onion, coarsely chopped
2 medium red or white new potatoes, left unpeeled and diced
2 medium carrots, coarsely chopped
1 medium rutabaga, peeled and cut into bite-size dice
1 heaping teaspoon dried dill, dried tarragon, or mixed herb blend, such as Italian herbs or Mrs. Dash
2 (3- to 4-inch-long) strips orange zest
$^1/_4$ cup dry red wine, such as Merlot or Pinot Noir, or cider vinegar
1 (32-ounce) container vegetable broth
2 tablespoons tomato paste
$^1/_4$ teaspoon freshly ground black pepper, or to taste
Sea salt
1 (16-ounce) container sour cream, imitation sour cream, or plain Greek yogurt, for serving

1. Place the porcini in a small bowl and add the hot water. Let soak until softened, about 20 minutes. Remove the mushrooms, reserving the soaking liquid, rinse, and chop. Strain the liquid through a fine mesh strainer lined with a paper towel or coffee filter into a bowl, reserving the liquid.

2. In a 5-to 7-quart pressure cooker, combine the beets, onion, potatoes, carrots, rutabaga, mushrooms, herbs, strips of zest, wine, reserved mushroom liquid, and vegetable broth. Add enough water just to cover. Plop the tomato paste on top of the vegetables; do not stir it in. Bring to a boil.

3. Close and lock the lid. Set the burner heat to high. When the cooker reaches HIGH pressure, reduce the burner heat as low as you can and still maintain HIGH pressure. Set a timer to cook for 10 minutes.

4. While the soup cooks, rinse the reserved beet greens well and chop.

5. Remove the pot from the heat. Open the cooker with the Quick Release method. Be careful of the steam as you remove the lid. Discard the strips of zest.

6. Stir in the beet greens. Cook over medium heat, uncovered, until they are heated through, about 2 minutes. Add the pepper and taste for salt.

7. To serve, ladle the hot soup into bowls and top with a big spoonful of cold sour cream. Serve immediately.

PEELING BEETS

Beets can be intimidating to peel, especially if they're gnarly and hairy. Here's our method. Cut off the root end and the stem end, where the greens were attached. Starting at the stem end and holding your fingers out of the way, peel the beet in strips from stem to root end. We like a Y-shaped peeler for beets—it takes a thicker strip, which seems to better catch the hairs and divots that beets have, and feels easier to control on the bumpy beet surface.

Indian Borscht

Serves 6 • Cooker: 5- to 7-quart • Time: 10 minutes at HIGH pressure

Borscht is usually associated with flavors like dill, red wine, and mushrooms. But here is a very different vegetarian version from Michael Romano's Union Square Café in New York. It is laced with Indian spices that are first warmed in hot oil to bring out their assertive flavors. The combination of beets and ginger is a true winner. Your cooked rice will be pink, but after blending, it will disappear into the puree to add body to the smooth soup. Serve with chapati or naan flatbread.

3 tablespoons olive oil
2 large white onions, coarsely chopped
3 tablespoons finely minced peeled fresh ginger
2 teaspoons ground cumin
1 teaspoon ground turmeric
1 teaspoon ground coriander
1 teaspoon sweet Hungarian paprika
$1/2$ teaspoon red pepper flakes
$1/3$ cup white basmati rice, rinsed until the water
    runs clear
1 (15.5-ounce) can diced tomatoes in juice,
    undrained
4 medium to large red beets (about $1^1/2$ pounds),
    greens trimmed off, rinsed well, and chopped;
    beets peeled and sliced $1/2$ inch thick
8 cups vegetable broth, or as needed
1 to 2 tablespoons honey, to taste
$3/4$ teaspoon garam masala, or to taste
Sea salt and freshly ground black pepper
1 (16-ounce) container sour cream, imitation sour
    cream, or plain Greek yogurt, for serving
$1/2$ cup chopped fresh cilantro, for serving

1. In a 5- to 7-quart pressure cooker, heat the oil over medium-high heat. Add the onions and cook, stirring a few times, until softened, about 4 minutes. Add the ginger and stir for a minute. Add all the spices and pepper flakes, stirring for a minute to warm them. Add the rice (it can be tossed in wet), tomatoes and their juices, beets and their greens, and just enough of the broth to cover the vegetables.
2. Close and lock the lid. Set the burner heat to high. When the cooker reaches HIGH pressure, reduce the burner heat as low as you can and still maintain HIGH pressure. Set a timer to cook for 10 minutes.
3. Remove the pot from the heat. Open the cooker with the Natural Release method; let stand for 10 minutes. Be careful of the steam as you remove the lid.
4. Puree the soup in the pot using an immersion blender. Blend in the honey and garam masala. Return to medium-low heat without the lid on. Season to taste with salt and pepper.
5. Serve immediately with big dollops of sour cream melting into the soup and chopped cilantro sprinkled over the top. Delicious!

PUREEING HOT SOUP IN A BLENDER

Take these precautions to avoid an accident that could send you to the hospital with third-degree burns:
• Let the soup cool a bit before transferring it from the pot to the blender.
• Don't fill the blender jar more than halfway full.
• Hold a folded dishtowel over the lid of the blender.
• Start the blender on a low speed.

Puree of Turnip Soup with Croutons

Serves 4 • Cooker: 5- to 7-quart • Time: 8 minutes at HIGH pressure

This is a lovely French-style winter root soup that is pureed after cooking, then blended with tangy crème fraîche. It was inspired by a description by Lulu Peyraud of Domaine Tempier, the wine growers who were neighbors to the idiosyncratic food and wine writer Richard Olney, who wrote his classic cookbooks from Provence, France. She spoke of cooking leek and potato soup for guests, but made it with turnips for herself when dining with her husband as a weeknight soup. Oh so very French. It is made with the all-purpose russet potato and turnips, a vegetable that looks much like a half-white half-purple spinning top. If you like, you can toss the well-rinsed tasty turnip greens into the soup to cook as well.

CROUTONS:

$1/2$ baguette, sliced diagonally into $1/2$-inch-thick slices

Extra virgin olive oil, or olive oil cooking spray, for drizzling

SOUP:

2 tablespoons unsalted butter

1 large white onion, chopped

$1^1/4$ pounds firm white turnips, peeled and sliced (4 to 5 turnips)

$1/2$ cup dry white wine

1 large or 2 medium russet potatoes, peeled and sliced

4 cups water or vegetable broth

Salt and freshly ground white pepper, to taste

$1/2$ to 1 cup crème fraîche, to taste

1. Make the croutons. Put a rack in the center of the oven. Preheat the oven to 400° F. Arrange the bread slices on a baking sheet. Drizzle or spray on both sides with olive oil. Bake until golden around the edges, 6 to 8 minutes, turning the slices halfway through the cooking time.

2. In a 5- to 7-quart pressure cooker, melt the butter over medium heat. When it begins to foam, add the onion, reduce the heat to medium-low, and cook, stirring a few times, until it begins to soften, about 2 minutes. Add the turnips and wine; cook until the wine reduces a little, a minute or so. Add the potato and water.

3. Close and lock the lid. Set the burner heat to high. When the cooker reaches HIGH pressure, reduce the burner heat as low as you can and still maintain HIGH pressure. Set a timer to cook for 8 minutes.

4. Remove the pot from the heat. Open the cooker with the Quick Release method. Be careful of the steam as you remove the lid.

5. Puree the soup in the pot using an immersion blender. Taste for salt and pepper. Stir in the crème fraîche and heat on low to bring back to serving temperature. Serve immediately in bowls, garnished with 2 or 3 of the French bread croutons.

Sweet Potato Vichyssoise with Whole Wheat Croutons

Serves 4 to 6 • Cooker: 5- to 7-quart • Time: 7 minutes at HIGH pressure

This soup is a variation on traditional leek and potato soup, a pale orange from the yams, and it is marvelous. You can use the Japanese white sweet potato instead of the bright orange Garnet yam if you want. Any sweet potato will work.

WHOLE WHEAT CROUTONS:
8 ounces whole wheat bread, sandwich style or artisan, torn into small uneven pieces to make about 4 cups
3 tablespoons unsalted butter
3 tablespoons olive oil

SOUP:
2 tablespoons butter
1 large white onion, chopped
3 medium leeks (white part only), trimmed, cut in half lengthwise, rinsed well, and sliced across about 3/4-inch thick
1 clove garlic, chopped
4 cups roughly chopped peeled sweet potatoes (about 1-inch chunks) (about 2 large sweet potatoes)
2 medium carrots, chopped
4 cups water or vegetable broth, or as needed
1/4 cup dry white wine
1/2 teaspoon sea salt
1/2 teaspoon ground white pepper
1 cup half-and-half or unsweetened soy milk
Minced fresh flatleaf parsley, for serving (optional)

1. Make the croutons. Preheat the oven to 375° F. Place the bread pieces on a parchment paper-lined baking sheet. Melt the butter in a small saucepan or in the microwave. Stir in the oil and pour over the bread pieces. Using a metal spatula, toss the bread to coat with the butter mixture. Make sure all the pieces are slightly moistened. Spread into a single layer. Bake until crunchy, 10 to 12 minutes. Stir once to assure even browning. Set aside on the baking sheet to cool.

2. Make the soup. In a 5- to 7-quart pressure cooker, melt the butter over medium heat. When it is foamy, add the onion and leeks, reduce the heat to medium-low, and cook, stirring a few times, until the leeks are aromatic and begin to soften, about 3 minutes. Add the garlic and stir 30 seconds. Add the sweet potatoes, carrots, water, and wine. The liquid should just barely cover the potatoes and leeks; it's okay if a few potato edges are exposed. Add a bit more water if need be. Stir in the salt and pepper and distribute the potatoes and leeks into as even a layer as possible.

3. Close and lock the lid. Set the burner heat to high. When the cooker reaches HIGH pressure, reduce the burner heat as low as you can and still maintain HIGH pressure. Set a timer to cook for 7 minutes.

4. Remove the pot from the heat. Open the cooker with the Quick Release method. Be careful of the steam as you remove the lid.

5. Puree the soup in the pot using an immersion blender until smooth. Stir in the half-and-half. Taste for salt and pepper. Serve immediately in deep soup bowls, garnished with a sprinkling of parsley if you like and a small handful of the croutons, or refrigerate until cold. If you are serving the soup cold, taste it again before serving, adding salt, pepper, and milk as desired.

Potato-Leek Soup

Serves 4 • Cooker: 5- to 7-quart • Time: 6 minutes at HIGH pressure

This versatile soup is the essence of simplicity. This soup is sustaining and warming when served hot, refreshing and rejuvenating when served cold. Some people like to prepare it with stock, but we find that making it with water lets the delicate flavors of the potato and leek shine through. Use a combination of Idaho, Maine, and Yukon Gold or red potatoes if you happen to have them in the pantry. Keep it lean with buttermilk or yogurt, go all out with cream, or compromise with half-and-half. To make it more substantial, top the hot soup with buttery homemade croutons fresh from the oven (page 62).

2 tablespoons butter
3 cups sliced (about $3/4$-inch thick) leeks (white and
    lightest green parts only)
3 cups cubed (1-inch) peeled russet potatoes
    (about 2 large potatoes)
4 to 5 cups water or chicken broth, as needed
$1/8$ teaspoon ground white pepper
1 cup buttermilk, plain yogurt, unsweetened soy
    milk, half-and-half, or cream
Salt
Minced fresh chives, for serving (optional)

1. In a 5 to 7-quart pressure cooker, melt the butter over medium heat. When it starts to foam, add the leeks, reduce the heat to medium-low, and cook, stirring a few times, until they are aromatic and begin to soften, about 3 minutes. Add the potatoes and enough of the water so that it just barely covers the potatoes and leeks; it's okay if a few potato edges are exposed. If you add too much liquid, it will make for watery soup. Stir in the white pepper and distribute the potatoes and leeks into as even a layer as possible.
2. Close and lock the lid. Set the burner heat to high. When the cooker reaches HIGH pressure, reduce the burner heat as low as you can and still maintain HIGH pressure. Set a timer to cook for 6 minutes.
3. Remove the pot from the heat. Open the cooker with the Quick Release method. Be careful of the steam as you remove the lid.

4. Puree the soup in the pot using an immersion blender. Stir in the buttermilk and heat over very low heat for 2 to 5 minutes to bring back up to a full simmer; do not boil. Taste for salt. Serve immediately, garnished with chives if you like, or set aside to cool to room temperature, then refrigerate in a covered container until cold. If you are serving the soup cold, taste it for salt and pepper again before serving, as refrigeration mutes flavors.

Potato, Leek, and Ham Soup: If you like, substitute the water with Ham Stock (page 42) but this is optional. Add 1 cup chopped celery with the leaves and $1 1/2$ tablespoons mustard seeds, crushed, in Step 1 to cook with the leeks. Add about 1 cup shredded or diced cooked ham along with the buttermilk in Step 4 to the pureed soup before tasting for salt.

Potato, Leek, and Spinach or Swiss Chard Soup: Add 1 pound spinach, rinsed well and stems removed, or Swiss chard, leaves separated from the stalk, then chopped, and stalks diced, in Step 1 along with the potatoes. Use chicken broth instead of water. A wonderful green soup.

Potato, Leek, and Cauliflower Soup: Use only 2 potatoes. Add 12 ounces cauliflower, broken into small florets and stems removed, along with the potatoes in Step 1. Use 3 cups vegetable broth instead of water.

Celery Root, Potato, and Leek Soup

Serves 4 to 6 • Cooker: 5- to 7-quart • Time: 8 minutes at HIGH pressure

This soup is another variation on traditional leek and potato soup with its own unique flavor and an elusive aroma that's almost like a perfume.

2 large leeks
2 tablespoons butter
2 tablespoons olive oil
3 pounds celery roots, peeled (see below) and cut into 1-inch cubes
5 Yukon Gold or white waxy potatoes, peeled and cut into 1-inch chunks
5 cups water or vegetable broth
$1/4$ cup dry white wine
1 tablespoon fine sea salt
$1/2$ teaspoon ground white pepper, or to taste
1 bay leaf
1 cup heavy cream
3 ribs celery with leaves, chopped and sautéed in 1 tablespoon olive oil until softened, for serving (optional)

THE SKINNY ON CELERY ROOT

Celery root is a sort of scary-looking hairy brown bulb, cultivated from a type of celery; it has an edible root that is quite mild in flavor. It can be eaten raw or cooked, stewed or mashed. It is low in carbohydrates and has a similar texture to potatoes, so it is nice in combination with them. Look for celery roots that feel heavy for their size. Celery root is notoriously difficult to peel, so search out bulbs with as smooth an exterior as possible.

To peel celery root, using a large, sharp knife, trim the rough ends squarely off the root. Place it flat end down on a cutting board and carefully trim off the remaining skin in thin strips from top to bottom. You can also use a vegetable peeler to do this. Use a paring knife to dig into the crevices, like peeling a pineapple.

1. Remove the tough outer layers and dark green tops of the leeks. Slice in half lengthwise and rinse under cold running water until all the dirt and grit is gone. Thinly slice the leeks against the grain.

2. In a 5- to 7-quart pressure cooker, melt the butter with the oil over medium heat. When the butter foams, add the leeks, reduce the heat to medium-low, and cook, stirring a few times, until they are aromatic and begin to soften, about 3 minutes. Add the celery root, potatoes, water, and wine. The liquid should just barely cover the vegetables and leeks if needed; it's okay if a few potato edges are exposed. Add a bit more water if need be. Stir the salt, pepper, and bay leaf and distribute the potatoes and leeks into as even a layer as possible.

3. Close and lock the lid. Set the burner heat to high. When the cooker reaches HIGH pressure, reduce the burner heat as low as you can and still maintain HIGH pressure. Set a timer to cook for 8 minutes.

4. Remove the pot from the heat. Open the cooker with the Quick Release method. Be careful of the steam as you remove the lid. Discard the bay leaves.

5. Puree the soup in the pot using an immersion blender until mostly smooth but still slightly chunky. Add the cream and heat through over medium heat; do not let it boil. Taste for salt and white pepper. Serve immediately, in deep soup bowls, topped with the sautéed celery if you like.

Creamy Roasted Red Pepper Soup

Serves 4 • Cooker: 5- to 7-quart • Time: 6 minutes at HIGH pressure

We were lucky to get this recipe. There was a popular eatery in Palo Alto called Fresco, around the corner from Julie's home—everyone went there for the red pepper soup. It was a culinary sensation in town. Eventually the restaurant closed and the new restaurant was besieged with so many requests for the red pepper soup they had to put it on the menu. A friend sent us a copy of the recipe, which must have appeared in the local freebie newspaper. It is the essence of simplicity. If you have time, char fresh peppers instead of using jarred. This soup is divine, probably from the heavy cream and butter. We changed the recipe slightly, adjusting the amounts of broth and cream. You can easily double this recipe.

¹/₄ cup (¹/₂ stick) unsalted butter
1 large white onion, chopped
1 (16-ounce) jar roasted red peppers, drained, or 6
    red bell peppers, roasted (see below)
2 large russet potatoes, peeled and cut into 1-inch
    cubes (about 3 cups)
1 jalapeño pepper, seeded
1 teaspoon Worcestershire sauce, or to taste
4 cups chicken or vegetable broth
2 cups organic heavy cream, or 1 cup heavy cream
    whisked with 1 cup plain Greek yogurt
Salt

1. In a 5- to 7-quart pressure cooker, melt the butter over medium heat. When it foams, add the onion, reduce the heat to medium-low, and cook, stirring a few times, until it begins to soften, about 3 minutes. Add the peppers, potatoes, jalapeño, Worcestershire, and broth. The broth should just barely cover the potatoes, peppers, and onion; it's okay if a few potato edges are exposed.

2. Close and lock the lid. Set the burner heat to high. When the cooker reaches HIGH pressure, reduce the burner heat as low as you can and still maintain HIGH pressure. Set a timer to cook for 6 minutes.

3. Remove the pot from the heat. Open the cooker with the Quick Release method. Be careful of the steam as you remove the lid.

4. Puree the soup in the pot using an immersion blender. Taste for salt. Stir in the cream and simmer over low heat 5 to 10 minutes to bring back to serving temperature. Do not boil. Serve immediately.

ROASTING PEPPERS

Char the skin over a gas flame (hold the pepper using a long fork to do this) or under the broiler or on a grill. Let the skin blacken all over, turning the pepper as needed. Once blackened, place the pepper in a plastic bag, seal it, and let it steam for about 5 minutes. The blistered skin will not slip off; remove it, the stem, and the seeds with your fingers. Slice as your recipe directs.

Cream of Artichoke Soup

Serves 6 • Cooker: 5- to 7-quart • Time: 8 minutes at HIGH pressure

South of Half Moon Bay, in Northern California, the coast is dotted with small communities and families that have lived in the area for generations, farming small plots of berry farms, artichoke fields, and cattle ranching. It is very pretty country, just over the hill from Silicon Valley. One of these hamlets is Pescadero, half a mile in from the foggy coast. The main attraction is Duarte's Tavern, a destination restaurant. The Duartes were Portuguese immigrants, and in 1894 they settled in Pescadero and paid $12 in gold for what is now Duarte's Tavern. The family has been running it using the same recipes and fresh seasonal coastal ingredients ever since. Duarte's is outright famous for their artichoke soup and olallieberry pie. On weekends, there is a special cioppino feast, and you might see a visiting movie star, a senator, or the mayor of San Francisco in the room. Emma Duarte never wrote down the recipes, but said she cooked by instinct. The recipes were passed on by practice in the kitchen. Emma originally made her artichoke soup from fresh artichokes, but with premium frozen artichoke hearts now available, you can make this soup in any season. The soup is rich, creamy, and a lovely pale green.

2 pounds frozen artichoke hearts, thawed
2 cups water
2 tablespoons extra virgin olive oil
2 tablespoons fresh lemon juice
2 tablespoons butter
2 cloves garlic, minced
1 medium white onion or $^1/_2$ large white onion, chopped
4 cups chicken or vegetable broth
$^1/_2$ cup cold water mixed with 2 tablespoons cornstarch
1 cup organic heavy cream
Sea salt and freshly ground white pepper
1 lemon cut into 6 wedges, for serving

1. Pulse the artichoke hearts in a food processor to chop. Add the water, oil, and lemon juice and process until smooth.
2. In a 5- to 7-quart pressure cooker, melt the butter over medium heat. When it foams, add the garlic and onion, reduce the heat to medium-low, and cook, stirring a few times until the onion begins to soften, about 3 minutes; be careful not to burn the garlic. Add the chopped artichoke hearts and broth.
3. Close and lock the lid. Set the burner heat to high. When the cooker reaches HIGH pressure, reduce the burner heat as low as you can and still maintain HIGH pressure. Set a timer to cook for 8 minutes.
4. Remove the pot from the heat. Open the cooker with the Quick Release method. Be careful of the steam as you remove the lid.
5. Stir the cornstarch slurry into the cream, then whisk into the soup. Puree the soup in the pot with an immersion blender until smooth. Taste for salt and pepper. Simmer, uncovered, over medium heat, whisking a few times, for 15 minutes to thicken.
6. To serve, grind some pepper over it, squeeze a wedge of lemon, and have some sourdough bread on the side.

Cream of Fresh Artichoke Soup: Cut 8 to 10 large fresh globe artichokes lengthwise into quarters. With a small knife, remove the thistly choke part and discard. Cut away the leaves from the artichoke hearts and reserve for steaming and eating later if desired. Cut or peel away the tough outside skin of the stems and discard. If you like, leave an inch or two of stem with each of the hearts. Slice the hearts or chop to a quarter-inch thickness. Add with the onion and garlic in Step 2. Increase the pressure cooker time to 10 minutes.

Pea and Watercress Soup

Serves 4 • Cooker: 5- to 7-quart • Time: 6 minutes at HIGH pressure

Beth used to live by a stream that had a patch of watercress growing in it. There would be a trek over a small hill to the stream, armed with kitchen shears and a plastic bag, to collect the precious peppery-flavored greens. Unknowingly, she was partaking in a ritual of food foraging that has gone on since antiquity, since watercress is one of the first leafy greens consumed by humans. Watercress is in the same family as the nasturtium, which has an edible flower and whose edible leaves have the same peppery bite as watercress. Look for watercress with the fresh herbs in your supermarket.

2 tablespoons butter
1 large white onion, chopped
2 large russet potatoes, peeled and quartered
4 cups vegetable or chicken broth
Sea salt and freshly ground white pepper
1 (12-ounce) package frozen petite peas, thawed
2 bunches watercress, rinsed well, tough stems
    removed, with 4 sprigs set aside for garnish
2 tablespoons white miso
1/2 cup half-and-half or unsweetened soy milk

1. In a 5- to 7-quart pressure cooker, melt the butter over medium heat. When it foams, add the onion, reduce the heat to medium-low, and cook, stirring a few times, until it begins to soften, about 3 minutes. Add the potatoes and broth. The broth should just barely cover the potatoes and onion; it's okay if a few potato edges are exposed. Stir in a pinch of salt and some white pepper and stir to distribute the potatoes and onion into as even a layer as possible.

2. Close and lock the lid. Set the burner heat to high. When the cooker reaches HIGH pressure, reduce the burner heat as low as you can and still maintain HIGH pressure. Set a timer to cook for 6 minutes.

3. Remove the pot from the heat. Open the cooker with the Quick Release method. Be careful of the steam as you remove the lid. Add the peas and watercress and cook, uncovered, over medium heat until the greens are wilted but still bright green, 3 to 4 minutes.

4. Puree the soup in the pot using an immersion blender. Place a little of the soup in a cup and add the miso. Mix well with a fork and return to the soup pot. Stir in the half-and-half and taste for salt. Serve immediately, garnished with a watercress sprig.

Split Pea Soup with Wild Rice

Serves 4 • Cooker: 5- to 8-quart • Time: 10 minutes at HIGH pressure

Split peas do not need to be soaked and they cook up in a flash in the pressure cooker, so you can think, "I'd like to have split pea soup for lunch" and be eating it 30 minutes later. Serve with crackers and cheese.

1$^1/_2$ cups dried green or yellow split peas, rinsed and picked over
1 large white onion, chopped
2 ribs celery, finely chopped
1 medium carrot, chopped
1 large russet potato, peeled and cut into 1-inch cubes (about 2 cups)
$^1/_2$ cup wild rice
8 cups water or vegetable broth
$^1/_2$ teaspoon dried Italian herb blend
3 tablespoons olive oil
Salt and a few grinds black pepper

1. In a 5- to 8-quart pressure cooker, combine the split peas, onion, celery, carrots, potato, and rice. Gradually pour in the water (this keeps the peas from clumping together), then sprinkle with the herbs. Do not stir; drizzle with the oil.
2. Close and lock the lid. Set the burner heat to high. When the cooker reaches HIGH pressure, reduce the burner heat as low as you can and still maintain HIGH pressure. Set a timer to cook for 10 minutes.
3. Remove the pot from the heat. Open the cooker with the Natural Release method; let stand for 10 minutes. Be careful of the steam as you remove the lid.
4. Season the soup with salt to taste (start with about $^1/_4$ teaspoon) and grind in some pepper. Serve hot in deep bowls.

Split Pea Soup with Ham

Serves 4 • Cooker: 5- to 7-quart • Time: 6 minutes at HIGH pressure

Some foods speak to your soul as well as your stomach, and therein lies the attraction of split pea soup. This thick pea and ham soup, known in French cuisine as the *potage St. Germain,* is so surprisingly easy, especially in a pressure cooker. It takes about 3 minutes of chopping, 6 minutes of pressure cooking time, and then 20 minutes to just let it sit to finish cooking. This particular version comes from popular blogger and cookbook writer Jaden Hair of steamykitchen.com, who got it from a friend, who got it from the back of a package of split peas. We also love our variation, adding white beans to the mix, since it is a natural marriage of texture and flavor.

1 pound (2¼ cups) dried green split peas, rinsed
   and picked over
3 cups chopped ham or smoked turkey
3 medium carrots, diced
3 ribs celery, diced
1 large white onion, diced
2 cloves garlic, minced
1 bay leaf
3 tablespoons chopped fresh flatleaf parsley
4 cups water
1 teaspoon fine sea salt
Freshly ground black pepper
2 tablespoons olive oil

1. In a 5- to 7-quart pressure cooker, combine the split peas, ham, carrots, celery, onion, garlic, bay leaf, and parsley. Gradually pour in the water (it keeps the peas from clumping up), then add the salt and a few grinds of pepper. Bring to a boil over high heat. Do not stir; drizzle with the oil.
2. Close and lock the lid. Set the burner heat to high. When the cooker reaches HIGH pressure, reduce the burner heat as low as you can and still maintain HIGH pressure. Set a timer to cook for 6 minutes.
3. Remove the pot from the heat. Open the cooker with the Natural Release method; let stand for 20 minutes. Be careful of the steam as you remove the lid.
4. Taste for salt and pepper. Serve hot, in deep soup bowls.

Split Pea Soup with Ham and White Beans: Add 1 (15-ounce) can white beans (such as Great Northern or navy), rinsed and drained, or 1¾ cups cooked white beans, in Step 3 after opening the pressure cooker. Simmer 5 to 8 minutes over medium heat, uncovered, to heat the beans.

Smoky Double Green Split Pea Soup

Serves 4 • Cooker: 5- to 7-quart • Time: 10 minutes at HIGH pressure

This vegetarian version of split pea soup is creamy, savory, and can be on your table in no time. If you like, serve with a spoonful of plain Greek yogurt on top and let it melt into the soup. Serve hot with warm whole wheat bread and butter, or crackers.

1¼ cups dried green split peas, rinsed and picked over
1 (10-ounce) package frozen peas (no need to defrost)
½ cup chopped shallots (3 medium to large)
1 medium white onion, chopped
1 large sweet potato, peeled and cut into 1-inch cubes
2 ribs celery, finely chopped
1½ teaspoons smoked sweet paprika (pimentón)
5 cups vegetable broth
1 (14-ounce) can diced tomatoes in juice, undrained
2 tablespoons olive oil
Salt

1. In a 5- to 7-quart pressure cooker, combine the split peas, frozen peas, shallots, onion, sweet potato, and celery. Add the paprika and stir to combine. Gradually pour in the broth and tomatoes with their juice. Do not stir; drizzle with the oil.
2. Close and lock the lid. Set the burner heat to high. When the cooker reaches HIGH pressure, reduce the burner heat as low as you can and still maintain HIGH pressure. Set a timer to cook for 10 minutes.
3. Remove the pot from the heat. Open the cooker with the Natural Release method; let stand for 10 minutes. Be careful of the steam as you remove the lid.
4. Puree the soup in the pot with an immersion blender. Season the soup with salt to taste (start with about ¼ teaspoon).

Doctor Frank-N-Furter's Yellow Split Pea Soup

Serves 4 • Cooker: 5- to 7-quart • Time: 10 minutes at HIGH pressure

A favorite of kids the world over. Great with bread, or biscuits and butter.

1 tablespoon butter
½ pound turkey, chicken, or kosher beef hot dogs, sliced on the diagonal into ¾-inch-thick rounds
1 large white onion, chopped
1½ cups dried yellow split peas, rinsed and picked over
1 large russet potato, peeled and diced
1 medium turnip, peeled and diced
6 cups chicken broth
2 tablespoons olive oil
Salt and freshly ground black pepper

1. In a 5- to 7-quart pressure cooker, melt the butter over medium heat. When it foams, add the hot dogs and slightly brown the slices on both sides; remove to a plate. Add the onion and cook, stirring a few times, until softened, about 3 minutes. Add the peas, potato, turnip, and broth. Return the hot dogs to the pot. Do not stir; drizzle with the oil.
2. Close and lock the lid. Set the burner heat to high. When the cooker reaches HIGH pressure, reduce the burner heat as low as you can and still maintain HIGH pressure. Set a timer to cook for 10 minutes.
3. Remove the pot from the heat. Open the cooker with the Natural Release method; let stand for 10 minutes. Be careful of the steam as you remove the lid. Taste for salt and pepper. Serve hot, in deep soup bowls.

Swedish Pea Soup with Smoked Turkey

Serves 6 • Cooker: 6- to 8-quart • Time: 22 minutes at HIGH pressure

Sweden has a particularly strong pea soup tradition. Pea soup—with pancakes for dessert—is the traditional Thursday night supper. The soup is generally made with pork in some form. Crispbread crackers are served on the side, and each diner stirs in prepared mustard to taste. Now that yellow and blue Ikea stores dot the United States' landscape, you can buy the special dried whole yellow peas used in Sweden. They take longer to cook than split peas, even if you soak them first. The pressure cooker cuts the time to a manageable 22 minutes. We made our Swedish soup with a whole smoked turkey leg. Because the smoked turkey is salty, no extra salt is needed.

18 ounces (about 2³/₄ cups) dried whole yellow peas, rinsed and picked over
1 medium white or yellow onion, chopped
3 ribs celery, chopped
2 medium carrots, chopped
1 teaspoon ground ginger
1 teaspoon dried marjoram
8 cups water
1 smoked turkey leg
Salt and freshly ground black pepper
Prepared brown mustard or cider vinegar, for serving

1. Place the peas in a large bowl and cover them generously with water. Let soak at least 12 hours or overnight.
2. Drain the peas and place them in a 6- to 8-quart pressure cooker. Add the onion, celery, carrots, ginger, marjoram, and water. Stir well. Add the turkey leg, nestling it down into the peas. (If the turkey leg is too big for the pressure cooker, you can use a cleaver to chop it in two, or simply slice off the meat and add that to the pot.)
3. Close and lock the lid. Set the burner heat to high. When the cooker reaches HIGH pressure, reduce the burner heat as low as you can and still maintain HIGH pressure. Set a timer to cook for 22 minutes.
4. Remove the pot from the heat. Open the cooker with the Quick Release method. Be careful of the steam as you remove the lid. Using tongs, remove the turkey leg to a cutting board. When the turkey has cooled a bit, cut the meat from the bone and chop it into bite-size pieces. Discard the skin.
5. Partly puree the soup in the pot using an immersion blender. Alternately, remove about 2 cups of the soup to a blender or food processor and process it smooth, then return it to the pot. Stir in the reserved turkey. Taste for salt and pepper.
6. Serve the soup hot, in soup plates or bowls. Traditionally, each diner stirs a bit of hearty mustard into his or her portion. A few drops of cider vinegar are a nice alternative.

Lemon Lentil Soup with Chard

Serves 4 to 6 • Cooker: 5- to 7-quart • Time: 8 minutes at HIGH pressure

Lentils are a good source of protein (they have the third highest level after soy and hemp). All you need is a simple green salad and crusty bread for a full meal. If you like, you can serve this soup over hot steamed rice or pasta. Top with plain yogurt or our Preserved Lemon Yogurt.

3 tablespoon olive oil
$^1/_2$ cup finely chopped onion
3 medium waxy potatoes, cut into $^1/_2$-inch dice
1 cup chopped celery
1 bunch Swiss chard, both stems and leaves
    chopped (about 4 cups)
1 tablespoon ground coriander
$^1/_2$ teaspoon ground cumin
$^1/_2$ teaspoon freshly ground black pepper
$1^1/_2$ cups dried brown lentils, rinsed and picked over
$^1/_4$ cup dried red lentils, picked over and rinsed in
    cold water until the water runs clear (this is very
    important or the lentils will get "scummy")
7 cups water
3 to 4 tablespoons fresh lemon juice, to taste
$^1/_4$ cup chopped fresh cilantro
$^1/_4$ cup chopped fresh flatleaf parsley
Sea salt
Preserved Lemon Yogurt (recipe follows), for serving

1. In a 5- to 7-quart pressure cooker, heat the oil over medium heat. Add the onion, potatoes, celery, and chard and cook, stirring a few times, until the onion and chard soften a bit, about 3 minutes. Add the spices, black pepper, and both lentils and stir until they are coated with the oil. Add the water. Stir well.
2. Close and lock the lid. Set the burner heat to high. When the cooker reaches HIGH pressure, reduce the burner heat as low as you can and still maintain HIGH pressure. Set a timer to cook for 8 minutes.
3. Remove the pot from the heat. Open the cooker with the Natural Release method; let for stand 15 minutes. Be careful of the steam as you remove the lid.
4. Stir in the lemon juice, cilantro, and parsley, which will wilt immediately in the hot soup. Add salt to taste. Serve hot, in deep soup bowls, topped with a dollop of the yogurt.

Preserved Lemon Yogurt

Makes about $1^1/_4$ cups

1 cup plain Greek yogurt
$^1/_4$ preserved lemon, pulp discarded, peel
    thoroughly rinsed and minced
1 tablespoon chopped fresh flatleaf parsley or
    cilantro
1 tablespoon fresh lemon juice or preserved lemon
    juice from jar
$^1/_2$ teaspoon finely grated lemon zest
$^1/_4$ teaspoon sea salt

Place all ingredients in a small bowl and stir with a fork until thoroughly blended. Cover and refrigerate for at least 1 hour to let the flavors develop before using. Keeps in an airtight container in the refrigerator for up to 1 week.

CUMIN

Cumin seeds are used for their distinctive aroma in North African, Middle Eastern, Western Chinese, Indian, Cuban, Brazilian, and Northern Mexican cooking. It is the second most popular spice in the world after black pepper.

Cumin is a critical ingredient in chili powder, and is found in achiote blends, adobos, *sofrito,* garam masala, curry powder, and *baharat.* In herbal medicine, cumin is classified as stimulant, carminative, and antimicrobial. Cumin is known for stimulating a healthy immune system.

Aromatic white cumin seeds are available in Indian food markets; do not substitute black cumin seed as it has a more assertive, complex flavor. Cumin can be used to season many dishes, either ground or as whole seeds, drawing out the natural sweetness of what it is added to. It is traditionally added to curries, enchiladas, and tacos. It is also used in making authentic Mexican guacamole.

Brown Lentil Tomato Soup

Serves 2 to 3 • Cooker: 5- to 7-quart • Time: 8 minutes at HIGH pressure

The type of broth you use to make this will affect the color and taste of the soup. We love using Mexican oregano in this. Use the plain ol' bag of generic lentils on your supermarket shelf or Pardina Spanish brown lentils, which are the favorite of many lentil lovers. The variation with mixed ancient grains is excellent as well. This recipe doubles or triples perfectly.

2 tablespoons olive oil
1 large white onion, finely chopped
1 medium carrot, diced
2 ribs celery, chopped
1 1/4 cups dried brown lentils, rinsed and picked over
1/2 to 1 teaspoon dried Italian herb blend, herbes de Provence, or Mexican oregano, to taste
4 cups chicken, vegetable, or beef broth (this is good with half chicken and half beef broth)
2 cups water
1 (14.5-ounce) can diced tomatoes in juice (can be fire roasted), undrained
1 tablespoon sherry vinegar, balsamic vinegar, or cider vinegar
1 1/2 teaspoons sea salt
Shredded Parmesan cheese, for serving

1. In a 5- to 7-quart pressure cooker, heat the oil over medium heat. Add the onion, carrot, and celery and cook, stirring a few times, until the vegetables begin to soften, about 3 minutes. Add the lentils and stir until they are coated with the oil. Add the herbs, broth, and water. Stir well.
2. Close and lock the lid. Set the burner heat to high. When the cooker reaches HIGH pressure, reduce the burner heat as low as you can and still maintain HIGH pressure. Set a timer to cook for 8 minutes.
3. Remove the pot from the heat. Open the cooker with the Natural Release method; let stand for 15 minutes. Be careful of the steam as you remove the lid.
4. Stir in the tomatoes with their juice, the vinegar, and salt. Thin with some water, if desired. Heat, uncovered, over medium heat until hot, about 10 minutes. Serve hot, in deep soup bowls, sprinkled with Parmesan if you like.

Brown Lentil Tomato Soup with Ancient Grains: Place 2 tablespoons *each* of red or white quinoa, whole millet, pearled or black barley, and amaranth in a small bowl. Cover with water and let soak 30 minutes to 1 hour. Drain. Add with the lentils in Step 1.

Brown Lentil Tomato Soup with Harissa: Substitute 1 to 2 tablespoons spicy harissa, or a combination of sweet and spicy harissa, for the dried herbs in Step 1.

Coconut Curry Red Lentil Soup

Serves 4 • Cooker: 5- to 7-quart • Time: 6 minutes at HIGH pressure

Red/pink lentils are the new darling of the lentil world, esteemed for their sweet, mild, nutty flavor. They cook in minutes to a nice mushy golden and are even good to feed to babies, they are so easily digested. Petite crimson/red lentils are marketed as *masoor* (red lentils). These are skinned and split whole greenish brown *masoor* lentils that are salmon-colored inside. The most common type of red lentil is the Red Chief. They are great for dal, soups, and for thickening other soups. Thai red curry paste is a potent mixture that embodies the taste of Thai food; it's a combination of coriander seeds, lemongrass, galangal, kaffir lime leaves, cilantro, shallots, garlic, fresh chiles, chili powder, coconut milk, lime juice, and shrimp paste. Look for it in the Asian section of your supermarket.

2 tablespoons olive oil, plus more for serving
1 medium or 1/2 large white onion, finely chopped
1 1/2 cups dried red lentils, picked over and rinsed in cold water until the water runs clear (this is very important or the lentils will get "scummy")
1 small clove garlic, minced
1 (1-inch) knob fresh ginger, peeled and grated
1 to 2 teaspoons Thai red curry paste, depending on how hot you like it
6 cups water
1 medium sweet potato, preferably a Japanese white sweet potato, peeled and cut into 1/2-inch dice
1/4 teaspoon turmeric
Sea salt
1/2 cup unsweetened coconut milk
1/3 cup chopped fresh cilantro, for garnish

1. In a 5- to 7-quart pressure cooker, heat the oil over medium heat until very hot. Add the onion and cook, stirring a few times, until it begins to soften, about 3 minutes. Add the lentils and stir to coat with the oil. Stir in the garlic, ginger, and curry paste, combining well with the lentils and heating until fragrant. Add the water, sweet potato, and turmeric.

2. Close and lock the lid. Set the burner heat to high. When the cooker reaches HIGH pressure, reduce the burner heat as low as you can and still maintain HIGH pressure. Set a timer to cook for 6 minutes.

3. Remove the pot from the heat. Open the cooker with the Natural Release method; let stand for 15 minutes. Be careful of the steam as you remove the lid.

4. Stir in the salt and coconut milk. Heat, uncovered, over medium heat for 5 minutes. Serve hot, in deep soup bowls, with a sprinkling of cilantro and a drizzle of oil.

Lentil Soup with Vegetables and Garden Herbs

Serves 4 to 6 • Cooker: 5- to 7-quart • Time: 12 minutes at HIGH pressure

The original recipe for this uniquely flavored lentil soup came from cookbook writer and radio personality, the late Dolores Kostelni, known to her radio audience as the Happy Cook. It was one she would teach in her classes about cooking with herbs; we've adapted it for the pressure cooker. "Lemon balm and lemon verbena grow profusely in my herb garden," said Dolores, "and I use them both with abandon. I grew up with lentil soup. My parents seasoned their bowls of lentil soup with plenty of olive oil and a little Parmesan cheese to give what they called 'the homely lentils a boost.' To this day, I do the same thing before I enjoy my bowl of lentil soup." Lemon verbena, a member of the mint family, is a really special flowering perennial herb, and you can find it at herbs & greens sellers at farmers' markets if you don't get delighted and grow it yourself. Verbena has a more assertive herbal lemon flavor than the balm, but both make excellent seasonings in butter cookies, simple syrups to drizzle on fruit salad, ice cream, infused vinegar, pesto, soups, and vegetable dishes.

^{1}/$_4$ cup olive oil, plus more for serving
1 large onion, halved and sliced into thin half
    moons
1^1/$_2$ cups dried brown lentils, rinsed and picked
    over
3 medium carrots, sliced into ^{1}/$_4$-inch-thick rounds
3 cloves garlic, minced
3 ribs celery, sliced
3 cups vegetable broth
3 cups water
Bouquet garni of 1 bay leaf and 1 small bunch
    lemon verbena, tied by stems
1 tablespoon chopped fresh lemon verbena
Grated zest of 1 lemon
^{1}/$_3$ cup chopped fresh flatleaf parsley
Salt and freshly ground black pepper
Grated Parmesan cheese, for serving

1. In a 5- to 7-quart pressure cooker, heat the oil over medium heat. Add the onion and cook, stirring a few times, until it begins to soften, about 3 minutes. Add the lentils and stir to coat them with the oil. Stir in the carrots, garlic, and celery, combining well with the lentils. Gradually pour in the broth and water to keep the lentils from clumping; bring to a simmer. Add the bouquet garni.

2. Close and lock the lid. Set the burner heat to high. When the cooker reaches HIGH pressure, reduce the burner heat as low as you can and still maintain HIGH pressure. Set a timer to cook for 12 minutes.

3. Remove the pot from the heat. Open the cooker with the Quick Release method. Be careful of the steam as you remove the lid. Discard the bouquet garni.

4. Stir in the lemon verbena, lemon zest, and parsley. Season with salt and pepper to taste. Pass the olive oil and Parmesan at the table.

Moong Dal with Vegetables

Serves 4 as a main dish • Cooker: 5- to 8-quart • Time: 18 minutes at HIGH pressure

Moong dal, a yellow split lentil, is considered in North India to be the best of the lentils, easy to digest, sweet, and nutritious. It is skinned and flat, making it easy to cook. Serve this with steamed basmati or jasmine brown rice and chapati or whole wheat paratha flatbread. You can also top each serving with a dollop of plain yogurt and a sprinkling of red New Mexican chile powder. This is a great dish to cook when you or a loved one has a cold or the flu.

1 cup dried moong dal
5 cups water
$1/2$ teaspoon turmeric
2 tablespons ghee or olive oil
1 teaspoon cumin seeds
1 (2-inch) piece fresh ginger, peeled and crushed or grated
2 medium plum tomatoes, seeded and chopped
2 teaspoons ground coriander
About 2 to 3 cups mixed vegetables, cut into even-sized small chunks, such as broccoli florets, cauliflower florets, green beans, radish, eggplant, Napa cabbage, potatoes, green bell pepper (do not use zucchini or Swiss chard; they don't taste good in this dal)
1 bunch fresh spinach, washed well, heavy stems discarded, and leaves cut across into thick ribbons
1 tablespoon tamarind juice or juice of 1 small lemon
Sea salt

1. Rinse the dal and remove any stones or debris. Place in a small bowl and cover with water; let soak 4 to 6 hours at room temperature.
2. Drain and place the dal in a 5- to 7-quart pressure cooker with the 5 cups water and turmeric.
3. Close and lock the lid. Set the burner heat to high. When the cooker reaches HIGH pressure, reduce the burner heat as low as you can and still maintain HIGH pressure. Set a timer to cook for 18 minutes. If using an Indian pressure cooker, pressure cook for three whistles (this is fast and will lead to a very creamy dal).
4. Meanwhile, in a deep skillet (because the cumin seeds will pop), heat the ghee over medium-high heat. Add the cumin seeds and let them sputter, then add the ginger. Stir in the tomatoes and sauté for a few minutes until soft.
5. Remove the pot from the heat. Open the cooker with the Quick Release method. Be careful of the steam as you remove the lid. Add the contents of the skillet to the pot. If the gravy is too thick, add some boiling water to thin it to your liking. Add the coriander and vegetable chunks. Partially cover (do not lock the lid) and simmer over low heat until the vegetables are tender, but not mushy, 15 to 20 minutes.
6. Stir in the spinach and tamarind juice. Taste for salt. Cover (do not lock the lid) and continue to simmer for another 5 minutes to cook the spinach. Stir once and serve. Keeps in an airtight container for 2 to 3 days in the refrigerator and up to 4 months in the freezer.

DAL

Dal, or *dahl,* refers to the dried peas and beans that have been part of Indian cuisine since ancient times. The brain twister is that all lentils are dal, but all dal are not lentils. The repertoire of dal cookery is staggering: soups, sauces, stews, pancakes, even desserts.

Dal soups are seasoned with ginger, to aid digestion, and a fried spice blend known as *tadka* or *chaun,* for added flavor. Some dals are prepared with garlic or onions, but traditional dals do not contain these, or any member of the onion family, in the manner of the ancient Hindu culinary laws.

The most popular dals for soup are the diminutive pale green or yellow mung dal *(moong dal),* whole or split without skins. Green or yellow split peas *(matar dal),* golden lentils *(toovar dal),* or black gram *(urad dal)* can be substituted, but will taste slightly different and have a different texture and color. *Chana dal* is the split chickpea.

Dal should be rinsed with cold water and sorted before soaking. We always make dal stews with split dals, as they take less time to cook. The hardness or softness of the water and the age of the dal can affect cooking times, so you may need to cook your dal a few extra minutes.

Black Bean and Sweet Potato Soup

Serves 6 • Cooker: 5- to 7-quart • Time: 40 minutes at HIGH pressure

The black bean and its New World relative the sweet potato combine for a creamy, hearty, flavorful bowl of goodness. Sweet potatoes are loved the world over and there are many varieties available. You can use either the yellow- or orange-fleshed types. We think the Japanese white sweet potatoes we get from a local organic farm are especially good. The two-step process of soaking, then cooking dried beans keeps so many people from preparing beans from scratch. Really, that is such a shame. Home-cooked beans are superior to canned ones in myriad ways—flavor, texture, cost, and sodium content, just to name a few. The pressure cooker really and truly solves this problem. Black beans cook go from dried to tender and creamy in a mere 40 minutes (no pre-soaking here!). A squeeze of lime juice adds zip, and don't knock the egg until you've tried it. The yolk bits almost melt into the soup, adding richness and depth.

1 1/2 cups dried black beans, rinsed and picked over
1 small sweet potato, peeled and roughly chopped
     (about 1 cup)
1 large yellow onion, roughly chopped
1 large rib celery, roughly chopped
A few tender celery leaves (2 to 3 tablespoons)
2 cloves garlic, peeled and smashed
4 cups chicken broth
4 cups water
2 tablespoons extra virgin olive oil
1/4 cup fresh flatleaf parsley leaves and tender
     stems (from about 2 to 3 medium sprigs)
1 teaspoon ground cumin
1/4 teaspoon ground coriander
4 large or extra-large eggs, for serving
Salt
Lime wedges, for serving (optional)

1. In a 5- to 7-quart pressure cooker, combine the beans, sweet potato, onion, celery rib and leaves, garlic, broth, water, oil, parsley, cumin, and coriander. Stir.
2. Close and lock the lid. Set the burner heat to high. When the cooker reaches HIGH pressure, reduce the burner heat as low as you can and still maintain HIGH pressure. Set a timer to cook for 40 minutes.
3. While the soup cooks, hard-boil the eggs. Place the eggs in a saucepan and add water to cover them by 1 inch. Bring to a boil over high heat. As soon as you see bubbles around the sides of the pot, remove the pan from the heat, cover, and let stand for 12 minutes. Drain the eggs and rinse under cold running water. Set aside to cool completely. Can be made the day before and refrigerated. Once the eggs have cooked and cooled, remove the shells by tapping each egg gently on the counter or sink all over to crackle it. Or roll each egg between your hands to loosen the shell. Peel, starting at the large end, while holding the egg under running cold water; this facilitates peeling and also removes any stray shell fragments. Coarsely chop and refrigerate until serving time.
4. Remove the pot from the heat. Open the cooker with the Natural Release method by turning off the heat or moving the cooker to another burner on an electric stove; let stand for 15 minutes. Be careful of the steam as you remove the lid. Add salt to taste.
5. Serve hot topped with 2 heaping tablespoons of chopped egg and lime wedges if you like for each bowl.

Vegetarian White Bean Soup

Serves 6 • Cooker: 5- to 7-quart • Time: 12 minutes at HIGH pressure

This wonderful fragrant soup should be called The Unbelievably Easy Bean Soup. It boasts three different types of white beans. Presoaking the beans makes for a very fast cook time. You can soak all the beans together if you like. If you use canned beans, cut the cook time in half. Seek out the Mexican oregano, one of our favorite all-purpose herbs, and use it instead of the Greek oregano, which is stronger. A great lunch soup.

1 cup dried Great Northern beans
1 cup dried cannellini (white kidney) beans
$1/2$ cup dried baby white beans
$1/4$ cup olive oil, plus more for serving
1 large white or yellow onion, chopped
3 ribs celery, chopped
2 medium carrots, chopped
$1/2$ teaspoon dried thyme
$1/2$ teaspoon dried oregano, preferably Mexican
1 (14.5-ounce) can diced tomatoes in juice,
   undrained
8 cups vegetable broth
2 medium zucchini, quartered lengthwise and sliced
   $1/2$ inch thick
Sea salt and freshly ground black pepper
Grated or shredded Parmesan cheese, for serving

1. Soak the beans (see page 405) and drain.
2. In a 5- to 7-quart pressure cooker, heat the oil over medium-high heat. Add onion, celery, carrots, and herbs and cook, stirring often, until the onion begins to soften, about 3 minutes. Stir in the beans, tomatoes with their juice, and broth.
3. Close and lock the lid. Set the burner heat to high. When the cooker reaches HIGH pressure, reduce the burner heat as low as you can and still maintain HIGH pressure. Set a timer to cook for 12 minutes.
4. Remove the pot from the heat. Open the cooker with the Quick Release method. Be careful of the steam as you remove the lid.
5. Add the zucchini to the pot and cook, uncovered, over low heat, until tender-crisp, 3 to 4 minutes. Season with salt and pepper to taste.
6. Serve the soup nice and hot with the grated cheese on the side and a drizzle of olive oil over the top.

Pressure Cooker Vegetable Bean Soup

Serves 3 to 4 • Cooker: 5- to 7-quart • Time: Consult pages 400–404 for your particular type of beans

Bean soups are hearty and nutritious and gloriously easy to prepare in the pressure cooker. It is a bean lover's delight, vegetarian or not, to be able to choose from dozens of dried beans. Don't pass up this recipe, thinking it's too basic. The character of the soup changes with each type of bean used—whether it be white, black, pinto, lima, or an heirloom bean. Use our universal bean chart on pages 400–404, to choose your bean and get its cook time. This is soup made with unsoaked beans, so you can whip it up any time, any season, *a la momento*. Great for lunch with cornbread or grilled cheese sandwiches.

1 cup dried beans of choice, rinsed and picked over
4 cups vegetable or chicken broth, or combination broth or water
1 large white or yellow onion, chopped
1 to 2 carrots, to taste, sliced $1/2$ inch thick ($1/2$ to 1 cup)
1 to 2 ribs celery, to taste, sliced $1/2$ inch thick ($1/2$ to 1 cup)
1 clove garlic, chopped
2 tablespoons chopped fresh flatleaf parsley
1 tablespoon light olive oil
1 teaspoon dried herbs, such as thyme, marjoram, Mexican oregano, poultry seasoning, Italian seasoning, etc., or salt-free herb blend
$1/2$ bay leaf
Meat, if desired (optional), such as 1 to 2 slices bacon cut into strips or $1/2$ cup diced ham or smoked turkey or sliced cooked sausage
$1/2$ teaspoon freshly ground black pepper
Sea salt
1 to 3 tablespoons good quality vinegar of your choice or fresh lemon or lime juice, to taste
Minced fresh herbs, such as parsley or cilantro

1. In a 5- to 7-quart pressure cooker, combine the beans, water, onion, carrots, celery, garlic, parsley, oil, and dried herbs. If you are using bacon, add it now. Stir to combine. Note the cooking time for your beans (unsoaked) from our chart.

2. Close and lock the lid. Set the burner heat to high. When the cooker reaches HIGH pressure, reduce the burner heat as low as you can and still maintain HIGH pressure. Set a timer to cook for the proper cooking time per the bean cooking chart.

3. Remove the pot from the heat. Open the cooker with the Natural Release method; let stand for 15 minutes. Be careful of the steam as you remove the lid. You will want the beans to be very soft for soup, so if they are not soft enough, relock the cooker, bring it back up to HIGH pressure, and cook for another 2 to 5 minutes.

4. If desired, puree part of the soup right in the pot with an immersion blender. If you are using a meat other than bacon, add it now. Add salt to taste. Let simmer, uncovered, a few minutes over medium heat. Stir in the vinegar.

5. Serve the soup hot in bowls, topped with a sprinkle of minced herbs. This will keep 4 to 5 days in the refrigerator or in the freezer up to 4 months.

Bean Soup Mixes in the Pressure Cooker

Mixed bean or bean and grain soup mixes seem to grow more popular and numerous every year. The vast majority of these mixes fall into two categories—quick or slow-cooking. The fast-cooking ones feature legumes such as split peas and lentils, and may include tiny pastas. These generally shouldn't be soaked before cooking. The slow-cooking ones include legumes like black beans, kidney beans, garbanzos, and the like. Anything called 10- or 13-bean soup mix is bound to be long-cooking!

How can you tell which is which? Look at the suggested cooking time on the package. The fast-cooking ones need about an hour by conventional methods; the slow ones usually call for soaking the beans, then a cook time of two hours or more. A good rule to remember is this: Let the longest-cooking bean in the mix be your guide. Once you have identified which type mix you have, and whether or not you want to soak it, select the appropriate recipe below.

If you have a dusty package of bean mix that has been on your shelf longer than you can remember, please toss it out and start fresh. When shopping, look for clean packages without a lot of debris on the bottom of the bag.

"Quick" Cooking Bean Mix Soup

Serves 6 • Cooker: 5- to 7-quart • Time: 13 minutes at HIGH pressure

1 cup "quick" bean or bean and grain mix (typically these include split peas, lentils, and the like)

4 cups unsalted or reduced-sodium chicken, beef or vegetable broth

1 cup water or 1 (14.5-ounce) can diced tomatoes in juice, undrained

1 medium onion, chopped into $^1/_2$-inch pieces, OR 1 leek (white and light green parts), trimmed, cut in half lengthwise, rinsed well, and sliced across $^1/_2$ inch thick

2 medium carrots, cut into $^1/_2$-inch-thick rounds, largest pieces halved crosswise

2 ribs celery, sliced $^1/_2$ inch thick, larger pieces halved

2 cloves garlic, chopped

1 ham bone; $^1/_2$ cup regular or turkey bacon, chopped; $^1/_2$ to 1 cup sliced smoked sausage, 1 cup diced stewing beef; OR 2 skinless, boneless chicken thighs, cut into small pieces (if using leftover cooked chicken, stir it in just before serving) (optional)

1 teaspoon salt-free seasoning or herb blend (we love Penzeys Forward for bean soups)

Salt

Juice of 1 lemon or 1 to 2 tablespoons vinegar of your choice (optional)

$^1/_2$ cup minced fresh flatleaf parsley or cilantro (optional)

1. If the package calls for rinsing the beans and grains, do so. Place the mix in a 5- to 7-quart pressure cooker. Add the broth, onion, carrots, celery, garlic, meat if using, and seasoning if using. Stir to combine.

2. Close and lock the lid. Set the burner heat to high. When the cooker reaches HIGH pressure, reduce the burner heat as low as you can and still maintain HIGH pressure. Set a timer to cook for 13 minutes.

3. Remove the pot from the heat. Open the cooker with the Quick Release method. Be careful of the steam as you remove the lid.

4. Taste the soup for salt. Add the lemon juice if using. Stir in the parsley. Ladle into bowls and serve hot. This will keep 4 to 5 days in the refrigerator or in the freezer up to 4 months.

"Slow" Cooking Bean Mix Soup with Unsoaked Beans: Substitute 1 cup "slow" bean or bean-and-grain mix for the "quick" mix. Increase the water to 2 cups or use 1 (14.5-ounce) can diced tomatoes in juice, undrained, plus 1 cup water. Follow the recipe as directed above, increasing the pressure cooker time to 35 minutes at HIGH pressure.

"Slow" Cooking Bean Mix Soup with Soaked Beans: Substitute 1 cup "slow" bean or bean-and-grain mix for the "quick" mix. Soak the bean mix (see page 406) and drain. Place in the pressure cooker and add the ingredients as directed above, omitting the water. If you like, add 1 (14.5-ounce) can diced tomatoes in juice, drained. Cook as directed, decreasing the pressure cooker time to 12 minutes.

Healing Chicken Soup for the Busy Soul

Serves 4 to 5 • Cooker: 6- to 8-quart • Time: 30 minutes at HIGH pressure

Homemade chicken soup is an expression of love and comfort, but finding the time to prepare it can be impossible, especially when a loved one is sick. Let your pressure cooker come the rescue. This soup takes several labor-saving shortcuts. It also makes one compromise—the 30-minute cooking time. For the richest, most flavorful broth, a longer cooking time would be required (see our Stocks and Broth chapter, page 21). But it's a small sacrifice for delicious chicken soup that doesn't come from a can.

1 (3¹/₂- to 4-pound) chicken
1 medium onion, halved lengthwise
1 medium carrot, halved crosswise
1 rib celery, halved crosswise
2 sprigs fresh flatleaf parsley
¹/₂ bay leaf
¹/₄ to ¹/₂ teaspoon peppercorns (use ¹/₄ teaspoon if you have only black pepper; ¹/₂ teaspoon if you have a blend of different colored peppercorns)
6 to 6¹/₂ cups water, or as needed
Sea salt
1 cup cooked rice or a small soup pasta such as orzo, for serving
Minced fresh flatleaf parsley, for serving (optional)

1. Rinse the chicken. Remove the bag of giblets from the cavity. Pull off and discard any large lumps of fat from inside the cavity or around the neck. Place the chicken in a 6- to 8-quart pressure cooker pot, breast side up. Add the neck, heart, and gizzard but not the liver. Tuck the onion, carrot, celery, parsley sprigs, bay leaf, and peppercorns around the chicken. Locate the "maximum fill" line on your pressure cooker. Add the water, stopping if you hit the "maximum fill" line. Depending on the shape of your cooker, the chicken should be just covered or almost covered. Add up to ¹/₂ cup more water if the chicken isn't covered if you can do so without exceeding the maximum capacity of your cooker.
2. Close and lock the lid. Set the burner heat to high. When the cooker reaches HIGH pressure,

reduce the burner heat as low as you can and still maintain HIGH pressure. Set a timer to cook for 30 minutes.
3. Remove the pot from the heat. Open the cooker with the Quick Release method. Be careful of the steam as you remove the lid. Put a sturdy wooden spoon in the cavity of the chicken and carefully lift it, tilting so that the broth runs out of the cavity into the pot. Place the chicken on a plate. Set a large colander or strainer lined with a double layer of cheesecloth over a large bowl and pour the broth through to strain it. Use tongs to set aside the carrot. Discard the remaining contents of the colander.
4. Taste the broth for salt. Slice the carrot and return it to the soup in the bowl, or distribute it among the serving bowls if you are serving the soup right away. Remove the skin from one side of the chicken breast with a sharp knife and fork, then chop or shred the meat. Add it to the soup or distribute among the bowls. Repeat with the second breast half if desired. Add the rice or pasta. Before serving, top each bowl of hot soup with minced parsley if desired.

Note: If you don't want to discard the remaining chicken meat, use it in a filling for enchiladas, cannelloni, or another use where a moist sauce and powerful flavors take center stage. The meat can be frozen in a ziptop plastic freezer bag up to 2 months.

Persian Chicken Soup for the Busy Soul: Wash 5 dried Persian limes well, then pierce them with a fork through to their centers (so that the cooking liquid can run through and they can distribute their pungent citrusy flavor). Add them and 2 to 3 white waxy new potatoes, cubed, in Step 2. Dried Persian limes, *limu omani*, are available from a Middle Eastern grocery or online.

French Chicken Soup

Serves 6 to 8 • Cooker: 6- to 8-quart • Time: 10 minutes at HIGH pressure

Tarragon and mustard, two French culinary staples, are the surprise aromatics in this chicken vegetable soup. If you like your broth a bit stronger, stir in a teaspoon or two of organic chicken Better Than Bouillon. This is marvelous with thick slices of fresh baguette for dunking, maybe a piece of hard cheese.

3 medium leeks
2 tablespoons olive oil
6 boneless, skinless chicken thighs (about 1^1/$_2$ pounds)
3 medium carrots, cut into ^{1}/$_2$-inch dice
2 ribs, chopped
6 baby new potatoes, left unpeeled and halved
8 cups chicken broth
1^1/$_2$ tablespoons Dijon mustard
2 teaspoons dried tarragon
^{1}/$_2$ teaspoon ground nutmeg
^{1}/$_2$ teaspoon ground white pepper
3 tablespoons chopped fresh flatleaf parsley
Sea salt

1. Remove the tough outer layers and dark green tops on the leeks. Slice in half lengthwise and rinse under cold running water until all grit and sand is gone. Slice into thick pieces against the grain.
2. In a 6- to 8-quart pressure cooker, heat the oil over medium-high heat until very hot. Add the chicken and brown on both sides, turning once, about 3 minutes. Add the leeks, carrots, celery, and potatoes and cook, stirring, for about 2 minutes. Add the broth, mustard, tarragon, nutmeg, and pepper. Stir to blend in the mustard. Bring to a boil and skim off the foam.
3. Close and lock the lid. Set the burner heat to high. When the cooker reaches HIGH pressure, reduce the burner heat as low as you can and still maintain HIGH pressure. Set a timer to cook for 10 minutes.
4. Remove the pot from the heat. Open the cooker with the Quick Release method. Be careful of the steam as you remove the lid. Transfer the chicken to a cutting board. Cut or shred it into bite-sized pieces. Return to the soup. Add the parsley. Taste for seasoning, maybe adding two nice pinches of sea salt, and serve hot.

ALL ABOUT LEEKS

We love the flavor of leeks and how they perform in our soups, so many of our recipes call for them. If you have never cooked with leeks before, they do require some special attention. Notice that the lower portion of the leek, nearest the root, is white, while the top portion is dark green. There is a transitional light green section in between. To get started, cut off the dark green portion and set it aside. Now halve the white and light green portion of the leek lengthwise and peek between the layers, leaving them attached at the stem end. You will find out very quickly if your leek has a lot of dirt trapped between its layers. If not, consider it your lucky day. Trim away and discard the root end, which frees the layers.

Rinse the leek under cold running water, letting it run between the layers to remove any bits of dirt but keeping the layers together for easy slicing. If your leek is very dirty, trim the root end, and carefully wash each layer under running water, removing the dirt with your fingers. Return the leek to the cutting board, flat side down, and slice it.

Now take a look at the dark green portion that you set aside earlier. Peel off the first couple of layers and you will likely see more light green. If you have the patience, continue to pull apart the leek, cutting as you go where light green meets dark green. These layers are likely to be dirtier and will have to be checked and washed carefully before slicing. (The dark green portion of a leek is a nice addition to the pot when making chicken stock. Wash it carefully and freeze it until your next stock-making session.)

Day-After-Thanksgiving Turkey Soup with Cilantro and Barley

Serves 4 • Cooker: 5- to 7-quart • Time: 10 minutes at HIGH pressure

It's part of the holiday ritual, picking the meat off the turkey so the carcass can be used to make turkey soup. Here is one of our favorite versions, with lemon and cilantro, which are great flavor complements to turkey.

3 tablespoons olive oil
1 large white onion, finely chopped
3 cloves garlic, minced
1 teaspoon turmeric
$1/2$ teaspoon ground cumin
Sea salt
6 cups homemade turkey stock (page 35–36) or
    chicken broth
Juice of 1 large lemon
3 long strips lemon zest (use a vegetable peeler)
$2/3$ cup pearl barley
2 to 3 cups chopped leftover turkey meat
$1/4$ cup chopped fresh flatleaf parsley
$1/4$ cup chopped fresh cilantro
Freshly ground black pepper

1. In a 5- to 7-quart pressure cooker, heat the oil over medium-high heat until very hot. Add the onion and cook, stirring a few times, until it begins to soften, about 3 minutes. Add the garlic and stir for 30 seconds, then stir in the turmeric, cumin, and a generous pinch of salt. Pour in the stock and lemon juice, and add the lemon zest. Bring to a simmer, then add the barley.

2. Close and lock the lid. Set the burner heat to high. When the cooker reaches HIGH pressure, reduce the burner heat as low as you can and still maintain HIGH pressure. Set a timer to cook for 10 minutes.

3. Remove the pot from the heat. Open the cooker with the Quick Release method. Be careful of the steam as you remove the lid. Discard the strips of lemon zest.

4. Stir in the turkey, parsley, and cilantro. Taste for salt and pepper, maybe adding two nice pinches of sea salt. Cook gently over medium heat just until the turkey is warmed through, 3 to 5 minutes. Serve hot.

Turkey Drumstick and Vegetable Soup

Serves 6 • Cooker: 6- to 8-quart • Time: 30 minutes at HIGH pressure

You don't have to have a turkey carcass to make turkey soup. Be sure to measure the turkey drumsticks to make sure they'll fit in your pressure cooker. It's okay if the end of the bone touches the lid of the cooker, as long as it doesn't block the vent. The meaty end will be submerged. This is delicious with homemade dinner rolls or cornbread and butter.

2 tablespoons olive oil
2 turkey drumsticks (about 2^1/$_2$ pounds), skin
    removed
1 large white onion, diced
4 large carrots, cut into bite-size pieces
2 ribs celery, finely diced
6 cups chicken broth
1 cup sliced white mushrooms
^{1}/$_4$ teaspoon dried oregano
^{1}/$_4$ teaspoon dried thyme
1 bay leaf
2 strips orange zest
Salt and freshly ground black pepper
1 cup frozen petite peas, thawed
1 cup chopped fresh green beans
3 to 4 tablespoons chopped fresh flatleaf parsley or
    cilantro, to taste

1. In a 6- to 8-quart pressure cooker, heat the oil over medium-high heat. Add the turkey legs and brown on all sides, about 5 minutes. Transfer to a plate. Add the onion, carrots, and celery to the pot and cook, stirring a few times until they begin to soften, about 3 minutes. Return the turkey legs to the pot, meaty side down, and add the broth. It's okay if the end of the bone touches the lid of the cooker, as long as it doesn't block the vent, but the meaty part should be submerged. Add the mushrooms, herbs, orange zest, and salt and pepper to taste.

2. Close and lock the lid. Set the burner heat to high. When the cooker reaches HIGH pressure, reduce the burner heat as low as you can and still maintain HIGH pressure. Set a timer to cook for 30 minutes.

3. Remove the pot from the heat. Open the cooker with the Quick Release method. Be careful of the steam as you remove the lid. Discard the orange zest and bay leaf. Transfer the turkey legs to a plate and let cool to lukewarm. Pick the meat off the legs and discard the sinews and bones. Cut or shred the meat into small pieces.

4. Skim the fat off the top of the broth. Add the reserved meat, peas, beans, and parsley, then simmer, uncovered, over medium heat for 5 to 8 minutes to heat the meat and cook the peas and beans. Taste for salt and pepper. Ladle into deep serving bowls and serve nice and hot.

Scotch Broth

Serves 6 • Cooker: 6- to 8-quart • Time: 30 minutes for stock, 8 minutes for soup at HIGH pressure

This classic winter soup, also called barley broth, is made from scratch with cracked lamb shanks, yielding a savory rich stock. No old mutton here! Beth got this recipe when she was working on the line inspecting lingerie at a small factory back in the 1970s. Women of all ages worked sorting and inspecting the garments, all the while talking about life, love, movie stars, and, of course, food. The married women would talk to the teens about food they cooked for their families. One of the women, a soup maven, gave Beth this recipe and she still makes it to this day. Because it took so long to make, the stock was originally made the day before, but with the pressure cooker, you can make the stock and soup in under 40 minutes total. Serve hot with Irish soda bread or biscuits and butter.

1 tablespoon olive oil
1 1/2 to 2 pounds cracked lamb shanks, trimmed of fat
8 cups cold water
1 teaspoon salt, plus more to taste
1 large yellow or white onion, chopped
2 large carrots, chopped
3 ribs celery, with leaves, chopped
1 medium turnip, peeled and diced
1/2 cup pearl barley
1/4 cup chopped fresh flatleaf parsley
Pinch dried thyme
Few grinds black pepper

1. In a 6- to 8-quart pressure cooker, heat the oil over medium-high heat until very hot. Add the lamb shanks and brown on all sides, about 3 minutes. Add the water and salt. Bring to a boil and skim the foam off the surface.
2. Close and lock the lid. Set the burner heat to high. When the cooker reaches HIGH pressure, reduce the burner heat as low as you can and still maintain HIGH pressure. Set a timer to cook for 20 minutes.
3. Remove the pot from the heat. Open the cooker with the Natural Release method; let stand for 15 minutes. Be careful of the steam as you remove the lid. Let the stock cool to lukewarm. Remove the shanks. Cut the meat off the bones; set aside. Discard the bones. Set a large colander lined with cheesecloth or fine mesh strainer over a large bowl and pour the broth through to strain. (If you make this the day before, store in the refrigerator, then lift the fat layer off the stock and discard.)
4. Quickly wash and dry the pressure cooker. Place the onion, carrots, celery, turnip, barley, parsley, and thyme in the cooker. Add the lamb stock. Close and lock the lid. Set the burner heat to HIGH. When the cooker reaches HIGH pressure, reduce the burner heat as low as you can and still maintain HIGH pressure. Set a timer to cook for 8 minutes.
5. Remove the pot from the heat. Open the cooker with the Quick Release method. Add the reserved meat and simmer, uncovered, over medium heat for 5 minutes to heat the meat. Taste for salt and pepper. Ladle into deep serving bowls.

Beef, Kale, and Brown Rice Soup

Serves 6 • Cooker: 6- to 8-quart • Time: 20 minutes for broth, 15 minutes for rice and vegetables at HIGH pressure

This hearty vegetable soup will warm a winter table. With its trio of cruciferous vegetables—kale, cabbage, and cauliflower—plus brown rice, it's a nutritional powerhouse. Make it in two easy steps.

1 pound chuck or other stew meat, trimmed of fat and cut into $3/4$-inch pieces
1 bay leaf
1 teaspoon dried oregano or 1 tablespoon chopped fresh oregano
$1/2$ large yellow or white onion, peeled
3 cloves garlic, peeled
10 cups water
3 medium carrots, sliced into $1/3$-inch-thick rounds, larger pieces halved crosswise
4 ribs celery, chopped into $1/2$-inch pieces
4 cups kale, thick stems discarded and leaves chopped into $1/2$-inch pieces
2 cups chopped ($1/2$-inch pieces) green cabbage
$3/4$ cup medium-grain brown rice
$1/2$ cup frozen corn kernels
1 (28-ounce) can diced tomatoes in juice, undrained
Salt and freshly ground black pepper

1. In a 6-to 8-quart pressure cooker, combine the meat, bay leaf, oregano, onion half, and garlic. Add 8 cups of the water.
2. Close and lock the lid. Set the burner heat to high. When the cooker reaches HIGH pressure, reduce the burner heat as low as you can and still maintain HIGH pressure. Set a timer to cook for 20 minutes.
3. Remove the pot from the heat. Open the cooker with the Quick Release method. Be careful of the steam as you remove the lid. Discard the onion half and garlic with a slotted spoon. Add the remaining ingredients, except the salt and pepper, to the pot, including the remaining 2 cups water.
4. Close and lock the lid. Set the burner heat to high. When the cooker reaches HIGH pressure, reduce the burner heat as low as you can and still maintain HIGH pressure. Set a timer to cook for 15 minutes.
5. Remove the pot from the heat. Open the cooker with the Quick Release method. Taste for salt and pepper. Serve the soup hot in deep soup bowls, as a warming first course or as a main course with a salad.

Beef Borscht with Butter Beans and Horseradish Cream

Serves 6 to 8 • Cooker: 5- to 7-quart • Time: 24 minutes at HIGH pressure

This delicious version of borscht is made with beef and butter beans. Serve this with toasted fresh dark rye bread from the bakery and butter.

BORSCHT:
3 tablespoons olive oil
1 pound beef stew meat, such as chuck, cut into
    $^1/_2$-inch cubes
1 large white onion, coarsely chopped
1 clove garlic, minced
3 ribs celery, sliced $^1/_2$ inch thick
2 large carrots, sliced $^1/_2$ inch thick
1 (14.5-ounce) can diced tomatoes in juice,
    undrained
$^1/_2$ teaspoon dried thyme
1 bunch red beets, greens trimmed off, rinsed well,
    and chopped; beets peeled and cut into bite-size
    pieces
4 cups beef broth
2 cups water, or as needed
$^1/_2$ small head green cabbage, cored and shredded
    into $^1/_2$-inch-wide strips (about 4 cups)
$^1/_3$ cup red wine vinegar (don't skip this, it makes
    the soup)
1 (15 ounce) can butter beans (large lima beans),
    drained and rinsed
$^1/_4$ cup chopped fresh dill
1 teaspoon Worcestershire sauce
$^1/_2$ teaspoon hot sauce, such as Tabasco or Sriracha
$^1/_4$ teaspoon freshly ground black pepper, or to
    taste
Sea salt

HORSERADISH CREAM:
1 (8-ounce) sour cream, imitation sour cream, or
    plain Greek yogurt
$^1/_2$ cup drained prepared horseradish (6 ounces)
$^1/_4$ cup minced fresh chives
Salt and freshly ground black pepper

1. In a 5- to 7-quart pressure cooker, heat 2 tablespoons of the oil over medium-high heat until very hot. Brown the beef on all sides, then transfer to a plate. Add the remaining 1 tablespoon oil and the onion, garlic, celery, and carrots; cook, stirring a few times, until the vegetables begin to soften, about 3 minutes. Add the tomatoes with their juice, thyme, beets and greens, broth, and water. Bring to a boil, then add the cabbage.
2. Close and lock the lid. Set the burner heat to high. When the cooker reaches HIGH pressure, reduce the burner heat as low as you can and still maintain HIGH pressure. Set a timer to cook for 24 minutes.
3. Remove the pot from the heat. Open the cooker with the Quick Release method. Be careful of the steam as you remove the lid.
4. Stir in the vinegar, butter beans, dill, Worcestershire, hot sauce, pepper, and salt to taste. Heat, uncovered, over medium heat for 5 minutes.
5. While the soup reheats, in a small bowl, mix the sour cream with the horseradish and chives; season lightly with salt and pepper.
6. To serve, ladle the hot soup into bowls and top with a big spoonful of the horseradish cream. Serve immediately.

BEETS

The beet, *Beta vulgaris,* is native to the Mediterranean coast. It is in the same family as Swiss chard. Its earthy flavor comes from a microorganism in the soil that it naturally absorbs to create a compound called geosmin, which is also found in the superfood blue-green algae. A bunch of beets usually includes 3 large or 5 to 6 small beets.

Escarole White Bean Sausage Soup

Serves 4 • Cooker: 5- to 7-quart • Time: 15 minutes for beans, 10 minutes for soup at HIGH pressure

Escarole, with its head of broad, pale green leaves, is a boutique vegetable these days in the sense that old becomes new again. It is a member of the endive family and the most mildly flavored of the clan. It is a green greatly favored in European-style soups; its flavor complements those of sausage, beans, and tomatoes. This thick and hearty soup is adapted from a recipe from Julia Wiley, a modern day farmer who owns Mariquita Farms with her husband (mariquita.com) and is a local at the farmers' markets. We originally found it on their charming e-newsletter called the Ladybug Letter. This soup is traditionally served with oversized garlic croutons made from a rustic day-old French bread or ciabatta.

SOUP:

1 1/4 cups (1/2 pound) dried cannellini beans, soaked (see page 406) and drained
2 tablespoons olive oil
1 pound mild or hot Italian sausage (pork or turkey), casings removed
1 large yellow or white onion, chopped
2 cloves garlic, chopped
4 cups chicken broth
1 (14.5-ounce) can diced tomatoes in juice, undrained
1 large head escarole (1 pound), cored and leaves chopped
1 rib celery, finely chopped
1 bay leaf
2 tablespoons chopped fresh flatleaf parsley
1/4 teaspoon dried oregano
1/4 teaspoon red pepper flakes
Sea salt and freshly ground black pepper

CIABATTA TOASTS:

2 to 3 tablespoons olive oil
8 (1/2-inch-thick) slices ciabatta (can be day old)
2 cloves garlic, cut in half
Grated or shredded Parmesan or Asiago cheese, for serving

1. In a 5- to 7-quart pressure cooker, cover the drained soaked beans with 2 inches of water and bring to a boil. Drizzle with the oil.
2. Close and lock the lid. Set the burner heat to high. When the cooker reaches HIGH pressure, reduce the burner heat as low as you can and still maintain HIGH pressure. Set a timer to cook for 15 minutes.
3. Remove the pot from the heat. Open the cooker with the Natural Release method; let stand for 15 minutes. Be careful of the steam as you remove the lid. Transfer the contents of the pot to a bowl.
4. Wipe out the pressure cooker. Add the sausage and cook over medium-high heat, breaking it up with a wooden spoon, until no pink remains. Drain off most of the fat and transfer the meat to a bowl. Add the onion to the sausage drippings, reduce the heat to medium, and cook, stirring a few times, until transparent, about 5 minutes. Add the garlic and cook, stirring, just until fragrant, 30 seconds. Add the broth, tomatoes with their juice, beans, escarole, celery, and bay leaf; bring to a low boil over medium heat, then add the sausage back to the pot. Add the parsley, oregano, and pepper flakes.
5. Close and lock the lid. Set the burner heat to high. When the cooker reaches HIGH pressure, reduce the burner heat as low as you can and still maintain HIGH pressure. Set a timer to cook for 10 minutes.
6. Remove the pot from the heat. Open the cooker with the Quick Release method. Season the soup with salt and pepper to taste.
7. Make the ciabatta toasts. In a large sauté pan, heat 1 tablespoon of the oil over medium-high heat. Fit 3 to 4 slices of the ciabatta in the pan and cook 1 to 2 minutes per side, turning once, until toasty and golden. Transfer to a plate. Toast the remaining slices, adding more of the oil as needed. Rub one side of the hot toasts with the cut side of a garlic half. Repeat while all the slices are hot.
8. To serve, ladle the hot soup into deep bowls and serve with 2 ciabatta toasts per diner and Parmesan cheese on the side.

Smoky Black Bean Soup with Crab

Serves 6 • Cooker: 5- to 7-quart • Time: 30 minutes at HIGH pressure

Make this super simple black bean soup, then top it with lemon, crab, cilantro, and chives. It is called *frijoles negro con jaibas* in Mexico.

2 tablespoons olive oil
1 large white onion, roughly chopped
1 clove garlic, peeled and smashed
$1/2$ red bell pepper, seeded and chopped
1 rib celery, diced
2 teaspoons ground chipotle or ancho chile, or to taste
1 teaspoon smoked paprika (pimentón)
2 cups dried black beans, soaked (page 406) and drained
7 cups chicken broth or water
1 tablespoon tomato paste
Salt, to taste
$1^1/2$ to 2 cups Dungeness crab meat, picked over for cartilage
$1/4$ cup chopped fresh cilantro
2 tablespoons minced fresh chives
Lime or lemon wedges, for serving

1. In a 5- to 7-quart pressure cooker, heat the oil over medium heat until very hot. Add the onion, garlic, red pepper, and celery and cook, stirring a few times, until the vegetables begin to soften, about 3 minutes. Add the chile powder and paprika. Add the beans and broth. Stir to combine. Place the tomato paste on top. Do not stir it in.
2. Close and lock the lid. Set the burner heat to high. When the cooker reaches HIGH pressure, reduce the burner heat as low as you can and still maintain HIGH pressure. Set a timer to cook for 30 minutes.
3. Remove the pot from the heat. Open the cooker with the Natural Release method; let stand for 15 minutes. Be careful of the steam as you remove the lid.
4. Puree the soup in the pot with an immersion blender until mostly smooth but still a little chunky. Taste for salt and if you want a bit more chipotle powder.
5. Place a heaping quarter cup of crab meat in the bottom of each soup bowl. Ladle the hot soup into the bowl, then sprinkle with cilantro and chives. Serve lime or lemon wedges on the side.

Creamy Shrimp Chowder with Lemon and Basil

Serves 6 • Cooker: 5- to 7-quart • Time: 5 minutes at HIGH pressure

It may not be as well known as clam chowder, but down in the Gulf States and Florida, creamy white shrimp chowder is a common sight and for good reason—it has a rich, extravagant flavor. You can leave the shrimp whole, as in the recipe, or coarsely chop them. Be sure to buy U.S. wild-caught or farmed shrimp for the best sustainable option. It's an excellent choice for special occasions—it's delicious and it makes an impressive show!

3 large russet potatoes, peeled and cut into $1/2$-inch cubes (about 4 cups)
1 large white onion, chopped
2 medium shallots, chopped
$1/2$ red bell pepper, seeded and finely chopped
2 ribs celery, chopped
3 (4-inch-long) strips lemon zest
1 bay leaf
3 cups chicken broth or Shrimp Stock (page 40)
2 cups whole milk
1 cup organic heavy cream
2 tablespoons all-purpose flour or rice flour mixed with 2 tablespoons softened unsalted butter
$1^1/2$ pounds medium (31–40 count) shrimp, peeled and deveined
2 tablespoons finely chopped fresh basil
Salt and freshly ground black or white pepper
Oyster crackers, for serving

1. In a 5- to 7-quart pressure cooker, combine the potatoes, onion, shallots, bell pepper, and celery. Tuck in the strips of zest and bay leaf. Slowly pour in the broth; it will just cover the vegetables. Add a bit more broth or water if needed.
2. Close and lock the lid. Set the burner heat to high. When the cooker reaches HIGH pressure, reduce the burner heat as low as you can and still maintain HIGH pressure. Set a timer to cook for 5 minutes.
3. Remove the pot from the heat. Open the cooker with the Natural Release method; let stand for 10 minutes. Quick Release any remaining pressure. Be careful of the steam as you remove the lid. Discard the bay leaf and zest strips.
4. Slightly mash the potatoes with a fork or potato masher, but leave some chunky texture. Add the milk and cream and let heat over medium-low heat. Whisk in the butter mixture and simmer 5 to 7 minutes until the flour is dissolved and the soup is slightly thickened. Add the shrimp and basil, stirring a few times. Let cook just until the shrimp turn pink and curl up (2 to 3 minutes). Don't let them overcook or they'll be tough. Taste for salt and pepper.
5. Serve immediately with lots of oyster crackers fresh out of the box.

Creamy Shrimp and Scallop Chowder: Reduce the amount of shrimp to 1 pound and add $3/4$ to 1 pound sea scallops, each one cut into 4 pieces, or bay scallops with the muscle removed on each, in Step 4.

Manhattan Clam Chowder

Serves 6 to 8 • Cooker: 5- to 7-quart • Time: 7 minutes at HIGH pressure

Manhattan clam chowder differs from New England in that it is tomato, not cream, based, sort of a humble relative of Italian cioppino and French bouillabaisse. The soup uses quahog clams, also known as chowder clams, which have a firmer texture and a stronger flavor than smaller littlenecks. We remember the first time we tasted homemade red clam chowder. It was a revelation it was so tasty. A natural briny broth comes from steaming the clams in water if you use fresh. Once the clams steam open, the meat pops out with minimal tugging.

1 (1-pound) container shucked clams with juice, or frozen clams, thawed (juices reserved) and rinsed, or 3 (6.5-ounce) cans minced clams, undrained
2 to 3 slices bacon or pancetta, to taste, coarsely chopped
1 large white onion, chopped
3 medium ribs celery with leaves, diced
1 medium carrot, cut into $1/2$-inch dice (1 cup)
1 small fennel bulb, trimmed of stalks, cored, and chopped (about 2 cups)
$1/2$ teaspoon dried thyme or 2 teaspoons Old Bay seafood seasoning
2 pinches cayenne pepper
$1^1/4$ pounds red or Yukon Gold potatoes, left unpeeled and cut into $1/2$-inch dice
1 (28-ounce) can whole plum tomatoes in juice, juices reserved, tomatoes chopped or crushed
3 cups bottled clam juice or Fresh Fish Stock (page 38), or as needed
2 cups chicken broth
Salt and freshly ground black pepper
Chopped fresh flatleaf parsley, for garnish
A very fruity extra virgin olive oil, for drizzling

1. Drain the clams through a strainer and add the drained liquid to the other liquids as part of the clam juice proportions; you want 3 cups total. Chop the clams if needed and set aside.
2. In a 5- to 7-quart pressure cooker, cook the bacon over medium heat until crisp and the fat is released. Using a slotted spoon, transfer it to paper towels to drain. If the bacon hasn't rendered 3 tablespoons fat, top it off with butter or oil. Add the onion and cook, stirring a few times until it begins to soften, about 3 minutes. Add the celery, carrot, fennel, thyme, and cayenne and cook for a moment more. Add the potatoes, reserved bacon, and tomatoes with their juices. Gradually pour in the clam juice and broth; it will just cover the vegetables.
3. Close and lock the lid. Set the burner heat to high. When the cooker reaches HIGH pressure, reduce the burner heat as low as you can and still maintain HIGH pressure. Set a timer to cook for 7 minutes.
4. Remove the pot from the heat. Open the cooker with the Natural Release method; let stand for 10 minutes. Quick Release any remaining pressure. Be careful of the steam as you remove the lid.
5. Add the clams and bring to a simmer over medium heat to just heat through. Taste for salt and pepper. Ladle into bowls and serve hot, sprinkled with parsley and drizzled with a swirl of olive oil.

Manhattan Clam Chowder with Fresh Steamed Clams: Substitute 36 fresh quahog or Long Island hard-shelled clams (which are smaller), scrubbed, for the clams called for above. Place a trivet and steamer rack or basket in a 6- to 8-quart pressure cooker. Add water to fill just even with the level of the rack. Place the clams on the rack, making sure the pot is no more than half full. If you have too many clams, steam in two equal batches; use the same steaming liquid for the second batch. Close and lock the lid. Set the burner heat to high. When the cooker reaches HIGH pressure, reduce the burner heat as low as you can and still maintain HIGH pressure. Set a timer to cook for 3 minutes. Open the cooker with the Quick Release method. Remove the opened clams with a slotted spoon or tongs to another bowl to cool slightly. Line a colander with a paper towel and set it over another bowl to strain the hot liquid and capture any unwanted sand. Reserve the strained liquid, which you will use instead of the bottled clam juice. Remove the meat from the cooled clams to a small bowl; discard the shells. Add any accumulated juice to the strained liquid. Coarsely chop the clams. Set aside. Follow the recipe above as directed from Step 2.

Smoked Salmon Chowder

Serves 4 • Cooker: 5- to 7-quart • Time: 6 minutes at HIGH pressure

Let's say this chowder hails from somewhere in between Norway, Scotland, and the West Coast of the U.S. It is very good served with a black Russian rye bread. If you wish the chowder a bit thicker, add $1/2$ cup instant mashed potato flakes with the milk and salmon in Step 4. If your market sells smoked salmon trimmings, this is a perfect use for them.

1 tablespoon unsalted butter
1 tablespoon olive oil
1 medium leek (white and palest green parts), trimmed, cut in half lengthwise, rinsed well, and thinly sliced across
1 medium carrot, diced
2 ribs celery, diced
1 clove garlic, minced
1 large russet potato, peeled and cut into $1/2$-inch cubes
1 teaspoon dried Italian herb blend
2 tablespoons all-purpose or rice flour
$1/2$ cup dry white wine
$1^3/4$ cups chicken broth, Fish Stock (page 38), or Salmon Stock (page 39)
2 cups whole milk
4 ounces smoked salmon, flaked
1 cup heavy cream
Salt and freshly ground black or white pepper
Oyster crackers, for serving
Minced fresh chives, for serving

1. In a 5- to 7-quart pressure cooker, melt the butter with the oil over medium heat. When it foams, add the leek, carrot, and celery and cook, stirring a few times, until the vegetables are softened, about 5 minutes. Add the garlic, potato, and herbs and cook for 2 minutes, stirring to coat the potato with the fat. Sprinkle in the flour and cook a few minutes, stirring. Gradually pour in the wine and broth; it will just cover the vegetables. Add a bit more broth or water if needed. Bring to a boil and simmer for a minute. Add the bay leaf if using.

2. Close and lock the lid. Set the burner heat to high. When the cooker reaches HIGH pressure, reduce the burner heat as low as you can and still maintain HIGH pressure. Set a timer to cook for 6 minutes.

3. Remove the pot from the heat. Open the cooker with the Quick Release method. Be careful of the steam as you remove the lid. The potato and carrot should be tender. Discard the bay leaf.

4. Stir in the milk and salmon and bring to a low simmer, uncovered. Stir in the cream and heat without letting the chowder boil. Taste for salt and pepper; go easy on the salt, as the salmon already has plenty. Serve immediately with lots of oyster crackers fresh out of the box and chives sprinkled on top.

Smoked Trout Chowder: Substitute smoked trout for the smoked salmon.

New England Clam Chowder: Substitute the salmon with 4 (6.5-ounce) cans chopped clams. Drain and measure the clam juice, then add chicken broth, Fish Stock, or Salmon Stock to equal $1^3/4$ cups. You can also fry 2 to 3 slices bacon until crisp, remove the bacon to paper towels, and use the rendered fat to cook the leek, carrot, and celery instead of the butter and olive oil; crumble the bacon into the chowder when you add the clams.

4

Bold Tomato Sauces

It is almost inconceivable to think about cooking without the tomato, and one of the most common uses of it is in tomato sauce. Tomatoes are rich in lycopene, a carotenoid antioxidant that may have beneficial health effects. The hitch is that lycopenes are hard to absorb raw, so cooking is the magic method of accessing them.

Different cuisines flavor tomato sauce in different ways, such as cinnamon or mint, or a mixture like herbes de Provence. Want sweet and sour? Add vinegar and brown sugar. Indian tomato sauce is rich with coconut milk and cilantro.

The pressure cooker loves tomato sauces of all types and we've presented you with a stellar collection in this chapter, with and without meat. For a stovetop pressure cooker, be sure to use a heat diffuser (this is not needed for the electric models). Tomatoes contain a lot of natural sugar and can easily scorch.

RAGÙ

Ragù is a derivative of the French word *ragoût,* or *ragoûter,* the arousing or enhancing of taste. Creating a ragù is a very personal thing. It can contain beef, veal, pork, sausages, lamb, pancetta, or even venison or ground turkey, a modern favorite variation. The most famous ragù is Ragù Bolognese, from Bologna, a cross between solid and liquid when cooked. It is a sauce that has captured the heart of Italian food lovers everywhere since its creation in the medieval kitchens of the country housewife. True Bolognese sauce does not use ground meat. Instead large pieces of meat such as veal, pork shoulder, beef ribs, or chicken sections are sliced/shredded into fine pieces after cooking in the sauce and combined with vegetables, olive oil, herbs, and white wine. One famous rich improvisation includes milk or even mascarpone cheese to make a creamy pink sauce.

Turkey Ragù with Fresh Herbs and Red Wine

Makes about 10 cups, enough for 3 pounds pasta • Cooker: 5- to 7-quart • Time: 10 minutes at HIGH pressure

Use dark meat rather than white for this, as the dark will cook up more tender and juicier, while the lean breast would be chewy and dry. Serve with a whole wheat or gluten-free rice spaghetti any day of the week.

2 tablespoons olive oil
1¹/₂ pounds ground turkey (dark meat preferred)
1 large white or yellow onion, finely chopped
1 large carrot, finely chopped
2 ribs celery, finely chopped
4 cloves garlic, finely chopped
1 (28-ounce) can organic peeled tomatoes in juice, undrained
1 (15-ounce) can organic tomato sauce
1 (6-ounce) can organic tomato paste
¹/₃ cup dry red wine, such as Merlot or Chianti (first pour it into the tomato cans and swirl it around to rinse down the inside), or more to taste
2 teaspoons dried Italian herb blend
¹/₄ cup torn fresh basil leaves
3 tablespoons chopped fresh flatleaf parsley
Sea salt and freshly ground black pepper

1. In a 5- to 7-quart pressure cooker, heat the oil over medium-high heat. Add the turkey and cook until it is no longer pink, stirring and breaking it up with a wooden spoon. Transfer to a plate. Add the onion and cook, stirring a few times, until it begins to soften, about 3 minutes. Add the carrot and celery and cook 1 minute. Add the garlic and stir for 1 minute. Add the tomatoes and their juice, tomato sauce, and tomato paste. Mash the whole tomatoes with the back of your spoon. Stir in the wine and dried and fresh herbs. Bring to a boil and let boil for 30 seconds. Return the cooked turkey to the pot with any accumulated juices. Add salt to taste and a few grinds of black pepper. Give a good stir.

2. Close and lock the lid. If you like, place a heat diffuser on the burner and the pressure cooker on the diffuser. Set the burner heat to high. When the cooker reaches HIGH pressure, reduce the burner heat as low as you can and still maintain HIGH pressure. Set a timer to cook for 10 minutes.

3. Remove the pot from the heat. Open the cooker with the Quick Release method. Be careful of the steam as you remove the lid. Stir and taste the sauce for salt and pepper. Use or let cool completely and store in an airtight container in the refrigerator up to 4 days or the freezer for up to 1 month.

Beef Ragù: Substitute lean ground beef for the turkey. Proceed as directed.

White Meat Ragù: Substitute the turkey with 1 pound ground veal and ¹/₂ pound ground chicken. Proceed as directed.

Venison Ragù: Substitute ground venison for the turkey. Proceed as directed, adding ¹/₄ cup red wine vinegar in Step 3.

Cheater's Bolognese Sauce

Makes 5 cups, enough for 1¹/₂ pounds pasta • Cooker: 5- to 7-quart • Time: 20 minutes at HIGH pressure

Salsa Bolognese is a primarily meat sauce flavored with a modest amount of tomato, as opposed to a tomato sauce flavored with a modest amount of meat. Our unconventional version is simpler, much lower in fat, and, thanks to the trusty pressure cooker, much quicker to prepare than the traditional classic, reducing the typical 1¹/₂ hours of simmering to a mere 20 minutes. Julie makes this with the ultra-lean, super-flavorful grass-fed beef her in-laws raise in rural Vermont. The tomato paste is important—look for recloseable tubes of Italian tomato sauce (like an old metal toothpaste tube) in better supermarkets. It lasts for ages in the refrigerator once opened. We like to serve this with a short and sturdy pasta such as the Slinky-like cellentani, gemelli, or rigatoni. And please use a good Parmesan for serving.

1 large yellow onion, quartered
1 large rib celery, lightly peeled or scraped to remove the outermost strings
1 large carrot, quartered
2 to 3 cloves garlic, to taste, peeled
2 to 3 tablespoons olive oil (you will need the larger amount if your beef is very lean)
1 pound very lean ground beef
4 slices turkey bacon, cut into ¹/₂-inch or smaller pieces
Leaves from 3 to 4 small sprigs fresh thyme, or ¹/₂ teaspoon dried thyme
Leaves from 1 small sprig fresh oregano, chopped, or ¹/₄ teaspoon dried oregano
¹/₂ cup dry white wine
1 cup chicken broth
2 tablespoons tomato paste
1 cup whole milk
Freshly ground black pepper
Freshly grated nutmeg
Salt (optional)

1. Place the onion, celery, carrot, and garlic in a food processor fitted with the metal blade and pulse until they are finely chopped. Alternately, chop the vegetables finely by hand.

2. In a 5- to 7-quart pressure cooker, heat the oil over medium-high heat. Add the chopped vegetables, reduce the heat to medium, and cook, stirring occasionally, until softened, 4 to 5 minutes. Do not let them brown; reduce the heat if necessary. Add the beef and bacon, breaking up the ground meat with a wooden spoon and stirring to combine it with the vegetables. Cook, stirring occasionally, until the beef is no longer pink. Stir in the herbs and wine. Cook for 1 to 2 minutes. Add the broth and tomato paste, stirring to distribute the paste evenly. Stir in the milk.

3. Close and lock the lid. If you like, place a heat diffuser on the burner and the pressure cooker on the diffuser. Set the burner heat to high. When the cooker reaches HIGH pressure, reduce the burner heat as low as you can and still maintain HIGH pressure. Set a timer to cook for 20 minutes.

4. Remove the pot from the heat. Open the cooker with the Quick Release method. Be careful of the steam as you remove the lid. Stir and taste the sauce, seasoning it with freshly ground pepper and just a dash of nutmeg. You may not need additional salt, as the turkey bacon is salty. Use or let cool completely and store in an airtight container in the refrigerator for up to 4 days or the freezer up to 1 month.

Rustic Two-Meat Ragù with Bacon

Makes 6 cups, enough for 1^1/$_2$ to 2 pounds pasta • Cooker: 5- to 7-quart • Time: 8 minutes at HIGH pressure

Got some spaghetti or penne or tortellini and want an aromatic chunky meat sauce to go with it? This is the sauce—on the table in 20 minutes. If you like, you could substitute meatloaf mix for the two ground meats. Don't skip the little bit of bacon—it's a real flavor enhancer. This is also nice spooned over polenta.

3 tablespoons olive oil
1 pound ground beef or veal
1 pound ground pork (make sure it is freshly
    ground that day)
3 slices bacon, chopped
1 large white onion, finely chopped
1 medium carrot, finely chopped
2 ribs celery, finely chopped
2 cloves garlic, minced
Leaves from 1 small bunch fresh basil, chopped
    (^{1}/$_2$ to ^{2}/$_3$ cup chopped)
^{1}/$_2$ teaspoon dried oregano
^{1}/$_2$ cup dry red wine
2 (14.5-ounce) cans diced tomatoes in juice,
    undrained
1 cup water or chicken broth
Salt and freshly ground black pepper
^{1}/$_2$ cup freshly grated Parmesan cheese

1. In a 5- to 7-quart pressure cooker, heat 1 tablespoon of the oil over medium-high heat. Add the ground meats, breaking them up with a wooden spoon, and cook, stirring occasionally, until the meat is no longer pink and a dash browned. With a slotted spoon, transfer the meat to a bowl. Drain off the fat. Add the remaining 2 tablespoons oil to the pot. Add the bacon, onion, garlic, carrot, and celery and cook, stirring occasionally, until the vegetables are softened and the bacon cooked through, 4 to 5 minutes. Add the garlic, basil, oregano, and wine. Bring to a boil and cook 1 minute. Add the tomatoes and their juice, browned meat, and water. Season with salt and a few grinds of black pepper.

2. Close and lock the lid. If you like, place a heat diffuser on the burner and the pressure cooker on the diffuser. Set the burner heat to high. When the cooker reaches HIGH pressure, reduce the burner heat as low as you can and still maintain HIGH pressure. Set a timer to cook for 8 minutes.

3. Remove the pot from the heat. Open the cooker with the Natural Release method and let stand 10 to 15 minutes. Be careful of the steam as you remove the lid. Taste for salt and pepper and stir in the Parmesan. Use or let cool completely and store in an airtight container in the refrigerator up to 4 days or the freezer up to 1 month.

Tomato Marsala Sauce with Italian Sausage and Garlic

Makes 10 cups, enough for 3 pounds pasta • Cooker: 5- to 7-quart • Time: 15 minutes at HIGH pressure

Use a sweet or hot, pork or turkey sausage here, as desired, and serve it with a drizzle of dark sweet balsamic vinegar. This is delicious with a chunky pasta such as cavatappi, shells, or penne rigate.

3 tablespoons olive oil
1 1/2 pounds ground beef
1 1/2 pounds pork or turkey Italian sausage, casings removed
1 large white or yellow onion, finely chopped
1 medium green bell pepper, seeded and chopped
4 to 6 cloves garlic, to taste, peeled
3 tablespoons chopped fresh basil
1/2 teaspoon dried oregano
1/2 cup dry Marsala
1 (24-ounce) can crushed tomatoes
1 (24-ounce) can plum tomatoes in juice, undrained
1/2 cup water
Salt and freshly ground black pepper

1. In a 5- to 7-quart pressure cooker, heat the oil over medium-high heat. Add the ground meat and sausage, breaking it up with a wooden spoon, and cook, stirring occasionally, until the meat is no longer pink and a dash browned. Add the onion, bell pepper, and whole garlic and cook until the garlic softens, 3 to 4 minutes longer, then mash it into a paste against the side of the pot and stir it in. Add the herbs and Marsala. Bring to a boil and let boil for 30 seconds. Add the crushed tomatoes, then the whole tomatoes and their juice, crushing the tomatoes with your hand as you add them to the pot. Add the water. Season with salt to taste and a few grinds of black pepper. Stir to combine.

2. Close and lock the lid. If you like, place a heat diffuser on the burner and the pressure cooker on the diffuser. Set the burner heat to high. When the cooker reaches HIGH pressure, reduce the burner heat as low as you can and still maintain HIGH pressure. Set a timer to cook for 15 minutes.

3. Remove the pot from the heat. Open the cooker with the Quick Release method. Be careful of the steam as you remove the lid. Stir the sauce and taste for salt and pepper. Use or let cool completely and store in an airtight container in the refrigerator up to 4 days or the freezer up to 1 month.

Tomato Meat Sauce with Porcini Mushrooms for a Crowd

Makes 10 cups, enough for 3 pounds pasta • Cooker: 8-quart • Time: 20 minutes at HIGH pressure

A Bolognese-style meat sauce, this is delicious served over hot pasta, potato gnocchi, or a mound of soft polenta. This is such an elegant sauce that we like to pair it with an elegant pasta. Look for an unusual medium or large shape, and try one of the artisan brands. Note that this requires an 8-quart pressure cooker.

$3/4$ cup dried porcini mushrooms (about $3/4$ ounce)
1 cup hot water
$1/4$ cup olive oil
2 pounds lean ground beef
1 large white onion, finely chopped
8 cloves garlic, chopped
2 (6-ounce) cans tomato paste
3 (14.5-ounce) cans diced tomatoes in juice, undrained
2 (15-ounce) cans tomato sauce
1 cup reduced-sodium chicken broth
2 tablespoons sugar or honey
$1/2$ cup coarsely chopped fresh basil (leaves from about $3/4$ bunch)
1 tablespoon dried oregano
1 bay leaf
2 teaspoons sea salt, or to taste
Freshly ground black pepper

1. Put the mushrooms in a small bowl and pour the hot water over them. Set aside to soak for 20 to 30 minutes. Drain, reserving the water. Strain the water through a fine mesh strainer lined with a coffee filter and reserve. If mushroom pieces are very large, chop them roughly.

2. In an 8-quart pressure cooker pot, heat the oil over medium-high heat. Add the beef, breaking it up with a wooden spoon, and cook until no longer pink. Transfer to a bowl. Add the onions and cook, stirring a few times, until softened, about 3 minutes. Add the garlic and cook until golden, a minute or so. Do not let it brown; reduce the heat if necessary. Add the tomato paste and cook 1 minute, stirring. Add the tomatoes and their juice, tomato sauce, broth, sugar, herbs, and salt. Return the beef to the pot and add the mushrooms and 1 cup of their soaking water.

3. Close and lock the lid. If you like, place a heat diffuser on the burner and the pressure cooker on the diffuser. Set the burner heat to high. When the cooker reaches HIGH pressure, reduce the burner heat as low as you can and still maintain HIGH pressure. Set a timer to cook for 20 minutes.

4. Remove the pot from the heat. Open the cooker with the Quick Release method. Be careful of the steam as you remove the lid. Taste the sauce, seasoning it with salt and a few grinds of pepper. If you prefer the sauce thicker, simmer, uncovered, to the desired thickness. Use or let cool completely and store in an airtight container in the refrigerator up to 5 days or in the freezer up to 1 month.

Lamb Ragù

Makes 5 cups, enough for 1¹/₂ pounds pasta • Cooker: 5- to 7-quart • Time: 10 minutes at HIGH pressure

We adapted this recipe from one we found in our local CUESA farmers' market weekly e-letter, adding more vegetables and parsley. Be sure to get freshly ground lamb from the butcher as it needs to be cooked the same day you buy it because it can go sour quickly. The spicy merguez is a fresh lamb sausage flavored with Moroccan spices like harissa and colored a lovely red from tomato paste and paprika. Look for them in your local specialty food market, farmers' market, or online. This is a marvelous and delightfully rich pasta sauce; serve it with rigatoni or bucatini.

2 tablespoons olive oil
1 large white or yellow onion, finely chopped
¹/₂ red bell pepper, seeded and finely chopped
1 pound very fresh ground lamb
4 lamb merguez sausages, casings removed
1 (28-ounce) can plum tomatoes in juice, crushed
    by hand into a bowl
Low-sodium chicken broth or water with a splash of
    dry red or white wine
Sea salt
1 cup petite frozen peas
3 tablespoons chopped fresh flatleaf parsley

1. In a 5- to 7-quart pressure cooker, heat the oil over medium-high heat. Add the onion, reduce the heat to medium, and cook, stirring a few times, until it begins to soften, about 3 minutes. Add the bell pepper and cook 1 minute. Do not let brown. Transfer the vegetables to a bowl and set aside. Add the ground lamb and sausage meat to the pot, breaking it up with a wooden spoon, and cook until the lamb is no longer pink. Return the vegetables to the pot and stir in. Add the tomatoes and their juice. Fill the tomato can halfway with broth or water and add to the pot along with a nice pinch of salt. Stir to combine.

2. Close and lock the lid. If you like, place a heat diffuser on the burner and the pressure cooker on the diffuser. Set the burner heat to high. When the cooker reaches HIGH pressure, reduce the burner heat as low as you can and still maintain HIGH pressure. Set a timer to cook for 10 minutes.

3. Remove the pot from the heat. Open the cooker with the Quick Release method. Be careful of the steam as you remove the lid.

4. Stir and taste the sauce for salt. Add the peas and parsley. Cook, uncovered, over medium heat 3 to 4 minutes to heat the peas. Use or let cool completely and store in an airtight container in the refrigerator up to 3 days or in the freezer up to 1 month.

Home-Style Pork Ragù with Fresh Basil and Mint

Makes 6 cups, enough for 1^1/$_2$ to 2 pounds pasta • Cooker: 5- to 7-quart • Time: 15 minutes at HIGH pressure

Basil and mint are a very Italian flavor combination, an eye opener to the palate. This simple meat sauce is best served over a tube pasta such as rigatoni or penne.

2 tablespoons extra virgin olive oil
1 medium-large white onion, finely chopped
1^1/$_2$ pounds ground pork (make sure it is freshly ground that day)
1 (28-ounce) can diced fire-roasted tomatoes in juice, undrained
1 (8-ounce) can tomato sauce
^{1}/$_2$ cup coarsely chopped fresh basil
^{1}/$_4$ cup coarsely chopped fresh mint
2 sprigs fresh thyme
Sea salt and freshly ground black pepper
^{1}/$_2$ cup water
^{1}/$_2$ cup dry red wine, such as Merlot or Chianti

1. In a 5- to 7-quart pressure cooker, heat the oil over medium-high heat. Add the onion, reduce the heat to medium, and cook, stirring a few times, until it begins to soften, about 3 minutes. Add the ground pork, breaking it up with a wooden spoon, and cook until the pork is no longer pink. Stir in the tomatoes and their juice, tomato sauce, herbs, salt and pepper to taste, water, and wine. Bring to a boil for 30 seconds.

2. Close and lock the lid. If you like, place a heat diffuser on the burner and the pressure cooker on the diffuser. Set the burner heat to high. When the cooker reaches HIGH pressure, reduce the burner heat as low as you can and still maintain HIGH pressure. Set a timer to cook for 15 minutes.

3. Remove the pot from the heat. Open the cooker with the Quick Release method. Be careful of the steam as you remove the lid. Stir and taste the sauce for salt. Discard the thyme sprigs. Use or let cool completely and store in an airtight container in the refrigerator up to 3 days or the freezer up to 1 month.

Pork Shoulder Ragù

Makes 12 cups, enough for 3¹/₂ pounds pasta • Cooker: 6- to 8-quart • Time: 45 minutes at HIGH pressure

This is a lesser known sauce, standing in the shadows of Bolognese and marinara. It is a winter dish, made when fresh basil and ripe tomatoes are nonexistent. The combination of wine and sweet vermouth is marvelous. It's a rustic Sunday dinner or brilliant dinner party dish for pork lovers. Serve it with pappardelle (think wide fettuccine) or rigatoni to stand up to the chunky sauce. Don't skip the fennel seeds.

1 (2- to 2¹/₂-pound) boneless pork shoulder roast (Boston butt), trimmed of fat and cut into 2-inch chunks
Sea salt and freshly ground black pepper
2 tablespoons olive oil
1 tablespoon butter
1 medium white onion, chopped
2 cloves garlic, minced
2 (28-ounce) cans whole or diced tomatoes in juice, undrained
1 (16-ounce) can tomato sauce
1 cup dry red wine
¹/₄ cup sweet Italian red vermouth
¹/₂ teaspoon dried thyme
¹/₂ teaspoon dried oregano
1 teaspoon fennel seeds
1 tablespoon hot sauce or pinch red pepper flakes

1. Liberally salt and pepper the pork. In a 6- to 8-quart pressure cooker, heat the oil and butter together over medium-high heat. When the butter has melted, brown the pork in batches on all sides, about 8 minutes per batch. Transfer the browned meat to a plate. Pour off all but 2 tablespoons of oil from the pot. Add the onion and garlic and cook for 1 minute. Add the tomatoes and their juice, tomato sauce, wine, vermouth, thyme, oregano, fennel, and hot sauce and bring to a boil. Boil for 1 minute.

2. Close and lock the lid. If you like, place a heat diffuser on the burner and the pressure cooker on the diffuser. Set the burner heat to high. When the cooker reaches HIGH pressure, reduce the heat as low as you can and still maintain HIGH pressure. Set a timer to cook for 45 minutes.

3. Remove the pot from the heat. Open the cooker with the Natural Release method; let stand for 15 minutes. Be careful of the steam as you remove the lid. Remove the pork to a cutting board and shred or cut into small pieces. Skim the fat off the top of the sauce, return the pork to the pot, and heat to a simmer. Taste for salt and pepper. Use or let cool completely and store in an airtight container in the refrigerator up to 4 days or the freezer up to 3 months.

White Wine Rabbit Ragù with Pancetta and Fresh Herbs

Makes 6 cups, enough for 1 1/2 to 2 pounds pasta • Cooker: 5- to 7-quart • Time: 12 minutes at HIGH pressure

Studies done by Louisiana State University show that rabbit meat contains the best ratio of lean to fat compared to other meat choices in the American diet. Domestic rabbit is all white meat, low in fat, and delicately flavored, so it goes with any number of spices and other ingredients. It is excellent for stewing and braising, which keeps the meat juicy and tender. Handle rabbit just like chicken and use a white wine instead of a red. Rabbit ragù is traditionally served with pappardelle but any wide egg noodle will work.

1 (2 1/2- to 3-pound) rabbit, cut into 6 pieces
1 cup white wine vinegar mixed with 1 cup water
Fine sea salt and freshly ground black pepper
1/4 cup olive oil
3 ounces pancetta or bacon, diced
1 large white onion, finely chopped
1 medium carrot, finely chopped
1 rib celery, finely chopped
4 cloves garlic, minced or pressed
2 (4- by 1-inch) strips orange zest
1 teaspoon dried thyme
1 cup dry white wine, such as Pinot Grigio
1 (28-ounce) can diced tomatoes in juice, undrained
1/4 cup tomato paste
1 cup water
1/3 cup chopped fresh flatleaf parsley
1/4 cup chopped fresh basil

1. In a medium bowl, combine the rabbit pieces with the vinegar-water mixture and marinate for 1 hour at room temperature. Drain. Pat the rabbit dry with paper towels and sprinkle with salt and pepper.
2. In a 5- to 7-quart pressure cooker, heat the oil over medium-high heat. Brown the rabbit pieces in batches on all sides, about 5 minutes per batch. Transfer the browned rabbit to a plate. Add the pancetta, onion, carrot, and celery to the pot, reduce the heat to medium, and cook, stirring a few times, until the pancetta is golden brown, 3 to 4 minutes. Add the garlic, zest, thyme, and wine and bring to a boil, scraping up any browned bits from the bottom of the pot, until most of liquid is evaporated, about 3 minutes. Stir in the tomatoes and their juice, tomato paste, and water and bring to a boil. Stir in the parsley and basil. Return the rabbit and any accumulated juices to the sauce.
3. Close and lock the lid. If you like, place a heat diffuser on the burner and the pressure cooker on the diffuser. Set the burner heat to high. When the cooker reaches HIGH pressure, reduce the burner heat as low as you can and still maintain HIGH pressure. Set a timer to cook for 12 minutes.
4. Remove the pot from the heat. Open the cooker with the Natural Release method; let stand for 15 minutes. Be careful of the steam as you remove the lid.
5. Transfer the rabbit pieces to a plate. When cool enough to handle, remove the meat from bones, discarding bones and gristle, and shred the meat. Return the meat along with any juices to the sauce. Stir and taste the sauce for salt and pepper. If you wish a thicker sauce, bring to a boil and cook 10 to 20 minutes with the lid off to evaporate some liquid. Use or cool completely and refrigerate in an airtight container up to 3 days or freeze up to 1 month.

White Wine Chicken Ragù with Pancetta and Fresh Herbs: Substitute a whole chicken, cut up, for the rabbit. Proceed with the recipe.

Mixed Seafood Marinara

Makes 3¹/₂ cups, enough for 1 pound pasta • Cooker: 5- to 7-quart • Time: 6 minutes at HIGH pressure

Simple and classic, this is best served over angel hair, linguine, or spaghetti. Seafood cooks quickly, so please pay special attention to the timing to avoid overcooking. Remember when buying seafood that it should have a glossy sheen and smell like the sea, not "fishy" or with any off odor; prepare it the day you buy it.

3 tablespoons olive oil
¹/₂ cup finely chopped white or yellow onion
1 clove garlic, minced
3 tablespoons tomato paste
1 (28-ounce) can crushed tomatoes
1 teaspoon dried Italian herb blend
¹/₂ cup dry white wine
¹/₂ cup water or bottled clam juice
Freshly ground black pepper
Sea salt
¹/₂ pound bay scallops (left whole) or sea scallops, cut into quarters, rinsed and patted dry
¹/₂ pound medium to large (23–30 count) shrimp, peeled and deveined
1 (6.5-ounce) can chopped clams
8 fresh basil leaves, chopped

CLEANING CALAMARI

Rinse the squid to remove dirt and debris from the outside. Lay flat on a plastic cutting board (so you can clean it in the dishwasher). Cut away the body of the squid below the eyes with a sharp knife or cleaver. Cut away the beak. Grasp the body and pinch the head with two fingers to pull the head off the body. The innards (known as the pen), which is a piece of triangular cartilage, is attached and will slide out; discard. Peel away the skin and cut off the tentacles from the eyes.

1. In a 5- to 7-quart pressure cooker, heat the oil over medium-high heat. Add the onion and cook, stirring a few times, until it begins to soften, about 3 minutes. Add the garlic and tomato paste. Stir and cook the tomato paste for 1 minute. Add the tomatoes, dried herbs, wine, and water. Bring to a boil and season with several grinds of black pepper.
2. Close and lock the lid. If you like, place a heat diffuser on the burner and the pressure cooker on the diffuser. Set the burner heat to high. When the cooker reaches HIGH pressure, reduce the burner heat as low as you can and still maintain HIGH pressure. Set a timer to cook for 6 minutes.
3. Remove the pot from the heat. Open the cooker with the Quick Release method. Be careful of the steam as you remove the lid. Taste the sauce for salt and pepper.
4. Stir in the scallops, shrimp, and clams. Add the basil. Cook, uncovered, over medium heat, just until the seafood is heated through, about 3 minutes, stirring occasionally. The shrimp will curl and turn pink, and the scallops turn opaque. Try to eat this dish the day it is made. Though you may reheat leftovers the following day, this doesn't keep well.

Lobster Marinara: Split lengthwise 2 (4- to 5-ounce) cooked lobster tails. Remove the meat and coarsely chop. Add to the sauce in Step 4 instead of the mixed seafood. Add ¹/₄ cup cognac or brandy. Simmer, uncovered, 3 to 5 minutes to heat through.

Calamari Marinara: Substitute 1 pound cleaned or 2 pounds uncleaned squid (calamari) for the mixed seafood. Cut the bodies into ¹/₂-inch-thick rings and the tentacles into 1-inch pieces. In Step 1, add 1 oil-packed anchovy along with the onion. When the onion is softened, add the squid and cook, stirring, for 30 seconds. Add the remaining ingredients as directed. Increase the pressure cook time to 15 minutes. Serve with lemon wedges. Abalone or conch can also be prepared in this manner.

Tomato-Basil Marinara

Makes 6 cups, enough for 1¹/₂ to 2 pounds pasta • Cooker: 5- to 7-quart • Time: 4 minutes at HIGH pressure

This is the basic marinara sauce that every pasta lover should know. This is a strong sauce with lots of olive oil and fresh basil. Extra virgin oil is a must here as you want the pronounced flavor. If you like, use only half the amount of olive oil called for here and then swirl in 2 tablespoons of butter at the end. For this is the recipe seek out San Marzano tomatoes. Great on spaghetti, spaghettini, or linguine.

¹/₃ cup extra virgin olive oil
1 to 4 cloves garlic, to taste, chopped
2 (28-ounce) cans plum tomatoes in juice,
    undrained
¹/₂ cup dry white wine or water
15 fresh basil leaves, cut across into chiffonade or
    torn
Sea salt and freshly ground black pepper

1. In a 5- to 7-quart pressure cooker, heat the oil over medium-high heat. Add the garlic and cook, stirring constantly, until golden, a minute or so. Do not let it brown; reduce the heat if necessary. Add the tomatoes (crushing them in your hand as you do) and their juice, wine, and half the basil. Bring to a boil and boil for 15 seconds.

2. Close and lock the lid. If you like, place a heat diffuser on the burner and the pressure cooker on the diffuser. Set the burner heat to high. When the cooker reaches HIGH pressure, reduce the burner heat as low as you can and still maintain HIGH pressure. Set a timer to cook for 4 minutes.

3. Remove the pot from the heat. Open the cooker with the Quick Release method. Be careful of the steam as you remove the lid. Stir in the remaining fresh basil, and taste the sauce for salt and pepper. Use or let cool completely and store in an airtight container in the refrigerator up to 5 days or the freezer up to 3 months, though the basil will suffer.

Tomato-Basil Marinara with Prosciutto: Add 2 ounces thinly sliced prosciutto, chopped, along with the garlic in Step 1. Proceed as directed.

Tomato-Basil Marinara with Cremini Mushrooms: Add 12 ounces sliced cremini mushrooms in Step 1 along with the garlic and cook until sizzling but not browned. If you like, substitute beef broth for the wine. Proceed as directed.

CREMINI MUSHROOMS

Cremini mushrooms, or baby bellas, are the step between white buttons and the large overgrown Portobello, and sold already sliced in well-stocked produce sections. Supermarket white button mushrooms and creminis are the same age, but different variants of *Agaricus bisporus.* It is a mushroom that is firmer and more flavorful than domestic white and great in stews and sauces since they hold their shape better.

Classic Marinara with Balsamic Vinegar for a Crowd

Makes 12 cups, enough for 3¹/₂ pounds pasta • Cooker: 8-quart • Time: 15 minutes at HIGH pressure

This is the recipe you want when the family is coming. It is adapted from a Weight Watchers recipe, and spiked with herbs, red pepper flakes, and balsamic vinegar. You can use this to serve over ravioli, to poach chicken tenders in, to make chicken Parmesan, or as the simmer sauce for meatballs. Note that this recipe requires an 8-quart pressure cooker.

¹/₄ cup olive oil
2 large white onions, finely chopped
7 cloves garlic, chopped
3 (28-ounce) cans crushed tomatoes
2 cups low-sodium vegetable or chicken broth
3 tablespoons balsamic vinegar
1 tablespoon sugar or honey
1 tablespoon dried Italian herb blend
1 teaspoon dried oregano
1¹/₂ teaspoons red pepper flakes
¹/₂ teaspoon fennel seeds, crushed in a mortar and pestle
2 teaspoons sea salt
Freshly ground black pepper

1. In an 8-quart pressure cooker, heat the oil over medium-high heat. Add the onions and cook, stirring occasionally, until softened, about 5 minutes. Add the garlic and cook until golden, a minute or so. Do not let it brown; reduce the heat if necessary. Add the tomatoes, broth, vinegar, sugar, herbs, pepper flakes, fennel seed, and salt.
2. Close and lock the lid. If you like, place a heat diffuser on the burner and the pressure cooker on the diffuser. Set the burner heat to high. When the cooker reaches HIGH pressure, reduce the burner heat as low as you can and still maintain HIGH pressure. Set a timer to cook for 15 minutes.
3. Remove the pot from the heat. Open the cooker with the Quick Release method. Be careful of the steam as you remove the lid. Taste the sauce for salt and pepper. Use or let cool completely and store in an airtight container in the refrigerator up to 5 days or the freezer 4 to 6 months.

Classic Marinara with Ricotta for a Crowd: Use 1 (8-ounce) container whole milk ricotta thinned with a bit of milk per each 4 servings. Spoon a scoop or two (about ¹/₄ cup) of the ricotta in a large shallow bowl, then portion the pasta on top, then ladle hot sauce over the pasta. Serve immediately. Swirl the ricotta while eating. If you love ricotta, especially über-creamy whole milk ricotta, you will love this.

THE MEANING OF MARINARA

Marinara is a southern Italian style of tomato sauce made with tomatoes, onions, olive oil, herbs, and garlic. *Marinara* derives from "mariner's," possibly because it is said to have been made on ships during lengthy voyages, perhaps because it was found to prevent scurvy because of the vitamin C in the tomatoes.

Fresh Tomato Sauce (Sugo di Pomodoro)

Makes 4 cups, enough for 1 pound pasta • Cooker: 5- to 8-quart • Time: 8 minutes at HIGH pressure

When tomatoes are in season, we celebrate and eat them every which way, including in this sauce. Make this in the summer when plump, ripe, juicy full-of-flavor tomatoes are abundant. Serve it with any shape pasta you like, from penne to farfalle to angel hair pasta—we love it over fresh pasta but if you use dried, splurge on a quality imported pasta. You can double this recipe but use an 8-quart pressure cooker and don't overfill it. Use a food mill to remove the seeds and skin; a food processor will grind them up, which is not what you want.

2 tablespoons olive oil
$3/4$ cup chopped yellow or white onion (optional)
2 cloves garlic, minced
3 pounds ripe, fresh tomatoes (12 to 15 large),
    coarsely chopped, with juices
3 tablespoons tomato paste
1 cup water
1 teaspoon salt, or to taste
Few grinds freshly ground black pepper
1 large pinch sugar, if needed
3 to 4 tablespoons chopped or torn fresh basil, to
    taste

1. In a 5- to 8-quart pressure cooker, heat the oil over medium-high heat. Add the onion if using and cook, stirring a few times, until it begins to soften, about 3 minutes. Add the garlic and cook 30 seconds. Add the tomatoes and their juice, tomato paste, water, salt, pepper, and sugar. Stir to combine.

2. Close and lock the lid. If you like, place a heat diffuser on the burner and the pressure cooker on the diffuser. Set the burner heat to high. When the cooker reaches HIGH pressure, reduce the burner heat as low as you can and still maintain HIGH pressure. Set a timer to cook for 8 minutes.

3. Remove the pot from the heat. Open the cooker with the Natural Release method; let stand for 15 minutes. Be careful of the steam as you remove the lid. Season to taste with salt and pepper. If it's not thick enough for you, simmer, uncovered, over medium heat until it reaches the desired thickness. Remove from the heat.

4. When cool enough to handle, ladle into a food mill set over a deep bowl to remove the skins and seeds. If using immediately, stir in the basil. If storing, let cool completely and transfer to an airtight container; it will keep in the refrigerator up to 5 days or in the freezer up to 2 months. Stir in the basil right before serving.

Winter Tomato Sauce

Makes 3¹/₂ cups, enough for 1 pound pasta • Cooker: 5- to 7-quart • Time: 10 minutes at HIGH pressure

With this recipe, you can have all the flavor of a long-simmering sauce in just 15 minutes (put on the water to boil for the pasta when you start this sauce). This versatile sauce works well with long pastas such as linguine or fettuccine.

3 tablespoons olive oil
1 cup finely chopped white or yellow onion
I cup finely chopped carrot
1 cup finely chopped celery
3 cloves garlic, minced
1 (28-ounce) can tomato puree
1 (28-ounce) can crushed tomatoes or whole plum
 tomatoes in puree, crushed with your hands
2 teaspoons dried Italian herb blend
1 teaspoon dried basil
1 teaspoon brown sugar
¹/₄ cup dry red or white wine
¹/₂ cup water or vegetable broth
Sea salt and freshly ground black pepper

1. In a 5- to 7-quart pressure cooker, heat the oil over medium-high heat. Add the onion, carrot, and celery and cook, stirring a few times, until they begin to soften, about 3 minutes. Stir in the garlic and tomato puree and cook, stirring, for 1 minute. Add the crushed tomatoes, herbs, sugar, wine, and water. Bring to a boil and season with a few grinds of pepper.

2. Close and lock the lid. If you like, place a heat diffuser on the burner and the pressure cooker on the diffuser. Set the burner heat to high. When the cooker reaches HIGH pressure, reduce the burner heat as low as you can and still maintain HIGH pressure. Set a timer to cook for 10 minutes.

3. Remove the pot from the heat. Open the cooker with the Quick Release method. Be careful of the steam as you remove the lid. Using an immersion blender, puree the sauce right in the pot. Taste the sauce for salt and pepper. Use or let cool completely and store in an airtight container in the refrigerator up to 3 days or the freezer 4 to 6 months.

Korean-Style Spicy Tomato Sauce: Substitute 2 tablespoons *gochujang* (Korean red chili pepper sauce) for the Italian herb blend and basil. *Gochujang* is a spicy, pungent, slightly sweet, dark red fermented chili paste that is a staple condiment in Korean cuisine and usually served with bibimbap. Look for it in the Asian section of large supermarkets or a specialty Asian food store. Enjoy the sauce with chewy soba or udon noodles.

Winter Tomato Sauce with White Beans: Add 2 to 3 cups fresh-cooked or 1 to 2 (15-ounce) cans drained cannellini, navy, Great Northern, or garbanzo beans in Step 3 after pureeing the sauce. Heat through, uncovered, for a few minutes over medium heat. This is a delicious sauce; use it with orecchiette or a shell-shaped pasta to catch the beans as well as the sauce.

Tomato Puttanesca Sauce

Makes 3$^1/_2$ cups, enough for 1 pound pasta • Cooker: 5- to 7-quart • Time: 10 minutes at HIGH pressure

This is adapted from Dr. Preston Maring's recipe for *sugo alla puttanesca*. He is the founding father of Kaiser Foundation's farmers' markets; he shared the recipe, when the markets launched in the Bay Area in 2003. If you have a few fresh plum tomatoes, cut them in half, remove seeds, chop, and toss them in. This sauce is traditionally served with spaghetti, but we like also it with penne or linguine.

3 tablespoons olive oil
1 cup finely chopped white or yellow onion
4 cloves garlic, minced
3 oil-packed anchovy fillets, chopped
$^1/_4$ teaspoon Aleppo or red pepper flakes
1 (35-ounce) can whole plum tomatoes in juice, crushed by hand, undrained
$^1/_4$ cup dry red wine
$^1/_4$ cup water
$^1/_3$ cup pitted oil-cured black olives (such as kalamata), coarsely chopped or in pieces
1 heaping tablespoon nonpareil capers, rinsed well and drained
$^1/_2$ teaspoon dried oregano or 2 teaspoons minced fresh oregano
$^1/_2$ teaspoon dried basil or 2 teaspoons minced fresh basil
Freshly ground black pepper
$^1/_4$ cup minced fresh flatleaf parsley

1. In a 5- to 7-quart pressure cooker, heat the oil over medium-high heat. Add the onion and cook, stirring frequently, until they begin to caramelize, about 10 minutes; turn the heat down if necessary to keep from burning. Add the garlic, anchovies, and pepper flakes and cook briefly, stirring, to melt the anchovies. Stir in the tomatoes and their juice, wine, water, olives, capers, and dried herbs (if using fresh, add at the end). Bring to a boil and season with a few grinds of black pepper.
2. Close and lock the lid. If you like, place a heat diffuser on the burner and the pressure cooker on the diffuser. Set the burner heat to high. When the cooker reaches HIGH pressure, reduce the burner heat as low as you can and still maintain HIGH pressure. Set a timer to cook for 10 minutes.

3. Remove the pot from the heat. Open with the Quick Release method. Be careful of the steam as you remove the lid. Add the parsley and fresh herbs, if using. Taste for pepper. You will not need salt. Use or let cool completely and refrigerate up to 3 days or freeze 4 to 6 months.

Tomato Puttanesca Sauce with Shrimp: In Step 3, add 1 pound medium peeled and deveined shrimp with the parsley. Simmer, uncovered, over medium heat, until they turn pink and curl, about 4 minutes.

Tomato Puttanesca Sauce with Tuna: In Step 3, add 2 (5-ounce) cans Italian solid-pack light tuna in olive oil or in water, drained well and broken up into chunks, with the parsley. Simmer, uncovered, over medium heat to heat through, about 4 minutes.

Spaghetti Squash Puttanesca: Here's a gluten-free alternative to serving the sauce with pasta. Place a 2- to 2$^1/_2$-pound spaghetti squash on the counter and, with a paring knife, make a $^1/_2$-inch-deep cut into the skin down the length of the squash and back up, from stem to stem. Pierce 8 times all over with the tip of the knife. Place in the pressure cooker with 2 cups water. Close and lock the lid. Set the burner heat to high. When the cooker reaches HIGH pressure, adjust the heat to maintain pressure. Set a timer to cook for 6 minutes at HIGH pressure. Open the cooker with the Natural Release method; let stand for 15 minutes. Using a chef's knife, cut the squash in half lengthwise along the slit you made; remove and discard seeds. With a fork, scrape the cooked flesh to separate the squash strands and place in a shallow serving bowl. Discard the shells. Top with the sauce and serve immediately.

ALEPPO PEPPER

Aleppo pepper is milder and more fruity-sweet than regular crushed red pepper. It is named after the city of the same name in Syria, a culinary mecca on the Silk Road near the Turkish border. You can order it online.

Sweet-and-Sour Tomato Pasta Sauce

Makes 6 cups, enough for 1¹/₂ to 2 pounds pasta • Cooker: 5- to 7-quart • Time: 7 minutes at HIGH pressure

The sweet and sour (a style known as *agradolce* in Italian) are supplied here by wine vinegar (try an assertive Cabernet vinegar) and brown sugar and honey. This is wonderful served with tortellini, shells, or fettuccine. It also makes a great cold dish in the summer, ladled over cold pasta and topped with grilled vegetables or shrimp.

¹/₄ cup extra virgin olive oil
2 tablespoons butter
1 medium shallot, minced
1 medium green bell pepper, seeded and cut into
    strips
2 (28-ounce) cans diced tomatoes in juice,
    undrained
¹/₄ cup red wine vinegar
2 tablespoons light brown sugar
2 tablespoons honey
1 cup hot water
3 tablespoons chopped fresh cilantro
Sea salt and freshly ground black pepper

1. In a 5- to 7-quart pressure cooker, heat the oil and butter together over medium-high heat until the butter melts. Add the shallot and cook, stirring a few times, until golden. Add the bell pepper and stir until limp. Add the tomatoes and their juice, vinegar, sugar, honey, and water.

2. Close and lock the lid. If you like, place a heat diffuser on the burner and the pressure cooker on the diffuser. Set the burner heat to high. When the cooker reaches HIGH pressure, reduce the burner heat as low as you can and still maintain HIGH pressure. Set a timer to cook for 7 minutes.

3. Remove the pot from the heat. Open the cooker with the Quick Release method. Be careful of the steam as you remove the lid. If the sauce is not thick enough for you, simmer, uncovered, over medium heat until it reaches the desired thickness. Mash the tomatoes against the side of the pot if you want a less chunky sauce. Stir in the cilantro. Taste the sauce for salt and pepper. Use or let cool completely and store in an airtight container in the refrigerator for 3 days or the freezer 4 to 6 months.

Italian Lentil Marinara

Makes 8 cups, enough for 2 pounds pasta • Cooker: 5- to 7-quart • Time: 8 minutes at HIGH pressure

This is a rich-flavored, hearty, low-fat sauce, delicious served over a whole-grain or gluten-free pasta, a variation of *pasta e fagioli,* pasta with beans, from southern Italy. You can use the diminutive earthy French Puy lentil, also known as green du Berry lentils (they get their blue-green marbling from being grown in volcanic soil), or organic brown Italian lentils, also known as Umbrian lentils, grown on the Castelluccio plain, both of which hold their shape during cooking, rather than becoming soupy. They are known for their exquisite flavor. You can add 1 cup Champagne or dry white wine in place of the water if you like but the sauce is great without it. Ladle the hot sauce over pasta (like medium shells, penne, or rigatoni) with a little drizzle of extra virgin olive oil before adding the cheese.

3 tablespoons olive oil
1 large white or yellow onion or 3 shallots, chopped
1/2 cup diced carrot
1 rib celery, chopped
4 cloves garlic, minced
2 bay leaves
2 pinches chili powder or red pepper flakes
2 (28-ounce) cans whole tomatoes in juice, crushed
    with your hands or pureed with an immersion
    blender inserted into the can
1 1/4 cups small green or brown lentils (*lentils du
    Puy* or *di Castelluccio di Norcia*), rinsed and
    picked over
2 cups water or vegetable broth
3 tablespoons tomato paste
Sea salt
3 tablespoons minced fresh flatleaf parsley
3 tablespoons minced fresh basil

1. In a 5- to 7-quart pressure cooker, heat the oil over medium-high heat. Add the onion and cook, stirring a few times until it just begins to soften, about 3 minutes. Add the carrot, celery, garlic, bay leaves, and chili powder, and cook, stirring constantly, until fragrant, about 30 seconds. Add the tomatoes and their juice, lentils, and water. Add the tomato paste on top; do not stir it in.
2. Close and lock the lid. If you like, place a heat diffuser on the burner and the pressure cooker on the diffuser. Set the burner heat to high. When the cooker reaches HIGH pressure, reduce the burner heat as low as you can and still maintain HIGH pressure. Set a timer to cook for 8 minutes.
3. Remove the pot from the heat. Open the cooker with the Quick Release method. Be careful of the steam as you remove the lid. Taste for salt, then stir in the parsley and basil. Add pasta cooking water to thin, if necessary. The lentils should be tender. Use or let cool and store in an airtight container in the refrigerator up to 3 days or the freezer 4 to 6 months. The sauce will thicken as it cools, so add a little water when reheating.

Creamy Lentil Marinara: In Step 3 before serving, add 1 cup heavy cream (you won't need the pasta water) to the sauce. Stir to combine. Simmer a few minutes to heat. This is really, really good.

Lentil Marinara with Pancetta: In Step 1, sauté 2 ounces chopped pancetta in 1 tablespoon of the oil over medium-high heat until crisp. Remove with a slotted spoon to a plate. Continue as directed, adding the remaining 2 tablespoons oil to the pot. Add the pancetta back to the pot with the tomatoes.

Cajun-Creole Tomato Vegetable Sauce

Makes 6 cups, enough for 1¹/₂ to 2 pounds pasta • Cooker: 5- to 7-quart • Time: 6 minutes at HIGH pressure

Cajun cooking, indigenous to South Louisiana, is French country cooking adapted to the local ingredients. Creole cooking is a mixture of French, Spanish, Italian, Native American, and Caribe African. It utilizes the holy trinity of onion, green pepper, and celery as a marvelously fresh flavor base and is an identifying mark of New Orleans food. This ever-so-spicy sauce is great on fettuccine.

¹/₂ pound small, slender fresh okra pods or 2 cups
    frozen sliced okra
Salt
¹/₄ cup cider vinegar
2 tablespoons olive oil
2 tablespoons butter
1 large green bell pepper, seeded and chopped
1 large white onion, chopped
2 cloves garlic, chopped
3 ribs celery, chopped
2 (28-ounce) cans whole plum tomatoes in juice,
    undrained
¹/₂ cup water
¹/₄ cup dry red wine
2 tablespoons Worcestershire sauce
2 teaspoons dried oregano
2 teaspoons hot pepper sauce, like Tabasco
¹/₄ teaspoon red pepper flakes
3 tablespoons chopped fresh flatleaf parsley
¹/₈ teaspoon ground white pepper
¹/₄ teaspoon cayenne pepper
Freshly ground black pepper

1. Trim the stems from the okra and place in a medium bowl. Salt generously and drizzle with the vinegar. Let sit for 30 minutes, tossing the okra a few times. This will reduce the stickiness during cooking. Drain the okra and rinse thoroughly. Cut each pod into 4 pieces.
2. In a 5- to 7-quart pressure cooker, heat the oil and butter together over medium-high heat until the butter melts. Add the bell pepper and onion and cook 1 minute. Add the garlic and cook another minute or so. Stir in the celery and okra. Stir in the tomatoes and their juice, water, wine, Worcestershire, oregano, hot sauce, pepper flakes, and parsley. Stir in the white pepper, cayenne, and a few grinds of black pepper. Bring to a boil and let boil for 1 minute. Crush the tomatoes with the back of a spoon but leave the sauce chunky.
3. Close and lock the lid. If you like, place a heat diffuser on the burner and the pressure cooker on the diffuser. Set the burner heat to high. When the cooker reaches HIGH pressure, reduce the burner heat as low as you can and still maintain HIGH pressure. Set a timer to cook for 6 minutes.
4. Remove the pot from the heat. Open the cooker with the Quick Release method. Be careful of the steam as you remove the lid. Taste for salt. Use or let cool completely and store in an airtight container in the refrigerator up to 5 days or the freezer 4 to 6 months.

ALL ABOUT OKRA

Also known as lady's fingers, okra is a member of the same botanical family as the cotton plant, hollyhocks, and hibiscus. It is a powerhouse of nutrients, a very good source of vitamins A, C, K, and B6, as well as calcium and dietary fiber. Okra likely originated in present-day Ethiopia and can still be found growing wild along the Nile. Cajuns took to the slender pod, exploiting its mucilaginous properties as a thickener in preparations like gumbo. For the best texture and flavor, buy the smallest pods you can find.

Roasted Red Pepper and Tomato Sauce

Makes 3¹/₂ cups, enough for 1 pound pasta • Cooker: 5- to 7-quart • Time: 10 minutes at HIGH pressure

This recipe is adapted from our Cuisinart hand blender instruction booklet. You can use your own roasted red peppers (page 65) or jarred for on the spot convenience. The peppers add a totally different flavor to the tomato sauce that is quite addictive. Serve it with spaghetti.

3 tablespoons olive oil
1 cup finely chopped white or yellow onions
1 cup finely chopped carrots
1 cup finely chopped celery
2 cloves garlic, minced
2 tablespoons tomato paste
2 whole roasted red bell peppers, chopped
2 (14.5-ounce) cans diced tomatoes in juice, undrained
1 teaspoon dried basil
¹/₂ cup water
¹/₃ cup dry vermouth or dry white wine
Freshly ground black pepper
Sea salt

1. In a 5- to 7-quart pressure cooker, heat the oil over medium-high heat. Add the onions, carrots, and celery and cook, stirring a few times, until they begin to soften, about 3 minutes. Stir in the garlic and tomato paste and cook for 1 minute. Add the peppers, tomatoes and their juice, basil, water, and vermouth. Bring to a boil and season with several grinds of black pepper.

2. Close and lock the lid. If you like, place a heat diffuser on the burner and the pressure cooker on the diffuser. Set the burner heat to high. When the cooker reaches HIGH pressure, reduce the burner heat as low as you can and still maintain HIGH pressure. Set a timer to cook for 10 minutes.

3. Remove the pot from the heat. Open the cooker with the Quick Release method. Be careful of the steam as you remove the lid. Using an immersion blender, puree the sauce right in the pot until smooth. Taste for salt and pepper. Use or let cool completely and store in an airtight container in the refrigerator up to 5 days or the freezer up to 3 months.

Roasted Eggplant and Garlic Tomato Sauce with Mushrooms

Makes 5 cups, enough for 1 1/2 pounds pasta • Cooker: 5- to 7-quart • Time: 8 minutes at HIGH pressure

With its meaty texture, eggplant makes a wonderful end-of-summer Italian-style vegetarian pasta sauce. You can use regular globe eggplants, white eggplant, or Japanese eggplants (which don't need to be peeled) interchangeably. If you like, you can sauté the eggplant right in the pressure cooker pot, but we prefer to roast it in the oven since it absorbs less oil. Serve on ziti and topped with sliced black olives and Parmesan.

1 (1 1/2-pound) eggplant, cut in half, sprinkled with salt, and drained on paper towels 30 minutes, then rinsed
3 cloves garlic, peeled
1/2 cup olive oil
2 large white or yellow onions, finely chopped
12 ounces white mushrooms, sliced
1 (6-ounce) can tomato paste
1 (28-ounce) can whole plum tomatoes in juice, crushed, undrained
1/2 cup dry red wine
1 1/2 teaspoons crumbled dried oregano or marjoram, or 1 tablespoon chopped fresh
1/4 cup minced fresh flatleaf parsley
Sea salt and freshly grated black pepper

1. Preheat the oven to 400° F. Arrange the eggplant and garlic cloves on an oiled baking sheet. Brush the halves with some of the oil and bake until tender, about 20 minutes. Let cool, remove the skin, and coarsely chop the pulp; smash the garlic into a paste.
2. In a 5- to 7-quart pressure cooker, heat the remaining oil over medium-high heat. Add the onions and cook, stirring a few times, until they begin to soften, about 3 minutes. Add the mushrooms and cook until they release their liquid. Add the tomato paste; stir for 1 minute until hot and coats the vegetables. Add the tomatoes and their juice, wine, and herbs. Bring to a boil and season with several grinds of black pepper. Add the eggplant and garlic; stir to combine.
3. Close and lock the lid. If you like, place a heat diffuser on the burner and the pressure cooker on the diffuser. Set the burner heat to high. When the cooker reaches HIGH pressure, reduce the burner heat as low as you can and still maintain HIGH pressure. Set a timer to cook for 8 minutes.
4. Remove the pot from the heat. Open the cooker with the Natural Release method; let stand for 15 minutes. Be careful of the steam as you remove the lid. Taste the sauce for salt and pepper. Use or let cool completely and store in the refrigerator up to 3 days or the freezer 4 to 6 months.

Mexican Spaghetti Sauce

Makes 5 cups, enough for 1¹/₂ pounds pasta • Cooker: 5- to 7-quart • Time: 7 minutes at HIGH pressure

Beth's friend, chef and great home cook Oscar Mariscal, shared his mother's recipe for Mexican spaghetti sauce, which was a weekly standard at his home growing up in the 1940s and '50s. Las Palmas brand enchilada chile sauce is the largest selling brand of cooking sauce in the U.S. and Mexican cooks swear by it, as it has an authentic flavor and color essential to traditional dishes. Serve with whole wheat spaghetti topped with freshly grated cotija anejo or crumbled fresh goat cheese.

2 tablespoons olive oil
1 large white or yellow onion, finely chopped
1 cup finely chopped celery
1 cup finely chopped green bell pepper
2 cloves garlic, minced
1 (28-ounce) can mild red enchilada sauce (we like the Las Palmas brand)
2 (14.5-ounce) cans diced tomatoes in juice, undrained
¹/₂ cup water
1¹/₂ teaspoons dried oregano, preferably Mexican
³/₄ cup chopped fresh cilantro
Sea salt and freshly ground black pepper

1. In a 5- to 7-quart pressure cooker, heat the oil over medium-high heat. Add the onion, celery, and bell pepper and cook, stirring a few times, until they begin to soften, about 3 minutes. Add the garlic and stir for 30 seconds. Add the enchilada sauce, tomatoes and their juices, water, and oregano. Add half the cilantro and stir.

2. Close and lock the lid. If you like, place a heat diffuser on the burner and the pressure cooker on the diffuser. Set the burner heat to high. When the cooker reaches HIGH pressure, reduce the burner heat as low as you can and still maintain HIGH pressure. Set a timer to cook for 7 minutes.

3. Remove the pot from the heat. Open the cooker with the Quick Release method. Be careful of the steam as you remove the lid. Leave the sauce chunky (that's how we like it) or use an immersion blender to puree the sauce right in the pot to the consistency you prefer. Stir in the rest of the cilantro. Taste for salt and pepper. Add more cilantro if you like. Use or let cool completely and store in an airtight container in the refrigerator up to 5 days or the freezer 4 to 6 months.

Mexican Spaghetti Sauce with Cicis: Add 1 (15-ounce) can drained and rinsed garbanzo beans, or 2 cups fresh cooked along with the cilantro in Step 3. Simmer, uncovered, over medium heat until heated through.

COTIJA CHEESE

Cotija is a hard, crumbly cheese from the state of Michoacan in southwestern Mexico and often used crumbled or grated as a topping for soups, tacos, beans, and enchilada casseroles. It is increasingly popular on pasta. Its similarity to Parmesan has earned it the nickname "Parmesan of Mexico." The aged version of cotija is referred to as *anejo*. Like Parmesan, it is often sold already grated, but it tastes so much better when you grate your own.

Saltsa Domato (Greek Tomato Sauce)

Makes 4 cups, enough for 1 pound pasta • Cooker: 5- to 7-quart • Time: 7 minutes at HIGH pressure

For authentic flavor, you want to prepare this with Greek—not Italian or Mexican—oregano, *rigani*, or "the joy of the mountain." Marjoram can be substituted. Greek olive oil, usually pressed from Kalamata olives, is considered the finest in the world, so for an authentic sauce, seek it out. This is a fabulous sauce to serve with long hollow pasta shapes like perciatelli, maccheroncelli, and ziti as well as rice or potatoes—either way, sprinkle the top with grated kefalotiri or Parmesan or crumbled fresh goat cheese. You can also use it in casseroles like moussaka or as a simmer sauce for lamb meatballs, zucchini, or artichokes. You can make it in large quantities, doubling or tripling the recipe. Allow it to cool, stir well to mix the oil back in (it will rise to the top), and freeze to use later.

1 (28-ounce) can whole plum tomatoes in juice, undrained
1 large white onion, chopped
1 to 4 large cloves garlic, to taste
1 medium green bell pepper, seeded and diced
1 medium red bell pepper, seeded and diced
8 ounces white mushrooms, sliced
$1/2$ cup Greek extra virgin olive oil
$1/2$ cup water
$1/2$ cup dry white wine or water
1 (8-ounce) can tomato sauce
2 teaspoons dried Greek oregano *(rigani)*
1 bay leaf
1 tablespoon sea salt
$1/2$ teaspoon freshly ground black pepper

1. In a 5- to 7-quart pressure cooker, with an immersion blender, puree the tomatoes and their juice, onion, and garlic together. Add the bell peppers, mushrooms, oil, water, wine, tomato sauce, oregano, and bay leaf. Stir and bring to a boil.
2. Close and lock the lid. If you like, place a heat diffuser on the burner and the pressure cooker on the diffuser. Set the burner heat to high. When the cooker reaches HIGH pressure, reduce the burner heat as low as you can and still maintain HIGH pressure. Set a timer to cook for 7 minutes.
3. Remove the pot from the heat. Open the cooker with the Quick Release method. Be careful of the steam as you remove the lid. Stir in the salt and pepper and remove the bay leaf. Let stand 10 minutes before using. Use or let cool completely and store in an airtight container in the refrigerator up to 5 days or the freezer up to 1 month.

Greek Tomato Sauce with Cinnamon: Add 2 teaspoons ground cinnamon or 2 (4-inch) cinnamon sticks and 1 pinch ground allspice with the oregano in Step 1.

Spicy Greek Tomato Sauce: Add $1^1/2$ teaspoons Aleppo pepper or $3/4$ teaspoon red pepper flakes with the oregano in Step 1.

Ancho Chile-Tomato Sauce with Roasted Garlic

Makes 4 cups, enough for 1 pound pasta • Cooker: 5- to 7-quart • Time: 7 minutes at HIGH pressure

This a delicious all-purpose tomato sauce for any type of Mexican cooking—with huevos rancheros, over chicken or rabbit, drizzled in tacos, in enchilada casseroles. There are a few steps before it all goes into the cooker, like roasting the garlic and grinding the chile, but don't skip them. This is adapted from a sauce Beth learned when she took a class from Ed Brown, author of the Tassajara cookbooks, in a private home in Mountain View, California. Brown made three tomato sauces, all from canned tomatoes, each with different spices to show how they made a totally different sauce each time. This is a great winter sauce.

1 (2^1/$_2$- to 3-ounce) head garlic, base cut off
Olive oil
2 ancho chiles
1 (28-ounce) can tomato puree
1 (14.5-ounce) can diced tomatoes in juice, undrained
^{1}/$_2$ cup water or vegetable broth
2 tablespoons tomato paste
^{1}/$_4$ teaspoon dried oregano, preferably Mexican
2 tablespoons sherry vinegar or cider vinegar
Pinch sugar
Sea salt

1. Preheat the oven to 350° F. Place the garlic on a baking sheet or in a gratin dish and brush it with oil. Bake until soft when squeezed, about 30 minutes. Place the chiles on the baking sheet at the same time and bake until puffy, about 3 minutes. Cool, then remove the stems, cut open, and remove the seeds; grind in a small food processor or coffee mill to make 2 to 3 tablespoons. This can all be done the day before and stored in an airtight container in the refrigerator.

2. In a 5- to 7-quart pressure cooker, combine the tomato puree, tomatoes and their juice, water, tomato paste, ground anchos, and oregano and stir to combine. Squeeze all of the garlic cloves out of their skins into the pot. Give a good stir.

3. Close and lock the lid. If you like, place a heat diffuser on the burner and the pressure cooker on the diffuser. Set the burner heat to high. When the cooker reaches HIGH pressure, reduce the burner heat as low as you can and still maintain HIGH pressure. Set a timer to cook for 7 minutes.

4. Remove the pot from the heat. Open the cooker with the Natural Release (let stand for 15 minutes) or Quick Release method. Be careful of the steam as you remove the lid. Use an immersion blender to puree the sauce right in the pot. Stir in the vinegar and sugar, then season to taste with salt. Use or let cool completely and store in an airtight container in the refrigerator up to 5 days or the freezer 4 to 6 months.

ANCHO CHILES

The ancho chile, which is a dried poblano, is deep red, with a rich, mild flavor, with underlying notes of dried raisins or prunes. Look for it with other dried chiles, usually in packages hanging on the wall in the produce section.

Smoky Chipotle Tomato Sauce

Makes 4 cups, enough for 1 pound pasta • Cooker: 5- to 7-quart • Time: 6 minutes at HIGH pressure

This sauce has a more pronounced tomato flavor. You can use as few or as many chiles as you wish to get the flavor you want. Remember, these chiles are hot, hot, hot. The sauce is excellent with cheese enchiladas and chiles rellenos as well as rice and beans and served over fettuccine. You can use an immersion blender at the end if you desire a totally smooth sauce.

3 tablespoons olive oil
$^2/_3$ cup diced white onion
2 cloves garlic, peeled
1 (28-ounce) can whole plum tomatoes in juice, undrained
1 (14.5-ounce) can diced tomatoes in juice, undrained
$^1/_2$ cup vegetable broth or water
$1^1/_4$ teaspoons dried oregano, preferably Mexican
2 to 4 canned chipotle chiles in adobo sauce, to taste, finely chopped
Pinch sugar
Sea salt

1. In a 5- to 7-quart pressure cooker, warm the oil over medium-high heat. Add the onion and cook, stirring a few times, until it begins to soften, about 3 minutes. Add the garlic cloves and stir until they soften, then crush them against the side of the pot and stir into the onion. Add the whole tomatoes and their juice, crushing them with your hand as you put them in the pot, the chopped tomatoes and their juice, broth, oregano, and chiles; stir to combine. Give a taste and add some of the adobo sauce if you want a bit more heat.

2. Close and lock the lid. If you like, place a heat diffuser on the burner and the pressure cooker on the diffuser. Set the burner heat to high. When the cooker reaches HIGH pressure, reduce the burner heat as low as you can and still maintain HIGH pressure. Set a timer to cook for 6 minutes.

3. Open the cooker with the Natural Release (let stand for 15 minutes) or Quick Release method. Be careful of the steam as you remove the lid. Add the sugar and taste for salt. Use or let cool completely and store in an airtight container in the refrigerator up to 3 days or the freezer 4 to 6 months.

CHIPOTLE CHILES

The chipotle chile is a jalapeño that's been left on the bush until ripe-red, then dried over a wood fire, so it's hot AND smoky at the same time. It has a thick skin and is smoked until it has the consistency of a prune. You can buy the dried whole chiles, the pure ground powder, or *chipotles en adobo* in a can, which are the dried chiles packed in a spicy adobo sauce, which is what we call for in this recipe.

Coconut Curry Tomato Sauce

Makes 5 cups, enough for 1$^1/_2$ pounds pasta • Cooker: 5- to 7-quart • Time: 6 minutes at HIGH pressure

Use any favorite curry powder you like here, from mild to the hotter Madras. This lovely pink sauce is delicious spooned over pasta—we like orzo, wagon wheels or spaghetti—rice, or potatoes. It is also good in complex dishes like a vegetable or meat curry. Try not to eat this by the spoonful out of the pot.

2 tablespoons light olive oil or plain sesame oil
1 large white onion, finely chopped
1 jalapeño pepper, seeded and chopped
2 cloves garlic, minced
1 tablespoon minced peeled fresh ginger
1$^1/_2$ tablespoons curry powder
1 (28-ounce) can whole plum tomatoes in juice, undrained
1 (8-ounce) can tomato sauce
1 (14-ounce) can unsweetened coconut milk
1 small cinnamon stick
1 teaspoon sugar or honey
Salt and freshly ground black pepper
$^1/_4$ cup chopped fresh cilantro

1. In a 5- to 7-quart pressure cooker, heat the oil over medium-high heat. Add the onion and cook, stirring a few times, until it begins to soften, about 3 minutes. Add the jalapeño, garlic, and ginger and stir for 1 minute. Add the curry powder and cook, stirring, until fragrant, about 1 minute. Add the tomatoes and their juice, crushing them with your hand as you put them in the pot. Add the tomato sauce, coconut milk, cinnamon, and sugar; stir to combine. Season to taste with salt and pepper and stir.

2. Close and lock the lid. If you like, place a heat diffuser on the burner and the pressure cooker on the diffuser. Set the burner heat to high. When the cooker reaches HIGH pressure, reduce the burner heat as low as you can and still maintain HIGH pressure. Set a timer to cook for 6 minutes.

3. Remove the pot from the heat. Open the cooker with the Natural Release (let stand for 15 minutes) or Quick Release method. Be careful of the steam as you remove the lid. Discard the cinnamon stick. Taste for salt and stir in the cilantro. If the sauce is not thick enough for you, simmer, uncovered, over medium heat until it reaches the desired consistency. Use or let cool completely and store in an airtight container in the refrigerator up to 3 days or the freezer 4 to 6 months.

Indian-Style Ginger Tomato Sauce

Makes 4 cups, enough for 1 pound pasta • Cooker: 5- to 7-quart • Time: 3 minutes at HIGH pressure

Redolent of Indian spices, this sauce has a bright, spicy flavor. Fennel is a natural in pasta sauces. You can make your own garam masala mixture if you like. This is very nice over penne or shells with a cucumber raita on the side.

1 1/2 teaspoons garam masala
1 heaping teaspoon fennel seeds
1/4 teaspoon red pepper flakes
1 (3-inch) chunk fresh ginger, peeled
1/3 cup water
2 tablespoons light olive oil or ghee
1 (28-ounce) can whole plum tomatoes in juice, undrained
1 (8-ounce) can tomato sauce
Sea salt and freshly ground black pepper
1/4 cup chopped fresh cilantro

1. Place the garam masala, fennel seeds, red pepper, and ginger in a food processor or blender. Add the water and puree until smooth.
2. In a 5- to 7-quart pressure cooker, heat the oil over low heat. Add the spice mixture and cook, stirring, until a thick paste is formed. Add the tomatoes and their juice, crushing them with your hand as you put them in the pot. Add the tomato sauce; stir to combine. Season to taste with salt and black pepper. Stir to combine.
3. Close and lock the lid. If you like, place a heat diffuser on the burner and the pressure cooker on the diffuser. Set the burner heat to high. When the cooker reaches HIGH pressure, reduce the burner heat as low as you can and still maintain HIGH pressure. Set a timer to cook for 3 minutes.
4. Remove the pot from the heat. Open the cooker with the Natural Release method; let stand for 15 minutes. Be careful of the steam as you remove the lid. Taste for salt and pepper, then stir in the cilantro. Use or let cool completely and store in an airtight container in the refrigerator up to 3 days or the freezer 4 to 6 months.

5

Seafood

The pressure cooker cooks fish fast in a clean, foolproof manner with minimal cleanup and, for many dishes, with no added cooking fat. Short cook times guarantee maximum moisture and flavor retention. It does a dynamite job with seafood stews, as well as poaching and steaming fish, including en papillote (in parchment), where the cooker really shines. Fish may also be cooked on a bed of vegetables for a one-pot meal.

If you are cooking up multiple portions all at once, select fish fillets and steaks of even thickness so they will cook in the same amount of time. You will usually use the Quick Release method, to stop the cooking as soon as the programmed time is reached to prevent overcooking.

MAKING SUSTAINABLE CHOICES AT THE FISH COUNTER

Whenever possible, choose sustainably raised or caught fish. What does "sustainable" mean? It's a word we see constantly now in relation to seafood. Monterey Bay Aquarium spokesman Ken Peterson explains, "Sustainable seafood comes from sources, whether fished or farmed, that can exist into the long term without jeopardizing the health of the fish population or the integrity of the surrounding ecosystem." Certain fishing practices destroy entire ecosystems and habitats. Harmful harvesting methods have the potential to sweep vast sections of ocean floor barren of life. Some fish, like Atlantic cod, have been overfished almost to the point of extinction.

Once fish markets had wraparound cold cases filled with selections of dozens of types of fish from the global seas on any one day. No longer. In order to prevent overfishing and maintain wild fish populations, fisheries are managed by quotas and other catch limits. Enter aquaculture. Farmed seafood, such as catfish, striped bass, and shellfish, are abundant in the market and safe, healthy foods to choose. Mussels, clams, and scallops take the lead for weeknight suppers. Fresh, local, and sustainably harvested catches include black cod, white seabass, sardines, anchovies, steelhead trout, halibut, squid, rockfish, and albacore tuna. Crabs, lobster, and squid are naturals in the pressure cooker. Wild salmon has a fat content that assures a succulent fish flavored by its poaching liquid.

Be an educated consumer at the fish counter. There are several very good online resources for determining the best choices when deciding what to buy, and they are constantly updated. We particularly recommend the Monterey Bay Aquarium's seafoodwatch.org.

Our selection of recipes makes use of sustainable seafood options, and we offer them here for you to master and enjoy.

THE SUPER GREEN LIST

The Monterey Bay Aquarium's Seafood Watch compiles a Super Green List each year of seafood choices. Those that are included must contain:

- Low levels of contaminants (below 216 parts per billion [ppb] mercury and 11 ppb PCBs)
- the daily recommended minimum of omega-3s (at least 250 milligrams per day)

Here are Seafood Watch's current "Best Choices":

The Best of the Best

- Albacore tuna (troll- or pole-caught from the U.S. and British Columbia)
- Freshwater Coho salmon (farmed in tank systems in the U.S.)
- Salmon (wild-caught from Alaska, and canned)
- Pacific sardines (wild-caught)
- Rainbow trout (farmed)
- Black cod/sablefish (wild-caught from Alaska and Canadian Pacific)
- Atlantic mackerel (purse-seined from Canada and the U.S.)
- Domestic catfish
- Striped bass
- Oysters (farmed)

Other Healthy "Best Choices"

- Arctic char (farmed; a relative of salmon)
- Barramundi (farmed, from the U.S.; similar to halibut and cod)
- Swordfish (harpoon and hand line caught)
- Dungeness crab (wild-caught, from California, Oregon, or Washington)
- Longfin squid (wild-caught, from the U.S. Atlantic)
- Mussels and clams (farmed)

Seafood to Avoid

The organization The Food & Water Watch has compiled a "Dirty Dozen" list of seafood to avoid because of depleted stocks and/or because they contain high levels of contaminants like mercury or PCBs.

1. Imported king crab
2. Caviar, especially from beluga and other wild-caught sturgeon
3. Atlantic bluefin tuna
4. Orange roughy
5. Atlantic flatfish (e.g. flounder, sole, and halibut)
6. American eel
7. Atlantic cod
8. Imported catfish
9. Chilean seabass
10. Shark
11. Farmed salmon, often sold as Atlantic salmon
12. Imported farmed shrimp

Fish Fillets in Parchment with Herbs

Serves 4 • Cooker: 5- to 7-quart • Time: 5 minutes at HIGH pressure

Cooking *en papillote* (French) or *al cartoccio* (Italian) means tightly wrapping something (usually fish, chicken, or vegetables) in parchment paper and, usually, baking it; the result is that the food steams in its own juices, yielding a fragrant, succulent result. It is an old technique that still works well in these modern days. Here the technique is used in the pressure cooker. You can assemble the packets in the morning and have them ready to steam in just a few minutes for dinner. Look for parchment paper next to the aluminum foil and plastic wrap in your supermarket. If you cannot find it, you can make the packets from foil—there is no flavor difference.

The components of this dish remain the same even though the specific ingredients vary:

- Choose a lean, tender protein, such as fish; shellfish; boneless, skinless chicken breast or thighs; or tofu.
- Add flavorful accompaniments, such as fresh garden herbs, chopped ginger, garlic, lemongrass, spice mixtures, citrus slices or zest, or sliced chiles.
- Add a splash of liquid. Try wine, vermouth, fish or chicken stock, soy sauce, mirin, sherry, or a combination.
- Use the steamer basket or double-stacked 6-inch bamboo steamer baskets.

4 (13-inch-square) sheets parchment paper
4 (4- to 6-ounce) skinless white fish fillets, such as bass, snapper, cod, catfish, salmon, or halibut, ³/₄ to 1 inch thick
4 tablespoons olive oil
Fresh herbs, such as sprigs of basil, dill, tarragon, marjoram, thyme, or chervil (you want 2 sprigs per packet)
4 green onions, trimmed and chopped
4 tablespoons (¹/₂ stick) unsalted butter
1 lemon or 2 limes, cut into 12 thin slices total
¹/₄ cup dry white wine, such as Pinot Grigio or Sauvignon Blanc
¹/₄ cup fresh lemon or lime juice
2 cups water

1. Make the fish packages: For each package, fold a piece of parchment in half to form a crease. Spray the lower half of the paper with some olive oil nonstick cooking spray. Place a fish fillet on the lower third of the parchment, about 3 inches from the bottom. Rub the top of the fillet with 1 tablespoon of oil. Top each with 2 herb sprigs, one quarter of the green onions, 1 tablespoon of the butter cut into small pieces, and 3 lemon or lime slices.

2. In a small bowl, combine the wine and lemon or lime juice. Drizzle 2 tablespoons of the mixture over the fillet. Fold the top half of the parchment down to meet the bottom edge. Starting on one side, fold and crimp the edges in small increments to form an airtight, half-moon-shaped packet that securely encloses the fish. Finish crimping the edges, then twist the pointed end around once and fold the "tail" underneath. (The packets can be prepared up to 3 hours in advance and refrigerated.)

3. Place a trivet and steamer basket in a 5- to 7-quart pressure cooker. Pour in the water. Stack the fish packets in the basket in a crisscross pile. You can also use double-stacked 6-inch bamboo steamer baskets.

4. Close and lock the lid. Set the burner heat to high. When the cooker reaches HIGH pressure, reduce the burner heat as low as you can and still maintain HIGH pressure. Set a timer to cook for 5 minutes.

5. Remove the pot from the heat. Open the cooker with the Quick Release method. Be careful of the steam as you remove the lid. Lift the packets out of the basket one at a time, holding one end with tongs and using a long plastic spatula. Transfer the packets to individual dinner plates. The fish should flake easily when a fork is inserted gently.

6. Serve immediately. Using a steak knife or scissors, let each diner tear open their own packet and dive in. Pour any accumulated juices over the fish.

Fish Fillets in Parchment with Herbs and Vegetables: Divide about 1 cup julienned zucchini and about 1 cup sliced white mushrooms equally between the 4 fillets (¹/₄ cup each) in Step 1, arranging them around the fillets.

Halibut in Parchment with Martini Butter

Serves 4 • Cooker: 5- to 7-quart • Time: 6 minutes at HIGH pressure

Here's another version of fish in parchment, a martini-inspired compound butter, complete with olives! Serve with plenty of hot crusty bread to sop up the butter sauce.

MARTINI BUTTER:
1 tablespoon gin
1 1/2 teaspoons dry vermouth
1/4 cup (1/2 stick) unsalted butter, at room temperature
1 green onion, trimmed and finely chopped
3 tablespoons chopped pimiento-stuffed green olives
1/4 teaspoon finely grated lemon zest
Dash cayenne pepper

HALIBUT:
4 (13-inch-square) sheets parchment paper
4 (6-ounce) skinless halibut fillets, about 1 inch thick
Salt and freshly ground black pepper
1 small red bell pepper, seeded and cut into julienne strips
2 cups water

1. Make the Martini Butter. In a small nonreactive saucepan, heat the gin and vermouth over medium-high heat until reduced to 1 1/2 teaspoons, 1 to 1 1/2 minutes. Remove from the heat and let cool.

2. In a small bowl, combine the gin mixture with the remaining martini butter ingredients and stir until well blended. Form the mixture into a log and wrap tightly in plastic wrap. Freeze until very firm, at least 1 hour. (Martini Butter can be frozen for several weeks, if desired.)

3. Make the fish packages. For each package, fold a piece of parchment in half to form a crease. Spray the lower half of the paper with some olive oil nonstick cooking spray. Place a fish fillet about 3 inches from the bottom, and season lightly with salt and pepper. Top with one quarter of the red pepper julienne and 1 generous tablespoon of the cold Martini Butter. Fold the top half of the parchment down to meet the bot-

tom edge. Starting on one side, fold and crimp the edges in small increments to form an airtight, half-moon-shaped packet that securely encloses the fish. Finish crimping the edges, then twist the pointed end around once and fold the "tail" under. Repeat with the remaining parchment and fish fillets. (The packets can be prepared up to 3 hours in advance and refrigerated.)

4. Place a trivet and steamer basket in a 5- to 7-quart pressure cooker. Pour in the water. Stack the fish packets in the basket in a crisscross pile. You can also use double-stacked 6-inch bamboo steamer baskets.

5. Close and lock the lid. Set the burner heat to high. When the cooker reaches HIGH pressure, reduce the burner heat as low as you can and still maintain HIGH pressure. Set a timer to cook for 6 minutes.

6. Remove the pot from the heat. Open the cooker with the Quick Release method. Be careful of the steam as you remove the lid. Using tongs and a plastic spatula, lift the packets out of the basket one at a time and transfer to individual dinner plates. The fish should flake easily when a fork is inserted gently.

7. Serve immediately. Using a steak knife or scissors, let each diner tear open his or her own packet.

Parchment-Wrapped Fish Fillets with Artichokes and Olives

Serves 4 • Cooker: 5- to 7-quart • Time: 5 minutes at HIGH pressure

We remember first discovering marinated artichoke hearts and how we wanted to use them in everything. Cooked with the fish *en papillote*, the flavors become wonderfully concentrated.

4 (13-inch-square) sheets parchment paper
4 (4- to 6-ounce) skinless white fish fillets, such as bass, snapper, cod, or halibut, ³/₄ to 1 inch thick
1 lemon, cut into 8 thin slices
16 black olives of your choice
2 (6-ounce) jars marinated artichoke hearts, drained
4 tablespoons dry white wine, such as Pinot Grigio or Sauvignon Blanc
2 cups water

1. Make the fish packages. For each packet, fold a piece of parchment in half to form a crease. Spray the lower half of the paper with some olive oil nonstick cooking spray. Place a fish fillet on the parchment about 3 inches from the bottom. Top each fillet with 2 lemon slices, 4 olives, a few artichoke hearts, and 1 tablespoon wine. Fold the top half of the parchment down to meet the bottom edge. Starting on one side, fold and crimp the edges in small increments to form an airtight, half-moon-shaped packet that securely encloses the fish. Finish crimping the edges, then twist the pointed end around once and fold the "tail" under. Repeat with the remaining parchment and fish fillets. (The packets can be prepared up to 3 hours in advance and refrigerated.)

2. Place a trivet and steamer basket in a 5- to 7-quart pressure cooker. Pour in the water. Stack the fish packets in the basket in a crisscross pile. You can also use double-stacked 6-inch bamboo steamer baskets.

3. Close and lock the lid. Set the burner heat to high. When the cooker reaches HIGH pressure, reduce the burner heat as low as you can and still maintain HIGH pressure. Set a timer to cook for 5 minutes.

4. Remove the pot from the heat. Open the cooker with the Quick Release method. Be careful of the steam as you remove the lid. Lift the packets out of the basket one at a time, holding one end with tongs and using a long spatula, and transfer to individual dinner plates. The fish should flake easily when a fork is inserted gently.

5. Serve immediately. Using a steak knife or scissors, let each diner tear open their own packet and dive in. Pour any accumulated juices over the fish.

Steamed Whole Brook Trout with Dill and Lemon

Serves 4 • Cooker: 5- to 7-quart • Time: 3 minutes at HIGH pressure

This method of stuffing the body of the trout with some lemon slices and herbs is borrowed from Beth's method of grilling whole salmon for parties. No need for a steamer basket, the fish is set on a bed of lettuce leaves. It is pure genius and gives a bit more room to the whole fish. You can fit four whole trout in a large pressure cooker. This is delicious served with roasted fingerling potatoes

LEMON MAYONNAISE:

1 cup mayonnaise or Vegenaise soy mayonnaise
Juice and grated zest of $1/2$ lemon
1 tablespoon low-sodium soy sauce
2 teaspoons Sriracha hot sauce, or to taste

TROUT:

1 good-size head butter lettuce, torn into large
   pieces
$3/4$ cup water
2 tablespoons dry white wine
4 (6- to 8-ounce) trout, gutted, cleaned, and boned,
   head and tail left on
Sea salt and freshly ground black or white pepper
4 tablespoons olive oil
2 lemons, thinly sliced
1 small bunch fresh dill

1. Make the Lemon Mayonnaise. In a small bowl, stir all the ingredients together until well combined. Taste for lemon juice and hot sauce. Store in an airtight container in the refrigerator for at least 1 hour to let the flavors develop and up to 1 week. Makes about 1 cup.

2. In a 6- to 8-quart pressure cooker, arrange about two-thirds of the lettuce leaves to make a bed that covers the entire bottom of the pot. Pour in the water and wine. Season each trout with salt and pepper to taste inside and out. Drizzle the cavity of each with 1 tablespoon of the oil. Stuff each with the lemon slices and dill. Set the trout, side by side, on top of the lettuce, curving them to fit. Cover with the remaining lettuce leaves.

3. Close and lock the lid. Set the burner heat to high. When the cooker reaches HIGH pressure, reduce the burner heat as low as you can and still maintain HIGH pressure. Set a timer to cook for 3 minutes.

4. Remove the pot from the heat and let stand for 3 minutes, no more. Open the cooker with the Quick Release method. Be careful of the steam as you remove the lid. Remove the top layer of lettuce with metal tongs, then use a spatula to transfer the fish to individual dinner plates. Peel away the skin with your fingers. Remove the heads, if desired. The meat should fall off the bone. Discard the bed of lettuce leaves. Serve immediately with the lemon mayonnaise on the side.

Steamed Red Snapper with Easy Black Bean Sauce

Serves 4 • Cooker: 5- to 8-quart • Time: 4 minutes at HIGH pressure

Steaming fish is a classic Cantonese technique, often used for whole fish, though we'll be cooking fillets. The fish needs to be put in a shallow heat-proof dish that will fit in the pressure cooker on the steamer plate, so that the juices can be collected. We added some rice wine to make more delicious juice for the rice to soak up. Use the domestically produced Hakusan sake for cooking; it is reasonably priced. Mirin is a sweet Japanese cooking wine (yes, we know, Japanese rice wine for a Chinese dish, but we always have some on the shelf for cooking). Be sure to read the label so that you are buying genuine mirin, not imitation mirin—the flavor difference is dramatic. This treatment will also work with salmon, halibut, and cod fillets, as well as shrimp.

This recipe comes from our ex-senior editor at the *San Jose Mercury News* (affectionately known as the Merc), Carolyn Jung, who is an accomplished cook as well as a James Beard award winner for her food journalism. She now runs the ever so popular blog Food Gal located in the San Francisco Bay Area. Says Carolyn, "I often just use the thick commercial black bean sauce in the jar, which tastes great with the garlic, chile, ginger, and soy sauce already in it, rather than the plain fermented dried black beans, which need more prep time with soaking. That makes this way of preparing fish even easier." The fermented black beans are soybeans, not black turtle beans, despite the resemblance.

Serve with steamed jasmine rice.

4 (6- to 8-ounce) skin-on red snapper fillets, ³/₄ to
   1 inch thick
About 4 teaspoons black bean garlic sauce
2 tablespoons slivered (2 to 3 inches long) peeled
   fresh ginger
4 green onions, trimmed and slivered
1 tablespoon sake
1 tablespoon mirin
2 cups water
4 tablespoons minced fresh cilantro, for garnish

1. Cut a piece of heavy-duty aluminum foil about 2 feet long. Fold in half twice to create a strip to move the dish in and out of the pot easily. Set aside.

2. Arrange the fish fillets in a single layer with a bit of space in between on a heat-proof dish, such as a small Pyrex pie pan or ceramic dish that will easily fit inside the pressure cooker on the steamer plate with ¹/₂ inch space all around the rim. If you have big fillets, cook them in two batches since they will cook so fast, and use half the toppings for each batch. You can also do this in a 6-inch stacked bamboo steamer lined with lettuce or cabbage leaves.

3. Smear 1 teaspoon black bean sauce over the top of each fillet. You don't want to overdo it, as the paste is quite salty. And you don't have to smear the entire fillet, as the natural juices from the fish will dilute the paste during the cooking process, creating more than enough black bean sauce for the fish. Sprinkle the fish with some ginger and slivered green onions. Drizzle with the sake and mirin.

4. Place a trivet and steamer rack in a 5- to 8-quart pressure cooker, then pour in the water. Place the uncovered heatproof dish over the foil strip and, holding the handles, lower it into the pressure cooker onto the steamer plate. Fold the handle edges loosely over the top.

5. Close and lock the lid. Set the burner heat to high. When the cooker reaches HIGH pressure, reduce the burner heat as low as you can and still maintain HIGH pressure. Set a timer to cook for 4 minutes.

6. Remove the pot from the heat. Open the cooker with the Quick Release method. Be careful of the steam as you remove the lid. The fish should be moist and no longer translucent and just flake. There will be accumulated liquid in the pie plate, which you can spoon over the fish as sauce.

7. Use a spatula to transfer each fillet to an individual dinner plate. Drizzle with the juices and sprinkle with 1 tablespoon of cilantro. Serve immediately.

Mahi-Mahi Poached in Coconut Milk

Serves 4 • Cooker: 5- to 7-quart • Time: 3 minutes at HIGH pressure

Poaching in a bath of seasoned coconut milk has to be one of the most fantastic flavor enhancers for fish (it works with chicken thighs as well). If mahi-mahi is not available, use a white-flesh fish as a substitute. Striped bass, halibut, black cod, grouper, snapper, and flounder are all similar in flavor and texture to mahi-mahi.

1 tablespoon olive oil or plain (not toasted) sesame oil
2 shallots, minced
2 tablespoons grated peeled fresh ginger
$1/2$ cup coarsely chopped fresh cilantro, including stems
1 stalk lemongrass (white and light green parts), chopped into pieces
1 tablespoon Asian fish sauce or soy sauce
1 (14-ounce) can unsweetened coconut milk
4 (6- to 8-ounce) mahi-mahi fillets or steaks, 1 inch thick
White or brown jasmine rice, for serving
Freshly ground black pepper
4 green onions, trimmed and cut into slivers, for serving
2 limes, quartered, for serving

1. In a 5- to 7-quart pressure cooker, heat the oil over medium heat. Add the shallots and cook, stirring, until soft, about 2 minutes. Add the ginger, cilantro, lemongrass, fish sauce, and coconut milk. Bring to a simmer. Lower the mahi-mahi into the hot liquid with a spatula.

2. Close and lock the lid. Set the burner heat to high. When the cooker reaches HIGH pressure, reduce the burner heat as low as you can and still maintain HIGH pressure. Set a timer to cook for 3 minutes.

3. Remove the pot from the heat. Open the cooker with the Natural Release method; let stand for 5 minutes. Quick Release any remaining pressure. Be careful of the steam as you remove the lid. The flesh should be opaque and flake easily.

4. Use a spatula to transfer the mahi-mahi to a serving platter with rice. Discard the lemongrass pieces and cilantro stems. Spoon the coconut sauce over the fish and rice, season to taste with pepper if you like, and garnish with the green onions and lime wedges. Serve immediately.

Salade Niçoise with Fresh Tuna

Serves 4 • Cooker: 5- to 7-quart • Time: 3 minutes at HIGH pressure

This is a substantial main-dish salad. The poaching liquid also works well for salmon and swordfish. You can prepare the vegetables and tuna the day before and refrigerate. Then all you have to do is arrange the salad.

COURT BOUILLON POACHING LIQUID:

2 cups water
$^1/_3$ cup cider vinegar
1 slice onion
4 black peppercorns
1 bay leaf
Fresh parsley stems (optional)
Sea salt and freshly ground black pepper

SALAD:

$^3/_4$ to 1 pound fresh tuna steaks
2 to 3 tablespoons olive oil
1 cup Niçoise Vinaigrette (recipe follows)
Assorted salad greens, such as butter lettuce, leaf lettuces, watercress, endive
Assorted seasonal vegetables, such as sliced beets, cauliflower and/or broccoli florets, or asparagus, blanched or steamed until crisp-tender
1 pound fresh green beans, trimmed, blanched until crisp-tender, refreshed in cold water, and drained
3 ripe Roma tomatoes, quartered
8 small red new potatoes, steamed or boiled just until tender
Marinated artichoke hearts or roasted red bell peppers
4 oil-packed anchovy fillets, drained just before serving and split in half lengthwise
2 hard-boiled eggs, quartered
$^1/_4$ cup Niçoise black olives
1 tablespoon nonpareil capers, rinsed
Freshly ground black pepper

1. Place the water, vinegar, onion slice, peppercorns, bay leaf, and parsley stems if using in a 5- to 7-quart pressure cooker. Bring to a simmer. Lower the tuna steaks into the hot liquid.
2. Close and lock the lid. Set the burner heat to high. When the cooker reaches HIGH pressure, reduce the burner heat as low as you can and still maintain HIGH pressure. Set a timer to cook for 3 minutes.

3. Open the cooker with the Natural Release method; let stand for 10 minutes. Quick Release any remaining pressure. Be careful of the steam as you remove the lid. Use a spatula to transfer the tuna to a plate. Let cool a bit, then rub with the olive oil. Cover with plastic wrap and refrigerate up to 24 hours.
4. Prepare the Niçoise Vinaigrette.
5. Shortly before serving, line a large, wide-rimmed salad bowl or a roomy platter with salad greens, drizzle a little olive oil on them, and sprinkle with salt. One at a time, toss the vegetables in some vinaigrette. Arrange the vegetables in piles on the lettuce. Drape the anchovy fillets over the potatoes. Drizzle a spoonful or two of the dressing over the tomatoes. Break the tuna into bite-sized pieces and toss with a little dressing; pile in the center. Ring the salad with the eggs. Spoon a little more vinaigrette over all; scatter on the olives and capers. Give a few turns of the pepper grinder over the whole salad. Serve as soon as possible.

Niçoise Vinaigrette

Makes about $1^1/_4$ cups

You can use all red wine vinegar, but the rice vinegar cuts the acid a bit. You can also use all olive oil, but the grapeseed oil is fantastic.

$^1/_4$ cup red wine vinegar
$^1/_4$ cup rice vinegar
1 tablespoon Dijon mustard
2 tablespoons fresh lemon juice
2 tablespoons minced shallot
$^1/_3$ cup grapeseed oil
$^1/_3$ cup olive oil
Sea salt and freshly ground black pepper

In a small bowl, combine all the ingredients except the oils and salt and pepper with a whisk. Slowly whisk in the oils to form an emulsion. You can also give a few pulses with an immersion blender. Taste and adjust the salt and pepper. It will keep in an airtight container in the refrigerator up to 2 days.

Miso-Honey Glazed Salmon in Parchment

Serves 4 • Cooker: 5- to 7-quart • Time: 5 minutes at HIGH pressure

Long one of the health food's staple ingredients, miso has moved into the mainstream. It pairs wonderfully with fish. Look for white miso, which is sweet and mild.

MISO-HONEY GLAZE:
2 tablespoons white miso paste
2 tablespoons honey
2 tablespoons unseasoned rice vinegar
2 teaspoons low-sodium soy sauce
2 teaspoons toasted sesame oil

SALMON:
4 (4- to 6-ounce) skin-on salmon fillets, $3/4$ to 1 inch thick
4 (13-inch-square) sheets parchment paper
2 cups water
3 green onions, trimmed and thinly sliced
2 teaspoons sesame seeds

1. Make the Miso-Honey Glaze. In a small bowl, stir all the ingredients together until smooth. Place the salmon on a plate, skin side down, and spread with half the glaze. Refrigerate 15 to 30 minutes.
2. Make the salmon packages. For each package, fold a piece of parchment in half to form a crease. Spray the lower half of the paper with olive oil nonstick cooking spray. Place a salmon fillet on the parchment, skin side down, about 3 inches from the bottom. Spread with some of the remaining glaze. Fold the top half of the parchment down to meet the bottom edge. Starting on one side, fold and crimp the edges in small increments to form an airtight, half-moon-shaped packet that securely encloses the fish. Finish crimping the edges, then twist the pointed end around once and fold the "tail" under. Repeat with the remaining parchment and fish fillets. (The packets can be prepared up to 3 hours in advance and refrigerated.)
3. Place a trivet and steamer basket in a 5- to 7-quart pressure cooker. Pour in the water. Stack the fish packets in the basket in a crisscross pile. You can also use double-stacked 6-inch bamboo steamer baskets.

4. Close and lock the lid. Set the burner heat to high. When the cooker reaches HIGH pressure, reduce the burner heat as low as you can and still maintain HIGH pressure. Set a timer to cook for 5 minutes.
5. Remove the pot from the heat. Open the cooker with the Quick Release method. Be careful of the steam as you remove the lid. Lift the packets out of the basket one at a time, holding one end with tongs and using a long plastic spatula, and transfer the packets to individual dinner plates. The fish should flake easily when a fork is inserted gently.
6. Using a steak knife or scissors, tear open each bag of salmon and sprinkle with the green onions and sesame seeds. Serve immediately.

ALL ABOUT SALMON

Meaty, enticingly pink-orange fleshed, and rich in flavor, salmon has become a favorite of American home cooks. A worknight meal becomes special with salmon. It is not only easy to prepare, but it is deliciously versatile as well as nutritious.

The fat in salmon is not something dieters need to shy away from. Salmon is touted as the most healthful of all fish due to the concentration of good fatty acids known as omega-3s.

Salmon is sold as a whole side (which makes for a dramatic presentation, especially for guests), fillets of various weights and thicknesses, and steaks, which are a cross-section of the whole fish. Thinner pieces cook faster than thicker pieces, no matter how large the overall piece is. If you have two thin fillets, you can cut off the tail section and overlap them to make one evenly thick piece. You can leave the skin on or off, as desired, but the skin does keep the fish together while cooking; just slip it off after cooking if you prefer. Salmon can be cooked to a variety of tastes, medium or rare, with no problem. Since it is a firm, high-fat fish, it takes to a wide variety of flavor enhancers.

Salmon in Parchment with Creamy Double Mustard Sauce and Chives

Serves 4 • Cooker: 5- to 7-quart • Time: 5 minutes at HIGH pressure

This piquant recipe has the ingredients spread onto the fish; under pressure, they will combine with the salmon's natural juices to make a creamy sauce.

CREAMY DOUBLE MUSTARD SAUCE:
$^1/_3$ cup crème fraîche
2 tablespoons Dijon or honey Dijon mustard
2 tablespoons whole-grain mustard
Juice of $^1/_2$ lemon
2 tablespoons olive oil

SALMON:
4 (13-inch-square) sheets parchment paper
4 (4- to 6-ounce) skin-on salmon fillets, $^3/_4$ to 1 inch thick
Sea salt and freshly ground black pepper
1 to 2 tablespoons minced fresh chives, to taste
1 lemon, cut into 8 thin slices
2 cups water

WILD VS. FARMED SALMON

Salmon was at one time all wild. They are carnivores, and wild salmon live on a diet of shrimp, squid, and small fish. The Pacific salmon fishing industry has made its fame on King salmon, also known as chinook, the largest of all salmon.

Coho salmon is less brilliant in color than King salmon and not as flavorful because it contains less fat. Coho salmon looks like trout, tastes similar to trout, and can be cooked like trout. Chum salmon is the last wild species of the year to be caught.

Atlantic salmon is a term used for salmon raised in floating saltwater feedlots. Environmental concerns have surfaced in the past years regarding farmed salmon its negative impact on the surrounding marine environments and wildlife. The flesh of farm-raised salmon is naturally pale and they are fed red food coloring to yield the bright red color consumers expect of salmon; their diet consists of ground-up cooked fishmeal.

Whether to eat wild or farm-raised salmon is a personal choice. One sound rule is to buy whichever looks and smells best that day.

1. Make the mustard sauce. In a small bowl, whisk all the ingredients together.
2. Make the salmon packages. For each packet, fold a piece of parchment in half to form a crease. Spray the lower half of the paper with olive oil nonstick cooking spray. Place the salmon fillet on the parchment, skin side down, about 3 inches from the bottom. Lightly season with salt and pepper. Spread one quarter of the mustard sauce on top of each salmon fillet with a rubber spatula. Top each fillet with a sprinkle of chives, then arrange 2 slices of lemon on top. Fold the top half of the parchment down to meet the bottom edge. Starting on one side, fold and crimp the edges in small increments to form an airtight, half-moon-shaped packet that securely encloses the fish. Finish crimping the edges, then twist the pointed end around once and fold the "tail" under. Repeat with the remaining parchment and fish fillets. (The packets can be refrigerated up to 3 hours.)
3. Place a trivet and steamer basket in a 5- to 7-quart pressure cooker. Pour in the water. Stack the fish packets in the basket in a crisscross pile. You can also use double-stacked 6-inch bamboo steamer baskets.
4. Close and lock the lid. Set the burner heat to high. When the cooker reaches HIGH pressure, reduce the burner heat as low as you can and still maintain HIGH pressure. Set a timer to cook for 5 minutes.
5. Remove the pot from the heat. Open the cooker with the Quick Release method. Be careful of the steam as you remove the lid. Lift the packets out of the basket one at a time, holding one end with tongs and using a long spatula, and transfer to individual dinner plates. The fish should flake easily when a fork is inserted gently.
6. Serve immediately. Using a steak knife or scissors, let each diner tear open their own bag of salmon and dive in.

Salmon Steaks Steamed in White Wine with Yogurt Tartar Sauce

Serves 4 • Cooker: 5- to 7-quart • Time: 4 minutes at HIGH pressure

This is the fastest and simplest salmon preparation, steamed in white wine on a bed of onions. In just a few minutes, you have perfectly cooked salmon. You can eat it plain, but we like our favorite yogurt tartar sauce on the side (keep Champagne vinegar and pickle relish on hand at all times to whip this up), which flatters the fish's natural taste and texture.

YOGURT TARTAR SAUCE:
$3/4$ cup mayonnaise, Miracle Whip, or Vegenaise soy mayonnaise
$3/4$ cup plain Greek yogurt
$1/3$ cup dill pickle relish, finely chopped dill pickles, or finely chopped cornichons
$1/4$ cup chopped green onion (white part and 1 inch of the green)
3 tablespoons nonpareil capers, rinsed and chopped
3 tablespoons finely chopped fresh flatleaf parsley
3 tablespoons fresh lemon juice or Champagne vinegar
1 teaspoon Dijon mustard
Pinch freshly ground black pepper or dash hot pepper sauce
Pinch turmeric

SALMON:
4 (6- to 8-ounce) skin-on salmon fillets or steaks, 1 inch thick
1 medium white onion, sliced into $1/2$-inch-thick rings
$3/4$ cup dry white wine, such as Sauvignon Blanc
1 teaspoon dried dillweed
Sea salt and ground white pepper
2 lemons, one sliced, the other cut into thick wedges, for serving
1 cup water

1. Make the Yogurt Tartar Sauce. In a small bowl, stir all the ingredients together until well combined. Store in an airtight container in the refrigerator at least 1 hour before serving, if possible, and up to 1 week. Makes about 2 cups.

2. Place a trivet and steamer basket in a 5- to 7-quart pressure cooker. Arrange the onion slices in an overlapping pattern in the basket; place the fish steaks on top. Pour the wine over the fish, then sprinkle with the dill, a little salt, and a few grinds of fresh pepper. Lay the lemon slices over the top of the fish. Pour over the water. Over high heat, bring the liquid in the pot to a boil. Boil 1 minute.

3. Close and lock the lid. Set the burner heat to high. When the cooker reaches HIGH pressure, reduce the burner heat as low as you can and still maintain HIGH pressure. Set a timer to cook for 4 minutes.

4. Remove the pot from the heat. Open the cooker with the Quick Release method. Be careful of the steam as you remove the lid. Remove the basket. Discard the lemon slices and use a spatula to transfer the fish to individual dinner plates. It should be firm and no longer translucent. Discard the bed of onions.

5. Serve immediately with the lemon wedges and tartar sauce.

Fabulous Fish Tacos with Lime Mayonnaise

Serves 4, 2 tacos per serving

What to do with leftover salmon, halibut, cod, tuna, or sea bass? I have found that, no matter what the glaze or cooking method, leftover cold fish, or even freshly cooked fish, makes a fabulous fish taco. You can certainly use a rub with some chili powder and cumin on the fish, but if not, don't sweat it; even the Asian glazes taste great the next day on a taco. The homemade mayonnaise is really special and whips up in a few minutes, so don't skip it because you think mayonnaise on a taco is weird (if you are pressed for time, add 3 tablespoons fresh lime juice and the zest of 1 lime into $^3/_4$ cup prepared mayonnaise). This recipe is made with pasteurized egg product for safety in place of a fresh egg, and the taste is spectacular, especially if you have not experienced homemade mayo before. The olive oil makes it a healthy food. The Mexican street stands of Baja and mainland, move over, the secret of a great fish taco is out. Serve with a side of refried beans.

LIME MAYONNAISE:

$^1/_4$ cup pasteurized liquid egg product (such as EggBeaters)
1 clove garlic, peeled
2 tablespoons fresh lime juice
1 teaspoon grated lime zest
$1^1/_2$ teaspoons Dijon mustard
$^1/_4$ teaspoon salt
Pinch chili powder
1 cup light olive oil or combination half olive oil and half vegetable oil

TACOS:

8 fresh corn tortillas
1 pound warm or cold cooked salmon, halibut, cod, tuna, or sea bass fillets, crumbled
$^1/_2$ red onion, thinly sliced
2 jarred whole roasted red peppers or whole roasted green chiles, rinsed, patted dry, and cut into strips
3 cups coleslaw mix
$^1/_3$ cup fresh cilantro leaves
1 ripe avocado, peeled, pitted, and thinly sliced
$^2/_3$ cup crumbled queso fresco
1 lime, quartered
Sea salt

1. Make the Lime Mayonnaise. In a food processor or 2-cup measure using an immersion blender, combine the egg product, garlic, lime juice and zest, mustard, salt, and chili powder. Process until the mixture begins to thicken, 15 to 20 seconds. Immediately begin to add the oil in a slow, steady stream. Continue processing, with an up-and-down motion if using an immersion blender, until thick and creamy, about another 30 seconds. Do not overmix or the mayonnaise can break. Refrigerate in an airtight container until ready to use or up to 2 days. Makes $1^1/_4$ cups.

2. Wrap the stack of tortillas in moistened paper towels and microwave on HIGH for 2 minutes, until steamy.

3. To assemble the tacos, place 2 warm tortillas on each plate and spread with 2 or 3 tablespoons of the mayonnaise. Layer in the following order, dividing the ingredients equally between the 8 tacos: fish, onion, pepper or chile strips, coleslaw mix, cilantro, avocado, and cheese. Squeeze over some lime juice and sprinkle with salt. Serve immediately.

Shrimp Boil in Beer with Our Own Remoulade Sauce

Serves 4 to 6 • Cooker: 6- to 8-quart • Time: 3 minutes at HIGH pressure

Use these in recipes calling for cooked shrimp or just sit, peel, and eat them with our luscious Louisiana-style remoulade sauce (our own—till now—secret sauce). Use the larger shrimp rather than the small—you want to be able to hold them by the tail to eat. These make for a great first course or appetizer. The sauce is also wonderful with crab cakes, fried green tomatoes, French fries, or po' boy sandwiches.

OUR OWN REMOULADE SAUCE:

$^1/_2$ cup Creole or other whole-grain mustard

$^1/_2$ cup Champagne vinegar or rice wine vinegar

2 teaspoons sweet paprika

$^1/_8$ teaspoon cayenne pepper, or to taste

Few pinches sea salt

1$^1/_4$ cups light olive oil

$^3/_4$ cup chopped green onions (white and part of green)

$^3/_4$ cup finely chopped celery

$^1/_2$ cup finely chopped fresh flatleaf parsley

SHRIMP:

2 (12-ounce) bottles beer, at room temperature

1 cup water

1 bay leaf

1 lemon, sliced, and 1 lemon, cut into thick wedges, for serving

2 pounds large (21–30) or extra-large prawns (16–20 count), unpeeled

1. In a medium bowl or 1-quart batter bowl (our favorite since it has a handle and its own lid), whisk the mustard, vinegar, paprika, cayenne, and salt together. Drizzle in the oil, whisking constantly to make a smooth thick sauce. You can also make this in the food processor like mayonnaise). Stir in the green onions, celery, and parsley. Cover and refrigerate for at least 4 hours to allow the flavor to develop or overnight. Taste for seasoning before serving. Makes about 3 cups.

2. Place the beer, water, bay leaf, and lemon slices in a 6-to 8-quart pressure cooker. Bring to a boil and let boil 1 minute. Add the shrimp.

3. Close and lock the lid. Set the burner heat to high. When the cooker reaches HIGH pressure, reduce the burner heat as low as you can and still maintain HIGH pressure. Set a timer to cook for 3 minutes.

4. Remove the pot from the heat. Open the cooker with the Quick Release method. Be careful of the steam as you remove the lid. The shrimp should be pink. Drain in a colander and cool with running water.

5. Place the shrimp in a large serving bowl or platter with the sauce on the side or refrigerate until ready to serve. Serve warm or chilled, peeling as you eat. If using for another recipe calling for cooked shrimp, you can peel and store in the refrigerator up to a day.

GUIDE TO SHRIMP SIZES

Probably one of the most frustrating things about recipes calling for shrimp is that many of them do not specify what size. So you are left visualizing the dish and figuring out what size seems most appropriate for the recipe. Our recipes always specify the exact size, which is calculated by how many shrimp make up a pound, called the "count." So, if you see a number that is high, such as 50, you know the shrimp are small. If you see a lower number, such as 10, you can tell they are jumbos, which are almost like mini-lobster tails. I usually call for large or extra-large shrimp with their tails left on. Here is a guideline for shrimp shopping:

- Medium: 31 to 40 count per pound
- Large: 21 to 30 count per pound
- Extra-large: 16 to 20 count per pound
- Jumbo: 10 to 15 count per pound

Mussels Fra Diavolo

Serves 2 to 3 • Cooker: 5- to 8-quart • Time: 4 minutes at HIGH pressure

Fra diavolo is the Neapolitan-style sauce of the devil, an Italian-American devil. It translates to "brother devil" or "devil monk," probably a reference to the hot pepper flakes that give the tomato sauce a kick. It was a 1930s' restaurant dish, popularized at the long defunct The Red Devil in New York City, made with calamari and served over spaghetti. The sauce is used for shrimp or lobster tails as well as mussels, infusing the seafood with its fiery flavor. Serve over fresh linguine and/or with fresh crusty bread for dipping.

1 (28-ounce) can crushed tomatoes
2 jalapeño peppers, seeded and chopped
$^1/_2$ cup chopped white onion or shallots
$^1/_4$ cup dry white wine
$^1/_4$ cup balsamic vinegar
$^1/_4$ cup extra virgin olive oil
2 tablespoons red pepper flakes
2 cloves garlic, minced
2 pounds mussels, rinsed and debearded if
    necessary (discard any with broken shells or that
    will not close)
$^1/_2$ cup chopped fresh basil
Sea salt
1 lemon, cut into thick wedges, for serving

1. Place the crushed tomatoes, jalapeños, onion, wine, vinegar, oil, pepper flakes, and garlic in a 5- to 8-quart pressure cooker pot. Stir to combine and bring to a boil. Stir in the mussels, making sure all are covered with the sauce.
2. Close and lock the lid. Set the burner heat to high. When the cooker reaches HIGH pressure, reduce the burner heat as low as you can and still maintain HIGH pressure. Set a timer to cook for 4 minutes.
3. Remove the pot from the heat. Open the cooker with the Quick Release method. Be careful of the steam as you remove the lid. Discard any mussels that have not opened.
4. Stir in the basil and taste for salt. Serve immediately with lemon wedges in shallow bowls or over pasta.

Calamari Fra Diavolo: Slice 2 pounds cleaned calamari squid into $^1/_2$-inch-wide rings and tentacles. Before combining all the ingredients in Step 1, heat the oil over high heat until very hot. Add the calamari and cook, stirring, for 4 minutes. Add the tomatoes, jalapeño, onion, wine, vinegar, pepper flakes, and garlic, stir to combine, and bring to a boil. Omit the mussels. Lock the lid and cook on HIGH pressure for 10 minutes. Use the Natural Release method to open the cooker; let stand for 10 minutes. Serve over spaghetti if desired.

Moules Dijonnaise

Serves 2 to 3 • Cooker: 5- to 8-quart • Time: 4 minutes at HIGH pressure

This version of Moules Dijonnaise, or mussels in the style of Dijon, is adapted from a recipe collection called *French in a Flash*. It uses a combination of two sharp mustards, which makes the luscious flavor. Serve these up with a side of French fries. *La moules marinieres magnifique!*

2 tablespoons olive oil
2 medium shallots, minced
1 small thin leek (white part only), trimmed, cut in half lengthwise, rinsed well, and thinly sliced across (about ¹/₂ cup)
Sea salt and freshly cracked black pepper
4 cloves garlic, chopped
1 cup dry white wine, such as Sauvignon Blanc or Pinot Grigio
1 cup water
4 to 6 sprigs fresh thyme, to taste
4 pounds mussels, rinsed and debearded if necessary (discard any with broken shells or that will not close)
1¹/₂ cups heavy cream
¹/₃ cup Dijon mustard
¹/₃ cup whole-grain mustard

1. In a 5- to 8-quart pressure cooker, heat the oil over medium heat. When the oil ripples, add the shallots and leek, and season to taste with salt and pepper. Cook, stirring often, until the vegetables are soft and fragrant, but not golden, about 3 minutes. Reduce the heat to low and add the garlic, stirring it around for about 45 seconds. Add the wine, water, and thyme. Bring to a boil; simmer for 3 minutes. Add the mussels.
2. Close and lock the lid. Set the burner heat to high. When the cooker reaches HIGH pressure, reduce the burner heat as low as you can and still maintain HIGH pressure. Set a timer to cook for 4 minutes.
3. Remove the pot from the heat. Open the cooker with the Quick Release method. Be careful of the steam as you remove the lid. Discard any mussels that have not opened. Transfer the mussels with tongs to a serving bowl. Discard the thyme.
4. Stir the cream and mustards into the broth in the pot until well combined. Taste the broth for seasoning, and adjust as needed. Pour over the mussels. Serve right away, in shallow bowls, with a baguette to tear apart or toasted baguette slices to dip into the broth.

MUSSELS AND CLAMS

Here's a tip for these two mollusks: Before cooking, if they're open and you can't get them to close (try tapping on them), throw them away. After cooking, if they haven't opened up at all, don't eat them.

Steamed Clams in Lemon Wine Broth

Serves 4 to 6 • Cooker: 6- to 8-quart • Time: 4 minutes at HIGH pressure

This is a lovely savory butter, garlic, wine liquid as the base for steaming clams, which will make a delicious broth to drizzle over the clams while eating. The ginger version is also wonderful. One hour before serving, scrub clams with a vegetable brush in cold water; rinse with water until free of sand (adding a little coarse salt to the water will help to remove the sand from the clams). If the shell is open, tap on it; discard if it does not close. There are 12 to 15 fresh clams per pound. Serve as a main dish meal with a green salad or as an appetizer with fresh crusty bread to dip in the broth.

1/4 cup (1/2 stick) unsalted butter
4 cloves garlic, minced
1 cup dry white wine, such as Pinot Grigio or
    Sauvignon Blanc
1 cup chicken broth
1 cup water
1 bunch green onions, trimmed and coarsely
    chopped, or 1 small white onion, coarsely
    chopped
6 parsley stems, plus 3 tablespoons chopped fresh
    flatleaf parsley, for serving
1 lemon, sliced, and 1 lemon, cut into thick wedges,
    for serving
3 pounds steamer, littleneck, or Manila clams,
    scrubbed

1. Melt the butter in a 6- to 8-quart pressure cooker over medium heat. When it starts to foam, add the garlic and cook, stirring, until fragrant, about 2 minutes. Add the wine, broth, and water; increase the heat to medium-high and bring to a boil; let boil for 1 minute. Add the onions, parsley stems, and lemon slices. Place a trivet and steamer basket in the pot. Fill the basket with the clams.

2. Close and lock the lid. Set the burner heat to high. When the cooker reaches HIGH pressure, reduce the burner heat as low as you can and still maintain HIGH pressure. Set a timer to cook for 4 minutes. Do not overcook or the clams will be tough.

3. Remove the pot from the heat. Open the cooker with the Quick Release method. Be careful of the steam as you remove the lid. Discard any clams that have not opened.

4. Transfer the clams to a serving bowl with tongs. If using the liquid, strain through a fine mesh strainer lined with cheesecloth; discard the solids. Serve immediately with the lemon wedges in shallow bowls with the clam juice ladled over, for dunking, if desired, sprinkled with the chopped parsley.

Steamed Garlic-Ginger Clams: Add 3 tablespoons minced peeled fresh ginger with the garlic in Step 1. Add 3 tablespoons oyster sauce along with the wine, broth, and water. Continue as directed.

Drunken Clams

Serves 4 to 6 • Cooker: 6- to 8-quart • Time: 4 minutes at HIGH pressure

Clams steamed in a simple beer-based broth with lots of fresh basil. Ale is an ancient style of beer fermented with naturally occurring yeasts and made from pale malts. They are not aged, so they are lighter in color, not bitter, and good for cooking. Look for Sierra Nevada Pale Ale and Anchor Liberty Ale. Serve with a crusty French baguette for dipping. A clam lover's nirvana!

^{1}/$_4$ cup olive oil
2 cloves garlic, minced
^{3}/$_4$ cup seeded and diced fresh plum tomato
^{1}/$_4$ cup finely chopped fresh basil
2 cups pale ale
1 cup water
^{1}/$_2$ cup chicken broth
^{1}/$_4$ cup dry white wine
2 tablespoons fresh lemon juice
3 pounds steamer, littleneck, or Manila clams, scrubbed

1. In a 6- to 8-quart pressure cooker, heat the oil over medium heat until hot. Add the garlic and cook, stirring, until fragrant, about 2 minutes. Stir in the tomato and basil. Add the ale, water, broth, wine, and lemon juice; increase the heat to medium-high and bring to a boil. Let boil for 1 minute. Arrange a trivet and steamer basket in the pot. Fill the basket with the clams.

2. Close and lock the lid. Set the burner heat to high. When the cooker reaches HIGH pressure, reduce the burner heat as low as you can and still maintain HIGH pressure. Set a timer to cook for 4 minutes. Do not overcook, as the clams will be tough.

3. Remove the pot from the heat. Open the cooker with the Quick Release method. Be careful of the steam as you remove the lid. Discard any clams that have not opened.

4. Transfer the clams to a serving bowl with tongs. Serve immediately in shallow bowls with some of the broth poured over them.

Pressure-Steamed Live Lobster

Serves 1 • Cooker: 6-quart or larger • Time: 3 minutes at HIGH pressure

Most people have never cooked a lobster. Steaming lobster is preferable to boiling it as the meat ends up more tender and retains all of its delicate flavor. The pressure cooker also has the advantage of cooking the lobster in a clean manner and without the use of gallons of water. If you feel queasy cooking a live lobster, remember that it does not feel pain and will be dead in less than 10 seconds.

Lobsters are sold live because when they die, the flesh disintegrates quickly. When buying a live lobster from a lobster tank, make sure that it is vigorous and lively. Observe its reaction when the fishmonger picks it up. If the lobster contracts unto itself, raising his claws and flapping his tail, that's a good sign it is fresh. If the lobster is lethargic and sluggish, don't buy it. Lobsters are loners and will fight each other constantly in an overcrowded tank, leading to atrophy. A fresh live lobster will keep one to two days in the coldest part of your refrigerator in a brown paper bag stuffed with seaweed or wet newspaper.

This recipe cooks one lobster at a time; do not add a second one. You can cook multiple lobsters at a time if have an oversized pressure canner.

4 cups water
Seaweed (optional, ask for some from your
    fishmonger)
1 (1^1/$_2$-pound) lobster, rinsed in cold water and
    rubber bands removed from claws, if possible
Lemon Lobster Butter (recipe follows), for serving

1. Put the water in a 6-quart or larger pressure cooker. Place the seaweed on the bottom of the pot if using, then place the lobster, head first, on top of the seaweed.
2. Close and lock the lid. Set the burner heat to high. When the cooker reaches HIGH pressure, reduce the burner heat as low as you can and still maintain HIGH pressure. Set a timer to cook for 3 minutes.
3. Remove the pot from the heat. Open the cooker with the Quick Release method. Be careful of the steam as you remove the lid. Use tongs to remove the lobster from the pot. Check the internal temperature of the lobster with an instant-read thermometer; the temperature should read 180° F. The lobster shell should be bright red. Tug on an antennae or one of the small legs; it should pull off easily. The meat will be white and firm, not opaque. The tomalley will be greenish yellow and fill the body cavity. The roe in females will be firm and bright orange; if it is dark, that means the lobster is undercooked. To stop the cooking process, place the lobster in a bowl of ice.
4. Place the lobster on a plate and serve with the Lemon Lobster Butter for dipping as you crack and liberate the delicious meat.

Lobster Steamed in Savory Herb Broth: Add a few cut stalks of celery, a few celery leaves, and a sprig of both fresh basil and dill to the cooking water before adding the lobster.

Lobster Steamed in Beer Broth: Substitute 1 cup beer for 1 cup of the water before adding the lobster.

Lemon Lobster Butter

Makes about 1¹/₄ cups, enough for dipping the meat of 1 or 2 lobsters

Clarified butter is the traditional dipping sauce for steamed lobster. Clarifying is a process to separate the milk solids from the oily butterfat (clarified butter is known as ghee in Indian cuisine). As you slowly melt the butter, watch for three layers to form: the foamy top layer made up of water and milk (it is skimmed off and discarded), the deep golden middle layer (this is the butterfat or clarified butter you want to use for sautéing or dipping), and on the bottom, the milk solids (which will also be discarded).

1¹/₂ cups (3 sticks) unsalted butter, cut into ¹/₂-inch pieces
Grated zest of 3 lemons

1. In a small, heavy-bottomed saucepan, melt the butter over medium-low heat. Pour into a 2-cup glass measuring cup. Let the melted butter stand at room temperature for 5 minutes.
2. Using a metal spoon, skim and discard the foam from the top of the butter. Place the lemon zest in small bowl. Spoon the warm clarified butter over the zest and discard the milk solids left in the bottom of the cup.
3. Divide the lobster butter into individual cups and serve on the side for dipping your fresh steamed lobster. Store any leftover in an airtight container in the refrigerator. Reheat before using.

HOW TO CRACK AND EAT YOUR COOKED LOBSTER

1. The head and intestines are not edible. First twist off the claws and crack each claw and knuckle with a nutcracker or lobster cracker. Remove the meat.
2. Separate the tail from the body and break off the tail flippers. Extract the meat from each flipper, then insert a fork and push the tail meat out in one piece. Remove and discard the black vein that runs the entire length of the tail meat.
3. Separate the shell of the body from the underside by pulling them apart. The green substance is called the tomalley, and is the liver of the lobster; some consider it a delicacy and it is used in sauces.
4. Open the underside of the body by cracking it apart in the middle, with the small walking legs on either side. Extract the meat from the leg joints and the legs themselves. The easiest way to do this is with your teeth, sticking a leg in your mouth, bearing down on it with your teeth, and slowly pulling the leg out of your mouth, leaving the meat behind. Many consider this to be the sweetest meat (probably because it takes the most effort to extract!).

Baby Lobster Tails with Vanilla-Shallot Dipping Sauce

Serves 4 • Cooker: 6- to 8-quart • Time: 5 minutes at HIGH pressure

With the advent of warehouse shopping, one of the great finds are bags of raw baby lobster tails. Be sure to defrost them before cooking (the best way is to put them in the fridge for 8 to 10 hours but you can also put them in a bowl of cold water); if you cook them frozen, you'll lose tenderness and succulence. They are great served on their own with a dipping sauce, or you can use them when you need fresh lobster meat without the hassle of cooking a whole lobster—think lobster rolls (see our recipe below), lobster risotto, lobster lasagna, lobster sauce on fish fillets, in a tomato sauce on linguine, even a lobster chowder. Always serve a dipping sauce with your lobster tails, even if it's simply clarified butter. Lemon wedges are also essential. This recipe serves one tail per person, but you might want to make 2 per person for big eaters. The cook time will not change.

VANILLA-SHALLOT DIPPING SAUCE:
$^1/_2$ cup (1 stick) butter
$^1/_4$ cup minced shallots
$^1/_3$ cup dry white wine
Pinch ground white pepper
$^1/_2$ vanilla bean, split in half lengthwise

LEMON BASTING SAUCE:
$^1/_4$ cup ($^1/_2$ stick) butter
$^1/_4$ cup fresh lemon juice
Pinch *each* salt and freshly ground black pepper

LOBSTER:
4 (6- to 8-ounce) lobster tails, thawed
1 cup water
1 lemon, cut into wedges, for serving

1. Make the Vanilla-Shallot Dipping Sauce. In a small bowl or 2-cup measure, combine the butter, shallots, wine, and white pepper. Scrape the seeds from the vanilla bean into the mixture. Partially cover and microwave on HIGH to melt the butter and warm the shallots and wine, about 4 minutes. Whisk well to combine. Keep warm. Makes about 1 cup.

2. Make the Lemon Basting Sauce. In a small bowl or 1-cup measure, combine the ingredients and microwave on HIGH for 1 minute to melt the butter. Whisk well. Keep warm

3. Lobster tails have two sides—the hard cup shell side and the soft flat underside. Remove the soft undercover of lobster shell. Using a bamboo skewer, insert it lengthwise through the tail, using one skewer per lobster. This will keep the tail from curling up when it cooks. Place a trivet and steamer basket in a 6- to 8-quart pressure cooker. Pour in the water. Spray the steamer basket with vegetable cooking spray and lay the tails in the basket. Clip the skewers if they are too long to fit in your pot. The tails can stand up or lay down. Brush the meat with the basting sauce.

4. Close and lock the lid. Set the burner heat to high. When the cooker reaches HIGH pressure, reduce the burner heat as low as you can and still maintain HIGH pressure. Set a timer to cook for 5 minutes.

5. Remove the pot from the heat. Open the cooker with the Quick Release method. Be careful of the steam as you remove the lid. Brush the tails with the basting sauce. Remove the basket from the pot and lift out the tails. They should be bright orange; the meat should be firm to the touch and have pulled away from the shell.

6. Reheat the dipping sauce in the microwave for a minute to warm. Serve the tails immediately, one per plate, with lemon wedges and a small bowl of dipping sauce on each plate.

Lobster Salad Roll

Makes 4 sandwiches

It used to be that to have a luscious lobster roll, you had to travel to New England. With the advent of warehouse shopping, big bags of lobster tails make preparing this sandwich as easy as 1-2-3. The lobster is the shining star, so the salad is bound together with a little mayonnaise and crunchy celery for contrasting texture. You'll need the meat from two baby lobster tails per sandwich, one from a regular size lobster. I like lots of meat piled up, and leave it nice and chunky. I like the soft long rolls, known as hoagie rolls, but if you want to go New England traditional, the only acceptable roll is the split-top hot dog roll, which is available in stores regionally or online.

2 to 3 cups cooked lobster tail meat, coarsely
    chopped
$^2/_3$ cup mayonnaise , or more to taste
2 teaspoons fresh lemon juice
2 ribs celery, finely chopped
Salt and ground white pepper or cayenne pepper
4 soft long rolls, split down the middle
1 to 1$^1/_2$ tablespoons butter
4 romaine lettuce leaves
Coleslaw, potato chips, lemon wedges, for serving

1. In a medium bowl, combine the lobster meat, mayonnaise, lemon juice, and celery; gently stir together, coating all the meat. Season to taste with salt and pepper.
2. In a heavy sautè pan or cast iron skillet, melt the butter over medium-high heat. Place the rolls in the hot butter, grilling the top, then the bottom until toasted and golden brown; do not toast interior, which will remain soft and warm up. Line the roll with a leaf of lettuce. Spoon the salad into the warm roll, mounding it high. Serve immediately with the coleslaw, potato chips, and lemon wedges.

New England Clambake in Your Kitchen

Serves 4 • Cooker: 6- to 8-quart • Time: 4 minutes at HIGH pressure

The sea defines New England and has amply fed its inhabitants. First enjoyed by the Native Americans, a summer clambake is traditionally done outdoors in a rock-lined pit dug into the sand and includes lobster, clams, potatoes, and corn on the cob. Here the clambake is reimagined for the pressure cooker, adapted from a recipe from the Presto pressure cooker website, a great resource for excellent recipes. If you can, get an assortment of different types of clams. The original recipe utilizes seaweed to separate the layers of shellfish and corn. Here we use potatoes as the bed and layer the seafood up from there.

1¹/₂ cups water

1 bay leaf

1 tablespoon *each* chopped fresh herbs such as parsley, chive, oregano, thyme, chervil (substitute with ¹/₂ teaspoon dried herbs), any combination (can be all parsley)

3 cloves garlic, slivered

Sea salt and freshly ground white pepper

2 or 3 large red potatoes, quartered

1 medium white onion, quartered

16 to 20 littleneck clams, scrubbed

1 (8- to 10-ounce) lobster tail, split in half (leave in shell)

4 large shrimp (21–30 count), deveined, shells left on

4 jumbo sea scallops or 4 more large shrimp

3 tablespoons butter, cut into thin slices

2 ears corn on the cob, each cut into four 1¹/₂-inch hunks

³/₄ cup (1¹/₂ sticks) butter, melted

2 lemons, cut into thick wedges, for serving

1. In a 6- to 8-quart pressure cooker, combine the water, bay leaf, herbs, garlic, and salt and pepper to taste. Arrange the potatoes and onion in an even layer. Add the clams, arranging them evenly over the potatoes and onion. Position the lobster halves, shrimp, and scallops over the clams. Place the butter slices evenly on top. Set the corn-on-the-cob pieces around the sides.

2. Close and lock the lid. Set the burner heat to high. When the cooker reaches HIGH pressure, reduce the burner heat as low as you can and still maintain HIGH pressure. Set a timer to cook for 4 minutes.

3. Remove the pot from the heat. Open the cooker with the Quick Release method. Be careful of the steam as you remove the lid. The lobster shell should be red-orange and the clams open. Do not overcook.

4. Using metal tongs, divide the lobster, clams, scallops, shrimp, corn, and potatoes between four large dinner plates or arrange on a large oval platter; drizzle with the steaming liquid to keep moist. Serve with individual portions of melted butter for dipping. Serve with lemon wedges and lots of napkins.

Seafood Chili

Serves 4 to 6 • Cooker: 6- to 8-quart • Time: 6 minutes at HIGH pressure

Coastal areas are a natural place to find seafood chili. While the use of seafood in chili is a new twist, the spices and sauce ingredients are similar to those of a beefy Texas cowboy trail driver chili. Serve with cornbread.

CHILI:
1/4 cup olive oil
1 large white onion, chopped
1 medium leek (white part only), trimmed, cut in half lengthwise, rinsed well, and thinly sliced
2 slices bacon, cut crosswise into strips
3 cloves garlic, chopped
2 red bell peppers, seeded and finely chopped
1 (28-ounce) can whole plum tomatoes in juice, undrained, cut into small pieces with a knife in the can
1 (4-ounce) can diced roasted green chiles, undrained
2 cups chicken broth or fish stock, or 1 cup bottled clam juice plus 1 cup water
1/4 cup chili powder
1 tablespoon ground cumin
1 teaspoon dried oregano, preferably Mexican
1/2 teaspoon cayenne pepper
1 (12-ounce) package frozen baby lima beans, thawed, or 1 (15-ounce) can cannellini beans, drained
1 pound medium (31–40 count) shrimp, peeled and deveined, or bay or sea scallops, quartered if large
1/2 pound firm white fish fillets, such as halibut, sea bass, or cod, cut into 1-inch pieces
1/4 cup finely chopped fresh cilantro
Salt and freshly ground black or white pepper

FOR SERVING:
Oyster crackers
Avocado slices
Sour cream
Chopped fresh cilantro
Lime wedges

1. In a 6- to 8-quart pressure cooker, heat the oil over medium-high heat. Add the onion and leek, then the bacon and cook, stirring occasionally, 8 to 10 minutes. Add the garlic and bell peppers and cook for 1 minute. Add the tomatoes and chiles with their juice, broth, chili powder, cumin, oregano, and cayenne and bring to a slow boil over medium heat. Add a bit more broth or water if needed to thin it out.

2. Close and lock the lid. Set the burner heat to high. When the cooker reaches HIGH pressure, reduce the burner heat as low as you can and still maintain HIGH pressure. Set a timer to cook for 6 minutes.

3. Remove the pot from the heat. Open the cooker with the Natural Release method; let stand for 15 minutes. Quick Release any remaining pressure. Be careful of the steam as you remove the lid. Add water to adjust the thickness if needed.

4. Return the pot to the burner and bring to a low simmer over medium heat, uncovered. Stir in the lima beans. Add the shrimp and fish, stirring a few times. When the shrimp have turned pink and curled up just a bit (about 5 minutes), stir in the cilantro. Taste for salt and pepper.

5. Serve immediately in large shallow bowls with lots of oyster crackers, sliced ripe avocado, sour cream, more chopped cilantro, and lime wedges.

Chinese Cioppino

Serves 4 • Cooker: 6- to 8-quart • Time: 10 minutes at HIGH pressure

San Francisco's North Beach, a haven for cioppino lovers since the 1930s, is a stone's throw from Chinatown. Cioppino, a mixed seafood stew, is served in every Italian restaurant and considered a signature dish of the city. It is delightfully versatile and many types of fish and shellfish can be used, originally utilizing the leftovers from the daily catch. Beth used to make cioppino for catering and once made the big mistake of leaving the sections of cracked crab in the stew, which was a fiasco for laptop diners and a white carpet. From then on, it was lump crabmeat all the way. This vegetable-rich version with a Chinese twist was inspired by San Francisco chef Martin Yan, and is every bit as fragrant as the Italian version, with lemongrass substituted for bay leaf, rice wine for the vineyard wine, and a salty miso swirl at the end. Serve it up for Christmas Eve dinner with sourdough bread.

2 tablespoons light olive oil or vegetable oil
1 medium white onion, chopped
1 cup chopped green bell pepper
2 ribs celery, chopped
2 cloves garlic, minced
2 teaspoons minced peeled fresh ginger
1/2 cup Chinese rice wine (shaoxing) or dry sherry
2 cups chicken broth or fish stock, or 1 cup bottled clam juice plus 1 cup water
1 (28-ounce) can plum tomatoes, undrained, cut into small pieces with a knife in the can
1 or 2 stalks lemongrass, to taste, tough outer leaves removed, trimmed to make a 5-inch stalk, and split lengthwise halfway up, OR 1 tablespoon prepared lemongrass paste
1/4 teaspoon sea salt
3 tablespoons tomato paste
8 small hard-shell clams, scrubbed
12 ounces skinless cod, halibut, red snapper, sea bass, monkfish, or other non-oily firm white fish fillets, cut into about l-inch pieces
8 ounces large (21–25 count) shrimp, peeled and deveined, with tails left on
8 ounces flaked Dungeness or lump blue crabmeat, picked over for cartilage
1/3 cup white miso

1/2 teaspoon chili garlic sauce (Chinese or Vietnamese *tuong ot toi*)
3 tablespoons chopped fresh cilantro, for garnish

1. In a 6- to 8-quart pressure cooker, heat the oil over medium-high heat. Add the onion, bell pepper, celery, garlic, and ginger and cook until softened, stirring a few times, about 2 minutes. Add the wine and bring to a boil. Add the broth, tomatoes, lemongrass, and salt. Spoon the tomato paste on top; do not mix in.

2. Close and lock the lid. Set the burner heat to high. When the cooker reaches HIGH pressure, reduce the burner heat as low as you can and still maintain HIGH pressure. Set a timer to cook for 10 minutes.

3. Remove the pot from the heat. Open the cooker with the Natural Release method; let stand for 10 minutes. Quick Release any remaining pressure. Be careful of the steam as you remove the lid. Remove the lemongrass stalk and discard. Add water to thin the sauce if necessary.

4. Return the pot to the burner and bring to a low simmer over medium heat, uncovered. Add the clams, fish, and shrimp. Cover and simmer until the clams open, the fish turns opaque, and the shrimp turns pink and curls, 3 to 4 minutes. Stir in the crab, miso, and chili garlic sauce; bring to a simmer to just heat through. The miso will dissolve into the broth. Do not overcook. Taste for seasoning and serve immediately, ladled into shallow bowls, portioning the seafood, and sprinkled with cilantro.

Even Quicker Seafood Cioppino with Mushrooms

Serves 4 • Cooker: 6- to 8-quart • Time: 5 minutes at HIGH pressure

One of the signature foods of San Francisco is cioppino, the Portuguese-Italian fisherman stew that originally utilized the leftovers from the daily catch. While the base sauce can cook for an extended period, this fabulous home version is on the table in 20 minutes. Serve with lots of sourdough bread to mop up the sauce.

3 tablespoons olive oil
1 large white onion, finely chopped
8 ounces white mushrooms, thickly sliced
2 cloves garlic, minced
1 (28-ounce) cans plum tomatoes, drained a bit (if packed in puree, don't drain)
$^1/_2$ teaspoon crumbled dried basil
$^1/_2$ teaspoon crumbled dried oregano, preferably Mexican
Pinch red pepper flakes
1 (8-ounce) can tomato sauce
I cup pale ale
Salt and freshly grated black pepper
12 littleneck clams, scrubbed
12 mussels, rinsed and debearded if necessary
12 to 16 ounces mixed firm non-oily white-flesh fish fillets, such as red snapper, sea bass, halibut, or monkfish, cut into chunks
12 large (21–25 count) shrimp, peeled and deveined, with tails left on

1. In a 6- to 8-quart pressure cooker, heat the oil over medium-high heat. Add the onion, mushrooms, and garlic, and cook, stirring a few times, until softened, about 2 minutes. Crush the plum tomatoes with your hands or the back of a spoon and add with their juices and the herbs. Bring to a boil, then stir in the tomato sauce and ale; bring back to a boil. Season to taste with salt and pepper.

2. Close and lock the lid. Set the burner heat to high. When the cooker reaches HIGH pressure, reduce the burner heat as low as you can and still maintain HIGH pressure. Set a timer to cook for 5 minutes.

3. Remove the pot from the heat. Open the cooker with the Natural Release method; let stand for 10 minutes. Quick Release any remaining pressure. Be careful of the steam as you remove the lid.

4. Return the pot to the burner and bring to a low simmer over medium heat, uncovered. Add the clams and cook 3 minutes. Add the mussels, fish, and shrimp, and simmer about 5 minutes, until the mollusks open, the fish is firm, and the shrimp are pink. Discard any clams or mussels that do not open.

5. Serve immediately in shallow bowls with a bowl on the side for the discarded shells.

Provençal Seafood and Vegetable Stew with Garlic Toasts

Serves 6 • Cooker: 6- to 8-quart • Time: 5 minutes at HIGH pressure

This is the Mediterranean version of the fisherman's stew, the seafood changing based on market availability. It is flavored with tarragon and fennel. Pernod or liqueur d'anis, a favorite salon drink of the Bohemian poets and artists in London and Paris and classic drink of the Mediterranean coast, is a licorice-flavored alcoholic beverage that adds a lovely dimension of flavor. You can substitute it with anisette

GARLIC TOASTS:

4 (^{3}/$_4$-inch-thick) slices crusty bread cut from a 9-inch round loaf

^{1}/$_2$ cup mayonnaise

1 heaping tablespoon minced fresh chives

2 teaspoons fresh lemon juice

2 teaspoons sweet Hungarian paprika

2 cloves garlic, halved lengthwise

STEW:

6 tablespoons light olive oil

1 large white onion, chopped

3 cloves garlic, minced

1 pound boiling potatoes, cut into ^{1}/$_2$-inch cubes

2 medium carrots, cut into ^{1}/$_4$-inch-thick rounds

1 fennel bulb, trimmed of stalks, sliced, and coarsely chopped

1 cup chopped green bell pepper

1 cup dry white wine

1 (28-ounce) can plum tomatoes in juice, undrained, cut into pieces with a knife in the can

2 cups bottled clam juice

Pinch sea salt

1 pound mussels, rinsed and debearded if necessary

1 pound non-oily firm white-flesh fish fillets, such as monkfish, cod, halibut, red snapper, or sea bass, cut into 1-inch pieces

8 ounces medium (31–40 count) shrimp, peeled and deveined, with tails left on

1 tablespoon finely chopped fresh tarragon

2 to 3 tablespoons Pernod or other anise-flavored liqueur, to taste

1. Preheat the broiler. Line a baking sheet with parchment paper or aluminum foil. In a small bowl, mix the mayonnaise, chives, lemon juice, garlic, and paprika together. Place the bread on the baking sheet 4 inches from the heat and toast, turning once, until golden brown on both sides. (Do not walk away; the slices will brown quickly.) Immediately rub each toast with the garlic, then, with a rubber spatula, spread the mayonnaise mixture over one side of each slice. Return the toasts to the broiler and broil until the topping is brown and bubbly, 20 to 30 seconds. Immediately remove from the oven. When cool enough to handle, cut across into 2-inch-wide strips for serving.

2. In a 6- to 8-quart pressure cooker, heat the oil over medium-high heat. Add the onion, garlic, potatoes, carrots, fennel, and green pepper and cook, stirring a few times, until softened, 3 to 4 minutes. Add the wine and bring to a boil. Add the tomatoes with their juice, clam juice, and salt.

3. Close and lock the lid. Set the burner heat to high. When the cooker reaches HIGH pressure, reduce the burner heat as low as you can and still maintain HIGH pressure. Set a timer to cook for 5 minutes.

4. Remove the pot from the heat. Open the cooker with the Natural Release method; let stand for 10 minutes. Quick Release any remaining pressure. Be careful of the steam as you remove the lid.

5. Return the pot to the burner and bring to a low simmer over medium heat, uncovered. Add the mussels, fish, and shrimp. Cover and simmer until the mussels open, the fish turns opaque, and the shrimp turns pink and curls, 2 to 3 minutes. Stir in the tarragon and Pernod; bring to a simmer to just heat through. Do not overcook; seafood continues to cook after it is removed from the pot. Taste for seasoning.

6. Serve immediately ladled into shallow bowls, portioning the seafood, and with the garlic toasts on the side.

6

Poultry, Game Birds, and Rabbit

Chicken and turkey are staples in the pressure cooker kitchen, whether for quick and easy meals or impressive party fare.

Both are available whole, in pieces, ground, bone in, or boneless. We especially like the thighs, as the dark meat holds up perfectly in the pressure cooker.

You'll also find in this chapter delicious recipes for Cornish game hens, duck, quail, pheasant, goose, and rabbit, as well as a sweetly piquant selection of cranberry sauces.

KNOW WHAT YOU'RE BUYING

The terms "organic" and "free range" are not standardized and are subject to different interpretations. Generally, **organic** poultry is raised without antibiotics or growth hormones and is given organically grown feed. Note that in order to carry the "organic" label, poultry must be certified, a process that costs time and money. Some small producers, therefore, do not apply for certification even though their products may conform to organic standards. Poultry allowed access to the outdoors can be labeled **free-range.** Some say the exercise and more varied diet of free-range birds translate to more flavorful and better-textured meat than that of cage-raised birds. **Kosher** birds are processed under rabbinical supervision. Their processing differs slightly from that of regular birds. Kosher birds are treated with salt; although they are rinsed before packaging, the salt does penetrate into the meat.

TIPS FOR HANDLING RAW POULTRY

- The sell-by stamp date is 7 days after the bird was processed and is the cutoff date for sale. Refrigerated, the bird will still be good. Never buy frozen poultry that has frozen liquid in the package, an indication of being frozen after sitting or refrozen. Freeze poultry 9 to 10 months maximum.
- Use refrigerated poultry within 2 to 3 days of purchase.
- Thaw frozen poultry in the refrigerator in its original wrapping with a plate underneath to catch any drips. It is important that the bird remain cold while thawing. Estimate 24 hours thaw time per 5 pounds; parts will thaw in half a day.
- Always handle raw poultry carefully to avoid cross-contamination of food-preparation surfaces and utensils, and never allow it to come into contact with foods that will be eaten raw or only partially cooked.
- All poultry is subject to contamination by harmful bacteria. Salmonella in particular has been found with raw or undercooked chicken and turkey, but it is killed at about 160° F. Cold temperatures inhibit bacterial growth, so refrigerate poultry as soon as possible after purchase. All poultry should be cooked to a minimum temperature of 165° F to kill food-borne bacteria such as salmonella. Be careful not to overcook poultry or the meat will be dry. To test for doneness, use an instant-read thermometer.

- It is a good idea to reserve one cutting board for raw poultry, meats, and seafood and another for produce and to wash the boards thoroughly with hot, soapy water and dry well between uses.

- Never use room-temperature poultry. Unless a recipe specifically calls for it, never put frozen poultry directly into the pressure cooker as it will change the cook time.

PRESSURE COOKING POULTRY AND GAME BIRDS

Type of Poultry	Pressure Level	Minutes Cooked	Release Method
Chicken breast, bone-in	High	8	Natural
Chicken breast, boneless	High	6	Quick
Chicken thigh, bone-in	High	8	Quick
Chicken thigh, boneless	High	6	Quick
Chicken leg with thigh	High	10	Natural
Chicken leg	High	6	Quick
Chicken, whole, quartered	High	15	Quick
Chicken, whole (4 to 5 pounds)	High	30	Quick or Natural
Turkey breast, bone-in, whole or half (4 to 6 pounds)	High	35	Quick
Turkey breast (3 to 3¹/₂ pounds), whole, rolled	High	25	Natural
Turkey breast half, rolled (2 pounds)	High	20	Quick
Turkey tenderloin	High	14	Natural
Turkey thighs	High	25 to 30	Natural
Turkey legs	High	18	Natural
Turkey wings	High	12	Natural
Turkey, ground	High	5	Natural
Cornish game hen, whole	High	10 to 12	Natural
Cornish game hen, halved	High	7	Natural
Quail, whole	High	8	Natural
Squab, whole	High	18 to 20	Natural
Duck pieces, bone-in	High	8	Natural
Pheasant, whole	High	15 to 20	Natural
Rabbit pieces, bone-in	High	14 to 18	Natural

Braised Whole Lemony Chicken with Garlic and Fresh Herbs

Serves 4 or makes 6 to 8 cups shredded or chopped chicken • Cooker: 5- to 8-quart • Time: 20 minutes at HIGH pressure

In 20 minutes or less (figure about 5 minutes per pound), you can be serving up a moist, tender chicken or use the cooked chicken in casseroles, burritos and wraps, sandwiches, salads, or soup. The key to success is to purchase a chicken that will comfortably fit in your pressure cooker (bring a tape measure to the market if you need to). You can substitute roasted garlic for the raw cloves; mash it up and slather it over the surface of the chicken.

1 (3^1/$_2$- to 4-pound) chicken
5 cloves garlic, peeled
1 tablespoon minced fresh oregano
1 tablespoon minced fresh flatleaf parsley
^{1}/$_2$ teaspoon minced fresh rosemary
^{1}/$_2$ teaspoon sweet Hungarian paprika
^{1}/$_2$ teaspoon mixed dried herbs or salt-free herb blend
^{1}/$_4$ teaspoon freshly ground black or white pepper
1 lemon, thinly sliced
4 sprigs fresh flatleaf parsley
2 cups reduced-sodium chicken broth
3 to 4 tablespoons fresh lemon juice, to taste
2 tablespoons cornstarch dissolved in 1 tablespoon water, for gravy, or 1 (1.8-ounce) package chicken gravy mix (optional)

1. Rinse the chicken. Remove the bag of giblets. Pull off and discard any large lumps of fat from inside the cavity or around the neck. Rinse and dry inside and out with paper towels.
2. Mash 3 cloves of the garlic with the minced oregano, parsley, and rosemary. Stir in the paprika, herb blend, and pepper. Rub the outside of the chicken with the mixture. Place the remaining 2 cloves garlic in the cavity along with half the lemon slices and the parsley sprigs.
3. Coat the inside of a 5- to 7-quart pressure cooker with olive oil spray. Place the chicken in the cooker, breast side up, and add the broth. Arrange the remaining lemon slices on top of the chicken.
4. Close and lock the lid. Set the burner heat to high. When the cooker reaches HIGH pressure, reduce the burner heat as low as you can and still maintain HIGH pressure. Set a timer to cook for 20 minutes.
5. Remove the pot from the heat; let stand for 10 minutes. Open the cooker with the Quick Release method. Be careful of the steam as you remove the lid. Insert a sturdy wooden spoon into the cavity of the chicken and, guiding with metal tongs, carefully lift it so it won't fall apart, tilting it so that the broth runs out of the cavity into the pot. Place on a platter and check the internal temperature at the thigh with an instant-read thermometer; it should be about 165° F. The juices should run clear when the thigh is pierced with a fork. Pour the lemon juice over the chicken, cover with foil, and let stand 10 minutes.
6. Pour the cooking liquid into a measuring cup and skim off any fat. Return the broth to the pot; bring to a boil. You can serve the chicken with just this broth or thicken it with the cornstarch slurry or add the chicken gravy mix; if making gravy, whisk for 2 minutes until it thickens.
7. Carve the chicken into serving pieces and serve with the jus or gravy. Refrigerate any leftover chicken or broth in an airtight container up to 2 days or freeze up to 2 months; store chicken and broth separately.

Braised Whole Chinese BBQ Chicken: In Step 2, instead of coating the chicken with the garlic mixture, combine ^{1}/$_3$ cup hoisin sauce, 2 tablespoons dry sherry or sake, ^{1}/$_2$ clove pressed garlic, and the juice from 2 tablespoons shredded peeled fresh ginger (use the large holes of a box grater and squeeze the juice in your hand to extract as much juice as possible; discard the shreds); stir to combine. Rub this paste over the chicken. Place in the cavity instead of the lemon slices and parsley: ^{1}/$_2$ bunch trimmed green onions; 6 coin-sized slices fresh ginger, bruised; 4 cloves peeled garlic, smashed; and 5 sprigs fresh cilantro. Continue as directed above. Once the chicken is cooked, omit the lemon juice; sprinkle with lightly toasted sesame seeds, if desired. Thicken the juices with cornstarch slurry; don't use the gravy mix. Serve with steamed jasmine rice.

Bollito of Whole Chicken with Two Sauces

Serves 4 to 5 • Cooker: 6- to 8-quart • Time: 20 minutes at HIGH pressure

A *bollito* is the Italian version of a French *pot au feu* or boiled dinner. The meat and vegetables are cooked in an aromatic broth, then served with some cold side sauces, such as *mostarda* candied fruits, horseradish with a dash of vinegar and olive oil, *salsa rossa* (plain fresh tomato sauce with vinegar and sugar), or *salsa verde* made with extra virgin olive oil so it's nice and flavorful. Here we add a cheese sauce, which melts into the chicken. It is a dish that usually takes hours, but in the pressure cooker it's ready in a fraction of the time. Serve with boiled or mashed potatoes, orzo, or steamed white rice, a bowl of sautéed mushrooms with garlic, and steamed spinach.

CHICKEN:

1 (3^1/$_2$- to 4-pound) chicken
^{1}/$_2$ teaspoon dried Italian herb blend
Sea salt and freshly ground black pepper
3 tablespoons olive oil
6 ribs celery, strings peeled away and cut into chunks
2 leeks (white part only), trimmed, cut in half lengthwise, rinsed well, and cut into 1-inch pieces
1 medium carrot, cut into 1-inch chunks
1 parsnip, peeled and cut into 1-inch chunks
3 sprigs fresh thyme
2 sprigs fresh flatleaf parsley
1 lemon, cut in half
1 cup chicken broth
^{3}/$_4$ cup dry white wine

GORGONZOLA SAUCE:

2 cups mayonnaise or Vegenaise soy mayonnaise
4 ounces Gorgonzola cheese, crumbled
1 tablespoon Dijon mustard
Few grinds black pepper

SALSA VERDE:

Leaves from 1 bunch fresh flatleaf parsley
2 small shallots, peeled
2 tablespoons nonpareil capers, rinsed
5 cornichon pickles
1 teaspoon hot sauce, or to taste
1 tablespoon sherry vinegar
^{1}/$_2$ cup extra virgin olive oil

1. Rinse the chicken. Remove the bag of giblets from the cavity. Pull off and discard any large lumps of fat from inside the cavity or around the neck. Rinse and dry inside and out with paper towels. Sprinkle the chicken with the herbs and salt and pepper to taste on all sides.

2. In a 6- to 8-quart pressure cooker pot, heat the oil over medium-high heat. Using metal tongs, place the chicken in the cooker, breast side up. Brown the bottom, then turn the chicken over and brown the other side. Add the celery, leeks, carrot, and parsnip. Tuck in the thyme and parsley sprigs. Squeeze in the lemon and add the rinds. Add the broth and wine. Bring to a boil.

3. Close and lock the lid. Set the burner heat to high. When the cooker reaches HIGH pressure, reduce the burner heat as low as you can and still maintain HIGH pressure. Set a timer to cook for 20 minutes.

4. Combine the Gorgonzola Sauce ingredients in a small bowl and mash with a fork until almost smooth. Cover with plastic wrap and refrigerate until serving. Makes 1^1/$_4$ cups.

5. Make the Salsa Verde. Place the parsley in a food processor and pulse to chop. Add the shallots, capers, and cornichons and pulse to finely chop. Do not puree. Transfer to a bowl and stir in the hot sauce, vinegar, and oil. Cover with plastic wrap and refrigerate until serving.

6. Remove the pressure cooker from the heat; let stand for about 10 minutes. Open the cooker with the Quick Release method. Be careful of the steam as you remove the lid. Insert a sturdy wooden spoon in the cavity of the chicken and, guiding it with metal tongs, carefully lift it so it won't fall apart, tilting so that the broth runs out of the cavity into the pot. Place the chicken on a platter. The internal temperature at the thigh should register about 165° F on an instant-read thermometer. The juices should run clear when the thigh is pierced with a fork. Cover with aluminum foil and let stand 10 minutes.

7. Discard the parsley and thyme. With a slotted spoon, place the vegetables in a serving bowl or around the chicken, and pour the cooking liquid into a small pitcher. Carve the chicken to serve with the two sauces and the jus on the side.

Chicken in Beer

Serves 4 • Cooker: 5- to 8-quart • Time: 8 minutes at HIGH pressure

Here chicken is braised in a beer-laced broth. Belgium-style beer is a nice choice, but really any good beer will do. Open the bottle and let it rest 30 minutes before using. As simple as this is, it is smashingly delicious. Serve with steamed brown rice or mashed potatoes and carrots.

$1/2$ cup all-purpose flour or potato starch flour
Sea salt and freshly ground black pepper
1 (3-pound) chicken, cut into 10 serving pieces
    (legs, thighs, wings, and each breast half cut into
    2 sections crosswise)
$1/4$ cup ($1/2$ stick) butter
1 large white onion, sliced $1/2$ inch thick
1 (12-ounce) bottle ($1 1/2$ cups) amber beer, at
    room temperature
$3/4$ cup heavy cream
2 tablespoons minced fresh flatleaf parsley

1. Combine the flour, salt, and pepper on a plate. Remove as much skin as possible from the chicken. Dredge the chicken pieces in the flour, coating them completely.

2. In a 5- to 8-quart pressure cooker, melt the butter over medium-high heat. Add the onion and cook, stirring a few times, until softened, about 3 minutes; push to the side. Brown the chicken in batches on both sides until golden, about 3 minutes per side. Transfer the browned chicken to a plate. Add the beer and bring to a boil, scraping up any browned bits on the bottom of the pot. Simmer 1 minute. Return the chicken to the pot along with any accumulated juice.

3. Close and lock the lid. Set the burner heat to high. When the cooker reaches HIGH pressure, reduce the burner heat as low as you can and still maintain HIGH pressure. Set a timer to cook for 8 minutes.

4. Remove the pot from the heat. Open the cooker with the Quick Release method. Be careful of the steam as you remove the lid. Transfer the chicken to a platter and tent with aluminum foil.

5. Add the cream and parsley to the pot and simmer over medium heat, uncovered, for 2 minutes, whisking until hot. Portion the chicken pieces on dinner plates and nap with the sauce.

Pomegranate Walnut Chicken *(Fesenjan)*

Serves 4 to 6 • Cooker: 5- to 7-quart • Time: 7 minutes for sauce, 7 minutes for chicken at HIGH pressure

We first encountered this rich and tangy chicken stew in one of our local Persian restaurants. *Fesenjan* is traditionally made for special occasions; one bite will tell you why. The flavors might be surprising—walnuts, pomegranate molasses, and a few carefully chosen spices. Walnuts comprise the bulk of the sauce, so check that yours are fresh-tasting before you begin. Take the time to toast them, as this enhances their flavor, but keep an eye on them, as they can quickly burn. If you have saffron, it's nice to use. We toast it—carefully wrapped in foil—along with the walnuts. Definitely serve this delicious dish over rice—a fragrant white or brown basmati. If fresh pomegranates are in season, use some of the brilliant red seeds as a garnish.

Pinch saffron threads (optional)
2 cups walnut pieces
1 (3-pound) chicken, cut into 10 serving pieces
     (legs, thighs, wings, and each breast half cut into
     2 sections crosswise)
$^1/_2$ teaspoon salt
$^1/_4$ teaspoon freshly ground black pepper
2 or 3 tablespoons olive oil
1 large onion, chopped
$^1/_2$ teaspoon ground cinnamon
$^1/_4$ teaspoon ground cardamom
$^3/_4$ cup water
$^2/_3$ cup pomegranate molasses
2 tablespoons sugar
Juice of $^1/_2$ lemon
Fresh pomegranate seeds, for garnish (optional)

1. If you are using the saffron threads, cut a small piece of aluminum foil about 2 inches by 1 inch. Place the saffron threads in the foil and fold into a neat package. Place the walnuts in a large non-stick skillet over medium-high heat. Toast the walnuts for about 5 minutes, until you can smell them, stirring frequently. If you are using saffron, add the foil package for the final minute of toasting. Transfer the walnuts to a food processor fitted with the metal blade and let cool. Set the saffron packet aside.
2. Remove as much skin as possible from the chicken and sprinkle with the salt and pepper. In a 5- to 7-quart pressure cooker, heat 2 tablespoons of the oil over medium-high heat until

very hot. Brown the chicken in batches on both sides until golden, about 3 minutes per side. Transfer the browned chicken to a plate.

3. Grind the walnuts in the food processor until no large pieces remain, but do not over-process or you will release their oil and the mixture will turn into walnut butter.
4. If the pot is dry after browning the chicken, add the remaining 1 tablespoon oil. Add the onion and cook over medium-high heat, stirring a few times, until softened, about 3 minutes. Add the cinnamon and cardamom and cook, stirring, for 1 minute. Unwrap the saffron threads and crumble them into the skillet. Add the water and scrape up any browned bits from the bottom of the pot. Stir in the walnuts, molasses, sugar, and lemon juice.
5. Close and lock the lid. Set the burner heat to high. When the cooker reaches HIGH pressure, reduce the burner heat as low as you can and still maintain HIGH pressure. Set a timer to cook for 7 minutes.
6. Remove the pot from the heat. Open with the Quick Release method. Be careful of the steam as you remove the lid. Return the chicken to the pot along with any accumulated juice, nestling the pieces into the sauce and spooning some sauce over them. Relock the cooker, bring it back up to HIGH pressure, and cook for another 7 minutes. Quick Release the pressure.
7. Taste the sauce, adding more sugar or lemon juice if needed. Serve the chicken over rice, each portion covered with a ladle of walnut sauce and sprinkled with a few fresh pomegranate seeds, if you have them.

POMEGRANATE MOLASSES

Pomegranate molasses is a thick reduction of pomegranate juice; it looks like a dark honey syrup. Look for it at a Middle Eastern market if your supermarket doesn't stock it. Pomegranate concentrate or pomegranate paste may be used as a substitute but not grenadine or other pomegranate syrups meant for cocktail drinks, which are too sweet.

Pressure Cooker Bourbon BBQ Chicken

Serves 2 to 4 • Cooker: 6- to 8-quart • Time: 10 minutes at HIGH pressure

The pressure cooker allows the cook to have the tastes of summer all winter long with this not-so-typical recipe. The chicken is fully cooked in the sauce in the pressure cooker, making for moist meat. If you like, you can then slather on a layer of the BBQ sauce and run the chicken under the broiler before serving it. If you want to make pulled chicken sandwiches, using two forks, pull the meat apart into shreds in a shallow dish. Serve spooned into warmed buns.

BOURBON BBQ SAUCE:
3 cups bottled BBQ sauce of your choice
2 tablespoons brown sugar
3 ounces bourbon
1 tablespoon sherry vinegar or red wine vinegar

CHICKEN:
2 tablespoons olive oil
1 large white onion, chopped
2 cloves garlic, chopped
1 1/2 cups Bourbon BBQ Sauce, plus 1/2 cup for glazing
1/2 cup water
2 tablespoons reduced-sodium soy sauce
2 teaspoons grated peeled fresh ginger
1 1/2 teaspoons tamarind concentrate
1 (4-pound) chicken, cut into quarters and skin removed

1. Make the Bourbon BBQ Sauce. Combine all the ingredients in a small saucepan and bring to a simmer over low heat. Let simmer, stirring occasionally, for about 6 minutes. Use immediately or let cool, then store in an airtight container in the refrigerator for up to 3 weeks. Makes about 3 1/2 cups, which is more than you will need.

2. In a 6- to 8- quart pressure cooker, heat the oil over medium heat. Add the onion and garlic and cook, stirring a few times until the vegetables soften, about 3 minutes. Stir in the BBQ sauce, water, soy sauce, ginger, and tamarind concentrate. Add the chicken, leg quarters first, then the breasts, meaty side up, nestling the pieces into the sauce.

3. Close and lock the lid. Set the burner heat to high. When the cooker reaches HIGH pressure, reduce the burner heat as low as you can and still maintain HIGH pressure. Set a timer to cook for 10 minutes.

4. Remove the pot from the heat. Open the cooker with the Quick Release. Be careful of the steam as you remove the lid.

5. Preheat the broiler. Transfer the chicken to an oiled broiler rack. Bring the sauce in the pot to a boil over medium-high heat. Cook, uncovered, stirring often to avoid scorching, until the sauce has thickened, about 3 minutes. Brush the chicken with the 1/2 cup reserved BBQ sauce. Position the broiler pan 6 inches from the heat and broil until the surface of the chicken is glazed, about 2 minutes. (Alternately you can fire up a gas grill and brown the chicken outside.) Serve hot, with the additional sauce on the side.

Chicken with Rice and Artichokes
(Arroz con Pollo y Alcachofas)

Serves 6 to 8 • Cooker: 5- to 7-quart • Time: 22 minutes at HIGH pressure

Arroz con pollo, chicken with rice, in its innumerable incarnations, is a popular party dish throughout the Spanish-speaking world. It's pretty and easily expansible, and most of the work is done before guests arrive. With a green salad, it's a complete meal. The pressure cooker simplifies cleanup and speeds cooking time. Best of all, the pressure cooker produces a moist and rich version, with an especially flavorful sauce, thanks to the fact that the chicken is cooked on the bone. You can make this with chicken parts but we don't use only breasts. The legs and thighs contribute substantially to add flavor to the sauce. We use a medium-grain brown rice, which is shorter and plumper than long grain and doesn't have the stickiness of short grain; it cooks to perfection in the moist heat of the pressure cooker. If saffron isn't in your budget, look in the Hispanic foods aisle of the supermarket for Bijol, an annatto-based seasoning that comes in a distinctive tiny yellow-orange canister.

1 (4- to 5-pound) chicken, or 3 to 3^1/$_2$ pounds bone-in chicken legs, thighs, and breasts
2 tablespoons olive oil, or more as needed
1 large white or yellow onion, chopped
2 cloves garlic, chopped
1 teaspoon sweet Hungarian paprika
^{3}/$_4$ teaspoon salt
^{1}/$_2$ teaspoon freshly ground black pepper
^{1}/$_2$ teaspoon dried marjoram, or 3 sprigs fresh marjoram
1 bay leaf, broken in half
About 10 saffron threads, or ^{1}/$_2$ teaspoon Bijol seasoning (see headnote)
2 cups medium-grain brown rice
1 cup dry white wine (leftover flat Champagne is nice if you have it)
1^3/$_4$ cups reduced-sodium chicken broth
1 (5-ounce) jar pimiento-stuffed green olives, drained
1 (6.5-ounce) jar marinated artichoke hearts, drained
16 ounces frozen peas (can be added frozen)
^{1}/$_4$ cup chopped fresh flatleaf parsley

1. If you are using a whole chicken, cut it into legs, thighs, breasts and wings. Remove and discard the skin from the thighs and breast pieces. Cut each breast in half crosswise so that you have four breast pieces total. In a 5- to 7-quart pressure cooker, heat the oil over medium-high heat until very hot. Brown the chicken in batches on both sides until golden, about 3 minutes per side. Transfer the browned chicken to a plate. Add the onion to the pot and cook, stirring a few times, until softened, about 3 minutes. Add 1 or 2 teaspoons more oil if the pot seems dry. Add the garlic and stir for 1 minute more. Stir in the paprika, salt, pepper, marjoram, bay leaf, and saffron or Bijol. Stir in the rice and cook, stirring, a moment more. Add the wine and cook, stirring and scraping up any browned bits from the bottom of the pot, until most of the liquid is absorbed by the rice. Stir in the broth, olives, and artichoke hearts. Return the chicken to the pot, nestling the pieces into the rice and turning them to coat with the liquid. Pour in any accumulated juices from the plate.

2. Close and lock the lid. Set the burner heat to high. When the cooker reaches HIGH pressure, reduce the burner heat as low as you can and still maintain HIGH pressure. Set a timer to cook for 22 minutes.

3. Remove the pot from the heat. Open the cooker with the Quick Release method. Be careful of the steam as you remove the lid.

4. Carefully stir in the frozen peas and parsley. Place the lid back on the cooker and let it stand for 5 minutes to cook the peas before serving.

Bone-in Chicken Breasts in Creamy Marinara

Serves 4 • Cooker: 5- to 7-quart • Time: 12 minutes at HIGH pressure

We use jarred marinara here, one of our culinary guilty pleasures. This recipe uses bone-in chicken breasts, nice and big, one per person. Though we don't tell you to do it here, you can add an extra layer of flavor to this dish by browning the breasts before setting them into the sauce. Serve this with a chunky pasta, like ziti. Start the water to boil so you can put the pasta in to cook right after you lock the lid on the pressure cooker; the chicken and pasta should be ready at about the same time. If you want a plain marinara, skip the addition of the crème fraîche, but it is oh so good.

2 tablespoons olive oil
4 cloves garlic, sliced
2 big pinches red pepper flakes
Pinch chili powder
2 cups jarred marinara sauce of your choice
3 tablespoons chopped fresh basil
2¹/₂ to 3 pounds (about 4) bone-in skin-on split
   chicken breasts, trimmed of fat
Sea salt
1¹/₂ cups grated Parmesan cheese
¹/₂ cup crème fraîche

1. In a 5- to 7-quart pressure cooker, heat the oil over medium-high heat. Add the garlic and pepper flakes and heat for 1 minute. Take the pot off the heat and add the marinara and basil (the sauce can spit and sputter when it hits the hot pot). Sprinkle the chicken breasts with some salt, but not too much as there is salt in the marinara and the cheese. Nestle the breasts down into the sauce.

2. Close and lock the lid. Set the burner heat to high. When the cooker reaches HIGH pressure, reduce the burner heat as low as you can and still maintain HIGH pressure. Set a timer to cook for 12 minutes.

3. Remove the pot from the heat. Open the cooker with the Quick Release method. Be careful of the steam as you remove the lid. Transfer the chicken to a serving platter, setting them on top of the hot pasta. Remove the skin and discard. Cover with aluminum foil to keep warm.

4. Spoon any fat off the surface of the sauce and stir in ³/₄ cup of the Parmesan and the crème fraîche. Pour the sauce over the chicken and pasta and serve the remaining ³/₄ cup Parmesan on the side for sprinkling.

Pressure-Poached Chicken Breasts

Makes 6 to 8 cups shredded or chopped chicken • Cooker: 5- to 7-quart • Time: 6 minutes at HIGH pressure

Many times when you are making a casserole, or enchiladas, or a main-course salad, the recipe will call for cooked chicken. You don't have to go out to buy a rotisserie chicken if you don't have leftovers on hand; poaching chicken in the pressure cooker couldn't be faster or easier. Make more than you need—what you don't use you can freeze.

Note: You can add the boneless chicken breasts to the pot still frozen. If you do, increase the cook time to 10 minutes. If you use bone-in breast halves instead of boneless, increase the cook time to 12 minutes.

6 to 10 boneless skinless chicken breast halves
1 rib celery, with leaves, cut into 3 chunks
1 sprig fresh flatleaf parsley
1 1/2 to 2 cups low-sodium chicken broth

1. Place the chicken, celery, and parsley in a 5- to 7-quart pressure cooker. Pour in enough of the broth to cover everything.
2. Close and lock the lid. Set the burner heat to high. When the cooker reaches HIGH pressure, reduce the burner heat as low as you can and still maintain HIGH pressure. Set a timer to cook for 6 minutes.
3. Remove the pot from the heat. Open the cooker with the Natural Release method; let stand for 15 minutes. Be careful of the steam as you remove the lid. The internal temperature of the chicken should register 165° F on an instant-read thermometer.
4. Set a large colander lined with a double layer of cheesecloth over a large bowl and pour the broth through to strain it. Use the chicken or let it cool a little, then store ziptop plastic bags in the refrigerator for 3 to 4 days or the freezer for up to 3 months. Pour the strained broth into an airtight container and let cool a bit before putting the lid on. Refrigerate up to 2 days or freeze up to 3 months and use in sauces or soups.

Mexican-Style Poached Chicken Breasts: In Step 1, omit the parsley and add the juice of 2 limes, along with the squeezed rind halves, and a few sprigs of fresh cilantro.

Chinese-Style Poached Chicken Breasts: In Step 1, omit the parsley and celery, add 1/2 bunch green onions, trimmed; 3 coin-sized slices fresh ginger, peeled and bruised; 1 clove garlic, smashed; 5 sprigs fresh cilantro; 1 star anise pod; and 1/4 cup reduced-sodium soy sauce in addition to the broth.

Salsa Lime Chicken with Goat Cheese

Serves 6 • Cooker: 5- to 7-quart • Time: 7 minutes at HIGH pressure

There is a wealth of fabulous jarred salsas on the market today. For this recipe, you can go with a plain salsa or one with black beans and corn in it. Whatever you decide, make sure it is a smooth liquidy jarred salsa, not a chunky fresh salsa fresca. Serve over steamed long-grain white or brown rice.

2 tablespoons olive oil
2 pounds (about 6) boneless, skinless chicken
    breast halves, trimmed of fat
1¹/₂ cups medium or spicy prepared salsa, your
    choice
1 teaspoon ground cumin
Pinch ground red chile powder of your choice
¹/₄ cup fresh lime juice
8 ounces fresh soft goat cheese, crumbled, for
    serving
2 limes, cut into wedges, for serving

1. In a 5- to 7-quart pressure cooker, heat the oil over medium-high heat until very hot. Lightly brown the breasts in batches on both sides. Transfer to a plate. Add the salsa, cumin, chile powder, and lime juice to the pot; stir, scraping up any browned bits from the bottom. Return the breasts and any accumulated juice to the pot, nestling the chicken into the sauce.

2. Close and lock the lid. Set the burner heat to high. When the cooker reaches HIGH pressure, reduce the burner heat as low as you can and still maintain HIGH pressure. Set a timer to cook for 7 minutes.

3. Remove the pot from the heat. Open the cooker with the Quick Release method. Be careful of the steam as you remove the lid. The chicken should be tender and make some of its own juice as well. Let stand 15 minutes, covered.

4. Transfer the chicken and its sauce to a platter of hot rice, sprinkle it with the goat cheese, and serve with the lime wedges on the side.

Chicken Breasts with Raspberry Vinegar

Serves 6 • Cooker: 5- to 7-quart • Time: 6 minutes at HIGH pressure

It is hard to even imagine the culinary world without fruit vinegars, but it wasn't until the 1980s that commercially made artisan berry wine vinegars hit the scene. We loved ruby-red red raspberry vinegar from the first sip. A zillion recipes promptly followed (it mates well with fruit, spinach salad, beets, pork, and lamb), and this recipe for chicken was one of the best.

2 pounds (about 6) boneless, skinless chicken
    breast halves
Salt and freshly ground black pepper
3 tablespoons olive oil
3 medium shallots, finely chopped
1 cup chicken broth
³/₄ cup red raspberry vinegar
³/₄ cup heavy cream or crème fraîche
³/₄ cup fresh or frozen whole raspberries

RASPBERRY VINEGAR

We have loved ruby-red red raspberry vinegar from the first sip. It is so delicious you can drink it as a tonic. The word vinegar comes from the French *vinaigre*, which means sour wine, and vinegar has been around as long as wine. Berries are mashed and macerated in white wine vinegar or cider vinegar with some sugar, then strained. Isabella Beeton had a recipe for raspberry vinegar in her 1861 cookbook, *Mrs. Beeton's Book of Household Management,* so home cooks have been loving berry-infused vinegars for a long time.

1. In a 5- to 7-quart pressure cooker, heat the oil over medium-high heat until very hot. Sprinkle the chicken breasts on both sides with salt and pepper. Lightly brown the chicken in batches on both sides. Transfer to a plate. Add the shallots to the pot and cook, stirring a few times, until softened, about 2 minutes. Pour in the broth and vinegar (keep your face away from the pot when you pour in the vinegar; when it hits the hot pot, vinegar steam can billow up and it will sting your eyes and nose). Scrape up any browned bits from the bottom of the pot.
2. Close and lock the lid. Set the burner heat to high. When the cooker reaches HIGH pressure, reduce the burner heat as low as you can and still maintain HIGH pressure. Set a timer to cook for 6 minutes.
3. Remove the pot from the heat. Open the cooker with the Quick Release method. Be careful of the steam as you remove the lid. Transfer the chicken to a platter and cover with aluminum foil.
4. Bring the broth in the pot to a boil over medium-high heat. Stir in the cream and raspberries. Taste for salt and pepper. Return the chicken to the sauce, turning to coat. Heat for a minute or two. Serve the chicken over rice, with plenty of sauce spooned over.

Pork Chops with Raspberry Vinegar: Substitute 6 boneless pork loin chops (1 inch thick) for the chicken breasts.

Indian Butter Chicken

Serves 6 • Cooker: 5- to 7-quart • Time: 5 minutes at HIGH pressure

With the popularity of Indian cuisine in the West comes one of its most famous savory dishes, Butter Chicken. As with all Indian recipes, the focus is on the spice combination. Garam masala, which means "warm-flavored mixture," is a spicy ground blend you can easily find in the supermarket or make your own. The characteristic anise flavor of Butter Chicken is provided by the herb fenugreek (though we make it optional here), which in India is most often used in leaf form. We use already ground since it is difficult to grind and it is easy to order from Penzeys (penzeys.com). Butter Chicken is mild and creamy, just the way we like it. This version contains both thick yogurt and heavy cream. Serve this over basmati rice, with a fruit chutney on the side (see pages 274–276).

$^1/_2$ cup plain Greek yogurt
2 tablespoons grated peeled fresh ginger
2 teaspoons sweet curry powder
$^1/_2$ teaspoon chili powder
$^1/_2$ teaspoon ground fenugreek (optional)
4 tablespoons ($^1/_2$ stick) butter
1$^1/_2$ pounds boneless skinless chicken breasts, cut into 1- to 1$^1/_2$-inch chunks
Salt and freshly ground black pepper
1 large white onion, finely chopped
1 jalapeño pepper, seeded and finely chopped
2 teaspoons garam masala
1 (6-ounce) can tomato paste
1$^1/_2$ cups low-sodium chicken broth
1 teaspoon sea salt
$^1/_2$ cup heavy cream
$^1/_4$ cup finely chopped fresh cilantro, for garnish

1. In a large bowl, whisk the yogurt, ginger, curry powder, chili powder, and fenugreek together.
2. Sprinkle the chicken on both sides with salt and pepper. In a 5- to 7-quart pressure cooker, melt 2 tablespoons of the butter over medium-high heat. When it foams, cook the chicken in batches in a single layer until you see no pink on the surface. Transfer the chicken as it is cooked to the bowl with the yogurt mixture with a slotted spoon. When all the chicken is added, stir gently until all the pieces are coated. Set aside.
3. Add the remaining 2 tablespoons butter to the hot pot, along with the onion. Cook, stirring, until it softens, about 3 minutes. Add the jalapeño and garam masala and cook, stirring, until it is fragrant, a couple of minutes. Add the tomato paste and broth. Using an immersion blender, pulse until the mixture is smooth. Add the chicken and yogurt mixture, and sea salt. Stir everything together.
4. Close and lock the lid. Set the burner heat to high. When the cooker reaches HIGH pressure, reduce the burner heat as low as you can and still maintain HIGH pressure. Set a timer to cook for 5 minutes.
5. Remove the pot from the heat. Open the cooker with the Quick Release method. Be careful of the steam as you remove the lid.
6. Stir in the cream and taste for seasoning. Heat for a minute or two over medium heat. Serve the chicken spooned over basmati rice with plenty of sauce, sprinkled with cilantro.

Indian Butter Potatoes and Chickpeas: In Step 1, add 6 large Yukon Gold potatoes, cut into large chunks (peeling is optional), to the yogurt mixture. Skip Step 2, omitting the chicken. In Step 3, melt all the butter before adding the onion. Proceed as directed, adding 2 cups cooked chickpeas when you stir in the cream; let simmer until hot, then serve.

Orange Chicken

Serves 4 • Cooker: 5- to 7-quart • Time: 6 minutes at HIGH pressure

Julie's dear friend Batia Rabec is a whiz in the kitchen. She loves to entertain friends in elegant style. Chicken with Orange Sauce is one of her specialties, originally made in the slow cooker. Imagine our delight when we discovered that the recipe works beautifully in the pressure cooker, cooking up in just 6 minutes with the same delectable, creamy sauce: Cointreau, orange zest, and orange juice contribute a triple threat of orange flavor. This recipe calls for flambéing. If you have never flamed alcohol, there's no need to be nervous. Just follow the directions carefully. If your pressure cooker has a nonstick pan, skip the flaming step, and simply follow the alternate directions, letting the Cointreau boil for a moment before covering the pressure cooker.

2 tablespoons unsalted butter
4 skin-on boneless chicken breast halves
$^3/_4$ teaspoon salt
$^1/_8$ teaspoon freshly ground black pepper
$^1/_3$ cup Cointreau or other orange-flavored liqueur
Juice and grated zest of 2 oranges
2 tablespoons cornstarch
$^1/_3$ cup whole milk
3 tablespoons heavy cream

1. Preheat the oven to 375 ° F. In a 5- to 7-quart pressure cooker, melt the butter over medium-high heat. When it foams, add 2 pieces of chicken to the pot, skin side down, and cook until deep golden brown on both sides, 5 to 7 minutes per side, sprinkling them with half the salt and pepper as they cook. Transfer the browned chicken to a plate. Brown the remaining 2 pieces of chicken in the same manner, using the remaining seasonings. Return all the chicken and any accumulated juice to the pressure cooker, skin side up. Add the Cointreau and bring it to a boil. Being careful of long sleeves and dangling hair, touch a long lit match to the liquid in the pot and turn off the stove. The liquid will catch fire and burn for about 30 seconds; the flames will extinguish themselves. (If you do not wish to flame the Cointreau or have a nonstick pressure cooker, simply allow the Cointreau to boil for 1 minute before proceeding.) Pour in the orange juice and sprinkle the orange zest over the chicken.

2. Close and lock the lid. Set the burner heat to high. When the cooker reaches HIGH pressure, reduce the burner heat as low as you can and still maintain HIGH pressure. Set a timer to cook for 6 minutes.

3. Remove the pot from the heat. Open the cooker with the Quick Release method. Be careful of the steam as you remove the lid. With a slotted spoon, transfer the chicken to a shallow baking dish and place in the oven to keep warm while you finish the sauce.

4. Stir the cornstarch into the milk to make a smooth slurry. Stir the cream with a whisk into the liquid in the pressure cooker and bring to a boil over high heat. Add the slurry and cook, stirring, until the sauce thickens, which will take only 1 to 2 minutes. Taste for salt and pepper. Serve the chicken hot with the sauce poured over the top or on the side.

Chicken Coconut Milk Curry

Serves 6 to 8 • Cooker: 5- to 8-quart • Time: 5 minutes at HIGH pressure

Serve this over basmati rice and set out garnishes in little bowls for diners to top their curry as they like: mango chutney, chopped cucumber, chopped cilantro, diced apple, toasted coconut, sieved hard-cooked egg, and/or coarsely chopped peanuts/cashews/pistachios in any combination you like. Or serve it with toasted pita or naan bread and a raita-style salad of chopped tomatoes, cucumbers, fresh mint, plain yogurt, and salt to taste.

4 tablespoon olive oil
3 pounds boneless, skinless chicken breasts, cut into $3/4$-inch-wide strips lengthwise down the breast, or chicken tenders
$1/2$ pound yellow or white onions, diced
$1/4$ cup curry powder of your choice, preferably Madras
1 (14-ounce) can unsweetened coconut milk
Pinch salt
1 cup mango chutney, pureed in the food processor or blender
$1/4$ cup chopped green onions, for garnish

1. In a 5- to 8-quart pressure cooker, heat 2 tablespoons of the oil over medium-high heat until very hot. Lightly brown the chicken strips in batches until you can no longer see any pink. Transfer the cooked chicken to a plate.
2. Add the remaining 2 tablespoons oil to the pot along with the onions and cook over medium-high heat, stirring a few times, until soft, 5 to 8 minutes. Add the curry powder, stir to combine with the onions, and cook until fragrant. Shake the can of coconut milk and pour into the onion curry. Add the salt and chutney. Return the chicken and any accumulated juices to the pot. Stir to combine.
3. Close and lock the lid. Set the burner heat to high. When the cooker reaches HIGH pressure, reduce the burner heat as low as you can and still maintain HIGH pressure. Set a timer to cook for 5 minutes.
4. Remove the pot from the heat. Open the cooker with the Quick Release method. Be careful of the steam as you remove the lid. Gently stir. If the curry is too thick for you, add some more coconut milk or heavy cream and simmer a minute to heat through.
5. Serve the chicken spooned over basmati rice with plenty of the coconut curry sauce spooned over, sprinkled with the green onions.

Mexican Soft Tacos with Shredded Chicken

Serves 6 • Cooker: 5- to 7-quart • Time: 6 minutes at HIGH pressure

This savory chicken is good not only for stuffing tacos, but rolling up in burritos, enchiladas, and tostadas as well. You could also spoon the filling into soft rolls for a sandwich.

FILLING:
2 tablespoons olive oil
1 large white onion, chopped
1 tablespoon chili powder
4 cloves garlic, minced
$^1/_2$ cup chicken broth
$^1/_3$ cup packed chopped fresh cilantro
6 boneless, skinless chicken breast halves
$1^1/_2$ teaspoons sea salt
10 grinds black pepper
Juice of 3 limes

TACOS:
12 taco-size flour tortillas, warmed
Shredded iceberg lettuce
Diced Roma tomato
Sliced ripe avocado
Chopped fresh cilantro
Chopped red onion
Shredded combination Cheddar and Monterey Jack
   cheeses or crumbled feta (an unconventional
   touch!)
Sour cream and medium or hot salsa (optional)

1. In a 5- to 7-quart pressure cooker, heat the oil over medium-high heat until very hot. Add the onion and cook, stirring a few times, until softened, about 3 minutes. Add the chili powder and garlic and stir for 1 minute. Add the broth and scrape up any browned bits from the bottom of the pot. Stir in the cilantro. Nestle the chicken breasts into the mixture, spooning some on top. Sprinkle with the salt and pepper. Pour in the lime juice.

2. Close and lock the lid. Set the burner heat to high. When the cooker reaches HIGH pressure, reduce the burner heat as low as you can and still maintain HIGH pressure. Set a timer to cook for 6 minutes.

3. Remove the pot from the heat. Open the cooker with the Natural Release method; let stand for 15 minutes. Be careful of the steam as you remove the lid.

4. Transfer the chicken to a plate or cutting board. Pull the chicken apart with your fingers into shreds or cut it into small dice. Pour the contents of the pot into a bowl and add the chicken; toss to combine. The chicken will stay juicy and moist. (At this point, you could let the chicken cool, then store in an airtight container in the refrigerator for up to 3 days or the freezer up to 3 months.)

5. To assemble the tacos, spoon the chicken into tortillas, then top as you prefer with lettuce, avocado, tomato, cilantro, onion, and/or cheese. Add a dollop of sour cream and salsa, too, if you like. Plan on two tacos per person.

Chinese Soy Chicken Wings

Serves 8 as a first or 3 to 4 as a main course • Cooker: 5- to 8-quart • Time: 14 minutes at HIGH pressure

These glossy, sticky chicken wings are braised in a mixture of soy sauce and aromatics. Serve as a main course (children love them) with rice and a green vegetable or as an appetizer.

$^1/_3$ cup reduced-sodium soy sauce
$^1/_3$ cup sake, mirin, or dry sherry
$^1/_3$ cup low-sodium chicken broth
2 **teaspoons** grated peeled fresh ginger
2 teaspoons Dijon mustard or tamarind pulp
1 small clove garlic, pressed
2 pinches red pepper flakes
2$^1/_2$ pounds chicken wings (about 25), with bony wing tips cut off (you can reserve for stock or discard)
$^1/_4$ cup apricot jam
1 tablespoon cornstarch mixed with 1 tablespoon cold water (optional)

1. In a large bowl or deep plastic refrigerator container with lid, combine the soy sauce, sake, broth, ginger, mustard, garlic, and red pepper. Add the wings and toss to evenly coat with the marinade. Marinate, covered, in the refrigerator for at least 2 hours or overnight. Stir twice to evenly coat the wings with marinade.

2. Transfer the wings and marinade to a 5- to 8-quart pressure cooker. Close and lock the lid. Set the burner heat to high. When the cooker reaches HIGH pressure, reduce the burner heat as low as you can and still maintain HIGH pressure. Set a timer to cook for 14 minutes.

3. Remove the pot from the heat; let stand for 5 minutes. Open the cooker with the Quick Release method. Be careful of the steam as you remove the lid.

4. Transfer the wings to a plate. Stir the jam into the liquid in the pot and stir with a whisk to melt. If you want to thicken the sauce, pour in the cornstarch mixture and stir. Add the wings back in and stir gently with a wooden spoon, bringing the wings on the top to the bottom to coat evenly with the sauce. Place the pot over medium heat, cover without locking the lid, and simmer until the sauce is thickened and translucent, about 2 minutes.

5. Remove the wings with tongs to dinner plates and serve immediately with lots of napkins.

French Chicken Wing Stew

Serves 4 • Cooker: 5- to 7-quart • Time: 24 minutes at HIGH pressure

When Beth lived in southwest France outside the small city of Tarbes near the Western Pyrenees National Park on the French/Basque Spanish border, she was introduced to the food of the region. The area is known for growing Tarbais beans, used in cassoulet, and there is plenty of local fresh poultry and game like duck and goose. The family she lived with ran a furniture business out of their farmhouse. Home-cooked dishes were amazingly delicious, crafted from thrifty and trustworthy ingredients, with nothing going to waste. Dinner at 9 p.m. was always a soup or stew with a fresh baguette and cheese for dessert. Use whatever vegetable you find fresh at the market. The classic fines herbes combination is a subtle and delicate blend of chervil, chives, parsley, and tarragon.

3 tablespoons olive oil (or rendered duck fat if you have it)

2^1/$_2$ pounds chicken wings (about 25), with bony wing tips cut off (you can reserve for stock or discard)

Sea salt and freshly ground black or white pepper

1 medium white onion, chopped

2 small leeks (white part only), trimmed, cut in half lengthwise, rinsed well, and thinly sliced across

2 cloves garlic, chopped

1 tablespoon all-purpose or rice flour

1 (14-ounce) can low-sodium chicken broth

1 (14.5-ounce) can diced tomatoes in juice, drained

1 medium fennel bulb, trimmed of stalks and cut into 1-inch chunks; or 3 carrots, peeled and cut into 1-inch chunks; or 2 medium turnips, peeled and chopped

1 teaspoon dried fines herbes

2 tablespoons chopped fresh flatleaf parsley

1. In a 5- to 7-quart pressure cooker, heat the oil over medium-high heat. Season the chicken wings with salt and pepper. Add to the oil in a single layer with metal tongs and lightly brown both sides, about 2 minutes each side. You will have to do this in batches. Remove the browned wings to a plate. Add the onion and leeks to the pot and cook, stirring a few times, until soft and browning on the edges, about 4 minutes. Add the garlic and heat for 30 seconds. Sprinkle with the flour and stir well. Add the broth and stir well, scraping up the browned bits from the bottom of the pot. Return the chicken wings to the pot along with any accumulated juice. Add the tomatoes, vegetable of choice, and fines herbes. Add a few grinds of black pepper. Stir gently to combine.

2. Close and lock the lid. Set the burner heat to high. When the cooker reaches HIGH pressure, reduce the burner heat as low as you can and still maintain HIGH pressure. Set a timer to cook for 24 minutes.

3. Remove the pot from the heat; let stand for 10 minutes. Open the cooker with the Quick Release method. Be careful of the steam as you remove the lid.

4. Taste for seasoning and stir in the parsley. Serve immediately in shallow bowls with mashed potatoes or egg noodles.

Chicken Legs with Two Chinese Sauces

Serves 4 • Cooker: 5- to 7-quart • Time: 6 minutes at HIGH pressure

Drumsticks are a tasty and economical alternative to breasts. Here they're served with two tasty dipping sauces, one made with hot chile paste, the other with mushroom soy sauce and vinegar. You need plain cold-pressed sesame oil for the sauce, not the amber-colored toasted sesame oil.

DIPPING SAUCE 1:
3 tablespoons reduced-sodium soy sauce
3 tablespoons low-sodium chicken broth
1 1/2 tablespoons cold-pressed sesame oil
1/2 teaspoon Asian chili-garlic paste

DIPPING SAUCE 2:
2 tablespoons balsamic vinegar
2 tablespoons reduced-sodium soy sauce
2 tablespoons mushroom soy sauce
2 teaspoons grated peeled fresh ginger
1 drop Worcestershire sauce

CHICKEN:
1 cup low-sodium chicken broth
1/2 cup water
1 strip orange or tangerine zest
2 green onions, trimmed
2 star anise pods
4 slices fresh ginger, crushed with the side of a knife
8 chicken drumsticks

1. Combine the dipping sauce ingredients in two separate small shallow bowls. Set both aside for 30 minutes to let the flavors develop.
2. In a 5- to 7-quart pressure cooker, combine the broth, water, zest, green onions, star anise, and ginger. Arrange the drumsticks in the liquid.
3. Close and lock the lid. Set the burner heat to high. When the cooker reaches HIGH pressure, reduce the burner heat as low as you can and still maintain HIGH pressure. Set a timer to cook for 6 minutes.
4. Remove the pot from the heat. Open the cooker with the Quick Release method. Be careful of the steam as you remove the lid.
5. Transfer the chicken to a small serving platter. Serve hot or refrigerate and eat cold with the dipping sauces.

Moroccan Lemon Chicken

Serves 4 to 6 • Cooker: 5- to 7-quart • Time: 6 minutes at HIGH pressure

Credit for this easy and festive recipe goes to Julie's husband's first cousin, Beth McIntosh Dusinberre, an archaeologist at the University of Colorado. She created it by combining several recipes that her housemate brought back after living for years in Morocco. Julie adapted it to the pressure cooker, which makes it a weeknight possibility. Save the parsley and cilantro stems in a freezer bag and use in making vegetable stock. Serve the chicken over steamed rice.

1 medium white or yellow onion, chopped
2 cloves garlic, chopped
Leaves from 1 medium bunch fresh parsley, chopped
Leaves from 1 medium bunch fresh cilantro, chopped
Pinch saffron threads
$1/4$ cup olive oil
2 teaspoons cumin seeds
2 teaspoons coriander seeds
1 teaspoon salt
$1/4$ teaspoon freshly ground black pepper
4 chicken drumsticks, skin removed
4 bone-in chicken thighs, skin removed
$1/3$ cup slivered blanched almonds
$1/3$ cup raisins
$1/3$ cup chopped dried apricots
1 (10-ounce) jar pitted Kalamata olives, drained
1 large or 2 small lemons, sliced across $1/4$ inch thick, ends discarded
2 cups water or chicken broth

1. In a 5- to 7-quart pressure cooker, combine the onion, garlic, parsley, cilantro, saffron, oil, and half of the spices: 1 teaspoon *each* cumin and coriander seeds, $1/2$ teaspoon salt, and $1/8$ teaspoon pepper. Nestle the chicken pieces on top of the onion mixture. Sprinkle with the remaining spices. Distribute the almonds, raisins, apricots, and olives over the chicken. Top with the lemon slices. Gently pour in the water so as not to disturb the ingredients.

2. Close and lock the lid. Set the burner heat to high. When the cooker reaches HIGH pressure, reduce the burner heat as low as you can and still maintain HIGH pressure. Set a timer to cook for 6 minutes.

3. Remove the pot from the heat. Open the cooker with the Natural Release method; let stand for 15 minutes. Be careful of the steam as you remove the lid.

4. Taste for salt and pepper. Serve the chicken over rice, being sure to give each person some of the fruit and almonds.

Braised Chicken with Mushrooms and Almonds

Serves 6 to 8 • Cooker: 6- to 8-quart • Time: 8 minutes at HIGH pressure

This one is for the mushroom lovers. The chicken braises on a bed of mushrooms and ground toasted almonds are used to thicken and flavor the sauce, reminding us of the fried almond tapas called *almendras fritas*.

$1/2$ cup blanched whole almonds
4 tablespoons olive oil
8 (about $2^{1}/2$ pounds) bone-in skin-on chicken thighs, patted dry
Sea salt and freshly ground black or white pepper
$1/3$ pound pancetta or bacon, cut into $1/2$-inch dice
1 large white onion, cut into julienne
Pinch red pepper flakes
2 to 3 cloves garlic, to taste, pressed
$1^{1}/2$ pounds mushrooms, such as cremini or domestic white, trimmed and sliced
1 cup dry white wine
1 to 2 cups low-sodium chicken broth
4 sprigs fresh thyme, tied in a bundle
Chopped fresh chives, for garnish

TOASTING NUTS IN THE MICROWAVE

To toast nuts in the microwave, place them on a microwave-safe plate and drizzle with a little olive oil. Spread the nuts around the outer edge of the plate, leaving the center open. Microwave on HIGH, stirring every minute, until lightly browned, 3 to 4 minutes.

1. Preheat the oven to 350° F. Place the almonds on a baking sheet in a single layer. Bake until evenly brown, 10 to 14 minutes, shaking the pan every 5 minutes. Cool, then grind in a food processor. Drizzle in 2 tablespoons of the oil while machine is running to make a loose paste. Set aside.

2. In a 6- to 8-quart pressure cooker, heat 2 tablespoons of the oil over medium-high heat until very hot. Sprinkle the chicken with salt and pepper. Brown the chicken in batches on both sides until golden. Transfer the browned chicken to a plate. Remove any excess fat from the pan.

3. Reduce the heat to medium. Add the pancetta and cook, stirring, until it renders its fat and begins to get crispy. Add the onion, increase the heat to medium-high, and cook, stirring a few times, until softened, about 3 minutes. Add the pepper flakes and garlic and stir until fragrant, about 30 seconds. Add the mushrooms and cook, stirring occasionally, until they release their juices, about 3 minutes. Don't let that liquid evaporate. Add the wine and bring to a boil. Add 1 cup of the broth and thyme. Return the chicken to the pot along with any accumulated juice, nestling the chicken into the mushrooms. Add a bit more broth to come just up the sides of the chicken. Bring to a boil.

4. Close and lock the lid. Set the burner heat to high. When the cooker reaches HIGH pressure, reduce the burner heat as low as you can and still maintain HIGH pressure. Set a timer to cook for 8 minutes.

5. Remove the pot from the heat. Open the cooker with the Quick Release method. Be careful of the steam as you remove the lid. Discard the thyme bundle. Transfer the chicken to a serving bowl and cover.

6. Taste the sauce for salt and pepper. Stir in the almond puree. Stirring, bring to a boil to thicken the juices. Remove from the heat. Place the chicken on individual dinner plates. Spoon the mushroom-almond sauce over and garnish with the chives.

Poulet au Vinaigre

Serves 6 to 8 • Cooker: 6- to 8-quart • Time: 8 minutes at HIGH pressure

Poulet au vinaigre (chicken with vinegar) is served in restaurants and bistros throughout France. The chicken literally takes minutes to make from start to finish, or you can make it ahead of time and reheat just before serving the next day. Apple cider vinegar is a delicious ingredient with meats, used just like wine. You want an organic, unfiltered, unpasteurized vinegar that has the mother starter, a bacterial raft that forms on the top of vinegar as it ferments. With a little time resting in its delicious juices, this chicken gets even more succulent and flavorful. Just reheat it gently. Serve with buttery mashed potatoes.

12 bone-in chicken thighs (3 to 4 pounds)
Salt and freshly ground black pepper
3 tablespoons unsalted butter
2 tablespoons olive oil
6 medium shallots, minced
6 cloves garlic, minced
$^1/_2$ cup cider vinegar
1 cup dry white wine
1 tablespoon tomato paste
1 cup low-sodium chicken broth
$^1/_2$ cup chopped fresh flatleaf parsley

1. Season the chicken generously with salt and pepper to taste. In a 6- to 8-quart pressure cooker, melt 2 tablespoons of the butter with 1 tablespoon of the oil over medium-high heat until it foams. Lightly brown the thighs in batches on both sides. Transfer the browned chicken to a deep, broad, platter.
2. Add the remaining 1 tablespoon butter and 1 tablespoon oil to the pot, along with the shallots and garlic. Cook, stirring, until they become translucent, about 1 minute. Add the vinegar and wine and scrape up any browned bits from the bottom of the pot. Allow the liquids to cook down a bit, stirring occasionally, for about 5 minutes. Whisk in the tomato paste and let the sauce simmer for about 2 minutes. Add the broth a little at a time and the parsley. Keep stirring to mix well. Return the chicken to the pot along with any accumulated juice, nestling the chicken into the sauce.
3. Close and lock the lid. Set the burner heat to high. When the cooker reaches HIGH pressure, reduce the burner heat as low as you can and still maintain HIGH pressure. Set a timer to cook for 8 minutes.
4. Remove the pot from the heat. Open the cooker with the Quick Release method. Be careful of the steam as you remove the lid.
5. With a slotted spoon, transfer the chicken to a platter or individual dinner plates. Over medium-high heat, bring the liquid in the pot to a boil to reduce it a bit if it's too thin. Serve the chicken with the juices on the side.

Chicken Thigh Bouillabaisse with Rouille

Serves 6 to 8 • Cooker: 5- to 7-quart • Time: 8 minutes at HIGH pressure

All along the Mediterranean coast of France succulent varieties of bouillabaisse are made by old and new cooks—Provence, Marseille, even Paris has its own version for city dwellers. It is said that bouillabaisse is of divine origin; the goddess of love Venus prepared the saffron-tinted stew for her husband, Vulcan, with fish only found in the Mediterranean.

Here we give you a California version made with chicken thighs in place of the fish. It is fabulously delicious and filling. Add a few quartered Yukon Gold potatoes if you like. Serve it in shallow bowls with the delicious sauce ladled over the chicken. Bouillabaisse is usually eaten with a crusty baguette, but here we use crunchy croutons spread with tasty garlic and pimiento spread known as a *rouille* that is the stew's traditional accompaniment. It is also good with buttery couscous.

ROUILLE:
6 cloves garlic, peeled
4 little pieces fresh bread
1 (4-ounce) jar pimientos, drained
1 egg yolk or pasteurized egg replacer equivalent
$1/2$ teaspoon crumbled dried herbes de Provence
1 cup olive oil
Few drops hot sauce, such as Tabasco or Sriracha

BOUILLABAISSE:
$1/4$ cup olive oil
1 large white onion, chopped
2 cloves garlic, minced
1 fennel bulb, trimmed of stalks and thinly sliced
$1/4$ cup finely chopped carrot
1 rib celery, finely chopped
1 (8-ounce) can tomato sauce
1 (28-ounce) can plum tomatoes in juice, undrained
1 cup chicken broth
1 cup dry white wine
2 pinches saffron threads
2 long strips orange or tangerine zest, cut in half
9 to 12 bone-in skinless chicken thighs (about 3 pounds), trimmed of fat
Bouquet garni of few sprigs fresh flatleaf parsley, 1 sprig fresh oregano, and $1/2$ bay leaf, wrapped in a double layer of cheesecloth and tied with kitchen twine

Salt and freshly ground black pepper
Chopped fresh flatleaf parsley, for serving

CROUTONS:
6 to 12 ($1/2$-inch) slices French bread or ciabatta, sliced on the diagonal
Olive oil (optional)

1. Make the rouille. Place the garlic in a food processor; pulse to chop. Add the bread and process to grind; you will have about 3 tablespoons. Add the remaining rouille ingredients and pulse until smooth and creamy. Remove to a bowl and refrigerate until serving. Preheat the oven to 400° F.

2. In a 5- to 7-quart pressure cooker, heat the oil over medium-high heat. Add the onion, garlic, fennel, carrot, and celery and cook, stirring a few times, until softened, about 3 minutes. Add the tomato sauce, tomatoes, broth, wine, saffron, and zest. Break up the tomatoes with the back of a spoon. Bring to a boil. Nestle the chicken thighs and bouquet garni into the sauce around the vegetables.

3. Close and lock the lid. Set the burner heat to high. When the cooker reaches HIGH pressure, reduce the burner heat as low as you can and still maintain HIGH pressure. Set a timer to cook for 8 minutes.

4. While the bouillabaisse cooks, place the bread slices on a baking sheet and brush with olive oil or leave plain. Bake until golden brown around the edges, 7 to 9 minutes. Remove and set aside.

5. Remove the pot from the heat. Open the cooker with the Natural Release method; let stand for 15 minutes. Be careful of the steam as you remove the lid. Discard the bouquet garni; season the bouillabaisse to taste with salt and pepper.

6. Spread the toasted bread with the rouille. Serve the bouillabaisse in shallow bowls, giving each portion 1 to 2 thighs, sprinkled with parsley, and 1 or 2 croutons on the side.

Peggy's Chicken, Black Beans, and Brown Rice

Serves 4 • Cooker: 5- to 7-quart • Time: 15 minutes at HIGH pressure

While Mexico favors pinto beans, Central America, the Caribbean, and Brazil all use the black bean as the main legume in their cuisine. This is a play on black beans and rice, prepared casserole style with chicken. The black beans must be cooked from scratch to get the right flavor. Do not omit the oil since it is necessary for cooking the beans in the pressure cooker. This is also delicious topped with cubes of ripe mango and toasted salted cashews. *Maravilhosa!*

²/₃ cup dried black beans
Green bell pepper slices (optional)
4 boneless skinless chicken thighs (about 1 pound), cut into 1-inch pieces
Sea salt and freshly ground black pepper
2¹/₂ cups low-sodium chicken or vegetable broth
1 medium red or white onion, coarsely chopped
2 ribs celery, chopped
3 cloves garlic, minced
²/₃ cup converted long-grain brown rice
1 (10-ounce) can tomatoes with green chiles, undrained
2 tablespoons olive oil
2 tablespoons finely chopped fresh cilantro
2 tablespoons finely chopped green onions
Hot sauce, for serving
³/₄ cup sour cream, for serving

1. Rinse the beans in a colander and sort through to remove any rocks. Place in a bowl with water to cover by about 2 inches. If you have a green bell pepper, add a few slices to the water for flavor. Let stand, uncovered, 6 to 12 hours, or overnight. Drain well in a colander before using. Rinse beans with cold water and discard the pepper slices.

2. Season the chicken with salt and pepper. In a 5- to 7-quart pressure cooker, combine the chicken, beans, broth, onion, celery, garlic, rice, tomatoes and their juice, and oil. Stir to combine.

3. Close and lock the lid. Set the burner heat to high. When the cooker reaches HIGH pressure, reduce the burner heat as low as you can and still maintain HIGH pressure. Set a timer to cook for 15 minutes.

4. Remove the pot from the heat. Open the cooker with the Quick Release method. Be careful of the steam as you remove the lid. Taste for salt and pepper.

5. Portion individual servings of the chicken, beans, and rice, sprinkle with the cilantro and green onions, and serve with hot sauce and sour cream on the side. If you have a nice flavorful green olive oil, drizzle a little over the individual servings.

Chicken Thighs with Shallots and Herbs

Serves 4 • Cooker: 5- to 7-quart • Time: 5 minutes at HIGH pressure

This a perfect weeknight dish. Serve it with couscous (try brown rice couscous), farro, rice, or a risotto.

2 tablespoons olive oil
8 boneless, skinless chicken thighs (about 2 pounds total)
Sea salt and freshly ground black or white pepper
2 medium shallots, minced
$^1/_2$ teaspoon dried mixed herbs, such as an Italian blend or herbes de Provence
$^1/_2$ cup chicken broth
$^1/_2$ cup dry white wine, red wine, or Prosecco sparkling wine left to go flat
2 tablespoons cold unsalted butter, cut into pieces

1. In a 5- to 7-quart pressure cooker, heat the oil over medium-high heat until very hot. Sprinkle the chicken thighs with salt and pepper. Lightly brown in batches on both sides. Transfer the browned chicken to a plate. Add the shallots, herbs, broth, and wine to the pot, scrape up any browned bits from the bottom, and bring to a boil. Return the chicken and any accumulated juice to the pot.

2. Close and lock the lid. Set the burner heat to high. When the cooker reaches HIGH pressure, reduce the burner heat as low as you can and still maintain HIGH pressure. Set a timer to cook for 5 minutes.

3. Remove the pot from the heat; let stand for 2 minutes. Open the cooker with the Quick Release method. Be careful of the steam as you remove the lid.

4. Transfer the chicken to a platter and cover with aluminum foil. Over medium-high heat, bring the liquid in the pot to a boil. Swirl in the butter pieces. Taste for salt and pepper, pour the sauce over the thighs, and serve.

Chicken Piccata with Lemon and Capers

Serves 4 • Cooker: 5- to 7-quart • Time: 8 minutes at HIGH pressure

Chicken piccata is traditionally prepared in a sauté pan using cutlets that have been pounded thin. For our pressure cooker version, we use plump skinless chicken thighs cooked in the same luscious lemon caper sauce. Be sure to allow a few hours to let the chicken marinate before cooking.

4 tablespoons olive oil
$1/2$ cup fresh lemon juice
Sea salt and freshly ground black pepper
8 boneless, skinless chicken thighs
2 tablespoons unsalted butter
2 tablespoons minced shallot
$3/4$ cup chicken broth
3 tablespoons nonpareil capers, rinsed
Grated zest of 1 lemon

1. In a shallow bowl, mix together 2 tablespoons of the oil, the lemon juice, and salt and pepper to taste. Add the chicken, turning it in the mixture to coat all sides, and marinate for 2 to 4 hours, covered, in the refrigerator.
2. Lift the chicken out of the marinade and blot it dry with paper towels. Reserve the marinade. Sprinkle the chicken lightly with the salt and pepper.
3. In a 5- to 7-quart pressure cooker, heat the remaining 2 tablespoons of oil with the butter over medium-high heat until the butter sizzles. Lightly brown the chicken in batches on both sides, about 3 minutes per side. Transfer the browned chicken to a plate. Add the shallots to the pot and cook, stirring a few times until softened, about 2 minutes. Pour the reserved marinade into the pot, along with the broth, and scrape up any browned bits from bottom. Return the chicken and any accumulated juice to the pot. Sprinkle in the capers.
4. Close and lock the lid. Set the burner heat to high. When the cooker reaches HIGH pressure, reduce the burner heat as low as you can and still maintain HIGH pressure. Set a timer to cook for 8 minutes.
5. Remove the pot from the heat. Open the cooker with the Quick Release method. Be careful of the steam as you remove the lid.
6. Stir in the lemon zest. Taste for salt and pepper. Transfer the chicken to individual dinner plates, topped with a few spoonfuls of the sauce.

Chicken Piccata with Lemon, Artichokes, and Capers: Add 1 (14-ounce) can artichoke hearts, drained and quartered, in Step 5 with the lemon zest. Simmer over medium heat for 3 minutes, uncovered, to heat through, then serve.

Braised Porcini Chicken

Serves 4 to 6 • Cooker: 5- to 7-quart • Time: 6 minutes at HIGH pressure

There are numerous versions of the hunter's chicken, a rustic chicken dish from Old Europe that always includes mushrooms and tomatoes. The pressure cooker is a long way from the open fire in the woods, but the flavor of this dish comes very close. This version features the aromatic and woodsy dried porcini mushroom.

$^1/_2$ ounce ($^1/_2$ cup) dried porcini mushrooms
1 cup hot water
8 boneless, skinless chicken thighs
$^1/_2$ teaspoon sea salt
$^1/_4$ teaspoon freshly ground black pepper
2 tablespoons olive oil
2 large shallots, finely chopped
1 clove garlic, minced
1 cup tomato puree
$^1/_2$ cup low-sodium chicken broth
2 tablespoons finely chopped fresh flatleaf parsley
2 tablespoons cold unsalted butter, cut into pieces

1. Place the dried mushrooms in a small heatproof bowl or glass and add the hot water. Let soak for 30 minutes. Remove the mushrooms from the water with a slotted spoon; rinse of any grit, then finely chop. Strain the liquid through cheesecloth to catch any dirt or solids and set aside.

2. Sprinkle chicken with the salt and pepper. In a 5- to 7-quart pressure cooker, heat the oil over medium-high heat until very hot. Brown the chicken in batches on both sides until golden. Transfer the browned chicken to a plate. Reduce the heat to medium, add the shallots and garlic to the pot, stir until fragrant, about 30 seconds. Stir in the tomato puree, broth, rehydrated mushrooms, parsley, and reserved mushroom liquid; heat to a simmer. Return the chicken pieces and any accumulated juice to the pot, nestling the chicken into the sauce.

3. Close and lock the lid. Set the burner heat to high. When the cooker reaches HIGH pressure, reduce the burner heat as low as you can and still maintain HIGH pressure. Set a timer to cook for 6 minutes.

4. Remove the pot from the heat. Open the cooker with the Quick Release method. Be careful of the steam as you remove the lid. Taste for salt. Transfer the chicken with a slotted spoon to a platter. Tent with aluminum foil to keep warm.

5. Bring the sauce to a simmer over medium heat and let simmer, uncovered, until thickened, 5 to 6 minutes, stirring occasionally. The sauce should be thick enough to coat the back of a spoon. When it is, swirl in the butter pieces until fully incorporated. Taste for salt again. Spoon the sauce over the chicken and serve.

Chicken Thighs with Artichokes and Black Olives

Serves 4 to 6 • Cooker: 5- to 7-quart • Time: 6 minutes at HIGH pressure

Another fast and scrumptious chicken braise—one of our best—Mediterranean style. It goes together in a flash.

2 tablespoons olive oil

8 boneless, skinless chicken thighs (about 2 pounds total)

Sea salt and freshly ground black or white pepper

2 medium shallots, minced

1 teaspoon dried mixed herbs, such as an Italian or Greek blend

1 (14.5-ounce) can diced tomatoes in juice (with basil and garlic if you can find it), undrained

^{1}/3 cup chicken broth

1 (10-ounce) package frozen artichoke hearts, thawed and patted dry

Juice of 1 lemon

18 pitted Kalamata or other favorite black olive

1 cup crumbled feta cheese, for serving

1. In a 5- to 7-quart pressure cooker, heat the oil over medium-high heat until very hot. Sprinkle the chicken thighs with salt and pepper. Lightly brown in batches on both sides, about 2 minutes each side. Transfer the browned chicken to a plate. Add the shallots to the pan and cook, stirring a few times, until softened, about 2 minutes. Return the chicken and any accumulated juice to the pot and sprinkle with the dried herbs. Add the tomatoes and their juices, broth, artichoke hearts, and lemon juice and sprinkle the olives over the top.

2. Close and lock the lid. Set the burner heat to high. When the cooker reaches HIGH pressure, reduce the burner heat as low as you can and still maintain HIGH pressure. Set a timer to cook for 6 minutes.

3. Remove the pot from the heat. Open the cooker with the Quick Release method. Be careful of the steam as you remove the lid.

4. Taste for salt and pepper and serve over rice or couscous sprinkled with feta.

Coq au Vin Blanc (Chicken in White Wine)

Serves 4 to 6 • Cooker: 6- to 8-quart • Time: 10 minutes at HIGH pressure

Coq au vin is without a doubt one of our favorites among the French bistro dishes. It conjures up visions of Julia Child and Simca Beck in their kitchens taking copious notes. It's a simple dish of mushrooms, onions, wine, herbs, and, of course, chicken, but the alchemy is spot on and it produces aroma while cooking and flavor that can't be beat.

Coq au vin is usually made with red wine, but this version uses only clear liquids to make a white version. Serve over rice or egg noodles, or with mashed or oven-roasted potatoes and a baguette for sopping up the sauce. *Bon appetit!*

4 boneless skinless chicken thighs (about 1 pound)
4 boneless skinless chicken breast halves (about 1 1/2 pounds)
Salt and freshly ground black pepper
1 (1/4-pound) thick-sliced pancetta, diced
3 tablespoons olive oil
3 medium shallots, chopped
1 clove garlic, minced
1 rib celery, finely chopped
1 pound white mushrooms, trimmed and halved or quartered according to size
3 sprigs fresh thyme or 1/2 teaspoon dried thyme or tarragon
1 bay leaf
1 1/2 cups dry white wine (such as a Riesling or white Burgundy) or dry vermouth
1 1/2 cup low-sodium chicken broth
2 tablespoons soft unsalted butter mashed with 2 tablespoons all-purpose flour, for thickening

1. Season the chicken generously with salt and pepper to taste. In a 6- to 8-quart pressure cooker over medium-high heat, cook the pancetta until crispy and it renders its fat. Remove with a slotted spoon to a plate. Add 1 tablespoon oil to the pot. Brown the chicken in batches on both sides. Transfer the browned chicken to the plate. Add the remaining 2 tablespoons oil to the pot along with the shallots and garlic and cook, stirring, until translucent, about 1 minute. Add the celery and mushrooms and cook, stirring, until the celery wilts and the mushrooms exude some liquid. Add the thyme and bay leaf, then the wine and broth. Bring to a boil, scraping up any browned bits from the bottom of the pot. Stir in the pancetta. Return the chicken and any accumulated juice to the pot and nestle the chicken into the sauce.

2. Close and lock the lid. Set the burner heat to high. When the cooker reaches HIGH pressure, reduce the burner heat as low as you can and still maintain HIGH pressure. Set a timer to cook for 10 minutes.

3. Remove the pot from the heat. Open the cooker with the Quick Release method. Be careful of the steam as you remove the lid. Discard the thyme and bay leaf. Taste for salt. Transfer the chicken pieces with a slotted spoon to a platter. Tent with aluminum foil to keep warm.

4. Over medium-high heat, bring the liquid to a boil. Whisk the butter mixture into the liquid and stir with a whisk or wooden spoon until thickened slightly. Serve the chicken with the sauce.

Coq au Vin Rouge (Chicken in Red Wine): Add 1/3 cup chopped carrot with the celery in Step 1. Substitute a strong dry red wine, such as a Burgundy or Cabernet, for the white wine. Proceed as recipe directs.

Chicken Paprikas

Serves 4 to 6 • Cooker: 5- to 7-quart • Time: 7 minutes at HIGH pressure

This is a marvelous example of Hungarian home cooking. We chose to make it with thighs rather than breasts because they are more flavorful and are less likely to dry out. The green pepper is essential to the flavor, so do not substitute another color pepper for it. You can double the amount of paprika if you like a strong flavor. If you have time, make the spätzle, a Hungarian tradition. Otherwise get the wide egg noodles found in the Jewish food section of the supermarket. And may we wish you, in proper Hungarian tradition, *Bort, Buzak, Bekesseget*—Wine, Wheat, and Peace.

2 to 3 tablespoons light olive oil
2 pounds boneless, skinless chicken thighs
1 medium white onion, chopped
1 large green bell pepper, seeded and chopped
1 tablespoon Hungarian paprika, sweet or hot
1 teaspoon dried dill
$1/4$ cup tomato sauce
1 cup chicken broth
Few pinches sea salt
$1^1/4$ cups sour cream
2 tablespoons all-purpose flour or rice flour
12 ounces extra-wide dry egg noodles, cooked according to package directions, drained, and buttered, or spätzle (recipe follows) for serving

1. In a 5- to 7- quart pressure cooker, heat the oil over medium-high heat until it begins to smoke. Brown the chicken in batches on both sides until golden, 4 to 5 minutes per side. Transfer the browned chicken to a plate. Add the onion, bell pepper, paprika, dill, tomato sauce, and broth to the pot and stir to mix. Return the chicken and any accumulated juice to the pot, nestling it down into the liquid. Add the salt.
2. Close and lock the lid. Set the burner heat to high. When the cooker reaches HIGH pressure, reduce the burner heat as low as you can and still maintain HIGH pressure. Set a timer to cook for 7 minutes.
3. Remove the pot from the heat. Open the cooker with the Natural Release method; let stand for 15 minutes. Be careful of the steam as you remove the lid. Transfer the chicken to a plate and cover with aluminum foil.
4. In a small bowl, whisk the sour cream and flour together until smooth. Whisk in $1/4$ cup of the liquid from the pot until smooth. Pour the sour cream mixture into the pot and whisk to mix. Cook, stirring, until the mixture simmers and thickens. Return the chicken to the pot. Reheat briefly over low heat without boiling.
5. Spread the warm egg noodles or spätzle on a serving platter. Arrange the chicken over the noodles and pour the sauce over all.

ALL ABOUT PAPRIKA

The signature spice of Hungarian cooking, paprika lends sweet, peppery flavor and rich color to an array of savory recipes. If you've never used true, imported paprika from Hungary, you are in for a treat. Notable for its sweet, gently spicy flavor and deep red hue, authentic Hungarian paprika is ideal as both a seasoning and garnish and holds up well to long braising times.

Spätzle

Serves 4 to 6

Soft spätzle dumplings are served as a side dish like noodles or rice and delicious with beef, veal, or pork stews. It is a real peasant dish from Alsace to Hungary. If you love these, invest in a spätzle maker, which looks like a hand grater; it is way easier than cutting them by hand.

3 cups all-purpose flour
1 teaspoon salt
3 large eggs
$2/3$ to 1 cup cold milk or water, as needed
1 tablespoon butter
Sour cream

1. In a medium bowl, combine the flour and salt. Make a well and add the eggs and milk to the center. Blend well with a wooden spoon until evenly moistened; the dough will be very thick and moist. If you use $2/3$ cup of liquid, you will have a firm dough; if you use a bit more, it will be softer. It can be made either way. Cover with plastic wrap and let rest at room temperature 30 to 45 minutes.

2. In a large stockpot, bring salted water to a rapid boil. Place the spätzle maker over the boiling water; it will rest on the rim of the pot. Place the dough in the hopper and slide the carriage back and forth, dropping pear-shaped bits of dough into the water. If shaping by hand, place the dough on a wet cutting board or plate and rest it on the rim of the pot. Using a damp paring knife or soup spoon, cut off little irregular portions the width of a pencil and about $1/2$ inch long at the edge of the plate and let them fall into the boiling water. Work quickly.

3. Simmer, uncovered, until they float back up to the surface, 1 to 2 minutes. Remove with a fine mesh strainer or slotted spoon, shake off the excess water, and place in a shallow casserole. Toss with 1 tablespoon of unsalted butter and dab of sour cream to keep them from sticking. Bake for 8 to 10 minutes in a 350° F oven. Serve immediately as a side dish to your chicken paprikas, or cover and refrigerate up to 8 hours and reheat in the oven at 300° F for 12 to 15 minutes.

Old-Fashioned Turkey Breast with Pan Gravy

Serves 4 to 6 • Cooker: 5- to 8-quart • Time: 25 minutes at HIGH pressure

Turkey is lean and tasty and with your pressure cooker, you can enjoy a boneless half-breast any night of the week. Because of its leanness, it's always been a challenge to keep turkey breast moist—not with the pressure cooker; all the natural juices are retained. Here we cook the breast in a simple braising liquid and serve with a flavorful gravy made from the juices. Serve with bakery-bought or homemade dinner rolls and cranberry sauce.

2 tablespoons olive oil
1 (2- to 2^1/$_2$-pound) boneless turkey breast (half a breast)
^{1}/$_2$ cup dry white wine
1 (14.5-ounce can) low-sodium chicken broth
^{1}/$_2$ large white or yellow onion, cut into thin wedges
1 teaspoon dried Italian herb mixture or herbes de Provence
1 (1.8-ounce) package turkey gravy mix (optional)

1. In a 5 to 8-quart pressure cooker, heat the oil over medium-high heat until very hot. Lightly brown the turkey breast on all sides, about 3 minutes per side. Transfer to a platter. Add the wine, broth, and herbs to the pot. Place a trivet in the pressure cooker and set the turkey breast on the trivet. Bring the braising liquid to a boil.

2. Close and lock the lid. Set the burner heat to high. When the cooker reaches HIGH pressure, reduce the burner heat as low as you can and still maintain HIGH pressure. Set a timer to cook for 25 minutes.

3. Remove the pot from the heat. Open the cooker with the Natural Release method; let stand for 15 minutes. Be careful of the steam as you remove the lid.

4. Using two wooden spoons or a pair of tongs, transfer the turkey breast to a cutting board. Turkey breast is done when the internal temperature in the center reaches 165° F on an instant-read thermometer. The breast will not be browned, but oh so moist. Tent the breast loosely with aluminum foil and let rest 10 to 15 minutes before slicing.

5. Remove the trivet from the pressure cooker. Strain the cooking liquid through a cheesecloth-lined colander and press to squeeze the juice from the onions. Return the broth to the pot. Bring to a boil and whisk in a packaged turkey gravy mix if you like, or you can just serve au jus. Simmer until thickened, about 5 minutes.

6. Remove the strings on the turkey with kitchen shears or a knife and discard. Slice the turkey breast on the diagonal, overlapping the pieces on a serving platter. Spoon a little gravy over the slices.

Butterflied Turkey Breast Stuffed with Ham and Herbs

Serves 8 • Cooker: 5- to 8-quart • Time: 25 minutes at HIGH pressure

One of the best methods for cooking a boneless turkey breast is in the pressure cooker. This recipe is from our friend, the late food writer Dolores Kostelni. It requires a modicum of fearless knife dexterity to butterfly the breast, as well as kitchen twine to tie up the rolled stuffed breast. Although a 5-quart pressure cooker or larger with a trivet cooks the turkey breast perfectly, you can also use a pressure fry pan with a dimpled bottom, eliminating the need for a trivet. Serve with cranberry sauce.

1 (3- to 3¹/₂-pound) whole boneless turkey breast
1 large shallot, peeled
6 thin deli slices boiled or baked ham, minced
Leaves from 4 sprigs fresh parsley
4 fresh chives, minced
¹/₄ cup (¹/₂ stick) unsalted butter, softened
¹/₄ cup instant flour, such as Wondra
4 tablespoons olive oil
¹/₂ cup dry white wine
¹/₄ cup chicken or vegetable broth
1 pound white mushrooms, trimmed and sliced

1. Place the breast on a work surface covered with aluminum foil or wax paper. Remove tendons and silver ligaments by placing the point of a sharp boning or paring knife under the beginning of the inedible parts and pulling them out with your other hand as you cut. Evaluate the turkey breast to determine the thickest side. Place that to your left. Using a sharp carving knife on the thinner side, cut a pocket three quarters of the way through the breast until it can be almost opened like a book. If there are parts of the turkey breast hanging loose from the sides, trim them off, chop with the knife, and mix with the ham and herbs in the next step.
2. Make the filling. Process the shallot, ham, parsley, and chives together in a food processor, using short pulses, until coarsely minced.
3. Spread the butter with a rubber spatula over the open turkey breast. Spread the ham mixture evenly over the butter. Fold the left side of the turkey breast over the filling, pressing down to seal. Slide a piece of kitchen twine measuring three times the length of the turkey breast under the turkey. Bring both ends of the twine together and tie in a knot at the top of the breast. Cut five more pieces measuring two times the width of the turkey breast. Beginning at the center, slide a piece under the turkey breast and bring to the top. Loop both ends of the twine under and over the lengthwise string, and tie a knot at the top of the breast. Repeat this with the remaining pieces, working out from the center to the ends. Tuck in any stray pieces of turkey and filling. Rub 1 tablespoon of the oil over the top of the turkey breast. Sprinkle the flour over the top, rubbing it in to evenly distribute.
4. In a 5- to 8-quart pressure cooker, heat the remaining 3 tablespoons oil over medium-high heat until hot but not smoking. Place the turkey breast, flour side down, in the oil and lightly brown, about 3 minutes. Turn the turkey breast over using two wooden spoons and lightly brown the underside, another 3 minutes. Remove the turkey breast from the oil with a meat fork and place on a platter.
5. Remove the pressure cooker from the heat. Add the wine and broth. Place a trivet in the pressure cooker. Place the turkey breast on the trivet. Return to the stove top and bring the liquid to a boil over medium-high heat
6. Close and lock the lid. Leave the burner heat at medium-high. When the cooker reaches HIGH pressure, reduce the burner heat as low as you can and still maintain HIGH pressure. Set a timer to cook for 25 minutes.
7. Remove the pot from the heat. Open the cooker with the Natural Release method; let stand for 15 minutes. Be careful of the steam as you remove the lid.
8. Using two wooden spoons or a pair of tongs, transfer the turkey breast to a cutting board and loosely tent with aluminum foil. Let rest 10 to 15 minutes before slicing.
9. Remove the trivet from the pressure cooker. Bring the liquid to a simmer and add the mushrooms. Close the lid, turn off the heat, and let stand for 10 minutes. Taste for salt and pepper.
10. Remove the strings from the turkey breast and slice the breast on the diagonal, overlapping the pieces on a serving platter. Spoon a little mushroom sauce over the slices. Serve immediately.

Turkey Verde

Serves 4 to 6 • Cooker: 6- to 8-quart • Time: 15 minutes at HIGH pressure

The turkey tenderloin is a long strip of white meat hidden under the breast, but they are sold separately. Because this strip of meat is an underused muscle of the turkey, it is very tender, but it can also dry out if not cooked properly. Keeping it moist and succulent is a snap in the pressure cooker. Here we braise the tenderloin in a classic Mexican-style green sauce, very mild and flavorful. When you see tomatillos in the produce section, grab some and make this dish. Serve this over rice. If you have any tenderloin left over, shred it to use in enchiladas, tacos, or burritos.

2 tablespoons olive oil
2 (¾-pound) turkey tenderloins
Sea salt and freshly ground black pepper
1 large white onion, chopped
2 cloves garlic, chopped
2 (4-ounce) cans chopped roasted green chiles, undrained
1½ pounds fresh tomatillos (8 to 10), paper husks removed and quartered
1½ teaspoons dried oregano
¼ teaspoon ground cumin
Pinch cayenne pepper
½ cup low-sodium chicken broth or turkey broth
Juice of 2 limes
Chopped fresh cilantro and lime wedges, for serving

1. In a 6- to 8-quart pressure cooker, heat the oil over medium-high heat until very hot. Sprinkle the tenderloins with salt and pepper. Brown them on both sides until golden, about 3 minutes per side, cooking one at a time if they are large. Transfer the browned tenderloins to a plate. Add the onion to the pot and cook, stirring a few times, until softened, about 3 minutes. Add the garlic, chiles, tomatillos, oregano, cumin, and cayenne and cook a few minutes, until softened a bit. Using an immersion blender, puree the mixture in the pot until smooth. Return the turkey tenderloins and any accumulated juice to the pot. Add the broth. Spoon the sauce over the tenderloins.

2. Close and lock the lid. Set the burner heat to high. When the cooker reaches HIGH pressure, reduce the burner heat as low as you can and still maintain HIGH pressure. Set a timer to cook for 15 minutes.

3. Remove the pot from the heat. Open the cooker with the Natural Release method; let stand for 15 minutes. Be careful of the steam as you remove the lid. Meat will be 160° F to 165° F on a meat thermometer.

4. Transfer the tenderloins to a platter. Taste the sauce for seasoning and sprinkle over the lime juice. Carve the loins into thick medallion slices. Drizzle the verde sauce over the top and sprinkle with cilantro. Serve with lime wedges.

Turkey Thighs Braised in Apple Cider

Serves 4 • Cooker: 6- to 8-quart • Time: 25 minutes at HIGH pressure

Apple cider (not hard cider) has a pleasant tang since it is usually a blend of different types of apples and is a great liquid for cooking. You need to refrigerate apple cider and use within a week as it will begin to ferment, giving it a carbonated edge as the sugar turns to alcohol. You can use an unfiltered, unsweetened apple juice in this turkey recipe as a substitute. Use a firm apple that will hold its shape in cooking, otherwise you'll end up with applesauce, though we suppose there are worse things! Rome Beauty, Winesap, Golden Delicious, Granny Smith, Braeburn, and Jonathan are all good choices. Use homemade turkey broth if you have it. It will make a difference.

2 tablespoons olive oil
4 bone-in turkey thighs (about 2 pounds), skin removed
Sea salt and freshly ground black pepper
2 large shallots, thinly sliced
4 Fuji or Granny Smith apples, peeled, quartered, and cored
1¹/₂ cups apple cider
1 (14.5-ounce) can low-sodium chicken broth or turkey broth
Juice and grated zest of 1 lemon

1. In a 6- to 8-quart pressure cooker, heat the oil until very hot. Sprinkle the thighs with salt and pepper. Brown the turkey thighs on both sides until golden, cooking them one at a time if they are large. Transfer to a plate as they are browned. Add the shallots and cook, stirring a few times, until softened, about 2 minutes. Add the apples and cook a few minutes, until they soften a bit. Return the turkey, skin side up, to the pot. Add the cider, broth, and lemon juice and zest. Position the apples around the thighs.
2. Close and lock the lid. Set the burner heat to high. When the cooker reaches HIGH pressure, reduce the burner heat as low as you can and still maintain HIGH pressure. Set a timer to cook for 25 minutes.
3. Remove the pot from the heat. Open the cooker with the Natural Release method; let stand for 15 minutes. Be careful of the steam as you remove the lid. Taste for salt and pepper.
4. Serve one thigh per person over rice, being sure to give each person some of the apples. You can also cut meat in large pieces from both sides of each thigh bone to give you 4 pieces. Place the pan juices in a pitcher to pour over the thigh.

Cranberry Sauces

Where there is turkey, there ought to be cranberries. But don't limit your enjoyment—cranberry sauce goes well with all sorts of proteins, particularly pork and duck. We absolutely love cranberries and buy extra bags in the fall. They'll keep in the fridge up to 2 weeks and in the freezer up to a year. You can use frozen berries for all these recipes; don't bother defrosting them, just increase the cook time by 2 minutes. And because of the cranberry's naturally high acidity, these sauces will keep well—up to 2 weeks in the refrigerator in an air-tight container.

One warning when making any of these recipes: Do not fill the pressure cooker pot more than half full, as the cranberries will produce foam as they cook.

Cranberry-Orange Sauce

Makes about 3 cups
Cooker: 5- to 7-quart
Cook Time: 4 minutes at HIGH pressure

1 (12-ounce) bag fresh cranberries, picked over
Scant 1 cup sugar
1/2 cup water
3 tablespoons orange-flavored liqueur, such as Grand Marnier or Triple Sec, or orange juice
Grated zest of 1 orange

1. In a 5- to 7-quart pressure cooker, combine all the ingredients.
2. Close and lock the lid. Set the burner heat to high. When the cooker reaches HIGH pressure, reduce the burner heat as low as you can and still maintain HIGH pressure. Set a timer to cook for 4 minutes.
3. Remove the pot from the heat. Open the cooker with the Natural Release method; let stand for 15 minutes. Be careful of the steam as you remove the lid. Transfer the sauce to serving bowl, cover, and refrigerate until chilled and set, at least 2 hours; it will keep for up to 2 weeks. Serve chilled or at room temperature.

Cranberry-Kumquat Sauce

Makes 2 1/4 cups
Cooker: 5- to 7-quart
Cook Time: 4 minutes at HIGH pressure

Kumquats, which are like miniature oval oranges, are eaten whole, skin and all. The juicy inside is quite sour, but the skin is sweet. Kumquats can be eaten raw or cooked. They share the season with cranberries.

1 (12-ounce) bag fresh cranberries, picked over
3 tablespoons sugar
2/3 cup cranberry juice cocktail or orange or cranberry juice
4 to 5 ounces (1 cup) kumquats, halved and seeded
1/3 cup crystallized ginger pieces, coarsely chopped
1/3 cup pecans pieces, toasted (see page 167) and coarsely chopped

1. In a 5- to 7-quart pressure cooker, combine the cranberries, sugar, juice, kumquats, and crystallized ginger.
2. Close and lock the lid. Set the burner heat to high. When the cooker reaches HIGH pressure, reduce the burner heat as low as you can and still maintain HIGH pressure. Set a timer to cook for 4 minutes.
3. Remove the pot from the heat. Open the cooker with the Natural Release method; let stand for 15 minutes. Be careful of the steam as you remove the lid. Stir. Transfer the sauce to serving bowl, cover, and refrigerate until chilled and set, at least 2 hours; it will keep for up to 2 weeks. Stir in the nuts just before serving. Serve chilled or at room temperature.

Cranberry Port Sauce with Tart Dried Cherries

Makes about 3 cups
Cooker: 5- to 7-quart
Cook Time: 4 minutes

1 cup ruby port
2 cinnamon sticks, broken in half
1 (12-ounce) bag fresh cranberries, picked over
1 cup dried tart cherries (about 6 ounces)
$1/2$ cup water
$1/3$ cup sugar

1. In a 5- to 7-quart pressure cooker, bring the port and cinnamon sticks to a boil. Reduce the heat and simmer 3 to 4 minutes. Add the remaining ingredients and stir until the sugar dissolves.
2. Close and lock the lid. Set the burner heat to high. When the cooker reaches HIGH pressure, reduce the burner heat as low as you can and still maintain HIGH pressure. Set a timer to cook for 4 minutes.
3. Remove the pot from the heat. Open the cooker with the Natural Release method; let stand for 15 minutes. Be careful of the steam as you remove the lid. Stir and discard the cinnamon sticks.
4. Transfer to serving bowl, cover, and refrigerate until chilled and set, at least 2 hours; it will keep up to 2 weeks. Serve chilled or at room temperature.

Maple-Apple-Cranberry Sauce

Makes about 3 cups
Cooker: 5- to 7-quart
Cook Time: 4 minutes at HIGH pressure

1 (12-ounce) bag fresh cranberries, picked over
1 large apple, peeled, quartered, cored, and cut into $1/2$-inch chunks
$1/2$ cup maple syrup
$1/4$ teaspoon ground ginger
$1/4$ teaspoon ground cinnamon
1 cup unsweetened apple juice or apple cider

1. In a 5- to 7-quart pressure cooker, combine all the ingredients. Stir to dissolve the spices and evenly combine.
2. Close and lock the lid. Set the burner heat to high. When the cooker reaches HIGH pressure, reduce the burner heat as low as you can and still maintain HIGH pressure. Set a timer to cook for 4 minutes.
3. Remove the pot from the heat. Open the cooker with the Natural Release method; let stand for 15 minutes. Be careful of the steam as you remove the lid. Stir. Transfer the sauce to serving bowl, cover, and refrigerate until chilled and set, at least 2 hours; it will keep up to 2 weeks. Serve chilled or at room temperature.

Turkey Thigh Osso Bucco with Cilantro Gremolata Crumbs

Serves 6 • Cooker: 6- to 8-quart • Time: 25 minutes at HIGH pressure

Osso bucco is a classic Italian dish, a beautiful braise of veal shanks that is traditional to Milan. The method used translates beautifully to a meaty turkey thigh and the pressure cooker. The dried mushrooms are applied as a paste to the meat with delicious results. The gremolata (an herb and citrus mix) is combined with crispy panko crumbs and sprinkled over the finished dish. Serve with polenta or risotto.

$^1/_2$ ounce dried porcini mushrooms ($^1/_2$ cup)
2 teaspoons unsalted butter, at room temperature
4 bone-in turkey thighs (about 2 pounds), skin removed
3 to 4 tablespoons all-purpose flour, as needed
4 tablespoons olive oil
Sea salt and freshly ground black pepper
1 large yellow or white onion, finely chopped
1 large carrot, finely chopped
3 ribs celery, finely chopped
2 (4-inch) strips lemon zest
$1^1/_2$ cups low-sodium chicken broth
$^1/_2$ cup dry white wine
2 tablespoons finely chopped fresh flatleaf parsley
2 teaspoons chopped fresh rosemary
1 bay leaf
2 tablespoons tomato paste

CILANTRO GREMOLATA CRUMBS:
1 medium shallot, peeled
2 cloves garlic, peeled
Pinch sea salt
Zest of 1 medium lemon, cut off in strips
Leaves from $^1/_2$ bunch fresh cilantro
Leaves from $^1/_2$ bunch fresh flatleaf parsley
Juice of $^1/_2$ lemon
1 to 2 tablespoons olive oil
$^3/_4$ cup plain panko bread crumbs

1. Place the dried porcini in a food processor and pulse until almost reduced to a powder. Place in a small bowl and mix in the butter with a fork. You can add an extra teaspoon of butter to make a more spreadable paste if you like. Rinse the turkey thighs and pat dry with paper towels. Rub the porcini butter in a thin layer over each turkey thigh. Sprinkle lightly with the flour.

2. In a 6- to 8-quart pressure cooker, heat $1^1/_2$ tablespoons of the oil over medium-high heat until very hot. Brown the thighs in two batches on both sides, about 3 minutes per side, adding another $1^1/_2$ tablespoons oil for the second batch. Season them to taste with salt and pepper. Transfer the browned thighs to a plate. Add the remaining 1 tablespoon oil and the onion, carrot, and celery and cook, stirring a few times, until softened, about 3 minutes. Add the lemon zest, broth, wine, parsley, rosemary, and bay leaf and bring to a boil, scraping up any browned bits from the bottom of the pot. Place the tomato paste in one lump on top of the liquid and vegetables. Return the turkey thighs and any accumulated juice to the pot.

3. Close and lock the lid. Set the burner heat to high. When the cooker reaches HIGH pressure, reduce the burner heat as low as you can and still maintain HIGH pressure. Set a timer to cook for 25 minutes.

4. Remove the pot from the heat. Use the Natural Release method; let stand for 15 minutes. Be careful of the steam as you remove the lid. Transfer the thighs to a serving bowl and pour over the pot juices and vegetables. Cover loosely with aluminum foil. Skim off any excess fat. Let rest 10 to 15 minutes while you make the crumbs.

5. Make the gremolata. In a small food processor, combine the shallot, garlic, salt, and lemon zest; pulse until finely chopped. Add the cilantro and parsley; pulse until finely chopped. Do not over-process or it will be mush. Remove to a bowl. Stir in the lemon juice. Makes about 1 cup.

6. In an 8-inch skillet, heat the oil over medium-high heat. Add the panko and cook until evenly and lightly toasted, stirring frequently. Remove from the heat and let cool. Stir in the herb mixture until evenly combined. Sprinkle lots of the gremolata crumbs over each turkey thigh before serving.

Braised Turkey Wings with Pantry Mexican Mole

Serves 4 • Cooker: 5- to 7-quart • Time: 15 minutes at HIGH pressure

Mole negro, also known as mole poblano or "chocolate sauce," is one of the characteristic sauces of Mexican cooking. A classic mole takes 3 to 4 hours. We don't have the time for that, but love the flavors. So enter the commercial jarred mole poblano paste, which you can find in Mexican markets or the Hispanic section of the supermarket. Mole is a natural accompaniment to turkey. Turkey wings are all white meat and are large enough to serve as a main course. You really want to use Mexican oregano if you can get it or Rancho Gordo Oregano Indio. Serve with steamed rice and cole slaw.

1 (8-ounce) jar prepared mole poblano paste (we like the Dona Maria brand)
1 tablespoon olive oil (optional)
4 turkey wings (2 to 3 pounds), separated at the joints, second and third joints only (reserve the wing tips for making stock or discard)
Sea salt and freshly ground black or white pepper
1/2 large white onion, chopped
2 cloves garlic, pressed
1 (14-ounce) can low-sodium chicken broth
1 cup hot water
2 tablespoons dark raisins
2 tablespoons dried cranberries
1/2 teaspoon chili powder
1/2 teaspoon unsweetened cocoa powder
1/4 teaspoon dried oregano, preferably Mexican
1/2 cup bottled favorite salsa
2 tablespoons chopped fresh cilantro
2 tablespoons green pepitas (pumpkin seeds) or 2 teaspoons sesame seeds, toasted lightly in a dry skillet, for serving
1 or 2 limes, quartered, for serving

1. In a 5- to 7-quart pressure cooker, pour the oil that has risen to the top of the jar of mole paste into the pot and heat over medium-high heat. Add the olive oil if you think you need it. Season the turkey wings with salt and pepper. Add two wings to the oil in a single layer and lightly brown both sides, about 2 minutes per side. Remove to a plate and brown the remaining wings in the same way.

2. Add the onion to the pot and cook, stirring a few times, until softened, about 2 minutes. Add the garlic and heat for 30 seconds. Add the mole paste, stirring until it softens, 2 to 3 minutes. Stir in the broth gradually. Stir in the water until the sauce is smooth. Bring to a boil. Return the turkey wings to the pot along with any accumulated juice. Add the dried fruit, chili powder, cocoa, and oregano. Stir gently to combine.

3. Close and lock the lid. If you like, place a heat diffuser on the burner and the pressure cooker on the diffuser. Set the burner heat to high. When the cooker reaches HIGH pressure, reduce the burner heat as low as you can and still maintain HIGH pressure. Set a timer to cook for 15 minutes.

4. Remove the pot from the heat; let stand for 10 minutes. Open the cooker with the Quick Release method. Be careful of the steam as you remove the lid. Check for doneness by inserting an instant-read thermometer in the thickest part of the wing, or by slicing through the thickest portion and checking for firm, white meat with no traces of pink. Turkey wings should have a minimum internal temperature of 165° F.

5. Taste for seasoning and stir in the salsa and cilantro. Serve immediately with a wing per person and lots of sauce. Remove the skin, if desired. Sprinkle with pumpkin seeds or sesame seeds (or both). Pass the lime wedges, which are also great squeezed onto the hot rice.

Better-with-Beer Turkey Sloppy Joes

Serves 6 • Cooker: 5- to 7-quart • Time: 5 minutes at HIGH pressure

Julie created this recipe to use up the last of a keg of excellent local beer after a party. Because it is made with mostly turkey breast, it is quite a bit leaner than most Sloppy Joe recipes (they are sometimes called Sloppy Janes due to the turkey). A mere five minutes under pressure yields a glossy, thick mélange that is at once spicy, sweet, salty, and pleasantly bitter. We love it on warmed or lightly toasted bakery brioche hamburger buns. Or use mini Hawaiian rolls for Sloppy Sliders. Have the rolls ready and waiting, since this cooks so fast. This is great football-watching food and, of course, it's even better with a glass of beer.

2 tablespoons extra virgin olive oil
1 large white or yellow onion, chopped into $1/2$-inch pieces
1 large yellow or red bell pepper, seeded and chopped into $1/2$-inch pieces
1 pound ground turkey breast
$1/2$ pound ground turkey thigh
2 to 3 cloves garlic, to taste, chopped
2 tablespoons chili powder
1 teaspoon salt
$1/2$ teaspoon freshly ground black pepper
$1/2$ teaspoon dry mustard (like Colman's)
1 (6-ounce) can tomato paste
3 tablespoons light brown sugar
1 (12-ounce) bottle Pilsner-style beer
1 tablespoon Worcestershire sauce
6 soft brioche hamburger buns or 12 mini buns, split and toasted

1. In a 5- to 7-quart pressure cooker, heat the oil over medium-high heat until very hot. Add the onion and bell pepper and cook, stirring a few times, until they just begin to soften, about 2 minutes. Add all the ground turkey and garlic. Stir to break up the meat and combine it with the vegetables. Cook, stirring occasionally, until the turkey is no longer pink. Stir in the chili powder, salt, pepper, and mustard and cook for just a minute or so to brown the chili. Stir in the tomato paste, brown sugar, and Worcestershire. Add the beer, stirring to evenly combine.

2. Close and lock the lid. Set the burner heat to high. When the cooker reaches HIGH pressure, reduce the burner heat as low as you can and still maintain HIGH pressure. Set a timer to cook for 5 minutes.

3. Remove the pot from the heat. Open the cooker with the Quick Release method. Be careful of the steam as you remove the lid.

4. Taste and adjust the seasonings as desired. Serve spooned onto the toasted buns.

Spaghetti with Herbed Parmesan Turkey Meatballs

Serves 6 • Cooker: 5- to 7-quart • Time: 15 minutes for sauce, 5 minutes for meatballs on HIGH pressure

Once upon a time, Italian-style meatballs were always made from ground beef and pork. Then around the 1970s, some ingenious turkey executive/rancher figured out that he could market Thanksgiving turkey cut into sections instead of just selling them whole during the holidays. The advent of ground turkey was upon us. Turkey burgers swept the nation, then turkey meatloaf and turkey meatballs followed. Please make these with ground dark meat, which will retain its moisture during braising to make a succulent meatball; white turkey meat is so lean that it dries out and gets chewy.

MEATBALLS:

1¹/₂ pounds ground lean dark meat turkey

¹/₂ cup plain dry bread crumbs (can be gluten free) or panko

¹/₂ cup grated Parmesan cheese

2 teaspoons onion powder

¹/₂ teaspoon dried Italian herb blend or 1 tablespoon grated peeled fresh ginger

¹/₄ cup milk

2 tablespoons ketchup

1 large egg, beaten

¹/₄ teaspoon freshly ground black pepper

2 pounds fresh or dried pasta, such as penne or spaghetti (can be gluten free)

SAUCE:

¹/₄ cup olive oil

2 large shallots, finely chopped, or ³/₄ cup chopped onion

1 rib celery, chopped

1 large carrot, chopped

2 cloves garlic, chopped

1 (28-ounce) can crushed tomatoes

1 (14-ounce) can diced tomatoes in juice, undrained

1 (3-ounce) package sundried tomatoes

1 cup dry red or white wine

1 cup water

¹/₄ teaspoon crushed Aleppo pepper or red pepper flakes

¹/₄ cup finely chopped fresh basil

3 tablespoons finely chopped fresh flatleaf parsley

Sea salt

1. Place the turkey in a large bowl. Make a well in the center of it and add the bread crumbs, Parmesan, onion powder, herbs, milk, ketchup, egg, and pepper. Using your fingers, gently mix all the ingredients until thoroughly combined. Add more crumbs or milk to adjust the consistency; it should be moist but hold its shape. Form into 1¹/₂- to 2-inch balls (22 to 24 meatballs about the size of a golf ball); a small metal ice cream scoop does this beautifully. Place on a waxed paper-lined baking sheet. Refrigerate, uncovered, until ready to add to the sauce.

2. In a 5- to 7-quart pressure cooker, heat the oil over medium-high heat. Add the shallots, celery, and carrot, reduce the heat to medium, and cook, stirring a few times, until softened, about 2 minutes. Add the garlic and stir for 30 seconds to warm. Add the crushed, diced, and sundried tomatoes, wine, water, Aleppo pepper, herbs, and salt to taste. Bring to a boil for 30 seconds.

3. Close and lock the lid. Set the burner heat to high. When the cooker reaches HIGH pressure, reduce the burner heat as low as you can and still maintain HIGH pressure. Set a timer to cook for 15 minutes.

4. While the sauce is cooking, bring a large pot of salted water to the boil for the pasta. Time it so that the pasta will be done just a minute or two after the meatballs cook in the sauce.

5. Remove the pressure cooker from the heat. Open it with the Quick Release method. Be careful of the steam as you remove the lid. Puree the mixture in the pot with an immersion blender. Taste for salt and pepper.

6. Bring the sauce to a high simmer over medium heat; add the meatballs one at a time, trying to get them in a single layer. If you need to pile some on top of one another, that's fine. Relock the cooker, bring back up to HIGH pressure, and cook for 5 minutes. Open the cooker with the Quick Release method.

7. Drain the pasta and portion onto dinner plates or in large shallow soup bowls. Top with sauce and meatballs. Serve with freshly grated Parmesan cheese on the side. The sauce and meatballs keep in an airtight container for up to 3 days in the refrigerator or 2 months in the freezer.

Super Shortcut Italian Turkey Mini-Meatball Sliders

Serves 10 to 15 • Cooker: 5- to 7-quart • Time: 18 minutes at HIGH pressure

Even the best cooks keep a secret stash of frozen cooked turkey meatballs for emergency entertaining. There are a number of brands in the freezer. The small meatballs are usually about one ounce each in weight. Combined with a quality store-bought marinara, you can have these on a table in no time. Enjoy the minis as a fun appetizer, or super-size it by putting the meatballs on a sub roll with melted cheese on top, drenched in sauce with a side of coleslaw for a great lunch.

2 (16-ounce) bags frozen cooked turkey meatballs
   (about 24 per bag)
2 (24-ounce) jars marinara sauce ($2^1/_4$ cups each)
1 (14.5-ounce) can low-sodium chicken broth
2 tablespoons balsamic vinegar
12 Hawaiian rolls, each cut in half, then split
   horizontally, or 12 small dinner rolls, split in half,
   warmed
6 to 12 slices mozzarella or provolone cheese, cut
   into quarters, for serving
24 fresh basil leaves

1. Coat the inside of a 5- to 7-quart pressure cooker with olive oil cooking spray. Add one bag of the frozen meatballs, then pour over a jar of the marinara. Add the other bag of meatballs and pour over the other jar of marinara. Pour in the broth and vinegar and gently stir to coat all the meatballs.

2. Close and lock the lid. Set a heat diffuser on the burner and the pressure cooker on the diffuser. Set the burner heat to high. When the cooker reaches HIGH pressure, reduce the burner heat as low as you can and still maintain HIGH pressure. Set a timer to cook for 18 minutes.

3. Remove the pot from the heat. Open the cooker with the Quick Release method. Be careful of the steam as you remove the lid. Gently stir and let rest 5 to 10 minutes.

4. To assemble the sliders, place 2 meatballs and a spoonful of sauce on each roll bottom half, add a piece or two of cheese and a basil leaf, then replace the top of the roll. If they are on a platter, you will need a toothpick to keep the sandwiches together. Serve warm with extra marinara on the side.

Cornish Game Hens with Fresh Herb Rub

Serves 4 • Cooker: 6- to 7-quart • Time: 10 minutes at HIGH pressure

Cornish hens bridge the gap between poultry and game birds, a cross between a Plymouth Rock hen and a Cornish game cock. They are a great alternative to a big turkey if you are serving 1 or 2 for a holiday dinner. Here we use a rub of the "song" herbs of parsley, rosemary, and thyme and braised them in a lovely wine broth. If you like, you can stuff the hens with a rice or couscous dressing. If you do, double the cook time.

2 (1¹/₂-pound) Cornish game hens, rinsed and
   dried
1 teaspoon sea salt
¹/₂ teaspoon freshly ground black pepper
2 tablespoons olive oil
1 cup dry vermouth or dry white wine
¹/₂ cup chicken broth
2 tablespoons fresh lemon juice

FRESH HERB RUB:
3 tablespoons olive oil
1 tablespoon minced or pressed garlic
1 tablespoon finely chopped fresh flatleaf parsley
1 teaspoon fresh rosemary needles, finely chopped
1 teaspoon fresh thyme, finely chopped
¹/₄ teaspoon ground fennel seeds
Pinch sweet paprika
2 tablespoons soft unsalted butter mashed with 2
   tablespoons all-purpose flour

CORNISH GAME HENS

Cornish game hens (4 to 5 weeks old) are a cross between a Plymouth Rock hen and a Cornish game cock. They are a great alternative to a big turkey if you are only serving 1 or 2 for a holiday dinner, but just as nice for a weekday dinner. If you buy them frozen, they'll keep in the freezer for 9 to 10 months. To thaw, place them on a plate in the refrigerator in the original wrapping; it'll take about 24 hours to thaw.

1. Sprinkle the Cornish hens on all sides with the salt and pepper. In a 6- to 7-quart pressure cooker over medium-high heat, heat the oil until very hot, then add the hens one at a time, breast side down. Cook until very light golden brown, about 3 minutes, then turn and cook the other side for 1 to 2 minutes. Remove to a plate and brown the other hen. If you are in a hurry, you can skip browning, but it adds a nice flavor.

2. In a small bowl, combine the herb rub ingredients. Press the herbs with the back of a spoon while mixing to release the oils and work into a paste. When the hens have cooled slightly, rub the mixture on all sides of each hen. Return the hens to the pot and arrange them side by side. Pour in the vermouth, broth, and lemon juice down the side of the pot so as not to wash the rub off the hens.

3. Close and lock the lid. Set the burner heat to high. When the cooker reaches HIGH pressure, reduce the burner heat as low as you can and still maintain HIGH pressure. Set a timer to cook for 10 minutes.

4. Remove the pot from the heat; let stand for 10 minutes. Open the cooker with the Quick Release method. Be careful of the steam as you remove the lid. Carefully transfer the hens to a platter and tent with aluminum foil. Let rest 5 minutes.

5. Bring the cooking liquid to a boil. Whisk the butter mixture into the liquid. Reduce the heat and stir until the sauce thickens slightly. Taste for salt and pepper. Serve in a gravy boat to pour over the hens. Portion one whole or one half hen (divide in half with sharp kitchen shears along the backbone) for each serving.

Indian-Style Game Hens Marinated in Yogurt and Spices

Serves 4 • Cooker: 6- to 7-quart • Time: 7 minutes at HIGH pressure

Game hens are marinated and then cooked in a spiced yogurt with super tender results. The sunny flavors meld well within the creamy sauce. Fresh game hens will last two days in the refrigerator, so plan to cook them as soon as you buy them. You can use this marinade and method with any poultry. Serve with plain or saffron basmati rice or farro.

2 (1 1/2-pound) Cornish game hens, rinsed and
    dried
2 cups plain yogurt
1/4 cup plain Greek yogurt
1/4 cup fresh lemon juice or lime juice
2 tablespoons olive oil
2 cloves garlic, pressed
2 teaspoons ground cumin
1 teaspoon sea salt
1/2 teaspoon chili powder or paprika
Pinch ground coriander
Pinch ground cardamom
3 tablespoons canola or grapeseed oil
3/4 cup low-sodium chicken broth
2 limes, quartered, for serving

1. Split the game hens in half, removing the backbone and tail with a sharp knife or kitchen shears. Cut on both sides of the backbone and discard. Cut off the wing tips. You can remove the skin, if you like, but it does add flavor. In a medium bowl, combine the two yogurts, citrus juice, olive oil, garlic, and spices and whisk until smooth. Place the game hens in 2-gallon ziptop freezer bag or a large square refrigerator container with lid. Pour the yogurt marinade over them and move them around to make sure they are fully coated. Seal or cover and refrigerate 4 to 12 hours.

2. Remove the hens from the marinade; reserve the marinade. In a 6- to 7-quart pressure cooker, heat the canola oil, 1 tablespoon at a time, over medium-high heat, then add the hen halves one at a time, breast side down. Cook until very light brown, 2 to 3 minutes, without turning over. Remove to a plate and brown the other hen halves in the same way. If you are in a hurry, you can skip browning, but it adds a nice flavor. Return all the hens to the pot along with any accumulated juice and pour over the reserved marinade and broth.

3. Close and lock the lid. Set the burner heat to high. When the cooker reaches HIGH pressure, reduce the burner heat as low as you can and still maintain HIGH pressure. Set a timer to cook for 7 minutes.

4. Remove the pot from the heat. Open the cooker with the Natural Release method; let stand for 15 minutes. Be careful of the steam as you remove the lid. Carefully transfer the hens to a platter and tent with aluminum foil. Let rest 5 minutes.

5. Bring the yogurt mixture in the pot to a boil over high heat. Cook for 1 to 2 minutes.

6. Portion one half hen for each serving, spooning over some sauce and serving with a lime wedge.

Duck Leg Chasseur

Serves 4 • Cooker: 5- to 7-quart • Time: 35 minutes at HIGH pressure

Duck legs have a beautiful rich meat which is particularly suited to slow cooking, in this case in a hunter's style tomato sauce with mushrooms. Duck legs have all the wonderful qualities that chicken does not: they're dark, moist, plump, and full of rich, meaty flavor. Duck has a bad reputation for being fatty, but you can trim the fat away, and it will cook just like chicken. Duck is becoming increasingly available, sold whole or, conveniently, in packages of breasts or duck legs with the thighs attached. If you don't see it with the refrigerated poultry, check in the freezer section. Completely defrost before braising. Serve this over polenta, a ribbon pasta like fettuccine or pappardelle, or spaghetti squash with a green salad to offset the rich, sweet duck meat.

1 tablespoon olive oil
4 duck leg-thigh sections, excess fat trimmed, skin scored all over, and pricked with a needle through the skin to release the fat
1 medium white onion, halved and thinly sliced
²/₃ cup dry white wine
¹/₂ cup chopped carrot
1 rib celery, chopped
8 ounces white or brown mushrooms, quartered
2 tablespoons nonpareil capers, drained
¹/₂ teaspoon dried Italian herb blend or 1 tablespoon chopped fresh oregano or marjoram
Pinch red pepper flakes
¹/₃ cup low-sodium chicken broth
2 cups tomato sauce
2 tablespoons chopped fresh flatleaf parsley
Sea salt and freshly ground black pepper

1. In a 5- to 7-quart pressure cooker, heat the oil over medium-high heat. Place two of the duck legs in the pressure cooker, skin side down. Cook until the skin has crisped and the meat feels springy, about 3 minutes per side. Transfer to a plate and repeat with the remaining legs.
2. Add the onion to the pot and cook, stirring a few times, until softened, about 3 minutes; do not brown. Add the wine and simmer to reduce slightly, 2 to 3 minutes, scraping up any browned bits from the bottom of the pot with a wooden spoon. Add the carrot, celery, mushrooms, capers, herbs, pepper flakes, broth, and tomato sauce and stir to combine. Return the duck legs to the pot, along with any accumulated juice, nestling them down into the sauce.
3. Close and lock the lid. If you like, place a heat diffuser on the burner and the pressure cooker on the diffuser. Set the burner heat to high. When the cooker reaches HIGH pressure, reduce the burner heat as low as you can and still maintain HIGH pressure. Set a timer to cook for 35 minutes.
4. Remove the pot from the heat. Open the cooker with the Natural Release method; let stand for 15 minutes. Be careful of the steam as you remove the lid. Sprinkle with the parsley and season to taste with salt and pepper.
5. Serve a duck leg per person with the sauce.

Duck Leg Chasseur with Olives: Add a handful of pitted black olives in Step 2.

Braised Duck for Tacos

Serves 4 or makes 2$^1/_2$ to 3 cups shredded meat • Cooker: 5- to 7-quart • Time: 35 minutes at HIGH pressure

Once you save the duck breasts for sautéing (it would drastically overcook braised), you have the legs and wings left, which are perfect for braising. You will pull the succulent cooked meat off the bones for use in tacos, enchiladas, burritos, or soup. The rich flavor of duck pairs beautifully with red and green salsas, as well as all sorts of fruit salsas, such as pineapple or mango, making it a natural filling for tacos. Mexican oregano is more fragrant than the stronger Greek oregano and a traditional addition to Mexican cooking.

4 duck leg-thigh sections
4 duck wings (optional)
Sea salt and freshly ground black pepper to taste
1 large white onion, halved and thinly sliced
1 teaspoon dried oregano, preferably Mexican
$^1/_4$ teaspoon crumbled dried thyme or epazote
1 (14.5-ounce) can diced tomatoes in juice, undrained
1 cup low-sodium chicken broth
2 tablespoons red wine vinegar

1. Trim the fat off the duck legs and wings. Trim the excess skin as well, leaving a small portion down the center of the meat. Season the duck all over with salt and pepper.

2. Heat a 5- to 7-quart pressure cooker over medium-high heat. Place two of the duck legs in the pressure cooker skin side down and cook about 5 minutes per side, until well browned and the skin is crisped. Transfer the legs to a plate. Repeat with the remaining legs.

3. Pour all but 2 tablespoons of fat from the pot. Add the onion to the pot and cook, stirring a few times, until softened, about 3 minutes; do not brown. Add the herbs, tomatoes and their juice, broth, and vinegar. Add the duck wings and return the legs to the pot with any accumulated juice.

4. Close and lock the lid. If you like, place a heat diffuser on the burner and the pressure cooker on the diffuser. Set the burner heat to high. When the cooker reaches HIGH pressure, reduce the burner heat as low as you can and still maintain HIGH pressure. Set a timer to cook for 35 minutes.

5. Remove the pot from the heat. Open the cooker with the Natural Release method; let stand for 15 minutes. Be careful of the steam as you remove the lid. The duck should be very tender and easy to pull off the bone.

6. When cool enough to handle, pull the meat off the bones. Discard the bones. Store with some liquid to keep the meat moist in an airtight container up to 3 days in the refrigerator or up to 3 months in the freezer.

Fried or Soft Tacos

Serves 4 to 6

There are two types of tacos. One is made using a crispy fried U-shaped shell, the other with a hot, soft tortilla, which works best wrapping around carnitas or fish tacos. Use the smaller, standard 6-inch corn tortilla, the size that fits in your hand. Made from yellow or white corn, they are gluten free.

$^1/_2$ cup cooking oil such as olive oil or grapeseed oil
    (for fried tacos)
12 fresh corn tortillas
2 to 3 cups shredded meat or other filling, such as
    Braised Duck for Tacos (above)

TOPPINGS (YOUR CHOICE):
$^1/_2$ head iceberg lettuce, $^1/_4$ of a ball of red or green
    cabbage, thinly shredded, or coleslaw
1 to 2 ripe tomatoes, diced
1 bunch green onions, trimmed and chopped, or $^1/_4$
    cup chopped red onion
1 cup salsa of choice (see page 301), such as Salsa
    Roja
2 cups grated Jack cheese
1 ripe avocado, peeled, pitted, and sliced or diced,
    or guacamole
Hot pepper sauce
Sprigs fresh cilantro
2 limes, cut into wedges

1. *For fried tacos,* in a small frying pan, heat the oil over medium-high heat until a drop of water sizzles immediately. One at a time, fry each tortilla lightly on one side. Turn and fry lightly on the other side. Before it becomes crisp, bend it in half with the tongs and a fork to hold it steady to crisp the folded end. Remove from the oil and drain on paper towel. Repeat with the remaining tortillas.

   For soft tacos, heat the tortillas in the oven or microwave in packs of four until hot and pliable. Depending on the filling, you might want to use two tortillas per taco to keep the filling from falling out.

2. Place 2 tablespoons of filling inside the taco. Add the toppings of your choice, garnishing the plate with a sprig of cilantro and a lime wedge.

Braised Duck with Sweet Cherry Sauce

Serves 4 • Cooker: 5- to 7-quart • Time: 35 minutes at HIGH pressure

When you start cooking duck, eventually you will get to *canard aux cerises*, duck with a seasonal fruit sauce of fresh cherries (as the season progresses, you can use apples, figs, persimmons, mangos, and winter dried fruit), the darling of the Michelin-starred restaurants. *Prunus avium* is botanic Latin for wild cherry and *avium* translates to "of or for the birds," which could refer to the birds eating the fruit off the tree or how the bird loves to be cooked with them. Serve this with egg noodles, farro, or wild rice.

4 duck leg-thigh sections, fat removed, excess skin trimmed away, skin scored all over, and pricked with a needle through the skin to release the fat
2 large shallots, sliced
$1/4$ cup dry white wine, such as Pinot Grigio
$1/4$ cup white balsamic vinegar
2 sprigs fresh thyme
1 small sprig fresh rosemary
1 cup low-sodium chicken broth
2 cups fresh or thawed frozen pitted Bing cherries (about 1 pound unpitted fresh)
$1/2$ cup dried tart or sweet cherries
1 tablespoon mild honey
2 tablespoons tawny or ruby port (or Cherry Marnier if you happen to have it)
1 tablespoon ice-cold unsalted butter
Sea salt and freshly ground black pepper

DUCK

Selective breeding has given today's ducks a nice layer of fat, large breasts, and tasty and succulent flesh, much subtler in flavor than wild duck. Muscovy ducks are the most widely available. Ducks are disease resistant and need no antibiotics, so it is a very clean meat. Ducks are sold 8 to 16 weeks old and will be labeled duckling, broiler, fryer, or roaster. The most tender ducks are no older than 8 weeks. Whole ducks are on the average about 4 pounds. You can also buy duck breasts or duck leg-thigh sections packaged separately.

1. Heat a 5- to 7-quart pressure cooker over medium-high heat. Place two duck legs in the pot, skin side down. Cook until well browned and the skin is crisped, about 5 minutes per side. Transfer to a plate. Brown the remaining legs in the same way.
2. Pour all but 2 tablespoons of fat from the pot (reserve the extra for another use). Add the shallots to the pot and cook, stirring a few times, until softened, about 2 minutes; do not brown. Add the wine, vinegar, herbs, and broth, scraping up the browned bits from the bottom of the pot with a wooden spoon. Return the duck legs along with any accumulated juice to the pot, nestling them down into the liquid. Bring to a boil for about 1 minute. Sprinkle half the fresh cherries and all of the dried cherries over the duck.
3. Close and lock the lid. Set the burner heat to high. When the cooker reaches HIGH pressure, reduce the burner heat as low as you can and still maintain HIGH pressure. Set a timer to cook for 35 minutes.
4. Remove the pot from the heat; let stand for 10 minutes. Open the cooker with the Quick Release method. Be careful of the steam as you remove the lid. The duck should be very tender. Transfer the duck legs to a rimmed serving platter. Discard the thyme and rosemary sprigs.
5. Add the honey and Port to the pot. Bring to a low boil over medium heat and let the sauce reduce until slightly thickened, about 2 minutes. Swirl in the butter pat. Add the remaining 1 cup fresh cherries and cook 2 minutes more to heat. Taste for salt and pepper. Add the duck legs back into the sauce to hold for serving, or pour the sauce over the duck to serve.

Duck with Tangerines and Turnips

Serves 4 • Cooker: 5- to 7-quart • Time: 35 minutes at HIGH pressure

Duck with citrus is a classic combination in French and Italian cooking. Duck thighs and legs are great because the meat is really dark, flavorful, tasty, and, amazingly, very low in fat. Now, the duck's skin, that's another matter. The top skin has quite a bit of fat underneath. Can scare off the uninitiated cook. You can actually get rid of almost all of that fat; use a knife and score the skin in a cross-hatch pattern. That will allow the heat to penetrate into the skin and render out the fat. Just make little cuts about halfway through the skin, in a cross-hatched pattern. Serve this with egg noodles.

4 duck leg-thigh sections, fat removed, excess skin trimmed, skin scored all over, and pricked with a needle all the way through to release the fat
2 medium leeks (white part only), trimmed, cut in half lengthwise, rinsed well, and chopped
1 cup chopped peeled turnips
2 ribs celery, chopped
Grated zest of 1 orange
3/4 cup dry white wine, such as Pinot Grigio
3/4 cup low-sodium chicken broth
Sea salt and freshly ground black pepper
1/3 cup fresh tangerine juice or orange liqueur, such as Grand Marnier or Cointreau, mixed with 1 tablespoon cornstarch
1/2 cup orange marmalade
3 tablespoons Champagne vinegar
2 small tangerines (Cuties or Clementines), peeled and sectioned

1. Heat a 5- to 7-quart pressure cooker over medium-high heat. Place two of the duck legs in the pot, skin side down, and cook until well browned and the skin is crisped, about 5 minutes per side. Transfer to a plate and repeat with the remaining duck legs.
2. Pour all but 3 tablespoons of fat from the pot (reserve the extra for another use). Add the leeks to the pot and cook, stirring a few times, until softened, about 3 minutes; do not brown. Add the turnips, celery, and zest, then the wine and broth, scraping up the browned bits from the bottom of the pot with a wooden spoon. Return the duck legs along with any accumulated juice to the pot, nestling them down in the liquid. Bring to a boil for about 1 minute.
3. Close and lock the lid. Set the burner heat to high. When the cooker reaches HIGH pressure, reduce the burner heat as low as you can and still maintain HIGH pressure. Set a timer to cook for 35 minutes.
4. Remove the pot from the heat; let stand for 10 minutes. Open the cooker with the Quick Release method. Be careful of the steam as you remove the lid. The duck should be very tender. Transfer the duck legs to a plate.
5. Add the tangerine juice mixture to the pot and simmer over medium heat, stirring, until the sauce is slightly thickened, about 2 minutes. Taste for salt and pepper, then stir in the marmalade and vinegar until the marmalade melts. Add the tangerine sections and heat through. Add the duck legs back to the sauce to hold for serving, or pour the sauce over the duck to serve.

Braised Goose Breast with Pomegranate and Lime

Serves 4 • Cooker: 5- to 7-quart • Time: 15 minutes at HIGH pressure

A goose is basically a big mallard duck and is cooked and handled as such. Goose is not as tender as duck, but has a rich flavor prized by game cooks. Goose fat is culinary gold and should not be discarded once it is rendered (think potatoes fried in goose fat). Goose pairs in the same sorts of combinations as duck: citrus, apples, berries, cherries, onions, root vegetables, sauerkraut, BBQ sauce, ginger, and dried fruit like prunes and raisins. While cooking a whole goose might not be for everyone, goose breasts are smaller, far more manageable, and faster cooking. Unlike the breasts of most poultry, goose breasts are all dark meat, with a full, intense flavor. You will prepare the goose breast the same as a duck breast, first searing it fatty skin side down. Goose fat melts at a lower temperature than that of duck, so you can pour it off earlier in the cooking process. Serve this with a bread and apple stuffing or wild rice with walnuts for the winter holidays.

¹/₂ cup unsweetened pomegranate juice
¹/₄ cup orange juice
1 boneless, skinless domestic goose breast (about 1 pound), cut into two sections
Sea salt and freshly ground black pepper
1 tablespoon rendered goose fat, unsalted butter, or olive oil
2 large shallots, finely chopped
2 ribs celery, finely chopped
1 cup reduced-sodium chicken broth
2 limes, zest finely grated, then limes cut into quarters
2 tablespoons lime marmalade or apricot jam
Pomegranate seeds, for serving (optional)

1. Place the pomegranate and orange juices in a shallow container with a lid or a ziptop plastic bag large enough to hold the two half goose breasts. Score the skin side in a crosshatch pattern with your sharpest knife. You want about 5 to 7 cuts on each angle; take care not to cut down into the meat. With your fingers, pull all but just a little of the visible fat off. (Save the fat to be melted down for cooking other dishes.) Salt and pepper the goose on both sides, then place in the marinade for 2 hours to overnight in the refrigerator.

2. Remove the breasts from the marinade; reserve the marinade. Let the breasts stand for 15 minutes at room temperature.

3. In a 5- to 7-quart pressure cooker over medium-high heat, melt the butter or oil. Pat the goose breasts dry with paper towels and place, skin side down, in the pot to sear lightly for 3 minutes. You want to do most of the browning on this side. Adjust the heat to get a steady sizzle. Turn the breasts and cook for 2 minutes. Also sear them on the cut side. Transfer to a plate and tent with aluminum foil.

4. Pour all but 2 tablespoons of fat from the pot (reserve the extra for another use). Add the shallots and celery and cook, stirring a few times, until softened, about 2 minutes; do not brown. Add the broth, marinade, and lime zest. Bring to a boil, scraping any browned bits from the bottom of the pot with a wooden spoon. Return the goose breasts along with any accumulated juice to the pot. Tuck the lime wedges in the spaces around the breasts.

5. Close and lock the lid. Set the burner heat to high. When the cooker reaches HIGH pressure, reduce the burner heat as low as you can and still maintain HIGH pressure. Set a timer to cook for 15 minutes.

6. Remove the pot from the heat. Open the cooker with the Quick Release method. Be careful of the steam as you remove the lid. Transfer the goose to a cutting board for 5 minutes. A goose breast is just like a steak: If you don't rest it, the juices will run out of it when you slice it.

7. Stir the marmalade into the pot. When serving a goose breast, *always* serve it skin side up, with its sauce underneath. Slice the breast against the grain into thin slices and serve with the pan juices. Sprinkle with pomegranate seeds, if you like.

Quail with Madeira

Serves 2 • Cooker: 6- to 8-quart • Time: 7 minutes

Quail are fast growing, need no hormones, and feast on a grain diet. They are incredibly tender and have a wild flavor. Quail are available year round and come four to a package. Here is a classic braise for quail, served on toast points. Be ready to use your fingers to eat the quail—you don't want to miss a single tasty morsel out of decorum! Serve with a side of White Beans with Mint (page 425) and a nice green salad vinaigrette with walnuts.

4 (6- to 8-ounce) quail, thawed
Sea salt and freshly ground black pepper
4 cherry tomatoes
3 green onions, trimmed and each cut into 4
    lengths
4 sprigs fresh flatleaf parsley
2 tablespoons olive oil
1/3 cup Madeira
1 cup reduced-sodium chicken broth
2 tablespoons cold unsalted butter, cut into pieces
2 slices white or whole-grain bread, toasted,
    buttered, and cut into 4 triangles, for serving

QUAIL

The Japanese quail, called *uzura* and raised for centuries, is now crossed with the common quail in order to create a hybrid that is used to restock the declining wild quail populations. Known as Coturnix, it is the most commonly available farm-raised quail in the U.S. Quail are fast growing, need no hormones, and feast on a grain diet. They are incredibly tender and have a mild flavor. Quail are sold frozen, bone in or partially boned. It is important not to overcook quail, which can happen easily, because they are so lean. For the best flavor, cook quail to medium rare. The meat should be slightly firm to the touch (similar to the feel of a cooked chicken breast) and the juices should run clear at the thigh; the meat looks like rich dark chicken thigh meat.

1. Season the quail inside and out with salt and pepper. Place a tomato, a few pieces of green onion, and a sprig of parsley in each of the 4 quail cavities. Truss the legs with kitchen twine.

2. In a 6- to 8-quart pressure cooker over medium-high heat, heat the oil. Sear the quail, two at a time, breast side down for 1 minute. Turn over and sear the other side for 1 minute. Transfer to a plate and repeat with the remaining quail. Add the Madeira and broth to the pot, bring to a boil and let boil for 1 minute, scraping up any browned bits on the bottom of the pot with a wooden spoon. Return the quail along with any accumulated juice to the pot, nestling them into the cooking liquid.

3. Close and lock the lid. Set the burner heat to high. When the cooker reaches HIGH pressure, reduce the burner heat as low as you can and still maintain HIGH pressure. Set a timer to cook for 7 minutes.

4. Remove the pot from the heat. Open the cooker with the Quick Release method. Be careful of the steam as you remove the lid. Transfer the quail to a deep serving dish.

5. Taste and adjust the seasoning, then stir in the cold butter. Make the toast and arrange on 2 dinner plates. Place 2 birds on each plate. Spoon the sauce over the quail. Serve immediately.

Quail Stuffed with Wild Rice, Pancetta, and Fruit

Serves 2 as a main or 4 as a first course • Cooker: 6- to 8-quart • Time: 7 minutes at HIGH pressure

The pressure cooker is one of the simplest and fastest ways to evenly cook the quail. Here they are stuffed with fruit and braised in sparkling wine. This is delicious served with a vegetable puree and a watercress and orange salad.

4 (6- to 8-ounce) quail, thawed
Sea salt and freshly ground black pepper
$1/4$ cup cooked brown rice or wild rice
1 teaspoon grated peeled fresh ginger
1 teaspoon grated orange zest
4 dried apricots, chopped
$1/2$ cup seedless green grapes
1 tablespoon olive oil
4 ounces sliced pancetta, chopped
2 large shallots, finely chopped
2 ribs celery, finely chopped
$3/4$ cup Prosecco, Asti Spumanti, or other sweet
    sparkling wine
$1/2$ cup low-sodium chicken broth
1 tablespoon balsamic vinegar

1. Season the quail inside and out with salt and pepper. In a small bowl, combine the rice, ginger, zest, apricots, and grapes. Divide the stuffing equally between the 4 quail cavities. Truss the legs with kitchen twine.

2. In a 6- to 8-quart pressure cooker over medium high heat, heat the oil. Sear the quail, two at a time, breast side down for 1 minute. Turn over and sear the other side for 1 minute. Transfer to a plate and repeat with the remaining quail. Add the pancetta, shallots, and celery to the pot and cook, stirring a few times, until the vegetables soften, about 2 minutes. Add the prosecco and broth, bring to a boil, and let boil for 1 minute, scraping up browned bits from the bottom of the pot with a wooden spoon. Return the quail along with any accumulated juice to the pot, nestling them in the cooking liquid.

3. Close and lock the lid. Set the burner heat to high. When the cooker reaches HIGH pressure, reduce the burner heat as low as you can and still maintain HIGH pressure. Set a timer to cook for 7 minutes.

4. Remove the pot from the heat. Open the cooker with the Quick Release method. Be careful of the steam as you remove the lid. Transfer the quail with metal tongs to a deep serving dish.

5. Puree the sauce in the pot with a handheld immersion blender. Taste for and adjust the seasoning with salt and pepper. Stir in the vinegar. Spoon the sauce over the quail and serve 1 per person for an appetizer or 2 as a main course.

OUR FAVORITE SIDE DISHES FOR GAME

Dark meat game likes assertive flavors; for lighter white meat game, look for more delicate flavors. For some meats, like bison or venison, you'll want a simpler side, like mashed potatoes or risotto, that will allow the meat's distinctive taste to be predominant. For milder quail, or duck, you'll want something heartier in texture to feature the meat, like polenta, pasta, beans, nuts, or wild rice.

*   Wild rice (Wild Rice with Chestnuts, page 328, is a classic combination)
*   Colored rices (we love Bhutanese Red Rice with Ginger and Green Onions, page 324, with game)
*   Risotto (such as saffron or butternut squash)
*   Farro
*   Pureed vegetables
*   Roasted or mashed potatoes, like Pressure Cooker "Roasted" Baby Potatoes (page 456)

*   Spaghetti squash
*   Potato dumplings or gnocchi
*   Polenta
*   Pappardelle, rigatoni, orzo, or egg noodles
*   Flavored white beans or white bean puree
*   Lentil salads
*   Minted White Beans with Pistachios
*   Sauerkraut (see Sauerkraut with Caraway, page 484)

Braised Pheasant and Cabbage

Serves 2 to 3 • Cooker: 6- to 7-quart • Time: 11 minutes for pheasant, 3 minutes for cabbage at HIGH pressure

Roy Andries de Groot, a food and wine writer for the *New York Times* in the 1960s and '70s, published a little-known pressure cooker book in 1978. He called pressure cookers "superspeed machines that do miraculous work in your kitchen." De Groot fashioned his recipes in the old French style, which was in vogue with the publication of Julia Child's *Mastering the Art of French Cooking* and the Kennedy White House hiring a French chef. He adapted his recipes from those he collected from small French inns, or auberges, tavern-style meals that utilized local, seasonal ingredients; this recipe is adapted from one of the dishes he collected. It is ironic that the pheasant was once the stuff of peasant meals, served more often than chicken until the chicken industry boom in the 1960s. The pheasant has the largest breast of all the game birds. Serve this with steamed rice and a tangy salad vinaigrette with black olives and feta. De Groot drank a California Gamay Beaujolais with this meal.

1 (3- to 3½-pound) pheasant, rinsed and patted dry
1 lemon, cut in half
3 tablespoons olive oil or butter-flavored olive oil
Sea salt and freshly ground black pepper to taste
6 tablespoons (¾ stick) cold unsalted butter
5 medium shallots, cut in half
¾ cup dry white wine
½ cup low-sodium chicken broth
1 (2-pound) head green cabbage, base trimmed, outer leaves removed, and quartered

1. Rub the pheasant inside and out with the cut lemon. In a 6- to 7-quart pressure cooker over medium-high heat, heat the oil. Add the pheasant to the pot and sear, about 3 minutes per side. Transfer to a plate. Season the pheasant all over with salt and pepper and place the butter inside the bird along with one of the lemon halves. Return the bird to the pot. Add the shallots, wine, and broth and bring to a boil.

2. Close and lock the lid. Set the burner heat to high. When the cooker reaches HIGH pressure, reduce the burner heat as low as you can and still maintain HIGH pressure. Set a timer to cook for 11 minutes.

3. Remove the pot from the heat. Open the cooker with the Quick Release method. Be careful of the steam as you remove the lid. Arrange the cabbage quarters around the bird. Relock the cooker, bring it back up to HIGH pressure, and cook another 3 minutes. Quick Release the pressure. Check the internal temperature of the pheasant with an instant-read thermometer inserted in the breast; it should register 180° F.

4. Transfer the pheasant to a platter and the cabbage and shallots to serving dish. Skim any fat off the top of the cooking juices. Carve the bird and serve with a wedge of cabbage, drizzled with the cooking juices.

Pinot Noir-Braised Rabbit and Dried Fruit

Serves 4 • Cooker: 5- to 7-quart • Time: 14 minutes at HIGH pressure

Rabbit tastes great with dried fruit and we like to serve this over a flat whole grain noodle. This is adapted from a recipe by Janie Hibler.

1 cup pitted large prunes, cut in half
$1/2$ cup mixed golden raisins and tart cherries
$2^1/2$ cups Pinot Noir
1 ($2^1/2$- to $3^1/2$-pound) rabbit, cut into 6 or 8 pieces
1 teaspoon sea salt
$1/2$ teaspoon freshly ground black pepper
2 tablespoons olive oil
2 large shallots, finely chopped
2 (4- x 1-inch) strips orange zest
1 teaspoon chopped fresh thyme
1 bay leaf
$1/2$ cup chicken broth
3 tablespoons red wine vinegar
12 ounces whole-grain ribbon pasta like pappardelle, tagliatelle, or fettuccine

RABBIT

Rabbit is considered a red meat and braises nicely. Small fryers are about 3 pounds, and roasters are 4 pounds and up. We usually have the butcher cut the rabbit into 6 or 8 pieces for easy handling in the pressure cooker—the loin, legs, ribs, and back or saddle. It is mild and tastes a lot like chicken. Rabbit is very lean and raised without steroids and hormones, making it a healthy alternative to chicken.

1. Place the dried fruit in a small bowl or glass and add 1 cup of the wine. Let soak for at least 1 hour or overnight, until the fruit has soaked up the wine.
2. Sprinkle the rabbit on all sides with the salt and pepper. In a 5- to 7-quart pressure cooker over medium-high heat, heat the oil, then add the rabbit and cook until very light golden brown, about 3 minutes. Turn the pieces and cook the other side for 1 to 2 minutes.
3. Add the shallots, reduce the heat to medium, and cook for about 30 seconds, stirring a few times, until fragrant. Stir in the zest, herbs, remaining 1 cup wine, the broth, vinegar, and soaked dried fruit; heat to a rapid simmer. Return the rabbit pieces and any accumulated juice to the pot, nestling them into the sauce.
4. Close and lock the lid. Set the burner heat to high. When the cooker reaches HIGH pressure, reduce the burner heat as low as you can and still maintain HIGH pressure. Set a timer to cook for 14 minutes.
5. While the rabbit cooks, bring a large pot of salted water to a boil.
6. Remove the pressure cooker from the heat; let stand for 10 minutes. Open the cooker with the Quick Release method. Be careful of the steam as you remove the lid. Discard the zest and bay leaf. Taste for salt. Transfer the rabbit pieces with a slotted spoon to a platter and tent with aluminum foil.
7. Add the pasta to the boiling water and cook to al dente. Bring the sauce to a boil and reduce by a third. Pour the sauce over the rabbit. Portion the pasta and top with the rabbit and sauce.

Rabbit with Mustard and Garlicky Sautéed Watercress

Serves 4 • Cooker: 5- to 7-quart • Time: 14 minutes at HIGH pressure

Rabbit in mustard, *lapin la moutarde,* is a French bistro classic and each home cook has their own variation. You want a French grainy mustard, which is sharp flavored and integral to the success of the dish. Serve with crusty bread and a nice big white wine like a California Chardonnay.

RABBIT:

1 (2¹/₂- to 3¹/₂-pound) rabbit, cut into 6 or 8 pieces
1 teaspoon sea salt
¹/₄ cup (¹/₂ stick) unsalted butter
3 large shallots, finely chopped
³/₄ cup dry white wine
¹/₂ cup chicken broth
¹/₂ cup grainy country mustard, such as Dijon
1 teaspoon dried herbes de Provence
¹/₂ teaspoon chopped fresh thyme
¹/₂ cup heavy cream or crème fraîche
3 tablespoons finely chopped fresh flatleaf parsley, or half parsley and chives

SAUTÉED WATERCRESS:

2 teaspoons olive oil
2 cloves garlic, minced
2 bunches fresh watercress, rinsed and dried
Pinch sea salt

1. Sprinkle the rabbit on all sides with the salt and set aside at room temperature, loosely covered with plastic wrap, for 30 minutes.

2. In a 5- to 7-quart pressure cooker, melt the butter over medium-high heat, then add the rabbit pieces and cook until very light golden brown, about 3 minutes. Turn the rabbit and cook the other side for 1 to 2 minutes. Remove to a plate. Add the shallots, reduce the heat to medium and cook until softened, about 3 minutes, stirring a few times. Add the wine and bring to a boil over high heat, scraping up any browned bits from the bottom of the pot with a wooden spoon. Stir in the broth, mustard, and herbs. Return the rabbit pieces and any accumulated juice to the pot, nestling them into the sauce.

3. Close and lock the lid. Set the burner heat to high. When the cooker reaches HIGH pressure, reduce the burner heat as low as you can and still maintain HIGH pressure. Set a timer to cook for 14 minutes.

4. Remove the pot from the heat; let stand for 10 minutes. Open the cooker with the Quick Release method. Be careful of the steam as you remove the lid. Taste for salt. With a slotted spoon, transfer the rabbit pieces to a platter and tent with aluminum foil. Add the cream and parsley to the juices in the pot and heat over low to warm. Do not let come to a boil.

5. Make the watercress. In a large skillet, heat the oil and add the garlic; cook, stirring constantly, for 30 to 60 seconds. Add the watercress and cook, stirring, until wilted. Sprinkle with the salt.

6. To serve, pour the sauce over the rabbit to evenly coat. Serve immediately on top of egg noodles or wild rice, with a side of the watercress.

Gypsy Rabbit Stew with Yellow Peppers and Oven Polenta

Serves 4 • Cooker: 5- to 7-quart • Time: 14 minutes at HIGH pressure

This is the dish to make at the end of summer when bell peppers are at their peak. Green and purple bell peppers have a slightly bitter flavor, while the red, orange and yellows are sweeter, almost fruity. The oven polenta, an amazing no-muss, no-fuss way to cook polenta, needs an hour to cook but can sit up to an hour in a low oven, so make it before the rabbit. Serve the rabbit on the polenta drizzled with the braising juices and a grating of Parmesan.

OVEN POLENTA:

1 cup coarse-grain yellow polenta or stoneground
    yellow or white cornmeal
3^1/$_2$ cups warm water or vegetable or chicken broth
^{3}/$_4$ teaspoon sea salt
3 tablespoons unsalted butter
^{1}/$_2$ cup grated Parmesan cheese (optional)

RABBIT:

1 (2^1/$_2$- to 3^1/$_2$-pound) rabbit, cut into 6 or 8 pieces
^{1}/$_2$ cup all-purpose flour or potato starch flour
1 teaspoon sea salt
4 tablespoons olive oil
4 large yellow bell peppers, or 2 yellow and 2 red,
    seeded and sliced into rings
1 cup chicken broth or vegetable broth
^{1}/$_3$ cup dry white wine
1 tablespoon tomato paste
2 tablespoons minced fresh flatleaf parsley
2 tablespoons minced fresh chives
1 teaspoon minced fresh sage
Pinch minced fresh marjoram
Salt and freshly ground black pepper

1. Combine the flour and salt in a shallow bowl and dredge the rabbit pieces in the mixture to fully coat. Set aside. Prepare the polenta.

2. Preheat the oven to 350° F. Grease an 8- or 9-inch square 2-quart baking dish with olive oil cooking spray. In a medium bowl, whisk together the water, polenta, and salt until smooth, no lumps. Pour into the baking dish. Cut the butter into small pieces and sprinkle them over the top; the butter will float. Cover with aluminum foil and bake for 40 minutes. Remove the foil and stir the polenta with a dinner fork. Return to the oven, uncovered, for another 20 minutes (1 hour total cook time, more if necessary), until the water is absorbed and the polenta has thickened and is creamy to the bite. If the polenta is too thick, add boiling water. Remove from the oven and stir in cheese, if using. Let rest at least 5 minutes before serving to allow it to further thicken.

3. In a 5- to 7-quart pressure cooker with the lid off, heat the oil, then add the rabbit and cook until very light golden brown, about 3 minutes. Turn the pieces and cook the other side for 1 to 2 minutes. Transfer to a plate. Add the wine and herbs to the pot and bring to a boil over high heat, scraping up any browned bits from the bottom of the pot with a wooden spoon. Return the rabbit pieces and any accumulated juice to the pot. Add the peppers, broth, wine, tomato paste, and herbs.

4. Close and lock the lid. Set the burner heat to high. When the cooker reaches HIGH pressure, reduce the burner heat as low as you can and still maintain HIGH pressure. Set a timer to cook for 14 minutes.

5. Remove the pot from the heat; let stand for 10 minutes. Open the cooker with the Quick Release method. Be careful of the steam as you remove the lid. Taste for salt and pepper. Serve immediately, nice and hot, with sauce spooned over the polenta.

7

Beef, Veal, and Bison

The tougher cuts of meat, those with the greatest muscle density, are the ones perfect for braises, stews, and pot roasts in the pressure cooker; a moist cooking environment under pressure does wonders for converting the long muscle fibers of these cuts into delicious succulence. This happens because the muscles are interwoven with connective tissue that dissolves into collagen as it is cooked, releasing incredible amounts of nutritious vitamins and minerals into the cooking liquid as well as flavor and producing a silky, fork-tender meat. A paleo's delight! These cuts include the shank, brisket, and short ribs, as well as bottom round, chuck roast, and boneless rump; these last three are all good choices for pot roast. Ground beef, in the form of meatballs and meatloaf, also works well in the pressure cooker.

When choosing a cut of beef, look for slightly moist meat with a light cherry red to red-brown hue, a clean smell, tight grain, marbled intramuscular fat (flecks of fat throughout the meat), and white external fat. Check expiration dates before buying packaged meat and always store beef in the refrigerator. You want to look for USDA Choice grade meats, as they are the juiciest and most flavorful, but often the lower grade, Select, while a lot leaner than Choice, is also fine for stewing and braising. If you buy with respect to religious restrictions, look for Kosher grading, which is subject to strict and specific Jewish handling laws. Shop at a reliable supermarket or small chain butcher shop. An excellent online source is Heritage Foods (look for them at heritagefoodsusa.com).

Veal, which is butchered from a four-month-old calf, is divided into the same sections as beef. Because the bones of the calf have not fully matured, all veal cuts contain goodly amounts of collagen and make for superior tender braises. When purchasing veal, you can choose formula-fed (sold as Provimi, translating to protein/vitamin/mineral), which is pale pink, or grass-fed (the animal was allowed to roam and graze); that meat has a ruddier color and is more flavorful. Veal takes to all sorts of spices, vegetables, and aromatic braising liquids because of its delicate taste, and it is the leanest of all meats. Veal breast, shoulder roasts, veal cheeks, and blade roasts are all good choices for cutting up into stew meat and the most economical. Veal shanks cook up almost silky tender. Please make our Veal Osso Bucco (page 232) and see for yourself. In the pressure cooker, veal should be cooked until falling off the bone.

Bison is the commercial name for buffalo meat. Yes, the same buffalo meat the Native Americans ate and the French explorers to the America West called *Les Boeufs*. Today bison are bred and raised on ranches. Grass-fed bison has a rich flavor very similar to that of beef but with a fraction of the fat. If your market doesn't carry bison, a great online source is US Wellness Meats in Monticello, Missouri (grasslandbeef.com). Bison can be substituted for beef in any of our beef stews; the cooking times will remain the same.

BEST CUTS FOR THE PRESSURE COOKER

Beef

- boneless chuck roast
- flank steak
- oxtails
- short ribs
- 7-bone blade roast
- corned beef
- brisket
- shoulder pot roast
- cross-cut beef shanks and shin
- beef cheeks

Veal

- shanks
- shoulder roast
- bone-in blade roast
- chuck shoulder roast
- veal breast
- veal cheeks

Bison

- rump roast
- brisket
- sirloin roast
- bottom and top round
- shanks
- short ribs

THE SCOOP ON BEEF LABELING

How is "organic" meat different from "natural" meat? Do "free range" and "grass fed" mean the same thing? And how do they differ from "pasture raised"? The world of meat has become a maze of sometimes ill-defined labels. What you need to know is that only some of these terms are legally regulated; others are simply marketing phrases created by clever PR firms. Let us shed some light on the matter:

Certified Organic

Meat must be certified by an independent organization accredited by the United States Department of Agriculture (USDA) to carry the label "organic." If a meat is certified organic, it means that the animal's feed was organic (produced without synthetic fertilizers, herbicides, pesticides, or GMO seeds) and that the animal was not given growth hormones or antibiotics. All organic livestock and milking cows graze on pasture at least four months of the year. Studies have shown that organic cuts of meat harbor significantly less antibiotic-resistant bacteria than those raised otherwise.

Grass Fed

The USDA has a grass-fed rule for ruminants such as cattle, sheep, goats, and bison. To carry the designation, these animals must be fed "grass (annual and perennial), forbs (e.g., legumes, Brassica), browse, or cereal grain crops in the vegetative (pre-grain) state." The "grass fed" designation also requires the animals to have "continuous access to pasture during the growing season." The American Grassfed Association has developed more stringent standards, which include the animal "must not be confined to a pen, feedlot or other area" during the growing season, the prohibition of antibiotics and synthetic hormones, and issues regarding the animals' welfare.

Free Range

The USDA only regulates the term "free range" as it applies to poultry meant for consumption, not to egg-laying hens or other animals.

Pasture Raised

Though the term is unregulated at present, most small farmers consider the designation "pasture raised" (or "pastured") the best way to describe animals raised outdoors without confinement.

Natural

Perhaps the most confusing meat labeling term regulated by the USDA is "natural," in part because of the discrepancy between "natural" and "naturally raised." At the moment, these terms mean two very different things and are, in fact, regulated by two separate agencies within the USDA. "Natural" refers only to post-harvest products that do not contain artificial ingredients or added color; "natural" animal products must be only minimally processed. "Natural" does not refer to the way the animal was raised, which is what the "naturally raised" label defines. As defined and regulated by the USDA, livestock that has been "naturally raised" has not been fed animal by-products or given growth hormones or antibiotics.

Humane

The USDA has no standardized definition of "humane," but many independent meat organizations have created their own labels and certification programs for animal welfare. These certifications not only evaluate access to pasture and exposure to growth hormones, but also things like sleep periods, litter management, castration, and methods of slaughter.

Meatballs in San Marzano Tomato Basil Sauce, Neapolitan Style

Makes 16 meatballs; serves about 4 • Cooker: 5- to 8-quart • Time: 5 minutes at HIGH pressure

The elusive flavor in these meatballs comes from the raisins, a Sicilian touch. The meatballs are cooked in a rich tomato marinara sauce, which keeps them moist. You can use this recipe with ground dark turkey; a combination of beef and turkey or pork and turkey; a meatloaf mix of beef, veal, and pork; or a combination of beef and veal. We love Italian seasoning blend, a mixture of dried basil, oregano, marjoram, thyme, and rosemary. You can also add a few tablespoons of pine nuts to the meat mixture if you like. Serve the meatballs in sauce over pasta, spaghetti squash, or polenta, or stuffed into fresh French or ciabatta rolls for a meatball sandwich.

SAN MARZANO TOMATO BASIL SAUCE:
$1/4$ cup extra virgin olive oil
2 cloves garlic, smashed
2 (28-ounce) cans San Marzano plum tomatoes in juice, crushed by hand
$1/2$ cup low-sodium chicken broth
$1/4$ cup dry red wine or vermouth
3 sprigs fresh basil
2 pinches dried Italian seasoning blend
Sea salt and freshly ground black pepper

MEATBALLS:
2 cups cubed dried crustless bread (4 slices, can be gluten-free)
About $1/4$ cup water or milk
$1 1/2$ pounds ground beef, or half ground beef and half ground pork
2 cloves garlic, minced
2 large eggs, beaten
$1/2$ cup grated Pecorino Romano cheese
3 tablespoons finely minced fresh flatleaf parsley
$2/3$ cup raisins or currants soaked in $1/3$ cup Marsala

1. Make the sauce. In a 5- to 8-quart pressure cooker, heat the oil over medium-high heat. Add the garlic and cook for 30 seconds. Add the crushed tomatoes with their juice, broth, wine, basil, and Italian seasoning. When the tomato sauce rapidly simmers, reduce the heat to medium-low and simmer, uncovered, while you make the meatballs.

2. In a medium bowl, combine the bread cubes and water. Let stand for 5 minutes. If you need to moisten the bread more, add a bit more water. If the bread is too wet, squeeze it out. Add the ground meat, garlic, eggs, cheese, parsley, and drained raisins. Blend the mix well with your hands or a fork. Form into 2-inch balls. You will get about 16. You can use a mini ice cream scoop for this or pat the meat into a 4-inch square and cut into 16 portions (4 across and 4 down), as you want the meatballs evenly sized so they cook in the same amount of time. As you make these, drop them into the simmering sauce. If you want to make the meatballs ahead, chill them in the refrigerator while you make the sauce. Chilling makes the meatballs hold together better.

3. Close and lock the lid. Set the burner heat to high. When the cooker reaches HIGH pressure, reduce the burner heat as low as you can and still maintain HIGH pressure. Set a timer to cook for 5 minutes.

4. Remove the pot from the heat. Open the cooker with the Natural Release method; let stand for 15 minutes. Be careful of the steam as you remove the lid. Discard the basil sprigs. Taste the sauce for salt and pepper.

5. Remove the meatballs with an oversized spoon to dinner plates and use a small ladle for the sauce. Serve the meatballs with some sauce spooned over.

Sweet and Sour Stuffed Savoy Cabbage

Serves 6 • Cooker: 5- to 7-quart • Time: 20 minutes at HIGH pressure

Stuffed cabbage is popular to eat—and not so popular to make because of the time it takes to make the rolls. If you doubt me, just Google "unstuffed cabbage" and you will find a bevy of shortcut recipes. One labor-saving trick is to use Savoy instead of regular green cabbage. The leaves of the Savoy are looser, rather elongated, and much easier to work with. Once you get the hang of stuffing them, you will be able to get this delicious meal into the pressure cooker in no time. Choose lean ground beef as you will have no opportunity to drain the fat from it (you can substitute ground lamb or ground turkey in place of the beef). Sometimes we like to use brown rice for extra flavor and fiber. If you do so, increase the cooking time to 25 minutes. Stuffed cabbage is often served with egg noodles but we like it with mashed potatoes, too.

FILLING:
1 medium head Savoy cabbage
1 pound lean ground beef
$^1/_2$ medium onion, finely chopped
3 tablespoons white long-grain rice
5 tablespoons dark raisins
1 teaspoon sea salt
$^1/_4$ teaspoon freshly ground black pepper
$^1/_4$ teaspoon ground ginger

SWEET AND SOUR SAUCE:
1 (28-ounce) can no-salt-added diced or whole
    tomatoes in juice
Juice of 1$^1/_2$ to 2 medium lemons, to taste
1$^1/_2$ to 2 tablespoons light brown sugar, to taste
Sea salt and freshly ground black pepper (optional)

1. Rinse the head of cabbage by holding it under cool running water. Leaving the cabbage wet, place the entire head in a plastic bag or wrap it in plastic wrap. Microwave it on HIGH power for 5 minutes. Carefully open the bag or the wrap and let it cool while you prepare the meat mixture.

2. Place the meat in a large bowl and gently break it up with a large fork. Add the onion, rice, 2 tablespoons of the raisins, the salt, pepper, and ginger. Mix gently but thoroughly with the fork, taking care not to compact the meat. Shape the meat into 12 meatballs. Keep them somewhat even but don't worry if they are not all exactly the same size. It will be useful to have some larger ones, some smaller ones, and some in-between ones.

3. When the cabbage is cool enough to handle, carefully peel away the outer leaves one by one, doing your best not to tear them. Stop when you have 12 reasonably intact ones. If the leaves seem stiff as you get near the center, return what is left of the cabbage head to the plastic bag or plastic wrap and microwave it for 2 minutes more. Once you have 12 leaves, you're ready to start stuffing.

4. Select the largest leaf and place the largest meatball in the lower third of it, centered across the spine of the leaf. Starting at the base of the leaf, enclose the meatball as follows: Fold up the bottom of the leaf, partially or fully covering the meatball. Fold in both sides of the leaf. Roll up the meatball, keeping the sides of the cabbage leaf neatly tucked in. Place the cabbage roll on a cutting board or large plate, loose side down.

5. Continue stuffing cabbage leaves until you have 12, working with the next largest leaf and the next largest meatball, and so on. If a leaf tears, either make a patch by placing a small piece of cabbage inside the roll to cover the tear or simply peel another leaf from the remaining cabbage head and start again.

6. Coarsely chop the remaining cabbage and spread it out on the bottom of a 5- to 7-quart pressure cooker to make a bed. Sprinkle the remaining 3 tablespoons raisins over the chopped cabbage. Stack the cabbage rolls in the pot, starting with a layer of the largest ones and being careful to tuck the loose end under each roll.

7. Make the sauce. Pour the tomatoes and their juice into a bowl. If you are using whole tomatoes, either crush them with your hands, or fish them out and chop them into rough chunks no larger than $3/4$ inch on a side, then return the chopped tomatoes to the bowl. Add the juice of $1^1/2$ lemons and 1 tablespoon of brown sugar and stir to combine. Taste and adjust the sour and sweet flavors to your liking. If desired, add a pinch of salt and a few grinds of pepper, but we like the pure tomato flavor on its own. When you are satisfied, pour the tomato sauce over the cabbage rolls in the pressure cooker.

8. Close and lock the lid. Set the burner heat to high. When the cooker reaches HIGH pressure, reduce the burner heat as low as you can and still maintain HIGH pressure. Set a timer to cook for 20 minutes.

9. Remove the pot from the heat. Open the cooker with the Quick Release method. Be careful of the steam as you remove the lid.

10. Carefully remove the cabbage rolls with an oversized spoon to a serving platter. Stir the bed of chopped cabbage and raisins into the tomato sauce, then pour the sauce over the cabbage rolls. Serve with egg noodles or mashed potatoes. Leftovers will keep in an airtight container in the refrigerator 4 to 5 days or the freezer up to 4 months.

Porcupine Meatballs

Serves 4 to 5 • Cooker: 5- to 8-quart • Time: 5 minutes at HIGH pressure

This is an iconic pressure cooker recipe. The recipe has appeared in all of the Presto cookbooks, old and current, for decades, adapted from Asian cooking. Generations of kids have been eating porcupine meatballs, with the rice sticking out all over like thorns, prepared by pressure-cooking moms needing to get dinner on the table as soon as possible.

Lorna Sass kept with the tradition and included the recipe in one of her pressure cooker collections. She recommends that the meatballs be arranged in a single layer in the water or else they won't have enough moisture to cook the rice. The tomato sauce gets poured over the top to avoid scorching as the cooker comes up to pressure. Make the meatballs in two separate batches, if necessary, rather than crowd them into the cooker. Also, avoid using a tomato sauce that has bits of solids in it, like mushrooms or sausage, as they have a tendency to stick to the bottom of the cooker. Enjoy our version, with a gussied-up tomato-lemon sauce.

LEMON-TOMATO SAUCE:

3 cups plain tomato sauce (such as Muir Glen)
1 tablespoon olive oil
Pinch chili powder
2 tablespoons tomato paste
$^1/_2$ teaspoon sea salt
Grated zest of 1 lemon
Juice of 1 large or 2 medium lemons

MEATBALLS:

$1^1/_2$ pounds ground beef, or a combination of 1 pound ground beef and $^1/_2$ pound ground pork, veal, or venison
$^1/_2$ cup raw long-grain white rice (don't try this with any other kind of rice)
$^1/_2$ cup finely chopped white onion or white part of green onions
$^1/_4$ cup finely chopped fresh flatleaf parsley
10 grinds black pepper
$^1/_2$ teaspoon sea salt, or to taste
1 cup water

TO FINISH:

1 tablespoon cornstarch (optional)
1 tablespoon water (optional)
Grated Parmesan cheese, for garnish (optional)

1. Make the sauce. In medium saucepan, combine the tomato sauce, oil, chili powder, tomato paste, salt, and lemon zest and lemon. Whisk to incorporate the tomato paste. Over medium-high heat, bring the tomato sauce to a rapid simmer. Reduce the heat to medium-low and simmer, uncovered, while you make the meatballs.

2. In a medium bowl, combine the ground meats, rice, onion, parsley, pepper, and salt. Blend well with your hands or a fork. Form into 2-inch balls (a mini ice cream scoop works nicely for this). You will get 17 to 18. If you want to make the meatballs ahead, refrigerate them while you make the sauce. Chilling makes the meatballs hold together better.

3. Pour the water into a 5- to 8-quart pressure cooker. Set the meatballs side by side in the water; don't stack them on top of each other. (You may have to cook the meatballs in two batches.) Pour the sauce on top. Do not stir.

4. Close and lock the lid. Set the burner heat to high. When the cooker reaches HIGH pressure, reduce the burner heat as low as you can and still maintain HIGH pressure. Set a timer to cook for 5 minutes.

5. Remove the pot from the heat. Open the cooker with the Natural Release method; let stand for 15 minutes. Be careful of the steam as you remove the lid. Check the meatballs for doneness by splitting one open and making sure that the rice on the inside is thoroughly cooked. If not, lock the lid back in place and let the meatballs steam in the residual heat for a minute or two without bringing them back to pressure.

6. Gently lift the meatballs from the pot with a slotted spoon and set in a warm serving dish. If the sauce is too thin for your taste, boil vigorously over high heat until reduced to the desired consistency. Alternatively, blend the cornstarch with the 1 tablespoon water and stir it into the sauce. Cook over medium-high heat, stirring frequently, until the sauce thickens. Pour over the meatballs. Serve the meatballs with some sauce spooned over, with Parmesan cheese on the side.

Ropa Vieja (Shredded Flank Steak)

Serves 6 • Cooker: 5- to 7-quart • Time: 30 minutes at HIGH pressure

Ropa vieja is often associated with Mexican food, but it is also the national dish of Venezuela, part of home cooking in Cuba and Puerto Rico, and really made throughout Latin and South America. It is usually prepared with flank steak or brisket and served with white rice, black beans, and pan-sautéed plantains (I've included the recipe because they are so incredibly good). It is also used as a taco filling or piled on tortillas along with sour cream, grated Jack cheese, and lots of fresh cilantro. Ropa vieja literally means "old clothes" in Spanish, referring to the long strands of the meat after it falls apart into shreds.

1 (2-pound) flank steak, 1 to 2 inches thick
Sea salt
1 medium white onion, sliced
1 large green bell pepper, seeded and chopped
2 cloves garlic, minced
$1/4$ teaspoon dried oregano, preferably Mexican
$1/4$ teaspoon ground cumin
1 bay leaf
$1/4$ teaspoon freshly ground black pepper
1 (10-ounce) can tomatoes and green chiles (Rotel brand), undrained
1 cup low-sodium chicken broth
3 tablespoons tomato paste
2 to 3 tablespoons fresh lime juice, to taste
2 to 4 teaspoons hot sauce (such as Cholula), to taste

FRIED PLANTAINS:
Canola or vegetable oil
1 ripe (black) plantain per person, peeled and cut across or on the diagonal into $1/4$-inch-thick slices
Sea salt (optional)

1. Season the meat all over with salt. Place the flank steak, onion, green pepper, garlic, oregano, cumin, bay leaf, pepper, tomatoes and chiles with their juice, and broth in a 5- to 7-quart pressure cooker. Bring to a boil over medium-high heat. Place the tomato paste on top; do not stir it in.

2. Close and lock the lid. Set the burner heat to high. When the cooker reaches HIGH pressure, reduce the burner heat as low as you can and still maintain HIGH pressure. Set a timer to cook for 25 minutes.

3. Remove the pot from the heat. Open the cooker with the Natural Release method; let stand for 15 minutes. Be careful of the steam as you remove the lid. Discard the bay leaf. Add the lime juice and hot sauce to taste, stirring it into the cooking liquid.

4. Remove the flank steak to a cutting board with tongs and let it rest briefly. Trim off any fat, pull the beef apart with two forks into shreds 2 inches wide, and coarsely chop the shreds. Skim any fat from the top of the sauce. Add the shredded meat back into the pot.

5. When ready to serve the ropa vieja, fry the plantains. Add enough oil to a large skillet to just coat the bottom of the pan and place over medium heat. When the oil begins to shimmer, add the plantain slices in a single layer (work in batches), and fry for $1^1/2$ minutes, then flip the slices over with a spatula and cook for 1 minute on the other side. Transfer the cooked plantains to paper towels to drain. Continue frying in batches until all the plantains are fried. Sprinkle lightly with sea salt, if you like.

6. Serve the ropa vieja from the pressure cooker with the fried plantains on the side.

Roast Beef with Madeira Butter Sauce, French Style

Serves 6 • Cooker: 6- to 8-quart • Time: 20 minutes at HIGH pressure

A friend from France mentioned how she uses her *la cocotte-minute,* the French name for the pressure cooker, almost every day and makes roast beef every week. We asked for her recipe, which was quite a simple affair and ready for the table in half an hour. It is hard to believe a rare *rosbif* can come out of a pressure cooker, which specializes in braises, but it, does. While you can do this with a tenderloin or prime rib, a much less expensive but still very tasty alternative is the top sirloin. Cut from the hip, it is known as the American chateaubriand. Lean and moderately tender when sliced thin, it has excellent flavor. Be sure to be exact with your timing. This is delicious served with a warm lentil salad and/or puree of cannellini beans.

1 (3-pound) sirloin beef roast
Sea salt and freshly ground black pepper
3 tablespoons olive oil
1 large white onion, finely chopped
4 ounces white mushrooms, sliced
2 medium carrots, cut into 1-inch pieces on the
    diagonal
2 tablespoons tomato paste
1¼ cups dry white wine
½ cup low-sodium chicken broth
Bouquet garni of 1 sprig fresh thyme, 1 bay leaf,
    and a few sprigs fresh parsley including stems
    sandwiched between 2 (2-inch) pieces celery
    and tied with kitchen twine
2 to 3 tablespoons Madeira, to taste
2 tablespoons cold unsalted butter

1. Pat dry the roast with paper towels and season the meat all over with salt and pepper. In a 6- to 8-quart pressure cooker, heat the oil over medium-high heat until very hot. Brown the meat on all sides, 6 to 8 minutes total. Transfer the roast to a plate.

2. Add the onion, mushrooms, and carrots to the pot and cook, stirring occasionally, until lightly browned at the edges, 3 to 5 minutes. Add the tomato paste and cook, stirring, 1 minute longer. Pour in the wine and broth, stirring to scrape up any browned bits from the bottom of the pot. Bring to a boil. Return the roast to the pot, pushing it down into the mixture. Tuck the bouquet garni to the side of the roast.

3. Close and lock the lid. Set the burner heat to high. When the cooker reaches HIGH pressure, reduce the burner heat as low as you can and still maintain HIGH pressure. Set a timer to cook for 20 minutes.

4. Remove the pot from the heat. Open the cooker with the Natural Release method; let stand for 15 minutes. Be careful of the steam as you remove the lid. Transfer the roast to a carving board and tent loosely with aluminum foil to retain the heat.

5. Skim any fat from the top of the sauce. Bring to a simmer. Whisk in the Madeira and butter. Taste, adding more salt if needed. Serve the sauce with the meat, sliced thinly across the grain.

Julie's Beef Stew

Serves 4 to 6 • Cooker: 5- to 7-quart • Time: 15 minutes for meat, onions and 5 minutes for vegetables at HIGH pressure

Here it is, the recipe that won us over to the pressure cooker! This story goes back a number years, to when we were just beginning to write our slow cooker series of books. We wanted to understand the subtleties of the slow cooker vs. the pressure cooker vs. conventional cooking methods. We prepped a batch of beef stew, then cooked half of it in the slow cooker and half in the pressure cooker. The slow cooker stew was absolutely delicious. Our big surprise was that the pressure cooker stew was just as delicious. One cooked unattended all day, the other was ready in minutes—two great ways to get dinner on the table at the end of a busy day. This stew is basic, well, what we mean is, it's basically fantastic. Serve it in shallow bowls on a chilly winter day.

1^1/$_2$ pounds boneless beef chuck roast, cut into 1^1/$_2$-inch cubes
^{1}/$_4$ cup all-purpose or whole-wheat pastry flour, lightly seasoned with salt and pepper
2 tablespoons olive oil
1 large yellow or white onion, chopped into ^{1}/$_2$-inch pieces
2 cloves garlic, chopped
^{1}/$_4$ cup dry red wine
2^1/$_2$ cups low-sodium beef broth
1 teaspoon sea salt
^{1}/$_2$ teaspoon freshly ground black pepper
^{1}/$_4$ teaspoon dried thyme
^{1}/$_4$ teaspoon dried rosemary
1 bay leaf
1^1/$_2$ cups sliced (^{1}/$_2$-inch-thick) celery, widest slices halved crosswise
4 medium carrots, cut into ^{1}/$_2$- to ^{3}/$_4$-inch-thick rounds
2 large russet potatoes, peeled and cut into 1-inch cubes
Chopped fresh flatleaf parsley, for serving

1. In a shallow bowl or plastic bag, toss the meat with the seasoned flour, shaking off any excess flour. In a 5- to 7-quart pressure cooker, heat 1 tablespoon of the oil over medium-high heat until very hot. Brown the meat in batches in a single layer, 1 to 2 minutes per side. (Do not crowd or the meat will not brown properly.) Transfer the browned meat to a plate.

2. Add the remaining 1 tablespoon oil to the pot. Add the onion and garlic, reduce the heat to medium, and cook gently until the onion begins to soften, 1 to 2 minutes. Add the wine and cook, scraping and stirring to dissolve any browned bits stuck to the bottom of the pan. Return the meat and any accumulated juice to the pot, along with the salt, pepper, thyme, rosemary, and bay leaf.

3. Close and lock the lid. Set the burner heat to high. When the cooker reaches HIGH pressure, reduce the burner heat as low as you can and still maintain HIGH pressure. Set a timer to cook for 15 minutes.

4. Remove the pot from the heat. Open the cooker with the Quick Release method. Be careful of the steam as you remove the lid.

5. Add the celery, carrots, and potatoes to the pot. Relock the cooker, bring back up to HIGH pressure, and cook for 5 minutes.

6. Remove the pot from the heat. Open the cooker with the Quick Release method. Taste for salt and pepper. Serve the stew in shallow bowls, topped with a sprinkling of parsley.

French Beef Stew with Mustard: In Step 2, add 3 chopped shallots along with the onion and garlic. In Step 6, stir in ^{1}/$_2$ cup Dijon mustard *and* ^{1}/$_4$ cup Pommery or whole-grain mustard before serving. *Voila!*

Beef Stew with Asian Flavors

Serves 6 • Cooker: 5- to 7-quart • Time: 25 minutes for stew, 5 minutes for carrots at HIGH pressure

Beef stew might be a culinary institution in America, but it is not immune to the vast influences of our melting pot culture. Here it meets up with the Asian flavors of star anise, lots of white-hot ginger, and shaoxing Chinese rice wine. Star anise is reddish brown, shaped like an irregular, eight-pointed star (its Chinese name means "eight points"), and it adds a whisper of licorice flavor to this dish. Dark-amber shaoxing rice wine been made since dynastic times and is used extensively for cooking meat dishes; you might find it sold as shao hsing. Look for the Pagoda brand, the cook's choice. It has a unique flavor and fragrance; a medium-dry sherry is a good substitute. This is a fabulous tasting stew.

$1/2$ cup Chinese rice wine (shaoxing)
$1/4$ cup reduced-sodium soy sauce
$3^1/_2$ pounds boneless beef chuck roast, cut into
    $1^1/_2$-inch cubes
2 tablespoons all-purpose or rice flour
$1/2$ teaspoon freshly ground white pepper
2 tablespoons olive oil
2 large white onions, chopped
1 teaspoon sea salt
6 cloves garlic, minced
$1^1/_2$ cups sliced ($1/2$-inch-thick) celery, widest slices
    halved crosswise
$1/3$ cup finely chopped peeled fresh ginger
$1/4$ teaspoon red pepper flakes
1 stalk lemongrass, trimmed of lower bulb and
    tough outer leaves removed; leave green stem
    intact and bruise by bending stalk in a few places
    to release its flavor
3 star anise pods
1 (3-inch) cinnamon stick
1 cup water
1 cup low-sodium chicken broth
4 large carrots, cut on a diagonal into $1/2$-inch-thick
    slices (about 2 cups)
6 green onions (whites and plenty of the green
    portion), thinly sliced
$1/2$ cup chopped fresh cilantro, for garnish
1 cup diced firm or extra-firm tofu, for garnish

1. In a medium bowl, mix 2 tablespoons each of the rice wine and soy sauce; add the beef, toss to coat, and let marinate at room temperature for 45 minutes. Drain the beef and blot dry. Wipe out the bowl and toss the beef, flour, and pepper together. In a 5- to 7-quart pressure cooker, heat 1 tablespoon of the oil over medium-high heat until very hot. Brown the meat in batches in a single layer on all sides, adding more oil as needed. Transfer the browned meat to a plate.

2. Reduce the heat to medium, add the onions and salt, and cook, stirring occasionally, until the onions are softened, about 4 minutes. Add the garlic, celery, ginger, red pepper flakes, lemongrass, star anise, and cinnamon and cook, stirring, until fragrant, about 45 seconds. Add the water and remaining 6 tablespoons rice wine, increase the heat to high, and, using a wooden spoon, scrape the bottom of the pot to loosen and dissolve any browned bits, about 1 minute. Add the broth, remaining 2 tablespoons soy sauce, and the beef with any accumulated juice, and bring to a boil.

3. Close and lock the lid. Set the burner heat to high. When the cooker reaches HIGH pressure, reduce the burner heat as low as you can and still maintain HIGH pressure. Set a timer to cook for 25 minutes.

4. Remove the pot from the heat. Open the cooker with the Quick Release method. Be careful of the steam as you remove the lid. Skim off any fat from the surface. Discard the lemongrass, star anise, and cinnamon stick.

5. Add the carrots to the pot. Relock the cooker, bring back up to HIGH pressure, and cook for 5 minutes. Remove the pot from the heat. Open the cooker with the Quick Release method. The carrots should be tender.

6. Stir in the green onions. Taste for seasoning and add salt and pepper if necessary. Serve immediately with steamed white rice, sprinkled with the cilantro and tofu. This is really good reheated the next day.

Chipotle Beef Stew

Serves 6 • Cooker: 5- to 7-quart • Time: 20 minutes at HIGH pressure

Back in 1999, Beth ripped out a page of *Gourmet* for a one-bowl chocolate cake recipe from the *Fannie Farmer Baking Book*. Fast forward all these years, and on the same page is a recipe for a Chipotle Beef Stew. It was a stew heralding the next trend, the chipotle chile, just a dash before its time. This is a straightforward, easy to make stew packed with that smoky flavor, not too much, just the right amount. Please, always use fresh garlic, not ever from a jar. The wet-packed posole/hominy shows up in the meat case of supermarkets, packed like a tray of meat, during the holiday season for making tamales. It is also available in Latin specialty markets. Serve with steamed rice and warm flour tortillas.

3 pounds boneless stewing beef or chuck roast, cut into 1-inch cubes
$^1/_3$ cup potato starch (not potato flour)
Salt and freshly ground black pepper
3 tablespoons olive oil
1 large yellow or white onion, finely chopped
4 cloves garlic, minced
2 teaspoons ground cumin
1 (28-ounce) can whole tomatoes in juice
2 canned chipotle chiles in adobo plus 2 tablespoons adobo sauce
1 cup water
1 (1-pound) package wet-packed posole, rinsed several times, or 1 (15.5-ounce) can hominy, drained and rinsed

1. In a large bowl, toss the beef with the potato starch, salt, and pepper to coat evenly.
2. In a 5- to 7-quart pressure cooker, heat half of the oil over medium-high heat until very hot. Brown the meat on all sides in batches in a single layer, 3 to 4 minutes per batch, adding the remaining oil as needed. Transfer the browned meat to the bowl.
3. Add the onion and garlic to the pot, reduce the heat to medium, and cook 1 to 2 minutes, stirring. Return the meat and any accumulated juice to the pot, and add the cumin. Cook 5 minutes.
4. Puree the tomatoes with their juice, the chiles and adobo sauce, and water in a blender or with an immersion blender until smooth. Add to the pot along with the posole and stir to combine.
5. Close and lock the lid. Set the burner heat to high. When the cooker reaches HIGH pressure, reduce the burner heat as low as you can and still maintain HIGH pressure. Set a timer to cook for 20 minutes.
6. Remove the pot from the heat. Open the cooker with the Quick Release method. Be careful of the steam as you remove the lid. Taste for salt. Serve immediately, but this is also really good reheated the next day.

Beef Curry with Apples and Bananas

Serves 4 • Cooker: 5- to 7-quart • Time: 20 minutes at HIGH pressure

This curry, with the unusual addition of chopped fresh fruit, came from a precious little book published in Australia called *How a Pressure Cooker Saved My Life* by Juanita Phillips. She wrote about a painful divorce and her adventures in the kitchen with her pressure cooker to keep busy while transitioning her life. Fast forward to a copy of Jacques Pepin's *Short Order Cook,* which was published in 1990 with his timesaving home-cooking recipes. And there was a recipe, designed for the pressure cooker, for a lamb curry with chopped fresh fruit. We had never seen a recipe like it before. So there was the original inspiration for this beef curry. Leave it to Jacques to add a banana to make a sauce for the warm spicy curry in place of the Indian use of mango in curries. The fruit will temper and complement the curry flavor as well as add texture to the *khari*, or sauce. Use a fresh curry powder blend, not one that has sat on your shelf for years. Ideally you should replace your tinned or jarred curry powder every 6 months.

2 tablespoons olive oil
2 pounds boneless stewing beef or chuck roast, cut
    into 2-inch cubes
1 large yellow or white onion, chopped
2 cloves garlic, minced
1 tablespoon grated peeled fresh ginger
2 teaspoons Madras curry powder, mild or hot
$^1/_2$ teaspoon ground cumin
2 cooking apples (such as McIntosh), cored and
    diced (don't peel)
1 firm ripe banana, peeled and cut into 1-inch-thick
    slices
1 (15.5-ounce) can diced tomatoes in juice
1 cup beef broth
2 tablespoons tomato paste
1 cup coconut cream (extra-thick coconut milk) or
    full-fat unsweetened coconut milk, can
    unshaken, and top poured off to measure
Sea salt and freshly ground black pepper

1. In a 5- to 7-quart pressure cooker, heat 1 tablespoon of the oil over medium-high heat until very hot. Add half the beef and brown on all sides in a single layer, 3 to 4 minutes total, then transfer to a bowl. Add the remaining 1 tablespoon oil and beef, brown, and transfer to the bowl.

2. Add the onion to the pot, reduce the heat to medium, and cook, stirring, 1 to 2 minutes. Return the meat and any accumulated juice to the pot, along with the garlic, ginger, curry powder, and cumin. Cook, stirring, for 2 minutes. Add the apple, banana, tomatoes with their juice, and broth. Add the tomato paste on top. Do not stir it in.

3. Close and lock the lid. Set the burner heat to high. When the cooker reaches HIGH pressure, reduce the burner heat as low as you can and still maintain HIGH pressure. Set a timer to cook for 20 minutes.

4. Remove the pot from the heat. Open the cooker with the Quick Release method. Be careful of the steam as you remove the lid.

5. Stir in the coconut cream, bring to a high simmer, and heat a few minutes, uncovered. Season to taste with salt and pepper. Serve immediately with basmati rice or noodles; this is also really good reheated the next day.

Guinness Beef Stew

Serves 4 to 6 • Cooker: 5- to 8-quart • Time: 20 minutes at HIGH pressure

For the meat, skip the extra lean stew meat for a nice chuck roast with a bit more fat. The flavor will be remarkably better blended with the Guinness. We have a bit of a love affair going with Guinness as our liquid of choice in meat stews. It is so much more satisfying than water, wine, or just broth, with a slightly bitter edge. Open the bottle of beer and let it sit 30 minutes before adding to the pot (you don't need all the fizzle). This is good as an alternative to corned beef for St. Patrick's Day.

2½ pounds beef chuck, fat trimmed and cut into
    1½-inch chunks
3 tablespoons all-purpose flour
3 teaspoons sea salt, plus more to taste if needed
Freshly ground black pepper
2 tablespoons olive oil
1 (18-ounce) bottle Guinness beer, at room
    temperature
1 large white onion, chopped
4 medium cloves garlic, minced
3 large carrots, cut into 1-inch chunks
4 ribs celery, diced
1½ cups beef broth
2 teaspoons Worcestershire sauce
1 bay leaf

1. In a large bowl, toss the beef with the flour, 1 teaspoon of the salt, and pepper to taste. In a 5- to 8-quart pressure cooker, heat 1 tablespoon of the oil over medium-high heat until very hot. Add enough of the beef cubes to the pot to form a single layer (about a third), being careful not to overcrowd the pot. Brown the meat on all sides, 5 to 6 minutes total, then transfer the meat to a large bowl. Brown the remaining beef in two batches and transfer to the bowl. If the meat or pan juices start to scorch, reduce the heat.

2. Add the bottle of Guinness to the pot. Scrape up any browned bits from the bottom. Pour the ale over the beef, return the empty pot to medium-high heat, and add the remaining 1 tablespoon oil to the pot. Add the onion and remaining 2 teaspoons salt; cook, stirring often, 2 minutes. Partially cover the pot (do not lock) and reduce the heat to low. Cook, stirring occasionally, until the onion has a hint of gold color, about 10 minutes.

3. Add the garlic, carrots, and celery and cook, stirring, for 2 minutes. Return the beef to the pot with the ale. Add the broth, Worcestershire, and bay leaf.

4. Close and lock the lid. Set the burner heat to high. When the cooker reaches HIGH pressure, reduce the burner heat as low as you can and still maintain HIGH pressure. Set a timer to cook for 20 minutes.

5. Remove the pot from the heat. Open the cooker with the Quick Release method. Be careful of the steam as you remove the lid. Skim off any fat and discard the bay leaf.

6. Season to taste with salt and pepper. Serve immediately or you can let cool and refrigerate in an airtight container up to 2 days or freeze up to 1 month.

Beef Stew with Turnips, Pearl Onions, and Mushrooms

Serves 4 • Cooker: 5- to 7-quart • Time: 15 minutes for stew, 5 minutes for vegetables at HIGH pressure

We say, eat more turnips! This hearty stew is a great way to start.

2 tablespoons olive oil
$1^1/_2$ pounds boneless beef chuck roast, cut into $1^1/_2$-inch cubes
2 cloves garlic, chopped
$1^1/_2$ cups sliced ($^1/_2$-inch-thick) celery, widest slices halved crosswise
$^1/_2$ pound small white or cremini mushrooms, halved or quartered
$2^1/_2$ cups water
1 teaspoon sea salt, plus more to taste
$^1/_2$ teaspoon freshly ground black pepper, plus more to taste
2 cups peeled turnip wedges (about 2 medium turnips)
4 medium carrots, cut into $^1/_2$- to $^3/_4$-inch rounds
1 (16-ounce) bag frozen whole pearl onions, thawed
2 large russet potatoes, peeled and cut into 1-inch cubes

TURNIPS

Turnips are a root vegetable commonly associated with potatoes, but their closest relatives are—surprisingly—peppery radishes and arugula, all three of them being members of the mustard family. Turnips are often overlooked, but they are fantastic in stews or mashed, so they are quite at home in the pressure cooker. Turnips are at their best in fall and spring, when they are small and at their sweetest; the larger bulbs can be quite hot. Baby turnips are a bit of a delicacy and look like somewhat large white spring radishes; these are great left whole in stews. Look for turnips with their greens attached, which says they are freshly harvested. Remove the greens to store in the produce drawer of your fridge.

1. In a 5- to 7-quart pressure cooker, heat 1 tablespoon of the oil over medium-high heat until very hot. Brown the meat in batches in a single layer, adding more of the oil as needed. Transfer the meat to a plate as it is browned.
2. Add the garlic and celery to the pot, reduce the heat to medium, and cook, stirring, 1 to 2 minutes. Return the meat and any accumulated juice to the pot, along with the mushrooms, water, salt, and pepper.
3. Close and lock the lid. Set the burner heat to high. When the cooker reaches HIGH pressure, reduce the burner heat as low as you can and still maintain HIGH pressure. Set a timer to cook for 15 minutes.
4. Remove the pot from the heat. Open the cooker with the Quick Release method. Be careful of the steam as you remove the lid. Skim off any fat.
5. Add the turnips, carrots, onions, and potatoes to the pot. Relock the cooker, bring back up to HIGH pressure, and cook for 5 minutes. Remove the pot from the heat. Open the cooker with the Quick Release method.
6. Season to taste with salt and pepper. Serve immediately or enjoy reheated the next day.

Our Best Pot Roast with Root Vegetables

Serves 4 to 6 • Cooker: 6- to 8-quart • Time: 35 minutes for meat, 2 minutes for vegetables at HIGH pressure

This simple, old-fashioned home-style pot roast is sublimely delicious and meltingly tender. If you see a nice chuck roast, grab it to make this. Some cooks like a rump roast for pot roast, but it takes double the cook time as chuck, which is also more tender and flavorful. Look for a thick piece. If it is too big to lay flat in your pressure cooker, cut it in half and stack the pieces one atop the other. Take the time to chop the vegetables properly. Don't forget fresh bread or dinner rolls to soak up the juices.

2 tablespoons olive oil, or as needed

1 (3- to 3^1/$_2$-pound) boneless chuck roast, trimmed of as much fat as possible and blotted dry

^{1}/$_2$ teaspoon salt

^{1}/$_4$ teaspoon freshly ground black pepper

^{1}/$_4$ pound thick-sliced pancetta, diced, OR ^{1}/$_2$ cup finely chopped thin-sliced prosciutto

3 cups beef broth

^{3}/$_4$ cup fruity dry red wine like Chianti, Barolo, or Pinot Noir

3 sprigs fresh thyme and a few parsley stems, tied securely together with kitchen twine

1 cup diced carrots (about 2 medium)

1 cup diced parsnips (about 2 medium)

1 cup diced celery, including some leaves (about 4 stalks)

1 cup diced turnips (1 or 2 medium)

1 medium leek (white part only), trimmed, cut in half lengthwise, rinsed well, and thinly sliced across

1 large white onion, cut into 8 wedges

4 medium red or Yukon Gold potatoes, each quartered

2 tablespoons all-purpose flour

1. In a 6- to 8-quart pressure cooker, heat the oil over medium heat until very hot. Add the beef and brown well on all sides. When well browned, remove the meat from the cooker, and season it with the salt and pepper. Add the pancetta to the pot and sauté over medium-high heat until browned and the fat is rendered, about 3 minutes. (If using prosciutto, just add with the liquid.) Add the broth, wine, and herb bundle; bring to a boil. Return the beef to the cooker.

2. Close and lock the lid. Set the burner heat to high. When the cooker reaches HIGH pressure, reduce the burner heat as low as you can and still maintain HIGH pressure. Set a timer to cook for 35 minutes.

3. Remove the pot from the heat. Open the cooker with the Quick Release method. Be careful of the steam as you remove the lid.

4. Add the carrots, parsnips, celery, turnips, leek, onion, and potatoes to the cooker. Relock the lid. Bring the cooker back up to HIGH pressure and cook for 2 minutes. Remove the pot from the heat. Open the cooker with the Natural Release method; let stand for 15 minutes. The root vegetables should be cooked through and the meat fork-tender.

5. Using a slotted spoon, transfer the meat and vegetables to a rimmed serving platter and tent with aluminum foil to keep warm. Discard the herb bundle.

6. Let the cooking liquid stand for 5 minutes. Skim any fat from the surface. Strain the cooking liquid through a cheesecloth-lined sieve into an oversized measuring cup or batter bowl. Discard the solids. Set aside ^{1}/$_4$ cup cooking liquid. Return the savory liquid to the pressure cooker and bring to a boil. Whisk the flour into the reserved ^{1}/$_4$ cup liquid and stir with a whisk to remove lumps. Pour into the hot liquid and whisk a few minutes to thicken the liquid.

7. Slice the pot roast into ^{1}/$_2$-inch-thick slices against the grain. Serve it with the vegetables and gravy.

Bison Pot Roast: Substitute 1 (2- to 2^1/$_2$-pound) bison inside round roast for the boneless chuck roast. Prepare as directed.

Beer-Braised Corned Beef and Cabbage

Serves 4 to 8 • Cooker: 6- to 8-quart • Time: 60 minutes for meat, 6 minutes for vegetables at HIGH pressure

Corned beef is one of the most popular dishes in the pressure cooker. Look for the flat piece of beef instead of the big roast. Cooking it with beer (I prefer Guinness or a craft beer like oatmeal stout) will make a much more flavorful broth than just water alone, but you can use chicken or vegetable broth instead if you want. No extra salt is needed for cooking; the cured meat has enough. Any leftovers make great Reuben sandwiches with sauerkraut and rye bread.

1 (12-ounce) bottle beer, strong or mild-flavored, as desired
2 cups water or as needed
2 large white or yellow onions, each cut into 6 wedges
3 cloves garlic, peeled and smashed
1 (3- to 4-pound) corned beef brisket with pickling spice seasoning packet, rinsed
6 medium red potatoes, quartered
4 medium carrots, cut into 2-inch chunks on the diagonal
1 medium head white cabbage, cut into 8 wedges, each securely tied with kitchen twine
Dijon mustard, for serving
Prepared horseradish, for serving

1. In a 6- to 8-quart pressure cooker, combine the beer, water, onions, garlic, and corned beef pickling spices (first wrap the spices in a double thickness of cheesecloth and tie it shut). Place the corned beef on top; don't worry if it touches the sides of the pot. If the meat is too big to lay flat in your cooker, cut it in half and stack the pieces one atop the other. Bring the liquid to a boil over medium-high heat.

2. Close and lock the lid. Set the burner heat to high. When the cooker reaches HIGH pressure, reduce the burner heat as low as you can and still maintain HIGH pressure. Set a timer to cook for 60 minutes.

3. Remove the pot from the heat. Open the cooker with the Natural Release method; let stand for 15 minutes. Be careful of the steam as you remove the lid. Discard the spice bag. Transfer the meat to a platter and, using a slotted spoon, remove the onions to a serving bowl; leave the garlic in the pot. Tent both with aluminum foil to keep warm.

4. Add the potatoes and carrots to the cooker and place the cabbage wedges on top. Close and lock the lid. When the cooker reaches HIGH pressure, reduce the burner heat as low as you can and still maintain HIGH pressure. Set a timer to cook for 6 minutes.

5. Remove the pot from the heat. Open with the Natural Release method; let stand for 15 minutes. Quick Release any remaining pressure. The root vegetables should be cooked through and cabbage crisp-tender. Using a slotted spoon, remove the vegetables to the bowl with the onions.

6. Serve the corned beef, sliced across the grain, in thin slices arranged over a bed of the vegetables. Spoon some of the broth over all and serve with the mustard, horseradish, a cabbage wedge for each serving, and more juices from the pot on the side. Good with fresh rye bread or Beth's Seeded Irish Soda Bread (page opposite).

Beth's Seeded Irish Soda Bread

Makes 2 round loaves

Soda bread is basically a large scone. This recipe comes from Beth's Irish side of the family, a few decades back. It is a must with corned beef or brisket. Day-old it makes great toast.

3 cups unbleached all-purpose flour, plus more for
    sprinkling
$^1/_4$ cup firmly packed light brown sugar
2 tablespoons *each* sunflower seeds, flax seeds,
    and pumpkin seeds
1 teaspoon *each* sesame seeds, poppy seeds, and
    fennel seeds or caraway seeds
1 tablespoon baking powder
1 teaspoon baking soda
1 teaspoon salt
$^1/_4$ cup ($^1/_2$ stick) cold unsalted butter, cut into
    pieces
1 to 1$^1/_4$ cups cold buttermilk, as needed
1 large egg
1 large egg yolk

1. Preheat the oven to 400° F. Line a baking sheet with parchment paper.
2. In the work bowl of a heavy duty stand mixer fitted with the paddle attachment, combine the flour, sugar, seeds, baking powder and soda, and salt. Add the butter pieces on low speed and mix just until soft, thick crumbs are formed.
3. Add 1 cup of the buttermilk, the whole egg, and egg yolk. Mix on medium-low speed until the dough forms a rough, soft mass. Adjust the consistency with a few more tablespoons of buttermilk, if necessary. You want the dough to be able to hold its own shape but still be soft and pliable.
4. Turn the dough out onto a lightly floured work surface and knead gently, sprinkling with flour as needed to prevent sticking, until the sticky dough just comes together and makes a smooth surface, no more than 5 to 10 times. You can leave the dough quite soft or a bit stiffer, depending on how dense you like your soda bread.
5. Divide the dough into 2 equal portions with a knife, and knead each a few times to make a smooth round. Do not overwork the dough. Dust 2 tablespoons of flour on the work surface and roll the top surface of the loaves in the flour to coat. Place the loaves on the prepared baking sheet about 6 inches apart and place another baking sheet of the same size underneath to prevent burning. With a small sharp knife or kitchen shears, slash the tops with a large X about $^1/_2$ inch deep. Bake until dark brown and crusty, 35 to 40 minutes. A cake tester inserted into the center of the X should come out clean.
6. Serve cut into thick slices with a serrated bread knife, warm or room temperature. Freeze in a large plastic freezer bag, whole or in slices, up to 1 month.

Beth's Irish Soda Bread with Golden Raisins and Tart Cherries: Omit all of the seeds. Add 1$^1/_4$ cups mixed golden raisins and dried tart cherries in Step 3 with the buttermilk.

Brisket with Mushrooms and Red Wine

Serves 8 • Cooker: 5- to 8-quart • Time: 60 minutes at HIGH pressure (plus 30 minutes in oven)

This is a mushroom-lovers' delight, with both fresh and dried varieties contributing their savory goodness. For the fresh mushrooms, use whatever looks best at your grocer. For the dried, porcini is a favorite, but the dried mushroom blends that are sometimes available are nice, too. Be sure to rinse the rehydrated mushrooms well before using to remove any unwanted grit. With brisket, for the best results, after the meat is pressure cooked to tenderness, slice it and heat it in the sauce so that its flavor permeates the meat. (Another option is to refrigerate the sliced brisket with the sauce overnight; then you can skim the fat off the top before reheating.)

$^1/_4$ cup dried porcini or wild mushroom blend
1 cup water
1 (4-pound) center-cut beef brisket (flat half)
$^3/_4$ teaspoon salt
$^1/_4$ teaspoon freshly ground black pepper
2 tablespoons olive oil
1 large onion, chopped into $^1/_2$-inch pieces
3 cloves garlic, chopped
2 medium carrots, sliced into $^1/_2$-inch-thick rounds
$^1/_2$ pound fresh white mushrooms, sliced
$2^1/_2$ cups red wine
2 cups reduced-sodium beef broth

1. Place the dried mushrooms in a microwave-safe medium bowl or 2-cup Pyrex measuring cup. Add the water and cover tightly with plastic wrap. Microwave on HIGH for 2 minutes. Remove the wrap. When the mushrooms are cool enough to touch, gently transfer them to a small plate, reserving the liquid. One or two pieces at a time, rinse the mushrooms under cool running water, rubbing them between your fingers to remove any grit. Once all of the mushrooms have been rinsed, carefully pour the soaking liquid through a strainer lined with a coffee filter or paper towel, stopping before you get to the last bit of the liquid, which will almost certainly be gritty.

2. Trim most of the visible fat away from the brisket and cut the meat into quarters. Season the meat with salt and pepper. In a 5- to 8-quart pressure cooker, heat the oil over medium-high heat until very hot. Add one or two pieces of brisket to the pot and brown, turning as necessary, about 3 minutes per side. As the brisket pieces are browned, remove them to a plate. Brown all the pieces.

3. Add the onion to the pot and cook 2 to 3 minutes, stirring. Add the garlic, carrots, and fresh mushrooms and continue to cook, stirring, until the mushrooms are fragrant. Stir in the reconstituted dried mushrooms. Using tongs, scoop out about two-thirds of the vegetables, placing them on the plate with the brisket. Stack the brisket pieces in the pot, tucking some of the vegetables in between the pieces of meat and spreading the remaining ones on top. Pour in the wine, broth, and strained mushroom soaking liquid.

4. Close and lock the lid. Set the burner heat to high. When the cooker reaches HIGH pressure, reduce the burner heat as low as you can and still maintain HIGH pressure. Set a timer to cook for 60 minutes.

5. Remove the pot from the heat. Open the cooker with the Quick Release method. Be careful of the steam as you remove the lid.

6. Preheat the oven to 350° F. Transfer the meat to a cutting board and slice it across the grain about $^1/_3$ inch thick. Arrange the sliced meat in a casserole dish and top with the sauce and vegetables, making sure that the sauce gets between the slices of meat. Cover with a lid or aluminum foil and bake for 30 minutes. Serve with noodles, mashed potatoes, rice, or couscous. Leftovers will keep in an airtight container in the refrigerator 4 to 5 days or in the freezer up to 4 months.

Barbecue-Style Brisket

Serves 8 • Cooker: 5- to 8-quart • Time: 60 minutes at HIGH pressure (plus 30 minutes in oven)

True barbecued brisket requires long cooking and some serious smoke. But with the magic of the pressure cooker, the cook time gets cut to an hour. For best results, the meat then should be sliced and heated in the cooking liquid so that its flavors permeate the meat. (If you can slice the meat, refrigerate it in the sauce overnight, and reheat it the next day, you can skim the fat and you will enhance the flavor further.) This brisket isn't really barbecued; rather it's pressure-cooked in a tangy tomato sauce that you stir together in moments. If you are a brisket newbie, two things to know: You will need to trim away a good deal of fat, and brisket shrinks quite a bit as it cooks. For that reason, we always figure close to one-half pound per person. If you're lucky, you might have enough left over for a sandwich the next day.

1 (4-pound) center-cut beef brisket (flat half)
1 teaspoon salt, plus more to taste
$^1/_4$ teaspoon freshly ground black pepper, plus
    more to taste
2 teaspoons smoked Spanish paprika (pimentón)
1 (28-ounce) can whole tomatoes in juice
$^1/_4$ cup firmly packed light brown sugar
3 tablespoons balsamic vinegar
1 tablespoon chili powder
1 teaspoon Worcestershire sauce
$^1/_2$ teaspoon dry mustard (like Colman's)
$^1/_2$ teaspoon garlic powder
$^1/_4$ teaspoon ground cumin
$^1/_4$ teaspoon ground ginger
$^1/_4$ teaspoon ground allspice
$^1/_8$ teaspoon ground cloves
2 tablespoons olive oil
1 large onion, sliced $^1/_2$ inch thick

1. Trim most of the visible fat away from the brisket and cut the meat into quarters. Season the meat with salt, pepper, and 1 teaspoon of the paprika.
2. In a blender or food processor, puree the canned tomatoes with their juice, brown sugar, vinegar, chili powder, Worcestershire, mustard, garlic powder, spices, and remaining 1 teaspoon paprika together until smooth.
3. In a 5- to 8-quart pressure cooker, heat the oil over medium-high heat until very hot. Add one or two pieces of brisket to the pot and brown, turning as necessary, about 3 minutes per side. As the brisket pieces are browned, remove them to a plate. Brown all the pieces.
4. Add the onion to the pot and cook for 2 to 3 minutes, stirring. Using tongs, scoop out about two-thirds of the onion, placing it on the plate with the brisket. Stack the brisket pieces in the pot, tucking onion in between the pieces of meat and spreading the remainder on top. Pour in the tomato sauce.
5. Close and lock the lid. Set the burner heat to high. When the cooker reaches HIGH pressure, reduce the burner heat as low as you can and still maintain HIGH pressure. Set a timer to cook for 60 minutes.
6. Remove the pot from the heat. Open the cooker with the Quick Release method. Be careful of the steam as you remove the lid.
7. Preheat the oven to 350° F. Transfer the meat to a cutting board and slice it across the grain about $^1/_3$ inch thick. Arrange the sliced meat in a casserole dish and top with the sauce and cooked onion, making sure that the sauce gets between the slices of meat. Cover with a lid or aluminum foil and bake for 30 minutes.
8. Serve with noodles, mashed potatoes, or latkes. Leftovers will keep in an airtight container in the refrigerator 4 to 5 days or in the freezer up to 4 months.

Our Horseradish Sauces

Horseradish sauce is a natural partner for beef, from roast beef, pot roast, and corned beef to brisket and prime rib. It is also good with salmon or cooked beets. Most of the recipes call for jarred prepared horseradish, which contains vinegar, but you can grate your own if you find horseradish root in your produce section. It is a white tapered root and member of the same family as mustard, wasabi, broccoli, and cabbage. You can store the root in the freezer and grate it as needed. Once you make the sauce, cover and let set in the refrigerator at least 2 hours to meld the flavors. Serve each portion with a tablespoon or two.

How to Grate Horseradish in a Food Processor

1. Wash the horseradish root thoroughly and peel well with a vegetable peeler. Cut the root into 2-inch pieces.
2. Place in a quart plastic freezer bag and place in the freezer for a few hours.
3. Fit the food processor bowl with a coarse grating wheel and put the horseradish pieces in the chute without overstuffing it. Turn on the machine and push the pieces through with the plunger. This is the best way to grate horseradish as it can be very potent once it is grated, so be prepared to open a window if necessary. Use immediately since it can darken and become bitter if not mixed with lemon or vinegar.

Yogurt Horseradish Sauce

Makes about 1$\frac{1}{4}$ cups

1 cup plain Greek yogurt or lowfat plain yogurt
2 tablespoons mayonnaise or Veganaise soy mayonnaise
1 to 3 tablespoons prepared horseradish, to taste
1$\frac{1}{2}$ tablespoons Champagne vinegar or orange juice
2 pinches sea salt
Few grinds black pepper

In a medium bowl, combine all the ingredients and whisk until smooth. Taste and adjust salt. Refrigerate in an airtight container for at least 2 hours and up to 2 days.

Light and Creamy Mustard Horseradish Sauce

Makes about 2 cups

1 cup reduced-fat sour cream
$\frac{3}{4}$ cup plain Greek yogurt or lowfat plain yogurt
$\frac{1}{4}$ cup freshly grated peeled horseradish
2 teaspoons Dijon mustard
2 pinches sea salt
Few grinds black pepper

In a medium bowl, combine all the ingredients and whisk until smooth. Taste and adjust the salt. Refrigerate in an airtight container for at least 2 hours and up to 3 days.

Lemon-Horseradish Whipped Cream

Makes about 1$\frac{1}{4}$ cups

$\frac{1}{2}$ cup chilled heavy cream
2 tablespoons prepared white horseradish
2 teaspoons freshly minced chives
2 tablespoons fresh lemon juice
Sea salt and freshly ground black pepper
Grated zest of $\frac{1}{2}$ lemon, for garnish

In a medium bowl with an electric mixer, beat the cream until almost stiff peaks form. Slowly add the horseradish, chives, and lemon juice and continue to beat together. Season to taste with salt and pepper. Garnish the top with the lemon zest. Refrigerate in an airtight container for at least 2 hours and up to 2 days.

Sour Cream Horseradish Sauce

Makes about 2$\frac{1}{2}$ cups

2 cups sour cream
$\frac{1}{4}$ to $\frac{1}{2}$ cup prepared horseradish, to your taste
3 tablespoons Champagne vinegar
2 pinches sea salt

In a medium bowl, combine all the ingredients and whisk until smooth. Taste and adjust the salt. Refrigerate in an airtight container for at least 2 hours and up to 2 days.

Apple Cider Brisket with a Kick

Serves 8 • Cooker: 5- to 8-quart • Time: 60 minutes at HIGH pressure (plus 30 minutes in oven)

When it comes to creamy horseradish sauce, there are mayonnaise people and there are sour cream people. We like it both ways—so make your own choice! As with all braised briskets, this one tastes better the second day.

BRISKET:
1 (4-pound) center-cut beef brisket (flat half)
1 teaspoon salt
$1/4$ teaspoon freshly ground black pepper
2 tablespoons olive oil
2 medium to large yellow onions, sliced $1/2$ inch thick
$1/2$ teaspoon dried rosemary
$1/2$ teaspoon dried thyme
1 (12-ounce) bottle or can hard cider
1 cup apple cider or apple juice

JULIE'S CREAMY HORSERADISH SAUCE:
$1/2$ cup mayonnaise or sour cream, regular or low-fat (not nonfat)
2 to 3 tablespoons prepared white horseradish, to taste
1 teaspoon cider vinegar
Pinch sugar

1. Trim most of the visible fat away from the brisket and cut the meat into quarters. Season the meat with salt and pepper. In a 5- to 8-quart pressure cooker, heat the oil over medium-high heat until very hot. Add one or two pieces of brisket to the pot and brown, turning as necessary, about 3 minutes per side. As the brisket pieces are browned, remove them to a plate. Brown all the pieces.

2. Add the onions to the pot and cook for 2 to 3 minutes, stirring. Using tongs, transfer out about two thirds of the onions to the plate with the brisket. Stack the brisket pieces in the pot, tucking some of the onions in between the pieces of meat and spreading the remaining ones on top. Pour in both ciders and sprinkle in the rosemary and thyme.

3. Close and lock the lid. Set the burner heat to high. When the cooker reaches HIGH pressure, reduce the burner heat as low as you can and still maintain HIGH pressure. Set a timer to cook for 60 minutes.

4. Prepare the horseradish sauce. In a small bowl, stir the mayonnaise or sour cream together with 2 tablespoons of the horseradish, the vinegar, and sugar. Taste the sauce and add more horseradish if desired. Cover and refrigerate until serving time.

5. Remove the pot from the heat. Open the cooker with the Quick Release method. Be careful of the steam as you remove the lid.

6. Preheat the oven to 350° F. Transfer the meat to a cutting board and slice it across the grain about $1/3$ inch thick. Arrange the sliced meat in a casserole dish and top with the cooking liquid and onions, making sure that the sauce gets between the slices of meat. Cover with a lid or aluminum foil and bake for 30 minutes.

7. Serve with mashed potatoes or egg noodles, with the horseradish sauce on the side. Leftovers will keep in an airtight container in the refrigerator 4 to 5 days or the freezer up to 4 months (Do not freeze the horseradish sauce.)

HARD CIDER

We have always enjoyed hard cider, so we feel the current renaissance in local hard ciders is something to be celebrated. Cider is pressed from apples specifically grown for the drink and there are only about ten varieties; traditionally it is made with one third each of sweet, bittersweet, and sharp apples. Hard cider is brewed in many styles, but the ones you are most likely to find on U.S. shelves are mildly fizzy and relatively low in alcohol. Some are sweeter; some are on the dry side. Pear cider is also popular. For this recipe, choose any hard apple or pear cider that you like, along with the fresh apple cider (unfiltered apple juice).

Brisket with Lemon, Dates, and Quince

Serves 8 • Cooker: 5- to 8-quart • Time: 55 minutes for brisket, 5 minutes for quince at HIGH pressure (plus 30 minutes in oven)

You can make this brisket with pears or apples instead of the quince, but those fruits do not hold their shapes as well.

1 (4-pound) center-cut beef brisket (flat half)
1 teaspoon salt
1 teaspoon sweet Hungarian paprika
$^{1}/_{4}$ teaspoon freshly ground black pepper
2 tablespoons olive oil
1 medium onion, sliced $^{1}/_{2}$ inch thick
1 lemon, washed and thinly sliced, rind and all
2 large dates (such as Medjool) or 3 smaller ones, pitted and roughly chopped
$2^{1}/_{2}$ cups water
1 (3-inch) cinnamon stick
4 or 5 saffron threads (optional)
2 large quinces or 3 large apples or firm-ripe pears

1. Trim most of the visible fat away from the brisket and cut the meat into quarters. Season the meat with the salt, paprika, and pepper on both sides. In a 5- to 8-quart pressure cooker, heat the oil over medium-high heat until very hot. Add one or two pieces of brisket to the pot and brown, turning as necessary, about 3 minutes per side. As the brisket pieces are browned, remove them to a plate. Brown all the pieces.
2. Add the onion to the pot and cook for 2 to 3 minutes, stirring. Using tongs, transfer about two thirds of the onion to the plate with the brisket. Place a few lemon slices and date pieces on the onion left in the pot, then stack the brisket pieces on top, tucking some more of the onion, the dates, and lemon slices in between the pieces of meat and spreading the remainder on top. Pour in the water and add the cinnamon stick and saffron threads if using.
3. Close and lock the lid. Set the burner heat to high. When the cooker reaches HIGH pressure, reduce the burner heat as low as you can and still maintain HIGH pressure. Set a timer to cook for 55 minutes.
4. When the 55 minutes are nearly up, cut the quinces in half, remove the seeds, and core them with a melon-ball cutter or sharp paring knife.

Peel the quinces, then cut the halves into $^{1}/_{2}$-inch-thick slices, or use the $^{1}/_{2}$-inch slicer disc on a food processor (frankly, this is a great way to cut all the hard fruit evenly and quickly).
5. Remove the pot from the heat. Open the cooker with the Quick Release method. Be careful of the steam as you remove the lid.
6. Add the fruit, distributing it as evenly as possible over the meat. Relock the cooker, bring it back up to HIGH pressure, and cook for 5 minutes. Remove the pot from the heat. Open the cooker with the Quick Release method.
7. Preheat the oven to 350° F. Carefully transfer the meat to a cutting board and slice it across the grain about $^{1}/_{3}$ inch thick. Arrange the sliced meat and fruit in a casserole dish and top with the sauce, making sure that the sauce gets between the slices of meat. Cover with a lid or aluminum foil and bake for 30 minutes.
8. Serve with rice or couscous. Leftovers will keep in an airtight container in the refrigerator 4 to 5 days or the freezer up to 4 months.

QUINCE

The fragrant quince is an ancient fruit, and today it is more appreciated in the Middle East, Europe, and Latin America than in the United States. In this country, the quince is almost completely eclipsed by its relatives, the apple and pear, which, granted, are easier to cut and core. Another difference is that quinces are inedible raw—they must be cooked before eating. We think it's a shame that the quince is a virtual unknown here, as it has an alluring aroma, gentle, spicy-sweet flavor, and a delightfully toothsome texture when cooked. Look for quince in the fall and winter; try a Middle Eastern market or farmers' market if they aren't in your supermarket.

Red Wine-Braised Beef Cheeks with Fennel and Sherry

Serves 4 • Cooker: 5- to 8-quart • Time: 90 minutes at HIGH pressure

Beef cheeks, a throwback to the days of nose to tail butchering, have been showing up on restaurant menus. It is a cut of meat you need to ask for at a butcher counter and might need to order ahead. It is a cut similar to brisket and osso bucco in that it is so lean that the only way to cook it is to braise it for a good long while (without the pressure cooker the cook time would be over 3 hours). The result is meat that is silky smooth in texture, deeply flavorful, and meltingly tender. Give the slices of beef plenty of room to brown. Pedro Ximenez sherry is a sweet dessert wine made from sun-dried raisins in the south of Spain. It is excellent with chocolate, so we've added a bit of unsweetened cocoa to the braise; use good quality cocoa for the best flavor. This dish really improves with some age in the fridge—we like to make it two days ahead of when we plan to serve it. If you do make it ahead, place a sheet of parchment or wax paper right on the surface. Cover with a lid and chill. Remove any solidified fat before reheating. Serve with mashed potatoes or polenta.

3 tablespoons olive oil or avocado oil
1 large white onion, finely chopped
1 clove garlic, chopped
2 medium carrots, finely chopped
1 rib celery, finely chopped
1 cup finely chopped fennel bulb
4 (12-ounce) beef cheeks, trimmed of excess fat
    and gristle
Sea salt and freshly ground black pepper
1 cup unbleached all-purpose flour, spelt flour, or
    potato starch, on a plate for dredging
1$^1/_2$ cups dry red wine
1 (28- to 32-ounce) can whole tomatoes in juice,
    crushed with your hands (3 cups)
3 tablespoons Pedro Ximenez sherry or port
1 tablespoon unsweetened cocoa powder
2 tablespoons tomato paste
1 bay leaf
4 strips orange zest

1. Heat half the oil in a wide sauté pan over medium-high heat. Add the onion, garlic, carrots, celery, and fennel and cook for a few minutes, stirring. Transfer to a 5- to 8-quart pressure cooker.

2. Season the beef with salt and pepper, then dredge in the flour, tapping off any excess. Heat the remaining oil in the sauté pan over medium-high heat until very hot, add one or two beef cheeks (if only one will fit, do one at a time) and brown on both sides, about 1 minute per side, no more. Take care not to crowd the pan. As the cheeks are browned, remove them to the pressure cooker, stacking them with some vegetables in between. Pour in the wine and bring to a boil. Boil a minute or two.

3. Add the crushed tomatoes with their juice, sherry, and cocoa and stir in. Add the tomato paste; do not stir in. Season to taste with salt and pepper, then tuck in the bay leaf and strips of orange zest.

4. Close and lock the lid. Set the burner heat to high. When the cooker reaches HIGH pressure, reduce the burner heat as low as you can and still maintain HIGH pressure. Set a timer to cook for 90 minutes Discard the bay leaf and orange zest strips.

5. Remove the cooker from the heat. Open the cooker with the Quick Release method. Be careful of the steam as you remove the lid. Discard the bay leaf and orange zest strips.

6. Carefully remove the meat to a deep, wide serving platter. Spoon the vegetables and sauce over the meat to serve.

Zinfandel-Braised Short Ribs with Salsa Verde

Serves 4 • Cooker: 5- to 7-quart • Time: 30 minutes at HIGH pressure

This quintessential wine-braised short rib recipe comes from the vastly creative culinary mind of Peggy Fallon. Serve with a mound of fluffy mashed potatoes or our Winter Root Mash (page 451).

SHORT RIBS:

2$^1/_2$ to 3 pounds bone-in beef short ribs (6 to 8 ribs), trimmed of excess fat and silverskin
2 teaspoons salt
12 grinds freshly ground black pepper
$^1/_4$ cup all-purpose flour
3 tablespoons olive oil
2 medium onions, halved and cut into $^1/_2$-inch-thick half moons
2 medium carrots, cut into 1-inch chunks
2 ribs celery, chopped
1 tablespoon tomato paste
1$^1/_2$ cups beef or chicken broth
1 cup Zinfandel or other dry red wine
1 tablespoon chopped fresh thyme
1 bay leaf

SALSA VERDE:

1 clove garlic, smashed with the flat side of a knife, peel removed
1 oil-packed anchovy fillet
Pinch salt, plus more to taste
1 cup packed fresh flatleaf parsley leaves
$^1/_2$ cup packed fresh mint leaves
$^1/_2$ cup packed fresh basil leaves
1 tablespoon capers, drained
1 teaspoon chopped fresh rosemary, marjoram, or oregano
$^1/_2$ cup extra-virgin olive oil (or more, if needed)
1 tablespoon fresh lemon juice
Freshly ground black pepper

1. Season the meat all over with the salt and pepper, then dredge in the flour, shaking off the excess. In a 5- to 7-quart pressure cooker, heat the oil over medium-high heat until very hot. Working in batches, brown the ribs in a single layer on all sides, 6 to 8 minutes per batch. Transfer the ribs to a platter. Pour off all but 1 tablespoon of fat.

2. Add the onions, carrots, and celery to the pot and cook over medium-high heat, stirring occasionally, until lightly browned at the edges, 3 to 5 minutes. Add the tomato paste and cook, stirring, 1 minute longer. Pour in the broth and wine, stirring to scrape up any browned bits from the bottom of the pot. Return the short ribs and any accumulated juice to the pot, pressing down on the meat so most of the ribs are covered with liquid. Add the thyme and bay leaf.

3. Close and lock the lid. Set the burner heat to high. When the cooker reaches HIGH pressure, reduce the burner heat as low as you can and still maintain HIGH pressure. Set a timer to cook for 30 minutes.

4. Make the salsa verde. In a food processor, combine the garlic, anchovy, and salt. Process, pulsing on and off, until coarsely chopped. Add the parsley, mint, basil, marjoram, and capers; pulse until finely chopped. With the machine running, slowly pour in the oil, then add the lemon juice and pepper to taste. If the mixture is too thick to pour, process in another tablespoon or two of oil. Taste for salt. Transfer to a bowl.

5. Remove the pot from the heat. Open the cooker with the Natural Release method; let stand for 15 minutes. Be careful of the steam as you remove the lid. The carrots should be cooked through and the meat fork-tender and falling off the bone. Discard the bay leaf.

6. Using a slotted spoon, transfer the meat and vegetables to a warm shallow serving bowl. Skim any fat from the top of the sauce. If you prefer a thicker sauce, boil, uncovered, over high heat to reach the desired consistency. (Alternatively, return the onions, carrots, and celery to the pot and puree with an immersion blender to thicken the sauce.) Taste for salt. Spoon the sauce over the meat. Drizzle about 2 teaspoons of salsa verde over each short rib, and pass the remainder at the table.

Zinfandel-Braised Short Ribs with Salsa Verde and Olives: Stir in $^1/_2$ cup pitted Nicoise olives to the beef in Step 5.

Chinese-Style Spicy Oxtails with Turnips

Serves 4 • Cooker: 5- to 7-quart • Time: 33 minutes for oxtails, 10 minutes for vegetables at HIGH pressure

We love braised oxtails for their silky tenderness and the delightfully thick sauce they produce, thanks to their high proportion of connective tissue. Oxtails take two to three hours to cook by conventional methods, but less than 45 minutes in the pressure cooker.

Half of a moderately hot medium-sized chile such as a red jalapeño or yellow Peruvian aji amarillo will produce a moderately spicy stew. If you have a really hot pepper such as a habanero, just use one slice, unless you really crave heat.

Serve over medium-grain brown rice, with a sprinkling of cilantro. Nestle steamed mustard greens or bok choy up against the rice for a complete meal.

1 tablespoon peanut oil
2 pounds oxtail pieces
$1/4$ teaspoon white pepper
$1/3$ cup sliced ($1/4$-inch-thick) green onions (white and light green parts)
2 large cloves garlic, chopped
3 cups water
$1/2$ cup Chinese rice wine (shaoxing) or dry sherry
$1/4$ cup reduced-sodium soy sauce
1 teaspoon brown sugar
3 nickel-size slices peeled fresh ginger
1 star anise pod
Peel of 1 tangerine or clementine, removed in as few pieces as possible, or 3 wide strips of orange peel, removed with a vegetable peeler
$1/2$ of a fresh red jalapeño or aji amarillo pepper, seeds and stem removed, sliced $1/4$ inch thick
3 medium turnips, peeled and cut into wedges
4 medium carrots, sliced into $1/2$-inch rounds
$1/4$ cup chopped fresh cilantro, for serving

1. In a 5- to 7-quart pressure cooker, heat the oil over medium-high heat until very hot. Season the oxtail pieces on both sides with the white pepper. Lightly brown the pieces in batches in a single layer on all sides, about 3 minutes per side. Take care not to crowd the pan. As the pieces are browned, remove them to a plate.
2. Add the green onions and garlic to the pot and cook for about a minute, stirring. Reduce the heat if they begin to burn. Return the oxtails and any accumulated juice to the pot, nestling them into the green onions. Add the water, rice wine, soy sauce, brown sugar, ginger, star anise, tangerine peel, and chile.
3. Close and lock the lid. Set the burner heat to high. When the cooker reaches HIGH pressure, reduce the burner heat as low as you can and still maintain HIGH pressure. Set a timer to cook for 33 minutes.
4. Remove the pot from the heat. Open the cooker with the Quick Release method. Be careful of the steam as you remove the lid.
5. Add the turnips and carrots to the pot and stir gently to combine. Relock the cooker, bring it back up to HIGH pressure, and cook for 10 minutes. Remove the pot from the heat. Open the cooker with the Quick Release method.
6. Ladle the stew over rice in shallow bowls, removing the star anise and ginger slices. (The tangerine peel will likely have disintegrated.) Top each portion with chopped cilantro. Leftovers will keep in an airtight container in the refrigerator 4 to 5 days or the freezer up to 4 months.

OXTAILS

As you can imagine, an oxtail (really the tail of a beef cow) has a thick end and a thinner, bonier end. Oxtail is typically sold cut into pieces about 2 inches long. In one oxtail, there will be some meaty pieces from the thick end, some pieces that are mostly bone, and some in between. Sometimes oxtails are sold prepackaged, but if you are buying oxtails from the butcher, ask for at least a few of the larger, meatier pieces. You'll no doubt have to take some bony ones, too, which seems only fair.

Oxtails contain a lot of collagen. Because of this, they respond really well to long, slow braising in the pressure cooker. The collagen melts into the broth, adding a robust, beefy flavor. Oxtails are usually served with the bone left in, so you can enjoy stripping off each piece of tender meat as you go.

Traditional Oxtail Stew with Cheddar Oven Drop Biscuits

Serves 4 • Cooker: 5- to 7-quart • Time: 45 minutes at HIGH pressure

Oxtails have long been considered poor people food. Now, what was economical has become trendy. Here the beefy flavor and tender texture of the oxtails shine, enhanced only by a bit of onion, carrot, tomato, salt, pepper, and a bay leaf.

OXTAILS:
2 pounds oxtail pieces
$1/4$ cup all-purpose flour
2 tablespoons vegetable oil
1 medium onion, thinly sliced
1 large carrot, diced
1 (14.5-ounce) can chopped tomatoes in juice
1 cup reduced-sodium beef broth
$1/2$ teaspoon freshly ground black pepper
1 small or $1/2$ large bay leaf

CHEDDAR OVEN DROP BISCUITS:
1 cup all-purpose flour
$1/4$ cup white or brown rice flour
1 teaspoon baking powder
$1/4$ teaspoon baking soda
$1/4$ teaspoon sea salt
1 cup shredded mild or sharp Cheddar cheese
3 tablespoons organic solid vegetable shortening or cold butter
$1/3$ to $1/2$ cup buttermilk, as needed

TO FINISH:
2 tablespoons dry or medium-dry sherry, or more to taste
Sea salt, if needed
2 tablespoons unsalted butter (optional)
2 tablespoons all-purpose flour (optional)
1 tablespoon minced fresh flatleaf parsley

1. In a plastic bag, toss the oxtails in the flour. In a 5- to 7-quart pressure cooker, heat the oil over medium-high heat until very hot. Shake the excess flour from the oxtail pieces. Brown the oxtail pieces well in batches in a single layer on all sides, about 10 minutes per batch for the larger pieces. Take care not to crowd the pan. As the oxtail pieces are browned, remove them to a plate.
2. Add the onion to the pot and cook for about 2 minutes, stirring. Add the carrot and cook for

about 1 minute more. Return the oxtails and any accumulated juice to the pot, nestling them into the vegetables. Add the tomatoes and their juice, broth, pepper, and bay leaf. If your broth was unsalted, add $1/2$ teaspoon salt. Stir to combine.
3. Close and lock the lid. Set the burner heat to high. When the cooker reaches HIGH pressure, reduce the burner heat as low as you can and still maintain HIGH pressure. Set a timer to cook for 45 minutes.
4. While the oxtails are cooking, make the Cheddar biscuits. Preheat the oven to 400° F (375° F if using a Pyrex pie plate). Lightly oil an 8-inch pie plate. Combine all the dry ingredients and Cheddar in a medium bowl and mix well. Add the shortening and buttermilk; stir until the dough comes together. The dough will be slightly sticky. Divide the dough into 4 equal portions and fashion each into a loose ball. Drop them into the pie plate. Bake in the center of the oven until lightly browned and firm to the touch, 25 to 30 minutes. Serve right from the oven.
5. Remove the pot from the heat. Open the cooker with the Quick Release method or the Natural Release method (let stand for 15 minutes). Be careful of the steam as you remove the lid. Stir in the sherry. Taste the broth and salt to taste.
6. If a thickened gravy is desired, heat the butter in a saucepan over medium-high heat. Add the flour and cook, stirring, until aromatic and lightly browned, 2 to 3 minutes. Ladle about $1/2$ cup of hot broth from the pressure cooker into the roux and stir until smooth and bubbly. Add $1/2$ cup more hot broth and again stir until smooth and bubbly. Pour the roux into the pressure cooker and stir carefully to combine. Bring the stew to a gentle boil, uncovered, and cook until the stew thickens, 2 to 3 minutes.
7. Serve the oxtail stew, sprinkled with the parsley, over egg noodles or mashed potatoes, and with a hot biscuit. Or refrigerate overnight, remove the layer of congealed fat, and reheat gently to serve. Leftovers will keep in an airtight container in the refrigerator 4 to 5 days or the freezer up to 4 months.

Jamaican Oxtail Stew

Serves 4 • Cooker: 5- to 7-quart • Time: 45 minutes at HIGH pressure

Oxtails are a favorite in Jamaica, where they are cooked into a stew with fava beans and a spicy Scotch bonnet or habanero chile. The main seasoning is allspice, familiar as the dominant flavor in jerk. Many Jamaican recipes make use of the pressure cooker, and it's clear why: without it, this is a dish that requires hours of slow cooking. If you can't find dried fava beans (try a Middle Eastern market), large lima beans are a good substitute. You may wonder why our recipe calls for either one tablespoon whole allspice berries or the same amount ground, when typically one would want to use less of a ground spice. The reason is that ground allspice declines in flavor fairly rapidly; if your jar of ground allspice is brand new, start with 2 teaspoons.

2 tablespoons vegetable or olive oil
2 pounds oxtail pieces
1 large onion, chopped
2 cloves garlic, chopped
1 bunch green onions (white and light green parts), trimmed and sliced 1/4 inch thick
2 large carrots, sliced 1/3 inch thick, larger pieces halved crosswise
1 tablespoon finely minced peeled fresh ginger
2 tablespoons all-purpose flour
2 cups reduced-sodium beef broth
2 cups water
2 teaspoons browning sauce or 1 tablespoon soy sauce
1 cup dried fava beans or dried large lima beans (no need to soak them)
1 Scotch bonnet or habanero pepper (for a milder dish, substitute 1 jalapeño pepper)
3 or 4 sprigs fresh thyme, tied together with string for easy removal, or 1/2 teaspoon dried thyme
1 tablespoon allspice berries or ground allspice
1/2 teaspoon freshly ground black pepper, plus more to taste
Sea salt

1. In a 5- to 7-quart pressure cooker, heat the oil over medium-high heat until very hot. Brown the oxtail pieces well in batches in a single layer on all sides, about 10 minutes per batch for the larger pieces. Take care not to crowd the pan. As the pieces are browned, remove them to a plate.

2. Add the onion to the pot and cook for about 2 minutes, stirring. Add the garlic, green onions, carrots, and ginger and cook for about 2 minutes. Sprinkle with the flour and cook, stirring, for about 2 minutes. Return the oxtails and any accumulated juice to the pot, nestling them into the vegetables. Add the broth, water, browning sauce, dried beans, chile, thyme, and black pepper and stir to combine.

3. Close and lock the lid. Set the burner heat to high. When the cooker reaches HIGH pressure, reduce the burner heat as low as you can and still maintain HIGH pressure. Set a timer to cook for 45 minutes.

4. Remove the pot from the heat. Open the cooker with the Quick Release method or the Natural Release method (let stand for 15 minutes). Be careful of the steam as you remove the lid. You are looking for a thick stew consistency, so let the stew simmer, uncovered, for 10 minutes or so on stovetop, if necessary. Taste the broth for salt and pepper. Remove and discard the bundle of thyme and the chile.

5. Serve the stew over rice in shallow bowls, or refrigerate it overnight, remove the layer of congealed fat, and reheat gently to serve. Leftovers will keep in an airtight container in the refrigerator 4 to 5 days or the freezer up to 4 months.

BROWNING SAUCE

Based on caramelized sugar and vegetable extracts, browning sauce adds both color and a savory note. Kitchen Bouquet or Gravy Master are two brands of browning sauce that are widely available in the U.S. Thanks to the magic of the Internet, you can easily order Jamaican brands online like Grace Browning and Benjamins Browning. If you don't want to use browning sauce, try substituting soy sauce. Or if you happen to be or know a dedicated pumpernickel bread baker, use "caramel color" liquid, which is just caramelized sugar.

Veal Ragout with Red Wine, Potatoes, and Carrots over Wide Noodles

Serves 4 • Cooker: 5- to 8-quart • Time: 20 minutes at HIGH pressure

The term "ragout" comes from the French *ragoûter*, which means "to revive the taste" and it is a main-dish stew. It is related to the word ragu, which is a sauce for pasta. Ragouts are usually made with meat of some sort, but they can also be prepared using all seasonal vegetables. Only use very fresh veal for this, bought the same day if possible. Veal is delicate and can go sour quickly.

2-pounds boneless veal stew meat or veal shoulder, cut into 1¹/₂-inch chunks
¹/₄ cup all-purpose flour
¹/₄ teaspoon salt
¹/₄ teaspoon freshly ground black pepper
3 tablespoons olive oil
1 medium yellow onion, chopped
2 cloves garlic, crushed
¹/₂ pound baby carrots, or 3 medium carrots, sliced ¹/₂ inch thick
¹/₂ pound new red potatoes, cut in half, or whole baby fingerlings
1 teaspoon dried thyme or 5 sprigs fresh thyme
1 cup low-sodium chicken broth
³/₄ cup dry white or red wine
¹/₂ cup frozen petite peas
4 sheets fresh lasagna noodles
¹/₂ cup shaved Parmesan cheese

1. Pat the veal dry with paper towels and sprinkle with the flour, salt, and pepper. In a 5- to 8-quart pressure cooker over medium-high heat, heat half the oil until very hot. Add half the veal cubes and brown on all sides in a single layer, 5 to 6 minutes total. Transfer the veal to a plate. Repeat with the remaining veal.

2. Add the remaining 1 tablespoon oil to the pot, then the onion, garlic, carrots, and potatoes and cook, stirring, until onion is tender, about 5 minutes. Add the thyme, broth, and wine. Bring to a boil and simmer for 1 minute, scraping up any browned bits from the bottom of the pot. Return the veal and any accumulated juice to the pot.

3. Close and lock the lid. Set the burner heat to high. When the cooker reaches HIGH pressure, reduce the burner heat as low as you can and still maintain HIGH pressure. Set a timer to cook for 20 minutes.

4. Remove the pot from the heat. Open the cooker with the Quick Release method. Be careful of the steam as you remove the lid.

5. Taste for salt. Stir in the peas and cover the pot partially; let sit for 5 minutes. Leave the veal chunky or shred slightly.

6. Meanwhile, cut each lasagna noodle into 4 squares. Cook the noodles in boiling salted water until al dente, about 4 minutes. Drain well.

7. To assemble, lay one sheet of pasta on each of four serving plates and spoon ¹/₂ cup veal ragout on top of each. Follow with two additional layers of pasta and ragout. Top with shaved Parmesan cheese, if desired. The ragout is also excellent reheated and served the next day.

Veal Marengo

Serves 8 • Cooker: 5- to 8-quart • Time: 20 minutes at HIGH pressure

Veal Marengo is a classic French braised bistro dish. This recipe is based on Pierre Franey's version. The original was created on June 14, 1800, after a battle between Napoleon Bonaparte's troops and the Austrians near the village of Marengo in northern Italy. The French and English have a long tradition of naming culinary delights after battles, especially when they win. After the battle was won, Napoleon was famished and asked his chef to whip up a meal; the result was Chicken Marengo. Or so the legend goes. The original dish has long since been altered to the modern palate and cooking methods, but it stays true to its Mediterranean roots.

4 pounds lean veal shoulder stew meat, cut into 2-inch cubes
Sea salt and freshly ground black pepper
4 tablespoons light olive oil
1 cup chopped yellow onion
1 teaspoon finely chopped garlic
1 cup chopped celery
2 long strips orange zest
1 bay leaf
$1/2$ teaspoon dried thyme
$1^1/2$ cups low-sodium chicken broth
1 cup plus 2 tablespoons dry white wine
2 (8-ounce) cans tomato sauce
2 sprigs fresh flatleaf parsley
2 teaspoons arrowroot or cornstarch
2 tablespoons butter
1 pound mushrooms of your choice, quartered
2 tablespoons fresh lemon juice
2 tablespoons finely chopped fresh flatleaf parsley, for garnish

1. Pat the veal dry with paper towels and sprinkle with salt and pepper. In a 5- to 8-quart pressure cooker over medium-high heat, heat 2 tablespoons of the oil until very hot. Brown the veal cubes in batches in a single layer on all sides, 5 to 6 minutes per batch. Transfer the veal to a plate as it is browned.

2. Add the remaining 2 tablespoons oil to the hot pot, along with the onion, garlic, and celery, and cook, stirring, until the onion is tender, about 5 minutes. Add the orange zest, bay leaf, thyme, broth, and 1 cup of the wine. Bring to a boil, then reduce the heat and simmer for 1 minute. Return the veal and any accumulated juice to the pot. Pour in the tomato sauce and set the parsley sprigs on top. Do not stir.

3. Close and lock the lid. Set the burner heat to high. When the cooker reaches HIGH pressure, reduce the burner heat as low as you can and still maintain HIGH pressure. Set a timer to cook for 20 minutes.

4. Remove the pot from the heat. Open the cooker with the Quick Release method. Be careful of the steam as you remove the lid. Remove the meat to a bowl with a slotted spoon. Discard the bay leaf and zest strips.

5. Use an immersion blender to puree the sauce. Taste for salt. Blend the arrowroot with the remaining 2 tablespoons wine in a small bowl. Stir into the pot and stir to thicken.

6. Meanwhile, melt the butter in a medium skillet; when hot, add the mushrooms and toss with the lemon juice. Sauté a few minutes to cook, then add to the pot along with the veal. Serve immediately with buttered wide egg noodles or Parsley New Potatoes (page 454), sprinkled with parsley. This can be made a day ahead and refrigerated.

Veal Osso Bucco

Serves 6 • Cooker: 5- to 8-quart • Time: 20 minutes at HIGH pressure

Osso bucco, or "bone with the hole," is the classic Milanese braised veal stew made with veal shanks, vegetables, wine, and broth. This version is dedicated to the memory of Marcella Hazan, who made the dish popular in the U.S. and would prepare it for her husband Viktor's lunch. You can serve osso bucco with its traditional Milanese accompaniment, Saffron Risotto (page 341) but it's also delicious with mashed potatoes, polenta, or over a tube pasta. Don't forget the delicious marrow—spread it on crusty bread—or the gremolata, the parsley/lemon/garlic garnish that really makes the dish. The gremolata is also excellent with fish, lamb shanks and chops, pork chops, green beans, asparagus, cauliflower, and steamed whole potatoes. An important tip from Marcella that is crucial to the success of the finished dish: don't remove the silver membranes around the shanks, as they help preserve the shape of the meat as it braises.

OSSO BUCCO:

6 (³/₄-pound) veal shanks (about 4 pounds total), tied with kitchen twine to prevent them from falling apart during cooking
3 to 4 tablespoons all-purpose flour
3 tablespoons olive oil
Sea salt, as needed
Freshly ground black pepper
3 tablespoon unsalted butter
2 large yellow onions, finely chopped
2 large carrots, finely chopped
3 ribs celery, finely chopped
2 (4-inch) strips lemon zest
1 cup dry white wine
1 cup low-sodium chicken broth
1 (15-ounce) can diced stewed tomatoes, drained
1 teaspoon chopped fresh thyme or 1 tablespoon minced fresh basil

GREMOLATA:

Zest of 2 medium lemons, cut off in strips
2 cloves garlic, peeled
³/₄ cup packed fresh flatleaf parsley leaves (about ³/₄ bunch)

1. Pat the veal dry with paper towels and sprinkle with the flour. In a 5- to 8-quart pressure cooker, heat half the oil over medium-high heat until very hot. Add 2 or 3 veal shanks (however many you can fit in a single layer) and brown on all sides, 3 minutes total. Transfer to a plate and tent with aluminum foil to keep warm. Repeat with the remaining oil and veal. Season to taste with salt and pepper. Discard the fat in the pot. Add the butter; when it has melted, add the onions, carrot, and celery and cook, stirring, until softened, about 5 minutes. Add the lemon zest, wine, broth, drained tomatoes, and thyme. Return the veal shanks and any accumulated juice to the pot, pushing them into the liquid.

2. Close and lock the lid. Set the burner heat to high. When the cooker reaches HIGH pressure, reduce the burner heat as low as you can and still maintain HIGH pressure. Set a timer to cook for 20 minutes.

3. Remove the pot from the heat. Open the cooker with the Natural Release method; let stand for 15 minutes. Be exact with your timing, so set a timer. Be careful of the steam as you remove the lid. Transfer the shanks to a bowl with tongs, snip off the string around the meat and discard, and cover loosely with foil. Skim off any excess fat. Let rest about 10 to 15 minutes while making the gremolata.

4. In a small food processor, combine the zest, garlic, and parsley; pulse until finely chopped. Pour the gremolata into the pot juices. Taste for salt and pepper. Serve the shanks with the pot juices poured over them. This is also very good served reheated the next day.

Bison Meatloaf with Mushrooms and Herbs

Serves 6 • Cooker: 5- to 8-quart • Time: 20 minutes at HIGH pressure

Buffalo meat is very lean and flavorful, and can be found sold ground in supermarkets, perfect to use in meatloaf and burgers just like beef. Buy the disposable aluminum loaf pans sold at the supermarket to make these smaller sized loaves. Use the fresh herbs if you can.

MEATLOAF:
2 tablespoons olive oil
$1/2$ cup finely chopped white onion
2 cloves garlic, minced
8 ounces fresh white or brown mushrooms, chopped
2 pounds ground bison
1 cup panko breadcrumbs or crushed saltine crackers
2 large eggs, beaten
$1/2$ cup milk
$1/3$ cup tomato paste whisked with 2 tablespoons balsamic vinegar
$1/4$ cup thick, smoky BBQ sauce, mild or spicy
3 tablespoons chopped fresh oregano or 1 tablespoon dried
3 tablespoons chopped fresh basil or 1 tablespoon dried
Sea salt and freshly ground black pepper

TOMATO-BROWN SUGAR TOPPING:
$3/4$ cup ketchup
1 tablespoon Dijon mustard
$1/4$ cup firmly packed brown sugar
$1^1/2$ teaspoons Worcestershire sauce
$1^1/2$ cups water

1. In a heavy skillet over medium-high heat, heat the oil and onion together and cook, stirring a few times, until just soft and starting to turn golden brown. Add the garlic and mushrooms and cook, stirring frequently, until all of the mushrooms' liquid has evaporated and the mushrooms are brown. Set aside to cool.

2. In a large bowl, using your hands or a fork, mix the bison and breadcrumbs together, then mix in the eggs, milk, tomato paste, BBQ sauce, herbs, and cooled mushroom mixture. Season to taste with salt and pepper. Divide the mixture equally between 3 or 4 disposable 6 x 3-inch loaf pans sprayed with olive oil cooking spray. Pack in and make level with the top rim. In a small bowl, combine the topping ingredients, then divide equally between the loaves and spread over the tops.

3. Place a trivet and then a steamer plate in a 5- to 8-quart pressure cooker. Add the water. Lower the loaf pans onto the steamer plate. Do not cover. You can stack the pans if necessary to make them fit or you can cook them in two batches.

4. Close and lock the lid. Set the burner heat to high. When the cooker reaches HIGH pressure, adjust the heat to maintain the pressure. Set a timer to cook for 20 minutes.

5. Remove the pot from the heat. Open the cooker with the Natural Release method; let stand for 15 minutes. Be exact with your timing, so set a timer. Be careful of the steam as you remove the lid. Let stand another for 5 minutes to let the juices settle. An instant-read thermometer inserted into the center of the loaf should read around 140° F.

6. Use tongs and an oven mitt to lift the loaf pans out of the pot. Slide the meatloaves out of their pans and place on a serving platter or serve sliced out of the pans. The loaves can be cooled, covered with plastic wrap, and refrigerated for up to 3 days and served cold. Do not freeze.

Bison Stew with Red Wine and Rosemary

Serves 4 • Cooker: 5- to 7-quart • Time: 20 minutes at HIGH pressure

This is a wonderfully deeply flavored dish, perfect for a dinner on a cold night.

6 ounces sliced bacon, chopped
1 1/2 pounds well-marbled chuck bison stew meat, cut into 1-inch cubes
1/4 cup potato starch (not potato flour) or rice flour
Sea salt and freshly ground black pepper, to taste
2 tablespoons olive oil
1 large yellow or white onion, finely chopped
2 sprigs fresh thyme
1 sprig fresh rosemary
2 bay leaves
2 cups dry red wine
3 medium carrots, cut into 1/2-inch-thick slices on the diagonal (if using baby carrots, trim and add whole)
3 ribs celery, sliced 1/2 inch thick
1/2 pound new red or white potatoes, cut into 1-inch chunks (small potatoes can be halved or quartered; don't peel them)
1/2 cup tomato paste
2 cups beef broth

1. In a large bowl or 1-gallon plastic ziptop bag, toss the bison with the potato starch, salt, and pepper to coat evenly.
2. In a 5- to 7-quart pressure cooker, heat 1 tablespoon of the oil over medium-high heat until very hot. Add the bacon and cook, stirring, until lightly browned. Transfer to paper towels to drain. Add half the bison to the pot in a single layer and brown on all sides, 3 to 4 minutes total. Transfer to the bowl with a slotted spoon. Add the remaining 1 tablespoon oil and brown the second batch of bison. Remove to the bowl.
3. Add the onion to the pot, reduce the heat to medium, and cook 1 to 2 minutes. Add the herbs and stir for 1 minute. Add the wine and bring to a low boil, scraping up any browned bits from the bottom of the pot. Return the meat and any accumulated juice to the pot, along with the carrots, celery, and potatoes. Stir the tomato paste into the broth and pour into the cooker.
4. Close and lock the lid. Set the burner heat to high. When the cooker reaches HIGH pressure, reduce the burner heat as low as you can and still maintain HIGH pressure. Set a timer to cook for 20 minutes.
5. Remove the pot from the heat. Open the cooker with the Quick Release method. Be careful of the steam as you remove the lid. Discard the whole herbs. Taste for salt and pepper.
6. If the liquid is too thin, transfer the bison and vegetables to a serving bowl or tureen, then turn the heat to high and simmer, uncovered, until the liquid is reduced to the desired consistency. Taste for seasoning. Pour the liquid over the bison and vegetables. Serve immediately or let cool, then refrigerate and enjoy reheated the next day.

8

Lamb, Goat, and Venison

Lamb is a relatively lean meat, yet delightfully tender and flavorful, with a subtle grassy flavor. The pressure cooker works best with the cuts suitable for stew (like shoulder or leg), shoulder chops, and shanks. Rolled and tied whole boneless leg of lamb also works in the pressure cooker.

Tenderness is determined more by the lamb's age when it was slaughtered than by marbling. Lamb comes from animals that are less than one year old. "Baby lamb" is less than 10 weeks old and weighs no more than 20 pounds. "Spring lamb" weighs 20 to 40 pounds. The smaller and younger the lamb, the milder the flavor will be. Young lamb is pale pink, tender, and mild. As the lamb ages, the meat darkens and toughens, gaining character and flavor.

Most lamb sold in supermarkets comes from animals that were fed grain and raised in feedlots. Grass-fed lamb is available at butcher shops and specialty-food stores, and is raised on a grass-only diet, with no feed supplements such as antibiotics, hormones, or steroids. It has a particularly tender texture and outstanding taste. Top grades of lamb are prime and choice. Prime has the greatest marbling and is reserved for restaurants, high-end retailers, and farmers' markets. Choice has less marbling, but is still high quality. Look for fresh lamb and a pink/red color, since that is an indication of how fresh it is.

Consume airtight, plastic-wrapped lamb from the supermarket within two days. Vacuum-sealed cuts may be kept longer. Well-marbled cuts take better to freezing than leaner cuts. Double wrap the meat tightly first in plastic, then in aluminum foil to freeze for up to six months. Safely defrost frozen lamb overnight in the refrigerator. Never thaw by microwave or with hot water.

To avoid an overly gamy flavor, trim away lamb fat more completely than you would other meats. A thick membrane called the fell is sometimes left intact on larger cuts to help retain their shape and juices as they cook, but you may still need to remove excess fat.

We have noticed more cooks working with specialty meats such as goat and that CSA boxes sometimes include goat, especially the shoulder cut for stew. If you are a traveler and have been to Baja, the Caribbean, Italy, or Greece, you will be familiar with goat meat. Goat is consumed around the world more than any other red meat. It tastes like lamb, but is far leaner and can hold its own with strong flavors like red wine, curry, and harissa. Easter is the time that baby goat (also called goat kid or cabrito) shows up in ethnic butcher shops. Online sources for pastured goat meat include Canyon Goat Company (canyongoat.com) and Salmon Creek Ranch (salmoncreekranch.com).

Venison has a flavor reminiscent of beef, sometimes with a gamy note, but it is richer and higher in moisture, but lower in fat. Because of its leanness, venison recipes will often include some type of bacon to replace some of that fat. The roasts, stew meat, sausages, and steaks are the most common cuts. Imported venison in restaurants and specialty grocers comes from New Zealand.

BEST CUTS FOR PRESSURE COOKING

Lamb
- shoulder (stew meat and chops)
- shank
- leg of lamb
- riblets
- neck

Goat
- shoulder
- bone-in leg roast
- ground lamb

Venison
- shoulder (stew meat and chuck roast)
- shank (osso bucco)
- bone-in leg roast
- spareribs
- ground venison

Lamb Dolmas with Tzatziki Sauce

Serves 6 to 8 as an appetizer; 4 as a main dish • Cooker: 5- to 7-quart • Time: 10 minutes at HIGH pressure

Stuffed grape leaves, or dolmas, are a favorite appetizer of ours, but we also love them cold for lunchboxes or picnics. Though available canned and in some delis, once you have made your own, you will not want to go back to store-bought. If you are lucky enough to have your own grapevine, follow the recipe below for prepping them for stuffing. Most of us, though, have to buy our grape leaves for stuffing—they are sold in jars, packed in brine. Pour off the liquid, slide out the bundle of leaves, carefully unroll them so as not to rip any, and rinse before using. This recipe makes enough filling for about half a jar of grape leaves. (There are usually at least 40 to 50 leaves per jar. You can put the unused leaves back in the jar and fill it with salt water. They will keep for several weeks.)

The pressure cooker makes dolmas perfectly. This recipe calls for cooked rice; you can use leftover rice that has been refrigerated or frozen.

TZATZIKI SAUCE:

1 large hothouse cucumber
Salt
2 cups plain 2% fat Greek yogurt
1 clove garlic, minced or pressed
1 tablespoon olive oil
2 tablespoons chopped fresh dill

DOLMAS:

1 recipe Fresh Grape Leaves in the Pressure Cooker (p. 238) or 1 (1-pound) jar grape leaves
1 quart water, brought to a boil
$^{1}/_{3}$ cup extra virgin olive oil
1 cup finely chopped white onion
3 tablespoons slivered almonds
$^{3}/_{4}$ pound lean ground lamb
2 cups cooked long-grain white or brown rice
$^{3}/_{4}$ cup grated carrot (1 large carrot)
3 tablespoons dried currants or minced dried apricots
2 tablespoons finely chopped fresh mint or cilantro
2 tablespoons finely chopped fresh flatleaf parsley
1 tablespoon grated lemon zest
$1^{1}/_{2}$ teaspoons salt
$^{1}/_{2}$ teaspoon freshly ground black pepper
2 cups water
$^{1}/_{2}$ cup fresh lemon juice
Lemon wedges, for serving

1. Make the Tzatziki Sauce. Cut the cucumber in half, remove the seeds, and cut into $1/2$-inch dice. Remove excess moisture from the cucumber; salt the dice generously and place in a colander. Let drain for 30 to 45 minutes, then rinse and pat dry. In a small bowl, beat the yogurt until smooth. Fold in the garlic, oil, and dill. Season to taste with salt. Fold in the cucumber. Chill at least 2 hours before serving to blend the flavors. Makes $2^1/2$ cups.

2. Make the dolmas. Drain the jarred grape leaves, carefully remove them from the jar, and place in a large heatproof bowl. Sort the leaves, selecting the most perfect to stuff, the rest to layer in the steamer basket. Pour the boiling water over them to cover and let soak 15 minutes. Drain and rinse under cold running water. Set aside in a colander to drain. (They are packed in brine and very salty so don't skip this step.)

3. In a large skillet, heat 4 tablespoons of the oil over medium-high heat until very hot. Add the onion and cook, stirring a few times, until softened, about 3 minutes. Add the almonds and cook, stirring, until they begin to brown, about 2 minutes more. Add the lamb and cook, breaking up any clumps with a spoon, until there is no pink. Transfer the onion-lamb mixture to a large bowl. Add the rice, carrot, mint, parsley, currants, lemon zest, 1 teaspoon of the salt, and the pepper to the bowl and mix gently with a fork to combine and coat the rice with the oil.

4. To stuff the leaves, line them up in a row, rib side up, on your work surface. Choose a perfect leaf. Trim off the stem, if there is one. Depending on the size of the leaf, place 2 teaspoons to 1 tablespoon of the filling in the center of the leaf. Shape it into a little log, running side to side across the leaf. Fold the stem over the filling, then bring the sides into the center as you would for an envelope and roll up jelly-roll fashion to make a small, tight, plump cylinder. If you have any tears, snip off a lobe and patch it from the inside. Repeat until the filling is used up. Place the stuffed leaves in a steamer basket as you make them, seam side down, making sure the loose ends are tucked firmly underneath the roll. Arrange them close, side by side, but don't jam them in. Make as many layers as necessary, separating the layers with extra or torn grape leaves.

5. Pour the water into a 5- to 7-quart pressure cooker and add the remaining $1/2$ teaspoon salt. Insert the filled basket. Pour the lemon juice and the remaining oil over the dolmas. Cover the leaves with a layer of heavy plastic wrap, pressing in around the edges of the basket.

6. Close and lock the lid. Set the burner heat to high. When the cooker reaches HIGH pressure, reduce the burner heat as low as you can and still maintain HIGH pressure. Set a timer to cook for 10 minutes.

7. Remove the pot from the heat. Open the cooker with the Natural Release method; let stand for 15 minutes. Be careful of the steam as you remove the lid. Remove the basket from the pot and let stand 10 minutes, still covered with wrap.

8. When you remove the dolmas, discard the extra leaves. Serve just slightly warm or at room temperature, although traditionally they are served cold. If not serving right away, refrigerate them. We like to serve them with lemon wedges (squeeze over the dolmas before serving), tzatziki sauce for dipping, and fresh pita bread, but they are good plain, too. They will keep in an airtight container in the refrigerator up to 3 days.

Fresh Grape Leaves in the Pressure Cooker

Cooker: 5- to 7-quart • Time: 10 to 13 minutes

If you have access to unsprayed grape vines, you can prepare fresh grape leaves for stuffing by blanching them in the pressure cooker. Pick young, light green, undamaged leaves in the spring or early summer, when they are tender. Look for medium or large leaves. The best are those below the new growth at the top of the plant and above the leaves close to the grapes. Rule of thumb: count down three leaves from the new growth at the end of the vine, and pick the next 2 to 3 leaves, then move on to the next stem. Grape leaves are also useful for wrapping fish or vegetables before grilling or pressure cooking.

1 pound fresh leaves = about 100 leaves
1 cup water
1 teaspoon salt

1. Cut the grape leaves off the vine at the stem (don't cut the leaf), if they are still attached. Since you will eventually stuff the leaves, make sure that they are at least as big as the palm of your hand so that they are large enough to hold the fillings.
2. Fill a clean sink with cold water and gently clean the leaves to wash off any dirt or residue under running water. Remove the stems. Drain the water and then fill the sink again. Clean the leaves one more time, then set them on a paper towel-covered wire rack to drain for at least 30 minutes.
3. Stack the cleaned and drained grape leaves together in stacks of 6 to 20 leaves. Roll each into a tight bundle. Secure each roll with kitchen twine or heavy-duty thread.
4. Add the 1 cup water and salt to a 5- to 7-quart pressure cooker. You can either submerge the bundles in the salted water or steam them on a rack or in the steaming basket.
5. Close and lock the lid. Set the burner heat to high. When the cooker reaches HIGH pressure, reduce the burner heat as low as you can and still maintain HIGH pressure. Set a timer to cook for 10 to 13 minutes. If you will be filling and cooking the leaves again, do not leave them in the pressure cooker for longer than 10 minutes. For use with a raw salad filling, cook the longer time.
6. Remove from the heat. Open the cooker with the Natural Release method; let stand for 15 minutes. Be careful of the steam as you remove the lid.
7. Transfer the bundles to a wire rack to cool. Untie the bundles and lay flat. Refrigerate the leaves that you are not going to use immediately by laying them flat on wax paper or parchment. Slide into a 1-quart ziptop bag and use them within 24 hours or freeze once they are completely cool. They keep for about 2 months.

Kofte in Cinnamon Tomato Sauce

Makes 18 mini meatballs; serves about 4 • Cooker: 5- to 8-quart • Time: 5 minutes at HIGH pressure

The word *kofta* in Turkish means "ball" and kofte are meatballs enriched with spices and onions. Instead of holding the meat together with bread-crumbs, this recipe uses bulgur wheat, which adds to the texture. Offer this as an appetizer with toothpicks or serve it over pasta as a main dish.

KOFTE:

1 cup uncooked bulgur

2 cups water

1^1/$_4$ pounds lean ground lamb

3 tablespoons chopped fresh flatleaf parsley

1 tablespoon snipped fresh dill or 1 teaspoon dried

^{1}/$_4$ teaspoon dried oregano

^{1}/$_2$ teaspoon sea salt

^{1}/$_2$ teaspoon freshly ground black pepper

2 cloves garlic, minced

1 large egg

CINNAMON TOMATO SAUCE:

2 tablespoons olive oil

1 cup finely chopped white onion

1 clove garlic, minced

^{1}/$_2$ cup dry red wine

^{1}/$_2$ cup water

^{1}/$_4$ teaspoon ground cinnamon

^{1}/$_8$ teaspoon ground cumin

1 cinnamon stick

1 (8-ounce) can tomato sauce

1 (28-ounce) can diced tomatoes in juice, undrained

1 cup grated kefalograviera (a firm Greek cheese made from sheep's milk or a mixture of sheep's and goat's milk), Parmesan, or Asiago, for serving

1. In a medium bowl, soak the bulgur in the water for 5 minutes to soften, then drain in a fine mesh strainer. Dry the bowl and return the bulgur to it. Add the lamb, herbs, salt, pepper, garlic, and egg. Blend the mix well with your hands or a fork. Cover and chill 30 minutes.

2. Form the chilled meat mixture into 1^1/$_2$-inch balls. You will get about 18. You can use a mini ice cream scoop for this, as you want the meat-balls evenly sized so they cook in the same amount of time. Cover and refrigerate for 30 minutes. Chilling makes the meatballs hold together better.

3. Make the sauce. While the meatballs are chill-ing, in a 5- to 8-quart pressure cooker, heat the oil over medium-high heat. Add the onion and cook, stirring a few times, until softened, about 3 minutes. Add the garlic, cook for 30 seconds. Add the wine and bring to a boil. Add the water, cinnamon, cumin, tomato sauce, and tomatoes with their juice. When the tomato sauce rapidly simmers, reduce the heat to medium-low and simmer, uncovered, until you are ready to cook the meatballs.

4. Add the meatballs to the simmering sauce. Close and lock the lid. Set the burner heat to high. When the cooker reaches HIGH pressure, reduce the burner heat as low as you can and still maintain HIGH pressure. Set a timer to cook for 5 minutes.

5. Remove the pot from the heat. Open the cooker with the Natural Release method; let stand for 15 minutes. Quick Release any remaining pres-sure. Be careful of the steam as you remove the lid. Remove and discard the cinnamon stick. Taste the sauce for salt and pepper.

6. Remove the meatballs with an oversized spoon to dinner plates and use a small ladle for the sauce. Serve the meatballs with some sauce spooned over and sprinkled with the cheese.

Lamb Stew with Irish Stout

Serves 4 • Cooker: 5- to 7-quart • Time: 17 minutes at HIGH pressure

This hearty one-pot meal requires nothing more than a crisp green salad to start and a crusty loaf of bread to sop up the juices. Guinness is one of the most popular beers in the world, certainly in Ireland. Its characteristic strong burnt flavor and dark ruby-black color come from the inclusion of roasted unmalted barley. It cooks into a delicious sauce for stews. If time permits, open the bottle of stout an hour or two before preparing the other ingredients so the sparklies can die down a bit. Doing this will dramatically reduce the amount of foam that forms when it's added.

2 pounds boneless lamb shoulder, trimmed of
    excess fat and cut into 2-inch chunks
1 teaspoon salt, plus more to taste
10 grinds freshly ground black pepper
$^{1}/_{4}$ cup all-purpose flour
3 tablespoons olive oil
2 medium onions, cut in half, then into $^{1}/_{2}$-inch-
    thick half moons
1 tablespoon tomato paste
4 red potatoes, cut into 4 or 8 wedges each,
    depending on size
3 medium carrots, cut into 1-inch chunks
2 medium turnips, peeled and cut into $^{3}/_{4}$-inch dice
1$^{3}/_{4}$ cups reduced-sodium chicken broth
1 (11.2-ounce) bottle Irish stout, such as Guinness
1 bay leaf
1$^{1}/_{2}$ cups fresh or frozen peas
2 tablespoons chopped fresh flatleaf parsley

1. Season the meat all over with the salt and pepper, then dredge in the flour, shaking off the excess. In a 5- to 7-quart pressure cooker, heat the oil over medium-high heat until very hot. Brown the meat in batches in a single layer on all sides, 5 to 7 minutes per batch. Use a slotted spoon to transfer the browned meat to a plate. Pour off all but 1 tablespoon of fat from the pot.

2. Add the onions to the pot and cook over medium-high heat, stirring a few times, until lightly browned at the edges, about 5 minutes. Add the tomato paste and cook, stirring, 1 minute longer. Stir in the potatoes, carrots, and turnips. Pour in the broth and stout, scraping up any browned bits from the bottom of the pot. Return the meat and any accumulated juices to the pot. Add the bay leaf.

3. Close and lock the lid. Set the burner heat to high. When the cooker reaches HIGH pressure, reduce the burner heat as low as you can and still maintain HIGH pressure. Set a timer to cook for 17 minutes.

4. Remove the pot from the heat. Open the cooker with the Natural Release method; let stand for 15 minutes. Be careful of the steam as you remove the lid. The vegetables should be cooked through and the meat fork-tender. Using a slotted spoon, transfer the meat and vegetables to a warm shallow serving bowl. Discard the bay leaf. Skim any fat from the top of the sauce.

5. If you prefer a thicker sauce, boil, uncovered, over high heat to reach the desired consistency. Reduce the heat to medium and stir in the peas and 1 tablespoon of the parsley; cook 5 minutes. Taste, adding more salt if needed.

6. Spoon the sauce over the meat and sprinkle with the remaining 1 tablespoon parsley. Serve at once.

Lemon Lamb Stew

Serves 6 • Cooker: 5- to 7-quart • Time: 15 minutes at HIGH pressure

It is a remarkable culinary pairing that lamb melds so well with lemon. It is the taste of spring. If you have a lemon tree, it will be a go-to recipe for you, as it cooks in a flash. Since this stew has only five ingredients, don't be tempted to substitute or leave one out. Serve with steamed rice or buttered whole wheat noodles sprinkled with grated Parmesan cheese and a green vegetable.

3 tablespoons olive oil
3 pounds lamb shoulder, with some bone, trimmed
    of excess fat and cut into 2-inch chunks
Salt and freshly ground black pepper
3 cloves garlic, chopped
$^1/_2$ cup fresh lemon juice
2 cups reduced-sodium chicken broth

1. In a 5- to 7-quart pressure cooker, heat the oil over medium-high heat until very hot. Brown the meat in batches in a single layer on all sides, 5 to 7 minutes per batch. Use a slotted spoon to transfer the browned meat to a plate. Return the meat and any accumulated juices to the pot. Season to taste with salt and pepper, and stir in the garlic. Add the lemon juice and broth.
2. Close and lock the lid. Set the burner heat to high. When the cooker reaches HIGH pressure, reduce the burner heat as low as you can and still maintain HIGH pressure. Set a timer to cook for 15 minutes.
3. Remove the pot from the heat. Open the cooker with the Natural Release method; let stand for 15 minutes. Be careful of the steam as you remove the lid. Skim any fat from the top of the sauce. Taste, adding more salt if needed. Serve immediately.

Lamb Cacciatore with Black Olives

Serves 6 • Cooker: 5- to 7-quart • Time: 18 minutes at HIGH pressure

Tori Ritchie, food writer and TV commentator, has a blog called Tuesday Recipe. She has the best recipes! Every one is so darn tasty. She also has her own pressure cooker book, published by Weldon Owen for Williams-Sonoma. Here is her lamb in the hunter's style with tomatoes and white wine, which we adapted for the pressure cooker. It is marvelous. Tori says when you shop for the lamb, ask the butcher where the meat was cut from. The most tender comes from the shoulder, but stew meat from the leg—which is leaner but also a bit drier—will work, too. The thickness of the sauce depends on the type of tomato product you use. If you want a thick, smooth sauce, use crushed tomatoes; for a lighter sauce, chopped or diced canned tomatoes (with their juice). A note from Tori regarding the olives: oil-packed black Saracena olives are a good choice (pitted or unpitted) or the shriveled ones usually labeled dry-cured olives. Kalamatas are too salty for this dish. Fresh rosemary, please—no substitute. Serve the cacciatore with buttered pappardelle, or other flat noodles and steamed broccolini dressed with a vinaigrette.

3 pounds boneless lamb stew, trimmed of excess
    fat and cut into 1-inch pieces
$^1/_2$ teaspoon salt
Several grinds freshly ground black pepper
1 cup packed fresh flatleaf parsley leaves
2 medium to large cloves garlic, peeled
3 tablespoons olive oil
1 large white or yellow onion, thinly sliced
1 tablespoon minced fresh rosemary
$1^1/_2$ cups Pinot Grigio or other dry white wine
1 (28-ounce) can diced or crushed plum tomatoes
$^1/_2$ cup water
4 ounces black Italian olives (see headnote), rinsed
    and halved

1. Place the meat in a bowl. Sprinkle with the salt and pepper and toss well. Mince together the parsley and garlic. Sprinkle over meat, toss again, then let stand, covered, at room temperature for 1 hour.

2. In a 5- to 7-quart pressure cooker, heat the oil over medium-high heat until very hot. Brown the meat in batches in a single layer on all sides, 5 to 7 minutes per batch, adding more oil if needed. Use a slotted spoon to transfer the browned meat to a bowl. Add the onion and rosemary to pot and cook, stirring, until softened, about 3 minutes. Add the wine and let boil until almost evaporated, scraping up any browned bits from the bottom of the pot. Stir in tomatoes and water and return the meat and any accumulated juices to the pot. Bring to a boil.

3. Close and lock the lid. Set the burner heat to high. When the cooker reaches HIGH pressure, reduce the burner heat as low as you can and still maintain HIGH pressure. Set a timer to cook for 18 minutes.

4. Remove the pot from the heat. Open the cooker with the Natural Release method; let stand for 15 minutes. Be careful of the steam as you remove the lid. The meat should be fork-tender. Skim any fat from the top of the sauce.

5. Stir in the olives and let stand, uncovered, until they are heated through, about 5 minutes. Serve immediately.

Lamb *Korma*

Serves 4 • Cooker: 6- to 8-quart • Time: 15 minutes at HIGH pressure

Lamb and goat are the primary meats used in Indian cooking. This recipe is adapted for the pressure cooker from one that appeared in an article about the author Salman Rushdie; it is a dish he makes for his son. The word *korma* means "braise" and the dish uses the classic technique of warming a mixture of spices, usually coriander and cumin, to release their essences, then cooking the meat or vegetables in yogurt, which makes its own sauce with the meat juices. If you end up with too much liquid, stir 1 teaspoon of cornstarch into the yogurt before adding it to the pot to thicken it slightly. Serve with plain basmati rice and a cucumber salad.

2 pounds lamb stew meat or lamb shoulder, trimmed of excess fat and cut into 2-inch chunks
1 tablespoon olive oil
1 teaspoon ground coriander
1 teaspoon chili powder
4 green cardamom pods, crushed with the back of a knife
$^1/_2$ cup (1 stick) butter
1 large white onion, chopped
1 ($1^1/_2$-inch) piece fresh ginger, peeled and grated
4 cloves garlic, chopped
$^3/_4$ cup low-sodium chicken or vegetable broth
Sea salt and freshly ground black or white pepper
1 cup thick plain whole-milk yogurt, whisked with a pinch of saffron

1. Rub the meat with oil. Mix the spices together, then rub them into the meat. Let sit at room temperature for an hour or overnight in the refrigerator.
2. In a 6- to 8-quart pressure cooker, melt the butter. When it starts to foam, add the onions, reduce the heat to medium, and cook until golden and soft, stirring occasionally, 6 to 8 minutes. Remove to a blender and puree. Add the lamb to the pot, browning it in batches in a single layer on all sides. Use a slotted spoon to transfer the browned meat to a plate. Add a bit more butter or oil if necessary between batches. When the meat is browned, add the ginger and garlic; cook 2 minutes, stirring. Return the meat and any accumulated juices to the pot. Add the broth. Season with salt and pepper to taste.
3. Close and lock the lid. Set the burner heat to high. When the cooker reaches HIGH pressure, reduce the burner heat as low as you can and still maintain HIGH pressure. Set a timer to cook for 15 minutes.
4. Remove the pot from the heat. Open the cooker with the Natural Release method; let stand for 15 minutes. Be careful of the steam as you remove the lid. The lamb should be fork-tender. Skim any fat from the top of the sauce.
5. Stir in the pureed onion, then the yogurt, and let simmer gently, uncovered, for 5 minutes. Taste for salt. Serve immediately over a nice mound of basmati rice.

Chuck Williams's Lamb Stew with Couscous

Serves 6 • Cooker: 6- to 8-quart • Time: 15 minutes at HIGH pressure

This delicious stew from master cook Chuck Williams, adapted for the pressure cooker, has just a hint of spice and tons of vegetables. You will be making a buttery couscous while the stew is cooking. A staple of North African cooking, couscous is fast and flavorful, perfect for weeknight dinners. Any leftover is good as a grain salad base the next day.

3 pounds lamb shoulder, trimmed of excess fat and
    cut into 2-inch chunks
Olive oil, for coating
1/2 teaspoon *each* ground ginger, turmeric, and
    allspice, mixed together
1/2 cup (1 stick) unsalted butter
2 tablespoons light olive oil
1 cup dry white or red wine
1 large white onion, coarsely chopped
5 large carrots, cut into 1-inch chunks
4 small to medium turnips or parsnips, peeled and
    cut into 1-inch chunks
1 (16-ounce) can tomato sauce
5 cups water, or to just reach the top of the
    vegetables
Sea salt and freshly ground black pepper
1 1/2 (10-ounce) boxes instant couscous (2 1/4 cups)
2 1/2 cups boiling water
1/2 pound green beans, trimmed and cut into 1-inch
    lengths
3 medium zucchini, cut into 1-inch chunks
Hot pepper sauce, such as Tabasco

1. Marinate the meat: Rub the meat with oil and the mixture of spices. Let sit at room temperature for an hour or overnight in the refrigerator.
2. In a 6- to 8-quart pressure cooker, melt 1/4 cup (1/2 stick) of the butter with the light olive oil over medium-high heat until foamy. Brown the meat in batches in a single layer on all sides, 5 to 7 minutes per batch. Transfer the browned meat to a plate. Add the wine and scrape up any browned bits on the bottom of the pot. Add the onion, carrots, and turnips, then the tomato sauce and water and bring to a boil. Return the meat and any accumulated juices to the pot. Season with salt and pepper to taste.
3. Close and lock the lid. Set the burner heat to high. When the cooker reaches HIGH pressure, reduce the burner heat as low as you can and still maintain HIGH pressure. Set a timer to cook for 15 minutes.
4. Spread the couscous in a layer in a 9 x 13-inch rectangular baking pan. Pour over the boiling water. Cut the remaining 1/4 cup (1/2 stick) butter into pieces and stir into the couscous along with 1/2 teaspoon salt. Cover tightly with aluminum foil, then a dish towel. Let stand 10 to 15 minutes. It will keep warm until the stew is ready. Makes about 8 cups couscous.
5. Remove the pot from the heat. Open the cooker with the Natural Release method; let stand for 15 minutes. Be careful of the steam as you remove the lid.
6. Stir in the green beans and zucchini and let simmer gently, uncovered, for 10 minutes over medium heat. Add hot sauce to taste. Skim any fat from the top of the sauce. Taste for salt.
7. Uncover the couscous and fluff with a fork. Serve the stew in shallow bowls over a nice mound of the couscous.

Navarin (Spring Lamb Stew)

Serves 6 • Cooker: 5- to 7-quart • Time: 15 minutes for lamb, 4 minutes for vegetables at HIGH pressure

Braised young lamb is the basis for this very classic French ragoût traditionally made with spring vegetables, known as *navarin a la printaniere,* or navarin in the style of spring. The vegetables will be cooked twice, first in butter and then a quick stint under pressure. Serve with crusty-fresh French baguette and butter, or with a side of mashed potatoes. Enjoy it with a glass of Bordeaux or Beaujolais.

2 tablespoons olive oil, as needed
2 pounds lamb shoulder, trimmed of excess fat and cut into 3-inch chunks
1 tablespoon sugar
1 tablespoon all-purpose flour
1 cup chicken broth
1 cup dry white wine
1 large white or yellow onion, cut into 8 wedges, then cut into slivers
2 plum tomatoes (canned are ok), seeded and chopped
3 tablespoons chopped fresh tarragon OR
    2 teaspoons dried herbes de Provence
2 cloves garlic, pressed
3 tablespoons butter
2 bunches baby carrots (14 to 16 carrots, about 10 ounces—not from a bag), peeled and stems trimmed down to $1/2$ inch (or 4 medium carrots, sliced $1/2$ inch thick)
$1/2$ pound baby turnips (10 to 12), peeled and left whole or halved (or 3 medium turnips, peeled and cubed)
$1^1/2$ cups fresh peas (about 1 pound unshelled peas) or thawed frozen petite peas
8 ounces green beans, ends trimmed and cut into 3-inch lengths
Salt and freshly ground black pepper

1. In a 5- to 7-quart pressure cooker, heat the oil over medium-high heat until very hot. Brown the meat in batches in a single layer on all sides, 5 to 7 minutes per batch. Use a slotted spoon to transfer the browned meat to a plate. Return the meat and any accumulated juices to the pot. Sprinkle with the sugar and stir to coat. Sprinkle with the flour and stir again. Cook, stirring, for 3 minutes. Add the broth and wine and bring to a boil, scraping up any browned bits from the bottom of the pot. Add the onion, tomatoes, tarragon, and garlic.
2. Close and lock the lid. Set the burner heat to high. When the cooker reaches HIGH pressure, reduce the burner heat as low as you can and still maintain HIGH pressure. Set a timer to cook for 15 minutes.
3. Remove the pot from the heat. Open the cooker with the Natural Release method; let stand for 15 minutes. Be careful of the steam as you remove the lid.
4. In a large sauté pan, melt the butter over medium heat until foamy, then add the carrots, turnips, peas, and green beans and cook for 10 minutes, stirring to coat all the vegetables with the butter. You are cooking them just slightly; do not brown. Add the vegetables to the meat in the pressure cooker.
5. Close and lock the lid. Set the burner heat to high. When the cooker reaches HIGH pressure, reduce the burner heat as low as you can and still maintain HIGH pressure. Set a timer to cook for 4 minutes.
6. Open the cooker with the Quick Release method. Be careful of the steam as you remove the lid. Skim any fat from the top of the sauce. Season to taste with salt and pepper. Serve immediately.

Lamb Stew with Pearl Onions and Mushrooms

Serves 6 • Cooker: 5- to 7-quart • Time: 16 minutes at HIGH pressure

When we were young and took plane trips via United Airlines around 1975, they always had copies of *Mainliner* magazine in the magazine pocket to read while waiting to take off. The first thing to read was the celebrity food column, which ran every month. Just after starring in Alfred Hitchcock's film *Deceit (Family Plot)*, Bruce Dern shared his favorite lamb stew, adapted here for the pressure cooker. This is one of those traditional style full-of-vegetables lamb stews, with no potatoes. Make it in the fall when the baskets of boiling onions appear (there are about 20 to 25 onions in a basket) or use frozen.

$1/4$ cup olive oil
1 large or 2 medium white onions, chopped
3 pounds lamb shoulder or boneless leg of lamb, trimmed of excess fat and cut into 2-inch chunks
Salt and freshly ground black pepper
$2^1/2$ cups reduced-sodium chicken broth
1 (8-ounce) can tomato sauce
1 clove garlic, peeled
2 pinches dried thyme
1 bay leaf
3 ribs celery, chopped
3 medium carrots, sliced $1/2$ inch thick
16 small fresh white pearl onions, peeled, or frozen, thawed
8 ounces white mushrooms, sliced
3 tablespoons chopped fresh flatleaf parsley

1. In a 5- to 7-quart pressure cooker, heat the oil over medium-high heat until very hot. Add the white onion(s) and cook, stirring a few times, until soft, about 3 minutes. Remove to a plate. Brown the meat in batches in a single layer on all sides, 5 to 7 minutes per batch. Use a slotted spoon to transfer the browned meat to a plate. Return the meat and accumulated juices to the pot. Season to taste with salt and pepper. Stir in the broth, tomato sauce, garlic, thyme, and bay leaf, add back the onions, and bring to a boil, scraping up any browned bits from the bottom of the pot. Add the celery, carrots, pearl onions, and mushrooms. Stir to combine.

2. Close and lock the lid. Set the burner heat to high. When the cooker reaches HIGH pressure, reduce the burner heat as low as you can and still maintain HIGH pressure. Set a timer to cook for 16 minutes.

3. Remove the pot from the heat. Open the cooker with the Natural Release method; let stand for 15 minutes. Be careful of the steam as you remove the lid. Skim any fat from the top of the sauce. Discard the garlic clove and bay leaf.

4. Taste for salt. Serve immediately with rice or mashed potatoes, sprinkled with the parsley.

Lamb and White Bean Stew with Herbes de Provence

Serves 4 • Cooker: 5- to 7-quart • Time: 25 minutes at HIGH pressure

Lamb and white beans are a classic combination and make for some mighty good eating. It's a one-bowl meal that only asks for a nice green salad. You do not need to soak the beans for this recipe.

2 tablespoons olive oil
4 lamb round-bone shoulder chops (about 2 pounds), trimmed of fat and cut in half
1 1/2 cups (about 1/2 pound) dried navy beans, rinsed and picked over
1 (14-ounce) can diced tomatoes in juice, undrained
1 medium white onion, diced
2 medium leeks (white part only), trimmed, cut in half lengthwise, rinsed well, and diced
2 ribs celery, chopped
2 tablespoons coarsely chopped garlic
1 teaspoon dried herbes de Provence
2 teaspoons Worcestershire sauce
1/2 cup dry white wine or dry vermouth
3 cups chicken broth
Sea salt and freshly ground black pepper
2 tablespoons unsalted butter mashed together with 2 tablespoons all-purpose flour (optional)

1. In a 5- to 7-quart pressure cooker, heat the oil over medium-high heat until very hot. Brown the meat in batches in a single layer on one side, about 3 minutes per batch. Use a slotted spoon to transfer the browned meat to a plate. Return the meat and any accumulated juices to the pot. Add the beans, tomatoes and their juice, onion, leeks, celery, garlic, herbs, Worcestershire, and wine and bring to a boil, scraping up any browned bits from the bottom of the pot. Add the broth and season with salt and pepper.

2. Close and lock the lid. Set the burner heat to high. When the cooker reaches HIGH pressure, reduce the burner heat as low as you can and still maintain HIGH pressure. Set a timer to cook for 25 minutes.

3. Remove the pot from the heat. Open the cooker with the Natural Release method; let stand for 15 minutes. Be careful of the steam as you remove the lid. Skim any fat from the sauce.

4. Taste the stew for salt. If you want a thicker sauce, remove the chops to a plate and cover with aluminum foil. Add the butter-and-flour mixture to the sauce and stir until thickened. Spoon the bean-and-vegetable mixture into large shallow bowls; top with a lamb chop and sauce.

Irish Pub Lamb Stew with Butternut Squash

Serves 4 • Cooker: 6- to 8-quart • Time: 22 minutes at HIGH pressure

Beth's mother liked to make this stew with round-bone shoulder chops and we were surprised to find that the Irish stew in Fran McCullough and Barbara Witt's fantastic cookbook *Classic American Without Fuss* (Villard, 1996) calls for them as well instead of the usual stew meat. We added their suggestion of seasoning the stew with parsley, bay leaf, garlic, and whole cloves á la Maxim's restaurant in Paris. (We like the idea of such a humble stew being served in such elegant surroundings!) And we've taken the liberty of using butternut squash in place of the carrots. Serve this with brown bread and butter and a pint of Guinness for the quintessential pub meal. It's best made a day ahead, chilled, and the fat lifted off the surface before reheating.

2 tablespoons olive oil
1 large yellow or white onion, sliced ¹/₂ inch thick
2 medium leeks (white part only), trimmed, cut in half lengthwise, rinsed well, and thinly sliced across
3 Yukon Gold or new white potatoes, cut into 1-inch-thick slices
3 tablespoons chopped fresh flatleaf parsley
4 lamb round-bone shoulder chops (about 2 pounds), trimmed of fat and cut into thirds (one section will have the flavorful round bone)
3 cups cubed (1-inch) peeled butternut squash
Sea salt and freshly ground black pepper
2 cloves garlic, sliced
6 whole cloves
1 bay leaf, broken in half
1¹/₂ cups chicken or vegetable broth

1. In a 6- to 8-quart pressure cooker, heat the oil over medium-high heat. Add the onion and leeks and cook, stirring a few times, until soft, about 3 minutes. Remove to a plate.

2. Layer the ingredients, beginning and ending with potatoes, in the pressure cooker: half of the potatoes (overlapping), leeks and onion, the parsley, 2 lamb chops, squash, the remaining 2 lamb chops, and the remaining potatoes. Lightly salt and generously pepper each layer as you go along, tucking in the garlic pieces, cloves, and bay leaf here and there. Pour over the broth.

3. Close and lock the lid. Set the burner heat to high. When the cooker reaches HIGH pressure, reduce the burner heat as low as you can and still maintain HIGH pressure. Set a timer to cook for 22 minutes.

4. Remove the pot from the heat. Open the cooker with the Natural Release method; let stand for 15 minutes. Be careful of the steam as you remove the lid. The vegetables and lamb should be tender. Discard the cloves and bay leaf. Skim any fat from the sauce. Serve in soup plates.

Braised Lamb Shoulder with Fennel and Peas

Serves 6 • Cooker: 5- to 7-quart • Time: 25 minutes at HIGH pressure

Fennel is very popular in Italian cooking. A member of the same family as parsley, carrots, dill, coriander, and caraway, its bulb, stalk, leaves, and seeds are all edible, and the crisp, anise-flavored bulb pairs very nicely with lamb.

2 tablespoons olive oil
4 lamb round-bone shoulder chops (about 2
    pounds), trimmed of fat and cut into thirds
Sea salt and freshly ground black pepper
1 medium leek or 2 baby leeks (white part only),
    trimmed, cut in half lengthwise, rinsed well, and
    thinly sliced across
4 cloves garlic, thinly sliced
1/2 cup dry white wine or dry vermouth
1 tablespoon minced fresh thyme
1 large fennel bulb, trimmed of stalks and cut into
    12 wedges
1 cup chicken or vegetable broth
1 1/2 cups frozen petite peas, thawed
2 tablespoons chopped fresh flatleaf parsley
Shaved Pecorino Romano cheese, for serving

1. In a 5- to 7-quart pressure cooker, heat the oil over medium-high heat until very hot. Season the lamb with salt and pepper. Brown the meat in batches in a single layer on one side, about 3 minutes per batch. Use a slotted spoon to transfer the browned meat to a plate. Add the leek and cook, stirring a few times, until soft, about 2 minutes. Add the garlic and cook 30 seconds. Add the wine and bring to a boil, scraping up any browned bits from the bottom of the pot. Return the meat and any accumulated juices to the pot. Add the thyme and fennel. Add the broth and season to taste with salt and pepper.

2. Close and lock the lid. Set the burner heat to high. When the cooker reaches HIGH pressure, reduce the burner heat as low as you can and still maintain HIGH pressure. Set a timer to cook for 25 minutes.

3. Remove the pot from the heat. Open the cooker with the Natural Release method; let stand for 15 minutes. Be careful of the steam as you remove the lid. The lamb and fennel should be fork tender. Be careful of the steam as you remove the lid. Skim any fat from the sauce.

4. Stir in the peas and parsley and let stand for a few minutes, covered, until heated through. Divide among bowls, garnishing each portion with a generous shower of cheese. Use a cheese grater or vegetable peeler to shave curls of cheese if you have a hunk. Serve immediately.

PECORINO ROMANO

Pecorino Romano is a dry grating cheese made from sheep's milk and it really complements vegetables. It is used in southern Italy and Sardinia instead of Parmigiano-Reggiano and has a tangier, more assertive taste. You can substitute Asiago or Grana Padano.

Braised Lamb Shanks with Lemon and Fresh Tomatoes

Serves 4 • Cooker: 5- to 8-quart • Time: 25 minutes at HIGH pressure

This is adapted from a recipe on the T-fal pressure cooker website. If the shanks are too large for your cooker, have the butcher cut them in half or in thirds. It won't affect the cooking process or the final product (a tip from our PC guru Lorna Sass). Look for nice, large fresh plum tomatoes for the best flavor. Make this the day before so you can skim the fat off before reheating. Serve with mashed potatoes and a green vegetable.

4 plum tomatoes, cored
4 (1^1/4-pound) lamb shanks, trimmed of as much
    fat and connective tissue as possible
1 teaspoon sea salt, plus more to taste
Freshly ground black pepper
^{1}/$_3$ cup all-purpose or rice flour
3 tablespoons olive oil
1 large white onion, chopped
3 medium carrots, thickly sliced
1 clove garlic, crushed
1 tablespoon chopped fresh oregano or 1 teaspoon
    dried
Finely grated zest of 1 lemon
4 long strips lemon zest
1 cup dry red wine
^{1}/$_4$ cup beef or vegetable broth

1. Drop the tomatoes into boiling water for 30 seconds, then remove with a slotted spoon and refresh in ice cold water. Place on a paper towel and slip off the skins. Cut in half, squeeze out the seeds, and crush with your hand. Set aside.

2. Season the shanks all over with the salt and pepper to taste. Place the flour in a plastic bag. One at a time, add the lamb shanks to the flour and shake until they are coated evenly. In a 5- to 8-quart pressure cooker, heat the oil over medium-high heat until very hot. Add one or two shanks to the pot at a time and brown them lightly on all sides, 2 to 3 minutes per side. Transfer the browned shanks to a plate. Add the onion, carrots, and garlic to the pot and cook, stirring a few times, until lightly browned at the edges, about 5 minutes. Add the crushed tomatoes, oregano, grated zest and strips, wine, and broth. Bring to a boil, scraping up any browned bits from the bottom of the pot. Return the shanks and any accumulated juices to the pot. Spoon some of the liquid and vegetables over the meat.

3. Close and lock the lid. Set the burner heat to high. When the cooker reaches HIGH pressure, reduce the burner heat as low as you can and still maintain HIGH pressure. Set a timer to cook for 25 minutes.

4. Remove the pot from the heat. Open the cooker with the Natural Release method; let stand for 15 minutes. Be careful of the steam as you remove the lid. The vegetables should be cooked through and the meat fork-tender. Using tongs and an oversized spoon, transfer the meat and vegetables to a storage container. Discard the lemon strips. Let cool. Cover and refrigerate overnight.

5. The next day, spoon off the congealed fat from the top of the sauce. Place the shanks and sauce in a deep saucepan and reheat. Taste for salt. Place a shank on each dinner plate and spoon the vegetables and sauce over the meat.

Spiced Lamb Shanks with Yogurt Sauce

Serves 4 • Cooker: 5- to 8-quart • Time: 30 minutes at HIGH pressure

Braised lamb shanks are often on the menu in Middle Eastern and Near Eastern restaurants, but few people prepare them at home. With a pressure cooker, there's no reason not to enjoy hearty, flavorful, and tender lamb shanks for a cozy weeknight supper or as the centerpiece of a company meal. This gently spiced rendition is braised in white wine, then served in a tangy yogurt-mint sauce. Serve it with brown or white basmati rice or a rice blend to soak up every bit of savory sauce.

$1/4$ cup plus 1 tablespoon all-purpose flour
$1/2$ teaspoon sea salt
$1/4$ teaspoon freshly ground black pepper
$1/4$ teaspoon ground cinnamon
$1/4$ teaspoon ground coriander
4 ($1 1/4$-pound) lamb shanks, trimmed of as much fat and connective tissue as possible
2 tablespoons olive or vegetable oil
1 large white onion, cut in half, then into $1/2$-inch-thick half moons
2 large cloves garlic, chopped
1 cup dry white wine
1 cup water
1 bay leaf
$3/4$ cup plain Greek yogurt (nonfat or lowfat works fine)
$1/4$ cup chopped fresh mint, for serving

1. In a plastic bag, shake together $1/4$ cup of the flour, the salt, pepper, cumin, and coriander. One at a time, add the lamb shanks to the seasoned flour and shake until they are coated evenly. In a 5- to 8-quart pressure cooker, heat the oil over medium-high heat until very hot. Add one or two shanks to the pot at a time and brown them lightly on all sides, 2 to 3 minutes per side. Transfer the browned shanks to a plate.

2. Add the onion to the pot and cook, stirring, for about 1 minute. Add the garlic and any leftover seasoned flour and cook, stirring, for 2 minutes. Add the wine and water and bring to a boil, scraping up any browned bits on the bottom of the pot. Return the shanks to the pot, stacking them as evenly as possible. Tuck in the bay leaf.

3. Close and lock the lid. Set the burner heat to high. When the cooker reaches HIGH pressure, reduce the burner heat as low as you can and still maintain HIGH pressure. Set a timer to cook for 30 minutes.

4. A few minutes before the timer sounds, preheat the broiler and arrange the rack over a broiler pan. In a small bowl, stir the remaining 1 tablespoon flour into the yogurt.

5. Remove the pot from the heat. Open the cooker with the Quick Release method. Be careful of the steam as you remove the lid. Using tongs, place the lamb shanks on the broiler pan. Skim any fat from the top of the sauce.

6. Stir the yogurt mixture into the pot liquid and let it come to a boil. Continue to boil, stirring occasionally, until the sauce reduces to the consistency of a creamy salad dressing, or even thicker, if you prefer. Stir in the mint.

7. Broil the lamb shanks for 2 minutes, turning as necessary to brown them nicely on all sides.

8. Serve each diner one lamb shank and a generous ladle of yogurt sauce.

Rosemary and Garlic Lamb Shanks

Serves 4 • Cooker: 5- to 8-quart • Time: 30 minutes at HIGH pressure

Gilroy, California, our backyard, calls itself the garlic capital of the world, and we felt the need to celebrate that in this recipe. As it cooks, the flavor of garlic mellows, so don't be put off by the amount of garlic called for. Serve these shanks on a bed of cauliflower puree.

4 (1¼-pound) lamb shanks, trimmed of as much
    fat and connective tissue as possible
1 teaspoon sea salt, plus more to taste
Freshly ground black pepper
3 tablespoons olive oil
4 leeks (white part with a little of the green),
    trimmed, cut in half lengthwise, rinsed well,
    and thickly sliced across
6 cloves garlic, sliced
1 cup chicken broth
½ cup dry red wine
¼ cup balsamic vinegar
1 teaspoon dried basil
1 teaspoon crumbled dried rosemary
2 tablespoons cold unsalted butter, cut into pieces

1. Season the shanks all over with the salt and pepper to taste. In a 5- to 8-quart pressure cooker, heat the oil over medium-high heat until very hot. Add one or two shanks to the pot at a time and brown them lightly on all sides, 2 to 3 minutes per side. Transfer the browned shanks to a plate. Add the leeks and garlic to the pot and cook, stirring a few times, until lightly browned at the edges, 2 to 3 minutes. Return the shanks and any accumulated juices to the pot. Add the broth, wine, vinegar, basil, and rosemary. Bring to a boil, scraping up any browned bits on the bottom of the pot.

2. Close and lock the lid. Set the burner heat to high. When the cooker reaches HIGH pressure, reduce the burner heat as low as you can and still maintain HIGH pressure. Set a timer to cook for 30 minutes.

3. Remove the pot from the heat. Open the cooker with the Natural Release method; let stand for 15 minutes. Be careful of the steam as you remove the lid. Skim any fat from the sauce.

4. Taste for salt. Place a shank on each dinner plate. Bring the liquid in the pot to a boil and let boil, uncovered, for 5 minutes to reduce and thicken the sauce. Whisk in the butter and spoon the sauce over the shanks.

French Lamb Shanks with Garlic and Prunes

Serves 4 • Cooker: 5- to 8-quart • Time: 30 minutes at HIGH pressure

This is adapted from a recipe from Kerry Saretsky's French Revolution, one of our very favorite blogs. Prunes are fantastic with lamb and help flavor the sauce. Serve with scalloped potatoes or mashed potatoes.

4 (1¼-pound) lamb shanks, trimmed of as much fat and connective tissue as possible
1 teaspoon sea salt
Freshly ground black pepper
2 tablespoons olive oil
2 medium yellow or white onions, cut in half and then into ½-inch-thick half moons
1 cup dry white wine
2 cups low-sodium chicken broth
12 large cloves garlic, unpeeled
20 pitted prunes
Equal portions of chopped fresh mint and flatleaf parsley, to serve

1. Season the shanks all over with the salt and pepper to taste. In a 5- to 8-quart pressure cooker, heat the oil over medium-high heat until very hot. Add one or two shanks to the pot at a time and brown them lightly on all sides, 2 to 3 minutes per side. Transfer the browned shanks to a plate. Add the onions to the pot, reduce the heat to low, and cook, stirring occasionally, until lightly caramelized, 10 to 15 minutes. Turn the heat to high, add the wine, and bring to a boil, scraping up any browned bits on the bottom of the pot; let boil for 2 minutes. Return the shanks and any accumulated juices to the pot. Add the broth, garlic, and prunes.

2. Close and lock the lid. Set the burner heat to high. When the cooker reaches HIGH pressure, reduce the burner heat as low as you can and still maintain HIGH pressure. Set a timer to cook for 30 minutes.

3. Remove the pot from the heat. Open the cooker with the Natural Release method; let stand for 15 minutes. Be careful of the steam as you remove the lid. Skim any fat from the sauce.

4. Taste for salt. Place a shank on each dinner plate along with 3 garlic cloves (diners can squeeze the garlic out of the skins to spread on bread) and 5 prunes; sprinkle with mint and parsley.

Red Wine Goat Ragù with Carrots and Shiitake Mushrooms

Serves 4 • Cooker: 5- to 7-quart • Time: 40 minutes at HIGH pressure

This is really good reheated the next day. Serve with Garlic Mashed Potatoes (page 446) and a nice salad vinaigrette.

1½ pounds boneless goat shoulder, trimmed of excess fat and cut into 1½-inch pieces
2 tablespoons olive oil
1 large red or white onion, finely chopped
2 sprigs fresh thyme
2 sprigs fresh marjoram
3 bay leaves
1½ cups dry red wine
1 bunch carrots, tops removed, peeled, and sliced ½ inch thick on the diagonal
8 ounces fresh shiitake mushrooms, stems discarded and quartered, or white mushrooms, quartered
1 (6-ounce) can tomato paste
1 teaspoon cornstarch
1 (10.5-ounce) can beef broth
Sea salt and freshly ground black pepper

1. In a 5- to 7-quart pressure cooker, heat 1 table-spoon of the oil over medium-high heat until very hot. Brown the meat in batches in a single layer on all sides, 3 to 4 minutes per batch, adding the remaining 1 tablespoon oil as needed. Use a slotted spoon to transfer the browned meat to a plate.
2. Add the onion to the hot oil, reduce the heat to medium, and cook, stirring a few times, 1 to 2 minutes. Add the herbs (you can tie them together) and wine and bring to a low boil, scraping up any browned bits from the bottom of the pot. Add the meat and any accumulated juices back to the pot, along with the carrots and mushrooms. Stir the tomato paste and cornstarch into the broth, then pour into the pot.
3. Close and lock the lid. Set the burner heat to high. When the cooker reaches HIGH pressure, reduce the burner heat as low as you can and still maintain HIGH pressure. Set a timer to cook for 40 minutes.
4. Remove the pot from the heat. Open the cooker with the Quick Release method. Be careful of the steam as you remove the lid. Discard the whole herbs. Skim any fat from the sauce.
5. Season to taste with salt and pepper and serve.

Jamaican Curry Goat

Serves 8 • Cooker: 5- to 8-quart • Time: 40 minutes at HIGH pressure

Curry goat is one of the most famous stews in the culinary world, usually prepared for holiday parties and celebrations. For authentic flavor, please seek out Jamaican hot curry powder. Jamaica was not introduced to curry powder until after the slaves were freed and indentured servants from India came during the 1830s to work on the sugar plantations. It was an instant hit and now flavors all sorts of meat dishes. What makes the Jamaican curry blend different from the Indian? The inclusion of allspice, also known as pimento in Jamaica. (Please note that store-bought Jamaican curry powder is not gluten free.) This stew produces an absolutely amazing aroma and it is even better the day after, or several days after, you make it. Serve with rice, peas, and roti or chapati.

1/4 cup olive oil
1/4 cup Jamaican hot curry powder, or to taste (if using regular curry powder, mix it with 2 teaspoons ground allspice)
3 pounds boneless goat shoulder, trimmed of excess fat
Sea salt
2 large white onions, chopped
1 to 2 habanero or Scotch bonnet peppers, to taste, seeded and chopped
1 (2-inch) piece fresh ginger, peeled and minced
1 head garlic, broken into cloves, peeled, and chopped
2 (15-ounce) cans unsweetened coconut milk
1 (15-ounce) can tomato sauce
1 tablespoon dried thyme
3 cups water
5 Yukon Gold potatoes, peeled and cut into 1-inch chunks, or 3 cups cooked garbanzo beans

1. Cut the meat into large chunks, maybe 2 to 3 inches across. Salt everything well and set aside to come to room temperature for about 30 minutes. Pat dry with paper towels.

2. In a 5- to 8-quart pressure cooker, heat the oil over medium-high heat until very hot. Add 2 tablespoons of the curry powder and stir until fragrant, about 30 seconds. Brown the meat in batches in a single layer on all sides in the curried oil. Transfer the browned meat to a bowl. It will take a while to do this, maybe 30 minutes or so total.

3. Add the onions and habanero to the pot and cook, stirring occasionally, until the onions just start to brown, about 5 minutes. Sprinkle some salt over them as they cook. Add the ginger and garlic, mix well, and cook, stirring, another 1 to 2 minutes. Return the meat and any accumulated juices to the pot. Mix well. Add the coconut milk, tomato sauce, and remaining curry powder. Stir to combine. Add the water and thyme and bring to a simmer, scraping up any browned bits from the bottom of the pot.

4. Close and lock the lid. Set the burner heat to high. When the cooker reaches HIGH pressure, reduce the burner heat as low as you can and still maintain HIGH pressure. Set a timer to cook for 40 minutes.

5. Remove the pot from the heat. Open the cooker with the Natural Release method; let stand for 15 minutes. Be careful of the steam as you remove the lid. The meat should be falling-apart tender. Skim any fat from the top of the sauce.

6. Taste the stew for salt. Add the potatoes. Recover and let steam (without bringing up the pressure) until they are just tender, about 10 minutes, then serve.

Venison Pot Roast with Bacon and New Potatoes

Serves 6 • Cooker: 5- to 8- quart • Time: 45 minutes at HIGH pressure

Because venison is so lean, bacon is often included, as it is here. It is a delicious, rich-tasting stew, a perfect choice for a chilly weekend.

1 (3-pound) venison shoulder roast
3 tablespoons all-purpose or rice flour
Sea salt and freshly ground black pepper, to taste
4 slices thick-cut bacon, chopped
1 tablespoon olive oil
2 large yellow onions, chopped
4 ribs celery, chopped
2 teaspoons minced garlic
2 cups reduced-sodium beef broth
$1/4$ cup low-sodium soy sauce
1 teaspoon dried thyme
1 bay leaf
$1/2$ cup red currant jelly
$1^{1}/2$ pounds fairly small Yukon Gold or red potatoes, left unpeeled and whole
4 medium carrots, cut into 3-inch chunks, or
   1 (16-ounce) bag baby carrots
2 tablespoons all-purpose flour mixed with $1/4$ cup water or white wine, for thickening

1. Pat the roast dry with paper towels and sprinkle with the flour, salt, and pepper. In a 5- to 8-quart pressure cooker over medium-high heat, cook the bacon, stirring, until brown. Transfer with a slotted spoon to paper towels to drain. Add the oil to the drippings and heat until very hot, then add the roast and brown on all sides, about 3 minutes total. Transfer to a plate and tent with aluminum foil to keep warm. Add the onions and celery to the pot and cook, stirring, until softened, about 2 minutes. Stir in the garlic, broth, soy sauce, bay leaf, and thyme. Add the jelly and stir to melt. Return the bacon, venison roast, and any accumulated juice to the pot. Tuck the potatoes and carrots around the roast.

2. Close and lock the lid. Set the burner heat to high. When the cooker reaches HIGH pressure, reduce the burner heat as low as you can and still maintain HIGH pressure. Set a timer to cook for 45 minutes.

3. Remove the pot from the heat. Open the cooker with the Natural Release method; let stand for 15 minutes. Be careful of the steam as you remove the lid. Transfer the meat and vegetables to a platter with tongs and a meat fork, and cover loosely with foil. Skim any fat from the top of the sauce. Let rest 10 to 15 minutes.

4. Taste the pot juices for salt and pepper. Give the flour slurry a brisk whisk to remix, then pour into the pot and stir to combine. Bring to a boil. The sauce will thicken. Carve the roast and serve with the vegetables. This is also good served the next day.

Venison Stew with Artichokes and Sundried Tomatoes

Serves 4 to 6 • Cooker: 5- to 7- quart • Time: 18 minutes at HIGH pressure

Serve this in shallow bowls on a chilly winter day over egg noodles or rice.

4 tablespoons olive oil
2 pounds boneless venison stew meat, cut into
    1 1/2-inch cubes
1 large white onion, chopped into 1/2-inch pieces
1 leek (white and light green parts), trimmed, cut in
    half lengthwise, rinsed well, and chopped
1 medium carrot, chopped
2 cups dry red wine
1 cup reduced-sodium beef broth
1 teaspoon sea salt
1/2 teaspoon freshly ground black pepper
Bouquet garni of 1 rib celery, cut to make 2 pieces,
    1 bay leaf, 1 sprig fresh thyme, 2 sprigs fresh
    parsley, tied together with kitchen twine
1/2 cup chopped drained oil-packed sundried
    tomatoes
2 (14-ounce) packages frozen artichoke hearts,
    thawed
1 tablespoon cornstarch mixed with 2 tablespoons
    water, for thickening
1/4 cup (1/2 stick) cold unsalted butter, cut into
    pieces
Grated zest of 1 lemon
1 clove garlic, minced
2 tablespoons finely chopped fresh flatleaf parsley

1. In a 5- to 7-quart pressure cooker, heat 1 tablespoon of the oil over medium-high heat until
   very hot. Brown the venison batches in a single
   layer, 1 to 2 minutes per side, adding more of
   the oil as needed. Transfer the meat to a plate as
   it browns.
2. Add the remaining oil to the pot. Add the onion,
   leek, and carrot, reduce the heat to medium, and
   cook, stirring a few times, until the onion begins
   to soften, 1 to 2 minutes. Add the wine and
   bring to a boil, scraping up any browned bits
   from the bottom of the pot. Add the meat and
   any accumulated juices to the pot, along with
   the broth, salt, pepper, bouquet garni, and sundried tomatoes. Add the artichokes.
3. Close and lock the lid. Set the burner heat to
   high. When the cooker reaches HIGH pressure,
   reduce the burner heat as low as you can and
   still maintain HIGH pressure. Set a timer to
   cook for 18 minutes.
4. Remove the pot from the heat. Open the cooker
   with the Quick Release method. Be careful of
   the steam as you remove the lid.
5. Drain off the cooking liquid into a saucepan and
   add the cornstarch mixture. Place the pan over
   medium heat and stir with a whisk until thickened. Whisk in the butter pieces, then the lemon
   zest, garlic, and parsley. Taste for salt and pepper. Pour back into the pot with the meat. Serve
   the stew in shallow bowls.

Venison Osso Bucco

Serves 6 • Cooker: 4- to 8-quart • Time: 20 minutes at HIGH pressure

This is based on a recipe that appeared in *Outdoor Life* magazine from restaurateur Lidia Bastianich (of Felidia and Becco in New York City and Lidia's in Kansas City, Missouri). It is just too delicious to pass up making in the pressure cooker. It contains carrot juice, which works great with tomatoes for flavor, and juniper berries, the classic spice for game stews. Serve with polenta or a risotto.

1 lemon
2 navel oranges
6 (8- to 10-ounce) venison shanks, cut from the hind shanks, tied with kitchen twine to prevent them from falling apart during cooking
$1/2$ cup all-purpose flour
4 tablespoons olive oil
Sea salt and freshly ground black pepper
2 large white onions, chopped
1 medium carrot, shredded
2 ribs celery, chopped
1 cup fruity red wine, such as Chianti
1 cup fresh carrot juice
1 (28-ounce can) San Marzano plum tomatoes in juice, drained and crushed with your hands
2 cups reduced-sodium chicken broth
2 bay leaves
4 whole cloves
1 sprig fresh rosemary
10 juniper berries
1 tablespoon tomato paste

1. Peel the zest from the oranges and lemon in wide strips with a vegetable peeler. Set the zest of 1 orange and lemon aside for the sauce. Slice the zest of the other orange into strips about $1/8$ inch wide and set aside for garnish. Remove and discard the pithy membrane of 1 orange, then slice into segments and reserve for garnish. Juice the second orange and set the juice aside.

2. Pat the venison dry with paper towels and sprinkle with the flour. In a 5- to 8-quart pressure cooker, heat 2 tablespoons of the oil over medium-high heat until very hot. Add 2 or 3 shanks (however many will fit in a single layer) and brown on all sides, about 3 minutes total. Transfer to a plate and tent with aluminum foil to keep warm. Repeat with the remaining 2 tablespoons oil and venison shanks. Season to taste with salt and pepper.

3. Add the onions, carrot, and celery to the pot and cook, stirring a few times, until softened, about 5 minutes. Add the wine, scraping up any browned bits from the bottom of the pot. Stir in the carrot juice, reserved orange juice, reserved wide strips of lemon and orange zest, tomatoes, and broth. Add the bay leaf, cloves, rosemary, and juniper berries. Return the veal shanks and any accumulated juices to the pot, pushing them down into the liquid. Place the tomato paste on top. Do not stir it in.

4. Close and lock the lid. Set the burner heat to high. When the cooker reaches HIGH pressure, reduce the burner heat as low as you can and still maintain HIGH pressure. Set a timer to cook for 20 minutes.

5. Remove the pot from the heat. Open the cooker with the Natural Release method; let stand for 15 minutes. Be exact with your timing, so set a timer. Be careful of the steam as you remove the lid. Skim off any fat from the top of the sauce. Let rest about 10 minutes. Discard the bay leaf, rosemary stalk, zest, and cloves.

6. Serve each osso bucco with plenty of vegetables and sauce. Garnish with the reserved orange segments and zest, and serve with polenta or a risotto, if you like.

9

Pork

Move over osso bucco, coq au vin, beef daube, and lamb stew. Pork cooks up like a champ in the pressure cooker, which is good news for the pork lover. Yes, we're talking pork stew and braised shoulder, but pork chops and loin roasts also work well in the pressure cooker.

High-quality outdoor pastured or heirloom pork is finding its way into the general market. Cooks looking for a better product than factory-farmed pork are seeking out crate-free, pastured pork, pigs that are allowed to do what they naturally do, which is root, dig, and graze in pastures and woods. While commercial pork is often fed anything cheap, pastured heritage hogs are given free range of pasture and supplemented with vegetables and grain, yielding a delicious meat. Look for Animal Welfare Approved pork, which is raised with no antibiotics, no steroids to hasten growth, and no medicated food. Organic pork is fed 100 percent organic corn and soy, and hormones are illegal. It can be raised indoors but must have some time pastured. Natural pork, which is minimally processed—meaning no synthetic ingredients or colorings can be added—is raised on organic feed. However, unless it states no antibiotics, natural pork can be raised indoors and given antibiotics.

When buying pork, look for firm, pink flesh and make sure pork is cooked to an internal temperature of 160° F.

THE BEST CUTS OF PORK FOR THE PRESSURE COOKER

- Boneless pork shoulder
- Pork rib eyes
- Center-cut pork loin chops
- Pork blade roast
- Pork loin roast
- Boston pork butt
- Picnic or smoked picnic pork
- Country-style pork ribs, spareribs, and baby back ribs
- Pork belly (fresh bacon)
- Boneless ham
- Ham hocks

Pork Tenderloin with Balsamic Cranberry Sauce

Serves 4 to 6 • Cooker: 6- to 8-quart • Time: 20 minutes at HIGH pressure

Pork tenderloin, the equivalent of the beef's filet mignon, is very popular because of its leanness. But in the pressure cooker, that means it cooks very quickly and can dry out. So we add broth and braise it whole so it will stay juicy and tender. Don't confuse the tenderloin with the loin roast. The tenderloin is a long slender strip that comes off the full loin. One pork tenderloin will serve 3 to 4 diners. This can be served hot or at room temperature for sandwiches or fanned over crisp greens with a tangy vinaigrette.

TENDERLOIN:

2 (12- to 16-ounce) pork tenderloins, trimmed of
     silverskin and patted dry with paper towels
$1/4$ teaspoon paprika
$1/4$ teaspoon garlic powder
$1/4$ teaspoon sea salt
$1/4$ teaspoon freshly ground black pepper
2 tablespoons olive oil
$1^1/2$ cups low-sodium chicken broth

BALSAMIC CRANBERRY SAUCE:

$1/3$ cup balsamic vinegar
1 small shallot, minced
1 (16-ounce) can whole-berry cranberry sauce
Sea salt

1. Season the tenderloin with the paprika, garlic, salt, and pepper. In a 6- to 8-quart pressure cooker, heat the oil over medium-high heat until very hot. Add one tenderloin to the pot and brown on all sides, about 4 minutes total. Transfer to a plate and brown the second tenderloin. Return the first tenderloin to the pot with any accumulated juices, curving them to fit the pot. Add the broth.

2. Close and lock the lid. Set the burner heat to high. When the cooker reaches HIGH pressure, reduce the burner heat as low as you can and still maintain HIGH pressure. Set a timer to cook for 20 minutes.

3. While the tenderloins are cooking, make the Balsamic Cranberry Sauce. Combine the vinegar and shallot in a small saucepan. Bring to a boil, reduce the heat to a simmer, and cook 3 to 4 minutes. Add the cranberry sauce, breaking it up with a spoon, and simmer until it melts, 6 to 8 minutes. Stir, then taste for salt. Cover, remove from the heat, and let stand until ready to serve. Add a few tablespoons of the braising liquid from the pork before serving. Simmer to reheat, if necessary.

4. Remove the pressure cooker from the heat. Open the cooker with the Natural Release method; let stand for about 15 minutes. Be careful of the steam as you remove the lid. An instant-read thermometer inserted into the center of the meat should read 150° F. Transfer the roast to a cutting board and cover loosely with aluminum foil for 5 minutes. (The temperature of the meat will rise another 5° to 10° F while sitting.)

5. Slice the meat into medallions and arrange on a warm platter. Serve with the hot sauce. The unsliced pork, well wrapped, will keep in the refrigerator for 3 days.

Green Sauce Pork Tenderloin

Serves 3 to 4 • Cooker: 6- to 8-quart • Time: 20 minutes at HIGH pressure

Pork tenderloin marinated and then braised in a green herb sauce is one of the fastest, most flavorful weeknight dinners we know. You can marinate the pork overnight, so all you have to do is place it in the pressure cooker. Serve with rice or whole wheat couscous.

1 clove garlic, peeled
$^1/_4$ cup fresh cilantro leaves
$^1/_4$ cup fresh flatleaf parsley leaves
$^1/_4$ cup coarsely chopped fresh chives or green
    onion tops
$^1/_4$ cup fresh lime juice or Meyer lemon juice
$^1/_4$ cup olive oil
$^1/_4$ to $^1/_2$ teaspoon red pepper flakes, to taste
Sea salt
1 (16-ounce) pork tenderloin, trimmed of silverskin
    and patted dry with paper towel
1 cup low-sodium chicken broth
1 small lime, thickly sliced
$^1/_2$ cup plain Greek yogurt (optional)

1. In a food processor fitted with the metal blade, process the garlic until finely chopped. Add the cilantro, parsley, and chives and pulse to chop. With the machine running, add the lime juice and oil through the feed tube and process until it forms a coarse puree. Add the red pepper and salt to taste. Place the tenderloin in a 1-gallon ziptop plastic bag and pour in the herb sauce. Seal and refrigerate for at least 4 hours or overnight.

2. Pour the broth into a 6- to 8-quart pressure cooker. Remove the tenderloin from the sauce and place it in the pot. Top with the lime slices, then pour the herb sauce over the top.

3. Close and lock the lid. Set the burner heat to high. When the cooker reaches HIGH pressure, reduce the burner heat as low as you can and still maintain HIGH pressure. Set a timer to cook for 20 minutes.

4. Remove the pot from the heat. Open the cooker with the Natural Release method; let stand for 15 minutes. Be careful of the steam as you remove the lid. The internal temperature should be 150° F. Transfer the roast with tongs to a carving board, cover loosely with aluminum foil, and let rest for 5 minutes (its temperature will rise to 160° F while it rests).

5. You can serve the pork with the green herb sauce straight from the pot, or stir in the yogurt, if you like, to make a creamy sauce. Slice the meat into medallions and arrange on a warm serving platter. Serve with the hot green herb sauce. The unsliced pork, well wrapped, will keep in the refrigerator for up to 3 days.

Pork Tenderloin and Sauerkraut with Goat Cheese Mashed Potatoes

Serves 4 to 6 • Cooker: 6- to 8-quart • Time: 20 minutes for tenderloin, 6 minutes for potatoes at HIGH pressure

Got a log of goat cheese in the fridge that needs to be used? Make these rich, tasty potatoes. Use the sauerkraut that comes in the bag for the best flavor. Gewürztraminer is a favorite cooking wine of ours, with its perfumed, floral flavor and aroma. While it is traditionally associated with Alsace in France, California has superb, reasonably priced Traminers from Monterey and Sonoma. Serve with a cranberry sauce (see pages 182–183) or Green Tomato Chutney (see page 276).

GOAT CHEESE MASHED POTATOES:

2 pounds (8 or 9) medium red or Yukon Gold potatoes, left unpeeled, halved
1 teaspoon salt
1/2 cup hot half-and-half
2 tablespoons butter
1 (6-ounce) log fresh goat cheese, crumbled
Few grinds freshly ground black or white pepper

PORK TENDERLOIN:

2 tablespoons olive oil
2 (12- to 16-ounce) pork tenderloins, trimmed of silverskin and patted dry with paper towel
1 cup low-sodium chicken broth
1/4 cup dry or sweet white wine, such as Gewürztraminer
1 1/2 teaspoons fennel seeds or caraway seeds
1 (16-ounce) package sauerkraut, drained and rinsed in a colander

1. Make the potatoes first unless you have two pressure cookers, then you can do the potatoes while the tenderloins cook. Place the potatoes in a 5- to 7-quart or 6- to 8-quart pressure cooker and fill with water to cover. It is okay if a few edges of the potatoes are peeking up out of the water. Sprinkle with the salt.

   Close and lock the lid. Set the burner heat to high. When the cooker reaches HIGH pressure, reduce the burner heat as low as you can and still maintain HIGH pressure. Set a timer to cook for 6 minutes.

2. Remove the pot from the heat. Open the cooker with the Quick Release method. Be careful of the steam as you remove the lid. The potatoes should be soft and tender when pierced with the tip of a knife but still hold their shape a bit. Drain in a colander. You can leave the potatoes in the pot or remove to a deep serving bowl. Add the half-and-half, butter and goat cheese. Mash with a fork or potato masher ONLY; these are supposed to be chunky. Season to taste with pepper and cover with plastic wrap. Set aside.

3. Make the pork tenderloin. In a 6- to 8-quart pressure cooker, warm the oil over medium-high heat until very hot. Add one tenderloin and brown on all sides, about 4 minutes total. Transfer to a plate and brown the second tenderloin. Return the tenderloins to the pot along with any accumulated juice, curving them to fit the pot. Add the broth, wine, and fennel seeds. Add the sauerkraut.

4. Close and lock the lid. Set the burner heat to high. When the cooker reaches HIGH pressure, reduce the burner heat as low as you can and still maintain HIGH pressure. Set a timer to cook for 20 minutes.

5. Remove the pot from the heat. Open the cooker with the Natural Release method; let stand for 15 minutes. Be careful of the steam as you remove the lid. The internal temperature should be 150° F. Transfer the roasts with tongs to a carving board, cover loosely with aluminum foil, and let rest for 5 minutes (their temperature will rise to 160° F while they rest).

6. Reheat the mashed potatoes in the microwave, if necessary. Slice the meat into medallions and portion on dinner plates. Serve with the hot sauerkraut and a scoop of mashed potatoes. The unsliced pork, well wrapped, will keep in the refrigerator up to 3 days.

Italian Braised Pork with Fresh Herbs

Serves 4 to 6 • Cooker: 5- to 7-quart • Time: 30 minutes at HIGH pressure

This is adapted from a recipe by Beth's friend Leslie Mansfield that appeared in her book *The Lewis and Clark Cookbook* (Celestial Arts, 2002), which translated historic American recipes into a modern format. Leslie traveled around the country hosting traditional Americana dinners in restaurants featuring her recipes, with tremendous success. This recipe was also made famous by the doyenne of Italian cooking, Marcella Hazan. The half-and-half used to braise the pork appears to curdle during the cooking, a technique that is very Italian, and that is exactly what you want, as it makes a scrumptious, creamy sauce. The herbs must be fresh; no substituting dried. We used rosemary and basil, which tasted divine.

3 tablespoons olive oil
1 (2^1/$_4$- to 2^1/$_2$-pound) boned and tied pork loin
   roast, trimmed of all but a thin layer of fat
1 teaspoon sea salt
10 turns freshly ground black pepper
2 cups half-and-half
2 teaspoons chopped fresh rosemary or marjoram
2 teaspoons chopped fresh tarragon or basil

1. In a 5- to 7-quart pressure cooker, heat the oil over medium-high heat until very hot. Season the roast all over with the salt and pepper and add it to the pot. Brown the meat on all sides, 6 to 8 minutes total. Add the half-and-half and herbs. The roast will be covered up to half its thickness.

2. Close and lock the lid. Set the burner heat to high. When the cooker reaches HIGH pressure, reduce the burner heat as low as you can and still maintain HIGH pressure. Set a timer to cook for 30 minutes.

3. Remove the pot from the heat. Open the cooker with the Quick Release method. Be careful of the steam as you remove the lid. An instant-read thermometer inserted into the center of the meat should read 150° F. Transfer the roast to a cutting board and cover loosely with foil while you finish the sauce. (The temperature of the meat will rise another 5° to 10° F while sitting.)

4. Spoon off any fat from the surface of the sauce. If you prefer a more homogenized sauce, use an immersion blender set right into the pot to puree the sauce until smooth. Taste the sauce, adding more salt if needed. Cut the roast into ^{1}/$_2$-inch-thick slices and arrange on a warm serving platter. Spoon the sauce over the top and serve.

Stuffed Pork Roast with Fresh Herbs, Spinach, Prosciutto, and Persimmon Chutney

Serves 6 • Cooker: 6- to 8-quart • Time: 12 minutes for chutney, 45 minutes for roast at HIGH pressure

Consider this dish foolproof. It is a butterflied roast rolled up with prosciutto and spinach, a favorite fall entertaining dish or special occasion meal on a weekend. You can make the chutney days ahead if you like.

PERSIMMON CHUTNEY:

8 Fuyu persimmons, peeled, seeded, and cut into small dice
3/4 cup sugar
1/2 cup cider vinegar
3/4 cup mixed golden raisin and dried tart cherry mix
1 tablespoon Sriracha hot sauce
2 tablespoons grated peeled fresh ginger
1 cup finely chopped white onions
3 tablespoons stone-ground mustard
2 teaspoons salt

PORK ROAST:

1 (3 1/2-pound) pork shoulder roast, butterflied and excess fat removed
1 tablespoon chopped fresh rosemary
1 tablespoon chopped fresh sage
1/4 pound thinly sliced prosciutto
1 bunch fresh spinach, stems removed, leaves washed well, and dried
Sea salt and freshly ground black pepper
1/4 cup olive oil
1/2 cup dry white wine
1/2 cup chicken broth

1. Make the Persimmon Chutney. Combine the ingredients in a 6- to 8-quart pressure cooker.
2. Close and lock the lid. Set the burner heat to high. When the cooker reaches HIGH pressure, reduce the burner heat as low as you can and still maintain HIGH pressure. Set a timer to cook for 12 minutes.
3. Remove the pot from the heat. Open the cooker with the Natural Release method; let stand for 15 minutes. Be careful of the steam as you re-move the lid. The persimmons should be very

tender. Let cool completely; the chutney will keep in an airtight container in the refrigerator up to 3 weeks. Wash and dry the pressure cooker.

4. Make the roast. Lay the pork flat on a work sur-face with the short side facing you. Sprinkle with half of the rosemary and sage. Arrange the prosciutto over it, covering its surface. Layer the spinach on top, overlapping the leaves. Starting at the side closest to you, roll up the roast and tie with kitchen string at 2-inch intervals. Sprin-kle the roast with the remaining rosemary and sage, and season with salt and pepper.
5. In the pressure cooker, heat the oil over medium-high heat until very hot. Add the roast and brown on all sides, 3 to 4 minutes total, then add the wine and broth. Bring to a boil.
6. Close and lock the lid. Set the burner heat to high. When the cooker reaches HIGH pressure, reduce the burner heat as low as you can and still maintain HIGH pressure. Set a timer to cook for 45 minutes.
7. Remove the pot from the heat. Open the cooker with the Natural Release method; let stand for 15 minutes. Be careful of the steam as you re-move the lid. An instant-read thermometer inserted into the center of the meat should read 150° F. Transfer the roast to a cutting board and cover loosely with aluminum foil for 5 minutes. (The temperature of the meat will rise another 5° to 10° F while sitting.) Remove the strings be-fore carving.
8. Skim the fat from the juices in the pot, season to taste, and transfer to a sauceboat. Slice the meat and arrange on a warm platter. Pass the juices and the persimmon chutney alongside.

Pork Chops with Apples, Thyme, and Dijon Mustard

Serves 4 • Cooker: 6- to 8-quart • Time: 7 minutes at HIGH pressure

Mustard pork is a French bistro dish known as *côtes de porc sauce moutarde*. For this, you must use the traditional smooth and creamy Dijon mustard, prepared with white wine and made since the fourteenth century in Burgundy, France, in combination with what is known as *moutarde a l'ancienne* or grainy mustard, black and brown mustard seeds ground with spices and vinegar. This dish is so easy to prepare and the chops stay delightfully moist. *Bon appetit!*

4 (8-ounce) bone-in pork loin or rib chops,
    $3/4$ to 1 inch thick
Sea salt and freshly ground black pepper
1 tablespoon olive oil
1 medium to large tart apple, such as Fuji,
    quartered, cored, and diced
2 medium shallots, chopped (about $1/3$ cup)
1 teaspoon chopped fresh thyme
$1/2$ cup dry white wine or dry hard apple cider
$1/2$ cup low-sodium chicken broth
1 tablespoon Dijon mustard
1 tablespoon grainy mustard, such as Pommery
    Moutarde de Meaux
3 tablespoons crème fraîche (optional)

1. Lightly season the chops with salt and pepper. In a 6- to 8-quart pressure cooker, heat the oil over medium-high heat until very hot. Brown the chops in batches on both sides. Use tongs to transfer the browned chops to a plate. Add the apples and shallots; stir for a minute. It's okay if they brown slightly. Add the thyme, cider, and broth and bring to a boil, scraping up any browned bits from the bottom of the pot. Return the chops and any accumulated juice to the pot, overlapping them to fit.

2. Close and lock the lid. Set the burner heat to high. When the cooker reaches HIGH pressure, reduce the burner heat as low as you can and still maintain HIGH pressure. Set a timer to cook for 7 minutes.

3. Remove the pot from the heat. Open the cooker with the Quick Release method. Be careful of the steam as you remove the lid. Transfer the chops to a platter and tent with aluminum foil.

4. Boil the liquid in the pot for a few seconds. Stir in the mustards and crème fraîche, if using. Once you add the mustard, do not boil again. Serve the chops immediately, with the sauce spooned over. Serve with rice or baked potatoes.

Pork Chops with Sour Cherries, Balsamic Vinegar, and Port

Serves 4 • Cooker: 6- to 8-quart • Time: 7 minutes at HIGH pressure

Pork chops work so well in the pressure cooker, it's worth it to have a variety of good recipes to fall back on. This one has a sweet edge, provided by the vinegar and Port. You want tart dried cherries for this, not the sweet ones like Bings.

$^2/_3$ cup dried tart cherries
$^1/_3$ cup Port wine
4 (8-ounce) bone-in pork loin or rib chops,
   $^3/_4$ to 1 inch thick
Sea salt and freshly ground black pepper
1 tablespoon olive oil
2 medium shallots, chopped (about $^1/_3$ cup)
$^2/_3$ cup low-sodium chicken broth
2 tablespoons balsamic vinegar
1 tablespoon cold unsalted butter

1. Place the cherries in a small microwave-safe bowl and add the Port. Heat in the microwave for a few minutes. Set aside to plump. Lightly season the chops with salt and pepper.
2. In a 6- to 8-quart pressure cooker, heat the oil over medium-high heat until very hot. Brown the chops in batches on both sides. Use tongs to transfer the browned chops to a plate. Add the shallots to the pot; stir for a minute. Add the broth and vinegar. Bring to a boil, scraping up any browned bits from the bottom of the pot. Return the chops and any accumulated juice to the pot, overlapping them to fit.
3. Close and lock the lid. Set the burner heat to high. When the cooker reaches HIGH pressure, reduce the burner heat as low as you can and still maintain HIGH pressure. When the cooker reaches HIGH pressure, reduce the burner heat as low as you can and still maintain HIGH pressure. Set a timer to cook for 7 minutes.
4. Remove the pot from the heat. Open the cooker with the Quick Release method. Be careful of the steam as you remove the lid. Transfer the chops to a platter and tent with aluminum foil.
5. Stir the cherries and Port into the liquid in the pot. Bring to a boil for 2 minutes. Swirl in the butter until fully incorporated. Serve the chops immediately, with the sauce spooned over.

Pork Chops with Yukon Gold Potatoes and Sauerkraut

Serves 4 • Cooker: 6- to 8-quart • Time: 12 minutes at HIGH pressure

Yukon Gold potatoes, with their thin skin and light yellow flesh, are wildly popular due to their high moisture, color, excellent storability, and wonderful flavor. Developed in Canada, the variety can hold up to both dry heat and moist heat cooking. If you find baby Yukon Golds, a harvest season specialty called Gold Creamers, just cut them in half. Serve with homemade applesauce and corn muffins on the side.

4 (8-ounce) bone-in or boneless pork loin chops,
$^3/_4$ to 1 inch thick
Sea salt and freshly ground black pepper
2 tablespoons Dijon mustard
2 tablespoons olive oil
$^1/_2$ cup dry white wine
$^1/_2$ cup reduced-sodium chicken broth
3 tablespoons sherry vinegar
4 Yukon Gold potatoes, left unpeeled and each cut
    into 6 wedges
1 teaspoon dried Italian herb blend
2 bay leaves
1 (16-ounce) pouch sauerkraut (about 2 cups),
    rinsed and drained

1. Lightly season the chops with salt and pepper, then spread one side with some mustard. In a 6- to 8-quart pressure cooker, heat the oil over medium-high heat until very hot. Brown the chops in batches, 1 minute per side. Use tongs to transfer the browned chops to a plate. Add the wine to the pot, scraping up any browned bits from the bottom, and bring to a boil. Add the broth and vinegar; stir to combine. Return the chops, mustard side up, and any accumulated juice to the pot, overlapping them to make them fit. Arrange the potato wedges on top and sprinkle with the Italian herbs. Tuck the bay leaves in the potatoes. Sprinkle with salt and pepper. Cover with the sauerkraut.

2. Close and lock the lid. Set the burner heat to high. When the cooker reaches HIGH pressure, reduce the burner heat as low as you can and still maintain HIGH pressure. Set a timer to cook for 12 minutes.

3. Remove the pot from the heat. Open the cooker with the Quick Release method. Be careful of the steam as you remove the lid.

4. Using tongs and an oversized spoon, portion the sauerkraut and potatoes on serving plates. Discard the bay leaves. Place a chop on each plate.

Hard Cider-Braised Pork Pot Roast with Cream Gravy

Serves 6 • Cooker: 6- to 8-quart • Time: 45 minutes at HIGH pressure

Less familiar than beef pot roast is a pork pot roast, which is more common in European cuisine. This has a lovely cream gravy, making the roast an excellent entertaining or family holiday meal. The roast uses hard cider instead of wine, and juniper berries, a secret herbal accent ingredient borrowed from game cookery to balance the meat's inherent sweetness. Look for them in the spice section of the supermarket. Serve this with peas and carrots and mashed potatoes.

2 tablespoons olive oil
4 tablespoons ($^1/_2$ stick) unsalted butter
1 (3$^1/_2$-pound) pork shoulder roast, excess fat removed and seasoned with salt and black pepper
4 shallots, chopped
1 large white onion, chopped
3 cloves garlic, chopped
8 ribs celery, finely chopped
8 juniper berries
2 sprigs fresh thyme
$^3/_4$ cup hard apple cider
$^3/_4$ cup low-sodium chicken broth
1 cup heavy cream
2 tablespoons all-purpose flour or potato starch flour

BEURRE MANIÉ

This recipe makes use of a beurre manié to thicken the gravy A French cooking term, beurre manié translates to "kneaded butter," which pretty much exactly describes what it is—equal amounts of butter and flour that are massaged together, then stirred into a sauce or gravy until the butter in the mixture fully melts into the liquid, thickening it as it is incorporated. The butter adds a bit of richness to the liquid and mixing the flour with the butter keeps it from clumping in the sauce.

1. In a 6- to 8-quart pressure cooker, heat the oil and 2 tablespoons of the butter over medium-high heat until the butter is foamy. Add the roast, fat side down, and brown on all sides, 3 to 4 minutes total. Transfer to a plate. Add the shallots and onion to the pot; cook, stirring, just until softened, about 1 minute. Add the garlic and cook for 30 seconds. Add the celery, juniper berries, thyme, cider, and broth. Return the roast and any accumulated juices to the pot. Bring to a boil.

2. Close and lock the lid. Set the burner heat to high. When the cooker reaches HIGH pressure, reduce the burner heat as low as you can and still maintain HIGH pressure. Set a timer to cook for 45 minutes.

3. Remove the pot from the heat. Open the cooker with the Natural Release method; let stand for 15 minutes. Be careful of the steam as you remove the lid. An instant-read thermometer inserted into the center of the meat should read 150° F. Transfer the roast to a cutting board and cover loosely with aluminum foil while you make the gravy. (The temperature of the meat will rise another 5° to 10° F while sitting.) Remove the strings before carving if your roast is tied.

4. Skim the fat from the juices and bring to a boil. Add the cream. Mash the remaining 2 tablespoons butter with the flour in a small bowl with a fork. Add to the pot and whisk until thickened, about 5 minutes. Season to taste and transfer to a sauceboat. Slice the meat at least $^1/_2$ inch thick and arrange on a platter. Pass the gravy boat.

Pork Carnitas Rápido

Serves 4 to 6 • Cooker: 5- to 7-quart • Time: 45 minutes at HIGH pressure

Mexican "little meats" (the literal translation of "carnitas") are traditionally cooked for hours until meltingly tender, then shredded and fried until crispy. To make the process easier—and considerably faster—we braise the pork in the pressure cooker, then brown it under the broiler. Serve carnitas over steamed rice, garnished with fresh cilantro sprigs, or piled into lettuce cups or warm tortillas along with all of your favorite taco fixings.

2^1/$_2$ pounds boneless pork butt or shoulder, trimmed of excess fat and sliced ^{3}/$_4$ inch thick
2 medium onions, coarsely chopped
2 cups reduced-sodium chicken broth
1 canned chipotle chile in adobo sauce, finely chopped
1 tablespoon olive oil
1 tablespoon chopped fresh oregano or 1 teaspoon dried
4 cloves garlic, finely chopped
1^1/$_2$ teaspoons salt
1^1/$_2$ teaspoons chili powder
1 teaspoon ground cumin
1 to 2 tablespoons fresh lime juice, to taste
Lime wedges, for serving

1. Cut the meat slices lengthwise into ^{3}/$_4$-inch-thick strips, then crosswise into ^{3}/$_4$-inch cubes. (Don't worry about removing any fat pockets within the roast. This fat will moisten and tenderize the meat as it cooks, and will be drained off later.)
2. In a 5- to 7-quart pressure cooker, combine the pork, onions, broth, chipotle, oil, oregano, garlic, salt, chili powder, and cumin. Stir to combine.
3. Close and lock the lid. Set the burner heat to high. When the cooker reaches HIGH pressure, reduce the burner heat as low as you can and still maintain HIGH pressure. Set a timer to cook for 45 minutes.
4. Remove the pot from the heat. Open the cooker with the Natural Release method; let stand for 15 minutes. Be careful of the steam as you remove the lid. The meat should be falling-apart tender. Use a slotted spoon to transfer the meat and onions to a large bowl, then use two forks to shred the meat. (At this point, the meat can be eaten as is or browned as described below.)
5. Line a rimmed baking sheet with aluminum foil and scrape the meat mixture (and any accumulated juices) on to it, forming an even layer. Position an oven rack about 4 inches from the heat source and preheat the broiler.
6. Pour the braising liquid from the pot into a fat separator or a 2-cup heatproof glass measuring cup. Set aside to let the fat rise to the top, then discard the fat.
7. Broil the meat on the baking sheet, stirring once or twice, until crisp and browned at the edges, 7 to 9 minutes. Stir in enough of the defatted braising liquid to keep the meat moist, and 1 tablespoon of the lime juice. (Any remaining braising liquid can be frozen to use in soups or stews, to cook rice, or in the braising liquid the next time you make carnitas.) Taste for seasoning, adding more lime juice or salt if needed. At the table, pass lime wedges to squeeze over the carnitas.

Pork Tamales

Makes 24 to 30 tamales, serves 8 to 16 • Cooker: 6- to 8-quart • Time: 20 minutes at HIGH pressure

While tamales are one of Mexico's most famous street foods, they are also one of its most popular party foods, which is fitting, since a tamal is packaged like a small gift waiting to be unwrapped. A pork filling is traditional. The dough, called *masa,* is made from masa harina or masa flour, corn that has been soaked in lime to make the kernels softer and more cohesive when dried and ground into cornmeal. The dough is made by kneading the masa harina with fat (you need a heavy-duty stand mixer for this, which will give a special fluffy texture). The tricky part of making tamales is mastering the technique for rolling and tying them.

Making tamales is a task often done in groups of seasoned tamale veterans. Consider it an honor if you are invited to a *tamalada,* the tamale fest where a group of family and friends make them together. It is an opportunity to make dozens of tamales, which keep well in the freezer. Using the pressure cooker shortens the steaming time by hours.

1 recipe Pork Carnitas Rápido (page 269)
3 (8-ounce) packages wide corn husks *(hojas de maiz)*

TAMALE DOUGH:
2^1/$_2$ cups masa para tamales/tamale-grind masa harina (we like the Maseca brand)
2 cups plus 3 to 6 tablespoons reserved cooking broth from the carnitas or chicken broth, simmering
^{3}/$_4$ cup vegetable shortening
1 teaspoon salt
1^1/$_2$ teaspoons baking powder
2 cups water, for steaming

1. The day before, prepare the pork carnitas filling. If making a vegetable filling, the filling and assembly can happen on the same day. After making, place in an airtight container and refrigerate until ready to use.
2. Prepare the corn husks. On the day you will be making the tamales, start by soaking the corn husks. Carefully remove the brittle husks from their packages and separate the individual

husks; there may be dust and grit. You will usually be using 2 husks per tamale (plan on 3 to 5 tamales per person, depending on the size), so plan on a few extra in case some are too small. Bring a large pot of water to a boil, then remove from the heat. Add the corn husks, making sure to submerge them underwater, and cover the pot. Soak the corn husks for 30 to 60 minutes, until the husks have absorbed the water and are pliable. They should be soft and flexible, and take on a deep beige color. Drain the husks in a colander, reserving 2 cups plus 6 tablespoons of the cooking water, and lay out on layers of clean tea towels or paper toweling. Tear a few of the husks into long, thin strips for the ties if not using twine.

3. Prepare the masa dough. In a medium bowl, combine the masa harina with 2 cups of the hot reserved cooking water and mix well. The masa should have the consistency of a stiff dough. Cover and set aside to cool completely, 15 to 20 minutes. It will soak up moisture as it sits.
4. In a heavy-duty stand mixer fitted with the paddle attachment, beat the shortening until light and fluffy, about 1 minute. On low speed, add dollops of the masa, slowly incorporating it. Stir the salt into the extra broth and drizzle it into the dough. Increase the speed to medium and whip for 3 minutes. To test the dough, drop ^{1}/$_2$ teaspoon of it into a glass of cold water; if it floats to the top, it is ready to go. If it sinks, continue to whip the dough for another few minutes. Add tablespoons of the reserved broth to adjust the texture and the remaining masa. On low speed, sprinkle in the baking powder. You want to be able to make a masa ball of dough.
5. To assemble the tamales, place a corn husk lengthwise in front of you with the wide side closest to you. Spread 2 tablespoons of the dough all over the bottom half (wide side) of the corn husk in an even layer, leaving about a 1-inch-wide border on the left and right sides. You can use a piece of plastic wrap on your fingers to spread the masa.

6. Place 2 heaping tablespoons of the filling lengthwise down the center of the dough. Drizzle with a bit of cooking liquid. Pick up the two long sides of the corn husk and fold them into the center to unite them. Allow the dough to surround the filling by pinching together the corn husk where the dough comes together. Fold up the bottom. Remember that the masa will not stick to the wet corn husk, so bring up the sides and pinch the masa so it touches the opposite side. Next, roll the husk over the log shape and fold up the bottom. Add a bit more masa to the end if the filling is exposed. Fold down the empty top section of the husk. You don't have to tie the tamales, but it is nice. Place a strip of corn husk under the tamal, wrap it around the middle (making sure that you have some of the tail underneath), and tie securely. The tamal will be about 6 inches in length. Repeat this process until all the corn husks and/or tamal dough are used up. You will make about 24 to 30. (The assembled but uncooked tamales can be frozen up to 4 months. When you are ready to serve them, steam them straight from the freezer for 35 to 40 minutes, twice the cooking time when not frozen.)

For a party appetizer, you can make the tamales in smaller bite-sizes that can be handled with fingers or as a one-bite item for an appetizer plate.

7. Steam the tamales. Place a trivet and steamer basket in a 6- to 8-quart pressure cooker. Add the water. Arrange the tamales standing up in the basket, top open side up, laying against each other against the side of the pot. You can stand tamales in front of each other; just make sure that the open ends of the tamales are facing upward. They can be laying a bit sideways, but not laying down. Expect to steam in two batches.

8. Close and lock the lid. Set the burner heat to high. When the cooker reaches HIGH pressure, reduce the burner heat as low as you can and still maintain HIGH pressure. Set a timer to cook for 20 minutes.

9. Remove the pot from the heat. Open the cooker with the Natural Release method; let stand for 15 minutes. Be careful of the steam as you remove the lid.

10. To test for doneness, quickly remove a tamale with tongs and replace the lid on the pot to continue the cooking. Put the tamale on the counter for a few minutes and then carefully unwrap it. The dough should be firm, no longer sticky or mushy. The masa should be set; if it pulls away easily from the husk, it is done; if it sticks, continue to steam in 10-minute intervals without pressure. Let the tamales rest for 5 to 10 minutes before serving to allow the masa to firm up. For softer tamales, let them rest in the pot, uncovered, with the heat off. For firmer tamales, let them rest out of the pot, covered with a cloth.

11. Transfer the tamales with a pair of tongs to a serving platter. At this point, the tamale is the most tender and delicate. Serve warm accompanied by Mexican crema, sliced avocados, salsa, Mexican rice, green salad, and refried beans.

The cooked tamales can be cooled in the steamer baskets, then stored in ziptop plastic bags in the refrigerator for up to 4 days. To reheat, place a whole tamale in its husk on a microwave-safe plate with a bit of water and microwave for 2 minutes.

Vegetarian Tamales: Combine in a bowl 1 (16-ounce) bag thawed frozen mixed vegetables; 2 steamed new potatoes, peeled and diced to make about 1 cup; 1 cup cooked black beans; and about $1/3$ cup salsa to moisten the mixture slightly. Use to fill the tamales in place of the pork filling.

CORN HUSKS

Dried corn husks come in plastic packages available in specialty food stores or the Latin food section of the supermarket. Melissa's corn husks, available from Amazon, are extra wide; 16 ounces yields about 100 husks and you will need them all since you use 2 to 3 per tamale.

Carnitas Buffet

Serves 8

Carnitas is a terrific fiesta dish. Set up piles of warm corn and flour tortillas and have guests make their own burritos/tacos with separate bowls full of carnitas, salsas, and beans. Make everything ahead.

1 recipe Pork Carnitas Rápido (page 269)
2 to 3 dozen warm corn and/or flour tortillas
1 recipe Frijoles de Olla (page 410)
2 cups chopped white onions
Leaves from 1 bunch fresh cilantro, chopped
2 bunches radishes, stems removed and chopped
1 recipe Avocado-Cilantro Sauce (recipe follows)
1 recipe Blender Tomato-Lime Salsa (recipe follows)
1 recipe Tomatillo Salsa Verde (recipe follows)

Place all the ingredients on the buffet table on platters and in separate bowls.

Avocado-Cilantro Sauce

Makes 2 cups

Avocado sauce is a staple of the Baja taco stands. It can be made up to 24 hours ahead.

$^1/_4$ cup fresh cilantro leaves
2 ripe avocados, peeled and pitted
$^3/_4$ to 1 cup milk or half-and-half
$1^1/_2$ teaspoons garlic salt

Place the cilantro in a food processor and pulse to chop. Add the avocado, milk, and garlic salt. Pulse until creamy. Do not overprocess. Add more milk if needed to make a creamy, pourable texture. Store in an airtight container in the refrigerator with the avocado pits set in the middle. Remove the pit and stir the sauce right before serving.

Blender Tomato-Lime Salsa

Makes about 2 cups

2 large ripe tomatoes or 4 ripe Roma tomatoes, seeded and chopped, or 1 (14-ounce) can chopped tomatoes with juice
Leaves from $^1/_3$ bunch fresh cilantro

$^1/_4$ large white onion, cut into chunks
Juice of 2 limes
2 tablespoons olive oil
$^1/_2$ to 1 fresh jalapeño, to taste, seeded and minced
Sea salt and freshly ground black pepper

Place the tomatoes, cilantro, and onion in a blender. Pulse until the onions are chopped. Remove to a small bowl and add the lime juice, oil, and jalapeño; season to taste with salt and pepper. Store in an airtight container in the refrigerator for up to 1 day.

Tomatillo Salsa Verde

Makes about 2 cups

Round, plump tomatillos, also known as *tomates verdes* or Mexican husk tomatoes, have a special tart flavor that complements the red sauces. Remove the paper husks, and place whole in freezer bags to store in the freezer. Thaw before using like fresh in cooked sauces.

1 pound tomatillos (about 12 average size), papery husks removed, rinsed
2 cloves garlic, unpeeled
1 small white onion, cut into sixths
1 to 2 jalapeño or serrano chiles, halved, and seeded (wear gloves if you have sensitive skin)
2 tablespoons olive oil
1 teaspoon fine sea salt
1 cup loosely packed fresh cilantro leaves
Juice of 2 limes

Preheat oven to 350° F. Place the tomatillos, unpeeled garlic, onion, and skin-up chile halves in a baking dish. Toss with the oil and salt. Roast in the center of the oven until the tomatillos are very soft and skin begins to split, 45 to 60 minutes, depending on the size. Transfer the roasted vegetables to a food processor and add cilantro. Squeeze the garlic out of its skin and add lime juice. Pulse on and off until a coarse puree is formed. Transfer to a serving bowl. Taste and add more salt or lime. Chill, covered, for up to 2 days, or serve at room temperature within 1 hour.

Pork and Sauerkraut with Potatoes and Caraway Seeds

Serves 4 to 5 • Cooker: 6- to 8-quart • Time: 25 minutes at HIGH pressure

Known as *szekelgulyas*, pork stew with sauerkraut is a classic Hungarian dish. Hungarian paprika is robust compared to the Spanish or Moroccan versions. Paprika releases its color and flavor when heated; we use just a bit of it here but its flavor and color still shine through. Buy fresh paprika every 6 to 9 months, as its potency deteriorates quickly. Only use a refrigerated sauerkraut to prepare this, such as Boar's Head, which has superlative flavor and texture.

2 to 2¹/₂ pounds boneless pork shoulder or butt, trimmed of excess fat and cut into 2-inch cubes
Salt and freshly ground black pepper
2 tablespoons olive oil
1 large white onion, diced
3 tablespoons all-purpose flour or potato starch
1 cup beef broth
1 cup low-sodium chicken broth
1 tablespoon Hungarian sweet paprika
¹/₂ teaspoon caraway seeds
¹/₂ cup tomato sauce
2 medium red or Yukon Gold potatoes, unpeeled and cubed
1 (16-ounce) pouch (about 2 cups) sauerkraut, rinsed and drained
1 (8-ounce) container sour cream (don't even consider using yogurt)

1. Sprinkle the meat with salt and pepper. In a 6- to 8-quart pressure cooker, heat the oil over medium-high heat until very hot. Brown the meat in batches in a single layer on all sides, 5 to 7 minutes per batch. Use a slotted spoon to transfer the browned meat to a platter. Add the onion and cook until soft, stirring a few times, about 3 minutes. Sprinkle with 2 tablespoons of the flour and stir for 1 minute. Return the meat and any accumulated juices to the pot. Add the broths, paprika, caraway, and tomato sauce. Stir in the sauerkraut and potatoes.

2. Close and lock the lid. Set the burner heat to high. When the cooker reaches HIGH pressure, reduce the burner heat as low as you can and still maintain HIGH pressure. Set a timer to cook for 25 minutes.

3. Remove the pot from the heat. Open the cooker with the Natural Release method; let stand for 15 minutes. Be careful of the steam as you remove the lid.

4. In a small bowl, whisk the sour cream and remaining 1 tablespoon flour together. Stir the sour cream into the stew. Heat for 1 minute, uncovered, over medium heat until the stew is slightly thickened and a lovely coral color. Do not boil. Taste for seasoning, but you probably will not need any salt since the broths and sauerkraut have plenty naturally. The aroma is mouthwatering. Serve immediately in soup plates with a light or dark rye bread.

Pork's Best Friend: Homemade Chutney

Homemade preserves have come back into favor in the last decade with the movements to preserve more traditional food preparation methods. Homemade chutneys are very popular as a condiment or ingredient paired with meats (particularly pork) and just minutes away in the pressure cooker. Small batches cut the tedious work of chopping and preparing the fruit.

Liquid does not evaporate when using the pressure cooker, so to finish off a chutney, you may need to bring the mixture to a low boil with the lid off to thicken it. Chutneys will thicken even more when cooled and refrigerated. Let the chutney rest overnight before serving. We suggest putting a flame tamer on your burner when making chutney to ensure the sugar does not burn.

Store your homemade chutney in an airtight container in the refrigerator, where it will keep for up to 1 month. You can also freeze chutney for up to 2 months. Even though sterilizing the jars is not necessary for short-term storage, we run them through the dishwasher or wash in hot sudsy water and dry completely before filling.

Dried Apricot Preserves with Toasted Almonds and Amaretto

Makes about 7 cups • Cooker: 5- to 7-quart • Time: 10 minutes at HIGH pressure

Certain preserves are made with dried fruit instead of fresh, to yield a thick and tremendously flavorful condiment or spread. This adult condiment is ideal to spread on bread or crackers; serve alongside Brie or goat cheese, or with roasted pork or grilled chicken. Please note the sugar is added after cooking the apricots to keep the flavor pure. This is from cook extraordinaire Peggy Fallon.

2$^1/_2$ cups water
4 cups coarsely chopped dried apricots (about 1$^1/_2$ pounds)
1 cup sliced almonds
2 tablespoons fresh lemon juice
$^1/_8$ teaspoon salt
4 cups sugar
$^1/_2$ cup Amaretto liqueur

1. In a 5- to 7-quart pressure cooker, bring the water to a boil over high heat. Stir in the apricots and remove from the heat. Let stand 1 hour, covered, to soften the apricots and infuse the water with flavor.
2. Meanwhile, toast the almonds: Preheat the oven to 350° F. Spread the almonds on a small baking sheet and bake, stirring once or twice, until fragrant and lightly toasted, 7 to 9 minutes.
3. Stir the lemon juice and salt into the apricots and their soaking liquid.
4. Close and lock the lid. Set the burner heat to high. When the cooker reaches HIGH pressure, reduce the burner heat as low as you can and still maintain HIGH pressure. Set a timer to cook for 10 minutes. Place a saucer in the freezer for testing the set later.
5. Remove the pot from the heat. Open the cooker with the Natural Release method; let stand for 15 minutes. Be careful of the steam as you remove the lid.
6. Return the pot to the stovetop and stir in the sugar and Amaretto. Cook, uncovered, over medium heat, stirring constantly, until the sugar is dissolved and the preserves have set to the desired consistency, about 5 minutes. To test the set, drop a spoonful of the preserves onto the ice-cold saucer; it should firm up immediately. For a thicker set, continue cooking a few minutes longer and test again. Skim off and discard any foam that has risen to the top. Stir in the toasted almonds.
7. Let cool completely and refrigerate overnight to develop the flavors before using.

Nectarine Chutney

Makes about 4 cups • Cooker: 5- to 7-quart • Time: 8 minutes at HIGH pressure

This is good with pork, ham, turkey, and lamb. You can also make it with peaches or plums instead of nectarines.

1 tablespoon olive oil
1 large white onion, chopped
2 cloves garlic, finely minced
2 tablespoons grated peeled fresh ginger
8 ripe nectarines, pitted and chopped into 1/2-inch pieces
1 cup firmly packed light brown sugar
1/2 cup cider vinegar
1 to 2 fresh jalapeño peppers, seeded and coarsely chopped, or more to taste
1/2 cup raisins
Grated zest of 2 limes
1 teaspoon ground cinnamon
1/2 cup water or dry white wine, such as Pinot Grigio

1. In a 5- to 7-quart pressure cooker, heat the oil over medium-high heat. Add the onion and cook, stirring a few times, until soft, about 3 minutes. Add the garlic and ginger and stir for 15 seconds. Add the remaining ingredients. Bring to a boil and stir to combine.
2. Close and lock the lid. Increase the burner heat to high. When the cooker reaches HIGH pressure, reduce the burner heat as low as you can and still maintain HIGH pressure. Set a timer to cook for 8 minutes.
3. Remove the pot from the heat. Open the cooker with the Natural Release method; let stand for 15 minutes. Be careful of the steam as you remove the lid.
4. Let cool completely and refrigerate overnight to develop the flavors before using.

Rhubarb and Golden Raisin Chutney

Makes about 4 cups • Cooker: 5- to 7-quart • Time: 8 minutes at HIGH pressure

Rhubarb has its season, the spring, and it has become a kind of boutique fruit, used in all sorts of sweet and savory preparations. Serve this with poultry, pork, or lamb.

4 cups thawed and drained frozen rhubarb, or about 8 stalks fresh rhubarb (trimmed completely of the leaf), cut into 1-inch pieces
1 large white onion, chopped
1/2 cup sugar
1/2 cup cider vinegar or sherry vinegar
3/4 cup golden raisins
1 to 2 jalapeño peppers, to taste, seeded and coarsely chopped
3 cloves garlic, finely minced
2 tablespoons grated peeled fresh ginger
8 green cardamom pods, tied together in cheesecloth or in a tea ball
1/2 cup water

1. In a 5- to 7-quart pressure cooker, combine all the ingredients.
2. Close and lock the lid. Set the burner heat to high. When the cooker reaches HIGH pressure, reduce the burner heat as low as you can and still maintain HIGH pressure. Set a timer to cook for 8 minutes.
3. Remove the pot from the heat. Open the cooker with the Natural Release method; let stand for 15 minutes. Be careful of the steam as you remove the lid. The rhubarb should be very tender. Discard the cardamom pods.
4. Let cool completely and refrigerate overnight to develop the flavors before using.

Pressure-Cooker Major Grey-Style Mango Chutney

Makes about 5 cups • Cooker: 5- to 7-quart • Time: 14 minutes at HIGH pressure

Major Grey's is a tangy mango chutney with lots of sweet spices. It is probably the most recognizable Indian style chutney in the West. It is an accompaniment to curries and it is famous spread on cheddar cheese and thick water crackers with tea in an English pub. Homemade is fantastic.

2¹/₄ pounds ripe mangos, peeled, pitted, and finely chopped
1 large white onion, finely chopped
1 cup cider vinegar
1 cup granulated sugar
³/₄ cup firmly packed light brown sugar
¹/₂ cup raisins
¹/₂ cup dried currants
¹/₄ cup finely chopped peeled fresh ginger
3 tablespoons fresh lime juice
2 teaspoons chili powder
1 teaspoon ground cinnamon
1 teaspoon sea salt
¹/₂ teaspoon ground cloves

1. In a 5- to 7-quart pressure cooker, combine all the ingredients.
2. Close and lock the lid. Set the burner heat to high. When the cooker reaches HIGH pressure, reduce the burner heat as low as you can and still maintain HIGH pressure. Set a timer to cook for 14 minutes.
3. Remove the pot from the heat. Open the cooker with the Natural Release method; let stand for 15 minutes. Be careful of the steam as you remove the lid. Stir to combine.
4. Let cool completely and refrigerate overnight to develop the flavors before using.

Green Tomato Chutney

Makes about 5 cups • Cooker: 5- to 7-quart • Time: 12 minutes at HIGH pressure

This is your end-of-the-summer chutney. It is a fantastic way to use up the hard unripe, green tomatoes once the tomato plants do not ripen anymore. This tastes better and better with age.

2 pounds green tomatoes, cored and diced
1 large white onion, quartered lengthwise and thinly sliced
2 red bell peppers, seeded and diced
²/₃ cup firmly packed brown sugar
²/₃ cup white wine vinegar or Champagne vinegar
¹/₂ cup dried currants
1 (4-inch) piece fresh ginger, peeled and grated
¹/₂ teaspoon sea salt

1. In a 5- to 7-quart pressure cooker, combine all the ingredients.
2. Close and lock the lid. Set the burner heat to high. When the cooker reaches HIGH pressure, reduce the burner heat as low as you can and still maintain HIGH pressure. Set a timer to cook for 12 minutes.
3. Remove the pot from the heat. Open the cooker with the Natural Release method; let stand for 15 minutes. Be careful of the steam as you remove the lid.
4. Let cool completely and refrigerate overnight to develop the flavors before using.

Tomato Pork and Lamb Ragout

Serves 6 to 8 • Cooker: 6- to 8-quart • Time: 25 minutes at HIGH pressure

Pork and lamb cook together to make a rich, hearty stew; we like to cut the meat into big chunks for this. Serve over a pasta like rotini, rigatoni, or farfalle, or polenta. It's also good with cornbread.

3 tablespoons olive oil
2 to 2^1/$_2$ pounds pork shoulder, trimmed of fat and cut into 2-inch chunks
1 to 1^1/$_2$ pounds lamb shoulder, trimmed of fat and cut into 2-inch chunks
1 large white onion, chopped
Sea salt and freshly ground black pepper
1 cup dry white wine
1 (28-ounce) can crushed tomatoes
1 (14.5-ounce) can diced tomatoes in juice, undrained
2 ribs celery, chopped
2 medium carrots, chopped
^{1}/$_2$ cup low-sodium chicken broth or water

1. In a 6- to 8-quart pressure cooker, heat the oil over medium-high heat until very hot. Brown the meat in batches in a single layer on all sides, 5 to 7 minutes per batch. Use a slotted spoon to transfer the browned meat to a platter. Add the onion and cook, stirring a few times, until soft, about 3 minutes. Return the meat and any accumulated juices to the pot. Season with salt and pepper to taste. Add the wine and bring to a simmer, scraping up any browned bits from the bottom of the pot. Stir in the tomatoes with their juice, celery, carrots, and broth and bring to a boil.

2. Close and lock the lid. Set the burner heat to high. When the cooker reaches HIGH pressure, reduce the burner heat as low as you can and still maintain HIGH pressure. Set a timer to cook for 25 minutes.

3. Remove the pot from the heat. Open the cooker with the Natural Release method; let stand for 15 minutes. Be careful of the steam as you remove the lid.

4. Skim any fat from the top of the sauce. Taste for seasoning. Serve immediately.

Pork Stew with Sherry and Red Wine

Serves 6 • Cooker: 6- to 8-quart • Time: 25 minutes at HIGH pressure

The addition of sherry and red wine here makes for an elegant stew. Serve with ciabatta rolls and butter, and a big green salad. As with all stews, this tastes better the next day, so don't hesitate to make it the day before and reheat.

3 tablespoons olive oil
2 to 2 1/2 pounds boneless pork shoulder, trimmed
    of fat and cut into 2-inch chunks
1 (16-ounce) bag frozen pearl onions, thawed
2 ribs celery, chopped
3 medium carrots, cut into 1-inch chunks
1 bay leaf
4 stems fresh parsley
1 or 2 sprigs fresh thyme
Sea salt and freshly ground black pepper
1 cup dry red wine
3/4 cup Amontillado dry sherry
3/4 cup low-sodium chicken broth
2 tablespoons butter mashed with 2 tablespoons
    all-purpose flour or rice flour
Juice of 1 lemon

1. In a 6- to 8-quart pressure cooker, heat the oil over medium-high heat until very hot. Brown the meat in batches in a single layer on all sides, 5 to 7 minutes per batch. Use a slotted spoon to transfer the browned meat to a plate. Add the onions to the pot and cook for 2 minutes. Add the celery, carrots, and herbs. Return the meat and any accumulated juices to the pot. Season to taste with salt and pepper. Add the wine, sherry, and broth and bring to a boil, scraping up any browned bits on the bottom of the pot.

2. Close and lock the lid. Set the burner heat to high. When the cooker reaches HIGH pressure, reduce the burner heat as low as you can and still maintain HIGH pressure. Set a timer to cook for 25 minutes.

3. Remove the pot from the heat. Open the cooker with the Natural Release method; let stand for 15 minutes. Be careful of the steam as you remove the lid. Discard the bay leaf, parsley, and thyme.

4. Skim any fat from the top of the sauce. Remove some of the meat and vegetables with a slotted spoon. Add the flour-and-butter mixture and stir over medium heat until the sauce is thickened. Taste for salt and pepper. Add the meat and vegetables back to the sauce and stir in the lemon juice.

SHERRY

There are two categories of sherry: fino and oloroso. Fino is the dry version, and includes Manzanilla and the potent and nutty Amontillado, which is considered a white wine despite its amber color. Oloroso sherry is more heavily fortified. The two are not interchangeable in recipes. Once opened, fino sherry should be stored in the refrigerator only up to 2 weeks, so plan to sip it after you make this stew. Oloroso sherry will keep at room temperature indefinitely.

Pork Stew with Kabocha Japanese Squash

Serves 4 to 5 • Cooker: 6- to 8-quart • Time: 20 minutes for stew, 3 minutes for squash at HIGH pressure

Kabocha squash has a nice strong flavor—sweeter than butternut—and a fluffy texture when cooked. It works great in soups and stews, and here it is combined with pork along with edamame. A dash of good quality cider vinegar is added to round out the sweet squash flavors. The natural starch from the kabocha will thicken the braising liquid, creating an unctuous sauce.

2 to 2^1/$_2$ pounds boneless pork shoulder, trimmed of fat and cut into 2-inch pieces
2 tablespoons all-purpose flour or rice flour
1 tablespoon paprika
Sea salt and freshly ground black pepper
3 tablespoons olive oil
1 large yellow or white onion, cut in half and thinly sliced into half moons (about 2 cups)
2 cloves garlic, minced
1^1/$_2$ cups low-sodium chicken broth
^{3}/$_4$ cup dry red wine
1 (14.5-ounce) can diced tomatoes in juice, undrained
1 bay leaf
1 (3- to 4-pound) kabocha squash or about 2 pounds butternut squash pieces
2 cups frozen edamame or baby lima beans, thawed
3 tablespoons cider vinegar

1. Pat the meat dry with paper towels and spread the chunks on a large piece of parchment or waxed paper. In a small bowl, combine the flour, paprika, a generous pinch of salt, and several grindings of pepper. Sprinkle the flour mixture over the meat and toss to coat. Set aside for an hour at room temperature or up to overnight, covered, in the refrigerator.

2. In a 6- to 8-quart pressure cooker, heat half of the oil over medium-high heat until very hot. Brown the meat in batches in a single layer on all sides, 3 to 5 minutes per batch, adding more of the oil as needed. Use a slotted spoon to transfer the browned meat to a plate. Add the onion and cook, stirring a few times, until soft, about 3 minutes. Add the garlic and cook for 30 seconds. Return the meat and any accumulated juices to the pot. Add the broth, wine, tomatoes with their juice, and bay leaf. Stir well.

3. Close and lock the lid. Set the burner heat to high. When the cooker reaches HIGH pressure, reduce the burner heat as low as you can and still maintain HIGH pressure. Set a timer to cook for 20 minutes.

4. Meanwhile, with a large, heavy knife, cut the kabocha in half through the stem end. Scoop out and discard the seeds and strings. Cut into chunks, then, with a small sharp knife, pare off the peel. Cut the flesh into 1^1/$_2$-inch cubes. You will have about 3 cups.

5. Remove the pot from the heat. Open the cooker with the Quick Release method. Be careful of the steam as you remove the lid. Add the squash. Relock the cooker, bring back up to HIGH pressure, and cook for 3 minutes.

6. Remove the pot from the heat. Open the cooker with the Natural Release method; let stand for 15 minutes. Taste for seasoning and stir in the vinegar and edamame. Simmer gently over medium heat 5 to 10 minutes. If the sauce is too thin, remove the meat and vegetables with a slotted spoon and bring the liquid to a boil. Simmer until the sauce is reduced to the consistency you prefer.

KABOCHA SQUASH

The kabocha, also known as the Japanese pumpkin, is a winter squash and a newcomer to most produce sections. You can substitute butternut squash for the kabocha, but not regular pumpkin, which is too watery. Here's a tip for cutting up an über-hard 3- to 4-pound kabocha. Microwave the whole squash for 1 to 3 minutes, until the nearly impenetrable exterior softens enough so that you can get a cleaver or the tip of a sharp, heavy-duty chef's knife into it without much trouble.

Pork Vindaloo with Pickled Raisins

Serves 6 • Cooker: 6- to 8-quart • Time: 25 minutes at HIGH pressure

Curry vindaloo is a complex sweet-and-tangy pork dish native to the west coast of India. If you travel to the Portuguese town of Goa on the Malabar Coast, you will find it in every beachfront restaurant with chicken, duck, or lamb instead of pork (Muslims and Hindus do not eat pork). It is spicy but not always a startling lip-burning hot curry. We use Penzeys' salt-free vindaloo seasoning (penzeys.com) instead of combining our own since it is so darn good and an incredible time saver. It contains a complex hand-mixed blend of coriander, garlic, cumin, ginger, Korintje cinnamon, crushed brown mustard, cayenne red pepper, jalapeño pepper, cardamom, turmeric, Tellicherry black pepper, and cloves.

PICKLED RAISINS:

1 cup water
$^1/_2$ cup cider vinegar
$^1/_2$ cup granulated cane or turbinado sugar
2 teaspoons brown mustard seeds
$1^1/_2$ cups golden raisins

PORK VINDALOO:

$2^1/_2$ to 3 pounds boneless pork shoulder, trimmed of excess fat and cut into 1-inch cubes
1 teaspoon sea salt
$^1/_4$ cup light olive oil
1 large white onion, finely chopped
4 cloves garlic, minced
1 (2-inch) piece fresh ginger, peeled and grated
2 tablespoons vindaloo seasoning or Madras curry
1 teaspoon sweet or hot paprika
$^1/_2$ teaspoon ground turmeric
3 tablespoons all-purpose or rice flour
$^1/_3$ cup Champagne vinegar or white wine vinegar
1 (14.5-ounce) can diced tomatoes in juice, undrained
1 cup low-sodium chicken broth
Steamed basmati white or basmati brown rice, for serving
$^1/_3$ cup loosely packed chopped fresh cilantro, plus more for serving

1. Make the Pickled Raisins. In a medium saucepan, combine the water, vinegar, sugar, and mustard seeds and bring to a boil, stirring until the sugar dissolves. Add the raisins. Remove from the heat and let stand to cool completely at room temperature, about 1 hour. It will keep in an airtight container in the refrigerator up to 2 weeks. Serve at room temperature or cold. Good in salads as well as a garnish.

2. Sprinkle the meat with the salt. In a 6- to 8-quart pressure cooker, heat 2 tablespoons of the oil over medium-high heat until very hot. Brown the meat in batches in a single layer on all sides, 5 to 7 minutes per batch. Use a slotted spoon to transfer the browned meat to a plate. Add the onion and cook, stirring a few times, until soft, 3 minutes. Add the garlic, ginger, and spices and cook, stirring, for 30 seconds. Sprinkle in the flour and stir to cook. Return the meat and any accumulated juices to the pot. Add the vinegar, tomatoes with their juice, and broth; stir well, scraping up any browned bits from the bottom of the pot, and bring to a boil.

3. Close and lock the lid. Set the burner heat to high. When the cooker reaches HIGH pressure, reduce the burner heat as low as you can and still maintain HIGH pressure. Set a timer to cook for 25 minutes.

4. Remove the pot from the heat. Open the cooker with the Natural Release method; let stand for 15 minutes. Be careful of the steam as you remove the lid.

5. Skim any fat from the top of the sauce. Stir in the cilantro. Serve immediately over the hot rice with a spoonful of Pickled Raisins and a sprinkling of chopped cilantro.

Pork Ragout with Cider and Root Vegetables

Serves 6 to 8 • Cooker: 6- to 8-quart • Time: 25 minutes at HIGH pressure

This is a winter stew flavored with the combination of hard cider and beer, an unusual combination, but works perfectly with the pork.

2^1/$_2$ to 3 pounds boneless pork shoulder, trimmed of excess fat and cut into 2-inch cubes
Salt and freshly ground black pepper
2 tablespoons butter
2 tablespoons olive oil
1 large white onion, cut in half and thinly sliced into half moons
2 cloves garlic, minced
3 tablespoons all-purpose flour or potato starch
1 cup hard apple cider
1 cup dark beer
2 tablespoons Dijon mustard
1 teaspoon ground coriander
1 teaspoon dried Italian herb blend
1 large sweet potato, peeled and cut into 2-inch chunks
4 parsnips, peeled and cut into 2-inch chunks
1 medium turnip, peeled and cubed, or 1 bunch baby turnips, trimmed (no need to peel babies)

1. Sprinkle the meat with salt and pepper. In a 6- to 8-quart pressure cooker, melt the butter with the oil over medium-high heat until foamy. Brown the meat in batches in a single layer on all sides, 5 to 7 minutes per batch. Use a slotted spoon to transfer the browned meat to a plate. Add the onion and cook, stirring a few times, until soft, about 3 minutes. Add the garlic, then sprinkle with the flour. Cook, stirring, for 1 minute. Return the meat and any accumulated juices to the pot. Add the cider, beer, mustard, coriander, herb blend, and root vegetables. Stir well, scraping up any browned bits from the bottom of the pot, and bring to a boil.

2. Close and lock the lid. Set the burner heat to high. When the cooker reaches HIGH pressure, reduce the burner heat as low as you can and still maintain HIGH pressure. Set a timer to cook for 25 minutes.

3. Remove the pot from the heat. Open the cooker with the Natural Release method; let stand for 15 minutes. Be careful of the steam as you remove the lid.

4. Skim any fat from the top of the sauce. Serve immediately over mashed potatoes or polenta with pumpernickel bread.

Red-Cooked Pork Shoulder

Serves 6 to 8 • Cooker: 6- to 8-quart • Time: 55 minutes at HIGH pressure

Red cooking is a traditional Chinese method of braising meats such as duck, chicken, beef, or pork in a savory-sweet mixture of soy sauce, wine, sugar, spices, and water that turns the food dark red-brown. This version for pork is loosely adapted from a recipe by Ming Tsai. He prepared this family recipe for *Iron Chef* and, because of time constraints, did it in the pressure cooker. Hours of braising were reduced to one, yielding up luscious, fork-tender pork. Tsai substituted red wine for the traditional shaoxing rice wine and added balsamic vinegar, both Western touches. Use an inexpensive balsamic vinegar. You need two types of soy sauce to get the proper flavor, light (*pak si yau*) and dark (*hak si yau*). Dark or double soy sauce is aged, rich in color, and slightly sweet. Light or thin soy is what is used whenever "soy sauce" is called for. Younger and paler than the dark, it has excellent flavor. Serve the pork sliced, with steamed rice and Chinese broccoli.

1 (3- to 3¹/₂-pound) piece boneless pork shoulder, skin discarded, trimmed of excess fat, and cut into a few large chunks
Freshly ground black pepper

RED-COOKING LIQUID:
1¹/₂ cups water
1¹/₂ cups dry red wine
1 cup light soy sauce (such as Kikkoman)
1 cup dark or double soy sauce (such as Koon Chun brand)
³/₄ cup balsamic vinegar
1¹/₄ cups firmly packed dark brown sugar
6 green onions (white and light green parts), trimmed and cut into 3-inch lengths
3 small dried red Thai chiles
1 (4-inch) piece fresh ginger, thinly sliced
4 cloves garlic, peeled
1 medium orange or tangerine, quartered
2 star anise pods, lightly crushed
1 (4-inch) cinnamon stick

1. Pat the pork dry and season lightly on all sides with the pepper.
2. In a 6- to 8-quart pressure cooker, combine all the red-cooking liquid ingredients. Bring to a boil, stirring to dissolve the sugar. Add the green onions, chiles, ginger, garlic, quartered orange or tangerine, anise, and cinnamon stick. Add the pork and settle it into the liquid.
3. Close and lock the lid. Set the burner heat to high. When the cooker reaches HIGH pressure, reduce the burner heat as low as you can and still maintain HIGH pressure. Set a timer to cook for 55 minutes.
4. Remove the pot from the heat. Open the cooker with the Quick Release method. Be careful of the steam as you remove the lid. The pork should be very tender. Transfer the pork to a cutting board and cover with aluminum foil.
5. Strain about 1 cup of the cooking liquid through a fine mesh strainer into a small saucepan. Discard the solids. Let the remaining liquid cool completely, then store in an airtight container in the refrigerator up to 1 week or the freezer up to 2 months if you would like to use it again. Bring the other liquid to a boil and continue to boil until it is reduced by two-thirds and thick, about 5 minutes. Brush a light coating of the sauce over each piece of pork to glaze it. Thinly slice the pork crosswise into ¹/₂-inch-thick slices and serve with a bit of the sauce on the side for drizzling.

Italian Sausages with Onions and Peppers

Serves 4 to 8 • Cooker: 5- to 7-quart • Time: 6 minutes at HIGH pressure

You want to seek out good Italian sausages for this, preferably from an Italian market with a meat department. Often they will make their own. You want the ones with fennel seeds added. You can use multi-colored peppers or even all green.

2 tablespoons olive oil
8 Italian sausages, sweet, hot, or half and half (about 2 pounds)
3 cloves garlic, minced
2 large sweet yellow onions, cut in half and sliced into $1/4$-inch-thick half moons
2 large green bell peppers, seeded and cut into thin strips
2 large red bell peppers, seeded and cut into thin strips
$1^1/2$ teaspoons dried Italian herb blend or oregano
$1/4$ cup dry white wine or dry Marsala
$2/3$ cup low sodium chicken broth

1. In a 5- to 7-quart pressure cooker, heat the oil over medium-high heat until very hot. Prick the sausages all over with the tip of a sharp knife to avoid bursting while cooking. Brown the sausages in batches on all sides, about 2 minutes per batch. Transfer the browned sausages to a plate. Add the garlic and cook for 30 seconds. Remove to the plate. Add the onions and cook until soft, stirring a few times, about 3 minutes. Remove to the plate with the sausages. Add the peppers and cook, stirring, until they soften, 3 to 5 minutes. Return the onions to the pot and toss with the peppers. Season with the herbs and add the wine. Scrape up any browned bits from the bottom of the pot and let the wine simmer until completely evaporated. Return the sausages to the pot with any accumulated juice and cover with the onions and peppers. Pour the broth over all.
2. Close and lock the lid. Set the burner heat to high. When the cooker reaches HIGH pressure, reduce the burner heat as low as you can and still maintain HIGH pressure. Set a timer to cook for 6 minutes.
3. Remove the pot from the heat. Open the cooker with the Quick Release method. Be careful of the steam as you remove the lid. The sausages should be cooked through.
4. Transfer the sausages and vegetables to a rimmed platter. Serve immediately with mashed potatoes, polenta, or a big pasta, or pile into rolls. This will keep, tightly covered, in the refrigerator up to 3 days.

Italian Sausages with Mushrooms, Onions, and Peppers: Add 6 ounces baby portabella mushrooms, sliced, when you add the onions.

Andouille and Chicken Red Jambalaya

Serves 4 to 6 • Cooker: 5- to 7-quart • Time: 7 minutes at HIGH pressure

Jambalaya is Louisiana's interpretation of Spanish paella, made with meat, vegetables, and rice, sometimes with seafood thrown in, all cooked together. This version is known as red jambalaya, for the addition of tomatoes. It is flavored with a bold and spicy seasoning blend (such as Emeril's Original Essence or Zatarain's Creole seasoning) and some cayenne for heat. Use only converted long-grain white rice for this, not regular long-grain white rice or brown rice. Jambalaya, usually cooked in a cast iron Dutch oven, is a great one pot meal. It can also be made with turkey thighs. Have the table set with a selection of hot pepper sauces, such as Tabasco, Crystal, and Frank's Red Hot.

2 tablespoons olive oil
$1/2$ pound smoked andouille sausage, sliced into $1/2$-inch-thick rounds
1 pound (about 5) boneless skinless chicken thighs, cut into 1- to $1 1/2$-inch pieces
1 large white onion (you want a sweet onion here), chopped
2 cloves garlic, chopped
1 green bell pepper, seeded and chopped
3 ribs celery, sliced $1/2$ inch thick
2 teaspoons Creole seasoning
1 teaspoon dried thyme
$1/8$ teaspoon cayenne pepper
1 cup converted long-grain white rice, such as Uncle Ben's
1 (14.5-ounce) can diced tomatoes in juice, undrained
1 cup low-sodium chicken broth
1 bay leaf
3 tablespoons minced fresh flatleaf parsley, for garnish
6 green onions, trimmed and chopped, for garnish

1. In a 5- to 7-quart pressure cooker, heat the oil over medium-high heat until very hot. Add the sausage and cook for 2 minutes, stirring a few times. Transfer to a plate. Add the chicken a few pieces at a time and brown slightly, about 3 minutes. Use a slotted spoon to transfer the browned chicken to the plate.
2. Add the onion, garlic, bell pepper, and celery to the pot and cook, stirring frequently, until soft, about 3 minutes. Sprinkle with the seasoning blend, thyme, and cayenne. Add the rice, stirring to coat the grains with the oil. Add the tomatoes with their juice, broth, and bay leaf. Return the chicken and sausage to the pot. Stir to combine.
3. Close and lock the lid. Set the burner heat to high. When the cooker reaches HIGH pressure, reduce the burner heat as low as you can and still maintain HIGH pressure. Set a timer to cook for 7 minutes.
4. Remove the pot from the heat. Open the cooker with the Quick Release method. Be careful of the steam as you remove the lid. Place the lid back on the pot and let stand for 5 minutes. Discard the bay leaf.
5. Transfer the jambalaya to a rimmed platter and garnish by sprinkling with the parsley and green onions. Serve immediately with the hot sauces. Dig in.

Andouille and Chicken Red Jambalaya with Shrimp: Add 1 pound cooked shrimp in Step 4 after releasing pressure from the pot. Cover and let heat through over medium heat, 5 to 10 minutes.

Andouille and Chicken Red Jambalaya with Ham: Add 1 heaping cup diced cooked ham in Step 4 after releasing pressure from the pot. Cover and let heat through over medium heat, about 5 minutes.

Pressure Cooker Spareribs with Smoky Tomato BBQ Sauce

Serves 6 • Cooker: 6- to 8-quart • Time: 15 minutes at HIGH pressure

You do not have to wait for summer to enjoy ribs. The pork ribs family includes spareribs, baby back ribs, and country-style ribs, spareribs being the most popular because of their meatiness and wonderful flavor. Spareribs are cut from the belly area after the bacon is removed and come in a slab of 2 to 3 pounds, with varying amounts of meat and fat attached, feeding two to three eaters. Carefully inspect your slab so you can get one with plenty of meat and the least amount of fat. We do not precook our ribs in boiling water; the pressure cooker does the job perfectly. Just load up the cooker and go. Serve these ribs with coleslaw, baked beans, corn on the cob, bean salads, and/or potato salad.

SMOKY TOMATO BBQ SAUCE:

1 clove garlic, pressed
1 cup ketchup
3 tablespoons tomato paste
$1/4$ cup apricot or peach preserves
$1/4$ cup cider vinegar or balsamic vinegar
2 tablespoons dry red wine
2 tablespoons light olive oil
2 tablespoons reduced-sodium soy sauce
1 tablespoon dry mustard (like Colman's)
1 tablespoon onion powder (not onion salt)
2 teaspoons smoked paprika

RIBS:

3 pounds pork spareribs, cut into serving pieces of
    3- to 4-rib sections
Sea salt and freshly ground black pepper
1 tablespoon olive oil
1 large white onion, thickly sliced
1 cup water

1. Make the BBQ sauce. Place all the ingredients in a small bowl and whisk until smooth. It will keep in an airtight container in the refrigerator for up to 2 weeks. Makes about $1^1/2$ cups.
2. Season the ribs with salt and pepper to taste. In a 6- to 8-quart pressure cooker, heat the oil over medium-high heat until very hot. Brown the ribs in batches in a single layer on both sides, 5 to 7 minutes per batch. Use tongs to transfer the browned ribs to a plate. Add the onion and cook until soft, stirring a few times, about 3 minutes. Return the ribs and any accumulated juice to the pot. Add the BBQ sauce and water and bring to a simmer.
3. Close and lock the lid. Place a heat diffuser on the burner and set the pressure cooker on top. Set the burner heat to high. When the cooker reaches HIGH pressure, reduce the burner heat as low as you can and still maintain HIGH pressure. Set a timer to cook for 15 minutes.
4. Remove the pot from the heat. Open the cooker with the Natural Release method; let stand for 15 minutes. Be careful of the steam as you remove the lid. The ribs should be tender and falling off the bone.
5. Skim any fat from the top of the sauce. Transfer the ribs to a serving platter and spoon the sauce over them. Serve with lots of napkins.

EVEN QUICKER

If you want a shortcut BBQ sauce, stir together $1^1/2$ cups of a favorite BBQ sauce, 1 tablespoon brown sugar, 1 tablespoon red wine vinegar or sherry vinegar, and 1 tablespoon bourbon.

Char Siu Pork Ribs

Serves 4 to 6 • Cooker: 6- to 8-quart • Time: 15 minutes at HIGH pressure

Char siu is the Chinese-style BBQ sauce used to make classic Chinese barbecue pork. It translates to "burn/roast," which describes the age-old cooking method. The sauce creates a shiny red layer. Just load up the cooker pot and go. You can marinate the ribs in the sauce overnight in the refrigerator, if you like. This is delicious or, as one would say in Cantonese, *hóusihk!* Serve with rice and sautéed Asian greens or baby bok choy.

2 tablespoons olive oil
2 to 2¹/₂ pounds country-style or baby back pork
    ribs, the baby backs cut into 2- to 3-rib sections
    or individual ribs
1 clove garlic, minced
3 tablespoons ketchup
3 tablespoons hoisin sauce
3 tablespoons reduced-sodium soy sauce
2 tablespoons honey
1 tablespoon mirin or sake
2 teaspoons grated peeled fresh ginger
Pinch Chinese five-spice or ground allspice
Pinch ground white pepper
¹/₃ cup low-sodium chicken broth

FOR SERVING:
3 green onions, trimmed and thinly sliced
2 tablespoons minced fresh cilantro

1. In a 6- to 8-quart pressure cooker, heat the oil over medium-high heat until very hot. Brown the ribs in batches in a single layer on both sides, 5 to 7 minutes per batch. Use tongs to transfer the browned ribs to a plate. Add the garlic to the pot and stir for 30 seconds. Add the ketchup, hoisin, soy sauce, honey, mirin, ginger, five spice, and pepper to the pot and stir to combine. Return the ribs and any accumulated juice to the pot.

2. Close and lock the lid. Place a heat diffuser on the burner, and set the pressure cooker on it. Set the burner heat to high. When the cooker reaches HIGH pressure, reduce the burner heat as low as you can and still maintain HIGH pressure. Set a timer to cook for 15 minutes.

3. Remove the pot from the heat. Open the cooker with the Natural Release method; let stand for 15 minutes. Be careful of the steam as you remove the lid. The ribs should be tender, with the meat falling off the bone.

4. Transfer the ribs to a platter and tent with aluminum foil to keep warm. Skim any fat from the top of the sauce. Stir in the cilantro and green onions. Spoon the sauce over the ribs and serve immediately with lots of napkins.

Braised Pork Belly and Kimchi Stew

Serves 4 • Cooker: 6- to 8-quart • Time: 40 minutes at HIGH pressure

All Korean cooks have their own recipe for *kimchi jigae*, a home-style stew made with pork belly, kimchi, and green onions. We have added aromatic seasonal vegetables for a heartier stew. Go to your local organic butcher and request pork belly, skin off, bone out. It might not be in the counter, but they likely will have it. When you're buying pork belly for this recipe, look for a piece that has plenty of meat in relation to the fat. This is delicious served with noodles, pasta, bread, or rice.

1 1/2 pounds slab pork belly, skin removed
Sea salt and freshly ground black pepper
1 large white onion, sliced
2 cups kimchi cut into pieces 2 inches long
2 medium carrots, cut into 1-inch chunks
8 ounces white mushrooms, sliced (at least 2 cups)
3 medium white or red new potatoes, cut into
   1-inch chunks or quartered
3 tablespoons mirin
1/2 cup kimchi juice
1 1/2 cups low-sodium chicken broth
Sliced green onions (white part and some of the
   green), for garnish

KIMCHI

With the resurgence of popularity of fermented foods, spicy sour kimchi, the Korean version of sauerkraut and the country's national dish, has become widely appreciated not only for its flavor, but its versatility. While kimchi is usually a side dish or eaten plain with steamed rice, it also is an ingredient in everything from pancakes to fried rice and porridge. Store-bought kimchi works just as well as homemade in this stew. You can find kimchi in the refrigerated section of the supermarket, usually near the tofu. For good *kimchi jigae,* you need overfermented (sour) kimchi. If your kimchi is not fermented enough, you can add 1 tablespoon cider vinegar for an extra kick of sour.

1. Slice the belly into 1-inch cubes. Season on all sides with salt and pepper. Remember that the more kimchi juice you add, the less salt you will need. Heat a 6- to 8-quart pressure cooker over medium heat. Add the pork belly cubes and sear on all sides until golden and brown, fat side down first for 5 minutes. You shouldn't need any oil as pork belly has plenty of fat. When the pork is golden, remove to a bowl. Drain off all but 2 tablespoons of the pork fat from the pot.

2. Increase the heat under the pot to medium-high. Add the onions and cook over medium heat until lightly browned and soft, about 5 minutes. Add the kimchi, carrots, and mushrooms and brown lightly, stirring as needed. The mushrooms will release some juice. Return the pork to the pot along with any accumulated juices and the potatoes, and mix well. Add the mirin, kimchi juice, and broth to barely cover the pork and bring to a gentle simmer.

3. Close and lock the lid. Set the burner heat to high. When the cooker reaches HIGH pressure, reduce the burner heat as low as you can and still maintain HIGH pressure. Set a timer to cook for 40 minutes.

4. Remove the pot from the heat. Open the cooker with the Natural Release method; let stand for 15 minutes. Be careful of the steam as you remove the lid. The pork should be incredibly tender. Taste and add more mirin or kimchi juice to your taste, if you like.

5. Transfer the pork to a small rimmed platter or a Dolsot ceramic stone bowl (the traditional serving bowl for kimchi stews, specially made to retain heat) and sprinkle with green onions. Pour the liquid from the pot into a sauceboat if you don't have a stone bowl and serve. Top each serving of pork belly with a generous ladle of the sauce.

Ham with Honey Mustard Glaze

Serves 4 to 10, depending on size of ham and side dishes • Cooker: 6- to 8-quart • Time: Depending on size, 11 or 15 minutes at HIGH pressure

Boneless hams, 2½ to 4 pounds, work best in the pressure cooker; make sure the ham you buy does not fill your cooker by more than two thirds. Figure on ⅓ pound per person. You can also cook spiral-cut hams in the pressure cooker but be mindful about size; most will be too large for the pot.

1 to 1½ cups ginger ale, beer, or sparkling apple cider, as needed
⅓ cup sweet-hot honey mustard or honey Dijon mustard (we like the Pommery brand)
¼ cup firmly packed brown sugar
Pinch ground cloves
1 (2½- to 4-pound) boneless fully cooked ham

1. In a 6- to 8-quart pressure cooker, place a trivet and steamer rack. Pour in the ginger ale. The liquid should just come up to the bottom of the rack. In a small bowl, whisk the mustard, brown sugar, and cloves together and spoon or spread with a pastry brush over the surface of the ham. Place the ham in a steamer basket, fat side up, and set the basket in the pot, making sure it does not exceed the two thirds full level.
2. Close and lock the lid. Set the burner heat to high. When the cooker reaches HIGH pressure, reduce the burner heat as low as you can and still maintain HIGH pressure. Set a timer to cook for 11 minutes for a small ham (2½ to 3 pounds) and 15 minutes for a larger ham.
3. Remove the pot from the heat. Open the cooker with the Natural Release method; let stand for 15 minutes. Be careful of the steam as you remove the lid.
4. Transfer the ham to a platter. Do not use sharp utensils, like a meat fork, to pierce the ham when trying to turn or lift it because the juices will escape. You can finish the ham off under the broiler for a minute or two to brown the top if you like. Cover with aluminum foil until ready to serve, at least 15 minutes. Slice the ham with a long, thin knife, and serve hot. Let the leftovers come to room temperature, then wrap tightly and refrigerate; it will keep up to 5 days. You can also freeze any leftovers up to 2 months.

White Beans and Ham

Serves 6 • Cooker: 5- to 7-quart • Time: 11 minutes at HIGH pressure

In lieu of making split pea soup, make a pot of white beans laced with the leftover ham, and serve with corn muffins and a salad. If you do not have time to soak the beans, increase the pressure cooker time to 25 minutes

1½ pounds dried navy beans, soaked (page 406) and drained
About 1 pound leftover ham, diced
5 cups water
1 medium yellow onion, diced
1 clove garlic, minced
2 tablespoons minced fresh flatleaf parsley
2 tablespoons minced celery
1 bay leaf
1 teaspoon sea salt
2 tablespoons light olive oil or other flavorless oil
Chopped fresh cilantro, for serving
Coarsely shredded Cheddar cheese, for serving

1. Place the drained soaked beans in a 5- to 7-quart pressure cooker. Add the ham, water, onion, garlic, parsley, celery, bay leaf, and salt. Drizzle in the oil.
2. Close and lock the lid. Set the burner heat to high. When the cooker reaches HIGH pressure, reduce the burner heat as low as you can and still maintain HIGH pressure. Set a timer to cook for 11 minutes.
3. Remove the pot from the heat. Open the cooker with the Natural Release method; let stand for 15 minutes. Be careful of the steam as you remove the lid. Discard the bay leaf.
4. Stir, then taste for salt. Serve hot with lots of cheese and cilantro, and warm corn muffins. It will keep in an airtight container in the refrigerator 4 to 5 days or in the freezer up to 4 months.

White Butter Beans and Ham: Substitute 1 (1-pound) package dried large lima beans for the navy beans. Cook for 6 minutes (23 minutes if unsoaked) at HIGH pressure.

10

Cha Cha Chilis

Chili is characterized by a flavor and color combination of spicy-hot red chili powder and Southwest herbs and spices like oregano and cumin, even sometimes accents of cinnamon and cloves. While chili has a reputation for heat, you can most certainly make a mild chili where all the individual subtle flavors are discernable and everyone can easily eat.

Chili is the child of invention. Chili stews appear with or without beans, with meat or without, tomatoes or not, wine or tequila, and with a variety of different types of beans. While all sorts of beans show up today, the traditional bean for chili is the pinto, also called the *frijol* bean or Mexican red bean, a faintly streaked reddish brown and pink bean grown in the Southwest. But today's chili makers do not limit themselves; there are chilis made with black turtle beans (popular in vegetarian chilis), Great Northerns (a favorite in white chilis), black-eyed peas, Anasazi beans, cannellini white kidneys, and so much more. In any of our recipes, feel free to substitute beans, even using heirloom American varieties like Anasazi, black-and-white Appaloosa, or Jacob's cattle beans, to vary the flavor. Mixing two or three different varieties is also popular, especially in vegetarian versions. Refer to our Bean Chart on pages 402–406 for substitutions and cook times.

We have assembled here a collection of chilis guaranteed to appeal to a wide range of cooks and diners. All of them can be made a day or two ahead; they just get better as they sit. They freeze great as well.

HOW TO THICKEN CHILI

Use dry masa harina, the cornmeal used for making tortillas (keep some in the freezer just for thickening your chilis); it is the traditional way and adds a wonderful flavor. Start with 2 tablespoons mixed with 4 tablespoons cold water to make a thin slurry; make sure there are no lumps. Pour into the hot chili and stir. The chili will thicken slightly within minutes. If you want it even thicker, repeat the process. If your chili is too thick, add more liquid and cook a bit longer to heat it through. Remember, though, that if your chili is too "sauce-y," you can serve it Cincinnati style—over spaghetti!

OUR QUICK GUIDE TO CHILES

There are dozens of chiles descended from their wild ancestors. But there are a few that are considered commercial crops. They are essential in making the oh-so-American stew called chili.

The most popular hot dried chile today is the complex flavored chipotle, the smoked-dried jalapeño, which is easily available canned in adobo sauce or dried in cellophane packages. A little bit of chipotle will give a so-so pot of chile that bit of hot and smoky. Jalapeño peppers are available fresh or canned *en escabeche* (pickled), which mellows the heat component considerably; if you like peppers but the heat is too much for you, try adding some jalapeño peppers *en escabeche* to your chili. Fresh green chiles, conveniently canned like the Anaheim, are a fast addition to chili without the hassle of roasting fresh chiles.

A few simple rules:

- The same kind of chile will be somewhat milder fresh and stronger when dried.
- Canned chiles will have a less pronounced flavor than fresh or dried.
- Every type of chile has a different level of heat and a slightly different flavor.
- Generally, the smaller the pepper, the hotter it is.
- Generally, the more pointed the shape, the hotter it is.
- The heat is in the membranes and seeds, not the meat of the chile; if you want the chile flavor but less of the heat, remove the seeds and membranes before adding the chile to your dish.
- Rehydrating dried chiles will develop their flavor.
- Don't rub your eyes while working with chiles.
- When handling chiles, if you think you might be sensitive to them, wear surgical gloves.

Here are the chiles we use most frequently:

Anaheim

This chile is also known as the California green chile and chile verde. When you buy canned chiles, this is what you're getting. They are labeled "roasted green chiles" and are sold whole or diced. They are mild in flavor and good for all types of cooking.

New Mexico Green Chile

New Mexico chile is a catch-all term for long, green chiles grown in that state. Popular varieties include Big Jims, Sandias, and 6-4s. Hatch is a town in New Mexico known for high quality chiles, hence the term "Hatch chiles" denotes the place where the chiles were grown, not the variety. When New Mexico green chiles are allowed to ripen to red before picking, then dried, they are sold as New Mexican red chiles.

New Mexico chiles range in heat from mild to quite hot. The ripened, dried chiles are sold in comely ristras throughout the Southwest in the fall. Red chile powder is made from the dried chiles, as are red pepper flakes. Red chile powder is often referred to as "the salt of the Southwest."

Poblano

Smaller than the Anaheim, the poblano is heart-shaped and dark green, with a thin, tough skin. It may be labeled "pasilla" in the supermarket. It is typically mild to medium hot. You can stuff poblanos as you would bell peppers. These chiles are difficult to roast and peel. When allowed to ripen to red and then dried, the poblano is called the ancho chile, which is sold both as a dried chile and a pure powder, which adds a lot of flavor without a lot of heat.

Jalapeño

Two inches long and bright dark green, the jalapeño is one of the most commonly used of the chiles, especially in fresh salsas. They are also sold canned or pickled *(en escabeche),* both of which are milder than the fresh. If you end up with a big batch from your garden, blanch them for 5 minutes in boiling water, drain on paper towels, cool, and store whole in plastic freezer bags in the freezer. When allowed to ripen to red and then smoke-dried, the jalapeño is known as the chipotle and has a distinctive smoky flavor. They are sold dried, as a pure powder, or canned with an adobo sauce, sold as *chipotles en adobo.*

Chile de Árbol

This little, pointed, dried red chile is sold in cellophane bags in the Latin section of the supermarket. They are extremely hot!

Serrano and Habanero

Both of these fresh chiles are smaller and lots hotter than jalapeños, these are an acquired taste and show up seasonally. The serrano looks like a little jalapeño and the habanero (also known as the Scotch bonnet) looks like a little golden lantern.

Southwestern Black Bean Chili

Serves 4 to 6 • Cooker: 5- to 8-quart • Time: 10 minutes at HIGH pressure

Black bean chili is the chili that made chili lovers out of a whole new generation of cooks and eaters from coast to coast. Serve bowls of this spicy vegetarian crowd-pleaser with tortilla chips or a big pile of warm tortillas, or over rice or soft polenta. Pass condiments at the table so everyone can customize their own chili. (The cheese and sour cream tame the heat.) This recipe yields a generous amount, so you'll likely have enough left over to freeze for another meal.

CHILI:
$1/4$ cup olive oil
2 medium white or yellow onions, chopped
2 medium or large bell peppers, preferably 1 red
    and 1 green or yellow, seeded and chopped
3 cloves garlic, finely chopped
1 (1-pound) package dried black beans, soaked
    (see page 406), drained, and rinsed in cold
    water
2 cups water
2 tablespoons chopped fresh oregano or 2 tea-
    spoons dried oregano, preferably Mexican
1 tablespoon chili powder
2 (10-ounce) cans diced tomatoes and green chiles,
    such as Rotel brand
2 teaspoons ground cumin
1 teaspoon salt, plus more to taste
$1/8$ teaspoon cayenne pepper

TOPPINGS:
Shredded Monterey jack or cheddar cheese
Sliced green onions
Sliced pickled jalapeño peppers
Sour cream
Sprigs fresh cilantro
Salsa and/or hot sauce
Lime wedges

1. In a 5- to 8-quart pressure cooker, heat the oil over medium-high heat. Add the onions and cook, stirring a few times, until they begin to soften, about 3 minutes. Add the bell peppers and garlic and cook, stirring a few times, until the garlic is fragrant, about 2 minutes. Add the beans, water, oregano, and chili powder. Stir to combine.

2. Close and lock the lid. Set the burner heat to high. When the cooker reaches HIGH pressure, reduce the burner heat as low as you can and still maintain HIGH pressure. Set a timer to cook for 10 minutes.

3. Remove the pot from the heat. Open the cooker with the Natural Release method; let stand for 10 minutes. Be careful of the steam as you remove the lid. The beans should be tender yet still slightly firm to the bite.

4. Add the tomatoes and chiles with their juices, cumin, salt, and the cayenne to the pot. Bring to a boil, uncovered, over medium-high heat and cook, stirring occasionally, until the liquid has reduced slightly, 8 to 10 minutes. Taste, adding more salt if needed.

5. Serve the chili warm, with the toppings in small bowls or plates for diners to customize their chili as they prefer.

MEXICAN OREGANO

Mexican oregano is, not surprisingly, native to Mexico and has an earthy fragrance. Though it tastes similar to the stronger Greek oregano, the two are not related botanically, though they can be used interchangeably in recipes. Mexican oregano belongs to the verbena family, while common Mediterranean oregano is part of the mint family.

Three-Bean Chili with Cilantro Cream

Serves 6 • Cooker: 5- to 8-quart • Time: 10 minutes for beans, 6 minutes for vegetables at HIGH pressure

This combination of dried beans is particularly flavorful. Smoked paprika supplies a dusky hint of heat along with fire-roasted tomatoes. The Cilantro Cream offers a nice counterpoint to the chili's spiciness. You can also serve this with slices of avocado and warm flour tortillas or cornbread.

CHILI:

$^3/_4$ cup dried white cannellini beans, rinsed and picked over

$^3/_4$ cup dried black beans, rinsed and picked over

$^3/_4$ cup dried cranberry beans (borlotti), rinsed and picked over

8 cups water

2 tablespoons olive oil

1 large white onion, chopped

2 cloves garlic, minced

1 medium carrot, chopped

2 ribs celery, chopped

1 medium sweet potato, peeled and cut into $^1/_2$-inch dice

2 cups frozen baby corn kernels, thawed

1 (4-ounce) can chopped roasted green chiles, drained

2 (14.5-ounce) cans diced tomatoes in juice, fire-roasted if possible, undrained

3 tablespoons sherry vinegar

2 tablespoons packed light brown sugar

4 teaspoons chili powder

1 tablespoon smoked paprika

2 teaspoons unsweetened cocoa powder

$^1/_4$ teaspoon cayenne pepper

2 teaspoons sea salt, or to taste

$^1/_2$ teaspoon ground white pepper or freshly ground black pepper

CILANTRO CREAM:

1 cup sour cream

$^1/_3$ cup minced fresh cilantro

3 tablespoons fresh lime juice

1. In a medium bowl, combine the three beans and cover with a few inches of water. Let soak overnight. The next day, drain and rinse the beans.

2. In a 5- to 8-quart pressure cooker, combine the soaked beans and 8 cups water. Bring to a boil.

3. Close and lock the lid. Set the burner heat to high. When the cooker reaches HIGH pressure, reduce the burner heat as low as you can and still maintain HIGH pressure. Set a timer to cook for 10 minutes.

4. Remove the pot from the heat. Open the cooker with the Quick Release method. Be careful of the steam as you remove the lid. Drain the beans, reserving the cooking liquid separately. Set aside.

5. In the pressure cooker (you don't need to wash it), heat the oil over medium-high heat. Add the onion and cook, stirring a few times, until it just begins to soften, about 3 minutes. Add the garlic, carrot, celery, and sweet potato and cook, stirring occasionally, until the vegetables are softened, about 5 minutes. Add the corn, green chiles, tomatoes with their juice, and 4 cups of the bean cooking liquid (add more water if you don't have enough bean liquid). Add the cooked beans. Stir in the vinegar, brown sugar, chili powder, paprika, cocoa, cayenne, salt, and black pepper.

6. Close and lock the lid. Set the burner heat to high. When the cooker reaches HIGH pressure, adjust the heat to maintain the pressure. Set a timer to cook for 6 minutes.

7. Remove the pot from the heat. Open the cooker with the Natural Release method; let stand for 15 minutes. Be careful of the steam as you remove the lid. The beans should be tender yet still be slightly firm to the bite. Stir, taste, and adjust the seasonings as desired.

8. Make the Cilantro Cream. Combine the sour cream, cilantro, and lime juice in a small bowl; stir until evenly combined. Cover and chill until serving.

9. Top each serving of the chili with a dollop of the Cilantro Cream.

Greengrocer Chili with Pinto Beans

Serves 6 to 8 • Cooker: 5- to 8-quart • Time: 10 minutes at HIGH pressure

This chili, inspired by a recipe from the always excellent *Southern Living* magazine, is a mild, tomato-based beauty. It's all about the fresh, nutritious, flavor-packed bevy of vegetables. Make it in late summer, when the zucchini and yellow squash are at their most prolific, using fresh corn instead of frozen and fresh basil. Sometimes we substitute two chayote squash for the zucchini and yellow squash—we like the way it stays a bit crunchy even after cooking.

CHILI:
2 tablespoons olive oil
1 medium sweet yellow onion (such as Walla Walla or Maui), chopped into $3/4$-inch pieces
2 large carrots, diced
2 ribs celery, diced
1 pound mushrooms, trimmed and sliced $1/2$ inch thick
1 large zucchini, chopped
1 medium or 2 small yellow squash, chopped
1 tablespoon chili powder, or more to taste
2 tablespoons chopped fresh basil or 1 teaspoon dried basil
$1/2$ teaspoon freshly ground black pepper
1 (8-ounce) can tomato sauce
2 cups tomato juice
1 (28-ounce) can diced tomatoes in juice, undrained
2 cups water
1 (1-pound) package dried pinto beans, soaked (see page 406), drained, and rinsed in cold water
1 cup fresh or frozen corn kernels
Salt

TOPPINGS:
Crumbled feta or cotija cheese
Slivered fresh basil
Sliced green onions
Sliced pickled jalapeño peppers
Lime wedges

1. In a 5- to 8-quart pressure cooker, heat the oil over medium-high heat. Add the onion, carrots, and celery and cook, stirring a few times, until they begin to soften, about 5 minutes. Add the mushrooms, zucchini, and summer squash and cook, stirring a few times, for 4 minutes. Add the chili powder, basil, and pepper and cook, stirring, for 1 minute, being careful not to burn the chili powder. Add the tomato sauce, tomato juice, tomatoes and juices, water, and pinto beans. Stir to combine.

2. Close and lock the lid. Set the burner heat to high. When the cooker reaches HIGH pressure, reduce the burner heat as low as you can and still maintain HIGH pressure. Set a timer to cook for 10 minutes.

3. Remove the pot from the heat. Open the cooker with the Natural Release method; let stand for 10 minutes. Be careful of the steam as you remove the lid. The beans should be tender yet still be slightly firm to the bite.

4. Add the corn to the pot. Bring to a boil, uncovered, over medium-high heat and cook, stirring occasionally, until the corn is warm, 2 to 3 minutes. Season to taste with salt.

5. Serve the chili warm, with the toppings in small bowls or plates for diners to customize their chili as they prefer.

RED CHILE POWDERS

We got introduced to Dixon chile powder by our Southwest cooking expert, Jacquie Hiquera McMahan. Dixon, named for Dixon, New Mexico, is known as the Rolls Royce of ground chiles for its incomparable flavor.

We also like ancho chile powder, for its lovely sweetness. It is often used in combination with other dried chiles to mellow their sharpness.

You can substitute ancho chile powder or Dixon anytime we call for chili powder.

Rainbow Chili with Black-Eyed Peas and Bulgur

Serves 6 to 8 • Cooker: 5- to 8-quart • Time: 10 minutes at HIGH pressure

Bulgur had a heyday in the U.S. in the 1970s and '80s, when tabbouleh was embraced by the masses and vegetarianism was being explored by a new generation. For many people, though, bulgur never got out of the salad bowl. What a shame—here it adds fiber, flavor, and great chewy texture to this colorful, mild vegetarian chili. Unlike many whole grains, bulgur is quick-cooking because it is parboiled before being dried and cracked into pieces. Look for a medium- or coarse-textured bulgur for chili. This is one of the quickest chili recipes we know! Serve with cornbread or a baguette and butter and a big green salad.

CHILI:

2 tablespoons olive oil

2 medium red onions, chopped

2 medium or large red, yellow, or orange bell peppers, or a combination, seeded and chopped

2 to 3 cloves garlic, to taste, minced

1 (28-ounce) can diced tomatoes in juice, undrained

1 (15-ounce) can tomato puree

1 cup water

$1/3$ cup bulgur wheat, medium- or coarse-grind

2 (12-ounce) packages frozen black-eyed peas, thawed

2 Anaheim or poblano peppers, seeded and chopped

1 to 2 teaspoons minced canned chipotle chile in adobo sauce, to taste

1 tablespoon chili powder

2 teaspoons sweet paprika

1 tablespoon dried oregano, crumbled

2 teaspoons ground cumin

$1/2$ teaspoon ground coriander

Salt

TOPPINGS:

Shredded Monterey Jack or cheddar cheese

Sour cream or plain Greek yogurt

Extra-firm tofu, rinsed and cut into cubes

Chopped radishes

Chopped fresh cilantro

Sliced black olives

Sliced ripe avocado

1. In a 5- to 8-quart pressure cooker, heat the oil over medium-high heat. Add the onions and cook, stirring a few times, until they begin to soften, about 3 minutes. Add the bell peppers and garlic and cook, stirring a few times, until the garlic is fragrant, about 2 minutes. Add the tomatoes and their juices, tomato puree, water, bulgur, black-eyed peas, Anaheims, chipotle, and spices. Stir gently but thoroughly to combine.

2. Close and lock the lid. Set the burner heat to high. When the cooker reaches HIGH pressure, reduce the burner heat as low as you can and still maintain HIGH pressure. Set a timer to cook for 10 minutes.

3. Remove the pot from the heat. Open the cooker with the Natural Release method; let stand for 10 minutes. Be careful of the steam as you remove the lid. The bulgur should be tender. Taste, adding salt if needed.

4. Serve the chili warm, with the toppings in small bowls or plates for diners to customize their chili as they prefer.

Lentil Chili with Lime Crema

Serves 6 • Cooker: 5- to 7-quart • Time: 10 minutes at HIGH pressure

Brown lentils, the kind found on the supermarket shelf, work best for this as they hold their shape even when tender. Lentils do not need to be soaked before cooking. Experiment with different chili powders, which can range from mild to hot spiciness.

CHILI:
2 tablespoons olive oil
1 medium yellow or white onion, chopped
1 large red bell pepper, seeded and chopped
2 ribs celery, sliced $^1/_4$ inch thick
4 cloves garlic, finely chopped
5 teaspoons chili powder
1 teaspoon ground cumin
1 teaspoon dried oregano, preferably Mexican
1 (16-ounce) package brown lentils, rinsed and
    picked over
7 cups vegetable broth
2 (14.5-ounce) cans diced tomatoes in juice,
    undrained
Sea salt
$^1/_2$ cup chopped fresh cilantro

LIME CREMA:
$^1/_2$ cup sour cream
$^1/_2$ cup plain Greek yogurt
Juice and grated zest of 2 limes

1. In a 5- to 7-quart pressure cooker, heat the oil over medium-high heat. Add the onion and bell pepper and cook, stirring occasionally, until they begin to soften, about 5 minutes. Add the celery and garlic and cook 1 minute, stirring. Add the chili powder, cumin, and oregano; stir until warmed. Add the lentils, broth, and tomatoes and their juices. Bring to a boil.

2. Close and lock the lid. Set the burner heat to high. When the cooker reaches HIGH pressure, reduce the burner heat as low as you can and still maintain HIGH pressure. Set a timer to cook for 10 minutes.

3. In a small bowl, whisk together the Lime Crema ingredients until smooth. Cover and refrigerate until using.

4. Remove the pot from the heat. Open the cooker with the Natural Release method; let stand for 10 minutes. Be careful of the steam as you remove the lid. Stir the chili and taste for salt. Stir in the cilantro.

5. Serve the chili warm in bowls, topped with a dollop of crema.

Chicken Chili with Chayote and Sweet Potato

Serves 6 to 8 • Cooker: 5- to 8-quart • Time: 10 minutes for beans, 5 minutes for chili at HIGH pressure

This is a colorful, low-fat chili, chock full of vegetables. We like to cook our pintos with epazote, the Mexican herb that is said to improve beans' digestibility. Whether or not it does that, we can vouch for the fact that it adds a delightful herbal flavor. If there are any large stems in your epazote, remove them before using. Freeze any leftovers in one-cup containers for lunches.

1 cup dried pinto beans, soaked (see page 406), drained, and rinsed with cold water
1 tablespoon dried epazote
$1/2$ cup white wine
1 pound ground chicken
1 medium red onion, chopped into $1/2$-inch pieces
2 cloves garlic, chopped
2 large ribs celery, strings scraped off and chopped into $1/2$-inch pieces
3 medium carrots, sliced $1/2$ inch thick, the largest slices halved
1 medium or large red bell pepper, seeded and chopped into $1/2$-inch pieces
1 medium sweet potato, peeled and chopped into $1/2$-inch pieces
1 medium chayote, peeled, any seeds discarded, and chopped into $1/2$-inch pieces
$1^1/2$ cups frozen corn kernels
1 (14.5-ounce) can diced tomatoes in juice, undrained
3 to 4 teaspoons chili powder, to taste
1 teaspoon sea salt
$1/2$ teaspoon freshly ground black pepper
2 to 4 tablespoons masa harina, as needed

1. In a 5- to 8-quart pressure cooker, combine the soaked beans and epazote. Add cold water to cover by $1^1/2$ inches.
2. Close and lock the lid. Set the burner heat to high. When the cooker reaches HIGH pressure, reduce the burner heat as low as you can and still maintain HIGH pressure. Set a timer to cook for 10 minutes.
3. Remove the pot from the heat. Open the cooker with the Quick Release method. Be careful of the steam as you remove the lid. If the beans are not done to your liking, relock the cooker, bring it back up to pressure, and cook for 2 to 5 min-

utes longer. Once done, carefully transfer the beans and their liquid to a bowl.

4. Add the white wine to the pressure cooker (no need to wash it). Bring it to a boil over medium-high heat. Add the ground chicken, onion, and garlic and cook, stirring occasionally, until the chicken is cooked through and the onion has softened, 3 to 4 minutes. Stir in the celery, carrots, and bell pepper and cook for about 2 minutes more. Add the sweet potato, corn, chayote, and tomatoes and their juice. Add the beans and their liquid. Stir in the chili powder.
5. Close and lock the lid. Set the burner heat to high. When the cooker reaches HIGH pressure, reduce the burner heat as low as you can and still maintain HIGH pressure. Set a timer to cook for 5 minutes.
6. Remove the pot from the heat. Open the cooker with the Natural Release method; let stand for 10 minutes. Be careful of the steam as you remove the lid. The beans should be tender yet still be slightly firm to the bite. Season with the salt and black pepper.
7. To thicken the chili, ladle out about $1/4$ cup of broth from the chili into a cup. Stirring with a fork, dissolve 2 tablespoons of the masa harina in the warm broth. Gently stir the mixture back into the chili. Bring the chili back to a boil and let it simmer, uncovered, for 4 to 5 minutes. If the chili still isn't as thick as you like it, repeat the process with 1 to 2 more tablespoons of masa harina and more broth.

MASA HARINA

Masa harina (also known as maseca) is a coarse-ground lime-treated cornflour blend used to make tortillas or tamales. It is also great for thickening chili. Look for it in the Hispanic section of your supermarket or next to the flour in the baking section. If you enclose the package in a heavy-duty ziptop plastic bag, it keeps almost indefinitely in the refrigerator or freezer. You can also thicken your chili with finely ground cornmeal, but it will be a bit gritty.

White Bean Chicken Chili

Serves 8 • Cooker: 5- to 8-quart • Time: 10 minutes for beans, 2 minutes for chili at HIGH pressure

This is adapted from one of Beth's favorite cookbooks, *Beyond Parsley* by the Junior League of Kansas City, Missouri. This is a mild chili and utilizes leftover cooked chicken or a store-bought rotisserie chicken combined with white beans such as Great Northern. If you like it spicy, add a jalapeño in Step 1. Everyone loves this chili, and the creamy version below. Serve it with warm flour tortillas or tortilla chips along with the suggested toppings.

CHILI:

1 (1-pound) package dried large white beans, such as Great Northern or cannellini, soaked (see page 406), drained, and rinsed with cold water
6 cups chicken broth
2 cloves garlic, minced
2 medium white onions, chopped
2 tablespoons olive oil
2 (4-ounce) cans chopped roasted green chiles, drained
2 teaspoons ground cumin
1 1/2 teaspoons dried oregano, preferably Mexican
1/4 teaspoon cayenne pepper
Leaves and tender stems from 1/2 bunch fresh cilantro, chopped
About 4 cups shredded cooked chicken breasts

TOPPINGS:

3 cups coarsely grated Monterey Jack cheese
1/2 cup chopped fresh cilantro
Chopped fresh tomatoes or salsa
Hot sauce of your choice
1/4 cup chopped green onions
1 ripe avocado, peeled, pitted, and chopped, or guacamole

1. In a 5- to 8-quart pressure cooker, combine the soaked beans, broth, garlic, and half of the chopped onions. Bring to a boil.
2. Close and lock the lid. Set the burner heat to high. When the cooker reaches HIGH pressure, reduce the burner heat as low as you can and still maintain HIGH pressure. Set a timer to cook for 10 minutes.
3. Remove the pot from the heat. Open the cooker with the Quick Release method. Be careful of the steam as you remove the lid.
4. In a skillet, heat the oil over medium-high heat until very hot. Add the remaining onion and cook, stirring a few times, until soft and a bit golden on the edges. Add to the cooked beans. Add the chiles, cumin, oregano, cayenne, chicken, and cilantro.
5. Close and lock the lid. Set the burner heat to high. When the cooker reaches HIGH pressure, reduce the burner heat as low as you can and still maintain HIGH pressure. Set a timer to cook for 2 minutes.
6. Remove the pot from the heat. Open the cooker with the Natural Release method; let stand for 10 minutes. The beans should be tender yet still be slightly firm to the bite. Taste for and adjust the seasonings as desired.
7. Serve the chili warm, with the toppings in small bowls or plates for diners to customize their chili as they prefer.

Creamy White Bean Chicken Chili: Just before serving, stir in 1 cup light or regular sour cream and 1/2 cup half-and-half until blended; cook over medium heat, uncovered, until heated through, about 10 minutes.

White Bean Turkey Chili: Add 4 cups shredded cooked turkey breast in place of the chicken.

Posole con Pollo

Serves 10 to 12 • Cooker: 5- to 8-quart • Time: 60 minutes at HIGH pressure

Posole is a spicy hominy stew, Native American in origin, found in Mexico and throughout the American Southwest. Perhaps the most famous posole in the world is served at The Shed in Santa Fe, a family-owned restaurant that is still serving New Mexican specialties near Santa Fe's picturesque plaza after 60 years in business. Julie has fond memories of eating there as a girl in the 1960s and '70s. When she went back to visit in 2012, the food was even better than she remembered. The Shed's posole is served as a soup or a side dish alongside the tacos and enchiladas. It is made with pork but beef is also common, as is lamb—remember that Native Americans have raised sheep in the Southwest for generations. We prefer lighter chicken or vegetarian versions—even lightened in this way, posole is extremely hearty food.

Most cooks like to boil the meat for posole separately, then combine it with the corn for final cooking but we think it's almost as good and so much easier to cook the whole stew at once in the pressure cooker. Traditional Southwestern versions of posole are seasoned very simply with some combination of chiles, oregano, garlic, salt, and pepper, perhaps with a squeeze of lime juice. Modern posole can be more elaborate—mushrooms were the star of a bowl of vegan posole that Julie enjoyed in downtown Oakland recently. Simple or elaborate, posole is party food, so follow the tradition and throw a posole party this winter!

POSOLE

Posole is made from field corn, which is starchy and tough, not the sweet corn we eat off the cob. The mature corn is dried and treated with lime (the mineral, not the fruit) in a process called nixtamalization, which softens the tough outer hull. When ground, nixtamalized corn is used to make tortillas and tamales. You can buy dried posole in cellophane bags or in the bulk section in Mexican markets throughout the U.S. or via mail order—even from The Shed if you like (www.sfshed.com). Don't be fooled by bags of dry "chicos" corn kernels. Chicos haven't been nixtamalized—they're different. Dried posole needs to be soaked for quite a long time before cooking—use one of our bean-soaking methods. Following a good soak, it still needs at least an hour in the pressure cooker to soften and "pop." We have noticed that Southwestern brands, such as Los Chileros de Nuevo Mexico or Bueno do cook in about an hour, but Mexican brands may take longer. If you happen to live in the Southwest, you can buy frozen posole, a time-saver because it has already been soaked. If all you can find in your town is canned hominy, go ahead and substitute if you must—just reduce the cooking time to 30 minutes under pressure.

CHILI:

2 or 3 dried New Mexican red chiles (each about 4 inches long), to taste, rinsed, stems removed, and most of the seeds shaken out and discarded, OR 3 tablespoons pure New Mexico red chile powder

1 cup hottest possible tap water

1 1/2 cups dried posole see page 382, soaked, drained, and rinsed with cold water, OR 3 cups frozen posole (no need to thaw), OR 2 (15.5-ounce) cans hominy, rinsed and drained

6 cups chicken broth

4 bone-in chicken thighs, skin removed

4 cloves garlic, peeled

1 1/2 teaspoons dried oregano

Juice of 1 lime

Sea salt and freshly ground black pepper

TOPPINGS:

Shredded lettuce

Diced fresh tomato

Cubed ripe avocado

Lime wedges

Chopped radishes

Crumbled dried oregano

Pure chile powder of your choice for sprinkling

Diced peeled jicama

Diced peeled cucumber

1. Place the dried chiles and hot water in a blender and blend until smooth. Be careful when you remove the lid, as a good whiff of the chile sauce can start a nasty coughing fit. Pour the chile sauce into a 5- to 8-quart pressure cooker. (If you are using ground chile, simply place it and the hot water in the pressure cooker.) Add the posole, broth, chicken, garlic, and oregano. Stir to combine.

2. Close and lock the lid. Set the burner heat to high. When the cooker reaches HIGH pressure, reduce the burner heat as low as you can and still maintain HIGH pressure. Set a timer to cook for 60 minutes. (If you are using canned hominy, you will cook the posole for only 30 minutes.)

3. Remove the pot from the heat. Open the cooker with the Natural Release method; let stand for 10 minutes. Be careful of the steam as you remove the lid. The posole should be tender, with almost all the kernels "popped" or "bloomed." If they are not, relock the cooker, bring it back to pressure, and cook 10 minutes longer. Repeat if necessary. If a neater presentation is desired, remove the chicken from the bones, discard the bones and cut the chicken into bite-size pieces

4. Stir in the lime juice and salt and pepper to taste. If your broth was salted, you might not need much.

5. Serve the posole warm, with the toppings in small bowls or plates for diners to customize their chili as they prefer.

Pork Posole: Substitute 1 pound boneless country-style pork ribs for the chicken. If desired, cut the meat into bite-size pieces after cooking to serve.

Lamb Posole: Substitute 3/4 pound cubed boneless lamb shoulder or leg of lamb for the chicken.

Buffalo-Style Cincinnati Chicken Chili

Serves 6 • Cooker: 5- to 8-quart • Time: 10 minutes for beans, 10 minutes for chili at HIGH pressure

Okay, we thought traditional Cincinnati-style chili (page 315) was a hoot, but then we heard about this fun hybrid—Cincinnati-style chili over pasta with a couple of Buffalo twists: chicken instead of beef, celery sticks, and blue cheese topping it instead of cheddar. We couldn't resist adapting it for the pressure cooker. When the Bengals play the Bills, you know what to serve!

CHILI:
1 cup dried white cannellini beans, soaked (see page 406), drained, and rinsed with cold water
3 cups water
3 tablespoons vegetable oil
1 medium onion, chopped
1 cup chopped celery
1 cup chopped carrots
2 cloves garlic, chopped
1 pound ground chicken breast
1 (14.5-ounce) can diced tomatoes in juice, undrained
1 cup light-tasting beer
1 cup chicken broth
1 teaspoon paprika
1 tablespoon chili powder
1 teaspoon dried oregano
1 teaspoon ground cumin
Salt and freshly ground black pepper

FOR SERVING:
1 pound spaghetti, cooked
1 cup crumbled blue cheese
Chopped onions
Cooked white kidney beans
Oyster crackers
Hot sauce of your choice
Celery sticks

1. In a 5- to 8-quart pressure, combine the soaked beans, water, and 1 tablespoon of the oil.
2. Close and lock the lid. Set the burner heat to high. When the cooker reaches HIGH pressure, reduce the burner heat as low as you can and still maintain HIGH pressure. Set a timer to cook for 7 minutes.
3. Remove the pot from the heat. Open the cooker with the Natural Release method; let stand for 10 minutes. Be careful of the steam as you remove the lid. The beans should be tender yet still slightly firm to the bite. Pour the beans and their liquid into a bowl and cover to keep warm.
4. Wipe out the pressure cooker, then heat the remaining 2 tablespoons oil over medium-high heat until very hot. Add the onion, celery, carrots, and garlic and cook, stirring a few times, until they begin to soften, about 3 minutes. Add the ground chicken and cook, stirring to break up any large chunks of meat, until the chicken is cooked through, 3 to 4 minutes. Add the tomatoes and their liquid, beer, broth, paprika, chili powder, oregano, and cumin. Stir to combine.
5. Close and lock the lid. Set the burner heat to high. When the cooker reaches HIGH pressure, reduce the burner heat as low as you can and still maintain HIGH pressure. Set a timer to cook for 10 minutes.
6. Remove the pot from the heat. Open the cooker with the Natural Release method; let stand for 10 minutes. Season to taste with salt and pepper.
7. Serve the chili warm over spaghetti, with the rest of the toppings in bowls for diners to customize their chili as desired.

Buffalo-Style Cincinnati Turkey Chili: Substitute ground turkey for the ground chicken.

Homemade Salsa with Your Chili

Whether we have listed it or not in the suggested toppings for the chilis in this chapter, salsa is always a welcome addition and even more so when it's homemade. Here are a few of our very favorites. Add a tablespoon or two per bowl of chili. These salsas all taste best the day they are made.

Pico de Gallo (Rooster's Beak or Salsa Fresca)

Makes 3 to 4 cups

Pico de gallo translates as "rooster's beak." It's also known as salsa fresca.

4 medium ripe tomatoes (about 1¹/₂ pounds), cored and diced
1 jalapeño pepper, seeded and finely chopped
1 clove garlic, finely chopped
1 small white or red onion, diced
¹/₂ cup chopped fresh cilantro
Juice of 2 limes
¹/₂ teaspoon dried oregano, preferably Mexican
Salt to taste

In a medium bowl, combine all the ingredients. Taste. If the chiles make the salsa too hot, add some more chopped tomato. If not hot enough, carefully add a few of the seeds from the chiles, or add some pure ground chile. Cover and refrigerate for a couple of hours to allow the flavors to develop.

Salsa Fresca with Sunflower Seeds: Add 3 tablespoons shelled raw sunflower seeds right before serving.

Winter Cilantro-Lime Salsa

Makes about 3 cups

2 (14.5-ounce) cans fire-roasted or plain diced tomatoes in juice, well drained
1 medium white onion, finely chopped
2 cloves garlic, finely chopped
¹/₂ cup chopped fresh cilantro
Juice of 2 limes
Grated zest of 1 lime
Salt to taste
1 to 2 jalapeño or serrano peppers, to taste, seeded and finely chopped

In a medium bowl, combine all the ingredients. Cover and refrigerate for a couple of hours to allow the flavors to develop.

Salsa Roja

Makes about 4 cups

Salsa roja is the salsa you'll find at taco stands and in Mexican restaurants for chips. It is thicker, less chunky, and more pourable than salsa fresca. This is a delicious salsa for tacos.

2 (14-ounce) cans fire-roasted canned tomatoes in juice
1 (4-ounce) can diced or whole roasted green chiles
¹/₂ cup packed fresh cilantro (leaves and stems)
4 green onions (white part and few inches of green), trimmed and cut into 2-inch pieces
1 roasted red pepper
¹/₂ to 1 small jalapeño, to taste, seeded (if you like a spicier flavor, leave the seeds in)
2 tablespoons fresh lime juice
¹/₂ teaspoon sea salt
¹/₄ teaspoon ground cumin

Drain the tomatoes, reserving the juice. Combine all ingredients except reserved tomato juice in a food processor. Pulse on and off until all the ingredients are finely chopped and as you prefer it, with a little bit of chunkiness or smooth. If you like a thinner salsa, add a small amount of the reserved tomato juice and pulse one or two more times.

Corn Salsa

Makes about 3 cups

2 cups frozen corn kernels, thawed
¹/₃ cup chopped red onion
¹/₄ cup chopped red bell pepper
¹/₄ cup chopped fresh cilantro
2 tablespoons fresh lime juice
1 to 2 tablespoons finely chopped jalapeño pepper, to taste
¹/₂ teaspoon sea salt, or to taste

In a medium bowl, combine all the ingredients. Cover and refrigerate for a couple of hours to allow the flavors to develop.

Turkey Tomatillo Chili

Serves 6 • Cooker: 5- to 8-quart • Time: 10 minutes for chili, 1 minute for tomatillos at HIGH pressure

This white turkey chili is light in both color and calories, thanks to the turkey breast, chicken broth, green chiles, and tomatillos. It is gently spiced with cumin and coriander, and the tomatillos add a citrus-y tang.

CHILI:
2 tablespoons olive oil
1 pound ground turkey breast
1 large onion, finely chopped
2 medium bell peppers, preferably 1 red and 1
    yellow, seeded and chopped
4 cloves garlic, minced
1 cup dried small white beans such as Great
    Northern or navy, soaked (see page 406),
    drained, and rinsed with cold water
2 cups water
1 tablespoon ground cumin
1 tablespoon ground coriander
1 tablespoon dried oregano, preferably Mexican
1 or 2 jalapeño peppers, to taste, seeded and diced
2 cups chopped fresh tomatillos (see below) OR 1
    (28-ounce) can tomatillos, drained and chopped
3 cups chicken broth
Salt and freshly ground black pepper

TOPPINGS:
Shredded Monterey Jack cheese
Sour cream or plain Greek yogurt
Chopped fresh cilantro
Sliced green onions
Lime wedges

1. In a 5- to 8-quart pressure cooker, heat the oil over medium-high heat. Add the turkey and cook, stirring to break up any clumps of meat, until it has lost most of its pink color, about 3 minutes. Add the onions and cook, stirring a few times, until it begins to soften, about 3 minutes. Add the bell peppers and garlic and cook, stirring a few times, until the garlic is fragrant, about 2 minutes. Add the soaked beans, water, cumin, coriander, and oregano. Stir to combine.

2. Close and lock the lid. Set the burner heat to high. When the cooker reaches HIGH pressure, reduce the burner heat as low as you can and still maintain HIGH pressure. Set a timer to cook for 10 minutes.

3. Remove the pot from the heat. Open the cooker with the Natural Release method; let stand for 15 minutes. Be careful of the steam as you remove the lid. The beans should be tender yet still slightly firm to the bite.

4. Add the jalapeños, tomatillos, and broth. Relock the cooker. Set the burner heat to high. When the cooker reaches HIGH pressure, reduce the burner heat as low as you can and still maintain HIGH pressure. Set a timer to cook for 1 minute.

5. Remove the pot from the heat. Open the cooker with the Natural Release method; let stand for 10 minutes. Season to taste with salt and pepper as desired.

6. Serve the chili warm, with the toppings in small bowls for diners to customize their own bowl.

TOMATILLOS

We think of tomatillos as small green tomatoes on a drizzly day—their green or brownish papery husks look like raincoats. They are pleasantly sweet and tart, and can be enjoyed raw in salsas or cooked in sauces or stews. If you can't find fresh tomatillos, look for canned, sold in the Hispanic section of the supermarket. If you are using fresh ones, choose firm tomatillos. Peel away the papery husks and rinse the tomatillos in cold water before using. A slight stickiness is normal.

Black Friday Turkey Chili

Serves 6 to 8 • Cooker: 5- to 8-quart • Time: 8 minutes at HIGH pressure

Black Friday, the day after Thanksgiving, is traditionally the start of the Christmas shopping season. Folks like to hit the stores early for special deals, and linger to enjoy the festive atmosphere. If you plan to make this hearty, warming chili with some of your leftover turkey, you can shop all day and have dinner on the table in no time.

CHILI:
1 tablespoon vegetable oil
1 large white onion, coarsely chopped
3 cloves garlic, minced
1 teaspoon chili powder
1 teaspoon sweet paprika
1 teaspoon ground cumin
1 teaspoon dried oregano, preferably Mexican
Pinch ground cloves
1 (28-ounce) can chopped tomatoes in juice, undrained
1 cup dried pinto beans, soaked (see page 406), drained, and rinsed in cold water
2 cups turkey or chicken stock OR 1 cup turkey gravy and 1 cup water
1 to 2 teaspoons chopped chipotle chiles canned in adobo sauce, to taste
3 cups shredded cooked turkey
Salt and freshly ground black pepper

TOPPINGS:
Sour cream or plain Greek yogurt
Chopped sweet onion
1 avocado, pitted, peeled, and chopped
Fresh salsa

1. In a 5- to 8-quart pressure cooker, heat the oil over medium-high heat. Add the onion and cook, stirring a few times, until it begins to soften, about 3 minutes. Add the garlic and cook, stirring, until it is fragrant, about 1 minute more. Add the chili powder, paprika, cumin, oregano, and cloves. Stir for 1 minute, until the spices are fragrant, but do not allow the chili powder to burn. Stir in the tomatoes and their juices, the soaked beans, broth, and chipotles.

2. Close and lock the lid. Set the burner heat to high. When the cooker reaches HIGH pressure, reduce the burner heat as low as you can and still maintain HIGH pressure. Set a timer to cook for 8 minutes.

3. Remove the pot from the heat. Open the cooker with the Natural Release method; let stand for 15 minutes. Be careful of the steam as you remove the lid. The beans should be tender yet still be slightly firm to the bite.

4. Add the turkey to the pot. Stir in and let heat through, uncovered, over medium-high heat, about 2 minutes. Season with salt and pepper to taste.

5. Serve the chili warm, with the toppings in small bowls for diners to customize their own chili.

Black Bean Turkey Chili

Serves 8 • Cooker: 5- to 8-quart • Time: 10 minutes for beans, 10 minutes for chili at HIGH pressure

Ground turkey and black bean chili is the most popular in the turkey chili genre, because their flavors are totally complementary. Be sure to use ground dark meat, as the white meat will dry out too much during cooking. In addition to the suggested toppings, serve with grilled fresh corn tortillas or tortilla chips.

CHILI:

1 cup dried black beans, soaked overnight (see page 406), drained, and rinsed in cold water
4 cups water
1 medium white onion, cut in half
2 cloves garlic, peeled
2 tablespoons olive oil
1 medium white onion, finely chopped
2 medium red bell peppers, preferably roasted, skinned, seeded, and cut into medium dice
1 to 2 jalapeño peppers, to taste, seeds and membranes removed and cut into fine dice
2 pounds dark ground turkey
2 tablespoons chili powder
1 teaspoon ground cumin
1 teaspoon dried oregano, preferably Mexican
1 (14.5-ounce) can chopped tomatoes in juice, undrained
1 (15-ounce) can tomato sauce
2 teaspoons sea salt, or to taste

TOPPINGS:

Shredded Monterey Jack cheese or Jack and Cheddar blend
Sour cream
Chopped sweet onion
Fresh salsa
Tortilla chips

1. In a 5- to 8-quart pressure cooker, combine the soaked beans, water, onion halves, and garlic. Bring to a boil.
2. Close and lock the lid. Set the burner heat to high. When the cooker reaches HIGH pressure, reduce the burner heat as low as you can and still maintain HIGH pressure. Set a timer to cook for 10 minutes.
3. Remove the pot from the heat. Open the cooker with the Quick Release method. Be careful of the steam as you remove the lid. Discard the garlic and onion pieces. Drain and reserve the bean cooking liquid separately. Set aside.
4. In a skillet over medium high heat, heat the oil over medium-high heat until very hot. Add the chopped onion and cook, stirring occasionally, until soft and a bit golden on the edges. Add the bell peppers and jalapeños and cook, stirring a few times, for 3 minutes. Add the turkey and cook, breaking up any clumps of meat, until it loses its pink color. Add the chili powder, cumin, and oregano; stir to combine. Add the tomatoes and their juices, tomato sauce, cooked beans, and 1 cup of the bean cooking liquid.
5. Close and lock the lid. Set the burner heat to high. When the cooker reaches HIGH pressure, reduce the burner heat as low as you can and still maintain HIGH pressure. Set a timer to cook for 10 minutes.
6. Remove the pot from the heat. Open the cooker with the Natural Release method; let stand for 10 minutes. Be careful of the steam as you remove the lid. Season to taste with salt.
7. Serve the chili with the toppings in small bowls for diners to customize their own.

Black Bean Meat Chili: Substitute 1 pound ground beef and 1 pound ground fresh pork for the turkey. Proceed as directed.

Beef and Chorizo Chili

Serves 4 to 6 • Cooker: 5- to 7-quart • Time: 4 minutes at HIGH pressure

This quick, simple chili is a mixture of ground beef and Mexican chorizo sausage, perfect for a satisfying meal on a chilly autumn evening. Mexican chorizo is uncooked pork; look for it in natural casings. This is especially good with some warm flour tortillas and a dark Mexican beer such as Negra Modelo.

CHILI:
1 pound ground beef chuck
1 pound fresh chorizo sausage, casings removed
1 tablespoon olive oil
2 large white onions, coarsley chopped
3 cloves garlic, crushed
2 tablespoons New Mexico chile powder
1 tablespoon mild paprika
1 teaspoon ground cumin
1 cup beef broth
1 (28-ounce) can crushed tomatoes
Salt
Taco shells (optional), for serving

TOPPINGS:
Saltine crackers or oyster crackers
Sour cream
Chopped fresh cilantro
Shredded sharp Cheddar cheese
Chopped red onions

1. In a 5- to 7-quart pressure cooker, heat the oil over medium-high heat. Add the onions and cook, stirring a few times, until they begin to soften. Add the beef and chorizo in small batches, mashing them with a fork until each batch is no longer pink, then adding the next batch. Add the garlic and spices. Stir in the broth and tomatoes and cook for about 2 minutes more.

2. Close and lock the lid. Set the burner heat to high. When the cooker reaches HIGH pressure, reduce the burner heat as low as you can and still maintain HIGH pressure. Set a timer to cook for 4 minutes.

3. Remove the pot from the heat. Open the cooker with the Natural Release method; let stand for 15 minutes. Be careful of the steam as you remove the lid. Taste for salt.

4. Serve the chili hot, in bowls or taco shells, and pile on the toppings.

Beef and Chorizo Chili with Beans: In Step 3, stir in 1½ cups firm-cooked pinto, kidney, or black beans, or 1 (15-ounce) can, drained and rinsed. Simmer, uncovered, 3 to 5 minutes to heat through.

Chili in Five

Serves 4 • Cooker: 5- to 7-quart • Time: 5 minutes at HIGH pressure

This is adapted from a Presto pressure cooker recipe and we love the name. You can use your pantry beans in this recipe, or those frozen extra beans in the freezer from your last bean cooking spree. While this couldn't be simpler, it is splendidly delicious and makes a great on-the-spot lunch or topping for hot dogs.

CHILI:
2 tablespoons olive oil
1 large white onion, chopped
1 medium green bell pepper, seeded and chopped
2 pounds coarse-ground beef round or ground venison
1 (8-ounce) can tomato sauce
1 cup water or beer
1 tablespoon your favorite chili powder
1 teaspoon ground cumin
$^1/_2$ teaspoon dried oregano, preferably Mexican
$^1/_8$ teaspoon cayenne pepper
$^1/_8$ teaspoon freshly ground black pepper
2 cloves garlic, finely chopped
1 teaspoon salt, or to taste
1 or 2 (16-ounce) cans kidney beans, drained and rinsed, or 2 cups fresh cooked beans

TOPPINGS:
Saltine crackers
Shredded sharp Cheddar cheese
Chopped fresh tomatoes
Chopped green onions
Sliced avocado

1. In a 5- to 7-quart pressure cooker, heat the oil over medium-high heat. Add the onion and bell pepper and cook, stirring a few times, until they begin to soften. Add the ground meat and cook, breaking up any clumps, until it is no longer pink. Stir in the tomato sauce, water, chili powder, cumin, oregano, peppers, and garlic and cook, stirring a few times, for about 2 minutes.
2. Close and lock the lid. Set the burner heat to high. When the cooker reaches HIGH pressure, reduce the burner heat as low as you can and still maintain HIGH pressure. Set a timer to cook for 5 minutes.
3. Remove the pot from the heat. Open the cooker with the Natural Release method; let stand for 10 minutes. Be careful of the steam as you remove the lid. Season to taste with salt.
4. Stir the beans into the pot and simmer, uncovered, over medium heat until they are heated through, 8 to 10 minutes.
5. Serve the chili hot, with the toppings in small bowls for diners to customize their own.

Beer and Mocha Lovers' Beef Chili

Serves 6 to 8 • Cooker: 5- to 8-quart • Time: 8 minutes at HIGH pressure

In most kitchens, beef chili is the perennial favorite, served on football Sundays or ski weekends and packed into lunchboxes all winter long. Beef chili can be rich; this version is meaty yet lean and satisfying. It gets its deep color and savory flavor from a combination of coffee, chocolate, and dark beer. We like to freeze leftovers in single-serving containers for lunches—just put a portion of shredded cheese or a dollop of sour cream on top before freezing. Pop a frozen chili into your lunch bag or box. It will keep the rest of your lunch cold, and thaws and reheats in the microwave in about 5 minutes, garnishes and all.

CHILI:
1 tablespoon olive oil
2 pounds extra-lean ground beef
2 medium white onions, chopped
2 medium red bell peppers, or 1 red and 1 green
4 cloves garlic, minced
1 (28-ounce) can diced tomatoes in juice, undrained
1 (8-ounce) can tomato sauce
1 cup strong brewed coffee
1 (12-ounce) bottle dark beer
1 cup dried red kidney beans, soaked (see page 406), drained, and rinsed in cold water
2 small wedges Mexican drinking chocolate (Abuelita is one brand) OR 1 tablespoon unsweetened cocoa powder and 2 teaspoons brown sugar
3 tablespoons chili powder
2 tablespoons ground cumin
2 teaspoons dried oregano, preferably Mexican
Sea salt and freshly ground black pepper

TOPPINGS:
Shredded cheddar cheese
Sour cream
Chopped onions
Sliced black olives

1. Coat the inside of a 5- to 8-quart pressure cooker with cooking spray. Add the oil and heat over medium-high heat. Add the ground beef and onions and cook, breaking up any clumps, until the beef has lost its pink color and the onions begin to soften, about 5 minutes. Add the bell peppers and garlic and cook, stirring a few times, about 2 minutes. Add the tomatoes and their juices, tomato sauce, coffee, beer, beans, chocolate, chili powder, cumin, and oregano.

2. Close and lock the lid. Set the burner heat to high. When the cooker reaches HIGH pressure, reduce the burner heat as low as you can and still maintain HIGH pressure. Set a timer to cook for 8 minutes.

3. Remove the pot from the heat. Open the cooker with the Natural Release method; let stand for 10 minutes. Be careful of the steam as you remove the lid. The beans should be tender yet still be slightly firm to the bite. Season to taste with salt and pepper.

4. Serve the chili warm, with the toppings in small bowls so diners can customize their own.

Pork and White Bean Chili

Serves 6 • Cooker: 6- to 8-quart • Time: 20 minutes for chili, 4 minutes for squash at HIGH pressure

This is a hearty chili, adapted from a recipe in *The Yankee Cook Book* (Amereon Ltd., 1939) by the late Imogene Woolcott, New England food writer and culinary radio host. Serve with cornbread.

CHILI:

2¹/₂ pounds pork shoulder (pork butt), patted dry and cut into 2-inch pieces
2 teaspoons sea salt, plus more to taste
³/₄ teaspoon freshly ground black pepper, plus more to taste
¹/₂ teaspoon ground allspice
¹/₄ teaspoon ground cloves
2 tablespoons olive oil
1 large white onion, diced
4 cloves garlic, minced
1 teaspoon cumin seeds or ¹/₄ teaspoon ground cumin
1 (28-ounce) can diced tomatoes in juice, undrained
2 (4-ounce) cans roasted green chiles, drained and diced
1¹/₂ cups dried navy or baby white beans, soaked (see page 405), drained, and rinsed in cold water
3 cups reduced-sodium chicken broth
1 medium butternut squash (about 2 pounds), peeled and cut into ¹/₂-inch cubes (about 1 pound flesh)
2 cups frozen corn kernels
Hot sauce

TOPPINGS:

2 cups crumbled feta or grated Monterey Jack cheese
1 cup packed fresh cilantro leaves, chopped

1. Spread meat on a large piece of parchment paper. In a small bowl, combine 1 teaspoon of the salt, the pepper, allspice, and cloves. Sprinkle this evenly all over the meat. In a 6- to 8-quart pressure cooker, heat 1 tablespoon of the oil over medium-high heat until very hot. Working in batches, brown the meat on all sides, 3 to 5 minutes per batch, and adding the remaining 1 tablespoon oil as needed. Use a slotted spoon to transfer the browned meat to a plate. Add the onion and cook, stirring a few times, until it begins to soften, about 3 minutes. Add the garlic and cumin seeds and stir for 30 seconds. Return the meat and any accumulated juices to the pot. Add the tomatoes, chiles, presoaked beans, and broth. Stir well.

2. Close and lock the lid. Set the burner heat to high. When the cooker reaches HIGH pressure, reduce the burner heat as low as you can and still maintain HIGH pressure. Set a timer to cook for 20 minutes.

3. Remove the pot from the heat. Open the cooker with the Quick Release method. Be careful of the steam as you remove the lid.

4. Add the squash and corn to the pot; stir to combine. Close and lock the lid. Set the burner heat to high. When the cooker reaches HIGH pressure, reduce the burner heat as low as you can and still maintain HIGH pressure. Set a timer to cook for 4 minutes.

5. Remove the pot from the heat. Open the cooker with the Natural Release method; let stand for about 10 minutes. Season to taste with salt, pepper, and hot sauce.

6. Serve the chili hot, with the toppings in bowls so diners can customize their own.

Bison Bean Chili with Corn Salsa

Serves 6 to 8 • Cooker: 5- to 8-quart • Time: 12 minutes at HIGH pressure

Bison, or buffalo, has definitely hit the mainstream in the U.S. If you don't see it in the meat case at your store, look in the freezer section. The meat looks like beef and tastes similar, but contains one-quarter of the fat of beef and is higher in protein; also, because it is raised grass fed, it contains no growth hormones or antibiotics. Because of its leanness, ground bison can cook up a bit dry, so chili is the perfect way to showcase it.

CHILI:

2 tablespoons olive oil

1¹/₂ pounds ground bison

1 large white onion, chopped

1 (28-ounce) can diced tomatoes in juice, undrained

3 tablespoons chili powder

2 teaspoons ground cumin

1 teaspoon ground coriander

¹/₂ teaspoon paprika

¹/₂ teaspoon ground allspice

1¹/₄ cups dried black beans, soaked (see page 402), drained, and rinsed in cold water

³/₄ cup dried pinto beans or kidney beans, soaked, drained, and rinsed in cold water

4 cups beef broth

2 canned chipotle peppers in adobo sauce, chopped

1 poblano pepper, seeded and chopped

TOPPINGS:

Corn Salsa (page 301)

Sour cream

Shredded Cheddar cheese

Corn chips

1. In a 5- to 8-quart pressure cooker, heat the oil over medium-high heat until very hot. Add the ground bison and onion and cook, breaking up any clumps, until the meat has lost its pink color and the onion begins to soften, about 5 minutes. Add the tomatoes and their juices, spices, beans, broth, and chiles. Stir to combine.

2. Close and lock the lid. Set the burner heat to high. When the cooker reaches HIGH pressure, reduce the burner heat as low as you can and still maintain HIGH pressure. Set a timer to cook for 12 minutes.

3. Remove the pot from the heat. Open the cooker with the Natural Release method; let stand for 15 minutes. Be careful of the steam as you remove the lid. The beans should be tender but still be slightly firm to the bite. Season to taste with salt and pepper.

4. Serve the chili hot, with the toppings in bowls for diners to customize their own.

CHIPOTLE CHILE PASTE

What to do once you've opened a can of chipotle chiles in adobo sauce? Pop the whole thing in the food processor or blender and pulse to create a paste. It'll keep in an airtight container in the refrigerator for up to 1 month. Or transfer it to a sandwich-size ziptop plastic bag and freeze it flat, so that the chile layer is quite thin. Then you can break off pieces while they're still frozen. About 1 teaspoon of puree equals 1 chile.

Chili and Cornbread

There isn't a bean dish that isn't enhanced by homemade cornbread on the side, preferably still warm from the oven. Because cornmeal is unique in flavor and texture, there is no substitute for it. The cornmeal sold in most supermarkets is a medium grind, very good in flavor, and will keep fresh a long time, so long as it is degerminated (and it usually will be). For an exceptional flavor, use stone-ground cornmeals, available from small local mills or a natural foods store, which will retain flecks of the flavorful germ. Store cornmeal—degerminated or not—in the refrigerator up to about 6 months or in the freezer up to a year. Fresh cornmeal will smell sweet, never sour or rancid.

Here are a few of our very favorite cornbread recipes. Wrapped tightly in plastic wrap and then foil or slipped into a 1-gallon plastic freezer bag, all of them can be frozen up to 2 months.

Best Cornbread

Makes one 8-inch round or square pan, serves 6

This is a great basic recipe, with lots of excellent variations if you want to get fancy. This will also make 10 standard-sized muffins.

To make this gluten-free, use a gluten-free baking mix.

1 cup fine-grind yellow cornmeal, preferably stone-ground
1 cup unbleached all-purpose flour or Bob's Red Mill Gluten-Free Baking Mix
$1/4$ cup firmly packed light brown sugar
$2^1/2$ teaspoons baking powder
$1/2$ teaspoon baking soda
$1/2$ teaspoon sea salt
2 large eggs
$1/2$ cup milk
$1/2$ cup sour cream
6 tablespoons ($3/4$ stick) unsalted butter, melted, or
$1/3$ cup light olive oil

1. Preheat the oven to 375° F (reduce the heat to 350° F if using Pyrex glass pan). Grease an 8-inch springform pan or square pan or 9-inch deep pie plate (ceramic or Pyrex).
2. In a deep, medium bowl, combine the cornmeal, flour, sugar, baking powder, and salt.
3. In a small bowl, whisk the eggs, milk, and sour cream together. Add to the dry ingredients and pour the melted butter over the top. Stir with a large rubber spatula just until all ingredients are moistened yet thoroughly blended. Take care not to overmix.
4. Pour the batter into the prepared pan. Bake until golden around the edges and a cake tester inserted into the center comes out clean, about 25 minutes. Let stand 15 minutes before cutting into wedges or squares to serve.

Feta Cornbread: Add 1 cup (4 ounces) crumbled feta cheese in Step 3.

Blueberry Cornbread: Gently fold in 1 cup fresh blueberries in Step 3.

Vegan Cornbread

Makes one 8-inch round or square pan, serves 6

Masarepa, white grits, are available in the Mexican section of the supermarket.

1 cup unbleached all-purpose flour or whole wheat flour

$^1/_2$ cup fine-grind yellow cornmeal, preferably stone-ground

$^1/_2$ cup white grits or Masarepa (fine white cornmeal)

3 tablespoons granulated or brown sugar

1 tablespoon baking powder

1 teaspoon sea salt

1 cup water or plain nondairy milk, such as almond milk, soy milk, or rice milk

$^1/_4$ cup light olive oil

1. Preheat the oven to 350° F (reduce the heat to 325° F if using a Pyrex pan). Grease an 8-inch springform pan or square pan or 9-inch deep pie plate (ceramic or Pyrex).
2. In a deep, medium bowl, combine the flour, cornmeal, grits, sugar, baking powder, and salt. Add the water and oil to the dry ingredients and stir with a large rubber spatula just until all ingredients are moistened yet thoroughly blended. Take care not to overmix.
3. Pour the batter into the prepared pan. Bake until golden around the edges and a cake tester inserted into the center comes out clean, 25 to 30 minutes. Let stand 15 minutes before cutting into wedges or squares to serve.

Whole-Grain Cornbread

Makes one 8-inch round or square pan, serves 6

$1^1/_4$ cups fine-grind yellow cornmeal, preferably stone-ground

$^3/_4$ cup white whole wheat flour or whole wheat pastry flour

$^3/_4$ cup frozen corn kernels, thawed

3 tablespoons sugar or honey

2 teaspoons baking powder

$^1/_2$ teaspoon sea salt

1 large egg, beaten

$^3/_4$ cup sour cream thinned with $^1/_4$ cup buttermilk or half-and-half

3 tablespoons light olive oil

1. Preheat the oven to 350° F (reduce the heat to 325° F if using a Pyrex pan). Grease an 8-inch springform pan or square pan or 9-inch deep pie plate (ceramic or Pyrex).
2. In a deep medium bowl, combine the cornmeal, flour, corn, sugar, baking powder, and salt. Add the egg, sour cream mixture, and oil and stir with a large rubber spatula just until all ingredients are moistened yet thoroughly blended. Take care not to overmix.
3. Pour the batter into the prepared pan. Bake until golden around the edges and a cake tester inserted into the center comes out clean, 25 to 30 minutes. Let stand 15 minutes before cutting into wedges or squares to serve.

Aunt Joan's Broccoli, Cottage Cheese, and Cheddar Cornbread

Makes 1 (10-inch) round springform pan or 9 x 19-inch pan, serves 12

Everyone wants to make this recipe even though it starts with a mix and uses frozen broccoli. Needs no embellishment; eat it perfectly plain.

1 (8.5-ounce) box corn muffin mix
$1/4$ teaspoon sea salt
$1/2$ cup (1 stick) unsalted butter
$1/2$ cup chopped white onion
1 (10-ounce) package frozen chopped broccoli, thawed but not drained
1 (8-ounce) container small-curd cottage cheese
4 large eggs
1 cup coarsely shredded Cheddar cheese

1. Preheat the oven to 375° F. Grease a 10-inch springform pan or 9 x 19-inch baking pan.
2. In a deep medium bowl, combine the corn muffin mix and salt. In a skillet over medium heat, melt the butter; add the onion and cook, stirring a few times, until it begins to soften, about 3 minutes. Add the broccoli and any liquid and cook for 1 minute. Set aside to cool 10 minutes.
3. Add the cottage cheese and eggs to the dry ingredients and combine with a whisk or Danish dough whisk. Add the sautéed vegetables and cheese and fold together with a large rubber spatula just until all the ingredients are moistened yet thoroughly blended. Take care not to overmix.
4. Pour the batter into the prepared pan. Bake until golden around the edge and a cake tester inserted into the center comes out clean, 30 to 35 minutes. Let stand 15 minutes before cutting into wedges or squares to serve.

Cheese and Double Corn Muffins

Makes 12 large muffins

Rich and cakelike, these savory corn muffins are positively addictive.

1 (15-ounce) can cream-style corn
$1/2$ cup (1 stick) unsalted butter, melted
2 large eggs, beaten
1 cup buttermilk
$1^3/4$ cups fine-grind yellow cornmeal, preferably stone-ground
1 cup unbleached all-purpose flour
$1^1/4$ cups coarsely shredded Monterey Jack cheese
2 tablespoons sugar
1 tablespoon baking powder
1 teaspoon sea salt
$1/2$ teaspoon baking soda

1. Preheat the oven to 400° F. Grease or spray with olive oil spray the cups of a standard ($2^3/4$-inch) muffin tin.
2. In medium bowl with a large spoon, stir the creamed corn, melted butter, eggs, and buttermilk together until well blended. In another bowl, combine the remaining ingredients, tossing to distribute the cheese. Add the cheese-flour mixture to the buttermilk mixture. Beat well to make a thick, creamy batter that falls off the spoon in clumps.
3. Spoon the batter into the muffin tin, filling each cup level with the top. You can use a spring-action ice cream scoop if you like. Bake until golden and the tops are dry and springy to the touch, 20 to 24 minutes. A cake tester will come out clean when inserted into the center. Cool in the pan 5 minutes before removing to cool on a rack. Serve warm or store in the refrigerator. Use within a day or freeze.

Two-Tone Maple Cornmeal Muffins

Makes 12 muffins

These muffins owe their colors to two batters, one made with blue cornmeal and the other yellow cornmeal. Blue cornmeal is ground from naturally blue maize and is considered a whole-grain cornmeal. You can find it at health food stores and online.

BLUE CORNMEAL BATTER:
3/4 cup whole wheat pastry flour
3/4 cup fine-to medium-grind blue cornmeal *(harina de maiz azul para tortillas)*
2 teaspoons baking powder
1/4 teaspoon sea salt
3 tablespoons light olive oil
3 tablespoons maple syrup
1 cup buttermilk

YELLOW CORNMEAL BATTER:
3/4 cup unbleached all-purpose flour
3/4 cup fine-grind yellow cornmeal, preferably stone-ground
2 teaspoons baking powder
1/4 teaspoon sea salt
3 tablespoons light olive oil
3 tablespoons maple syrup
1 cup buttermilk

1. Preheat the oven to 350° F. Grease or coat with olive oil spray the cups of a standard (2³/₄-inch) muffin tin.
2. Make the blue batter. In a medium bowl, combine the dry ingredients. In a small bowl or measuring cup, whisk the oil, maple syrup, and buttermilk together. Add the wet ingredients to the dry and, with a large rubber spatula, stir just until all ingredients are moistened yet thoroughly blended. Take care not to overmix. Set aside.
3. Prepare the yellow batter in the same manner. The batters will be thin and pourable.
4. Using an oversized spoon, fill each muffin cup first halfway with the blue batter, then fill with the yellow batter, filling each cup level with the top. With a knife, draw a spiral through to the bottom of the cup. Bake until golden and the tops are dry and springy to the touch, 25 to 30 minutes. A cake tester will come out clean when inserted into the center. Cool in the pan 5 minutes before removing to a wire rack. Serve warm or store in the refrigerator. Keep a bag in the freezer for impromptu dining.

Navajo Lamb Chili with Black Beans and Yams

Serves 6 • Cooker: 5- to 8-quart • Time: 12 minutes at HIGH pressure

A specialty of the American Southwest, lamb chili is real comfort food.

CHILI:

2 pounds boneless leg of lamb, trimmed of fat and cut into $1/2$-inch cubes

1 teaspoon sea salt

$1/2$ teaspoon freshly ground black pepper

2 tablespoons olive oil

2 cups cubed ($3/4$-inch) peeled yams (about 2 yams)

1 medium white onion, chopped

2 tablespoons ancho chile powder

1 tablespoon chopped garlic

1 teaspoon ground cumin

1 teaspoon dried oregano, preferably Mexican

1 (14.5-ounce) can diced tomatoes in juice, undrained

1 (14-ounce) can reduced-sodium chicken broth

1 (15-ounce) can black beans, rinsed and drained, or $13/4$ cups freshly cooked black beans

TOPPINGS:

Crumbled feta cheese

Sliced green onions

1. In medium bowl, combine the lamb, salt, and pepper; toss to evenly coat. In a 5- to 8-quart pressure cooker, heat the oil over medium-high heat until very hot. Add the lamb, yams, onion, ancho chile powder, garlic, cumin, and oregano. Cook, stirring frequently, for 5 minutes. Do not brown the meat. You can do this in batches. Stir in the tomatoes and their juices and broth.

2. Close and lock the lid. Set the burner heat to high. When the cooker reaches HIGH pressure, reduce the burner heat as low as you can and still maintain HIGH pressure. Set a timer to cook for 12 minutes.

3. Remove the pot from the heat. Open the cooker with the Natural Release method; let stand for 15 minutes. Be careful of the steam as you remove the lid.

4. Stir in the beans and simmer, uncovered, over medium heat until heated through. Taste for salt and pepper.

5. Serve the chili hot, topped with feta and green onions.

ANCHO CHILE POWDER

Ancho chile powder has a dark, somewhat smoky flavor, with mild heat. It is an integral part of authentic Mexican cooking and is a perfect partner with lamb. Because of its mildness, you can use it as liberally as you would salt and black pepper.

Cincinnati-Style Chili

Serves 6 • Cooker: 5- to 8-quart • Time: 8 minutes for beans, 15 minutes for chili at HIGH pressure

Cincinnati-style chili is unique—a true testament to chili's ability to pack its bags, move and happily settle in to new surroundings, reinventing itself to please the locals. Cincinnati-style chili is traditionally made with beef, and it has a thin consistency. It's served over spaghetti, which never fails to surprise the uninitiated, or over a hot dog, chili-dog style. The seasonings tend to the warm spices—allspice, cloves, cinnamon, coriander—often with a bit of unsweetened chocolate or cocoa for good measure. But don't be bound by tradition—try ladling your own favorite chili over pasta. Ever accommodating, chili won't mind.

CHILI:
1 cup dried kidney beans, soaked (see page 406), drained, and rinsed in cold water
3 cups water
3 tablespoons oil
1 medium onion, chopped
2 cloves garlic, chopped
1 pound lean ground beef
2 cups beef broth
1 (14.5-ounce) can diced tomatoes in juice, undrained
2 tablespoons paprika
1 tablespoon chili powder
1 teaspoon ground cumin
1 teaspoon ground cinnamon
$^1/_2$ teaspoon ground allspice
$^1/_2$ teaspoon ground coriander
Pinch ground cloves
1 tablespoon unsweetened cocoa powder
1 tablespoon cider vinegar
Sea salt and freshly ground black pepper

FOR SERVING:
1 pound spaghetti, cooked
1 pound shredded Cheddar cheese
Chopped onions
Cooked kidney beans
Oyster crackers
Bottled hot sauce

1. In a 5- to 8-quart pressure cooker, combine the soaked beans, water, and 1 tablespoon of the oil.

2. Close and lock the lid. Set the burner heat to high. When the cooker reaches HIGH pressure, reduce the burner heat as low as you can and still maintain HIGH pressure. Set a timer to cook for 8 minutes.

3. Remove the pot from the heat. Open the cooker with the Natural Release method; let stand for 10 minutes. Be careful of the steam as you remove the lid. The beans should be tender but still be slightly firm to the bite. Pour the beans and liquid into a bowl and keep warm.

4. Wipe out the pressure cooker. Heat the remaining 2 tablespoons oil over medium-high heat until very hot. Add the onion and garlic and cook, stirring a few times, until they begin to soften, about 3 minutes. Add the beef and cook, until browned, 3 to 4 minutes. Spoon off excess fat. Stir in the broth, tomatoes and their juices, spices, cocoa, and vinegar.

5. Close and lock the lid. Set the burner heat to high. When the cooker reaches HIGH pressure, reduce the burner heat as low as you can and still maintain HIGH pressure. Set a timer to cook for 15 minutes.

6. Remove the pot from the heat. Open the cooker with the Natural Release method; let stand for 15 minutes. Season to taste with salt and pepper.

7. Serve as you prefer, with hot sauce on the side.

CINCINNATI-STYLE CHILI, THE WAY YOU WANT IT

In Cincinnati, chili speaks its own language. The diner orders it as "bowl" or plain, or with add-ons in the following way:

"One-way": Over spaghetti

"Two-way": Over spaghetti, topped with cheddar

"Three-way": Over spaghetti, topped with cheddar and onions

"Four-way": Over spaghetti, topped with cheddar, onions, and kidney beans

"Five-way": All of the above, plus the final addition of oyster crackers for crunch

Venison Chili with Blue Cheese Toasts

Serves 6 to 8 • Cooker: 5- to 8-quart • Time: 8 minutes at HIGH pressure

If you're a hunter, or you have one in the family, you are probably well-acquainted with the rich flavor and lean texture of venison. If you're not, you're in luck because venison is more available to shoppers than ever before. Chile is the perfect showcase for ground venison—the savory flavor of the meat stands up perfectly to the chile, smoky paprika and vinegar. The blue cheese toasts take this chili directly into gourmet territory! If your butcher doesn't stock ground venison (check the freezer case), you can easily order it online.

2 tablespoons olive oil
2 large white onions, chopped
1 green bell pepper, seeded and diced
2 cloves garlic, minced
2 pounds ground venison
3 tablespoons red wine vinegar
1 (28-ounce) can crushed tomatoes
4 tablespoons tomato paste
1 (12-ounce) bottle dark beer
2 tablespoons chili powder
1 to 1^1/$_4$ teaspoons ground cumin, to taste
1 to 1^1/$_4$ teaspoons smoked paprika, to taste
1 to 1^1/$_4$ teaspoons ancho chile powder, to taste
Few dashes hot sauce
Sea salt and freshly ground black pepper
Salsa of your choice (page 301)
Blue Cheese Toasts (recipe follows)

1. In a 5- to 8-quart pressure cooker, heat the oil over medium-high heat until very hot. Add the onions and cook, stirring a few times, until they begin to soften, about 5 minutes. Add the bell pepper and garlic; cook, stirring, 1 minute. Remove the vegetables to a plate. Brown the ground venison in batches in the pot, breaking up any clumps, until there is no pink and it is nicely browned. Stir in the vinegar, then return the sautéed onions and pepper to the pot. Add the tomatoes and their juices, tomato paste, beer, spices, and hot sauce. Stir to combine.
2. Close and lock the lid. Set the burner heat to high. When the cooker reaches HIGH pressure, reduce the burner heat as low as you can and still maintain HIGH pressure. Set a timer to cook for 8 minutes.

3. Remove the pot from the heat. Open the cooker with the Natural Release method; let stand for 15 minutes. Make the Blue Cheese Toasts while the pressure comes down. Be careful of the steam as you remove the lid. Season to taste with salt and black pepper.
4. Serve the chili warm topped with salsa with a few blue cheese toasts on the side.

Blue Cheese Toasts

Makes 12 toasts

^{1}/$_2$ cup (1 stick) unsalted butter, softened
4 ounces blue cheese, softened
^{1}/$_4$ cup finely chopped pecans
12 baguette slices, ^{1}/$_2$ to 1 inch thick

Preheat the oven to 350° F. In a small bowl, combine the butter and blue cheese with a fork until blended. Mash in the pecans. Spread a layer of the cheese mixture evenly on one side of each baguette slice. Place in a single layer on a parchment paper-lined rimmed baking sheet. Bake until the cheese mixture is melted and the toasts are heated through, 5 to 7 minutes. Serve immediately.

VENISON

When prepared properly, free-range venison is one of the most beautiful, flavorful meats you'll ever eat. Whether farm raised or hunted, the key elements for producing great meat are the same: cooling the meat as quickly as possible, keeping the meat clean, aging it properly, and packaging and freezing it well. Many people shy away from venison because they are intimidated by the cooking process. Nothing could be further from the truth. While there are a variety of ways to prepare venison, you can use it in recipes that you are already familiar with. Typically you can replace beef, pork, or even lamb with venison in all of your favorite recipes.

11

Rice East and West

Thousands of varieties of rice are grown throughout the world. Most varieties we will never see as they are never exported beyond the locales where they are cultivated. Luckily there are small companies like Lotus Foods that have brought to the Western market a whole rainbow of colored rices from Southeast Asia. In fact, America now grows many Asian varieties, responding to growing demand for these rices at home.

Rice can be divided broadly into three categories—long-, medium-, and short-grain—and then again into many subdivisions, such as color (brown, white, red, or black) and texture (dry or sticky).

Long-grain rice can be either brown (with its husk intact) or white (husk removed). Its texture is light and fluffy, its flavor mild, and the grains tend to remain separate when cooked. Long-grain white rices are the fastest cooking rices.

Short- and medium-grain rices are shorter, plumper, and tend to be stickier and moister when cooked due to their higher starch content. They are available as either brown or white.

RICE IN THE PRESSURE COOKER

- Generally, allow $1^1/_2$ cups of water to 1 cup long- or medium-grain white rice, and for long-, medium-, and short-grain brown rices $1^1/_2$ to $1^3/_4$ cups to 1 cup of rice. The liquid proportions are higher for softer risotto and porridges. You are using quite a bit less liquid in the pressure cooker since there is less evaporation.
- A bit of oil (any mild or neutral-tasting oil is fine) or butter is added to keep down the foaming.
- Many cooks use a heat diffuser for cooking rice so it won't burn or stick. When the pressure comes up, place a preheated flame deflector under the cooker and reduce the heat to low. This will keep the heat evenly distributed.
- Do not overcook rice; use the Natural Release method to allow the rice time to finish steaming.
- One cup of raw rice yields about $2^1/_2$ to 3 cups of cooked rice.
- Plain rices keep up to 3 days in the refrigerator in a covered container or plastic storage bag. Rice can be frozen up to 2 months.

Pressure-Steamed Long-Grain White Rice

Cooker: 5- to 7-quart • Time: 4 minutes at HIGH pressure

This basic recipe is for regular domestic long-grain white rice, brands like Mahatma and Pacific International, and the non-aromatic Indian extra-long grain white rice (look for the finest, which is called *patna* for the region where it is grown), NOT an aromatic rice like basmati. Domestic long-grain white rice does not have to be washed or soaked before cooking, but the Indian rice should be rinsed until the water runs clear. Use this recipe to make rice to refrigerate overnight for stir-fried rice. Serve with tamari and butter for a great umami taste adventure.

FOR 3 CUPS COOKED:
1 cup long-grain white rice
1 (1-finger) pinch sea salt
1 tablespoon oil or butter
1^1/$_2$ cups spring or filtered water

FOR 4^1/$_2$ CUPS COOKED:
1^1/$_2$ cups long-grain white rice
1 (2-finger) pinch sea salt
1 tablespoon oil or butter
2^1/$_4$ cups spring or filtered water

FOR 6 CUPS COOKED:
2 cups long-grain white rice
1 (3-finger) pinch sea salt
2 tablespoons oil or butter
2^3/$_4$ cups spring or filtered water

1. In a 5- to 7-quart pressure cooker, combine the rice, salt, oil, and water.
2. Close and lock the lid. Place a heat diffuser on the burner and the pressure cooker on top. Set the burner heat to high. When the cooker reaches HIGH pressure, reduce the burner heat as low as you can and still maintain HIGH pressure. Set a timer to cook for 4 minutes.
3. Remove the pot from the heat. Open the cooker with the Natural Release method; let stand for 10 minutes. At time, if the pressure is not all released, open the valve. Be careful of the steam as you remove the lid. Fluff the rice with a fork.
4. Spoon out the rice to a serving bowl to serve hot or into a storage container. Let stand, uncovered, at room temperature until cooled before refrigerating. It is okay if this is a few hours.

Our White Jasmine Blend: Use half long-grain white rice and half white Thai jasmine rice. Proceed as directed in the recipe.

Pressure-Steamed Basmati Rice

Cooker: 5- to 7-quart • Time: 3 minutes at HIGH pressure

Cooks appreciate basmati for its short cooking time and lovely texture and flavor, but many special diets restricting fiber rely on basmati. Basmati is considered the one white rice suitable for diabetics compared to other white rices.

FOR 3 CUPS COOKED:
1 cup basmati rice
1^1/$_2$ tablespoons butter
1 (3 finger) pinch sea salt
1^1/$_4$ cups spring or filtered water

FOR 5^1/$_2$ CUPS COOKED:
2 cups basmati rice
3 tablespoons butter
2 (3-finger) pinches sea salt
2^1/$_4$ cups spring or filtered water

1. Place the rice in a fine mesh strainer or bowl and rinse with cold water and drain 2 to 4 times. The first rinse water will be chalky and slightly foamy; continue rinsing until the water runs clear. Spread the wet rice out with your hands on a clean tea towel on the counter. Let air-dry at least 1 hour, until cooking time.
2. In a 5- to 7-quart pressure cooker, melt the butter over medium heat. Add the rice over, stir to coat the grains with the butter, and cook until the grains turn opaque. Add the salt and water.
3. Close and lock the lid. Place a heat diffuser on the burner and the pressure cooker on top. Set the burner heat to high. When the cooker reaches HIGH pressure, reduce the burner heat as low as you can and still maintain HIGH pressure. Set a timer to cook for 3 minutes.
4. Remove the pot from the heat. Open the cooker with the Natural Release method; let stand for 10 minutes. At time, if the pressure is not all released, open the valve. Be careful of the steam as you remove the lid. Fluff the rice with a fork.
5. Spoon out the rice to a serving bowl to serve hot or a storage container. Let stand, uncovered, at room temperature until cooled before refrigerating. It is okay if this is a few hours.

Basmati Rice with Raisins and Whole Spices: If starting with 1 cup raw rice, in Step 2, add 3 cracked black cardamom pods, 4 whole cloves, 1 cinnamon stick broken in half, 1 small bay leaf, and 2 tablespoon golden raisins along with the rice. If starting with 2 cups, add 6 cloves, a larger bay leaf, and ^{1}/$_4$ cup raisins. You don't need to increase the cinnamon. Proceed as directed.

BASMATI RICE

Just ten years ago, Indian-grown basmati white rice was virtually a culinary secret to American cooks unless they had traveled in India or had a palate for ethnic world cuisine. Basmati is today a favorite long-grain rice for everyday cooking because of its distinctive mild flavor and firm, extra-long grains that increase in length by more than three times after cooking.

Literally translating to the "queen of fragrance," basmati rice is so delicious it can be eaten plain. It has been cultivated in the river flood plains of the Indian Himalayan foothills and Pakistan for thousands of years. The key to its flavor is that the grains are aged in burlap bags for at least one year. This develops its translucent, milk-white color as well as its almost musty scent.

The Mississippi Delta and Northern California have developed high-yield domestic basmati crops using Indian seed strains, but because of the differences in soil and climate, domestic basmati looks and tastes more like regular long-grain white rice than Indian-grown basmati. The rice has a nutty aroma, but the fragrance is lost after cooking. American-grown basmati does not require the washing that basmati imported from India does.

We consider domestic basmati a totally different rice than the imported brands, but still a satisfying rice that holds up well in rice dishes like jambalaya, casseroles, and pilafs. It's also excellent after refrigeration for reheating the next day and in cold salads and fried rice dishes. Keep your Indian basmati as your special table rice.

Pressure-Steamed Thai Jasmine Rice

Serves 4 to 6 • Cooker: 5- to 7-quart • Time: 3 minutes at HIGH pressure

Thai jasmine rice is pearl white, with a plump, elongated shape, rather than round like short-grain rice, or thin and long like long-grain. The rice cooks up fluffy and moist, with a delicate floral aroma. Considered the most delicate of all the rices, it is harvested in December during the dry months and marketed fresh. Thai jasmine rice loses its fragrance as the raw rice ages, so often it is stored in the refrigerator. Thai jasmine is not the same as long-grain Thai sticky rice, *kao neuw,* which is eaten in the north of the country, steamed in a spittoon-shaped rice pot, and eaten only with the hands.

2 cups Thai jasmine rice
2¼ cups water
1 tablespoon oil
¼ teaspoon salt

1. In a 5- to 7-quart pressure cooker, combine the rice, water, oil, and salt.
2. Close and lock the lid. Place a heat diffuser on the burner and the pressure cooker on top. Set the burner heat to high. When the cooker reaches HIGH pressure, reduce the burner heat as low as you can and still maintain HIGH pressure. Set a timer to cook for 3 minutes.
3. Remove the pot from the heat. Open the cooker with the Natural Release method; let stand for 10 minutes. At time, if the pressure is not all released, open the valve. Be careful of the steam as you remove the lid. Fluff the rice with a fork.
4. Spoon out the rice to a serving bowl to serve hot.

Pressure-Steamed Long-Grain Brown Rice

Serves 4 • Cooker: 5- to 7-quart • Time: 20 minutes at HIGH pressure

This is the everyday brown rice. Nothing fancy, just toss it into the pressure cooker while you are preparing the rest of the dinner and voila, you have your grain side. Brown rice in the pressure cooker takes half the time to cook and uses less water than stovetop or rice cooker. Use these proportions for long-grain rice blends, brown basmati (rinse it several times first), and any generic brand of long-grain brown rice at the supermarket.

1 cup long-grain brown rice
1 (3-finger) pinch sea salt
1 tablespoon oil
1½ cups spring or filtered water or vegetable or chicken broth

1. In a 5- to 7-quart pressure cooker, combine the rice, salt, oil, and water.
2. Close and lock the lid. Place a heat diffuser on the burner and the pressure cooker on top. Set the burner heat to high. When the cooker reaches HIGH pressure, reduce the burner heat as low as you can and still maintain HIGH pressure. Set a timer to cook for 20 minutes.
3. Remove the pot from the heat. Open the cooker with the Natural Release method; let stand for 10 minutes. At time, if the pressure is not all released, open the valve. Be careful of the steam as you remove the lid.
4. Spoon out the rice to a serving bowl to serve hot. Brown rice freezes perfectly for up to 2 months; let it cool completely before storing.

Pressure-Steamed Long-Grain Brown Jasmine Rice: Follow the above directions but pressure cook for 18 minutes at HIGH pressure.

Pressure-Steamed Short-Grain Brown Rice

Cooker: 5- to 8-quart • Time: 22 minutes at HIGH pressure

Beth learned to make short-grain brown rice from her friend Andrew Whitfield. Up to that time, it seemed to never cook right. The secret? Never lift the lid to peek. Here in the pressure cooker we don't have to worry about peeking. Short-grain brown rice is the foundation of the macrobiotic diet. Short-grain brown rice is a dash stronger flavored and moister than long-grain rices, its flavor described as nutty. We call it good health in a bowl. One cup of raw rice will cook up to serve 4 to 6. The proportions and timing here will also work for multicolored mixed rice blends.

FOR 2¹/₄ CUPS COOKED:

1 cup short-grain brown rice

1²/₃ cups water

1 (1-finger) pinch sea salt or 1 postage stamp-size square kombu seaweed

1 tablespoon butter or light olive oil

FOR 5 CUPS COOKED:

2 cups short-grain brown rice

2²/₃ cups water

1 (2-finger) pinch sea salt or 2 postage stamp-size squares kombu seaweed

2 tablespoons butter or light olive oil

FOR 7 CUPS COOKED:

3 cups short-grain brown rice

4 cups water

1 (3-finger) pinch sea salt or 3 postage stamp-size squares kombu seaweed

3 tablespoons butter or light olive oil

FOR 10 CUPS COOKED:

4¹/₂ cups short-grain brown rice

5 cups water

2 (2-finger) pinches sea salt or 4 postage stamp-size squares kombu seaweed

¹/₄ cup butter or light olive oil

1. Place the rice in a bowl and cover with cold water. Rinse the rice with your hands, stirring from top to bottom. Drain, using a fine mesh strainer to keep from losing any grains. Repeat this process two to three more times until the rinse water is clear.
2. In a 5- to 8-quart pressure cooker, combine the rice, measured water, salt, and butter.
3. Close and lock the lid. Place a heat diffuser on the burner and the pressure cooker on top. Set the burner heat to high. When the cooker reaches HIGH pressure, reduce the burner heat as low as you can and still maintain HIGH pressure. Set a timer to cook for 22 minutes at HIGH pressure.
4. Remove the pot from the heat. Open the cooker with the Natural Release method; let stand for 12 to 15 minutes. At time, if the pressure is not all released, open the valve. Be careful of the steam as you remove the lid.
5. Portion out the rice with a wooden or plastic rice paddle to serve hot to eat or to a storage container. The top rice is yin and dry; the bottom rice is yang and soft.

Soaked Short-Grain Brown Rice: Soaking brown rice is an optional step but if you plan ahead and can do it, go ahead! You will find that the rice has a more even, more pleasant texture. Drain the last rinse water in Step 1, add the measured water minus ¹/₂ cup to the bowl. Cover with plastic wrap or a clean tea towel. The rice can be left to soak overnight on the counter and then transferred to the pressure cooker pot to be cooked in this water. Continue with Step 2.

The Ohsawa Pot

The Japanese Ohsawa pot is a thick-walled earthenware pot designed specifically for the pressure cooker by a Japanese man named George Ohsawa. He advocated the concepts of macrobiotic eating, which he believed would lead to a healthier, more balanced life.

The macrobiotic diet is built around grains, supplemented with vegetables, lightly fermented food, beans, and legumes. The modern macrobiotic approach is about eating foods that are minimally processed; steaming is the preferred cooking method. Enter the pressure cooker and what it does best.

The ceramic material of the Ohsawa pot is nonreactive with food and lead free. Each pot is individually hand thrown and fired. The pots transfer heat slowly, much slower than stainless steel insert pans. When completely elevated out of the steaming water the pot heats uniformly all around, not just from the bottom.

The Ohsawa pot is very easy to use. It has a rope handle for sliding it in and out of your pressure cooker, and a built-in raised ridge that allows the pot to be set on a rack or trivet without tipping over.

These truly attractive pots offer stove-to-table convenience, while at the same time providing you with the ultimate in flavorful and healthful foods.

Your Ohsawa pot and lid should be seasoned before its first use by simmering it in water to cover for an hour in a metal saucepan with a tight-fitting lid. Ohsawa pots can be put in the dishwasher.

Guide to Ohsawa Pot Sizes

Before you purchase an Ohsawa pot, make sure it will fit in your pressure cooker. Here are the dimensions for the different sized pots:
- Small: $1^1/_2$ cups to $1^3/_8$ quarts – $7^3/_8$" wide – $4^1/_4$" high
- Medium: $2^1/_2$ cups to $1^7/_8$ quarts – $7^3/_8$" wide – $5^1/_2$" high
- Intermediate: $3^1/_2$ cups to 3 quarts – $8^1/_4$" wide – 6" high
- Large: $4^1/_2$ cups to 4 quarts – $8^1/_4$" wide – $7^3/_4$" high

Short-Grain Brown Rice in an Ohsawa Pot

Serves 4 • Cooker: 5- to 7-quart • Time: 20 minutes at HIGH pressure

1 cup short-grain brown rice
$1^1/_2$ cups spring or filtered water
1 postage stamp-size piece kombu seaweed or
   pinch sea salt

1. Rinse the rice in a colander, then soak in the water for 30 minutes to 2 hours at room temperature.
2. Place the kombu in the bottom of the Ohsawa pot, then add the rice and soaking water. Fasten the lid on the pot by pulling the rope tightly up over the top to hold the lid in place. Tie the rope tightly, twisting the rope around the top knob, which will secure the lid down onto the pot.
3. Fill a 5- to 8-quart pressure cooker (whatever size works with your Ohsawa pot) with about 1 inch of water. Place a trivet or steamer rack in the cooker to keep the Ohsawa pot from scratching the bottom. Place the Ohsawa pot on the trivet or rack. The water should not touch the pot.
4. Close and lock the lid. Set the burner heat to high. When the cooker reaches HIGH pressure, reduce the burner heat as low as you can and still maintain HIGH pressure. Set a timer to cook for 20 minutes.
5. Remove the pot from the heat. Open the cooker with the Natural Release method; let stand for 20 minutes. At time, if the pressure is not all released, open the valve. Be careful of the steam as you remove the lid. Carefully lift the Ohsawa pot out of the cooker with pot holders. Untie the rope. Remove the lid of the Ohsawa pot and use a wooden or plastic rice paddle to scoop the rice into a serving bowl. Cover with a bamboo mat until serving.

Barley in the Ohsawa Pot: Substitute pearled barley for the rice and pressure cook 15 minutes at HIGH pressure with a Natural Release of 10 minutes. You can also combine half brown rice and half barley, cooking at HIGH pressure for 20 minutes.

Pressure-Steamed Wehani Rice

Serves 4 • Cooker: 5- to 7-quart • Time: 20 minutes at HIGH pressure

Wehani is a strain of rice developed by Lundberg Family Farms in California. It is a nutty, honey-red rice; use it for side dishes or in stuffings.

1 cup wehani rice
1 (3-finger) pinch sea salt
1 tablespoon oil or butter
1 1/2 cups spring or filtered water or vegetable broth

1. In a 5- to 7-quart pressure cooker, combine the rice, salt, oil, and water.
2. Close and lock the lid in place. Place a heat diffuser on the burner and the pressure cooker on top. Set the burner heat to high. When the cooker reaches HIGH pressure, reduce the burner heat as low as you can and still maintain HIGH pressure. Set a timer to cook for 20 minutes at HIGH pressure.
3. Remove the pot from the heat. Open the cooker with the Natural Release method; let stand for 10 minutes. At time, if the pressure is not all released, open the valve. Be careful of the steam as you remove the lid.
4. Spoon out the rice to a serving bowl to serve hot or a storage container. Let stand, uncovered, at room temperature until cooled before refrigerating. It is okay if this is a few hours.

Pressure-Steamed Thai Ruby Red Jasmine or Bhutanese Red Rice: Substitute Thai ruby red jasmine or Bhutanese red rice for the wehani rice. Decrease the water or vegetable broth to 1 1/3 cups. Decrease the pressure-cook time to 9 minutes. Otherwise, follow the recipe as directed.

Pressure-Steamed Forbidden Black Rice

Serves 4 to 6 • Cooker: 5- to 7-quart • Time: 16 minutes at HIGH pressure

Forbidden rice is a nonsticky short-grain rice from Southern China and Indonesia, first introduced to this country by Lotus Foods, based in the San Francisco Bay area. It is a rice that was so expensive it was reserved for special occasions and royalty. Well, those days are over. It is deemed a superfood, with antioxidant values similar to those of blueberries. Forbidden rice has a great, ever so whole grainy, assertive flavor. It is versatile and can be eaten as a plain bowl of rice or in soups or a salad, and its color adds drama to the plate. Forbidden rice has been used to develop some new strains of rice, including a cross with Arborio rice, producing *riz nero,* which is grown in the Po Valley of Northern Italy.

1 cup Forbidden black rice
1 (3-finger) pinch sea salt
1 tablespoon oil
1 1/2 cups spring or filtered water, vegetable broth, or chicken broth

1. In a 5- to 7-quart pressure cooker, combine the rice, salt, oil, and water.
2. Close and lock the lid. Place a heat diffuser on the burner and the pressure cooker on top. Set the burner heat to high. When the cooker reaches HIGH pressure, reduce the burner heat as low as you can and still maintain HIGH pressure. Set a timer to cook for 16 minutes at HIGH pressure.
3. Remove the pot from the heat. Open the cooker with the Natural Release method; let stand for 10 minutes. At time, if the pressure is not all released, open the valve. Be careful of the steam as you remove the lid.
4. Spoon out the rice to a serving bowl to serve hot or a storage container. Let stand, uncovered, at room temperature until cooled. It is okay if this is a few hours.

French-Style Rice Pilaf

Serves 6 • Cooker: 5- to 7-quart • Time: 4 minutes at HIGH pressure

This is an all-purpose pilaf and the recipe is easily cut in half for two people with some leftovers to reheat the next day.

2 tablespoons light olive oil
$1/3$ cup minced onion or shallots
$1^1/2$ cups long-grain white rice
2 (3-finger) pinches fine sea salt
$2^1/4$ cups spring or filtered water or vegetable or chicken broth

1. In a 5- to 7-quart pressure cooker, heat the oil over medium heat. Add the onion and rice and cook, stirring a few times, until the onion is soft and translucent and rice is completely coated with the oil. Add the salt and water.
2. Close and lock the lid. Place a heat diffuser on the burner and the pressure cooker on top. Set the burner heat to high. When the cooker reaches HIGH pressure, reduce the burner heat as low as you can and still maintain HIGH pressure. Set a timer to cook for 4 minutes at HIGH pressure.
3. Remove the pot from the heat. Open the cooker with the Natural Release method; let stand for 10 to 20 minutes. At time, if the pressure is not all released, open the valve. Be careful of the steam as you remove the lid.

Bhutanese Red Rice with Ginger and Cilantro

Serves 4 • Cooker: 5- to 7-quart • Time: 9 minutes at HIGH pressure

Bhutan is a Himalayan country and this delightful russet-brown ancient rice is a local crop and dietary staple. It is considered an heirloom rice and imported to the U.S. by Lotus Foods. Also sold as Himalayan whole-grain rice, it is nutty flavored, with an ivory interior, and has a soft texture, as it is partially milled. It's particularly delicious with game birds and rabbit and other foods you would pair with brown rice.

1 tablespoon unsalted butter
2 teaspoons minced peeled fresh ginger
$1/2$ cup chopped green onions
1 cup Bhutanese red rice, rinsed
1 (3-finger) pinch sea salt
$1^1/4$ cups low-sodium chicken or vegetable broth
$1/3$ cup chopped fresh cilantro
Juice of 1 lime

1. In a 5-to 7-quart pressure cooker over medium-high heat, melt the butter. Add the ginger and green onions and cook, stirring a few times, until softened, about 2 minutes. Add the rice and stir to coat with the butter. Add the salt and broth.
2. Close and lock the lid. Set the burner heat to high. When the cooker reaches HIGH pressure, reduce the burner heat as low as you can and still maintain HIGH pressure. Set a timer to cook for 9 minutes.
3. Remove the pot from the heat. Open the cooker with the Natural Release method; let stand for 10 minutes. At time, if the pressure is not all released, open the valve. Be careful of the steam as you remove the lid.
4. Spoon the rice into a serving bowl, stir in the cilantro and lime juice, and serve.

Our Yellow Rice

Serves 6 • Cooker: 5- to 7-quart • Time: 5 minutes at HIGH pressure

Why buy packaged yellow rice when you can make your own from scratch in minutes? Serve this plain or top it with chopped cilantro.

2 cups white basmati rice
1 tablespoon butter
1 tablespoon olive oil
2 teaspoons turmeric
2 (3-finger) pinches sea salt
2^1/$_2$ cups chicken broth or spring or filtered water
2 to 3 tablespoons chopped fresh cilantro, for
   serving (optional)

1. Place the rice in a fine mesh strainer or bowl, rinse with cold water, and drain two to four times. At first the water will be chalky and slightly foamy; continue until the water runs clear. Spread the wet rice out with your hands on a clean tea towel on the counter. Let air-dry at least 1 hour, until cooking time.

2. In a 5- to 7-quart pressure cooker, heat the butter and oil over medium heat until the butter melts. Add the rice and turmeric; cook, stirring, until the rice is ever so slightly golden and shiny and coated with the fat, about 1 minute. Add the salt and broth. Stir.

3. Close and lock the lid. Set the burner heat to high. Place a heat diffuser on the burner and the pressure cooker on top. Set the burner heat to high. When the cooker reaches HIGH pressure, reduce the burner heat as low as you can and still maintain HIGH pressure. Set a timer to cook for 5 minutes at HIGH pressure.

4. Remove the pot from the heat. Open the cooker with the Natural Release method; let stand for 10 minutes. At time, if the pressure is not all released, open the valve. Be careful of the steam as you remove the lid.

5. Spoon out the rice to a serving bowl and top with the cilantro if using.

TURMERIC

Turmeric is a rhizome, like ginger, to which it is botanically related, and grown in tropical areas like India, the Philippines, Indonesia, and Taiwan. It is turmeric that gives curry powder as well as American ballpark yellow mustard their color; it has a warm, bitter flavor. Turmeric contains a powerful antioxidant, curcumin, and has been used in Ayurvedic and Chinese medicine as an anti-inflammatory and as a treatment for digestive ailments.

Diane's Creamy Coconut Rice with Curry

Serves 6 • Cooker: 5- to 7-quart • Time: 5 minutes at HIGH pressure

Diane is Diane Phillips, author of *The Easy Pressure Cooker Cookbook* (Chronicle, 2011) and the inspiration for this rice side dish. Diane is a marvelous cook and has written many excellent books on entertaining and holiday cooking. This rice is so simple and so good. We love cooking the rice in coconut milk with a dash of hot curry powder. This is a vegan recipe.

3 tablespoons light olive oil
2 cups white basmati rice
2 teaspoons your favorite curry powder
2 (3-finger) pinches sea salt
1 cup unsweetened coconut milk (not light)
1¹/₂ cups vegetable broth
3 tablespoons minced fresh cilantro

1. In a 5- to 7-quart pressure cooker, heat the oil over medium heat until hot. Add the rice and curry powder and cook, stirring, until the rice is ever so slightly golden, shiny, and coated with the oil, about 1 minute. Add the coconut milk, broth, and salt; stir.
2. Close and lock the lid. Place a heat diffuser on the burner and the pressure cooker on top. Set the burner heat to high. When the cooker reaches HIGH pressure, reduce the burner heat as low as you can and still maintain HIGH pressure. Set a timer to cook for 5 minutes at HIGH pressure.
3. Remove the pot from the heat. Open the cooker with the Quick Release method; let stand for 2 to 3 minutes. Be careful of the steam as you remove the lid. Taste for seasoning.
4. Spoon out the rice to a serving bowl and sprinkle with the cilantro.

Gingery Brown Jasmine Rice and Lentils

Serves 4 to 6 • Cooker: 5- to 7-quart • Time: 18 minutes at HIGH pressure

Rice and lentils are a natural pairing. Here we partner brown jasmine, one of our favorite rices, with French *lentils du Puy*.

1 tablespoon olive oil
1 tablespoon minced peeled fresh ginger
2 cloves garlic, minced
2 cups brown jasmine rice
¹/₂ cup dried French green lentils
2 (3-finger) pinches sea salt
3¹/₄ cups vegetable broth or spring or filtered water
1 tablespoon sesame seeds, for serving

1. In a 5- to 7-quart pressure cooker, heat the oil over medium heat until hot. Add the ginger and garlic and stir for 30 seconds. Add the rice and cook, stirring, until it is ever so slightly golden, shiny, and coated with the oil, about 1 minute. Add the lentils, salt, and broth. Stir.
2. Close and lock the lid. Place a heat diffuser on the burner and the pressure cooker on top. Set the burner heat to high. When the cooker reaches HIGH pressure, reduce the burner heat as low as you can and still maintain HIGH pressure. Set a timer to cook for 18 minutes.
3. Remove the pot from the heat. Open the cooker with the Natural Release method; let stand for 10 minutes. At time, if the pressure is not all released, open the valve. Be careful of the steam as you remove the lid.
4. Spoon out the rice to a serving bowl and sprinkle with sesame seeds.

Spiced Brown Rice and Pepper Pilaf with Feta

Serves 8 • Cooker: 5- to 7-quart • Time: 17 minutes at HIGH pressure

Even though we have all been told how valuable whole grains are to our diets, brown rice pilafs are not so common—no doubt because of the longer cooking time. The pressure cooker solves that issue! This easy pilaf pairs well with yogurt-marinated grilled chicken, plain roast chicken, and Mexican food.

3 tablespoons olive oil
1 cup chopped onions
1 cup chopped yellow, orange, or red bell peppers
1 clove garlic, minced
2 cups long-grain brown rice
3 cups chicken broth
$^1/_2$ teaspoon salt, if broth is unsalted
$^1/_4$ teaspoon freshly ground black pepper
Dash ground cinnamon
Dash ground allspice
3 tablespoons minced fresh flatleaf parsley or dill
$^1/_2$ cup crumbled feta cheese

1. In a 5- to 7-quart pressure cooker, heat the oil over medium-high heat until very hot. Add the onions, bell peppers, and garlic and cook, stirring a few times, until the vegetables begin to soften, about 3 minutes. Add the rice and cook, stirring, until the rice is fragrant, about 2 minutes. Add the broth, salt, pepper, cinnamon, and allspice and stir to combine well.
2. Close and lock the lid. Place a heat diffuser on the burner and the pressure cooker on top. Set the burner heat to high. When the cooker reaches HIGH pressure, reduce the burner heat as low as you can and still maintain HIGH pressure. Set a timer to cook for 17 minutes.
3. Remove the pot from the heat. Open the cooker with the Quick Release method. Let the rice rest for 2 to 3 minutes before opening the cooker. Be careful of the steam as you remove the lid.
4. Fluff the rice with a wooden spoon or heat-proof spatula and gently stir in the parsley and cheese.

Thai Brown Rice Salad with Fresh Herbs

Serves 4 to 6

This is a fantastic, fresh-tasting salad. The combination of basil, cilantro, and mint will wake up your taste buds. Serve the salad room temperature or nice and cold.

THAI VINAIGRETTE:
$^1/_2$ cup seasoned rice vinegar
3 tablespoons light olive oil
1 tablespoon reduced-sodium soy sauce
1 tablespoon brown sugar
$^1/_2$ teaspoon hot chili oil
Juice and grated zest of 1 lime

SALAD:
4 cups cooked long-grain brown rice (page 320), at room temperature
1 medium hothouse cucumber, thickly sliced into rounds, then cut into quarters
3 green onions (white and part of green), trimmed and thinly sliced

1 cup frozen petite peas, thawed
$^1/_2$ cup shredded carrots
$^1/_3$ cup loosely packed chopped fresh basil
$^1/_3$ cup loosely packed chopped fresh cilantro
$^1/_4$ cup loosely packed chopped fresh mint

1. In a small bowl, whisk together the vinaigrette ingredients. Cover and refrigerate if not using right away.
2. Place the rice in a medium salad bowl. Add the cucumber, green onion, peas, carrots, and herbs. With a large rubber spatula, fold and combine the salad ingredients and all of the vinaigrette to lightly coat and evenly distribute all the ingredients. Serve at room temperature or store in the refrigerator at least 3 hours and serve the salad chilled.

Pressure-Steamed Wild Rice

Cooker: 5- to 7-quart • Time: 22 minutes at HIGH pressure

Wild rice should have a smoky-rich, nutty flavor. It has only its hull removed, so when cooking, the water will always be dark because of the rich bran layer. During cooking you want the grains to swell and split just slightly down the side to show the gray-white interior. If the grains split and curl out like a butterfly, the rice is overcooked and you will need to adjust your timing for the next batch. If you make this with a hand-harvested wild rice, add 3 minutes to the pressure-cook time.

FOR 6 SERVINGS:

1 cup wild rice, rinsed

1 (3-finger) pinch sea salt

2^1/$_4$ cups spring or filtered water or vegetable, beef, or chicken broth

FOR 8 SERVINGS:

1^1/$_2$ cups wild rice, rinsed

1 (3-finger) pinch sea salt

3^1/$_3$ cups spring or filtered water, vegetable, beef, or chicken broth

1. In a 5- to 7-quart pressure cooker, combine the wild rice, salt, and water.
2. Close and lock the lid. Place a heat diffuser on the burner and the pressure cooker on the diffuser. Set the burner heat to high. When the cooker reaches HIGH pressure, reduce the burner heat as low as you can and still maintain HIGH pressure. Set a timer to cook for 22 minutes.
3. Remove the pot from the heat. Open the cooker with the Natural Release method; let stand for 10 minutes. At time, if the pressure is not all released, open the valve. Be careful of the steam as you remove the lid. Drain any excess liquid.
4. Spoon out the rice to a serving bowl to serve hot or a storage container. Let stand, uncovered, at room temperature until cooled before refrigerating. It is okay if this is a few hours. Keeps in an airtight container in the refrigerator up to 3 days or the freezer up to 4 months.

WILD RICE

Wild rice is the only grain native to North America. It grows in the lakes and shallow moving waters along the American-Canadian border (western Ontario, eastern Manitoba, Wisconsin, and Minnesota). French fur traders and Jesuit missionaries in the New World adopted wild rice into their diets, calling it "crazy oats" because it grows where maize can't. Some wild rice is still harvested in the old way by Native tribespeople: balanced in birch bark ricing canoes sewn together with strips of spruce roots that are so light they float like corks, beating the plants with flexible forked flails fashioned from saplings.

Hand-gathered lake rice is quite expensive, but cultivated wild rice (sometimes called tame rice) is very affordable, though different in flavor. It's less assertive than lake rice (some refer to it as "real rice"), which we love because lake rice is so strong that it often needs to be mixed half and half with white or brown rice. Labels will tell you if the rice is hand-harvested or cultivated, but you'll also know from the color; hand-harvested rice is distinctly matte colored and paddy rice is a very shiny sable-black. Paddy rice is left to cure out in the weather longer, causing the characteristic shiny, dark kernels, while hand-harvested rice is parched immediately over open fires, resulting in distinctly matte colors that range from ruddy red-brown or deep chocolate to tan and subtle gray-green.

Each brand of wild rice has its own particular taste (in general, the darker the grain, the stronger the flavor), so if you have experienced a brand that was too husky or bitter for your palate, experiment with others, or use it in combination with other rices for a milder taste.

Wild Rice and Chicken Salad with Tarragon and Green Grapes

Serves 6 to 8

This salad is adapted from one originally sold at the deli at Byerly's gourmet supermarket in Wisconsin. It can be made the day before to give the flavors time to meld. It's creamy, cool, crunchy, earthy, sweet, and savory all at one time. Turkey can be substituted for the chicken.

CREAMY TARRAGON DRESSING:
³/₄ cup mayonnaise
¹/₃ cup whole milk
2 tablespoons fresh lemon juice
¹/₂ teaspoon crumbled dried tarragon
Salt and freshly ground black pepper, to taste

SALAD:
4 cups cooked wild rice (page 328), at room temperature
3 cups shredded or diced cooked chicken

1 bunch green onions (white part with some of the green), trimmed and chopped
2 ribs celery, thinly sliced
1 (8-ounce) can water chestnuts, drained and sliced
2 to 3 cups seedless green grapes, to taste, halved

1. In a medium bowl, whisk the Creamy Tarragon Dressing ingredients together until combined. Cover and refrigerate.
2. Place the wild rice in a large salad bowl. Add the chicken, green onions, celery, water chestnuts, and grapes. With a large rubber spatula, fold and combine the salad ingredients with the dressing to lightly coat all the ingredients. Cover, store in the refrigerator at least 3 hours, and serve the salad chilled.

Wild Rice with Mushrooms

Serves 6 • Cooker: 5- to 7-quart • Time: 25 minutes at HIGH pressure

The deep flavor and chewy texture of wild rice melds perfectly with mushrooms of any type.

3 tablespoons butter
3 tablespoons olive oil
1 large or 2 small shallots, minced
1 cup wild rice, rinsed
1 (3-finger) pinch sea salt, plus more to taste
2¹/₄ cups chicken or beef broth
1 pound white or brown mushrooms, sliced
Few tablespoons finely shredded carrot
Freshly ground black pepper

1. In a 5- to 7-quart pressure cooker, heat 1 tablespoon each of the butter and oil over medium heat until the butter melts. Add the shallots and cook, stirring a few times, until they begin to soften, about 2 minutes. Add the wild rice, salt, and broth; stir.

2. Close and lock the lid. Place a heat diffuser on the burner and the pressure cooker on the diffuser. Set the burner heat to high. When the cooker reaches HIGH pressure, reduce the burner heat as low as you can and still maintain HIGH pressure. Set a timer to cook for 25 minutes.
3. While the rice cooks, heat the remaining 2 tablespoons butter with the 2 tablespoons oil over medium-high heat in a large skillet until the butter melts. Add the mushrooms and cook, stirring, until they begin to brown. Set aside.
4. Remove the pot from the heat. Open the cooker with the Quick Release method. Be careful of the steam as you remove the lid.
5. Add the sautéed mushrooms and grated carrot to the rice and stir gently to combine. Taste for salt and pepper. Spoon out the rice to a serving bowl to serve hot.

Wild Rice Pilaf with Mango and Macadamias

Serves 6 • Cooker: 5- to 7-quart • Time: 25 minutes at HIGH pressure

Wild rice is extra delicious when combined with dried fruit and nuts, and here it is partnered with the sweet-tart flavor of dried mango. Look for unsalted macadamias in the bulk bins.

$^1/_2$ cup finely chopped dried mango or apricots
2 tablespoons water
3 tablespoons butter or olive oil
1 large or 2 small shallots, minced
1 cup wild rice, rinsed
1 (3-finger) pinch sea salt
$2^1/_4$ cups chicken broth
$^1/_2$ cup chopped unsalted macadamia nuts

1. In a small bowl or quart plastic food bag, combine the mango and water. Let soften 1 to 4 hours. Drain.
2. In a 5- to 7-quart pressure cooker, heat the butter over medium heat until melted. Add the shallots and cook, stirring a few times, until they begin to soften, about 2 minutes. Add the wild rice, salt, and broth; stir.
3. Close and lock the lid. Place a heat diffuser on the burner and the pressure cooker on top. Set the burner heat to high. When the cooker reaches HIGH pressure, reduce the burner heat as low as you can and still maintain HIGH pressure. Set a timer to cook for 25 minutes.
4. Remove the pot from the heat. Open the cooker with the Quick Release method. Be careful of the steam as you remove the lid.
5. Add the mango and macadamias to the rice, cover and let stand 5 to 10 minutes. Stir gently to combine.
6. Spoon out the rice to a serving bowl to serve hot or a storage container. Let stand, uncovered, at room temperature until cooled before refrigerating. It is okay if this is a few hours. Keeps in an airtight container in the refrigerator up to 3 days or the freezer up to 4 months.

Wild Rice with Chestnuts

Makes about 4 cups • Cooker: 5- to 7-quart • Time: 22 minutes at HIGH pressure

An excellent flavor combination with game of all sorts.

12 chestnuts, peeled and shelled (see below)
1 cup wild rice, rinsed
1 (3-finger) pinch sea salt
2^1/$_4$ cups vegetable or chicken broth

1. Crumble the peeled chestnuts.
2. In a 5- to 7-quart pressure cooker, combine the chestnuts, wild rice, salt, and broth.
3. Lock the lid in place. Place a heat diffuser on the burner and the pressure cooker on the diffuser. Set the burner heat to high. When the cooker reaches HIGH pressure, reduce the burner heat as low as you can and still maintain HIGH pressure. Set a timer to cook for 22 minutes.
4. Remove the pot from the heat. Open the cooker with the Natural Release method; let stand for 10 minutes. At time, if the pressure is not all released, open the valve. Be careful of the steam as you remove the lid.
5. Spoon out the rice to a serving bowl to serve hot or portion on dinner plates. Leftovers will keep in an airtight container for up to 3 days in the refrigerator and up to 3 months in the freezer.

PEELING CHESTNUTS

Many cooks avoid fresh chestnuts as they are difficult to peel. No more, with the microwave oven at hand. With a sharp knife, cut across the chestnut or make a deep X on the flat side. Rinse with water and drain. Place 6 at a time on a plate and microwave on HIGH for exactly 1 minute. Remove from the microwave and let stand until cool enough to handle but still warm. (Have a thin dishtowel to hold the chestnut if necessary while using your fingers.) Rinse your fingers in cold water, then insert them into the cracks in the shell and peel away the shell. It should come away easily. The fuzzy inner skin (called the pellicle) should come away with shell. The chestnut is now ready to cook. If you are not using them immediately, refrigerate in an airtight container.

When purchasing chestnuts, look for ones with firm shells. Fresh chestnuts appear around November and December, their harvest time.

White Sushi Rice

Makes enough for 6 sushi rolls • Cooker: 5- to 7-quart • Time: 2 minutes at HIGH pressure

The type of rice you use is important; you want a Japanese-style short- or medium-grain rice, not a risotto or Carolina medium-grain rice. For white rice, our top-of-the-charts favorites for sushi are Tamaki Gold from Williams Rice Milling Co. of Williams, California, and the Japanese heirloom varieties *Koshihikari* and *Akitakomachi*. We also like Nishiki and Kokuho Rose brands. If you can't find them, look for rice labeled "new variety" or "sushi rice." There are also organic brands in health food groceries.

The amount of the vinegar dressing you add to the rice—and the amounts of salt and sugar you use in the dressing—is subject to your own personal taste. The dressing gives the sushi rice its pearly sheen and mildly sweet flavor.

2 cups high-quality short- or medium-grain
    Japanese-style rice (see Sushi, on page 335)
2 cups water
2 tablespoons sake or mirin
$^1/_4$ cup unseasoned rice vinegar
$1^1/_2$ to 2 tablespoons sugar, to taste
1 teaspoon salt

1. Wash the rice thoroughly. Place the rice in a bowl and fill it about half-full of cold tap water. Swirl the rice in the water with your hand. Carefully pour off most of the water, holding one cupped hand under the stream to catch any grains of rice carried away with the water. Holding the bowl steady with one hand, use the other to rub and squeeze the wet rice, turning the bowl as you go so that all rice is "scrubbed." (One friend calls this giving the rice a massage, and you definitely do want to use some muscle power.) The small amount of water in the bowl will turn chalky white. Run cold water into the bowl, give the rice a quick swish, and carefully drain off the water as before. Repeat the scrubbing and pouring-off process twice more. By the third time, the water you pour off will be nearly clear.

2. In a 5- to 7-quart pressure cooker, combine the washed rice and 2 cups water. If you have time, let the rice soak for 30 minutes. Add the sake.

3. Close and lock the lid. Set the burner heat to high. When the cooker reaches HIGH pressure, reduce the burner heat as low as you can and still maintain HIGH pressure. Set a timer to cook for 2 minutes.

4. Remove the pot from the heat. Open the cooker with the Natural Release method; let stand for 15 minutes. At time, if the pressure is not all released, open the valve. Be careful of the steam as you remove the lid.

5. While the rice stands, prepare the vinegar mixture. In a small saucepan, combine the vinegar, sugar, and salt. Simmer over medium heat, stirring until the salt and sugar dissolve. Or you can heat the vinegar mixture in a microwave oven. Remove from the heat and allow to cool to room temperature.

6. Lay out the following items around your workspace. When the rice is done, you will have to act quickly, so everything should be assembled and available within arm's reach.
    • a plastic or wooden rice spatula or a wide wooden spatula, rinsed in cool water
    • your mixing bowl, wooden (if it is pristine), plastic, metal, or glass; if your bowl is wooden, rinse it out with cool water to prevent the rice from sticking
    • the vinegar mixture, at room temperature
    • an electric fan or a hair dryer with a "cool" setting.
    • a clean dishcloth or cloth napkin, rinsed in cool water and wrung out

7. When the pressure has fully dropped, remove the lid away from you to avoid the steam. Use the spatula to scoop all the rice into the bowl. Holding the spatula in one hand over the rice and the pan with the vinegar mixture in the other, slowly pour the vinegar over the spatula, letting it run off and fall lightly onto the rice. Move the spatula around the bowl as you pour. The net effect will be to sprinkle the vinegar as evenly as possible over the surface of the rice.

Gently nestle the damp cloth over the rice, covering it completely and bunching up the cloth against the side of the bowl. Wait 2 minutes.

8. Mix and cool the rice. You want rice that is shiny, body temperature or a bit cooler, mostly dry, and fairly sticky. The grains should be distinct, not mashed. Force-cooling the rice keeps it from absorbing the vinegar and getting too sticky. Aim the electric fan at the rice in the bowl (or get your hair dryer ready), but don't turn it on yet. Mix the rice with the spatula, holding the spatula vertically and using it like a knife, gently and repeatedly cutting through and lifting sections of rice. (If you stirred the rice in the traditional manner, you would quickly make rice mush.) Rotate the bowl so that all of the rice gets mixed. After 1 minute of mixing, turn the fan to low or medium speed (or begin to use the hair dryer or to fan the rice by hand). Continue "cutting," lifting, fanning, and turning the bowl until the rice is shiny and about body temperature (feel it with your palm). The rice is now ready to use.

If you are not ready to assemble your sushi, just set the spatula on top of the rice and cover the rice with the damp towel. The rice can wait, covered, for about an hour or so.

White and Red Quinoa Sushi Rice: Substitute $1/2$ cup red quinoa with $1/2$ cup of the short- or medium-grain Japanese-style rice. Wash the quinoa along with the rice. Proceed as directed.

TOOLS FOR MAKING SUSHI RICE

You will need a large bowl to mix the cooked sushi rice with its vinegar dressing. The traditional mixing tub, called a *han giri*, looks like half of a very flat wooden wine barrel. The wood absorbs the excess moisture from the rice. You can use any large wooden bowl that doesn't smell like salad dressing. If you don't have a wooden bowl that is pristine, a plastic, metal, or glass bowl works fine.

You will also need something to blow cool air on the rice while you mix it. We usually set up an electric fan so it blows directly on the bowl. A hair dryer set on "cool" delivers a nicely focused stream of air and is especially good if you have a friend willing to hold it steady.

Brown Sushi Rice

Makes enough for 6 sushi rolls • Cooker: 5- to 7-quart • Time: 18 minutes at HIGH pressure

For brown sushi rice, look for brown versions of Tamaki Gold from Williams Rice Milling Co. of Williams, California, and from Lundberg, Nishiki, and Kokuho Rose. Partially milled brown rices (where the outer bran layer is only partly removed during processing) are becoming increasingly popular; these are often labeled "Quick-Cooking Brown Rice" or something similar. These are also a good choice for sushi—you will simply adjust the water slightly as noted in the variation below.

Brown rice for sushi is best prepared by steaming the rice in a heatproof bowl set on a trivet or rack inside the pressure cooker. We have a stainless steel mixing bowl that we like to use; a heatproof glass bowl is another option.

2 cups high-quality short- or medium-grain
  Japanese-style brown rice (not "Quick Cooking"
  or partially milled)
5 cups water (3 cups for cooking the rice, 2 cups
  water to create the steam)
2 tablespoons sake or mirin
$1/4$ cup plus 2 tablespoons unseasoned rice vinegar
$1^1/2$ to 2 tablespoons sugar, to taste
1 teaspoon salt

1. Wash the rice as directed in Step 1 for White Sushi Rice (page 332).
2. Transfer the rice to the bowl you will use for steaming and add 3 cups of the water. Place a trivet or steamer rack in 5- to 7-quart pressure cooker. Add the remaining 2 cups water to the cooker. Place the bowl of rice and water on top of the trivet. If you have time, let the rice soak for 30 minutes. Add the sake to the rice.
3. Close and lock the lid. Set the burner heat to high. When the cooker reaches HIGH pressure, reduce the burner heat as low as you can and still maintain HIGH pressure. Set a timer to cook for 18 minutes.
4. Remove the pot from the heat. Open the cooker with the Natural Release method; let stand for 15 minutes. At time, if the pressure is not all released, open the valve. Be careful of the steam as you remove the lid.

5. While the rice is cooking, prepare the vinegar mixture. In a small saucepan, combine the vinegar, sugar, and salt. Simmer over medium heat, stirring just until the salt and sugar dissolve. Or you can heat the vinegar mixture in a microwave oven. Remove from the heat and allow to cool to room temperature.
6. Lay out the items you will need as instructed in Step 5 of White Sushi Rice (page 332).
7. Add the seasoned vinegar to the rice as instructed in Step 6 of White Sushi Rice.
8. Mix and cool the rice as instructed in Step 7 of White Sushi Rice.

"Quick Cooking" Brown Rice for Sushi: The Japanese brown rices labeled "Quick Cooking" have been partially milled to break up the outer bran layer of the rice kernel and thus speed cook times. Some Japanese markets carry a whole line of partially milled brown rices that display a percentage on the label—that's the percentage of the bran layer that has been milled away. You may use 30 percent milled rice in this recipe. Substitute "Quick Cooking" Japanese brown rice for the short- or medium-grain Japanese-style brown rice. Decrease the water added to the rice in the bowl to $2^1/2$ cups. Decrease the pressure-cook time to 12 minutes. Otherwise, follow the recipe as directed.

Your trusty pressure cooker can help you prepare sushi so good that you might just break the take-out habit. Surprised? You shouldn't be. The pressure cooker is an excellent method of cooking both white and brown rice, and cooking the rice properly is the first step on the road to tasty homemade sushi.

In fact, the word "sushi" has nothing to do with fish but instead refers to the vinegar-dressed rice that is the basis for a wide variety of sushi dishes. Japanese home cooks make sushi often, but typically not the little fish-topped rice logs, called *nigiri* sushi, that come to mind first when one thinks about sushi. *Nigiri* sushi is left to professionally trained sushi chefs. Home cooks have their own types of sushi. Perhaps the most popular are *maki*—seaweed-wrapped rolls that are sliced to expose the carefully arranged fillings inside—and hand rolls. For hand rolls, the sushi rice is spread on a piece of seaweed, topped with fillings, and rolled up in an ice-cream cone shape to be eaten out of hand. This is popular party food.

MAKI SUSHI

Maki are seaweed-wrapped rolls of rice with something tasty centered inside. The rolls are sliced to expose a cross-section of the fillings. Be as creative as you want but remember that anything used to stuff *maki* sushi should be soft and no thicker around than a pencil. (And if you want to try raw fish in your sushi, please purchase sashimi grade fish, from a Japanese market if possible. Use it the day you buy it.) Simple or lavish, the variations are endless.

The only piece of special equipment you will need is a *maki-su,* the little bamboo-and-string mat used to support the seaweed while you roll it around the rice and fillings (it looks like a miniature window shade). You can use a piece of heavy-duty aluminum foil as a substitute. The dried seaweed wrappers, *yaki sushi nori*, wasabi, and ginger are all sold in Asian markets, health food stores, and in the Asian food aisle of many large supermarkets. Japanese cucumbers are small and thin, resembling the Persian ones. If you can't find these, use an English cucumber. All three types are less watery than the standard American ones. If you have a choice, the smooth, rich Hass avocados are the best for sushi. They should be ripe but not as soft as for guacamole. Japanese sesame seeds are sold in a plastic shaker canister. They are larger and more flavorful than the ones used for baking and have been toasted. (If you have time, toast them again in a small skillet to bring out the flavor.)

Arrange around your work surface for assembly:
- the sheets of nori
- the cucumber slivers, the avocado slices and the sesame seeds
- a bamboo rolling mat for forming the rolls, or a 9 x 10-inch sheet of heavy-duty aluminum foil
- 2 forks
- a clean, damp dishcloth
- a sharp chef's knife
- a plastic or wooden cutting board
- a small saucer of unseasoned rice vinegar (may be needed to seal the rolls)
- a serving platter (a cake plate or small square platter works nicely)
- condiments in serving bowls

Cucumber, Avocado, and Sesame Rolls

Makes 6 rolls; serves 4 to 8

2 Japanese or Persian cucumbers or 1 English
  cucumber
2 firm-ripe medium avocados
1 recipe White or Brown Sushi Rice (page 332 or
  334)
6 sheets *yaki sushi nori* (roasted seaweed sheets)
Japanese sesame seeds
Soy sauce, ready-to-eat wasabi (sold in a plastic
  tube or as a powder that you mix with water to
  make the paste), and slices of pickled ginger, for
  serving

1. Cut an unpeeled cucumber on the diagonal into
   slices about $1/4$ inch thick, forming long ovals.
   Stack the ovals and cut into thin matchsticks. If
   using an English cucumber, you will only need
   about one-third to one-half of it. Also, you may
   want to let the pieces wait for you on a double
   layer of paper towel so that any extra moisture is
   absorbed.
2. Cut each avocado in half the long way, working
   your knife around the pit. Remove the pit and
   use a knife to score the avocado into slices
   about $1/3$ inch thick. Don't cut all the way
   through the skin. Use a large soup spoon to
   scoop the slices right out of the avocado shell. If
   the avocado is large, you may wish to halve the
   slices lengthwise.
3. Arrange the rolling mat in front of you, with the
   pieces of bamboo running horizontally (parallel
   to the edge of the work surface). Place a piece
   of nori on the mat, with the smoother side down.
4. Uncover the rice and use the spatula to section
   the rice into 6 parts. Scoop out one section and
   place it on the bottom half of the sheet of nori.
   Re-cover the remaining rice to keep it from drying out. Hold a fork in each hand, tines down,
   rounded side up. Use the forks like garden rakes
   to spread out the rice as evenly as possible over
   the bottom two thirds of the nori. Don't leave
   any margins; spread the rice all the way to the
   edges.

5. Pick up a clump of cucumber slivers and arrange them in a line about 1 inch up from the
   edge of the nori closest to you. You want the
   cucumber slivers to be about $1/2$ inch thick and
   go all the way across the piece of nori (parallel
   to the edge). It is okay to mound the cucumber
   up a bit. You will compress it as you complete
   the roll. (You will quickly learn how much filling to use to produce a roll that is neither
   skimpy nor bulging.)
6. Add a row of avocado slices on top of or alongside the cucumber. Sprinkle the cucumber and
   avocado with sesame seeds.
7. Slide the nori to the edge of the mat closest to
   you. Lifting the mat, not the nori, begin the roll
   by bringing the strip of rice closest to you to
   meet the strip of rice on the other side of the filling. Squeeze the mat gently but firmly, move
   your hands along the entire length of the mat, to
   create a nice, even log shape. Now complete the
   roll, stopping every so often to gently squeeze
   the mat and shape the roll. At the end, give a
   final squeeze, hard enough to firm and seal the
   roll but not so hard that the filling oozes out the
   ends. If the nori doesn't seal, dip your finger in
   vinegar and wet the edge of the nori. Repeat
   with the remaining rice, nori, and fillings
8. Moisten a sharp knife with water and cut each
   roll in half. Cut each half in thirds, moistening
   the knife each time before cutting and using a
   back-and-forth sawing motion. You should now
   have 6 equal size pieces of sushi. Arrange the
   rolls cut side up, on the serving platter. Serve
   with the soy sauce, wasabi, and slices of pickled
   ginger.

Salmon Salad Rolls

Makes 6 rolls; serves 4 to 8

If you keep a can of salmon in the cupboard and lettuce in the fridge, you can make Salmon Salad Rolls anytime.

1 tall can salmon or 2 small cans (12 to 15 ounces total)
2 to 4 tablespoons mayonnaise, to your taste
1 to 2 teaspoons Chinese (hot) mustard, to your taste
1/2 teaspoon soy sauce
1 recipe White or Brown Sushi Rice (page 332 or 334)
6 sheets *yaki sushi nori* (toasted seaweed sheets)
About 12 tender inner leaves of Romaine lettuce

SOY AND WASABI DIPPING SAUCE:
1 tablespoon wasabi powder
1 1/4 teaspoons hot water
1/2 cup water
3 tablespoons soy sauce or tamari

1. Drain the salmon and flake it into a bowl with a fork, picking out any large pieces of skin and bones. Mix the salmon with just enough mayonnaise to hold it together. Stir in 1 teaspoon of the mustard and the soy sauce. Add more mustard if you want a spicier flavor.

2. For each Salmon Salad roll, spread the rice on the nori as described on page 336. Lay the lettuce leaves in a line across the rice, about 1 inch up from the edge of the nori that is closest to you. Top the lettuce with one-sixth of the salmon salad, nudging it into a line. Roll up carefully. Moisten a sharp knife with water and cut the roll in half. Cut each half in thirds, for 6 pieces, wiping the knife with a damp towel between cuts.

3. Make the dipping sauce. Place the wasabi in a small bowl or tea cup. Stir in the hot water to make a mound of thick paste. Let rest 5 minutes to develop the flavor. Heat the 1/2 cup water in a small saucepan or in a bowl to microwave to heat without boiling. Add the soy sauce and simmer for 1 minute. Pour the sauce into small individual dipping bowls. Drop equal pieces of wasabi paste into each bowl. Mix and serve with the sushi.

RISOTTO IN THE PRESSURE COOKER

The one thing everyone knows about risotto is that you have to stir it nonstop until it is done, which can take up to 30 minutes. It turns out that risotto takes to the pressure cooker like a fish to water. It's ready in just minutes, nary a wooden spoon in sight. You will be using less liquid than in traditional risotto recipes because there is less evaporation with the pressure cooker. Depending on your stove and your pressure cooker, you may find that the risotto has a tendency to scorch. If this is the case, using a flame tamer is the answer.

The Basics

There are three distinct steps to making risotto: cooking the onion and rice, adding the stock and other ingredients, and adding the butter and cheese to finish, known as "creaming."

1. Risotto is made by first sautéing chopped onion in butter (or half butter and half olive oil), then the rice. Place the butter, in pieces, in the uncovered pot over medium-high heat on the stovetop. Butter as the cooking fat is traditional, but these days a bit of olive oil is often added and maybe some pancetta or bacon. Add the chopped onion, leek, or shallot; cook until soft and any liquid the aromatics exude is evaporated.

2. Add the measured amount of rice to the hot butter and onion; stir with a wooden spoon. The rice will gradually heat up and gently sizzle. Stir occasionally and gently to coat all the grains. Give the rice a full 1 to 2 minutes to cook. At first the grains will be translucent; when they turn pure white again, they are ready for the next step. This precooking will allow the grains to release their amylopectin (which results in the creaminess) and stay separate as they slowly absorb the stock. If using wine or vermouth, add and cook for a minute or so. This is an important step; if you don't evaporate the alcohol, the flavor will be bitter and affect the delicate taste of your risotto.

3. Add the stock (never water) all at once, with no preheating, and any other ingredients as specified in the recipe. You will have three times the amount of liquid to rice and there will be less evaporation with the cover closed than when you cook stovetop. Stir a few times. Cover the pressure cooker and lock the lid in place. Set the burner heat to high. When the cooker reaches HIGH pressure, adjust the heat to maintain the pressure. Set your timer as directed in the specific recipe.

4. Remove the pot from the heat and open the cooker with the Quick Release method. If it is not sufficiently cooked or the risotto is too soupy, place the pot over medium-high heat and cook, uncovered, stirring constantly, until the desired consistency is reached. With a heat-resistant spatula or plastic or wooden spoon, stir the risotto a few times, adding the butter and cheese, or cream. The bit of butter stirred in at the end of cooking is very traditional, but optional. Risotto is best served immediately (it thickens dramatically as it stands at room temperature). We prefer to serve risotto in a warm shallow soup bowl with a soup spoon, but the correct etiquette is a fork, with more Parmesan cheese on hand for sprinkling (use as much as you like) as well as a pepper grinder.

Classic White Risotto

Serves 3 to 4 • Cooker: 5- to 7-quart • Time: 7 minutes at HIGH pressure

The wine you use will add to the dish considerably—Sauvignon Blanc and Chenin Blanc are tasty white wines, Chardonnay is oaky, and the popular Vermouth has an herbal aftertaste. Be sure to refrigerate the opened bottle and use within three months. Add the cheese after the release method is completed and off the burner so it melts properly. If the risotto is just a little wet, don't worry as it will absorb more liquid by the time you serve it. If it is still very wet, put the open pressure cooker back over medium heat for a few minutes until the right consistency is achieved. Salt after cooking. Always let risotto rest a few minutes off the heat so it can continue to cook in its own heat to finish the cooking process and not overcook.

2 tablespoons olive oil
2 tablespoons butter
$^{1}/_{4}$ cup finely chopped shallots
$1^{1}/_{2}$ cups Arborio, Carnaroli, or Vialone Nano rice
$3^{1}/_{2}$ cups chicken or vegetable broth
$^{1}/_{2}$ cup dry white wine or dry vermouth
$^{3}/_{4}$ to 1 cup freshly grated Parmesan cheese, to
    taste, plus more for sprinkling
Salt and freshly ground black pepper

1. In a 5- to 7-quart pressure cooker or $2^{1}/_{2}$-quart skillet pressure cooker, heat the oil and 1 tablespoon of the butter together over medium heat until the butter melts. Add the shallots and cook until softened, about 1 minute. Add the rice and cook 1 minute, stirring constantly, to evenly coat the grains of rice. Add the broth and wine.

2. Close and lock the lid. If you like, place a heat diffuser on the burner and the pressure cooker on the diffuser. Set the burner heat to high. When the cooker reaches HIGH pressure, reduce the burner heat as low as you can and still maintain HIGH pressure. Set a timer to cook for 7 minutes.

3. Remove the pot from the heat. Open the cooker with the Quick Release method. Be careful of the steam as you remove the lid. If the rice is not sufficiently cooked or the risotto is too soupy, place the pot over medium-high heat and cook, uncovered, stirring constantly, until the desired consistency is reached, 1 to 2 minutes.

4. Stir in the cheese, the remaining 1 tablespoon butter, and pepper to taste. Replace the cover and let stand a few minutes to thicken and set up. Taste for salt.

5. Spoon out the rice with an oversized spoon to a serving bowl to serve hot, with extra cheese for sprinkling and the pepper grinder on the side.

Ginger-Sweet Potato Risotto: In Step 1, add 1 tablespoon grated peeled fresh ginger and 1 to $1^{1}/_{2}$ cups cubed ($^{1}/_{2}$-inch) peeled sweet potato with the shallots. In Step 3, add another 2 teaspoons grated fresh ginger with the butter.

Green Risotto: In Step 3, add 14 ounces baby spinach, $^{1}/_{4}$ cup chopped fresh basil, and 2 teaspoons chopped fresh mint. Stir in before adding the cheese and butter, letting it wilt.

7-Minute Lemon Risotto with Prosecco and Parmesan

Serves 3 to 4 as a main or 6 as a first course • Cooker: 5- to 7-quart • Time: 7 minutes at HIGH pressure

We tried this with Carnaroli and Arborio; we liked the forgiving nature of Carnaroli, which remained al dente, while Arborio rice produced a slightly softer grain in the pressure cooker. Don't worry if the rice is a tad runny after cooking—it thickens as it stands before serving.

1/4 cup (1/2 stick) butter
2 large shallots, finely chopped
1 1/2 cups Arborio or Carnaroli rice
1 cup Prosecco sparkling white wine
Grated lemon zest of 1 medium lemon
3 cups reduced-sodium chicken broth
1 cup freshly grated or shredded Parmigiano-
  Reggiano cheese, plus more for sprinkling
1/4 teaspoon freshly ground black or white pepper

1. In a 5- to 7-quart pressure cooker or 2 1/2-quart skillet pressure cooker, melt the butter over medium heat. Add the shallots and cook until softened, about 1 minute. Add the rice and cook 1 minute, stirring constantly, to evenly coat the grains of rice. Add 1/2 cup of the Prosecco and stir until the wine is absorbed and evaporated. Add the rest of the Prosecco and lemon zest. Add the broth.

2. Close and lock the lid. If you like, place a heat diffuser on the burner and the pressure cooker on the diffuser. Set the burner heat to high. When the cooker reaches HIGH pressure, reduce the burner heat as low as you can and still maintain HIGH pressure. Set a timer to cook for 7 minutes.

3. Remove the pot from the heat. Open the cooker with the Quick Release method. Be careful of the steam as you remove the lid. If the rice is not sufficiently cooked or the risotto is too soupy, place the pot over medium-high heat and cook, uncovered, stirring constantly, until the desired consistency is reached, 1 to 2 minutes.

4. Stir in half the cheese and the pepper. Replace the cover and let stand a few minutes to thicken.

5. Spoon out the rice with an oversized spoon to serving bowls to serve hot, with extra cheese for sprinkling on top, and the pepper grinder on the side.

RICE FOR RISOTTO

There is a family of Italian short- and medium-grain rices grown for risotto that includes Carnaroli, Vialone Nano, and Arborio and they can be used interchangeably. All of these rices contain more starch than other types of rice and it's this starch that is responsible for the creamy texture of risotto (for that reason, don't ever rinse risotto rice before cooking it). These rices also have the capacity to swell to over three times their size, which is why the liquid to rice ratio for risotto is so much higher than for other rices; of the three mentioned, Vialone has the greatest capacity for absorption. There are now domestically produced Arborio rices available.

Carnaroli, known as the king of rice, is often grown alongside Arborio. It is a short-grained *superfino* Italian rice that is slightly elongated and looks rather elegant. Carnaroli rice does not become mushy or lose its shape during the cooking process. As a result, this rice is the perfect base for risotto in the pressure cooker or in other creamy rice dishes since it blends with creamy ingredients without becoming too soft. A new hybrid of Carnaroli is just starting to be exported from Argentina by Lotus Foods and is considered equal, even superior, to Arborio.

In Venice and Verona, Vialone Nano is cooked until *all'onde,* or "wavy," which is a bit looser texture than usually directed in most risotto recipes.

For those who no longer eat white rice, in the last few years, the Italians have brought brown risotto rices to the market. There is Integrale (brown Arborio), Riso Venere (black risotto, which is Arborio crossed with Chinese Forbidden Black Rice), and Brown Carnaroli.

Risotto alla Milanese

Serves 2 to 3 as a main or 4 as a first course • Cooker: 5- to 7-quart • Time: 7 minutes at HIGH pressure

Risotto Milanese, or risotto with saffron, is one of the trademark dishes of Italian cuisine. It is usually eaten as a first course and washed down with a nice Chianti. Less common than Arborio rice, Vialone Nano is a hybrid that was developed in the Veneto region of Italy in the 1930s. It became popular in the U.S. when the infamous Harry's Bar opened its restaurant in New York, where the chef used only Vialone Nano to make his risotto. It tends to absorb more liquid than Arborio—resulting in a more flavorful dish. If you substitute Arborio or Carnaroli rice, reduce the stock to $2^{1}/_{4}$ cups. Serve as a side dish to veal *osso bucco* or *carbonata,* Italian beef stew.

1 tablespoon butter
1 tablespoon olive oil
1 small onion, chopped
$^{3}/_{4}$ teaspoon salt, plus more to taste
1 cup Vialone Nano or Carnaroli rice
$^{1}/_{3}$ cup dry white wine
$2^{1}/_{2}$ cups low-sodium chicken or vegetable broth
Large pinch saffron threads
$^{1}/_{3}$ cup freshly grated Grana Padano or Parmigiano-
    Reggiano cheese, plus extra for serving
6 to 8 grinds black pepper

1. In a 5 to 7-quart pressure cooker, heat the butter and oil over medium-high heat until the butter melts. Add the onion and salt and cook, stirring a few times, until the onion begins to soften, about 3 minutes. Add the rice, stirring to coat with the butter and oil. Pour in the wine. Rub the saffron threads between your fingers and add to the broth; pour into the pot.
2. Close and lock the lid. If you like, place a heat diffuser on the burner and the pressure cooker on the diffuser. Set the burner heat to high. When the cooker reaches HIGH pressure, reduce the burner heat as low as you can and still maintain HIGH pressure. Set a timer to cook for 7 minutes.
3. Remove the pot from the heat. Open the cooker with the Quick Release method. Be careful of the steam as you remove the lid. If the rice is not sufficiently cooked or the risotto is too soupy, place the pot over medium-high heat and cook, uncovered, stirring constantly, until the desired consistency is reached, 1 to 2 minutes.
4. Stir in the cheese and season with pepper. Taste, adding salt if needed.
5. Spoon out the rice with an oversized spoon to serving bowls to serve hot, with extra cheese for sprinkling on top, and the pepper grinder on the side.

Mixed Mushroom Risotto with Fresh Thyme and Asiago

Serves 2 to 3 as a main or 4 as a first course • Cooker: 5- to 7-quart • Time: 7 minutes at HIGH pressure

Restaurant-quality risotto is so easy—and inexpensive—to make at home, you'll want to add it to your weekly repertoire. In this version, even a modest number of wild mushrooms in the mix elevate the flavor off the charts. Cremini—which are baby portobellos—are ever so yummy.

2 tablespoons butter
1 tablespoon olive oil
$^1/_4$ cup finely chopped shallots
8 to 10 ounces mixed fresh mushrooms, such as chanterelles, shiitake (discard the stems), and/or cremini, sliced
2 teaspoons chopped fresh thyme
$^1/_2$ teaspoon salt, plus more to taste
1 cup Arborio or Carnaroli rice
$^1/_3$ cup dry white wine
$2^1/_4$ cups low-sodium chicken or vegetable broth
$^1/_3$ cup freshly grated Asiago cheese, plus extra for serving
6 to 8 turns freshly ground black pepper

1. In a 5 to 7-quart pressure cooker, heat the butter and oil together over medium-high heat until the butter melts. Add the shallots and cook until softened, 1 to 2 minutes. Stir in the mushrooms, 1 teaspoon of the thyme, and the salt. Add the rice, stirring to coat. Pour in the wine, scraping up any browned bits from the bottom of the pot. Stir in the broth.

2. Close and lock the lid. If you like, place a heat diffuser on the burner and the pressure cooker on the diffuser. Set the burner heat to high. When the cooker reaches HIGH pressure, reduce the burner heat as low as you can and still maintain HIGH pressure. Set a timer to cook for 7 minutes.

3. Remove the pot from the heat. Open the cooker with the Quick Release method. Be careful of the steam as you remove the lid. If the rice is not sufficiently cooked or the risotto is too soupy, place the pot over medium-high heat and cook, uncovered, stirring constantly, until the desired consistency is reached, 1 to 2 minutes.

4. Stir in the remaining 1 teaspoon thyme, then the cheese and season to taste with pepper. Taste, adding salt if needed.

5. Spoon out the rice with an oversized spoon to serving bowls to serve hot, with extra cheese for sprinkling on top, and the pepper grinder on the side.

Risotto with Italian Sausage and Kale

Serves 2 to 3 as a main or 4 as a first course • Cooker: 5- to 7-quart • Time: 7 minutes at HIGH pressure

Zesty Italian flavors make this a popular choice for casual weeknight dinners. A tossed green salad, crusty bread, and a glass of dry red wine round out the meal nicely.

1 tablespoon olive oil
8 ounces sweet or hot Italian sausage, removed from casings, if necessary
1 tablespoon butter
1 small onion, chopped
3 cups chopped fresh kale leaves
$^1/_2$ teaspoon salt, plus more to taste
$^1/_4$ teaspoon red pepper flakes
1 cup Arborio or Carnaroli rice
$^1/_3$ cup dry white wine
$2^1/_4$ cups low-sodium chicken or vegetable broth
$^1/_3$ cup freshly grated Parmesan cheese, plus extra for serving

1. In a 5- to 7-quart pressure cooker, heat the oil over medium-high heat until very hot. Add the sausage meat and cook, stirring and breaking it into bite-size pieces with a wooden spoon, until nicely browned and no longer pink, 5 to 7 minutes. Drain off all but 1 tablespoon of fat from the pot and add the butter. When the butter has melted, add the onion and cook, stirring a few times, until softened, about 3 minutes. Stir in the kale, salt, and pepper flakes. Add the rice, stirring to coat. Pour in the wine, scraping up any browned bits from the bottom of the pot. Stir in the broth.

2. Close and lock the lid. If you like, place a heat diffuser on the burner and the pressure cooker on the diffuser. Set the burner heat to high. When the cooker reaches HIGH pressure, reduce the burner heat as low as you can and still maintain HIGH pressure. Set a timer to cook for 7 minutes.

3. Remove the pot from the heat. Open the cooker with the Quick Release method. Be careful of the steam as you remove the lid. If the rice is not sufficiently cooked or the risotto is too soupy, place the pot over medium-high heat and cook, uncovered, stirring constantly, until the desired consistency is reached, 1 to 2 minutes.

4. Stir in the cheese and taste, adding more salt if needed.

5. Serve at once in warm shallow bowls. Pass more cheese at the table.

CHEESE, PLEASE

The Italians are sticklers for the right cheese to be used with risotto: Parmigiano-Reggiano. Buy a chunk of imported, even just a little bit, if you can, otherwise domestic is okay. You can also use Romano Pecorino (it is quite a bit stronger than Parmesan), Asiago (known as the poor man's Parmesan), Grana Padano or a Parmesan-Romano combination, if you like. We like it shredded as well as finely grated. Nontraditionalists should feel free to experiment.

Lemony Artichoke Risotto with Olives

Serves 2 to 3 as a main or 4 as first course • Cooker: 5- to 7-quart • Time: 7 minutes at HIGH pressure

Frozen artichoke hearts are always a time-saver; and even more so when paired with the pressure cooker. Due to the intense heat that builds up under pressure, it is not necessary to thaw them before adding to the pot. If the artichoke hearts are frozen together, simply break them apart.

1 tablespoon butter
1 tablespoon olive oil
$^1/_4$ cup finely chopped shallots
9 to 12 ounces frozen artichoke hearts
$^3/_4$ teaspoon salt, plus more to taste
2 teaspoons chopped fresh lemon thyme or basil
1 cup Arborio or Carnaroli rice
$^1/_3$ cup dry white wine
$2^1/_4$ cups low-sodium chicken or vegetable broth
$^1/_3$ cup coarsely chopped pitted Kalamata olives
Finely grated zest and juice of 1 lemon
$^1/_3$ cup freshly grated Pecorino Romano cheese, plus extra for serving
6 to 8 grinds black pepper, to taste

1. In a 5- to 7-quart pressure cooker, heat the butter and oil together over medium-high heat until the butter melts. Add the shallots and cook, stirring a few times, until softened, 1 to 2 minutes. Stir in the artichoke hearts, salt, and 1 teaspoon of the thyme. Add the rice, stirring to coat. Pour in the wine, broth, olives, and lemon zest and juice.
2. Close and lock the lid. If you like, place a heat diffuser on the burner and the pressure cooker on the diffuser. Set the burner heat to high. When the cooker reaches HIGH pressure, reduce the burner heat as low as you can and still maintain HIGH pressure. Set a timer to cook for 7 minutes.
3. Remove the pot from the heat. Open the cooker with the Quick Release method. Be careful of the steam as you remove the lid. If the rice is not sufficiently cooked or the risotto is too soupy, place the pot over medium-high heat and cook uncovered, stirring constantly, until the desired consistency is reached, 1 to 2 minutes.
4. Stir the cheese and remaining 1 teaspoon thyme into the risotto. Season with pepper. Taste, adding salt if needed.
5. Serve at once in warm shallow bowls. Pass more cheese at the table.

Black Rice, Fava, and Cauliflower Risotto

Serves 2 as a main or 4 as a first course • Cooker: 5- to 7-quart • Time: 18 minutes for risotto, 2 minutes for cauliflower at HIGH pressure

The season is short for fresh fava beans, so feel free to use frozen ones, or substitute frozen shelled edamame (green soy beans). Fresh fava beans have to be removed from their large green, outer pods, then blanched and the translucent inner skin removed from each bean. It's a bit labor-intensive but they are delicious. We give the method for that here.

1 tablespoon olive oil
2 tablespoons butter
$1/4$ cup minced shallots
1 cup Riso Venere
$1/4$ cup dry white wine
2 cups low-sodium chicken or vegetable broth
2 cups water
$2^1/2$ cups bite-size cauliflower florets
$1/2$ cup fresh or frozen shelled fava beans or frozen shelled edamame
$1/4$ cup freshly grated Grana Padano or Parmigiano-Reggiano cheese, plus extra for serving
$1/4$ teaspoon freshly black ground pepper
Sea salt

1. In a 5- to 7-quart pressure cooker, heat the oil and 1 tablespoon of the butter over medium-high heat until the butter melts. Add the shallots and cook, stirring a few times, until softened, about 2 minutes. Add the rice and cook about 2 minutes, stirring constantly, to evenly coat the grains. Add the wine and stir until the wine is absorbed. Add the broth and water.
2. Close and lock the lid. If you like, place a heat diffuser on the burner and the pressure cooker on the diffuser. Set the burner heat to high. When the cooker reaches HIGH pressure, reduce the burner heat as low as you can and still maintain HIGH pressure. Set a timer to cook for 18 minutes.
3. Meanwhile, if you are using fresh fava beans, this is a good time to prepare them. Remove the beans from their pods. Bring a saucepan of salted water to a boil, add the beans, and blanch for 1 minute. Drain the beans and cool them quickly in a bowl of ice water. Using your fin-

gernails or a small paring knife, slit the translucent skin of each bean, remove, and discard it, leaving just the bright green bean. Set the prepared beans aside.
4. Remove the pot from the heat. Open the cooker with the Quick Release method. Be careful of the steam as you remove the lid.
5. Stir in the cauliflower. Relock the cooker and bring back up to HIGH pressure. Set a timer for 2 minutes.
6. Remove from the heat. Open the cooker with the Quick Release method. Stir in the fava beans or edamame. Top with the remaining 1 tablespoon butter, the cheese, and pepper. Replace the cover and let stand a few minutes to melt the butter and let the risotto thicken. Stir the risotto, taste, and add salt if desired.
7. Serve hot, with extra cheese for sprinkling and the pepper grinder on the side.

BLACK VENUS RICE

One of our favorite things about living and cooking in this foodie age is the development of exciting and healthful new foods. Riso Venere, or Black Venus rice, is one of these foods. A cross between Chinese Black Forbidden rice and an Italian variety, Riso Venere is a medium-grain, oval-shaped black grain cultivated in Italy alongside Arborio. Riso Venere is a whole grain—in other words, the outer bran layer is intact—so for cooking, it is comparable to a brown rice. You will also be using more liquid than with white risotto rices. We were thrilled when we discovered that it makes a lovely and strikingly beautiful risotto—and in only 20 minutes in the pressure cooker. A heads up: Riso Venere will slightly discolor whatever ingredients you add during cooking—in the case of this particular risotto, it will turn the cauliflower pale pink. The fava beans are added after cooking to keep them bright green.

Black Rice Risotto with Fire-Roasted Tomatoes and Mozzarella

Serves 2 as a main or 4 as a first course • Cooker: 5- to 7-quart • Time: 20 minutes at HIGH pressure

A tomato risotto for when you have the winter blues, with our favorite cheese, mozzarella, streaked through, all nice and melted. You can substitute smoked mozzarella if you can find it.

1 tablespoon olive oil
2 tablespoons butter
$1/4$ cup minced shallots
1 cup Riso Venere
$1/2$ cup dry white wine
$3^1/2$ cups vegetable broth
1 (14.5-ounce) can fire-roasted tomatoes in juice, undrained
Sea salt
3 to 4 tablespoons chopped fresh basil leaves
3 ounces whole-milk mozzarella, cut into small dice
$1/4$ cup freshly grated Parmigiano-Reggiano cheese, for serving
Freshly ground black ground pepper

1. In a 5- to 7-quart pressure cooker, heat the oil and 1 tablespoon of the butter together over medium-high heat until the butter melts. Add the shallots and cook, stirring a few times, until softened, about 2 minutes. Add the rice and cook about 2 minutes, stirring constantly, to evenly coat the grains of rice. Add the wine and stir until it is absorbed. Add the broth and tomatoes with their juices.
2. Close and lock the lid. If you like, place a heat diffuser on the burner and the pressure cooker on the diffuser. Set the burner heat to high. When the cooker reaches HIGH pressure, reduce the burner heat as low as you can and still maintain HIGH pressure. Set a timer to cook for 20 minutes.
3. Remove the pot from the heat. Open the cooker with the Quick Release method. Be careful of the steam as you remove the lid.
4. Taste for salt and stir in the basil and remaining butter. Fold in the mozzarella. Replace the cover; let stand a few minutes to melt the cheese and let the risotto thicken.
5. Serve hot, with the cheese for sprinkling and the pepper grinder on the side.

Black Rice Risotto with Shrimp and Fresh Basil

Serves 4 as a main or 8 as a first course • Cooker: 5- to 7-quart • Time: 20 minutes at HIGH pressure

Slightly nutty, chewy black Riso Venere pairs beautifully with shrimp in this simple risotto, which gets bright notes of flavor from a sprinkle of fresh basil. Because the black pigment in the rice will turn shrimp a gray-black color, a special technique is required. Chop about one-third of the shrimp and cook with the rice. Reserve the remaining shrimp and sauté them separately in a skillet while the risotto finishes cooking. Before serving, divide the sautéed shrimp among the plates. This way you get the best of both worlds—shrimp flavor in the rice and beautiful, pink and white shrimp atop each serving.

3 tablespoons olive oil
3 tablespoons unsalted butter
$1/3$ cup minced shallots
$1^1/2$ cups Riso Venere
$1/2$ cup dry white wine
3 cups low-sodium chicken broth
3 cups water
1 pound medium (31–40 count) shrimp, peeled and deveined
$1/2$ teaspoon freshly ground black pepper
Salt
$1/2$ cup fresh basil leaves, sliced across into fine ribbons

1. In a 5- to 7-quart pressure cooker, heat 2 tablespoons each of the oil and butter over medium-high heat until the butter melts. Add the shallots and cook, stirring a few times, until softened, about 2 minutes. Add the rice and cook about 2 minutes, stirring constantly, to evenly coat the grains of rice. Add the wine and stir until it is absorbed. Add the broth and water. Chop about one third of the shrimp into $1/2$-inch pieces. Stir the pieces into the rice mixture.

2. Close and lock the lid. If you like, place a heat diffuser on the burner and the pressure cooker on the diffuser. Set the burner heat to high. When the cooker reaches HIGH pressure, reduce the burner heat as low as you can and still maintain HIGH pressure. Set a timer to cook for 20 minutes.

3. When there is about 5 minutes left on the timer, sauté the remaining shrimp. Heat the remaining 1 tablespoon oil and butter in a 12-inch skillet over medium-high heat until sizzling. Add the shrimp and cook until they are just pink and opaque throughout, 2 to 4 minutes, stirring a few times.

4. Remove the pot from the heat. Open the cooker with the Quick Release method. Be careful of the steam as you remove the lid.

5. Season with the pepper, stir, and add salt to taste. Replace the cover and let stand a moment or two to let the risotto thicken.

6. Divide the risotto among four plates or shallow bowls. Top each serving with one-quarter of the sautéed shrimp, nestling some of them gently into the risotto and leaving the rest on top where they will keep their color. Sprinkle each serving with basil ribbons. Serve immediately.

Parmesan Risotto with Brown Carnaroli

Serves 3 as a main or 6 as a first course • Cooker: 5- to 7-quart • Time: 22 minutes at HIGH pressure

Brown Carnaroli rice has the outer bran left on so the finished rice is chewier than white Arborio or regular Carnaroli. It also has a slightly more distinct flavor and holds it shape since it is a bit larger grain. Brown Carnaroli has more starch than other types of brown rices, but don't expect a risotto made with it to be quite as creamy and delicate as one made with a white rice. In fact, the rice will not turn creamy until the very end of cooking. As with other brown rices, you will be using more liquid and triple the cooking time.

2 tablespoons olive oil
$^{1}/_{4}$ cup ($^{1}/_{2}$ stick) butter
$^{1}/_{4}$ cup finely chopped shallots
$1^{1}/_{2}$ cups Brown Carnaroli rice
3 cups low-sodium chicken or vegetable broth
3 cups water
$^{1}/_{2}$ cup dry white wine
$^{3}/_{4}$ to 1 cup freshly grated Parmesan cheese, to taste, plus extra for serving
Salt and freshly ground black pepper

1. In a 5- to 7-quart pressure cooker or $2^{1}/_{2}$-quart skillet pressure cooker, heat the oil and 2 tablespoons of the butter together over medium heat until the butter melts. Add the shallots and cook, stirring a few times, until softened, about 2 minutes. Add the rice and cook 1 minute, stirring constantly, to evenly coat the grains. Add the broth, water, and wine.
2. Close and lock the lid. If you like, place a heat diffuser on the burner and the pressure cooker on the diffuser. Set the burner heat to high. When the cooker reaches HIGH pressure, reduce the burner heat as low as you can and still maintain HIGH pressure. Set a timer to cook for 22 minutes.
3. Remove the pot from the heat. Open the cooker with the Quick Release method. Be careful of the steam as you remove the lid.
4. Stir in the cheese, the remaining 2 tablespoons butter, and pepper to taste. Replace the cover and let stand a few minutes to thicken and set up. Taste for salt.

5. Spoon out the rice to shallow serving bowls to serve hot, with extra cheese for sprinkling and the pepper grinder on the side.

Parmesan Risotto with Pesto: In Step 4, also stir in 3 tablespoons of your favorite pesto until evenly combined.

Parmesan Risotto with Four Cheeses: In Step 4, substitute for the Parmesan $^{1}/_{2}$ cup grated Gruyère cheese, $^{1}/_{2}$ cup diced fontina cheese, $^{1}/_{2}$ cup crumbled Gorgonzola, and $^{1}/_{2}$ cup grated or shredded Parmesan. Stir gently to melt the cheeses. Sprinkle with chopped fresh flatleaf parsley and black pepper.

Parmesan Risotto with Poached Eggs: Bring a large frying pan of water to simmer over medium-low heat. Sprinkle the water with salt. Working with 1 egg at a time, crack 6 large eggs into a small bowl and slide each egg into the simmering water. Cook the eggs until the whites are opaque but the yolks are still runny, 3 to 4 minutes. Top each bowl of risotto with a poached egg, transferring it with a slotted spoon. Sprinkle the egg with salt and pepper to taste, minced fresh flatleaf parsley, and additional cheese. This is an unconventional but delicious breakfast treat with crispy bacon strips on the side.

Brown Carnaroli Risotto with Zucchini, Arugula, and Peas

Serves 3 as a main or 6 as a first course • Cooker: 5- to 7-quart • Time: 22 minutes at HIGH pressure

Rich and creamy, this vegetable risotto is Italian-style comfort food. This is also good with baby spinach leaves in place of the arugula.

4 tablespoons olive oil
$1/4$ cup finely chopped shallots or white onion
$1^1/2$ cups Brown Carnaroli rice
$3^1/2$ cups low-sodium chicken or vegetable broth
3 cups water
1 large or 2 medium zucchini (10 to 12 ounces), cut into $1/2$-inch dice
1 cup frozen petite peas, thawed
1 ($1/2$-pound) bunch arugula, large stems discarded and leaves coarsely chopped
Salt and freshly ground black pepper
2 tablespoons butter
$3/4$ to 1 cup freshly grated Parmesan cheese, to taste

1. In a 5- to 7-quart pressure cooker or $2^1/2$-quart skillet pressure cooker, heat 2 tablespoons of the oil over medium heat until hot. Add the shallots and cook, stirring a few times, until softened, about 2 minute. Add the rice and cook 1 minute, stirring constantly, to evenly coat the grains. Add 3 cups of the broth and the water.

2. Close and lock the lid. If you like, place a heat diffuser on the burner and the pressure cooker on the diffuser. Set the burner heat to high. When the cooker reaches HIGH pressure, reduce the burner heat as low as you can and still maintain HIGH pressure. Set a timer to cook for 22 minutes.

3. Meanwhile, in a large skillet, heat the remaining 2 tablespoons over medium-high heat. Add the zucchini and cook until just tender, about 2 minutes, stirring constantly. Add the peas and arugula and cook until the arugula is wilted, about 1 minute. Add the remaining $1/2$ cup broth, season to taste with salt and pepper and bring to a simmer. Remove from the heat and set aside until the risotto is done.

4. Remove the pot from the heat. Open the cooker with the Quick Release method. Be careful of the steam as you remove the lid.

5. Stir in the butter. Replace the cover and let stand a few minutes to thicken and set up.

6. Stir the vegetables and their liquid into the risotto and heat, uncovered, over medium heat until the rice is creamy, about 1 minute. Season the risotto with salt and pepper to taste.

7. Spoon the risotto into shallow bowls and serve with the Parmesan on the side for sprinkling.

Asparagus Risotto with Brown Carnaroli

Serves 3 as a main or 6 as a first course • Cooker: 5- to 7-quart • Time: 22 minutes at HIGH pressure

Carnaroli rice is considered the premium risotto rice of Italy. It was developed by a Milanese rice grower who successfully crossed the plump Vialone Nano white risotto rice with a Japanese rice. It is characterized by the outer layer that dissolves in cooking, leaving the ever so al dente inner grain. Use the thin stalks of asparagus if you can find them.

2 tablespoons olive oil
4 tablespoons butter
$^1/_4$ cup finely chopped shallots
1 bunch thin fresh asparagus, bottoms trimmed and
    stalks cut into 1-inch pieces
1$^1/_2$ cups Brown Carnaroli rice
3 cups vegetable broth
3 cups water
$^1/_2$ cup dry white wine
2 tablespoons fresh lemon juice
1 cup frozen petite peas, thawed
$^1/_2$ cup chopped fresh flatleaf parsley
$^1/_2$ cup freshly grated Parmesan cheese, plus extra
    for serving
Salt and freshly ground black pepper

1. In a 5- to 7-quart pressure cooker or 2$^1/_2$-quart skillet pressure cooker, heat the oil and 2 tablespoons of the butter together over medium heat until the butter melts. Add the shallots and asparagus, and cook, stirring a few times, until the shallots are softened, about 2 minutes. Add the rice and cook 1 minute, stirring constantly, to evenly coat the grains. Add the broth, water, and wine.

2. Close and lock the lid. If you like, place a heat diffuser on the burner and the pressure cooker on the diffuser. Set the burner heat to high. When the cooker reaches HIGH pressure, reduce the burner heat as low as you can and still maintain HIGH pressure. Set a timer to cook for 22 minutes.

3. Remove the pot from the heat. Open the cooker with the Quick Release method. Be careful of the steam as you remove the lid.

4. Stir in the lemon juice, peas, parsley, cheese, the remaining 2 tablespoons butter, and pepper to taste. Replace the cover and let stand a few minutes to thicken and set up. Taste for salt.

5. Serve the risotto in shallow serving bowls, with extra cheese for sprinkling on top and the pepper grinder on the side.

White Bean Risotto with Brown Carnaroli

Serves 3 as a main or 6 as a first course • Cooker: 5- to 7-quart • Time: 22 minutes at HIGH pressure

This is one of our favorite main-dish risottos. It has flavor and fragrance, and is very filling. It only needs a salad as accompaniment.

2 tablespoons olive oil
4 tablespoons ($^1/_2$ stick) butter
$^1/_2$ cup finely chopped white onion
$^1/_2$ fennel bulb, stalks discarded, bulb chopped
$1^1/_2$ cups Brown Carnaroli rice
3 cups reduced-sodium vegetable broth
3 cups water
2 tablespoons fresh lemon juice
1 (15-ounce) can white beans, such as Great Northern or navy, drained and rinsed, or $1^3/_4$ to 2 cups fresh cooked white beans
$^1/_3$ cup chopped fresh flatleaf parsley
Salt and freshly ground black pepper
$^1/_2$ to 1 cup freshly shaved Parmesan cheese, to taste

1. In a 5- to 7-quart pressure cooker or $2^1/_2$-quart skillet pressure cooker, heat the oil and 2 tablespoons of the butter over medium heat until the butter melts. Add the onion and fennel and cook, stirring a few times, until softened, about 3 minutes. Add the rice and cook 1 minute, stirring constantly, to evenly coat the grains. Add the broth and water.
2. Close and lock the lid. If you like, place a heat diffuser on the burner and the pressure cooker on the diffuser. Set the burner heat to high. When the cooker reaches HIGH pressure, reduce the burner heat as low as you can and still maintain HIGH pressure. Set a timer to cook for 22 minutes.
3. Remove the pot from the heat. Open the cooker with the Quick Release method. Be careful of the steam as you remove the lid.
4. Stir in the lemon juice, beans, parsley, the remaining 2 tablespoons butter, and pepper to taste. Cook, uncovered, over medium heat a few minutes to heat the beans. Taste for salt.
5. Serve the risotto in shallow serving bowls with the shaved Parmesan cheese on top and the pepper grinder on the side.

White Bean Risotto with Butternut Squash: Substitute $1^1/_2$ cups diced peeled butternut squash for the fennel bulb. Sauté with the onion and proceed with the recipe.

SHAVING PARMESAN CHEESE

This is ever so easy to do with a vegetable peeler and makes for a very elegant presentation.

Jook (Chinese Rice Porridge)

Serves 4 as a light main dish or 6 as a snack or side dish • Cooker: 5- to 7-quart • Time: 15 minutes at HIGH pressure

Jook, also known as congee, is the definition of Chinese comfort food. It is simple as can be: white rice cooked in plenty of broth or water until it falls apart. It is eaten for breakfast, as a late-night snack, or anytime a creamy and sustaining dish is in order. Flavor comes from slivers of meat or vegetables, a dash of this or that (soy sauce and sesame oil are popular additions), and toppings that range from the simple (green onions or sesame seeds) to those that require a trip to the Chinese market (preserved or "century eggs"). Jook takes a long time to cook on the stove, but with the pressure cooker you will be spooning up warming bites before you know it. Don't try to use the Quick Release function with jook—you will create a sputtering mess. Use a short-, medium-, or long-grain white rice, but not any of the risotto rices or basmati. Medium-grain Calrose rice is a nice choice.

1 cup short-, medium-, or long-grain white rice, or combination of the three
4 cups reduced-sodium chicken or vegetable broth
1 cup water
4 quarter-size slices peeled fresh ginger
Salt and white or black pepper

TO SERVE, ANY OR ALL OF THE FOLLOWING:
$^1/_2$ cup thin matchsticks of ham or leftover cooked chicken
$^1/_2$ cup frozen peas
2 tablespoons thinly sliced green onions (white and tender green parts) or chopped fresh cilantro
A few drops of sesame oil per serving

1. In a 5- to 7-quart pressure cooker, combine the rice, broth, and water. Add the ginger.
2. Close and lock the lid. Place a heat diffuser on the burner and the pressure cooker on the diffuser. Set the burner heat to high. When the cooker reaches HIGH pressure, reduce the burner heat as low as you can and still maintain HIGH pressure. Set a timer to cook for 15 minutes.
3. Remove the pot from the heat. Open the cooker with the Natural Release method; let stand for 20 minutes. At time, if the pressure is not all released, open the valve. Be careful of the steam as you remove the lid.
4. Stir the porridge briskly; most of the rice should have broken down and the porridge should be the consistency of a thick soup or oatmeal. If it's not quite done, simmer it for a few minutes, uncovered. Using tongs or a pair of chopsticks, remove the ginger slices. Season the porridge with salt and pepper to taste. Stir in the ham or chicken if using and frozen peas (which will thaw very quickly in the hot porridge).
5. Serve in bowls, topped with a sprinkle of scallions and a drizzle of sesame oil.

Creamy Jook: Add 1 cup plain soy milk in Step 4 and simmer a few minutes to heat, for an ultra-creamy consistency.

Turkey and Shiitake Jook

Serves 4 • Cooker: 6- to 8-quart • Time: 25 minutes at HIGH pressure

One familiar kind of jook in Chinese-American households is made with a turkey carcass over Thanksgiving weekend. Our friend and former food editor at the *San Jose Mercury News,* Carolyn Jung, always makes her family recipe for jook with the carcass and a ham bone, which she keeps in the freezer waiting for jook day. We couldn't fit the bones and 21 cups of liquid into our pressure cooker, but love the turkey version, so here is one adapted for our pressure cooker by the late Shirley Fong-Torres, one of our beloved local San Francisco culinary specialists, from a *Cooking Light* recipe some years ago. Shirley was a best-selling food writer, dim sum lover, and culinary tour guide and known as the unofficial mayor of San Francisco's Chinatown for her Wok Wiz Chinatown Tours tourist walking tours, educating everyone who was interested about the Chinese immigrants and their culture. She knew her jook.

4 dried shiitake mushrooms
1 cup long-grain white rice, such as jasmine
8 cups water
1 fresh turkey wing (about 1 pound)
4 quarter-size slices peeled fresh ginger
2 teaspoons sea salt

TO SERVE:
1/4 cup thinly sliced green onions (white and tender green parts)
Chopped fresh cilantro or flatleaf parsley
Reduced-sodium soy sauce
White pepper

1. In a small bowl, soak the shiitake mushrooms in hot water to cover for 20 minutes. Drain, discard the tough stems, rinse, and coarsely chop. Set aside.
2. In a 6- to 8-quart pressure cooker, combine the rice, water, turkey wing, ginger, and salt. Add the ginger.
3. Close and lock the lid. Place a heat diffuser on the burner and the pressure cooker on the diffuser. Set the burner heat to high. When the cooker reaches HIGH pressure, reduce the burner heat as low as you can and still maintain HIGH pressure. Set a timer to cook for 25 minutes at HIGH pressure.
4. Remove the pot from the heat. Open the cooker with the Natural Release method; let stand for 20 minutes. At time, if the pressure is not all released, open the valve. Be careful of the steam as you remove the lid.
5. Remove the turkey from the soup; place it on a cutting board or work surface. Discard the ginger. Stir in the shiitakes. Let cool 10 minutes. Meanwhile, remove the skin from the turkey, discard. Remove the meat from the bones; discard the bones. Chop the meat into bite-size pieces and stir into the soup. Stir the porridge briskly; most of the rice should have broken down and the porridge should be a creamy consistency. Season with white pepper to taste.
6. Ladle the jook into deep bowls, ones you can hold in your hands and drink from, sprinkle with the green onions and cilantro, and serve with soy sauce. Leftover jook will keep in the refrigerator for a few days. If after reheating, the jook seems too thick, add a little water or stock to thin it to desired consistency. You also can freeze jook in an airtight container for up to 3 months.

Dev's Kitchari with Cumin Seeds

Serves 4 • Cooker: 6- to 8-quart • Time: 15 minutes at HIGH pressure

Kitchari is a favorite Indian vegetarian breakfast porridge, savory instead of sweet. It is often eaten after a fast, or along with extremely simple foods and lots of water to rest the digestive tract. Cleanses of one meal to several days featuring this simple, nourishing porridge are popular. Almost every Indian cookbook has a recipe for it, but it is practically unknown in American cooking circles. It is comfort food, Eastern style, tasting like a cross between lentil soup and rice cereal. Serve it with a dollop of plain Greek yogurt on top or a pat of butter or ghee swirled in, sprinkled with chopped cilantro if you happen to have some, and/or lemon or lime wedges and warm chapati or flour tortillas.

2 to 3 tablespoons ghee or neutral-tasting oil
1 heaping teaspoon white cumin seeds
1 cup split moong dal, rinsed and picked over for stones and debris
1 cup basmati rice, rinsed until the water runs clear
7 cups water
Few pinches salt, plus more to taste
About 2 to 3 cups mixed vegetables, cut into small, even-sized chunks, such as carrot and red potato (a favorite); or cauliflower, green beans, and peas; or zucchini and green bell pepper.
1 bunch fresh spinach, rinsed well, leaves separated, thick stems discarded, and leaves cut across into thick ribbons

1. In a 6- to 8-quart pressure cooker, heat the ghee over medium-high heat until very hot. Add the cumin seeds and cook just until they start to pop and sputter; let sizzle for a few seconds. Add the rice and dal into the pot, stirring to coat with the ghee. Add the water and salt. Bring to a boil. Stir and skim off any froth with a large spoon.

2. Close and lock the lid. Set the burner heat to high. When the cooker reaches HIGH pressure, reduce the burner heat as low as you can and still maintain HIGH pressure. Set a timer to cook for 15 minutes.

3. Remove the pot from the heat. Open the cooker with the Natural Release method; let stand for 15 minutes. At time, if the pressure is not all released, open the valve. Be careful of the steam as you remove the lid. If the kitchari is too thick, add about 1 cup boiling water to thin. The porridge should be like thin oatmeal in consistency.

4. Add the vegetables and spinach and stir. Simmer, uncovered, over low heat until the vegetables are tender, but not mushy, about 10 minutes. (The smaller you chop the vegetables, the faster they will cook.) Taste for salt. Stir once. Serve in deep bowls.

Hot Cinnamon Rice and Quinoa with Breakfast Fruit Salad

Serves 4 • Cooker: 5- to 7-quart • Time: 12 minutes at HIGH pressure

Sweet brown rice is a glutinous short-grain brown rice grown in the U.S. It is used for Asian mochi, snacks, sushi, and desserts like rice pudding (it is not the same as regular short-grain brown rice). It makes a marvelous breakfast rice, cooking up to a consistency similar to that of risotto, rich and filling. Here it is mixed with quinoa and topped with a fresh fruit salad. Red quinoa has twice the protein of rice and is very easy to digest. It has a slightly more pronounced flavor than white quinoa. Be sure to give it a good rinse (until the water is clear) before cooking to avoid bitterness. It is available from Lundberg Farms and Purcell Mountain Farms.

2 cups sweet brown rice
1 cup red quinoa, rinsed in a fine mesh strainer
$1/2$ to 1 teaspoon ground cinnamon, to taste
1 teaspoon sea salt
$5^1/2$ cups water
3 tablespoons unsalted butter
$1/4$ cup honey or maple syrup, plus extra for serving
Almond milk, dairy milk, half-and-half, or rice milk, for serving

BREAKFAST FRUIT SALAD:
1 cup fresh blueberries
1 cup fresh strawberries
$1/2$ cup fresh raspberries
$1/2$ cup fresh blackberries
1 ripe plum, pitted and chopped, or 1 small tangerine, peeled and sections cut in half
1 kiwi fruit, peeled, sliced, and slices cut into fourths
1 small banana (optional), sliced

1. In a 5- to 7-quart pressure cooker, combine the rice, quinoa, cinnamon, salt, and water. Stir.
2. Close and lock the lid. Place a heat diffuser on the burner and the pressure cooker on the diffuser. Set the burner heat to high. When the cooker reaches HIGH pressure, reduce the burner heat as low as you can and still maintain HIGH pressure. Set a timer to cook for 12 minutes at HIGH pressure.
3. Remove the pot from the heat. Open the cooker with the Natural Release method; let stand for 15 minutes. At time, if the pressure is not all released, open the valve. The rice should be creamy and the quinoa melted into it, turning light brown and slightly transparent, its curly string-like germ separated from the circular part. Stir in the butter and honey.
4. Prepare the fruit salad while waiting for the grains. Rinse the berries and let drain in a small colander. Hull the strawberries and cut in half or quarters. Place the berries in a medium bowl. Add the plum, tangerine, and kiwi. Toss to mix.
5. Stir the cereal well and scoop into serving bowls. Serve with a few splashes of the milk of your choice and top with plenty of the fruit salad. Drizzle the top with more honey or maple syrup if you want the fruit sweeter.

Hot Rice and Oatmeal with Dried Fruit and Coconut

Serves 4 to 6 • Cooker: 5- to 7-quart • Time: 7 minutes at HIGH pressure

This is a breakfast favorite.

1 cup old-fashioned or thick-cut rolled oats
$^2/_3$ cup short- or long-grain brown rice, soaked 4 hours or overnight in water to cover and drained
2 tablespoons oat bran or toasted wheat germ
$^1/_2$ teaspoon apple pie spice or ground cinnamon with a pinch of cloves, nutmeg, and allspice added
Pinch sea salt
5 cups water
$^1/_2$ cup golden raisins or dried cherries, blueberries, or cranberries
$^1/_4$ cup chopped dried pitted prunes
$^1/_4$ cup chopped dried apricots
1 tablespoon butter
$^2/_3$ cup shredded sweetened coconut, for serving
Milk, half-and-half, almond milk, coconut milk, or rice milk, for serving

1. In a 5- to 7-quart pressure cooker, combine the oats, rice, oat bran, spice, salt, and water. Stir in the dried fruit and butter.
2. Close and lock the lid. Place a heat diffuser on the burner and the pressure cooker on the diffuser. Set the burner heat to high. When the cooker reaches HIGH pressure, reduce the burner heat as low as you can and still maintain HIGH pressure. Set a timer to cook for 10 minutes.
3. Remove the pot from the heat. Open the cooker with the Natural Release method; let stand for 20 minutes. At time, if the pressure is not all released, open the valve.
4. Stir well and scoop into serving bowls. Sprinkle each serving with the coconut. Serve with a few splashes of the milk of your choice.

OATS

Today nearly half of the world's oat crop, more than 4 billion bushels a year, is grown in the U.S. and Canada. Oat kernels look very much like wheat in structure. They have an outer covering of bran, which protects the starchy endosperm and the germ that sits at the bottom of the grain. Because the oat kernel is soft, the nutritious bran is not removed. Oatmeal is considered a health food because of the beta-glucan soluble fiber, B vitamins, and complex carbohydrates it contains. All that and it tastes great! Quaker Oats Company sets the industry standard for rolled oat thickness, so theirs is considered REGULAR old-fashioned rolled oats. If they are thicker, they are called THICK old-fashioned rolled oats. We love Bob's Red Mill and they also carry gluten-free rolled oats along with regular rolled oats. Remember that, as with everything, the better the quality of the food that you put into your body, the better your body will feel.

Breakfast Risotto with Apples and Dried Cranberries

Serves 4 to 6 • Cooker: 5- to 7-quart • Time: 7 minutes at HIGH pressure

A tasty way to start the day! The pressure cooker cooks this risotto up so fast that you can enjoy it for breakfast, especially if you have the ingredients laid out and ready. It's delicious topped with plain Greek yogurt.

2 tablespoons butter
1 1/2 cups Arborio or Vialone Nano medium-grain rice
Grated zest of 1 orange
2 tart large apples, peeled, cored, and chopped
1 teaspoon ground cinnamon
1/2 cup firmly packed light brown sugar
1 cup unsweetened apple juice or apple cider
3 cups whole milk (can be part half-and-half)
2/3 cup dried cranberries
Plain Greek yogurt, for serving
Milk or half-and-half, for serving
Slivered almonds, for serving

1. In a 5- to 7-quart pressure cooker or 2 1/2-quart skillet pressure cooker over medium heat, melt the butter. Add the rice and stir for 1 minute to evenly coat the grains. Add the orange zest, apples, cinnamon, apple juice, and milk. Bring to a boil and stir.
2. Close and lock the lid. Place a heat diffuser on the burner and the pressure cooker on the diffuser. Set the burner heat to high. When the cooker reaches HIGH pressure, reduce the burner heat as low as you can and still maintain HIGH pressure. Set a timer to cook for 7 minutes at HIGH pressure.
3. Remove the pot from the heat. Open the cooker with the Natural Release method; let stand for 7 minutes. At time, if the pressure is not all released, open the valve and use Quick Release. Stir in the cranberries, which will plump in the hot cereal.
4. Serve in bowls with a spoonful of plain Greek yogurt and sprinkled with slivered almonds, if desired. If you like your cereal soupy, pour over some milk or half-and-half at eating time.

12

Global Grains and Pastas

A pressure cooker makes quick work of grains, heart-healthy ingredients that often require lots of soaking and long cooking times. Check your pressure cooker's manual for any specific guidelines about handling grains in your model, as whole grains will foam as they cook.

You'll find a selection of recipes for some of our favorite grains in this chapter (also be sure to check out the rice recipes—including wild rice—on pages 317–357). You'll find a complete listing of grains in our Pressure Cooking Grains chart.

WHAT IS A WHOLE GRAIN?

In order for a grain to be labeled whole, it must retain 100% of its bran (the fiber), germ (vitamins and EFAs), and endosperm (starchy carbs). There's one main exception to this rule; because barley is extremely high in protein and other nutrients throughout even its endosperm, many consider it a whole grain even when it may not *technically* qualify. Corn, rye, and wheat are what are referred to as "naked" grains, meaning that they're made up of 100% edible parts right from the stalk. But most of the grains we eat are encased in an inedible hull. Some are more easily removed than others; in certain cases, as with barley, it's exceedingly difficult to hull the grain without removing some or all of the bran and germ.

TIPS FOR COOKING WITH GRAINS IN THE PRESSURE COOKER

- Store whole grains in the freezer to prevent them from going rancid.
- Some grains need cleaning before cooking; each recipe will be specific.
- Most grains will create foam when cooked in the pressure cooker; adding a bit of oil or butter to the pot will keep this from happening. If making a dish that contains some fat, you do not need to add extra.
- Do not fill the pressure cooker more than one-half full before cooking; you need to leave room for expansion.
- Many grains' starches harden when they are chilled after cooking. If you plan to use grains in salads served cold, cook them as you normally would, drain and rinse, then either cool at room temperature (rather than refrigerating), or toss with a bit of olive oil or dressing before refrigerating to avoid this.
- The cooking liquid can be water or your choice of broth.
- If the grain is not done at the end of the cook time indicated, lock the lid, bring the pot back to pressure, and steam a few minutes longer.
- For all of these grains, open the cooker using the Natural Release method.
- For these amounts, use a 5- to 7-quart pressure cooker.
- Adding salt to the cooking liquid is optional.

PRESSURE COOKING GRAINS

Grain (1 cup)	Liquid	Cook Time at High Pressure
Amaranth	2$\frac{1}{4}$ cups	4 minutes
Barley, hulled or pot	3 cups	20 to 25 minutes
Barley, pearled	2$\frac{3}{4}$ cups	18 minutes
Barley, purple	3 cups	25 minutes
Buckwheat groats (kasha)	2 cups	5 minutes
Couscous, regular	1$\frac{1}{2}$ cups	1 to 2 minutes
Couscous, whole wheat and brown rice	1$\frac{3}{4}$ cups	3 to 4 minutes
Cracked bulgur wheat	2 cups	4 to 6 minutes
Einkorn (farro piccolo)	2 cups	5 minutes
Farro, perlato (emmer) (rinse before cooking)	2$\frac{1}{2}$ cups	8 to 10 minutes
Freekeh, cracked	2 cups	6 to 7 minutes
Freekeh, whole-grain	2 cups	10 to 12 minutes
Job's tears (hato mugi)	2$\frac{1}{2}$ cups	16 minutes
Kamut berries (rinse before cooking)	2$\frac{1}{2}$ cups	22 to 25 minutes
Kañiwa	1$\frac{1}{4}$ cups	4 minutes
Millet (rinse before cooking)	2 cups	8 to 10 minutes
Oats, rolled	2$\frac{1}{2}$ cups	6 minutes
Oats, steel-cut	3 cups	8 to 10 minutes
Posole/hominy	3 cups	60 minutes
Quinoa, white, red and black (rinse before cooking if needed)	1$\frac{1}{4}$ cups	5 minutes
Rye berries	2$\frac{1}{2}$ cups	20 to 25 minutes
Sorghum, whole-grain	3 cups	20 minutes
Spelt (farro grande)	2$\frac{1}{2}$ cups	20 to 25 minutes
Teff, whole-grain	2 cups	4 to 5 minutes
Triticale berries	4 cups	20 to 25 minutes
Wheat berries	3 cups	20 to 30 minutes
Wild rice (rinse before cooking)	2$\frac{1}{4}$ cups	22 to 25 minutes

Important notes: For these amounts, use a 5- to 7-quart pressure cooker; use the Natural Release method to open the cooker. Include 1T of butter or oil in the pot to prevent foaming, unless the recipe already calls for butter or oil.

PASTA IN THE PRESSURE COOKER

Pasta can be cooked in the pressure cooker. We make only dishes that contain both the pasta and sauce ingredients for a one-pot meal, as cooking pasta alone in boiling water is just as efficient. Pasta in a pressure cooker requires only the amount of liquid that the pasta will absorb to become soft. The rule of thumb is to use just enough water or broth to barely cover the pasta and do not drain. The sauce won't cling if the residual starch is rinsed away. The pasta and its water should not fill the pot more than halfway because the pasta will almost double in size when cooked. You need to add a little oil or butter to discourage foaming, so don't skip this ingredient.

Don't walk away from your pressure cooker unless it is programmable to release pressure automatically once the timer goes off; this goes really fast. Use the Quick Release function on your cooker to reduce pressure once the timer goes off. Do not overcook pasta or it will be mushy. We like the short shapes best in the pressure cooker, such as penne, macaroni, shells, bowties, rotini, and orzo. You'll also find recipes for couscous here.

ONLINE AND MAIL ORDER GRANARY

All these resources are organic, using sustainable agricultural practices, and processed and handled in accordance with applicable standards. Look for heirloom grains and grain products (such as buckwheat groats and hull-less barley) and ancient grains (such as teff, quinoa, amaranth, and spelt) for variety.

Anson Mills (ansonmills.com): Farro piccolo, hominy, stone-cut oats, Carolina Gold Rice
Arrowhead Mills (arrowheadmills.com): Amaranth, buckwheat groats, millet, pearled barley, quinoa
AlterEco Foods (alterecofoods.com): Quinoa and specialty rices
Birkett Mills (thebirkettmills.com): Buckwheat groats and kasha
Bluebird Grain Farm (bluebirdgrainfarms.com): Farro (emmer) and wheat berries
Bob's Red Mill (bobsredmill.com): We love this employee-owned co-op in Oregon and its wonderful products
Gibbs Wild Rice (gwrice.com)
Goldmine Natural Foods Company (goldminenaturalfoods.com): Heirloom grains and macrobiotic foods
Great River Organic Milling (greatrivermilling.com): Wide range of grains
Lundberg Family Farms (lundberg.com): Wide range of rices
Purcell Mountain Farms (purcellmountainfarms.com): Grains and beans
Rancho Gordo (ranchogordo.com): Heirloom grains and beans
Texas Best Organics (texasbestorganics.com): Organic rices
Village Harvest (villageharvestrice.com): Freekeh, imported rices, farro perlato, and quinoa
Zürsun Idaho Heirloom Beans (zursunbeans.com): Grains as well as legumes

Basic Pearl Barley

Makes about 4 cups; serves 6 • Cooker: 5- to 7-quart • Time: 18 minutes at HIGH pressure

Pearl barley gets its name because of the pearling process it goes through, which removes all of the bran and polishes the grain. Pot barley goes through this process for a shorter time and some of the bran remains. Hulled barley has the tough outer covering of the grain removed; that process also removes some of the bran. When cooked, no matter the type, the barley should still be chewy. Use this in salads (see the recipe that follows) or as part of a filling for stuffed peppers.

1^1/$_2$ cups pearl barley, rinsed and drained
1 tablespoon olive oil
1 teaspoon salt
4 cups water or vegetable broth

1. Combine the barley, oil, salt, and water in a 5- to 7-quart pressure cooker that has been sprayed with nonstick cooking spray.
2. Close and lock the lid. Set the burner heat to high. When the cooker reaches HIGH pressure, reduce the burner heat as low as you can and still maintain HIGH pressure. Set a timer to cook for 18 minutes.
3. Remove the pot from the heat. Open the cooker with the Natural Release method; let stand for 10 minutes. At time, if the pressure is not all released, open the valve. Be careful of the steam as you remove the lid. Drain.
4. Spoon out the cooked grain to a serving bowl to serve immediately or cool to room temperature and store in an airtight container in the refrigerator up to 3 days.

Barley Fruit Salad with Almonds and Coconut

Serves 8

Barley is a great grain choice for fruit salads.

CREAMY ORANGE DRESSING:
5 tablespoons plain Greek yogurt
1 tablespoon mayonnaise or Vegenaise soy mayonnaise
1 tablespoon light olive oil
2 tablespoons orange juice
Grated zest of ^{1}/$_2$ orange
1 tablespoon rice wine vinegar

SALAD:
1^1/$_2$ cups pearl barley, pressure cooked (facing page)
1^1/$_2$ cups fresh blueberries, picked over
1^1/$_2$ cups green and red grapes, halved
3 baby tangerines (Cuties, Sweethearts, or Clementines), peeled and broken into sections
^{3}/$_4$ cup slivered almonds, lightly toasted
^{3}/$_4$ cup sweetened shredded coconut
^{1}/$_2$ cup thinly sliced celery

1. In a small bowl, whisk together the dressing ingredients. Cover and refrigerate until needed.
2. Place the warm barley in a medium salad bowl. Let cool to room temperature if necessary. Add the fruit, almonds, and coconut. Toss the ingredients with the dressing to lightly coat. Store in the refrigerator and serve salad chilled.

Pearl Barley Risotto with Corn, Chiles, and Cheese

Serves 4 to 6 as a first, or 3 to 4 as a main course • Cooker: 5- to 7-quart • Time: 18 minutes at HIGH pressure

Mild Mexican flavors spice things up for this hearty one-pot meal. There's no need to thaw the corn; but if large clumps of kernels are frozen together, break them into smaller pieces before adding to the pot.

2 tablespoons olive oil
1 medium onion, chopped
1 or 2 jalapeño peppers, to taste, seeded if desired, finely chopped
1 clove garlic, finely chopped
1 cup pearl barley, rinsed and drained
2$\frac{1}{4}$ cups chicken or vegetable broth
1$\frac{1}{2}$ cups water
1 cup frozen corn kernels
$\frac{3}{4}$ cup grated dry Monterey Jack cheese or shredded Cheddar cheese
$\frac{1}{3}$ cup coarsely chopped fresh cilantro
4 to 6 grinds black pepper
Salt
Salsa, for serving

1. In a 5- to 7-quart pressure cooker, warm the oil over medium-high heat until hot. Add the onion and cook, stirring a few times, until soft, about 3 minutes. Add the jalapeño and garlic and cook, stirring, until the garlic is fragrant, about 1 minute. Add the barley, stirring until lightly toasted, 1 to 2 minutes. Stir in the broth and water.

2. Close and lock the lid. Set the burner heat to high. When the cooker reaches HIGH pressure, reduce the burner heat as low as you can and still maintain HIGH pressure. Set a timer to cook for 18 minutes.

3. Remove the pot from the heat. Open the cooker with the Quick Release method. Be careful of the steam as you remove the lid. The barley should be cooked, but a bit chewy. The mixture should be fairly loose; but if more than about $\frac{1}{3}$ cup liquid remains in the pot, drain it off and discard. Add the corn and cover without pressure. Let stand 5 minutes.

4. Stir in the cheese and cilantro and season with pepper. Taste, adding salt as needed. Serve at once in warm shallow bowls. Pass salsa at the table to spoon over each serving.

Barley Risotto with Mushrooms and Fresh Herbs

Serves 4 to 6 as a first or 3 to 4 as a main course • Cooker: 5- to 7-quart • Time: 20 minutes at HIGH pressure

We love hulled barley cooked in the manner of risotto. Barley, known as *orzo* in Italy, cooked in this manner is called *orzotto*.

2 tablespoons olive oil
2 shallots, chopped
8 ounces cremini mushrooms, sliced
1 cup hulled barley or pot barley, picked over and
    rinsed in a colander
3 cups low-sodium chicken broth
$^3/_4$ cup water
$^1/_2$ teaspoon turmeric
Sea salt
4 to 6 grinds black pepper
$^1/_2$ cup grated Parmesan cheese, plus more for
    serving
1 tablespoon chopped fresh chives
1 tablespoon chopped fresh flatleaf parsley
1 tablespoon chopped fresh basil
1 tablespoon butter

1. In a 5- to 7-quart pressure cooker, heat the oil over medium-high heat until hot. Add the shallots and cook, stirring a few times, until softened, about 2 minutes. Add the mushrooms and cook 3 minutes. Add the barley and stir until lightly toasted, 1 to 2 minutes. Stir in the broth, water, turmeric, and a few pinches salt. Bring to a boil.

2. Close and lock the lid. Set the burner heat to high. When the cooker reaches HIGH pressure, reduce the burner heat as low as you can and still maintain HIGH pressure. Set a timer to cook for 20 minutes.

3. Remove the pot from the heat. Open the cooker with the Natural Release method; let stand for 10 minutes. At time, if the pressure is not all released, open the valve. Be careful of the steam as you remove the lid. The barley should be cooked, but still a bit chewy. If it is too soupy or the barley is not cooked, set the pot, without the cover, over high heat and cook, stirring frequently, until the barley is tender (but still slightly chewy) and the mixture has thickened to a porridge consistency, about 5 minutes. If too dry, you can add more boiling water or broth to adjust the consistency. The mixture should be a fairly loose consistency.

4. Season with pepper and stir in the cheese, herbs, and butter. Taste, adding more salt as needed. Serve at once in warm shallow bowls. Pass more Parmesan at the table.

Barley Risotto with Wilted Greens

Serves 4 to 6 as a first or 3 to 4 as a main course • Cooker: 5- to 7-quart • Time: 20 minutes at HIGH pressure

Wolfgang Puck had a Mediterranean-Asian fusion restaurant for some time in downtown San Francisco called Postrio, his first outside of Los Angeles. That was the first place we saw barley risotto on a menu and this is a twist on that dish.

2 tablespoons olive oil
1 cup finely chopped yellow onion
$^1/_2$ cup finely chopped carrot
$^1/_2$ cup finely chopped celery
2 teaspoons finely chopped garlic
$^1/_4$ cup dry white wine
1 cup hulled or pot barley, picked over and rinsed in a colander
3 cups low-sodium chicken or vegetable broth
$^3/_4$ cup water
2 teaspoons minced fresh thyme
Sea salt
4 cups baby spinach leaves or torn leafy greens, such as Swiss chard
4 to 6 grinds black pepper, to taste
$^1/_2$ cup grated Romano cheese, plus more for serving
3 tablespoons mascarpone (optional)

1. In a 5- to 7-quart pressure cooker, heat the oil over medium-high heat until hot. Add the onion, carrot, and celery and cook, stirring a few times, until soft, about 3 minutes. Stir in the garlic, then add the wine and cook, stirring constantly, until it is absorbed. Add the barley and stir well until hot. Stir in the broth, water, thyme, and a few pinches salt. Bring to a boil
2. Close and lock the lid. Set the burner heat to high. When the cooker reaches HIGH pressure, reduce the burner heat as low as you can and still maintain HIGH pressure. Set a timer to cook for 20 minutes.
3. Remove the pot from the heat. Open the cooker with the Natural Release method; let stand for 10 minutes. At time, if the pressure is not all released, open the valve. Be careful of the steam as you remove the lid. The barley should be cooked but still chewy. If it is too soupy or the barley is not cooked, set the cooker, without the cover, over high heat and cook, stirring frequently, until the barley is tender and the mixture has thickened to a porridge consistency, about 5 minutes. If too dry, you can add more boiling water or broth to adjust the consistency. The mixture should have a fairly loose consistency.
4. Stir in the greens. Remove the pot from the heat and let the greens wilt. Season with the pepper and stir in the cheese. Taste, adding more salt as needed. If you want the orzotto creamy, stir in the mascarpone. Serve at once in warm shallow bowls. Pass more Romano cheese at the table.

Basic Bulgur Cracked Wheat

Makes about 5 cups; serves 6 • Cooker: 5- to 7-quart • Time: 6 minutes at HIGH pressure

Cracked wheat is the whole, raw wheat berry that has been broken into pieces, while bulgur cracked wheat is made from whole wheat berries that have been hulled, steamed, and kiln-dried before cracking. We have found that plain cracked wheat (which is not precooked) is virtually impossible to find, but bulgur cracked wheat is available in every supermarket. It is available in three grades, fine, medium, and coarse (known as grade C), with the supermarket variety being medium unless otherwise labeled. Since the wheat berries are initially steamed, the cooking process is shortened considerably; the box gives instructions for simply soaking with boiling water, but cooking it in the pressure cooker makes for an even better, more tender grain.

Plain cooked bulgur has one of the most appealing flavors of all the grains and is, sadly, rarely served as a side dish. Serve this in place of rice with your stews, or with a pat of butter as a side dish. It's also delicious in salads; to get out of the tabbouleh rut, try the one that follows.

2 cups bulgur cracked wheat, rinsed and drained
2 teaspoons sea salt
2 tablespoons olive oil
4 cups water

1. Combine the bulgur, oil, and water in a 5- to 7-quart pressure cooker.
2. Close and lock the lid. Set the burner heat to high. When the cooker reaches HIGH pressure, reduce the burner heat as low as you can and still maintain HIGH pressure. Set a timer to cook for 6 minutes.
3. Remove the pot from the heat. Open the cooker with the Natural Release method; let stand for 10 minutes. At time, if the pressure is not all released, open the valve. Be careful of the steam as you remove the lid. Drain if necessary.
4. Fluff the bulgur with a fork. Spoon out the cooked grain to a serving bowl to serve immediately or let cool to room temperature and store in an airtight container up to 3 days.

Bulgur Salad with Garden Vegetables and Pine Nuts

Serves 6

Chop or dice all the vegetables into $1/4$- to $1/2$-inch pieces.

SALAD:
3 cups cooked Basic Bulgur Cracked Wheat (left), at room temperature
1 red bell pepper, seeded and chopped
1 medium or 2 small zucchini, cubed
1 yellow summer squash, cubed
2 ribs celery, chopped
$1/2$ cup chopped red onion
$1/3$ cup pine nuts, toasted (see below)

DILL AND LIME DRESSING:
$1/3$ cup olive oil
Grated zest of 1 lime
Juice of 2 limes
3 tablespoons minced fresh dill or 2 teaspoons dillweed
Sea salt and freshly ground black pepper to taste

1. In a large serving bowl, combine the bulgur, red pepper, squashes, celery, onion, and pine nuts.
2. In a small bowl, whisk the dressing ingredients together. Pour the dressing over the salad and toss to coat the vegetables. Serve at room temperature.

TOASTING PINE NUTS AND ALMONDS

Toast these nuts in a dry skillet over medium-low heat, stirring and shaking the pan frequently, until golden in spots, about 3 minutes. Heat releases and intensifies their rich flavor.

Winter Tabbouleh

Serves 6 • Cooker: 5- to 7-quart • Time: 6 minutes at HIGH pressure

Tabbouleh is one of the most popular salads in France, served as part of family dinners as well as school lunches. It is delicious alongside roasted poultry, duck, lamb, or as a complement side dish with a vegetable offering like ratatouille. Here is the ultimate winter version, substituting apples for tomatoes, from Chateau de Leavault in Orly, France, from friend and feng shui practitioner Marina Lighthouse.

BULGUR:

1¼ cups bulgur cracked wheat, rinsed and drained
1 teaspoon sea salt
1 teaspoon ground cumin
Pinch cayenne pepper
2½ cups water
2 tablespoons olive oil

SALAD:

½ small red onion, minced
1 (8-ounce) cucumber, seeded and diced to make 2
    cups (peel if skin is thick or waxed; if you use a
    hothouse or Persian cucumber, you do not need
    to peel)
2 ribs celery, minced (can add the leaves, if you
    like)
1 large firm apple, cored but unpeeled, finely
    chopped
½ cup minced fresh flatleaf parsley
¼ cup pine nuts (optional), toasted (see page 365)
⅓ cup fresh lemon juice
⅓ cup olive oil
Sea salt and freshly ground black pepper

1. Place the bulgur, salt, cumin, and cayenne in a 5- to 7-quart pressure cooker. Add the water and oil.
2. Close and lock the lid. Set the burner heat to high. When the cooker reaches HIGH pressure, reduce the burner heat as low as you can and still maintain HIGH pressure. Set a timer to cook for 6 minutes.
3. Remove the pot from the heat. Open the cooker with the Natural Release method; let stand for 10 minutes. At time, if the pressure is not all released, open the valve. Be careful of the steam as you remove the lid. Let stand, uncovered, on the counter for 1 hour. You will have about 3 cups cooked grain.
4. Fluff the bulgur with a fork and place in a medium serving bowl. Add the onion, cucumber, celery, and apple; toss together.
5. In a small bowl, whisk the lemon juice and oil together. Pour over the salad. Add the parsley and pine nuts, then stir with a large spoon or spatula to moisten everything evenly. Season to taste with salt and pepper. Serve at room temperature.

Tabbouleh in Grape Leaves: You'll need 1 (1-pound) jar pickled grape leaves (dolma), which contains about 50 leaves, or use room-temperature pressure-cooked fresh grape leaves if you have access (see page 238). Refrigerate the salad until you are ready to stuff the grape leaves. Rinse the brine off the leaves. Tuck in the sides and roll each grape leaf tightly around about 2 heaping tablespoons of the tabbouleh. Arrange on a serving platter or in a covered refrigerator container until serving time. These are great for including in your lunch box, for bite-sized appetizers, or for a picnic.

Basic Semi-Pearled Farro

Makes about 2^1/$_2$ cups cooked; serves 4 to 6 • Cooker: 5- to 7-quart • Time: 8 minutes at HIGH pressure

A member of the wheat family, farro (also known as emmer wheat) is an ancient grain, having been cultivated in Italy, particularly in the regions of Tuscany and Abruzzo, since ancient Roman times. Farro is sold whole, semi-pearled (semiperlato), and pearled (perlato), the two pearled options having been polished of their germ and bran to a lesser and greater degree. We prefer the semi-pearled.

Farro is a different species of wheat than the one that produces plain wheat berries; the grains are larger and shiny red-brown, with a chewy texture and pleasantly nutty flavor. It is also a softer wheat, so it cooks faster, needs less water, and is more digestible than regular wheat. Use farro exactly as you would regular wheat berries—in casseroles, soups, stuffings, pilafs, salads, or sautéed in olive oil with garlic for a simple side. While farro is not gluten-free, it is considerably lower in gluten than commercial wheat varieties. This recipe can be doubled; increase the salt to 1^1/$_2$ teaspoons, not 2 teaspoons.

1 cup semi-pearled farro (labeled *farro semiperlato*), rinsed and drained
1 tablespoon olive oil
1 teaspoon salt
2^1/$_2$ cups water or vegetable broth

1. Combine the farro, oil, salt, and water in a 5- to 7-quart pressure cooker.
2. Close and lock the lid. Set the burner heat to high. When the cooker reaches HIGH pressure, reduce the burner heat as low as you can and still maintain HIGH pressure. Set a timer to cook for 8 minutes.
3. Remove the pot from the heat. Open the cooker with the Natural Release method; let stand for 15 minutes. At time, if the pressure is not all released, open the valve. Be careful of the steam as you remove the lid. Drain.
4. Spoon out the cooked berries to a serving bowl to serve immediately or let cool to room temperature and store in an airtight container in the refrigerator up to 3 days.

Toasted Farro: Place the farro in a dry skillet over medium-high heat. Toast, stirring constantly, until the grains pop and deepen in color, about 4 minutes, then proceed with the recipe.

Aleta's Farro Salad with Radishes and Beet Greens

Serves 4 • Cooker: 5- to 7-quart • Time: 8 minutes at HIGH pressure

Aleta Watson was a member of our food team at the *San Jose Mercury News.* She ran a great blog giving discourse on her particular palate. This is a grain salad she re-created after having it at the café at the Museum of Modern Art in New York. Says Aleta, "This salad starts with a base of chewy farro, dressed with a simple vinaigrette made with good olive oil. Crunchy radishes, barely blanched carrots, and a handful of tender beet greens add layers of color and texture to perk up the palate. I've thrown in shaved shallots and a spoonful of salty capers. The flavor is best if you dress the salad at least half an hour before serving. This allows it to soak into the farro and there are no worries about wilting." You will need to buy a bunch of beets with their greens attached to get the fresh beet greens. If there are any leftovers, they refrigerate nicely overnight.

FARRO:

1 cup semi-pearled farro (labeled *farro semiperlato*), rinsed and drained
1 tablespoon olive oil
1 teaspoon salt
2$^1/_2$ cups water or vegetable broth

SALAD:

4 slender carrots, cut into matchsticks about 1$^1/_2$ inches long
1 bunch small radishes, trimmed and quartered
Generous handful of tender beet greens, washed well and torn into bite-size pieces
2 medium shallots, very thinly sliced
1 tablespoon sherry vinegar
$^1/_3$ cup extra virgin olive oil
Sea salt and freshly ground black pepper
1 tablespoon nonpareil capers, rinsed

1. Combine the farro, oil, salt, and water in a 5- to 7-quart pressure cooker.
2. Close and lock the lid. Set the burner heat to high. When the cooker reaches HIGH pressure, reduce the burner heat as low as you can and still maintain HIGH pressure. Set a timer to cook for 8 minutes.
3. Remove the pot from the heat. Open the cooker with the Natural Release method; let stand for 10 minutes. At time, if the pressure is not all released, open the valve. Be careful of the steam as you remove the lid. Drain. The farro should be just tender to the bite. Drain and spread out in a single layer on a sheet pan to cool thoroughly.
4. In the same pot, bring 3 to 4 cups of water to a boil and blanch the carrot sticks until crisp tender, about 2 minutes. Drain and plunge into bowl of ice water to stop the cooking. When the carrots have cooled completely, drain and pat dry with a clean dishtowel.
5. Combine the farro, carrots, radishes, beet greens, and shallots in a medium serving bowl. Whisk together the vinegar and oil and season to taste with salt and pepper. Toss the salad with the dressing, sprinkle with the capers and serve.

GREAT GRAINS FOR SALADS

Not too many years ago, a salad book would have a grain salad chapter tacked onto the end and have only a few recipes, such as tabbouleh. Now with so many grain choices, there is no excuse not to prepare a grain-based salad every week. The following grains are the best for making salads, sturdy enough to stand up to all sorts of dressings.

- Barley
- Black rice
- Bulgur
- Farro (emmer)
- Kamut
- Long-grain brown rice
- Quinoa
- Spelt
- Wheat berries
- Wild rice

Tuscan Farro and Baby White Beans con Pecorino

Serves 6 • Cooker: 5- to 7-quart • Time: 10 minutes at HIGH pressure

When beans and grains cook in the same amount of time, a one-pot meal is a natural evolution. If the flavor of the Pecorino Romano is too piquant for you, use Parmesan instead.

3 tablespoons olive oil
1 white onion, finely chopped
1 clove garlic, minced
3 ribs celery, finely chopped
1 medium carrot or parsnip, finely chopped
¼ cup finely chopped red or yellow bell pepper
4 canned whole San Marzano plum tomatoes, chopped or crushed with your hands
4 cups vegetable or low-sodium chicken broth
1 cup dry white wine, such as Pinot Grigio
2 tablespoons chopped fresh flatleaf parsley
1 cup dried baby white beans, soaked (page 406) and drained
1½ cups semi-pearled farro (labeled *farro semiperlato*), rinsed and drained
Sea salt and freshly ground black pepper
¾ cup freshly grated Pecorino Romano cheese, for serving
Extra virgin olive oil, for serving

1. Heat the oil in a 5- to 7-quart pressure cooker over medium-high heat. Add the onion, garlic, celery, carrot, and bell pepper, and cook, stirring a few times, until softened, 3 to 4 minutes. Stir in the tomatoes, broth, wine, and parsley. Stir in the drained beans and farro. The liquid should be at least a full inch over the solids. If not, add some water.

2. Close and lock the lid. Set the burner heat to high. When the cooker reaches HIGH pressure, reduce the burner heat as low as you can and still maintain HIGH pressure. Set a timer to cook for 10 minutes.

3. Remove the pot from the heat and let stand for 5 minutes. Open the cooker with the Quick Release method. Be careful of the steam as you remove the lid. The farro should be al dente (tender but chewy) and the beans tender. If not cooked, relock the cooker, bring back up to HIGH pressure, and cook another 5 minutes. Quick Release the pressure again and gently stir.

4. Transfer to a serving bowl and serve hot, topped with the Pecorino cheese and a drizzle of extra virgin olive oil. Serve with crusty bread, preferably Tuscan, which is saltless.

Farro Risotto with Red Wine and Parmesan

Serves 4 as a main course or 6 as a first course • Cooker: 5- to 7-quart • Time: 8 minutes at HIGH pressure

Farro is grown in Italy and a popular second choice to Arborio rice and its short-grain cousins for risotto. In Italy, a risotto made with farro is called a *farrotto*. Farro is chewier than Arborio and doesn't release starch when it's cooked, so there's no need to stir. This is an excellent winter risotto.

2 tablespoons extra virgin olive oil
2 large shallots, finely chopped (about $1/3$ cup)
$1^1/4$ cups semi-pearled farro (labeled *farro semiperlato*), rinsed and drained
$1^1/2$ cups Chianti Classico or other good, fruity Italian red wine
$2^1/2$ cups vegetable or low-sodium chicken broth, or Vegetable Parmesan Broth (page 25)
$1/2$ cup freshly grated or shredded Parmigiano-Reggiano cheese, plus more for serving
Freshly ground black pepper
2 tablespoons butter

1. Heat the oil in a 5- to 7-quart pressure cooker over medium-high heat. Add the shallots and cook until softened, about 1 minute. Add the farro and cook 1 minute, stirring constantly, until the grains are evenly coated with oil and fragrant. Add 1 cup of the Chianti and stir until it is absorbed. Add the rest of the Chianti and the broth.

2. Close and lock the lid. Set the burner heat to high. When the cooker reaches HIGH pressure, reduce the burner heat as low as you can and still maintain HIGH pressure. Set a timer to cook for 8 minutes.

3. Remove the pot from the heat. Open the cooker with the Quick Release method. Be careful of the steam as you remove the lid. Stir in $1/4$ cup of the cheese and a few grindings of pepper. Replace the cover and let stand a few minutes to thicken and set up. The farro should be al dente (tender but chewy) and the cooked grains suspended in the thick liquid.

4. Stir in the butter and the rest of the cheese over medium heat. Taste for seasoning. The finished *farrotto* should be slightly runny as it will continue to thicken as it sits on the plate. Spoon out with an oversized spoon, with extra cheese for sprinkling on top, and the pepper grinder on the side.

Creamy Farro Risotto with Fresh Herbs

Serves 4 as a main or 6 as a first course • Cooker: 5- to 7-quart • Time: 8 minutes at HIGH pressure

Risotto alle erbe, what we consider a green risotto, is about aromatic fresh herbs. We like a combination that includes a large percentage of basil, watercress or arugula, and Italian flatleaf parsley, plus smaller amounts of one or two other herbs. We give you three different choices for adding the creamy factor—heavy cream, cream cheese, or mascarpone—each is delicious, each brings its own particular flavor.

2 tablespoons extra virgin olive oil
2 large shallots, finely chopped (about $^1/_3$ cup)
$^1/_4$ cup minced celery
1$^1/_4$ cups semi-pearled farro (labeled *farro semiperlato*), rinsed and drained
$^1/_2$ cup dry white wine or vermouth
3 cups vegetable or low-sodium chicken broth
1 cup finely chopped fresh herbs, such as equal parts basil, watercress or arugula, and flatleaf parsley plus small amounts of oregano, marjoram, thyme, tarragon, or rosemary
$^1/_3$ cup freshly grated Parmigiano-Reggiano cheese
Sea salt and freshly ground black pepper
$^1/_2$ cup heavy cream, 3 ounces cream cheese, or $^1/_3$ cup mascarpone

1. In a 5- to 7-quart pressure cooker or 2$^1/_2$-quart skillet pressure cooker, heat the oil over medium-high heat. Add the shallots and celery and cook until softened, about 1 minute. Add the farro and cook 1 minute, stirring constantly, until the grains are evenly coated with oil and fragrant. Add the wine and stir until absorbed. Add the broth.

2. Close and lock the lid. Set the burner heat to high. When the cooker reaches HIGH pressure, reduce the burner heat as low as you can and still maintain HIGH pressure. Set a timer to cook for 8 minutes.

3. Remove the pot from the heat. Open the cooker with the Quick Release method. Be careful of the steam as you remove the lid. Stir in half the cheese and some pepper. Replace the cover and let stand a few minutes to thicken and set up. The farro should be al dente (tender but chewy), the cooked grain suspended in the thick liquid.

4. Stir in the cream and remaining cheese (if using cream cheese or mascarpone, stir until melted). Cook a few minutes over medium heat, uncovered. The finished *farrotto* should be slightly runny as it will continue to thicken as it sits on the plate. Taste for seasoning. Spoon out with an oversized spoon, with extra cheese for sprinkling on top, and the pepper grinder on the side.

Farrotto with Asparagus and Peas

Serves 4 as a main or 6 as a first course • Cooker: 5- to 7-quart • Time: 8 minutes at HIGH pressure

Feel free to mix and match your own combination of vegetables. If you use a homemade broth, the flavor will soar. Go with authentic Parmigiano-Reggiano cheese.

2 tablespoons extra virgin olive oil
1 cup finely chopped white onion or leek
1¼ cups semi-pearled farro (labeled *farro semiperlato*), rinsed and drained
½ cup dry white wine or Prosecco (left to go flat)
3 cups vegetable or low-sodium chicken broth
1 teaspoon minced fresh tarragon or basil
½ pound thin fresh asparagus, tough bottoms trimmed and cut into 1-inch pieces, with the tips reserved separately
½ cup freshly grated Parmigiano-Reggiano cheese
1 cup frozen petite peas, thawed
Sea salt and freshly ground black pepper

1. In a 5- to 7-quart pressure cooker, heat the oil over medium-high heat. Add the onion and cook, stirring a few times, until softened, about 3 minutes. Add the farro and cook 1 minute, stirring constantly, until the grains are evenly coated with oil and fragrant. Add the wine and stir until it is absorbed. Add the broth, herb, and asparagus pieces (reserve the tips to add at the end).
2. Close and lock the lid. Set the burner heat to high. When the cooker reaches HIGH pressure, reduce the burner heat as low as you can and still maintain HIGH pressure. Set a timer to cook for 8 minutes.
3. Remove the pot from the heat. Open the cooker with the Quick Release method. Be careful of the steam as you remove the lid. Stir in half the cheese and some pepper. Replace the cover without locking and let stand a few minutes to thicken and set up. The farro should be al dente (tender but chewy) and the cooked grains suspended in the thick liquid.
4. Stir in the asparagus tips, the remaining cheese, and peas. Cook over medium-high heat a few minutes, partially covered, to cook the vegetables and thicken. Taste for salt and pepper. The finished *farrotto* should be slightly runny as it will continue to thicken as it sits on the plate. Spoon out with an oversized spoon, with extra cheese for sprinkling on top, and the pepper grinder on the side.

Farrotto with Fennel and Peas: Replace the asparagus with 4 to 5 ounces (½ medium bulb) fresh fennel, fernlike tops removed, bulb cut into ½-inch-thick slices. Add in Step 1 along with the onion or leek.

Farro Risotto Primavera with Goat Cheese

Serves 4 as a main or 6 as a first course • Cooker: 5- to 7-quart • Time: 8 minutes at HIGH pressure

The primavera touch of early season mixed vegetables is really about making the risotto with whatever you can find that looks fresh. A classic primavera is based on a soffritto of onion, garlic, celery, and carrot in olive oil, which we use here. Formaggio di capra, caprino, or chévre, young fresh goat's milk cheese without a rind, works like a charm, melting quickly into the risotto.

2 tablespoons extra virgin olive oil
$1/2$ cup finely chopped white onion or leek
1 clove garlic, minced
$1/2$ cup finely diced zucchini
$1/2$ cup very small cauliflower florets
2 ounces cremini mushrooms, quartered
$1/4$ cup minced carrot
$1/4$ cup minced celery
$1^1/4$ cups semi-pearled farro (labeled *farro semiperlato*), rinsed and drained
$1/2$ cup dry white wine or vermouth
$3^1/2$ cups vegetable or low-sodium chicken broth
4 ounces fresh goat cheese, cut into small pieces
1 tablespoon butter
$1/4$ cup chopped fresh flatleaf parsley
Sea salt and freshly ground black pepper
Grated lemon zest, for garnish
Freshly grated Parmesan cheese, for serving (optional)

1. In a 5- to 7-quart pressure cooker, heat the oil over medium-high heat. Add the onion, garlic, zucchini, cauliflower, mushrooms, carrot, and celery and cook , stirring a few times, until softened, 2 to 3 minutes. Add the farro and cook 1 minute, stirring constantly, until the grains are evenly coated with the butter and fragrant. Add the wine and stir until it is absorbed. Add the broth.

2. Close and lock the lid. Set the burner heat to high. When the cooker reaches HIGH pressure, reduce the burner heat as low as you can and still maintain HIGH pressure. Set a timer to cook for 8 minutes.

3. Remove the pot from the heat. Open the cooker with the Quick Release method. Be careful of the steam as you remove the lid.

4. Stir in the goat cheese, butter, and parsley. Cook, uncovered, over medium heat a few minutes to melt the cheese. Stir and taste for salt and pepper. The finished *farrotto* should be slightly runny as it will continue to thicken as it sits on the plate. Spoon out into serving bowls and garnish with a little sprinkling of lemon zest. If you want more cheese, sprinkle with Parmesan.

Herbed Freekeh Tabbouleh with Lemon Tahini Sauce

Serves 6 • Cooker: 5- to 7-quart • Time: 6 minutes at HIGH pressure

Also known as *farik* or *frikeh* in the Middle East, freekeh is roasted green wheat. The name freekeh is derived from the Arabic word *al-freek*, which means "what is rubbed," referring to the rubbing of the wheat grains to rid them of their shells. It is harvested when it is still young, wet, and "green" in the spring. It is then slow roasted over coals, and de-hulled, polished, and cracked, resulting in a beautiful, and gently perfumed, green wheat berry. Whole-grain freekeh can be cooked like a risotto with vegetables, used in breads, soups, and as an alternative to rice. Cracked freekeh is used like bulgur in salads. Nutritionally freekeh is a powerhouse. It is considered a low-glycemic index food with four times the fiber content of brown rice. It has a high protein content compared to other grains.

FREEKEH:
1 1/2 cups cracked freekeh
3 cups water
1 tablespoon olive oil
2 teaspoons cider vinegar
3/4 cup chopped fresh flatleaf parsley
1/4 cup chopped fresh mint
2 tablespoons chopped fresh dill
1 medium tomato, seeded and diced
1/4 cup finely chopped red onion
1/4 cup chopped green onion
1 jalapeño pepper, seeded and minced
Juice of 2 limes
2 tablespoons pomegranate molasses
2 tablespoons olive oil

LEMON TAHINI SAUCE:
2 small cloves garlic, peeled
1 cup tahini
Warm water, as needed
Juice of 2 lemons
Sea salt and freshly ground black pepper, to taste
Salted roasted sunflower seeds or chopped
   pistachios, for garnish

1. In a 5- to 7-quart pressure cooker, combine the freekeh, water, oil, and vinegar. You do not need to stir.
2. Close and lock the lid. Set the burner heat to high. When the cooker reaches HIGH pressure, reduce the burner heat as low as you can and still maintain HIGH pressure. Set a timer to cook for 6 minutes.
3. Remove the pot from the heat. Open the cooker with the Natural Release method; let stand for 10 minutes. At time, if the pressure is not all released, open the valve. Be careful of the steam as you remove the lid. Let stand, uncovered, for 10 minutes. Fluff gently so it won't become mushy. The freekeh should be tender. Transfer to a wide bowl to cool completely.
4. Make the Lemon Tahini Sauce. Place the garlic cloves in a food processor and pulse a few times until finely chopped. Add the tahini, then start adding warm water through the feed tube while the food processor is running until it reaches a pourable consistency. Add the lemon juice, season to taste with salt and pepper, and pulse a couple of times to combine. Set aside.
5. When the freekeh is cool, add the herbs, tomato, onion, green onion, and jalapeños. Drizzle with the lime juice, molasses, and oil. To serve, pour the tahini sauce over the salad in the bowl, or spread 2 tablespoons of the sauce on a serving platter and arrange the tabbouleh over it to create a firm pyramid shape, then drizzle with the rest of the sauce. Garnish with sunflower seeds or pistachios and serve.

Freekeh Hot Breakfast Cereal

Serves 6 • Cooker: 5- to 7-quart • Time: 10 minutes at HIGH pressure

Humble green wheat freekeh, with its subtle smoky flavor (from roasting the wheat), is a delightful whole-grain breakfast cereal. If all you have is whole freekeh, crack it yourself in a blender by pulsing it a few times. The grain turns rancid quickly, so store it in the freezer. Serve this with the sweetener of your choice, such as maple syrup, honey, brown sugar, or agave nectar, and half-and-half or nondairy milk, such as rice milk, coconut milk, soy milk, or almond milk. It's also delicious topped with fresh seasonal fruit like blueberries, strawberries, or sliced nectarines.

4^1/$_2$ cups water
1^1/$_2$ cups cracked freekeh
2 tablespoons butter or coconut oil
1 (2-finger) pinch sea salt

1. In a 5- to 7-quart pressure cooker, combine the ingredients. You do not need to stir.
2. Close and lock the lid. Set the burner heat to high. When the cooker reaches HIGH pressure, reduce the burner heat as low as you can and still maintain HIGH pressure. Set a timer to cook for 10 minutes.
3. Remove the pot from the heat. Open the cooker with the Natural Release method; let stand for 15 minutes. At time, if the pressure is not all released, open the valve. Be careful of the steam as you remove the lid. Stir. The mixture should be fairly loose, the grains soft and creamy. Serve at once in warm shallow bowls.

Basic Kamut Berries

Makes about 3 cups, serves 4 to 5 • Cooker: 5- to 7-quart • Time: 22 minutes if unsoaked or 12 minutes if soaked at HIGH pressure

Kamut® is a trademark for Khorasan wheat, originally cultivated in Central Asia, the Near East, and North Africa, and now grown primarily in Montana and Canada. The berries are double the size of regular wheat berries, with a firm texture and nutty taste. Serve Kamut in place of rice or with a pat of butter as a side dish. You can also use this recipe to cook regular wheat berries, spelt, and rye berries.

You have the option of soaking the berries in water overnight. It's not necessary, but if you do, it will cut the pressure cooker time by 10 minutes.

1 cup Kamut berries, rinsed and drained
2 tablespoons olive oil
1 teaspoon salt
2^1/$_2$ cups water

1. Combine the ingredients in a 5- to 7-quart pressure cooker.
2. Close and lock the lid. Set the burner heat to high. When the cooker reaches HIGH pressure, reduce the burner heat as low as you can and still maintain HIGH pressure. Set a timer to cook for 22 minutes. If you soaked the berries overnight, cooking time will be 12 minutes.
3. Remove the pot from the heat. Open the cooker with the Natural Release method; let stand for 15 minutes. At time, if the pressure is not all released, open the valve. Be careful of the steam as you remove the lid. Drain.
4. Spoon out the cooked berries to a serving bowl to serve immediately or let cool to room temperature and store in an airtight container in the refrigerator up to 3 days.

Braised Mushroom and Onion Kasha

Serves 4 • Cooker: 5- to 7-quart • Time: 6 minutes at HIGH pressure

This easy and delicious pilaf is adapted from a back-of-the-box recipe from Wolff's brand kasha, which is gluten-free. Serve this as a side dish for poultry, topped with a fried egg for breakfast, or with smoked salmon for brunch. Refrigerated leftovers can be fried in patties and topped with sour cream or used in sandwiches.

$^{1}/_{2}$ ounce dried porcini mushrooms
$^{1}/_{3}$ cup boiling water
1 cup buckwheat groats (kasha), shaken in a fine
    mesh strainer to remove the chaff
1 large egg, lightly beaten
4 tablespoons butter
1 tablespoon olive oil
1 medium white onion, finely chopped
1$^{1}/_{2}$ cups vegetable broth
$^{1}/_{2}$ teaspoon sea salt
8 ounces cremini mushrooms, sliced
1 jarred roasted red bell pepper, diced
2 tablespoons chopped fresh dill
2 tablespoons chopped fresh flatleaf parsley
Sea salt and freshly ground black pepper

KASHA

Kasha, or roasted, hulled buckwheat groats (hulled kernels), is not a type of wheat; in fact, it is not a grain at all but the fruit of a red-stemmed annual bush related to rhubarb and sorrel. After roasting, the creamy triangular seed turns an earthy red-brown. It is a strong flavored grain, an acquired taste but a comforting food, described by food writer Elizabeth Schneider as the "love-it-or-leave-it" grain. Buckwheat is high in protein and all eight amino acids (especially lysine), B vitamins (it has double the amount of wheat), making it a good dietary addition for vegetarians. Store kasha in the refrigerator, where it will last up to 3 months, or in the freezer for 6 months.

1. Place the porcini in a small bowl with $^{1}/_{3}$ cup boiling water. Let soak until the mushrooms are soft, about 1 hour. Remove the mushrooms from the liquid; squeeze dry and set aside. Strain soaking liquid through a coffee filter, leaving any sediment behind. Reserve the soaking liquid.

2. In a small bowl, combine the kasha and beaten egg. Stir to evenly coat the grains.

3. Melt 1 tablespoon of the butter with the oil in a 5- to 7-quart pressure cooker over medium heat. Add the onion and cook, stirring a few times, until soft, 3 to 4 minutes. Stir in the kasha-egg mixture and cook 4 to 5 minutes over medium heat, stirring constantly, until the egg is set and the grains lightly browned, dry, and separate. Stir in the broth, reserved mushroom liquid, porcinis, and salt. Bring to a boil.

4. Close and lock the lid. Set the burner heat to high. When the cooker reaches HIGH pressure, reduce the burner heat as low as you can and still maintain HIGH pressure. Set a timer to cook for 6 minutes.

5. Remove the pot from the heat. Open the cooker with the Natural Release method; let stand for 15 minutes. At time, if the pressure is not all released, open the valve. Be careful of the steam as you remove the lid. The kasha should be tender and the liquid absorbed.

6. Meanwhile, in a large skillet over high heat, melt the remaining 3 tablespoons butter. When sizzling, add the fresh mushrooms and cook until they release their liquid and they begin to brown on the edges. Add the roasted pepper and dill and stir 1 minute. Fluff the kasha with a fork and stir in the mushrooms and parsley. Taste for salt and pepper. Serve immediately

Kasha Porridge

Serves 2 to 3 • Cooker: 5- to 7-quart • Time: 6 minutes at HIGH pressure

Nutty flavored kasha makes a soul-satisfying hot breakfast cereal and it's gluten free! It combines particularly well with flavors like maple, chocolate, bacon, prunes, and nuts. The cacao nibs included here, pieces of cacao beans that have been roasted and hulled, contribute a crunchy texture and dash of chocolate bitterness.

2$^1/_4$ cups water
$^1/_2$ cup half-and-half or almond milk
1$^1/_4$ cups buckwheat groats (kasha), shaken in a
   fine mesh strainer to remove the chaff
1 tablespoon butter

TOPPINGS (YOUR CHOICE):
Sliced banana
Berries
Almond butter or tahini
Cottage cheese
Pumpkin seeds, sunflower seeds, and cacao nibs
1 (2-finger) pinch sea salt

1. In a 5- to 7-quart pressure cooker, combine the water, half-and-half, kasha, and butter. You do not need to stir.
2. Close and lock the lid. Set the burner heat to high. When the cooker reaches HIGH pressure, reduce the burner heat as low as you can and still maintain HIGH pressure. Set a timer to cook for 6 minutes.
3. Remove the pot from the heat. Open the cooker with the Natural Release method; let stand for 10 minutes. At time, if the pressure is not all released, open the valve. Be careful of the steam as you remove the lid. Stir. The mixture should be fairly loose, the grains fluffy and creamy.
4. Serve at once in warm shallow bowls with your choice of, or all of, the toppings.

"GRAINS" THAT AREN'T GRAINS

These are what are known as pseudograins and include quinoa, amaranth, buckwheat, millet, and wild rice. These grains are all gluten free, along with oats, corn, rice, and teff.

Millet-Cauliflower Mash

Serves 2 as a side dish • Cooker: 5- to 7-quart • Time: 10 minutes at HIGH pressure

Millet, one of the smallest of the whole grains, is at its best combined with other ingredients, in this case, mashed with cauliflower to yield a puree with the same mouth-feel as mashed potatoes, but without the starch. If you make a lot of purees, you will want to invest in a hand immersion blender so you can puree right in the pot instead of transferring it to a food processor. Serve topped with a pat of butter, a dollop of sour cream, or a few cloves of roasted garlic stirred in as a side dish.

²/₃ cup millet, rinsed in a fine mesh strainer and
    drained
1 tablespoon olive oil
2 cups water
2 heaping cups cauliflower florets and sliced stems

1. Combine the millet, oil, and water in a 5- to 7-quart pressure cooker. Pile in the cauliflower.
2. Close and lock the lid. Set the burner heat to high. When the cooker reaches HIGH pressure, reduce the burner heat as low as you can and still maintain HIGH pressure. Set a timer to cook for 10 minutes.
3. Remove the pot from the heat. Open the cooker with the Natural Release method; let stand for 10 minutes. At time, if the pressure is not all released, open the valve. Be careful of the steam when you lift the lid. Stir to combine. The millet should be soft.
4. With an immersion blender or in a food processor, puree until smooth and fluffy.

GLUTEN-FREE GRAINS: THE BIG TEN

These grains, and their flours, do not contain gluten, if they are processed in a gluten-free environment.
- Amaranth
- Buckwheat
- Corn
- Millet
- Oats
- Quinoa
- Rice
- Sorghum
- Teff
- Wild rice

Basic Steel-Cut Oats

Serves 3 to 4 • Cooker: 5- to 7-quart • Time: 8 minutes at HIGH pressure

Steel-cut oats, also known as Irish or Scottish oats, are hulled oat kernels (also called groats) cut into chunks on a steel burr mill. They are considered one of the optimum sources of carb nutrition in the grain world. They are less processed than rolled oats and need more liquid and more time to cook. Usually steel-cut oats need to be soaked overnight, but this is not necessary in the pressure cooker.

1 cup steel-cut oats
3 tablespoons butter
$1/2$ teaspoon salt
3 to $3^1/2$ cups water, depending if you want a
    looser oatmeal

1. Combine the ingredients in a 5- to 7-quart pressure cooker.
2. Close and lock the lid. Set the burner heat to high. When the cooker reaches HIGH pressure, reduce the burner heat as low as you can and still maintain HIGH pressure. Set a timer to cook for 8 minutes.
3. Remove the pot from the heat. Open the cooker with the Natural Release method; let stand for 15 minutes. At time, if the pressure is not all released, open the valve. Be careful of the steam when you remove the lid.
4. Spoon out the cooked grain to a serving bowl to serve immediately. Top with milk, half-and-half, nondairy milk, almond milk, fresh fruit (sliced strawberries or peaches, grated apple), dried fruit (such as dried cranberries, blueberries, raisins, or cherries), $1/2$ cup pumpkin puree, chopped raw or toasted nuts (macadamia nuts, almonds, or pecans), seeds (sunflower or pumpkin—not salted), granola, sweetener of choice such as brown sugar, maple syrup, honey, agave syrup, or Splenda.

Steel-Cut Oatmeal with Cinnamon, Vanilla, and Dried Fruit

Serves 4 to 6 • Cooker: 5- to 7-quart • Time: 8 minutes at HIGH pressure

Steel-cut oats cook down into a sweet, creamy porridge. Any leftover oatmeal can be refrigerated for up to 3 days in an airtight container and reheated in the microwave. This is also delicious served with blueberries and sunflower seeds.

3 cups water
3 cups nondairy milk, such as rice milk, coconut
    milk, soy milk, almond milk, or oat milk
2 cups steel-cut oats
2 tablespoons butter
1 cinnamon stick or $1/4$ teaspoon ground cinnamon
$1/2$ vanilla bean or $1/2$ teaspoon vanilla extract
$1/2$ to $3/4$ cup dried currants, cranberries, cherries,
    raisins, or a mixture, to taste

1. Combine the ingredients in a 5- to 7-quart pressure cooker. If using the vanilla bean, remove the seeds, and add both the seeds and the bean. You do not need to stir.
2. Close and lock the lid. Set the burner heat to high. When the cooker reaches HIGH pressure, reduce the burner heat as low as you can and still maintain HIGH pressure. Set a timer to cook for 8 minutes.
3. Remove the pot from the heat. Open the cooker with the Natural Release method; let stand for 15 minutes. At time, if the pressure is not all released, open the valve. Be careful of the steam as you remove the lid. The mixture should be fairly loose and creamy. Serve at once.

Breakfast Steel-Cut Oatmeal and Quinoa with Cinnamon, Vanilla, and Dried Fruit: Add $1/2$ cup rinsed white or red quinoa in Step 1.

Savory Steel-Cut Oat Porridge with Mushrooms

Serves 6 • Cooker: 5- to 7-quart • Time: 8 minutes at HIGH pressure

We are conditioned to oats being served as a sweet breakfast cereal. But they translate to a savory porridge as well, cooked in the manner of a risotto, thick with vegetables and cheese. Enjoy this for breakfast or as a side dish with roasted meats and poultry.

2 tablespoons butter
1 tablespoon olive oil
2 large shallots, chopped
2 medium carrots or parsnips, peeled and chopped
3 ribs celery, chopped
12 ounces white mushrooms, sliced
2 teaspoons minced fresh thyme
2 cloves garlic, minced
2 cups steel-cut oats
$1/2$ cup dry white wine or white French vermouth
6 cups low-sodium chicken broth
2 tablespoons chopped fresh flatleaf parsley
1 tablespoon fresh lemon juice
$1/2$ cup grated Parmesan cheese
Sea salt and freshly ground black pepper
Worcestershire sauce (optional)

1. In a 5- to 7-quart pressure cooker, melt the butter with the oil over medium-high heat. Add the shallots and cook 1 minute. Add the carrots, celery, and mushrooms; cook 3 minutes, stirring a few times. Add the thyme and garlic. Cook, stirring occasionally, until the liquid from the mushrooms is reabsorbed. Add the oats, stirring to coat them with the butter and oil. Add the wine and let boil until completely evaporated, stirring constantly. Add the broth and bring to a boil.

2. Close and lock the lid. Set the burner heat to high. When the cooker reaches HIGH pressure, reduce the burner heat as low as you can and still maintain HIGH pressure. Set a timer to cook for 8 minutes.

3. Remove the pot from the heat. Open the cooker with the Natural Release method; let stand for 15 minutes. At time, if the pressure is not all released, open the valve. Be careful of the steam when you remove the lid. The mixture should be fairly loose and creamy like risotto but still a dash of bite left in the oats.

4. Stir in the parsley, lemon juice, and cheese. Season to taste with salt and pepper and add a splash of Worcestershire, if desired. Serve hot in bowls.

Oat Risotto with Peas and Sautéed Shrimp

Serves 4 • Cooker: 5- to 7-quart • Time: 8 minutes at HIGH pressure

This is adapted from a recipe created by Chef Art Smith, while he was on the Lyfe Kitchen panel in Palo Alto, California, a few years ago. This is a marvelous choice for brunch or dinner, a combination of harmonious flavors and textures.

OAT RISOTTO:
1 tablespoon extra virgin olive oil
$1/2$ cup minced white onion
2 cloves garlic, minced
1 cup steel-cut oats
3 to $3^1/2$ cups chicken broth or water
$1^1/4$ cups frozen peas, thawed
$1/3$ cup grated Parmesan cheese
3 tablespoons chopped fresh chives
Sea salt and freshly ground black pepper, to taste

SHRIMP:
1 tablespoon extra virgin olive oil
12 large (26–30 count) shrimp, peeled and
    deveined
1 tablespoon chopped fresh marjoram or basil
1 tablespoon fresh lemon juice

1. In a 5- to 7-quart pressure cooker, heat the oil over medium-high heat. Add the onion and garlic, and cook until fragrant, stirring a few times, about 2 minutes; do not brown. Add the oats and cook for 1 minute. Add the broth, stir, and bring to a boil.
2. Close and lock the lid. Set the burner heat to high. When the cooker reaches HIGH pressure, reduce the burner heat as low as you can and still maintain HIGH pressure. Set a timer to cook for 8 minutes.
3. Remove the pot from the heat. Open the cooker with the Natural Release method; let stand for 10 minutes. At time, if the pressure is not all released, open the valve. Be careful of the steam as you remove the lid. The mixture should be fairly loose and creamy like risotto but still a dash of bite left in the oats.
4. While the risotto is cooking, prepare the shrimp. Heat a large sauté pan over medium-high heat, then add the oil and let warm for a minute. Add the shrimp and cook until they curl and turn pink, about 2 minutes per side. Remove from the heat and stir in the herbs and lemon juice. Set aside until ready to serve.
5. Stir the peas, Parmesan, and chives into the oats. Taste for salt and pepper. Serve the oat risotto hot in bowls topped with three shrimp for each portion. Serve immediately.

Basic Dried Posole/Hominy

Makes about 4 cups • Cooker: 5- to 7-quart • Time: 60 minutes at HIGH pressure

Posole, or hominy, are whole corn kernels that have been soaked in a lime bath, then dried again, a method of preservation that gives the corn a distinctive flavor. It can then be ground into *masa harina,* which is used for making corn tortillas. This is how to prepare dried hominy you would use instead of canned in soups, chili, and posole stew. One cup (about 6 ounces) dried hominy will cook up to equal two 14.5-ounce cans. Home cooked is again much more flavorful than canned. Hominy is great served hot with a red chile sauce and cheese. Look for dried posole in Mexican markets called *maiz para posole* in bulk, or Los Chileros brand white corn posole in 12-ounce bags from New Mexico. Frozen posole, available in the Southwest, does not need to be soaked.

2 cups dried hominy/posole (about 12 ounces),
    soaked and drained
1 tablespoon sea salt
6 cups water, to cover

1. Combine the posole, salt, and water in a 5- to 7-quart pressure cooker.
2. Close and lock the lid. Set the burner heat to high. When the cooker reaches HIGH pressure, reduce the burner heat as low as you can and still maintain HIGH pressure. Set a timer to cook for 60 minutes.
3. Remove the pot from the heat. Open the cooker with the Natural Release method; let stand for 15 minutes. At time, if the pressure is not all released, open the valve. Be careful of the steam as you remove the lid. Check the kernels and if still hard, return to a boil, relock the cooker, bring back up to HIGH pressure, and cook for 10 minutes, 20 if they are still quite hard. Keep cooking in 10-minute increments this way until the kernels are tender.
4. Drain and rinse. (You can reserve the cooking liquid to add to posole stew or soup.) The grains may or may not open up and blossom like popcorn, but should still be slightly firm to the bite. (They will have a firmer texture than canned hominy.) Serve immediately or let cool to room temperature and store in an airtight container in the refrigerator up to 2 days or the freezer for 3 months.

Basic Quinoa

Cooker: 5- to 7-quart • Time: 5 minutes at HIGH pressure

Quinoa turns translucent and fluffy when cooked. A hoop-like bran layer surrounds each grain, and it looks like a curly tail after cooking (a sure sign it is cooked enough). Quinoa is very light and extremely digestible, with a surprising crunch despite the tiny size. It is a great choice in grain salads and a nice substitute for rice and pasta.

FOR 3 CUPS COOKED:
1 cup red, white, or black quinoa
1 (2-finger) pinch sea salt
1 tablespoon olive oil
1¼ cups spring or filtered water

FOR 4½ CUPS COOKED:
1½ cups red, white, or black quinoa
1 (2-finger) pinch sea salt
1½ tablespoons olive oil
2⅓ cups spring or filtered water

FOR 6 CUPS COOKED:
2 cups red, white, or black quinoa
1 (3-finger) pinch sea salt
2 tablespoons olive oil
3 cups spring or filtered water

1. If necessary, rinse the quinoa well in a fine mesh strainer under cold running water, rubbing the grains with your fingers until no suds appear when you rub the grains. Combine the quinoa, salt, oil, and water in a 5- to 7-quart pressure cooker.
2. Close and lock the lid. Set the burner heat to high. When the cooker reaches HIGH pressure, reduce the burner heat as low as you can and still maintain HIGH pressure. Set a timer to cook for 5 minutes.
3. Remove the pot from the heat. Open the cooker with the Natural Release method; let stand for 10 minutes. At time, if the pressure is not all released, open the valve. Be careful of the steam as you remove the lid. The quinoa should be tender and translucent; each grain should have a little crescent-shaped thread protruding from it (this is the bran). Fluff the quinoa with a fork.
4. Serve or let cool to room temperature and store in an airtight container in the refrigerator for 2 days or in the freezer up to 1 month.

QUINOA

Quinoa (keen-wah) poetically translates to "mother" in Quechua, one of the languages of the native Andean peoples and descendants of the Incas. This ancient grain has been in cultivation for over 6,000 years and there are hundreds of strains. Quinoa is actually the edible seed of a plant that is related to beets and spinach and is gluten-free. The seed is a round, flat disc, smaller than millet, and can be white, red, or black. White quinoa has a very mild flavor with a gentle, tangy aftertaste; the red and black are slightly more assertive in flavor.

Nutrition-wise, quinoa has awesome benefits. One cup contains eight grams of protein; in comparison, brown rice only has five. It's a complete protein, so there's no need to combine it with beans or lentils in order to get all nine essential amino acids. Because it contains protein and fats, quinoa is slightly more perishable than rice or other grains, so use it within three months of purchase or store in the freezer. Quinoa expands during the cooking process to several times its original size, so a little goes a long way.

Pea and Watercress Quinoa Salad with Lemon Vinaigrette and Feta

Serves 6 • Cooker: 5- to 7-quart • Time: 5 minutes at HIGH pressure

The peppery bitter flavor of watercress, a member of the mustard and radish family, is a flavorful culinary counterpoint to the sweet peas and roasted red pepper. It combines with most all vegetables, both raw and cooked. Watercress is an integral vegetable in the commercial V-8 juice blend. This lovely power salad with its variety of textures is an excellent way to get more leafy watercress into your diet. Be sure to rinse watercress in cold water and use a knife to trim the stems. Blot the leaves dry with paper towel.

QUINOA:
1 cup red quinoa
1 (2-finger) pinch sea salt
1 tablespoon olive oil
1 1/4 cups spring or filtered water

SALAD:
2 Persian cucumbers, diced (about 1 cup)
1 medium carrot, shredded
2 jarred roasted red peppers, diced
1 bunch fresh watercress, stems discarded and
   leaves chopped to make about 2 cups
1 (10-ounce) package petite frozen peas, thawed
1 cup crumbled feta cheese

LEMON VINAIGRETTE:
1/4 cup fresh lemon juice
1/3 cup olive oil
1/2 teaspoon sea salt

1. If necessary, rinse the quinoa well in a fine mesh strainer under cold running water, rubbing the grains with your fingers until no suds appear. Combine the quinoa, salt, and water in a 5- to 7-quart pressure cooker.

2. Close and lock the lid. Set the burner heat to high. When the cooker reaches HIGH pressure, reduce the burner heat as low as you can and still maintain HIGH pressure. When the cooker reaches HIGH pressure, reduce the burner heat as low as you can and still maintain HIGH pressure. Set a timer to cook for 5 minutes.

3. Remove the pot from the heat. Open the cooker with the Natural Release method; let stand for 10 minutes. At time, if the pressure is not all released, open the valve. Be careful of the steam as you remove the lid. Spoon out the quinoa to a serving bowl and let cool to room temperature. You will have about 3 cups cooked grain.

4. Add the cucumbers, carrot, red peppers, watercress, and peas to the quinoa. Toss with a rubber spatula to combine. Add the feta. In a small bowl, whisk the lemon juice, oil, and salt together. Pour over the salad and, with the spatula, gently toss to evenly coat the dressing. Serve immediately or cover and store in the refrigerator and serve chilled.

Red Quinoa Salad with Cucumbers and Tomatoes

Serves 4 • Cooker: 5- to 7-quart • Time: 5 minutes at HIGH pressure

The red quinoa is really flavorful but not too strong. If you use a long English cucumber, use half, and you will not need to peel it. You want an equal amount of cucumbers and tomatoes.

QUINOA:

1 cup red quinoa
1 (2-finger) pinch sea salt
1 tablespoon olive oil
1 1/4 cups spring or filtered water
Juice and grated zest of 1 lime

SALAD:

1 cucumber, seeded and diced (about 2 cups; peel if skin is thick or waxed)
2 ribs celery, coarsely chopped
2 ripe Roma tomatoes, seeded and diced (about 2 cups)
About 1/2 cup packed chopped fresh cilantro
Juice of 2 limes
2 tablespoons red wine vinegar or sherry vinegar
1/4 cup olive oil

1. If necessary, rinse the quinoa well in a fine mesh strainer under cold running water, rubbing the grains with your fingers until no suds appear when you rub the grains. Combine the quinoa, salt, oil, water, and lime juice and zest in a 5- to 7-quart pressure cooker.

2. Close the cooker and lock the lid. Set the burner heat to high. When the cooker reaches HIGH pressure, reduce the burner heat as low as you can and still maintain HIGH pressure. Set a timer to cook for 5 minutes.

3. Remove the pot from the heat. Open the cooker with the Natural Release method; let stand for 10 minutes. At time, if the pressure is not all released, open the valve. Be careful of the steam as you remove the lid. Spoon out the quinoa to a serving bowl and let stand, uncovered, at room temperature until cooled. You will have about 3 cups cooked grain.

4. Add the cucumber, celery, tomatoes, and cilantro to the quinoa. Pour over the lime juice, then the vinegar and oil. With a rubber spatula, gently toss the ingredients together until well combined. Serve immediately or cover and store in the refrigerator and serve chilled.

RINSING QUINOA

The grains of quinoa are coated with a resiny natural pesticide and preservative compound called saponin that is bitter and soapy flavored. If the quinoa you buy hasn't already been rinsed (it should say so on the package, be sure to rinse it well before cooking to remove this coating. Place it in a fine mesh strainer and rub the grains under cold running water until no suds appear.

Mexican-Style Red Quinoa and Black Bean Salad with Avocado and Cilantro

Serves 4 to 6 • Cooker: 5- to 7-quart • Time: 5 minutes at HIGH pressure

Quinoa mixed with black beans, cumin spice, and lots of lime juice makes for a delicious salad. Cook the black beans first; you can even do it the day before. We prefer to use red quinoa in salads as it doesn't clump like the white variety.

QUINOA:
1 1/2 cups red quinoa
1 (2-finger) pinch sea salt
1 1/2 tablespoons olive oil
2 1/3 cups spring or filtered water
Juice and grated zest of 1 lime (you want some
    long, thin strips of zest)

DRESSING:
Juice of 3 limes
1/2 cup olive oil
1/2 teaspoon ground cumin
Pinch chili powder
1 small clove garlic (optional), pressed
Pinch sea salt

SALAD:
1 1/2 cups Black Beans for Salads (recipe follows) or
    1 (15-ounce) can, drained
1 1/2 cups fresh or thawed frozen corn kernels)
1 1/2 cups quartered cherry tomatoes
1 red bell pepper, seeded and diced
1 to 2 firm ripe avocadoes, to taste, peeled, pitted,
    and diced
4 green onions (white part and some of the green),
    chopped
About 1/3 cup chopped fresh cilantro

1. If necessary, rinse the quinoa well in a fine mesh strainer under cold running water, rubbing the grains with your fingers until no suds appear. Combine the quinoa, salt, oil, water, and lime juice and zest in a 5- to 7-quart pressure cooker.
2. Close and lock the lid. Set the burner heat to high. When the cooker reaches HIGH pressure, reduce the burner heat as low as you can and still maintain HIGH pressure. Set a timer to cook for 5 minutes.
3. Remove the pot from the heat. Open the cooker with the Natural Release method; let stand for 10 minutes. At time, if the pressure is not all released, open the valve. Be careful of the steam as you remove the lid. The quinoa should be tender. Spoon it out onto a clean baking sheet or wide storage container and let cool to room temperature. You will have about 4 cups cooked grain.
4. In a small bowl, whisk the dressing ingredients together.
5. In a medium salad bowl, combine the salad ingredients. Add the quinoa and fold in with a rubber spatula. Pour the dressing over the top and, with the spatula, gently toss to evenly coat the salad with it. Serve immediately or cover and store in the refrigerator and serve chilled. If serving later, add the avocado right before serving.

Black Beans for Salads

Makes about 3 cups • Cooker: 5- to 7-quart • Time: 3 minutes at HIGH pressure

Once you start making fresh beans for salads, casseroles, and soups, you will never go back to canned. They just do not taste anywhere near the same. This addition of the kombu seaweed keeps the foaming down (you won't taste it).

1 cup dried black beans, soaked (page 402) and
    drained
6 cups water
1 (4- to 6-inch) square piece kombu seaweed
1 to 2 cloves garlic, to taste, peeled
2 sprigs fresh cilantro
Sea salt, if desired

1. Place the drained beans in a 5- to 7-quart pressure cooker. Add the water, kombu, garlic, and cilantro. Never fill the pot past halfway to allow room for the beans to expand during cooking.

2. Close and lock the lid. Set the burner heat to high. When the cooker reaches HIGH pressure, reduce the burner heat as low as you can and still maintain HIGH pressure. Set a timer to cook for 3 minutes.

3. Remove the pot from the heat. Open the cooker with the Natural Release method; let stand for 15 minutes. Be careful of the steam as you remove the lid. The beans should be soft and the water a chocolaty brown. If the beans are too hard, cook a few minutes longer on the stovetop or relock the cooker and return to HIGH pressure for a few minutes if very underdone. If there is too much liquid for your taste, simmer the beans with the lid off for a few minutes to reduce it. Discard the kombu, garlic, and cilantro. Taste for salt.

4. Use or let cool to room temperature and store in an airtight container in the refrigerator for 4 to 5 days or in the freezer up to 3 months.

Quinoa Risotto with Arugula

Serves 3 • Cooker: 5- to 7-quart • Time: 5 minutes at HIGH pressure

This recipe is adapted from one developed by Dr. Preston Maring for the Recipes for Health column that appears in Kaiser Permanente's monthly flyer. You can make this vegan by leaving out the Parmesan or using a vegan cheese. Arugula's peppery bite pairs well with the nutty flavor of quinoa. This recipe can be doubled.

1 cup white quinoa
2 tablespoons olive oil
1 cup finely chopped white onion
1 clove garlic, minced
1/4 cup dry white wine
2 1/4 cups vegetable broth
1/2 cup thinly sliced cremini mushrooms
1/2 bunch skinny asparagus, bottoms trimmed and cut into 1-inch pieces
2 cups coarsely chopped arugula
1 medium carrot, shredded
1/4 to 1/2 cup grated Parmesan cheese, to taste (optional)
1/2 teaspoon sea salt
1/4 teaspoon freshly ground black or white pepper

1. If necessary, rinse the quinoa well in a fine mesh strainer under cold running water, rubbing the grains with your fingers until no suds appear.

2. In a 5- to 7-quart pressure cooker, heat 1 tablespoon of the oil over medium heat. Add the onion and cook, stirring a few times, until softened, about 4 minutes. Stir in the quinoa and garlic and cook, stirring, for about a minute. Pour in the wine, increase the heat to medium-high, and let the wine bubble until evaporated. Add the broth and bring to a boil.

3. Close and lock the lid. Set the burner heat to high. When the cooker reaches HIGH pressure, reduce the burner heat as low as you can and still maintain HIGH pressure. Set a timer to cook for 5 minutes.

4. Meanwhile, in a nonstick skillet over medium-high heat, heat the remaining 1 tablespoon oil. Add the mushrooms and asparagus and cook until all the liquid from the mushrooms evaporates, the mushrooms have browned on one side, and the asparagus is crunchy tender. Remove from the heat.

5. Remove the pressure cooker from the heat and open with the Natural Release method; let stand for 10 minutes. At time, if the pressure is not all released, open the valve. Be careful of the steam as you remove the lid. The mixture will be loose, the quinoa tender and translucent; each grain should have a little thread (the bran) protruding from it.

6. Stir the arugula, carrot, mushrooms, and asparagus into the quinoa with a large rubber spatula and simmer over medium heat with the lid off for a couple minutes to warm the vegetables. Stir in the cheese, if using, salt, and pepper and serve.

Basic Wheat Berries

Makes about 4^1/$_2$ cups • Cooker: 5- to 7-quart • Time: 2 minutes at HIGH pressure

Wheat berries, chewy whole grain wheat with all its natural bran and germ intact, are a popular grain, especially in salads, due to their sweet flavor and enticing aroma. If you cook wheat berries as you would for a risotto, it's called a *granotto*. Varieties (hard, soft, spring, or winter) can be used interchangeably. They can be sweet or savory with equal eating pleasure. The timing will vary due to the age of the berries and where they are grown. Do not fill the pressure pot more than one-half full before cooking to leave room for expansion: 1^1/$_2$ cups dry grain/ 5 cups liquid per 4 quart cooker; 3 cups dry grain/ 8 cups liquid per 5 to 6-quart cooker; 4 cups dry grain/10 cups liquid per 8-quart cooker. There are 2^1/$_2$ cups wheat berries to a pound. Find them in natural-foods markets and online at kingarthurflour.com.

2 cups wheat berries, sorted, discarding any stones
6 cups water
2 tablespoons olive oil

1. Place the wheat berries in a dry skillet over medium-high heat. Toast, stirring constantly, until the grains pop and deepen in color, about 4 minutes. This step is optional, but many cooks like this flavor a bit better than the raw grain.
2. Rinse the wheat berries well under cool running water. Combine with the water and oil in a 5- to 7-quart pressure cooker.
3. Close and lock the lid. Set the burner heat to high. When the cooker reaches HIGH pressure, reduce the burner heat as low as you can and still maintain HIGH pressure. Set a timer to cook for 25 minutes. If you soak the berries overnight, cook time will be 10 minutes.
4. Remove the pot from the heat. Open the cooker with the Natural Release method; let stand for 15 minutes. At time, if the pressure is not all released, open the valve. Be careful of the steam as you remove the lid.
5. Drain well in a fine mesh strainer and rinse off the starch. Spoon out the cooked grain to a serving bowl to serve immediately, or let stand, uncovered, at room temperature until cooled and place in a storage container in the refrigerator up to 2 days, or freeze up to 2 months, to use in salads, chili, breakfast cereal, or soups.

Wheat Berry Pilaf with Edamame, Corn, and Mushrooms

Serves 4 • Cooker: 5- to 7-quart • Time: 18 minutes at HIGH pressure

Edamame (their name translates to "beans on branches") are young soybeans and have a consistency similar to that of baby lima beans. They are a wonderful addition to this pilaf, with its mixture of tastes and textures.

2 tablespoons extra virgin olive oil
$^1/_2$ cup minced white onion or leek (white part only)
3 ounces cremini mushrooms, sliced
$^1/_4$ cup sliced green onions
$^1/_3$ cup finely chopped red bell pepper
1$^1/_4$ cups wheat berries, sorted, discarding any stones, rinsed, and drained
2$^1/_2$ cups chicken or vegetable broth
$^1/_2$ of a 12-ounce package frozen shelled edamame, thawed
$^1/_2$ cup frozen petite white corn kernels, thawed
Sea salt and freshly ground black pepper

1. In a 5- to 7-quart pressure cooker, heat the oil over medium-high heat. Add the onion and cook, stirring a few times, until soft, about 3 minutes. Stir in the mushrooms and cook for 2 minutes. Add the green onions, bell pepper, and wheat berries. Stir and cook for 1 minute. Add the broth and bring to a boil.
2. Close and lock the lid. Set the burner heat to high. When the cooker reaches HIGH pressure, reduce the burner heat as low as you can and still maintain HIGH pressure. Set a timer to cook for 18 minutes.
3. Remove the pot from the heat. Open the cooker with the Natural Release method; let stand for 15 minutes. At time, if the pressure is not all released, open the valve. Be careful of the steam as you remove the lid.
4. Stir the corn and edamame into the wheat berries. Let stand a few minutes, with the lid on but not locked, to heat the vegetables. Season to taste with salt and pepper. Serve immediately.

Wheat Berry Salad with Dried Cranberries and Pomegranate Vinaigrette

Serves 8

Dried cranberries are made from what is left of the cranberries after they have been pressed for juice, sweetened with sugar to tame their bitterness and then oven-dried. Look for low-sugar dried cranberries, if you can find them. Dried cranberries have a chewy texture and tart-sweetness that complement the nutty wheat berries.

POMEGRANATE VINAIGRETTE:
$^1/_4$ cup raspberry vinegar
$^1/_4$ cup pomegranate juice
$^1/_3$ cup fruity olive oil
Sea salt and freshly ground black pepper, to taste

SALAD:
4$^1/_2$ cups pressure-cooked wheat berries (page 389), at room temperature

1$^1/_4$ cups dried cranberries, soaked in hot water 15 minutes and drained
1$^1/_2$ cups grated carrots
1 cup finely chopped red onion
3 tablespoon minced fresh flatleaf parsley

1. In a small bowl, whisk the vinaigrette ingredients together.
2. In a large serving bowl, combine the wheat berries, cranberries, carrots, onion, and parsley. Toss the salad with enough of the vinaigrette so it is lightly coated. Store in the refrigerator, covered, 30 minutes to 2 hours, to let the flavors meld. Serve the salad chilled or room temperature.

Wheat Berry Waldorf

Serves 8

The crunchy, fresh Waldorf Salad has a history. It was created by Oscar Tschirky. Known throughout the world as Oscar of the Waldorf, he worked as maitre d'hotel of the Waldorf Astoria Hotel in New York City from 1893 to 1943 (50 years!) and contributed to the recipes served in the restaurant dining room. In 1896, Waldorf Salad appeared in *The Cook Book* by "Oscar of the Waldorf." A delightful 1931 profile called "Oscar the Epicure" declared, "Whenever people, in America at least, speak of the art of eating, they invariably mention Oscar." We've added wheat berries to the mix, as well as yogurt to the dressing. It's a great side salad on the holiday table.

2 to 3 cups pressure-cooked wheat berries (page 389), at room temperature

WALDORF DRESSING:
1 cup plain yogurt (not Greek)
1 cup mayonnaise or Vegenaise
$^{1}/_{3}$ cup sour cream
$^{1}/_{4}$ cup orange or tangerine juice

SALAD:
2 large Fuji or Granny Smith apples, cored and chopped
2 Honeycrisp or Braeburn apples, cored and chopped
Juice of 1 lemon
3 ribs celery, chopped
1 cup red or green seedless grapes, halved, or pomegranate seeds
$^{1}/_{2}$ cup slivered blanched almonds
$^{1}/_{2}$ cup dried tart cherries

1. In a small bowl, whisk the dressing ingredients together until smooth.
2. In a large serving bowl, combine the wheat berries and apples, then add the lemon juice and toss. Add the celery, grapes, almonds, and cherries and toss with just enough of the dressing to lightly coat all the salad ingredients; you might not use all the dressing. Store in the refrigerator, covered, 30 minutes to 2 hours, to let the flavors meld. Serve the salad chilled.

Multi-Grain Rice (Japgok-bap)

Serves 6 to 8 • Cooker: 5- to 7-quart • Time: 6 minutes at HIGH pressure

Visit any Korean household these days and you will find most families are serving a pressure-cooked multi-grain rice called *japgok-bap* instead of plain rice for their daily meal. If you go to any major Asian grocery store you will find the bags of mixed grains, from 5 up to 20 different grains and legumes per package, next to the rices. The most common grains are brown rice, glutinous brown rice, black rice, rice bran, oats, barley, sorghum, and millet in combination with split peas and all sorts of beans (red, black, kidney, soy, etc.). You don't want the bag with mostly red beans, you want a nice mixture. White rice is included in the dish as it adds stickiness and helps to create a soft chewing texture. If you are using an electric pressure cooker, use the multi-grain or brown rice button. This is best eaten the day it is made.

1¹/₂ cups mixed grains and legumes
2 cups white short-grain Japanese-style rice, rinsed
1¹/₂ tablespoons olive oil or plain sesame oil
1 or 2 (3-finger) pinch(es) sea salt or Himalayan
    pink salt
4 cups spring or filtered water

1. Rinse the mixed grains several times until the water runs clear and soak them in water to cover for 30 minutes to 1 hour. Drain.
2. Combine the soaked mixed grains and legumes, rice, oil, salt, and water in a 5 to 7-quart pressure cooker that has been sprayed with nonstick cooking spray.
3. Close and lock the lid. Place a heat diffuser on the burner and the pressure cooker on the diffuser. Set the burner heat to high. When the cooker reaches HIGH pressure, reduce the burner heat as low as you can and still maintain HIGH pressure. Set a timer to cook for 6 minutes.
4. Remove the pot from the heat. Open the cooker with the Natural Release method; let stand for 15 minutes. Be careful of the steam as you remove the lid. Gently stir to fluff and combine the grains and legumes and serve.

Three-Grain Pilaf with Porcini Mushrooms

Serves 6 • Cooker: 5- to 7-quart • Time: 20 minutes at HIGH pressure

When you have grains with the same cook time, you can mix and match. This is one of our favorite combinations, wheat berries, barley, and wild rice. It's a great partner for roasted meats and game and braised tofu, topped with a little plain Greek yogurt or crumbled goat cheese. It also makes a delicious stuffing for acorn squash halves sprinkled with toasted Marcona almonds.

$^1/_3$ cup wheat berries
$^1/_3$ cup hulled barley
$^1/_4$ ounce dried porcini mushrooms (about $^1/_4$ cup)
$^3/_4$ cup warm water
2 tablespoons olive oil
$^3/_4$ cup finely chopped white onion
$^3/_4$ cup diced celery
$^1/_3$ cup wild rice, rinsed
1$^1/_2$ cups low-sodium chicken or vegetable broth
3 tablespoons chopped fresh flatleaf parsley
2 tablespoons fresh lemon juice
$^1/_4$ teaspoon sea salt, or to taste
Freshly ground black pepper

1. Soak the wheat berries and barley together in water to cover for 2 to 12 hours. Drain.
2. Place mushrooms in a small bowl and cover with the warm water. Let soak for 15 minutes. Lift out mushrooms with a slotted spoon. Rinse and coarsely chop. Strain the soaking liquid through a sieve lined with a paper coffee filter or cheesecloth. Reserve $^1/_2$ cup mushroom liquid. Place the chopped mushrooms in a 5- to 7-quart pressure cooker, then stir in the wild rice, wheat berries, and barley. Stir 1 minute to warm. Add the broth and reserved mushroom liquid.
3. Close and lock the lid. Place a heat diffuser on the burner and the pressure cooker on the diffuser. Set the burner heat to high. When the cooker reaches HIGH pressure, reduce the burner heat as low as you can and still maintain HIGH pressure. Set a timer to cook for 20 minutes.
4. Remove the pot from the heat. Open the cooker with the Natural Release method; let stand for 15 minutes. Be careful of the steam as you remove the lid. Gently stir to fluff the grains.
5. Add the parsley, lemon juice, salt, and pepper to taste to the pilaf and fluff again to combine. Serve immediately. Store the leftover rice in a ziptop plastic bag in the freezer up to 1 month.

Pressure Cooker Macaroni and Four Cheeses

Serves 4 to 6 • Cooker: 5- to 7-quart • Time: 6 minutes at HIGH pressure

With this recipe, you will never reach for a box again; it goes together so fast, it might as well be sleight of hand. Mac and cheese takes to all sorts of additions if you want to make it fancier. You can stir in 1 cup thawed frozen peas along with the cheese or 8 to 12 ounces sliced smoked sausage, such as a chicken apple. Fold in 8 ounces chopped cooked lobster meat, or a combination of cooked shrimp and crab meat. Instead of the cream cheese and goat cheese you can substitute a 5.2-ounce package of Boursin cheese with garlic and herbs (this is a favorite of ours; it melts like a dream). If you use whole wheat or spelt macaroni, increase the cook time to 7 minutes. Serve with a green salad.

2³/₄ cups dry elbow macaroni, mini penne, or small
    shells (10 to 12 ounces)
2 cups low-sodium chicken or vegetable broth
1 cup water
2 pinches sea salt
2 tablespoons olive oil
1¹/₂ cups shredded cheddar cheese
1¹/₂ cups shredded Fontina or cubed mozzarella
    cheese
2 ounces cream cheese
2 ounces fresh goat cheese
¹/₄ cup half-and-half
2 teaspoons Dijon mustard
Freshly ground black pepper
Salt
Grated Parmesan cheese, for serving

1. In a 5- to 7-quart pressure cooker, combine the pasta, broth, water, salt, and oil.
2. Close and lock the lid in place. Set the burner heat to high. When the cooker reaches HIGH pressure, reduce the burner heat as low as you can and still maintain HIGH pressure. Set a timer to cook for 6 minutes.
3. Remove the pot from the heat. Open the cooker with the Quick Release method. Be careful of the steam as you remove the lid. Do not drain. Stir in the cheeses, half-and-half, mustard, and pepper to taste until the cheeses are melted and combined. Replace the cover and let stand a few minutes to thicken and set up. Taste for salt.
4. Portion the mac and cheese into shallow bowls or on dinner plates and serve with Parmesan for sprinkling and the pepper grinder on the side.

Pressure Cooker Penne with Creamy Tomato Vodka Sauce

Serves 4 • Cooker: 5- to 7-quart • Time: 7 minutes at HIGH pressure

While our recipes feature fresh foods, there are a few convenience items we find handy, like jarred marinara sauce. This pasta is on the table in less than 15 minutes, so have the table set and the salad tossed.

3 cups dry penne (about 12 ounces)
1 (26-ounce) jar plain marinara sauce
1 (14.5-ounce) can diced tomatoes in juice, drained
$^1/_4$ teaspoon red pepper flakes
$1^1/_2$ cups water
$^1/_4$ cup vodka
3 tablespoons olive oil
1 cup heavy cream, heated
3 tablespoons minced fresh basil
Freshly ground black pepper
Salt
1 cup freshly grated Parmesan cheese, for serving

1. In a 5- to 7-quart pressure cooker, combine the pasta, marinara sauce, tomatoes, pepper flakes, water, vodka, and oil. Bring to a boil.
2. Close and lock the lid. Set the burner heat to high. When the cooker reaches HIGH pressure, reduce the burner heat as low as you can and still maintain HIGH pressure. Set a timer to cook for 7 minutes.
3. Remove the pot from the heat. Open the cooker with the Quick Release method. Be careful of the steam as you remove the lid. Stir in the cream, basil, and pepper to taste. Replace the cover and let stand a few minutes to thicken and set up. Taste for salt.
4. Portion the penne into shallow bowls or on dinner plates and serve with the Parmesan for sprinkling and the pepper grinder on the side.

Whole-Grain Penne, Ragu, and Mozzarella One Pot

Serves 4 to 6 • Cooker: 5- to 7-quart • Time: 20 minutes at HIGH pressure

This is an adaptation of a recipe Deb Murray makes every time she demos the Wolfgang Puck electric pressure cooker on QVC. It is one of those "I have to feed the kids, oh what can I do" or "I am so hungry what can I eat that will be hot and filling ASAP" kind of recipes. What is remarkable about this pantry concoction is that it starts with frozen ground meat. Don't be tempted to use a larger pasta or string pastas like spaghetti; it won't work (but you can substitute ziti or medium shells).

1 pound frozen ground dark meat turkey (do not thaw)
1³/₄ cups water or chicken broth
¹/₄ cup dry red or white wine
2 cups penne rigate (you can make this with regular pasta or whole wheat, spelt, low-carb, brown rice, or quinoa pasta)
1 (24- to 26-ounce) jar marinara sauce
6 to 8 ounces whole-milk mozzarella cheese, to taste, cut into ¹/₂-inch dice
1 (2.25-ounce) can sliced California black olives, drained, for garnish (optional)
¹/₂ cup shredded or grated Parmesan cheese, for sprinkling (optional)

LEMON RICOTTA (OPTIONAL):
1¹/₄ cups whole-milk ricotta cheese
2 tablespoons olive oil
Grated zest of 1 lemon
1 tablespoon minced fresh flatleaf parsley or basil
Few grinds black pepper

1. Place the frozen turkey meat in a 5- to 7-quart pressure cooker. Pour in the broth and wine. Layer the dry pasta over and around the meat and flatten into a layer with the back of a large spoon. Pour in the marinara sauce. You want the pasta completely submerged in the sauce.

2. Close and lock the lid. Set the burner heat to high. When the cooker reaches HIGH pressure, reduce the burner heat as low as you can and still maintain HIGH pressure. Set a timer to cook for 20 minutes.

3. Make the Lemon Ricotta, if using. In a small bowl, whisk the ricotta, oil, lemon zest, parsley, and pepper together. Cover and refrigerate until serving.

4. Remove the pot from the heat. Open the cooker with the Quick Release method. Be careful of the steam as you remove the lid. The pasta should be tender. Using a large spoon, break up the ground meat and gently stir to evenly distribute. The meat should be fully cooked.

5. With a heat-resistant spatula, fold the mozzarella cubes into the mixture. Set the lid askew on top of the cooker (do not lock it) for 5 minutes to let the cheese melt into scrumptious pockets in the pasta. Serve immediately topped with some black olives and Parmesan or with a dollop of Lemon Ricotta.

Basic Couscous

Serves 6 to 8 • Cooker: 5- to 7-quart • Time: 2 minutes at HIGH pressure

Couscous resembles a grain, but is actually a pasta, made from granules of semolina. It is a staple in Moroccan and North African cuisine. Plain, buttery couscous is piled into a dramatic mound on a communal platter and served on its own or with a tagine or roasted meat and freshly made flatbreads. The instant, parboiled couscous is very easy to prepare for even a novice cook as it only needs boiling water to swell. It is a great alternative to pasta or rice. A 10 ounce box of couscous equals $1^1/_2$ cups uncooked.

3 cups (two 10-ounce boxes) instant couscous
$4^1/_2$ cups water
2 tablespoons olive oil
3 tablespoons butter, cut into pieces
1 teaspoon sea salt

1. Combine the couscous, water, oil, butter, and salt in a 5- to 7-quart pressure cooker. Bring to a boil.
2. Close and lock the lid. Set the burner heat to high. When the cooker reaches HIGH pressure, reduce the burner heat as low as you can and still maintain HIGH pressure. Set a timer to cook for 2 minutes.
3. Remove the pot from the heat. Open the cooker with the Natural Release method; let stand for 15 minutes. Be careful of the steam as you remove the lid. Set the lid askew on the pot and let stand another 5 minutes.
4. Fluff the couscous with a fork. Spoon out the cooked grain to a serving bowl to serve immediately or let cool to room temperature. Will keep in an airtight container in the refrigerator for 2 days.

Saffron Couscous: Crush 16 saffron threads with the salt in a mortar and pestle or using the flat side of a chef's knife on a cutting board until a coarse powder is formed. Add in Step 1. Heat $1/_2$ cup slivered blanched almonds in a sauté pan with 2 teaspoons olive oil over medium-high heat. Stir and cook until the nuts are just turning golden. Remove from the pan and drain on paper towels. Serve the saffron couscous sprinkled with the almonds.

Breakfast Couscous: Combine 1 (10-ounce) box instant couscous, $2^1/_4$ cups almond or coconut milk, 1 tablespoon butter, $1/_2$ teaspoon sea salt, 1 (4-inch) cinnamon stick, broken in half, a pinch or two of ground ginger, and 3 cardamom pods in the pressure cooker. Cook as directed for Basic Couscous. Serve topped with fresh fruit, such as chopped mango, peaches, sliced banana, or berries. Serves 2 to 4.

Lemon Whole-Wheat Couscous

Serves 5 to 6 • Cooker: 5- to 7-quart • Time: 3 minutes at HIGH pressure

If you do not want to eat the traditional semolina couscous, you have the option of whole-wheat, barley, and gluten-free brown rice couscous. All three will work in this recipe.

2 cups instant whole-wheat couscous
3¹/₂ cups low-sodium chicken broth
2 tablespoons olive oil
¹/₄ cup fresh lemon juice
1 tablespoon grated lemon zest
¹/₂ teaspoon sea salt
¹/₄ cup chopped fresh chives or cilantro (optional)
¹/₄ preserved lemon (optional), pulp discarded, peel rinsed and minced

1. Combine the couscous, broth, oil, lemon juice and zest, and salt in a 5- to 7-quart pressure cooker. Bring to a boil.
2. Close and lock the lid. Set the burner heat to high. When the cooker reaches HIGH pressure, reduce the burner heat as low as you can and still maintain HIGH pressure. Set a timer to cook for 3 minutes.
3. Remove the pot from the heat. Open the cooker with the Natural Release method; let stand for 15 minutes. Be careful of the steam as you remove the lid. Set the lid askew on the pot and let stand for another 5 minutes.
4. Fluff the couscous with a fork and stir in the chives and preserved lemon, if using. Spoon out the cooked grain to a serving bowl to serve immediately or let cool to room temperature and store in an airtight container in the refrigerator for up to 2 days.

Lemon Whole-Wheat Couscous with Currants and Green Onions: Add ¹/₄ teaspoon turmeric and ³/₄ cup currants in Step 1. Substitute chopped green onions for the chives or cilantro in Step 4.

Moroccan Seven-Vegetable Couscous

Serves 4 to 6 • Cooker: 5- to 7-quart • Time: 1 minute at HIGH pressure

There are umpteen versions of Seven-Vegetable Couscous. While the ingredient list looks long, it is very easy to put in the pot. You can substitute seasonal vegetables to be creative, keeping the number at seven. Traditionally this dish is cooked in a two-tiered cooking vessel called a couscoussier, which features a large base and a steamer basket that fits snugly atop the pot. It turns out that the pressure cooker does a fine job of mimicking the couscoussier. This is a great dish for relaxed entertaining, served with a big green salad and a grated carrot salad. The leftovers are good eating the next day.

2 tablespoons olive oil
1 tablespoon unsalted butter
1 large white onion, coarsely chopped
1 rib celery, thinly sliced
1 medium to large turnip, peeled and cut into
  $1/2$-inch cubes
Pinch saffron threads or sweet paprika
Pinch red pepper flakes or cayenne pepper
$1/2$ teaspoon turmeric
$1/2$ teaspoon ground cumin
1 tablespoon grated peeled fresh ginger
1 pound butternut squash, peeled, seeded, and cut
  into $1^{1}/_{2}$-inch chunks
8 ounces green beans, ends trimmed and cut into
  $1^{1}/_{2}$-inch lengths
$1/4$ cup dried currants or golden raisins
2 tablespoon minced dried apricots
1 (14.5-ounce) can diced tomatoes in juice, drained
2 cups vegetable broth
1 stick cinnamon, broken in half
$1^{1}/_{2}$ cups couscous (any kind)
1 medium zucchini or yellow summer squash,
  sliced $1/4$ inch thick
$3/4$ cup frozen petite peas, thawed
Sea salt
$1/4$ cup chopped fresh cilantro
$1/2$ cup blanched slivered almonds, toasted (see
  page 167)
2 lemons, each cut into 6 wedges, for serving
Extra virgin olive oil, for drizzling

1. In a 5- to 7-quart pressure cooker over medium high heat, melt the butter with the oil. Add the onion, carrot, celery, and turnip, and cook, stirring occasionally, until soft, about 5 minutes. Stir in the saffron, red pepper, turmeric, cumin, and ginger. Cook 1 to 2 minutes, stirring, until fragrant. Add the butternut squash, green beans, currants, apricots, and tomatoes, then pour in the broth and add cinnamon stick. Bring to a boil.

2. Close and lock the lid. Set the burner heat to high. When the cooker reaches HIGH pressure, reduce the burner heat as low as you can and still maintain HIGH pressure. Set a timer to cook for 1 minute.

3. Remove the pot from the heat. Open the cooker with the Natural Release method; let stand for 5 minutes. At time, if the pressure is not all released, open the valve. Be careful of the steam as you remove the lid.

4. Stir in the couscous, zucchini, and peas. Cover without bringing to pressure and let stand for about 10 minutes, until the couscous is tender. Fluff the couscous with a fork and gently stir to distribute the vegetables.

5. Taste for salt. Stir in the cilantro and sprinkle with the almonds. Serve with lemon wedges on the side and fresh flatbread, like naan or pita bread. Have a cruet of olive oil at the table for drizzling to substitute for *smen* or preserved butter, a finishing touch integral to Moroccan cooking.

13

The Bean Eater: Dried Beans and Lentils

Dried beans are the kind of good and good-for-you food that doesn't get much publicity. They are an important source of protein, are gluten-free, heart-healthy, and a complex carbohydrate suitable for diabetics.

Cooking your own dried beans and lentils is absolutely the cheapest way to serve them. A 1-pound bag generally costs less than $2. That one bag yields more than 6 cups of beans or lentils and broth. A 15-ounce can of beans, at about the same price, yields less than 2 cups. It doesn't take a genius to do the math. And the pressure cooker is a dried bean's best friend. Cook up at least double the amount you will need and freeze the rest.

Refer to our Pressure Cooker Bean and Lentil Cooking Time chart on pages 402–406 as a guide, which includes cook times for beans soaked and unsoaked. Cooking beans in the pressure cooker significantly cuts their cook time, but if you soak the beans prior to cooking, you can cut that time even more. Lentils require no soaking at all. Don't be afraid to cook just 1 cup of dry beans at a time. You can use any size pressure cooker to cook a small amount of beans.

BEANS AND LENTILS THE PRESSURE COOKER WAY

Soaking vs. not soaking. The pressure cooker handles both soaked and unsoaked beans beautifully. Some beans should not be soaked, and lentils do not need soaking; if there is no time given in the chart for soaked beans that means they don't need it or we don't recommend it.

Quick Release or Natural Release. Generally speaking, use Natural Release for cooking beans. Most pressure-cooked beans and lentils work fine with Natural or Quick Release, so your choice depends on convenience or the steps in the recipe you are choosing. The exceptions are noted in the chart—if there is no time given for Quick Release that means we don't recommend it. Natural Release takes about 3 to 5 minutes off the overall cooking time. Natural Release is also gentler on the beans, preserving their shape, which sometimes makes a noticeable difference with thin-skinned beans such as black-eyed peas.

Controlling the foam. When you cook beans, and particularly lentils, they can produce a good amount of foam. Adding a tablespoon or so of oil to the bean pot helps greatly with that. It's *essential* for lentils and split peas, but we like to add it to every pot of beans. Some cooks spray the surface of the water with vegetable cooking spray to prevent boil ups and foaming. A 4- to 6-inch piece of kombu seaweed cooked with the beans will do the same job. Discard it after cooking.

When to salt. The accepted wisdom is that beans should be salted after cooking; if they are salted before cooking, they will never fully soften. We haven't felt the need to test out this tenet, but just in case salt does really toughen the skins or slow down cooking, you'll find our recipes adding the salt after cooking, except in the cases of thin-skinned beans or where there is a danger of overcooking the bean. In those cases, salt is added up front to preserve the integrity of the bean.

Aiding digestibility. There are a whole host of suggestions for controlling the inner turbulence that some feel after enjoying a plate of beans. The one most commonly offered up is adding epazote, known as the "bean herb" of Mexico, to the cooking pot. We haven't noticed any difference in digestibility, but its grassy flavor is nice addition to most beans. Sage is used in Mediterranean cuisines. Some cooks add a peeled whole potato to the pot, then throw it out after cooking. We've tried this as well and again, can't say we noticed a difference. Other tips include soaking, then rinsing the beans and cooking them in fresh water with ginger and turmeric or eating the cooked beans with yogurt. The good news is that if you eat beans frequently, your body will adjust.

SOAKING BEANS

With just a few exceptions (see the chart), soaking beans is completely optional. The benefit of doing it is that it decreases your cook time in pressure cooker even more.

If you choose to soak, there are three methods, all interchangeable, although many cooks swear by the conventional overnight soak. Always drain off the soaking water before adding the fresh water you will cook the beans in. The drained soaked beans can also be frozen, then defrosted and cooked.

Before you use any of these methods, rinse the beans under cold running water until the water runs clean, then pick through them to remove any small stones or wrinkled or deformed beans.

Pressure Cooker Quick-Soak Method: Place the beans in the pressure cooker with 4 cups water and 1 teaspoon salt per 1 cup dried beans. Cover the pressure cooker, lock the lid in place, and bring to HIGH pressure over high heat. Reduce the heat to maintain the pressure and cook for 2 minutes. Open the cooker with the Quick Release method. Drain the beans and they're ready for cooking.

Regular Quick-Soak Method: Place the beans in the pressure cooker pot or a saucepan with water to cover by about 2 inches. Bring to a boil, boil for 1 minute, then cover loosely and remove from the heat to another burner. Let soak for at least 1 hour and up to 8 hours. Drain the beans and they are ready for cooking.

Overnight Method: Place the beans in a bowl with cold water to cover by about 2 inches. Let stand, uncovered, 8 to 12 hours, or overnight. Drain the beans and they are ready for cooking. Use this method for black beans.

COOKING BEANS AND LENTILS NOT INCLUDED IN OUR CHART

Over the past decade, there has been an explosion in the number of beautiful heirloom varieties available in farmers' markets and specialty markets, as well as online. They are delightfully delicious, each with its own flavor profile, ranging from sweet to robust to earthy. For varieties you don't find on our chart, use the following guidelines to convert conventional stovetop cook times to the pressure cooker times.

- No matter the recipe, **do not fill the pressure cooker more than one half full** when cooking beans or lentils. That is beans/lentils plus cooking liquid.

- For beans or lentils that cook in 1 hour or less by conventional methods: Try 10 minutes soaked or 20 minutes unsoaked. Open with Quick Release and test for doneness.

- For beans that cook in 1 to 1 1/2 hours by conventional methods: Try 15 minutes soaked or 30 minutes unsoaked. Open with Quick Release and test for doneness.

- For beans that cook in 1 1/2 hours or longer by conventional methods: Try 25 minutes soaked or 40 minutes unsoaked. Open with Quick Release and test for doneness.

DRY BEAN MATH

1 pound dry beans = 2 cups dry beans = 5 to 6 cups cooked beans

1 pound dry beans = 3 (15.5-ounce) cans drained beans

1/2 cup dry beans = 1 (15.5-ounce) can drained beans = about 1 1/2 cups drained cooked beans

1 cup dry beans = 2 1/2 to 3 cups cooked beans

1 cup dried garbanzo, large lima, or Great Northern beans = 2 1/2 to 3 cups cooked beans

1 (19-ounce) can beans = 2 1/4 cups drained cooked beans

COOKING TIMES FOR BEANS AND LENTILS IN THE PRESSURE COOKER

All cooking times are based on 1 cup dried beans or lentils and 4 cups liquid OR 1 cup dried beans, soaked, and 3 cups liquid. Also we add 1 tablespoon olive oil to every pot of beans or lentils we cook. For lentils, the oil is absolutely necessary to control the foaming.

Bean	Soaked Quick Release/Cooking Time	Soaked Natural Release/Cooking Time	Unsoaked Quick Release/Cooking Time	Unsoaked Natural Release/Cooking Time	Notes
Adzuki	4 minutes	Just bring to pressure, then remove from heat	15 minutes	13 to 14 minutes	Quick Release not recommended as beans will sputter.
Anasazi	6 minutes	1 minute	16 minutes	13 minutes	Best not to soak these mild-flavored beans as they are quick-cooking and don't hold their shape well if soaked.
Black, tampico, turtle	9 to 10 minutes	7 minutes	30 minutes	24 minutes	Excellent results even unsoaked.
Black valentine	11 to 12 minutes	8 minutes	43 minutes	40 minutes	These are twice the size of normal black beans, shaped like a kidney bean.
Black-eyed peas, cow peas	2 minutes	Just bring to pressure, then remove from heat	10 minutes	6 minutes	
Calypso	11 minutes	7 minutes	27 minutes	25 minutes	Mild and delicious, with a potato flavor. Black markings fade to gray/pink when cooked.
Cannellini, white kidney	10 minutes	7 minutes	33 minutes	30 minutes	Soaking is recommended for better color.
Channa dal, Bengal gram, split baby garbanzo			10 minutes	6 minutes	Larger than toor dal but otherwise looks similar, corn-like flavor.

COOKING TIMES FOR BEANS AND LENTILS IN THE PRESSURE COOKER

Bean	Soaked Quick Release/Cooking Time	Soaked Natural Release/Cooking Time	Unsoaked Quick Release/Cooking Time	Unsoaked Natural Release/Cooking Time	Notes
Chestnut, chestnut lima, Christmas lima	34 to 35 minutes	30 minutes	45 minutes	40 minutes	Taste so much like chestnuts that they are good absolutely plain and cold. Eat as a snack. If cooking unsoaked, be sure to use plenty of water (5 cups or more per cup of beans).
Corona, corona runner, sweet white	9 minutes	6 minutes	33 minutes	32 minutes	Substitute for gigante. If cooking unsoaked, be sure to use plenty of water (5 cups or more per cup of beans).
Cranberry, borlotti, Romano	10 minutes	7 minutes	35 minutes	32 minutes	Plump and creamy. A nice change from pintos.
Eye of the goat (ojo de cabra)	22 minutes	19 minutes	55 minutes	53 minutes	Plump and flavorful. Beautiful cream and brown color.
Fava beans, peeled and split	10 to 11 minutes	6 minutes			Best to let the pressure release naturallly.
Flageolet	9 minutes	6 minutes	41 minutes	38 minutes	Long slender white and pale green. Taste vegetable-like and fresh.
Garbanzo, chickpeas, ceci, kabuli chana	20 minutes	17 minutes	43 to 45 minutes	41 minutes	
Good Mother Stallard	21 minutes	18 minutes	50 minutes	44 minutes	Plump, almost spherical, mottled bean, very flavorful, almost sweet tasting.
Great Northern	10 minutes	7 minutes	42 minutes	40 mintues	One of the trio of white beans found in most supermarkets.

COOKING TIMES FOR BEANS AND LENTILS IN THE PRESSURE COOKER

Bean	Soaked Quick Release/Cooking Time	Soaked Natural Release/Cooking Time	Unsoaked Quick Release/Cooking Time	Unsoaked Natural Release/Cooking Time	Notes
Lentils, black, caviar, Beluga			9 minutes for salads, 11 for soups or dal	6 minutes for salads, 7 to 8 for soup or dal	Nutty flavor. Use 2 cups liquid to cook 1 cup dried lentils. Adding oil to the cooking liquid is a must.
Lentils, brown and Castelluccio			10 minutes for salads, 12 to 14 for soup or dal	6 minutes for salads, 8 to 10 for soup or dal	Use 2 cups liquid to cook 1 cup dried. Adding oil to the cooking liquid is a must.
Lentils, green (de Puy)			10 minutes	6 minutes	Use 2 cups liquid to cook 1 cup dried lentils. Adding oil to the cooking liquid is a must. Natural release is far preferred to Quick Release to prevent splitting.
Lentils, green sprouted			3 minutes	1 to 2 minutes	Use 2 cups liquid to cook 1 cup sprouted lentils. Adding oil to the cooking liquid is a must. They're so quick-cooking, they are a convenience food.
Lentils, split orange, red			4 minutes	Just bring to pressure	Use 2 cups liquid to cook 1 cup dried lentils. Adding oil to the cooking liquid is a must.
Lima, baby	8 minutes	6 minutes	25 minutes	23 minutes	Limas really benefit from soaking.
Lima, large, butter	5 minutes	3 minutes	23 minutes	21 minutes	Soaking is recommended for better shape and even cooking.

COOKING TIMES FOR BEANS AND LENTILS IN THE PRESSURE COOKER

Bean	Soaked Quick Release/Cooking Time	Soaked Natural Release/Cooking Time	Unsoaked Quick Release/Cooking Time	Unsoaked Natural Release/Cooking Time	Notes
Lupini			20 minutes	17 minutes	These coin-shaped beans, which are naturally so bitter as to be inedible, are a favorite Italian snack and must be soaked both before and after cooking. After cooking, soak in refrigerator for 5 to 14 days, changing water daily. When bitterness is gone, add salt to fresh water and brine the beans for day before eating.
Mung			8 minutes	5 minutes	
Mung, sprouted			2 to 3 minutes	Just bring to pressure	If you think regular mung beans are quick-cooking, the sprouted ones will really amaze you.
Navy, white haricot, pea beans	6 to 7 minutes	3 minutes	25 minutes	22 minutes	Soaking is recommended for even cooking.
Peas, split green			8 minutes	6 minutes	Adding oil to the cooking water is a must.
Peas, split yellow			9 minutes	7 minutes	Adding oil to the cooking water is a must.
Peruano, canary, mayocoba	6 minutes	3 minutes	24 minutes	22 minutes	Nice mild flavor. Soaking is recommended for even cooking.
Pigeon peas, split (toor dal, gandules)			9 minutes	7 minutes	Looks like chana dal but smaller.
Pink (pinquito, chili beans)	8 minutes	5 minutes	40 minutes	37 minutes	Mild and small. Popular BBQ bean on California's Central Coast.

COOKING TIMES FOR BEANS AND LENTILS IN THE PRESSURE COOKER

Bean	Soaked Quick Release/Cooking Time	Soaked Natural Release/Cooking Time	Unsoaked Quick Release/Cooking Time	Unsoaked Natural Release/Cooking Time	Notes
Pinto	12 minutes	8 minutes	35 to 40 minutes	30 to 35 minutes	Cook extra and make your own refried beans.
Red kidney	11 minutes	8 minutes	33 minutes	30 minutes	Freshly cooked kidney beans are far superior to the canned ones.
Red small (red)	8 minutes	4 minutes	29 minutes	25 minutes	Nice for chili.
Runner cannellini	16 minutes	12 minutes	54 minutes	52 minutes	Huge, delicioius, and meaty. Use 6 cups liquid for cooking 1 cup of these large beans unsoaked and 4 cups if soaked.
Scarlet runner	14 to 15 minutes	9 minutes	55 minutes	53 minutes	Amazing potato flavor. Use 5 cups liquid for cooking 1 cup of these large beautiful beans unsoaked and 4 cups if soaked.
Small white beans	9 minutes	5 minutes	33 minutes	29 minutes	
Snow cap	13 to 14 minutes	9 to 10 minutes	49 to 50 minutes	45 to 46 minutes	An attractive heirloom bean. Great for bean salads.
Soybeans	10 minutes	6 minutes	30 minutes	25 minutes	Soaking is recommended for even cooking and fewer broken beans. Adding oil to the cooking water is a must.
Tarbais (haricot tarbais, coco)	20 to 22 minutes	17 minutes	51 minutes	48 minutes	The traditional beans for cassoulet, these keep their shape after long cooking in the oven.

Note: Soaking is not recommended/needed for some beans and lentils.

Pressure Cooker Pot o' Beans (Soaked)

Makes about 3 cups cooked beans • Cooker: 5- to 7-quart • Time: Depends

1 cup dried beans of your choice, soaked (page 401) and drained
3 cups water or combination of unsalted or low-sodium broth and water
1 tablespoon olive oil
Optional flavorings:
1 small onion, peeled (stuck with 1 to 2 cloves, if desired)
1 clove garlic, peeled
1 large sprig fresh parsley
1 rib celery with leaves, broken into 2 pieces
1 carrot, broken into 2 pieces
1 dried red chile, rinsed and seeds shaken out and discarded
1 teaspoon dried herbs or salt-free herb or herb-and-spice blend such as thyme, marjoram, poultry seasoning, etc.
$1/2$ bay leaf
1 to 3 teaspoons epazote, to taste (optional)
1 to 2 slices bacon, to taste, chopped or $1/4$ to $1/2$ cup diced ham or smoked turkey or a ham or smoked turkey bone (optional)
$1/4$ teaspoon freshly ground black pepper
Sea salt

1. Place the drained soaked beans in a 5- to 7-quart pressure cooker. Add the water, oil, and any flavorings you are using. Stir to combine.
2. Close and lock the lid. Set the burner heat to high. When the cooker reaches HIGH pressure, reduce the burner heat as low as you can and still maintain HIGH pressure. Set a timer to cook for the proper cooking time as indicated on the Pressure Cooker Bean Cooking Time chart at HIGH pressure.
3. Remove the pot from the heat. Use Quick Release or Natural Release as indicated on the chart to open the cooker. Be careful of the steam as you remove the lid.
4. If there is too much liquid for your taste in the pot, simmer the beans for a few minutes to reduce it. Taste and add salt only to taste, if desired. Serve hot or warm. Keeps 4 to 5 days in an airtight container in the refrigerator or up to 4 months in the freezer.

Pressure Cooker Pot o' Beans (Unsoaked): Follow the directions above, using unsoaked beans that have been picked over for debris and increasing the amount of cooking water to 4 cups. Follow the Pressure Cooker Bean Cooking Time chart for timing.

Chipotle Pinto Beans

Serves 8 • Cooker: 5- to 7-quart • Time: 8 minutes at HIGH pressure

These beans are great for bean tacos. The chipotle gives them a smoky edge and they cook up nice and creamy. Instead of pintos, you can substitute one of the heirloom beans that are part of the pinto family: rattlesnake, Appaloosa, Anasazi, cranberry, borlotti, or eye of the goat (*ojo de cabra* beans); consult the bean cooking chart on pages 402–406 for cook times.

2 cups (1 pound) dried pinto beans, soaked using the Overnight Method (page 401) and drained
6 cups water
1 tablespoon olive oil
1 cup chopped onion
1 tablespoon minced garlic
1¹/₂ teaspoons ground cumin
1 teaspoon chili powder
1 teaspoon dried oregano, preferably Mexican
1 canned chipotle chile packed in adobo sauce
1 (14.5-ounce) can diced tomatoes, drained
¹/₂ cup chopped fresh cilantro
Sea salt

1. Place the drained soaked beans in a 5- to 7-quart pressure cooker. Add the water. Drizzle in the oil. Add the onion, garlic, cumin, chili powder, oregano, and chipotle.
2. Close and lock the lid. Set the burner heat to high. When the cooker reaches HIGH pressure, reduce the burner heat as low as you can and still maintain HIGH pressure. Set a timer to cook for 8 minutes.
3. Remove the pot from the heat. Open the cooker with the Natural Release method; let stand for 10 minutes. Be careful of the steam as you remove the lid.
4. Remove the whole chipotle and stir in the tomatoes and chopped cilantro. Season to taste with salt. If you like your beans spicier, you can chop up the chipotle and stir it back into the pot. Serve hot in soup bowls. Keeps in an airtight container 4 to 5 days in the refrigerator or up to 4 months in the freezer.

Feijão Preto (Brazil) or Caraotas Negras (Venezuela): Use black beans in place of the pintos.

Frijoles Borrachos (Drunken Beans): Substitute 1 (12-ounce) bottle of Mexican beer for some of the water. Crumbled bacon is also sometimes stirred in at the end. This is popular in northern Mexico.

Mexican Yellow Beans

Serves 6 to 8 • Cooker: 5- to 7-quart • Time: 6 minutes at HIGH pressure

While the pinto bean is the bean that comes to mind when discussing Mexican food, there are others that figure into the regional cuisines of the country. One is the sweet and creamy Peruano, or "yellow bean" (also known as the mayocoba), popular in Sonora and Jalisco. It is said that once you eat the Peruano, you'll never eat the pinto again.

For the best results, these beans need to soak. They can be used in any recipe that calls for navy, cannellini, or pinto beans. Yellow beans make a fantastic salad with avocado, tomato, and cilantro, but they're also delicious served hot with lots of chopped cilantro in warm corn tortillas.

2 cups (1 pound) dried Peruano yellow beans, soaked (page 401) and drained
6 cups water
2 tablespoons light olive oil or other flavorless cooking oil
1 teaspoon to 1 tablespoon sea salt, to taste

1. Place the drained soaked beans in a 5- to 7-quart pressure cooker. Add the water. Drizzle in the oil.
2. Close and lock the lid. Set the burner heat to high. When the cooker reaches HIGH pressure, reduce the burner heat as low as you can and still maintain HIGH pressure. Set a timer to cook for 6 minutes.
3. Remove the pot from the heat. Open the cooker with the Natural Release method; let stand for 15 minutes. Be careful of the steam as you remove the lid.
4. If there is too much liquid in the pot for your taste, simmer the beans for a few minutes to reduce it. Check the seasoning and add the salt to taste. Simmer another 5 minutes. Keeps in an airtight container 4 to 5 days in the refrigerator or up to 4 months in the freezer.

Frijoles de Olla

Serves 8 • Cooker: 5- to 7-quart • Time: 35 minutes for pinto, and 30 minutes for black beans at HIGH pressure

Frijoles de olla (which translates to "beans from the pot") are usually served alone at the end of the main course, sometimes on the same plate but most often in their own small bowl. These are the staple beans of Mexico: pintos or black beans cooked until tender. They are nourishing and comforting on their own, but corn or flour tortillas or rice are their natural partners. Some people make very plain beans—the better to serve as a blank canvas for other foods—while others prefer to spice them up. This recipe falls in between. Also, remember that yesterday's (or today's) beans can easily become *refritos,* the basis of many more Mexican meals. We include recipes for two of our favorites—*molletes* and *enfrijoladas.* Most Mexican cooks don't presoak beans, so that is how we have prepared them here. If you do decide to soak them, adjust the cooking time and reduce the water to 6 cups.

2 cups (1 pound) dried pinto or black beans, rinsed and picked over
8 cups water
1 small onion or $1/2$ medium onion, peeled but left in one piece for easier removal
2 cloves garlic, peeled
1 tablespoon oil, lard, or bacon drippings
1 tablespoon dried epazote (optional)
2 teaspoons ground pure chile powder (mild California chile or hot New Mexican chile) OR 1 whole dried chile, rinsed, stem removed, and seeds shaken out and discarded
1 teaspoon dried oregano, preferably Mexican
Sea salt and freshly ground black pepper

1. Rinse and drain the beans in a colander, then pick over for any small rocks or dirt clods and beans that look wrinkled or deformed. Place the beans in a 5- to 7-quart pressure cooker. Add the water, onion, garlic, oil, epazote if using, ground or whole chile, and oregano. Stir to combine.
2. Close and lock the lid. Set the burner heat to high. When the cooker reaches HIGH pressure, reduce the burner heat as low as you can and still maintain HIGH pressure. Set a timer to cook for 35 minutes for pinto beans or 30 minutes for black beans.
3. Remove the pot from the heat. Open the cooker with the Quick Release method. Be careful of the steam as you remove the lid. If the beans are not done to your liking, relock the cooker, bring back up to pressure, and cook for 2 to 5 minutes longer.
4. Remove the onion, garlic cloves, and whole chile, if you used one. Season with salt and pepper to taste. Serve hot, warm, or cold, on their own in a bowl, or with rice, tortillas, or other dishes. Keeps in an airtight container 4 to 5 days in the refrigerator or up to 4 months in the freezer.

Refritos (Refried Beans)

Makes 4 cups

If you're making beans regularly, refritos should become part of your repertoire, to enjoy as is or to be used as an ingredient in other Mexican or Tex-Mex recipes (see below). You can mash the beans with a potato masher or a wooden bean masher from Mexico, which looks like a club with a flat bottom. Your heaviest wooden spoon will work well, too.

About 6 cups Frijoles de Olla (page 410) or Mexican Yellow Beans (page 409), including the cooking liquid
2 tablespoons oil, lard, or bacon drippings
2 cloves garlic (optional), chopped
Salt and freshly ground black pepper

1. Drain the beans, reserving the cooking liquid. Heat the fat over medium-low heat in a large skillet, preferably a cast-iron one. Add the garlic, if using, and cook it gently, being carefully not to let it burn.
2. Add about 1 cup of the beans, turn the heat up to medium-high, and mash the beans against the pan, stirring. Add a splash of the cooking liquid and stir. Continue in this manner, adding the beans gradually, mashing and stirring them, and adding more cooking liquid as needed so the beans don't scorch or dry out completely. You are aiming for an oatmeal-like texture in the end. When all of the beans are incorporated and everything is bubbling, the beans are ready. Taste them and add salt and pepper if desired.

Molletes: *Molletes* (mo-YET-tays) are Mexican comfort food—a torpedo-shaped white bread roll (*bolillo*), somewhat crisp on the outside and soft within), split and topped with hot refried beans, melted cheese, and a spoonful of salsa. Lacking bolillos, use a baguette cut into 5- to 6-inch sections and split as directed. The traditional choice would be a mild white cheese that melts smoothly, such as asadero or Monterey Jack. Mozzarella works as well, as does Cheddar. The salsa fresca can make or break the mollete; use your favorite store-bought or make your own. To make them, split the rolls in half lengthwise. Lightly butter the cut sides, if desired. Place cut side up and toast them lightly under the broiler, watching carefully so they don't burn. Remove from the oven and reduce the oven tempera-ture to 350° F. Spread $^1/_4$ to $^1/_2$ cup warm refried beans on each toasted half, all the way out to the edges of the roll. Top with a generous sprinkling of grated cheese. Bake until the beans are hot and the cheese is completely melted, 4 to 7 minutes. Remove from the oven and top each with a dollop of salsa.

Enfrijoladas: In *enfrijoladas* (en-free-hoe-la-das), refried beans are transformed into a sauce into which corn tortillas are dipped and enjoyed as you would crepes. In a blender or food processor, puree 2 cups refried beans and $1^1/_2$ cups bean cooking liquid or chicken broth. Set aside. In a medium skillet, heat 1 tablespoon oil over medium-high heat. Add $^1/_2$ onion, chopped, and 1 clove garlic, chopped, and cook, stirring, until the onion is lightly browned, 3 to 4 minutes. Add 1 Roma tomato, chopped; $^1/_2$ to 1 serrano or jalapeño pepper, minced and seeded, $^1/_2$ teaspoon dried oregano, and $^1/_4$ teaspoon ground cumin and cook, stirring, until the tomato softens and the oregano is fragrant, 2 to 4 minutes. Scrape into the blender with the beans and puree again. Taste the sauce and add salt to taste. The sauce should be pourable, about the consistency of canned tomato sauce. If it is too thick, thin it with broth, water, or milk. If it is too thin, you can reduce it on the stove in the next step. If the sauce is too spicy, add a splash of milk. If it is too bland, add some ground chile. Pour as much of the bean sauce into the skillet as will comfortably fit and heat it over medium-high heat. When it is bubbling, you are ready to begin. Have the toppings of your choice in small bowls at the ready: crumbled queso fresco or feta cheese, grated Parmesan, shredded cooked chicken, crumbled cooked Mexican chorizo, salsa fresca, crema Mexicana or sour cream. Using a pair of tongs, dip a 6-inch corn tortilla into the warm bean sauce, pushing it down into the sauce and flipping it rather quickly to coat the other side. If the tortilla disintegrates, you are working too slowly. Place the tortilla on an oven-safe plate, tuck a bit of cheese or meat inside, if desired, and quickly fold the tortilla into quarters, using the tongs. Repeat with 1 or 2 more tortillas. Ladle more bean sauce on top of the folded tortillas, top with a bit of cheese, and place the plate in a preheated 350° F oven for a few minutes, until the cheese melts. Serve the enfrijoladas hot from the oven, topped with salsa fresca or crema, if desired.

Christmas Limas with Mango Chutney

Serves 6 • Cooker: 5- to 7-quart • Time: 35 minutes at HIGH pressure

If you like your beans with a little pep, this is your dish. If you have never tasted the mildly spicy Thai sweet chili sauce, you are in for a pleasant surprise. Look for the Mae Ploy brand. You can also use as a dipping sauce for spring rolls, in barbecue sauce, or like ketchup with meatloaf and grilled meats. Christmas limas are large, flat white beans, with a beautiful maroon pattern that doesn't fade with cooking. They have an appealing flavor reminiscent of chestnuts.

1 cup dried Christmas lima beans, soaked (page 401) and drained
1 medium onion, chopped
1 clove garlic, chopped
2 tablespoons mango chutney
1 tablespoon Thai sweet chili sauce
1 teaspoon Dijon mustard
1/4 cup chopped ham (optional)
4 cups water
Juice of 1 large or 2 small limes
Sea salt (optional)

1. Place the drained soaked beans in a 5- to 7-quart pressure cooker. Add the onion, garlic, chutney, chili sauce, mustard, ham, if using, and water. Stir to combine.
2. Close and lock the lid. Set the burner heat to high. When the cooker reaches HIGH pressure, reduce the burner heat as low as you can and still maintain HIGH pressure. Set a timer to cook for 35 minutes.
3. Remove the pot from the heat. Open the cooker with the Natural Release or Quick Release; let stand for 15 minutes. Be careful of the steam as you remove the lid.
4. If there is too much liquid for your taste, simmer the beans for a few minutes to reduce it. Stir in the lime juice. Taste and add salt only if needed. Serve hot or warm. Keeps in an airtight container 4 to 5 days in the refrigerator or up to 4 months in the freezer.

Feijao (Brazilian Black Beans)

Serves 6 • Cooker: 5- to 7-quart • Time: 7 minutes at HIGH pressure

In Brazil, a fresh batch of black beans to be eaten with white rice is made every day. The cooking time for black beans can vary a lot. With a pressure cooker, it is possible to overcook, therefore, check them out after 7 minutes, and continue cooking if needed. Try out different brands and decide which is your favorite. Dry black beans sold in 500 gram bags are equal to about 2 cups.

2 cups (1 pound) dried black beans, soaked (page 401) and drained
6 cups water
5 tablespoons olive oil
1 medium or $1/2$ large white onion, chopped
2 to 4 cloves garlic, to taste, chopped
2 bay leaves
Sea salt (optional)
2 large limes, cut into wedges, for serving
Chopped fresh cilantro, for serving

1. Place the drained soaked beans in a 5- to 7-quart pressure cooker. Add the water and 2 tablespoons of the oil.
2. Close and lock the lid. Set the burner heat to high. When the cooker reaches HIGH pressure, reduce the burner heat as low as you can and still maintain HIGH pressure. Set a timer to cook for 7 minutes.
3. Remove the pot from the heat. Open the cooker with the Natural Release method; let stand for 15 minutes. Be careful of the steam as you remove the lid. The beans should be soft and the water chocolaty brown.
4. If the beans are still too hard, simmer a few minutes longer on the stovetop or relock the cooker and bring back to pressure for a few minutes if very underdone. If there is too much liquid for your taste, simmer the beans with the lid off for a few minutes to reduce it. Set aside.
5. In a large skillet, warm the remaining 3 tablespoons oil over medium-high heat. Add the onion and garlic and cook, stirring, until fully softened, 5 to 8 minutes. You want them well cooked. Add 2 to 3 ladles full of the black beans to the skillet. Stir until evenly combined, then pour the contents of the skillet back into the pot of cooked beans. Add the bay leaves and salt to taste, about 2 teaspoons. Simmer, uncovered, over medium heat for 15 to 30 minutes.
6. Serve hot with the lime wedges and cilantro. Keeps in an airtight container 4 to 5 days in the refrigerator or up to 4 months in the freezer.

Citrus Feijao: Add $1/3$ cup fresh lime juice, $1/3$ cup thawed orange juice concentrate, and 1 tablespoon pureed canned chipotle chile in adobo to the sautéed onions in Step 5 before you add the beans. Serve with the cilantro; omit the lime wedges.

Feijao with Tropical Fruit: Add 2 ripe mangos, peeled, pitted, and chopped, and 1 to 2 firm-ripe bananas, peeled and cut into $1/2$-inch slices, after the beans and onions have been combined. Omit the bay leaves and season with salt. Just heat through and serve immediately with the lime wedges and cilantro.

Feijao with Tadka and Smoked Provolone

Serves 6 • Cooker: 5- to 7-quart • Time: 7 minutes at HIGH pressure

In Europe and South America, there is a trend for eco-villages, communities that use sustainable methods for living. This recipe comes from a working farm in one of the villages, Vila Sao Francisco, which is located on the Atlantic coast, not far from Rio de Janeiro. *Tadka,* also called *chounk* in Hindi, means tempering and is a cooking technique used in Indian cuisine. Whole and/or powdered spices are fried briefly to release their essential oils and enhance their flavor. Serve this with rice or roti.

2 cups (1 pound) dried black beans, soaked (page 401) and drained

6 cups water

2 tablespoons olive oil

Sea salt (optional)

3 tablespoons ghee or olive oil

1 tablespoon sweet paprika

3 (2-finger) pinches asafoetida powder

2 teaspoons ground cumin

1 to 1^1/$_2$ teaspoons turmeric

3 to 4 ripe tomatoes, to taste, seeded and chopped

^{1}/$_4$ to ^{1}/$_2$ cup cubed smoked provolone cheese *per serving*

Fresh cilantro leaves, for serving

1. Place the drained soaked beans in a 5- to 7-quart pressure cooker. Add the water and oil.
2. Close and lock the lid. Set the burner heat to high. When the cooker reaches HIGH pressure, reduce the burner heat as low as you can and still maintain HIGH pressure. Set a timer to cook for 7 minutes.
3. Remove the pot from the heat. Open the cooker with the Natural Release method; let stand for 15 minutes. Be careful of the steam as you remove the lid. The beans should be soft and the water chocolaty brown.
4. If the beans are too hard, simmer for a few minutes on the stovetop or relock the cooker and bring back to pressure for a few minutes if very underdone. If there is too much liquid for your taste, simmer the beans, uncovered, to evaporate some of it. Set aside.
5. In a small skillet, warm the ghee over medium-high heat. Add the paprika, asafoetida, cumin, and turmeric and cook a few seconds. Add the tomatoes and cook for 10 minutes, cooking the mixture down to a "gravy." Pour the mixture into the beans and stir well to combine.
6. Top each serving with cheese and cilantro. Keeps in an airtight container 4 days in the refrigerator or up to 4 months in the freezer (store the beans without the cheese).

Southwestern-Style Baked Black Beans with Bacon and Green Chiles

Serves 6 • Cooker: 5- to 7-quart • Time: 7 minutes at HIGH pressure

These are great stuffed into a pita or served up with warm corn tortillas. Our favorite way to enjoy them is with corn muffins.

5 slices bacon, chopped
2 tablespoons olive oil
1 medium white onion, finely chopped
1 large green bell pepper, seeded and chopped
3 cloves garlic, minced
2 teaspoons ground cumin
1 (4-ounce) can diced roasted green chiles, undrained
1 (14-ounce) can tomato sauce
$1/2$ cup dry sherry or dry red wine
$2^1/2$ cups water
2 cups (1 pound) dried black beans, soaked (see page 401) and drained
Sea salt and freshly ground black pepper

1. In a 5- to 7-quart pressure cooker over medium heat, cook the bacon pieces until just crisp. Leave the bacon in the pot but use paper towels to blot up the extra fat. Add the oil, onion, bell pepper, and garlic, stir to evenly coat the vegetables with the oil, and cook, stirring a few times, until softened, 3 to 4 minutes. Sprinkle with the cumin and stir it in. Add the chiles with their liquid, tomato sauce, sherry, and water. Stir in the drained soaked beans. Bring to a rolling boil.

2. Close and lock the lid. Set the burner heat to high. When the cooker reaches HIGH pressure, reduce the burner heat as low as you can and still maintain HIGH pressure. Set a timer to cook for 7 minutes.

3. Remove the pot from the heat. Open the cooker with the Natural Release method; let stand for 15 minutes. Be careful of the steam as you remove the lid. If there is too much liquid in the pot, simmer, uncovered, to evaporate some of it. Season to taste with salt and pepper. Keeps in an airtight container in the refrigerator up to 4 days and in the freezer 3 months.

Black Soy Beans and Wild Rice

Serves 4 • Cooker: 5- to 7-quart • Time: 20 minutes at HIGH pressure

Soybeans come in many colors, including black, buff, and yellow. Black soybeans, an integral part of macrobiotic cooking, are considered the most edible of the soybeans. They are also very high in antioxidants and sweeter than the other soybeans, with a silky texture. They have a delicate skin; for that reason, they are soaked in salted water prior to cooking, to firm them up, and then salt is added again, to the cooking water. Paired with the wild rice, this makes a great holiday dish. When buying wild rice, look for hand-harvested brands rather than paddy rice; the taste is entirely different.

1 cup dried black soy beans, soaked (page 401),
    adding $1/2$ teaspoon salt to the soaking water,
    and drained
4 cups low-sodium vegetable broth
1 cup raw wild rice
1 tablespoon olive oil
1 teaspoon sea salt
$1/2$ medium white onion, halved
1 large sprig fresh parsley
1 rib celery with leaves, broken into 2 pieces
Gomasio sesame salt

1. Place the drained soaked beans in a 5- to 7-quart pressure cooker. Add the broth and bring to a boil. Skim off the bubbly foam on the surface. Bring to a boil a second time and skim again. Add the wild rice, oil, sea salt, onion, parsley, and celery. Stir to combine.

2. Close and lock the lid. Set the burner heat to high. When the cooker reaches HIGH pressure, reduce the burner heat as low as you can and still maintain HIGH pressure. Set a timer to cook for 20 minutes.

3. Remove the pot from the heat. Open the cooker with the Natural Release method; let stand for 10 minutes. Be careful of the steam as you remove the lid. Discard the onion, parsley, and celery. Sprinkle with sesame salt to taste. Keeps in an airtight container for 3 days in the refrigerator or up to 3 months in the freezer.

Vegetarian Louisiana-Style Red Beans and Rice

Serves 6 to 8 • Cooker: 5- to 7-quart • Time: 8 minutes at HIGH pressure

Because it could simmer all day, red beans and rice was a dish traditionally made on wash day throughout South Louisiana; the women could put the beans on to cook in the morning and would only need to cook up the rice to have dinner ready after the work was done. Though it is usual to make it with meat (ham hocks, andouille, and/or ham), red beans and rice is just as tasty *sans animaux*. You can add liquid smoke or a bit of chipotle chile to get the smokiness. (Colgin Company makes a vegetarian liquid smoke.)

1/4 cup extra virgin olive oil
1 large yellow or white onion, chopped
4 cloves garlic (or to taste), minced
4 ribs celery, chopped
1 medium green bell pepper, seeded and chopped
2 cups (1 pound) dried red kidney beans, soaked using the Overnight Method (page 401) and drained
1 (32-ounce) box vegetable broth
2 bay leaves
1 teaspoon dried thyme or 3 sprigs fresh
1 teaspoon dried oregano or 1 sprig fresh
1 (3-inch) stick cinnamon
Few pinches Creole seasoning
1/4 to 1/2 teaspoon red pepper flakes, to taste
1 tablespoon vegetarian Worcestershire sauce
1 1/2 teaspoons liquid smoke or 1 canned chipotle chile in adobo sauce, finely chopped
Sea salt and freshly ground black pepper
3 tablespoons chopped fresh flatleaf parsley
1/2 teaspoon to 1 tablespoon Louisiana hot sauce, such as Tabasco or Crystal, plus more for serving
4 cups cooked white or brown long-grain rice, for serving
1/2 cup sliced green onions, for garnish

1. In a 5- to 7-quart pressure cooker, heat the oil over medium-high heat. Stir in the onion and cook, stirring a few times, until it just begins to soften, about 2 minutes. Do not let it brown; reduce the heat if necessary. Add the garlic and cook 30 seconds. Add the celery and green pepper. Cook 2 minutes, coating them with the oil. Add the drained soaked beans. Add the broth and, if necessary, enough water so the liquid is 1 inch above the beans. Add the bay leaves, herbs, cinnamon stick, Creole seasoning, red pepper, Worcestershire, and liquid smoke and stir to combine.

2. Close and lock the lid. Set the burner heat to high. When the cooker reaches HIGH pressure, reduce the burner heat as low as you can and still maintain HIGH pressure. Set a timer to cook for 8 minutes.

3. Remove the pot from the heat. Open the cooker with the Natural Release method; let stand for 10 minutes. Be careful of the steam as you remove the lid. Discard the bay leaves, cinnamon stick, and herb sprigs, if using. Taste for salt and pepper. Stir in the parsley and hot sauce.

4. For an authentic texture, use a large spoon and mash half the beans against the side of the pot or use a hand immersion blender to puree some, leaving the remainder whole. Serve ladled over cooked rice sprinkled with the green onions. Pass the bottle of hot sauce.

Rajma (North Indian Red Bean Masala Stew)

Serves 4 • Cooker: 5- to 7-quart • Time: 12 minutes at HIGH pressure

Rajma, or *rajma chawal*, is classic comfort food in India. The spices vary from household to household, but are generally kept rather light so the flavor of the beans dominates. This is the Kashmiri version of rajma, without onion and garlic. If you prefer it with, add 1 chopped red onion and 2 minced cloves garlic prior to adding the tomatoes and sauté until softened.

In India there are three different kinds of kidney beans, grown in different regions. Typically, the dark red largish variety (which is the one we use in the West) is used to make this dish, but if you can find them, you can also make it with the slightly smaller Kashmiri rajma bean (also called *badarwahi rajma* and grown in the hills of Kashmir and the Punjab) or the variegated pink rajma beans instead. Serve this with plain or saffron rice, roti, and raita.

1 1/2 cups dried red kidney beans or rajma beans, soaked using the Overnight Method (page 401), adding pinch baking soda to the water, and drained
2 bay leaves
4 1/2 cups water
3 tablespoons olive oil
1 teaspoon cumin seeds
1 (2-finger) pinch asafoetida
1 (2-inch) piece fresh ginger, peeled and minced
1 (15-ounce) can peeled whole tomatoes in juice, crushed by hand
1 teaspoon ground coriander
1 teaspoon garam masala
1 teaspoon red chili or chile powder or 1/2 teaspoon red pepper flakes
1 heaping tablespoon ghee
1/4 cup chopped fresh cilantro
4 cups cooked white or brown basmati rice, for serving
1/2 cup thinly sliced green onions or lemon wedges, for garnish (optional)

1. In a 5- to 7-quart pressure cooker, combine the drained soaked beans and bay leaves with 4 1/2 cups water.
2. Close and lock the lid. Set the burner heat to high. When the cooker reaches HIGH, reduce the burner heat as low as you can and still maintain HIGH pressure. Set a timer to cook for 12 minutes.
3. Remove the pot from the heat. Open the cooker with the Natural Release method; let stand for 12 minutes. Be careful of the steam as you remove the lid. The beans will look cracked. Drain in a colander over a bowl to reserve the cooking liquid. Discard the bay leaves. Place the beans back in the pot. Set the beans and liquid aside.
4. In a large skillet over medium-high heat, heat the oil and cumin seeds. When the seeds change color, stir in the asafoetida and ginger to warm. Stir in the tomato pulp and juice. Add the coriander, garam masala, and chili powder. Cook, stirring, over medium heat until you see some oil collect around the side of the pan. Add about 1/2 cup of the beans and, with a large spoon, mash half the beans against the side of the pot. Add the contents of the skillet to the rest of the beans in the pot. You can adjust the consistency of the beans by adding as much of the reserved cooking water as you like. Stir in a few big pinches sea salt to taste, the ghee, and cilantro. (The ghee will enhance the flavor of the spices.) Over medium heat, bring to a boil, then reduce the heat to a simmer. Simmer, uncovered, for 10 minutes to thicken the gravy.
5. Serve ladled over cooked rice sprinkled with the green onions or with lemon wedges.

Classic "Braised" Flageolets with Roast Leg of Lamb

Serves 4 to 6 • Cooker: 5- to 7-quart • Time: 6 minutes for beans at HIGH pressure

The flageolet is a small bean, shaped like a little kidney bean (though they are not related), with a lovely muted green color that ranges from celadon to mint green, a delightful fragrance, and a mild taste, similar to that of fresh peas. Flageolets get soft and creamy when cooked, without being mushy.

In France, flageolets are the traditional side dish to roast leg of lamb. This is one of the simplest versions of this classic dish. While the lamb is roasting, cook the beans in the pressure cooker and toss the salad.

ROAST LEG OF LAMB:
6 cloves garlic, pressed
1 tablespoon fresh thyme leaves
1/3 cup Dijon mustard
1/3 cup fresh lemon juice
3 tablespoons reduced-sodium soy sauce
3/4 cup olive oil
1 small bone-in leg of lamb (4 to 5 pounds), trimmed of as much of the fat as possible

FLAGEOLETS:
2 to 3 tablespoons olive oil, as needed
2 large shallots, finely diced
2 cups (1 pound) dried flageolet vertes, soaked (see page 401) and drained
1 bouquet garni (two 4-inch pieces celery, 1 bay leaf, stems from 1 bunch fresh parsley, 1 sprig fresh thyme or rosemary, and a few black peppercorns tied in a cheesecloth)
1 (4-inch-wide) strip lemon zest
1/2 cup dry white wine
4 cups water
Sea salt and freshly ground black pepper

1. In a small bowl, whisk the garlic, thyme, Dijon, lemon juice, soy sauce, and oil together. Place the lamb in a deep bowl and pour the marinade over. Cover and refrigerate for at least 2 hours or overnight, turning the lamb a few times.
2. Preheat the oven to 400° F.
3. Lift the lamb out of the marinade and place in a roasting pan. Roast for 30 minutes, then reduce the oven temperature to 350° F and continue to roast until a meat thermometer inserted into the thickest part of the leg registers about 130° to 135° F (be careful that the thermometer does not touch the bone) for a pink center, about 1 hour, or 145° for medium-well (temperature will rise 5° F while it sits). While the lamb is roasting, pressure cook the flageolets.
4. Heat the oil in a 5- to 7-quart pressure cooker over medium heat and cook the shallots, stirring, until softened, 3 to 5 minutes. Do not brown. Add the drained soaked beans, bouquet garni, and lemon zest. Add the wine and water. Bring to a rolling boil.
5. Close and lock the lid. Set the burner heat to high. When the cooker reaches HIGH pressure, reduce the burner heat as low as you can and still maintain HIGH pressure. Set a timer to cook for 6 minutes.
6. Remove the pot from the heat. Open the cooker with the Natural Release method; let stand for 15 minutes. Be careful of the steam as you remove the lid. The beans should be tender. Discard the bouquet garni and lemon zest.
7. If there is too much liquid for your taste, simmer the beans for a few minutes to reduce it. Taste and season to taste with salt and pepper. Keeps in an airtight container for 3 days in the refrigerator or up to 4 months in the freezer.
8. Baste the lamb with the pan juices. Remove the lamb from the pan to a carving board, cover with aluminum foil, and let rest for 10 to 15 minutes.
9. Skim off any excess fat from the pan juices. Stir the juices from the roast lamb into the beans, if you like. Place beans in an earthenware or porcelain gratin, slice the lamb into medium-thick slices, and arrange the slices over the beans. Serve immediately.

Fusion Baked Beans

Serves 6 • Cooker: 5- to 7-quart • Time: 35 minutes at HIGH pressure

Baked beans is one of America's favorite foods, a tradition at summertime cookouts as well as winter potlucks. We created this super-quick, super-easy recipe to reflect today's eclectic refrigerator and pantry, adding maple syrup in homage to its New England roots, hoisin sauce because it imparts a complex barbecue flavor to the quick-cooking beans, and bourbon just because! Julie's beloved mother-in-law, Sue, always makes her baked beans with more than one type of bean and we think that's a grand idea. We do think it works best to include one large bean in the mix, such as Christmas lima beans or scarlet runner beans. Stay away from the slowest-to-soften beans such as garbanzos and soybeans and the quick-cooking lentils and split peas. Enjoy this as a hearty luncheon dish or side. You can also use for franks (or more upscale sausages) and beans.

1 cup dried beans (a blend of two or more of the
    following: pinto, kidney, pinquito, black, Peruano,
    scarlet runner, and/or Christmas lima beans),
    soaked (page 401) and drained
1 medium onion, chopped
1 clove garlic, chopped
1 large or 2 small slices bacon, chopped
1 tablespoon bourbon
1 tablespoon maple syrup
1 tablespoon honey mustard
1 tablespoon hoisin sauce
1 tablespoon tomato paste
1 tablespoon chopped crystallized ginger
3 cups water
Salt (optional)

1. Place the drained soaked beans in a 5- to 7-quart pressure cooker. Add the remaining ingredients (except the salt) and stir to combine.
2. Close and lock the lid. Set the burner heat to high. When the cooker reaches HIGH, reduce the burner heat as low as you can and still maintain HIGH pressure. Set a timer to cook for 35 minutes.
3. Remove the pot from the heat. Open the cooker with the Natural Release or Quick Release method. Be careful of the steam as you remove the lid. If there is too much liquid for your taste, simmer the beans for a few minutes to reduce it.
4. Taste and add salt only if needed (the hoisin, bacon, and mustard all are salty). Keeps in an airtight container for 4 to 5 days in the refrigerator or up to 4 months in the freezer.

New England–Style Ham and Beans

Serves 6 • Cooker: 5- to 7-quart • Time: 8 minutes at HIGH pressure

Here are your classic molasses Boston Baked Beans, adapted for the pressure cooker. If you like, you can use diced turkey bacon instead of ham or omit the ham entirely if you want this to be vegetarian. Petite French white beans, Steuben yellow eyes, or Swedish brown beans can be substituted for the navy beans. Enjoy this with steamed brown bread.

$^1/_3$ cup light or dark molasses (but not blackstrap)
$^1/_3$ cup ketchup
$^1/_3$ cup firmly packed brown sugar
1 tablespoon Dijon mustard
3 cups water
1 medium white onion, finely chopped
2 cups (1 pound) dried navy beans, soaked (page 401) and drained
8 ounces ham, diced
Sea salt and freshly ground black pepper

1. In a 5 to 7-quart pressure cooker, combine the molasses, ketchup, brown sugar, mustard, and water. Stir to dissolve the sugar and molasses. Add the onion, drained soaked beans, and ham. Stir to evenly coat the beans with the mixture.

2. Close and lock the lid. Set the burner heat to high. When the cooker reaches HIGH pressure, reduce the burner heat as low as you can and still maintain HIGH pressure. Set a timer to cook for 8 minutes.

3. Remove the pot from the heat. Open the cooker with the Natural Release method; let stand for 15 minutes. Be careful of the steam as you remove the lid. Season with salt and pepper to taste. Keeps in an airtight container in the refrigerator up to 4 days and in the freezer up to 3 months.

Pressure-Steamed Breads

Steamed breads have a long history, and steamed brown bread has long been a traditional accompaniment to bean dishes. They were originally farm breads, rustic, slightly sweetened with molasses, and made from whole grains that could grow in poor soils: crunchy cornmeal, fragrant graham flour, rich whole wheat flour, slightly sour rye flour. On stovetop, they are cooked in a tightly covered mold set in simmering water, which makes for an exceptionally moist, almost spongy-textured yet dense bread that goes perfectly with bean dishes.

These breads come out just as moist in the pressure cooker, at a fraction of the cook time. As many folks do, we cook ours in clean 1-pound (or almost 1-pound) food cans. We used to use coffee cans but a lot of those are no longer made of metal. If you do use a can instead of a mold, be sure it is food safe. We take our lead from PC guru Lorna Sass and use Eden brand bean cans, which are lead-free and enamel-lined.

Steamed Boston Brown Bread

Makes 3 small loaves • Cooker: 5- to 8-quart • Time: 20 minutes at HIGH pressure

3/4 cup graham or whole-wheat flour
3/4 cup rye flour
3/4 cup yellow cornmeal
1/4 cup firmly packed light brown sugar
1/2 teaspoon baking soda
1/2 teaspoon baking powder
1/2 teaspoon salt
1/3 cup light molasses (not blackstrap)
1 cup sour cream
1/2 cup buttermilk
1/2 cup golden or dark raisins, dried blueberries, or dried cranberries (optional), soaked in hot water for 10 minutes and drained if not moist
3 to 4 cups boiling water

1. Generously coat the inside of 3 (15-ounce) Eden bean cans or a lidded 4-cup pudding mold with nonstick cooking spray.
2. In a large bowl, combine the graham flour, rye flour, cornmeal, brown sugar, baking soda, baking powder, and salt. Stir and make a well in the center. Add the molasses, sour cream, buttermilk, and raisins. Scrape the sides with a large rubber spatula. Stir well until the dry ingredients are evenly moistened. The batter will be thick.
3. Divide the batter between the prepared cans, filling each no more than three-fourths full. Cover tightly with a sheet of aluminum foil and secure at the top with a thick rubber band so no condensation forms inside as the breads cook.
4. Place a steamer rack or basket in a 5- to 8-quart pressure cooker. Place the cans on the rack as far away as they can be from one another without touching the side of the cooker. Do not place the molds directly on the bottom of the pot; they must be on a rack. Add boiling water so that it comes 2 inches up the sides of the molds.

5. Close and lock the lid. Set the burner heat to high. When the cooker reaches HIGH pressure, reduce the burner heat as low as you can and still maintain HIGH pressure. Set a timer to cook for 20 minutes. (If you use a single 4-cup mold, steam for 35 minutes.)
6. Remove the pot from the heat. Open the cooker with the Natural Release method; let stand for 10 minutes. Quick Release any remaining pressure. Be careful of the steam as you remove the lid. Remove one can with metal tongs or a folded dish towel to a cooling rack. Let stand to cool for about 15 minutes, then remove the foil. Run a knife around the edge and turn upside down onto the rack. The loaf will slide out. A cake tester inserted into the center should come out clean. If not, return it to the mold, re-cover it with the foil, and replace in the pot. Relock the cooker, bring back up to HIGH pressure, and cook for 5 minutes. Repeat the Natural Release.
7. Remove the cans to a rack. Let stand to cool about 15 minutes and remove the foil as soon as it is comfortable to touch the can. Run a knife around the edge and turn upside down onto the rack. Give a gentle shake. The warm loaf will slide out. If it does not, cut out the bottom of the can and push it out. Serve warm, sliced into rounds, or cool to room temperature to serve later reheated, slathered with butter. Use a serrated knife to cut; try to cut it without pressing down. Once cooled to room temperature, store in plastic storage bags in the refrigerator up to 4 days or the freezer up to 3 months.

Steamed Maple Brown Bread: Substitute the molasses with Grade B maple syrup.

Gluten-Free Boston Brown Bread

Makes 2 small loaves • Cooker: 5- to 8-quart • Time: 30 minutes at HIGH pressure

Steamed brown bread translates perfectly to gluten-free with a lovely sweet flavor provided by the sorghum and rice flours. Soft and moist (despite the absence of added fat), steamed brown bread complements baked beans, the salty/sharp flavor of a hot dog with mustard, or just slathered with cream cheese for breakfast. This is adapted from a recipe from gluten-free diva baker Elizabeth Barbone of glutenfreebaking.com.

³/₄ cup brown rice flour
³/₄ cup sorghum flour
³/₄ cup yellow cornmeal
¹/₂ teaspoon baking soda
¹/₂ teaspoon baking powder
¹/₂ teaspoon salt
¹/₄ teaspoon xanthan gum
¹/₂ cup light molasses (not blackstrap) or sorghum molasses
1 cup buttermilk
¹/₂ cup chopped pitted dates (optional)
3 to 4 cups boiling water

1. Generously grease two empty, clean 28-ounce tomato cans with nonstick cooking spray.
2. In a large bowl, combine the flours, cornmeal, baking soda and powder, salt, and xanthan gum. Stir and make a well in the center. Add the molasses, buttermilk, and dates, if using. Stir well until the dry ingredients are evenly moistened. The batter will be thick.
3. Divide the batter between the two prepared cans, filling each no more than three-fourths full. Cover tightly with a piece of parchment paper and secure with thick rubber bands so that the water cannot get in. Place a piece of heavy-duty aluminum foil over the top.
4. Put a trivet and steamer rack or basket in a 5- to 8-quart pressure cooker. Position the cans so they do not touch one another or the side of the pot. The can cannot sit directly on the bottom of the pot; they must be elevated. Add boiling water so that it comes 2 inches up the sides of the cans.

5. Close and lock the lid. Set the burner heat to high. When the cooker reaches HIGH pressure, reduce the burner heat as low as you can and still maintain HIGH pressure. Set a timer to cook for 30 minutes.
6. Remove the pot from the heat. Open the cooker with the Natural Release method; let stand for 10 minutes. Quick Release any remaining pressure. Be careful of the steam as you remove the lid. Remove one can with metal tongs or a folded dish towel to a cooling rack. Let cool about 15 minutes, then remove the foil, run a knife around the edge, and turn the can upside down onto the rack. The loaf will slide out. Insert a cake tester in the center to test for doneness; it should come out clean. If it is not done, return the bread to the mold, relock the lid, bring back up to HIGH pressure, and cook for 5 minutes. Open the cooker with the Natural Release method.
7. Remove the cans to a rack. Let cool about 15 minutes, then remove from the cans. If they won't come out, cut out the bottom of the can and slide it out. Serve warm, sliced into rounds, or cool to room temperature to serve later reheated, slathered with butter. Use a serrated knife to cut without pressing down. Store in plastic storage bags in the refrigerator up to 4 days or freezer up to 3 months.

Steamed Zucchini-Walnut Corn Bread

Makes 3 small loaves • Cooker: 5- to 8-quart • Time: 20 minutes at HIGH pressure

If you don't want to use a commercial corn muffin mix, here is the equivalent of one 8.5-ounce box dry ingredients: $^3/_4$ cup all-purpose flour or gluten-free flour mixture, $^1/_2$ cup yellow cornmeal, 1 tablespoon sugar, 1 tablespoon baking powder, and $^1/_2$ teaspoon sea salt.

1 (8.5-ounce) package corn muffin mix (such as Jiffy)
$^1/_2$ cup chopped walnuts
$^1/_4$ cup firmly packed light brown sugar
$1^1/_4$ teaspoons ground cinnamon
1 cup tightly packed shredded zucchini
1 large egg
$^1/_4$ cup plain Greek yogurt
2 tablespoons light olive oil
3 to 4 cups boiling water

1. Generously coat the inside of 3 (15-ounce) Eden bean cans, or a lidded 4-cup pudding mold, with nonstick cooking spray.

2. In a large bowl, combine the corn muffin mix, walnuts, brown sugar, and cinnamon. Stir and make a well in the center. Add the zucchini, egg, yogurt, and oil. Scrape the sides with a large rubber spatula. Stir well until the dry ingredients are evenly moistened. The batter will be thick.

3. Divide the batter between the prepared cans or mold, filling each no more than two-thirds full. Cover each can tightly with a sheet of aluminum foil and secure at the top with a thick rubber band so that no condensation forms inside as the breads cook. If using a mold, put the lid on.

4. Place a steamer rack or basket in a 5- to 8-quart pressure cooker. Place the mold or the cans on the rack so they are as far away as they can be from one another without touching the side of the cooker. Do not place the mold or cans directly on the bottom of the pot; they must be on a rack. Add boiling water so it comes 2 inches up the sides of the molds.

5. Close and lock the lid. Set the burner heat to high. When the cooker reaches HIGH pressure, reduce the burner heat as low as you can and still maintain HIGH pressure. Set a timer to cook for 20 minutes. (If you use the 4-cup mold, steam for 35 minutes.)

6. Remove the pot from the heat. Open the cooker with the Natural Release method; let stand for 10 minutes. Quick Release any remaining pressure. Be careful of the steam as you remove the lid. Remove one can with metal tongs or a folded dish towel to a cooling rack. Let stand to cool about 15 minutes and remove the foil. Run a knife around the edge and turn upside down onto the rack. The loaf will slide out. A cake tester inserted into the center should come out clean. If not, return it to the mold, re-cover with foil, and replace in the pot. Relock the cooker, bring back up to HIGH pressure, and cook for 5 minutes. Repeat the Natural Release.

7. Remove the cans to a rack. Let stand to cool about 15 minutes and remove the foil as soon as it is comfortable to touch the can. Run a knife around the edge and turn upside down onto the rack. Give a gentle shake. The warm loaves will slide out. If they do not come out, cut out the bottom of the can and push it out. Serve warm, sliced into rounds, or cool to room temperature to serve later reheated, slathered with butter. Use a serrated knife to cut; try to cut without pressing down. Once cooled to room temperature, store in plastic storage bags in the refrigerator up to 4 days or the freezer up to 3 months.

Steamed Pumpkin-Walnut Bread: For the zucchini, substitute $^1/_2$ cup canned pumpkin puree and add $^1/_2$ tablespoon thawed orange juice concentrate.

Garlicky White Beans with Sage

Serves 8 • Cooker: 5- to 7-quart • Time: 7 minutes at HIGH pressure

Sage has a savory, slightly peppery flavor and it works wonderfully with beans. Be sure to use fresh sage here, not dried. Cut fresh sage leaves should be stored in the refrigerator in a plastic bag, or you may wrap them in a damp paper towel; they will usually last for three or four days.

2 cups (1 pound) dried Great Northern white
    beans, soaked using the Overnight Method (page
    401) and drained
2 (14-ounce) cans chicken or vegetable broth
5 tablespoons olive oil, plus more for serving
1 medium onion, quartered
6 fresh sage leaves
12 cloves garlic, or to taste, minced
Sea salt and freshly ground black pepper
2 tablespoons chopped fresh flatleaf parsley

1. Place the drained soaked beans in a 5- to 7-quart pressure cooker. Add the broth and enough water so the liquid is 1 inch above the beans. Drizzle in 1 tablespoon of the oil. Add the onion and sage leaves.
2. Close and lock the lid. Set the burner heat to high. When the cooker reaches HIGH pressure, reduce the burner heat as low as you can and still maintain HIGH pressure. Set a timer to cook for 7 minutes.
3. Remove the pot from the heat. Open the cooker with the Natural Release method; let stand for 10 minutes. Be careful of the steam as you remove the lid. Drain the beans and discard the onion pieces and sage leaves.
4. Gently heat the remaining 4 tablespoons oil in a medium skillet over low heat. Add the garlic and cook until it is straw-colored, stirring often to prevent it from becoming overcooked. Turn off the heat and season with salt. Combine the garlic and oil with the beans, stirring gently to avoid breaking the tender beans. Garnish with freshly ground pepper and the parsley. Drizzle the beans with more oil before serving.

Minted White Beans with Pistachios

Makes about 4 cups • Cooker: 5- to 7-quart • Time: 10 minutes at HIGH pressure

Beth met Ralph Tingle while he was head chef at Fetzer Vineyards in Northern California. The vineyard had just planted a gigantic kitchen garden for the chef's use in the restaurant, a new concept at the time. This recipe, deceptively simple, was served with duck in the restaurant. You can make this the day before.

1 1/2 cups (1 pound) dried Great Northern or navy
    white beans, soaked (page 401) and drained
2 (14-ounce) cans vegetable broth
2 tablespoons olive oil
3 tablespoons finely chopped fresh mint
Sea salt and freshly ground black or white pepper
1/2 cup toasted pistachios, chopped

1. Place the drained soaked beans in a 5- to 7-quart pressure cooker. Add the broth, oil, and water to cover if necessary but not past the halfway mark of the pot.
2. Close and lock the lid. Set the burner heat to high. When the cooker reaches HIGH pressure, reduce the burner heat as low as you can and still maintain HIGH pressure. Set a timer to cook for 10 minutes.
3. Remove the pot from the heat. Open the cooker with the Natural Release method; let stand for 15 minutes. Be careful of the steam as you remove the lid. The beans should be tender but not mushy. Let cool completely. If not using immediately, store the beans in their cooking liquid in the refrigerator and drain before making the salad.
4. In a medium serving bowl, combine the drained cooled beans and mint. Season with salt and pepper to taste. Cover with plastic wrap and let stand at room temperature until serving. Just before serving, stir in the pistachios (you want them to stay crunchy).

Our Pressure Cooker Cassoulet

Serves 8 to 10 • Cooker: 8-quart or larger • Time: 20 minutes at HIGH pressure (then 1 hour in oven)

Cassoulet, the hearty white bean and mixed meat casserole, originated in the Languedoc region of France, and it is made differently from place to place and person to person. Like any traditional country-side dish, the ingredients vary based on what is plentiful and available locally, and the techniques by each individual cook. Traditionally, cassoulet is made in several steps: The beans and meats are prepared separately, then combined for a long, slow bake in the oven under a crust of breadcrumbs. Our decidedly nontraditional version is made quickly in the pressure cooker, then baked for just 1 hour. As for the meats, there really is no official "right" choice. Duck or goose confit is often used as are sausage and chunks of pork or lamb (mutton in the old days). Older recipes are incredibly rich—Julia Child's version from *Mastering the Art of French Cooking* includes 7^1/$_2$ pounds of meat (and meat fat) to serve 10 to 12 people!

We chose our cuts of meat based on what was available in our local higher-end supermarkets. That means we used shoulder lamb chops instead of a whole lamb shoulder, and veal stew meat instead of veal shank. Ready-made duck confit was right there in the supermarket freezer section. For the beans, Beth ordered Tarbais beans online, used for cassoulet in and grown around the city of Tarbes in Southwest France (the Label Rouge on the label means they are the real deal). They look like small limas, have a nutty, mild flavor, and, very important, don't turn to mush in cassoulet. Other popular choices in France are lingot and coco beans. In the U.S., many recipes call for Great Northern beans, cannellini beans, or flageolets. Rancho Gordo now offers a "cassoulet bean" which is a white runner bean.

Even with a pressure cooker and shortcuts like purchased duck confit, cassoulet is a project, so share it with a table full of people you really like. We think you and your guests will be pleased. Also, you can make this in two steps—do the pressure cooking one day, then bake the cassoulet the next day. (You will need to add an extra 20 minutes to the baking time.) One last note: This recipe requires a large pressure cooker—6 quarts or larger. If you have a smaller cooker, reduce the quantities or pressure-cook it in two batches, then combine in a big casserole or Dutch oven for baking.

CASSOULET:

2 cups (1 pound) dried Tarbais, lingot, coco, cannellini, Great Northern, or flageolet beans, soaked (see page 401) and drained
4 cups unsalted or reduced-sodium chicken broth
^{1}/$_2$ pound sliced bacon, cut into ^{3}/$_4$-inch pieces
1 to 1^1/$_2$ pounds lamb shoulder chops, the thickest in the case, trimmed of fat
1 pound pork shoulder or veal stew meat, trimmed of fat and cut into 1^1/$_2$- to 2-inch chunks
Olive or sunflower oil, as needed
2 confit duck legs
2 large onions, chopped
4 cloves garlic, chopped
4 medium carrots, sliced ^{1}/$_2$ inch think
2 ribs celery, chopped into ^{1}/$_2$-inch pieces, leafy tops reserved for bouquet garni
^{1}/$_2$ pound sweet Italian sausages
1 cup dry white wine
1 (28-ounce) can whole tomatoes packed in juice, undrained
^{1}/$_2$ teaspoon freshly ground black pepper
1 teaspoon dried thyme or 3 to 4 sprigs fresh thyme
2 big sprigs fresh flatleaf parsley
1 bay leaf
Salt

BREAD CRUMB TOPPING:

3 cups soft, fresh bread crumbs (grind several slices of a good quality firm country bread such as a boule or a ciabatta)
^{1}/$_4$ cup minced fresh flatleaf parsley
2 tablespoons butter, melted and cooled, or olive oil

1. Place the drained soaked beans in an 8-quart or larger pressure cooker. Add the broth.
2. Heat a large, heavy skillet, preferably cast iron, over medium-high heat. Add the bacon and cook, stirring, until some of the fat has rendered, about 2 minutes; you do not want to fully cook it. Use a slotted spoon to transfer the bacon to the pressure cooker. Stir gently to combine with the beans.
3. Brown the lamb chops well in the fat in the skillet, 2 to 3 minutes per side, then set them atop the beans in the pressure cooker.
4. If the skillet is dry, add about 1 tablespoon of oil. Brown the pork or veal in the skillet, about 2 minutes per side. As the pieces are browned, transfer them to the pressure cooker.
5. Brown the duck legs well, about 2 minutes per side. If yours came with a great deal of fat, scrape some of the excess off before adding the legs to the pan. If not, you may need to add a bit more oil to the pan. Place the browned legs in the pressure cooker.
6. Add the onions and garlic to the skillet and cook, stirring, until they are fragrant and beginning to brown, about 2 minutes. Add the carrots and celery and continue to cook, stirring, for another 2 to 3 minutes. Transfer the vegetables to the pressure cooker.
7. Place the sausages in the skillet and brown them on all sides. Pour in the wine, bring it to a boil, and scrape up all the flavorful brown bits stuck to the bottom of the skillet with a wooden spoon. Cover the skillet, reduce the heat to medium-low, and cook for a minute to allow the sausages to plump up. Uncover the skillet and transfer the sausages to the pressure cooker.
8. Add the tomatoes and their juice to the skillet, using a wooden spatula or spoon to break up the tomatoes. Stir in the pepper and thyme, if you are using dried thyme. Bring the mixture to a boil and cook, stirring, for 1 to 2 minutes to allow the liquid to reduce slightly. Pour the contents of the skillet into the pressure cooker.
9. Use a piece of twine to tie together the parsley, celery tops, and thyme sprigs, if you are using them. Tuck this bouquet garni into the pressure cooker, submerging it. Tuck in the bay leaf.
10. Close and lock the lid. Set the burner heat to high. When the cooker reaches HIGH pressure, reduce the burner heat as low as you can and still maintain HIGH pressure. Set a timer to cook for 20 minutes.
11. Remove the pot from the heat. Open the cooker with the Natural Release method; let stand for 15 minutes. Meanwhile, preheat the oven to 350° F. Be careful of the steam as you remove the lid.
12. Using tongs, transfer the bouquet garni, sausages, pork, duck confit, and lamb chops to a plate. Discard the bouquet garni (and the bay leaf when you find it). Slice the sausages 3/4 inch thick. Remove and discard the lamb bones. Remove and discard the bones and skin from the duck.
13. Grease a large earthenware or enameled cast iron casserole or Dutch oven. Carefully ladle the contents of the pressure cooker into the casserole, watching for any stray bones or herb stems. Taste for salt and pepper. Gently stir in the sliced sausages, lamb, and duck, leaving the meat in large pieces. The liquid should come up just to the top of the beans, or a bit higher. If there is too much liquid, reserve some of it. If there is not enough, pour in additional broth.
14. In a medium bowl, combine the bread crumbs, parsley, and butter, working the butter into the mixture. Sprinkle the crumbs on top of the casserole as evenly as possible. Bake for 1 hour, checking it every 20 minutes. If the beans dry out too much, add a bit more broth or water. The crumbs will form a crust on top. If that happens within the first 40 minutes or so, use a wooden spoon to break it up and push it under the surface. A new crust will form. If no crust has formed when the cooking time is almost up, turn the oven to broil and brown the crumbs under the broiler.
15. Serve the cassoulet hot, in flat soup plates. A green salad dressed with a tart vinaigrette is a nice accompaniment to cut the richness. Keeps in an airtight container 4 to 5 days in the refrigerator, and is delicious reheated. You may freeze cassoulet up to 3 months but the bread crumb topping will suffer.

White Bean Puree

Serves 8 • Cooker: 5- to 7-quart • Time: 10 minutes at HIGH pressure

This puree makes an elegant side dish to serve with roasted meats. You can also spread it over bruschetta or garlic toast and use it as a dip with crudités. If you are a garlic lover, roasted garlic is a delicious addition.

2 cups (1 pound) dried white emergo, haricot lingot, Royal Corona, Great Northern, or other large white bean, soaked (page 401) and drained
$1/2$ onion, diced, or 1 fat leek (white part only), trimmed, cut in half lengthwise, rinsed well, and thinly sliced
2 cloves garlic, cut in half
2 (14-ounce) cans chicken or vegetable broth
3 tablespoons olive oil
Sea salt and freshly ground black or white pepper

1. Place the drained soaked beans in a 5- to 7-quart pressure cooker. Add the onion, garlic, broth, and 1 tablespoon of the oil. If needed, add water so the liquid comes even with the surface of the beans.
2. Close and lock the lid. Set the burner heat to high. When the cooker reaches HIGH pressure, reduce the burner heat as low as you can and still maintain HIGH pressure. Set a timer to cook for 10 minutes.
3. Remove the pot from the heat. Open the cooker with the Natural Release method; let stand for 15 minutes. Remove the lid away from you to avoid the steam. The beans should be very tender, but not mushy. Drain in a colander, reserving $1/4$ cup of the cooking liquid.
4. In a food processor or with a handheld immersion blender, pulse to mash the beans, drizzling in some of the reserved cooking liquid and the remaining 2 tablespoons oil to adjust the consistency. You want the puree to be smooth but still firm enough that you can mound it a bit on the plate. If you prefer, you can mash only half of the beans, leaving the rest whole.

   Taste for salt and pepper. Place in a serving bowl and cover with plastic wrap to keep warm. Keeps in an airtight container 4 days in the refrigerator or up to 4 months in the freezer.

Our Simple Bean Salad

Serves 4

You can make this little salad with a few ingredients or make it a full meal, depending on what you have in your pantry and fridge.

3 cups just-cooked beans of your choice (from 1 cup dried)

VINAIGRETTE:
2 tablespoons vinegar of your choice, fresh lemon or lime juice, or a combination
6 tablespoons olive oil or another salad oil
1 teaspoon sea salt, or to taste
$1/2$ teaspoon freshly ground black pepper, or to taste
1 clove garlic or $1/2$ shallot, minced
$1/4$ teaspoon dry mustard or $1/2$ to 1 teaspoon Dijon mustard, to taste

SALAD (ADD ANY OR ALL, AS YOU PREFER):
Chopped soft, raw vegetables, such as: cucumbers, radish, celery, or jicama
Cooked and cooled harder vegetables, such as chopped carrots or cauliflower
Chopped fresh herbs, such as parsley, cilantro, mint, or a combination
Cubed or crumbled cheese, such as feta or queso fresco
Cooked or canned fish or seafood, such as tuna, shrimp, or scallops
Sliced pitted olives
Sieved hard-boiled eggs
A bed of salad greens

1. Immediately after cooking the beans, drain them in a colander.
2. Shake, whisk, or blend the vinaigrette ingredients together. Gently toss about one third of the vinaigrette with the warm beans, taking care not to mash or break them up too much. A large rubber spatula works well here.
3. Add the vegetables, herbs, and/or any other ingredients to the beans. Toss with half of the remaining vinaigrette. Add salt and pepper to taste. If needed, add the remaining vinaigrette. Serve at room temperature or chilled on a bed of greens. Keeps in an airtight container in the refrigerator for 2 to 3 days.

Greek Garbanzo Bean Salad with Feta, Tomato, and Parsley

Serves 4 to 6 • Cooker: 5- to 7-quart • Time: 40 minutes at HIGH pressure

Garbanzos take a long time to cook but you also want to be careful not to overcook them, or they will fall apart. For that reason we add some salt to the cooking liquid to help avoid this. This is a delicious and filling salad.

BEANS:
1 1/2 cups (9 ounces) dried garbanzo beans, rinsed and picked over
6 cups water
1 bay leaf
2 cloves garlic, peeled
1/2 teaspoon sea salt
1 tablespoon olive oil

SALAD:
1/4 cup minced fresh flatleaf parsley
2 cloves garlic, pressed
1 tablespoon grated lemon zest
1 ripe medium tomato, seeded and diced
1/4 to 1/2 red onion, to taste, diced
2 tablespoons fresh lemon juice
1/4 cup olive oil
1/3 cup crumbled feta cheese
6 sliced Kalamata olives
Sea salt and freshly ground black pepper

1. Place the beans in a 5- to 7-quart pressure cooker. Add the water, bay leaf, garlic cloves, and salt and drizzle the top with the oil.
2. Close and lock the lid. Set the burner heat to high. When the cooker reaches HIGH pressure, reduce the burner heat as low as you can and still maintain HIGH pressure. Set a timer and cook for 40 minutes.
3. Remove the pot from the heat. Open the cooker with the Natural Release method; let stand for 15 minutes. Be careful of the steam as you remove the lid. The chickpeas should be very tender. If they are still too hard, relock the cooker, bring back to HIGH pressure, and cook for another 5 minutes, then Quick Release the steam.
4. Drain the chickpeas in a colander, reserving 1 cup of the cooking liquid. Discard any loose skins that came off during cooking and the bay leaf and garlic. Let cool to room temperature. Keeps in an airtight container 2 to 3 days in the refrigerator in the reserved liquid; you can also drain the beans and freeze up to 4 months.
5. Place the beans in a medium salad bowl. Combine the parsley, garlic, and lemon zest on a cutting board and chop them together. Add to the beans, along with the tomato and onion. Pour the lemon juice and oil over the mixture. With a rubber spatula, toss to coat. Add the feta and olives, then taste for salt and pepper. This salad can be made 4 hours ahead and served chilled or at room temperature.

Crunchy Kidney Bean Salad with Lemon and Garlic

Serves 4 to 6 • Cooker: 5- to 7-quart • Time: 8 minutes at HIGH pressure

This salad is a riot of colors. Be sure to chop the onion and peppers the same size as the beans. There will be an equal amount of raw vegetables and cooked beans.

BEANS:
1 cup dried red kidney beans, soaked using
    Overnight Method (page 401) and drained
3 cups water
1 tablespoon olive oil

SALAD:
1 medium red onion, diced
1 large red bell pepper, seeded and diced
1 large yellow bell pepper, seeded and diced
$^3/_4$ to 1 cup loosely packed fresh flatleaf parsley
    leaves, to taste, chopped
2 cloves garlic, minced or pressed
3 to 4 tablespoons olive oil
Juice from 2 lemons
Sea salt and freshly ground black pepper

1. Place the drained soaked beans in a 5- to 7-quart pressure cooker. Add the water and drizzle with the oil.
2. Close and lock the lid. Set the burner heat to high. When the cooker reaches HIGH pressure, reduce the burner heat as low as you can and still maintain HIGH pressure. Set a timer to cook for 8 minutes.
3. Remove the pot from the heat. Open the cooker with the Natural Release method; let stand for 10 minutes. Be careful of the steam as you remove the lid. Drain the beans in a colander. Discard any loose skins that came off during cooking. Let cool to room temperature. Keeps in the reserved liquid in an airtight container 1 day in the refrigerator; you can also drain the beans and freeze up to 4 months.
4. Place the beans in a medium salad bowl. Add the onion, bell peppers, parsley, and garlic and pour over the oil and lemon juice. With a rubber spatula, toss to coat, then taste for salt and pepper. This salad can be made 4 hours ahead; serve chilled or at room temperature.

Tuscan Cannellini Salad with Garlic Toast

Serves 4 • Cooker: 5- to 7-quart • Time: 8 minutes at HIGH pressure

Cannellini are often confused with Great Northern white beans as they are the same size and shape. They are available year round, cook up fluffy and creamy, and are very versatile, delicious in salads, soups, stews, and much more. Cannellini beans benefit from presoaking, if you have the time. This is a nice salad to serve as an accompaniment to grilled meats or fish. If you want to dress it up, add diced Roma tomato, chopped black olives, and grated Pecorino cheese.

BEANS:

1 cup dried white cannellini or white kidney beans, soaked using Overnight Method (page 401) and drained
About 3 cups water
1 tablespoon olive oil

SALAD:

1 clove garlic, minced
2 ribs celery, diced
$^1/_4$ cup loosely packed chopped fresh flatleaf parsley or basil
3 to 4 tablespoons olive oil
2 tablespoons red wine vinegar
Sea salt and freshly ground black pepper

GARLIC TOAST:

4 thick slices country-style bread
1 to 2 cloves garlic, to taste, halved
$^1/_4$ cup extra virgin olive oil

1. Place the drained soaked beans in a 5- to 7-quart pressure cooker. Add enough water to come 1 inch above the beans. Drizzle with the oil.
2. Close and lock the lid. Set the burner heat to high. When the cooker reaches HIGH pressure, reduce the burner heat as low as you can and still maintain HIGH pressure. Set a timer to cook for 8 minutes.
3. Remove the pot from the heat. Open the cooker with the Natural Release method; let stand for 10 minutes. Be careful of the steam as you remove the lid. Drain the beans in a colander. Let cool to room temperature. The beans will keep in their cooking liquid in an airtight container 1 day in the refrigerator; you can also drain the beans and freeze up to 4 months.
4. Place the beans in a medium salad bowl. Add the garlic, celery, and parsley. Pour over the oil and vinegar. With a rubber spatula, toss to coat, then taste for salt and pepper. This salad can be made 4 hours ahead.
5. Right before serving, toast the bread, then rub it on one side with the cut side of the halved garlic clove. Drizzle each toast on one side with 1 tablespoon oil. Serve the salad, chilled or at room temperature, with a piece of toast.

Tuscan Tuna, Pasta, and Cannellini Salad: Add 1 to 2 (7-ounce) cans tuna packed in olive oil, drained and flaked into chunks; 6 ounces small shell pasta cooked to al dente and drained; 4 cornichons, sliced, or 2 tablespoons diced dill pickle; 3 tablespoons capers; and $^1/_2$ cup diced red onion to the cannellini salad. Add more olive oil and vinegar if necessary. This is delicious, nutritious, and filling.

Texas Caviar

Serves 6 • Cooker: 5- to 7-quart • Time: 7 minutes at HIGH pressure

Somewhere along the way, black-eyed peas got a bad rap among the gourmet set. In fact, they are terrifically delicious and easy to cook, requiring no presoaking. African slaves brought seeds for black-eyed peas to the New World and the creamy little bean with the black spot soon became a Southern staple, including in Texas, where it became an integral part of chuck wagon and rancho cooking.

This chunky salsa (which is more like a salad) is adapted from a recipe from cookbook author Helen Corbitt, the mother of modern Texas cooking. Helen was a food consultant to the restaurant at Neiman Marcus in Dallas in the 1950s and her recipes are popular to this day. If you haven't tasted this vegetarian bean appetizer, dubbed "caviar," you are in for a delightful surprise. You won't be able to stop eating it.

1 cup dried black-eyed peas, picked over and rinsed
6 cups water
4 tablespoons olive oil
1 heaping cup frozen yellow corn kernels, thawed
1 bunch green onions, including green tops halfway
   up, thinly sliced
2 cloves garlic, minced
1 pint cherry or grape tomatoes, quartered or
   halved
1 to 2 jalapeño peppers, to taste, seeds removed
   and minced
1/2 large red bell pepper, seeded and finely
   chopped
3 tablespoons cider vinegar
2 tablespoons fresh lime juice
1/2 teaspoon ground cumin
Sea salt and freshly ground black pepper
1/2 cup loosely packed fresh cilantro leaves,
   chopped (from about 1/2 bunch)

1. In a 5- to 7-quart pressure cooker, combine the black-eyed peas, water, and 1 tablespoon of the oil.
2. Close and lock the lid. Set the burner heat to high. When the cooker reaches HIGH pressure, reduce the burner heat as low as you can and still maintain HIGH pressure. Set a timer to cook for 7 minutes.
3. Remove the pot from the heat. Open the cooker with the Natural Release method; let stand for 15 minutes. Be careful of the steam as you remove the lid. The peas should be very tender. Drain in a colander and set aside to cool to room temperature.
4. In a large bowl, mix the drained cooked peas, corn, green onions, garlic, tomatoes, chiles, and bell pepper. In a small bowl, whisk the remaining 3 tablespoons oil, the vinegar, lime juice, cumin, and salt and pepper to taste together (or shake together in a small jar). Pour the dressing over the pea mixture and stir to evenly coat the ingredients. Taste for salt. Cover the bowl with plastic wrap and chill for at least 4 hours or overnight to allow the flavors to come together. The peas get tastier over several days; they will keep for up to 4 days and can be frozen up to 2 months.
5. Just before serving, add the cilantro and gently stir with a spatula to combine. Serve the peas chilled, with tortilla chips as a party dip or on a bed of butter lettuce leaves as a salad.

Val's Mediterranean Hummus

Makes about 3 cups • Cooker: 6- to 8-quart • Time: 40 minutes (unsoaked chickpeas) or 17 minutes (soaked)

Beth met Val Bushell at the beginning of her pressure cooker adventures. Her hummus is a combination of three recipes, a result of wanting to get the perfect recipe: Lorna Sass's recipe for cooking the chickpeas and mixing the hummus in the food processor, a traditional smooth and creamy recipe from *Cook's Illustrated* (which uses water and no olive oil), and the hummus from a local Lebanese bakery, which has a looser consistency. Val prefers the flavor of Lebanese tahini.

Val does not soak her chickpeas prior to cooking but you certainly can if you like. Use the Overnight Method and then reduce the pressure cooker time to 17 minutes.

In the Middle East, hummus is served fresh from the pot, on a big communal plate, drizzled with olive oil and sprinkled with paprika and cumin. The plate has to be big enough and flat enough so that you can comfortably wipe up the hummus with a pita. Serve with warm pita bread or oven-baked pita chips. It's also tasty with the inner leaves of romaine lettuce, crudités, and pear or apple slices. You can also use it in sandwiches and wraps and as a topping for bruschetta.

CHICKPEAS:

1$^1/_4$ cups dried chickpeas, picked over and rinsed
7 cups water
1 tablespoon olive oil
$^1/_2$ teaspoon baking soda (if you have hard water)

HUMMUS:

Juice from 2$^1/_2$ lemons
$^3/_4$ cup chickpea cooking liquid
$^1/_4$ tablespoon unroasted tahini paste
1 tablespoon olive oil, plus more for drizzling
Heaping $^1/_2$ teaspoon garlic salt, or 4 cloves roasted garlic, smashed

1. Place the unsoaked chickpeas in a 6- to 8-quart pressure cooker with the water and oil. Add the baking soda if you have hard water; it will help loosen the skins.
2. Close and lock the lid. Set the burner heat to high. When the cooker reaches HIGH pressure, reduce the burner heat as low as you can and still maintain HIGH pressure. Set a timer to cook for 40 minutes.
3. Remove the pot from the heat. Open the cooker with the Natural Release method; let stand for 15 minutes. Be careful of the steam as you remove the lid. The chickpeas should be very tender, with a melting softness, breaking easily when pressed between your thumb and finger. Drain in a colander, reserving the cooking liquid. Pick out and discard any loose skins that came off during cooking. You will have about 3$^2/_3$ cups beans. Let cool for 30 minutes. Reserve $^1/_2$ cup whole cooked beans if you like to sprinkle them over your hummus.
4. Make the hummus. Place the still warm chickpeas in a food processor and grind them up a bit. With the motor running, pour in the lemon juice through the feed tube, then 1 cup of the still slightly warm cooking liquid. Add the tahini in a stream, and then the oil. Be sure to add each ingredient one at a time and to pour it in slowly so it has the opportunity to thicken and emulsify, like a good salad dressing. If the mixture is too dry, add a bit more warm cooking liquid. The end result should be smooth and creamy. Then add the garlic salt and pulse a few times to combine. Depending on your taste, you might want to add some more cooking water or lemon juice.
5. Scrape into a small bowl and make an indentation on top with the back of a spoon or spatula. Fill this with a drizzle of olive oil so you have a little pool on the top. Sprinkle with whole cooked beans if you like. Cover with plastic wrap and let rest at room temperature for 30 minutes, then enjoy or refrigerate. Make sure to take it out of the fridge at least 30 minutes before serving. Keeps in an airtight container 4 days in the refrigerator or up to 4 months in the freezer.

Creamy Hummus: For a more whipped consistency, beat in 1 cup plain Greek yogurt right before serving.

Red Pepper Hummus: Add 1 (14- to 18-ounce) jar roasted red peppers, well drained and patted dry with paper towels, along with the chickpeas to the food processor. Complete the recipe as directed. This makes a nice bright red dip.

Chipotle Hummus: Add 1 to 2 canned chipotle chiles in adobo sauce (to your taste and seeds removed if you prefer for less heat) and $^1/_4$ cup loosely packed fresh cilantro leaves along with the chickpeas to the food processor. Substitute lime juice for the lemon juice if desired. Complete the recipe as directed. This is a smoky, spicy dip.

Black Olive and Walnut Hummus: Add about $^2/_3$ cup pitted black olives of choice (canned or oil-cured), $^3/_4$ cup toasted walnuts, and $^1/_4$ cup chopped fresh parsley or cilantro along with the chickpeas to the food processor. Complete the recipe as directed.

Nut Butter Hummus: Add $^1/_2$ cup creamy peanut butter along with the chickpeas to the food processor. Complete the recipe as directed.

Avocado-Cilantro Hummus: Add 2 ripe avocados, peeled, pitted, and diced, $^1/_4$ cup loosely packed fresh cilantro leaves, and $^1/_2$ teaspoon ground cumin along with the chickpeas to the food processor. Complete the recipe as directed.

Tofu Hummus: Add 8 ounces silken or soft tofu, well drained and patted dry with a paper towel, along with the chickpeas to the food processor. Complete the recipe as directed.

Green Chile and Cilantro Hummus: Add $^1/_4$ cup canned fire-roasted green chiles and $^1/_3$ cup loosely packed fresh cilantro leaves along with the chickpeas to the food processor. Complete the recipe as directed, adding a garnish of chopped cilantro.

Pumpkin Hummus: Add 1 cup canned unsweetened pumpkin puree and $^1/_2$ teaspoon smoked paprika along with the chickpeas to the food processor. Complete the recipe as directed, omitting the garlic salt.

Artichoke Hummus: Add 1 (14-ounce) can drained artichoke hearts along with the chickpeas to the food processor. Complete the recipe as directed.

TAHINI

The secret to the flavor of a good hummus is the peanut butter–like, almost bitter, raw sesame paste known as tahini or *tehina*. You can find it shelved with the health foods next to the peanut butter or with the kosher or Middle Eastern foods (some brands are imported.) There is a Chinese sesame paste, but it is toasted and has a totally different flavor—you do not want that for hummus. As with unhomogenized peanut butter, the oil separates out of tahini when it stands and should be stirred back in before using. For easy mixing when the jar is full, stir with a table knife instead of a spoon. If the tahini is too stiff to stir easily, and is in a glass or other microwave-safe container, warm it in the microwave, removing the lid first. About 15 to 30 seconds on medium-high power should do the trick. Tahini will keep for months, but it must be refrigerated after opening.

Bessara (Moroccan Fava Bean Dip)

Makes about 3 cups • Cooker: 6- to 8-quart • Time: 8 minutes at HIGH pressure

Do you like hummus? You will love *bessara,* which has been described as fava bean hummus even though it doesn't contain tahini. If you are a fan of za'atar seasoning, with its citrusy flavor of sumac, you can add some or sprinkle it on top at serving time, but it's optional.

FAVA BEANS:

1¹/₂ cups (about 8 ounces) skinless, split dried fava beans, picked over and rinsed
6 cups water or vegetable broth
1 tablespoon olive oil
¹/₂ teaspoon sea salt

BESSARA:

1 teaspoon ground cumin
¹/₂ teaspoon sweet paprika
Pinch hot paprika or cayenne pepper
¹/₂ to 1 teaspoon sea salt, to taste
2 cloves garlic, peeled
¹/₄ cup fresh lemon juice (about 2 lemons)
¹/₃ cup olive oil or cold-pressed sesame oil
Olive oil, for drizzling
¹/₂ cup chopped fresh cilantro leaves, for garnish

FAVA BEANS

Favas, also known as broad beans, were a staple in the ancient world and have remained popular in the Middle East, Egypt, North Africa, Italy, and generally around the Mediterranean. These broad, flat beans are one of the largest and brawniest in the dried bean family. They range in color from khaki to green, and the largest of them boast a tough brown outer skin that has to be removed. We skip that step and use split and skinless favas, known as *habas.* They do not need soaking and they cook remarkably quickly in the pressure cooker.

1. Place the unsoaked favas in a 6- to 8-quart pressure cooker with the water (which will come about 2 inches above the beans), oil, and salt.
2. Close and lock the lid. Set the burner heat to high. When the cooker reaches HIGH pressure, reduce the burner heat as low as you can and still maintain HIGH pressure. Set a timer to cook for 8 minutes.
3. Remove the pot from the heat. Open the cooker with the Natural Release method; let stand for 15 minutes. Be careful of the steam as you remove the lid. The favas should be very tender, but not mushy. Drain in a colander, reserving ¹/₂ to 1 cup of the cooking liquid in a measuring cup; set aside. Let cool for 20 minutes. You want to process them while they are still warm, as the heat will tame the edge of the raw garlic.
4. In a food processor, combine the cooked favas, spices, ¹/₂ teaspoon salt, and garlic. Pulse to mash the beans and chop the garlic. With the motor running, through the feed tube and one at a time, slowly pour in the lemon juice, 2 to 4 tablespoons of the slightly warm cooking liquid, and the oil. It's important to do this slowly so it has the chance to thicken and emulsify, like a salad dressing. Taste the bessara, and adjust the seasoning, adding more salt it needed. Traditionally, bessara should be a bit thinner than hummus—thin enough to slowly pour from the food processor, but thick enough to scoop it up with bread, but you can adjust the thickness to your own preference.
5. Transfer the bessara to a saucepan and heat over low heat. Traditionally, it should be served hot, but some people prefer it warm. Pour onto a warmed plate or into individual small bowls like a soup and make an indentation on top with the back of a spoon or spatula. Fill this with a little drizzle of olive oil and sprinkle with the cilantro and more paprika, if you like. Serve bessara with hot pita bread triangles or pita chips. Keep in an airtight container in the refrigerator up to 4 days and in the freezer for 3 months.

Black Bean Cilantro Dip

Makes about 1¹/₂ cups • Cooker: 5- to 7-quart • Time: 8 minutes at HIGH pressure

Here is any casy bean dip with the taste of the Southwest. You want to use a smooth jarred cooked salsa for this dip, not a raw salsa fresca. Double the recipe for a party.

1 cup dried black beans, soaked (page 401) and
    drained
4 cups water
1 tablespoon olive oil
3 tablespoons chopped fresh cilantro
¹/₄ teaspoon ground cumin
¹/₂ teaspoon salt, plus more to taste
²/₃ cup jarred salsa, hot or mild
3 tablespoons fresh lime juice
Freshly ground black pepper

1. Place the drained soaked beans in a 5- to 7-quart pressure cooker along with the water and oil.
2. Close and lock the lid. Set the burner heat to high. When the cooker reaches HIGH pressure, reduce the burner heat as low as you can and still maintain HIGH pressure. Set a timer to cook for 8 minutes.
3. Remove the pot from the heat. Open the cooker with the Natural Release method; let stand for 15 minutes. Be careful of the steam as you remove the lid. The beans should be very tender, but not mushy. Drain in a colander, reserving ¹/₄ cup of the cooking liquid; set aside to cool for 20 minutes.
4. In a food processor, combine the cooked black beans, cilantro, cumin, salt, salsa, and lime juice. Add a few grinds of black pepper. Pulse to mash the beans, drizzling in some cooking liquid to adjust the consistency to your liking. You want flecks of cilantro in smooth, fluffy beans. Taste for seasoning. Serve at room temperature. Keeps in an airtight container for up to 2 days in the refrigerator; do not freeze.

White Bean Dip with Walnuts and Artichokes

Makes about 3 cups • Cooker: 5- to 7-quart • Time: 8 minutes at HIGH pressure

The Middle Eastern tradition of combining nuts and beans yields a delicious dip that can also be used as a sandwich spread.

BEANS:

1 cup dried cannellini beans, soaked (see page 401) and drained
4 cups water
1 tablespoon olive oil

WHITE BEAN DIP:

4 to 6 green onions, to taste, trimmed
Leaves from $^1/_2$ bunch fresh cilantro
1 to 2 cloves garlic, to taste, peeled
$^3/_4$ cup walnut pieces
1 (6.75-ounce) jar marinated artichoke hearts, drained well
$^1/_4$ cup white wine vinegar or Champagne vinegar
3 tablespoons olive oil
$^1/_2$ teaspoon sea salt
Freshly ground black pepper
$^1/_4$ teaspoon pure chile powder of your choice
$^1/_4$ cup chopped roasted red pepper
Pita crisps or seeded crackers, for serving

1. Place the drained soaked beans in a 5- to 7-quart pressure cooker with the water and 1 tablespoon of the oil.

2. Close and lock the lid. Set the burner heat to high. When the cooker reaches HIGH pressure, reduce the burner heat as low as you can and still maintain HIGH pressure. Set a timer to cook for 8 minutes.

3. Remove the pot from the heat. Open the cooker with the Natural Release method; let stand for 15 minutes. Be careful of the heat as you remove the lid. The beans should be very tender, but not mushy. Drain in a colander, reserving $^1/_4$ cup of the cooking liquid; set aside to cool for 20 minutes.

4. In a food processor, chop the green onions and cilantro. Remove to a bowl. Add the garlic to the processor and chop. Add the walnuts and pulse until chopped. Add the cooked cannellini beans, artichoke hearts, vinegar, the remaining 4 tablespoons oil, salt, few grinds of black pepper, and chile powder. Pulse to mash the beans, drizzling in some cooking liquid to adjust the consistency to your liking. You want to leave the mixture a bit coarse. Stir in half of the green onions and cilantro. Place in a serving bowl and cover with plastic wrap. Refrigerate for up to 2 hours to let the flavors develop; this is best eaten within hours of being made.

5. Serve at room temperature, sprinkled with the rest of the green onions and cilantro and the roasted red pepper. Serve with pita crisps or seeded crackers.

Basic Pressure Cooker Lentils and Split Peas

Serves 4 to 6 as a side dish • Cooker: 5- to 7-quart • Time: 6 to 10 minutes at HIGH pressure, depending on type

It used to be that it was not recommended to cook lentils in the pressure cooker because they foam as they cook and would clog the vent. With this second generation of cookers, just add 1 tablespoon of oil per 1 cup of lentils and don't fill the pot more than half full.

1 cup dried lentils or split peas
2 cups water
1 tablespoon olive oil or neutral oil
Sea salt

1. Sift through the lentils to remove pebbles or other debris. Discard any that are shriveled or discolored. Put the lentils in a sieve and rinse them thoroughly under cold running water until the water runs clear.
2. In a 5- to 7-quart pressure cooker, combine the lentils, water, and oil.
3. Close and lock the lid. Set the burner heat to high. When the cooker reaches HIGH, reduce the burner heat as low as you can and still maintain HIGH pressure. Set a timer to cook for 8 to 10 minutes at HIGH pressure for brown lentils, 6 to 10 minutes for French green and Castelluccio brown lentils and split peas, 6 to 9 minutes for black lentils, 4 to 5 minutes for red lentils, and 4 to 6 minutes for yellow lentils. Use the lesser time for a firmer lentil destined for a salad.
4. Remove the pot from the heat. Open the cooker with the Quick Release method. Be careful of the steam as you remove the lid. If they are not quite tender, relock the cooker, bring back up to HIGH pressure, and cook for 1 to 2 minutes longer. Add a pinch of sea salt per cup of lentils if you wish. If not using right away, cool to room temperature by spreading out on a clean baking sheet, then store in an airtight container in the refrigerator up to 3 days; do not freeze.

LOVING LENTILS

Lentils were one of the first crops to be domesticated in the Near East and India. Today lentils are grown commercially in over 35 countries; most of the lentils sold in this country are imported from India. The waist-high lentil plants are grown in fields much like alfalfa. The pods that hold the lentils are left to mature and dry on the plants, and then are mechanically harvested.

Lentils are versatile, flavorful, and nutritious. They have a distinctive nutty, earthy taste that pairs well with a host of spices and aromatics.

Lentils are available in many colors—pink, red, yellow, brown, green, black—vary in size, and are round, oval, or heart-shaped. They do not need soaking before cooking.

Lentil & Split Pea Math

1 (16-ounce) package lentils = $2^1/_3$ cup dry lentils = 7 to 8 cups cooked
$^1/_2$ cup dried lentils = $1^1/_2$ cups cooked lentils

Cheesy Lentil Tacos

Serves 4 to 6 as a side dish • Cooker: 5- to 7-quart • Time: 9 minutes at HIGH pressure

This is a smashingly good vegetarian taco. Brown lentils are best in fillings for tacos, burritos, and tostadas. Serve with Chipotle Style Lime and Cilantro Rice.

1 to 2 tablespoons olive oil, as needed
1 cup chopped white onion
2 cloves garlic, chopped
3 teaspoons chili powder
1 teaspoon dried oregano, preferably Mexican
1 cup dried brown lentils, picked over and rinsed
2$^1/_2$ cups low-sodium vegetable or chicken broth
Sea salt (optional)

FOR SERVING:
12 soft corn or multi-grain tortillas
Sour cream or plain Greek yogurt
2 cups shredded extra-sharp Cheddar cheese
Shredded lettuce
Chopped fresh cilantro
Salsa fresca

HEATING TORTILLAS

There are three ways to heat tortillas. Use tongs to flip them.
1. Throw them on the grill until slightly charred and pliable, about 20 seconds per side.
2. Turn one of your stovetop burners on low. Place a tortilla on top of the grate and cook for about 20 seconds per side or until it is browned to your liking.
3. Heat up a dry, heavy skillet (cast iron works great) over medium-high heat. Place a tortilla in the hot skillet and heat until browned to your liking on both sides.

1. In a 5- to 7-quart pressure cooker heat the oil over medium heat. Add the onion and garlic and cook, stirring a few times, until soft, 1 to 2 minutes. Add the chili powder and oregano and stir until fragrant. Add the lentils and broth. Bring to a boil.
2. Close and lock the lid. Set the burner heat to high. When the cooker reaches HIGH pressure, reduce the burner heat as low as you can and still maintain HIGH pressure. Set a timer to cook for 9 minutes.
3. Remove the pot from the heat. Open the cooker with the Quick Release method. Be careful of the steam as you remove the lid. If they are not quite tender, relock the cooker, bring back up to HIGH pressure, and cook for 1 to 2 minutes longer. If too wet, simmer the lentils, uncovered, to evaporate the liquid but take care not to overcook. Add a pinch of sea salt per cup of lentils if you wish. If using right away, top with some of the cheese and let it melt.
4. When ready to serve, heat up the tortillas. Lay out the hot tortillas, one to two per person, along with all the possible fillings in small bowls. Let the diners top their tortillas as they like with the lentils, sour cream, more cheese, lettuce, cilantro, and plenty of salsa.

Lentil-Portobello Tacos: In a large skillet, heat 3 tablespoons olive oil over medium heat. Add 2 large portobello mushroom caps, sliced, and cook, stirring a few times, until slightly browned, 6 to 8 minutes. The mushrooms will stay quite firm. Layer them into the tacos over the lentils. Yum!

Brown Lentils with Herbes de Provence

Serves 4 to 6 as a side dish • Cooker: 5- to 7-quart • Time: 9 minutes at HIGH pressure

Herbes de Provence, the quintessential herb blend from France, adds a burst of flavor to this hearty dish. Serve as a side or enjoy for lunch with goat cheese melted on top.

2 tablespoons extra virgin olive oil
1 medium white onion, finely chopped
2 medium carrots, chopped into $1/4$-inch pieces
2 teaspoons dried herbes de Provence
$2^1/_2$ cups chicken broth
1 cup dried brown lentils, picked over and rinsed
Salt and freshly ground black pepper

1. In a 5- to 7-quart pressure cooker, heat the oil over medium-high heat. Add the onion and cook, stirring occasionally, until it just begins to soften, about 2 minutes; don't let it brown. Add the carrots, herbes de Provence, broth, and lentils and stir to combine well and coat the lentils with the oil.

2. Close and lock the lid. Set the burner heat to high. When the cooker reaches HIGH pressure, reduce the burner heat as low as you can and still maintain HIGH pressure. Set a timer to cook for 9 minutes.

3. Remove the pot from the heat. Open the cooker with the Quick Release method. Be careful of the steam as you remove the lid. Stir and taste for salt and pepper. The lentils should still be firm but tender. If they are not quite tender, re-lock the cooker, bring back up to HIGH pressure, and cook for 1 to 2 minutes longer.

Italian-Style Lentils with Pancetta, Fennel, and Mozzarella

Serves 4 to 6 as a side dish • Cooker: 5- to 7-quart • Time: 8 minutes at HIGH pressure

This makes for a rich, delicious, and nutritious side or you can enjoy for lunch or as a light dinner with a crisp green salad.

3 tablespoons light olive oil
2 ($1/2$-inch-thick) slices pancetta (4 ounces), cut into $1/2$-inch dice
2 shallots, finely chopped
1 rib celery, chopped
$1/4$ cup finely chopped fennel bulb
1 (14.5-ounce) can diced tomatoes in juice, undrained
2 teaspoons Dijon mustard
2 cups vegetable broth or water
$1^1/_4$ cup dried brown or Castelluccio lentils, picked over and rinsed
Sea salt and freshly ground black pepper
Diced fresh mozzarella cheese, for serving

1. In a 5- to 7-quart pressure cooker, heat the oil over medium heat. Add the pancetta and shallots and cook, stirring a few times, until the fat has been rendered from the pancetta, about 4 minutes. Add the celery and fennel and cook 2 minutes. Add the tomatoes with their juice, mustard, broth, and lentils and stir to combine well and coat the lentils.

2. Close and lock the lid. Set the burner heat to high. When the cooker reaches HIGH pressure, reduce the burner heat as low as you can and still maintain HIGH pressure. If using brown lentils, set a timer to cook for 8 minutes; for Castelluccio lentils, set it for 10 minutes.

3. Remove the pot from the heat. Open the cooker with the Quick Release method. Be careful of the steam as you remove the lid. If the lentils are not quite tender, relock the cooker, bring back up to HIGH pressure, and cook for 1 to 2 minutes longer. Stir and taste for salt and pepper. Top the lentils immediately with the mozzarella and serve.

Indian Lentils with Spinach

Serves 4 as a main course • Cooker: 5- to 7-quart • Time: 10 minutes at HIGH pressure

Served with chapati or naan and a salad, this makes for a wonderful lunch or light dinner. The toppings are optional but delicious. The crunchy toasted coconut mix was inspired by a recipe from Melissa Clark.

2 tablespoons light olive oil
1 medium white onion, finely chopped
1 to 2 cloves garlic, to taste, minced
1 tablespoon grated peeled fresh ginger
$1/2$ to 1 teaspoon turmeric, to taste
1 cup canned diced tomatoes in juice, undrained, or
   1 Roma tomato, seeded and diced
2 cups vegetable broth
1 cup dried brown lentils, picked over and rinsed
1 to $1^1/2$ cups frozen chopped spinach, to taste,
   thawed and squeezed dry (about half a 10-
   ounce box)
Sea salt and freshly ground black pepper
$2/3$ cup unsweetened coconut flakes (they look like
   chips; optional)
2 teaspoons poppy seeds (optional)
Plain yogurt, for serving (optional)
Chopped fresh cilantro, for serving (optional)

1. In a 5- to 7-quart pressure cooker, heat the oil over medium-high heat. Stir in the onion and cook, stirring a few times, until it just begins to soften, about 2 minutes. Add the garlic, ginger, and turmeric and heat for 30 seconds. Add the tomatoes, broth, and lentils; stir to combine well.
2. Close and lock the lid. Set the burner heat to high. When the cooker reaches HIGH pressure, reduce the burner heat as low as you can and still maintain HIGH pressure. Set a timer to cook for 10 minutes.
3. Remove the pot from the heat. Open the cooker with the Quick Release method. Be careful of the steam as you remove the lid. Stir and taste for salt and pepper. Stir in the spinach and simmer, uncovered, over medium heat for about 3 minutes to heat through.
4. If using, in a small dry skillet over medium heat, toast the coconut and poppy seeds until the coconut is golden, about 2 minutes, stirring a few times or shaking the pan for even browning.
5. Serve the lentils topped with a dollop of yogurt, sprinkling of cilantro, and a spoonful of the toasted coconut mix, if you like.

Insalata di Lenticchie with Sherry-Mustard Vinaigrette

Serves 4 to 6 as a side dish • Cooker: 5- to 7-quart • Time: 6 minutes at HIGH pressure

Castelluccio lentils are special. Named after the area where they are grown in the Apennine Mountains in Umbria, Italy, they are harvested by hand, which is why they are double the price of common lentils. Even though they have a relatively thin skin, Castelluccio lentils hold their shape after cooking, and they are cooked al dente, which makes them great for salads. Don't ever cook them until they are soft and mushy. If you can't find them, substitute a French green lentil. This is a very simple salad, but terrifically flavorful; if you like, you can also add bits of Gorgonzola. Be sure to make it the same day you plan to eat it and don't refrigerate—it loses flavor and texture when it's chilled.

LENTILS:
2 cups dried Castelluccio lentils, picked over and
    rinsed
4 cups water
2 tablespoons olive oil

SHERRY-MUSTARD VINAIGRETTE:
Juice of $^1/_2$ small lemon
2 tablespoons sherry wine vinegar
2 teaspoons Dijon mustard
Sea salt and freshly ground black pepper
$^1/_2$ cup extra virgin olive oil

SALAD:
8 cherry tomatoes, halved
1 yellow bell pepper, seeded and finely chopped
2 to 3 cloves garlic, to taste, finely chopped
$^1/_4$ cup finely chopped fresh basil
Sea salt and freshly ground black pepper

1. In a 5 to 7-quart pressure cooker, combine the lentils, water, and oil.
2. Close and lock the lid. Set the burner heat to high. When the cooker reaches HIGH pressure, reduce the burner heat as low as you can and still maintain HIGH pressure. Set a timer to cook for 6 minutes.
3. Remove the pot from the heat. Open the cooker with the Quick Release method. Be careful of the steam as you remove the lid. Drain the lentils and place in a shallow salad bowl. Let stand at room temperature until warm.
4. In a small bowl, combine the lemon juice, vinegar, mustard, and salt and pepper to taste. Whisk in the oil in a slow stream until the mixture thickens and emulsifies. (This can also be made with an immersion blender.) Makes about $^3/_4$ cup.
5. Add the salad ingredients to the lentils. Drizzle with the vinaigrette and toss to coat. Taste for salt and pepper. You won't use all the vinaigrette, and it can be stored in an airtight container in the refrigerator for a week. Serve at room temperature with crusty Pugliese style bread or baguette.

French Green Lentil and Brown Rice Salad with Walnuts

Serves 4 as a side dish • Cooker: 5- to 7-quart • Time: 6 minutes at HIGH pressure

Lentils and brown rice are a fantastic combination in a salad. Walnuts are especially complementary. For this salad use the tiny dark green or French lentils, which hold their shape well and cook quickly. There's no need to cook the peas, which will thaw right in the bowl. Use any leftovers in pita bread or wraps.

SALAD:

1^1/$_2$ cups dried French or green lentils, picked over and rinsed
3 cups water
1 tablespoon olive oil
1 cup cooked brown rice (fresh cooked or leftover)
^{1}/$_2$ cup chopped walnuts
2 cups frozen petit peas, thawed
Sea salt and freshly ground black pepper
^{1}/$_2$ cup crumbled feta cheese (optional)

VINAIGRETTE:

1^1/$_2$ tablespoons white balsamic vinegar
3 tablespoons olive oil

1. In a 5- to 7-quart pressure cooker, combine the lentils, water, and oil.
2. Close and lock the lid. Set the burner heat to high. When the cooker reaches HIGH pressure, reduce the burner heat as low as you can and still maintain HIGH pressure. Set a timer to cook for 6 minutes.
3. Remove the pot from the heat. Open the cooker with the Quick Release method. Be careful of the steam as you remove the lid. The lentils should be soft, yet slightly chewy. Drain and place in a shallow salad bowl. Let stand at room temperature until warm.
4. Add the brown rice, walnuts, and peas to the lentils and gently toss to thoroughly combine and break any clumps of rice up into grains. Drizzle with the vinegar and oil, and gently toss to coat. Season with salt and pepper to taste and add the cheese, if using. Let stand for 10 minutes to let the rice absorb the dressing. Serve warm, at room temperature, or chilled; it will keep in an airtight container in the refrigerator up to 2 days.

14

Everyday to Gourmet Potatoes

Potatoes are the ultimate comfort food. They are so versatile and cook so well in the pressure cooker that we decided to give them their own chapter! They can be steamed, mashed, made into salads, or cooked whole, with or without the peel. Since potatoes are a blank canvas flavor-wise, you can flavor them in myriad ways.

Potatoes come in a variety of sizes, colors, and textures; there are several hundred cultivars commercially available. Potatoes can be divided into two main categories—starchy and waxy. Starchy potatoes, such as russets, are fluffy and floury when cooked. Waxy varieties, like new potatoes and fingerlings, are low in starch, have a creamy texture, and hold their shape well when cooked. Choose potatoes that are uniform in size, so that they will take the same amount of time to cook when you prepare them.

The pressure cooker also loves sweet potatoes and yams, which come in colors from white to orange to bright garnet. Raw sweet potatoes can seem hard as rocks—the pressure cooker's speed and moist heat seem to us to be the perfect cooking environment for them

PROPER POTATO STORAGE

Do not store potatoes in the refrigerator (sweet potatoes and yams, however, can go in the fridge) or in airtight plastic bags. If they are sold in plastic, the bag should have cut-outs to enable breathing. Do not store potatoes near onions; proximity to onions causes them to sprout more quickly. Shield potatoes from light, otherwise they become green-tinged, which is a sign of the presence chlorophyll and toxic alkaloids.

Buttermilk Mashed Potatoes

Serves 4 to 6 • Cooker: 5- to 7-quart • Time: 6 minutes at HIGH pressure

Everyone wants to know how to make mashed potatoes in the pressure cooker. While we like to steam our potatoes for salads or serving whole, for mashed we prefer boiling them, which takes about a third of the time to do in the pressure cooker vs. stovetop. Use just enough water to cover the potatoes and do not fill the pot more than two-thirds full, water included. And when mashing, the more milk, the fluffier the potatoes.

2¼ pounds russet potatoes (5 to 6), peeled and
    cut into 2-inch chunks
¾ to 1 teaspoon salt, to taste
3 tablespoons butter, cut into pieces
¾ cup buttermilk, or as needed, shaken or whisked
Few grinds black or white pepper

1. Place the potatoes in a 5- to 7-quart pressure cooker and fill with water to cover. It is okay if a few edges of the potatoes are peeking up out of the water. Sprinkle with the salt.
2. Close and lock the lid. Set the burner heat to high. When the cooker reaches HIGH pressure, reduce the burner heat as low as you can and still maintain HIGH pressure. Set a timer to cook for 6 minutes.
3. Remove the pot from the heat. Open the cooker with the Quick Release method. Be careful of the steam as you remove the lid. The potatoes should be soft and tender when pierced with the tip of a knife and still hold their shape. Drain in a colander. You can leave the potatoes in the pot, shaking to dry them a bit, or transfer to a deep serving bowl.
4. Using a ricer, potato masher, or handheld electric mixer on low speed, mash the potatoes; do not use a food processor. Add the butter and then the buttermilk. Beat to the desired consistency, very smooth or a bit chunky (smashed), adding more buttermilk 1 tablespoon at a time as needed. Taste for salt and pepper. Serve immediately.

Julie's Creamy Garlic Buttermilk Mashed Potatoes: Add 2 to 3 peeled cloves garlic with the potatoes in Step 1. Reduce the butter to 2 tablespoons and add 2 tablespoons cream cheese in Step 4.

Crème Fraîche Mashed Potatoes: Substitute ¾ cup crème fraîche for the buttermilk. Heat it in a small saucepan over low heat until hot and add in Step 4, along with the butter. Divine!

WHY NOT USE THE FOOD PROCESSOR?

The food processor is fantastic for oh-so-many kitchen tasks. One it just can't handle well is mashing potatoes. As the sharp blades rupture the potato cell walls, the potatoes will turn gluey in a flash. Mash your potatoes with an old-fashioned potato masher, a ricer (which looks like a giant garlic press), a food mill, or an electric mixer.

Rich and Creamy Mashed Potatoes

Serves 6 to 8 • Cooker: 5- to 7-quart • Time: 8 minutes at HIGH pressure

Using warm organic heavy cream, a true luxury, really brings the flavor out of potatoes. Gently warm the milk and cream in a saucepan (you can do this mixed together if you like) or in the microwave. White pepper is also a special treat, with a heat and flavor ever so slightly different than that of black pepper. These can be your special-occasion mashers with a big WOW factor.

3 pounds russet potatoes, peeled and quartered
1¹/₂ teaspoons salt, or to taste
6 tablespoons (³/₄ stick) butter, at room
   temperature
1 cup warm heavy cream, organic preferred
1 cup warm whole milk
Freshly ground white pepper

1. Place the potatoes in a 5- to 7-quart pressure cooker and fill with water to cover. It is okay if a few edges of the potatoes are peeking up out of the water. Sprinkle with the salt.

2. Close and lock the lid. Set the burner heat to high. When the cooker reaches HIGH pressure, reduce the burner heat as low as you can and still maintain HIGH pressure. Set a timer to cook for 8 minutes.

3. Remove the pot from the heat. Open the cooker with the Quick Release method. Be careful of the steam as you remove the lid. The potatoes should be soft and tender when pierced with the tip of a knife and still hold their shape. Drain in a colander. You can leave the potatoes in the pot or transfer to a deep serving bowl.

4. Using a ricer, potato masher, or handheld electric mixer on low speed, mash the potatoes, gradually adding the butter pieces, then ³/₄ cup of the warm cream, ³/₄ cup of the warm milk, and white pepper to taste. Adjust the consistency with the remaining cream and milk as needed. Serve immediately.

Home-Style Mashed Potatoes for Two

Serves 2 • Cooker: 4- to 7-quart • Time: 6 minutes at HIGH pressure

These are the ones you remember from your childhood.

2 large or 4 medium russet potatoes, peeled and
   cut into 2-inch chunks
Pinch salt
¹/₄ cup milk, or as needed
2 tablespoons butter, or as needed, at room
   temperature
Few grinds black pepper

1. Place the potatoes in a 4- to 7-quart pressure cooker and fill with water to cover. It is okay if a few edges of the potatoes are peeking up out of the water. Sprinkle with the salt.

2. Close and lock the lid. Set the burner heat to high. When the cooker reaches HIGH pressure, reduce the burner heat as low as you can and

still maintain HIGH pressure. Set a timer to cook for 6 minutes.

3. Remove the pot from the heat. Open the cooker with the Natural Release method; let stand for 15 minutes. Be careful of the steam as you remove the lid. The potatoes should be soft and tender when pierced with the tip of a knife and still hold their shape. Drain in a colander. Place the milk and butter in the pot and heat over medium heat until bubbles form around the edge.

4. Add the potatoes back to the pot. Using a potato masher or handheld electric mixer on low speed, beat until to the desired consistency, very smooth or a bit chunky (smashed), adding more milk 1 tablespoon at a time as needed. Taste for salt and pepper. You can add more butter if you like as well. Serve immediately.

Garlic Yukon Gold Mashed Potatoes

Serves 6 • Cooker: 5- to 7-quart • Time: 6 minutes at HIGH pressure

An entirely different mashed potato is made with the medium- to high-starch Yukon Gold variety. A very popular all-purpose potato, its smooth yellow flesh is great for mashing. Two cloves of garlic per pound of potatoes make for a mild garlic flavor. The ricer is the preferred manner of mashing here.

3 pounds Yukon Gold potatoes (10 to 12), peeled, cut into 2-inch chunks, and rinsed
6 cloves garlic, peeled
3/4 cup milk or potato cooking water
3 to 5 tablespoons butter
Sea salt and a few grinds black pepper

1. Place the potatoes and garlic in a 5- to 7-quart pressure cooker and fill with water to cover. It is okay if a few edges of the potatoes are peeking up out of the water.

2. Close and lock the lid. Set the burner heat to high. When the cooker reaches HIGH pressure, reduce the burner heat as low as you can and still maintain HIGH pressure. Set a timer to cook for 6 minutes.

3. In a saucepan or microwave-safe measuring cup, heat the milk until small bubbles appear around the edges.

4. Remove the pot from the heat. Open the cooker with the Quick Release method. Be careful of the steam as you remove the lid. The potatoes should be soft and tender when pierced with the tip of a knife and still hold their shape. Drain in a colander. You can leave the potatoes in the pot or remove to a deep serving bowl.

5. Using a ricer, mash the potatoes. Add the hot milk and butter and beat to the desired consistency, very smooth or a bit chunky. Taste for salt and pepper. Serve immediately.

Whipped New Potatoes with Almond Milk

Serves 6 • Cooker: 5- to 7-quart • Time: 6 minutes at HIGH pressure

Low-starch new potatoes are a nice alternative to russets for mashed potatoes. You can use red or white new potatoes or blue potatoes interchangeably.

3 pounds red potatoes (10 to 12), peeled and cut into 2-inch chunks
Sea salt
1/2 cup plain almond milk
3 tablespoons butter or Earth Balance (to make vegan)
Freshly ground black pepper

1. Place the potatoes with a pinch or two of salt in a 5- to 7-quart pressure cooker and fill with water to cover. It is okay if a few edges of the potatoes are peeking up out of the water.

2. Close and lock the lid. Set the burner heat to high. When the cooker reaches HIGH pressure, reduce the burner heat as low as you can and still maintain HIGH pressure. Set a timer to cook for 6 minutes.

3. In a saucepan or microwave-safe measuring cup, heat the almond milk until small bubbles appear around the edges.

4. Remove the pot from the heat. Open the cooker with the Quick Release method. Be careful of the steam as you remove the lid. The potatoes should be soft and tender when pierced with the tip of a knife and still hold their shape. Drain in a colander. Return the potatoes to the pot and allow to dry a bit.

5. Using a ricer, potato masher, or handheld electric mixer on low speed, mash the potatoes. Add the hot milk and butter. Beat to the desired consistency, very smooth or a bit chunky. Taste for salt and pepper. Serve immediately.

Kefir Mashed Potatoes

Serves 4 to 6 • Cooker: 5- to 7-quart • Time: 6 minutes at HIGH pressure

Kefir, which means "feel good" in Turkish, is a relative of yogurt and used as a substitute for buttermilk. With a consistency like thin yogurt, kefir is excellent for babies and people with digestive concerns. It tastes slightly sour but also has a tingly quality from the natural carbonation created by the wild yeasts used to make it. You can find it in well-stocked supermarkets and natural food stores.

2 pounds (4 to 6) russet potatoes, peeled and cut
     into 2-inch chunks
$3/4$ to 1 teaspoon salt, to taste
$1/4$ cup ($1/2$ stick) butter
$1/4$ cup milk, or as needed
$1/3$ cup plain kefir, or as needed
Few grinds black pepper

1. Place the potatoes in in a 5- to 7-quart pressure cooker and fill with water to cover. It is okay if a few edges of the potatoes are peeking up out of the water. Sprinkle with the salt.

2. Close and lock the lid. Set the burner heat to high. When the cooker reaches HIGH pressure, reduce the burner heat as low as you can and still maintain HIGH pressure. Set a timer to cook for 6 minutes.

3. Remove the pot from the heat. Open the cooker with the Quick Release method. Be careful of the steam as you remove the lid. The potatoes should be soft and tender when pierced with the tip of a knife and still hold their shape. Drain in a colander. You can leave the potatoes in the pot or remove to a deep serving bowl.

4. Using a ricer, potato masher, or handheld electric mixer on low speed, mash the potatoes. Add the butter and then the milk and kefir. Beat to the desired consistency, very smooth or a bit chunky (smashed), adding more milk or kefir 1 tablespoon at a time as needed. Taste for salt and pepper. Serve immediately.

Dairy-Free Olive Oil Mashed Potatoes with Chives

Serves 6 • Cooker: 5- to 7-quart • Time: 6 minutes at HIGH pressure

Olive oil comes in many colors—the green is sharp and tart, and golden is smooth tasting—and makes for a delicious vegan alternative to regular mashed potatoes.

3 pounds Yukon Gold potatoes, peeled or unpeeled
     and cut into 2-inch chunks
1 teaspoon sea salt
About $1/2$ cup extra virgin olive oil of your choice
Freshly ground white pepper
2 tablespoons minced fresh chives

1. Place the potatoes in a 5- to 7-quart pressure cooker and fill with water to cover. It is okay if a few edges of the potatoes are peeking up out of the water. Sprinkle with the salt.

2. Close and lock the lid. Set the burner heat to high. When the cooker reaches HIGH pressure, reduce the burner heat as low as you can and still maintain HIGH pressure. Set a timer to cook for 6 minutes.

3. Remove the pot from the heat. Open the cooker with the Quick Release method. Be careful of the steam as you remove the lid. The potatoes should be soft and tender when pierced with the tip of a knife and still hold their shape. Drain in a colander and remove to a deep serving bowl.

4. Using a ricer, potato masher, or handheld electric mixer on low speed, roughly mash the potatoes, gradually drizzling in the oil and white pepper to taste. Taste for salt. Serve immediately sprinkled with the chives; pass the pepper grinder.

Halfsies Mashed Potatoes (Potato-Cauliflower Mash)

Serves 6 • Cooker: 5- to 7-quart • Time: 7 minutes at HIGH pressure

When a co-worker of Julie's brought mashed potatoes to a healthy holiday potluck at the office, they were voted best recipe. The secret? They were really half mashed potato, half mashed cauliflower. It's a great concept—once you mash and season it, cauliflower tastes quite a lot like potato. Here's a pressure cooker adaptation that you can whip up in no time for a dinner side.

1³/₄ pounds russet potatoes (2 very large or 3 medium), peeled and cut into 1¹/₂-inch chunks
1 head cauliflower, cut into large florets
2 tablespoons butter
¹/₂ teaspoon salt, or to taste
¹/₈ teaspoon freshly ground white pepper
¹/₂ cup buttermilk, or as needed

1. Place the potatoes in a 5- to 7-quart pressure cooker pot and fill with water to cover. Top with the cauliflower. It's okay if the cauliflower isn't covered all the way.

2. Close and lock the lid. Set the burner heat to high. When the cooker reaches HIGH pressure, reduce the burner heat as low as you can and still maintain HIGH pressure. Set a timer to cook for 7 minutes.

3. Remove the pot from the heat. Open the cooker with the Quick Release method. Be careful of the steam as you remove the lid. The potatoes should be soft and tender when pierced with the tip of a knife and still hold their shape. Drain in a colander and remove to a deep bowl.

4. Add the butter, salt, and pepper. Using a hand-held electric mixer or stand mixer (use the paddle attachment), mix on low speed until the potatoes and cauliflower are smooth. Add the buttermilk and incorporate it on low speed. Whip the potatoes for about 2 minutes (for a stand mixer, change to the whisk attachment to do this). If the potatoes are too stiff for your taste, add more buttermilk 2 tablespoons at a time. Taste and adjust the seasonings if desired. Serve immediately.

Winter Root Mash

Serves 6 • Cooker: 5- to 7-quart • Time: 5 minutes at HIGH pressure

Nearly every root vegetable is delicious mashed and they become truly special in combination with other roots, so why not mix them together? This combination is traditionally served with braised short ribs. It is also good sprinkled lightly with smoked paprika instead of the chives.

1 pound sweet potatoes, peeled and cut into 1-inch chunks

1 pound Yukon Gold potatoes, peeled and cut into 1-inch chunks

1 pound red potatoes, peeled and cut into 1-inch chunks

$^1/_2$ pound celery root (celeriac), peeled and cut into 1-inch chunks

$^1/_2$ pound rutabaga or turnips, peeled and cut into 1-inch chunks

3 cloves garlic, peeled

3 cups water

Pinch or two sea salt, plus more to taste

$^1/_4$ cup ($^1/_2$ stick) unsalted butter, cut into pats

1 cup plain Greek yogurt

$^1/_2$ cup grated Parmesan cheese

3 tablespoons minced fresh chives, for garnish

1. Place all the roots and garlic cloves in a 5- to 7-quart pressure cooker and add the water. Sprinkle with the salt.

2. Close and lock the lid. Set the burner heat to high. When the cooker reaches HIGH pressure, reduce the burner heat as low as you can and still maintain HIGH pressure. Set a timer to cook for 5 minutes.

3. Remove the pot from the heat. Open the cooker with the Quick Release method. Be careful of the steam as you remove the lid. The roots should be soft and tender when pierced with the tip of a knife and hold their shape.

4. Drain in a colander, reserving 1 cup of the cooking water. Puree the roots, either in a food processor or by returning them to the pot and using an immersion blender or handheld electric mixer. Add the butter and yogurt, and slowly add some of the reserved cooking water. Beat until the desired consistency, either very smooth or a bit chunky (smashed). The more of the reserved cooking water you add, the creamier the puree will be. Season to taste with salt and pepper. Stir in the Parmesan and serve immediately sprinkled with the chives. Pass the pepper mill.

Rustic Mashed Potatoes and White Beans with Ricotta

Serves 4 • Cooker: 5- to 7-quart • Time: 8 minutes at HIGH pressure

This is a pressure-cooker adaptation of a Skinnygirl recipe. Skinnygirl, aka Bethenny Frankel, was a private cook for many Hollywood celebrities (before she became a TV celebrity herself) and is at the forefront of preparing healthy, delicious foods that are low in fat. This recipe leaves on the skins, but you can peel the potatoes if you prefer.

1¼ pounds (about 4) russet potatoes, left
    unpeeled and quartered
1 (15-ounce) can white beans (navy, Great
    Northern, or cannellini), drained and rinsed, or
    2 cups cooked white beans (page 402)
¼ cup (½ stick) butter, at room temperature
½ cup low-fat or nonfat milk, soy milk, or other
    nondairy milk
⅓ cup whole-milk ricotta cheese
2 teaspoons salt
Few grinds black pepper

1. Place the potatoes in a 5- to 7-quart pressure cooker and fill with water to cover. It is okay if a few edges of the potatoes are peeking up out of the water.
2. Close and lock the lid. Set the burner heat to high. When the cooker reaches HIGH pressure, reduce the burner heat as low as you can and still maintain HIGH pressure. Set a timer to cook for 8 minutes.
3. Meanwhile, pulse the beans in a food processor until smooth.
4. Remove the pot from the heat. Open the cooker with the Quick Release method. Be careful of the steam as you remove the lid. The potatoes should be soft and tender when pierced with the tip of a knife and still hold their shape. Drain in a colander and transfer to a deep bowl.
5. Add the butter, then the pureed beans, milk, and ricotta to the potatoes, using a potato masher or handheld electric mixer on low speed to mix them together. Beat to the desired consistency, very smooth or a bit chunky. Add the salt and pepper. Return the potatoes to the pot and reheat over medium heat until steaming hot. Serve immediately.

NO NEED TO EXPLODE!

Always pierce potatoes in a few places or peel a strip off with a vegetable peeler or paring knife around the middle to avoid bursting if cooking them whole.

Gourmet Mashed Potatoes for a Crowd

Serves 10 • Cooker: 7- to 8-quart • Time: 6 minutes at HIGH pressure

What was life like before Chuck Williams opened his first Williams-Sonoma on the Sonoma town square in 1954? Chuck is responsible for bringing the potato ricer to the U.S., which seems like it has always been here. You will put the potatoes through the ricer before adding the hot half-and-half and butter to create the fluffiest potatoes ever. This is a large-quantity recipe for family gatherings and holiday meals. You can cut it in half if you prefer.

5 pounds russet potatoes, peeled and cut into 2-
    inch chunks
2 teaspoons salt
1 1/2 cups half-and-half
1/2 cup (1 stick) unsalted butter, cut into pieces, at
    room temperature
Few grinds white pepper

1. Place the potatoes in a 7- to 8-quart pressure cooker pot and fill with water to cover. It is okay if a few edges of the potatoes are peeking up out of the water. Sprinkle with the salt.
2. Close and lock the lid. Set the burner heat to high. When the cooker reaches HIGH pressure, reduce the burner heat as low as you can and still maintain HIGH pressure. Set a timer to cook for 6 minutes.
3. Remove the pot from the heat. Open the cooker with the Natural Release method; let stand for 15 minutes. Be careful of the steam as you remove the lid. The potatoes should be soft and tender when pierced with the tip of a knife and still hold their shape. Drain in a colander.
4. Set the ricer over the pot and pass the potatoes through in batches. Gradually add the half-and-half and butter, beating with a large spoon or rubber spatula to the desired consistency. Taste for salt and white pepper. Serve immediately.

Goat Cheese and Chive Mashed Potatoes for a Crowd

Serves 12 • Cooker: 7- to 8-quart • Time: 6 minutes at HIGH pressure

The sour cream and goat cheese make for fluffy, flavorful mashed potatoes perfect for entertaining.

5 pounds russet potatoes, peeled and cut into 2- to
    3-inch chunks
5 cloves garlic, peeled
2 teaspoons salt
1 (10-ounce) log fresh plain goat cheese
1 cup sour cream
1/2 cup (1 stick) unsalted butter, cut into pieces, at
    room temperature
1/2 cup finely chopped fresh chives
Few grinds black pepper

1. Place the potatoes and garlic in a 7- to 8-quart pressure cooker pot and fill with water to cover. It is okay if a few edges of the potatoes are peeking up out of the water. Sprinkle with the salt.
2. Close and lock the lid. Set the burner heat to high. When the cooker reaches HIGH pressure, reduce the burner heat as low as you can and still maintain HIGH pressure. Set a timer to cook for 6 minutes.
3. In a microwave-safe bowl, heat the goat cheese and sour cream in the microwave for 2 minutes.
4. Remove the pot from the heat. Open the cooker with the Natural Release method; let stand for 15 minutes. Be careful of the steam as you remove the lid. The potatoes should be soft and tender when pierced with the tip of a knife and still hold their shape. Drain in a colander. Return the potatoes to the hot pot to dry out a bit.
5. Use a ricer, potato masher, or handheld electric mixer on low speed to mash the potatoes; do not use a food processor. Slowly add the goat cheese, sour cream, and butter and beat until fluffy. Beat in the chives. Taste for salt and pepper. Serve immediately.

Smashed Potatoes with Green Onions and Sour Cream

Serves 4 • Cooker: 5- to 7-quart • Time: 6 minutes at HIGH pressure

The true name of this recipe is Beth's Little Sister's Outrageously Good Chunky, Smashed Potatoes. There have been volumes written on the best way to make rustic smashed potatoes. Smashed potatoes are mashed with a fork and left chunky and uneven in texture, which, surprisingly, yields an entirely different taste. It is important not to peel the potatoes; you want the bits of skin in these. We are saying this serves four, but it has been known to feed only two if you are craving potatoes.

2 pounds (8 or 9) medium red or Yukon Gold
    potatoes, left unpeeled and halved
1 teaspoon salt, or to taste
2 tablespoons butter
1 cup sour cream, imitation sour cream, or plain
    Greek yogurt, or as needed
6 green onions (white part and some of the green),
    trimmed and chopped
Few grinds black or white pepper

1. Place the potatoes in a 5- to 7-quart pressure cooker and fill with water to cover. It is okay if a few edges of the potatoes are peeking up out of the water. Sprinkle with the salt.
2. Close and lock the lid. Set the burner heat to high. When the cooker reaches HIGH pressure, reduce the burner heat as low as you can and still maintain HIGH pressure. Set a timer to cook for 6 minutes.
3. Remove the pot from the heat. Open the cooker with the Quick Release method. Be careful of the steam as you remove the lid. The potatoes should be soft and tender when pierced with the tip of a knife and still hold their shape. Drain in a colander. You can leave the potatoes in the pot or remove to a deep serving bowl.
4. Add the butter and sour cream. Mash with a fork or potato masher ONLY; these are supposed to be chunky. Add the green onions and mix well to distribute throughout the potatoes. Season to taste with salt and pepper and serve.

Parsley Whole New Potatoes

Serves 4 • Cooker: 5- to 7-quart • Time: 5 minutes at HIGH pressure

We especially love to make this with diminutive creamer red potatoes, which show up in the fall freshly dug (they cook in 3 minutes rather than 5) but use whichever type you prefer, including fingerlings. If you get the larger new potatoes, quarter them.

1 cup water
2^1/$_2$ pounds small new potatoes or fingerlings, 2 to
    3 inches in diameter (2 to 3 ounces each), left
    unpeeled and pricked a few times with a knife
^{1}/$_4$ cup (^{1}/$_2$ stick) butter, cut into pieces
^{1}/$_4$ cup finely chopped fresh flatleaf parsley
Sea salt and freshly ground black pepper

1. Place a trivet in a 5- to 7-quart pressure cooker pot and add the water. Pile the potatoes in a steamer basket and place in the pot.

2. Close and lock the lid. Set the burner heat to high. When the cooker reaches HIGH pressure, reduce the burner heat as low as you can and still maintain HIGH pressure. Set a timer to cook for 5 minutes.
3. Remove the pot from the heat. Open the cooker with the Natural Release method; let stand for 15 minutes. Be careful of the steam as you remove the lid. The potatoes should be soft and tender when pierced with the tip of a knife and still hold their shape. Drain; leave in the pot.
4. Add the butter to the pot and roll the potatoes around to evenly coat. Add the parsley, season to taste with salt and pepper, and toss to coat. Transfer the potatoes to a serving bowl; serve.

Potatoes with Chiles Poblanos and Goat Cheese (Papas con Rajas)

Serves 4 to 6 • Cooker: 5- to 7-quart • Time: 6 minutes at HIGH pressure

Rajas are chile strips. In Mexican cooking, rajas show up in many dishes. Here we add them to potatoes. Serve this as a filling in warm corn tortillas, as an alternative to hash browns for breakfast, or as a dinner side dish. A note about the chiles: Fresh, dark green poblano chiles are sometimes sold as "pasillas" in California.

1¼ pounds (about 4) russet potatoes, peeled and cut into 1½-inch chunks
1 tablespoon olive oil
1 medium white onion, cut in half and then into ¼-inch-thick half moons
4 to 6 green poblano chiles, to taste
1 cup crumbled soft goat cheese or queso fresco
3 tablespoons chopped fresh cilantro
Salt and freshly ground black pepper

1. Place the potatoes in a 5- to 7-quart pressure cooker and fill with water to cover. It is okay if a few edges of the potatoes are peeking up out of the water.
2. Close and lock the lid. Set the burner heat to high. When the cooker reaches HIGH pressure, reduce the burner heat as low as you can and still maintain HIGH pressure. Set a timer to cook for 6 minutes.
3. While the potatoes cook, heat the oil in a large skillet over medium-high heat. Add the onion slices and cook, stirring occasionally, until they soften, become fragrant, and brown on the edges a bit, about 10 minutes. Cut the stems off the chiles, then cut in half lengthwise and remove the seeds with a spoon. Remove the veins if you want milder rajas, then slice the chiles crosswise into ½-inch strips. Add the chiles to the onions halfway through cooking. Reduce the heat to low and season with salt and pepper to taste.
4. Remove the pot from the heat. Open the cooker with the Quick Release method. Be careful of the steam as you remove the lid. The potatoes should be soft and tender when pierced with the tip of a knife and still hold their shape. Drain in a colander.
5. Add the potatoes to the skillet with the onions and chiles and cook for another 8 to 10 minutes to combine the flavors and slightly mash the potatoes. Stir in the goat cheese and cilantro; taste for salt and pepper.

Quesadillas with Papas con Rajas: Divide the potato mixture among 3 (10-inch) flour tortillas. You can sprinkle with Monterey jack cheese if you like it really cheesy. Place another tortilla on top of each and press down. Heat a medium sauté pan over medium heat. Add 1 quesadilla and cook until the cheese melts and the bottom tortilla gets a few golden brown spots, 3 to 4 minutes. Flip over and cook the other side 2 to 3 minutes. Repeat with the remaining quesadillas. Let rest 5 minutes, then cut each quesadilla into 8 pieces and serve.

Pressure Cooker "Roasted" Baby Potatoes

Serves 4 • Cooker: 5-to 7-quart • Time: 5 minutes at HIGH pressure

Early harvest potatoes that appear during the summer or early fall are called *new potatoes*, or sometimes creamers or fingerlings. When selecting them, be careful not to pick any with patches of green under the skin. New potatoes have a short shelf life so cook within a few days of purchase. They are perfect cooked whole and unpeeled since the skin is thin as well as nutritious. A thorough browning will get these potatoes as close to oven roasted as can be without ever heating up the oven, a technique we learned from pressure cooker diva Laura Pazzaglia. Be sure to prick the potato skin before cooking so they hold their shape and don't explode.

6 tablespoons olive or grapeseed oil

1$^1/_2$ to 2 pounds baby new potatoes (red, blue, white, or yellow; about 24), 1$^3/_4$ to 2 inches in diameter, left unpeeled and each pierced a few times with the tip of a knife

$^1/_2$ cup vegetable broth

Sea salt, to taste

Hungarian sweet paprika, dried herbes de Provence, chopped fresh chives or green onions, grated Parmesan cheese, and/or freshly ground black pepper, for garnishing (optional)

1. In a 5-to 7-quart pressure cooker over medium-high heat, heat 3 tablespoons of the oil. Add as many of the potatoes that will fit in the pot in a single layer and brown on all sides. With a slotted spoon, transfer to a shallow bowl. Add more oil and potatoes and cook in the same way until they have all been browned. Return all the potatoes to the pot and add the broth.

2. Close and lock the lid. Set the burner heat to high. When the cooker reaches HIGH pressure, reduce the burner heat as low as you can and still maintain HIGH pressure. Set a timer to cook for 5 minutes.

3. Remove the pot from the heat. Open the cooker with the Natural Release method; let stand for 15 minutes. Be careful of the steam as you remove the lid. The potatoes should be soft and tender when pierced with the tip of a knife and hold their shape a bit. Drain and sprinkle with salt to taste. Transfer the potatoes to a serving bowl and garnish, if desired. Serve immediately.

Raclette with Fingerling Potatoes

Serves 4 • Cooker: 5- to 7-quart • Time: 6 minutes at HIGH pressure

Raclette is similar to fondue and also finds its origins in Switzerland, where mountain farmers would make a meal of small potatoes and melted cheese over an open campfire or hearth. The word "raclette" comes from the French *racler,* to scrape, describing the melted cheese scraped from the unmelted part onto the plate. It is the name of the dish, as well as the name of the cow's milk cheese used to make it. Look for Gomser, Conches, or Bagnes if you can find it, named for the alpine villages they are produced in. They have exceptional melting quality—key to the success of this dish—and will give the authentic flavor. Raclette is a popular entertaining meal, especially during the winter holidays, and there are electric raclette makers, but here we utilize the oven. Fingerling potatoes are a great choice for this; they hold their shape and have a marvelous flavor. A nice way to serve this is with a green salad and plates of cold cuts or leftover holiday ham, accompanied by hot tea or chilled white wine.

1 pound (about 12) fingerling potatoes, left unpeeled and pierced with a knife in several places

2 teaspoons salt, or as needed

12 ounces raclette or good-melting French hard mountain cheese like Emmenthaler or Gruyère, rind removed and thinly sliced

Freshly ground black pepper

3 green onions, trimmed and sliced diagonally in $^{1}/_{8}$-inch strips

Cornichons, pickled onions, caper berries (the big ones), and/or pickled cauliflower (optional), for serving

1. Place the potatoes in a 5- to 7-quart pressure cooker pot and fill with water to cover. It is okay if a few edges of the potatoes are peeking up out of the water. Sprinkle with the salt.
2. Close and lock the lid. Set the burner heat to high. When the cooker reaches HIGH pressure, reduce the burner heat as low as you can and still maintain HIGH pressure. Set a timer to cook for 6 minutes.
3. Remove the pot from the heat. Open the cooker with the Quick Release method. Be careful of the steam as you remove the lid. The potatoes should be soft and tender when pierced with the tip of a knife and still hold their shape. Drain in a colander.
4. If you have oven-proof plates, preheat a broiler. If you don't, preheat the oven to 250° F. When cool enough to handle, cut the potatoes in half lengthwise. Divide the warm potatoes, cut side up, evenly among four plates, arranging them in a pinwheel pattern.
5. Arrange one quarter of the cheese slices in a single layer over each portion of potatoes, taking care to completely cover all of the potatoes. Broil or bake until the cheese melts and is almost liquidy, about 3 minutes in a broiler or 10 minutes in the oven.
6. Season with a few grinds of pepper to taste. Serve immediately while hot, with the green onions sprinkled on top. Cornichons, pickled onions and pickled cauliflower are optional accompaniments.

Summer Potato Salad with Olive Oil and Green Onions

Serves 6 • Cooker: 5- to 7-quart • Time: 7 minutes at HIGH pressure

This is a vinaigrette-style potato salad rather than mayonnaise style. It is a marvelous homey side dish in summer. Keep this salad chunky, as slices will fall apart. The waxy new potatoes will hold their shape, so don't be tempted to substitute russet or baking potatoes, which are better for mashing.

1 1/2 cups water
3 pounds new red or white potatoes, left unpeeled and halved or quartered, depending on their size
1/3 cup cider vinegar
Leaves from 1/2 bunch fresh flatleaf parsley, finely chopped
1 bunch green onions (white parts and a few inches of the green), trimmed and chopped
1/4 cup olive oil
Sea salt and freshly ground black pepper

1. Place a trivet in a 5- to 7-quart pressure cooker. Add the water. Place the potatoes in a steamer basket and place in the pot. The water should not touch the potatoes (pour some out if there is too much).
2. Close and lock the lid. Set the burner heat to high. When the cooker reaches HIGH pressure, reduce the burner heat as low as you can and still maintain HIGH pressure. Set a timer to cook for 7 minutes.
3. Remove the pot from the heat. Open the cooker with the Natural Release method; let stand for 15 minutes. Be careful of the steam as you remove the lid. The potatoes should be tender when pierced with the tip of a knife and still hold their shape.
4. Transfer the hot potatoes to a serving bowl or storage container. Pour the vinegar over the potatoes. Let stand, uncovered, at room temperature until cooled and the vinegar is absorbed, about 30 minutes minimum.
5. Add the parsley, green onions, oil, and salt and pepper to taste. With a rubber spatula, gently toss the potatoes to evenly coat with the ingredients. Serve immediately or cover and store in the refrigerator up to 3 days.

Summer Potato Salad with Tuna: Substitute Champagne vinegar or sherry vinegar for the cider vinegar. If using sherry vinegar, look for the Spanish brand Ortiz, a 100-year-old company. Add one 6-ounce can or jar olive oil-packed tuna, drained and broken into chunks, in Step 5. This is a really elegant and tasty salad.

Classic Potato Salad

Serves 6 to 8 • Cooker: 5- to 7-quart • Time: 7 minutes at HIGH pressure

This is your quintessential American mayonnaise potato salad. If you like, add a few chopped hard-boiled eggs.

1 1/2 cups water
3 pounds medium red or Yukon Gold potatoes, left unpeeled and halved or left whole if small and pierced in several places with a knife
3/4 to 1 cup mayonnaise, as needed
2 tablespoons cider vinegar or Champagne vinegar
2 teaspoons Dijon mustard
1 teaspoon sea salt
Freshly ground black pepper
4 green onions (white and light green parts), trimmed and thinly sliced
3 ribs celery, cut into 1/4-inch dice

1. Place a trivet in a 5- to 7-quart pressure cooker. Add the water. Place the potatoes in a steamer basket and set in the pot. The water should not touch the potatoes (pour some out if there is too much).

2. Cover and lock the lid in place. Set the burner heat to high. When the cooker reaches HIGH pressure, reduce the burner heat as low as you can and still maintain HIGH pressure. Set a timer to cook for 7 minutes.

3. Remove the pot from the heat. Open the cooker with the Natural Release method; let stand for 15 minutes. Be careful of the steam as you remove the lid. Transfer the potatoes to a medium bowl. Loosely cover and refrigerate until cooled. Cut the potatoes in half if you cooked them whole.

4. When you're ready to assemble the salad, whisk together the mayonnaise, vinegar, mustard, salt, and pepper to taste in a serving bowl. Add the potatoes, green onions, and celery and toss until well combined. Chill thoroughly in the refrigerator before serving; it can be made the day before.

Whipped Jewel Yams

Serves 5 to 6 • Cooker: 5- to 8-quart • Time: 15 minutes at HIGH pressure

The Jewel yam is, in fact, not a yam, but an orange-fleshed sweet potato, the root of a vigorous-growing vine. It has a lovely deep rose color with brilliant orange flesh and its flavor is delightfully sweet and satisfying. This is a recipe adapted from the Kuhn Rikon cookbook *Quick Cuisine,* which came with Beth's Duromatic pressure cooker. The potatoes are steamed whole and will slip easily out of their skins, which saves on prep and clean-up time. Use the larger size pressure cooker if you decide to make a double batch or use giant yams.

1 cup water for the 5- to 7-quart pot OR 2 cups
    water for the 8-quart pot
5 medium Jewel yams (about 2^1/$_2$ pounds)
6 tablespoons (^{3}/$_4$ stick) butter, cut into pieces, at
    room temperature
Freshly grated nutmeg
Salt

1. Place a trivet in the pressure cooker and add the water. Pierce the yams in several places with a knife and cut off the ends. Pile them in a steamer basket and place in the pot.
2. Close and lock the lid. Set the burner heat to high. When the cooker reaches HIGH pressure, reduce the burner heat as low as you can and still maintain HIGH pressure. Set a timer to cook for 15 minutes.
3. Remove the pot from the heat. Open the cooker with the Natural Release method; let stand for 15 minutes. Be careful of the steam as you remove the lid. The potatoes should be soft and tender when pierced with the tip of a knife and still hold their shape. Remove from the pot with tongs to a bowl.
4. When cool enough to handle, slip the yams out of their skins. Add the butter and grate nutmeg to taste (do this a little at a time, tasting as you go) over the top. Beat with a handheld electric mixer on low speed (do not use a food processor) just until fluffy. Taste for salt. Serve immediately.

Yams with Orange and Indian Spices

Serves 4 • Cooker: 5- to 7-quart • Time: 7 minutes at HIGH pressure

Mashed yams take beautifully to the warm flavors of garam masala. Most large supermarkets carry garam masala in their ethnic foods section.

1 cup water
4 medium-large Jewel yams (about 2 pounds),
    peeled and cut into 2-inch chunks
1 to 2 tablespoons butter, to taste
^{1}/$_3$ cup orange juice
1 teaspoon garam masala
Salt

1. Place a trivet in a 5- to 7-quart pressure cooker and add the water. Pile the yams in a steamer basket and place in the pot.
2. Close and lock the lid. Set the burner heat to high. When the cooker reaches HIGH pressure, reduce the burner heat as low as you can and still maintain HIGH pressure. Set a timer to cook for 7 minutes.
3. Remove the pot from the heat. Open the cooker with the Natural Release method; let stand for 15 minutes. Be careful of the steam as you remove the lid. The potatoes should be soft and tender when pierced with the tip of a knife and still hold their shape a bit. Remove the basket from the pot.
4. Melt the butter in a wide sauté pan, add the yams, and mash with a potato masher or fork, adding the orange juice and garam masala and mixing thoroughly. Season to taste with salt. Serve immediately.

Maple Mashed Sweet Potatoes

Serves 4 • Cooker: 5- to 7-quart • Time: 7 minutes at HIGH pressure

We would be remiss not to include a recipe for mashed sweet potatoes with maple syrup, a classic combination.

4 medium-large Jewel yams (about 2 pounds), peeled and cut into 1- to 2-inch chunks
Sea salt
2 to 3 tablespoons butter, to taste
2 to 3 tablespoons maple syrup, to taste
Pinch ground cinnamon
1/4 cup half-and-half or sour cream

1. Place the potatoes in a 5- to 7-quart pressure cooker and fill with water to cover. It is okay if a few edges of the potatoes are peeking up out of the water. Sprinkle with salt to taste.

2. Close and lock the lid. Set the burner heat to high. When the cooker reaches HIGH pressure, reduce the burner heat as low as you can and still maintain HIGH pressure. Set a timer to cook for 7 minutes.

3. Remove the pot from the heat. Open the cooker with the Quick Release method. Be careful of the steam as you remove the lid. The potatoes should be soft and tender when pierced with the tip of a knife and still hold their shape a bit. Drain in a colander and transfer to a bowl.

4. Using a ricer, potato masher, or handheld electric mixer on low speed, mash the potatoes; do not use a food processor. Slowly add the butter, maple syrup, cinnamon, and half-and-half and beat until fluffy. Taste for salt. Serve immediately.

White Lotus Kitchen Savory Yams with Coconut Milk

Serves 4 to 6 • Cooker: 5- to 7-quart • Time: 7 minutes at HIGH pressure

White Lotus Foundation in Santa Barbara specializes in training yoga teachers and yoga retreats for advanced practitioners. It is also known for its excellent food, prepared onsite for the staff and students. The long-time resident chef, Beatrix, makes this mashed yam dish, adapted here for the pressure cooker and a favorite side dish on the White Lotus table. Feed the body. Feed the mind.

5 to 6 medium-large Jewel yams (2 to 3 pounds), peeled and cut into 3-inch chunks
Sea salt
1/2 to 3/4 cup unsweetened coconut milk, as needed
1 tablespoon light olive oil
1/2 clove garlic, minced
1 teaspoon crumbled dried Italian herb blend

1. Place the potatoes in a 5- to 7-quart pressure cooker and fill with water to cover. It is okay if a few edges of the potatoes are peeking up out of the water. Sprinkle with salt to taste.

2. Close and lock the lid. Set the burner heat to high. When the cooker reaches HIGH pressure, reduce the burner heat as low as you can and still maintain HIGH pressure. Set a timer to cook for 7 minutes.

3. Remove the pot from the heat. Open the cooker with the Quick Release method. Be careful of the steam as you remove the lid. The potatoes should be soft and tender when pierced with the tip of a knife and still hold their shape a bit. Drain in a colander and transfer to a bowl.

4. Use a ricer, potato masher, or handheld electric mixer on low speed to mash the potatoes; do not use a food processor. Slowly add 1/2 cup of the coconut milk, beating on low speed until smooth.

5. In a small sauté pan, heat the oil over medium heat. Add the garlic and herbs; sauté until the garlic is soft and fragrant, 1 minute. Add to the yams and beat until fluffy, adding more of the coconut milk as needed. Taste for salt. Serve immediately.

Mashed Sweet Potatoes with Smoked Paprika

Serves 6 to 8 • Cooker: 5- to 8-quart • Time: 7 minutes at HIGH pressure

The sweet potato combines beautifully with so many different spices. Here smoked paprika, also known as pimentón, is the star of the show. To make it, the peppers are dried slowly over oak fires for several weeks and then stone ground, which gives it a special silky texture. It's a great way to add a smoky flavor with no heat. Instead of milk, goat cheese adds the creaminess to the mashed potatoes. This recipe is perfect for Thanksgiving and Christmas holiday meals.

6 medium-large Jewel yams (about 3 pounds), peeled and cut into 2-inch chunks
Sea salt
4 ounces soft fresh goat cheese
$^1/_2$ teaspoon smoked paprika, or to taste

1. Place the potatoes in a 5- to 8-quart pressure cooker pot and fill with water to cover. It is okay if a few edges of the potatoes are peeking up out of the water. Sprinkle with salt.

2. Close and lock the lid. Set the burner heat to high. When the cooker reaches HIGH pressure, reduce the burner heat as low as you can and still maintain HIGH pressure. Set a timer to cook for 7 minutes.

3. Remove the pot from the heat. Open the cooker with the Quick Release method. Be careful of the steam as you remove the lid. The potatoes should be soft and tender when pierced with the tip of a knife and still hold their shape. Drain in a colander and transfer to a medium bowl.

4. Add the goat cheese and paprika and, with a ricer, potato masher, or handheld electric mixer on low speed, beat until you have the consistency you prefer. Taste for salt. Serve immediately.

Candied Sweet Potatoes

Serves 6 to 8 • Cooker: 5- to 8-quart • Time: 9 minutes at HIGH pressure

This is an old Betty Crocker recipe adapted for the pressure cooker. The candying process is done stovetop after the potatoes are cooked. Use smaller potatoes; you don't want the slices too large.

6 to 8 small to medium (they need to fit in the pressure cooker whole) Jewel yams (about 2 pounds), left unpeeled, pierced in several places with a knife and ends trimmed
$^2/_3$ cup firmly packed light brown sugar
Pinch sea salt
5 tablespoons unsalted butter
$^1/_2$ cup water

1. Place the potatoes in a 5- to 8-quart pressure cooker pot and fill with water to cover. It is okay if a few edges of the potatoes are peeking up out of the water.

2. Close and lock the lid. Set the burner heat to high. When the cooker reaches HIGH pressure, reduce the burner heat as low as you can and still maintain HIGH pressure. Set a timer to cook for 9 minutes.

3. Remove the pot from the heat. Open the cooker with the Quick Release method. Be careful of the steam as you remove the lid. The potatoes should be firm but tender when pierced with the tip of a knife and hold their shape. Drain in a colander. When cool enough to handle, slip off the skins and cut across into $^3/_4$-inch-thick slices. Set aside.

4. In a deep 10-inch skillet, combine the brown sugar, salt, butter, and water. Melt over medium-low heat, stirring constantly with a heatproof spatula, until just bubbly and smooth. Add the sliced potatoes and gently stir until all the slices are glazed and hot, 2 to 3 minutes. Transfer to a warmed serving bowl. Serve immediately.

Gingered Sweet Potato Salad with Mandarins, Dates, and Pecans

Serves 6 • Cooker: 5- to 7-quart • Time: 4 minutes at HIGH pressure

There was a time when you could only find sweet potato salad at Southern and Pennsylvania Dutch picnics. But then everyone discovered how super nutritious they are and recipes for all manner of sweet potatoes started popping up everywhere. This recipe is adapted for the pressure cooker from one found in a pamphlet collection called *Hellman/Best Foods Favorite Recipes* (CPC International, 1990). Every bite bursts with flavor.

1¹/2 cups water
2 pounds large sweet potatoes, peeled and cubed
Juice of 1 lemon
1¹/4 cups mayonnaise
1 tablespoon Champagne vinegar
1 tablespoon orange juice
1 teaspoon grated orange zest
2 teaspoons grated peeled fresh ginger
¹/4 teaspoon sea salt
¹/8 teaspoon ground nutmeg
1 cup chopped pecans
1 (11-ounce) can mandarin orange sections, drained, or 3 fresh mandarins, peeled and sectioned
¹/3 cup chopped pitted dates
3 ribs celery, cut into ¹/4-inch dice

1. Place a trivet in a 5- to 7-quart pressure cooker. Add the water. Place the potato cubes in a steamer basket and place in the pot. The water should not touch the potatoes (pour some out if there is too much). Sprinkle with the lemon juice.

2. Cover and lock the lid in place. Set the burner heat to high. When the cooker reaches HIGH pressure, reduce the burner heat as low as you can and still maintain HIGH pressure. Set a timer to cook for 4 minutes.

3. Remove the pot from the heat. Open the cooker with the Natural Release method; let stand for 15 minutes. Be careful of the steam as you remove the lid. Transfer the potatoes to a medium bowl. Loosely cover and refrigerate until cooled.

4. When you're ready to assemble the salad, whisk together the mayonnaise, vinegar, orange juice and zest, ginger, salt, and nutmeg in a serving bowl. Add the potatoes, pecans, mandarins, dates, and celery and, using a large rubber spatula, fold gently together. Serve immediately or transfer to an airtight container and store in the refrigerator; it can be made a day ahead.

Sweet Potato Stew with Green Chard

Serves 4 to 6 • Cooker: 5- to 7-quart • Time: 3 minutes at HIGH pressure

This is adapted from a recipe by Ayurvedic vegetarian cooking teacher and holistic living caterer Nalini Mehta of Route to India (routetoindia.com) cooking school and meditation center in San Francisco. Serve this ladled over cooked rice, quinoa, or other grain of your choice.

2 tablespoons olive oil
1 teaspoon cumin seeds
1 medium white onion, diced
1 jalapeño pepper, seeded and minced (adjust quantity to suit your taste)
$^1/_2$ teaspoon turmeric
1 tablespoon peeled minced fresh ginger
1 teaspoon sea salt, plus more to taste
2 medium sweet potatoes, peeled and cut into $^1/_2$-inch cubes
1 teaspoon ground coriander
$^3/_4$ cup water
1 bunch Swiss chard, both stems and leaves coarsely chopped
1 (14-ounce) can unsweetened coconut milk
$^1/_4$ cup finely chopped fresh cilantro
Lime wedges, for serving

1. In a 5- to 7-quart pressure cooker, heat the oil over medium heat. Add the cumin seeds. Once they start to dance in the oil, add the onion. Cook and stir for about 3 minutes. Add the jalapeño, turmeric, ginger, salt, and sweet potatoes and cook, stirring, for 3 minutes. Add the coriander and stir until you smell its fragrance. Add the water and a bit more salt. Add the chard and coconut milk, pushing the chard down into the pot to wilt.

2. Close and lock the lid. Set the burner heat to high. When the cooker reaches HIGH pressure, reduce the burner heat as low as you can and still maintain HIGH pressure. Set a timer to cook for 3 minutes.

3. Remove the pot from the heat. Open the cooker with the Quick Release method. Be careful of the steam as you remove the lid.

4. Serve sprinkled with the cilantro and a wedge of lime.

AYURVEDIC COOKING

Preparing Ayurvedically balanced meals is about the combining of six tastes—sweet, sour, salty, astringent, bitter, and pungent—to create balance in the body. For this reason the Ayurvedic style of food preparation is referred to as the yoga of cooking.

15

Garden Variety: Vegetables

Of all the foods prepared in the pressure cooker, vegetables have the most variables due to their different densities. Hard vegetables like winter squashes and tubers like parsnips and carrots are excellent in the pressure cooker, as are the tougher greens, such as kale and collards. Softer vegetables, like summer squash, green beans, and corn, need only a whisper of pressurized heat to cook through. Some vegetables are best pressure-cooked in the steamer basket, others boiled under pressure in liquid to cover, and still others braised in a little bit of liquid. In addition to saving time, cooking vegetables under pressure retains their natural bright colors, flavor, and nutrients.

TIPS FOR COOKING VEGETABLES IN THE PRESSURE COOKER

- Use good quality ingredients in perfect condition. The taste of vegetables past their prime is accentuated (in a bad way) when cooked under pressure.
- When steaming, the steamer basket or steamer plate can be sprayed with nonstick cooking spray or lined with parchment paper, cheesecloth, whole cabbage or chard leaves, or corn husks to keep the food from sticking or dripping (beets, for instance).
- When steaming, arrange the foods in the steamer basket as directed in the recipe for proper circulation of the steam during cooking.
- Make certain the vegetables are of a similar size or cut to a similar size so that they cook in the same amount of time.
- Do not fill the pot more than two-thirds full, including the liquid.
- Check your food for doneness. If not completely cooked through or to your liking, put the lid back on the cooker, without locking it for pressure, and let it finish cooking to your liking over medium heat to medium-low.
- Open the cooker using the Quick Release method to avoid overcooking unless otherwise directed.

GUIDE TO STEAMING VEGETABLES IN THE PRESSURE COOKER

Use a trivet and steamer rack or basket to elevate the vegetables above the steaming liquid. Most any size pressure cooker will work with this amount of vegetables, from 3 to 8 quarts.

Vegetable (1 to 1¹/₂ pounds; serves 4 as side dish)	Steaming Liquid	Cooking Time at High Pressure
Artichokes (see pages 470–472)		
Asparagus	³/₄ cup	2 to 2¹/₂ minutes
Beans, green or wax string	³/₄ cup	2 minutes
Beans, lima (fresh)	³/₄ cup	2 minutes
Beets, small, whole	1 cup	10 minutes
Beets, (large, whole)	1¹/₂ cups	15 to 20 minutes
Bok choy, baby, or sliced mature bok choy	³/₄ cup	1 minute
Broccoli, cut into florets	1 cup	2 minutes
Broccoli stalks, sliced	1 cup	3 minutes
Brussels sprouts, trimmed	1 cup	4 minutes
Cabbage, green, shredded	1 cup	3 minutes
Cabbage, green or red, cut into wedges	1 cup	5 to 8 minutes
Cabbage, red, shredded	1 cup	4 minutes
Carrots, sliced, or small baby carrots	¹/₂ cup	2¹/₂ to 3 minutes
Cauliflower, cut into florets	³/₄ cup	2 minutes
Cauliflower, whole (see page 479)		
Celery, sliced	³/₄ cup	3 to 5 minutes
Corn on the cob (see page 485)		
Corn, kernels	³/₄ cup	3 minutes
Eggplant, cubed	³/₄ cup	3 minutes
Escarole/endive, coarsely chopped or thick cut	³/₄ cup	1 to 2 minutes
Fennel bulb, sliced	³/₄ cup	3 to 4 minutes
Green beans, trimmed	³/₄ cup	2 to 3 minutes
Kale or collard greens, heavy stems cut out	³/₄ cup	4 to 6 minutes
Okra, whole pods	³/₄ cup	3 minutes
Onions, sliced	³/₄ cup	3 minutes
Onions, medium whole	1 cup	7 to 10 minutes
Parsnips, sliced	³/₄ cup	2 minutes
Parsnips, cut in half	1 cup	2 minutes
English peas	³/₄ cup	2 to 3 minutes
Potatoes, sliced	1¹/₄ cups	2¹/₂ minutes

GUIDE TO STEAMING VEGETABLES IN THE PRESSURE COOKER

Vegetable (1 to 1¹/₂ pounds; serves 4 as side dish)	Steaming Liquid	Cooking Time at High Pressure
Potatoes, medium, cut in half	2 cups	8 minutes
Potatoes, medium, whole	2 cups	12 to 15 minutes
Potatoes, sweet or yams, cubed	1¹/₂ cups	6 minutes
Potatoes, sweet or yams, cut in half	1¹/₂ cups	8 to 10 minutes
Rutabagas, cubed	1 cup	5 minutes
Sauerkraut	³/₄ cup	12 minutes
Spinach	³/₄ cup	1 minutes
Swiss chard & other greens	³/₄ cup	2 minutes
Squash, butternut or acorn, halved or quartered	1 cup	6 to 7 minutes
Squash, Hubbard, cut in half or quartered	1 cup	8 to 10 minutes
Squash, pumpkin, cut in half or quartered	1¹/₂ cups	8 to 10 minutes
Squash, summer or zucchini, sliced	1 cup	1 to 2 minutes
Tomatoes, whole	¹/₂ cup	2¹/₂ minutes
Turnips, cubed, quartered, or thick sliced	1 cup	3 minutes

Bacon-Braised Mixed Greens

Serves 6 • Cooker: 5- to 8-quart • Time: 8 minutes at HIGH pressure

We love the combination of collards, kale, and mustard greens for this but feel free to experiment with your own partnerings.

4 slices bacon, diced
¹/₂ white onion, diced
2 cloves garlic, crushed
1 bunch kale, washed well, center ribs removed, and chopped
1 bunch collard greens, washed well, stems trimmed off, and chopped
1 bunch mustard greens, washed well and chopped
Pinch sugar
3 cups chicken broth
Sea salt and freshly ground black pepper
2 to 3 tablespoons cider vinegar or juice of 1 lemon

1. Place the bacon and onion in a 5- to 8-quart pressure cooker. Turn the heat to medium-high and cook for 3 minutes to crisp the bacon slightly, stirring a few times. Stir in the garlic, then add the greens, sugar, and broth, pushing down on the greens until they wilt enough to fit in the pot.
2. Close and lock the lid. Set the burner heat to high. When the cooker reaches HIGH pressure, reduce the burner heat as low as you can and still maintain HIGH pressure. Set a timer to cook for 8 minutes.
3. Remove the pot from the heat. Let stand for 6 minutes, then open the cooker with the Quick Release method. Be careful of the steam as you remove the lid. Do not drain. Stir. Taste for salt and pepper and stir in the vinegar.

Garlicky Braised Escarole with Red Pepper

Serves 3 to 4 • Cooker: 5- to 7-quart • Time: 1 minute at HIGH pressure

Escarole comes in a big leafy head and is far milder than the other chicories (including radicchio and curly endive) it is related to, which can be quite bitter. When serving this, be sure to have a hunk of Parmesan and a hand grater at the ready. You can use this method to cook any number of leafy greens, including Swiss chard, broccoli rabe, kale, chicory, or any mix of them; the cooking time will be the same for all of them. Delicious hot, warm, or at room temperature.

1 head escarole (about 1 pound)
$1/4$ cup extra virgin olive oil, plus more for serving
1 to 3 cloves garlic, to taste, chopped
$1/4$ teaspoon red pepper flakes
$1/2$ cup water
Sea salt and freshly ground black pepper

1. Cut the root ends off the escarole and remove any unsightly outside leaves. Rinse well. Divide the head lengthwise into halves or thirds, depending on its size. Discard the core. Rinse in a colander with several changes of cold water, leaving the leaves a little moist but eliminating all excess water. Cut the leaves across into 2-inch ribbons, then into bite-size pieces

2. Place the oil and garlic in a 5- to 7-quart pressure cooker, then turn on the heat to medium-high and heat the oil until the garlic is fragrant and the oil just starts to sizzle around it; do not let the garlic brown. Add the red pepper flakes and stir for 15 seconds. Add the escarole and toss with the oil. The leaves will be bulky at first, then begin to wilt. Add the water. Season to taste with salt and black pepper. Bring to a simmer.

3. Close and lock the lid. Set the burner heat to high. When the cooker reaches HIGH pressure, reduce the burner heat as low as you can and still maintain HIGH pressure. Set a timer to cook for 1 minute.

4. Remove the pot from the heat. Open the cooker with the Quick Release method. Be careful of the steam as you remove the lid. The escarole should be tender.

5. Simmer over medium heat (without pressure) to evaporate most of the liquid. Taste and adjust the salt and pepper. Serve hot drizzled with a little bit of oil.

Kale in Coconut Milk

Serves 4 • Cooker: 5- to 8- quart • Time: 4 minutes at HIGH pressure

This is like a healthy cousin to creamed spinach. Be sure to wash the kale leaves well in the sink with lots of water. Discard yellowed or tough leaves, and the fibrous stem. This is adapted from a Whole Foods recipe.

2 tablespoons olive oil
1 medium white onion, thinly sliced
2 bunches kale (about 1 pound), washed well, stemmed, and roughly chopped
1 cup unsweetened coconut milk
2 tablespoons fresh lemon juice
Sea salt and freshly ground black pepper

1. Place the oil and onion in a 5- to 8-quart pressure cooker. Turn the heat to medium-high and cook, stirring a few times, until the onion is translucent, 3 to 5 minutes. Add the coconut milk and lemon juice, then the kale, pushing down on it until it wilts enough to fit in the pot.

2. Close and lock the lid. Set the burner heat to high. When the cooker reaches HIGH pressure, reduce the burner heat as low as you can and still maintain HIGH pressure. Set a timer to cook for 4 minutes.

3. Remove the pot from the heat. Let stand 6 minutes, then open the cooker with the Quick Release method. Be careful of the steam as you remove the lid. Do not drain. Stir. Taste for salt and pepper. Serve immediately.

Tale of Two Kales

Serves 6 to 8 • Cooker: 6- to 8-quart • Time: 2 minutes at HIGH pressure

We knew kale before it was famous. Suddenly our better grocery stores and winter farmers' markets are stocked with not just kale but kales—multiple varieties of this super-nutritious, sturdy, leafy green member of the cabbage family. The most common types are red Russian or black kale, Lacinato or Tuscan kale (also known as elephant kale, and popular for its flavor, which is sweeter than other kales), dinosaur kale with large, rough leaves, and Scotch curly leaf kale. Each type looks and tastes a little different from the others. This recipe is designed to showcase two types, so look for a contrast in leaf texture and color, if you can; red kale isn't as rare as it used to be. Of course, you can make this with two bunches of the same type of kale, or 1 bunch of kale and one of chard or another sturdy green. In the pressure cooker, kale cooks to silky tenderness in just 2 minutes. Some people discard the stems but we like them and find they are easy to cook and eat as long as you chop them into $^3/_4$-inch pieces along with the leaves. This goes for chard stems, too.

2 bunches kale (different varieties if possible)
1 tablespoon extra virgin olive oil
1 medium onion, chopped into $^1/_2$-inch pieces
  (about 1 cup)
Pinch red pepper flakes
$^1/_2$ cup chicken or vegetable broth
Salt and freshly ground black pepper

1. Trim ends from each bunch of kale stems and wash kale well in a colander under cold running water, running your fingers along the leaves. If you find any grit or sand, wash the kale by swishing it in a large bowl of cold water and lifting out the leaves so that the grit can fall to the bottom of the bowl. Shake the excess water from the leaves and chop the kale crosswise into $^3/_4$-inch ribbons. Chop the stems, too.

2. In a 6- to 8-quart pressure cooker, heat the oil over medium-high heat. Add the onion and cook, stirring a few times, until soft, about 3 minutes; do not brown. Add the red pepper flakes and stir for 15 seconds. Add the broth and stir. Add the kale. You may have to push it down with your hands to get the lid on the cooker.

3. Close and lock the lid. Set the burner heat to high. When the cooker reaches HIGH pressure, reduce the burner heat as low as you can and still maintain HIGH pressure. Set a timer to cook for 2 minutes.

4. Remove the pot from the heat. Open the cooker with the Quick Release method. Be careful of the steam as you remove the lid.

5. Stir well to distribute the onions and broth throughout the kale. Taste the kale and add salt and black pepper, if desired. Serve hot.

Pressure-Steamed Baby Artichokes

Makes 4 to 6 side-dish or 12 appetizer servings • Cooker: 6- to 8-quart • Time: 6 minutes at HIGH pressure

During artichoke season, baby artichokes show up in packages of 6 or 8. They are a seasonal specialty and can easily be prepped and then frozen. When artichokes are cooked on the stove top, lemon juice is squeezed into the water to prevent discoloration, but also to add a hint of citrus flavor. In the pressure cooker, the artichokes turn out their same bright cooked-artichoke color, and the steaming lemon water imbues the leaves with far more lemon taste than in stove-top cooking. Keep in mind, the artichokes must be baby ones, and they are cooked whole.

¹/₄ cup fresh lemon juice (keep the reamed-out rinds)
3 cups cold water
24 baby artichokes (about 2 pounds)

1. Combine the lemon juice and water in a large bowl; add the rinds. You will drop the artichokes into the water as you trim them to prevent discoloring. Bend back the lower, outer petals until they snap off easily near the base. Continue to snap off the leaves until you reach the point where the leaves are half green at the top and half yellow. Using a paring knife, cut off the top cone of leaves at the crown where the yellow color meets the green. Cut off the stem level with the base and trim any remaining green from the base. Rinse under cold water. Toss into the lemon bath.
2. Pour the lemon water into a 6- to 8-quart pressure cooker. Set a trivet or steamer basket on the bottom and pile the artichokes on top (they don't need to be in a single layer).
3. Close and lock the lid. Set the burner heat to high. When the cooker reaches HIGH pressure, reduce the burner heat as low as you can and still maintain HIGH pressure. Set a timer to cook for 6 minutes.
4. Remove the pot from the heat. Let sit for 10 minutes for soft artichokes or 6 minutes if you prefer them firmer (if, for example, you will be using them in a recipe and they will cook a bit more), then open the cooker with the Quick Release method. Be careful of the steam as you remove the lid. When the steam subsides, pour off the liquid, taking care not to break the artichokes apart. Set aside without disturbing until cool enough to handle.
5. When ready to serve, transfer the artichokes to a serving dish and serve with your choice of an artichoke dipping sauce or melted butter. They will keep 4 to 5 days in the refrigerator in a zip-top plastic bag and up to 2 months in the freezer.

Medium Artichokes

Serves 2 to 6 • Cooker: 6- to 8-quart • Time: 12 minutes at HIGH pressure

In between the baby artichokes and the jumbos are the medium size, often coming in clamshell plastic boxes of 4 to 6 artichokes. Serve with one of our artichoke dipping sauces (page 473) or plain mayonnaise.

4 to 6 medium artichokes (6 to 8 ounces each)
2 lemons, cut in half
$1^1/_2$ cups water
2 tablespoons olive oil

1. Trim the artichoke: Pull off and discard any small leaves on the artichoke stem. Place the artichoke on a cutting board on its side and use a large knife to cut off about a third of the top. Use scissors to trim off the sharp points of any remaining whole tough leaves. Trim off and discard about $1/_2$ inch from the base of the stem. A further, optional step, is to open up the leaves at the top and remove the choke (the inner thorny leaves and fuzz) with a melon baller or spoon. Rub the cut parts of the artichoke with 2 of the lemon halves.

2. Place the water and juice of 1 lemon in a 6- to 8-quart pressure cooker. Set a trivet or steamer basket on the bottom. Place the artichokes in the pressure cooker, stem side up. Drizzle each with the oil.

3. Close and lock the lid. Set the burner heat to high. When the cooker reaches HIGH pressure, reduce the burner heat as low as you can and still maintain HIGH pressure. Set a timer to cook for 12 minutes.

4. Remove the pot from the heat. Open the cooker with the Natural Release method; let stand for 15 minutes. Be careful of the steam as you remove the lid.

5. Using tongs, remove the artichokes to a plate, allowing any liquid to drip out as you remove them. Serve the artichokes warm, at room temperature, or cold. Eat by pulling off individual leaves and scraping them with your teeth to enjoy the tender portions. Discard the top, fibrous portion of each leaf. When you reach the spiky center "choke," which is inedible, use a soup spoon to remove it, if you didn't when you were prepping the artichokes for cooking. Trim the dark green portions from the remaining tender "heart" and cut the heart into bite-size pieces. You will find that the center portion of the stem is also tender and delicious. They will keep 4 to 5 days in the refrigerator in a ziptop plastic bag.

Jumbo Artichokes

Serves 1 to 2 • Cooker: 6- to 8-quart • Time: 27 minutes at HIGH pressure

We live in the San Francisco Bay Area, just over the hill from acres of cool, coastal artichoke fields. So when it comes to artichokes, we are definitely spoiled. They are inexpensive, abundant, super fresh, and available practically year round. Nevertheless, spring is peak artichoke season and the time of year when the extra-large jumbo monster chokes—over 1 pound each—are in the markets. If you have never seen a jumbo artichoke, you will do a double-take the first time you encounter one! They are fun to share—really, it can take two people to eat one—that is, if you want to share! They tend to be addictive since there is so much excellent flesh to feed on. The pressure cooker is our absolute favorite way to cook them to delicious tenderness.

1 jumbo artichoke (1 pound or larger)
$1/2$ lemon
1 tablespoon olive oil
$1^1/2$ cups water
2 cloves garlic, peeled

1. Trim the artichoke: Pull off and discard any small leaves on the artichoke stem. Place the artichoke on a cutting board on its side and use a large knife to cut off about 1 inch from the top. Use scissors to trim off the pointed tips of any remaining whole leaves. Trim off and discard about $1/2$ inch from the base of the stem.
2. Cut the lemon half in half. Holding the artichoke over a 6- to 8-quart pressure cooker, squeeze the lemon pieces over the artichoke, aiming to cover most of it with lemon juice. Drop the lemon pieces into the pressure cooker. Now repeat the process with the oil, drizzling it over the artichoke and allowing it to drip into the pressure cooker. Place the artichoke in the pressure cooker, stem side up or sideways if the stem is too long to fit. Add the water and drop in the garlic cloves.
3. Close and lock the lid. Set the burner heat to high. When the cooker reaches HIGH pressure, reduce the burner heat as low as you can and still maintain HIGH pressure. Set a timer to cook for 27 minutes.
4. Remove the pot from the heat. Open the cooker with the Quick Release. Be careful of the steam as you remove the lid.
5. Using tongs, remove the artichoke to a plate, tipping it upside down to allow any liquid to drip out as you remove it. Serve the artichoke hot, at room temperature, or cold. Eat by pulling off individual leaves and scraping them with your teeth to enjoy the tender portions. Discard the top, fibrous portion of each leaf. When you reach the spiky center "choke," which is inedible, use a soup spoon to remove it. Trim the dark green portions from the remaining tender "heart" and cut the heart into bite-size pieces. You will find that the center portion of the stem is also tender and delicious. Keeps 4 to 5 days in the refrigerator in a ziptop plastic bag.

Artichoke Dipping Sauces

S erve steamed artichokes warm, at room temperature, or chilled with melted butter or one of the sauces below.

Mustard-Lemon Aioli

Makes about 1 cup

1 clove garlic, peeled
Pinch sea salt
1 cup mayonnaise
2 tablespoons coarse-grained Dijon mustard
1 tablespoon fresh lemon juice

Using a mortar with pestle, mash the garlic with the salt until a paste forms (or mince the garlic and mix it with salt). Transfer the garlic mixture to small bowl. Mix in the remaining ingredients. Will keep in an airtight container in the refrigerator up to 2 days.

Yogurt Dill Dip

Makes 1 cup

1 cup plain Greek yogurt
1 to 2 cloves garlic, to taste, pressed
Squeeze of fresh lemon juice
2 tablespoons chopped fresh dill or 2 teaspoons
   dillweed
Sea salt and freshly ground black or white pepper

In a small bowl, whisk the yogurt, garlic, lemon juice, and dill together. Season to taste with salt and pepper. Will keep in an airtight container in the refrigerator overnight.

Skordalia (Greek Potato and Garlic Dip)

Makes about 2 cups
Pressure Cooker: 5- to 7-quart
Pressure Time: 6 minutes at HIGH pressure

There are many versions of this thick, garlicky Greek sauce, considered a cousin to French aioli and used on everything from fish and roast turkey to steamed artichokes and fried vegetables (try it with fried zucchini strips or sliced steamed beets). While Greeks like lots of garlic in their skordalia, here we give you a range to fit your palate.

1 pound russet potatoes, peeled and cut into 2-inch
   chunks
4 to 12 cloves garlic, to taste, peeled
1 teaspoon sea salt
1/3 cup blanched almonds, whole or slivered, or
   pine nuts
1 cup extra virgin olive oil
1 tablespoon red wine vinegar
Freshly ground black pepper

1. Place the potatoes in a 5- to 7-quart pressure cooker pot and fill with water to cover. It is okay if a few edges of the potatoes are peeking up out of the water.
2. Close and lock the lid. Set the burner heat to high. When the cooker reaches HIGH pressure, reduce the burner heat as low as you can and still maintain HIGH pressure. Set a timer to cook for 6 minutes.
3. Remove the pot from the heat. Open the cooker with the Quick Release method. Be careful of the steam as you remove the lid. The potatoes should be soft and tender when pierced with the tip of a knife. Drain in a colander. Return the potatoes to the pot, shaking to dry them a bit.
4. Place the garlic and salt in a food processor and pulse to grind. Add the nuts and pulse to grind. Dump the hot potatoes into the processor and add the oil and vinegar; blend until smooth. Taste for salt and pepper. This is best served the day it is made. If not serving immediately, cover and refrigerate until ready to serve.

Asparagus with Lime Hollandaise

Serves 5 (sauce makes 1¹/₄ cups) • Cooker: 5- to 7-quart • Time: 2 to 3 minutes at HIGH pressure

Asparagus retains its bright green color in the pressure cooker. It will be tender from top to bottom. We add sour cream to our version of hollandaise, which stabilizes it, allowing the sauce to sit in a warm water bath for hours before serving or even to be made a day ahead, with no danger of breaking. The best!

ASPARAGUS:

2 pounds asparagus, bottom 2 inches snapped off (use a vegetable peeler to peel the bottom of the stalk if large)
1 cup water

LIME HOLLANDAISE SAUCE:

4 large egg yolks
1 tablespoon fresh lime juice
1 teaspoon grated lime zest
Dash sea salt
Ground white pepper
1 cup (2 sticks) unsalted butter, melted and hot
¹/₃ cup sour cream (low-fat, IMO imitation sour cream, or crème fraîche acceptable)

1. In a 5- to 7-quart pressure cooker, lay the asparagus spears in a flat pile on the steamer plate or stand them upright tied in one or two bunches with kitchen twine or foil. Add the water.
2. Close and lock the lid. Set the burner heat to high. When the cooker reaches HIGH pressure, reduce the burner heat as low as you can and still maintain HIGH pressure. Set a timer to cook for 1¹/₂ minutes for thin stalks, 2 minutes for medium stalks, and 3 minutes for giant fat stalks.
3. Remove the pot from the heat and let stand 1 minute, no more. Open the cooker with the Quick Release method. Be careful of the steam as you remove the lid. Transfer the asparagus to a serving platter.
4. To make the sauce, place the yolks, lime juice and zest, salt, and pepper to taste in a food processor or a blender. Process to combine. With the motor running, add the hot melted butter in a slow, steady stream, drop by drop at first, until the sauce becomes creamy and thick. Whisk in the sour cream. Use immediately or hold in the top of a double boiler over low heat until serving time. Can be made the day ahead and reheated slowly in the double boiler.
5. Drizzle the asparagus with the hollandaise. Serve immediately.

Hungarian Green Beans with Paprika

Serves 6 • Cooker: 5- to 7-quart • Time: 2 minutes at HIGH pressure

Haricots vert means "green bean" in French but they are a dash longer and thinner, looking like a baby green bean, than regular green beans. You can also make this with older, less tender green beans; increase the pressure cook time to 3 minutes. Serve this creamy side dish with beef stew or broiled fish.

3 tablespoons butter
1 tablespoon olive oil
1 large white onion, diced
1 1/2 pounds tender young green beans or haricots vert, ends trimmed and cut into 2-inch pieces on the diagonal
1 teaspoon sea salt, plus more to taste
Freshly ground black pepper
1 cup water
3/4 to 1 cup sour cream, to taste
1 1/4 teaspoons sweet Hungarian paprika
2 tablespoons chopped fresh chives

1. In a 5- to 7-quart pressure cooker over medium-high heat, melt the butter with the oil. Add the onion and cook, stirring a few times, until soft, about 3 minutes; do not brown. Add the green beans, salt, a few grinds of pepper, and the water.
2. Close and lock the lid. Set the burner heat to high. When the cooker reaches HIGH pressure, reduce the burner heat as low as you can and still maintain HIGH pressure. Set a timer to cook for 2 minutes.
3. Remove the pot from the heat. Open the cooker with the Quick Release method. Be careful of the steam as you remove the lid. The beans should be just tender when pierced with the tip of a knife.
4. Drain the beans in a colander and return to the pot. Combine the sour cream and paprika. Add this to the pot and gently stir it into the beans, coating them completely. Warm through over low heat; do not boil. Taste for salt and pepper. Transfer to a serving dish, sprinkle with the chives, and serve immediately.

Italian-Style Braised Green Beans

Serves 6 • Cooker: 5- to 7- quart • Time: 4 minutes at HIGH pressure

Green beans prepared this way taste incredible—they're buttery soft, with a deep, earthy flavor and a rich sauce. This is the perfect recipe for older, tougher green beans. Serve as a side dish with roast chicken or meatloaf, sprinkled with some Parmesan.

2 tablespoons olive oil
1 large white onion, diced
1 clove garlic, minced
2 pounds older green beans, ends trimmed
4 ripe plum tomatoes, seeded and diced, or 1 (14.5-ounce can) diced tomatoes in juice, drained
1 cup water (for added flavor, you can sub some of water out for juice from the can of tomatoes, if using)
2 tablespoons dry rosé or white wine
Sea salt and freshly ground black pepper

1. In a 5- to 7-quart pressure cooker over medium-high heat, heat the oil. Add the onion and cook, stirring a few times, until soft, about 3 minutes; do not brown. Add the garlic and cook for 30 seconds. Add the green beans, tomatoes, water, and wine.
2. Close and lock the lid. Set the burner heat to high. When the cooker reaches HIGH pressure, reduce the burner heat as low as you can and still maintain HIGH pressure. Set a timer to cook for 4 minutes.
3. Remove the pot from the heat. Open the cooker with the Quick Release method. Be careful of the steam as you remove the lid. The green beans should be tender.
4. Season the beans to taste with salt and pepper. Serve hot or at room temperature with a slotted spoon.

Green Beans with Shiitake Mushrooms and Ginger

Serves 4 to 6 as a side dish • Cooker: 5- to 7-quart • Time: 2 minutes at HIGH pressure

The shiitake is a delicious, meaty mushroom and pairs well with green beans in this dish, sparked up with the addition of fresh ginger.

1 tablespoon extra virgin olive oil
2 medium shallots, chopped
5 ounces fresh shiitake mushrooms (about 1 1/2 cups), tough stems removed and caps thinly sliced
1 tablespoon grated peeled fresh ginger
1 1/2 pounds tender young green beans or haricots vert, ends trimmed and cut into 2- to 3-inch pieces on the diagonal
1/2 cup water or vegetable broth
2 tablespoons reduced-sodium soy sauce
1 tablespoon rice vinegar or brown rice vinegar

1. In a 5- to 7-quart pressure cooker pot, heat the oil over medium-high heat. Add the shallots and cook, stirring a few times, until soft, about 3 minutes; do not brown. Add the mushrooms and ginger and cook, stirring a few times, for 2 minutes. Add the green beans, water, soy sauce, and vinegar.
2. Close and lock the lid. Set the burner heat to high. When the cooker reaches HIGH pressure, reduce the burner heat as low as you can and still maintain HIGH pressure. Set a timer to cook for 2 minutes.
3. Remove the pot from the heat. Open the cooker with the Quick Release method. Be careful of the steam as you remove the lid. Serve immediately.

Greek Lima Beans

Serves 4 • Cooker: 5- to 7-quart • Time: 3 minutes at HIGH pressure

This is adapted from a deceptively simple recipe we found in *Gourmet*. The lima beans cook up creamy and comforting. The broth is delicious, so be sure to serve this with some crusty bread to soak up the juices. You can also use this recipe to prepare frozen edamame or fava beans.

1 (10-ounce) package frozen baby lima beans (no need to thaw)
2 tablespoons coarsely chopped fresh flatleaf parsley
1 tablespoon minced garlic
1/2 teaspoon sea salt, plus more to taste
1 cup vegetable broth or water
2 to 3 tablespoons good-quality olive oil, to taste
Freshly ground black pepper
1 lemon, halved or quartered, plus wedges for serving

1. Place the lima beans, parsley, garlic, and 1/2 teaspoon salt in a 5- to 7-quart pressure cooker. Add the broth and oil. Bring to a boil.
2. Close and lock the lid. Set the burner heat to high. When the cooker reaches HIGH pressure, reduce the burner heat as low as you can and still maintain HIGH pressure. Set a timer to cook for 3 minutes.
3. Remove the pot from the heat and let stand a few minutes. Open the cooker with the Quick Release method. Be careful of the steam as you remove the lid. The beans should be tender when pierced with the tip of a knife. If the beans are not totally cooked, cover the pot and cook without pressure for a few minutes over medium heat.
4. Stir, season to taste with salt and pepper, and squeeze in the juice from halved or quartered lemon. Serve immediately with lemon wedges, if you like.

Romano Beans Braised with Peppers and Tomatoes

Serves 4 • Cooker: 5- to 7-quart • Time: 1 minute at HIGH pressure

Julie's friends Karin Schlanger and David Winsberg own Happy Quail Farms in East Palo Alto, California, where they grow dozens of specialty crops, including a bounty of peppers. David's red-flecked Romano beans and skinny, mild Piment d'Anglet peppers (sometimes called Basque fryers) were the inspiration for this late-summer dish. Mild Italian frying peppers work well, too. Also feel free to substitute red, yellow, or orange bell pepper strips. If you like some heat, slip in a few strips of a hot pepper, too. The Romano is a flat, rather tough, green snap bean that shows up in farmers' markets at the end of summer. They are great braised since they hold their shape and the pressure cooking brings out their natural sweetness. This is delicious with grilled or baked fish.

$^1/_2$ pound sweet frying peppers such as Piment d'Anglet (Basque fryers) or Italian frying peppers, OR 1 large red, yellow, or orange bell pepper

1 tablespoon olive oil

1 medium onion, chopped

1 clove garlic, chopped

$^1/_2$ pound Romano beans, ends trimmed

3 ripe medium tomatoes, chopped into $^1/_2$-inch pieces

1 teaspoon smoked Spanish paprika, sweet or hot (pimentón)

$^1/_2$ teaspoon ground coriander

$^1/_2$ teaspoon ground cumin

$^1/_2$ teaspoon salt

$^1/_4$ teaspoon freshly ground black pepper

$^1/_2$ cup water

1. Split the peppers lengthwise and remove the stem, seeds, and veins, using the tip of a teaspoon if necessary. If the peppers are on the large side, slice each half lengthwise into strips no wider than $^1/_2$ inch. If they are very long (more than about 4 inches), cut the strips in half crosswise. If you are using a bell pepper, halve it, remove the seeds and stem, and slice into $^1/_2$-inch-wide strips.

2. In a 5- to 7-quart pressure cooker over medium-high heat, heat the oil. Add the onion and garlic and cook, stirring a few times, until the onion just begins to soften, about 2 minutes. Add the peppers and cook for 2 minutes more. Add the beans, tomatoes, spices, salt, and black pepper, and cook, stirring, for an additional minute. Pour in the water.

3. Close and lock the lid. Set the burner heat to high. When the cooker reaches HIGH pressure, reduce the burner heat as low as you can and still maintain HIGH pressure. Set a timer to cook for 1 minute.

4. Remove the pot from the heat. Open the cooker with the Quick Release method. Be careful of the steam as you remove the lid. Stir and taste and adjust seasonings as desired. Serve immediately.

PIMENT D'ANGLET PEPPERS

This pepper is also known as Basque fryer or Doux des Landes ("Sweet from Landes," Landes referring to an area of Southwest France, where it was developed). It is one of the longest peppers (it can grow over a foot long) and is delightfully sweet and mild, scoring a 0 on the Scoville scale of hotness. It is used in Basque cooking and notably in piperade, a stewy dish of tomatoes and peppers.

Peas and Onions with Turmeric

Serves 6 • Cooker: 5- to 7-quart • Time: 4 minutes at HIGH pressure

This recipe is from frenchrevolutionfood.com, adapted for the pressure cooker, cutting the cook time from 40 minutes down to 4. It's so good and so simple.

3 tablespoons olive oil
1 large white onion, finely diced
1¹/₂ teaspoons turmeric
2 pounds frozen petit peas (no need to thaw)
¹/₂ cup water
Dash sea salt

1. In a 5- to 7-quart pressure cooker over medium-high heat, heat the oil. Add the onion and cook, stirring a few times, until really soft, about 5 minutes; do not brown. Stir in the turmeric, then add the peas, water, and salt and stir to combine.
2. Close and lock the lid. Set the burner heat to high. When the cooker reaches HIGH pressure, reduce the burner heat as low as you can and still maintain HIGH pressure. Set a timer to cook for 4 minutes.
3. Remove the pot from the heat and let stand for 10 minutes, no more. Open the cooker with the Quick Release method. Be careful of the steam as you remove the lid. Stir gently and serve immediately.

Broccoli Sauce for Pasta

Makes about 3¹/₂ cups, enough for 1 pound pasta • Cooker: 5- to 7-quart • Time: 3 minutes at HIGH pressure

Beth watched Laura Pazzaglia, author of *Hip Pressure Cooking*, demo a super-green zucchini pesto when she was visiting Northern California, and it reminded her of a thick green broccoli sauce she was served at a pasta buffet some years back. Here is her taste memory of it, rebooted for the pressure cooker. The broccoli is cooked slightly longer than you would if you were going to eat it as a side dish. Put on the water to boil for the pasta before you make the sauce. Beth likes it with semolina spaghetti or cariole, which is double the width of spaghetti and square cut instead of round.

3 tablespoons olive oil
1 cup chopped white or yellow onion
2 cloves garlic, chopped
2 large heads broccoli (1³/₄ to 2 pounds), stems peeled and stems and florets coarsely chopped
¹/₃ cup dry vermouth or dry white wine
¹/₂ cup water
Freshly ground black pepper
Leaves from 1 bunch fresh basil
Sea salt
Freshly grated Parmesan cheese, for serving

1. In a 5- to 7-quart pressure cooker pot, heat the oil over medium-high heat. Add the onion; cook until just soft, stirring a few times, about 3 minutes. Add the garlic; stir 30 seconds. Add the broccoli, vermouth, and water. Bring to a boil and add several grinds of pepper.
2. Close and lock the lid. Set the burner heat to high. When the cooker reaches HIGH pressure, reduce the burner heat as low as you can and still maintain HIGH pressure. Set a timer to cook for 3 minutes.
3. Remove the pot from the heat. Open the cooker with the Quick Release method. Be careful of the steam as you remove the lid.
4. Add the basil. Puree with an immersion hand blender in the pot using an up and down motion for 30 seconds. Season to taste with salt and pepper. The sauce will be thick and smooth. Serve immediately on hot pasta with lots of grated Parmesan on the side, or let cool and store in an airtight container in the refrigerator up to 3 days. We don't recommend freezing this.

Pressure-Steamed Whole Cauliflower

Serves 4 to 6 • Cooker: 5- to 7-quart • Time: 5 minutes at HIGH pressure

It is important not to overcook cauliflower, otherwise it will develop an overly strong taste. Pressure steaming it whole is a good way to prepare it. You can then slice the head into wedges and serve with a cheese sauce or a generous drizzle of good quality olive oil, or cut it into florets and use it in a salad.

2 cups water
1 head cauliflower (2 to 4 pounds), leaves trimmed and cored

1. Place the water in a 5- to 7-quart pressure cooker. Position a trivet and steamer basket in the pot. Place the cauliflower in the steamer basket, stem side down. The water should not touch it.
2. Close and lock the lid. Set the burner heat to high. When the cooker reaches HIGH pressure, reduce the burner heat as low as you can and still maintain HIGH pressure. Set a timer to cook for 5 minutes.
3. Remove the pot from the heat. Open the cooker with the Quick Release method. Be careful of the steam as you remove the lid. Using a heavy-duty oven mitt, lift up the steamer basket, taking care not to get burned by the steam and hot water.

Cauliflower and Romanesco Broccoli with Olive Oil and Lemon

Serves 4 to 6 • Cooker: 5- to 7-quart • Time: 2 minutes at HIGH pressure

The Italian heirloom broccoli known as Romanesco (as well as Romanesque cauliflower and broccoflower) is very beautiful and its flavor is less assertive than cauliflower. Both cook the same way. You want to taste the oil in this recipe, so pick a nice green extra virgin olive oil. If you have access to Meyer lemons, use them here.

1 cup water
1 head cauliflower (2 pounds), leaves trimmed, cored, and cut into equal size florets
1 head Romanesco broccoli (2 pounds), leaves trimmed, cored, and cut into equal size florets
6 tablespoons good-quality extra virgin olive oil, a local press if available
1 lemon, cut in half
Sea salt, such as Maldon

1. Place the water in a 5- to 7-quart pressure cooker. Position the trivet and steamer basket in the pot. Pile the cauliflower and Romanesco florets in the steamer basket. The water should not touch it.
2. Close and lock the lid. Set the burner heat to high. When the cooker reaches HIGH pressure, reduce the burner heat as low as you can and still maintain HIGH pressure. Set a timer to cook for 2 minutes.
3. Remove the pot from the heat and let stand 1 minute. Open the cooker with the Quick Release method. Be careful of the steam as you remove the lid. The florets should be very tender. Using a heavy-duty oven mitt, lift up the steamer basket, taking care not to get burned by the steam and hot water.
4. Transfer the vegetables to a medium bowl. Add the oil, squeeze over the lemon halves, and season to taste with salt, then toss to mix the florets well with everything. Check the seasoning again before serving.

Cauliflower, Green Peas, and Potatoes with Fresh Ginger and Spices

Serves 4 to 6 • Cooker: 5- to 7-quart • Time: 3 minutes at HIGH pressure

This is the dish to make when you see nice extra-fresh, firm heads of pure white cauliflower with no little brown spots at the market. You want an equal weight of potatoes and cauliflower. Serve with basmati or saffron rice, if you like, and a nice green salad with radishes and cucumbers. We also like warm naan or flour tortillas.

2 tablespoons light olive oil, ghee, or melted butter
1 teaspoon cumin seeds
1 clove garlic (optional), minced
1 (2-inch) piece fresh ginger, peeled and grated
2 medium ripe plum tomatoes, seeded and diced
1 teaspoon turmeric
$^1/_2$ teaspoon ground coriander
$^1/_4$ teaspoon sea salt, plus more to taste
$^1/_4$ teaspoon red pepper flakes
$^3/_4$ cup water
4 Yukon Gold potatoes (about 1$^1/_2$ pounds), diced (do not peel)
1 small head cauliflower (about 1$^1/_2$ pounds), leaves trimmed, cored, and broken into 1-inch florets
1$^1/_2$ cups frozen green peas, thawed
3 tablespoons chopped fresh cilantro
Freshly ground black pepper

1. In a 5- to 7-quart pressure cooker, heat the oil over medium heat. Add the cumin seeds and garlic and cook, stirring, until fragrant, 30 to 60 seconds. Add the ginger and tomatoes and cook, stirring, until the oil separates out. Stir in the turmeric, coriander, salt, red pepper, and water. Add the potatoes and stir to combine. Layer the cauliflower over the top of the mixture. Do not stir.

2. Close and lock the lid. Set the burner heat to high. When the cooker reaches HIGH pressure, reduce the burner heat as low as you can and still maintain HIGH pressure. Set a timer to cook for 3 minutes.

3. Remove the pot from the heat. Open the cooker with the Quick Release method. Be careful of the steam as you remove the lid. The potatoes and cauliflower should be tender, not mushy.

4. Stir the peas and cilantro into the mixture, and heat through over low heat. Season to taste with black pepper and more salt. Serve hot or at room temperature.

Bok Choy with Ginger

Serves 4 • Cooker: 5- to 7-quart • Time: 5 minutes at HIGH pressure

Bok choy, a member of the cabbage family, looks like a cross between romaine lettuce and celery. It's sold as a full-sized head or as smaller baby bok choy. Look for firm, crisp stalks and store wrapped in a paper towel in your crisper drawer; it's best to buy bok choy close to when you plan to cook it to avoid any wilt in the leaves.

1 full-size head bok choy or 6 to 8 baby bok choy
1 to 2 tablespoons julienned peeled fresh ginger, to taste
1 cup water, as needed
2 tablespoons mirin or shaoxing rice wine
Reduced-sodium soy sauce, oyster sauce, toasted sesame oil, or salt, for serving
3 tablespoons chopped green onions (white and a few inches of green part), for serving

1. Cut off the stem end of the full-size bok choy and separate the leaves. Wash the leaves in cold water to remove any grit. Cut the stems out of the leaf and shred or cut into strips. Chop the leaves. If using baby bok choy, slice off a little of the stem end, then cut the bunch in half lengthwise.
2. Place the stems or halved baby bok choy with the ginger in a 5- to 7-quart pressure cooker. Add the water and mirin. The liquid should just cover the bok choy; if it doesn't add a few more tablespoons of water. If using full-size bok choy, arrange the leaves on top and pat down.
3. Close and lock the lid. Set the burner heat to high. When the cooker reaches HIGH pressure, reduce the burner heat as low as you can and still maintain HIGH pressure. Set a timer to cook for 5 minutes.
4. Remove the pot from the heat. Open the cooker with the Quick Release method. Be careful of the steam as you remove the lid. The leaves will be wilted but still bright green.
5. Use tongs to transfer the bok choy to a serving bowl. The stems, leaves, and little strips of ginger will be mixed up. Drizzle with some soy sauce, oyster sauce, or sesame oil, or season with salt and leave plain. Sprinkle with the green onions and serve immediately.

Bacon and Mustard Braised Brussels Sprouts

Serves 4 • Cooker: 5- to 7-quart • Time: 4 minutes at HIGH pressure

The quick cook time in the pressure cooker is perfect for brussels sprouts, bringing out their nutty flavor. Dill might seem an unusual choice for brussels sprouts but it complements them perfectly. Choose vibrantly green sprouts and select heads about the same size so they cook evenly. One inch in diameter is perfect and they will be sweet. Prepare them as soon as possible, within two days of buying them.

$1/2$ cup diced bacon (about 3 slices)
1 to 2 small shallots, to taste, chopped
1 to $1^1/4$ pounds brussels sprouts, trimmed of some outer leaves and stem, and cut in half lengthwise
1 cup chicken or vegetable broth
2 tablespoons dry vermouth or dry white wine
1 heaping tablespoon Dijon mustard
Freshly ground black pepper
1 tablespoon chopped fresh dill
2 tablespoons unsalted butter
Sea salt

1. In a 5- to 7-quart pressure cooker, cook the bacon just until soft, stirring, about 3 minutes. Add the shallots and cook 2 minutes. Add the brussels sprouts, broth, vermouth, and mustard. Bring to a boil and add several grinds of pepper.
2. Close and lock the lid. Set the burner heat to high. When the cooker reaches HIGH pressure, reduce the burner heat as low as you can and still maintain HIGH pressure. Set a timer to cook for 4 minutes.
3. Remove the pot from the heat. Open the cooker with the Quick Release method. Be careful of the steam as you remove the lid. The sprouts should still be a dash crisp-tender, not mushy.
4. Stir in the dill and butter until the butter melts and coats all the sprouts. Season to taste with salt. Serve immediately.

Chinese-Style Brussels Sprouts with Hoisin Glaze

Serves 4 • Cooker: 5- to 7-quart • Time: 4 minutes at HIGH pressure

This is a dish created by our dear friend, editor and writer Carolyn Jung, the Food Gal (foodgal.com), after having a similar dish at Straits restaurant in San Jose's Santana Row. The sweet, salty, spicy, tangy flavor of the hoisin sauce really works with the brussels sprouts.

2 tablespoons olive oil
3 tablespoons minced peeled fresh ginger
1 cup diced white onion
2 cloves garlic, thinly sliced
$1^1/2$ pounds brussels sprouts, trimmed of some outer leaves and stem, and cut in half lengthwise
$1/2$ cup chicken or vegetable broth
3 tablespoons mirin
1 tablespoon low-sodium soy sauce
$1/3$ cup hoisin sauce
Toasted sesame oil, for serving

1. In a 5- to 7-quart pressure cooker, heat the olive oil over medium-high heat. Add the ginger and onion; cook until just soft, stirring a few times, about 2 minutes. Add the garlic; cook 30 seconds. Add the brussels sprouts, broth, mirin, and soy sauce and bring to a simmer.
2. Close and lock the lid. Set the burner heat to high. When the cooker reaches HIGH pressure, reduce the burner heat as low as you can and still maintain HIGH pressure. Set a timer to cook for 4 minutes.
3. Remove the pot from the heat. Open the cooker with the Quick Release method. Be careful of the steam as you remove the lid. The sprouts should still be a dash crisp-tender, not mushy.
4. Place the cooker over medium heat and stir in the hoisin until all the sprouts are coated with it. Drizzle with a little sesame oil and serve immediately.

Cabbage and Apples with Fresh Goat Cheese

Serves 6 • Cooker: 5- to 7-quart • Time: 4 minutes at HIGH pressure

Soft goat cheese is amazingly compatible flavorwise with cabbage. This is a really tasty side dish with sausage or roast chicken.

1 small head red cabbage
1 small head green cabbage
1 medium white onion, thinly sliced
1 large tart cooking apple, peeled, cored, and
    chopped
$1/2$ cup chicken or vegetable broth
2 tablespoons frozen apple juice concentrate
Salt and freshly ground black pepper
4 ounces fresh soft goat cheese, crumbled

1. Remove the outermost leaves from the cabbages, then cut them in quarters through the stem. Cut out the core from each quarter, then shred. You should have about 8 cups total.
2. In a 5- to 7-quart pressure cooker, combine the cabbage, onion, and apple. Pour over the broth and apple juice concentrate.
3. Close and lock the lid. Set the burner heat to high. When the cooker reaches HIGH pressure, reduce the burner heat as low as you can and still maintain HIGH pressure. Set a timer to cook for 4 minutes.
4. Remove the pot from the heat. Open the cooker with the Quick Release method. Be careful of the steam as you remove the lid.
5. Season with salt and pepper to taste. Transfer to a serving platter or shallow bowl, sprinkle with the cheese, and serve.

Red Cabbage with Red Vermouth and Grapes

Serves 4 to 6 • Cooker: 5- to 7-quart • Time: 4 minutes at HIGH pressure

Most people are familiar with the dry white vermouth, but sweet red vermouth or "rosso" is an excellent choice for cooking cabbage.

2 tablespoons olive oil
1 small white onion, chopped ($1/2$ cup)
1 small head red cabbage, outermost leaves
    removed, quartered, cored, and coarsely
    shredded
$1/3$ cup chicken or vegetable broth
$1/3$ cup sweet red vermouth
1 tablespoon honey
Pinch sea salt, plus more to taste
$1 1/2$ cups halved seedless green or red grapes
Juice of $1/2$ lemon

1. In a 5- to 7-quart pressure cooker, heat the oil over medium-high. Add the onion and cook until soft, stirring a few times, about 3 minutes. Add the cabbage and toss to combine with the oil and warm through. Stir in the broth, vermouth, honey, and salt and bring to a boil.
2. Close and lock the lid. Set the burner heat to high. When the cooker reaches HIGH pressure, reduce the burner heat as low as you can and still maintain HIGH pressure. Set a timer to cook for 4 minutes.
3. Remove the pot from the heat. Open the cooker with the Quick Release method. Be careful of the steam as you remove the lid.
4. Add the grapes and lemon juice to the pot. Cover partially with the lid (don't lock it) and let the heat of the cabbage warm the grapes through for 1 minute. Taste for salt and serve immediately.

Cabbage and Bacon with Crème Fraîche

Serves 6 • Cooker: 5- to 7-quart • Time: 3 minutes at HIGH pressure

This is a luxurious, special-occasion cabbage dish. There is simply no substitute for crème fraîche here—sour cream is less rich and more sour.

3 slices bacon, chopped
1 medium white onion, chopped
1 small head green cabbage, outermost leaves
    removed, quartered, and cored
1 cup chicken broth or water
$^1/_2$ to $^3/_4$ cup crème fraîche, to taste
Salt and freshly ground black pepper

1. In a 5- to 7-quart pressure cooker over medium-high heat, cook the bacon, stirring, until it begins to crisp. Add the onion and cook, stirring a few times, until it softens, about 3 minutes.

While the onion cooks, cut each cabbage quarter into 1- to 2-inch pieces. Add to the pot and stir to combine. Add the broth.

2. Close and lock the lid. Set the burner heat to high. When the cooker reaches HIGH pressure, reduce the burner heat as low as you can and still maintain HIGH pressure. Set a timer to cook for 3 minutes.

3. Remove the pot from the heat. Open the cooker with the Quick Release method. Be careful of the steam as you remove the lid.

4. Stir in the crème fraîche and season to taste with salt and pepper. Warm for 5 minutes over low heat, uncovered. Serve hot.

Sauerkraut with Caraway

Serves 6 to 8 • Cooker: 5- to 7-quart • Time: 8 minutes at HIGH pressure

This is delicious with braised game and potatoes.

2 tablespoons unsalted butter
2 slices bacon, chopped
1 small onion, thinly sliced
$1^1/_2$ teaspoons caraway seeds
3 (16-ounce) pouches sauerkraut (about 6 cups),
    rinsed and drained (we like Boar's Head brand)
1 cup vegetable broth
$^3/_4$ cup dry white wine

1. In a 5-to 7-quart pressure cooker over medium heat, melt the butter and let cook until it starts to brown, about 2 minutes. Add the onion and cook, stirring a few times, until softened, about 2 minutes. Add the caraway and sauerkraut and stir to combine. Add the broth and wine. Bring to a boil.

2. Close and lock the lid. Set the burner heat to high. When the cooker reaches HIGH pressure, reduce the burner heat as low as you can and still maintain HIGH pressure. Set a timer to cook for 8 minutes.

3. Remove the pot from the heat. Open the cooker with the Natural Release method; let stand for 10 minutes. Be careful of the steam as you remove the lid. Any leftovers will keep in an airtight container in the refrigerator for at least a week.

CARAWAY

Caraway seed is a member of the parsley family, along with dill, cilantro, cumin, and fennel, and it adds a pungent aroma and spicy flavor to the foods it graces. Its distinctive taste deliciously counterbalances the rich fattiness of pork, duck, and goose. It is especially nice paired with cabbage and pickled foods. Store caraway seeds in the freezer until needed for the best flavor.

Pressure Cooker Corn on the Cob

Serves 4 to 6 • Cooker: 5- to 7- quart • Time: 4 minutes at HIGH pressure

The pressure cooker is one of the most efficient methods of cooking corn on the cob. You must do the Quick Release method or else the corn will overcook and get mushy. If you steam fewer than 4 ears of corn, you can use $1/2$ cup water for the steaming. This is served with olive oil instead of butter, so be sure to buy a flavorful one.

4 to 6 ears fresh corn
1 cup water
1 tablespoon good-quality extra virgin olive oil per
    ear of corn
Salt and freshly ground black pepper

1. Husk the corn by removing the husk and the silk from the ears of corn. Brushing downward on a cob of corn with a damp paper towel (instead of trying to strip down each bit of silk with your fingers) will remove every strand of silk. Cut or break the larger ears of corn in half. The size of your pressure cooker will determine how large the pieces can be.

2. Place a trivet and steamer basket in a 5- to 7-quart pressure cooker. Add the water. Arrange the corn in the steamer basket on their sides in layers. The water should not touch the corn.

3. Close and lock the lid. Set the burner heat to high. When the cooker reaches HIGH pressure, reduce the burner heat as low as you can and still maintain HIGH pressure. Set a timer to cook for 4 minutes.

4. Remove the pot from the heat. Open the cooker with the Quick Release method. Be careful of the steam as you remove the lid.

5. Transfer the corn to a serving platter. Drizzle 1 tablespoon of oil over each ear, then sprinkle with salt and pepper. Cover with a damp clean dishcloth until serving if you are serving warm or room temperature.

Corn Maque Choux

Serves 4 to 6 • Cooker: 5- to 7- quart • Time: 3 minutes at HIGH pressure

Maque choux (pronounced *mock-shoe*) is a fresh-tasting stewy tomato-corn side dish made with fresh summer corn and the savory flavor base known as "the trinity" in Louisiana: sautéed onion, celery and green pepper. Our version calls for a bit of tasso (TAH-so), a spiced ham native to Louisiana that is usually used as a flavor ingredient in other dishes. (If you can't find it locally, you can order it online.) The dish is finished with salt and a combination of red and black pepper. Have a bottle of hot sauce on the table for your diners.

6 ears fresh corn, shucked and silks removed
$1/4$ cup ($1/2$ stick) butter
$1/3$ cup finely diced tasso (optional)
1 cup finely diced white onion
1 cup finely diced green bell pepper
1 cup finely diced celery
2 cloves garlic, minced
1 tablespoon fresh thyme
Salt
1 cup chicken broth
2 Roma tomatoes, seeded and diced
$1/8$ teaspoon cayenne pepper
Freshly ground black pepper
$1/2$ cup loosely packed fresh cilantro leaves, chopped
$1/2$ cup thinly sliced green onions

1. With a sharp or serrated knife, cut down the length of each ear to remove the kernels from the cob. Then, scrape each cob using the top of the knife or the thicker, dull edge, to extract the milk and additional pulp from the corn cob into a separate bowl. Set the corn and corn milk aside.

2. In a 5- to 7-quart pressure cooker over medium-high heat, melt the butter. Add the tasso and cook until slightly browned, stirring a few times. Add the corn, onion, bell pepper, celery, garlic, thyme, and a healthy pinch of salt and reduce the heat to medium. Cook, stirring often, until the vegetables are just tender, about 3 minutes. Add the broth, tomatoes, and reserved corn milk.

3. Close and lock the lid. Set the burner heat to high. When the cooker reaches HIGH pressure, reduce the burner heat as low as you can and still maintain HIGH pressure. Set a timer to cook for 3 minutes.

4. Remove the pot from the heat. Open the cooker with the Quick Release method. Be careful of the steam as you remove the lid.

5. Stir in the cayenne, black pepper to taste, cilantro, and green onions. Taste for salt. Serve hot over steamed rice. Leftovers will keep in an airtight container in the refrigerator up to 3 days.

Chicken Maque Choux: Add 3 to 4 cups cooked chicken, torn into bite-sized pieces, in Step 5. Stir in and heat through over medium heat. A great main dish.

French Quarter Eggplant Stew with Okra

Serves 4 • Cooker: 5- to 7- quart • Time: 3 minutes at HIGH pressure

The trinity of onion, celery, and green pepper is the flavor base for this eggplant, tomato, and okra stew. When buying fresh okra, feel the pod; if it is sticky, it is too old.

4 Japanese eggplant, unpeeled, or 2 regular
   eggplant, peeled
2 teaspoons sea salt
1/4 cup olive oil
1 large white onion, chopped
4 cloves garlic, minced
1/4 cup vegetable broth
1 green bell pepper, seeded and finely chopped
2 ribs celery, chopped
1 (28-ounce) can peeled whole tomatoes in juice,
   crushed with your hands
1 teaspoon fresh oregano leaves or 1/2 teaspoon
   dried oregano
Freshly ground black pepper
1 pound okra, washed, ends trimmed, and cut into
   1-inch pieces (2 cups)
2 tablespoons red wine vinegar

1. Cut the eggplant into 2-inch cubes and transfer it to a paper towel-lined colander. Sprinkle with 1 teaspoon of the salt and leave it to drain for 30 minutes. Rinse the salt thoroughly from the drained eggplant and pat dry.
2. In a 5- to 7-quart pressure cooker pot, heat 1 tablespoon of the oil over medium-high heat. Reduce the heat to medium-low, add the onion, and cook, stirring a few times, until soft, about 5 minutes. Add the rest of the oil, the eggplant and garlic and cook, stirring occasionally, until soft and the onions are golden, about 5 minutes. Add the broth, then the pepper, celery, the tomatoes with their juice, oregano, the remaining 1 teaspoon salt, and black pepper to taste.
3. Close and lock the lid. Set the burner heat to high. When the cooker reaches HIGH pressure, reduce the burner heat as low as you can and still maintain HIGH pressure. Set a timer to cook for 3 minutes.
4. Remove the pot from the heat. Open the cooker with the Quick Release method. Be careful of the steam as you remove the lid. Stir. The eggplant and peppers should be tender but not mushy. If there is too much liquid, simmer with the lid off to evaporate some.
5. Add the okra, partially cover, and cook over medium heat (without pressure) until the okra is tender, about 10 minutes. Drizzle with the vinegar. This is delicious hot, at room temperature, or even cold.

Baba Ghanoush Under Pressure

Makes 1^1/$_3$ cups • Cooker: 5- to 7-quart • Time: 4 minutes at HIGH pressure

This version of the smoky eggplant dip adds tahini, an Israeli touch.

3 tablespoons olive oil
1 large eggplant (about 1^1/$_4$ pounds), peeled and cut into 1-inch cubes
1 to 2 cloves garlic, to taste, halved
^{1}/$_2$ cup water
2 tablespoons chopped fresh flatleaf parsley
^{1}/$_2$ teaspoon sea salt
^{1}/$_2$ teaspoon smoked paprika
3 tablespoons fresh lemon juice
2 tablespoons tahini paste
^{1}/$_2$ teaspoon crushed Aleppo or other red pepper flakes, for garnish
1 Roma tomato, seeded and diced, for garnish

1. In a 5- to 7-quart pressure cooker, heat 2 tablespoons of the oil over medium-high heat. Add the eggplant and garlic and cook, stirring occasionally, until soft and golden, about 5 minutes. Pour in the water.
2. Close and lock the lid. Set the burner heat to high. When the cooker reaches HIGH pressure, reduce the burner heat as low as you can and still maintain HIGH pressure. Set a timer to cook for 4 minutes.
3. Remove the pot from the heat. Open the cooker with the Quick Release method. Be careful of the steam as you remove the lid.
4. Drain the eggplant in a colander. Add the parsley, salt, paprika, lemon juice, and tahini and, using a fork or immersion blender, mash or process into a coarse puree. Add the remaining tablespoon oil and work it into the mixture. Taste for your preferred balance of salt, tahini, and lemon juice. Spread out in a shallow dish and garnish with the Aleppo pepper and tomatoes.

Baba Ghanoush with Roasted Red Pepper: Add 1 whole roasted red pepper in Step 4 and puree with the eggplant.

CHOOSING EGGPLANT

Select ones without soft spots or bruises; bruises often mean the flesh will be unpleasantly bitter. Also, ripe eggplants are sweeter and less bitter than under-ripe ones; a ripe eggplant is firm to the touch, but not hard—it should yield a little when pressed with your finger. The stem should be green, with no trace of mold or softening, and firmly attached. If possible, select smaller eggplants—the smaller they are, the more intense the flavor and less watery the flesh. And if you can, opt for female eggplants, which are less bitter than male: they have an indented little belly button at the bottom end.

Mediterranean Vegetable Garden Ratatouille with Couscous

Serves 4 • Cooker: 5- to 7-quart • Time: 3 minutes at HIGH pressure

Hailing from Provence, ratatouille is an aromatic summer stew that makes use of seasonally plentiful eggplant, pepper, tomato, zucchini, and fresh herbs. Classic versions of the dish from Julia Child and Jacques Pepin involve a multi-step process of simmering each vegetable separately. In the pressure cooker, we cook it all together; in addition to saving time, this method preserves the vibrant colors of all the vegetables. Fluffy couscous is a marvelous accompaniment. One 10-ounce box contains 1^1/$_2$ cups instant couscous.

RATATOUILLE:
4 Japanese eggplant, unpeeled, or 2 regular
    eggplant, peeled
2 teaspoons sea salt
^{1}/$_4$ cup olive oil
1 medium onion, chopped
3 cloves garlic, minced
^{1}/$_4$ cup chicken or vegetable broth
4 small zucchini, quartered lengthwise and cut
    across into 1-inch pieces
2 medium bell peppers of any color, seeded and
    sliced into strips
3 cups seeded and diced plum tomatoes, or 2
    (14.5-ounce) cans chopped tomatoes in juice,
    drained
2 teaspoons chopped fresh basil or 1 teaspoon
    dried basil
1 teaspoon chopped fresh marjoram or ^{1}/$_2$
    teaspoon dried marjoram
1 teaspoon fresh thyme leaves or ^{1}/$_2$ teaspoon
    dried thyme
Freshly ground black pepper
2 tablespoons Champagne vinegar

COUSCOUS PILAF:
2^1/$_2$ cups chicken or vegetable broth
2 tablespoons butter
^{1}/$_2$ teaspoon sea salt
2^1/$_2$ cups couscous
^{3}/$_4$ cup crumbled feta or soft goat cheese

1. Cut the eggplant into 2-inch cubes and transfer it to a paper towel-lined colander. Sprinkle with 1 teaspoon of the salt and leave it to drain for 30 minutes. Rinse the salt thoroughly from the drained eggplant and pat dry.

2. In a 5- to 7-quart pressure cooker, heat 1 tablespoon of the oil over medium-high heat. Reduce the heat to medium-low, add the onion, and cook, stirring a few times, until soft, about 5 minutes. Add the rest of the oil, eggplant, and garlic and cook, stirring occasionally, until soft and golden, about 5 minutes. Add the broth, then the zucchini, peppers, tomatoes, herbs, black pepper to taste, and remaining 1 teaspoon salt.

3. Close and lock the lid. Set the burner heat to high. When the cooker reaches HIGH pressure, reduce the burner heat as low as you can and still maintain HIGH pressure. Set a timer to cook for 3 minutes.

4. Remove the pot from the heat. Open the cooker with the Quick Release method. Be careful of the steam as you open the lid. Stir. The eggplant and zucchini should be tender but not mushy. If there is too much liquid, simmer with the lid off to evaporate some. Drizzle with the vinegar.

5. Make the couscous. Combine the broth, butter, and salt in a medium saucepan and bring to a boil. Remove from the heat, add the couscous, stir, cover, and set aside for 5 to 10 minutes. Mound the couscous on large serving platter or portion into the center of individual dinner plates, and make a well in center. Use slotted spoon to transfer the ratatouille vegetables on top of the well. Ladle some juice over the vegetables and couscous. Sprinkle with the cheese and serve immediately.

Moroccan Ratatouille with Dates: Add 10 ounces pitted dates, sliced in half lengthwise, in Step 2 with the tomatoes. Substitute 2 to 3 teaspoons ras el hanout spice mixture (available in Middle Eastern groceries) for the basil, marjoram, and thyme.

Ratatouille with Olives: Add 12 pitted black olives (such as Greek) and 12 pitted green olives (such as Sicilian), halved, in Step 4 along with the vinegar.

White Eggplant Ratatouille with Parmesan Polenta Rounds

Serves 4 • Cooker: 5- to 7-quart • Time: 3 minutes at HIGH pressure

This simple stew is adapted from a recipe by one of our favorite food writers, Tori Ritchie, of tuesdayrecipe.com. If you haven't used the prepared polenta yet, you are in for a treat. It is delightfully delicious without any work at all. Serve this warm or at room temperature with lamb, grilled chicken, or even scrambled eggs.

WHITE EGGPLANT RATATOUILLE:
$1/4$ cup olive oil
1 large white onion, chopped
Sea salt
2 large white eggplants (about $3/4$ pound total), peeled and cut into 1-inch cubes
1 pound zucchini, cut into 1-inch cubes
$1/2$ teaspoon dried herbes de Provence
1 pound ripe Roma tomatoes, seeded and chopped
1 cup dry white wine
Freshly ground black pepper
Handful chopped fresh basil or flatleaf parsley (optional)

PARMESAN POLENTA ROUNDS:
1 (16-ounce) tube plain prepared polenta, patted dry, cut crosswise into 8 slices
$3/4$ cup freshly shredded Parmesan cheese

1. In a 5- to 7-quart pressure cooker, heat the oil over medium-high heat. Reduce the heat to medium-low, add the onion, sprinkle with a little salt, and cook, stirring a few times, until soft, about 5 minutes. Add the eggplant, zucchini, and herbes de Provence and cook, stirring, for a minute. Add the tomatoes, wine, and pepper to taste and bring to a boil.

2. Close and lock the lid. Set the burner heat to high. When the cooker reaches HIGH pressure, reduce the burner heat as low as you can and still maintain HIGH pressure. Set a timer to cook for 3 minutes.

3. Remove the pot from the heat and let stand 15 minutes, no more. Preheat the oven to 350° F. Open the cooker with the Quick Release method. Be careful of the steam as you remove the lid. Stir. The eggplant and zucchini should be tender.

4. Arrange the polenta slices on a parchment-lined baking sheet. Sprinkle each slice with 1 tablespoon of the Parmesan. Bake until the cheese is melted and the polenta is slightly crisped, 12 to 15 minutes.

5. Stir a handful of basil or parsley into the stew. For each serving, ladle the stew over two polenta rounds and garnish with more cheese, if desired.

WHITE EGGPLANT

Those white eggplant that show up for a short time at the end of summer are beguiling. Eggplants were originally all white in color, hence the name. White eggplant are dense textured, less bitter than their purple kin and more delicate in flavor. The skin is tough, though, so it is important to peel it.

Milk-Poached Fennel

Serves 4 • Cooker: 5- to 7-quart • Time: 4 minutes at HIGH pressure

Fennel is a highly aromatic vegetable and herb at the same time, with a slightly sweet, little-bit-spicy anise flavor that sweetens considerably when poached in milk. Serve as a side dish with simple roasted meats, poultry, and game.

2 to 3 medium to large fennel bulbs
2 tablespoons unsalted butter
1 teaspoon rice flour or all-purpose flour
1 (3-finger) pinch sea salt
Freshly grated nutmeg
2 cups half-and-half
Grated Parmesan cheese, for serving

1. Cut the green frond tops and stalks off the fennel bulbs and trim the root slightly. If the outer thick layers of the bulbs look tough and scarred, take a slice off the base and remove them. Cut the bulb in half lengthwise from top. Lay each half flat and cut in half to make a wedge, leaving a bit of root core on each wedge to help it hold together.

2. In a 5- to 7-quart pressure cooker over medium heat, melt the butter. Add the fennel pieces, cut side down, and brown, about 2 minutes. Turn them over and sprinkle with the flour, salt, and a few gratings of nutmeg. Don't be tempted to add more flour. Pour over the half-and-half. Bring to a simmer.

3. Close and lock the lid. Set the burner heat to high. When the cooker reaches HIGH pressure, reduce the burner heat as low as you can and still maintain HIGH pressure. Set a timer to cook for 4 minutes.

4. Remove the pot from the heat. Let stand for 1 minute, then open the cooker with the Quick Release method. Be careful of the steam as you remove the lid. Serve immediately, sprinkled with Parmesan.

Braised Leeks with Shallot Mustard Vinaigrette

Serves 4 • Cooker: 5- to 7-quart • Time: 3 minutes at HIGH pressure

These tender leeks with their sharp Dijon vinaigrette make a great side dish for almost any meat, poultry or seafood recipe.

4 medium to large leeks, tough outer leaves
    discarded and leeks trimmed to about 7 inches
    in length, including an inch of green, or 12 baby
    leeks, trimmed
1 cup water or vegetable broth
2 teaspoons chopped fresh thyme
1 bay leaf
3 sprigs fresh flatleaf parsley
1 rib celery, sliced $^1/_2$ inch thick

SHALLOT MUSTARD VINAIGRETTE:
2 tablespoons fresh lemon juice, sherry vinegar, or
    red wine vinegar
1 medium shallot, minced
1 tablespoon capers, rinsed
$^1/_4$ teaspoon sea salt
1 tablespoon Dijon mustard
2 tablespoons crème fraîche or sour cream
$^1/_3$ cup olive oil
Pinch freshly ground black pepper
1 tablespoon snipped fresh chives
1 tablespoon minced fresh flatleaf parsley

1. Using a sharp knife, trim most of the roots off the leeks, then cut the leeks in half lengthwise. Rinse well under running water-using your fingers to loosen and remove any dirt or sand from between the leaves. If you like, you can cut each leek in half again lengthwise.
2. Place the water in a 5- to 7-quart pressure cooker. Lay the leeks side by side in the pot and place the aromatics and celery on top of them.
3. Close and lock the lid. Set the burner heat to high. When the cooker reaches HIGH pressure, reduce the burner heat as low as you can and still maintain HIGH pressure. Set a timer to cook for 3 minutes.
4. Remove the pot from the heat. Open the cooker with the Quick Release method. Be careful of the steam as you remove the lid. The leeks should be very tender. Discard the aromatics and celery. Transfer the leeks to a small serving platter, arranging them cut side up.
5. In a small bowl, combine the lemon juice, shallots, capers, and salt. Whisk in the mustard, crème fraîche, and oil. Taste for salt and add a few grindings of pepper. Pour the vinaigrette over the leeks and sprinkle with the chives and parsley. Serve immediately or at room temperature.

Pressure-Roasted Whole Garlic

Makes 4 heads • Cooker: 5- to 7-quart • Time: 9 minutes at HIGH pressure

Make this when garlic is freshly harvested and get a nice bulb with big cloves that fill their peels. It is quite remarkable that steamed garlic could taste so similar to oven-roasted garlic. Use it in mashed potatoes or tomato sauce; stir it into sour cream or yogurt to use as a topping for vegetables or baked potatoes, a sauce for pasta, a sandwich spread, or salad dressing; or serve it as an appetizer, squeezing and mashing the cloves onto slices of baguette.

4 heads garlic
About $1/4$ cup olive oil
1 cup water

1. Peel and discard the papery outer layers of the head of garlic, leaving intact the skins of the individual cloves. Using a sharp knife, cut $1/2$ inch from the top stem end, exposing the tops of the individual cloves of garlic. Cut 4 pieces of aluminum foil three times the size of the garlic bulb. Set each head of garlic in the center of one of the pieces of foil. Drizzle a few teaspoons of olive oil over the exposed part of each head and rub the oil all over the outside. You can also spray the head with olive oil cooking spray but definitely pour some good olive oil into the cut cloves. Wrap the garlic completely in the foil and twist the top to seal tight.

2. Place a trivet and steamer basket in a 5- to 7-quart pressure cooker. Add the water. Arrange the garlic packets in the basket in a single layer, top side up. The water should not touch them.

3. Close and lock the lid. Set the burner heat to high. When the cooker reaches HIGH pressure, reduce the burner heat as low as you can and still maintain HIGH pressure. Set a timer to cook for 9 minutes.

4. Remove the pot from the heat and let stand for 10 minutes, no more. Open the cooker with the Quick Release method. Be careful of the steam as you remove the lid. Wearing a heavy-duty oven mitt, lift up the steamer basket, taking care not to get burned by the steam and hot water, or transfer the packets with metal tongs to a plate.

5. Let cool 10 minutes before opening the packets. The cloves will feel soft when pressed. With a small knife, cut the skin slightly around each clove. Use your fingers or a cocktail fork to pull or squeeze the roasted garlic cloves out of their skins. Enjoy warm or let cool and store in an airtight container in the refrigerator for up to 1 week.

Multi-Colored Peperonata

Serves 4 to 6 • Cooker: 5- to 7-quart • Time: 3 minutes at HIGH pressure

Peperonata is a stew of fried peppers with onions, fresh plum tomatoes and herbs, and a hint of garlic (the cloves are cooked with the peppers left in their peels). It's great as a side dish with grilled sausage and meats of all kinds, as a topping for pasta, crostini, or baked potatoes, and as a filling for omelettes.

2 red bell peppers
2 yellow bell peppers
1 green bell pepper
2 ripe medium Roma tomatoes
2 tablespoons olive oil, plus more for drizzling
1 small red onion, sliced into thin strips from top to
  bottom
2 cloves garlic, unpeeled
Sea salt and freshly ground black pepper
1 clove garlic, pressed, for garnish (optional)
$^{1}/_{4}$ cup chopped fresh basil, for garnish
$^{1}/_{4}$ cup chopped fresh flatleaf parsley, for garnish

1. Cut the peppers in half lengthwise and remove the stems, seeds and white ribbing. Cut the halves into strips lengthwise, then cut the strips in half. Cut the tomatoes in half, squeeze out the seeds, and chop finely, reserving any juices.

2. In a 5- to 7-quart pressure cooker, heat the oil over medium-high heat. Add the onion and cook, stirring a few times, until soft, about 3 minutes. Add the peppers and unpeeled garlic. Brown one side of the peppers, then add the tomatoes and any juice and season to taste with salt and black pepper; mix well.

3. Close and lock the lid. Set the burner heat to high. When the cooker reaches HIGH pressure, reduce the burner heat as low as you can and still maintain HIGH pressure. Set a timer to cook for 3 minutes.

4. Remove the pot from the heat. Open the cooker with the Quick Release method. Be careful of the steam as you remove the lid. Remove the garlic cloves. Discard or squeeze out the garlic to use later. Let the peppers cool completely. This is best made a few hours ahead. When ready to serve, gently reheat in the pot; it's also good served at room temperature or cold.

5. Transfer the peppers to a platter. Garnish with the pressed garlic, if using, grindings of black pepper, the basil and parsley, and a drizzle of olive oil. Serve on toast.

Salad of Beets with Blue Cheese and Walnuts

Serves 4 • Cooker: 5- to 7-quart • Time: 15 minutes at HIGH pressure

Delicious beets—white, golden, Chioggia, or Bull's Blood—have their fresh greens attached. Stick to the medium to large beets for this, which are usually in a bunch of three. The gigantic beets tend to be woody. You can substitute feta or soft goat cheese for the blue cheese. Or you can keep it super simple and serve the sliced steamed beets hot with butter.

1 1/2 pounds beets (about 4, 4 inches in diameter,
    5 to 6 ounces each), any variety
2 cups water
1 tablespoon cider vinegar
1 tablespoon fresh lemon juice
1 1/2 teaspoons Dijon mustard
3 tablespoons extra virgin olive oil
8 cups loosely packed baby spinach or mixed baby
    greens
Sea salt and freshly ground black pepper
6 ounces firm blue cheese, shredded on the large
    holes of a box grater
1/2 cup finely chopped toasted walnuts

1. Leave the root tail and a 2-inch stem on the beets; scrub with a brush. In a 5- to 7-quart pressure cooker, place a trivet and steamer basket in the bottom and arrange the beets in the basket. Add the water.
2. Close and lock the lid. Set the burner heat to high. When the cooker reaches HIGH pressure, reduce the burner heat as low as you can and still maintain HIGH pressure. Set a timer to cook for 15 minutes.
3. In a salad bowl, combine the vinegar, lemon juice, mustard, and oil. Whisk to combine. Season with salt and pepper to taste. Set aside.
4. Remove the pot from the heat. Open the cooker with the Quick Release. Be careful of the steam as you remove the lid. The beets should be tender when pierced with the tip of a knife. Transfer the beets to a plate to cool.
5. Trim off the roots and stems with a paring knife. Slip the skins off with your fingers; they should peel away easily. Rinse under cold running water and drain. Cut the beets in half vertically and then each half into 4 wedges.
6. When ready to serve the salad, toss the greens with vinaigrette, along with a couple of large pinches of salt and several grinds of pepper. Divide the greens among 4 plates. Arrange the wedges of each beet on top of each plate of greens. Sprinkle each with one quarter of the blue cheese and 2 tablespoons walnuts. Serve immediately.

CUTTING BEETS

Beet juice will stain your fingers and counter red, so wear gloves if this is an issue for you. To keep the mess to a minimum, place a sheet of parchment paper over your cutting board. When you're done peeling and slicing the beets, wrap the peels and trimmings up in the paper and discard. All you will need to do is wash the knife.

Braised Carrots and Peas

Serves 6 • Cooker: 5- to 7-quart • Time: 2 minutes at HIGH pressure

Here the traditional peas and carrots mix gets the French treatment, cooked with lettuce. If you can make this with fresh green peas, so much the better!

1 tablespoon butter
1 bunch green onions (white and few inches of green part), chopped
1 pound baby carrots, sliced in half lengthwise
3/4 cup vegetable broth
1 (16-ounce) bag frozen petite peas, thawed, or 2 pounds fresh peas in their pod, shelled (2 cups)
1 small head romaine lettuce heart, stem end cut off, shredded
Sea salt and freshly ground black pepper

1. In a 5- to 7-quart pressure cooker, melt the butter over medium heat. Add the green onions and cook for 1 or 2 minutes only. Add the carrots and broth, then add the peas and lettuce on top.
2. Close and lock the lid. Set the burner heat to high. When the cooker reaches HIGH pressure, reduce the burner heat as low as you can and still maintain HIGH pressure. Set a timer to cook for 2 minutes.
3. Remove the pot from the heat. Open the cooker with the Quick Release method. Be careful of the steam as you remove the lid.
4. Season to taste with salt and pepper. Drain or serve with a slotted spoon.

Buttery Carrot and Rutabaga Puree

Serves 6 • Cooker: 5- to 7-quart • Time: 5 minutes at HIGH pressure

Purees are a delicious grown-up version of baby food and welcome on any dinner plate. This puree is so simple and so tasty and is easy to scale up for family holiday dinners and buffet parties. The rutabaga, like the turnip, is a strong-flavored root, so it works nicely in tandem with another root that will mellow out the dish. You will not be able to stop eating this. Promise.

1 pound carrots, peeled and cut into 2-inch chunks
1 pound rutabagas, peeled and cut into 2-inch chunks
Dash sea salt and freshly ground black pepper
3 tablespoons unsalted butter

1. Place the carrots and rutabagas in a 5- to 7-quart pressure cooker and fill with water to cover. It is okay if a few edges of the vegetables are peeking up out of the water. Sprinkle with the salt.
2. Close and lock the lid. Set the burner heat to high. When the cooker reaches HIGH pressure, reduce the burner heat as low as you can and still maintain HIGH pressure. Set a timer to cook for 5 minutes.
3. Remove the pot from the heat. Open the cooker with the Quick Release method. Be careful of the steam as you remove the lid. The roots should be soft and tender when pierced with the tip of a knife and hold their shape a bit.
4. Drain the vegetables in a colander. Puree them, either in a food processor or return to the pot and use an immersion blender or handheld electric mixer. Add the butter and beat to the desired consistency, very smooth or a bit chunky (smashed). Taste for salt and pepper. Serve immediately.

Buttery Carrot and Potato Puree: Substitute 1 pound Yukon Gold potatoes for the rutabagas.

Carrot and Parsnip Puree with Cumin

Serves 6 • Cooker: 5- to 7-quart • Time: 3 minutes at HIGH pressure

The parsnip is often overlooked as a weekday vegetable. It looks and cooks just like carrots, with a sweet flavor like carrots as well. This is a favorite winter mash.

1 teaspoon cumin seeds
$^1/_2$ pound carrots (2 large), peeled and cut into 2-inch chunks
$1^1/_2$ pounds parsnips (8), peeled and cut into 2-inch chunks
$^1/_2$ cup vegetable broth
3 tablespoons unsalted butter
Dash sea salt and freshly ground black pepper

1. In a dry skillet over medium heat, toast the cumin seeds until fragrant. Set aside to cool. Grind in a spice grinder.
2. Place the carrots and parsnips in a 5- to 7-quart pressure cooker and add the broth.
3. Close and lock the lid. Set the burner heat to high. When the cooker reaches HIGH pressure, reduce the burner heat as low as you can and still maintain HIGH pressure. Set a timer to cook for 3 minutes.
4. Remove the pot from the heat. Open the cooker with the Quick Release method. Be careful of the steam as you remove the lid. The roots should be soft and tender when pierced with the tip of a knife and hold their shape a bit.
5. Drain the vegetables in a colander, reserving the cooking liquid. Puree them, either in a food processor or return them to the pot and use an immersion blender or handheld electric mixer. Add the butter, and slowly add some of the reserved cooking water. Beat to the desired consistency, either very smooth or a bit chunky (smashed). The more of the reserved cooking water you add, the creamier the puree will be. Season to taste with salt and pepper. Serve immediately.

Braised Carrots with Marsala and Basil

Serves 4 as a side dish • Cooker: 5- to 7-quart • Time: 3 minutes at HIGH pressure

If you love chicken Marsala and tiramisu, you will love these carrots.

3 tablespoons unsalted butter
$^1/_3$ cup dry Marsala
$^1/_2$ cup chicken or vegetable broth
2 teaspoons Dijon mustard
Pinch sugar
Freshly grated nutmeg
1$^1/_2$ pounds carrots (8 to 10 medium), peeled and cut into $^1/_2$-inch-thick rounds, or 1$^1/_2$ pounds whole baby carrots
Dash sea salt, plus more to taste
2 tablespoons olive oil
Freshly ground black pepper
$^1/_3$ cup chopped fresh basil

1. In a 5- to 7-quart pressure cooker over medium-high heat, melt the butter. Add the Marsala, broth, mustard, sugar, and nutmeg and stir to combine. Add the carrots and stir to coat with the mixture. Sprinkle with the salt. Bring to a boil and let boil for a full minute.
2. Close and lock the lid. Set the burner heat to high. When the cooker reaches HIGH pressure, reduce the burner heat as low as you can and still maintain HIGH pressure. Set a timer to cook for 3 minutes for sliced carrots and 4 minutes for whole baby carrots.
3. Remove the pot from the heat. Open the cooker with the Quick Release method. Be careful of the steam as you remove the lid. The carrots should be tender when pierced with the tip of a knife.
4. With the pot uncovered, simmer over medium heat until the liquid reduces by half. Drizzle with the oil and season to taste with pepper. Add the basil and toss to combine. Serve hot.

MARSALA

Marsala is an aged fortified wine, which means it has some brandy added to it, like sherry. It is best known for its culinary uses and it really blends well with the sweet flavors. It keeps a long time at room temperature so don't worry about buying a bottle and using only a small amount at a time.

Sherried Carrots with Raisins and Pine Nuts

Serves 4 • Cooker: 5- to 7-quart • Time: 2$^1/_2$ minutes at HIGH pressure

This is a delicious combination to serve with grilled or roast chicken, or pork dishes.

3 tablespoons pine nuts
$^1/_4$ cup olive oil or rendered duck fat
1$^1/_2$ pounds carrots (8 to 10 medium), peeled and
    cut into $^1/_2$-inch-thick rounds
$^1/_3$ cup golden raisins
$^3/_4$ cup water
Dash sea salt
2 tablespoons sherry vinegar
Freshly ground black pepper

1. Put the nuts in a dry skillet and cook over medium-low heat, stirring frequently, until pale golden in spots, about 2 minutes. Remove from the pan to a bowl. Set aside to cool.
2. In a 5- to 7-quart pressure cooker over medium-high heat, heat the oil. Add the carrots and toss to coat for 2 minutes. Add the raisins and water. Sprinkle with the salt.
3. Close and lock the lid. Set the burner heat to high. When the cooker reaches HIGH pressure, reduce the burner heat as low as you can and still maintain HIGH pressure. Set a timer to cook for 2$^1/_2$ minutes.
4. Remove the pot from the heat. Open the cooker with the Quick Release method. Be careful of the steam as you remove the lid. The carrots should be tender when pierced with the tip of a knife.
5. Stir to mix everything, then transfer to a serving bowl. Add the pine nuts, drizzle with the vinegar, and give a few grinds of pepper. Taste for salt. Serve hot.

Celery Root Puree, French Style

Serves 6 • Cooker: 5- to 7-quart • Time: 4 minutes at HIGH pressure

Celery root, also known as celeriac or knob celery, is a variety of celery. It tastes like celery and can be enjoyed raw or cooked. Its rough, knobby appearance is pretty ugly as vegetables go, but don't pass it by. Select firm roots that have no soft spots. They are best bought during the winter months. Refrigerate and use within a week.

3/4 to 1 pound celery root (celeriac)
1 cup water
Pinch sea salt, plus more to taste
1 tablespoon unsalted butter
Juice of 1/2 lemon
1/4 cup heavy cream
Freshly ground black pepper
Freshly grated nutmeg

1. Cut the foliage and stalks off the root ball with a sharp paring knife and discard. Peel completely so only the white interior portion of the root remains. Cut the root into 2-inch cubes. Place the cubes in a 5- to 7-quart pressure cooker and add the water and salt.
2. Close and lock the lid. Set the burner heat to high. When the cooker reaches HIGH pressure, reduce the burner heat as low as you can and still maintain HIGH pressure. Set a timer to cook for 4 minutes.
3. Remove the pot from the heat. Open the cooker with the Quick Release method. Be careful of the steam as you remove the lid. The celery root should be soft and tender when pierced with the tip of a knife and hold their shape a bit. Drain in a colander, retaining some of cooking water.
4. Puree the celery root, either in a food processor or return it to the pot and use an immersion blender or electric mixer. Add the butter, lemon, and cream and process or beat to the consistency you like, either very smooth or a bit chunky (smashed), adding a bit of the reserved cooking water to adjust the texture. Season to taste with salt and pepper. Transfer to a serving dish, sprinkle with nutmeg, and serve.

Celery Root Puree with Orange: Substitute orange juice for half of the water or add a few tablespoons orange juice concentrate to the cooking water and use some of the cooking water when whipping. Substitute orange juice for the lemon juice. Omit the nutmeg; instead, garnish with finely grated orange zest.

Chayote al Vapor with Chile and Cilantro

Serves 4 • Cooker: 5- to 7-quart • Time: 2¹/₂ minutes at HIGH pressure

Whether you call it mirliton (as it's known in Louisiana), vegetable pear, or ishkus (in India), chayote is a member of the squash family and native to Mexico. In Mexico and Baja, a lovely fish dinner will have a side of steamed chayote as the vegetable. *Al vapor* means steamed in its own juices.

2 tablespoons butter
1 pound chayote, peeled and thinly julienned
1 small serrano pepper, seeded and finely chopped
¹/₄ cup water or vegetable broth
Sea salt and freshly ground black pepper
2 tablespoons chopped fresh cilantro
2 tablespoons finely grated Parmesan cheese or
    queso anejo (optional)

1. In a 5- to 7-quart pressure cooker pot, melt the butter over medium-high heat. Add the chayote and chile and cook for 1 minute, stirring to coat the vegetable with the butter. Add the water.
2. Close and lock the lid. Set the burner heat to high. When the cooker reaches HIGH pressure, reduce the burner heat as low as you can and still maintain HIGH pressure. Set a timer to cook for 2¹/₂ minutes.
3. Remove the pot from the heat. Open the cooker with the Quick Release method. Be careful of the steam as you remove the lid. The chayote should be al dente, not mushy. Season to taste with salt and pepper, then stir in the cilantro.
4. Spoon onto a small rimmed serving platter or shallow bowl. Sprinkle with the cheese if you like. Serve hot.

Braised Italian-Style Zucchini

Serves 4 to 6 • Cooker: 5- to 7-quart • Time: 2 minutes at HIGH pressure

If you are a vegetable gardener or participate in a CSA, this is a good recipe to use with large zucchini or you can use other types of summer squash or mix and match them.

2 tablespoons olive oil
1 cup chopped white or red onion
2 cloves garlic, crushed
4 to 5 medium zucchini (about 1 pound), cut into
    ¹/₄- to ¹/₂-inch-thick rounds (4 to 5 cups)
1 cup diced fresh or canned tomatoes
¹/₄ cup water or vegetable broth
Handful fresh basil leaves, chopped, or 1 table-
    spoon pesto sauce
Freshly ground black pepper
Sea salt
Lemon wedges, or sherry vinegar, or toasted bread
    crumbs and grated Parmesan, for serving

1. In a 5- to 7-quart pressure cooker pot, heat the oil over medium-high heat. Add the onion and cook until just soft, stirring a few times, about 3 minutes. Add the garlic; stir 30 seconds. Add the zucchini, tomatoes, and water. Bring to a boil and add several grinds of pepper.
2. Close and lock the lid. Set the burner heat to high. When the cooker reaches HIGH pressure, reduce the burner heat as low as you can and still maintain HIGH pressure. Set a timer to cook for 2 minutes.
3. Remove the pot from the heat and let stand for 2 minutes, no more. Open the cooker with the Quick Release method. Be careful of the steam as you remove the lid. Stir in the basil. Season to taste with salt and pepper.
4. Serve hot or at room temperature with lemon wedges, or drizzled with sherry vinegar, or sprinkled with breadcrumbs and Parmesan.

Braised Italian Squash with Tofu: Slice 8 ounces firm or extra firm tofu into thick slabs, and lay them on top of the squash before you close the lid. Cook time is the same.

Fresh Pumpkin Puree

Makes about 5 cups puree • Cooker: 5- to 8-quart • Time: 10 minutes at HIGH pressure

Opening a can is the easiest way to use pumpkin puree, but making it in the pressure cooker is a close second. Be sure to choose a sugar pumpkin, which is small and compact (5 to 8 inches across) rather than a big jack-o-lantern, whose flesh will be stringy and watery. Pumpkins don't yield a large amount of puree, about 1 cup of cooked puree per two pounds of pumpkin. Use this in any recipe that calls for canned pumpkin.

2 pie pumpkins (about 4 pounds), stem removed, cut in half with a serrated knife, and seeds and fiber removed with a spoon
2 cups water

1. Place a steamer basket in a 5- to 8-quart pressure cooker. Add the water. The water will touch the bottom of the basket. Cut each pumpkin half into 4 pieces. Place the pumpkin in the steamer, piling the pieces on top of one another. You can do one or two pumpkins at a time depending on the size of your pressure cooker.

2. Close and lock the lid. Set the burner heat to high. When the cooker reaches HIGH pressure, reduce the burner heat as low as you can and still maintain HIGH pressure. Set a timer to cook for 10 minutes.

3. Remove the pot from the heat. Open the cooker with the Quick Release method. Be careful of the steam as you remove the lid. Using a sharp knife, test the squash to see if it is cooked through; it should slide all the way in with no resistance. If still hard, cover and let steam a few more minutes without locking for pressure. Do not overcook.

4. Let the pumpkin rest in the pot for a minute, then transfer the pieces to a plate. When it is cool enough to handle, use a soup spoon to scoop the soft flesh from the peel. Puree in a food processor or use an immersion blender until smooth and creamy. It will keep in an airtight container in the refrigerator up to 3 days or in the freezer up to 6 months.

Pressure-Steamed Whole Winter Squash

Serves 4 to 6 as a side dish, or makes 2 to 2$\frac{1}{2}$ cups puree • Cooker: 5- to 7-quart, depending on size of squash • Time: 7 to 9 minutes at HIGH pressure

Pressure-steaming winter squash is so much better than baking it, if you need to use it in a soup or pie. Not only do you avoid the crusty edges you get from baking, you also don't have to hack the raw squash in two, which can be intimidating. Just pop it into the pressure cooker whole! Be sure to check the important tips below before you do.

1 hard-skinned winter squash, about 1$\frac{1}{2}$ pounds (choose one that will fit in your pressure cooker, on top of the steamer rack)
2 cups water

TIPS FOR STEAMING WINTER SQUASH WHOLE

- For best results, choose a squash that is symmetrical, like one of the hollow round or oval winter squashes, such as acorn, delicata, or kabocha.
- Choose a squash that fits very comfortably in your pressure cooker on top of the steaming rack, without touching the lid. If you need a larger quantity of cooked squash, buy two or three small ones and cook them one after the other. It will still be quicker than baking.
- Use a steaming rack or the flat perforated steaming disk that came with your cooker. Do not place the whole squash on the bare bottom of the cooker pot.
- Poke a few holes in the squash with a sharp skewer or knife before you begin so that the steam that will build up inside of them can escape. We've never had a squash burst inside the pressure cooker, and want to keep it that way.

1. Using the tip of a sharp knife or a sharp metal skewer, poke 6 to 8 slits or holes around the body of the squash.
2. Place a steamer basket in a 5- to 7-quart (or size needed to fit the squash) pressure cooker. Add the water. The water will touch the bottom of the basket. Place the squash in the basket.
3. Close and lock the lid. Set the burner heat to high. When the cooker reaches HIGH pressure, reduce the burner heat as low as you can and still maintain HIGH pressure. Set a timer to cook for 7 minutes.
4. Remove the pot from the heat. Open the cooker with the Quick Release method. Be careful of the steam as you remove the lid. Using a sharp knife, test the squash to see if it is cooked through; it should slide all the way in with no resistance. If the squash is not quite tender, relock the cooker, bring it back up to HIGH pressure, and cook for another 1 or 2 minutes. Open the cooker with Quick Release again.
5. Let the squash rest in the pot for a moment or two. Carefully transfer it to a cutting board with a large pair of metal tongs or with potholder-protected hands. Cut the squash in half, let it cool a bit, and use a soup spoon to scoop out the seeds. The cooked flesh will easily lift away from the skin. Mash with a fork to serve as a side dish or puree in a food processor or with an immersion blender to use in recipes. It will keep in an airtight container in the refrigerator up to 3 days or in the freezer up to 6 months.

Steamed Butternut Squash

Serves 4 to 6 as a side dish or makes 2 to 2$\frac{1}{2}$ cups puree • Cooker: 5- to 7-quart • Time: 5 minutes at HIGH pressure

Butternut squash is probably the most popular of the winter squashes.

1 butternut squash (about 1$\frac{1}{2}$ pounds)
2 cups water

1. Wipe down the squash with a damp paper towel to remove any dirt. If using a whole squash, set it on a cutting board and, with a sharp knife, cut it in half or quarters as needed to fit your pressure cooker. With a spoon, remove and discard the seeds.
2. Place a steamer basket in a 5- to 7-quart pressure cooker. Add the water. The water will just touch the bottom of the basket. Place the squash in the steamer basket.
3. Close and lock the lid. Set the burner heat to high. When the cooker reaches HIGH pressure, reduce the burner heat as low as you can and still maintain HIGH pressure. Set a timer to cook for 5 minutes.
4. Remove the pot from the heat. Open the cooker with the Quick Release method. Be careful of the steam as you remove the lid. Using a sharp knife, test the squash to see if it is cooked through; it should slide all the way in with no resistance. If still hard, cover (without locking for pressure) and steam a few more minutes.
5. Let the squash rest in the pot for a minute. Transfer to a deep bowl with a large pair of metal tongs. Use a soup spoon to scoop the flesh from the skin. Mash with a fork to serve as a side dish or puree in a food processor or with an immersion blender to use in recipes. It will keep in an airtight container up to 2 days in the refrigerator or up to 2 months in the freezer.

STORAGE OF WINTER SQUASHES

Winter squashes are so hard and dense, you might think you can store them indefinitely at room temperature. Not so. Here is a guide to cooking these squashes while they still have the best flavor. Look for squash that still have their stems; they'll store better.

- **Acorn:** Can store up to 3 months
- **Buttercup:** Is sweeter after being stored for a few weeks after harvest; keeps up to 4 months
- **Butternut and Hubbard:** Best a few weeks after harvest; will store up to 6 months
- **Delicata and similar types:** Stores up to 4 months
- **Kabocha:** Gets sweeter when stored for a few weeks after harvest; green varieties keep from 4 to 5 months, gray varieties up to 6 months
- **Spaghetti squash:** Lasts up to 3 months
- **Sugar pumpkin:** Best a few weeks after harvest; will store up to 4 months

Miso-Braised Butternut Squash

Serves 4 • Cooker: 5- to 7-quart • Time: 3 minutes at HIGH pressure

A great recipe to use with the bags of pre-cubed butternut squash you can find in the produce section, a nutty sweet winter squash. This is delicious served over steamed rice or quinoa.

2 pounds butternut squash, peeled and diced into
    1-inch hunks (4 cups)
2 cloves garlic, minced
1 tablespoon grated peeled fresh ginger
2 tablespoons mirin
3 tablespoons white miso
1 cup vegetable broth
$^1/_2$ cup unsweetened coconut milk

1. Place the squash cubes in a 5- to 7-quart pressure cooker and add the garlic, ginger, mirin, 1 tablespoon of the miso, the broth, and coconut milk. Bring to a boil.
2. Close and lock the lid. Set the burner heat to high. When the cooker reaches HIGH pressure, reduce the burner heat as low as you can and still maintain HIGH pressure. Set a timer to cook for 3 minutes.
3. Remove the pot from the heat. Open the cooker with the Quick Release method. Be careful of the steam as you remove the lid. The squash will have softened and the liquid thickened. Stir in the remaining 2 tablespoons miso. Serve immediately.

MISO

Miso has become a secret ingredient when braising vegetables. It is savory and salty at the same time, similar to soy sauce, so you don't need to add extra salt. White miso, made from fermented soy beans and rice, is the mildest miso, and tasty dissolved in hot water to drink like tea. The color also varies with length of fermentation, with white or light-colored miso associated with shorter fermentation and a milder flavor, and brown miso associated with a longer fermentation and a more robust flavor. Look for miso in the refrigerated area of the produce section.

Curried Butternut Squash, Spinach, and Chickpeas

Serves 4 • Cooker: 5- to 7-quart • Time: 4 minutes at HIGH pressure

Easy, quick, and healthy, this is an amazingly tasty one-pot meal. Serve this with couscous, bulgur, quinoa, or steamed rice. If you have preserved lemons, add some, finely chopped, along with the raisins. This is delicious the day after.

2 tablespoons olive oil
1 large yellow or white onion, finely chopped
1¹/₂ pounds butternut squash, peeled and cut into chunks
2 to 3 tablespoons Madras curry powder, to taste
2 cups vegetable stock
1 (14.5-ounce) can diced tomatoes (can be fire roasted), drained
3 cups cooked garbanzo beans or 2 (15-ounce) cans chickpeas, drained
¹/₂ cup dark raisins
1¹/₄ teaspoons sea salt
1 teaspoon freshly ground black pepper
3 to 4 cups baby spinach leaves
Chopped fresh cilantro, for garnish (optional)
Toasted slivered almonds, for garnish (optional)

1. In a 5- to 7-quart pressure cooker, heat the oil over medium-high heat. Reduce the heat to medium-low, add the onion, and cook, stirring a few times, until soft, about 5 minutes. Add the squash and cook, stirring a few times, until golden around the edges, about 3 minutes. Sprinkle with the curry powder. Add the broth, then the tomatoes, beans, raisins, and salt and pepper to taste.

2. Close and lock the lid. Set the burner heat to high. When the cooker reaches HIGH pressure, reduce the burner heat as low as you can and still maintain HIGH pressure. Set a timer to cook for 4 minutes.

3. Remove the pot from the heat. Open the cooker with the Quick Release method. Be careful of the steam as you remove the lid. Stir. If there is too much liquid from the vegetables, simmer with the lid off to evaporate some.

4. Add the spinach, cover partially (without pressure), and wilt the leaves, about 2 minutes. Serve immediately, sprinkled with cilantro and almonds.

MADRAS CURRY

Madras curry is a mild blend of ground herbs and spices that can include turmeric (the source of its gold color), coriander, cumin, cloves, cinnamon, bay leaves, fenugreek, all-spice, black pepper, chiles, and curry leaves.

Spaghetti Squash Primavera

Serves 4 • Cooker: 5- to 8-quart • Time: 10 minutes at HIGH pressure

Spaghetti squash, a football-shaped squash with a stringy interior, has become an alternate to pasta for those allergic to wheat or on a low-carb diet. Serve it like you would angel hair pasta. Here is one of our favorite summer versions, with an uncooked room-temperature tomato sauce/salad originally served over pasta at the Four Seasons in New York City based on an old Italian recipe from Ed Giobbi.

1 vegetable spaghetti squash (2 to 2^1/$_2$ pounds)
2 cups water
1 pound ripe tomatoes (2 to 3 tomatoes)
^{1}/$_3$ cup olive oil
1 teaspoon minced garlic
1 cup shredded fresh basil
Sea salt and fresh ground black pepper
^{1}/$_2$ cup grated Parmesan cheese

1. Place the squash on the counter and, with a paring knife, make a ^{1}/$_2$ inch-deep cut down into the skin, then halve the squash lengthwise all the way around. Pull the halves apart and scoop out and discard the seeds and fibers.

2. Place a steamer basket in a 5- to 8-quart pressure cooker. Pour in the water. The water will touch the bottom of the basket. Set the squash halves in the steamer basket, cut side down.

3. Close and lock the lid. Set the burner heat to high. When the cooker reaches HIGH pressure, reduce the burner heat as low as you can and still maintain HIGH pressure. Set a timer to cook for 10 minutes.

4. While the squash is steaming, prepare the tomato sauce/salad. Cut the tomatoes in half crosswise and gently squeeze the seeds out. Chop the flesh into ^{1}/$_2$-inch pieces and place them in a shallow serving bowl large enough to hold the finished dish. Add the oil, garlic, basil, and salt and pepper to taste and toss well. Set aside.

5. Remove the pot from the heat. Open the cooker with the Quick Release method. Be careful of the steam as you remove the lid.

6. Remove the steamer basket. Let the squash cool until easy to handle. With a fork, scrape the cooked flesh to separate the squash into strands, then combine with the tomato sauce in the serving bowl. Discard the shells. Toss gently and thoroughly with the sauce. Serve from the bowl or divide among 4 soup plates. Sprinkle with the cheese and serve immediately.

Spaghetti Squash with Herb Butter and Vegetable Noodles

Serves 4 • Cooker: 5- to 8-quart • Time: 10 minutes at HIGH pressure

Here spaghetti squash is combined with an herb butter and zucchini ribbons. You can chop the zucchini if you cannot make the long ribbon strips.

1 vegetable spaghetti squash (2 to 2$\frac{1}{2}$ pounds)
2 cups water
2 tablespoons butter
2 zucchini
3 tablespoons olive oil
2 medium shallots, chopped
3 tablespoons chopped fresh basil
3 tablespoons chopped fresh flatleaf parsley
Grated zest of 1 lemon
Sea salt and fresh ground black pepper

1. Place the squash on the counter and, with a paring knife, make a $\frac{1}{2}$ inch-deep cut down into the skin, then halve the squash lengthwise all the way around. Pull the halves apart and scoop out and discard the seeds and fibers.
2. Place a steamer basket in a 5- to 8-quart pressure cooker. Pour in the water. The water will touch the bottom of the basket. Set the squash halves in the steamer basket, cut side down.
3. Close and lock the lid. Set the burner heat to high. When the cooker reaches HIGH pressure, reduce the burner heat as low as you can and still maintain HIGH pressure. Set a timer to cook for 10 minutes.
4. While the squash is steaming, prepare the herb butter. Slice the zucchini into long ribbon-like noodles with a Spiralizer, Vegetti, or mandoline. You want thin to medium ribbons about the same size as the strands of the spaghetti squash. In a sauté pan, melt the butter with the oil over medium-high heat. Add the shallots and cook, stirring a few times, until soft, about 3 minutes. Add the zucchini and toss to coat with the butter and oil mixture. Cook about 1 minute. Stir in the basil, parsley, and lemon zest. Season to taste with salt and pepper. Set aside.
5. Remove the pot from the heat. Open the cooker with the Quick Release method. Be careful of the steam as you remove the lid.
6. Remove the steamer basket. Let the squash cool until easy to handle. With a fork, scrape the cooked flesh to separate the squash into strands, then combine with the zucchini and herb butter in the serving bowl. Discard the shells. Toss gently and thoroughly with the herb butter. Serve from the bowl or divide among 4 soup plates.

Soy-Simmered Shiitake Mushrooms

Makes about 3¹/₂ cups • Cooker: 5- to 7-quart • Time: 3 minutes at HIGH pressure

When fully hydrated, dried mushrooms taste exactly like their fresh counterparts, only more intense, with a wonderful meaty yet tender texture. And after cooking dried mushrooms, you're left with a hearty vegetarian mushroom broth you can use to boost the flavor of sauces, braises, and miso soups. You can use these mushrooms to add to fillings for sushi and spring rolls, as pizza toppings, in soups and stews, stir-fries, or just enjoy them as is for an appetizer. They will keep in an airtight container in the refrigerator for at least 2 weeks.

4 ounces dried shiitake mushrooms, woody stems cut off with kitchen shears
4 (¹/₄-inch-thick) slices fresh ginger
3 tablespoons mirin
2 tablespoons sake
1 tablespoon packed light brown sugar
¹/₄ cup reduced-sodium soy sauce

1. Brush the dried mushrooms with a vegetable brush or rub them between your fingers while holding them under cool water to remove any grit clinging to them. Pour 4 cups boiling water over mushrooms in bowl. Cover with plastic wrap and soak 30 minutes at room temperature. Drain, reserving 1¹/₂ cups of the soaking liquid. If there is grit, pour through a sieve lined with a coffee filter set over a bowl. You can reserve the rest of the leftover liquid for broths, soups, or reductions (it can be frozen).

2. In a 5- to 7-quart pressure cooker, place the mushrooms, ginger, mirin, sake, brown sugar, and reserved soaking liquid. Bring to a simmer over medium-high heat.

3. Close and lock the lid. Set the burner heat to high. When the cooker reaches HIGH pressure, reduce the burner heat as low as you can and still maintain HIGH pressure. Set a timer to cook for 3 minutes.

4. Remove the pot from the heat. Open the cooker with the Natural Release method; let stand for 15 minutes. Be careful of the steam as you remove the lid. Add the soy sauce and simmer, uncovered, for 5 minutes to thicken the sauce slightly. Serve warm or chilled, whole or sliced.

Mushroom Bourguignon

Serves 6 • Cooker: 6- to 8-quart • Time: 10 minutes at HIGH pressure

This is a vegetarian delight that makes for a filling main course. It's adapted from a recipe Beth first enjoyed at a yoga retreat. Serve over al dente-cooked wide egg noodles. If you are a chive person, sprinkle with fresh chives.

5 tablespoons olive oil
2 large portobello mushrooms, stems and black
    gills removed, thickly sliced, then cut into chunks
2 pounds cremini mushrooms, sliced
Sea salt and freshly ground black pepper
1 large yellow or white onion, finely chopped
1 pound carrots, cut into 1-inch pieces on the
    diagonal
2 cloves garlic, finely chopped
2 tablespoons potato starch (not potato flour) or
    rice flour
1 pound baby new white or red potatoes, scrubbed,
    unpeeled, and quartered
1 rib celery, cut into $1/2$-inch-thick slices on the
    diagonal
2 cups dry red wine
3 cups beef, chicken, or vegetable broth
1 teaspoon dried herbes de Provence
2 bay leaves
2 tablespoons tomato paste
2 tablespoons cornstarch dissolved in 2 tablespoons
    cold water

1. In a 6- to 8-quart pressure cooker, heat half the oil over medium-high heat. Add half the mushrooms and brown on all sides, 3 to 4 minutes. Transfer to a bowl with a large spoon to catch the accumulated juices. Add the remaining oil and brown the remaining mushrooms. Remove to the bowl. Season to taste with salt and pepper. Set aside.

2. Add the onion to the hot pot, reduce the heat to medium, and cook 1 to 2 minutes. Add the carrots and garlic. Sprinkle with the potato starch, stir to coat the carrots, and let stand a minute to be absorbed. Return the mushrooms to the pot. Add the potatoes and celery, then the wine, broth, and herbs. Stir the tomato paste into the liquid. Bring to a low boil and simmer for 5 minutes, uncovered.

3. Close and lock the lid. Set the burner heat to high. When the cooker reaches HIGH pressure, reduce the burner heat as low as you can and still maintain HIGH pressure. Set a timer to cook for 10 minutes.

4. Remove the pot from the heat. Open the cooker with the Quick Release method. Be careful of the steam as you remove the lid. Discard the bay leaves.

5. Taste for seasoning. If the liquid is too thin, add the cornstarch slurry and stir over medium heat until thickened, about 2 minutes. This is good reheated the next day.

Mixed Vegetables in Parchment with Garlic Cream

Serves 4 • Cooker: 5- to 7-quart • Time: 6 minutes at HIGH pressure

Cooking *en papillote* works beautifully with vegetables. Bring the fat vegetable packages to the table on individual dinner plates and enjoy unfolding the wrapping to release the savory steam.

GARLIC CREAM:

^{1}/₃ cup crème fraîche or plain Greek yogurt
Grated zest of ^{1}/₂ lemon
1 clove garlic, pressed

VEGETABLE PACKETS:

4 (13-inch-square) sheets parchment paper
6 ounces fresh mushrooms, a mixture of types or just one, thickly sliced or quartered
1 small garnet yam, peeled and cut into ^{1}/₂-inch-thick slices
2 small red new potatoes, unpeeled and cut into ^{1}/₂-inch-thick slices
1 medium zucchini, cut into ^{1}/₄-inch-thick slices on the diagonal
1 small leek (white part only), cut into quarters lengthwise, washed well, then cut in half lengthwise
^{3}/₄ to 1 cup frozen edamame or peas
Dried thyme or favorite salt-free herb blend
Sea salt and freshly ground black pepper
4 tablespoons chicken or vegetable broth
4 tablespoons Madeira
4 teaspoons olive oil
2 cups water

1. Make the Garlic Cream. In a small bowl, whisk together the crème fraîche, lemon zest, and garlic. Set aside.

2. Make the vegetable packages. Fold each sheet of parchment in half to form a crease. Spray the lower half of the paper with some olive oil cooking spray. You will be dividing all the vegetables among the four packages. Arrange the mushrooms over one half of the parchment. Top with a few slices of yam, then potato, then arrange 3 slices of zucchini overlapping on top. Spread with 1 tablespoon of Garlic Cream. Place 2 pieces of leek and a few edamame on top. Sprinkle with thyme and season lightly with salt and pepper. Sprinkle 1 tablespoon each of the broth and Madeira over the top of each, then 1 teaspoon of the oil. Fold over the top of the parchment to enclose the vegetables. Starting at the right side, fold ^{1}/₂ inch of the parchment over toward you in 2-inch increments, crimping the edges and making sure the previous fold is covered a bit with the succeeding fold to securely wrap the vegetables airtight. Finish crimping the edges, then twist the pointed end around once and fold the "tail" under.

3. Place a trivet and steamer basket in a 5- to 7-quart pressure cooker. Add the water. Stack the vegetable packets in the basket in a crisscross pile. You can also use double-stacked 6-inch bamboo steamer baskets.

4. Close and lock the lid. Set the burner heat to high. When the cooker reaches HIGH pressure, reduce the burner heat as low as you can and still maintain HIGH pressure. Set a timer to cook for 6 minutes.

5. Remove the pot from the heat. Open the cooker with the Quick Release method. Be careful of the steam as you remove the lid.

6. Lift the packets out of the basket one at a time, holding one end with tongs and using a long plastic spatula. Transfer each package to an individual dinner plate. Serve immediately. Using a steak knife or scissors, let each diner tear open his or her own bag of vegetables.

Garmugia (Spring Fresh Vegetable Stew)

Serves 4 • Cooker: 5- to 7-quart • Time: 5 minutes at HIGH pressure

Make this traditional French mixed vegetable stew after a trip to the farmers' market when the baby artichokes are in season. Serve ladled over rice or with bread to sop up the juices.

Juice from ¹/₂ lemon
2 cups cold water
5 baby artichokes, trimmed and cut into sixths (about ¹/₂ pound)
2 thick slices pancetta, cut across into strips
8 ounces shelled fresh baby favas
8 ounces asparagus, bottoms trimmed and cut into 3-inch lengths
2 pounds fresh peas in the pod, shelled (2 cups)
¹/₄ cup thinly sliced new green garlic (white part only) or 2 cloves garlic, chopped
2 tablespoons coarsely chopped fresh flatleaf parsley
1 cup water
¹/₂ cup extra virgin olive oil
Sea salt
Lemon wedges, for serving (optional)

1. Combine the lemon juice and water in a large bowl. You will drop the artichokes into the water as you trim them to prevent discoloring. Bend back the lower, outer petals until they snap off easily near the base. Continue to snap off the leaves until you reach the point where the leaves are half green at the top and half yellow. Using a paring knife, cut off the top cone of leaves at the crown where the yellow color meets the green. Cut off the stem level with the base and trim any remaining green from the base. Cut into sixths. Toss into the lemon water.

2. Place the pancetta in a 5- to 7-quart pressure cooker. Turn the heat to medium-high and cook for 2 minutes, stirring a few times. Add the artichokes, favas, asparagus, peas, garlic, and parsley. Add the 1 cup water and oil. Bring to a boil.

3. Close and lock the lid. Set the burner heat to high. When the cooker reaches HIGH pressure, reduce the burner heat as low as you can and still maintain HIGH pressure. Set a timer to cook for 5 minutes.

4. Remove the pot from the heat. Open the cooker with the Quick Release method. Be careful of the steam as you remove the lid. Do not drain. Stir. Taste for salt. Serve immediately with lemon wedges, if you like.

Vegetarian Tzimmes

Serves 10 • Cooker: 5- to 7-quart • Time: 5 minutes at HIGH pressure

Tzimmes, a sweet mélange of sturdy winter vegetables and fruit, is a treasured part of the festive Jewish repertoire, often making an appearance on the Passover table. Tzimmes has another meaning as well. The expression "to make a tzimmes" over something means to make a fuss. When you look at traditional tzimmes recipes, you will see why. They call for long baking, basting, and careful stirring. But the pressure cooker makes tzimmes a quick and easy dish. In other words, you can make a tzimmes without making a tzimmes! Tzimmes is sometimes flavored with meat (usually a chunk of brisket) but we like this vegetarian version better. Serve as a side dish with roast chicken or a braised brisket.

4 medium sweet potatoes, peeled and cut into 1-inch slices
5 large carrots, peeled and sliced into 1-inch chunks
2 cups butternut squash, peeled and diced into 1-inch pieces
2 cups pitted prunes
1 cup dried apricot halves
$^1/_2$ cup golden raisins
1 teaspoon ground cinnamon
$^1/_2$ teaspoon ground nutmeg
$^1/_4$ teaspoon ground cardamom
2 tablespoons brown sugar
1 cup orange juice

1. Place the sweet potatoes, carrots, squash, prunes, apricots, and raisins in a 5- to 7-quart pressure cooker. Sprinkle on the cinnamon, nutmeg, cardamom, and brown sugar and gently stir to blend. Pour in the orange juice.
2. Close and lock the lid. Set the burner heat to high. When the cooker reaches HIGH pressure, reduce the burner heat as low as you can and still maintain HIGH pressure. Set a timer to cook for 5 minutes.
3. Remove the pot from the heat. Open the cooker with the Quick Release method. Be careful of the steam as you remove the lid. If you are not serving the tzimmes right away, place it in a baking dish, cover it with foil, and keep warm in a 250° F oven for up to 30 minutes. It will keep in an airtight container in the refrigerator 4 to 5 days or the freezer up to 4 months.

Summer Vegetable Succotash

Serves 4 • Cooker: 5- to 7-quart • Time: 2 minutes at HIGH pressure

The word "succotash" derives from the Narragansett Indian word for "boiled corn kernels." Although lima beans and corn are the defining ingredients, feel free to add in or substitute fava beans or edamame for the limas. This summer version uses all fresh vegetables but it's still super good using frozen vegetables in winter and swapping winter squash for the summer squash. Enjoy it with grilled or roasted meats or as a topping for a giant baked potato.

3 ears fresh corn, shucked
1 tablespoon olive oil
1 cup white onion, diced
1 to 2 cloves garlic, to taste, minced
1 cup (about 7 ounces) fresh or frozen baby lima beans
2 medium/large zucchini, trimmed, cut in half lengthwise, then cut into $^1/_2$-inch-thick half moons
1 medium sunburst or yellow crookneck squash, trimmed and cut into chunks
2 Roma tomatoes, seeded and diced
1 to 2 teaspoons chopped fresh thyme, to taste
$^1/_2$ cup chicken or vegetable broth
2 tablespoons coarsely chopped fresh flatleaf parsley
Sea salt and freshly ground black pepper
Umeboshi plum vinegar or red wine vinegar

1. With a sharp or serrated knife, cut down the length of each cob to remove the kernels. Then, scrape each cob using the top of the knife, or the thicker, dull edge, to extract the milk and additional pulp from the cob. You should have about 2 cups.
2. In a 5- to 7-quart pressure cooker, heat the oil over medium-high heat. Add the onion and garlic and cook, stirring often, until just tender, about 2 minutes. Add the corn, lima beans, squash, tomatoes, thyme, and broth.
3. Close and lock the lid. Set the burner heat to high. When the cooker reaches HIGH pressure, reduce the burner heat as low as you can and still maintain HIGH pressure. Set a timer to cook for 2 minutes.
4. Remove the pot from the heat. Open the cooker with the Quick Release method. Be careful of the steam as you remove the lid.
5. Stir in the parsley. Season to taste for salt and pepper. Splash with some vinegar. Leftovers will keep in an airtight container in the refrigerator up to 3 days.

16

Fantastic Desserts

The pressure cooker makes beautiful creamy-sweet desserts like custard and flan and delightful old-fashioned desserts like bread, rice, and steamed puddings. It's also the perfect vehicle for making the creamiest ever cheesecake and poaching whole fruit. We also love it for making stewed fruit and all kinds of applesauce. We've assembled a scrumptious selection of our favorites.

Nutmeg Cup Custard

Serves 6 • Cooker: 5- to 7-quart • Time: 8 minutes at HIGH pressure

With the pressure cooker, you can have a rich and creamy dessert in no time at all. Don't think of making this with anything but freshly grated nutmeg—the flavor of already ground nutmeg doesn't begin to compare. Whole nutmegs keep indefinitely at room temperature; you can use any kind of grater with them or get a special nutmeg grater that has a spot to keep a nutmeg at the ready to grate. To make the foil cover, use a 6-inch piece of foil, then cut it in half to make two squares. Be sure to try the variations—they're all winners.

2 cups whole milk, or 1 cup whole milk and 1 cup heavy cream, or 1 cup half-and-half and 1 cup heavy cream
2 large eggs
$1/3$ cup sugar
$1^1/2$ teaspoons vanilla extract
Whole nutmeg for grating
2 cups water
Whipped cream, for serving

1. Scald the milk in a small saucepan just until steaming (don't allow it to boil) or in the microwave in a glass measuring cup and allow to cool slightly. In a medium bowl, whisk together eggs and sugar, then add the milk slowly in a thin stream, whisking constantly so the eggs do not cook. Add the vanilla. Pour into 6 individual $1/2$- or $3/4$-cup (4- or 6-ounce) capacity custard cups, grate a sprinkling of nutmeg over the top of each, and cover each cup tightly with aluminum foil.
2. Place a trivet and steamer basket or rack in a 5- to 7-quart pressure cooker. Add the water. Arrange 3 of the foil-covered custard cups in the basket or on the rack. Place a rack on top of the cups and arrange the other 3 cups on it. It is okay if they touch.
3. Close and lock the lid. Set the burner heat to high. When the cooker reaches HIGH pressure, reduce the burner heat as low as you can and still maintain HIGH pressure. Set a timer for 8 minutes.
4. Remove the pot from the heat. Open the cooker with the Natural Release; let stand for 15 minutes. Be careful of the steam as you remove the

lid. Remove the cups from the pot with metal tongs and discard the foil. Let the custards cool at room temperature on a wire rack for about 1 hour. Cover with plastic wrap and chill in the refrigerator 4 hours to overnight before serving.
5. Serve the custards with a dollop of whipped cream.

Chocolate Cup Custard: Whisk $1/3$ cup unsweetened cocoa powder OR 3 ounces chopped bittersweet chocolate or chocolate chips into the scalded milk until smooth and melted in Step 1. Omit the nutmeg.

Chocolate-Orange Cup Custard: Whisk 4 ounces chopped bittersweet chocolate or $2/3$ cup chocolate chips into the scalded milk until smooth and melted in Step 1. Add a few strips of orange zest and let sit in the milk mixture. Omit the nutmeg. Stir in 2 teaspoons orange juice or orange liqueur, such as Grand Marnier. Discard the zest strips before portioning into the molds.

Butterscotch Cup Custard: Whisk $1/2$ cup butterscotch chips into the scalded milk until smooth and melted in Step 1. Substitute light brown sugar for the granulated sugar.

Cappuccino Cup Custard: Add 1 tablespoon instant espresso powder in Step 1.

Lemon Cup Custard: Add the grated zest of 1 large lemon and substitute lemon extract or lemon oil for the vanilla to the scalded milk.

CUSTARD IN THE PRESSURE COOKER

Custards are either cooked on the stovetop in a double boiler or baked in a water bath in the oven. The pressure cooker steamer basket melds both methods. Steam cooking insures that the custards cook evenly, so the eggs don't curdle or get rubbery. They don't dry out either.

Maple Pumpkin Custard

Serves 6 • Cooker: 5- to 7-quart • Time: 10 minutes at HIGH pressure

If you love pumpkin pie, you will love creamy pumpkin custard, which is basically the filling without the crust. We include a nondairy variation, made with coconut milk.

1^1/$_2$ cups whole milk, or 1 cup whole milk and
   ^{1}/$_2$ cup heavy cream
4 large eggs
^{3}/$_4$ cup canned pumpkin puree (not pumpkin pie
   filling)
^{2}/$_3$ cup maple syrup
^{1}/$_2$ teaspoon ground cinnamon
^{1}/$_2$ teaspoon freshly grated nutmeg, plus more
   for sprinkling
^{1}/$_4$ teaspoon salt
2 cups water
Whipped cream, for serving
3 tablespoons finely chopped crystallized ginger,
   for serving

1. Scald the milk in a small saucepan until steaming (do not let it boil) or in the microwave in a glass measuring cup and allow to cool slightly. In a medium bowl, whisk together eggs, pumpkin puree, and maple syrup until smooth, then add the milk slowly in a thin stream, whisking constantly so the eggs do not cook. Add the spices and salt. Pour into 6 individual ^{3}/$_4$-cup (6-ounce) capacity custard cups, sprinkle the tops lightly with nutmeg, and cover each cup tightly with aluminum foil.

2. Place a trivet and steamer basket or rack in a 5- to 7-quart pressure cooker. Add the water. Arrange 3 of the foil-covered custard cups in the basket or on the rack. Place a rack on top of the cups and arrange the other 3 cups on it. It is okay if they touch.

3. Close and lock the lid. Set the burner heat to high. When the cooker reaches HIGH pressure, reduce the burner heat as low as you can and still maintain HIGH pressure. Set a timer for 10 minutes.

4. Remove the pot from the heat. Open the cooker with the Natural Release method; let stand for 15 minutes. Be careful of the steam as you remove the lid. Remove the molds with metal tongs and let cool at room temperature on a wire rack for about 1 hour. Cover with plastic wrap and chill in the refrigerator for 4 hours to overnight before serving.

5. Serve the puddings with a dollop of whipped cream and a sprinkle of crystallized ginger.

Coconut-Pumpkin Custard: For the milk, substitute (13.5-ounce) can unsweetened coconut milk (shake well before opening). Use sugar instead of maple syrup. Add ^{1}/$_2$ teaspoon coconut extract.

THE BEST DISHES FOR STEAMING CUSTARD

You can make a single batch of custard in the pressure cooker or use individual molds. There are three main types of heat-proof individual dishes suitable for steaming custards. The following recipes are designed to be used in this type of container and all are able to be used interchangeably.

Apilco and Emile Henry brands are heatproof ceramic ramekins that come in 3^1/$_2$-inch diameter with a ^{1}/$_2$-cup (4-ounce) capacity. Three of these will fit comfortably in the steamer basket. Apilco, really a miniature soufflé dish, is always plain white French porcelain, while Emile Henry ceramics come in a range of earthy colors.

Pyrex heatproof custard cups, easily available in most supermarkets and hardware stores, are 4 inches in diameter with a ^{3}/$_4$-cup (6-ounce) capacity. One-half cup of custard fits in this size as well. Three of these will fit comfortably in the steamer basket. You can stack two in tandem on top or cover and refrigerate the extra custard, steaming in shifts. You can also use half-pint Mason jars with the wide mouth or stainless steel cups if you can find them.

Vanilla-Almond Flan

Serves 8 • Cooker: 5- to 7-quart or larger • Time: 15 minutes at HIGH pressure

The caramel-topped custard known as flan is a favorite throughout the Spanish-speaking world. Typically, flan is baked in the oven in a water bath or cooked on top of the stove like a steamed pudding. We first heard of preparing flan in the pressure cooker when Julie's family hosted a Mexican exchange student. Truly, we're converted. It's so much easier to cook a flan after dinner when it takes only 15 minutes in the pressure cooker rather than an hour or more in the oven. Then you can pop it into the fridge, go to bed, and serve a wonderful dessert the following evening.

There are truly infinite flavor varieties of flan. This is one of the most basic, and certainly the easiest. It has proven incredibly popular with flan lovers and flan doubters alike. If you make only one type of flan, choose this one.

$^3/_4$ cup sugar
3 large eggs
1 (12-ounce) can evaporated milk
1 (14-ounce) can sweetened condensed milk
1 teaspoon vanilla extract
$^1/_2$ teaspoon almond extract
2 to 3 cups water

1. Place the sugar in a small saucepan over medium heat. Cook until the sugar melts, stirring occasionally with a wooden spoon or a silicone spatula. Watch it carefully. When the sugar turns golden brown, pour it into a $1^1/_2$-quart (6-cup) pan or *flanera*. Holding the mold with potholders, carefully swirl the hot caramel to cover the bottom of the mold. Tilt the mold and carefully coat the sides with caramel, too, bringing the caramel one-half or two-thirds of the way up the side. Set the mold aside to cool.

2. In a medium bowl, beat the eggs with an electric mixer or a whisk. Beat in the evaporated milk and condensed milk. Stir in the extracts. Pour the milk mixture through a wire fine-mesh strainer into the caramel-coated flan mold. This step will keep your flan smooth. Cover the flan mold tightly—with the lid of the *flanera* or with a triple layer of foil, tied on tightly with string.

3. Place a trivet and steamer rack inside a 5- to 7-quart or larger pressure cooker. Pour 2 or 3 cups of water into the pressure cooker—2 cups if you are using a flat steamer rack, 3 cups if your steamer sits up off the base or if your pressure cooker is larger than 7 quarts. If you wish, construct a foil sling to help remove the finished flan from the pressure cooker: Tear two pieces of foil about 18 inches long. Fold each piece lengthwise toward the center, and fold the sides in again to create two long foil straps. Arrange the strips crosswise on top of the steamer. Place

THE PROPER PAN FOR FLAN

You need a proper cooking vessel for your flan. A cake pan covered with a triple layer of foil (and tied around with kitchen string) works fine. If you truly love flan, buy yourself a proper *flanera*, which looks like an English pudding mold with a clamp-on lid. It is stainless steel, has a $1^1/_2$-quart (6-cup) capacity, and comes in a round flat or pyramid shape; you can find them online. Before buying one, check its dimensions to be sure it will fit inside your pressure cooker.

If your flan mold is a fairly tight fit inside the cooker, you will want to construct a foil sling to aid in removing it from the hot pot; we've included directions for doing that in each recipe.

the covered flan mold in the pressure cooker on top of the strips, making sure the ends of all four extend over the top of the mold.

4. Close and lock the lid. Set the burner heat to high. When the cooker reaches HIGH pressure, reduce the burner heat as low as you can and still maintain HIGH pressure. Set a timer to cook for 15 minutes.

5. Remove the pot from the heat. Open the cooker with the Quick Release method. Be careful of the steam as you remove the lid. Let cool for 5 minutes or so, then carefully remove the flan mold from the pot, keeping it as level as you can and using the foil sling. Uncover the mold. Your flan should look set around the edge but may be a bit jiggly in the center. Refrigerate the flan. When it has cooled, you may cover it. Refrigerate 8 hours or overnight for the best taste.

6. To serve the flan, find a serving plate with a lip that will contain the caramel. Uncover the flan and run a table knife around the edge. Place the plate on top of the mold and carefully flip it. You will hear the flan slip out of the mold and onto the plate. Cut the flan into thin wedges to serve, spooning some of the caramel over the top of each slice.

Ginger-Lime Flan: Substitute the finely grated zest of 2 limes for the vanilla and almond extracts. Peel and coarsely grate a large chunk of fresh ginger, about 5 inches long. Take the grated ginger in your fist and squeeze out as much of the juice as you can into the milk mixture with the rest of the ingredients. Some cooks place the ginger in cheesecloth to do this. Discard the pulp. Stir to combine and pour the flan into the prepared mold.

Cappuccino Flan: Omit the almond extract. Add 2 tablespoons instant espresso or instant coffee powder dissolved in 1 tablespoon hot water to the milk mixture and stir to combine. This is one of the most popular flans.

Pumpkin Pie Flan

Serves 8 • Cooker: 5- to 7-quart or larger • Time: 15 minutes at HIGH pressure

This is a wonderful alternative to the usual pumpkin pie during the holidays.

1 cup sugar
6 large eggs
1 (12-ounce) can evaporated milk
1 (14-ounce) can sweetened condensed milk
1 cup canned pumpkin puree (not pumpkin pie filling)
1 tablespoon vanilla extract
1 1/2 teaspoons pumpkin pie spice
2 or 3 cups water

1. Place the sugar in a small saucepan over medium heat. Cook until the sugar melts, stirring occasionally with a wooden spoon or a silicone spatula. Watch it carefully. When the sugar turns golden brown, pour it into a 1 1/2-quart (6-cup) pan or *flanera*. Holding the mold with potholders, carefully swirl the hot caramel to cover the bottom of the mold. Tilt the mold and carefully coat the side with caramel, too, bringing the caramel one-half or two-thirds of the way up the side. Set the mold aside to cool.

2. In a medium bowl, beat the eggs with an electric mixer or a whisk. Beat in the evaporated milk, condensed milk, and pumpkin. Stir in the vanilla and spices. Pour the milk mixture through a fine-mesh strainer into the caramel-coated flan mold. This step will keep your flan smooth. Cover the flan mold tightly with the lid or with a triple layer of foil, tied on tightly with string.

3. Place a trivet and steamer rack in a 5- to 7-quart or larger pressure cooker. Pour the water into the pressure cooker—2 cups if you are using a flat steamer rack, 3 cups if your steamer sits up off the base or if your pressure cooker is larger than 7 quarts. If you wish, construct a foil sling to help in removing the finished flan from the pressure cooker: Tear two pieces of foil about 18 inches long. Fold each piece lengthwise toward the center and fold the sides in again to create two long foil strips. Arrange the strips crosswise on top of the steamer. Place the covered flan mold in the pressure cooker on top of the strips, making sure the ends of all four extend over the top of the mold.

4. Close and lock the lid. Set the burner heat to high. When the cooker reaches HIGH pressure, reduce the burner heat as low as you can and still maintain HIGH pressure. Set a timer to cook for 15 minutes.

5. Remove the pot from the heat. Open the cooker with the Quick Release method. Be careful of the steam as you remove the lid. Let cool for 10 minutes or so, then carefully remove the flan mold from the pressure cooker, keeping it as level as you can and using the foil sling if you made one. Uncover the mold. Your flan should look set around the edge but may be a bit jiggly in the center. Refrigerate the flan. When it has cooled, you may cover it. Refrigerate 8 hours or overnight for the best taste.

6. To serve the flan, find a serving plate with a lip that will contain the caramel. Uncover the flan and run a table knife around the edge of the flan. Place the plate on top of the mold and carefully flip it. You will hear the flan slip out of the mold and onto the plate. Cut the flan into thin wedges to serve, spooning some of the caramel over the top of each slice.

Creamy Vanilla and Lemon Rice Pudding

Serves 6 • Cooker: 5- to 7-quart • Time: 11 minutes at LOW or 4 minutes at HIGH pressure

Be sure to use a medium- or short-grain white rice to make this; the extra starchiness is needed to thicken the pudding. Goya sells it, or you can use Italian risotto rices (Arborio and Carnaroli), or Calrose, grown in California. Serve with whipped cream or pour cold heavy cream over each portion.

2 cups whole milk
2 cups half-and-half
1 1/2 cups medium- or short-grain white rice
3/4 cup sugar
1 (3-finger) pinch sea salt
Finely grated zest of 1 lemon
1/4 cup diced dried mango, chopped dried apricots, or dried cranberries (optional)
1 tablespoon vanilla extract
Freshly grated nutmeg

1. Coat the bottom third of a 5- to 7-quart pressure cooker with nonstick cooking spray. Combine the milk, half-and-half, rice, sugar, salt, and lemon zest in the pot.
2. Close and lock the lid. Place a heat diffuser on the burner and the pressure cooker on the diffuser. Set the burner heat to high. When the cooker reaches HIGH pressure, adjust the heat to maintain pressure at LOW or HIGH pressure. Set a timer to cook for 11 minutes at LOW or 4 minutes at HIGH.
3. Remove the pot from the heat. Open the cooker with the Quick Release method. Be careful of the steam as you remove the lid. If the rice is not done enough for you, replace the lid and let stand 10 minutes off the heat, then check again. It will cook in the residual heat.
4. Stir in the dried fruit if using and vanilla. Portion into individual serving bowls to eat warm, sprinkled with nutmeg, or pour into a refrigerator storage bowl, cool to lukewarm, cover, and refrigerate 3 hours to overnight. When chilled, the pudding will firm up.

THE BEST RICE PUDDING

The key to making rice pudding is not to overcook it, so follow our timings exactly. The starch in rice breaks down during the cooking process and, along with eggs if included, gently thickens the mixture. Different rice types contain different amounts of starch, so follow our recommendations. Serve your rice pudding warm. Chilling hardens the starch in the rice kernel, which means you'll end up with a stiffer pudding after refrigeration.

Triple Coconut Rice Pudding

Serves 6 • Cooker: 5- to 7-quart • Time: 11 minutes at LOW or 4 minutes at HIGH pressure

Coconut milk has become one of the darlings of the food world. Long a staple in tropical cuisines, it is now an integral part of American dessert cooking as well. Canned coconut milk is rich and smooth and the flavor is fantastically addicting. You can find coconut extract next to the vanilla extract in the supermarket spice aisle.

1 cup shredded sweetened coconut
1¹/₂ cups half-and-half
1 cup whole milk
1 (14-ounce) can unsweetened coconut milk
1¹/₂ cups medium- or short-grain white rice
³/₄ cup sugar
1 (3-finger) pinch sea salt
1 teaspoon vanilla extract
¹/₂ teaspoon coconut extract

1. Spread the coconut on a parchment paper-lined baking sheet and place in a preheated 350° F oven. Bake until lightly browned, about 8 minutes, stirring halfway through.
2. Coat the bottom third of a 5- to 7-quart pressure cooker with nonstick cooking spray. Combine the half-and-half, milk, coconut milk, rice, sugar, and salt in the pot.
3. Close and lock the lid. Place a heat diffuser on the burner and the pressure cooker on the diffuser. Set the burner heat to high. When the cooker reaches HIGH pressure, adjust the heat to maintain pressure at LOW or HIGH pressure. Set a timer to cook for 11 minutes at LOW or 4 minutes at HIGH.
4. Remove the pot from the heat. Open the cooker with the Quick Release method. Be careful of the steam as you remove the lid. If the rice is not tender enough for you, replace the lid and let stand 10 minutes, then check again. It will cook in the residual heat.
5. Stir in the toasted coconut and extracts. Portion into serving bowls to eat warm, or pour into a refrigerator storage bowl, cool to lukewarm, cover, and refrigerate 3 hours to overnight. When chilled, the pudding will firm up.

Basmati Rice Pudding with Crystallized Ginger

Serves 4 • Cooker: 5- to 7-quart • Time: 8 minutes at HIGH pressure

There is no rice with a flavor and aroma like Indian basmati rice. It is one of the most coveted rices in the world and has been grown for centuries in the foothills of northern India. All our friends from India prefer basmati over any other white rice. Long-grain rice has less starch than short or medium grain, so it makes a rice pudding with a slightly lighter consistency.

2 tablespoons unsalted butter, softened
3 cups whole milk
1 cup basmati white rice, rinsed until the water runs clear
$1/2$ cup sugar
1 (2-finger) pinch sea salt
$1/4$ cup heavy cream
1 large egg, beaten
1 teaspoon vanilla extract
2 tablespoons finely chopped crystallized ginger
Whipped cream

1. Coat the bottom of a 5- to 7-quart pressure cooker with the butter. Add the milk and rice. Stir in the sugar and salt.
2. Close and lock the lid. Place a heat diffuser on the burner and the pressure cooker on the diffuser. Set the burner heat to high. When the cooker reaches HIGH pressure, reduce the burner heat as low as you can and still maintain HIGH pressure. Set a timer to cook for 8 minutes.
3. Remove the pot from the heat. Open the cooker with the Natural Release method; let stand for 15 minutes. At time, if the pressure is not all released, open the valve.
4. In a small bowl, beat the cream, egg, and vanilla with a fork. Spoon a bit of the hot rice into the cream mixture. Stir back into the pot, then cook, uncovered, over medium heat for a few minutes. Stir a few times. Stir in the ginger.
5. Portion into individual serving bowls to eat warm, or pour into a refrigerator storage bowl, cool to lukewarm, cover, and refrigerate 3 hours to overnight. When chilled, the pudding will firm up. Serve with whipped cream.

CRYSTALLIZED GINGER

There is not much in the food world that crystallized ginger can't enhance the flavor of, from baking to salads and chutneys. To make it, fresh ginger is cooked in sugar water until tender, then rolled in coarse sugar for a crunchy shell that preserves it practically for eternity. It has a sweet taste with a slight afterburn of gingery heat. Look for it online or in the spice section of the supermarket.

Black and Blue Coconut Rice Pudding

Serves 4 • Cooker: 5- to 7-quart • Time: 12 minutes at HIGH pressure

We simply adore the black Chinese Forbidden rice from Lotus Foods. It's a nutritious whole grain with a sweet, nutty flavor that is more delicate than that of regular brown rice. It's rich in antioxidants as well as fiber. Loook for it at upscale grocers. It's also available online. When we saw a Forbidden Rice pudding recipe in a *New York Times* article by Martha Rose Shulman, who credits it to pastry chef Sherry Yard, formerly of Spago Beverly Hills, we just had to adapt it to the pressure cooker. A few small tweaks and it worked perfectly. This is a nondairy recipe.

$^1/_2$ cup Forbidden rice (Chinese black rice)
1 cup water
1 cup vanilla-flavored almond milk
1 cup unsweetened light coconut milk
3 tablespoons sugar
Pinch salt
1 cup blueberries
1 teaspoon vanilla extract

1. In a 5- to 7-quart pressure cooker, combine the rice, water, almond milk, coconut milk, sugar, and salt.
2. Close and lock the lid. Place a heat diffuser on the burner and the pressure cooker on the diffuser. Set the burner heat to high. When the cooker reaches HIGH pressure, adjust the heat to maintain the pressure. Set a timer to cook for 12 minutes.
3. Remove the pot from the heat. Open the cooker with the Natural Release method; let stand for 15 minutes. At time, if the pressure is not all released, open the valve.
4. Stir in the blueberries and vanilla and simmer the pudding, uncovered, over low heat for 5 minutes.
5. Transfer the pudding to one large bowl or 6 small ones. Cover with plastic wrap and chill for at least 2 hours before serving.

Jeweled Dessert Risotto

Serves 4 to 6 • Cooker: 5- to 7-quart • Time: 7 minutes at HIGH pressure

This dessert risotto contains no added sugar. You can also enjoy it for breakfast, topped with a dollop of plain Greek yogurt.

2 tablespoons unsalted butter
1^1/$_2$ cups medium- or short-grain rice (Arborio or Vialone Nano)
Grated zest of 1 orange (about 1 tablespoon)
3^1/$_2$ cups whole milk
^{2}/$_3$ cup mixed golden raisins and dried tart cherries
^{1}/$_2$ cup heavy cream mixed with 2 teaspoons vanilla extract
Paradise Cream (recipe follows; optional)

1. In a 5- to 7-quart pressure cooker or 2^1/$_2$-quart skillet pressure cooker, melt the butter over medium heat. Add the rice and cook 1 minute, stirring constantly, to evenly coat the grains. Add the orange zest, milk, and dried fruit. Bring to a boil and stir.
2. Cover and lock the lid in place. Place a heat diffuser on the burner and the pressure cooker on the diffuser. Set the burner heat to high. When the cooker reaches HIGH pressure, reduce the burner heat as low as you can and still maintain HIGH pressure. Set a timer to cook for 7 minutes.
3. Remove the pot from the heat. Open the cooker with the Natural Release method; let stand for 10 minutes. At time, if the pressure is not all released, open the valve. Stir in the heavy cream. Cover and let stand a few minutes to thicken and set up.
4. Spoon out the rice with an oversized spoon to serving bowls to serve hot. Serve with a spoonful of Paradise Cream, if desired.

Paradise Cream

Makes 2^1/$_4$ cups

1 cup cold whipping cream
^{1}/$_2$ cup sour cream or crème fraîche

Place a medium bowl and the beaters from an electric mixer in the freezer for at least 1 hour to thoroughly chill. Place the cream in the bowl. Whip on high speed until soft peaks form, about 3 minutes. Whisk in the sour cream gently. Cover and refrigerate until serving.

Seasonal Fresh Fruit Risotto

Serves 4 to 6 • Cooker: 5- to 7-quart • Time: 7 minutes at HIGH pressure

This is the queen of rice puddings.

2 tablespoons unsalted butter
1 cup medium- or short-grain rice (Arborio or
   Vialone Nano)
1 (14-ounce) can unsweetened coconut milk
1 cup whole milk
$^1/_4$ cup sugar
Grated zest of 1 lemon
2 teaspoons vanilla extract
2 cups fresh berries (strawberries, blueberries,
   blackberries, or combination), sliced peaches,
   sliced mango, tangerine sections, pineapple
   chunks, and/or sliced banana (use all of one fruit
   or a combination)

1. In a 5- to 7-quart pressure cooker or $2^1/_2$-quart skillet pressure cooker, melt the butter over medium heat. Add the rice and cook 1 minute, stirring constantly, to evenly coat the grains. Add the coconut milk, milk, sugar, lemon zest, and vanilla. Bring to a boil and stir.
2. Cover and lock the lid in place. Place a heat diffuser on the burner and the pressure cooker on the diffuser. Set the burner heat to high. When the cooker reaches HIGH pressure, reduce the burner heat as low as you can and still maintain HIGH pressure. Set a timer to cook for 7 minutes.
3. Remove the pot from the heat. Open the cooker with the Natural Release method; let stand for 15 minutes. At time, if the pressure is not all released, open the valve.
4. Let the risotto cool slightly before adding the fruit; you want it to retain its shape. Replace the cover and let stand a few minutes to thicken and set up. Spoon out the rice with an oversized spoon to serving bowls to serve warm, or chill and serve cold with whipped cream.

Frozen Fruit Risotto: Yes, we love using fresh fruit but sometimes the fruit we want isn't in season and frozen is the better choice. Make the risotto exactly as directed using the same amount of IQF (individually quick frozen) fruit—no need to thaw. Add the fruit as soon as you open the cooker, then cover and let stand as directed in Step 4.

Old-Fashioned New World Indian Pudding

Serves 6 • Cooker: 5- to 7-quart • Time: 28 minutes at HIGH pressure

Indian pudding is often served at Thanksgiving. It was originally baked in a stone crock for at least 7 hours in a fireplace oven. It is similar to a baked cornmeal mush or polenta pudding, sweet and spicy. The flavor is outstanding, comforting and rich. Serve with a dollop of whipped cream or vanilla ice cream on the top so it can melt down the sides, or pour a bit of organic heavy cream around the outer edges.

3 cups whole milk
$1/3$ cup fine-ground yellow cornmeal
1 teaspoon ground cinnamon
$1/2$ teaspoon sea salt
$1/2$ teaspoon ground ginger
$1/4$ teaspoon ground cloves
$1/3$ cup light molasses
2 tablespoons light brown sugar
2 tablespoons unsalted butter, plus more for greasing the dish
2 cups water

1. In a large saucepan, combine the milk and cornmeal with a whisk, slowly pouring in the cornmeal in a steady stream while whisking to avoid lumps. Heat over medium-high heat just to a low simmer, whisking constantly. Whisk in the salt and spices. Bring to a boil over low heat, whisking until the cornmeal thickens to the consistency of oatmeal, about 15 minutes. If the mixture gets clumpy, use an immersion blender to smooth it out. Whisk in the molasses, brown sugar, and butter. Remove from the heat.

2. Place a trivet in a 5- to 7-quart pressure cooker. Add the water. Butter or coat with butter-flavored cooking spray a $1^1/2$- or 2-quart (6- or 8-cup) soufflé dish that fits comfortably in the cooker with an inch of space all the way around the edge. Pour the cornmeal mixture into the dish. Cover the dish tightly with aluminum foil and tuck it underneath a bit. If you wish, construct a foil sling to help in removing the dish from the pressure cooker when the pudding is done: Tear two pieces of foil about 18 inches long. Fold each piece lengthwise toward the center and fold the sides in again to create two long foil straps. Arrange the strips crosswise on top of the cooker. Place the covered soufflé dish in the pressure cooker on top of the strips, making sure the ends of all four extend over the top of the dish.

3. Close and lock the lid. Set the burner heat to high. When the cooker reaches HIGH pressure, reduce the burner heat as low as you can and still maintain HIGH pressure. Set a timer to cook for 28 minutes.

4. Remove the pot from the heat. Open the cooker with the Natural Release method; let stand for 15 minutes. Be careful of the steam as you remove the lid. Remove the soufflé dish from the pressure cooker, using the foil handles to carefully lift it out, and place on a wire rack. Remove the foil from the dish and let cool for about an hour to warm, which is the perfect temperature for serving. It is okay if the center is not quite set, as it will firm up as it sits. Use an oversized spoon for portioning.

Vanilla Bread Pudding with Wild Turkey Sauce

Serves 6 to 8 • Cooker: 6- to 8-quart • Time: 20 minutes at HIGH pressure

This bread pudding is so addictive you might find yourself eating it right out of the dish before it cools and the heck with the sauce. This is a grand dessert for company after a light meal. If you use fresh bread, place it on a baking sheet and toast for 10 to 15 minutes at 350° F.

VANILLA BREAD PUDDING:
6 to 7 cups cubed stale French bread, crusts removed
2 cups half-and-half
$^1/_2$ cup granulated sugar
$^1/_3$ cup firmly packed light brown sugar
3 large eggs
$^1/_2$ cup (1 stick) unsalted butter, melted and cooled
1 teaspoon ground cinnamon
1 teaspoon ground nutmeg
2 tablespoons vanilla extract
1 tablespoon cold unsalted butter, cut into little pieces
2 cups water

WILD TURKEY SAUCE:
$^1/_2$ cup (1 stick) unsalted butter
$1^1/_2$ cups confectioners' sugar
$^1/_3$ cup heavy cream
$^1/_4$ cup Wild Turkey bourbon, or to taste

1. Butter or coat with butter-flavored cooking spray a 2-quart (8-cup) soufflé dish that fits comfortably in a 6- to 8- quart pressure cooker with an inch of space all the way around the edge. Place the bread in the dish. In a large bowl, whisk the milk, sugars, eggs, melted butter, spices, and vanilla together until smooth. Pour it over the bread. Let the mixture stand at room temperature for 15 minutes. Push down the bread to evenly moisten it. Dot the top with the bits of cold butter. Cover the dish with foil, leaving some room for expansion, and tuck the foil underneath a bit.
2. Place a trivet in the pressure cooker. Add the water. If you wish, construct a foil sling to help

in removing the dish from the pressure cooker when the pudding is done: Tear two pieces of foil about 18 inches long. Fold each piece lengthwise toward the center and fold the sides in again to create two long foil strips. Arrange the straps crosswise on top of the cooker. Place the dish in the pressure cooker on top of the foil strips, making sure the ends of all four extend over the top of the dish. Fold the strips over the top.

3. Close and lock the lid. Set the burner heat to high. When the cooker reaches HIGH pressure, reduce the burner heat as low as you can and still maintain HIGH pressure. Set a timer to cook for 20 minutes.

4. Make the Wild Turkey Sauce. Place the butter and confectioners' sugar in a medium saucepan over medium heat and melt the butter. Beat with an immersion blender or whisk until smooth; beat in the cream. Remove from the heat and slowly beat in the bourbon to taste. The sauce will thicken as it cools. Makes 1 cup.

5. Remove the pot from the heat. Open the cooker with the Natural Release method; let stand for 15 minutes. Be careful of the steam as you remove the lid. Remove the soufflé dish from the pressure cooker, using the foil handles to carefully lift it out, and place on a wire rack. Loosen the foil. A toothpick or cake tester inserted into the center of the pudding, which will be puffed, will come out clean.

6. Let the pudding cool before serving warm or at room temperature with the warm whiskey sauce.

Banana-Vanilla Bread Pudding: Peel and cut 2 firm-ripe bananas into $^1/_2$-inch-thick slices. Layer them in the soufflé dish with the bread cubes, having the top layer be bread. Proceed as directed.

Blueberry-Vanilla Bread Pudding: Toss 2 cups fresh blueberries with the bread cubes. Proceed as directed.

Eggnog Bread Pudding with Golden Raisins and Pecans

Serves 6 • Cooker: 6- to 8-quart • Time: 20 minutes at HIGH pressure

Ready-made eggnog shows up around Christmas, and it's a wonderful ingredient in puddings, cakes, and ice cream. The rum extract is amazingly delicious. Your bread must be at least a day old and thoroughly dry to make a successful bread pudding. You will need about a 1¼-pound loaf.

3 tablespoons unsalted butter, melted, plus soft
    butter for greasing the soufflé dish
7 to 8 (1-inch-thick) slices day-old French or Italian
    bread, crusts trimmed, cut into cubes to make 6
    cups
½ cup golden raisins
½ cup chopped pecans
2 cups commercial eggnog
4 large eggs, lightly beaten
¼ cup firmly packed light brown sugar
½ teaspoon freshly grated nutmeg
1 teaspoon vanilla extract
½ teaspoon imitation rum extract
2 cups water
Whipped cream, for serving

THE BEST BREAD PUDDING

Firm breads, those you would choose to make French toast, make the best bread pudding because the cut pieces hold up to all of the liquid ingredients without becoming mushy. Think raisin bread, panettone holiday bread, brioche, challah, croissants. Although firm bread is best for bread pudding, avoid artisan or rustic breads with a very crisp or hard crust. Always remove the crusts. To dry bread cubes, spread the cubes in a single layer on a baking sheet. Bake, uncovered, in a 300° F oven until the cubes are dry, 10 to 15 minutes, stirring twice. Cubes will continue to dry and crisp as they cool. Alternately, the bread can be left to air dry overnight. When making bread pudding in the pressure cooker, be certain not to overcook it. If you want to serve the pudding warm, follow Lorna Sass's tip: Cut a few slits in the top of the foil and let it remain sitting in the warm pressure pot with the lid ajar for up to an hour.

1. Butter or coat with butter-flavored cooking spray a 1½-quart (6-cup) soufflé dish that fits comfortably in a 6- to 8-quart pressure cooker with an inch of space all the way around the edge.
2. In the soufflé dish, toss the melted butter, bread cubes, raisins, and pecans together. In a medium bowl, whisk the eggnog, eggs, brown sugar, nutmeg, and extracts together. Pour the milk mixture over the bread. Press down to make sure all the bread is soaked. Let stand 10 minutes. Cover the dish with foil, leaving some room for expansion, and tuck the foil underneath a bit.
3. Place a trivet in the pressure cooker. Add the water. If you wish, construct a foil sling to help in removing the dish from the pressure cooker when the pudding is done: Tear two pieces of foil about 18 inches long. Fold each piece lengthwise toward the center and fold the sides in again to create two long foil strips. Arrange the strips crosswise on top of the cooker. Place the dish in the pressure cooker on top of the strips, making sure the ends of all four extend over the top of the dish. Fold the strips over the top.
4. Close and lock the lid. Set the burner heat to high. When the cooker reaches HIGH pressure, reduce the burner heat as low as you can and still maintain HIGH pressure. Set a timer to cook for 20 minutes.
5. Remove the pot from the heat. Open the cooker with the Natural Release method; let stand for 15 minutes. Be careful of the steam as you remove the lid. Remove the soufflé dish from the pressure cooker, using the foil handles to carefully lift it out, and place on a wire rack. A toothpick or cake tester inserted into the center of the pudding will come out clean. Serve with whipped cream.

Chocolate Bread Pudding with Dried Cherries and Sweetened Crème Fraîche

Serves 6 • Cooker: 6- to 8-quart • Time: 20 minutes at HIGH pressure

The original idea for this recipe came from Lissa Doumani, the co-owner and pastry chef of Terra restaurant, in St. Helena, California. Unlike the original, this includes sour cream, which creates a slightly firmer custard. Please use a good quality chocolate.

2 cups water

CHOCOLATE BREAD PUDDING:
$^1/_2$ cup dried sour cherries
$^1/_3$ cup brandy, Cognac, or Cherry Marnier
8 ounces bittersweet chocolate, chopped or broken
    into pieces, or 1 $^1/_3$ cups chocolate chips
1 cup heavy cream
$^1/_2$ cup sour cream
$^1/_2$ cup granulated sugar
3 large eggs, lightly beaten
$^1/_4$ teaspoon ground cinnamon
1 teaspoon vanilla extract
4 to 5 ($^1/_2$-inch-thick) slices day-old challah egg
    bread or soft French bread, crusts trimmed and
    cut in $^1/_2$-inch cubes to make 4 cups

SWEETENED CRÈME FRAÎCHE:
1 cup crème fraîche or sour cream
1 tablespoon confectioners' sugar
$^1/_4$ teaspoon vanilla extract

1. Butter a 2-quart (8-cup) soufflé dish that fits comfortably in a 6- to 8-quart pressure cooker with an inch of space all the way around the edge. Place a trivet in the pressure cooker. Add the water. If you wish, construct a foil sling to help in removing the dish from the pressure cooker when the pudding is done: Tear two pieces of foil about 18 inches long. Fold each piece lengthwise toward the center and fold the sides in again to create two long foil strips. Arrange the strips crosswise on top of the cooker.
2. In a small bowl, combine the cherries and brandy. Let stand 20 minutes to soften. In another small bowl, melt the chocolate in the microwave or in the top of a double boiler over simmering water; stir until smooth.
3. In a large bowl, whisk the cream, sour cream, granulated sugar, eggs, cinnamon, and vanilla together until smooth. Whisk in the warm chocolate. Stir in the bread cubes and cherries with their soaking liquid; let mixture stand at room temperature 15 minutes.
4. Pour the mixture into the soufflé dish. Cover the dish with foil, leaving some room for expansion, and tuck it underneath a bit. Place the dish in the pressure cooker on top of the foil strips, making sure the ends of all four extend over the top of the dish. Fold the strips over the top.
5. Close and lock the lid. Set the burner heat to high. When the cooker reaches HIGH pressure, reduce the burner heat as low as you can and still maintain HIGH pressure. Set a timer to cook for 20 minutes.
6. Remove the pot from the heat. Open with the Natural Release method; let stand for 15 minutes. Be careful of the steam as you remove the lid. Remove the dish from the pressure cooker, using the foil handles to carefully lift it out, and place on a wire rack. Loosen the foil. A toothpick or cake tester inserted into the center of the firm pudding should come out clean.
7. In a small bowl, whisk the crème fraîche, confectioners' sugar, and vanilla together until smooth and soft peaks form. Serve the bread pudding warm with a spoonful of the sweetened crème fraîche on top.

MELTING CHOCOLATE IN THE MICROWAVE

Since the microwave heats food from the inside out, you can't see the progress of chocolate melting the way you can when you melt it over heat, which means you can burn chocolate in the microwave if you're not paying attention. Use the lowest heat setting you can with your microwave. Place the chocolate in a microwavable bowl, then microwave it in short increments (10 to 20 seconds) and stir the chocolate after each blast; repeat until the chocolate is fully melted and smooth.

Lemon Bread Pudding

Serves 4 • Cooker: 6- to 8-quart • Time: 20 minutes at HIGH pressure

Give us lemon anything. Maybe it's the color; the bright yellow lifts the spirits as well as piquing the palate. Limoncello, a popular liqueur from Italy that is now also made domestically, imparts a strong lemon flavor without the sourness of lemon juice and gives a bit more of a citrus punch.

3 tablespoons unsalted butter, melted, plus soft butter for greasing the soufflé dish
4 to 5 (1-inch-thick) slices day-old French or Italian bread, crusts trimmed and cut into $^1/_2$-inch cubes to make 3 to $3^1/_2$ cups
Grated zest of 2 to 3 lemons ($1^1/_2$ tablespoons)
1 cup heavy cream
1 cup whole milk
4 large eggs, lightly beaten
$^3/_4$ cup granulated sugar
Pinch salt
$^1/_2$ cup fresh lemon juice
3 tablespoons limoncello liqueur (optional but nice)
2 cups water
Confectioners' sugar and fresh berries, for serving

1. Butter or coat with butter-flavored cooking spray a 2-quart (8-cup) soufflé dish that fits comfortably in a 6- to 8- quart pressure cooker with an inch of space all the way around the edge. In the dish, toss the bread cubes with the lemon zest. In a medium bowl, whisk the cream, milk, 3 of the eggs, the sugar, melted butter, and salt together. In a small bowl, beat the remaining egg, lemon juice, and limoncello if using together. Pour into the milk mixture and beat well.

Pour the milk mixture into the soufflé dish over the bread. Press down to make sure all the bread is soaked. Let stand 10 minutes. Cover the dish with foil and tuck it underneath a bit, leaving some room for expansion.

2. Place a trivet in the pressure cooker. Add the water. If you wish, construct a foil sling to help in removing the dish from the pressure cooker when the pudding is done: Tear two pieces of heavy-duty foil about 18 inches long. Fold each piece lengthwise toward the center and fold the sides in again to create two long foil strips. Arrange the strips crosswise on top of the cooker. Place the dish in the pressure cooker on top of the strips, making sure the ends of all four extend over the top of the dish. Fold the strips over the top.

3. Close and lock the lid. Set the burner heat to high. When the cooker reaches HIGH pressure, reduce the burner heat as low as you can and still maintain HIGH pressure. Set a timer to cook for 20 minutes.

4. Remove the pot from the heat. Open the cooker with the Natural Release method; let stand for 15 minutes. Be careful of the steam as you remove the lid. Remove the dish from the cooker, using the foil handles to carefully lift it out, and place on a wire rack. Loosen the foil. A toothpick or cake tester inserted into the center of the pudding should come out clean.

5. Serve sprinkled with confectioners' sugar and some fresh seasonal berries.

SOUFFLÉ DISHES FOR PRESSURE COOKER STEAMED PUDDINGS

In making bread puddings, we call for heatproof soufflé dishes. We use a tall version of the classic white porcelain pleated soufflé dish made by the French ceramic company Pillivuyt. It comes in five sizes: 4-inch diameter holds $1^1/_2$ cups for a dramatic individual serving; $5^3/_4$-inch diameter holds 4 cups; $6^1/_2$-inch diameter holds 6 cups; $7^1/_4$-inch diameter holds 8 cups, and $7^3/_4$-inch diameter holds 11 cups. The 6- or 8-cup capacity dishes, at around 7 inches in diameter, will fit in the pressure cooker pot with plenty of room around to let the steam surround the pudding. You will love owning these dishes, they are incredibly versatile for cooking and serving.

Persimmon Bread Pudding

Serves 6 • Cooker: 6- to 8-quart • Time: 20 minutes at HIGH pressure

For real ginger lovers, serve with our fantastic extra-quick ginger ice cream (recipe follows).

2 cups water
3 soft, ripe Hachiya persimmons
1 cup heavy cream
1 cup milk
3 large eggs, lightly beaten
³/₄ cup firmly packed light brown sugar
1 teaspoon grated orange zest
¹/₂ teaspoon ground cloves
¹/₂ teaspoon ground nutmeg
¹/₂ teaspoon ground cinnamon
1 teaspoon vanilla extract
7 to 8 (1-inch-thick) slices day-old challah egg bread, Texas toast, or soft French bread, crusts trimmed and cut into 1-inch cubes to make 6 to 7 cups
1¹/₂ tablespoons cold unsalted butter, cut into small pieces

1. Butter a 2-quart (8-cup) soufflé dish that fits comfortably in a 6- to 8-quart pressure cooker with an inch of space all the way around the edges. Place a trivet in the cooker. Add the water. If you wish, construct a foil sling to help in removing the dish from the pressure cooker when the pudding is done: Tear two pieces of heavy-duty foil about 18 inches long. Fold each piece lengthwise toward the center and fold the sides in again to create two long foil strips. Arrange the strips crosswise on top of the cooker.
2. Peel the persimmons, cut in half, and remove the seeds and cores. Discard the dried green or brown calyxes. You will need 1¹/₄ to 1¹/₂ cups persimmon goop. Place it in a large bowl, add the cream, milk, brown sugar, eggs, zest, spices, and vanilla and whisk together until smooth. Stir in the bread cubes and let the mixture stand at room temperature 15 minutes.
3. Pour the mixture into the prepared soufflé dish and dot the top with the bits of butter. Cover the dish with foil and tuck it underneath a bit, leaving some room for expansion. Place the dish in the pressure cooker on top of the strips, making sure the ends of all four extend over the top of the dish. Fold the strips over the top.

4. Close and lock the lid. Set the burner heat to high. When the cooker reaches HIGH pressure, reduce the burner heat as low as you can and still maintain HIGH pressure. Set a timer to cook for 20 minutes.
5. Remove the pot from the heat. Open the cooker with the Natural Release method; let stand for 15 minutes. Be careful of the steam as you remove the lid. Remove the dish from the pressure cooker, using the foil handles to carefully lift it out, and place on a wire rack. Loosen the foil. A toothpick or cake tester inserted into the center of the pudding should come out clean.

Quick Ginger Ice Cream

Makes 1 quart

¹/₄ cup chopped crystallized ginger
¹/₄ cup water
1 quart vanilla ice cream

1. In a small saucepan over medium-low heat, simmer the candied ginger in the water until softened; the liquid will evaporate and thicken a bit. Set aside to cool to room temperature.
2. Soften the ice cream in the refrigerator 15 to 30 minutes, until soft and malleable, but not melted. With an electric mixer or by hand, beat the ice cream quickly until just creamy. Pour in the ginger and soaking liquid; blend until evenly distributed. Working quickly, scrape the ice cream back into the carton. Return the ice cream to the freezer to firm up at least 6 hours.

PERSIMMONS

You can buy two types of persimmons in the fall—the larger, pointed Hachiya and the smaller, more rounded Fuyu. Fuyu are ripe when firm, but Hachiya should be jelly-soft. To ripen, let sit at room temperature and do their thing. This can take days, or even weeks. You can freeze ripe persimmons, whole, up to 3 months, or just the pulp up to 1 month.

Cranberry-Date Pudding with Brandy Butter

Serves 8 • Cooker: 5- to 7-quart • Time: 25 minutes at HIGH pressure

This is a classic English-style steamed pudding traditionally served during the winter holidays. Even though the pudding contains no eggs or butter, it is luscious and moist. Use unsulfured sweet Barbados molasses rather than blackstrap, which is bitter. Serve with a dollop of oh-so-very traditional Brandy Butter, which can be used on any manner of steamed pudding.

CRANBERRY-DATE PUDDING:

1^1/$_3$ cups all-purpose flour
2 teaspoons baking soda
^{1}/$_2$ teaspoon sea salt
2 cups fresh or thawed frozen cranberries
^{3}/$_4$ cup golden raisins
^{3}/$_4$ cup snipped pitted dates
^{1}/$_2$ cup light molasses
^{1}/$_3$ cup hot water
3 cups water

BRANDY BUTTER:

1^1/$_2$ cups confectioners' sugar
^{1}/$_2$ cup (1 stick) unsalted butter, softened
3 tablespoons brandy
1 teaspoon vanilla extract
^{1}/$_4$ teaspoon almond extract
Pinch ground nutmeg

1. Generously butter or coat with butter-flavored cooking spray a 1- or 1^1/$_2$-quart (4- or 6-cup) pudding mold with clip-on lid.
2. In a large bowl, combine the flour, baking soda, and salt. Add the cranberries, raisins, and dates. Add the molasses and hot water and stir well with a large rubber spatula with a folding motion until the ingredients are evenly moistened. Scrape the batter into the mold, filling it no more than two-thirds full. Snap on the lid.
3. Place a trivet and steamer rack in a 5- to 7-quart pressure cooker. Add the water. Set the mold on the rack, making sure it is centered and will not tip.
4. Close and lock the lid. Set the burner heat to high. When the cooker reaches HIGH pressure, reduce the burner heat as low as you can and still maintain HIGH pressure. Set a timer to cook for 25 minutes.
5. Remove the pot from the heat. Open the cooker with the Natural Release method; let stand for 15 minutes. Be careful of the steam as you remove the lid. Wearing oven mitts, carefully lift the mold out of the cooker by the lid handles to a wire rack. Remove the cover; let cool for about 20 minutes. Place a plate on top of the mold and invert to unmold the pudding.
6. Make the Brandy Butter while the pudding cools. Place the sugar in a food processor and pulse to sift and aerate. Add the butter in pieces, the brandy, and extracts. Pulse until smooth, fluffy, and creamy. You can also mix this in a stand electric mixer on low speed. Place in a small serving bowl and sprinkle with the nutmeg or place in an airtight container and refrigerate until serving (remove 30 to 60 minutes before serving to soften).
7. Serve the pudding still warm, cut in wedges, or at room temperature, with the Butter. It will keep, wrapped in plastic, in the refrigerator up to 1 week.

Steamed Gingerbread Pudding

Serves 8 • Cooker: 5- to 7-quart • Time: 45 minutes at HIGH pressure

This pudding is a classic for the holidays, especially Christmas. Use plenty of fresh ground ginger (buy a new bottle every 6 to 9 months) to get the most out of its concentrated hot and fiery flavor. The combination of the Guinness and ginger is fantastic. Some Guinness leftover in the bottle? Drizzle it over vanilla ice cream.

²/₃ cup unsalted butter, softened
1¹/₃ cups firmly packed light brown sugar
3 large eggs
2¹/₃ cups all-purpose flour
1¹/₂ teaspoons baking powder
¹/₄ teaspoon baking soda
2 teaspoons ground ginger
1 teaspoon ground cinnamon
¹/₄ teaspoon ground cloves
¹/₄ teaspoon ground nutmeg
¹/₂ teaspoon sea salt
1¹/₂ cups stout, such as Guinness
1 cup golden raisins
1 cup chopped walnuts
¹/₂ cup chopped candied or crystallized ginger
3 cups water

FOR SERVING:

2 cups cold heavy cream
3 tablespoons sifted powdered sugar
1¹/₂ teaspoons vanilla extract, or ³/₄ teaspoon orange oil, or 1 teaspoon orange extract

1. Generously butter or coat with a butter-flavored cooking spray a 1¹/₂-quart (6-cup) pudding mold with clip-on lid.
2. In a large bowl, using an electric mixer at medium speed, cream the butter and brown sugar together until light and fluffy. Add the eggs one at a time, beating well after each addition. In a medium bowl, combine the flour, baking powder, baking soda, spices, and salt. Add alternately with the stout on low speed to the butter mixture until evenly moistened. Gently fold in the raisins, walnuts, and chopped ginger. Scrape the batter into the mold, filling it no more than two-thirds full. Snap on the lid.
3. Place a trivet and steamer rack in a 5- to 7-quart pressure cooker. Add the water. Set the mold on the rack, centered so it won't tip.
4. Close and lock the lid. Set the burner heat to high. When the cooker reaches HIGH pressure, reduce the burner heat as low as you can and still maintain HIGH pressure. Set a timer to cook for 45 minutes.
5. Meanwhile, using clean, dry beaters, whip the cream until just thickened; add the confectioners' sugar and vanilla. Beat until soft peaks are formed. Refrigerate, covered, until serving.
6. Remove the pot from the theat. Open the cooker with the Natural Release method; let stand for 15 minutes. Be careful of the steam as you open the lid. Wearing oven mitts, carefully lift the mold out of the cooker by the lid handles to a wire rack. Remove the cover and let cool for about 20 minutes. Place a plate on top of the mold and invert to unmold the pudding.
7. Serve the pudding in slices still warm or at room temperature, with spoonfuls of the whipped cream. Pass the extra whipped cream separately.

STEAMED PUDDING IN THE PRESSURE COOKER

Steamed pudding is a cross between cake and bread. They are moist, dense, sweet, and sometimes have an accompanying sauce. Traditionally they are baked in flowerpot-like ceramic bowls, known as English china pudding molds or basins, or decorative tin molds.

The technique for steaming is simple. The mold is buttered and never filled past two-thirds to allow for expansion. Snap on the lid and lower it onto the trivet in the water.

The mold is of paramount importance here. It has to fit in the pressure cooker, so it must be more tall and narrow, and is should have a lid. You can find them online in 3-, 4-, and 6-cup capacities. You can also use lidded kugelhopf tube molds. Our recipes use a 4- or 6-cup mold; if you have a 3-cup mold, cut the recipe in half. If your mold doesn't have a lid, cover it with heavy-duty aluminum foil and secure it in place with a rubber band.

Lemon and Vanilla Yogurt Cheesecake

Makes 1 (7-inch) cheesecake; serves 6 • Cooker: 5- to 7-quart • Time: 20 minutes at HIGH pressure

This is your basic cheesecake, deli style. The citrus and vanilla are complementary spring flavors. Use Meyer lemons if you have them. Serve with sliced fresh berries or berry sauce poured over the top.

$3/4$ cup graham cracker crumbs or biscotti cookie crumbs
3 tablespoons unsalted butter, melted
$1/2$ cup plus 1 tablespoon sugar
Sea salt
2 cups water
4 (3-ounce) packages cream cheese, at room temperature
1 tablespoon cornstarch
2 large eggs
1 tablespoon fresh lemon juice (from 1 lemon)
1 teaspoon grated lemon zest (organic lemon, please)
2 teaspoons vanilla extract
1 cup plain Greek yogurt
Our Berry Sauce, for serving (recipe on page 540)

1. Make the crust. In a medium bowl, mix the crumbs with the melted butter, 1 tablespoon of the sugar and a pinch of salt. Wrap the bottom of a 7-inch-diameter, 3-inch-deep springform pan with heavy-duty aluminum foil. Coat the inside of the pan with nonstick cooking spray. Press the crumbs over the bottom and 1 inch up the side. Chill in the freezer 30 minutes.

2. Place a trivet in a 5- to 7-quart pressure cooker. Add the water. Cut a piece of heavy-duty aluminum foil about 2 feet long. Fold in half twice lengthwise to create a strip to move the pan in and out of the pot.

3. Make the filling. In a stand mixer fitted with the paddle attachment, combine the cream cheese with the cornstarch, remaining $1/2$ cup sugar, and $1/4$ teaspoon salt. Beat at medium-high speed until smooth, about 2 minutes. Scrape down the sides of the bowl and add the eggs, lemon juice and zest, and vanilla. Beat at medium speed until blended. Add the yogurt and beat until smooth. Pour the batter over the crust in the springform pan. Tap the pan on the countertop to break any large air bubbles. Tightly cover the pan with foil that has been buttered or sprayed with nonstick cooking spray to prevent sticking, pinching the edges to seal. Leave some room for expansion.

4. Set the pan on the center of the foil sling, pressing the foil strip up against the sides. Pull the ends of both sides as handles. You can scrunch them for an easier grip. Set the foil-wrapped pan on the trivet, slowly lowering it into the pot. Loosely fold the foil ends over the pan.

5. Close and lock the lid. Set the burner heat to high. When the cooker reaches HIGH pressure, reduce the burner heat as low as you can and still maintain HIGH pressure. Set a timer to cook for 20 minutes.

6. Remove the pot from the heat. Open the cooker with the Natural Release method; let stand for 15 minutes. Be careful of the steam as you remove the lid. Using the handles, lift the pan out of the pressure cooker and place on a wire rack. Remove all the foil. If there is a small pool of condensed water in the middle of the cake, blot it up gently with a paper towel. Cool to room temperature on the rack, about 1 hour.

7. Cover the cheesecake with plastic wrap and refrigerate until chilled, at least 4 hours or overnight.

8. To serve, heat a sharp, thin-bladed knife under hot water; dry the knife by wiping with a clean dish cloth. Carefully run the knife around the edge of the cheesecake. Release and remove the rim of the springform pan and lift the cheesecake out of the mold. Slide a metal cake spatula under the cake and remove to a serving platter. Cut into wedges and serve with berry sauce. It will keep, wrapped in plastic, in the refrigerator up to 3 days and in the freezer up to 3 months.

Orange or Tangerine Yogurt Cheesecake: Substitute orange or tangerine juice and zest for the lemon juice and zest. Proceed as directed.

FOUR SEASONS OF CHEESECAKES IN THE PRESSURE COOKER

There are two types of cheesecakes: New York style, which is dense and rich with cream cheese and cream (and the kind we feature here), and Italian style, which is lighter and coarser in texture and made from ricotta cheese or other soft curd cheese. Flavorings for the filling are almost infinite: lemon, vanilla, almond, chocolate, praline, mixed candied fruits, cappuccino, pumpkin, blueberry. These desserts are so popular that some restaurants make a different flavor every day for their menus.

Crumb crusts vary from crushed chocolate wafers, graham crackers, Walker's shortbread, and vanilla wafers, to gingersnaps and biscotti, or perhaps none at all, where the cheesecake bakes up into a thick outer layer to support the creamy center.

Cheesecakes are cooked in springform pans, as they are usually too delicate to be turned out like a cake. Although they look just fine plain, if we are entertaining or serving them for catering, we decorate with fancy borders of whipped cream accented with chocolate coffee beans, chopped nut brittle, chocolate shavings, miniature marzipan fruits, even chocolate-dipped fresh strawberries or a dash of gold leaf. Our all-purpose favorite tip is a large open star; it makes rosettes or swirling borders in a snap. Some cakes lend themselves well to an accompanying berry sauce or a thick layer of fruit topping.

Cheesecakes cooked in the pressure cooker come out über-creamy since the cake steams as it bakes. Baked in a 7-inch springform pan, which will fit in every size pot, the entire cook time process takes about 20 minutes, then it cools and is refrigerated to set the texture. Be sure to follow the directions exactly for wrapping the cake pan in foil, making a sling to remove the hot cheesecake from the pot, and the cook time.

Tips for Cheesecake Success

- Be sure the ingredients for the cheesecake batter are at room temperature (keep the cream cheese wrapped until you use it to prevent it from drying out while it comes to room temperature).
- Mix the batter on low speed to minimize air incorporation. Too much air mixed into the batter will cause the cheesecake to puff up and deflate during cooking, resulting in a cracked top.
- Cheesecake will jiggle a bit in the center when removed from the pressure cooker; that's okay because it will continue to cook for a bit from residual heat. The internal temperature in the center of the cheesecake should reach about 150° F.
- Cheesecakes aren't firm enough to cut until they are completely chilled—overnight is best.
- Cheesecakes will absorb lingering odors from the fridge, so be sure to cover it tightly.
- For tidy looking slices, rinse your knife with hot water and dry between each cut.

Chocolate Heaven Cheesecake with Mocha Whipped Cream

Makes 1 (7-inch) cheesecake, serves 6 • Cooker: 5- to 7-quart • Time: 20 minutes at HIGH pressure

This rich and decadent winter cheesecake is adapted from a recipe we found on the paper insert of our new 7-inch springform pan by Professional Essentials. We upgraded to a chocolate crust. Decorate and serve with the mocha-flavored whipped cream.

$^2/_3$ cup finely ground chocolate wafers
1 tablespoon plus $^1/_2$ cup sugar
2 tablespoons unsalted butter, melted, plus butter for coating pan
10 ounces semisweet chocolate, chopped
2 cups water
2 (8-ounce) packages cream cheese, at room temperature
2 large eggs
2 teaspoons vanilla extract
Mocha Whipped Cream, for serving (recipe on page 540)

1. Make the crust. In a medium bowl, mix the crumbs, 1 tablespoon of the sugar, and melted butter until all the crumbs are moistened. Wrap the bottom and halfway up the side of a 7-inch-diameter, 3-inch-deep springform pan with heavy-duty aluminum foil. Coat the inside of the pan with butter. Press the crumbs over the bottom and 1 inch up the side. Chill in the freezer 30 minutes.

2. Meanwhile, melt the chocolate in the top of a double boiler over simmering water or in a microwave (see page 530). Stir until smooth; let cool.

3. Set a trivet in a 5- to 7-quart pressure cooker. Add the water. Cut a piece of heavy-duty aluminum foil about 2 feet long. Fold in half twice lengthwise to create a strip to move the pan in and out of the pot.

4. Make the filling. In a stand mixer fitted with the paddle attachment, combine the cream cheese and remaining $^1/_2$ cup sugar. Beat at medium-high speed until smooth, about 2 minutes. Scrape down the sides of the bowl and add the eggs, one at a time, beating well on medium speed after each. Add the vanilla and chocolate, and beat until smooth. Pour the batter over the crust in the springform pan. Tap the pan on the countertop to break any large air bubbles. Tightly cover the pan with foil that has been buttered or coated with nonstick cooking spray to prevent sticking, pinching the edges to seal. Leave some room for expansion.

5. Set the pan on the center of the foil sling, pressing the foil strip up against the sides. Pull the ends of both sides as handles. You can scrunch them for an easier grip. Set the foil-wrapped pan on the trivet, slowly lowering it into the pot. Loosely fold the foil ends over the pan.

6. Close and lock the lid. Set the burner heat to high. When the cooker reaches HIGH pressure, reduce the burner heat as low as you can and still maintain HIGH pressure. Set a timer to cook for 20 minutes.

7. Remove the pot from the heat. Open the cooker with the Natural Release method; let stand for 15 minutes. Be careful of the steam as you remove the lid. Using the foil handles, lift the pan out of the pressure cooker to a wire rack. Remove all the foil. If there is a small pool of condensed water in the middle of the cake, blot it up gently with a paper towel. Cool to room temperature on the rack, about 1 hour.

8. Cover the cheesecake with plastic wrap and refrigerate until chilled, at least 4 hours or overnight.

9. To serve, heat a sharp, thin-bladed knife under hot water; dry the knife by wiping with a clean dishcloth. Carefully run the knife around the edge of the cheesecake. Release and remove the rim of the springform pan and lift the cheesecake out of the mold. Slide a metal cake spatula under the cake and remove to a serving platter. Cut into wedges and serve with the Mocha Whipped Cream. It will keep, wrapped in plastic, in the refrigerator up to 3 days and in the freezer up to 3 months.

Chocolate Chip Chocolate Heaven Cheesecake: Add $^1/_2$ cup (3 ounces) miniature semisweet chocolate chips in Step 3, mixing in with the vanilla and melted chocolate. Proceed as directed.

Margarita Cheesecake with Pretzel Crust

Makes 1 (7-inch) cheesecake; serves 6 • Cooker: 5- to 7-quart • Time: 20 minutes at HIGH pressure

This is a cheesecake for summer entertaining. It is adapted from one by Martha Stewart that uses some of the most complementary of flavors. A pretzel crust? Positively addictive. Keep one of those miniature airplane-size bottles of tequila in the liquor cabinet just for this cheesecake if you are not a tequila drinker. We like it with a cherry sauce on top!

3 ounces salted pretzels (regular or gluten-free brand)
2 tablespoons unsalted butter, melted
2 tablespoons plus 1/2 cup sugar
Sea salt
4 (3-ounce) packages cream cheese, at room temperature
1 tablespoon cornstarch
2 large eggs
2 tablespoons orange liqueur, such as Grand Marnier or Triple Sec
2 teaspoons grated lime zest
2 teaspoons tequila
3/4 cup sour cream
2 cups water
Dark Sweet Cherry Sauce, for serving (recipe on page 540)

1. Make the crust. In a food processor, pulse the pretzels into fine crumbs. In a small bowl, mix with the melted butter and 2 tablespoons of the sugar until the crumbs are evenly moistened. Wrap the bottom of a 7-inch-diameter, 3-inch-deep springform pan with heavy-duty aluminum foil. Coat the inside of the pan with nonstick cooking spray. Press the crumbs over the bottom and 1 inch up the side. Chill in the freezer 30 minutes.
2. Set a trivet in a 5- to 7-quart pressure cooker. Add the water. Cut a piece of heavy-duty aluminum foil about 2 feet long. Fold in half twice lengthwise to create a strip to move the pan in and out of the pot.
3. Make the filling. In a stand mixer fitted with the paddle attachment, combine the cream cheese with the cornstarch and remaining 1/2 cup sugar. Beat at medium-high speed until smooth, about

2 minutes. Scrape down the sides and add the eggs, liqueur, lime zest, and tequila. Beat at medium speed until blended. Add the sour cream and beat until smooth. Pour the batter over the crust in the springform pan. Tap the pan on the countertop to break any large air bubbles. Tightly cover the pan with foil that has been buttered or coated with nonstick cooking spray to prevent sticking, pinching the edges to seal. Leave some room for expansion.
4. Set the pan on the center of the foil sling, pressing the foil strip up against the sides. Pull the ends of both sides as handles. You can scrunch them for an easier grip. Set the foil-wrapped pan on the trivet, slowly lowering it into the pot. Loosely fold the foil ends over the pan.
5. Close and lock the lid. Set the burner heat to high. When the cooker reaches HIGH pressure, reduce the burner heat as low as you can and still maintain HIGH pressure. Set a timer to cook for 20 minutes.
6. Remove the pot from the heat. Open the cooker with the Natural Release method; let stand for 15 minutes. Be careful of the steam as you remove the lid. Using the foil handles, lift the pan out of the pressure cooker to a wire rack. Remove all the foil. If there is a small pool of condensed water in the middle of the cake, blot it up gently with a paper towel. Cool to room temperature on the rack, about 1 hour.
7. Cover the cheesecake with plastic wrap and refrigerate until chilled, at least 4 hours or overnight.
8. To serve, heat a sharp, thin-bladed knife under hot water; dry the knife by wiping with a clean dish cloth. Carefully run the knife around the edge of the cheesecake. Release and remove the rim of the springform pan and lift out the cheesecake. Slide a metal cake spatula under the cake and remove to a serving platter. Cut into wedges and serve with a spoonful of the sauce. It will keep, wrapped in plastic, in the refrigerator up to 3 days and in the freezer up to 3 months.

Pumpkin Cheesecake with White Chocolate Chantilly

Makes 1 (7-inch) cheesecake; serves 6 • Cooker: 5- to 7-quart • Time: 20 minutes at HIGH pressure

This is our fall cheesecake. It is ravishingly good. Don't miss the white chocolate whipped cream garnish, which is so delicious and a counterpoint to the rich cheesecake texture.

²/₃ cup gingersnap cookie crumbs (15 to 18 cookies)

2 tablespoons unsalted butter, melted

4 (3-ounce) packages cream cheese, at room temperature

¹/₂ cup sugar

1 tablespoon cornstarch

¹/₂ teaspoon ground cinnamon

¹/₂ teaspoon ground ginger

¹/₄ teaspoon ground cloves

¹/₄ teaspoon ground nutmeg

¹/₂ cup pumpkin puree (not pumpkin pie filling)

1 tablespoon maple syrup

2 large eggs

2 cups water

White Chocolate Chantilly, for serving (recipe on page 540)

1. Make the crust. In a medium bowl, mix the crumbs and melted butter until all the crumbs are moistened. Wrap the bottom of a 7-inch-diameter, 3-inch-deep springform pan with heavy-duty aluminum foil. Coat the inside of the pan with nonstick cooking spray. Press the crumbs over the bottom and 1 inch up the side. Chill in the freezer 30 minutes.

2. Place a trivet in a 5- to 7-quart pressure cooker. Add the water. Cut a piece of heavy-duty aluminum foil about 2 feet long. Fold in half twice lengthwise to create a strip to move the pan in and out of the pot.

3. Make the filling. In a stand mixer fitted with the paddle attachment, combine the cream cheese, sugar, and cornstarch. Beat at medium-high speed until smooth, about 2 minutes. Scrape down the sides and add the spices, pumpkin puree, maple syrup, and eggs. Beat at medium speed until blended. Pour the batter over the crust in the springform pan. Tap the pan on the countertop to break any large air bubbles.

Tightly cover the pan with foil that has been buttered or coated with nonstick cooking spray to prevent sticking, pinching the edges to seal. Leave some room for expansion.

4. Set the pan on the center of the foil sling, pressing the foil strip up against the sides. Pull the ends of both sides as handles. You can scrunch them for an easier grip. Set the foil-wrapped pan on the trivet, slowly lowering it into the pot. Loosely fold the foil ends over the pan.

5. Close and lock the lid. Set the burner heat to high. When the cooker reaches HIGH pressure, reduce the burner heat as low as you can and still maintain HIGH pressure. Set a timer to cook for 20 minutes.

6. Remove the pot from the heat. Open the cooker with the Natural Release method; let stand for 15 minutes. Be careful of the steam as you remove the lid. Using the foil handles, lift the pan out of the pressure cooker to a wire rack. Remove all the foil. If there is a small pool of condensed water in the middle of the cake, blot it up gently with a paper towel. Cool to room temperature on the rack, about 1 hour.

7. Cover the cheesecake with plastic wrap and refrigerate until chilled, at least 4 hours or overnight.

8. To serve, heat a sharp, thin-bladed knife under hot water; dry the knife by wiping with a clean dish cloth. Carefully run the knife around the edge of the cheesecake. Release and remove the rim of the springform pan and lift out the cheesecake. Slide a metal cake spatula under the cake and remove to a serving platter. Cut into wedges and serve with spoonfuls of White Chocolate Chantilly. It will keep, wrapped in plastic, in the refrigerator up to 3 days and the freezer up to 3 months.

Pumpkin-Ginger Cheesecake: Add ¹/₄ cup finely chopped crystallized ginger in Step 3 with the eggs and pumpkin. Proceed as directed.

Favorite Cheesecake Toppings

Cheesecakes become a specialty when served drizzled with a complementary homemade sweet fruit sauce or topped with a small mound of flavored whipped cream. These sauces are delightfully easy to make, can be made ahead and refrigerated the day before, and are served cold.

Our Berry Sauce

Makes about 2¹/₄ cups

2 cups fresh or frozen unsweetened strawberries, blackberries, or raspberries
2 to 3 tablespoons sugar, or to taste
2 tablespoons raspberry liqueur, such as Chambord

In a small bowl, sprinkle the berries with the sugar. Let stand 1 hour at room temperature. Pass through a sieve to remove the seeds; stir in the liqueur. Refrigerate until serving; it will keep up to 3 days.

Mocha Whipped Cream

Makes about 3¹/₂ cups

2 cups chilled heavy cream
3 tablespoons superfine sugar
1 tablespoon unsweetened cocoa powder
2 teaspoons instant espresso powder
1 teaspoon vanilla extract
¹/₈ teaspoon ground cinnamon

1. In a large chilled bowl, whisk the cream, sugar, cocoa, and instant espresso to combine. Cover and refrigerate at least 1 hour.
2. Add the vanilla and cinnamon. With an electric mixer, whip until firm peaks are formed. Use to decorate the cake immediately or dollop on individual slices.

Dark Sweet Cherry Sauce

Makes 2 cups

1 (16-ounce) package IQF pitted Bing cherries (no need to thaw)
¹/₂ cup sugar
¹/₂ cup water or cherry juice
2 tablespoons fresh lemon juice
1 tablespoon cornstarch

1. In a medium saucepan, bring the cherries, sugar, and water to a boil over medium-high heat, stirring a few times.
2. In a small bowl, with a fork, whisk the lemon juice and cornstarch together until smooth. Whisk this into the boiling cherry mixture. Return to a boil, stirring constantly to avoid scorching on the bottom. Cook until the liquid has thickened, which should take about 1 minute.
3. Remove from the heat and taste for sweetness. Allow the sauce to cool to room temperature. Refrigerate until serving; it will keep for up to 3 days.

White Chocolate Chantilly

Makes about 2¹/₂ cups

This stuff is really luscious.

1¹/₄ cups chilled heavy cream
¹/₂ teaspoon vanilla extract
3¹/₂ ounces white chocolate, chopped, or white chocolate chips, melted and tepid (80° to 84° F)

In a chilled bowl with an electric mixer, whip the cream and vanilla together until soft peaks form. On low speed, gradually pour in the tepid melted white chocolate and beat just until the chocolate is incorporated. Cover and chill until needed.

Red Wine and Vanilla Stewed Dried Fruit

Serves 8 • Cooker: 5- to 8-quart • Time: 8 minutes at HIGH pressure

Dried fruit is great stewed until nice and plump and then served at the winter buffet table with baked ham or turkey. You can also enjoy it as a topping for cottage cheese at breakfast or for ice cream, with a final dollop of whipped cream. It is one of our favorite ways to dress up a slice of pound cake or chiffon cake. Any combination of dried fruit will do. Consider apples, pears, and/or peaches in addition to what we suggest here.

3 cups Zinfandel or Merlot wine
1 cup water
³/₄ cup sugar
¹/₂ to ³/₄ vanilla bean, split in half lengthwise but left attached at the end
1 cinnamon stick
1 (12-ounce) package dried apricot halves
1 (12-ounce) package dried pitted prunes
1 (12-ounce) package dried whole Mission figs
¹/₂ cup mixed dried tart cherries and golden raisins

1. In a 5- to 8-quart pressure cooker, combine the wine, water, sugar, cinnamon stick, and vanilla bean. Bring to a boil, stirring until the sugar dissolves, then simmer for 2 minutes. Add the dried fruit and return to a boil.
2. Close and lock the lid. Set the burner heat to high. When the cooker reaches HIGH pressure, reduce the burner heat as low as you can and still maintain HIGH pressure. Set a timer to cook for 8 minutes.
3. Remove the pot from the heat. Open the cooker with the Natural Release method; let stand for 15 minutes. Be careful of the steam as you remove the lid. Remove the cinnamon stick and vanilla bean.
4. Transfer the fruit and the stewing liquid to a glass storage bowl with cover and chill at least 4 hours; it will keep for 3 to 4 days. Serve cold.

FRUIT DESSERTS IN THE PRESSURE COOKER

The pressure cooker, with its even heat source and steamy cooking environment, is the perfect vehicle for making lovely fruit desserts that are the essence of soothing simplicity.

Stewed, steamed, and poached fruit desserts are wonderful in the cooker. Poached fresh and dried fruit have a charm all their own. Depending on the type of fruit, they can be poached whole, halved, or in pieces, in water, wine, fruit juice, a sugar syrup, or a combination thereof. Be scrupulous with the timing, though; you want the fruit to retain its shape, not be reduced to puree.

You can make compote out of a single fruit or combination of two or more fruits, called a *compote composée.* They are just plain gorgeous in a serving bowl surrounded by their syrup. Or purchase a *compotier,* a special glass or porcelain raised footed bowl.

Cooked fruits are traditionally served still gently warm or room temperature the day they are made with whipped cream, but are also good cold as a garnish to vanilla cheesecake and a battery of plain old-fashioned cakes like angel food cake, sponge cake, gold cake, and pound cake.

We love simple fruit sauces like applesauce, pear sauce, and peach sauce, so we offer many recipes here. These preparations need only a few tablespoons of liquid; the fruit itself has plenty and when it breaks down in the cooking process, you get a nice, naturally thick puree of fruit. Enjoy them over ice cream, on their own, or as a delicious fruity alternative for breakfast.

Honey and Vanilla Poached Dried Pears

Serves 8 to 10 • Cooker: 5- to 7-quart • Time: 7 minutes at HIGH pressure

Pears are dried with no added sugar and are a favorite of folks with home dehydrators. Poached pears are an elegant addition to rice pudding and custard, as well as for serving alongside roast lamb, turkey, or pork. The poaching liquid can be used to drizzle over vanilla ice cream.

1¼ cups water
1 cup cream sherry
2 tablespoons sugar
2 tablespoons honey
1 cinnamon stick
2 thick lemon slices
½ vanilla bean, split
10 to 12 dried pear halves

1. In a 5- to 7-quart pressure cooker, combine the water, sherry, sugar, honey, cinnamon stick, lemon slices, and vanilla bean (first scraping the seeds out and adding them to the pot along with the bean). Bring to a boil and simmer for 2 minutes. Add the pears and return to a boil.

2. Close and lock the lid. Set the burner heat to high. When the cooker reaches HIGH pressure, reduce the burner heat as low as you can and still maintain HIGH pressure. Set a timer to cook for 7 minutes.

3. Remove the pot from the burner. Open the cooker with the Natural Release method; let stand for 15 minutes. Be careful of the steam as you remove the lid. Remove the cinnamon stick, lemon slices, and vanilla bean. You should be able to pierce the pear easily with the tip of a knife.

4. With a slotted spoon, transfer the cooked pears to a plate lined with parchment paper so they do not stick or to a glass storage bowl with a cover. Return the uncovered pressure cooker to the heat. Bring to a low boil and continue to simmer until the liquid thickens and is reduced by about a third. Pour over the poached pears. Cover and chill at least 4 hours; it will keep for 3 to 4 days. Serve warm, at room temperature, or cold, with, if you wish, its liquid or whipped cream.

Spiced Pears in Black Cherry Juice

Serves 6 • Cooker: 5- to 7-quart • Time: 2 minutes at HIGH pressure

The trick to poaching fresh pears is selecting fruit that is firm, otherwise it will turn to mush during cooking. Pears are harvested unripe, never ripened on the tree or they will become mushy. Judge ripeness by gently pressing on the neck end of the pear to see if it will yield ever so slightly. The cherry juice will color the pears a lovely pink, just like the wine-poached version but without the alcohol.

4 cups unsweetened black cherry juice
6 whole cloves
2 green cardamom pods
2 long strips orange zest
2 (4-inch) cinnamon sticks
$^3/_4$ cup granulated sugar
$^1/_4$ cup firmly packed light brown sugar
6 firm, ripe unblemished pears, such as Bartlett, Red Bartlett, Bosc, or Anjou, the stems left on, carefully peeled, and placed in lemon water to prevent discoloration

1. Pour the juice into a 5- to 7-quart pressure cooker. Add the spices and sugars. Bring to a simmer, stirring until the sugars dissolve. Add the pears to the liquid and spoon the liquid over them.
2. Close and lock the lid. Set the burner heat to high. When the cooker reaches HIGH pressure, reduce the burner heat as low as you can and still maintain HIGH pressure. Set a timer to cook for 2 minutes.
3. Remove the pot from the burner. Open the cooker with the Quick Release method. Be careful of the steam as you remove the lid.
4. Transfer the pears with a slotted spoon to a storage bowl. Set aside. Return the uncovered pressure cooker to the heat and bring to a boil over medium-high heat. Continue to boil until the liquid thickens and reduces by half. Pour the syrup over the pears and let cool completely. Refrigerate for at least 4 hours; it will keep for up to 3 days.
5. Serve the chilled pears in a dessert bowl with the syrup spooned over. Serve with a fork, knife, and dessert spoon.

Pressure-Poached Nectarines in White Wine

Serves 4 • Cooker: 5- to 7-quart • Time: 2 minutes at HIGH pressure

Serve these glistening nectarines slightly warm, at room temperature, or chilled, topped with a dollop of sweetened crème fraîche. As an accompaniment, pass a plate of plain butter cookies at the table.

2 cups Moscato or other fruity white wine
$^1/_2$ cup sugar
1 (3-inch) cinnamon stick
1 (3-inch) strip lemon zest
4 firm but ripe nectarines (about 1$^1/_4$ pounds),
   skins left on, halved, and stoned

1. In a 5- to 7-quart pressure cooker, combine the wine, sugar, cinnamon stick, and lemon zest. Cook over medium-high heat, stirring until the sugar has dissolved, about 1 minute. Carefully add the nectarine halves, cut side down, in a single layer.
2. Close and lock the lid. Set the burner heat to high. When the cooker reaches HIGH pressure, reduce the burner heat as low as you can and still maintain HIGH pressure. Set a timer to cook for 2 minutes.
3. Remove the pot from the burner. Open the cooker with the Natural Release method; let stand for 15 minutes. Be careful of the steam as you remove the lid.
4. Transfer the nectarines with a slotted spoon, cut side up, to a pie plate or other baking dish just large enough to hold them.
5. Return the uncovered pressure cooker to high heat and boil the liquid until it is reduced to 1 cup, about 5 minutes. Discard the cinnamon stick and lemon zest.
6. To serve, place 2 nectarine halves in each of 4 individual compotes or other dessert bowls and drizzle with the sauce. Serve slightly warm or chilled.

NECTARINES

The nectarine is a relative of the peach and is almost identical to it, except for its smooth skin. Its perfumed flesh poaches up juicy, sweet, and slightly tart. Store nectarines at room temperature and handle with care, as they damage easily.

Honey and Ginger-Poached Fuyu Persimmons

Serves 4 • Cooker: 5- to 7-quart • Time: 3 minutes at HIGH pressure

Fuyu persimmons are usually eaten raw, chopped in fruit salads. Unlike their over-the-top-sweet cousin the Hachiya, the Fuyu persimmon is delicately flavored. Here they're poached and can be used as a garnish for custard or plain gold cake, or served chilled with whipped cream.

1¼ cups water
3 tablespoons honey or agave nectar
1 (3-inch) cinnamon stick
3 slices fresh ginger
¼ teaspoon ground allspice
¼ teaspoon ground ginger
4 Fuyu persimmons

1. In a 5- to 7-quart pressure cooker, combine the water, honey, cinnamon stick, ginger slices, allspice, and ground ginger. Cook over medium-high heat, stirring until the sugar has dissolved, about 1 minute.

2. Cut the stem end tops off the persimmons. Peel and slice the fruits in half horizontally. Carefully add the persimmon halves, cut side down, in a single layer in the pressure cooker.

3. Close and lock the lid. Set the burner heat to high. When the cooker reaches HIGH pressure, reduce the burner heat as low as you can and still maintain HIGH pressure. Set a timer to cook for 3 minutes.

4. Remove the pot from the burner. Open the cooker with the Natural Release method; let stand for 15 minutes. Be careful of the steam as you remove the lid.

5. Transfer the persimmons with a slotted spoon, cut side up, to a pie plate or other rimmed baking dish just large enough to hold them. Return the uncovered pressure cooker to high heat and boil the poaching liquid for a few minutes to concentrate the flavor. Remove the cinnamon stick and ginger slices, and discard. Spoon the warm sauce over the persimmons. Let cool at least 10 minutes.

6. Serve the persimmons slightly warm, or cover and refrigerate. To serve, place 2 persimmon halves in each of 4 dessert bowls and drizzle with the sauce.

Apple and Wine-Poached Fresh Figs with Raspberries

Serves 3 to 4 • Cooker: 5- to 7-quart • Time: 1 minute at HIGH pressure

The fig tree was brought to the New World along with the grape by the Spanish. Use the pale Calimyrna or the dark purple Mission fig. The figs will soften in hot apple juice syrup and turn a lovely mahogany.

2 cups unsweetened apple juice
$^1/_2$ cup dry white wine or water
$^2/_3$ cup sugar
1 cinnamon stick
3 whole cloves
2 (3-inch) strips lemon zest
Juice of 1 lemon
9 firm, ripe fresh figs (about 1 pound)
$^1/_2$ pint fresh raspberries or IQF raspberries (no need to thaw)

1. In a 5- to 7-quart pressure cooker, combine the apple juice, wine, sugar, cinnamon stick, cloves, and lemon zest and juice. Bring to a boil over medium-high heat, uncovered, stirring occasionally, until the sugar has dissolved and syrup is reduced slightly, about 5 minutes.
2. Trim a small piece from the bottom of each fig so they stand up straight. Remove stems and score a $^1/_4$-inch-deep "X" into the top of each fig. Add the whole figs in a single layer to the poaching liquid.
3. Close and lock the lid. Set the burner heat to high. When the cooker reaches HIGH pressure, reduce the burner heat as low as you can and still maintain HIGH pressure. Set a timer to cook for 1 minute.
4. Remove the pot from the burner. Open the cooker with the Natural Release method; let stand for 15 minutes. Be careful of the steam as you remove the lid.
5. Gently transfer the figs with a slotted spoon to a glass or ceramic bowl. Let the poaching liquid cool. Pour the liquid over the figs and add the raspberries. Cover and refrigerate at least 30 minutes before serving chilled.

Madeira-Poached Fresh Cherries with Honeyed Mascarpone

Serves 4 • Cooker: 5- to 7-quart • Time: 3 minutes at HIGH pressure

The cherry season is short, so we say, make the most of it. This can be served as is or used as a filling for crepes or a topping for ice cream. Sweet sherry, Marsala, and Madeira can be used interchangeably here; the flavors are different, but they share the same intensity and will all work in this recipe. Warn your diners that the cherries still have their pits.

$2^1/_4$ cups Madeira wine
$^3/_4$ cup water
$^3/_4$ cup sugar
2 (3-inch) strips orange zest
1 tablespoon orange juice
2 pounds sweet cherries (about 5 cups), stemmed
1 cup mascarpone cheese
2 tablespoons honey

1. In a 5- to 7-quart pressure cooker, combine the wine, water, sugar, and orange zest and juice. Bring to a boil over medium-high heat, stirring until the sugar has dissolved, about 1 minute. Add the cherries.
2. Close and lock the lid. Set the burner heat to high. When the cooker reaches HIGH pressure, reduce the burner heat as low as you can and still maintain HIGH pressure. Set a timer to cook for 3 minutes.
3. Remove the pot from the burner. Open the cooker with the Natural Release method; let stand for 15 minutes. Be careful of the steam as you remove the lid. The cherries should be tender. Transfer them with a slotted spoon to a glass or ceramic bowl. Pour the liquid over the cherries. Let cool at least 10 minutes. Cover and refrigerate at least 30 minutes.
4. In a small bowl, combine the mascarpone with the honey. Cover and chill until serving. Serve the cherries and syrup in bowls or stemmed glasses, topped with a large dollop of the mascarpone.

Madeira-Poached Fresh Plums with Honeyed Mascarpone: Substitute $1^1/_2$ pounds (about 10) fresh small to medium red plums, such as Santa Rosa, for the cherries. Cook them whole with their skins on. Cook time is the same.

Fresh Kumquat Compote with Strawberries and Crystallized Ginger

Serves 3 to 4 • Cooker: 5- to 7-quart • Time: 5 minutes at HIGH pressure

Kumquats are like oval oranges the size of an olive. You eat them whole—peel and all—usually raw in salads, but they also make a marvelous summer compote with fresh strawberries.

2 cups Lillet Blanc
1/2 cup water
2/3 cup sugar
2 tablespoons honey
3 tablespoons minced crystallized ginger
1 cinnamon stick
Seeds from 6 green cardamom pods, seeds crushed
    with a mortar and pestle
2 (3-inch) strips lemon zest
12 to 14 ounces kumquats, thinly sliced and seeded
1/2 pint fresh strawberries, hulled and sliced

1. In a 5- to 7-quart pressure cooker, combine the Lillet, water, sugar, honey, ginger, cinnamon stick, cardamom seeds, and lemon zest and juice. Bring to a boil, uncovered, over medium-high heat and cook, stirring occasionally, until the sugar has dissolved and syrup is reduced slightly, about 3 minutes. Add the kumquats.

2. Close and lock the lid. Set the burner heat to high. When the cooker reaches HIGH pressure, reduce the burner heat as low as you can and still maintain HIGH pressure. Set a timer to cook for 5 minutes.

3. Remove the pot from the burner. Open the cooker with the Natural Release method; let stand for 15 minutes. Be careful of the steam as you remove the lid. The kumquats should be translucent. Gently transfer the compote to a glass or ceramic bowl. Discard the cinnamon stick and zest. Cool to room temperature.

4. When cool, stir in the strawberries. Cover and refrigerate at least 30 minutes before serving chilled.

LILLET BLANC

Lillet Blanc is a fruity aperitif wine that combines a wine from the Bordeaux region of France with bitter orange peel from Haiti and cinchona bark (quinine) from Peru. It became popular in the Roaring Twenties and has experienced a revival, set off by its use in the Vesper martini ordered by James Bond in *Casino Royale*. It makes a great poaching liquid for the kumquats.

Biscotti-Stuffed Peaches

Serves 6 • Cooker: 5- to 7-quart • Time: 2 minutes at HIGH pressure

Peaches steamed over sparkling Prosecco wine are divine. You will need a steamer basket for this recipe. You can use stale biscotti in this recipe. These are delicious topped with a scoop of gelato or whole-milk ricotta.

3 large firm, ripe peaches, peeled, cut in half and stoned
1 cup Prosecco
3 tablespoons sugar
2 long strips lemon zest
1$^1/_2$ cups crumbled almond biscotti cookies (6 to 7 cookies depending on size)
3 tablespoons unsalted butter, melted

1. With the large end of a melon baller, dig out a bit more space around the pit for the filling.
2. In a 5- to 7-quart pressure cooker, combine the wine, sugar, and lemon zest. Place a trivet and steamer basket in the cooker. Bring to a boil over medium-high heat, stirring until the sugar has dissolved, about 1 minute.
3. In a small bowl, combine the crumbs and melted butter, mixing until the crumbs are evenly moistened. Divide the filling among the 6 peach halves, mounding it slightly. Gently arrange the stuffed peaches side by side in the steamer basket, then set the basket in the pressure cooker.
4. Close and lock the lid. Set the burner heat to high. When the cooker reaches HIGH pressure, reduce the burner heat as low as you can and still maintain HIGH pressure. Set a timer to cook for 2 minutes.
5. Remove the pot from the burner. Open the cooker with the Quick Release method. Be careful of the steam as you remove the lid. Remove the steamer basket from the cooker. Carefully transfer the peaches to a plate to cool.
6. Return the uncovered pressure cooker to medium-high heat, bring the liquid to a boil, and let continue to boil until reduced by a third if you want to use the syrup.
7. Serve the peaches with a tablespoonful of syrup pooled on the plate and a peach half on top. Serve with a fork and knife.

Our Homemade Cinnamon Applesauce

Makes 4 cups • Cooker: 5- to 7-quart • Time: 2 minutes at HIGH pressure

Making applesauce in a pressure cooker takes mere minutes. You can use all of one type of apple, like a firm cooking apple, or a combination of tart and softer sweet apples. Applesauce makes a great quick dessert or snack, or served with yogurt or cottage cheese, breakfast. It is even good slathered on buttered toast or served warm over waffles.

2¹⁄₂ to 3 pounds apples (6 to 7 large apples),
    peeled, cored, and cut into wedges or chunks
¹⁄₄ cup firmly packed brown sugar
1¹⁄₂ teaspoons ground cinnamon
1 cup unsweetened apple juice, apple cider, or
    water
1 tablespoon fresh lemon juice

1. In a 5- to 7-quart pressure, combine all the ingredients.
2. Close and lock the lid. Set the burner heat to high. When the cooker reaches HIGH pressure, reduce the burner heat as low as you can and still maintain HIGH pressure. Set a timer to cook for 2 minutes.
3. Remove the pot from the burner. Open the cooker with the Natural Release method; let stand for 15 minutes. Be careful of the steam as you remove the lid.
4. With a wooden spoon or potato masher, briskly stir or crush the apples, breaking up large chunks, until you achieve the desired consistency. You can leave some chunks for a rustic texture. If you like a very smooth applesauce, puree it right in the pot with an immersion blender. Use immediately or let cool completely and store in an airtight container in the refrigerator up to 5 days or in the freezer up to 1 month.

Our Homemade Cinnamon-Apricot Applesauce: Add ³⁄₄ cup chopped dried apricots in Step 1. If the apricots are very dry, soak for 1 to 2 hours in water, then drain and add to the apples.

IMPORTANT TIPS FOR MAKING APPLESAUCE IN THE PRESSURE COOKER

Manufacturers of old warned against preparing applesauce in the pressure cooker. We make it without a problem in the spring top pressure cooker, with the following caveats:

• Do not fill the cooker more than halfway.
• Stay nearby and listen while you are cooking. If the steam stops escaping or there is any other sound change, immediately turn off the stove and let the cooker cool by the Natural Release method (NOT the Quick Release method). Open it carefully once the pressure has fully released. Finish the applesauce by simmering it gently on the stove conventionally, with the lid off.
• Clean the vent carefully after use and visually inspect it to make sure it is clear before using the pressure cooker again.

Beth's Natural Applesauce

Makes 8 cups • Cooker: 6- to 8-quart • Time: 4 minutes at HIGH pressure

For those who don't want or need sugar in their applesauce, and like lots of cinnamon, this is the recipe. Check the produce department and see what apples look good to you. The base should always be Granny Smith. If you have some extra fruit around, like a few over-ripe pears or apricots, 1 or 2 peaches, or berries, go ahead and toss them in with the apples.

2^1/$_2$ to 3 pounds Granny Smith apples (6 to 7 large apples), peeled, cored, and cut into wedges or chunks

2^1/$_2$ to 3 pounds red apples like McIntosh or Fuji (6 to 7 large apples), peeled, cored, and cut into wedges or chunks

2 teaspoons ground cinnamon or apple pie spice

^{3}/$_4$ cup water

2 tablespoons fresh lemon juice or organic cider vinegar

^{1}/$_4$ cup (^{1}/$_2$ stick) unsalted butter, cut into pieces

1. In a 6- to 8-quart pressure cooker, combine the apples, cinnamon, and water.
2. Close and lock the lid. Set the burner heat to high. When the cooker reaches HIGH pressure, reduce the burner heat as low as you can and still maintain HIGH pressure. Set a timer to cook for 4 minutes.
3. Remove the pot from the heat. Open the cooker with the Natural Release method; let stand for 15 minutes. Be careful of the steam as you remove the lid.
4. Mash the apples with a potato masher or pulse with an immersion blender until you achieve the desired consistency. You can leave some chunks for a rustic texture. Stir in the lemon juice and butter until the butter melts. Use immediately or let cool completely and store in an airtight container in the refrigerator up to 5 days or in the freezer up to 1 month.

APPLES FOR APPLESAUCE

The best apples to use for applesauce are tart cooking apples like Golden Delicious, Granny Smith, Rome Beauty, McIntosh, Macon, Winesap, Fuji, Haralson, Jonathan, and Greening.

Pink Cranberry Applesauce

Makes 6 cups • Cooker: 6- to 8-quart • Time: 3 minutes at HIGH pressure

Apples belong to the Rose family, which includes some very familiar fruits, including apricots, plums, cherries, peaches, pears, and raspberries. All of them can be added in a small proportion to the apples in this recipe to vary the flavor. The applesauce will be slightly colored if you don't peel the apples and include the dried cranberries. This is a good time to buy a bag of apples rather then select them individually (they are usually small to medium sized). Delicious!

4 pounds apples (8 to 10 large apples), peeled or
    unpeeled, cored, and cut into wedges or chunks
1³/₄ cups dried cranberries
2 teaspoons ground cinnamon
²/₃ cup water
Juice of 1 lemon

1. In a 6- to 8-quart pressure cooker, combine the ingredients.
2. Close and lock the lid. Set the burner heat to high. When the cooker reaches HIGH pressure, reduce the burner heat as low as you can and still maintain HIGH pressure. Set a timer to cook for 3 minutes.
3. Remove the pot from the heat. Open the cooker with the Natural Release method; let stand for 15 minutes. Be careful of the steam as you remove the lid.
4. With an immersion blender, pulse until you have the consistency you prefer; it is okay if there are bits of the cranberries. Use immediately or let cool completely and store in an airtight container in the refrigerator up to 5 days or in the freezer up to 1 month.

Peachy Pink Applesauce: Add 4 ripe peaches, peeled, stoned, and chopped, in Step 1 with the apples. Reduce the cranberries to 1 cup.

Plum Good Applesauce

Makes 5 cups • Cooker: 5- to 7-quart • Time: 2 minutes at HIGH pressure

Plums are great paired with apples. They come in various sizes and shapes and the best for cooking have black or red skin and flesh. When selecting fruit, ripe plums will feel soft when given a gentle squeeze.

2 pounds apples (4 to 5 large apples), peeled,
    cored, and cut into wedges or chunks
10 medium red or black plums (1¹/₄ to 1¹/₂
    pounds), cut in half, stoned, and sliced or
    chopped
¹/₂ cup water
¹/₃ cup sugar
Grated zest and juice of 1 lemon
2 to 3 tablespoons orange marmalade (optional,
    but oh so good)

1. In a 5- to 7-quart pressure cooker, combine the apples, plums, water, sugar, and lemon juice and zest.
2. Close and lock the lid. Set the burner heat to high. When the cooker reaches HIGH pressure, reduce the burner heat as low as you can and still maintain HIGH pressure. Set a timer to cook for 2 minutes.
3. Remove the pot from the heat. Open the cooker with the Natural Release method; let stand for 15 minutes. Be careful of the steam as you remove the lid.
4. With an immersion blender, puree the sauce in pot to the thick and chunky or smooth consistency you prefer. If using, stir in the marmalade while the sauce is still hot. Use immediately or let cool completely and store in an airtight container in the refrigerator up to 5 days or in the freezer up to 1 month.

Spice-Scented Pineapple Guava Applesauce

Makes 4 cups • Cooker: 5- to 7-quart • Time: 1 minute at HIGH pressure

Applesauce provides a marvelous background for other fruits. Here we pair it up with the pineapple guava, or feijoa, a fruit grown in California, Texas, and Florida that looks like a green egg.

2 pounds apples (4 to 5 large apples), peeled, cored, and cut into wedges or chunks
2 dozen pineapple guavas, cut in half and fruit scooped out with a teaspoon
$^1/_3$ cup sugar
$^2/_3$ cup water
2 cinnamon sticks
3 green cardamom pods, crushed
$^1/_2$ vanilla bean, split

1. In a 5- to 7-quart pressure cooker, combine the ingredients.
2. Close and lock the lid. Set the burner heat to high. When the cooker reaches HIGH pressure, reduce the burner heat as low as you can and still maintain HIGH pressure. Set a timer to cook for 1 minute.
3. Remove the pot from the heat. Open the cooker with the Natural Release method; let stand for 15 minutes. Be careful of the steam as you remove the lid.
4. Remove the spices and discard. Use a potato masher, wooden spoon, or immersion blender to crush or puree the sauce to the consistency you prefer. Use immediately or let cool completely and store in an airtight container in the refrigerator up to 5 days or in the freezer up to 1 month.

PINEAPPLE GUAVA

The flesh of this egg-shaped fruit has a jelly consistency and tastes delicately sweet and tart, an aromatic pineapple-papaya-piney combination. Pineapple guavas are eaten raw or used in preserves, and cook up great in applesauce. If they aren't quite ripe when you buy them, let them ripen on the counter at room temperature. When ripe, they are very fragrant and give slightly to finger pressure. You can refrigerate them for a week or two once ripe.

Applesauce with Pineapple and Berries

Makes 5 cups • Cooker: 5- to 7-quart • Time: 4 minutes at HIGH pressure

Apples have an amazing flavor affinity for berries and pineapple. Add sugar to taste, especially if you use fresh pineapple, as the sweetness of a fresh pineapple varies from fruit to fruit.

3 pounds apples (6 to 7 large apples), peeled, cored, and cut into wedges or chunks

1 cup fresh or IQF (no need to thaw) blueberries or halved strawberries

1 (4-ounce) can crushed pineapple in juice or 1 cup finely chopped peeled fresh pineapple

³/₄ cup water

¹/₄ cup granulated sugar or light brown sugar, or to taste

2 tablespoons unsalted butter

1 teaspoon ground cinnamon (optional)

1. In a 5- to 7-quart pressure cooker, combine the apples, berries, pineapple, and water.
2. Close and lock the lid. Set the burner heat to high. When the cooker reaches HIGH pressure, reduce the burner heat as low as you can and still maintain HIGH pressure. Set a timer to cook for 4 minutes.
3. Remove the pot from the heat. Open the cooker with the Natural Release method; let stand for 15 minutes. Be careful of the steam as you remove the lid.
4. Stir in the sugar, adding it to taste, particularly if you're using fresh pineapple. Stir in the butter until melted. Add the cinnamon if using. With an immersion blender, puree the sauce in the pot to the consistency you prefer. Use immediately or let cool completely and store in an airtight container in the refrigerator up to 5 days or in the freezer up to 1 month.

Apple-Pear Sauce with Honey

Makes 5 cups • Cooker: 6- to 8-quart • Time: 2 minutes at HIGH pressure

The combination of aromatic apples and pears is pure comfort food. You can use Bartlett, Comice, Seckel, or Anjou (Green or Red); all are naturally juicy. The honey adds a flavor dimension, but it is optional. The pears are sweet enough as they contain lots of natural sugar, more than any other fruit. Cut the apples first, then the pears, because the pears will brown faster.

2¹/₂ pounds Granny Smith apples (6 large apples), peeled, cored, and cut into wedges or chunks
2¹/₂ pounds pears (6 to 7 pears), peeled, cored, and cut into wedges or chunks
1 cup water
¹/₄ cup honey or agave syrup (optional)
3 tablespoons unsalted butter

1. In a 6- to 8-quart pressure cooker, combine the apples, pears, and water.
2. Close and lock the lid. Set the burner heat to high. When the cooker reaches HIGH pressure, reduce the burner heat as low as you can and still maintain HIGH pressure. Set a timer to cook for 2 minutes.
3. Remove the pot from the heat. Open the cooker with the Natural Release method; let stand for 15 minutes. Be careful of the steam as you remove the lid.
4. Stir in the honey if using and butter. With a wooden spoon, potato masher, or immersion blender, briskly stir, crush, or pulse the fruit until you've achieved the desired consistency. Use immediately or let cool completely and store in an airtight container in the refrigerator up to 5 days or in the freezer up to 1 month.

RIPENING PEARS

Don't worry about buying hard pears. Leave them at room temperature and they will slowly ripen from the inside out. Apply pressure to the neck at the stem end with your thumb; if it yields lightly to pressure, the pear is ready to eat. If not using that day, ripe pears can be kept refrigerated for a few days. Wash the fruits with cold water even if you plan on peeling them.

Rhubarb Applesauce

Makes 5 cups • Cooker: 5- to 7-quart • Time: 4 minutes at HIGH pressure

Rhubarb has come to our backyard gardens from the rarified altitudes of the Himalayas, where it grows with alpine flowers. Ripe rhubarb has a shiny red stem. Never eat the leaves, which contain a concentration of oxalic acid and can make you very sick. If you grow your own rhubarb, completely trim away the leaves and discard them (rhubarb is usually sold already trimmed to just the stalk).

2 pounds apples (4 to 5 large apples), peeled, cored, and cut into wedges or chunks
1 pound trimmed rhubarb stalks, cut into 1-inch pieces
1 cup water or white grape juice
3/4 cup sugar
3 tablespoons orange liqueur, such as Grand Marnier (optional)
1 teaspoon ground cinnamon (optional)

1. In a 5- to 7-quart pressure cooker, combine the apples, rhubarb, and water.
2. Close and lock the lid. Set the burner heat to high. When the cooker reaches HIGH pressure, reduce the burner heat as low as you can and still maintain HIGH pressure. Set a timer to cook for 4 minutes.
3. Remove the pot from the heat. Open the cooker with the Natural Release method; let stand for 15 minutes. Be careful of the steam as you remove the lid.
4. Stir in the sugar and liqueur if using. Taste for sweetness. Stir in the cinnamon if using. With an immersion blender, puree the sauce in the pot to the consistency you prefer. Cool to room temperature, cover, and refrigerate. Use immediately or let cool completely and store in an airtight container in the refrigerator up to 5 days or in the freezer up to 1 month.

Strawberry-Rhubarb Applesauce: Add 1 pint hulled and halved strawberries in Step 1.

Rhubarb Applesauce with Ginger: Grate a 1- to 2-inch peeled piece of fresh ginger. Add that or 1/4 cup chopped crystallized ginger in Step 1.

17

Little Foodie: Baby Food

When Julie was expecting her first child more than a quarter-century ago, her dear colleague Marcie gave her a small hand-held food grinder. It was the perfect gift and the start of a special adventure: preparing food for an appreciative and unspoiled little "consumer."

Making your own baby food is easy, efficient, and economical. Instead of spending money on prepackaged baby food, you can use fresh produce, grains, and meat that you have on hand. With the pressure cooker on your side, cooking for baby can be even faster. Best of all, you'll know exactly what you're feeding your baby and have full control over all the ingredients.

In addition to your pressure cooker, you'll also need an appliance for pureeing and food-safe storage containers to refrigerate and/or freeze extra portions.

According to the American Academy of Pediatrics, solid food should not be introduced to babies younger than 4 months. When making your own baby food, we recommend that you use organic produce and filtered or bottled water instead of tap water. Talk to your pediatrician about which solids to introduce and when.

Even though it's a good idea to get your baby accustomed to eating a wide variety of foods, it'll take time for him or her to get used to each new taste and texture. Never introduce more than one new food at a time. With each recipe, puree or mash the food based on how your baby is chewing

BEST BEGINNER FOODS FOR BABY

Vegetables
- sweet potatoes
- winter squash
- peas
- carrots
- rice and vegetables (try basmati, as it's easy to digest and flavorful)

Fruits
- pears
- avocado
- apples
- plums
- peaches
- nectarines

Meats
- chicken
- turkey
- lamb

557

MAKING BABY FOOD PUREE

- **ALWAYS** consult your pediatrician prior to beginning any new food for your infant.
- **ALWAYS** use clean hands, clean cooking utensils, counter preparation surface(s), clean pressure cooker, etc. when preparing homemade baby food.
- You can use any size pressure cooker to make a small quantity of baby food. The smallest size is 2¹/₂ quarts and works great for this purpose.

1. Cook the food by either steaming or boiling in the pressure cooker. Steaming retains the most nutrients in foods. Steaming and boiling all allow for relatively large batches of foods to be made at onc time. You will use either a steamer basket or trivet and steamer plate, or boil the food in liquid directly in the pot. Each recipe is specific as to what technique to use. DO NOT use salt or sugar. We call for filtered water.

    Choose the freshest fruits and vegetables (we recommend you use organic), and try to use what you buy in a day or two. When fresh isn't available, frozen is a fine option. Good fruits to start with include apples, apricots, bananas, blueberries, mangos, peaches, pears, plums, and prunes. Vegetables to include are asparagus tips, avocados, carrots, peas, potatoes, sweet peppers, sweet potatoes, and the array of winter squashes (try winter squash puree mashed with some cooked quinoa).

2. Transfer the cooked food to a blender, food processor, or food mill.

3. Set aside the liquid that the food was cooked in. You will need this when making the puree and adding it (instead of filtered water, for example) helps to preserve any nutrients that may have leached into the water. You may also thin with breast milk, formula, or plain filtered water.

4. With the appliance or utensil of your choice, puree the food until smooth. As you are doing this, you can add the liquid of your choice to achieve the consistency you prefer, or add no liquid at all at this point. Many parents prefer to thin the puree right before serving it to baby. You may wish to push pureed peas or green beans through a sieve or fine mesh strainer to get rid of any remaining skins or strings.

5. If you do make small batches and store in the refrigerator, please keep in mind that you should *never* feed your baby from the container and then re-store. Saliva may contaminate the food and bacteria can take root. Always take the portion you are serving out of the container and transfer to a feeding bowl.

FREEZING BABY FOOD PUREE

Plastic ice cube trays are a convenient way to freeze the puree (each cube is equivalent to 1 ounce), and now there are specially made trays with lids for baby food freezer storage. Look for Tupperware and OXO in the houseware aisle of the supermarket, where the sippy cups are sold. OXO also sells Tot Baby Blocks. Each single-portion container fits into a freezing tray and multiple trays can be stacked to save space in the freezer. These clear containers are airtight, watertight, and leak-proof and have measurement markings that make portioning a breeze. The 2-ounce size is perfect for children in the early feeding stages, and the 4-ounce size is great for a growing appetite.

Never freeze homemade baby food in glass that is not specifically labeled as "safe to freeze"; for example, old baby food jars are not meant for freezing.

Transfer the puree to your storage containers within two to three hours of making it. If you are using an ice cube tray, fill each cube with the puree, as though you were filling the tray with water to make ice cubes. If the tray does not have its own lid, cover it with plastic wrap. Repeat this process until you have filled all the trays and no puree remains. If the puree is still hot, let it cool off at room temperature before putting the trays in the freezer.

Once the cubes have frozen, you can pop them out and store them in ziptop freezer bags. Be sure to label each bag with the date of preparation and what it contains. The baby food cubes should be used within 1 to 3 months of freezing; each recipe will indicate its storage time.

When it is time to feed baby, simply take out the number of food cubes needed, thaw, and serve. **To thaw:** Set the cube(s) out on the counter to thaw until soft, or put in the microwave for 20 to 30 seconds. Make sure to check for hot spots when microwaving frozen cubes. If you are going to be out of the house at mealtime, put each food cube in a small plastic lidded container. The cubes are so small they will defrost quickly, but if you find yourself with a hungry baby and frozen food, just shake the container, holding the lid in place. The food will be thawed in moments.

Baby Pear Sauce

Makes 1¹/₂ cups or 12 (1-ounce) ice-cube tray servings • Cooker: Any size • Time: 2 minutes at HIGH pressure

This is a perfect first food for your baby and you might soon find yourself sampling it—you know, "one for baby, one for mommy." This really is delicious. To vary it, you can add 1 cup pitted fresh Bing cherries for a pear-cherry sauce, add pieces of peeled ripe mango for mango-pear sauce, or substitute apples for two of the pears for an apple-pear sauce.

4 medium pears
³/₄ cup filtered water

1. Peel and core the pears, taking care to cut out and discard any bruised parts. Discard the cores.
2. Place a trivet and steamer rack in the pressure cooker. Add the water. Arrange the pear chunks on the rack as evenly as possible.
3. Close and lock the lid. Set the burner heat to high. When the cooker reaches HIGH pressure, reduce the burner heat as low as you can and still maintain HIGH pressure. Set a timer to cook for 2 minutes at HIGH.
4. Remove the pot from the heat. Open the cooker with the Natural Release method; let stand for 15 minutes. Be careful of the steam as you remove the lid.
5. Lift out the steamer and transfer the pears to a bowl with an oversized spoon. They should be soft enough to puree them by stirring with a fork or a silicone spatula. Use or let cool completely and store in the refrigerator for 1 to 2 days or the freezer up to 3 months.

Baby Peaches

Makes 1¹/₂ cups or 12 (1-ounce) ice-cube tray servings • Cooker: Any size • Time: 1 minute at HIGH pressure

With their sunny color and warm fragrance, peaches almost scream summer. They are also a beloved baby classic. When peaches are out of season, buy frozen unsweetened sliced peaches. You don't need to thaw them and the cooking time will not change. Peaches for baby should be peeled. You can peel firm peaches with a sharp knife. With ripe, soft ones, the easier way is to dip them into a pot of boiling water for 30 seconds. The pits on freestone varieties will pop right out; cling peaches need to be cut away from the pit.

3 medium firm-ripe peaches
¹/₂ cup filtered water

1. Peel the peaches and cut into slices or 1-inch chunks, discarding the pit and any bruised parts.
2. Place a trivet and steamer rack in the pressure cooker. Add the water. Arrange the peach pieces on the rack as evenly as possible.

3. Close and lock the lid. Set the burner heat to high. When the cooker reaches HIGH pressure, reduce the burner heat as low as you can and still maintain HIGH pressure. Set a timer to cook for 1 minute at HIGH.
4. Remove the pot from the heat. Open the cooker with the Natural Release method; let stand for 15 minutes. Be careful of the steam as you remove the lid. The peaches should be soft and tender when pierced with the tip of a knife.
5. Transfer the peaches to a food processor, blender, or food mill and process to a smooth puree, adding a tablespoon or two of the steaming water if needed. Use or let cool completely and store in the refrigerator for 1 to 2 days or the freezer up to 3 months.

Baby Applesauce

Makes 1¹/₄ cups or 10 (1-ounce) ice-cube tray servings • Cooker: Any size • Time: 2 minutes at HIGH pressure

Applesauce is a favorite of all ages. When you taste this warm from your blender, you will wonder why anyone feels the need to add sugar to applesauce. The variety of apple you use is up to you, but we especially like Gravenstein, Fuji, Gala, Rome Beauty, and Golden Delicious. Use two or three different types of apples to mix and match flavors and textures if you have them. The apples cook up so soft that you don't even need an appliance to puree them—a fork or spatula works just fine. When baby is ready for new flavors, sprinkle some cinnamon over the apple chunks in the steamer before you cook them.

3 large apples
¹/₂ cup filtered water

1. Peel the apples, taking care to cut out and discard any bruised parts. Cut the apples into wedges and remove and discard the cores. Cut each wedge into 2 or 3 pieces crosswise.
2. Place a trivet and steamer rack in the pressure cooker. Add the water. Arrange the apple chunks on the rack as evenly as possible.
3. Close and lock the lid. Set the burner heat to high. When the cooker reaches HIGH pressure, reduce the burner heat as low as you can and still maintain HIGH pressure. Set a timer to cook for 2 minutes.
4. Remove the pot from the heat. Open the cooker with the Natural Release method; let stand for 15 minutes. Be careful of the steam as you remove the lid.
5. Transfer the apples to a bowl. They should be soft enough to puree them by stirring with a fork or a silicone spatula. Use or let cool completely and store in the refrigerator for 1 to 2 days or the freezer up to 3 months.

Baby Apple and Fennel Puree

Makes 2 cups or 16 (1-ounce) ice-cube tray servings • Cooker: Any size • Time: 3 minutes at HIGH pressure

A member of the same family as carrots and parsley, fennel has plenty of aroma and a gentle taste of anise. Fennel is made into a syrup to treat infants with colic, so it is good for the digestion. Serve fennel to babies over a year old and no more than once every other week. Breastfeeding moms should avoid eating fennel as it contains natural estrogens.

1 cup filtered water
2 large apples, peeled, cored, and sliced
1 medium to large fennel bulb, fronds trimmed and discarded and white bulb chopped
1 cup filtered water

1. Place a trivet and steamer rack in the pressure cooker. Add the water. Arrange the apple slices on the rack as evenly as possible, covering the rack. Arrange the chopped fennel on top.
2. Close and lock the lid. Set the burner heat to high. When the cooker reaches HIGH pressure, reduce the burner heat as low as you can and still maintain HIGH pressure. Set a timer to cook for 3 minutes.
3. Remove the pot from the heat. Open the cooker with the Quick Release method. Be careful of the steam as you remove the lid. Remove the steamer rack and transfer the fennel and apples to a food processor, blender, or food mill and puree until smooth, adding the steaming water as needed to get the consistency you prefer. Use or let cool completely and store in the refrigerator 1 to 2 days or the freezer up to 3 months.

Baby Blapple-Pear Sauce

Makes 1¹/₄ cups or 10 (1-ounce) ice-cube tray servings • Cooker: Any size • Time: 2 minutes at HIGH pressure

Applesauce lends itself to myriad seasonal variations. This one combines the familiar—apples—with the distinctive texture and haunting sweetness of pears and the fun color and supercharged nutrition of blueberries. When fresh berries aren't in season, choose unsweetened frozen ones. Select a pear that is ripe and sweet but not mushy (it is considered the perfect first fruit for baby). D'Anjou, Comice, and Bosc all work well. The crisp Asian pears are not ideal for this recipe. A dash of cinnamon is a nice addition when baby is ready for it.

1 large apple
1 large firm pear
¹/₂ cup filtered water
1 cup (¹/₂ pint) blueberries

1. Peel the apple and pear, taking care to cut out and discard any bruised parts. Cut the apple and pear into wedges and remove and discard the cores. Cut each wedge into 2 or 3 pieces crosswise.
2. Place a trivet and steamer rack in the pressure cooker. Add the water. Arrange the apple and pear chunks on the rack as evenly as possible, covering it totally, and sprinkle the blueberries on top so they don't fall into the water.
3. Close and lock the lid. Set the burner heat to high. When the cooker reaches HIGH pressure, reduce the burner heat as low as you can and still maintain HIGH pressure. Set a timer to cook for 2 minutes.
4. Remove the pot from the heat. Open the cooker with the Natural Release method; let stand for 15 minutes. Be careful of the steam as you remove the lid.
5. Lift out the steamer and transfer the fruit to a food processor, blender, or food mill and puree until smooth, adding a tablespoon or two of the steaming water if needed to get the consistency you prefer. Use or let cool completely and store in the refrigerator for 1 to 2 days or the freezer up to 3 months.

Baby Summer Orchard Sauce: Substitute 1 to 2 ripe peaches for the blueberries. Cut a small cross in the top and bottom of each one and place in a heat-proof bowl. Cover with boiling water and let stand for 30 seconds, then drain and plunge in cold water. Slip off the skins. Cut the peaches into quarters, remove the pits, and dice the flesh. Add to the apple and pears in Step 2 and pressure cook and puree as directed.

Baby Plum Puree

Makes 4 cups or 32 (1-ounce) ice-cube tray servings • Cooker: Any size • Time: 3 minutes at HIGH pressure

You can use unsweetened apple or pear juice as the poaching liquid since plums can be quite tart (the tartness is in the skin), and you will need a food mill to remove the skins after cooking. Plums mix well with apricots, apples, pears, blueberries, banana, peaches, and baby rice cereal or brown rice.

³/₄ cup unsweetened fruit juice or filtered water
6 to 8 ripe plums, such as Santa Rosa, pitted and
    halved or cut into chunks
Dash ground cinnamon or vanilla extract (optional)

1. Place a trivet and steamer rack in the pressure cooker. Add the juice. Arrange the plums on the rack as evenly as possible.
2. Close and lock the lid. Set the burner heat to high. When the cooker reaches HIGH pressure, reduce the burner heat as low as you can and still maintain HIGH pressure. Set a timer to cook for 3 minutes.
3. Remove the pot from the heat. Open the cooker with the Natural Release method; let stand for 15 minutes. Be careful of the steam as you remove the lid.
4. With an oversized spoon, transfer the fruit to a food mill set over a bowl and process to remove the skins. Add the cinnamon or vanilla, if using. Use or let cool completely and store in the refrigerator for 1 to 2 days or the freezer up to 3 months.

ALL ABOUT PLUMS

Plums are a delicate, juicy fruit, related to almonds, nectarines, and peaches, and one of the fruits on the minimal pesticide exposure list. They come in a rainbow of colors—blue, black, green, red, yellow—with flesh that is orange, pink, or yellow. Santa Rosa plums are the sweetest. Store ripe plums in the refrigerator and cook within a few days. To remove the pit, cut the fruit in half, then twist the two halves in opposite directions; they will fall apart. Remove the pit, using a paring knife, if necessary.

Baby Prune Puree

Makes 1 cup or 8 (1-ounce) ice-cube tray servings • Cooker: Any size • Time: 3 minutes at HIGH pressure

Stewed prunes aren't commonly found on breakfast menus these days but they are as popular as ever with the baby set! Prunes are nutritious, sweet on the lips, and packed with fiber, which can help keep little digestive systems on track. Prune puree is a great baby food by itself, but many parents also mix it with cereal or other fruits like apple or mango.

1 cup filtered water
1 cup pitted prunes

1. Place a trivet and steamer rack in the pressure cooker. Add the water. Arrange the prunes on the rack as evenly as possible, making sure they don't stick together.

2. Close and lock the lid. Set the burner heat to high. When the cooker reaches HIGH pressure, reduce the burner heat as low as you can and still maintain HIGH pressure. Set a timer to cook for 3 minutes.

3. Remove the pot from the heat. Open the cooker with the Natural Release method; let stand for 15 minutes. Be careful of the steam as you remove the lid.

4. Transfer the prunes to a food processor, blender, or food mill and process until smooth, adding steaming water as needed to achieve the consistency you prefer. Use or let cool completely and store in the refrigerator for 1 to 2 days or the freezer up to 3 months.

Baby Tropical Treat

Makes 1 1/2 cups or 12 (1-ounce) ice-cube tray servings • Cooker: Any size • Time: 1 minute at HIGH pressure

Bananas and peaches are common early foods for babies—some experts advise waiting till about 8 months to introduce mango. If your banana isn't quite ripe, cook it with the rest of the fruit.

1/2 cup filtered water
1 large ripe peach, peeled, pitted, and cut into
    1-inch chunks
1/2 cup peeled and pitted ripe mango chunks
1 ripe banana

1. Place a trivet and steamer rack in the pressure cooker. Add the water. Arrange the peach and mango pieces on the rack as evenly as possible.

2. Close and lock the lid. Set the burner heat to high. When the cooker reaches HIGH pressure, reduce the burner heat as low as you can and still maintain HIGH pressure. Set a timer to cook for 1 minute.

3. Remove the pot from the heat. Open the cooker with the Natural Release method; let stand for 15 minutes. Be careful of the steam as you remove the lid.

4. Lift out the steamer and transfer the fruit to a food processor, blender, or food mill. Add the banana and puree until smooth, adding a tablespoon or two of the steaming water if needed to get the consistency you prefer. Use or let cool completely and store in the refrigerator for 1 to 2 days or the freezer up to 1 month.

ALL ABOUT MANGOS

A ripe mango is fragrant and soft without being mushy. Green ones will ripen at home on the counter. If you can't find a fresh mango that looks nice, unsweetened frozen mango works well. Mangos vary widely in size, with the small Manila mangos yielding about 1/2 cup of fruit.

Soft Vegetable Puree

Makes 2 cups or 16 (1-ounce) ice-cube tray servings • Cooker: Any size • Time: 3 minutes at HIGH pressure

This recipe will work with summer squash (including zucchini), asparagus, and green beans. If your green beans are on the old side, add an extra minute cook time. You can also use frozen organic green beans. Fresh thin asparagus work best with this.

1 cup filtered water
1 pound zucchini or summer squash (ends trimmed), asparagus tips (remove fibrous stem), or green beans (ends trimmed), all cut into small pieces

1. Place a trivet and steamer rack in the pressure cooker. Add the water. Arrange the vegetable pieces on the rack as evenly as possible.
2. Close and lock the lid. Set the burner heat to high. When the cooker reaches HIGH pressure, reduce the burner heat as low as you can and still maintain HIGH pressure. Set a timer to cook for 3 minutes.
3. Remove the pot from the heat. Open the cooker with the Quick Release method. Be careful of the steam as you remove the lid.
4. Transfer the vegetable to a food processor, blender, or food mill and process until smooth, adding the steaming water as needed to achieve the consistency you prefer. Use or let cool completely and store in the refrigerator for 1 to 2 days or the freezer up to 3 months.

Baby Tuscan Green Vegetable Puree

Makes 2 cups or 16 (1-ounce) ice-cube tray servings • Cooker: Any size • Time: 2 minutes at HIGH pressure

Green vegetables are pureed, then mixed with a little tomato sauce and Parmesan to create a treat for baby with an Italian flair. You can serve this with cooked pastina or stars pasta. Delightfully tasty!

1 cup filtered water
2 small zucchini, ends trimmed and sliced or cubed
1 to 2 cups chopped broccoli florets
$1/3$ cup organic tomato sauce or marinara sauce
2 to 3 tablespoons grated Parmesan cheese (optional)

1. Place a trivet and steamer rack or basket in the pressure cooker. Add the water. Arrange the zucchini and broccoli on the rack as evenly as possible.
2. Close and lock the lid. Set the burner heat to high. When the cooker reaches HIGH pressure, reduce the burner heat as low as you can and still maintain HIGH pressure. Set a timer to cook for 2 minutes.
3. Remove the pot from the heat. Open the cooker with the Quick Release method. Be careful of the steam as you remove the lid.
4. Lift out the steamer and transfer the vegetables to a bowl with an oversized spoon. They should be soft enough to puree them by mashing with a fork or a silicone spatula, or use a handheld immersion blender. Add the sauce and cheese, if using, and stir to combine. The puree will keep in an airtight container in the refrigerator for 3 days or can be frozen up to 3 months.

Baby Brocco-Cauliflower Puree

Makes 2 cups or 16 (1-ounce) ice-cube tray servings • Cooker: Any size • Time: 3 minutes at HIGH pressure

Cauliflower and broccoli are very tasty in combination. You will have about 2 cups of each vegetable chopped.

1 pound broccoli
1 pound cauliflower
1 cup filtered water

1. Cut the broccoli into florets and peel the stems, then chop everything. Cut the cauliflower into florets, discarding the stems. Chop the florets.
2. Place a trivet and steamer rack in the pressure cooker. Add the water. Arrange the vegetable pieces on the rack as evenly as possible.
3. Close and lock the lid. Set the burner heat to high. When the cooker reaches HIGH pressure, reduce the burner heat as low as you can and still maintain HIGH pressure. Set a timer to cook for 3 minutes.
4. Remove the pot from the heat. Open the cooker with the Quick Release method. Be careful of the steam as you remove the lid.
5. Transfer the vegetables to a food processor, blender, or food mill and process until smooth, adding the steaming water as needed to achieve the consistency you prefer. Use or let cool completely and store in the refrigerator for 1 to 2 days or the freezer up to 3 months.

Baby Spinach Puree

Makes 2 cups or 16 (1-ounce) ice-cube tray servings • Cooker: Any size • Time: 1 minute at HIGH pressure

Spinach is in the same family as quinoa, beets, and chard and is loaded with antioxidants and vitamin K. You want to cook spinach quickly to maximally retain its nutrients and vibrant color. When making baby food, use baby spinach (makes sense, right?) instead of mature leaves for a finer texture. Popeye the sailor man certainly knew his healthy vegetables!

1 cup filtered water
4 (10-ounce) bags pre-washed baby spinach, rinsed well
1 tablespoon olive oil or unsalted butter

1. Set a trivet in the pressure cooker. Add the water. Pack the spinach into a steamer basket and place in the pot. Place a metal lid on top to weight down the leaves.
2. Close and lock the lid. Set the burner heat to high. When the cooker reaches HIGH pressure, reduce the burner heat as low as you can and still maintain HIGH pressure. Set a timer to cook for 1 minute.
3. Remove the pot from the heat. Open the cooker with the Quick Release method. Be careful of the steam as you remove the lid. Discard the cooking liquid as it has a concentration of oxalic acids removed from the leaves in the steaming process.
4. Transfer the spinach to a food processor, blender, or food mill and add the oil or butter. Puree until smooth, adding hot filtered water if needed to thin the mixture to the consistency you prefer. Use or let cool completely and store in the refrigerator for 1 to 2 days or the freezer up to 3 months.

White Beans with Spinach and Brown Rice: Combine $1/2$ cup spinach puree with $1/2$ cup cooked white beans and $1/4$ cup cooked brown rice. Puree in the food processor.

Baby Peas

Makes 2 cups or 16 (1-ounce) ice-cube tray servings • Cooker: Any size • Time: 1 minute at HIGH pressure

Unless you have a surplus of garden peas—and really, who does?—frozen peas are the way to go. They are picked and processed at their peak and widely available. Be sure to buy plain frozen peas—leave the ones with sauce or flavorings for later, when baby has joined the family table. Once baby's palate has matured a bit, and he or she is eating a wider variety of foods, you can slip in a couple of mint leaves and a thin slice of butter (about 1 teaspoon). Cooking the peas for just 1 minute and using the Quick Release method keep the color bright. If using fresh peas, available in the spring, open the pods and scrape out the peas from the pod.

16 ounces (1 pound) frozen petite peas
$^1/_2$ cup filtered water

1. Place the peas in the pressure cooker. Add the water.
2. Close and lock the lid. Set the burner heat to high. When the cooker reaches HIGH pressure, reduce the burner heat as low as you can and still maintain HIGH pressure. Set a timer to cook for 1 minute.
3. Remove the pot from the heat. Open the cooker with the Quick Release method. Be careful of the steam as you remove the lid.
4. Transfer the peas and their cooking liquid to a food processor, blender, or food mill and process until smooth. Use or let cool completely and store in the refrigerator for 1 to 2 days or the freezer up to 3 months.

Baby Green Peas and Green Beans with Mint

Makes 2 cups or 16 (1-ounce) ice-cube tray servings • Cooker: Any size • Time: 3 minutes at HIGH pressure

This is a marvelous combination of green vegetables with a hint of garden mint.

2 cups frozen petite peas or shelled fresh peas
1 cup frozen or fresh green beans, ends trimmed
3 fresh mint leaves
$^1/_2$ cup filtered water

1. Place the peas, green beans, and mint leaves in the pressure cooker. Add the water.
2. Close and lock the lid. Set the burner heat to high. When the cooker reaches HIGH pressure, reduce the burner heat as low as you can and still maintain HIGH pressure. Set a timer to cook for 3 minutes.
3. Remove the pot from the heat. Open the cooker with the Quick Release method. Be careful of the steam as you remove the lid. Transfer the vegetables and their cooking liquid to a food processor, blender, or food mill and puree until smooth. Use or let cool completely and store in the refrigerator for 1 to 2 days or the freezer up to 3 months.

FOR A SMOOTHER PUREE

Plunging the hot cooked peas into a bowl of ice cold water is known to help make a smoother puree. You may wish to push the peas through a sieve or fine mesh strainer to get rid of any remaining skins.

Baby Butternut Squash

Makes 2 cups or 16 (1-ounce) ice-cube tray servings • Cooker: Any size • Time: 4 minutes at HIGH pressure

While this recipe specifies butternut, you can use any hard winter squash and prepare it with this timing. These winter squashes can be cooked using this recipe: Acorn, Delicata, Hubbard, Kabocha, Red Kuri, Sugar Pie Pumpkin, Turban.

1 cup filtered water
2 to 3 cups cubed peeled butternut squash
1 tablespoon olive oil

1. Place a trivet and steamer rack in the pressure cooker. Add the water. Arrange the squash cubes on the rack as evenly as possible.
2. Close and lock the lid. Set the burner heat to high. When the cooker reaches HIGH pressure, reduce the burner heat as low as you can and still maintain HIGH pressure. Set a timer to cook for 4 minutes.
3. Remove the pot from the heat. Open the cooker with the Natural Release method; let stand for 15 minutes. Be careful of the steam as you remove the lid. Lift out the steamer rack and transfer the squash to a food processor, blender, or food mill. Add the oil and a few tablespoons of the steaming water and process until smooth. Use or store in the refrigerator for 1 to 2 days or freezer up to 3 months.

Baby Butternut Squash and Sweet Potato: Add 1 cubed peeled sweet potato to the squash in Step 1. Pressure cook and puree as directed.

PREPPING WINTER SQUASH

Fresh winter squash is often sold already peeled and cubed and cryo-wrapped in the produce department, which will save you time and effort. But if you do need to work with a whole winter squash, first, cut the ends off the squash, then microwave it for about 3 minutes. The skin will now come off easily using a vegetable peeler or paring knife. Cut the squash in half lengthwise. With a spoon or melon baller, remove the seeds and membranes. The squash is now ready to be cut and added according to your recipe. If you need chunks, slice the squash half into strips and then cut those strips into chunks.

Baby Pumpkin and Parsnip Puree

Makes 3¹/₂ cups or 28 (1-ounce) ice-cube tray servings • Cooker: Any size • Time: 4 minutes at HIGH pressure

Look for the small, compact pumpkins the size of a nice cantaloupe known as Sugar Pies. They have a smooth, delightfully sweet flesh with minimum fiber. To prep them, cut the pumpkin in half. With a pumpkin scraper or small ice cream scoop, scrape out the stringy membranes and seeds. One pound raw pumpkin will yield about 1 cup puree.

1 cup filtered water
1 (8- to 12-ounce) Sugar Pie pumpkin, peeled and
    cubed
1 large or 2 medium parsnips (8 to 12 ounces
    total), peeled and cut into pieces

1. Place a trivet and steamer rack in the pressure cooker. Add the water. Arrange the pumpkin and parsnip pieces on the rack as evenly as possible.
2. Close and lock the lid. Set the burner heat to high. When the cooker reaches HIGH pressure, reduce the burner heat as low as you can and still maintain HIGH pressure. Set a timer to cook for 4 minutes.
3. Remove the pot from the heat. Open the cooker with the Natural Release method; let stand for 15 minutes. Be careful of the steam as you remove the lid. Lift out the steamer and transfer the vegetables to a bowl with an oversized spoon. They should be soft enough to puree by mashing them with a fork or a silicone spatula, or use an immersion blender. Use or let cool completely and store in the refrigerator for 3 days or the freezer up to 3 months.

ALL ABOUT PARSNIPS

Sometimes it is hard to distinguish the difference between a white parsnip and an orange carrot—they are both long taproots and both can be cooked and mashed like potatoes. Parsnips need to be peeled before cooking and, if they are extra large, slice lengthwise into quarters and trim out the bitter core. Firm, small to medium parsnips, 5 to 10 inches long, are best.

Baby Sweet Potatoes

Makes 1¹/₄ cups or 10 (1-ounce) ice-cube tray servings • Cooker: Any size • Time: 5 minutesat HIGH pressure

Sweet potatoes are one of the very first foods for many babies, and it's easy to see why. They are naturally sweet and blend into a velvety smooth puree. For a slightly older baby, skip the pureeing step and thoroughly freeze the 1-inch-thick slices on a cookie sheet before popping them into a zipper-top plastic bag. They will be a familiar flavor in a fun, new shape, a perfect early finger food. Use a steaming rack on a trivet here—the flat perforated steaming disk won't keep the sweet potatoes out of the water.

³/₄ pound sweet potatoes (about 2 smallish ones)
1 cup filtered water

1. Peel the sweet potatoes carefully, being sure to dig out and discard any eyes. Trim and discard the ends and any discolored portions. Cut the sweet potatoes crosswise into 1-inch-thick slices.

2. Place a trivet and steamer rack in the pressure cooker. Add the water. Arrange the sweet potato slices on the rack as evenly as possible.

3. Close and lock the lid. Set the burner heat to high. When the cooker reaches HIGH pressure, reduce the burner heat as low as you can and still maintain HIGH pressure. Set a timer to cook for 5 minutes.

4. Remove the pot from the heat. Open the cooker with the Natural Release method. Be careful of the steam as you remove the lid.

5. Transfer the sweet potato slices to a food processor, blender, or food mill and process until smooth, adding the steaming water as needed to achieve the consistency you prefer (start with 2 tablespoons). Use or let cool completely and store in the refrigerator for 1 to 2 days or the freezer up to 3 months.

Baby Sweet Potato and Pear Puree

Makes 5 cups or 40 (1-ounce) ice-cube tray servings • Cooker: Any size • Time: 7 minutes at HIGH pressure

This is a combination of two first foods, both sweet but with different textures.

1 cup filtered water
2 large or 4 small sweet potatoes, peeled and cut into ¹/₂-inch slices
1 to 2 firm-ripe pears, peeled and cored
1 tablespoon olive oil or unsalted butter

1. Set a trivet and steamer rack in the pressure cooker. Add the water. Arrange the sweet potatoes on the rack as evenly as possible.

2. Close and lock the lid. Set the burner heat to high. When the cooker reaches HIGH pressure, reduce the burner heat as low as you can and still maintain HIGH pressure. Set a timer to cook for 7 minutes.

3. Remove the pot from the heat. Open the cooker with the Natural Release method; let stand for 15 minutes. Be careful of the steam as you remove the lid. The potatoes should be soft and tender when pierced with the tip of a knife.

4. Lift out the steamer rack and transfer the sweet potatoes to a food processor, blender, or food mill. Add the pear and oil or butter. Puree, adding the steaming water as needed to thin the mixture to the consistency you prefer. This puree is very nice left thick. Use or let cool completely and store in the refrigerator for 1 to 2 days or the freezer up to 3 months.

Baby Mashed Potatoes

Makes 3 to 4 cups or 24 to 32 (1-ounce) ice-cube tray servings • Cooker: 4- to 7-quart • Time: 6 minutes at HIGH pressure

This recipe is written for a russet, but you can use any type of potato. Do not use the food processor for this, otherwise you'll reduce the puree to a sticky mess. The yield for this is more than usual as we think you'll find this ends up being a favorite for baby.

2 large or 4 medium russet potatoes (about 1 1/2 pounds total), peeled and cut into 1-inch chunks
Filtered water as needed
About 1/2 to 2/3 cup milk
2 tablespoons butter, at room temperature
Pinch white pepper

1. Place the potatoes in a 4- to 7-quart pressure cooker and fill with water to cover. It is okay if a few edges of the potatoes are peeking up out of the water.
2. Close and lock the lid. Set the burner heat to high. When the cooker reaches HIGH pressure, reduce the burner heat as low as you can and still maintain HIGH pressure. Set a timer to cook for 6 minutes.
3. In a separate saucepan or microwave measuring cup, heat the milk until small bubbles appear around the edges.
4. Remove the pot from the heat. Open the cooker with the Natural Release method; let stand for 10 minutes. Be careful of the steam as you remove the lid. The potatoes should be soft and tender when pierced with the tip of a knife and hold their shape a bit. Drain in a colander and return to the pot or place in a deep bowl.
5. Use a potato masher, fork, or handheld electric mixer or immersion blender on low speed to mash the potato and butter together until smooth, drizzling in the hot milk as needed. Taste for salt and pepper. Use or let cool completely and store in the refrigerator for 1 to 2 days or the freezer up to 3 months.

Baby Mashed Potatoes and Turnips: Add a small turnip for each potato; peel and cut into chunks. Pressure cook with the potatoes and continue as directed.

Baby Mashed Potatoes and Carrots: Add 1 large carrot, peeled and cut into chunks. Pressure cook with the potatoes and continue as directed. This is excellent mashed with 3 1/2 to 4 ounces steamed salmon fillet.

Baby Yukon Gold and Zucchini Puree

Makes 2 cups or 16 (1-ounce) ice-cube tray servings • Cooker: Any size • Time: 3 minutes at HIGH pressure

The yellow-fleshed Yukon Gold potato, named for the Yukon River and the gold rush country of Northern Canada, looks like a waxy new potato and can be used for boiling, baking, roasting, grilling, even frying. Boiled with summer squash, the mash is sweet and nutritious. White potatoes will not give the same texture, so seek out the Yukon Gold.

4 small zucchini, ends trimmed and cubed
1 large Yukon Gold potato, finely diced (peeling is optional)
$1/2$ cup filtered water
3 to 4 tablespoons grated Parmesan cheese
1 tablespoon olive oil

1. Place the zucchini and potato in the pressure cooker. Add the water.
2. Close and lock the lid. Set the burner heat to high. When the cooker reaches HIGH pressure, reduce the burner heat as low as you can and still maintain HIGH pressure. Set a timer to cook for 3 minutes.
3. Remove the pot from the heat. Open the cooker with the Quick Release method. Be careful of the steam as you remove the lid.
4. Transfer the vegetables and their cooking liquid to a food processor, blender, or food mill and add the Parmesan and oil. Puree until smooth. Use or let cool completely and store in the refrigerator for 1 to 2 days or the freezer up to 3 months.

Baby Turkey Puree

Makes 2 cups or 16 (1-ounce) ice-cube tray servings • Cooker: Any size • Time: 5 minutes at HIGH pressure

This is perfect for combining with vegetables and rice.

1 pound organic ground turkey (can be mixed white and dark)
1 cup filtered water or salt-free chicken broth

1. Place the turkey and water in the pressure cooker. Using a plastic spatula, break up the clumps of meat.
2. Close and lock the lid. Set the burner heat to high. When the cooker reaches HIGH pressure, reduce the burner heat as low as you can and still maintain HIGH pressure. Set a timer to cook for 4 minutes.
3. Remove the pot from the heat. Open the cooker with the Quick Release method. Be careful of the steam as you remove the lid.
4. Using a slotted spoon, transfer the cooked meat to a food processor, blender, or food mill. Add 1 tablespoon of the cooking liquid and puree; you want the final consistency to be smooth and fluffy. Add more liquid if needed. Use or let cool completely and store in the refrigerator for 1 to 2 days or the freezer up to 3 months.

Baby Lamb Puree: Substitute 1 pound organic ground lamb for the turkey.

Baby Veal Puree: Substitute 1 pound organic ground veal for the turkey. Be sure the veal is ground fresh that day, as it can go sour quickly. Veal is easier for baby to digest than beef.

Our Favorite Baby Chicken Puree

Makes 4 cups or 32 (1-ounce) ice-cube tray servings • Cooker: Any size • Time: 5 minutes at HIGH pressure

This is a recipe by Annabel Karmel (annabelkarmel .com) adapted for the pressure cooker. It is so very delicious and an excellent introduction to chicken for hungry babies. Meat from the thigh is softer than that from the breast and the sweet potato and dried fruit add a special sweetness. This can be introduced from 6 to 9 months.

1 tablespoon olive oil
2 organic free-range boneless chicken thighs, fat
   and skin discarded (4 to 5 ounces) and cut into
   chunks
1 (2-inch) chunk of a small leek (white part only),
   halved lengthwise, rinsed well, and sliced across
   $^1/_2$ inch thick
1 large sweet potato, peeled and cut into 1-inch
   pieces (about 2 cups)
1 cup filtered water or salt-free chicken broth
$^1/_4$ cup dried apricot halves, coarsely chopped
$^2/_3$ cup tomato puree

1. Heat the oil over medium heat in a pressure cooker of any size. Add the chicken and leek and cook for about 3 minutes, turning the pieces as they lose their pink color on each side. Add the sweet potato and cook until it just begins to soften, about 1 minute. Add the water or broth, apricots, and tomato puree, stirring to combine.

2. Close and lock the lid. Set the burner heat to high. When the cooker reaches HIGH pressure, reduce the burner heat as low as you can and still maintain HIGH pressure. Set a timer to cook for 5 minutes.

3. Remove the pot from the heat. Open the cooker with the Quick Release method. Be careful of the steam as you remove the lid.

4. Transfer the contents to a food processor, blender, or food mill and puree until smooth. Use or let cool completely and store in the refrigerator for 1 to 2 days or the freezer up to 3 months.

Baby Chicken Stock

Makes about 8 cups (2 quarts) • Cooker: 5- to 7-quart or larger • Time: 50 minutes at HIGH pressure

Stock is a culinary magic potion, adding rich taste, moisture, and nutrition to everything from stew to pilaf to vegetable soups. In the old days, poultry and meat were not on the list of earliest foods, but the American Academy of Pediatrics changed its nutrition recommendations in 2008. Stock for baby should be quite plain, made with a few vegetables that baby has already "met" if desired, and no added salt. The relatively long cooking time extracts maximum flavor and nutrition. Our local markets generally have chicken backs in stock, even if they're not on display. If yours doesn't, you might have to phone a couple of days ahead. We recommend making a big batch of stock in the pressure cooker and freezing it in 1-cup portions for babyfood making. (You can always season some of it for the rest of the family but be sure to mark your packages.) Use it for cooking pastina or to thin cooked vegetables.

5 pounds chicken backs or a combination of backs,
    necks, and wing tips or whole wings
1 onion (optional), peeled and quartered
1 carrot (optional), peeled and roughly chopped
1 rib celery (optional), roughly chopped
1 large sprig fresh flatleaf parsley (optional)
4 black peppercorns
About 8 cups cold filtered water

1. Place the chicken in a 5- to 7-quart or larger pressure cooker. Add the onion, celery, carrot, and parsley, if using. Add the peppercorns. Add 8 cups cold water if possible, but do not exceed the "maximum fill" line on your pressure cooker. If the chicken isn't submerged, add up to 1 cup more water if you can do so without exceeding the maximum capacity of your cooker.

2. Close and lock the lid. Set the burner heat to high. When the cooker reaches HIGH pressure, reduce the burner heat as low as you can and still maintain HIGH pressure. Set a timer to cook for 50 minutes.

3. Remove the pot from the heat. Open the cooker with the Natural Release method; let stand for 15 minutes. Be careful of the steam as you remove the lid.

4. Ladle or pour the contents of the cooker into a colander set over a large bowl in the sink. Discard the contents of the colander. Let the stock cool to room temperature, then cover and refrigerate overnight.

5. The next day, remove and discard the layer of solidified fat from the top. The stock is now ready to use. It will keep 3 to 4 days in the refrigerator, but we recommend freezing it in 1-cup portions (it will keep for up to 3 months) which will thaw quickly in the microwave or on the stovetop.

Red Lentil Soup for Baby

Makes 3^1/$_2$ cups or 28 (1-ounce) ice-cube tray servings • Cooker: 5- to 7-quart or larger • Time: 4 minutes at HIGH pressure

Usually sold split, the red lentil is very small and a powerhouse of vitamins, minerals, and plant protein. It is naturally low in calories and contains both soluble and insoluble dietary fiber. Unlike dried beans, red lentils require no soaking. They will turn golden and mushy after cooking. You can substitute 1 cup coconut milk for the same amount of water or stock if you want a creamy mixture.

1 cup red lentils (masoor dal), picked over and rinsed
^{1}/$_2$ cup finely chopped or grated carrot, celery, or zucchini (or combination)
3^1/$_2$ cups water or Baby Chicken Stock (page 573)
^{1}/$_2$ teaspoon turmeric
1 tablespoon olive oil
Pinch sea salt (optional)

1. Place the lentils, carrot, water or stock, turmeric, and oil in a 5- to 7-quart or larger pressure cooker.
2. Close and lock the lid. Set the burner heat to high. When the cooker reaches HIGH pressure, reduce the burner heat as low as you can and still maintain HIGH pressure. Set a timer to cook for 4 minutes.
3. Remove the pot from the heat. Open the cooker with the Natural Release method; let stand 10 to 15 minutes. Be careful of the steam as you remove the lid. Using an immersion blender, blend into a puree or use a whisk and beat hard to mash. Taste for seasoning. Use or let cool completely and store in the refrigerator up to 1 day or the freezer up to 2 months.

Baby Fresh Fish Puree

Makes ^{1}/$_2$ cup or 4 (1-ounce) ice-cube tray servings • Cooker: Any size • Time: 1 minute at HIGH pressure

Fish is brain food, and these are the most important months/years in brain development for a child. According to the American Academy of Pediatrics, by 9 months you can safely introduce some white fish to baby. Fish contains all nine amino acids, so it is a complete protein. It also contains Omega-3s, the healthy fat needed for overall growth. Choose very fresh white fish to start, then you can move to salmon and Arctic char (the salmon family). Check Seafood Watch online for the most up-to-date information on sustainable seafood choices. DO NOT serve baby shark, mackerel, or swordfish, which all contain high levels of methylmercury. DO NOT serve baby mollusks or crustaceans—lobster, oysters, mussels, crab, shrimp—until after 3 years of age due to high allergy possibilities. Consult your pediatrician.

4 ounces skinless fresh fish fillet, such as haddock, black cod, sole, tilapia, flounder, or salmon
^{1}/$_2$ cup filtered water
1 green onion, trimmed
2 sprigs fresh flatleaf parsley or cilantro

1. Rinse the fish and pat dry. Set a trivet or steamer basket that has been coated with nonstick olive oil cooking spray in the pressure cooker. Add the water, then set the fish on the trivet and add the green onion and parsley.
2. Close and lock the lid. Set the burner heat to high. When the cooker reaches HIGH pressure, reduce the burner heat as low as you can and still maintain HIGH pressure. Set a timer to cook for 1 minute.
3. Remove the pot from the heat. Open the cooker with the Quick Release method. Be careful of the steam as you remove the lid. The fillet should flake easily.
4. Discard the green onion and parsley and transfer the fish and a few tablespoons of the steaming water to a food processor, blender, or food mill and puree until smooth. You may need to add a little more water for a smoother puree. Use or let cool completely and store in the refrigerator for 1 to 2 days. Do not freeze this.

Baby Spring Lamb Stew

Makes 2¹/₂ cups or 20 (1-ounce) ice-cube tray servings • Cooker: Any size • Time: 15 minutes at HIGH pressure

Here's a bit of French home cooking. With its tender lamb, new potatoes, turnip, and carrots, it's a perfect starter stew for baby. Stir in the peas at the last minute so they don't overcook. We call for a lamb shoulder chop for convenience, but boneless leg of lamb works well, too. Lamb is often fatty—trim it as well as you can before cooking. Another characteristic of lamb is that it makes a very light broth, even when the bones are cooked for a long time. If you enjoy a more full-flavored broth, use chicken stock instead of water in this recipe. Make lamb stew just for baby, or make a triple recipe and serve two thirds of it—unpureed and seasoned to taste with salt and pepper—to the rest of the family. As baby grows, adjust the chunkiness of the puree.

1 (¹/₂-pound) lamb shoulder chop
1 teaspoon unsalted butter
1 (2-inch) chunk leek (white part only), trimmed, halved lengthwise, rinsed well, and sliced ¹/₂ inch thick
1 cup water or Baby Chicken Stock (page 573)
1 medium new white potato, peeled and cut into 1-inch pieces (about ³/₄ cup)
1 medium turnip, peeled and cut into 1-inch pieces (about ¹/₂ cup)
1 medium carrot, peeled and cut into 1-inch pieces (about ¹/₂ cup)
1 tablespoon minced fresh flatleaf parsley
¹/₄ cup frozen green peas

1. Cut the lamb chop into ³/₄-inch pieces, leaving the pieces on the bone. You will remove the bones after the stew is cooked. Trim away and discard any large chunks of fat. Count the pieces of meat and jot down the number.

2. Melt the butter over medium heat in the pressure cooker. When it starts to foam, add the meat and brown it lightly for about 2 minutes, turning the pieces as they lose their pink color. Add the leek and cook, stirring, until it just begins to soften, about 2 minutes. Add the water, potato, turnip, carrot, and parsley, stirring to combine.

3. Close and lock the lid. Set the burner heat to high. When the cooker reaches HIGH pressure, reduce the burner heat as low as you can and still maintain HIGH pressure. Set a timer to cook for 15 minutes.

4. Remove the pot from the heat. Open the cooker with the Quick Release method. Be careful of the steam as you remove the lid.

5. Using tongs, remove the meat to a plate, counting to be sure you have removed all of the pieces. Place the plate in the refrigerator for a few minutes. While the lamb cools, carefully stir the frozen peas into the stew remaining in the pressure cooker. When the lamb is cool enough to handle, use your fingers to remove any bones or hard pieces of gristle. Discard any large pieces of fat. Stir the meat back into the stew.

6. Transfer the stew to a food processor, blender, or food mill and puree until smooth. Use or let cool completely and store in the refrigerator 1 to 2 days or the freezer up to 3 months.

Baby Buffalo Cottage Pie

Makes 1³/₄ cups or 14 (1-ounce) ice-cube tray servings • Cooker: Any size • Time: 5 minutes at HIGH pressure

Cottage pie is English comfort food, a one-dish wonder consisting of a savory stew topped with a layer of mashed potatoes. The stew is generally made with ground meat, which makes it quick and easy. Here cottage pie gets an American makeover with lean and flavorful buffalo meat, also called bison. If you can't find it in your store, choose lean ground beef (10% to 15% fat) or lamb. The ground lamb found in U.S. supermarkets is usually quite high in fat, so be prepared to drain it well. Made with your own super-flavorful Baby Chicken Stock (page 573), this dish really shines. Make this version for baby, or make a quadruple recipe and serve three-fourths of it—unpureed—to the rest of the family. As baby grows, adjust the chunkiness of the puree.

1 teaspoon light olive oil or butter (optional)
¹/₄ pound 4 ounces lean ground buffalo (bison), or ground beef, or ground lamb
1 small shallot, minced
1 small carrot, peeled and chopped into ¹/₂-inch pieces (¹/₃ cup)
1 small potato, peeled and chopped into ¹/₂ inch pieces (³/₄ cup)
³/₄ cup unsalted chicken broth
Small pinch dried or fresh thyme
8 fresh green beans, ends trimmed and cut into ¹/₂-inch pieces (¹/₃ cup)
¹/₄ cup frozen green peas

1. If you are using very lean meat, heat the butter or oil over medium heat in the pressure cooker until melted or very hot. Add the meat and shallot and cook gently, stirring to break up lumps, until the meat has just lost its pink color, about 2 minutes. If there is a lot of fat, drain off and discard it before continuing. Add the carrot, potato, broth, and thyme, stirring to combine.

2. Close and lock the lid. Set the burner heat to high. When the cooker reaches HIGH pressure, reduce the burner heat as low as you can and still maintain HIGH pressure. Set a timer to cook for 4 minutes.

3. Remove the pot from the heat. Open the cooker with the Quick Release method. Be careful of the steam as you remove the lid.

4. Carefully stir in the green beans and frozen peas. Relock the cooker, bring back up to HIGH pressure, and cook for 1 minute.

5. Remove the pot from the heat and open with the Quick Release method. Transfer the mixture to a food processor, blender, or food mill and puree until smooth. Use or let cool completely and store in the refrigerator 1 to 2 days or the freezer up to 3 months.

Pressure Cooker Manufacturer Contact Information

The following is a list of the major pressure cooker manufacturers to contact for customer service and product information.

Calphalon (manufactured in China)
888-626-9112
www.calphalon.com

Cuisinart (manufactured in Costa Rica)
800-726-0190
www.cuisinart.com
customerservice@cuisinart.com

Elite Platinum/Maxi-Matic USA (manufactured in China)
800-365-6133, ext. 120
www.maxi-matic.com
info@maxi-matic.com

Fagor America, Inc. (manufactured in Spain)
800-207-0806
www.fagoramerica.com
info@fagoramerica.com

Fissler Pressure Cooker (manufactured in Germany)
704-545-2287
www.fisslerstore.com

Hawkins Futura (manufactured in India)
91-22-2218 6607 (Mumbai, India)
www.hawkinscookers.com
enquiry@hawkinscookers.com

Kuhn Rikon Corporation (Switzerland)
415-461-3927
www.kuhnrikon.com
kuhnrikon@kuhnrikon.com

Magafesa (Spain)
888-787-9991
www.e-magafesa.com
napl@interaccess.com

Manttra (India)
877-962-6887
www.manttra.com

Mirro Consumer Center (WearEver Cookwear-USA)
800-527-7727
www.mirro.com
moreinfo@mirro.com

Nordic Ware (USA)
877-466-7342
www.nordicware.com

Prestige (Royal Prestige India)
800-279-3373
www.royalprestige.com
CustomerCare@hycite.com

Presto (USA)
800-877-0441
www.presto.net.com
contact@GoPresto.com

Salton/Farberware (USA)
800-233-9054
www.salton-maxim.com

Sitram America (France)
805-383-4165
www.sitram.fr
customerservice@sitramcookware.com

T-Fal/Wearever (France)
800-395-8325
www.t-falusa.com
askt-fal@t-fal.com

WMF Americas Group Inc. (manufactured in Germany)
704-882-3998/800-966-3009
www.wmfamericas.com
consumer@WMFAmericas.com

Metric Equivalents

WEIGHTS

1 ounce = 28 grams
4 ounces ($^1/_4$ pound) = 113 grams
8 ounces ($^1/_2$ pound) = 227 grams
16 ounces (1 pound) = 454 grams

VOLUME MEASURES

$^1/_4$ teaspoon = 1.25 ml
$^1/_2$ teaspoon = 2.5 ml
1 teaspoon = 5 ml
1 tablespoon = $^1/_2$ fluid ounce = 15 ml
2 tablespoons = 1 fluid ounce = 30 ml
$^1/_4$ cup = 2 fluid ounces = 60ml
$^1/_3$ cup = 3 fluid ounces = 80 ml
$^1/_2$ cup = 4 fluid ounces = 120ml
$^2/_3$ cup = 6 fluid ounces = 160ml
$^3/_4$ cup = 6 fluid ounces = 180ml
1 cup = 8 fluid ounces = 235 ml
1 pint = 16 fluid ounces = 475 ml
1 quart = 32 fluid ounces = 945 ml
1 gallon = 128 fluid ounces = 3,755 ml ($3^3/_4$ liters)

LENGTH MEASURES

1 inch = 2.5 cm
1 foot = 30.5 cm

TEMPERATURE EQUIVALENTS		
(rounded to the nearest 5 degrees)		
°F	°C	*Gas Mark*
90	30	
100	40	
110	45	
125	50	
135	55	
250	120	$^1/_2$
275	135	1
300	150	2
325	165	3
350	175	4
375	190	5
400	205	6
425	220	7
450	230	8
475	245	9
500	260	10

Index

Page numbers in italics indicate sidebars, tables, and charts.

579

MODERN GUNS

Identification & Values

8th Revised Edition

Russell C. Quertermous
Steven C. Quertermous

1991

COLLECTOR BOOKS

A Division of Schroeder Publishing Co., Inc.

The current values in this book should be used only as a guide. They are not intended to set prices, which vary from one section of the country to another. Auction prices as well as dealer prices vary greatly and are affected by condition as well as demand. Neither the Authors nor the Publisher assumes responsibility for any losses that might be incurred as a result of consulting this guide.

For the purpose of estimating values, the firearm's condition is the first and fore-most consideration. Conditions of guns evaluated in this guide are considered to be in accordance with the National Rifle Association (NRA) definitions, taken from its magazine, *The American Rifleman*. This evaluation system is generally accepted in the firearms trade.

New Discontinued – same as new, but discontinued model. The following defini-tions will apply to all second hand articles.

Perfect – in new condition in every aspect.

Excellent – new condition, used little, no noticeable marring of wood or metal, bluing perfect (except at muzzle or sharp edges).

Very Good – in perfect working condition, no appreciable wear on working surfaces, no corrosion or pitting, only minor surface dents or scratches.

Good – in safe working condition, minor wear on working surfaces, no broken parts, no corrosion or pitting that will interfere with proper functioning.

Fair – in working condition, but well worn, perhaps requiring replacement of minor parts or adjustments, no rust but may have corrosion pits which do not render article unsafe or inoperable.

Values in this guide are for guns in the following conditions:

New (retail) – suggested retail prices still in production.

Excellent and Very Good or Very Good and Good – second hand items.

The illustrations included are from gun manufacturer's promotional photos, advertisements, catalogs and brochures. Since they are from a number of sources, relative size cannot be determined by comparing photos.

Contents

Acknowledgments

The companies included for the use of catalogs, advertisements and promotional material.

A special thanks to the following gun manufacturers for additional photos, information and assistance: Beretta Arms Co., Inc. for material on Beretta handguns and shotguns; Browning for material on Browning handguns, rifles and shotguns; Charter Arms Corporation for material on Charter Arms handguns; Colt Industries, Firearms Division for material on Colt handguns and rifles; Commercial Trading Imports, Inc. for material on Baikal shotguns; Harrington & Richardson, Inc. for material on Harrington & Richardson handguns, rifles & shotguns; Heckler & Koch for material on Heckler & Koch rifles and handguns; Interarms for material on Mark X rifles, Valmet rifles, Whitworth rifles, Walther handguns and rifles, Star handguns and Astra handguns; Ithaca Gun Co. for material on Ithaca shotguns; Iver Johnson Arms, Inc. for material on Iver Johnson handguns, Kleinguenther, Inc. for materials on Kleinguenther rifles; Mannlicher for materials on Mannlicher rifles and shotguns; Marlin for material on Marlin and Marlin-Glenfield rifles and shotguns; O.F. Mossberg & Sons, Inc. for material on Mossberg and New Haven rifles and shotguns; Remington for material on Remington rifles, shotguns and handguns; Richland Arms Co. for material on Richland shotguns; Savage Arms for material on Savage rifles and shotguns, Stevens rifles and shotguns, Fox shotguns and Anschutz rifles; Sears, Roebuck & Co. for material on Sears rifles and shotguns and Ted Williams rifles and shotguns; Smith & Wesson for material on Smith & Wesson handguns, rifles and shotguns; Speer Inc. Advertising for material on Mossberg firearms; Sterling Arms Corporation for material on Sterling handguns; Universal Firearms for material on Universal rifles; Weatherby, Inc. for material on Weatherby rifles and shotguns; Winchester-Western for material on Winchester rifles and shotguns; U.S. Repeating Arms for material on Winchester rifles and shotguns.

Petersen Publishing Company for the use of the following photographs from *Guns and Ammo Annual*, 1977, 1982 and *Hunting Annual* 1983:

Shotguns:

Beretta BL4, 680 Trap, 685, MKII Trap, GR-2; 410, AL-2; Bernardelli Game Cock; Browning Super Light, Citori Trap, B-SS, BPS, 2000; Charles Daly Field III, Auto Superior; Fox FA-1; Franchi Standard; Harrington & Richardson 176, 1212; Ithaca 37 Standard, 37 DV Deluxe, 37 Bicentennial, 51 Deluxe Trap, 51 Magnum, 51 Deerslayer; Mannlicher Oxford, Mossberg 500 ATP8, 500 AHTD, Slugster, Richland 200; Smith & Wesson 916, 1000, 3000; Valmet 412K; Weatherby Orion, Athena, 92, 82; Winchester 1200 Defender

Rifles:

Anschutz 1422D, 520/61; Browning BAR; Harrington & Richardson 750; Heckler & Koch 770, 940; Mossberg 321K, 341, 353, 800, 810; New Haven 453T; Remington 541 S, 700 ADL; Salo Classic, Safari; Stevens 35, 125; Valmet 412, M62/S, M71/S; Walther KKJ, KKM, UIT, Moving Target; Winchester 70 XTR Featherweight, 70 Western, 70XTR Sporter Magnum, Super Xpress

Handguns:

Beretta 951; Browning Challenger II, Challenger III; Charter Arms Explorer II, Bulldog Tracker; Colt S-4 Targetsman, Target S-3; Dan Wesson 9-2, 44V; Heckler & Koch HK4, P9S; Iver Johnson TP22; Llama Comanche; Ruger Redhawk; Smith & Wesson 30, 1953 22/32, 25-1955, 10, 31, 27, 28, 58, 38, 547 M & P, 586; Sterling MKII 400

Stackpole Books for the use of the following photographs from W.H.B. Smith's *Book of Pistols and Revolvers* and *Book of Rifles*: Astra 1911-Patent, 1915 Patent, 1924, 300, 600, 400; Bayard 1908, 1923, 1930; Beretta 1915, 1923, 1931; Browning, FN, 1900, 1903 Military, 1910, 1922; CZ 22, 1945; Colt 1900, 1902, 1905, Model M, 1911; Fiala Single Shot; Harrington & Richardson 32; Japanese Military pistols; Lignose 2A, 2 Pocket; MAB C; Mauser 2; Sauer 1913, WTM, H; Savage 1907, 1915, 1917; Smith & Wesson 32 & 35, No. 3 Frontier, Doubled Action Frontier, Military & Police 32-20, New Century; Star 1919; Steyr Solothurn, Vest Pocket; Walther 5, 4, 7, 9; Webley & Scott 1906, Mark I; Military rifles

Shotguns

AYA

AYA Matador
Gauge: 10, 12, 16, 20, 20 magnum
Action: Box lock; top lever break-open; hammerless; selective single trigger & automatic ejector
Magazine: None
Barrel: Double barrel, 26", 28", 30" any choke combination
Finish: Blued; checkered walnut pistol grip stock & beavertail forearm
Approximate wt.: 7 lbs.
Comments: Made from 1953 until 1963. Replaced by Matador II.
Estimated Value: Excellent: $435.00
                   Very good: $345.00

AYA Matador II
Same as the Matador with ventilated rib. Produced from about 1963 to 1970.
Estimated Value: Excellent: $460.00
                   Very good: $365.00

AYA Bolero
Same as the Matador except non-selective single trigger & extractors; 28 & 410 gauges. Made from the mid 1950's until 1963.
Estimated Value: Excellent: $360.00
                   Very good: $280.00

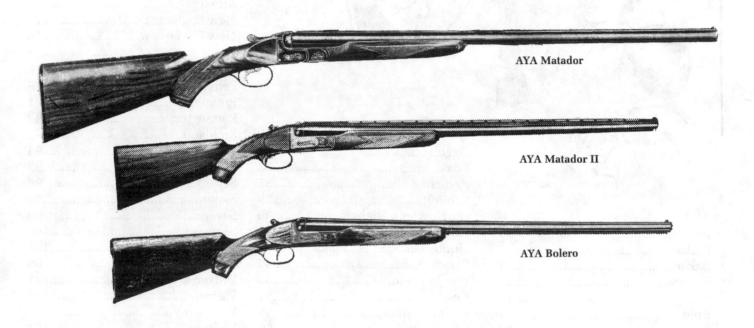

AYA Matador

AYA Matador II

AYA Bolero

Armalite

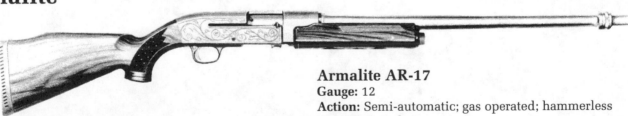

Armalite AR-17

Armalite AR-17
Gauge: 12
Action: Semi-automatic; gas operated; hammerless
Magazine: 2-shot
Barrel: 24" aluminum alloy; interchangeable choke tubes; improved modified & full chokes
Finish: Gold anodized or black anodized; plastic stock & forearm
Approximate wt.: 5½ lbs.
Comments: Barrel & receiver housing made of high tensile aluminum alloy. Made from about 1963 to 1965. Approximately 2,000 manufactured.
Estimated Value: Excellent: $675.00
                   Very good: $500.00

Baikal

Baikal Model IJ-27IC and IJ-27EIC

Gauge: 12, 20
Action: Box lock; top lever break-open; hammerless; selective single trigger
Magazine: None
Barrel: Over & under double barrel; 26", 28", 30" improved cylinder & modified or modified & full chokes; ventilated rib
Finish: Blued; engraved receiver; hand checkered walnut pistol grip stock & forearm
Approximate wt.: 7½ lbs.
Comments: Made in Soviet Union; IJ-37EIC has selective ejectors, add $40.00.
Estimated Value:　Excellent:　　$350.00
　　　　　　　　　　　Very good:　　$280.00

Baikal Model IJ-27EIC Silver

Same as the Model IJ-27EIC with silver inlays and fancy engraving.
Estimated Value:　Excellent:　　$450.00
　　　　　　　　　　　Very good:　　$365.00

Baikal Model IJ-12

Less fancy but similar to the IJ-27IC. No engraving, no recoil pad; 28" barrel only. Imported in the early 1970's.
Estimated Value:　Excellent:　　$230.00
　　　　　　　　　　　Very good:　　$185.00

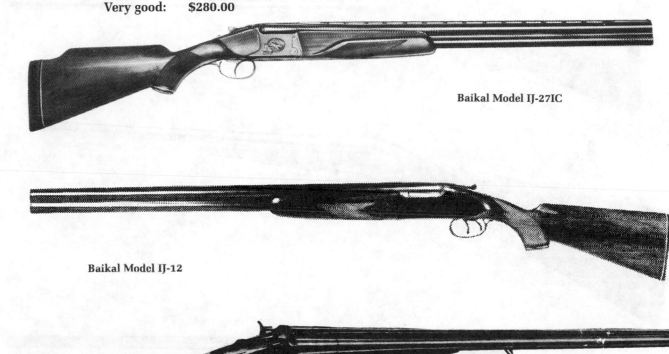

Baikal Model IJ-27IC

Baikal Model IJ-12

Baikal TOZ-66

Baikal TOZ-66

Gauge: 12
Action: Box lock; top lever break-open; exposed hammers
Magazine: None
Barrel: Double barrel; 28" chrome lined, variety of chokes
Finish: Blued; checkered wood pistol grip stock & short tapered forearm; engraving
Approximate wt.: 8 lbs.
Comments: Imported during the 1970's.
Estimated Value:　Excellent:　　$260.00
　　　　　　　　　　　Very good:　　$205.00

Baikal Model TOZ-34E Souvenir

Gauge: 12, 20, 28
Action: Box lock; top lever break-open; hammerless
Magazine: None
Barrel: Over and under double barrel; 26" or 28" improved cylinder & modified or modified & full; ventilated rib on 12 and 20 gauge; solid rib on 28 gauge
Finish: Blued; select walnut, hand checkered and pistol grip stock and forearm; engraved receiver
Approximate wt.: 7 lbs.
Comments: Imported from the Soviet Union. It features selective ejectors and cocking indicators.
Estimated Value:　Excellent:　　$600.00
　　　　　　　　　　　Very good:　　$450.00

Baikal Model IJ-18 and IJ-18E

Gauge: 12, 20
Action: Box lock; top lever break-open; hammerless; single shot; cocking indicator
Magazine: None
Barrel: 26", 28" modified, 30" full choke
Finish: Blued; checkered walnut-stained hardwood, pistol grip stock and tapered forearm; engraved receiver
Approximate wt.: 6 lbs.
Comments: IJ-18E has selective ejector, add $6.00.
Estimated Value: Excellent: $75.00
                        Very good: $55.00

Baikal IJ-58MA and 58MAE

Gauge: 12, 20 magnum
Action: Box lock; top lever break-open; hammerless
Magazine: None
Barrel: Double barrel; 26" improved cylinder & modified, 28" modified & full chokes; chrome lined
Finish: Blued; checkered walnut pistol grip stock and short tapered forearm; engraved receiver. IJ-58MAE has selective ejectors, add $28.00.
Approximate wt.: 7 lbs.
Comments: Imported in 1970's.
Estimated Value: Excellent: $250.00
                        Very good: $200.00

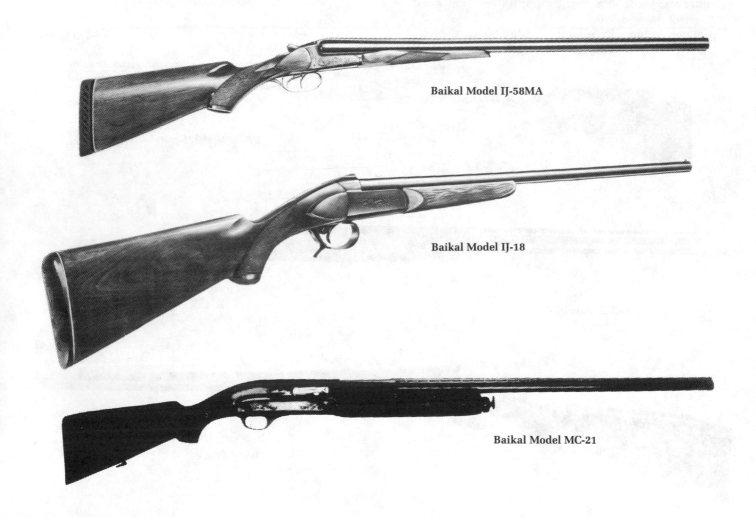

Baikal Model IJ-58MA

Baikal Model IJ-18

Baikal Model MC-21

Baikal Model MC-8

Gauge: 12
Action: Box lock; top lever break-open; hammerless
Magazine: None
Barrel: Over and under double barrel; trap, skeet, 26" or 28", modified or full chokes; chrome lined barrels
Finish: Blued; checkered walnut Monte Carlo pistol grip stock and forearm; engraved receiver
Approximate wt.: 8½ lbs.
Comments: Imported during the 1970's.
Estimated Value: Excellent: $1,800.00
                        Very good: $1,300.00

Baikal Model MC-21

Gauge: 12
Action: Semi-automatic; hammerless; side ejection
Magazine: 5-shot tubular
Barrel: 26" improved cylinder; 28" modified; 30" full chokes; ventilated rib
Finish: Blued; checkered walnut, pistol grip stock and forearm; engraved receiver
Approximate wt.: 7½ lbs.
Comments: Imported in the 1970's.
Estimated Value: Excellent: $325.00
                        Very good: $250.00

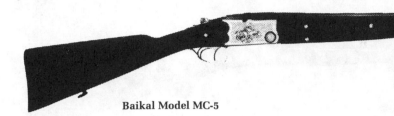

Baikal Model MC-5

Baikal Model MC-5
Gauge: 20
Action: Box lock; top lever break-open; hammerless; double triggers
Magazine: None
Barrel: Over and under double barrel; 26" or 28" improved cylinder & modified or skeet chokes; ribbed
Finish: Blued; checkered walnut pistol grip or straight stock and forearm; engraved receiver.
Approximate wt.: 5¾ lbs.
Comments: Imported during the 1970's.
Estimated Value: Excellent: $850.00
Very good: $650.00

Baker

Baker Batavia Leader

Baker Black Beauty Special
Similar to Baker Batavia Leader except higher quality wood and finish. Add $75.00 for automatic extractors.
Estimated Value: Excellent: $675.00
Very good: $500.00

Baker Black Beauty Special

Baker Batavia Leader
Gauge: 12, 16, 20
Action: Slide lock; hammerless
Magazine: None
Barrel: 26", 28", 30", 32" double barrel; any standard choke combination
Finish: Blued; walnut pistol grip stock and forearm.
Approximate wt.: 7-8 lbs.
Comments: Made from about 1900 to 1930. Add $75.00 for automatic extractors.
Estimated Value: Excellent: $450.00
Very good: $360.00

Beretta

Beretta Companion FS-1
Gauge: 12, 16, 20, 28, 410
Action: Underlever; hammerless; single shot
Magazine: None
Barrel: 26", 28" full choke
Finish: Blued; checkered walnut pistol grip stock and forearm.
Approximate wt.: 5 lbs.
Comments: A folding shotgun made from about 1960 to the late 1970's.
Estimated Value: Excellent: $120.00
Very good: $ 90.00

Beretta Model 412
Gauge: 12, 20, 28, 410
Action: Underlever, break-open, hammerless, single shot
Magazine: None
Barrel: 28" full choke
Finish: Blued; checkered walnut semi-pistol grip stock and forearm.
Approximate wt.: 5 lbs.
Comments: A lightweight shotgun designed for beginners, campers and backpackers.
Estimated Value: New (retail): $215.00
Excellent: $160.00
Very good: $130.00

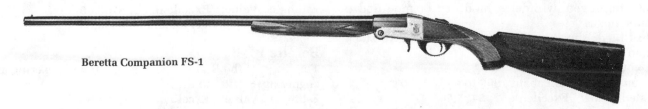

Beretta Companion FS-1

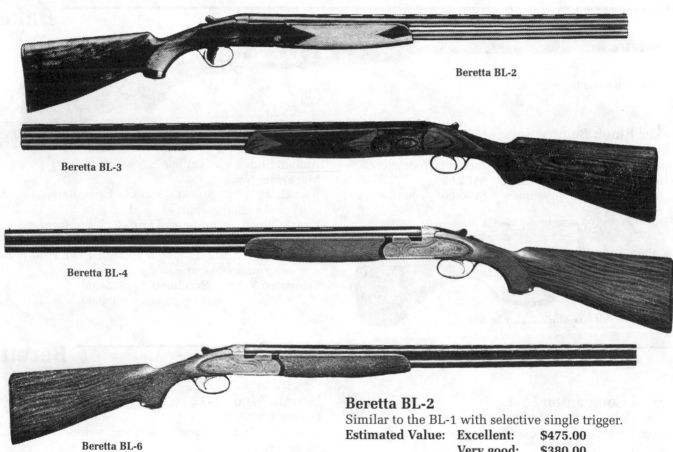

Beretta Mark II Trap

Gauge: 12
Action: Box lock; top lever break-open; hammerless; single shot
Magazine: None
Barrel: 32", 34" full choke; ventilated rib
Finish: Blued; checkered walnut Monte Carlo pistol grip stock and forearm; recoil pad; engraving
Approximate wt.: 8 lbs.
Comments: Made from the mid 1970's to early 1980's.
Estimated Value: Excellent: $500.00
**   Very good: $375.00**

Beretta Mark II Trap

Beretta BL-2

Beretta BL-3

Beretta BL-4

Beretta BL-6

Beretta BL-1

Gauge: 12
Action: Box lock; top lever break-open; hammerless; double triggers
Magazine: None
Barrel: Over and under double barrel; chrome steel; 26"-30" improved cylinder & modified or modified & full chokes
Finish: Blued; checkered walnut semi-pistol grip stock and forearm
Approximate wt.: 7 lbs.
Comments: Made from about 1969 to early 1970's.
Estimated Value: Excellent: $425.00
**   Very good: $340.00**

Beretta BL-2
Similar to the BL-1 with selective single trigger.
Estimated Value: Excellent: $475.00
**   Very good: $380.00**

Beretta BL-3
Similar to the BL-2 with ventilated rig; engraving.
Estimated Value: Excellent: $600.00
**   Very good: $480.00**

Beretta BL-4 and BL-5
Similar to the BL-3 with deluxe engraving and checkering; automatic ejectors. Add $200.00 for BL-5.
Estimated Value: Excellent: $700.00
**   Very good: $560.00**

Beretta BL-6
The finest of the BL line. Highest quality checkering and engraving. Similar to the BL-4.
Estimated Value: Excellent: $1,200.00
**   Very good: $ 960.00**

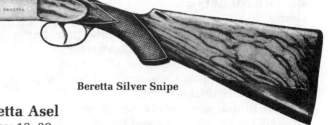

Beretta Silver Snipe

Gauge: 12, 20, regular or magnum
Action: Box lock; top lever break-open; hammerless
Magazine: None
Barrel: 26"-30" improved cylinder & modified, modified & full, full or skeet chokes; ribbed; over and under double barrel
Finish: Blued; nickel receiver; checkered walnut pistol grip stock and forearm
Approximate wt.: 7½ lbs.
Comments: Made from mid 1950's to late 1960's. Add $25.00 for single selective trigger.
Estimated Value: Excellent: $500.00
Very good: $400.00

Beretta Silver Snipe

Beretta Asel

Gauge: 12, 20
Action: Box lock; top lever break-open; hammerless; automatic ejector; single trigger
Magazine: None
Barrel: Over and under double barrel; 25", 28", 30" improved cylinder & modified or modified & full chokes
Finish: Blued; checkered walnut semi-pistol grip stock and forearm
Approximate wt.: 7 lbs.
Comments: Made from late 1940's to mid 1960's.
Estimated Value: Excellent: $1,020.00
Very good: $ 815.00

Beretta Golden Snipe

Similar to the Silver Snipe with ventilated rib; automatic ejectors. Discontinued in the mid 1970's.
Estimated Value: Excellent: $650.00
Very good: $520.00

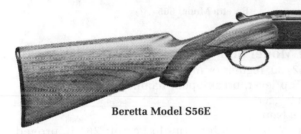

Beretta Model S56E

Beretta Model S55B

Gauge: 12, 20, regular or magnum
Action: Box lock; top lever break-open; hammerless
Magazine: None
Barrel: Over and under double barrel; chrome lined; ventilated rib; 26" improved cylinder and modified; 28" or 30" modified & full; 30" full in 12 gauge
Finish: Blued; checkered walnut pistol grip stock and beavertail forearm; recoil pad on magnum
Approximate wt.: 6-7 lbs.
Comments: Made from late 1970's to early 1980s.
Estimated Value: Excellent: $660.00
Very good: $520.00

Beretta Model S56E

Similar to Model S55B with scroll engraving on the receiver; selective automatic ejectors.
Estimated Value: Excellent: $725.00
Very good: $580.00

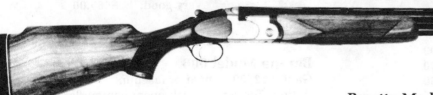

Beretta Model 680 Trap

Beretta Model 680 Trap

Similar to the Model 680 Skeet with a Monte Carlo stock, recoil pad; 30" or 32" improved modified & full choke barrels.
Estimated Value: Excellent: $1,220.00
Very good: $ 975.00

Beretta Model 680 Mono Trap

Similar to the Model 680 Trap with a single high ventilated rib barrel; 32" or 34" full choke barrel.
Estimated Value: Excellent: $1,250.00
Very good: $1,000.00

Beretta Model 680 Competition Skeet

Gauge: 12
Action: Top lever, break-open; hammerless; automatic ejector; single selective trigger
Magazine: None
Barrel: Over and under double barrel; 26" or 28" skeet choke barrels; ventilated rib
Finish: Blued; checkered walnut pistol grip stock and forearm; silver grey receiver with engraving; gold-plated trigger
Approximate wt.: 7 lbs.
Comments: Interchangeable barrel capacity; price includes luggage-style case.
Estimated Value: Excellent: $1,200.00
Very good: $ 960.00

Beretta Model 625

Gauge: 12, 20, regular or magnum
Action: Box lock; top lever break-open; hammerless; double barrel; mechanical extractor
Magazine: None
Barrel: 26" improved cylinder/modified; 28" or 30" modified/full; double barrel
Finish: Blued; grey receiver; checkered walnut pistol grip or straight stock and tapered forearm
Approximate wt.: 6 to 7 lbs.
Comments: Produced in the mid 1980's.
Estimated Value: Excellent: $750.00
                          Very good: $600.00

Beretta Model 626; 626 Onyx

Similar to the Model 625 with selective automatic ejectors. Add 30% for Onyx model. (Regular Model discontinued 1990)
Estimated Value: New (retail): $995.00
                          Excellent: $745.00
                          Very good: $600.00

Beretta Model 627EL, 627EELL

Similar to the Model 626 with higher grade finish and engraved sideplate. Add 70% for EELL Model.
Estimated Value: New (retail): $2,600.00
                          Excellent: $1,950.00
                          Very good: $1,560.00

Beretta Model 685

Beretta Model 687L

Gauge: 12, 20, regular or magnum
Action: Top lever, break-open; hammerless; selective automatic ejectors; single selective trigger
Magazine: None
Barrel: Over and under double barrel; 26" or 28" with interchangeable choke tubes; ventilated rib
Finish: Blued; greyed receiver with engraving; checkered walnut pistol grip stock and forearm
Approximate wt.: 6 to 6¾ lbs.
Comments: Add 25% for Golden Onyx Model; 38% for Sporting Clays Model.
Estimated Value: New (retail): $1,573.00
                          Excellent: $1,180.00
                          Very good: $ 945.00

Beretta Model 685

Gauge: 12, 20, regular or magnum
Action: Top lever, break-open; hammerless; single selective trigger
Magazine: None
Barrel: Over and under double barrel; 26" improved cylinder & modified, 28" or 30" modified & full, 30" full & full; ventilated rib
Finish: Blued; checkered walnut pistol grip stock and fluted forearm; silver grey receiver with light engraving
Approximate wt.: 8 lbs.
Comments: Available until late 1980's.
Estimated Value: Excellent: $700.00
                          Very good: $565.00

Beretta Model 687EL, 687 EELL

Similar to the Model 687L with higher quality finish, extensive engraving on receiver and engraved sideplate. Add 50% for EELL Model; 50% for Sporting Clays Model.
Estimated Value: New (retail): $2,607.00
                          Excellent: $1,955.00
                          Very good: $1,565.00

Beretta Model 686

Gauge: 12, 20, regular or magnum
Action: Top lever, break-open; hammerless; single selective trigger; selective automatic ejectors
Magazine: None
Barrel: Over and under double barrel; 26" improved cylinder & modified, 28" or 30" modified & full, or 30" full & full; ventilated rib; multi-choke tubes available
Finish: Blued; checkered walnut pistol grip stock and fluted forearm; silver grey receiver with engraving; recoil pad on magnum
Approximate wt.: 8 lbs.
Comments: Currently available. Add 2% for Onyx model; 44% for Sporting Clays model.
Estimated Value: New (retail): $1,147.00
                          Excellent: $ 860.00
                          Very good: $ 690.00

Beretta GR-2

Beretta GR-2

Gauge: 12, 20
Action: Box lock, top lever, break-open; hammerless
Magazine: None
Barrel: Double barrel; 26"-30"; variety of choke combinations
Finish: Blued; checkered walnut semi-pistol grip stock and forearm
Approximate wt.: 6 to 8 lbs.
Comments: Made from the late 1960's to mid 1970's.
Estimated Value: Excellent: $525.00
Very good: $425.00

Beretta GR-3

Similar to the GR-2 with single selective trigger.
Estimated Value: Excellent: $575.00
Very good: $460.00

Beretta GR-4

Similar to the GR-3 with automatic ejector; engraving and deluxe wood work.
Estimated Value: Excellent: $700.00
Very good: $560.00

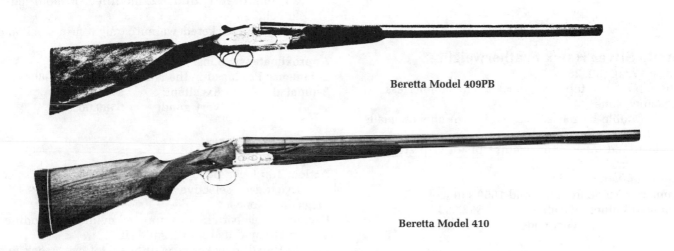

Beretta Model 409PB

Beretta Model 410

Beretta Model 409PB

Gauge: 12, 16, 20, 28
Action: Box lock, top lever, break-open; hammerless; double triggers
Magazine: None
Barrel: Double barrel 27½", 28½", 30" improved cylinder & modified or modified & full chokes
Finish: Blued; checkered walnut straight or pistol grip stock and small tapered forearm; engraved
Approximate wt.: 6 to 8 lbs.
Comments: Made from mid 1930's to mid 1960's.
Estimated Value: Excellent: $600.00
Very good: $480.00

Beretta Model 410E

Similar to the 409PB with higher quality finish and engraving; automatic ejector.
Estimated Value: Excellent: $750.00
Very good: $600.00

Beretta Model 411E

Similar to 410E with higher quality finish.
Estimated Value: Excellent: $1,025.00
Very good: $ 820.00

Beretta Model 410

Gauge: 10 magnum
Action: Box lock; top lever, break-open; hammerless; double triggers
Magazine: None
Barrel: Double barrel; 27½", 28½", 30" improved cylinder & modified or modified & full chokes
Finish: Blued; checkered walnut pistol stock & short tapered forearm
Approximate wt.: 10 lbs.
Comments: Made from the mid 1930's to early 1980's.
Estimated Value: Excellent: $1,000.00
Very good: $800.00

Beretta Model 410E

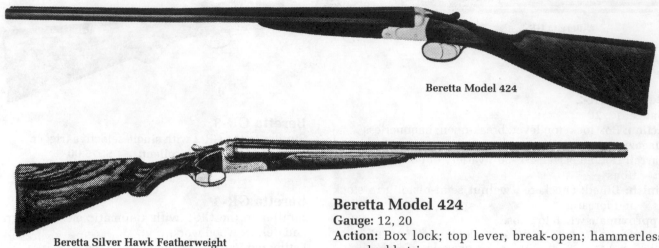

Beretta Model 424

Beretta Silver Hawk Featherweight

Beretta Silver Hawk Featherweight

Gauge: 12, 16, 20, 28
Action: Box lock; top lever, break-open; hammerless
Magazine: None
Barrel: Double barrel; 26"-32" variety of chokes; matted rib
Finish: Blued; checkered walnut pistol grip stock and forearm
Approximate wt.: 7¼ lbs.
Comments: Made from the mid 1950's to late 1960's.
Estimated Value: Excellent: $525.00
                    Very good: $420.00

Beretta Silver Hawk Featherweight Magnum

Similar to the Silver Hawk Featherweight in 10 or 12 gauge magnum; chrome lined 30" or 32" barrels; ventilated rib; recoil pad.
Estimated Value: Excellent: $600.00
                    Very good: $480.00

Beretta Model 424

Gauge: 12, 20
Action: Box lock; top lever, break-open; hammerless; double trigger
Magazine: None
Barrel: Double barrel; chrome lined; matted rib; 26" or 28" improved cylinder & modified or modified & full chokes
Finish: Blued; checkered walnut straight grip stock and forearm
Approximate wt.: 6 lbs.
Comments: Produced in the late 1970's to mid 1980s.
Estimated Value: Excellent: $725.00
                    Very good: $580.00

Beretta Model 426

Gauge: 12, 20, magnum
Action: Top lever, break-open; hammerless; single selective trigger; selective automatic ejector
Magazine: None
Barrel: Double barrel; 26" improved cylinder & modified or 28" modified & full; solid rib
Finish: Blued; checkered walnut pistol grip stock and tapered forearm; silver grey engraved receiver; silver pigeon inlaid
Approximate wt.: 8 lbs.
Comments: Discontinued mid 1980's.
Estimated Value: Excellent: $920.00
                    Very good: $735.00

Beretta Silver Pigeon

Beretta Silver Pigeon

Gauge: 12
Action: Slide action; hammerless
Magazine: 5-shot tubular
Barrel: 26"-32", various chokes
Finish: Blued; engraved and inlaid with silver pigeon; chrome trigger; checkered walnut pistol grip stock and slide handle
Approximate wt.: 7 lbs.
Comments: Made from about 1960 for 6 years.
Estimated Value: Excellent: $300.00
                    Very good: $240.00

Beretta Gold Pigeon

Similar to the Silver Pigeon with heavy engraving; gold pigeon inlaid; ventilated rib; gold trigger.
Estimated Value: Excellent: $630.00
                    Very good: $500.00

Beretta Ruby Pigeon

Similar to the Gold Pigeon with deluxe engraving and ruby eye in inlaid pigeon.
Estimated Value: Excellent: $725.00
                    Very good: $580.00

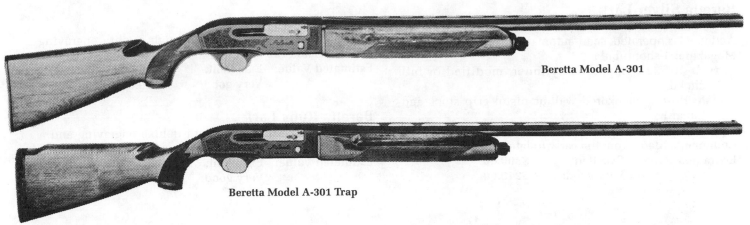

Beretta Model A-301

Beretta Model A-301 Trap

Beretta Model A-301

Gauge: 12, 20, regular or magnum
Action: Gas operated, semi-automatic; hammerless
Magazine: 3-shot tubular
Barrel: 26" improved cylinder; 28" modified or full; 30" full in 12 gauge; ventilated rib; chrome molybdenum
Finish: Blued; checkered walnut pistol grip stock and forearm; decorated alloy receiver; recoil pad on magnum model
Approximate wt.: 6¼-7 lbs.
Comments: Made from the late 1970's to early 1980's. Add $45.00 for magnum.
Estimated Value: Excellent: $375.00
Very good: $300.00

Beretta Model A-301 Trap

Similar to the A-301 with Monte Carlo stock, recoil pad & gold plated trigger; 12 gauge only; 30" full choke.
Estimated Value: Excellent: $400.00
Very good: $320.00

Beretta Model A-301 Skeet

Similar to the A-301 Trap with a 26" skeet choke barrel.
Estimated Value: Excellent: $400.00
Very good: $320.00

Beretta Model A-301 Deer Gun

Similar to the A-301 with a 22" slug barrel; adjustable open sights.
Estimated Value: Excellent: $375.00
Very good: $300.00

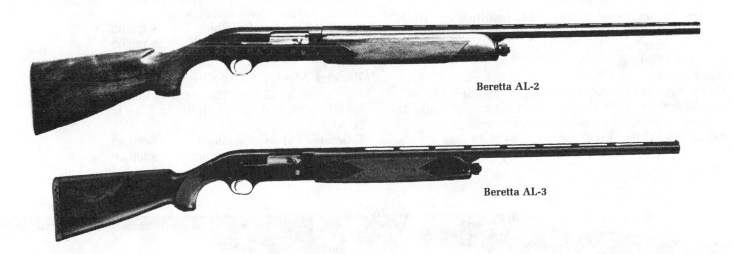

Beretta AL-2

Beretta AL-3

Beretta AL-1

Gauge: 12, 20, regular or magnum
Action: Gas operated, semi-automatic; hammerless
Magazine: 3-shot tubular
Barrel: 26"-30" skeet, improved cylinder, modified or full shokes; ventilated rib
Finish: Blued; checkered walnut pistol grip stock and forearm
Approximate wt.: 6½-7¾ lbs.
Comments: Made from the late 1960's to mid 1970's.
Estimated Value: Excellent: $300.00
Very good: $240.00

Beretta AL-2

Similar to the AL-1 with ventilated rib; recoil pad; chrome lined bores.
Estimated Value: Excellent: $340.00
Very good: $270.00

Beretta AL-3

Similar to the AL-2 with light engraving.
Estimated Value: Excellent: $350.00
Very good: $280.00

Beretta Silver Lark

Gauge: 12
Action: Gas operated, semi-automatic; hammerless
Magazine: 5-shot tubular
Barrel: 26"-32", improved cylinder, modified or full chokes
Finish: Blued; checkered walnut pistol grip stock and forearm
Approximate wt.: 7 lbs.
Comments: Made from the early to late 1960's.
Estimated Value: Excellent: $300.00
                        Very good: $240.00

Beretta Gold Lark

Similar to the Silver Lark with high quality engraving and ventilated rib.
Estimated Value: Excellent: $400.00
                        Very good: $320.00

Beretta Ruby Lark

Similar to the Silver Lark with deluxe engraving and a stainless steel barrel.
Estimated Value: Excellent: $550.00
                        Very good: $440.00

Beretta Model A302 Mag-Action

Beretta Model A302 Mag-Action

Gauge: 12, 20, regular or magnum
Action: Gas operated, semi-automatic
Magazine: 3-shot tubular
Barrel: 26" improved cylinder; 28" modified or full; 30" full; ventilated rib
Finish: Blued; checkered walnut pistol grip stock and fluted forearm
Approximate wt.: 7 lbs.
Comments: Interchangeable barrel capacity, 2¾" or 3" chambering. Produced from 1982 to 1987; add 5% for multi-choke model with four choke tubes.
Estimated Value: Excellent: $435.00
                        Very good: $340.00

Beretta Model A302 Skeet

Similar to the Model A302 Mag-Action except 26" skeet choke barrel.
Estimated Value: Excellent: $465.00
                        Very good: $370.00

Beretta Model A302 Trap

Similar to the Model A302 Mag-Action with Monte Carlo stock & 30" full choke barrel.
Estimated Value: Excellent: $470.00
                        Very good: $380.00

Beretta Model A302 Slug

Similar to the Model A302 Mag-Action with a 22" slug barrel; adjustable front sight, folding leaf rear sight; swivels.
Estimated Value: Excellent: $450.00
                        Very good: $360.00

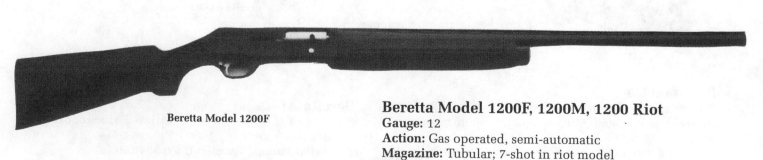

Beretta Model 1200F

Beretta Model 1200F, 1200M, 1200 Riot

Gauge: 12
Action: Gas operated, semi-automatic
Magazine: Tubular; 7-shot in riot model
Barrel: 28" modified; 20" cylinder bore on Riot Model
Finish: Blued; non-glare; synthetic stock & forearm
Approximate wt.: 7 lbs.
Comments: Introduced in 1988. Add 10% for Riot Model.
Estimated Value: New (retail): $527.00
                        Excellent: $395.00
                        Very good: $315.00

Beretta Model 303

Beretta 303 Slug

Beretta Model 303

Gauge: 12, 20, regular or magnum
Action: Gas operated, semi-automatic
Magazine: 2-shot plugged tubular
Barrel: 26", 28", 30" or 32" in a variety of chokes or interchangeable choke tubes; 24" barrel on youth model
Finish: Blued; checkered walnut pistol grip stock & forearm; recoil pad on youth model
Approximate wt.: 6 to 7 lbs.
Comments: Replaced the 302 series. Deduct 10% for shotguns without interchangeable choke tubes; add 12% for Sporting Clays Model.

Estimated Value:	New (retail):	$653.00
	Excellent:	$490.00
	Very good:	$390.00

Beretta Model 303 Slug

Similar to the Model 303 with a 22" cylinder bore barrel, rifle sights.

Estimated Value:	New (retail):	$680.00
	Excellent:	$510.00
	Very good:	$410.00

Beretta Model 303 Skeet

Similar to the Model 303 with a 26" skeet choke barrel.

Estimated Value:	New (retail):	$673.00
	Excellent:	$505.00
	Very good:	$400.00

Beretta Model 303 Trap

Similar to the Model 30 with a 30" or 32" full choke barrel or interchangeable choke tubes. Add 8% for interchangeable choke tubes.

Estimated Value:	New (retail):	$673.00
	Excellent:	$505.00
	Very good:	$400.00

Bernardelli

Bernardelli Roma

Bernardelli Roma

Gauge: 12, 16, 20, 28
Action: Anson & Deeley type; top lever break-open; hammerless; double trigger; automatic ejector
Magazine: None
Barrel: Double barrel; 27½" or 29½" modified & full choke
Finish: Blued; checkered walnut straight or pistol grip stock & forearm
Approximate wt.: 5 to 7 lbs.
Comments: Produced in three grades from the mid 1940's. Add $50.00 for single trigger.

Estimated Value:	Roma 3	Roma 4	Roma 5
Excellent:	$800.00	$1,000.00	$1,025.00
Very good:	$600.00	$ 750.00	$ 825.00

Bernardelli Game Cock

Bernardelli Game Cock Deluxe

Same as the Game Cock with light scroll engraving; single trigger; automatic ejector.

Estimated Value: **Excellent:** $760.00
                       Very good: $575.00

Bernardelli Game Cock Premier

Same as the Game Cock with more engraving; selective single trigger; automatic ejector.

Estimated Value: **Excellent:** $875.00
                       Very good: $650.00

Bernardelli Game Cock

Gauge: 12, 20
Action: Box lock; top lever break-open; double trigger; hammerless
Magazine: None
Barrel: Double barrel, 25" improved & modified or 28" modified & full chokes
Finish: Blued; checkered walnut straight stock & forearm; light engraving
Approximate wt.: 6½ lbs.
Comments: Produced in the early 1970's.
Estimated Value: **Excellent:** $690.00
                       Very good: $520.00

Bernardelli Italia

Bernardelli Italia

Gauge: 12, 16, 20
Action: Top lever break-open; exposed hammer; double trigger
Magazine: None
Barrel: Double barrel; chrome lined 30" modified & full chokes
Finish: Blued; engraved receiver; checkered walnut straight grip stock & forearm
Approximate wt.: 7 lbs.
Comments: Still in production.
Estimated Value: **New (retail):** $1,420.00
                       Excellent: $1,065.00
                       Very good: $ 850.00

Bernardelli Brescia

Bernardelli Brescia

Same as the Italia but available in 28" barrels or 20 gauge in 26" barrels; modified & improved cylinder bore.

Estimated Value: **Excellent:** $750.00
                       Very good: $560.00

Bernardelli Holland

Bernardelli Holland

Gauge: 12
Action: Slide lock; top lever break-open; hammerless; double trigger; automatic ejector
Magazine: None
Barrel: Doubel barrel, 26" to 32" any choke combination
Finish: Blued; straight or pistol grip stock & forearm; engraving
Approximate wt.: 7 lbs.
Comments: Produced from the mid 1940's to the early 1970's.
Estimated Value: **Excellent:** $2,000.00
                       Very good: $1,500.00

Bernardelli Holland Deluxe

Bernardelli Holland Deluxe

Same as the Holland with engraved hunting scene.

Estimated Value: **Excellent:** $2,500.00
                       Very good: $1,900.00

Bernardelli St. Uberto
Gauge: 12, 16, 20, 28
Action: Box lock; top lever break-open; double triggers; hammerless
Magazine: None
Barrel: Double barrel, 26" to 32", any choke combination
Finish: Blued; checkered walnut straight or pistol grip stock & forearm
Approximate wt.: 7 lbs.
Comments: Made from the mid 1940's to present.
Estimated Value: New (retail): $1,210.00
                        Excellent: $910.00
                        Very good: $725.00

Bernardelli St. Uberto

Breda

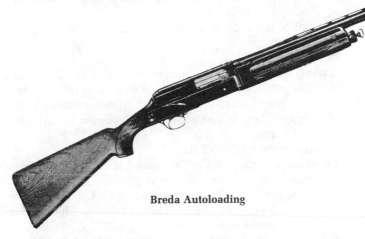

Breda Autoloading

Breda Autoloading
Gauge: 12, 12 magnum
Action: Semi-automatic; hammerless
Magazine: 4-shot tubular
Barrel: 25½" or 27½"
Finish: Blued; checkered walnut straight or pistol grip stock & forearm; available with ribbed barrel; engraving on grades 1, 2 & 3
Approximate wt.: 7¼ lbs.
Comments: Engraved models worth more, depending on grade & quality of engraving. Add 30% for magnum.
Estimated Value: Excellent: $350.00
                        Very good: $275.00

Browning

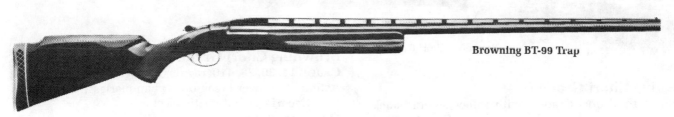

Browning BT-99 Trap

Browning BT-99 Trap
Gauge: 12
Action: Top lever break-open; automatic ejector; hammerless; single shot
Magazine: None
Barrel: 32" or 34" full, modified or improved modified choke; high post ventilated rib; some models have choke tubes
Finish: Blued; wide rib; checkered walnut pistol grip stock & forearm, some with Monte Carlo stock; recoil pad; some engraving; Pigeon grade is satin grey steel with deep relief hand engraving
Approximate wt.: 8 lbs.
Comments: Introduced in the early 1970's. Add 2% for choke tubes.
Estimated Value: New (retail): $981.00
                        Excellent: $735.00
                        Very good: $590.00

Browning Model BT-99 Plus
Gauge: 12
Action: Top lever, break-open; automatic ejector; single shot
Magazine: None, single shot
Barrel: 32" or 34", choke tubes; high post, ventilated, tapered target rib with matted sight plane; front & center sight beads; ported barrel available
Finish: Blued; receiver engraved with rosette & scrolls; select walnut, checkered pistol grip stock & modified beavertail forearm; Monte Carlo style comb with recoil reducer system; adjustable for drop, recoil pad cant, cast & length of pull; recoil pad
Approximate wt.: 8¾ lbs.
Comments: A trap shotgun with adjustable stock & patented recoil reduction system. Introduced in 1989. Add $50.00 for ported barrel.
Estimated Value: New (retail): $1,600.00
                        Excellent: $1,200.00
                        Very good: $ 950.00

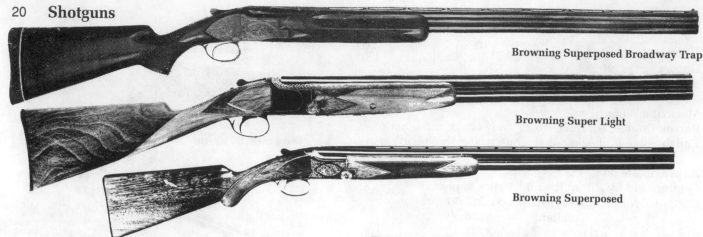

Browning Superposed Broadway Trap

Browning Super Light

Browning Superposed

Browning Super Light

Similar to Superposed except: lightweight; 26½" barrel; straight grip stock. Introduced in the late 1960's in many grades.

Estimated Value: **Excellent:**   **$2,000.00 - $5,000.00**
                      Very good: **$1,500.00 - $4,000.00**

Browning Superposed Broadway Trap Grade I

Similar to Superposed but with wide ventilated rib. Introduced in 1960 in many grades.

Estimated Value: **Excellent:**   **$1,800.00 - $4,000.00**
                      Very good: **$1,400.00 - $3,200.00**

Browning Superposed Magnum Grade I

Same gun as the Superposed except chambered for 3" magnum 12 gauge & with recoil pad.

Estimated Value: **Excellent:**   **$1,600.00 - $3,600.00**
                      Very good: **$1,200.00 - $2,800.00**

Browning Superposed

Gauge: 12; 20 added following World War II; 28 & 410 added in early 1960's

Action: Non-selective trigger; twin single triggers; selective trigger

Magazine: None

Barrel: Browning over & under double barrel; 26½", 28", 30", 32" choice of chokes; ventilated or matted rib

Finish: Blued; hand-checkered European walnut pistol grip stock & forearm; fluted comb; recoil pad; engraving

Approximate wt.: 6 to 8 lbs.

Comments: This gun first appeared in 1931 & has been made in a dozen different grades. More inlays & engraving is added on higher grades. Some expensive, highly decorative grades were produced. Belgium made until 1973.

Estimated Value: **Excellent:**   **$1,000.00 - $5,000.00**
                      Very good: **$ 750.00 - $3,700.00**

Browning Citori Grade I

Browning Citori Grade II

Similar to the Citori Grade I with select walnut stock, satin grey receiver engraved with Canada Goose & Ringneck Pheasant scenes. Add 5% for 410 or 28 gauge.

Estimated Value: **Excellent:**   **$975.00**
                      Very good: **$730.00**

Browning Citori Grade III

Similar to the Grade II with greyed receiver, scroll engraving & mallards & ringnecks decoration; 20 gauge, 28 gauge & 410 bore have quail & grouse. Add 10% for 28 gauge or 410.

Estimated Value: **New (retail):**   **$1,455.00**
                      Excellent: **$1,090.00**
                      Very good: **$ 875.00**

Browning Citori Grade V

Similar to the Citori Grade II with hand-checkered wood, hand-engraved receiver with Mallard Duck & Ringneck Pheasant scenes. Add 5% for 410 or 28 gauge; 3% for "Invector" choke tubes.

Estimated Value: **Excellent:**   **$1,475.00**
                      Very good: **$1,100.00**

Browning Citori Grade I

Gauge: 12, 20, 28, 410; regular & magnum

Action: Top lever break-open; hammerless; single selective trigger; automatic ejector

Magazine: None

Barrel: Over & under double barrel; 26" or 28", variety of choke combinations in 420, 28 or 20 gauge; 26", 28" or 30" variety of choke combinations in 12 gauge; ventilated rib; some models have choke tubes

Finish: Blued; checkered walnut stock & forearm; Hunting Model has pistol grip stock & beavertail forearm; Sporter has straight stock & lipped forearm; engraved receiver; high polish finish on Hunting Model, oil finish on Sporter; Upland Special has straight stock; Lighting model has rounded pistol grip

Approximate wt.: 6½ to 7¾ lbs.

Comments: Similar to the Browning Superposed. Introduced in the early 1970's & currently produced. In 1982 a Superlight Model was added in 12 or 20 gauge with straight stock & scaled-down forearm. Add 3% for 410 or 28 gauge; 2% for Superlight or Upland Special.

Estimated Value: **New (retail):**   **$1,035.00**
                      Excellent: **$ 775.00**
                      Very good: **$ 620.00**

Browning Citori Trap

Browning Citori Sideplate

Similar to the Citori Grade V in 20 gauge Sporter style only; 26" improved cylinder & modified or modified & full choke; sideplates & receiver are decorated with etched upland game scenes of doves, Ruffed Grouse, quail, pointing dog; trigger guard tang is decorated & engraved. Introduced in 1981. Discontinued in 1984.

Estimated Value: Excellent: $1,475.00
                   Very good: $1,100.00

Browning Citori Skeet

Similar to the Citori with 26" or 28" skeet choke barrels; high post target rib. Add 30% for Grade II or Grade III decoration; 80% for Grade IV, Grade V or Grade VI.

Estimated Value: New (retail): $1,155.00
                   Excellent: $ 865.00
                   Very good: $ 690.00

Browning Citori Trap

A trap version of the Citori in 12 gauge only; high post target rib; 30", 32" or 34" barrel; Monte Carlo stock. Add 30% for Grade II or Grade III decoration; 80% for Grade V or Grade VI.

Estimated Value: New (retail): $1,160.00
                   Excellent: $ 870.00
                   Very good: $ 695.00

Browning Citori Grade VI

Similar to the Grade V Citori with greyed or blued receiver, deep relief engraving, gold plating & engraving of ringneck pheasants, mallard drakes & English Setter. Add 10% for 28 gauge or 410.

Estimated Value: New (retail): $2,095.00
                   Excellent: $1,570.00
                   Very good: $1,250.00

Browning Citori Plus

Gauge: 12
Action: Top lever, break-open; hammerless; automatic ejectors
Magazine: None
Barrel: 30" or 32" over & under double barrel with high post, ventilated, tapered target rib; matted sight plane; choke tubes; front & center sight beads; ported barrel available
Finish: Blued; receiver engraving; select walnut checkered pistol grip stock & modified beavertail forearm; Monte Carlo style comb with recoil reduction system adjustable for drop, recoil pad cant, cast & length of pull
Approximate wt.: 9¼ to 9½ lbs.
Comments: A trap shotgun with adjustable stock & patented recoil reduction system. Introduced in 1990. Add $50.00 for ported barrel.

Estimated Value: New (retail): $1,575.00
                   Excellent: $1,180.00
                   Very good: $ 950.00

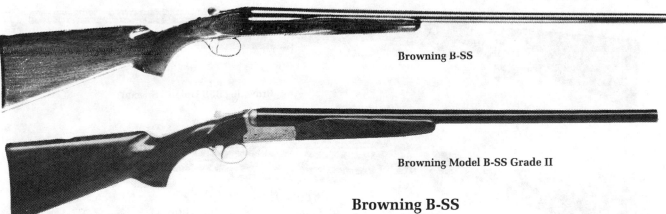

Browning B-SS

Browning Model B-SS Grade II

Browning Model B-SS Grade II

Similar to the B-SS with engraved satin grey frame featuring a pheasant, duck, quail & ducks. Discontinued 1984.

Estimated Value: Excellent: $850.00
                   Very good: $650.00

Browning B-SS Sidelock

Similar to the Model B-SS with sidelock action, engraved grey receiver, double triggers, small tapered forearm & straight grip stock.

Estimated Value: Excellent: $1,280.00
                   Very good: $ 915.00

Browning B-SS

Gauge: 12, 20
Action: Top lever break-open; hammerless; automatic ejector
Magazine: None
Barrel: Double barrel; in 12 gauge, 30" full & full or modified & full chokes; in 12 & 20 gauge, 28" modified & full chokes; 26" modified & full or improved cylinder & modified chokes
Finish: Blued; checkered walnut pistol grip stock & forearm
Approximate wt.: 7-7½ lbs.
Comments: Made from the early 1970's to 1988. Add 5% for barrel selector.

Estimated Value: Excellent: $580.00
                   Very good: $435.00

Browning BPS

Browning BPS

Gauge: 12, 20; 2¾" or 3"; 10 (added 1988); 3½" magnum (added 1989)

Action: Slide action; concealed hammer; bottom ejection

Magazine: 4-shot; 3-shot in magnum

Barrel: 26" improved cylinder bore, 28" modified choke, 30" or 32" full choke; ventilated rib; 20 gauge added in 1982 with variety of chokes; choke tubes available on later models

Finish: Blued; checkered walnut pistol grip stock & slide handle. Trap model has Monte Carlo stock; Stalker model has graphite-fiberglass composite stock, matte finish

Approximate wt.: 7½ lbs.

Comments: Produced since the late 1970's. Add 25% for 3½" magnum; add 5% for Trap Model (discontinued); add 25% for 10 gauge.

Estimated Value:	New (retail):	$433.50
	Excellent:	$325.00
	Very good:	$260.00

Browning BPS Upland Special

Similar to the BPS with a straight grip stock, 22" barrel and "Invector" choke tubes. Introduced in 1984.

Estimated Value:	New (retail):	$433.50
	Excellent:	$325.00
	Very good:	$260.00

Browning BPS Buck Special

Similar to the BPS with a 24" barrel for slugs, rifle sights. Add 5% for strap & swivels.

Estimated Value:	New (retail):	$439.50
	Excellent:	$330.00
	Very good:	$265.00

Browning BPS Youth and Ladies

Similar to the Model BPS in 20 gauge only with 22" barrel, compact stock & recoil pad. Introduced in 1986.

Estimated Value:	New (retail):	$433.50
	Excellent:	$325.00
	Very good:	$260.00

Browning BPS Youth and Ladies

Browning BPS Upland Special

Browning Model 12

Browning Model 12

Gauge: 20, 28 (added 1990)

Action: Slide action, repeating; concealed hammer

Magazine: 5-shot tubular; 2-shot with plug

Barrel: 26" modified, high ventilated rib

Finish: Blued; checkered walnut pistol grip stock & slide handle; steel grip cap. Grade V has engraved receiver with gold plated scenes.

Approximate wt.: 7 lbs.

Comments: A reintroduction of the popular Winchester Model 12 designed by John Browning. Introduced in 1988. Add 5% for 28 gauge; add 60% for Grade V.

Estimated Value:	New (retail):	$734.95
	Excellent:	$550.00
	Very good:	$440.00

Browning B.A.A.C. No. 1 Regular

Gauge: 12
Action: Semi-automatic, hammerless
Magazine: 4-shot
Barrel: 28"
Finish: Blued; walnut straight stock & grooved forearm
Approximate wt.: 7¾ lbs.
Comments: This gun was sold in the U.S. from 1902 to 1905. Made in Belgium.
Estimated Value: Excellent: $325.00
                        Very good: $260.00

Browning B.A.A.C. No. 2 Trap

Trap grade version of the No. 1 with some checkering.
Estimated Value: Excellent: $350.00
                        Very good: $280.00

Browning B.A.A.C. Two Shot

Similar to the No. 1 in 2-shot model.
Estimated Value: Excellent: $275.00
                        Very good: $220.00

Browning B.A.A.C. No. 0 Messenger

A short, 20" barrel, version of the No. 1, made for bank guards, etc.
Estimated Value: Excellent: $300.00
                        Very good: $250.00

F.N. Browning Automatic

Similar to the B.A.A.C. No. 1 sold only overseas. Some models carried swivels for sling. Produced until Browning's American sales began in 1931.
Estimated Value: Excellent: $375.00
                        Very good: $300.00

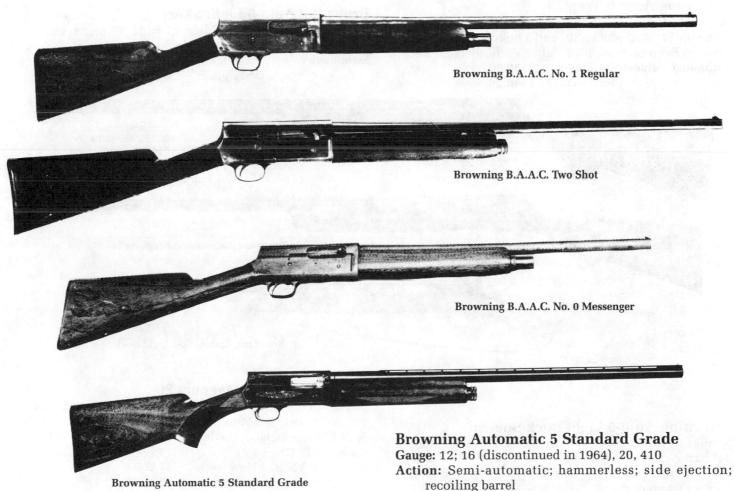

Browning B.A.A.C. No. 1 Regular

Browning B.A.A.C. Two Shot

Browning B.A.A.C. No. 0 Messenger

Browning Automatic 5 Standard Grade

Browning Automatic 5 Standard Grade

Gauge: 12; 16 (discontinued in 1964), 20, 410
Action: Semi-automatic; hammerless; side ejection; recoiling barrel
Magazine: 4-shot, bottom load; 3-shot model also available
Barrel: 26"-32" full choke, modified or cylinder bore; plain, raised matted rib or ventilated rib
Finish: Blued; checkered walnut, pistol grip stock & forearm
Approximate wt.: 7 to 8 lbs.
Comments: Made from about 1931 to 1973 in Belgium. Add 13% for ventilated rib.
Estimated Value: Excellent: $575.00
                        Very good: $475.00

Browning Automatic 5 Grades II, III, IV

Basically the same shotgun as the Standard Grade with engraving & improved quality on higher grades. Discontinued in the early 1940's. Add $25.00 for rib.

Estimated Value:	Gr. II	Gr. III	Gr. IV
Excellent:	$750.00	$1,000.00	$1,500.00
Very good:	$575.00	$ 750.00	$1,200.00

Browning Automatic-5 Light 12

Browning Automatic-5 Light 20

Browning Auto-5 Light 20

Basically the same as the Standard Grade except: 20 gauge only; a lightweight 26" or 28" barrel. Made from the late 1950's to present. Add 35% for Belgian made; rounded pistol grip reintroduced in 1987.

Estimated Value: New (retail): $719.95
                Excellent: $540.00
                Very good: $430.00

Browning Auto-5 Trap

Basically the same as the Standard Grade except 12 gauge only; trap stock; 30" full choke; ventilated rib; made in Belgium until 1971. Add 35% for Belgian made.

Estimated Value: Excellent: $550.00
                Very good: $440.00

Browning Auto-5 Light 12

Basically the same as the Standard Grade except 12 gauge only & light weight. Made from about 1948 to present. Add 35% for Belgian made; rounded pistol grip reintroduced in 1987.

Estimated Value: New (retail): $719.95
                Excellent: $540.00
                Very good: $430.00

Browning Auto-5 Light Skeet

Similar to the Light 12 & Light 20 with 26" or 28" skeet choke barrel. Add 35% for Belgian made.

Estimated Value: Excellent: $450.00
                Very good: $360.00

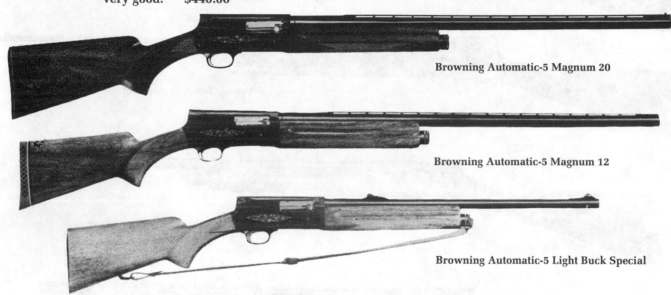

Browning Automatic-5 Magnum 20

Browning Automatic-5 Magnum 12

Browning Automatic-5 Light Buck Special

Browning Auto-5 Light Buck Special

Similar to the Standard Model, 12 or 20 gauge; special 24" barrel choked & bored for slug. Made from the early 1960's to present. Add 4% for strap & swivels; add 35% for Belgian made.

Estimated Value: New (retail) $724.95
                Excellent: $545.00
                Very good: $435.00

Browning Auto-5 Buck Special Magnum

Same as the Buck Special, for 3" magnum shells, in 12 & 20 gauge. Add 4% for strap & swivels; add 35% for Belgian made.

Estimated Value: New (retail): $747.95
                Excellent: $560.00
                Very good: $450.00

Browning Auto-5 Magnum 20

Similar to the Standard Model except 20 gauge magnum; 26" or 28" barrel. Made from the late 1960's to present. Add 35% for Belgian made; rounded pistol grip reintroduced in 1987.

Estimated Value: New (retail): $742.95
                Excellent: $560.00
                Very good: $445.00

Browning Auto-5 Magnum 12

Similar to the Standard Model except 12 gauge magnum, equipped with recoil pad. Made from the late 1950's to present. Also equipped with a 32" full choke barrel. Add 35% for Belgian made; rounded pistol grip reintroduced in 1987.

Estimated Value: New (retail): $742.95
                Excellent: $560.00
                Very good: $445.00

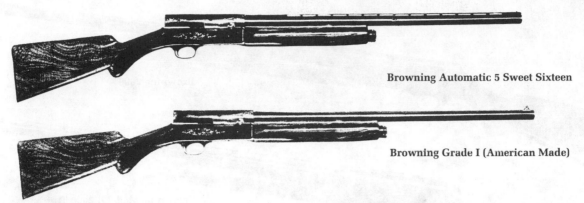

Browning Automatic 5 Sweet Sixteen

Browning Grade I (American Made)

Browning Auto-5 Sweet Sixteen

A lightweight 16 gauge version of the Standard Model with a gold plated trigger. Made from about 1936 to 1975 in Belgium. Reintroduced in 1987; add 35% for Belgium made.

Estimated Value: New (retail): $719.95
                  Excellent: $540.00
                  Very good: $430.00

Browning Grade I (American Made)

Similar to Browning Standard Grade. Made by Remington from 1940 until about 1948. World War II forced the closing of the Fabrique Nationale plant in Belgium.

Estimated Value: Excellent: $330.00
                  Very good: $260.00

Browning Special (American Made)

Similar to Grade I with a matted or ventilated rib.

Estimated Value: Excellent: $375.00
                  Very good: $300.00

Browning Special Skeet (American Made)

Same as the Grade I with a Cutts Compensator.

Estimated Value: Excellent: $325.00
                  Very good: $260.00

Browning Utility (American Made)

Similar to Grade I with Poly Choke.

Estimated Value: Excellent: $290.00
                  Very good: $230.00

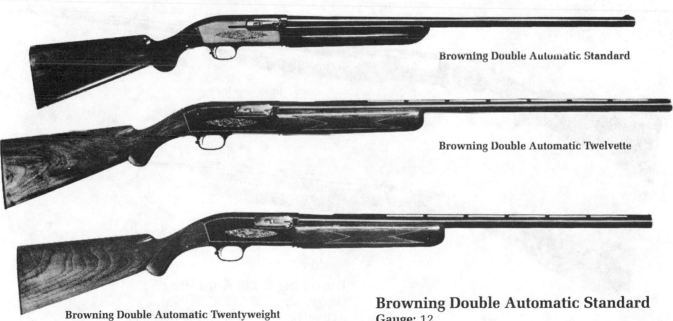

Browning Double Automatic Standard

Browning Double Automatic Twelvette

Browning Double Automatic Twentyweight

Browning Double Automatic Twelvette

Basically the same as the Standard with lightweight aluminum receiver. Made until the early 1970's.

Estimated Value: Excellent: $400.00
                  Very good: $300.00

Browning Double Automatic Twentyweight

A still lighter version of the Standard with 26½" barrel. Made until the early 1970's.

Estimated Value: Excellent: $410.00
                  Very good: $320.00

Browning Double Automatic Standard

Gauge: 12
Action: Semi-automatic; short recoil, side ejection; hammerless; 2 shot
Magazine: 1-shot
Barrel: 30" or 28" full choke; 28" or 26" modified choke; 28" or 26" skeet; 26" cylinder bore or improved cylinder
Finish: Blued; checkered walnut pistol grip stock & forearm
Approximate wt.: 7¾ lbs.
Comments: Made from the mid 1950's to the early 1960's. Add 8% for ventilated rib.
Estimated Value: Excellent: $375.00
                  Very good: $290.00

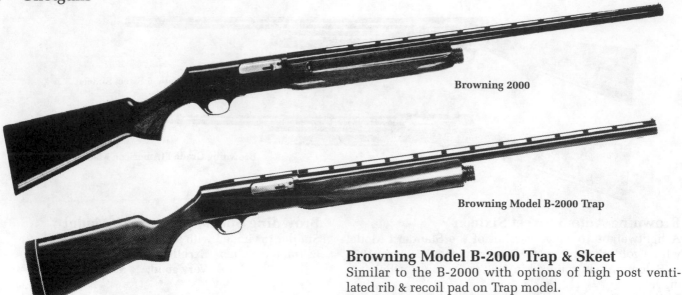

Browning 2000

Browning Model B-2000 Trap

Browning 2000 or B-2000

Similar to the Automatic 5 shotgun except gas operated. Introduced in the early 1970's in 12 & 20 gauge regular or magnum. Discontinued about 1981.

Estimated Value: Excellent: $375.00
                       Very good: $280.00

Browning Model B-2000 Trap & Skeet

Similar to the B-2000 with options of high post ventilated rib & recoil pad on Trap model.

Estimated Value: Excellent: $400.00
                       Very good: $300.00

Browning 2000 Buck Special

Similar to the 2000 except; 24" barrel; adjustable rifle sights; swivels.

Estimated Value: Excellent: $425.00
                       Very good: $350.00

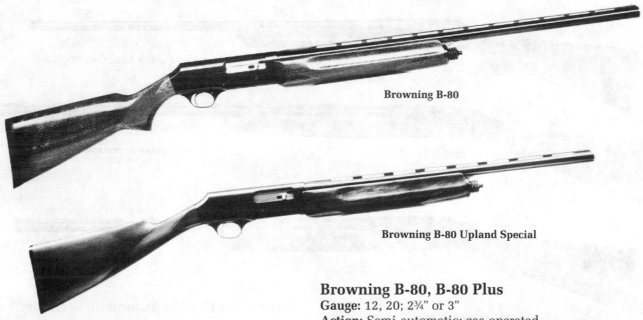

Browning B-80

Browning B-80 Upland Special

Browning B-80 Buck Special

Similar to the B-80 with 24" slug barrel, rifle sights. Add $20.00 for strap & swivels.

Estimated Value: Excellent: $425.00
                       Very good: $325.00

Browning B-80 Upland Special

Similar to the Model B-80 with a straight grip stock & 22" barrel. Introduced in 1986.

Estimated Value: New (retail): $561.95
                       Excellent: $420.00
                       Very good: $335.00

Browning B-80, B-80 Plus

Gauge: 12, 20; 2¾" or 3"
Action: Semi-automatic; gas-operated
Magazine: 3-shot, 2-shot in magnum
Barrel: 26", 28", 30" or 32" in a variety of chokes; internally chrome plated; ventilated rib; choke tubes available
Finish: Blued; checkered walnut semi-pistol grip stock & fluted, checkered forearm; alloy receiver on Superlight model
Approximate wt.: 6 to 8 lbs.
Comments: Introduced in 1981. Superlight model added in 1982.
Estimated Value: New (retail): $561.95
                       Excellent: $420.00
                       Very good: $335.00

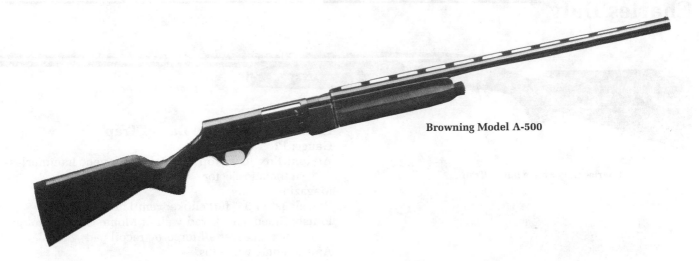

Browning Model A-500

Browning Model A-500

Gauge: 12, regular or magnum
Action: Short recoil operated semi-automatic
Magazine: 4-shot tubular; 3-shot in magnum; plug included; magazine cut-off allows chambering of shell independent of magazine
Barrel: 26", 28", 30" choke tubes; ventilated rib; 24" Buck Special barrel available
Finish: Blued; checkered walnut pistol grip stock & forearm; recoil pad
Approximate wt.: 7¼ lbs.
Comments: Introduced in 1987.
Estimated Value: New (retail): $552.00
Excellent: $415.00
Very good: $330.00

Browning Model A-500G

Gauge: 12, regular or magnum
Action: Gas operated, semi-automatic
Magazine: 4-shot; 3-shot with magnum shells; 2-shot with plug installed
Barrel: 26", 28" or 30" barrel; ventilated rib with matted sighting surface; choke tubes
Finish: Blued; gold accents on receiver; select checkered walnut, pistol grip & forearm; recoil pad; gold trigger
Approximate wt.: 7¾ to 8½ lbs.
Comments: Introduced in 1990.
Estimated Value: New (retail): $639.00
Excellent: $480.00
Very good: $385.00

Browning Model A-500G

Browning Model A-500 Buck Special

Similar to the Model A-500G with a 24" slug barrel & adjustable rear, ramp front sights.
Estimated Value: New (retail): $639.00
Excellent: $480.00
Very good: $385.00

Browning Model M-500R

Gauge: 12, regular or magnum
Action: Recoil operated, semi-automatic
Magazine: 4-shot; 3-shot with magnum shells; 2-shot with plug installed
Barrel: 26", 28" or 30" with choke tubes; ventilated rib with matted sighting surface
Finish: Blued; red accents on receiver; select checkered walnut pistol grip stock & forearm; gold trigger
Approximate wt.: 7¾ to 8 lbs.
Comments: Introduced in 1990.
Estimated Value: New (retail): $559.95
Excellent: $420.00
Very good: $335.00

Browning Model A-500R Buck Special

Similar to the Model A-500R with a 24" slug barrel, adjustable rear & ramp front sights.
Estimated Value: New (retail): $559.00
Excellent: $420.00
Very good: $335.00

Charles Daly

Charles Daly Single Barrel Trap

Charles Daly Commander 100

Gauge: 12, 16, 20, 28, 410
Action: Box lock; top lever, break-open; hammerless; automatic ejector
Magazine: None
Barrel: Over & under double barrel; 26", 28", 30" improved cylinder & modified or modified & full chokes
Finish: Blued; checkered walnut straight or pistol grip stock & forearm; engraved
Approximate wt.: 5 to 7½ lbs.
Comments: Made from the mid 1930's to about 1939.
Estimated Value: **Excellent:**   **$600.00**
                        Very good: **$450.00**

Charles Daly Commander 200

This is a fancier version of the Commander 100 with select wood, more engraving & a higher quality finish.
Estimated Value: **Excellent:**   **$700.00**
                        Very good: **$525.00**

Charles Daly Single Barrel Trap

Gauge: 12
Action: Box lock; top lever, break-open; hammerless; automatic ejector
Magazine: None
Barrel: 32" or 34" full choke; ventilated rib
Finish: Blued; checkered walnut Monte Carlo pistol grip stock & beavertail forearm; recoil pad
Approximate wt.: 8 lbs.
Comments: Made from late 1960's to mid 1970's. This model should not be confused with the Single Barrel Trap Models made in the 1930's that are worth several times more.
Estimated Value: **Excellent:**   **$450.00**
                        Very good: **$360.00**

Charles Daly Hammerless Double

Gauge: 10, 12, 16, 20, 28, 410
Action: Box lock; top lever, break-open; hammerless; automatic ejector (except Superior)
Magazine: None
Barrel: Double barrel; 26", 28", 30", 32"; choice of choke combinations
Finish: Blued; checkered walnut pistol grip stock & short tapered forearm; engraving
Approximate wt.: 4 to 8 lbs.
Comments: Manufactured in differing grades, alike except for quality of finish & amount of engraving. Made from 1920 to 1935.

Estimated Value:	**Excellent**	**Very Good**
Diamond:	$3,000.00	$2,250.00
Empire:	$2,200.00	$1,650.00
Superior:	$1,500.00	$1,150.00

Charles Daly Field Grade

Charles Daly Field Grade

Gauge: 12, 20, 28, 410, 12 magnum, 20 magnum
Action: Box lock; top lever, break-open; hammerless; single trigger
Magazine: None
Barrel: Over & under double barrel; 26", 28", 30", various choke combinations; ventilated rib
Finish: Blued; engraved; checkered walnut pistol grip stock & forearm; 12 gauge magnum has recoil pad
Approximate wt.: 6 to 8 lbs.
Comments: Manufactured from the early 1960's to mid 1970's.
Estimated Value: **Excellent:**   **$550.00**
                        Very good: **$410.00**

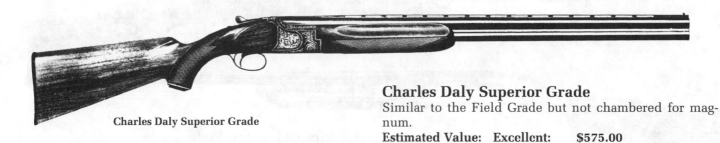

Charles Daly Superior Grade

Charles Daly Superior Grade
Similar to the Field Grade but not chambered for magnum.
Estimated Value: Excellent: $575.00
Very good: $430.00

Charles Daly Diamond Grade

Charles Daly Diamond Grade
Similar to the Superior with select wood & fancier engraving.
Estimated Value: Excellent: $650.00
Very good: $490.00

Charles Daly Field III

Charles Daly Field III
Similar to the Field Grade with some minor changes; double trigger. Currently available.
Estimated Value: New (retail): $450.00
Excellent: $337.00
Very good: $255.00

Charles Daly Superior II
Similar to the Field III but higher quality. Currently available.
Estimated Value: New (retail): $700.00
Excellent: $525.00
Very good: $420.00

Charles Daly Venture Grade

Charles Daly Venture Grade
Gauge: 12, 20
Action: Box lock; top lever, break-open; hammerless; automatic ejector
Magazine: None
Barrel: Over & under double barrel; 26", 28", 30", various chokes; ventilated rib
Finish: Blued; checkered walnut pistol grip stock & forearm
Approximate wt.: 7 to 8 lbs.
Comments: Made since the early 1970's to mid 1980's. Add $25.00 for Skeet model; $35.00 for Trap model.
Estimated Value: Excellent: $425.00
Very good: $340.00

Charles Daly Auto

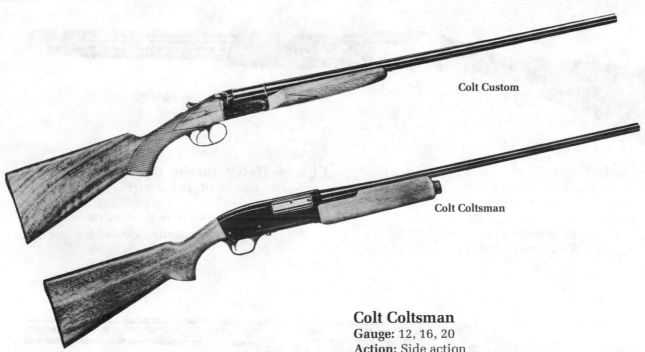

Charles Daly Auto Superior

Charles Daly Auto Field
Gauge: 12, 12 magnum
Action: Semi-automatic, recoil operated
Magazine: 5-shot tubular
Barrel: 26" improved cylinder or skeet, 28" modified or full, 30" full, chokes; ventilated rib
Finish: Blued; checkered walnut pistol grip stock & forearm
Approximate wt.: about 7½ lbs.
Comments: Made from the mid 1970's to present.
Estimated Value: New (retail): $386.00
                    Excellent: $290.00
                    Very good: $215.00

Charles Daly Auto Superior
Similar to the Auto Field but higher quality.
Estimated Value: Excellent: $300.00
                    Very good: $225.00

Colt

Colt Custom

Colt Coltsman

Colt Custom
Gauge: 12, 16
Action: Box lock; top lever, break-open; hammerless; double trigger; automatic ejector
Magazine: None
Barrel: Double barrel; 26" improved & modified, 28" modified & full or 30" full chokes
Finish: Blued; checkered walnut pistol grip stock & tapered forearm
Approximate wt.: 7 to 8 lbs.
Comments: Produced in the early 1960's.
Estimated Value: Excellent: $375.00
                    Very good: $280.00

Colt Coltsman
Gauge: 12, 16, 20
Action: Side action
Magazine: 4-shot
Barrel: 26" improved, 28" modified, 30" full chokes
Finish: Blued; plain walnut pistol grip stock & slide handle
Approximate wt.: 6½ to 7 lbs.
Comments: Made from the early to mid 1960's in takedown models.
Estimated Value: Excellent: $200.00
                    Very good: $150.00

Colt Coltsman Custom
A fancier version of the Coltsman with checkering & a ventilated rib.
Estimated Value: Excellent: $250.00
                    Very good: $200.00

Colt Ultra Light

Colt Ultra Light

Gauge: 12, 20
Action: Semi-automatic
Magazine: 4-shot
Barrel: Chrome lined, 26" improved or modified, 28" modified or full, 30", 32" full chokes; rib available
Finish: Blued; checkered walnut pistol grip stock & forearm; alloy receiver
Approximate wt.: 6½ lbs.
Comments: A takedown shotgun produced during the mid 1960's. Add $15.00 for solid rib; $25.00 for ventilated rib.
Estimated Value: Excellent: $250.00
Very good: $190.00

Colt Ultra Light Custom

This is the same as the Ultra Light Auto with select wood, engraving & ventilated rib.
Estimated Value: Excellent: $300.00
Very good: $225.00

Colt Magnum Auto

Same as the Ultra Light Auto in magnum gauges & of heavier weight. Add $15.00 for solid rib; $25.00 for ventilated rib.
Estimated Value: Excellent: $250.00
Very good: $190.00

Colt Magnum Auto Custom

Same as Magnum Auto with select wood, engraving & ventilated rib.
Estimated Value: Excellent: $310.00
Very good: $230.00

Darne

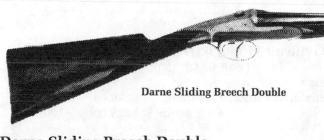

Darne Sliding Breech Double

Darne Sliding Breech Double

Gauge: 12, 16, 20, 28
Action: Sliding breech; selective ejectors; double trigger
Magazine: None
Barrel: Doubel barrel; 25½" or 27½" modified & improved cylinder, raised rib
Finish: Blued; checkered walnut straight or pistol grip stock & forearm
Approximate wt.: 5¾ to 6¼ lbs.
Comments: A French shotgun.
Estimated Value: Excellent: $800.00
Very good: $600.00

Darne Deluxe

Same as the Sliding Breech Double with engraving & 28" modified & full choke barrels.
Estimated Value: Excellent: $1,100.00
Very good: $ 825.00

Darne Supreme

Same shotgun as the Darne Deluxe except in 20 or 28 gauge; 25½" barrels; elaborate engraving & swivels.
Estimated Value: Excellent: $1,500.00
Very good: $1,200.00

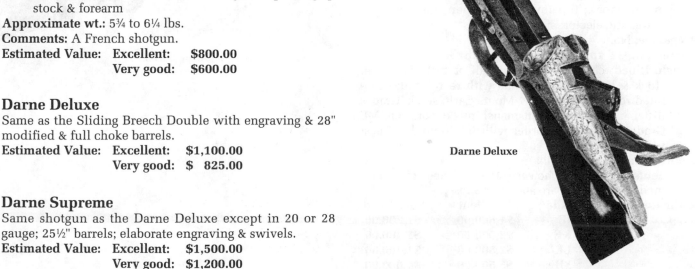

Darne Deluxe

Davidson

Davidson Model 73 Stagecoach

Davidson Model 69SL

Gauge: 12, 20 magnum

Action: Box lock; top lever break-open; exposed hammers

Magazine: None

Barrel: Doubel barrel; 20" improved cylinder & modified or modified & full chokes; matted rib

Finish: Blued; checkered walnut pistol grip stock & forearm; sights; engraved receiver

Approximate wt.: 7 lbs.

Comments: Made from early to late 1970's.

Estimated Value: Excellent: $220.00
Very good: $175.00

Davidson Model 69 SL

Gauge: 12, 20

Action: Side lock

Magazine: None

Barrel: Doubel barrel; 26"-30", variety of chokes

Finish: Blued or nickel; checkered walnut pistol grip stock & forearm; gold trigger; bead sights; engraved

Approximate wt.: 6 to 7 lbs.

Comments: Made from early 1960's to late 1970's.

Estimated Value: Excellent: $275.00
Very good: $220.00

Davidson Model 63B

Davidson Model 63B

Gauge: 12, 16, 20, 28, 410

Action: Box lock; top lever break-open; double triggers

Magazine: None

Barrel: Double barrel; 26", 28"; 25" in 410; 30" in 12 gauge; improved cylinder & modified, modified & full, full & full chokes

Finish: Blued or nickel; checkered walnut pistol grip stock & forearm; bead sights; some engraving

Approximate wt.: 6 to 7 lbs.

Comments: Produced in Spain.

Estimated Value: Excellent: $250.00
Very good: $200.00

Davidson Model 63B Magnum

Davidson Model 63B Magnum

Same as Model 63B in 10, 12 or 20 gauge magnum. Available with 32" barrel in 10 gauge.

Estimated Value: Excellent: $280.00
Very good: $225.00

Fox

Fox Trap (Single Barrel)

Gauge: 12

Action: Box lock; top lever break-open; hammerless; automatic ejector; single shot

Magazine: None

Barrel: 30", 32" trap bore; ventilated rib

Finish: Blued; checkered walnut half or full pistol grip stock & large forearm; some with recoil pad; decorated receiver; after 1931 Monte Carlo stock. Grades differ in quality of craftsmanship & decoration. ME Grade was made to order with inlaid gold & finest walnut wood.

Approximate wt.: 7 to 8 lbs.

Comments: Made until the early 1940's. Prices for grades made before 1932 are about 20% less.

Fox Trap (Single Barrel)

Estimated Value:	Grade	Excellent	Very Good
	JE	$1,600.00	$1,200.00
	KE	$2,000.00	$1,400.00
	LE	$2,500.00	$1,400.00
	ME	$5,500.00	$4,000.00

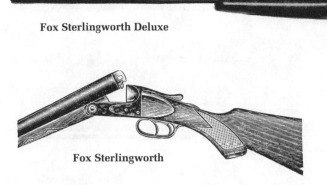

Fox Sterlingworth Deluxe

Fox Sterlingworth

Fox Sterlingworth

Gauge: 12, 16, 20
Action: Box lock; top lever break-open; hammerless; double trigger or selective single trigger; some with automatic ejector
Magazine: None
Barrel: Double barrel; 26"-30"; full & full, modified & full, cylinder & modified chokes
Finish: Blued; checkered walnut pistol grip stock & forearm
Approximate wt.: 5¾ to 8 lbs.
Comments: Made until the early 1940's. Add $50.00 for selective trigger; $75.00 for automatic ejector.
Estimated Value: Excellent: $550.00
Very good: $445.00

Fox Sterlingworth Deluxe

This is a fancy model Sterlingworth with ivory bead; recoil pad; 32" barrels; selective single trigger. Add $75.00 for automatic ejector.
Estimated Value: Excellent: $625.00
Very good: $500.00

Fox Sterlingworth Skeet

Basically the same as the Sterlingworth with skeet bore; 26" or 28" barrels; straight grip stock. Add $75.00 for automatic ejector.
Estimated Value: Excellent: $600.00
Very good: $480.00

Fox Skeeter

Similar to Sterlingworth with 28" skeet bored barrels; ventilated rib; ivory bead; recoil pad, 12 or 20 gauge; automatic ejector.
Estimated Value: Excellent: $1,000.00
Very good: $ 750.00

Fox Model B

Fox Hammerless Doubles

These are very similar to the Sterlingworth models, in varying degrees of increased quality. All have automatic ejectors except Grade A. Add $50.00 for selective single trigger; $125.00 for ventilated rib.

Estimated Value:	Grade	Excellent	Very Good
	A	$ 850.00	$ 650.00
	AE	$1,200.00	$ 950.00
	BE	$1,600.00	$1,200.00
	CE	$1,700.00	$1,290.00
	DE	$3,000.00	$2,275.00

Fox Super Fox

Gauge: 12
Action: Box lock; top lever break-open; hammerless; double trigger; automatic ejector
Magazine: None
Barrel: Double barrel; 30" or 32" full choke
Finish: Blued; checkered walnut pistol grip stock & forearm
Approximate wt.: 7¾ to 9¾ lbs.
Comments: This is a long range gun produced from the mid 1920's to early 1940's.
Estimated Value: Excellent: $500.00
Very good: $400.00

Fox Model B, BE

Gauge: 12, 16, 20, 410
Action: Box lock; top lever break-open; hammerless; double triggers; plain ejector
Magazine: None
Barrel: Double barrel; 24"-30" full & full, modified & full, cylinder & modified chokes; ventilated rib
Finish: Blued; checkered walnut pistol grip stock & forearm; case hardened receiver on current model
Approximate wt.: 7½ lbs.
Comments: Made from the early 1940's to 1988. 16 gauge discontinued in the late 1970's. Model BE has automatic ejector.
Estimated Value: Excellent: $275.00
Very good: $210.00

Fox Model B Lightweight

Same as the Model B with 24" cylinder bore & modified choke barrels in 12 & 20 gauge.
Estimated Value: Excellent: $250.00
Very good: $200.00

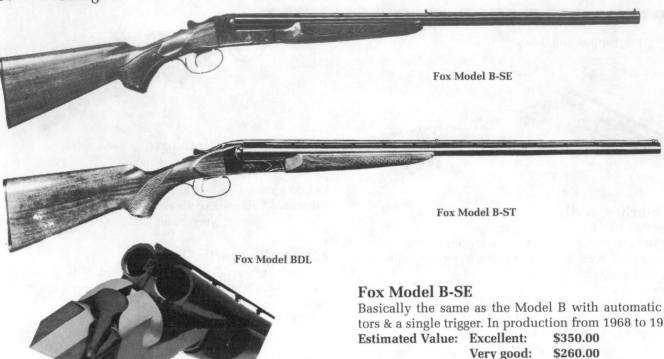

Fox Model B-SE

Fox Model B-ST

Fox Model BDL

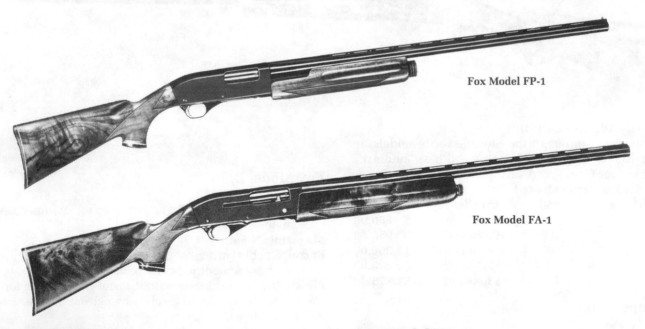

Fox Model B-DL & B-DE
Similar to the B-ST with chrome frame & beavertail forearm. Made from the early 1960's to early 1970's.

Estimated Value: Excellent: **$350.00**
                       Very good: **$275.00**

Fox Model B-SE
Basically the same as the Model B with automatic ejectors & a single trigger. In production from 1968 to 1988.

Estimated Value: Excellent: **$350.00**
                       Very good: **$260.00**

Fox Model B-ST
This is the same as Model B with gold plated nonselective single trigger. Made from the mid 1950's to mid 1960's.

Estimated Value: Excellent: **$325.00**
                       Very good: **$250.00**

Fox Model FP-1

Fox Model FA-1

Fox Model FP-1
Gauge: 12; 2¾" or 3"
Action: Slide action, hammerless
Magazine: 4-shot tubular; 3-shot with 3" shells
Barrel: 28" modified, 30" full choke; ventilated rib
Finish: Blued; checkered walnut pistol grip stock & slide handle; rosewood cap with inlay
Approximate wt.: 7¼ lbs.
Comments: Produced from 1981 to 1983.
Estimated Value: Excellent: **$260.00**
                       Very good: **$200.00**

Fox Model FA-1
Gauge: 12; 2¾"
Action: Semi-automatic; gas operated
Magazine: 3-shot tubular
Barrel: 28" modified; 30" full choke; ventilated rib
Finish: Blued; checkered walnut pistol grip stock & forearm; rosewood cap with inlay
Approximate wt.: 7½ lbs.
Comments: Produced from 1981 to 1983.
Estimated Value: Excellent: **$285.00**
                       Very good: **$220.00**

Franchi

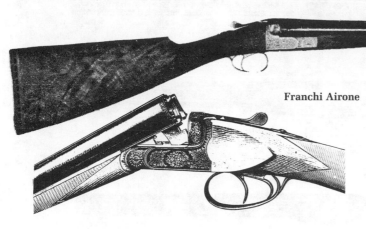

Franchi Airone

Franchi Astore

Franchi Airone

Gauge: 12
Action: Box lock; top lever, break-open; hammerless; automatic ejector
Magazine: None
Barrel: Double barrel; several lengths & choke combinations available
Finish: Blued; checkered walnut straight grip stock & short tapered forearm; engraved
Approximate wt.: 7 lbs.
Comments: Made from the mid 1940's to late 1950's.
Estimated Value: **Excellent:** **$800.00**
Very good: **$640.00**

Franchi Astore

Gauge: 12
Action: Box lock; top lever, break-open; hammerless; double triggers
Magazine: None
Barrel: Double barrel; several lengths & choke combinations available
Finish: Blued; checkered walnut straight grip stock & short tapered forearm
Approximate wt.: 7 lbs.
Comments: Made from the mid 1950's to late 1960's.
Estimated Value: **Excellent:** **$775.00**
Very good: **$620.00**

Franchi Astore S

Same as the Astore with higher quality wood & engraving.
Estimated Value: **Excellent:** **$1,250.00**
Very good: **$1,000.00**

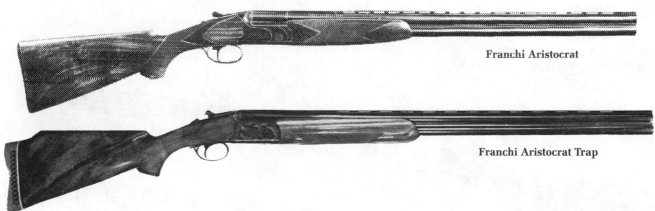

Franchi Aristocrat

Franchi Aristocrat Trap

Franchi Aristocrat

Gauge: 12
Action: Box lock; top lever, break-open; hammerless; automatic ejector; single trigger
Magazine: None
Barrel: Over & under double barrel; 24" cylinder bore & improved cylinder; 26" improved cylinder & modified, 28", 30" modified & full chokes; ventilated rib
Finish: Blued; checkered walnut pistol grip stock & forearm; engraved
Approximate wt.: 7 lbs.
Comments: Made from the early to late 1960's.
Estimated Value: **Excellent:** **$540.00**
Very good: **$430.00**

Franchi Aristocrat Trap

Similar to the Aristocrat with Monte Carlo stock; chrome lined barrels; case hardened receiver; 30" barrels only.
Estimated Value: **Excellent:** **$600.00**
Very good: **$480.00**

Franchi Aristocrat Skeet

Same as the Aristocrat Trap with 26" skeet barrels.
Estimated Value: **Excellent:** **$580.00**
Very good: **$465.00**

Franchi Aristocrat Silver King

Similar to the Aristocrat with higher quality finish; select wood; engraving.
Estimated Value: **Excellent:** **$690.00**
Very good: **$550.00**

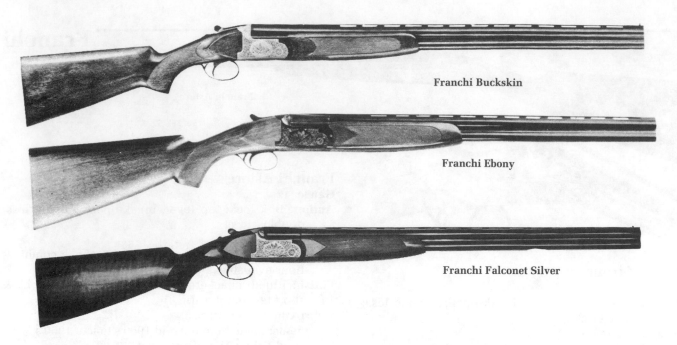

Franchi Buckskin

Franchi Ebony

Franchi Falconet Silver

Franchi Falconet Buckskin & Ebony

Gauge: 12, 20
Action: Box lock; top lever, break-open; hammerless
Magazine: None
Barrel: Over & under double barrel; 24"-30" barrels in several choke combinations; ventilated rib; chrome lined
Finish: Blued; colored frame with engraving; epoxy finished checkered walnut pistol grip stock & forearm
Approximate wt.: 6-7 lbs.
Comments: Made from about 1970 to late 1970's. Buckskin & Ebony differ only in color of receiver & engraving.
Estimated Value: Excellent: $545.00
                       Very good: $410.00

Franchi Falconite Silver

Same as the Buckskin & Ebony except: 12 gauge only; pickled silver receiver.
Estimated Value: Excellent: $575.00
                       Very good: $430.00

Franchi Falconet Super

Similar to the Falconet Silver except slightly different forearm; 12 gauge only; 27" or 28" barrels. Currently manufactured.
Estimated Value: Excellent: $650.00
                       Very good: $485.00

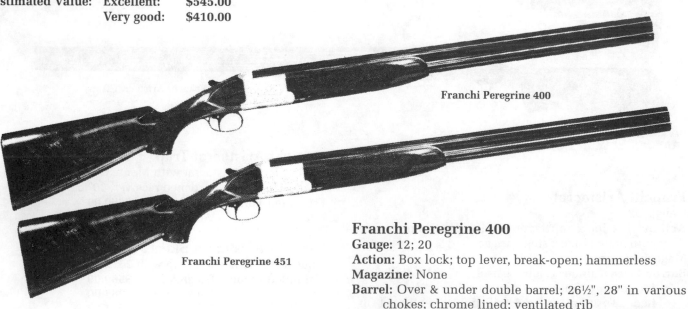

Franchi Peregrine 400

Franchi Peregrine 451

Franchi Peregrine 400

Gauge: 12; 20
Action: Box lock; top lever, break-open; hammerless
Magazine: None
Barrel: Over & under double barrel; 26½", 28" in various chokes; chrome lined; ventilated rib
Finish: Blued; checkered walnut pistol grip stock & forearm
Approximate wt.: 7 lbs.
Comments: Made from the mid to late 1970's.
Estimated Value: Excellent: $550.00
                       Very good: $440.00

Franchi Peregrine 451

Similar to the 400 except: alloy receiver; lightweight.
Estimated Value: Excellent: $500.00
                       Very good: $400.00

Franchi Diamond

Gauge: 12
Action: Box lock; top lever, break-open; hammerless; single selective trigger; automatic extractors
Magazine: None
Barrel: Over & under double barrel; 28" modified & full choke; ventilated rib
Finish: Blued; checkered walnut pistol grip stock & forearm; silver plated receiver
Approximate wt.: 6¾ lbs.
Comments: Produced in Italy.
Estimated Value: Excellent: $675.00
Very good: $540.00

Franchi Alcione

Gauge: 12, 3" magnum
Action: Box lock; top lever, break-open; hammerless; single selective trigger; automatic split selective ejectors
Magazine: None
Barrel: Over & under double barrel; 26" improved cylinder & modified; 28" modified & full choke; ventilated rib
Finish: Blued; coin-finished steel receiver with scroll engraving; checkered walnut pistol grip stock & forearm; recoil pad
Approximate wt.: 7 lbs.
Comments: Produced in Italy.
Estimated Value: New (retail): $669.95
Excellent: $500.00
Very good: $400.00

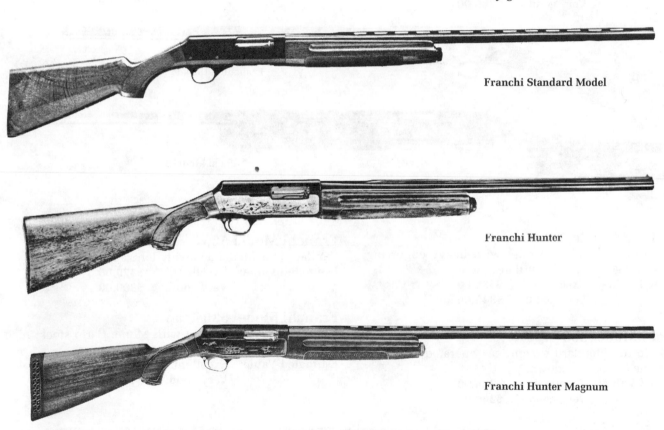

Franchi Standard Model

Franchi Hunter

Franchi Hunter Magnum

Franchi Standard Model, 48AL

Gauge: 12, 20, 28
Action: Semi-automatic; recoil operated
Magazine: 5-shot tubular
Barrel: 24", 26" improved cylinder, modified or skeet, 28" modified or full chokes; ventilated rib on some models; chrome lined
Finish: Blued; checkered walnut pistol grip stock with fluted forearm
Approximate wt.: 5 to 6¼ lbs. One of the lightest autoloaders available
Comments: Manufactured in Italy from about 1950 to present; 28 gauge discontinued.
Estimated Value: New (retail): $439.95
Excellent: $330.00
Very good: $260.00

Franchi Hunter, 48AL

Similar to the Standard Model; 12 or 20 gauge; higher quality wood; engraving; ventilated rib.
Estimated Value: New (retail): $474.95
Excellent: $355.00
Very good: $285.00

Franchi Hunter Magnum

Same as the Hunter with recoil pad & chambered for magnum shells.
Estimated Value: Excellent: $350.00
Very good: $280.00

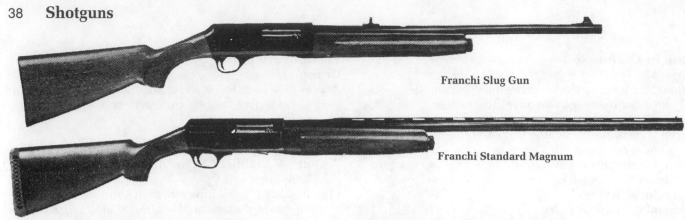

Franchi Slug Gun

Franchi Standard Magnum

Franchi Standard Magnum, 48AL

Similar to the Standard with recoil pad; chambered for magnum shells; 12 or 20 gauge.

Estimated Value: New (retail): $474.95
                  Excellent: $355.00
                  Very good: $285.00

Franchi Slug Gun, 48AL

Similar to the Standard Model with a 22" cylinder bore barrel; sight; swivels; alloy receiver. Made from the mid 1950's to early 1980's; 12 or 20 gauge.

Estimated Value: Excellent: $325.00
                  Very good: $260.00

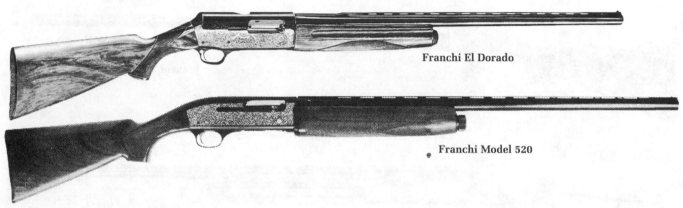

Franchi El Dorado

Franchi Model 520

Franchi Eldorado

Similar to the Standard Model with heavy engraving; select wood; gold trigger; ventilated rib.

Estimated Value: Excellent: $435.00
                  Very good: $345.00

Franchi Model 500

Similar to the Standard except: gas operated; 12 gauge only; made for fast takedown.

Estimated Value: Excellent: $325.00
                  Very good: $260.00

Franchi Model 520

Similar to the Model 500 with deluxe features.

Estimated Value: Excellent: $375.00
                  Very good: $300.00

Franchi Model 530 Trap

Similar to the Model 520 with Monte Carlo stock; high ventilated rib; 3 interchangeable choke tubes.

Estimated Value: Excellent: $525.00
                  Very good: $400.00

Franchi Prestige

Franchi Elite

Similar to the Prestige with higher quality finish. Receiver has acid-etched wildlife scenes.

Estimated Value: New (retail): $524.95
                  Excellent: $390.00
                  Very good: $315.00

Franchi Prestige, PG 85MA

Gauge: 12, regular or magnum
Action: Gas operated, semi-automatic
Magazine: 5-shot tubular (2¾" shells)
Barrel: 24" slug, 26" improved cylinder or modified, 28" modified or full, 30" full; chrome lined; ventilated rib
Finish: Blued; checkered walnut pistol grip stock & fluted forearm; sights on slug barrel
Approximate wt.: 7½ lbs.
Comments: Introduced in the late 1980's.

Estimated Value: New (retail): $474.95
                  Excellent: $355.00
                  Very good: $285.00

Greifelt

Greifelt Model 22

Gauge: 12, 16
Action: Box lock; top lever, break-open; hammerless; double trigger
Magazine: None
Barrel: Double barrel; 28" or 30" modified or full choke
Finish: Blued; checkered walnut straight or pistol grip stock & forearm; cheekpiece
Approximate wt.: 7 lbs.
Comments: Made from the late 1940's.
Estimated Value: **Excellent:**   **$1,400.00**
                        Very good: **$1,120.00**

Greifelt Model 22E

Same as Model 22 with automatic ejector.
Estimated Value: **Excellent:**   **$1,400.00**
                        Very good: **$1,120.00**

Greifelt Model 103

Gauge: 12, 16
Action: Box lock; top lever, break-open; hammerless; double triggers
Magazine: None
Barrel: Double barrel; 28" or 30" modified & full
Finish: Blued; checkered walnut straight or pistol grip stock & forearm; cheekpiece
Approximate wt.: 7 lbs.
Comments: Maded from the late 1940's.
Estimated Value: **Excellent:**   **$1,250.00**
                        Very good: **$1,000.00**

Greifelt Model 103E

Same as the Model 103 with automatic ejector.
Estimated Value: **Excellent:**   **$1,350.00**
                        Very good: **$1,080.00**

Greifelt Model 22

Harrington & Richardson

Harrington & Richardson No. 3

Gauge: 12, 16, 20, 410
Action: Box lock; top lever, break-open; hammerless; single shot; automatic extractors
Magazine: None
Barrel: 26"-32" full choke
Finish: Blued; walnut semi-pistol grip stock & tapered forearm
Approximate wt.: 5½ to 6½ lbs.
Comments: Made from about 1908 until World War II.
Estimated Value: **Excellent:**   **$80.00**
                        Very good: **$65.00**

Harrington & Richardson No. 5

Gauge: 20, 28, 410
Action: Box lock; top lever, break-open; exposed hammer; single shot; automatic extractors
Magazine: None
Barrel: 26", 28" full choke
Finish: Blued; walnut semi-pistol grip stock & tapered forearm
Approximate wt.: 4½ lbs.
Comments: Made from about 1908 until World War II.
Estimated Value: **Excellent:**   **$90.00**
                        Very good: **$70.00**

Harrington & Richardson No. 3

Harrington & Richardson No. 5

Harrington & Richardson No. 6

Harrington & Richardson No. 6

Similar to the No. 5 in 10, 12, 16 & 20 gauge; heavier design & barrel lengths of 28"-36". Weighs 5 to 8 lbs.
Estimated Value: **Excellent:**   **$85.00**
                        Very good: **$65.00**

Harrington & Richardson No. 8

Similar to the No. 6 with different style forearm & in 12, 16, 20, 24, 28 & 410 gauges.

Estimated Value:	Excellent:	$80.00
	Very good:	$65.00

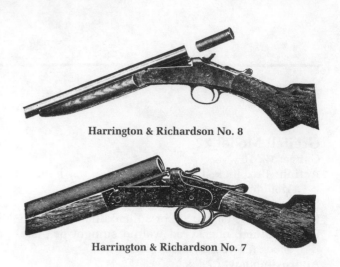

Harrington & Richardson No. 8

Harrington & Richardson No. 7 or No. 9

Similar to the No. 8 with smaller forearm & more rounded pistol grip. Not available in 24 gauge.

Estimated Value:	Excellent:	$80.00
	Very good:	$65.00

Harrington & Richardson No. 7

Harrington & Richardson Topper No. 48

Harrington & Richardson Topper No. 48

Similar to the No. 8. Made from the mid 1940's to the late 1950's.

Estimated Value:	Excellent:	$75.00
	Very good:	$60.00

Harrington & Richardson Topper No. 488 Deluxe

Similar to the No. 48 with chrome frame; recoil pad; black lacquered stock & forearm.

Estimated Value:	Excellent:	$80.00
	Very good:	$65.00

Harrington & Richardson Folding Model

Harrington & Richardson No. 148

Gauge: 12, 16, 20, 410
Action: Box lock; top lever, break-open; hammerless; single shot; automatic extractor
Magazine: None
Barrel: 28"-36" full choke
Finish: Blued; walnut semi-pistol grip stock & forearm; recoil pad
Approximate wt.: 5 to 6½ lbs.
Comments: Made from the late 1950's to early 1960's.

Estimated Value:	Excellent:	$75.00
	Very good:	$60.00

Harrington & Richardson Topper Jr. 480

Youth version of the No. 48; 410 gauge; 26" barrel; smaller stock.

Estimated Value:	Excellent:	$65.00
	Very good:	$50.00

Harrington & Richardson Topper Jr. 580

Similar to the Topper Jr. 480 with color finish similar to 188 Deluxe.

Estimated Value:	Excellent:	$70.00
	Very good:	$55.00

Harrington & Richardson Folding Model

Gauge: 28, 410 with light frame; 12, 16, 20, 28, 410 with heavy frame
Action: Box lock; top lever, break-open; exposed hammer; single shot
Magazine: None
Barrel: 22" in light frame; 26" in heavy frame; full choke
Finish: Blued; walnut semi-pistol grip stock & tapered forearm; sight
Approximate wt.: 5½ to 6¾ lbs.
Comments: This shotgun has a hinged frame; barrel folds against stock for storage. Made from about 1910 until World War II.

Estimated Value:	Excellent:	$110.00
	Very good:	$ 85.00

Harrington & Richardson Topper 188 Deluxe

Similar to the No. 148 with black, red, blue, green, pink, yellow or purple lacquered finish; chrome plated frame; 410 gauge only.

Estimated Value:	Excellent:	$70.00
	Very good:	$55.00

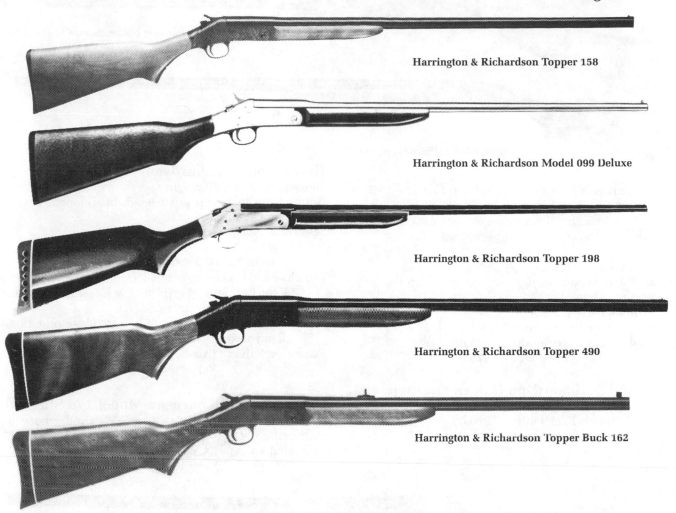

Harrington & Richardson Topper 158

Harrington & Richardson Model 099 Deluxe

Harrington & Richardson Topper 198

Harrington & Richardson Topper 490

Harrington & Richardson Topper Buck 162

Harrington & Richardson Topper 158 or 058

Gauge: 12, 16, 20, 28, 410; currently 20 gauge only
Action: Box lock; side lever, break-open; exposed hammer; single shot
Magazine: None
Barrel: 28"-36", variety of chokes
Finish: Blued; plain wood, straight or semi-pistol grip stock & tapered forearm; recoil pad on early models
Approximate wt.: 5½ to 6½ lbs.
Comments: Made from the early 1960's to mid 1970's as Model 158, mid 1970's to 1985 as 058. Also available is 058 combination with 22" rifle barrel in 22 Hornet or 30-30 Win. (Add 20%.)
Estimated Value: Excellent: $90.00
Very good: $65.00

Harrington & Richardson Model 099 Deluxe

Similar to the Model 158 with electro-less matte nickel finish. Introduced in 1982, discontinued in 1984.
Estimated Value: Excellent: $75.00
Very good: $60.00

Harrington & Richardson Topper 198 or 098

Similar to the Model 158 or 058 except; 20 or 410 gauge only; black lacquered stock & forearm; nickel plated frame. Discontinued 1982.
Estimated Value: Excellent: $90.00
Very good: $70.00

Harrington & Richardson Model 258 Handy Gun

Similar to the Model 058 combination shotgun/rifle with nickel finish, 22" barrel; 20 gauge with 22 Hornet, 30-30, 44 magnum, 357 magnum or 357 Maximum rifle barrel; includes case. Produced in the mid 1980's.
Estimated Value: Excellent: $160.00
Very good: $120.00

Harrington & Richardson Topper 490 & 490 Greenwing

A youth version of the Model 158 & 058 with 26" barrel; shorter stock; 20, 28 & 410 gauges only. Greenwing has higher quality finish.
Estimated Value: Excellent: $75.00
Very good: $60.00

Harrington & Richardson Topper 590

Similar to the 490 with chrome plated frame & color lacquered stock & forearm. Production ended in the mid 1960's.
Estimated Value: Excellent: $80.00
Very good: $60.00

Harrington & Richardson Topper Buck 162

Similar to the Model 158 & 058 with a 24" cylinder bore barrel for slugs; equipped with sights.
Estimated Value: Excellent: $90.00
Very good: $65.00

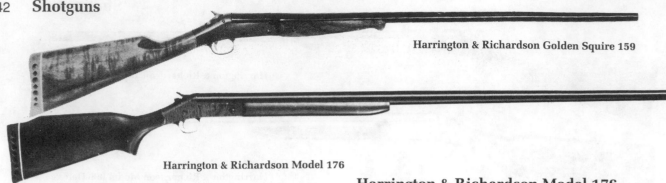

Harrington & Richardson Golden Squire 159

Harrington & Richardson Model 176

Harrington & Richardson Golden Squire 159
Gauge: 12, 20
Action: Box lock; top lever, break-open; exposed hammer; single shot; automatic ejectors
Magazine: None
Barrel: 28", 30" full choke
Finish: Blued; wood, straight grip stock & lipped forearm; recoil pad
Approximate wt.: 6½ lbs.
Comments: Made in the mid 1960's.
Estimated Value: Excellent: $95.00
                       Very good: $70.00

Harrington & Richardson Golden Squire Jr. 459
Similar to the 159 with a 26" barrel & shorter stock.
Estimated Value: Excellent: $90.00
                       Very good: $70.00

Harrington & Richardson Model 176
Gauge: 10, 12, 16, 20 magnum
Action: Box lock; top push lever, break-open; exposed hammer; single shot
Magazine: None
Barrel: 32" or 36" full choke in 10 or 12 gauge; 32" full choke in 16 or 20 gauge
Finish: Blued; case hardened frame; plain hardwood Monte Carlo pistol grip stock & forearm; recoil pad
Approximate wt.: 8 to 10 lbs.
Comments: Produced from the late 1970's to mid 1980's. All guns except 10 gauge discontinued in 1982.
Estimated Value: Excellent: $95.00
                       Very good: $70.00

Harrington & Richardson Model 176 Slug
Similar to the Model 176 with a 28" cylinder bore slug barrel; rifle sights; swivels. Produced from 1982 to 1985.
Estimated Value: Excellent: $110.00
                       Very good: $ 80.00

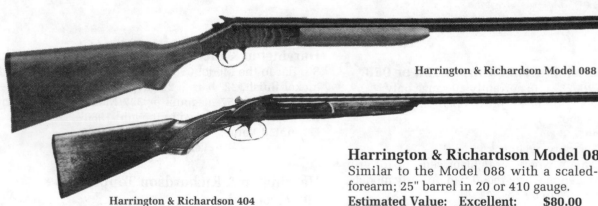

Harrington & Richardson Model 088

Harrington & Richardson 404

Harrington & Richardson Model 088
Gauge: 12, 16, 20, 410, regular or magnum
Action: Box lock; top lever, break-open; exposed hammer; single shot
Magazine: None
Barrel: 28" modified or full in 12 gauge; 28" modified in 16 gauge; 26" modified or full in 20 gauge; 25" full in 410
Finish: Blued; case hardened frame; plain hardwood semi-pistol grip stock & forearm
Approximate wt.: 6 lbs.
Comments: An inexpensive line of all purpose shotguns produced from the late 1970's to mid 1980's.
Estimated Value: Excellent: $80.00
                       Very good: $60.00

Harrington & Richardson Model 088 Jr.
Similar to the Model 088 with a scaled-down stock & forearm; 25" barrel in 20 or 410 gauge.
Estimated Value: Excellent: $80.00
                       Very good: $60.00

Harrington & Richardson Model 404
Gauge: 12, 20, 410
Action: Box lock; side lever, break-open
Magazine: None
Barrel: Double barrel; 26", 28" variety of choke combinations
Finish: Blued; checkered wood semi-pistol grip stock & forearm
Approximate wt.: 5¾ to 7½ lbs.
Comments: Made from the late 1960's to early 1970's.
Estimated Value: Excellent: $190.00
                       Very good: $145.00

Harrington & Richardson Model 404C
Similar to the 404 with Monte Carlo stock.
Estimated Value: Excellent: $200.00
                       Very good: $150.00

Harrington & Richardson Model 1212

Harrington & Richardson Model 1212

Gauge: 12
Action: Box lock; top lever, break-open; single selective trigger
Magazine: None
Barrel: Over & under double barrel; 28" improved modified over improved cylinder; ventilated rib
Finish: Blued; decorated frame; checkered walnut pistol grip stock & forearm
Approximate wt.: 7 lbs.
Comments: Introduced in the late 1970's. Manufactured in Spain for H & R.
Estimated Value: Excellent: $325.00
                       Very good: $250.00

Harrington & Richardson Model 1212 Waterfowl

Similar to the Model 1212 in 12 gauge magnum; 30" full choke over modified barrel; ventilated recoil pad.
Estimated Value: Excellent: $350.00
                       Very good: $290.00

Harrington & Richardson Gamester 348

Gauge: 12, 16
Action: Bolt action; repeating
Magazine: 2-shot
Barrel: 28" full choke
Finish: Blued; plain wood, semi-pistol grip stock & forearm
Approximate wt.: 7 lbs.
Comments: Made from about 1950 to 1954.
Estimated Value: Excellent: $80.00
                       Very good: $65.00

Harrington & Richardson Gamester 349 Deluxe

Similar to the 348 Model with adjustable choke; 26" barrel; recoil pad.
Estimated Value: Excellent: $90.00
                       Very good: $75.00

Harrington & Richardson Huntsman 351

Gauge: 12, 16
Action: Bolt action; repeating
Magazine: 2-shot tubular
Barrel: 26" adjustable choke
Finish: Blued; plain Monte Carlo semi-pistol grip stock & forearm; recoil pad
Approximate wt.: 7 lbs.
Comments: Made from the mid to late 1950's.
Estimated Value: Excellent: $85.00
                       Very good: $70.00

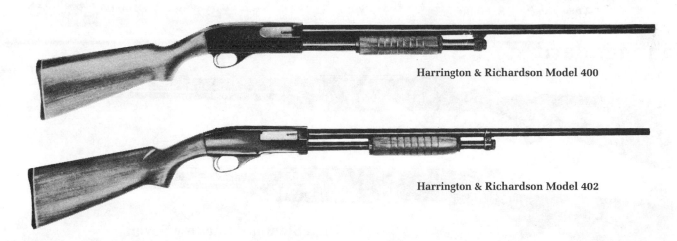

Harrington & Richardson Model 400

Harrington & Richardson Model 402

Harrington & Richardson Model 400

Gauge: 12, 16, 20
Action: Slide action; hammerless; repeating
Magazine: 5-shot tubular
Barrel: 28" full choke
Finish: Blued; semi-pistol grip stock & grooved slide handle; recoil pad on 12 & 16 gauges
Approximate wt.: 7½ lbs.
Comments: Made from the mid 1950's to the late 1960's.
Estimated Value: Excellent: $150.00
                       Very good: $115.00

Harrington & Richardson Model 401

Similar to the 400 with adjustable choke. Made to the early 1960's.
Estimated Value: Excellent: $145.00
                       Very good: $105.00

Harrington & Richardson Model 402

Similar to the 400 in 410 gauge only.
Estimated Value: Excellent: $160.00
                       Very good: $120.00

Harrington & Richardson 440

Harrington & Richardson 442

Harrington & Richardson 403

Harrington & Richardson Model 440
Gauge: 12, 16, 20
Action: Slide action; hammerless; repeating
Magazine: 4-shot clip
Barrel: 24"-28" variety of chokes
Finish: Blued; walnut semi-pistol grip stock & forearm; recoil pad
Approximate wt.: 7 lbs.
Comments: Made from the early to mid 1970's.
Estimated Value: Excellent: $150.00
                      Very good: $115.00

Harrington & Richardson Model 403
Gauge: 410
Action: Semi-automatic
Magazine: 4-shot tubular
Barrel: 26" full choke
Finish: Blued; wood semi-pistol grip stock & fluted forearm
Approximate wt.: 5¾ lbs.
Comments: Made from the mid 1960's.
Estimated Value: Excellent: $210.00
                      Very good: $160.00

Harrington & Richardson Model 442
Similar to the 440 with a ventilated rib & checkering.
Estimated Value: Excellent: $175.00
                      Very good: $140.00

High Standard

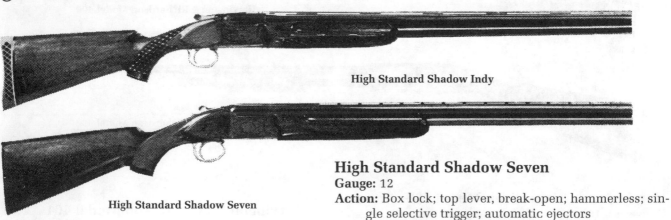

High Standard Shadow Indy

High Standard Shadow Seven

High Standard Shadow Seven
Gauge: 12
Action: Box lock; top lever, break-open; hammerless; single selective trigger; automatic ejectors
Magazine: None
Barrel: Over & under double barrel; 27½", 29½", variety of chokes; ventilated rib
Finish: Blued; checkered walnut pistol grip stock & forearm; gold plated trigger
Approximate wt.: 8 lbs.
Comments: Made to the late 1970's.
Estimated Value: Excellent: $500.00
                      Very good: $375.00

High Standard Shadow Indy
Similar to Shadow Seven with higher quality finish; chrome lined barrels; engraving; recoil pad.
Estimated Value: Excellent: $600.00
                      Very good: $450.00

High Standard Flite-King Field

High Standard Flite-King Special

High Standard Flite-King Deluxe Rib

High Standard Flite-King Trophy

High Standard Flite-King Brush

High Standard Flite-King Skeet

High Standard Flite-King Trap

High Standard Flite-King Field
Gauge: 12, 16, 20, 410
Action: Slide action; hammerless; repeating
Magazine: 5-shot tubular; 4-shot tubular in 20 gauge
Barrel: 26" improved cylinder; 28" modified; 30" full chokes
Finish: Blued; plain walnut semi-pistol grip stock & grooved slide handle
Approximate wt.: 6 to 7¼ lbs.
Comments: Made to the early 1960's to late 1970's.
Estimated Value: Excellent: $150.00
                       Very good: $115.00

High Standard Flite-King Special
Similar to Flite-King Field with an adjustable choke & 27" barrel. No. 410 gauge.
Estimated Value: Excellent: $155.00
                       Very good: $120.00

High Standard Flite-King Deluxe Rib
Similar to the Flite-King Field with ventilated rib & checkered wood.
Estimated Value: Excellent: $170.00
                       Very good: $130.00

High Standard Flite-King Trophy
Similar to the Deluxe Rib model with an adjustable choke & 27" barrel. No. 410 gauge.
Estimated Value: Excellent: $175.00
                       Very good: $135.00

High Standard Flite-King Brush
Similar to Flite-King Field with an 18" or 20" cylinder bore barrel; rifle sights. 12 gauge only.
Estimated Value: Excellent: $185.00
                       Very good: $140.00

High Standard Flite-King Skeet
Similar to the Deluxe Rib model with a skeet choke; 26" ventilated rib barrel. Not available in 16 gauge.
Estimated Value: Excellent: $180.00
                       Very good: $135.00

High Standard Flite-King Trap
Similar to the Deluxe Rib model with a 30" full choke barrel; ventilated rib; recoil pad; trap stock. 26" barrel on 410 gauge.
Estimated Value: Excellent: $190.00
                       Very good: $145.00

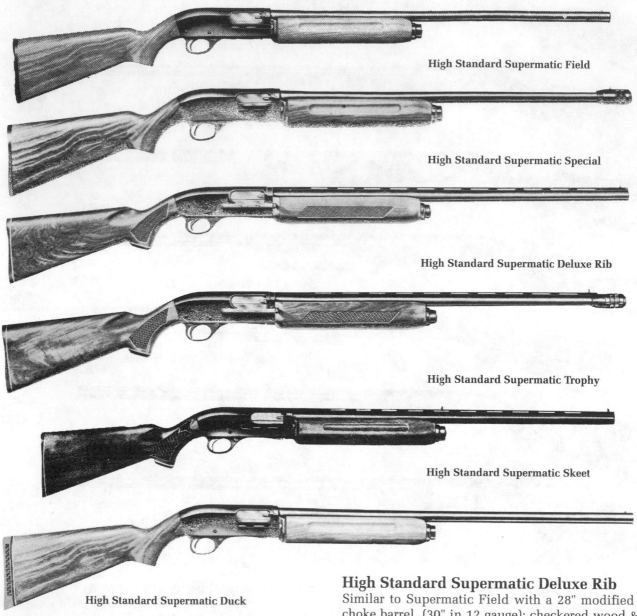

High Standard Supermatic Field

High Standard Supermatic Special

High Standard Supermatic Deluxe Rib

High Standard Supermatic Trophy

High Standard Supermatic Skeet

High Standard Supermatic Duck

High Standard Supermatic Field

Gauge: 12, 20, 20 magnum
Action: Semi-automatic, gas operated; hammerless
Magazine: 4-shot tubular; 3-shot tubular in 20 magnum
Barrel: In 12 gauge: 26" improved; 28" modified or full, 30" full chokes. In 20 gauge: 26" improved; 28" modified or full chokes
Finish: Blued; plain walnut semi-pistol grip stock & fluted forearm
Approximate wt.: 7 to 7½ lbs.
Comments: Available from about 1960 to late 1970's; 20 gauge magnum from 1963 to late 1970's.
Estimated Value: Excellent: $200.00
                       Very good: $150.00

High Standard Supermatic Special

Similar to the Supermatic Field with adjustable choke & 27" barrel.
Estimated Value: Excellent: $210.00
                       Very good: $155.00

High Standard Supermatic Deluxe Rib

Similar to Supermatic Field with a 28" modified or full choke barrel, (30" in 12 gauge); checkered wood & ventilated rib.
Estimated Value: Excellent: $215.00
                       Very good: $160.00

High Standard Supermatic Trophy

Similar to the Supermatic Field with a 27" barrel; adjustable choke; ventilated rib; checkering.
Estimated Value: Excellent: $220.00
                       Very good: $160.00

High Standard Supermatic Skeet

Similar to Field Model with a 26" ventilated rib barrel; skeet choke; checkered wood.
Estimated Value: Excellent: $225.00
                       Very good: $165.00

High Standard Supermatic Duck

Similar to the Supermatic Field in 12 gauge magnum with a 30" full choke barrel & recoil pad. Made from the early 1960's to mid 1960's.
Estimated Value: Excellent: $215.00
                       Very good: $160.00

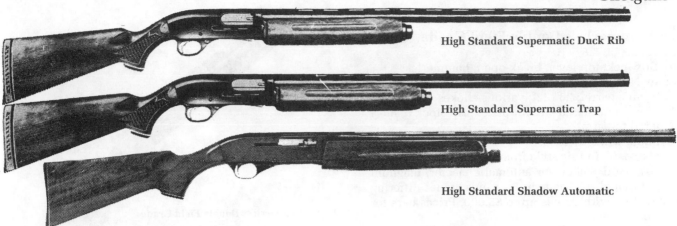

High Standard Supermatic Duck Rib

High Standard Supermatic Trap

High Standard Shadow Automatic

High Standard Supermatic Duck Rib
Similar to the Supermatic Duck with checkered wood & ventilated rib.

Estimated Value:	Excellent:	$220.00
	Very good:	$160.00

High Standard Supermatic Trap
Similar to the Supermatic Field in 12 gauge only; 30" full choke; ventilated rib; checkered trap stock & forearm; recoil pad.

Estimated Value:	Excellent:	$225.00
	Very good:	$165.00

High Standard Shadow Automatic
Gauge: 12, 20, regular or magnum
Action: Semi-automatic; gas operated; hammerless
Magazine: 4-shot tubular
Barrel: 26", 28", 30"; variety of chokes; rib
Finish: Blued; walnut pistol grip stock & forearm; sights; recoil pad available
Approximate wt.: 7 lbs.
Comments: Made to the late 1970's.

Estimated Value:	Excellent:	$250.00
	Very good:	$200.00

Hunter

Hunter Fulton
Gauge: 12, 16, 20
Action: Box lock; top lever, break-open; hammerless; double or single trigger
Magazine: None
Barrel: Double barrel; 26" to 32" any choke
Finish: Blued; checkered walnut pistol grip stock & forearm
Approximate wt.: 6½ to 7½ lbs.
Comments: Made from the early 1920's until shortly after World War II in the United States. Add $50.00 for single trigger.

Estimated Value:	Excellent:	$600.00
	Very good:	$450.00

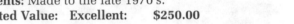

Hunter Fulton

Hunter Special
Very similar to Hunter Fulton but somewhat higher quality. Add $50.00 for single trigger.

Estimated Value:	Excellent:	$650.00
	Very good:	$490.00

Ithaca

Ithaca Victory
Gauge: 12
Action: Box lock; top lever, break-open; hammerless; single shot
Magazine: None
Barrel: 34" full choke; ventilated rib; trap grade
Finish: Blued; engraving; checkered pistol grip stock & forearm
Approximate wt.: 8 lbs.
Comments: Made from the early 1920's to World War II. Other grades in higher quality available, valued up to $4,000. Prices here are for standard grade. Made in 5 grades.

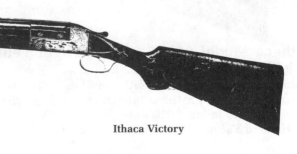

Ithaca Victory

Estimated Value:	Excellent:	$1,100.00
	Very good:	$ 825.00

Ithaca Hammerless Double Field Grade
Gauge: 12, 26, 20, 28, 410
Action: Box lock; top lever, break-open; hammerless
Magazine: None
Barrel: Double barrel; 26"-32"; various chokes
Finish: Blued; checkered walnut pistol grip stock & short tapered forearm
Approximate wt.: 6 to 10 lbs.
Comments: Made in this style from the mid 1920's to late 1940's. Add $50.00 for automatic ejector, magnum or ventilated rib. Made in 8 various grades differing in quality, with values up to $5,000. Prices here for standard grade.

Estimated Value:	Excellent:	$550.00
	Very good:	$400.00

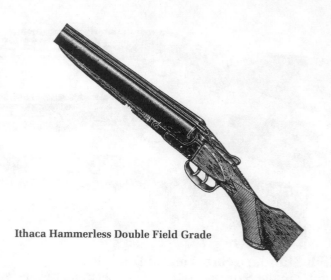
Ithaca Hammerless Double Field Grade

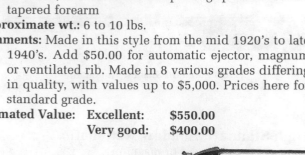
Ithaca Model 66 Supersingle

Ithaca Model 66 Supersingle Youth

Ithaca Model 66 Supersingle
Gauge: 20, 410
Action: Lever action; exposed hammer; single shot
Magazine: None
Barrel: 26" full choke; 28" full or modified choke, 30" full choke
Finish: Blued; plain or checkered straight stock & forearm
Approximate wt.: 7 lbs.
Comments: Made from 1963 to late 1970's.

Estimated Value:	Excellent:	$80.00
	Very good:	$60.00

Ithaca Model 66 Supersingle Youth
Similar to the 66 with shorter stock; 410 gauge; 25" barrel; recoil pad.

Estimated Value:	Excellent:	$75.00
	Very good:	$55.00

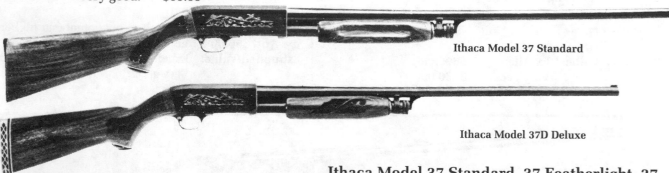
Ithaca Model 37 Standard

Ithaca Model 37D Deluxe

Ithaca Model 37V, 37 Featherlight Vent, 37 Field Grade Vent
Similar to the Model 37 with ventilated rib. Currently manufactured with three interchangeable choke tubes; discontinued in late 1980's.

Estimated Value:	Excellent:	$320.00
	Very good:	$240.00

Ithaca Model 37D Deluxe
Similar to the 37 with checkered stock & slide handle. Made from the mid 1950's to 1970's.

Estimated Value:	Excellent:	$260.00
	Very good:	$200.00

Ithaca Model 37 Standard, 37 Featherlight, 37 Field Grade Standard
Gauge: 12, 16, 20, 28
Action: Slide action; hammerless; repeating; bottom ejection
Magazine: 4-shot tubular
Barrel: 26"-30" various chokes
Finish: Blued; walnut, semi-pistol grip stock & grooved slide handle; some with checkering
Approximate wt.: 6 to 7 lbs.
Comments: Made from 1937 to 1985; add 25% for magnum with interchangeable choke tubes.

Estimated Value:	Excellent:	$250.00
	Very good:	$185.00

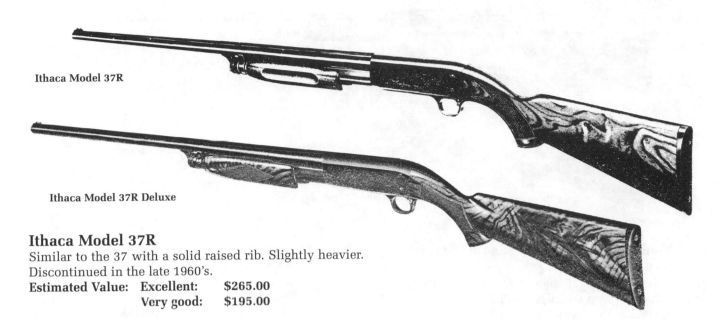

Ithaca Model 37R

Ithaca Model 37R Deluxe

Ithaca Model 37R
Similar to the 37 with a solid raised rib. Slightly heavier. Discontinued in the late 1960's.

Estimated Value: Excellent: $265.00
                    Very good: $195.00

Ithaca Model 37R Deluxe
Similar to the 37 Deluxe with a raised solid rib. Made to the early 1960's.

Estimated Value: Excellent: $300.00
                    Very good: $225.00

Ithaca Model 37DV Deluxe Vent, 87 Deluxe Vent
Similar to the 37D with ventilated rib. Renamed Model 87 in 1987.

Estimated Value: New (retail): $520.00
                    Excellent: $390.00
                    Very good: $310.00

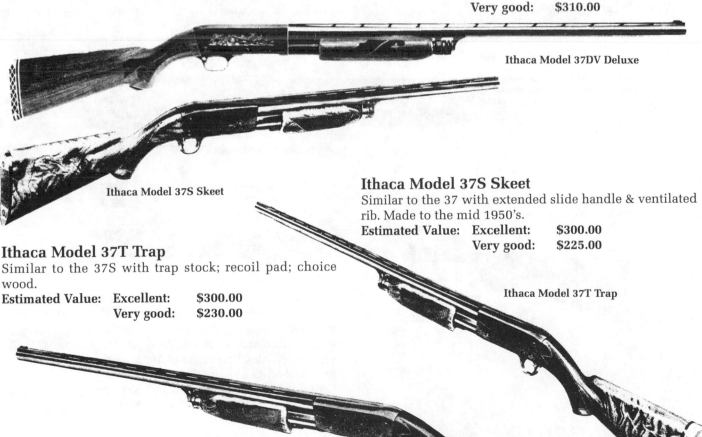

Ithaca Model 37DV Deluxe

Ithaca Model 37S Skeet

Ithaca Model 37S Skeet
Similar to the 37 with extended slide handle & ventilated rib. Made to the mid 1950's.

Estimated Value: Excellent: $300.00
                    Very good: $225.00

Ithaca Model 37T Trap
Similar to the 37S with trap stock; recoil pad; choice wood.

Estimated Value: Excellent: $300.00
                    Very good: $230.00

Ithaca Model 37T Trap

Ithaca Model 37T Target
Available in skeet or trap version with high quality finish & select wood. Replaced the 37S & 37T Trap. Made from the mid 1950's to about 1961.

Estimated Value: Excellent: $325.00
                    Very good: $245.00

Ithaca Model 37T Target

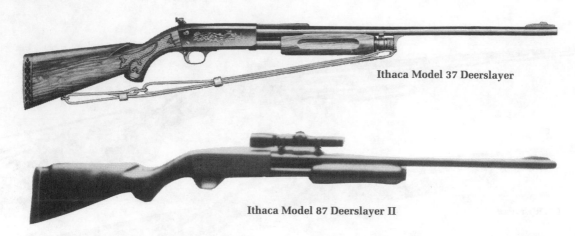

Ithaca Model 37 Deerslayer

Ithaca Model 87 Deerslayer II

Ithaca Model 37 Supreme, 37 Featherlight Supreme, 87 Supreme

Similar to the 37T Target. Renamed Model 87 in 1987.

Estimated Value: New (retail): $819.45
                  Excellent: $615.00
                  Very good: $490.00

Ithaca Model 37 Deerslayer, 87 Deerslayer

Similar to the Model 37 with a 20" or 25" barrel & rifle sights. Made from the 1960's to present; 12 or 20 gauge; renamed Model 87 in 1987.

Estimated Value: New (retail): $427.00
                  Excellent: $320.00
                  Very good: $255.00

Ithaca Model 87 Deerslayer II

Similar to the Model 87 Deerslayer with uncheckered stock & forearm, Monte Carlo stock & rifle barrel. Introduced in 1988.

Estimated Value: New (retail): $550.00
                  Excellent: $410.00
                  Very good: $330.00

Ithaca Model 37 Deerslayer Super Deluxe

Similar to the Model 37 Deerslayer with higher quality finish. Discontinued 1985.

Estimated Value: Excellent: $350.00
                  Very good: $260.00

Ithaca Bear Stopper

Ithaca Model 37 M&P

Ithaca Model 37 DSPS, DSPS II, 87 DSPS

A law enforcement version of the Model 37 Deerslayer; grooved slide handle; available in regular, parkerized, or chrome finished. Add 5% for 8-shot magazine; 15% for chrome finish (discontinued 1985); 5% less for DSPS II; renamed Model 87 in 1987.

Estimated Value: Excellent: $250.00
                  Very good: $200.00

Ithaca Model 37 M&P, 87 M&P

Similar to the Model 37 for law enforcement use; 18" or 20" cylinder bore barrel; non-glare tung oil finish; parkerized or chrome finish metal; 5 or 8-shot magazine. Add 10% for chrome (discontinued 1985); 7% for hand grip. Renamed Model 87 in 1987.

Estimated Value: Excellent: $250.00
                  Very good: $200.00

Ithaca Bear Stopper

A short barrelled version of the Model 37; 18½" or 20" barrel; 12 gauge; one-hand grip & grooved slide handle; 5- or 8-shot magazine; blued or chrome finish. Add 5% for 8-shot; 10% for chrome. Produced in early 1980's.

Estimated Value: Excellent: $300.00
                  Very good: $225.00

Ithaca Model 37 Camo Vent, 87 Camo Vent
Similar to the Model 37 Field Grade Vent with a rust-resistant camo finish in spring (green) or fall (brown); sling & swivels; 12 gauge, 26" or 28" full choke barrel. Introduced in 1986. Renamed Model 87 in 1987.

Estimated Value: New (retail): $550.00
Excellent: $410.00
Very good: $330.00

Ithaca Model 37 Ultra Deerslayer, 87 Ultra-light Deerslayer
Similar to the Ultra Featherlight with a 20" barrel for slugs; sights; recoil pad; swivels. Renamed Model 87 in 1987.

Estimated Value: Excellent: $315.00
Very good: $250.00

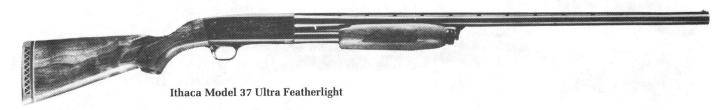

Ithaca Model 37 Ultra Featherlight

Ithaca Model 37 Basic Featherlight
Similar to the Model 37 without cosmetic finish; no checkering; finished in non-glare tung oil; grooved slide handle; "vapor blasted" metal surfaces with a non-glare finish; add 2% for ventilated rib, 30% for magnum. Introduced in 1979, discontinued in the mid 1980's.

Estimated Value: Excellent: $260.00
Very good: $200.00

Ithaca Model 37 Ultra Featherlight, Ultralite, 87 Ultralite
A 20 gauge lightweight version of the Model 37; 25" ventilated rib barrel; recoil pad, gold trigger; special grip cap. Introduced in 1979. Currently available with interchangeable choke tubes. Renamed Model 87 in 1987.

Estimated Value: Excellent: $320.00
Very good: $260.00

Ithaca English-Ultra Featherlight
Gauge: 12, 20
Action: Slide action; hammerless; repeating
Magazine: 3-shot tubular
Barrel: 25" full, modified or improved cylinder bore; ventilated rib
Finish: Blued; checkered walnut straight grip stock & slide handle; waterfowl scene on receiver
Approximate wt.: 4¾ lbs.
Comments: A lightweight English stock version of the Model 37 series. Introduced in 1982. Available with interchangeable choke tubes.

Estimated Value: Excellent: $390.00
Very good: $295.00

Ithaca Model 300

Ithaca Model 900 Deluxe Slug

Ithaca Model 900 Deluxe
Similar to the 300 except: ventilated rib on all models; gold filled engraving; nameplate in stock; gold trigger.

Estimated Value: Excellent: $275.00
Very good: $205.00

Ithaca Model 900 Deluxe Slug
Similar to the 900 Deluxe with a 24" barrel for slugs; rifle sights.

Estimated Value: Excellent: $285.00
Very good: $215.00

Ithaca Model 300
Gauge: 12, 20
Action: Semi-automatic; recoil operated; hammerless
Magazine: 3-shot tubular
Barrel: 26" improved cylinder; 28" modified or full, 30" full chokes
Finish: Blued; checkered walnut pistol grip stock & fore-arm
Approximate wt.: 6½ to 7 lbs.
Comments: Made from 1970 to 1973. Add $10.00 for ventilated rib.

Estimated Value: Excellent: $225.00
Very good: $170.00

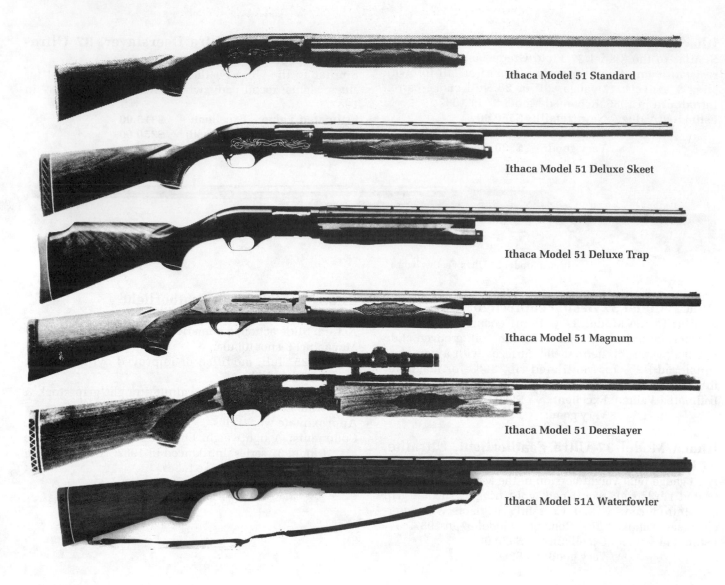

Ithaca Model 51 Standard

Ithaca Model 51 Deluxe Skeet

Ithaca Model 51 Deluxe Trap

Ithaca Model 51 Magnum

Ithaca Model 51 Deerslayer

Ithaca Model 51A Waterfowler

Ithaca Model 51 Standard, 51 Featherlight, 51A

Gauge: 12, 20
Action: Gas operated, semi-automatic
Magazine: 3-shot tubular
Barrel: 26"-30", various chokes; some with ventilated rib
Finish: Blued; checkered walnut pistol grip stock & forearm; decorated receiver
Approximate wt.: 7½ lbs.
Comments: Manufactured from 1970 until 1986.
Estimated Value: Excellent: $350.00
                        Very good: $260.00

Ithaca Model 51 Magnum

Similar to the 51 but chambered for magnum shells; ventilated rib.

Estimated Value: Excellent: $390.00
                        Very good: $310.00

Ithaca Model 51 Deerslayer

Similar to the Model 51 with 24" barrel for slugs; sights; recoil pad; 12 gauge only.

Estimated Value: Excellent: $350.00
                        Very good: $260.00

Ithaca Model 51 Deluxe Skeet, 51A Supreme Skeet

Similar to the 51 with recoil pad; ventilated rib; 28" or 29" skeet choke barrel, 26" after 1985. Discontinued in late 1980's.

Estimated Value: Excellent: $645.00
                        Very good: $480.00

Ithaca Model 51 Deluxe Trap, 51A Supreme Trap

Similar to the Model 51 except: 12 gauge only; select wood; 28" or 30" barrel; recoil pad. Add 5% for Monte Carlo stock. Discontinued in late 1980's.

Estimated Value: Excellent: $650.00
                        Very good: $490.00

Ithaca Model 51A Waterfowler, 51A Turkey Gun

Similar to the Model 51A with matte-finish metal & flat-finish walnut. The Turkey model has a 26" ventilated rib barrel, the Waterfowler has a 30" ventilated rib barrel. Introduced in 1984. Add10% camo finish with vent rib. Discontinued in late 1980's.

Estimated Value: Excellent: $465.00
                        Very good: $350.00

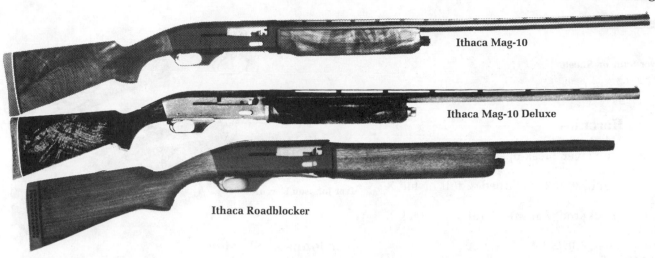

Ithaca Mag-10

Ithaca Mag-10 Deluxe

Ithaca Roadblocker

Ithaca Mag-10 Deluxe
Gauge: 10 magnum
Action: Semi-automatic; gas operated
Magazine: 3-shot tubular
Barrel: 32" full choke; ventilated rib
Finish: Blued; checkered walnut pistol grip stock & fore-arm; recoil pad; swivels
Approximate wt.: 11½ lbs.
Comments: Deduct 15% to 20% for Ithaca Mag-10 Standard.
Estimated Value: Excellent: $700.00
                 Very good: $525.00

Ithaca Mag-10 Supreme
Similar to the Magnum 10 Deluxe with higher quality finish & select wood.
Estimated Value: Excellent: $840.00
                 Very good: $630.00

Ithaca Mag-10 Roadblocker
A law enforcement version of the Mag-10 with a 20" barrel; plain stock; "vapor blasted" metal finish. Add 5% for ventilated rib.
Estimated Value: Excellent: $560.00
                 Very good: $420.00

Iver Johnson

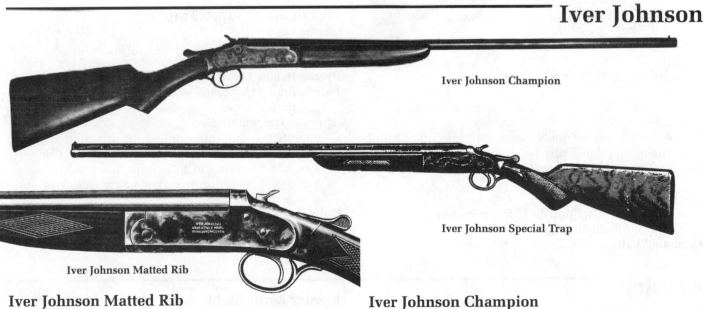

Iver Johnson Champion

Iver Johnson Special Trap

Iver Johnson Matted Rib

Iver Johnson Matted Rib
Similar to the Champion with a matted rib & checkering. Discontinued in the late 1940's.
Estimated Value: Excellent: $125.00
                 Very good: $ 95.00

Iver Johnson Special Trap
Similar to the Champion with a 32" ribbed barrel; checkered stock; 12 gauge only. Manufactured until the early 1940's.
Estimated Value: Excellent: $175.00
                 Very good: $130.00

Iver Johnson Champion
Gauge: 12, 20, 410
Action: Box lock; top lever, break-open; hammerless; single shot; automatic ejectors
Magazine: None
Barrel: 26"-30", full choke
Finish: Blued; hardwood semi-pistol grip stock & short tapered forearm
Approximate wt.: 7 lbs.
Comments: Made from about 1910 to the late 1970's.
Estimated Value: Excellent: $100.00
                 Very good: $ 75.00

Iver Johnson Skeeter

Iver Johnson Hercules

Gauge: 12, 16, 20, 410
Action: Box lock; top lever, break-open; hammerless
Magazine: None
Barrel: Double barrel, 26"-32" modified & full or full & full chokes
Finish: Blued; checkered walnut pistol grip stock & tapered forearm
Approximate wt.: 6 to 8 lbs.
Comments: Made from about 1920 to 1949. Available with some extras. Prices are for Standard grade. Add $75.00 for single trigger or automatic ejectors.
Estimated Value: Excellent: $400.00
Very good: $320.00

Iver Johnson Hercules

Iver Johnson Skeeter

Similar to the Hercules with addition of 28 gauge; 26"-28" barrels; wide forearm. Add $75.00 for automatic ejectors; $75.00 for single selective trigger.
Estimated Value: Excellent: $500.00
Very good: $400.00

Iver Johnson Silver Shadow

Iver Johnson Super Trap

Iver Johnson Silver Shadow

Gauge: 12
Action: Box lock; top lever, break-open; hammerless
Magazine: None
Barrel: Over & under double barrel; 28" modified & full choke; ventilated rib
Finish: Blued; checkered walnut pistol grip stock & forearm
Approximate wt.: 8¼ lbs.
Comments: Manufactured in Italy for Iver Johnson. Add $75.00 for single trigger.
Estimated Value: Excellent: $375.00
Very good: $300.00

Iver Johnson Super Trap

Gauge: 12
Action: Box lock; top lever, break-open; hammerless
Magazine: None
Barrel: Double barrel; 32" full choke; ventilated rib
Finish: Blued; checkered walnut pistol grip stock & forearm; recoil pad
Approximate wt.: 8½ lbs.
Comments: Production stopped on this model during World War II. Available with some extras. Prices for Standard grade; add $35.00 for non-selective single trigger; $75.00 for selective single trigger or automatic ejectors.
Estimated Value: Excellent: $550.00
Very good: $410.00

Kessler

Kessler 3-Shot

Gauge: 12, 16, 20
Action: Bolt action; hammerless; repeating
Magazine: 2-shot detachable box
Barrel: 26", 28", full choke
Finish: Blued; plain pistol grip stock & forearm; recoil pad
Approximate wt.: 6 to 7 lbs.
Comments: Made for a few years only in the early 1950's.
Estimated Value: Excellent: $85.00
Very good: $65.00

Kessler Lever Matic

Gauge: 12, 16, 20
Action: Lever action
Magazine: 3-shot
Barrel: 26", 28", 30", full choke
Finish: Blued; checkered walnut straight stock & forearm; recoil pad
Approximate wt.: 7 lbs.
Comments: Produced for only a few years in the early 1950's.
Estimated Value: Excellent: $150.00
Very good: $110.00

Kleinguenther

Kleinguenther Condor

Kleinguenther Condor

Gauge: 12, 20

Action: Double lock; top lever break-open; hammerless; selective single trigger; automatic ejectors

Magazine: None

Barrel: Over & under double barrel; ventilated rib; 26" improved & modified or skeet; 28" modified or modified & full; 30" modified & full or full in 12 gauge

Finish: Blued; checkered walnut pistol grip stock & forearm; recoil pad

Approximate wt.: 7½ lbs.

Comments: An Italian shotgun produced in the 1970's.

Estimated Value: Excellent: $550.00
Very good: $415.00

Kleinguenther Condor Skeet

A skeet version of the Condor with a wide rib.

Estimated Value: Excellent: $575.00
Very good: $430.00

Kleinguenther Condor Trap

A trap version of the Condor with a Monte Carlo stock, wide rib; available in 32" barrel.

Estimated Value: Excellent: $590.00
Very good: $440.00

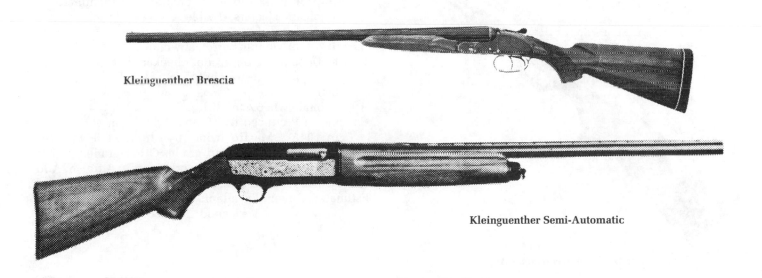

Kleinguenther Brescia

Kleinguenther Semi-Automatic

Kleinguenther Brescia

Gauge: 12, 20

Action: Box lock; top lever, break-open; hammerless; double trigger

Magazine: None

Barrel: Double barrel; chrome lined, 28" improved or modified or modified & full chokes

Finish: Blued; checkered walnut pistol grip stock & tapered forearm

Approximate wt.: 7½ lbs.

Comments: Manufactured in Italy.

Estimated Value: Excellent: $275.00
Very good: $205.00

Kleinguenther Semi-Automatic

Gauge: 12

Action: Semi-automatic; hammerless; side ejection

Magazine: 3-shot tubular

Barrel: Chrome lined; 25" skeet, 26" improved cylinder, 28" & 30" full chokes; ventilated rib

Finish: Blued; smooth walnut pistol grip stock & grooved forearm; engraved

Approximate wt.: 7½ lbs.

Comments: Made from the early to mid 1970's.

Estimated Value: Excellent: $300.00
Very good: $225.00

L.C. Smith

L.C. Smith Single Barrel

Gauge: 12
Action: Box lock; top lever, break-open; automatic ejectors, hammerless
Magazine: None, single shot
Barrel: 32", 34" choice of bore; ventilated rib
Finish: Blued; checkered walnut pistol grip stock & forearm; recoil pad
Approximate wt.: 8 lbs.
Comments: Produced by Hunter Arms from about 1890 to 1945 & Marlin from about 1946 to 1951.
Estimated Value:

	Olympic	Specialty	Crown
Excellent:	$1,450.00	$2,000.00	$3,200.00
Very good:	$1,050.00	$1,450.00	$2,500.00

L.C. Smith Single Barrel

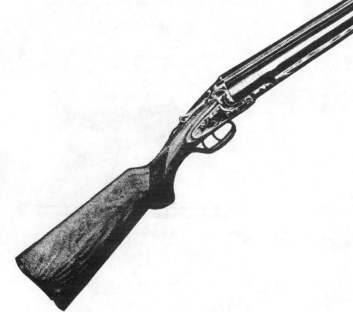

L.C. Smith Double Barrel (Hunter Arms)

L.C. Smith Double Barrel (Hunter Arms)

Gauge: 12, 16, 20, 410
Action: Side lock, top lever break-down; hammerless; automatic ejectors; double or single trigger
Magazine: None
Barrel: 26"-32" double barrel, any choke
Finish: Depending on grade, checkered walnut pistol, semi-pistol or straight grip stock & forearm; blued barrels
Approximate wt.: 6½ to 8½ lbs.
Comments: Produced by Hunter Arms from about 1890 to 1945 & Marlin from 1946 to 1951. Prices for Hunter Arms in field grade. Other grades higher due to higher quality of workmanship & finish. Add $50.00 for single trigger.

Estimated Value:	**Excellent:**	**$650.00**
	Very good:	$560.00

L.C. Smith Field Grade (Marlin)

L.C. Smith Field Grade (Marlin)

Same as the Deluxe Model with standard checkered walnut pistol grip stock & forearm & extruded ventilated rib. Made from about 1946 to 1951.

Estimated Value:	**Excellent:**	**$475.00**
	Very good:	$360.00

L.C. Smith Deluxe (Marlin)

Gauge: 12, regular or magnum
Action: Top lever break-open; hammerless; side lock; double triggers
Magazine: None
Barrel: Double barrel; 28" modified & full chokes; floating steel ventilated rib
Finish: Top quality, hand-fitted, hand-checkered walnut pistol grip stock & beavertail forearm; blued; case hardened side plates
Approximate wt.: 6¾ lbs.
Comments: Made from about 1968 to mid 1970's.

Estimated Value:	**Excellent:**	**$500.00**
	Very good:	$375.00

Lefever

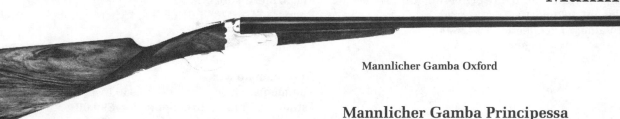

Lefever Long Range

Lefever Trap

Lefever Nitro Special

Lefever Long Range
Gauge: 12, 16, 20, 410
Action: Box lock, top lever, break-open; hammerless; single shot
Magazine: None
Barrel: 26", 28", 30", 32"; any choke
Finish: Blued; plain or checkered walnut pistol grip stock & forearm; bead sight
Approximate wt.: 5 to 7 lbs.
Comments: Made from the early 1920's to the early 1940's.
Estimated Value: Excellent: $200.00
                      Very good: $160.00

Lefever Trap
Gauge: 12
Action: Box lock; top lever break-open; hammerless; single shot
Magazine: None
Barrel: 30" or 32" full choke; ventilated rib
Finish: Blued; checkered walnut pistol grip stock & forearm; recoil pad
Approximate wt.: 8 lbs.
Comments: Made from the early 1920's to the early 1940's.
Estimated Value: Excellent: $400.00
                      Very good: $320.00

Lefever Nitro Special
Gauge: 12, 16, 20, 410
Action: Box lock; top lever, break-open; hammerless; double triggers
Magazine: None
Barrel: Double barrel; 26", 28", 30", 32"; any choke
Finish: Blued; checkered walnut pistol grip stock & forearm
Approximate wt.: 5½ to 7 lbs.
Comments: Made from the early 1920's to late 1940's. Add $75.00 for single trigger.
Estimated Value: Excellent: $500.00
                      Very good: $400.00

Lefever Excellsior
Similar to Nitro-Special with light engraving & automatic ejector.
Estimated Value: Excellent: $525.00
                      Very good: $420.00

Mannlicher

Mannlicher Gamba Oxford

Mannlicher Gamba Oxford
Gauge: 12, 20, 20 magnum
Action: Top lever break-open; hammerless; single or double trigger
Magazine: None
Barrel: Double barrel; 26½" improved cylinder & modified or 27½" modified & full
Finish: Blued; engraved receiver; checkered walnut straight grip stock & tapered forearm
Approximate wt.: 5½ to 6½ lbs.
Comments: Add $140.00 for single trigger.
Estimated Value: Excellent: $1,325.00
                      Very good: $ 995.00

Mannlicher Gamba Principessa
Gauge: 28
Action: Top lever break-open; hammerless; single or double trigger
Magazine: None
Barrel: Double barrel; 26" improved cylinder & modified or 28" modified & full
Finish: Blued; case hardened receiver with engraved scrollwork; checkered walnut straight grip stock & tapered forearm; beavertail forearm available; recoil pad
Approximate wt.: 5½ lbs.
Comments: Add $130.00 for single trigger.
Estimated Value: Excellent: $1,175.00
                      Very good: $ 880.00

Marlin

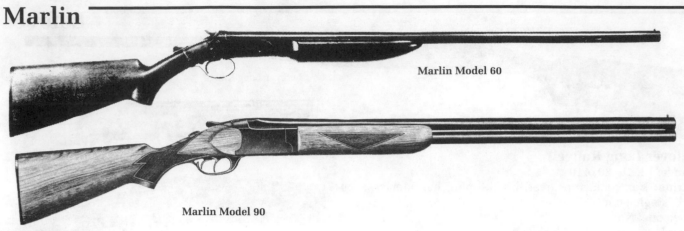

Marlin Model 60

Marlin Model 90

Marlin Model 60

Gauge: 12
Action: Box lock; take down breech-loaded; automatic ejector; exposed hammer; single shot
Magazine: None
Barrel: 30" or 32" full choke; matted top; 2¾" chamber
Finish: Blued; walnut pistol grip stock & beavertail forearm
Approximate wt.: 6½ lbs.
Comments: This shotgun was made in 1923, a combination of Marlin & Hopkins & Allen parts. Less than 1,000 were manufactured.
Estimated Value: Excellent: $175.00
                                      Very good: $130.00

Marlin Model 410

Gauge: 410
Action: Lever action; exposed hammer
Magazine: 5-shot tubular
Barrel: 22" or 26", 2½" chamber
Finish: Blued; walnut pistol grip stock & beavertail forearm
Approximate wt.: 6 lbs.
Comments: A solid frame lightweight shotgun produced from about 1929 to 1932.
Estimated Value: Excellent: $425.00
                                      Very good: $325.00

Marlin Model 90

Gauge: 12, 16, 20, 410 (also .22 caliber & .222)
Action: Top lever break down; box lock; double trigger (single trigger available prior to World War II); hammerless; non-automatic extractors
Magazine: None
Barrel: Over & under double barrel, 26", 28" or 30" rifle; shotgun barrels available in 26"; 2¾" chamber, 3" chamber in 410; full, modified, skeet or improved cylinder bore
Finish: Blued; plain or checkered walnut pistol grip stock & forearm; recoil pad
Approximate wt.: 6 to 7½ lbs.
Comments: This shotgun or combination was manufactured from about 1937 to 1958. Add $40.00 for 410 gauge; $50.00 for single trigger.
Estimated Value: Excellent: $400.00
                                      Very good: $300.00

Marlin Model 55 Hunter

Gauge: 12, 16, 20
Action: Bolt action; repeating
Magazine: 2-shot clip
Barrel: 26" or 28" full choke; "Micro Choke" available; 2¾" or 3" chamber
Finish: Blued; walnute pistol grip stock & forearm; recoil pad optional
Approximate wt.: 7¼ lbs.
Comments: Made from about 1950 to 1965.
Estimated Value: Excellent: $90.00
                                      Very good: $70.00

Marlin Model 410

Marlin Model 55 Hunter

Marlin Model 55G

Marlin Glenfield 50

Marlin Glenfield 60G

Marlin Model 55 Swamp Gun

Marlin Model 55 Goose Gun

Marlin Model 55 Swamp Gun
The same shotgun as the Model 55 except barrel is shortened with "Micro Choke," recoil pad is standard & it has swivels. It weighs about 6½ lbs. & is chambered for 3" 12 gauge magnum shells. It was produced for two years beginning in 1963.

Estimated Value: **Excellent:**   **$90.00**
                Very good: **$70.00**

Marlin Model 55 Goose Gun
Same shotgun as the Model 55 except: swivels; extra long 36" barrel; chambered for 3" 12 gauge magnum shells; weighs 8 lbs.; recoil pad standard. It has been in production since 1966.

Estimated Value: **New (retail):** **$242.95**
                Excellent: **$185.00**
                Very good: **$145.00**

Marlin 55G, Glenfield 55G & Glenfield 50
The same basic shotgun as the Marlin Model 55 Hunter. It was produced from about 1961 to 1966 as the 55G & Glenfield 55G & in 1966 it became the Glenfield 50.

Estimated Value: **Excellent:**   **$85.00**
                Very good: **$65.00**

Marlin Model 59

Marlin Model 55S Slug Gun

Marlin Model 59, 60G, 61G
Gauge: 410
Action: Bolt action; self-cocking
Magazine: None; single shot
Barrel: 24" full coke; chambered for 2½" or 3" shells
Finish: Blued; walnut pistol grip or semi-pistol grip stock & forearm
Approximate wt.: 5 lbs.
Comments: This takedown model was produced from about 1959 to 1961. It was replaced by Model 61G in 1962 which was replaced by the Model 60G in 1963 & discontinued in 1970.
Estimated Value: **Excellent:**   **$75.00**
                        Very good: **$60.00**

Marlin Model 55S Slug Gun
Basically the same as Model 55, this gun has rifle sights & a 24" barrel that is chambered for 2¾" & 3" shells. It has swivels & a recoil pad. In production since 1973.
Estimated Value: **Excellent:**   **$100.00**
                        Very good: **$ 75.00**

Marlin Model 5510 Supergoose 10

Marlin Model 5510 Supergoose 10
Gauge: 10 gauge magnum
Action: Bolt action
Magazine: 2-shot clip (2⅞" shells must be loaded singly)
Barrel: 34" full choke; chambered for 2⅞" or 3½" shells
Finish: Blued; black walnut semi-pistol grip stock & forearm; swivels; recoil pad
Approximate wt.: 10½ lbs.
Comments: This is a more powerful version of the Marlin Goose Gun. Produced from 1976 to 1986.
Estimated Value: **Excellent:**   **$195.00**
                        Very good: **$150.00**

Marlin Model 1898
Gauge: 12 (2¾")
Action: Slide action; exposed hammer; side ejection
Magazine: 5-shot tubular
Barrel: 26", 28", 30" or 32"
Finish: Blued; walnut pistol grip stock & grooved slide handle
Approximate wt.: 7¼ lbs.
Comments: This shotgun was produced in many grades from 1898 to 1905. Price for grade A (Field Grade).
Estimated Value: **Excellent:**   **$375.00**
                        Very good: **$300.00**

Marlin Model 1898

Marlin Model 19

Marlin Model 19 & 19G
Similar to the Model 1898 with improvements. Made from 1906-1907; 19G produced until 1915.
Estimated Value: **Excellent:**   **$300.00**
                        Very good: **$240.00**

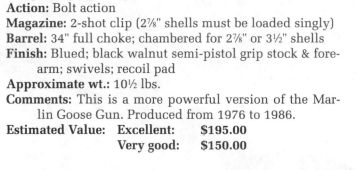

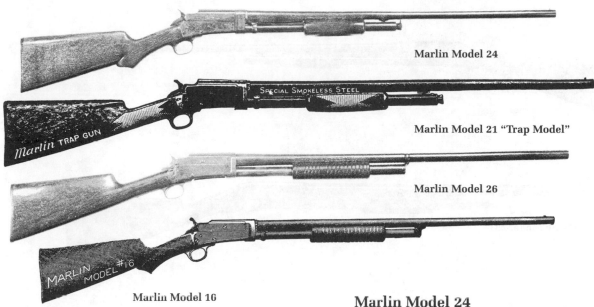

Marlin Model 24

Marlin Model 21 "Trap Model"

Marlin Model 26

Marlin Model 16

Marlin Model 16
Gauge: 16 (2¾")
Action: Slide action; exposed hammer
Magazine: 5-shot tubular
Barrel: 26" or 28"
Finish: Blued; walnut pistol grip stock & forearm; some checkered, some with grooved slide handle
Approximate wt.: 6¼ lbs.
Comments: This takedown model was made from about 1904 to 1910.
Estimated Value: Excellent: $325.00
                       Very good: $245.00

Marlin Model 24
An improved version of the Model 19 made from 1908 to 1915.
Estimated Value: Excellent: $275.00
                       Very good: $210.00

Marlin Model 21 "Trap Model"
This shotgun is very similar to the Model 24 with trap specifications. Made from 1907 to 1909.
Estimated Value: Excellent: $325.00
                       Very good: $245.00

Marlin Model 26
Very similar to the Model 24 except: stock is straight grip; solid frame. Made from about 1909 to 1915.
Estimated Value: Excellent: $300.00
                       Very good: $225.00

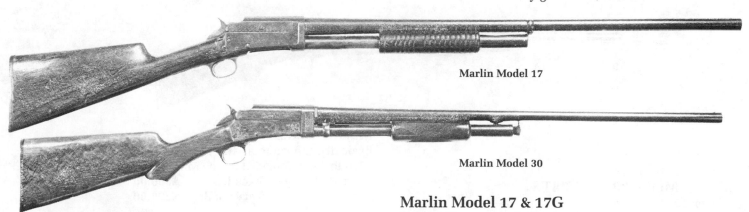

Marlin Model 17

Marlin Model 30

Marlin Model 30 & 30G
Gauge: 16 & 20
Action: Slide action; exposed hammer
Magazine: 5-shot tubular
Barrel: 25", 26", 28" modified choke, 2¾" chamber
Finish: Blued; checkered walnut straight or pistol grip stock, grooved or checkered slide handle
Approximate wt.: 6¾ lbs.
Comments: Made from about 1910 to 1915. In 1915 it was called the Model 30G.
Estimated Value: Excellent: $280.00
                       Very good: $210.00

Marlin Model 17 & 17G
Gauge: 12
Action: Slide action; exposed hammer
Magazine: 5-shot tubular
Barrel: 30" or 32" full choke; others available by special order
Finish: Blued; walnut pistol grip stock & grooved slide handle
Approximate wt.: 7½ lbs.
Comments: This solid frame shotgun was made from about 1906 to 1908; from 1908 to 1915 as Model 17G.
Estimated Value: Excellent: $300.00
                       Very good: $225.00

Marlin Model 28

Marlin Model 28T

Marlin Model 28A

Marlin Model 31

Marlin Model 31A

Marlin Model 28, 28T, 28TS

Gauge: 12
Action: Slide action; hammerless; side ejection
Magazine: 5-shot tubular
Barrel: 26" or 28" cylinder bore or modified choke; 30" or 32" full choke
Finish: Blued; checkered walnut pistol grip stock & slide handle
Approximate wt.: 8 lbs.
Comments: This takedown shotgun was produced from about 1913 to just before World War I. The Model 28T & 28TS were Trap grade guns with an available straight stock. Add $100.00 for 28T, 28TS.

Estimated Value: Excellent: $325.00
Very good: $245.00

Marlin Model 28A

Basically the same as the Model 28. Made from about 1920 to 1922; replaced by the Model 43A.

Estimated Value: Excellent: $300.00
Very good: $225.00

Marlin Model 31

This shotgun is much like the Model 28 except: 20 or 16 gauge. Made from about 1915 to 1917 & 1920 to 1922.

Estimated Value: Excellent: $360.00
Very good: $270.00

Marlin Model 31A

Very similar to the Model 28A in 20 gauge only. Replaced by the Model 44A.

Estimated Value: Excellent: $350.00
Very good: $265.00

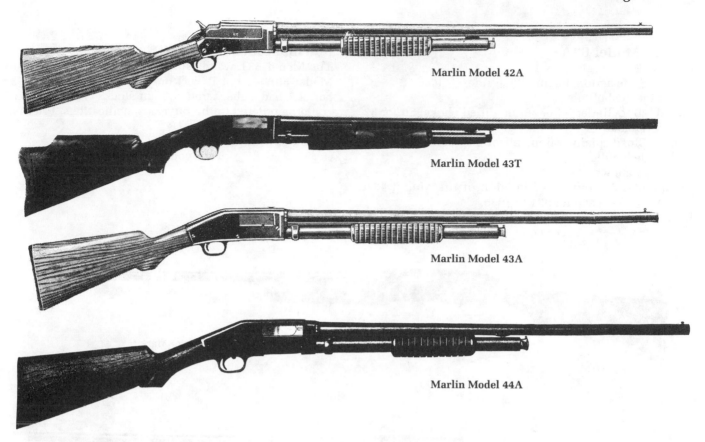

Marlin Model 42A

Marlin Model 43T

Marlin Model 43A

Marlin Model 44A

Marlin Model 42A

Gauge: 12

Action: Slide action; exposed hammer; side ejection

Magazine: 5-shot tubular; bottom load

Barrel: 26" cylinder bore, 28" modified, 30" & 32" full choke; 2¾" chamber; round matted barrel

Finish: Blued; black walnut semi-pistol grip stock, grooved slide handle

Approximate wt.: 7½ lbs.

Comments: A takedown shotgun manufactured from about 1922 to 1934.

Estimated Value: Excellent: $280.00
Very good: $210.00

Marlin Model 49

This shotgun is similar to the Model 42A. It was given away with stock in the corporation. It was produced from about 1925 to 1928.

Estimated Value: Excellent: $375.00
Very good: $275.00

Marlin Model 43A

Gauge: 12

Action: Slide action; hammerless; side ejection

Magazine: 5-shot tubular

Barrel: 26" cylinder bore, 28" modified, 30" & 32" full choke; 2¾" chamber

Finish: Blued; walnut pistol grip stock & grooved slide handle

Approximate wt.: 8 lbs.

Comments: Made from about 1923 to 1930. It was a new style takedown. Replaced by Model 53.

Estimated Value: Excellent: $240.00
Very good: $180.00

Marlin Model 43T & 43TS

Same basic shotgun as the Model 43A except it has checkered Monte Carlo stock & forearm with recoil pad. The Model 43TS had a choice of many options & the value is dependent on the number & type of extras.

Estimated Value: Excellent: $350.00
Very good: $265.00

Marlin Model 53

Similar to Model 43A. Made in standard grade only, from 1929 to 1931 & replaced by Model 63A.

Estimated Value: Excellent: $350.00
Very good: $280.00

Marlin Model 44A

Gauge: 20

Action: Slide action; hammerless; side ejection

Magazine: 4-shot tubular; bottom load

Barrel: 25" or 28" cylinder bore, modified or full choke; 2¾" chamber

Finish: Blued; walnut pistol grip stock & grooved slide handle

Approximate wt.: 6 lbs.

Comments: A takedown model produced from about 1923 to 1935.

Estimated Value: Excellent: $325.00
Very good: $245.00

Marlin Model 44S

Same basic shotgun as the Model 44A except it came with either straight or pistol grip checkered stock & forearm.

Estimated Value: Excellent: $350.00
Very good: $260.00

Marlin Model 63A

Gauge: 12
Action: Slide action; hammerless; side ejector
Magazine: 5-shot tubular
Barrel: 26" cylinder bore, 28" modified choke, 30" or 32" full choke
Finish: Blued; plain walnut pistol grip stock & grooved slide handle
Approximate wt.: 8 lbs.
Comments: An improved version of the Model 43A. Made from about 1931 to 1935.
Estimated Value: Excellent: $275.00
                        Very good: $200.00

Marlin Model 63T & 63TS

The Model 63T was basically the same shotgun as the Model 63A except it was only produced in 30" or 32" barrel & had a checkered straight stock. The Model 63TS could be ordered to the buyer's specifications. Prices are for standard trap gun.
Estimated Value: Excellent: $325.00
                        Very good: $240.00

Marlin Model Premier Mark I

Marlin Model Premier Mark II

Marlin Model Premier Mark IV

Marlin Model Premier Mark I

Gauge: 12
Action: Slide action; hammerless; side ejection
Magazine: 3-shot tubular
Barrel: 26" cylinder bore, 28" modified, 30" full choke; ventilated rib available; 28" slug barrel with rifle sights available; 2¾" chamber
Finish: Blued; walnut pistol grip stock & forearm; recoil pad optional
Approximate wt.: 7 lbs.
Comments: Made from about 1960 to 1963.
Estimated Value: Excellent: $160.00
                        Very good: $120.00

Marlin Model Premier Mark II

This is basically the same shotgun as the Premier Mark I except the stock & forearm are checkered & the receiver is engraved.
Estimated Value: Excellent: $205.00
                        Very good: $155.00

Marlin Model Premier Mark IV

This is basically the same shotgun as the Mark II except the wood is more elaborate & the engraving heavier.
Estimated Value: Excellent: $270.00
                        Very good: $200.00

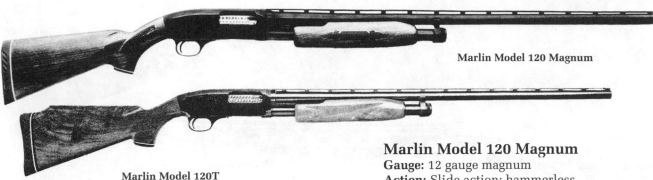

Marlin Model 120 Magnum

Marlin Model 120T

Marlin Deluxe 120 Slug Gun

Similar to the Marlin 120 with a 20" slug barrel & rifle sights. Produced from the late 1970's to 1986.

Estimated Value: Excellent: $275.00
               Very good: $210.00

Marlin Model 120T

This is basically the same shotgun as Model 120 with a Monte Carlo stock & 30" full choke or 30" modified trap choke barrel. This gun was offered from 1973 to the late 1970's.

Estimated Value: Excellent: $280.00
               Very good: $210.00

Marlin Model 120 Magnum

Gauge: 12 gauge magnum
Action: Slide action; hammerless
Magazine: 5-shot tubular (4-shot with 3" shells)
Barrel: 26" cylinder bore, 28" modified or 30" full choke
Finish: Blued; ventilated rib; checkered walnut, pistol grip stock & forearm; recoil pad
Approximate wt.: 7¾ lbs.
Comments: This gun was first offered in 1971. In 1973 a 40" MXR Magnum barrel & a choked 26" slug barrel were offered for the first time. Discontinued in 1986.

Estimated Value: Excellent: $275.00
               Very good: $210.00

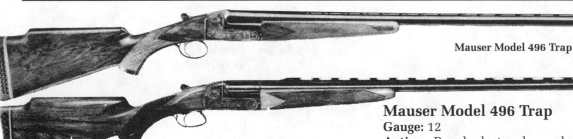

Marlin Glenfield 778

Marlin Glenfield 778

Gauge: 12, regular or magnum
Action: Slide action; hammerless; repeating
Magazine: 5-shot tubular; 4-shot with 3" magnum
Barrel: 26" improved cylinder; 28" modified; 30" full choke; ventilated rib available; 38" MXR full choke barrel available without rib
Finish: Blued; checkered hardwood, semi-pistol grip stock & fluted slide handle; recoil pad
Approximate wt.: 7¾ lbs.
Comments: Made from about the late 1970's to early 1980's. Add $50.00 for ventilated rib or MXR barrel.

Estimated Value: Excellent: $175.00
               Very good: $130.00

Marlin Glenfield 778 Slug

Similar to the Glenfield 778 with a 20" slug barrel & rifle sights.

Estimated Value: Excellent: $200.00
               Very good: $150.00

Mauser

Mauser Model 496 Trap

Mauser Model 496 Competition

Mauser Model 496 Competition

Similar to the Model 496 with select wood; higher ventilated rib.

Estimated Value: Excellent: $625.00
               Very good: $475.00

Mauser Model 496 Trap

Gauge: 12
Action: Box lock; top lever, break-open; hammerless; automatic ejectors; single shot
Magazine: None
Barrel: 32" modified or 34" full chokes; ventilated rib
Finish: Blued; checkered walnut Monte Carlo pistol grip stock & tapered forearm; engraved; recoil pad
Approximate wt.: 8½ lbs.
Comments: Imported in the 1970's.

Estimated Value: Excellent: $500.00
               Very good: $375.00

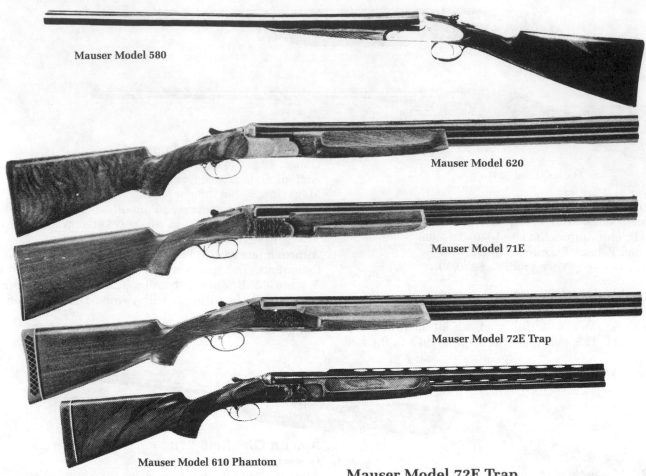

Mauser Model 580

Mauser Model 620

Mauser Model 71E

Mauser Model 72E Trap

Mauser Model 610 Phantom

Mauser Model 580

Gauge: 12
Action: Side lock; top lever break-open; hammerless
Magazine: None
Barrel: Double barrel; 28"-30", various chokes
Finish: Blued; checkered walnut straight stock & tapered forearm; engraved
Approximate wt.: 7¾ lbs.
Comments: Imported in the 1970's.
Estimated Value: Excellent: $825.00
                       Very good: $620.00

Mauser Model 620

Gauge: 12
Action: Box lock; top lever, break-open; hammerless; automatic ejectors; single trigger
Magazine: None
Barrel: Over & under double barrel; 28", 30" improved cylinder & modified or modified & full or skeet chokes; ribbed
Finish: Blued; plain walnut pistol grip stock & forearm; recoil pad
Approximate wt.: 7½ lbs.
Comments: Imported from the early to mid 1970's.
Estimated Value: Excellent: $875.00
                       Very good: $650.00

Mauser Model 71E

Similar to the Model 620 with double triggers & no recoil pad; 28" barrel.
Estimated Value: Excellent: $420.00
                       Very good: $315.00

Mauser Model 72E Trap

Similar to the Model 71E with large recoil pad; engraving; wide rib; single trigger.
Estimated Value: Excellent: $575.00
                       Very good: $430.00

Mauser Model 610 Phantom

Gauge: 12
Action: Box lock; top lever, break-open; hammerless
Magazine: None
Barrel: Over & under double barrel; ventilated rib between barrels & on top barrel; 30", 32" various chokes
Finish: Blued; case hardened frame; checkered walnut pistol grip stock & forearm; recoil pad
Approximate wt.: 8 lbs.
Comments: Made in the mid 1970's.
Estimated Value: Excellent: $900.00
                       Very good: $675.00

Mauser Contest

Gauge: 12
Action: Top lever break-open; automatic ejectors; single selective trigger
Magazine: None
Barrel: Over & under double barrel; 27½" improved cylinder & improved modified
Finish: Blued; engraved grey sideplates; checkered walnut pistol grip stock & lipped forearm
Approximate wt.: 7½ lbs.
Comments: Add $500.00 for trap model.
Estimated Value: Excellent: $1,000.00
                       Very good: $ 750.00

Mossberg

Mossberg Model 83D

Mossberg Model 183K

Mossberg Model 183K

Similar to the 183D with adjustable choke & recoil pad.
Made from the early 1950's to mid 1980's.

Estimated Value: Excellent: $110.00
                      Very good: $ 80.00

Mossberg Model 83D, 183D

Gauge: 410
Action: Bolt action; repeating
Magazine: 2-shot, top loading; fixed magazine
Barrel: 23" on 83D, 24" on 183D; interchangeable choke
          fittings
Finish: Blued; hardwood Monte Carlo semi-pistol grip
          one-piece stock & forearm
Approximate wt.: 5½ lbs.
Comments: Made as the 83D from about 1940 to 1947 &
          as the 183D from 1948 until the early 1970's.

Estimated Value: Excellent: $85.00
                      Very good: $65.00

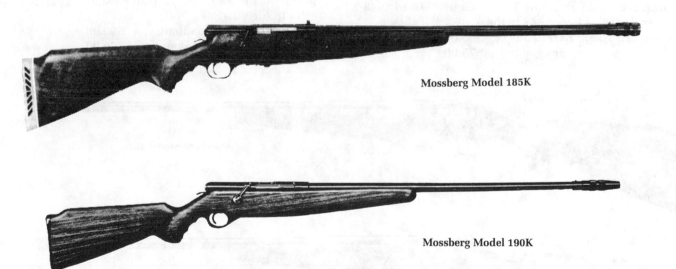

Mossberg Model 185K

Mossberg Model 190K

Mossberg Model 190K

Similar to the 183K in 16 gauge. Made from the mid
1950's to early 1960's.

Estimated Value: Excellent: $90.00
                      Very good: $70.00

Mossberg Model 185K

Similar to the 183K in 20 gauge. Made from about 1950
to early 1960's.

Estimated Value: Excellent: $85.00
                      Very good: $65.00

Mossberg Model 195K

Similar to the 183K in 12 gauge. Made from the mid
1950's to early 1960's.

Estimated Value: Excellent: $90.00
                      Very good: $70.00

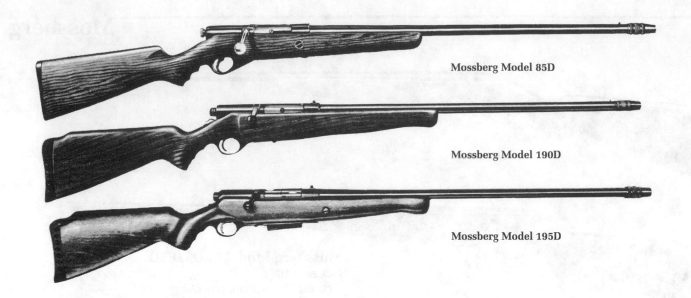

Mossberg Model 85D

Mossberg Model 190D

Mossberg Model 195D

Mossberg Model 85D, 185D

Gauge: 20
Action: Bolt action; repeating
Magazine: 2-shot detachable box
Barrel: 25" on 85D, 26" on 185D; interchangeable choke fittings
Finish: Blued; hardwood pistol grip one-piece stock & forearm
Approximate wt.: 6½ lbs.
Comments: Made as the 85D from about 1940 to 1948 & as the 185D from 1948 to the early 1970's.
Estimated Value: Excellent: $95.00
                        Very good: $75.00

Mossberg Model 190D

Similar to the 185D in 16 gauge. Made from the mid 1950's to early 1960's.
Estimated Value: Excellent: $85.00
                        Very good: $65.00

Mossberg Model 195D

Similar to the 185D in 12 gauge. Made from the mid 1950's to early 1970's.
Estimated Value: Excellent: $90.00
                        Very good: $70.00

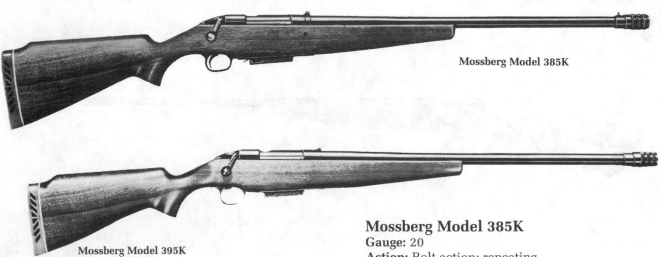

Mossberg Model 385K

Mossberg Model 395K

Mossberg Model 385K

Gauge: 20
Action: Bolt action; repeating
Magazine: 2-shot detachable box
Barrel: 26" adjustable choke
Finish: Blued; wood Monte Carlo semi-pistol grip one-piece stock & tapered forearm; recoil pad
Approximate wt.: 6½ lbs.
Comments: Made from the early 1960's to early 1980's.
Estimated Value: Excellent: $100.00
                        Very good: $ 75.00

Mossberg Model 395K

Similar to the 385K in 12 gauge. Weighs 7½ lbs.
Estimated Value: Excellent: $100.00
                        Very good: $ 75.00

Mossberg Model 390K

Mossberg Model 585

Similar to the Model 385K with improved safety. Produced in mid 1980's.

Estimated Value: Excellent: $120.00
　　　　　　　　　Very good: $ 90.00

Mossberg Model 390 K

Similar to the 385K with a 28" barrel in 16 gauge. Discontinued in the late 1970's.

Estimated Value: Excellent: $95.00
　　　　　　　　　Very good: $75.00

Mossberg Model 595

Similar to the Model 395K with improved safety. Introduced in 1984. Available with 28" adjustable choke barrel or 38" waterfowl barrel. Add $20.00 for Waterfowl model.

Estimated Value: Excellent: $120.00
　　　　　　　　　Very good: $ 90.00

Mossberg Model 395 SPL

Similar to the Model 395K with a 38" full choke barrel for waterfowl; swivels. Introduced in 1982.

Estimated Value: Excellent: $115.00
　　　　　　　　　Very good: $ 90.00

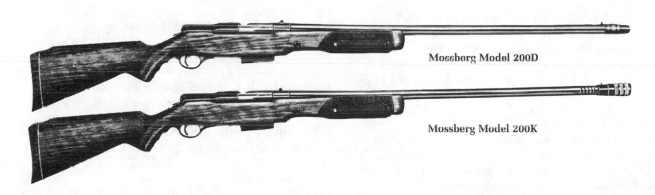

Mossberg Model 200D

Mossberg Model 200K

Mossberg Model 3000 Field

Gauge: 12, 20; regular or magnum
Action: Slide action; hammerless; repeating
Magazine: 4-shot tubular, 3-shot in magnum
Barrel: 26" improved cylinder, 28" modified or full, 30" full; ventilated rib; "Multi choke" available
Finish: Checkered walnut pistol grip stock & slide handle
Approximate wt.: 6¼ to 7½ lbs.
Comments: Produced in the mid 1980's. Add $25.00 for "Multi choke."

Estimated Value: Excellent: $265.00
　　　　　　　　　Very good: $200.00

Mossberg Model 3000 Waterfowler

Similar to the Model 3000 with 30" full choke barrel & Parkerized, oiled finish or camo finish with "Speedfeed" storage stock (add 10%). Add 10% for "Multi choke."

Estimated Value: Excellent: $290.00
　　　　　　　　　Very good: $215.00

Mossberg Model 3000 Slug

Similar to the Model 3000 with a 22" slug barrel & rifle sights. Add $35.00 for black finish with "Speedfeed" storage stock.

Estimated Value: Excellent: $250.00
　　　　　　　　　Very good: $185.00

Mossberg Model 200D

Gauge: 12
Action: Slide action; hammerless; repeating; slide handle is metal cover over wood forearm
Magazine: 3-shot detachable box
Barrel: 28" interchangeable choke fittings
Finish: Blued; wood Monte Carlo semi-pistol grip one-piece stock & forearm
Approximate wt.: 7½ lbs.
Comments: Made from the mid to late 1950's.

Estimated Value: Excellent: $110.00
　　　　　　　　　Very good: $ 85.00

Mossberg Model 200K

Similar to the 200D with adjustable choke.

Estimated Value: Excellent: $120.00
　　　　　　　　　Very good: $ 90.00

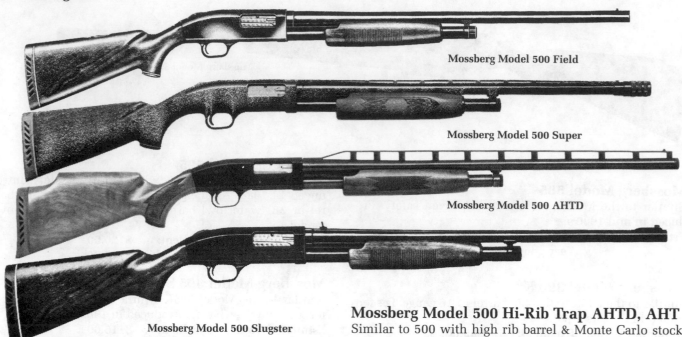

Mossberg Model 500 Field

Mossberg Model 500 Super

Mossberg Model 500 AHTD

Mossberg Model 500 Slugster

Mossberg Model 500 Field

Gauge: 12, 16, 20, 410
Action: Slide action; hammerless; repeating
Magazine: 6-shot tubular
Barrel: 26" adjustable choke or improved cylinder; 28" modified or full; 30" full choke in 12 gauge only; available with "Accu-Choke" after 1984. Vent rib available. 24" in Junior Model
Finish: Blued; walnut pistol grip stock & grooved slide handle; recoil pad; camo finish & "Speedfeed" stock available in 1986
Approximate wt.: 6 to 8 lbs.
Comments: Manufactured from about 1960 to present. Add 8% for vent rib; add 3% for "Accu-Choke"; add 25% for camo finish & "Speedfeed" stock.

Estimated Value:	New (retail):	$275.00
	Excellent:	$205.00
	Very good:	$165.00

Mossberg Model 500 Super

Similar to the 500 Field with checkered stock & slide handle & ventilated rib. 12 gauge magnum.

Estimated Value:	Excellent:	$200.00
	Very good:	$150.00

Mossberg Model 500 Hi-Rib Trap AHTD, AHT

Similar to 500 with high rib barrel & Monte Carlo stock. AHT full choke; AHTD had adjustable choke; 28" or 30" barrel.

Estimated Value:	Excellent:	$270.00
	Very good:	$200.00

Mossberg Model 500 Slugster

Similar to 500 with 18" or 24" slug barrel & rifle sights. Add 20% for removable choke; add 15% for Trophy Model.

Estimated Value:	Excellent:	$200.00
	Very good:	$160.00

Mossberg Model 500 ALDR, CLDR, ALDRX

Similar to 500 in 12 gauge (ALDR) & 20 gauge (CLDR) with removable choke. Add $50.00 for additional slugster barrel (ALDRX).

Estimated Value:	Excellent:	$200.00
	Very good:	$150.00

Mossberg Model 500 ALMR Duck Gun

Similar to 500 in 12 gauge with 30" or 32" vent rib barrel for 3" magnum. Discontinued in the early 1980's.

Estimated Value:	Excellent:	$190.00
	Very good:	$140.00

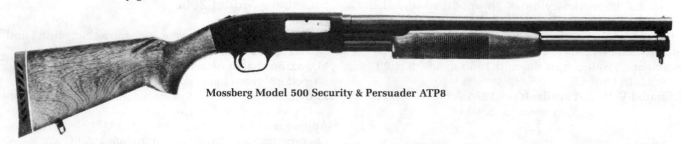

Mossberg Model 500 Security & Persuader ATP8

Mossberg Model 500 Security & Persuader ATP6

Similar to the Model 500, built in several models for law enforcement use. 12 gauge, 6-shot, 18½" barrel. Add 17% for Parkerized finish; 9% for rifle sights; 26% for nickel finish; 13% for "Speedfeed" stock; 22% for camo finish.

Estimated Value:	Excellent:	$190.00
	Very good:	$150.00

Mossberg Model 500 Security & Persuader ATP8

Similar to the Model 500 ATP6 series with a 20" barrel, 8-shot capacity. Add 8% for rifle sights; 16% for Parkerized finish; 24% for nickel finish; 12% for "Speedfeed" stock; 20% for camo finish.

Estimated Value:	Excellent:	$200.00
	Very good:	$160.00

Mossberg Model 500 Mariner

Similar to the Persuader series except it has a special Teflon & metal coating that is resistant to salt water spray. Stock & slide handle are synthetic. Available in 6- or 8-shot version. Add 7% for 8-shot model, 10% for "Speedfeed" stock. Introduced in 1987.

Estimated Value: Excellent: $260.00
Very good: $210.00

Mossberg Model 500 Camper

Similar to the Model 500 Cruiser in 12 gauge, 20 gauge or 410 bore; 18½" barrel; synthetic grip & slide handle; camo carrying case. Introduced in the late 1980's.

Estimated Value: Excellent: $210.00
Very good: $170.00

Mossberg Model 500 APR Pigeon

Similar to the 500 Field except; engraving; ventilated rib. Made from the late 1960's to the late 1970's.

Estimated Value: Excellent: $260.00
Very good: $190.00

Mossberg Model 500 ARTP Trap

Similar to the 500 APR with a 30" full choke barrel; Monte Carlo stock. Discontinued in the late 1970's.

Estimated Value: Excellent: $275.00
Very good: $200.00

Mossberg 500 Security & Persuader CTP6, ETP6

Similar to the other 500 series law enforcement shotguns in 20 gauge (CTP6) or 410 bore (ETP6); 18½" barrel; 6-shot.

Estimated Value: Excellent: $190.00
Very good: $150.00

Mossberg Model 500 Persuader Cruiser

Similar to the Model 500 ATP6 and ATP8 series law enforcement shotguns with one-hand grip. Add 6% for 20" barrel; 26% for nickel finish.

Estimated Value: Excellent: $190.00
Very good: $150.00

Mossberg Model 500 ER

Mossberg Model 500 ER, ELR

Similar to the 500 Field in 410 gauge; 26" barrel; skeet version has checkering & ventilated rib. Discontinued in the early 1980's.

Estimated Value: Excellent: $200.00
Very good: $150.00

Mossberg Model 500 Regal

Similar to the Model 500 with deluxe finish, crown design on receiver. Produced in mid 1980's. Add $20.00 for "Accu-Choke."

Estimated Value: Excellent: $210.00
Very good: $165.00

Mossberg Model 5500

Mossberg Model 5500

Gauge: 12, regular or magnum
Action: Gas operated semi-automatic
Magazine: 4-shot tubular
Barrel: 26" improved cylinder, 28" modified, 30" full; 28" "Accu-Choke" with interchangeable tubes; ventilated rib available; 25" on youth model
Finish: Blued; checkered hardwood semi-pistol grip stock & forearm; aluminum alloy receiver; small stock on youth model
Approximate wt.: 7½ lbs.
Comments: Produced from the early to mid 1980's. Add $20.00 for "Accu-Choke"; $15.00 for magnum.

Estimated Value: Excellent: $330.00
Very good: $250.00

Mossberg Model 5500 Slugster

Similar to the Model 5500 with 18½" or 24" slug barrel, rifle sights & swivels.

Estimated Value: Excellent: $335.00
Very good: $255.00

Mossberg Model 1000 Field

Mossberg Model 1000 Super

Gauge: 12 or 20, regular or magnum
Action: Gas-operated semi-automatic
Magazine: 3-shot tubular
Barrel: 26", 28", 30" "Multi choke"; ventilated rib
Finish: Blued; checkered walnut pistol grip stock & fore-
    arm; recoil pad; scrolling on receiver
Approximate wt.: 6¾ to 7¾ lbs.
Comments: Produced in the mid 1980's.
Estimated Value: Excellent: $400.00
                    Very good: $300.00

Mossberg Model 1000 Super Waterfowler

Similar to the Model 1000 Super with dull wood & Parkerized finish; 12 gauge only.
Estimated Value: Excellent: $420.00
                    Very good: $315.00

Mossberg Model 1000 Super Slug

Similar to the Model 1000 Super with 22" slug barrel.
Estimated Value: Excellent: $395.00
                    Very good: $295.00

Mossberg Model 1000 Super Skeet

Similar to the Model 1000 Super with 25" barrel.
Estimated Value: Excellent: $495.00
                    Very good: $370.00

Mossberg Model 1000 Field

Similar to the Model 1000 Super with alloy receiver; various chokes available including a 26" skeet barrel; add
$30.00 for "Multi choke"; Junior model has 22" barrel
with "Multi choke" (add $25.00).
Estimated Value: Excellent: $330.00
                    Very good: $245.00

Mossberg Model 1000 Slug

Similar to the Model 1000 Field with 22" slug barrel, rifle
sights.
Estimated Value: Excellent: $320.00
                    Very good: $240.00

Mossberg Model 1000 Trap

Similar to the Model 1000 Field with a 30" "Multi
choke" barrel, recoil pad, Monte Carlo stock & high-rib
barrel.
Estimated Value: Excellent: $420.00
                    Very good: $315.00

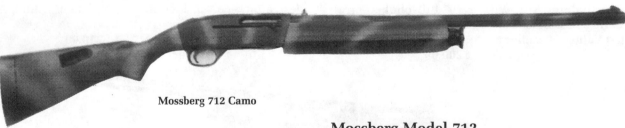

Mossberg 712 Camo

Mossberg Model 712 Camo

Similar to the Model 712 with camo finish & "Speedfeed" storage stock. Add $20.00 for "Accu-Choke." Pro-
duced in mid 1980's.
Estimated Value: Excellent: $290.00
                    Very good: $220.00

Mossberg Model 712 Regal

Similar to the Model 712 with deluxe finish, crown
design on receiver. Produced in mid 1980's. Add $20.00
for "Accu-Choke."
Estimated Value: Excellent: $275.00
                    Very good: $200.00

Mossberg Model 712

Gauge: 12, regular or magnum
Action: Gas-operated semi-automatic
Magazine: 4-shot tubular, 3-shot in magnum
Barrel: 30" full, 28" modified, 24" "Accu-choke," 24"
    slug; ventilated rib available
Finish: Alloy receiver with anodized finish; checkered
    walnut finish semi-pistol grip stock & forearm;
    recoil pad; junior model has 13" stock
Approximate wt.: 7½ lbs.
Comments: This shotgun was designed to handle any 12
    gauge shell interchangeably. Produced from 1986 to
    late 1980's; add $15.00 for slug model with rifle
    sights; $15.00 for ventilated rib; $40.00 for "Accu-
    choke."
Estimated Value: Excellent: $260.00
                    Very good: $205.00

New England

New England Pardner

New England Pardner
Gauge: 12, 16, 20, 410; 12 magnum
Action: Break-open, side lever release, single shot; exposed hammer
Magazine: None, single shot
Barrel: 24", 26" or 28"; full, modified or cylinder bore
Finish: Blued with color case hardened frame; hardwood walnut finish pistol grip, smooth stock & lipped forearm
Approximate wt.: 5 to 6 lbs.
Comments: Introduced in 1989.
Estimated Value: New (retail): $150.70
Excellent: $110.00
Very good: $ 90.00

New England Youth Pardner
Same as the Pardner except 20 or 410 gauge only with 22" barrel & straight grip, shorter stock with recoil pad. Introduced in 1989.
Estimated Value: New (retail): $160.00
Excellent: $120.00
Very good: $ 95.00

New England Deluxe Pardner
Same as the Pardner except 12 or 20 gauge only with special double back-up butt stock (holds two spare shells) & recoil pad. Introduced in 1989.
Estimated Value: New (retail): $165.00
Excellent: $120.00
Very good: $ 95.00

New England Mini-Pardner
Same as the Pardner except 20 or 410 gauge only, 18½" barrel with short butt stock; weighs 4¾ lbs.; equipped with swivel studs. Introduced in 1989.
Estimated Value: New (retail): $150.00
Excellent: $110.00
Very good: $ 90.00

New England Protector
Gauge: 12
Action: Break-open, side release, single shot exposed; hammer
Magazine: None, single shot
Barrel: 18½"
Finish: Blued or nickel; smooth hardwood walnut finish; pistol grip stock & lipped forearm; recoil pad; special double back-up butt stock holds two spare shells; swivels
Approximate wt.: 5¾ lbs.
Comments: Introduced in 1990; add 8% for nickel finish
Estimated Value: New (retail): $165.70
Excellent: $125.00
Very good: $100.00

New England 10 Gauge Magnum
Gauge: 10 gauge, 3½" chamber
Action: Break-open, side lever release, single shot; exposed hammer
Magazine: None, single shot
Barrel: 32" full choke
Finish: Blued; hardwood walnut finish, smooth, pistol grip stock & extended forearm; recoil pad
Approximate wt.: 10 lbs.
Comments: Introduced in 1989.
Estimated Value: New (retail): $170.70
Excellent: $125.00
Very good: $100.00

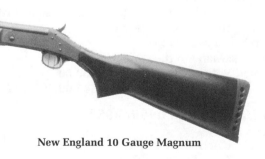

New England 10 Gauge Magnum

New England Handi-Gun Combination
See Handi-Gun Combination in Rifle section.

New Haven (Mossberg)

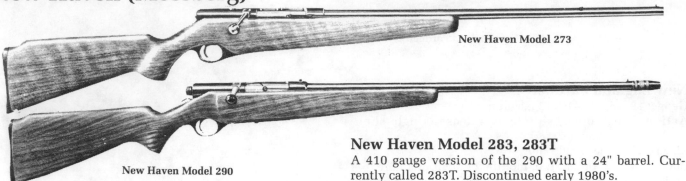

New Haven Model 273

New Haven Model 290

New Haven Model 290

Gauge: 16
Action: Bolt action; hammerless; repeating
Magazine: 2-shot detachable box
Barrel: 28" removable full choke
Finish: Blued; walnut Monte Carlo pistol grip one-piece stock & tapered forearm
Approximate wt.: 6½ lbs.
Comments: Made in the early 1960's.
Estimated Value: Excellent: $85.00
                       Very good: $65.00

New Haven Model 283, 283T

A 410 gauge version of the 290 with a 24" barrel. Currently called 283T. Discontinued early 1980's.
Estimated Value: Excellent: $90.00
                       Very good: $70.00

New Haven Model 295

A 12 gauge version of the 290.
Estimated Value: Excellent: $80.00
                       Very good: $60.00

New Haven Model 285

A 20 gauge version of the 290 with 24" barrel.
Estimated Value: Excellent: $85.00
                       Very good: $65.00

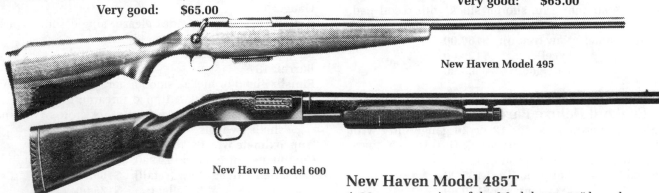

New Haven Model 495

New Haven Model 600

New Haven Model 273

Gauge: 20
Action: Bolt action; hammerless; single shot
Magazine: None
Barrel: 24" full choke
Finish: Blued; plain walnut Monte Carlo semi-pistol grip one-piece stock & forearm
Approximate wt.: 6¼ lbs.
Comments: Made in the early 1960's.
Estimated Value: Excellent: $60.00
                       Very good: $45.00

New Haven Model 495, 495T

Gauge: 12
Action: Bolt action; hammerless; repeating
Magazine: 2-shot detachable box
Barrel: 28" full choke
Finish: Blued; walnut Monte Carlo semi-pistol grip stock & tapered forearm
Approximate wt.: 7½ lbs.
Comments: Made from the mid 1960's to early 1980's.
Estimated Value: Excellent: $110.00
                       Very good: $ 85.00

New Haven Model 485T

A 20 gauge version of the Model 495; 26" barrel.
Estimated Value: Excellent: $120.00
                       Very good: $ 90.00

New Haven Model 600

Gauge: 12, 20, 410
Action: Slide action; hammerless; repeating
Magazine: 6-shot tubular
Barrel: 26" improved cylinder, 28" modified or full, 30" full chokes. Ventilated rib, adjustable choke & interchangeable choke available
Finish: Blued; walnut semi-pistol grip stock & slide handle
Approximate wt.: 7½ lbs.
Comments: Made from the early 1960's to early 1980's. Add $30.00 for ventilated rib; $20.00 for adjustable choke; $10.00 for interchangeable choke.
Estimated Value: Excellent: $175.00
                       Very good: $140.00

New Haven Model 600 AST

Similar to Model 600 with 24" barrel & rifle sights.
Estimated Value: Excellent: $180.00
                       Very good: $145.00

Noble

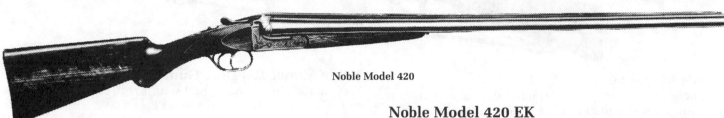

Noble Model 420

Noble Model 420

Gauge: 12, 16, 20
Action: Box lock; top lever, break-open; hammerless; double triggers
Magazine: None
Barrel: Double barrel, 28" modified & full choke
Finish: Blued; checkered walnut pistol grip stock & forearm
Approximate wt.: 6¾ lbs.
Comments: Made from the late 1950's to the early 1970's.
Estimated Value: Excellent: $225.00
Very good: $180.00

Noble Model 420 EK

A fancy version of the Model 420 with automatic ejectors; select walnut; recoil pad; engraving; sights; gold inlay. Made in the late 1960's.
Estimated Value: Excellent: $300.00
Very good: $240.00

Noble Model 450E

Very similar to Model 420 EK. Made from the late 1960's to the early 1970's.
Estimated Value: Excellent: $325.00
Very good: $255.00

Noble Model 40

Noble Model 420 EK

Basically the same gun as the Model 40 without recoil pad or "Multi-Choke."
Estimated Value: Excellent: $125.00
Very good: $ 95.00

Noble Model 40

Gauge: 12
Action: Slide action; hammerless
Magazine: 5-shot tubular
Barrel: 28" with multi-choke
Finish: Blued; plain walnut pistol grip stock & grooved slide handle; recoil pad
Approximate wt.: 7½ lbs.
Comments: Made from the early to mid 1950's.
Estimated Value: Excellent: $140.00
Very good: $110.00

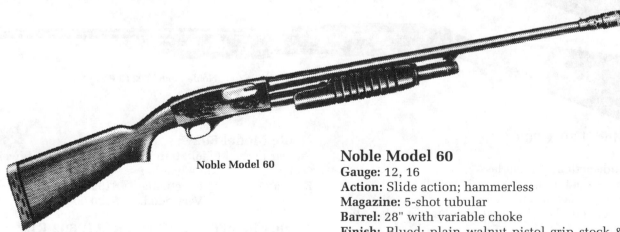

Noble Model 60

Noble Model 60 ACP

Very similar to Model 60 with a ventilated rib. Made from late 1960's to early 1970's.
Estimated Value: Excellent: $140.00
Very good: $110.00

Noble Model 60

Gauge: 12, 16
Action: Slide action; hammerless
Magazine: 5-shot tubular
Barrel: 28" with variable choke
Finish: Blued; plain walnut pistol grip stock & grooved slide handle; recoil pad
Approximate wt.: 7½ lbs.
Comments: Manufactured in takedown version from the mid 1950's to late 1960's.
Estimated Value: Excellent: $130.00
Very good: $100.00

Noble Model 60 AF

Noble Model 160 Deer Gun

Noble Model 60 AF

A fancier version of the Model 60 with special steel barrel; select wood; fluted comb. Made only during the mid 1960's.

Estimated Value: Excellent: $145.00
                      Very good: $115.00

Noble Model 160 Deer Gun, 166L Deer Gun

Very similar to the Model 60 with a 24" barrel; sights; swivels. Made in the mid 1960's as 160 & from late 1960's to early 1970's as 166L.

Estimated Value: Excellent: $150.00
                      Very good: $120.00

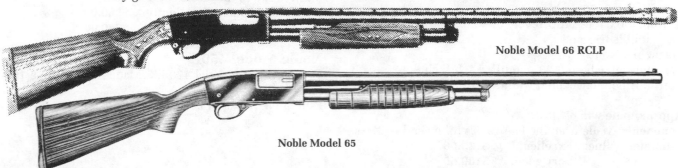

Noble Model 66 RCLP

Noble Model 65

Noble Model 65

Basically the same as the Model 60 without the recoil pad or adjustable choke.

Estimated Value: Excellent: $120.00
                      Very good: $ 90.00

Noble Model 66 RCLP

Similar to the Model 60 ACP with a fancier checkered stock.

Estimated Value: Excellent: $145.00
                      Very good: $110.00

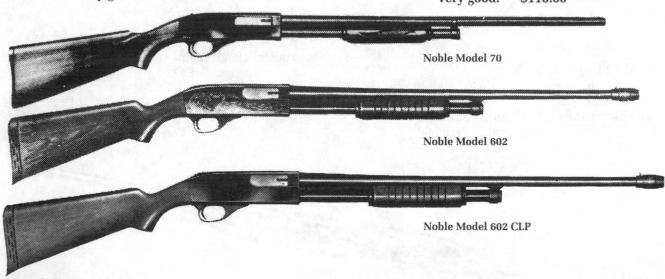

Noble Model 70

Noble Model 602

Noble Model 602 CLP

Noble Model 70 & 70X

Gauge: 410
Action: Slide action; hammerless
Magazine: 5-shot tubular
Barrel: 26" modified or full choke
Finish: Blued; checkered walnut pistol grip stock & slide handle
Approximate wt.: 6 lbs.
Comments: Made from the late 1950's to late 1960's as Model 70 & from the late 1960's to early 1970's as 70X.

Estimated Value: Excellent: $150.00
                      Very good: $115.00

Noble Model 602

Similar to the Model 70 in 20 gauge & 28" barrel; weighs 6½ lbs. Grooved slide handle.

Estimated Value: Excellent: $155.00
                      Very good: $120.00

Noble Model 602 CLP, 602 RCLP, 602 RLP

The 602 CLP is same as 602 with adjustable choke & recoil pad; 602 RCLP is same as 602 with recoil pad; 602 RLP is same as 602 with recoil pad & ventilated rib. Add $20.00 for ventilated rib.

Estimated Value: Excellent: $160.00
                      Very good: $125.00

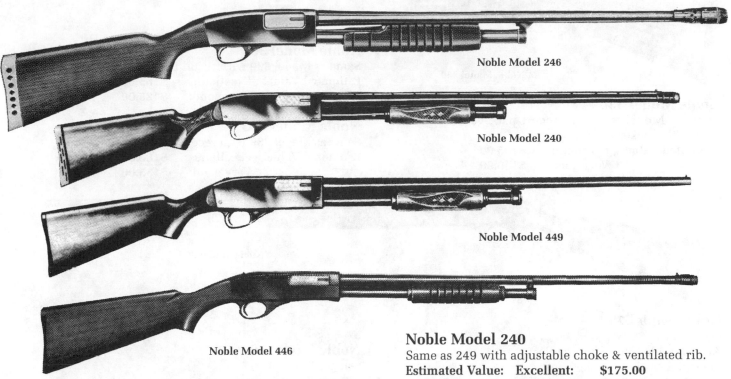

Noble Model 246

Noble Model 240

Noble Model 449

Noble Model 446

Noble Model 249
Gauge: 20
Action: Slide action; hammerless
Magazine: 5-shot tubular
Barrel: 28" modified or full choke
Finish: Blued; checkered walnut pistol grip stock & slide handle; recoil pad
Approximate wt.: 6½ lbs.
Comments: Produced in the early 1970's.
Estimated Value: Excellent: $150.00
Very good: $115.00

Noble Model 246
Same as 249 with adjustable choke.
Estimated Value: Excellent: $160.00
Very good: $120.00

Noble Model 243
Same as 249 with ventilated rib.
Estimated Value: Excellent: $165.00
Very good: $125.00

Noble Model 240
Same as 249 with adjustable choke & ventilated rib.
Estimated Value: Excellent: $175.00
Very good: $130.00

Noble Model 449
Similar to Model 249 without recoil pad & in 410 bore.
Estimated Value: Excellent: $160.00
Very good: $120.00

Noble Model 446
Similar to Model 246 without recoil pad & in 410 bore.
Estimated Value: Excellent: $165.00
Very good: $125.00

Noble Model 443
Similar to Model 243 without recoil pad & in 410 bore.
Estimated Value: Excellent: $170.00
Very good: $130.00

Noble Model 440
Similar to Model 240 without recoil pad & in 410 bore.
Estimated Value: Excellent: $180.00
Very good: $135.00

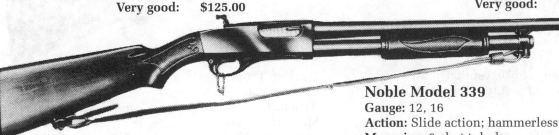

Noble Model 390 Deer Gun

Noble Model 390 Deer Gun
Similar to Model 339 with a 24" slug barrel; sights; swivels.
Estimated Value: Excellent: $160.00
Very good: $120.00

Noble Model 339
Gauge: 12, 16
Action: Slide action; hammerless
Magazine: 6-shot tubular
Barrel: 28" modified or full choke
Finish: Blued; checkered walnut pistol grip stock & slide handle
Approximate wt.: 7½ lbs.
Comments: Made in the early 1970's.
Estimated Value: Excellent: $155.00
Very good: $115.00

Noble Model 330

Noble Model 330

Same as Model 339 with recoil pad, ventilated rib & adjustable choke.

Estimated Value: **Excellent:**   **$185.00**
                Very good: **$140.00**

Noble Model 336

Same as Model 339 with recoil pad & adjustable choke.

Estimated Value: **Excellent:**   **$165.00**
                Very good: **$125.00**

Noble Model 333

Same as Model 339 with recoil pad & ventilated rib.

Estimated Value: **Excellent:**   **$180.00**
                Very good: **$135.00**

Noble Model 80

Noble Model 757

Gauge: 20
Action: Slide action; hammerless
Magazine: 5-shot tubular
Barrel: 28" aluminum; adjustable choke
Finish: Black anodized aluminum; decorated receiver; checkered walnut pistol grip stock & slide handle; recoil pad
Approximate wt.: 4½ lbs.
Comments: A very light gun made in the early 1970's.
Estimated Value: **Excellent:**   **$175.00**
                Very good: **$130.00**

Noble Model 80

Gauge: 410
Action: Semi-automatic; hammerless
Magazine: 5-shot tubular
Barrel: 26" full choke
Finish: Blued; plain walnut pistol grip stock & forearm
Approximate wt.: 6 lbs.
Comments: Made in the mid 1960's.
Estimated Value: **Excellent:**   **$200.00**
                Very good: **$150.00**

Parker

Parker Single Barrel Trap

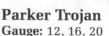

Parker Single Barrel Trap

Gauge: 12
Action: Slide action; hammerless; top lever break-open; box lock
Magazine: None
Barrel: 30", 32", 34", any choke; ventilated rib
Finish: Blued; checkered walnut straight, full or semi-pistol grip stock
Approximate wt.: 6½ to 7½ lbs.
Comments: Grades differ according to workmanship, checkering & engraving. Made from about 1917 to 1941. Manufacture of Parker guns was taken over by Remington in 1934 & this gun was called Remington Parker Model 930. There is a wide range of values for this gun. Prices for pre-1934 models.
Estimated Value: **Excellent:**   **$3,000.00 - $12,000.00**
                Very good: **$2,000.00 - $10,000.00**

Parker Trojan

Parker Trojan

Gauge: 12, 16, 20
Action: Top lever break-open; hammerless; box lock
Magazine: None
Barrel: Double barrel; 26", 28", 30", full & full or modified & full chokes
Finish: Blued; checkered walnut pistol grip stock & forearm
Approximate wt.: 6½ to 8 lbs.
Comments: Made from about 1915 to 1939.
Estimated Value: **Excellent:**   **$1,200.00**
                Very good: **$1,000.00**

Parker Hammerless Double

Gauge: 10, 12, 16, 20, 28, 410
Action: Box lock; top lever, break-open; hammerless; selective trigger & automatic ejectors after 1934
Magazine: None
Barrel: Double barrel; 26", 28", 30", 32"; any choke combination
Finish: Blued; checkered walnut straight, full or semi-pistol grip stock & forearm
Approximate wt.: 6½ to 8½ lbs.
Comments: Grades vary according to workmanship, checkering & engraving. Manufacture of Parker guns was taken over by Remington in 1934 & this gun was called Remington Parker Model 920 until it was discontinued in 1941. Prices for pre-1934 models.
Estimated Value: Excellent: $2,100.00 - $50,000.00
Very good: $1,200.00 - $20,000.00

Parker Hammerless Double G.H.E.

Parker Hammerless Double A.H.E.

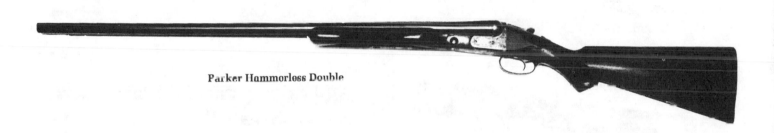

Parker Hammerless Double

Pedersen

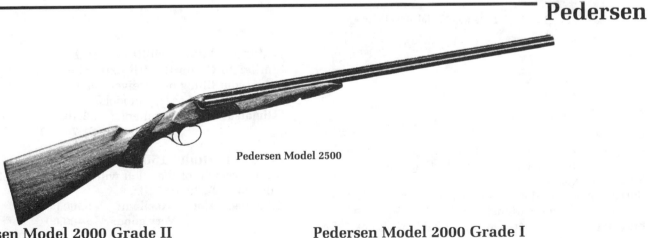

Pedersen Model 2500

Pedersen Model 2000 Grade II

Gauge: 12, 20
Action: Box lock; top lever, break-open; hammerless; automatic ejectors; single selective trigger
Magazine: None
Barrel: Double barrel; length to customer's specifications
Finish: Blued; checkered walnut pistol grip stock & tapered forearm; engraved
Approximate wt.: 7½ lbs.
Comments: Made in the mid 1970's.
Estimated Value: Excellent: $1,500.00
Very good: $1,200.00

Pedersen Model 2000 Grade I

Similar to Grade II with fancier engraving, gold filling on receiver, select walnut.
Estimated Value: Excellent: $1,800.00
Very good: $1,450.00

Pedersen Model 2500

A field version of the 2000; no engraving; blade front.
Estimated Value: Excellent: $400.00
Very good: $320.00

Pedersen Model 1000 Grade II

Pedersen Model 1000 Grade I

Pedersen Model 1500

Pedersen Model 4000 Deluxe

Pedersen Model 1000 Grade II

Gauge: 12, 20
Action: Box lock; top lever, break-open; hammerless; automatic ejectors; single selective trigger
Magazine: None
Barrel: Over & under double barrel; length made to customers specifications; ventilated rib
Finish: Blued; checkered walnut pistol grip stock & forearm; recoil pad
Approximate wt.: 7½ lbs.
Comments: Produced in the mid 1970's.
Estimated Value: Excellent: $800.00
                        Very good: $600.00

Pedersen Model 1000 Grade II

Similar to Grade III with engraving & fancier wood; made to customers specs. Add $15.00 for magnum.
Estimated Value: Excellent: $1,725.00
                        Very good: $1,400.00

Pedersen Model 1000 Grade I

Similar to Grade II with extensive engraving, select wood, gold filling on receiver; made to customers specs; in hunting, skeet or trap models.
Estimated Value: Excellent: $2,100.00
                        Very good: $1,750.00

Pedersen Model 1500

A field version of the 1000 with standard barrel lengths only (26", 28", 30" or 32").
Estimated Value: Excellent: $500.00
                        Very good: $400.00

Pedersen Model 4000 Deluxe

Gauge: 10, 12, 410
Action: Slide action; hammerless; side ejection
Magazine: Tubular
Barrel: 26", 28", 30", variety of chokes; ventilated rib
Finish: Blued; checkered walnut pistol grip stock & slide handle; recoil pad; floral engraving on receiver
Approximate wt.: 6¾ lbs.
Comments: Made in the mid 1970's.
Estimated Value: Excellent: $375.00
                        Very good: $300.00

Premier

Premier Regent

Gauge: 12, 16, 20, 28, 410
Action: Box lock; top lever, break-open; hammerless; double triggers
Magazine: None
Barrel: Double barrel; 26", 28" modified & full chokes; matte rib
Finish: Blued; checkered walnut pistol grip stock & tapered forearm
Approximate wt.: 7 lbs.
Comments: Produced in the 1970's.
Estimated Value: Excellent: $250.00
 Very good: $200.00

Premier Brush King

Similar to Regent 12 & 20 gauge only; 22" improved cylinder & modified choke barrels; straight stock. Still in production.
Estimated Value: Excellent: $260.00
 Very good: $205.00

Premier Magnum

Similar to Regent except: 10 gauge magnum with 32" barrels or 12 gauge magnum with 30" barrels; both gauges in full & full choke; recoil pad; beavertail forearm. Add $25.00 for 20 gauge magnum.
Estimated Value: Excellent: $285.00
 Very good: $225.00

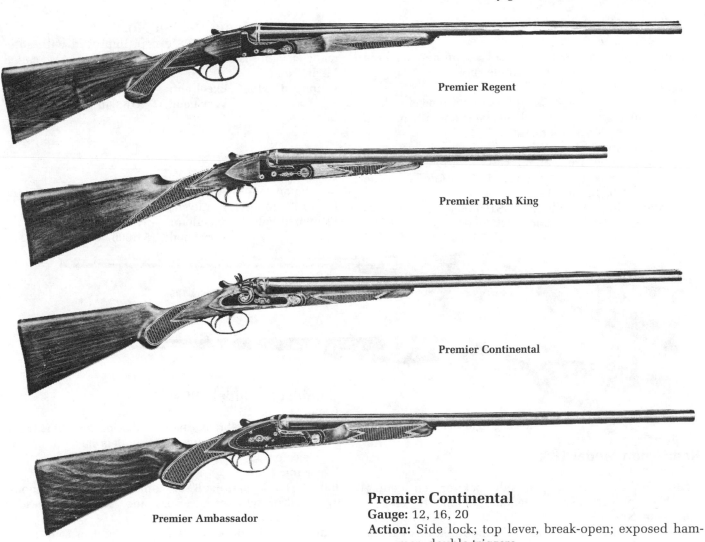

Premier Regent

Premier Brush King

Premier Continental

Premier Ambassador

Premier Ambassador

A hammerless version of the Continental. Also available in 410 gauge.
Estimated Value: Excellent: $325.00
 Very good: $260.00

Premier Continental

Gauge: 12, 16, 20
Action: Side lock; top lever, break-open; exposed hammer; double triggers
Magazine: None
Barrel: Double barrel; 26" modified & full choke
Finish: Blued; checkered walnut pistol grip stock & tapered forearm
Approximate wt.: 7 lbs.
Comments: Produced in the 1970's.
Estimated Value: Excellent: $300.00
 Very good: $240.00

Remington

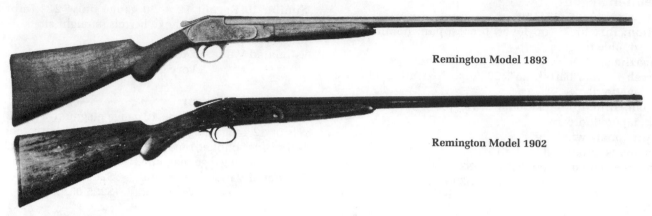

Remington Model 1893

Remington Model 1902

Remington Model 1893

Gauge: 10, 12, 16, 20

Action: Top lever break-open; semi-hammer (cocking lever on left), takedown; single shot

Magazine: None

Barrel: 28", 30", 32" or 34"; plain barrel with bead sight

Finish: Blued; case hardened receiver; smooth walnut, pistol grip stock & forearm

Approximate wt.: 5½ to 6½ lbs.

Comments: Made from about 1893 to 1906. Approximately 25,000 were produced. Also known as the Model No. 3 & the '93.

Estimated Value: Excellent: $195.00

Very good: $155.00

Remington Model 1902 or No. 9

Similar to the Model 1893 except improved with automatic ejector. Made from about 1902 to 1912. Also called Model No. 9.

Estimated Value: Excellent: $200.00

Very good: $165.00

Remington Parker 930

Remington took over production of the Parker shotguns from 1934 to 1941; single shot hammerless.

Estimated Value: Excellent: $1,500.00 - $2,500.00

Very good: $1,000.00 - $2.000.00

Remington Model 1889

Remington Model 1894

Remington Model 1894

Gauge: 10, 12, 16

Action: Top lever break-open; concealed hammer; triple lock; double triggers; some models have automatic ejectors

Magazine: None

Barrel: Double barrel; 26"-32" tapered barrels; full, modified or cylinder bore; ordnance steel or Damascus barrels with concave matted rib

Finish: Blued; checkered walnut, straight or semi-pistol grip stock & short tapered forearm; special engraving & inlays on higher grades

Approximate wt.: 7½ to 8½ lbs.

Comments: Made from about 1894 to 1910 in seven grades. Receivers marked Remington Arms Co. on left side. Prices for Standard Grade. Deduct $125.00 - $150.00 for Damascus barrels.

Estimated Value: Excellent: $700.00

Very good: $525.00

Remington Model 1889

Gauge: 10, 12, 16

Action: Top lever break-open; side lock; breech loading black powder; exposed hammer; double trigger

Magazine: None

Barrel: Double barrel; 28"-32" full, modified or cylinder bore; Damascus or steel

Finish: Blued; checkered walnut semi-pistol grip stock & short forearm

Approximate wt.: 7½ to 9 lbs.

Comments: Made from about 1889 to 1909 in seven grades. Approximately 30,000 produced. Prices are for Standard Grade.

Estimated Value: Excellent: $550.00

Very good: $440.00

Remington Model 1900

Remington Parker 920

Remington took over production of Parker shotguns from 1934 to 1941; double barrel hammerless; double triggers; 12 gauge.

Estimated Value: Excellent: $1,000.00
Very good: $ 750.00

Remington Model 1900

Gauge: 12, 16
Action: Top lever; break-open; concealed hammer; double triggers; automatic ejectors optional
Magazine: None
Barrel: Double barrel; 28" or 32" steel or Damascus in standard chokes; matted rib
Finish: Checkered walnut pistol grip stock & short tapered forearm with gap at front for disassembly
Approximate wt.: 8 to 9 lbs.
Comments: Similar to Model 1894 except lower grade; takedown model; internal forearm release. Made from about 1900 to 1910. Deduct $100.00 for Damascus barrels.

Estimated Value: Excellent: $500.00
Very good: $400.00

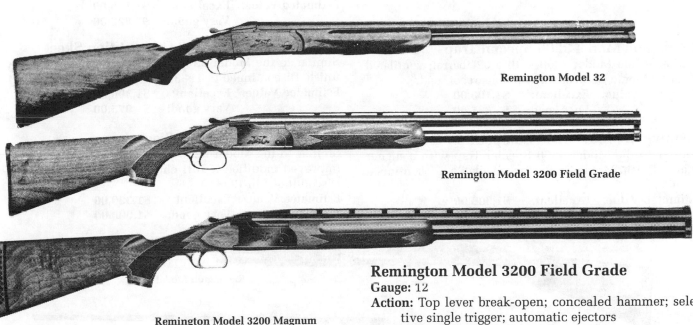

Remington Model 32

Remington Model 3200 Field Grade

Remington Model 3200 Magnum

Remington Model 3200 Field Grade

Gauge: 12
Action: Top lever break-open; concealed hammer; selective single trigger; automatic ejectors
Magazine: None
Barrel: 26"-30" over & under doubel barrel; ventilated rib; modified & full or improved cylinder & modified chokes
Finish: Blued; pointing dogs engraved on receiver; checkered walnut pistol grip stock & matching forearm
Approximate wt.: 7¾ to 8¾ lbs.
Comments: A modern version of the Model 32 started back in production in the early 1970's. Still available in Trap & Skeet models. Other models valued higher than Field Grade.

Estimated Value: Excellent: $860.00
Very good: $685.00

Remington Model 32

Gauge: 12
Action: Top lever; break-open; concealed hammer; single selective trigger; automatic ejectors
Magazine: None
Barrel: Over & under double barrel; 26-32" plain, solid or ventilated rib; full & modified choke standard but any combination available
Finish: Blued; engraved receiver; checkered walnut pistol grip stock & forearm
Approximate wt.: 7¾ to 8½ lbs.
Comments: One of the first modern American over & under double barrel shotguns produced. Made from about 1932 to 1942. Made in about six grades, high grades with fancier wood & engravings. Add $35.00 for solid rib; $50.00 for ventilated rib.

Estimated Value: Excellent: $720.00
Very good: $575.00

Remington Model 3200 Magnum

Similar to the Model 3200 Field Grade except: chambered for 12 gauge magnum; 30" barrels in full & full or modified & full chokes; receiver decorated with engraved scrollwork.

Estimated Value: Excellent: $990.00
Very good: $790.00

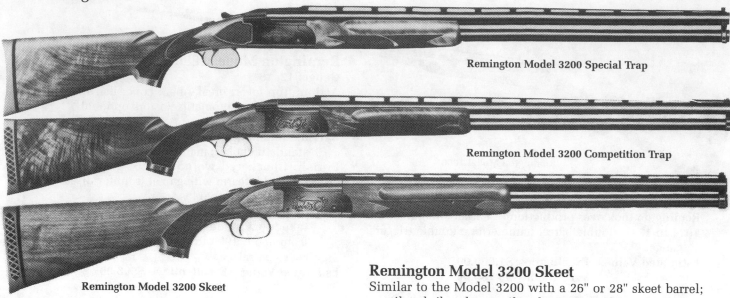

Remington Model 3200 Special Trap

Remington Model 3200 Competition Trap

Remington Model 3200 Skeet

Remington Model 3200 Skeet

Similar to the Model 3200 with a 26" or 28" skeet barrel; ventilated rib only; recoil pad; Monte Carlo stock.

Estimated Value: Excellent: $1,100.00
　　　　　　　　　　Very good: $ 825.00

Remington Model 3200 Special Trap

Similar to the Model 3200 with a 32" barrel; ventilated rib only; Monte Carlo stock available; recoil pad.

Estimated Value: Excellent: $1,100.00
　　　　　　　　　　Very good: $ 825.00

Remington Model 3200 Competition Trap

Similar to the Model 3200 Special Trap with a higher quality finish. Monte Carlo stock available. Discontinued in 1983.

Estimated Value: Excellent: $1,300.00
　　　　　　　　　　Very good: $ 975.00

Remington Model 3200 Competition Skeet

Similar to the Model 3200 Skeet with a higher quality finish. Discontinued in 1983.

Estimated Value: Excellent: $1,300.00
　　　　　　　　　　Very good: $ 975.00

Remington Model 3200 Pigeon

Similar to the Model 3200 Competition Skeet with 28" improved modified & full choke barrels for live birds. Discontinued in 1983.

Estimated Value: Excellent: $1,320.00
　　　　　　　　　　Very good: $1,000.00

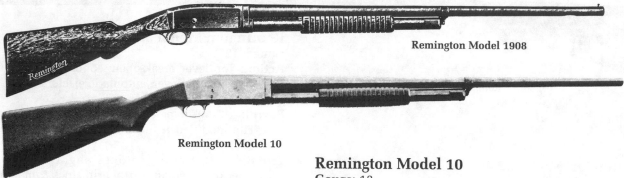

Remington Model 1908

Remington Model 10

Remington Model 1908

Gauge: 12

Action: Slide action; hammerless; bottom ejection; repeating

Magazine: 5-shot tubular

Barrel: 26"-32" steel barrel in full, modified or cylinder bore

Finish: Blued; plain or checkered walnut straight or pistol grip stock & forearm

Approximate wt.: 7½ to 8 lbs.

Comments: Made from about 1908 to 1910 in six grades with fancy checkering & engraving on higher grades. Marking on top of barrel "Remington Arms Co." & patent date. About 10,000 made.

Estimated Value: Excellent: $360.00
　　　　　　　　　　Very good: $280.00

Remington Model 10

Gauge: 12

Action: Slide action; hammerless; bottom ejection; repeating

Magazine: 5-shot tubular

Barrel: 26"-32" steel barrel in full, modified or cylinder bore

Finish: Blued; plain or checkered walnut straight or pistol grip stock & forearm

Approximate wt.: 7½ to 8 lbs.

Comments: Made from about 1910 to 1929, an improved version of the Model 1908. Made in seven grades with fancy checkering & engraving on higher grades. Also produced in 20" barrel riot gun. Solid rib optional from 1910-1922; ventilated rib optional from 1922-1928. Prices are for Standard Grade.

Estimated Value: Excellent: $280.00
　　　　　　　　　　Very good: $210.00

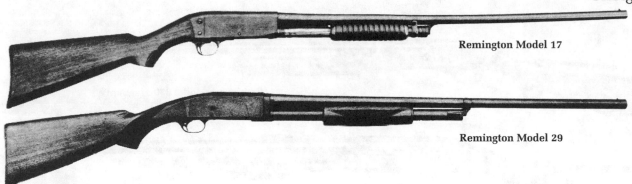

Remington Model 17

Remington Model 29

Remington Model 17

Gauge: 20

Action: Slide action; hammerless; bottom ejection; repeating

Magazine: 3-shot tubular

Barrel: 26"-32" steel in full, modified or cylinder bore; matted sighting groove on receiver or optional solid rib; 20" barrel on riot gun

Finish: Blued; plain or checkered walnut pistol grip stock & forearm

Approximate wt.: 7½ to 8 lbs.

Comments: Made from about 1917 to 1933 in seven grades. Higher grades have higher quality finish.

Estimated Value: Excellent: $275.00

Very good: $205.00

Remington Model 29

Gauge: 12

Action: Slide action; hammerless; bottom ejection; repeating

Magazine: 5-shot tubular

Barrel: 26"-32" steel in full, modified or cylinder bore; optional solid or ventilated rib; 20" barrel on riot gun

Finish: Blued; plain or checkered walnut pistol grip stock & forearm

Approximate wt.: 7½ to 8 lbs.

Comments: Made from about 1929 to 1933 in nine grades. Higher grades have higher quality finish. Prices are for Standard Grade.

Estimated Value: Excellent: $250.00

Very good: $200.00

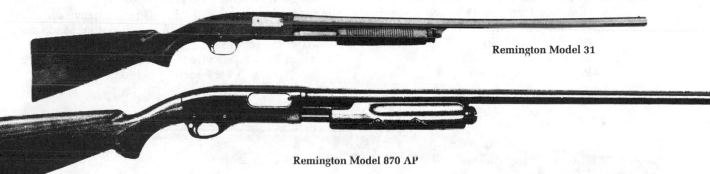

Remington Model 31

Remington Model 870 AP

Remington Model 31

Gauge: 12, 16, 20

Action: Slide action; hammerless; side ejection; repeating

Magazine: 3-shot tubular or 5-shot tubular

Barrel: 26", 32" steel; full, modified, cylinder or skeet chokes; optional solid or ventilated rib

Finish: Blued; slightly groove on receiver; plain or checkered pistol grip stock & forearm; forearm checkered or grooved

Approximate wt.: 6½ to 8 lbs.

Comments: Made from about 1931 to 1949 in eight grades. Higher grades differ in quality of finish. Prices for Standard Grades. Add $20.00 for solid rib; $25.00 for ventilated rib.

Estimated Value: Excellent: $250.00

Very good: $200.00

Remington Model 31 R Riot Gun

Similar to the Model 31 in 12 gauge only with 20" plain barrel.

Estimated Value: Excellent: $225.00

Very good: $170.00

Remington Model 31 Skeet

Similar to the Model 31 except: 12 gauge only; 26" barrel; solid or ventilated rib; skeet choke. Add $20.00 for ventilated rib.

Estimated Value: Excellent: $425.00

Very good: $320.00

Remington Model 870 AP

Gauge: 12, 16, 20

Action: Slide action; hammerless; side ejection; repeating

Magazine: 4-shot tubular

Barrel: 26", 28", 30" in 12 gauge; 26" or 28" in 16 & 20 gauge; full, modified or improved cylinder bore; plain or ventilated rib

Finish: Blued; plain or fancy; fluted comb, pistol grip stock & grooved slide handle

Approximate wt.: 6½ to 8 lbs.

Comments: Made in many styles, grades & variations from about 1950 to 1964. Higher grades have higher quality finish. Prices for standard grade. Add $25.00 for ventilated rib.

Estimated Value: Excellent: $250.00

Very good: $185.00

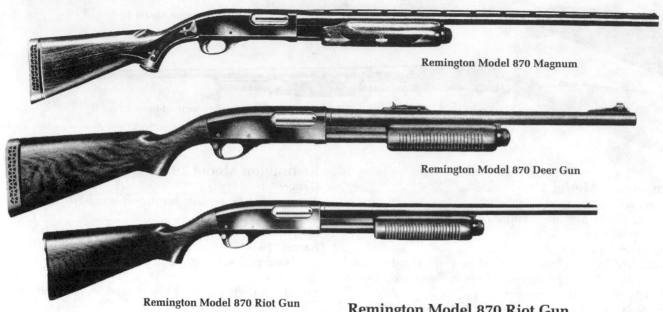

Remington Model 870 Magnum

Remington Model 870 Deer Gun

Remington Model 870 Riot Gun

Remington Model 870 Riot Gun

Same as the Model 870 AP except: 12 gauge only; 20" plain barrel; improved cylinder bore.

| Estimated Value: | Excellent: | $225.00 |
| | Very good: | $180.00 |

Remington Model 870 Magnum

Similar to the Model 870 AP except: 12 gauge magnum; 30" full choke barrel; recoil pad. Made from about 1955 to 1964. Add $25.00 for ventilated rib.

| Estimated Value: | Excellent: | $260.00 |
| | Very good: | $195.00 |

Remington Model 870 Deer Gun

Similar to the Model 870 AP except: 12 gauge only; 26" barrel for slugs; rifle type adjustable sights. Made from about 1959 to 1964.

| Estimated Value: | Excellent: | $240.00 |
| | Very good: | $190.00 |

Remington Model 870 Wingmaster

Remington Model 870 Special Purpose

Similar to the Model 870 with oil-finish wood & Parkerized metal; recoil pad & nylon camo strap; 12 gauge; ventilated rib, 26" or 30" barrel. Introduced in 1985. "Rem Choke."

Estimated Value:	New (retail):	$469.00
	Excellent:	$350.00
	Very good:	$280.00

Remington Model 870 SP Deer Gun

Similar to the 870 Special Purpose with 20" improved cylinder barrel & rifle sights. Introduced in 1986.

Estimated Value:	New (retail):	$443.00
	Excellent:	$335.00
	Very good:	$265.00

Remington Model 870 Wingmaster Field Gun

Gauge: 12, 16, 20 from 1964 to present; 28 & 410 added in 1969

Action: Slide action; hammerless; side ejection; repeating

Magazine: 4-shot tubular

Barrel: 26"-30" in 12 gauge; 26" or 28" in 16 & 20 gauge; 25" in 28 & 410 bore; full, modified or improved cylinder bore; plain barrel or ventilated rib

Finish: Blued; checkered walnut pistol grip stock with matching slide handle; recoil pad

Approximate wt.: 5½ to 7¼ lbs.

Comments: Improved version of the Model 870AP. Made in many grades & styles from about 1964 to present. Left hand models available & also lightweight models. Prices for standard grades. Add 10% for left hand model.

Estimated Value:	New (retail):	$469.00
	Excellent:	$350.00
	Very good:	$280.00

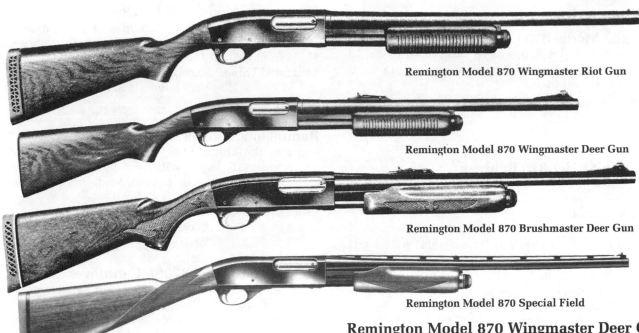

Remington Model 870 Wingmaster Riot Gun

Remington Model 870 Wingmaster Deer Gun

Remington Model 870 Brushmaster Deer Gun

Remington Model 870 Special Field

Remington Model 870 Wingmaster Riot Gun, Police

Similar to the Model 870 Wingmaster except: 12 gauge only; 18" or 20" improved cylinder barrel; plain stock & grooved slide handle; designed for law enforcement use. Add 8% for rifle sights. Blued or Parkerized finish.

Estimated Value: Excellent: $235.00
                    Very good: $190.00

Remington Model 870 Wingmaster Magnum

Same as the Model 870 Field Grade except: 12 or 20 magnum gauge only; full or modified choke. Add $30.00 for left hand model; add 10% for "Rem Choke."

Estimated Value: Excellent: $325.00
                    Very good: $260.00

Remington Model 870 Wingmaster Deer Gun

Same as Model 870 Wingmaster except: 12 gauge only; 20" barrel; rifle sights. Produced from 1964 to mid 1980's.

Estimated Value: Excellent: $300.00
                    Very good: $225.00

Remington Model 870 Brushmaster Deer Gun

Same as the Model 870 Wingmaster Deer Gun except: 12 & 20 gauge; checkered stock & slide handle; recoil pad. Left hand version introduced in 1983.

Estimated Value: New (retail): $443.00
                    Excellent: $335.00
                    Very good: $265.00

Remington Model 870 Special Field

Similar to the Model 870 with a straight grip stock, 21" ventilated rib barrel; 12 or 20 gauge; 3" chamber. Introduced in 1984. Some models have "Rem Choke."

Estimated Value: New (retail): $469.00
                    Excellent: $350.00
                    Very good: $280.00

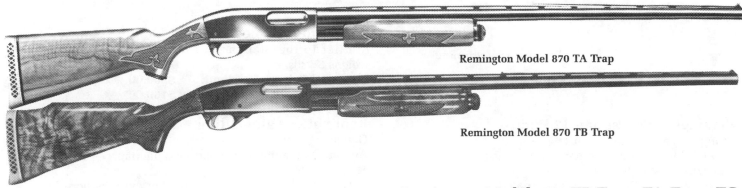

Remington Model 870 TA Trap

Remington Model 870 TB Trap

Remington Model 870SA Skeet

Similar to the Model 870 in skeet choke; ventilated rib only; recoil pad. Made from the late 1970's to early 1980's; 25" or 26" barrel.

Estimated Value: Excellent: $275.00
                    Very good: $220.00

Remington Model 870 TB Trap, TA Trap, TC Trap

Similar to the Model 870 with a 30" full choke barrel; ventilated rib; recoil pad; choice of Monte Carlo stock (add $10.00).

Estimated Value: Excellent: $400.00
                    Very good: $320.00

Remington Model 870 Competition Trap

Similar to the Model 870; single shot; 30" full choke; ventilated rib barrel; recoil pad; non-glare matte finish receiver. Introduced in 1982.

Estimated Value: Excellent: $570.00
                     Very good: $425.00

Remington Model 870 Express

Gauge: 12, magnum
Action: Slide action; hammerless; side ejection repeating
Magazine: 4-shot tubular
Barrel: 28" ventilated rib; "Rem Choke"
Finish: Blued; checkered hardwood semi-pistol grip stock & forearm
Approximate wt.: 7¼ lbs.
Comments: Introduced in 1987.

Estimated Value: New (retail): $223.00
                     Excellent: $165.00
                     Very good: $135.00

Remington Model 870 Ltd. 20

Same as the Model 870 Wingmaster Field except: 20 gauge only; 23" barrel with ventilated rib; lightweight. Made from 1980 to 1984.

Estimated Value: Excellent: $310.00
                     Very good: $250.00

Remington Model 870 Youth Gun

Same as the Model 870 Wingmaster Field except: 20 gauge only; 21" barrel with ventilated rib; lightweight; short stock (12½" length of pull). Made from 1984 to present; changeable choke tubes after 1985.

Estimated Value: New (retail): $452.00
                     Excellent: $340.00
                     Very good: $270.00

Remington Model 870SP Cantilever

Same as the Model 870SP Deer Gun except: no sights; equipped with cantilever scope mount, rings & changeable choke tubes (rifled choke tub for slugs & improved cylinder choke tube). Introduced in 1989

Estimated Value: New (retail): $496.00
                     Excellent: $375.00
                     Very good: $295.00

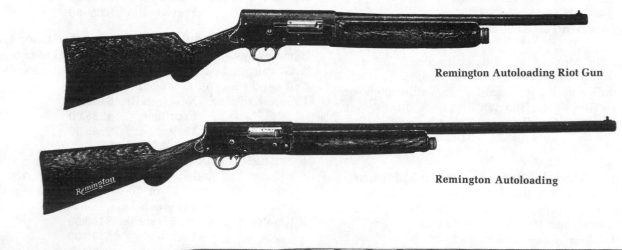

Remington Autoloading Riot Gun

Remington Autoloading

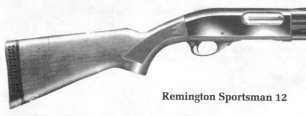

Remington Sportsman 12

Remington Sportsman 12 Pump

Gauge: 12, regular or magnum
Action: Slide action; hammerless; side ejection; repeating
Magazine: 4-shot tubular
Barrel: 28" modified, 30" full; ventilated rib
Finish: Blued; checkered walnut semi-pistol grip stock & slide handle; steel receiver; recoil pad
Approximate wt.: 6½ to 7½ lbs.
Comments: Introduced in 1984. Add $25.00 for "Rem Choke." Discontinued in late 1980's.

Estimated Value: Excellent: $230.00
                     Very good: $170.00

Remington Autoloading Riot Gun

Similar to the Standard Grade except: 20" barrel & weighs 6¾ lbs.

Estimated Value: Excellent: $200.00
                     Very good: $160.00

Remington Autoloading

Gauge: 12
Action: Semi-automatic; concealed hammer
Magazine: 5-shot tubular
Barrel: 26", 28" steel; full, modified or cylinder bore
Finish: Blued; matted sight groove; plain or checkered straight or pistol grip stock & forearm
Approximate wt.: 7¾ lbs.
Comments: Made from about 1905 to 1910 in six grades. Prices for Standard Grade.

Estimated Value: Excellent: $225.00
                     Very good: $180.00

Remington Model 11

Remington Model 11 Sportsman

Remington Model 11 Riot Gun

Remington Model 11 Sportsman

Same as the Model 11 with a 2-shot magazine. Made from about 1931 to 1948 in six grades. Prices for the Standard Grade. Add $15.00 for solid rib; $25.00 for ventilated rib.

Estimated Value: Excellent: $325.00
                       Very good: $250.00

Remington Model 11 Riot Gun

Same as the Model 11 except with a 20" plain barrel.

Estimated Value: Excellent: $240.00
                       Very good: $180.00

Remington Model 11

Gauge: 12 only to 1931; 12, 16, 20 1931-1948
Action: Semi-automatic; concealed hammer; side ejection; repeating
Magazine: 4-shot, bottom load
Barrel: 26" or 28" to 1931; 26", 28", 30", 32" 1931-1948; full, modified or cylinder
Finish: Blued; wood semi-pistol grip stock; straight grip on Trap grades; checkering & fancy wood on higher grades
Approximate wt.: 7½ to 8½ lbs.
Comments: Made from about 1911 to 1948 in six grades. Optional solid or ventilated rib available; rounded grip ends on stock from 1911 to 1916. Prices are for Standard Grade. Add $15.00 for ribbed barrel.

Estimated Value: Excellent: $260.00
                       Very good: $200.00

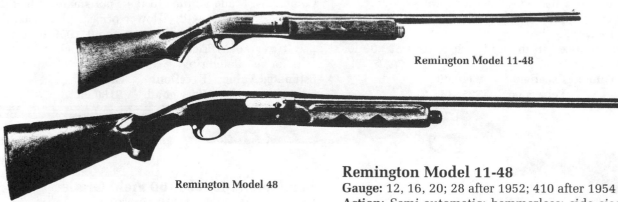

Remington Model 11-48

Remington Model 48

Remington Model 11-48 Riot Gun

Same general specifications as the Model 11-48 except: 12 gauge only; 20" plain barrel. Made from about 1954-1968.

Estimated Value: Excellent: $240.00
                       Very good: $190.00

Remington Model 48

Similar to the Model 11-48 except: 2-shot magazine; 12, 16, 20 gauge. Made from about 1948-1959 in several grades to replace the Model 11 Sportsman. Prices for Standard Model. Add $30.00 for ventilated rib.

Estimated Value: Excellent: $225.00
                       Very good: $180.00

Remington Model 11-48

Gauge: 12, 16, 20; 28 after 1952; 410 after 1954
Action: Semi-automatic; hammerless; side ejection; take down; cross bolt safety
Magazine: 4-shot tubular; 3-shot in 28 & 410 gauge
Barrel: 26", 28", 30" in 12, 16, & 20 gauge; 25" in 28 & 410 bore; full, modified or improved cylinder
Finish: Checkered walnut pistol grip stock with fluted comb, matching semi-beavertail forearm; higher grades are fancier
Approximate wt.: 6½ to 7½ lbs.
Comments: Made from about 1949 to 1968 in about seven grades. Replacing the Model 11, it had an improved action & the rear of the receiver was rounded off flush with the stock. Prices are for Standard Model. Add $30.00 for ventilated rib.

Estimated Value: Excellent: $265.00
                       Very good: $215.00

Remington Sportsman 58

Remington Sportsman 58 Magnum

Similar to the Sportsman 58 except: 12 gauge magnum; 30" barrel; recoil pad. Made from the late 1950's to early 1960's. Add $30.00 for ventilated rib.

| Estimated Value: | Excellent: | $240.00 |
| | Very good: | $180.00 |

Remington Sportsman 58 Rifled Slug Special

Same as the Sportsman 58 except: 12 gauge only; 26" barrel for slugs; equipped with rifle sights.

| Estimated Value: | Excellent: | $250.00 |
| | Very good: | $185.00 |

Remington Sportsman 58

Gauge: 12, 16, 20
Action: Semi-automatic; hammerless; side ejection; solid breech; gas operated sliding bolt; fixed barrel
Magazine: 2-shot tubular
Barrel: 26", 28", 30"; plain or ventilated rib; full, modified, improved cylinder or skeet chokes
Finish: Blued; checkered walnut pistol grip stock with fluted comb & matching semi-beavertail forearm
Approximate wt.: 6½ to 7½ lbs.
Comments: Made from about 1956 to 1963. Prices for Standard Model. Add $30.00 for ventilated rib.

| Estimated Value: | Excellent: | $260.00 |
| | Very good: | $195.00 |

Remington Sportsman 878 Automaster

Remington Sportsman 12 Auto

Gauge: 12
Action: Gas operated semi-automatic
Magazine: 4-shot tubular
Barrel: 28" modified, 30" full; ventilated rib; "Rem Choke" available
Finish: Checkered hardwood semi-pistol grip stock & forearm
Approximate wt.: 7¾ lbs.
Comments: Produced in the mid 1980's. Add $30.00 for "Rem Choke."

| Estimated Value: | Excellent: | $340.00 |
| | Very good: | $255.00 |

Remington Model 878 Automaster

Gauge: 12
Action: Semi-automatic; gas operated; hammerless
Magazine: 2-shot tubular
Barrel: 26"-30"; full, modified, improved cylinder or skeet chokes
Finish: Blued; plain or checkered walnut pistol grip stock & forearm
Approximate wt.: 7 lbs.
Comments: Made similar to the Sportsman 58 to fill in the sales line with a lower priced, plain, standard grade shotgun. Made from about 1959 to 1962 in two grades. Prices for Standard Model. Add $30.00 for ventilated rib.

| Estimated Value: | Excellent: | $240.00 |
| | Very good: | $180.00 |

Remington Model 1100 Field Grade

Remington Model 1100 Ltd. 20

Same as the Model 1100 Field except: 20 gauge only; 23" ventilated rib barrel; lightweight; made from 1980 to 1984.

| Estimated Value: | Excellent: | $395.00 |
| | Very good: | $315.00 |

Remington Model 1100 Youth Gun

Same as the Model 1100 Field except: 20 gauge only; 21" ventilated rib barrel; lightweight; short stock (12½" length of pull). Made from 1984 to present. Changeable choke tubes after 1985.

Estimated Value:	New (retail):	$566.00
	Excellent:	$425.00
	Very good:	$340.00

Remington Model 1100 Field Grade

Gauge: 12, 16, 20; 28 & 410 after 1970
Action: Semi-automatic; gas operated sliding bolt; fixed barrel; solid breech; hammerless; takedown
Magazine: 4-shot tubular
Barrel: 26", 28" in 16 & 20 gauge; 26", 28", 30" in 12 gauge; 25" in 28 & 410; full, modified, improved cylinder & skeet chokes; ventilated rib available
Finish: Blued; checkered wood pistol grip stock with fluted comb & matching forearm; engraved receiver
Approximate wt.: 6½ to 7½ lbs.
Comments: An improved, low-recoil shotgun to replace the 58, 11-48 & 878. Made from about 1963 to 1987 in several grades. Add $30.00 for left hand model, $30.00 for "Rem Choke."

| Estimated Value: | Excellent: | $420.00 |
| | Very good: | $315.00 |

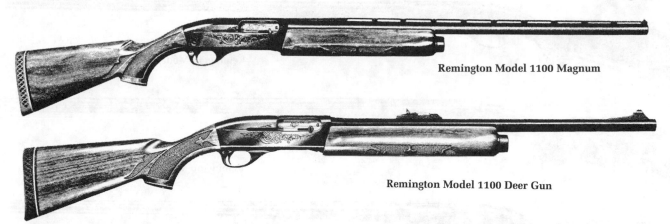

Remington Model 1100 Magnum

Remington Model 1100 Deer Gun

Remington Model 1100 Magnum
Similar to the Model 1100 except: 12 or 20 gauge magnum; 28" or 30" barrel; full or modified chokes; recoil pad. Add $30.00 for left hand model; $30.00 for "Rem Choke."

Estimated Value:	Excellent:	$400.00
	Very good:	$320.00

Remington Model 1100 Deer Gun
Similar to the Model 1100 with a 22" plain barrel & adjustable rifle sights; bored for rifle slugs; 12 or 20 gauge lightweight. Left hand version introduced in 1983.

Estimated Value:	New (retail):	$525.00
	Excellent:	$395.00
	Very good:	$315.00

Remington Model 1100 Special Purpose
Similar to the Model 1100 with oil-finished wood & Parkerized metal; recoil pad & nylon camo strap; 12 gauge only; ventilated rib barrel. Introduced in 1985. Add $30.00 for 26" "Rem Choke." Discontinued 1987.

Estimated Value:	Excellent:	$460.00
	Very good:	$345.00

Remington Model 1100 SP Deer Gun
Similar to the Model 1100 Special Purpose with a 21" improved cylinder barrel & rifle sights. Produced in mid 1980's.

Estimated Value:	Excellent:	$360.00
	Very good:	$270.00

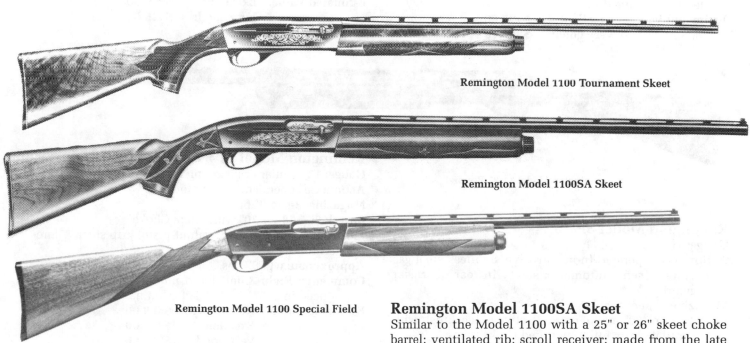

Remington Model 1100 Tournament Skeet

Remington Model 1100SA Skeet

Remington Model 1100 Special Field

Remington Model 1100 Special Field
Similar to the Model 1100 with straight grip stock & 21" ventilated rib barrel; 12 gauge or LT 20 Model, 2¾" chamber. Introduced in 1983.

Estimated Value:	New (retail):	$583.00
	Excellent:	$435.00
	Very good:	$350.00

Remington Model 1100SA Skeet
Similar to the Model 1100 with a 25" or 26" skeet choke barrel; ventilated rib; scroll receiver; made from the late 1970's to 1987. Add $30.00 for left hand model.

Estimated Value:	Excellent:	$425.00
	Very good:	$340.00

Remington Model 1100 Tournament Skeet
Similar to the Model 1100SA Skeet with higher quality finish.

Estimated Value:	Excellent:	$440.00
	Very good:	$350.00

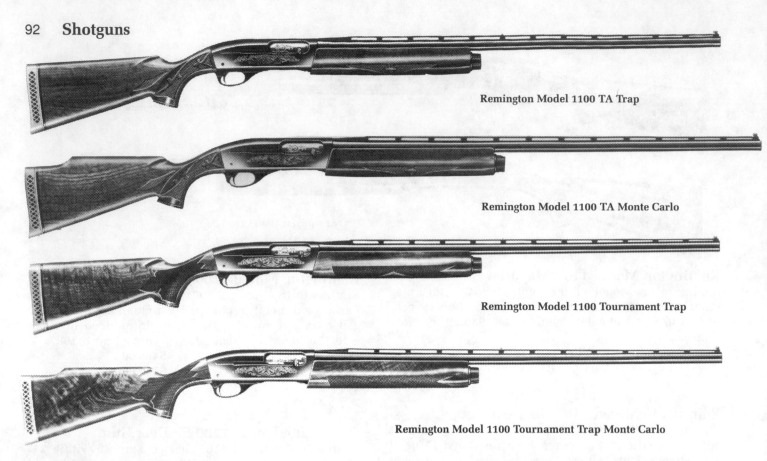

Remington Model 1100 TA Trap

Remington Model 1100 TA Monte Carlo

Remington Model 1100 Tournament Trap

Remington Model 1100 Tournament Trap Monte Carlo

Remington Model 1100TA Trap

Similar to the Model 1100 with a 30" full or modified trap barrel; ventilated rib only; recoil pad; choice of Monte Carlo stock (add $10.00). Add $30.00 for left hand model. Discontinued in 1987.

Estimated Value: Excellent: $475.00
Very good: $360.00

Remington Model 1100 Tournament Trap

Similar to the Model 1100 TA Trap with higher quality finish. Add $10.00 for Monte Carlo stock. Discontinued in 1987.

Estimated Value: Excellent: $565.00
Very good: $425.00

Remington Model 11-87 Premier

Remington Model SP-10

Gauge: 10
Action: Gas operated (non-corrosive stainless steel gas system) semi-automatic; safety in rear of trigger guard
Magazine: 3-shot tubular
Barrel: 26" or 30" matte, non-reflective blued finish with ventilated rib; full & modified choke tubes
Finish: Checkered walnut pistol grip stock & forearm with low gloss satin finish to reduce glare
Approximate wt.: 11 lbs. (26" barrel); 11¼ lbs. (30" barrel)
Comments: Introduced in 1989. Some critical components of the Model SP-10 & other Remington 10 gauge shotguns are not interchangeable.
Estimated Value: New (retail): $1,265.00
Excellent: $ 950.00
Very good: $ 760.00

Remington Model 11-87 Premier

Gauge: 12, regular or magnum, interchangeably
Action: Gas operated, semi-automatic
Magazine: 3-shot tubular
Barrel: 26", 28" or 30" with "Rem Choke"
Finish: Blued; checkered walnut pistol grip stock & forearm
Approximate wt.: 8¼ lbs.
Comments: Right & left hand models available. Introduced in 1987. Add 10% for left hand model.
Estimated Value: New (retail): $599.00
Excellent: $450.00
Very good: $360.00

Remington Model 11-87 Premier Trap

Similar to the Model 11-87 with 30" barrel. Available in full choke or with "Rem Choke." Monte Carlo or regular stock. Add $13.00 for "Rem Choke" or Monte Carlo stock.

Estimated Value: Excellent: $425.00
Very good: $340.00

Remington Model 11-87 Cantilever

Same as the Model 11-87 Special Purpose Deer Gun except: no sights; equipped with cantilever scope mount, rings & changeable choke tubes (rifled choke tube for slugs & improved cylinder tube). Introduced in 1989.

Estimated Value:	New (retail):	$621.00
	Excellent:	$465.00
	Very good:	$375.00

Remington Model 11-87 Premier Skeet

Similar to the Model 11-87 Premier with 26" skeet or "Rem Choke" barrel. Weight 7¾ lbs. Add $13.00 for "Rem Choke."

Estimated Value:	Excellent:	$475.00
	Very good:	$335.00

Remington Model 11-87 Special Purpose

Similar to the Model 11-87 Premier with a 26" or 30" "Rem Choke" barrel, non-glare finish, recoil pad, ventilated rib & camo strap. Introduced in 1987.

Estimated Value:	New (retail):	$599.00
	Excellent:	$450.00
	Very good:	$360.00

Remington Model 11-87 Special Purpose Deer Gun

Similar to the Model 11-87 Special Purpose except it has a 21" improved cylinder barrel & rifle sights.

Estimated Value:	New (retail):	$580.00
	Excellent:	$435.00
	Very good:	$350.00

Richland

Richland Model 200

Richland Model 200

Gauge: 12, 16, 20, 28, 410
Action: Box lock; top lever, break-open; hammerless; double trigger
Magazine: None
Barrel: Double barrel; 22" improved cylinder & modified in 20 gauge; 26", 28" improved & modified or modified & full chokes
Finish: Blued; checkered walnut pistol grip stock & tapered forearm; cheekpiece; recoil pad
Approximate wt.: 6 to 7 lbs.
Comments: Manufactured from the early 1960's to mid 1980's.

Estimated Value:	Excellent:	$255.00
	Very good:	$190.00

Richland Model 202

This is the same shotgun as the Model 200 with an extra set of barrels. Produced until the mid 1970's.

Estimated Value:	Excellent:	$375.00
	Very good:	$290.00

Richland Model 707 Deluxe

Gauge: 12, 20
Action: Box lock; top lever, break-open; hammerless; double trigger
Magazine: None
Barrel: Double barrel; 26", 28", 30" variety of chokes
Finish: Blued; checkered walnut pistol grip stock & tapered forearm; recoil pad
Approximate wt.: 7 lbs.
Comments: Made from the mid 1960's to the mid 1970's.

Estimated Value:	Excellent:	$310.00
	Very good:	$250.00

Richland Model 707 Deluxe

Richland Model 711 Long Range Waterfowl

Richland Model 711 Long Range Waterfowl

Gauge: 10, 12, magnum
Action: Box lock; top lever, break-open; hammerless; double trigger
Magazine: None
Barrel: Double barrel; 30", 32" full choke
Finish: Blued; checkered walnut pistol grip stock & tapered forearm
Approximate wt.: 8 to 10 lbs.
Comments: Made from the early 1960's to present. Made in 10 gauge magnum only from 1981 to 1983.

Estimated Value:	Excellent:	$295.00
	Very good:	$220.00

Richland Model 747

Gauge: 12 or 20, magnum
Action: Box lock; top lever, break-open; hammerless; single selective trigger
Magazine: None
Barrel: Over & under double barrel; 22" or 26" improved cylinder & modified, 28" modified & full
Finish: Blued; grey receiver; checkered walnut pistol grip stock & forearm; ventilated rib on top & between barrels
Approximate wt.: 7 lbs.
Comments: Introduced in the mid 1980's.

Estimated Value:	Excellent:	$340.00
	Very good:	$255.00

Richland Model 808
Gauge: 12
Action: Box lock; top lever, break-open; hammerless; non-selective single trigger
Magazine: None
Barrel: Over & under double barrel; 26" improved cylinder & modified; 28" modified & full; 30" full & full
Finish: Blued; checkered walnut pistol grip stock & forearm; ribbed barrel
Approximate wt.: 7 lbs.
Comments: Made from the early to late 1960's.
Estimated Value: Excellent: $375.00
Very good: $300.00

Richland Model 844
Gauge: 12 magnum
Action: Box lock; top lever, break-open; hammerless; non-selective single trigger
Magazine: None
Barrel: Over & under double barrel; 26" improved cylinder & modified; 28" modified & full; 30" full & full
Finish: Blued; checkered walnut pistol grip stock & forearm; ribbed barrel
Approximate wt.: 7 lbs.
Comments: Made in the early 1970's.
Estimated Value: Excellent: $290.00
Very good: $220.00

Richland Model 828

Richland Model 808

Richland Model 828
Gauge: 28
Action: Box lock; top lever, break-open; hammerless
Magazine: None
Barrel: Over & under double barrel; 26" improved & modified; 28" modified & full chokes
Finish: Blued; case hardened receiver; checkered walnut pistol grip stock & forearm; ribbed barrel
Approximate wt.: 7 lbs.
Comments: Made in the early 1970's.
Estimated Value: Excellent: $350.00
Very good: $260.00

Richland Model 41 Ultra
Gauge: 410
Action: Box lock; top lever, break-open; hammerless; over & under double barrel; single non-selective trigger
Magazine: None
Barrel: Over & under double barrel; 26" chrome lined, modified & full; ventilated rib
Finish: Blued; grey engraved receiver; checkered walnut pistol grip stock & forearm
Approximate wt.: 6 lbs.
Comments: A lightweight 410 shotgun first announced in 1985.
Estimated Value: New (retail): $289.00
Excellent: $215.00
Very good: $160.00

Ruger

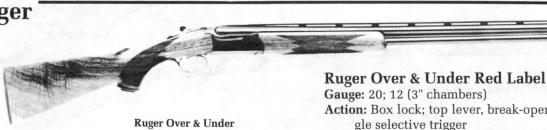

Ruger Over & Under

Ruger Over & Under Red Label
Gauge: 20; 12 (3" chambers)
Action: Box lock; top lever, break-open; hammerless; single selective trigger
Magazine: None
Barrel: Over & under double barrel; 26" or 28" variety of choke combinations; ventilated tib; stainless steel receiver on 12 gauge beginning in 1986; stainless steel receiver or 20 gauge beginning in 1990
Finish: Checkered walnut pistol grip stock & semi-beavertail forearm; pistol grip cap; recoil pad
Approximate wt.: 7 lbs.
Comments: Introduced in the late 1970's; 12 gauge model introduced in 1982.
Estimated Value: New (retail): $1,102.50
Excellent: $ 825.00
Very good: $ 660.00

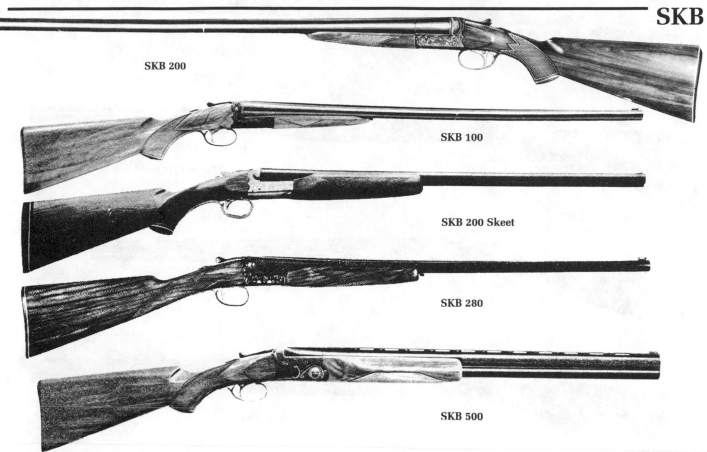

SKB 200

SKB 100

SKB 200 Skeet

SKB 280

SKB 500

SKB Model 100

Gauge: 12, 12, magnum, 20
Action: Box lock; top lever, break-open; hammerless; single selective trigger
Magazine: None
Barrel: Double barrel; 26", 28" improved cylinder & modified or 30" full & full choke in 12 gauge
Finish: Blued; checkered hardwood pistol grip stock & short tapered forearm
Approximate wt.: 6 to 7 lbs.
Comments: Made from the mid 1960's to mid 1970's.
Estimated Value: Excellent: $300.00
Very good: $225.00

SKB Model 200 & 200E

Similar to the SKB 100 with engraved silverplate frame; wide forearm; select walnut; automatic selective ejectors; 200E has straight grip stock.
Estimated Value: New (retail): $895.00
Excellent: $670.00
Very good: $530.00

SKB Model 200 Skeet

Similar to the 200 with 25" skeet choke barrels & recoil pad.
Estimated Value: Excellent: $525.00
Very good: $420.00

SKB Model 280

Similar to the 200 without silver frame. Has straight grip stock.
Estimated Value: Excellent: $500.00
Very good: $375.00

SKB Model 400

Similar to the Model 200 with sideplate receiver; straight stock available.
Estimated Value: New (retail): $1,195.00
Excellent: $ 895.00
Very good: $ 715.00

SKB Model 500, 505F & 505CF

Gauge: 12, 12 magnum, 20, 28, 410
Action: Box lock; top lever, break-open; hammerless
Magazine: None
Barrel: Over & under double barrel; 26" improved cylinder & modified; 28", 30" modified & full; ventilated rib; chrome lined. 505CF has "inter" choke system in 1980's
Finish: Blued; checkered walnut pistol grip stock & forearm; recoil pad on magnum; front sight; engraved receiver on Model 500
Approximate wt.: 6½ to 8 lbs.
Comments: Made from the mid 1960's to mid 1980's as Model 500.
Estimated Value: New (retail): $1,165.00
Excellent: $ 875.00
Very good: $ 700.00

SKB Model 505 Trap

Similar to the Model 505; 12 gauge only, 30" or 32" "Inter Choke" barrels. Single Barrel Trap available with ventilated rib.
Estimated Value: New (retail): $1,180.00
Excellent: $ 885.00
Very good: $ 710.00

SKB 600

SKB 600 Trap

SKB 600 Skeet

SKB 680

SKB 700

SKB Model 885
Similar to the Model 505 in an engraved silver-receiver sideplate version. Add 3% for Trap or Skeet Model.

Estimated Value:	New (retail):	$1,450.00
	Excellent:	$1,085.00
	Very good:	$ 870.00

SKB Model 500 Skeet & 505 CSK
Similar to the Model 500 with 26" or 28" skeet choke barrels. Model 500 discontinued in mid 1980's & replaced by Model 505CSK.

Estimated Value:	New (retail):	$1,220.00
	Excellent:	$ 915.00
	Very good:	$ 730.00

SKB Model 600 & 605F
Similar to the 500 with select wood; trigger mounted barrel selector; silverplate receiver; middle sight.

Estimated Value:	New (retail):	$975.00
	Excellent:	$730.00
	Very good:	$585.00

SKB Model 600 Trap & 605 Trap
Similar to the 600 with regular or Monte Carlo stock; 12 gauge only; recoil pad, 30" or 32" full choke barrels on Model 600; "inter" choke system available on Model 605 Trap (late 1980's).

Estimated Value:	New (retail):	$995.00
	Excellent:	$745.00
	Very good:	$600.00

SKB Model 600 Skeet & 605 CSK
Similar to the 600 with 26" or 28" skeet choke barrels (Model 600) & recoil pad; "inter" choke system available on 605CSK (late 1980's).

Estimated Value:	New (retail):	$995.00
	Excellent:	$745.00
	Very good:	$600.00

SKB Model 680
Similar to the 600 with a straight grip stock.

| Estimated Value: | Excellent: | $700.00 |
| | Very good: | $560.00 |

SKB Model 700
Similar to the 600 with higher quality finish & more extensive engraving.

| Estimated Value: | Excellent: | $725.00 |
| | Very good: | $585.00 |

SKB Model 1300

Gauge: 12, 20, regular or magnum
Action: Semi-automatic
Magazine: 5-shot; 3-shot with plug
Barrel: 26" or 28" "Inter Choke"; ventilated rib; slug barrel with rifle sights available
Finish: Blued, black receiver; checkered walnut pistol grip stock & forearm
Approximate wt.: 6½ to 7¼ lbs.
Comments: Add 1% for slug barrel with rifle sights.
Estimated Value: New (retail): $719.00
Excellent: $540.00
Very good: $430.00

SKB Model 1900

Similar to the Model 1300 with light receiver featuring engraved hunting scene, gold trigger. Add 5% for 30" barrel Trap Model; slug barrel with rifle sights also available.
Estimated Value: New (retail); $550.00
Excellent: $410.00
Very good: $330.00

SKB Model 3000

A presentation deluxe version of the Model 1900. High-back receiver. A trap version is available (add 2%).
Estimated Value: New (retail); $585.00
Excellent: $435.00
Very good: $350.00

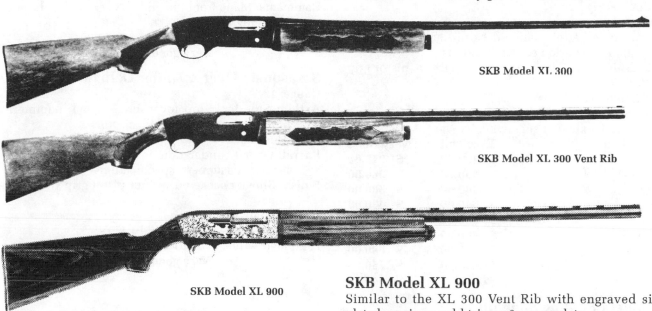

SKB Model XL 300

SKB Model XL 300 Vent Rib

SKB Model XL 900

SKB Model XL 300

Gauge: 12, 20
Action: Gas operated; semi-automatic; hammerless
Magazine: 5-shot tubular
Barrel: 26" improved cylinder or skeet; 28" modified or full; 30" modified or full chokes
Finish: Blued; decorated receiver; checkered walnut pistol grip stock & forearm
Approximate wt.: 6 to 7 lbs.
Comments: Made from the early to late 1970's.
Estimated Value: Excellent: $275.00
Very good: $220.00

SKB XL 300 Vent Rib

Similar to the XL 300 with front sights & ventilated rib.
Estimated Value: Excellent: $300.00
Very good: $240.00

SKB Model XL 100 Slug

A no-frills slug gun with 20" barrel; rifle sights; swivels; similar to the XL 300.
Estimated Value: Excellent: $235.00
Very good: $175.00

SKB Model XL 900

Similar to the XL 300 Vent Rib with engraved silver-plated receiver; gold trigger & name plate.
Estimated Value: Excellent: $325.00
Very good: $260.00

SKB Model XL 900 Slug

Similar to the XL 900 with a 24" barrel for slugs; rifle sights; swivels.
Estimated Value: Excellent: $310.00
Very good: $230.00

SKB Model XL 900 Trap

Similar to the XL 900 with middle sight; no silver receiver; recoil pad; choice of regular or Monte Carlo stock.
Estimated Value: Excellent: $350.00
Very good: $280.00

SKB Model XL 900 Skeet

Similar to the XL 900 Trap with skeet stock & skeet choke barrel.
Estimated Value: Excellent: $330.00
Very good: $250.00

SKB Model XL 900 MR

Similar to the XL 900 for 3" magnum shells; recoil pad; deduct $35.00 for slug model.
Estimated Value: Excellent: $350.00
Very good: $260.00

Sarasqueta

Sarasqueta Sidelock

Sarasqueta Sidelock Grades 4 to 12

Gauge: 12, 16, 20, 28
Action: Side lock; top lever, break-open; hammerless; double triggers
Magazine: None
Barrel: Double barrel; standard barrel lengths & chokes available to customer specifications
Finish: Blued; checkered walnut straight or pistol grip stock & forearm
Approximate wt.: Varies
Comments: A Spanish shotgun. Grades differ as to quality & extent of engraving.

Estimated Value:	Grade	Excellent	Very Good
	4	$ 400.00	$ 315.00
	5	$ 450.00	$ 360.00
	6	$ 480.00	$ 385.00
	7	$ 540.00	$ 430.00
	8	$ 800.00	$ 640.00
	9	$ 960.00	$ 765.00
	10	$1,100.00	$ 890.00
	11	$1,440.00	$1,150.00
	12	$1,800.00	$1,440.00

Sarasqueta Folding Shotgun

Gauge: 410
Action: Box lock; top lever, break-open; exposed hammer
Magazine: None
Barrel: Double barrel; 26" choice of chokes
Finish: Blued; case-hardened frame; walnut pistol grip stock & forearm
Approximate wt.: Varies
Comments: A "folding" shotgun produced in the 1970's.
Estimated Value: Excellent: $150.00
                        Very good: $115.00

Sauer

Sauer Royal

Sarasqueta Model 2 & 3

Gauge: 12, 16, 20, 28
Action: Box lock; top lever, break-open; hammerless; double triggers
Magazine: None
Barrel: Double barrel; standard barrel lengths & chokes available to customer specifications
Finish: Blued; checkered walnut straight grip stock & forearm
Approximate wt.: Varies
Comments: Made from the mid 1930's. Grades differ only in engraving style.
Estimated Value: Excellent: $375.00
                        Very good: $300.00

Sarasqueta Over & Under Deluxe

Gauge: 12
Action: Side lock; top lever, break-open; hammerless; double triggers; automatic ejectors
Magazine: None
Barrel: Over & under double barrel; lengths & chokes made to customer's specifications
Finish: Blued; checkered walnut pistol grip stock & forearm
Approximate wt.: Varies
Comments: Made from the mid 1930's.
Estimated Value: Excellent: $1,200.00
                        Very good: $ 850.00

Sarasqueta Folding Shotgun

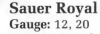

Sauer Royal

Gauge: 12, 20
Action: Box lock; top lever, break-open; hammerless; automatic ejectors; single selective trigger
Magazine: None
Barrel: Double barrel; 28" modified & full, 26" improved & modified in 20 gauge; 30" full in 12 gauge
Finish: Blued; engraved frame; checkered walnut pistol grip stock & tapered forearm; recoil pad
Approximate wt.: 6 to 7 lbs.
Comments: Produced in Germany from the mid 1950's to late 1970's.
Estimated Value: Excellent: $1,000.00
                        Very good: $800.00

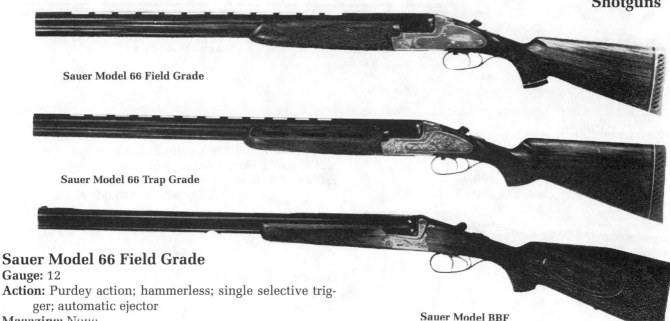

Sauer Model 66 Field Grade

Sauer Model 66 Trap Grade

Sauer Model BBF

Sauer Model 66 Field Grade

Gauge: 12
Action: Purdey action; hammerless; single selective trigger; automatic ejector
Magazine: None
Barrel: Over & under doubel barrel; 28" modified & full choke; ventilated rib
Finish: Blued; checkered walnut pistol grip stock & forearm; recoil pad; engraving
Approximate wt.: 7 lbs.
Comments: Made from the mid 1950's. Prices are for Grade I. Fancier Grades II & III differ in quality & extent of engraving.
Estimated Value: Excellent: $1,500.00
Very good: $1,200.00

Sauer Model 66 Trap Grade

Basically the same as the Field Grade with 30" barrels & a trap stock. Also produced in three grades.
Estimated Value: Excellent: $1,550.00
Very good: $1,240.00

Sauer Model 66 Skeet

Basically the same as the Trap Model with 25" barrel in skeet choke. Prices are for Grade I.
Estimated Value: Excellent: $1,525.00
Very good: $1,220.00

Sauer Model BBF

Gauge: 16
Caliber: 30-30, 30-06, 7 x 65
Action: Kersten lock; Blitz action; top lever, break-open; hammerless; double trigger
Magazine: None
Barrel: Over & under rifle-shotgun combination; 25" Krupp barrels; rifle barrel & full choke shotgun barrel
Finish: Blued; checkered walnut Monte Carlo pistol grip stock & forearm; engraved; sights; swivels
Approximate wt.: 6 lbs.
Comments: Made from the mid 1950's. Also available in deluxe model with extensive engraving.
Estimated Value: Excellent: $1,600.00
Very good: $1,200.00

Savage

Savage Model 220

Savage Model 220

Gauge: 12, 16, 20, 28, 410
Action: Top lever, break-open; single shot; hammerless; automatic ejector
Magazine: None
Barrel: Full choke; 28" 30", 32" in 12 & 16 gauge; 26", 28", 30", 32" in 20 gauge; 28" & 30" in 28 gauge; 26" & 28" in 410 bore
Finish: Blued; plain wood, pistol grip stock & forearm
Approximate wt.: 6 lbs.
Comments: Made from 1930's until late 1940's. Reintroduced in the mid 1950's with 36" barrel. Replaced by 220L in mid 1960's.
Estimated Value: Excellent: $80.00
Very good: $65.00

Savage Model 220L

Savage Model 220P

Basically the same as 220 except no 410 gauge, has "PolyChoke" & recoil pad.

Estimated Value: Excellent: $90.00
Very good: $70.00

Savage Model 220L

Similar to Model 220 except has side lever. Made from mid 1960's to early 1970's.

Estimated Value: Excellent: $85.00
Very good: $65.00

Savage Model 311

Savage Model 311

Gauge: 12, 20; regular or magnum
Action: Top lever, break open; hammerless, double trigger
Magazine: None
Barrel: Double barrel; 28" modified & full; matted rib
Finish: Blued; hardwood, semi-pistol grip stock & tapered forearm
Approximate wt.: 7 lbs.
Comments: The Model 311 was originally a Stevens shotgun. In 1988 Savage dropped the Stevens designation; discontinued in late 1980's.

Estimated Value: Excellent: $230.00
Very good: $185.00

Savage Model 311 Waterfowler

Similar to the Model 311 with parkerized finish.

Estimated Value: Excellent: $230.00
Very good: $185.00

Savage Model 24D

Savage Model 24 Combination

Gauge: 20, 410
Caliber: 22 short, long, long rifle; 22 magnum
Action: Top lever, break open; exposed hammer; single trigger; bottom opening lever in mid 1980's
Magazine: None
Barrel: Over & under double barrel; 24" rifle barrel over shotgun barrel
Finish: Blued; checkered walnut finish hardwood pistol grip stock & forearm; sporting rear & ramp front sights; case hardened receiver
Approximate wt.: 6 lbs.
Comments: Made from the early 1950's to late 1980's.

Estimated Value: Excellent: $175.00
Very good: $140.00

Savage Model 24D

Deluxe version of the Model 24. Discontinued in mid 1980's.

Estimated Value: Excellent: $190.00
Very good: $150.00

Savage Model 24F Combination

Gauge: 20, 12 gauge with 3" chamber
Caliber: 222 Rem., 223 Rem., 30-30 Win.
Action: Top lever, break open; exposed hammer with barrel selector; hammer block safety
Magazine: None
Barrel: 24" rifle barrel over 24" shotgun barrel; any combination of rifle caliber & shotgun gauge; shotgun barrel in modified choke; modified & full choke tubes available
Finish: DuPont Rynite® two-piece stock & forearm
Approximate wt.: 7½ lbs.
Comments: Introduced in the late 1980's; add 4% for choke tube; 4% for Camo Rynite® stock on 12 gauge with 222 Rem. or 223 Rem.

Estimated Value: New (retail): $375.85
Excellent: $280.00
Very good: $225.00

Savage Model 24V Combination

Same as the Model 24F Combination except: walnut finish hardwood stock & forearm; 20 gauge, 3" chamber under 222 Rem., 223 Rem. or 30-30 Win. rifle barrel. Introduced in the late 1980's.

Estimated Value: New (retail): $335.00
Excellent: $250.00
Very good: $200.00

Savage Model 24C Camper

Savage Model 242

Savage Model 24C Camper, 24CS

A shorter version of the Model 24; 20" barrel; 5¾ lbs.; 22LR over 20 gauge barrel; buttplate opens for ammo storage area. Add $45.00 for satin nickel finish (24CS) & extra pistol grip stock; discontinued late 1980's.

| Estimated Value: | Excellent: | $180.00 |
| | Very good: | $140.00 |

Savage Model 242

Similar to the Model 24 with 410 gauge over & under shotgun barrels; full choke; bead sights; made only in late 1970's.

| Estimated Value: | Excellent: | $150.00 |
| | Very good: | $120.00 |

Savage Model 389

Gauge: 12, regular or magnum
Caliber: 222 or 308
Action: Top lever, break-open; hammerless; double trigger; shotgun barrel over rifle barrel; tang safety
Magazine: None
Barrel: 25¾" over & under doubel barrel; changeable choke tubes
Finish: Blued; checkered walnut pistol grip stock & matching forearm; sling studs
Approximate wt.: 8 lbs.
Comments: Introduced in the late 1980's.

Estimated Value:	New (retail):	$919.20
	Excellent:	$670.00
	Very good:	$550.00

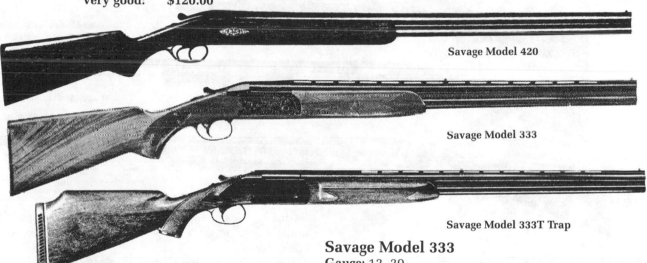

Savage Model 420

Savage Model 333

Savage Model 333T Trap

Savage Model 420

Gauge: 12, 16, 20
Action: Box lock; top lever, break-open; hammerless; double triggers or non-selective single trigger
Magazine: None
Barrel: Over & under double barrel; 26" to 30" modified & full or cylinder bore & modified chokes
Finish: Blued; plain walnut pistol grip stock & forearm
Approximate wt.: 6¾ to 7¾ lbs.
Comments: Made from the mid 1930's until World War II. Add $25.00 for single trigger.

| Estimated Value: | Excellent: | $400.00 |
| | Very good: | $320.00 |

Savage Model 430

Similar as Model 420 with special checkered walnut stock & forearm; matted upper barrel; recoil pad. Add $25.00 for single trigger.

| Estimated Value: | Excellent: | $450.00 |
| | Very good: | $360.00 |

Savage Model 333

Gauge: 12, 20
Action: Top lever, break-open; hammerless; single trigger
Magazine: None
Barrel: Over & under double barrel; 26" to 30"; variety of chokes; ventilated rib
Finish: Blued; checkered walnut pistol grip stock & forearm
Approximate wt.: 6¼ to 7¼ lbs.
Comments: Made from the early to late 1970's.

| Estimated Value: | Excellent: | $500.00 |
| | Very good: | $375.00 |

Savage Model 333T Trap

Similar to 333 with Monte Carlo stock & recoil pad in 12 gauge, 30" barrel.

| Estimated Value: | Excellent: | $525.00 |
| | Very good: | $395.00 |

Savage Model 330

Similar to 333 without ventilated rib.

| Estimated Value: | Excellent: | $450.00 |
| | Very good: | $340.00 |

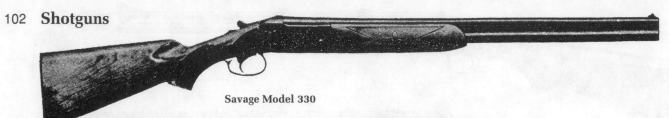

Savage Model 330

Savage Model 312T

Same as Model 312 Field except: 30" barrels; 2 full & 1 modified choke tubes; Monte Carlo stock; approximate wt., 7¼ lbs. Introduced in 1990.

Estimated Value: New (retail): $828.25
                 Excellent: $620.00
                 Very good: $495.00

Savage Model 312 SC

Same as the Model 312 Field except: 28" barrels only; seven choke tubes included (1 full, 2 improved cylinder, 2 modified, 1 #1 skeet & 1 #2 skeet); "Sporting Clays" engraved on receiver. Introduced in 1990.

Estimated Value: New (retail): $850.00
                 Excellent: $640.00
                 Very good: $510.00

Savage Model 312 Field

Gauge: 12, regular or magnum
Action: Top lever, break-open; concealed hammers; single trigger with safety acting as barrel selector
Magazine: None
Barrel: Over & under double barrel; 26" or 28"; ventilated rib; ivory bead front sight & bead middle sight; changeable choke tubes in full, modified & improved cylinder with wrench
Finish: Blued barrels; satin chrome receiver; cut-checkered walnut pistol grip stock & matching forearm; recoil pad
Approximate wt.: 7 lbs.
Comments: Introduced in 1990.

Estimated Value: New (retail): $779.00
                 Excellent: $585.00
                 Very good: $470.00

Savage Model 28A

Savage Model 28D Trap

Savage Model 30

Savage Model 28A & B Standard

Gauge: 12
Action: Slide action; hammerless; solid breech; side ejection
Magazine: 5-shot tubular
Barrel: 26", 28", 30" or 32" cylinder, modified or full choke; raised rib on 28B
Finish: Blued; checkered wood pistol grip stock & grooved slide handle
Approximate wt.: 7½ lbs.
Comments: Made from the late 1920's until mid 1930's. Add $10.00 for matted rib.

Estimated Value: Excellent: $200.00
                 Very good: $160.00

Savage Model 28C Riot

Basically the same as 28A except with a 20" cylinder bore barrel. This was for use by police, bank guards, etc., for protection.

Estimated Value: Excellent: $175.00
                 Very good: $140.00

Savage Model 28D Trap

Basically the same as 28B except: special straight checkered walnut stock & checkered slide handle; 30" full choke barrel.

Estimated Value: Excellent: $240.00
                 Very good: $190.00

Savage Model 28S Special

Basically the same as 28B except: ivory bead front sight; checkered pistol grip stock; checkered forearm.

Estimated Value: Excellent: $225.00
                 Very good: $180.00

Savage Model 30

Gauge: 12, 20, 410
Action: Slide action; hammerless
Magazine: 4-shot tubular
Barrel: 26", 28", 30"; cylinder bore, modified or full choke; ventilated rib
Finish: Blued; decorated receiver; walnut pistol grip stock & grooved slide handle
Approximate wt.: 6½ lbs.
Comments: Made from late 1950's to late 1960's.

Estimated Value: Excellent: $190.00
                 Very good: $140.00

Savage Model 30 FG

Savage Model 30D

Savage Model 30 AC

Savage Model 30 AC
Same as Model 30 FG with adjustable choke.

Estimated Value: Excellent: $170.00
              Very good: $135.00

Savage Model 30 FG (Field Grade)
Similar to Model 30 with plain receiver, no ventilated rib & horizontal groove in slide handle.

Estimated Value: Excellent: $150.00
              Very good: $110.00

Savage Model 30 FG Slug Gun
Same as Model 30 FG with 22" barrel & rifle sights, 12 gauge. Introduced in 1971, discontinued in the late 1970's.

Estimated Value: Excellent: $160.00
              Very good: $120.00

Savage Model 30D (Deluxe)
1970's version of the Model 30 FG with recoil pad & horizontal groove in slide handle. Discontinued in the late 1970's.

Estimated Value: Excellent: $175.00
              Very good: $130.00

Savage Model 30T Trap
Fancy version Model 30 in 12 gauge; 30" full choke barrel; Monte Carlo stock; grooved slide handle; recoil pad. Introduced in mid 1960's.

Estimated Value: Excellent: $180.00
              Very good: $135.00

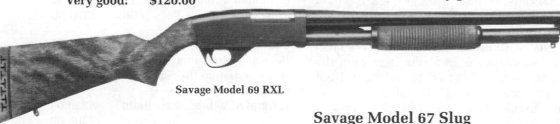

Savage Model 69 RXL

Savage Model 67
Gauge: 12, 20, regular or magnum
Action: Slide action; hammerless; side ejecting; repeating
Magazine: 4-shot tubular, 3-shot in magnum
Barrel: 28" modified
Finish: Blued; hardwood, semi-pistol grip stock & grooved slide handle
Approximate wt.: 6¼ to 7½ lbs.
Comments: The Model 67 was originally a Stevens shotgun. In 1988 Savage dropped the Stevens designation; discontinued late 1980's.

Estimated Value: Excellent: $170.00
              Very good: $135.00

Savage Model 67 VRT
Similar to the Model 67 with a ventilated rib barrel, interchangeable choke tubes & recoil pad. Discontinued late 1980's.

Estimated Value: Excellent: $195.00
              Very good: $155.00

Savage Model 67 Slug
Similar to Model 67 with a 21" cylinder bore barrel, recoil pad, rifle sights & scope mount. Discontinued in late 1980's.

Estimated Value: Excellent: $185.00
              Very good: $145.00

Savage Model 69R, 69N, 69RXL, 69RXG
Gauge: 12, regular or magnum
Action: Slide action; hammerless; top tang safety
Magazine: 6-shot tubular, 4-shot on 69R
Barrel: 18¼" cylinder bore, 20" on 69R
Finish: Blued; walnut stock & grooved slide handle; recoil pad, swivels; 69N has satin nickel finish; 69RXG has plastic pistol grip & sling
Approximate wt.: 6½ lbs.
Comments: A law enforcement shotgun introduced in 1982. Add 30% for model 69N. (69R & 69N discontinued in mid 1980's) Discontinued late 1980's.

Estimated Value: Excellent: $185.00
              Very good: $150.00

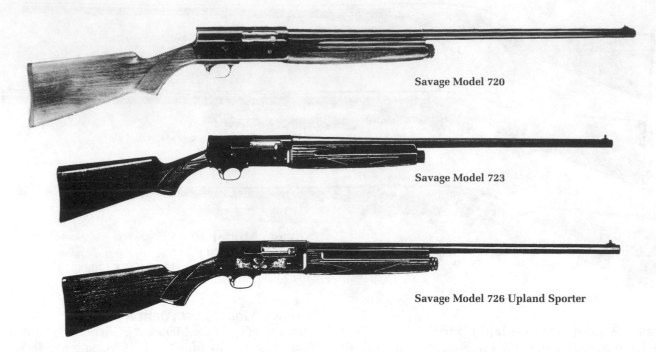

Savage Model 720

Savage Model 723

Savage Model 726 Upland Sporter

Savage Model 720

Gauge: 12
Action: Browning patent; semi-automatic; hammerless
Magazine: 4-shot tubular
Barrel: 28", 30" or 32" cylinder bore, modified or full choke
Finish: Blued; checkered walnut pistol grip stock & forearm; after 1940, engraved receiver
Approximate wt.: 8½ lbs.
Comments: Originally a Springfield shotgun, this takedown model was made from about 1930 until the late 1940's. In the early 1940's, Model 720R (Riot Gun) was introduced with a 20" barrel.
Estimated Value: Excellent: $265.00
Very good: $210.00

Savage Model 720-P

Basically the same as 720 with "Poly-Choke" produced from the late 1930's to 1940's; 3 or 5-shot; 12 gauge only.
Estimated Value: Excellent: $260.00
Very good: $205.00

Savage Model 721

Same as 720 with matted rib.
Estimated Value: Excellent: $270.00
Very good: $215.00

Savage Model 722

Same as 720 except with ventilated rib.
Estimated Value: Excellent: $280.00
Very good: $220.00

Savage Model 723

Same as 720 except no 32" barrel; available in 16 gauge. Weighs about 7½ lbs.
Estimated Value: Excellent: $255.00
Very good: $200.00

Savage Model 724

Same as 723 except with matted rib.
Estimated Value: Excellent: $260.00
Very good: $205.00

Savage Model 725

Sve as 723 except with ventilated rib.
Estimated Value: Excellent: $270.00
Very good: $215.00

Savage Model 726 Upland Sporter

Basically the same as 720 except no 32" barrel; 2-shot tubular magazine; available in 16 gauge; decorated receiver.
Estimated Value: Excellent: $250.00
Very good: $200.00

Savage Model 727 Upland Sporter

Same as Model 726 except with matted rib.
Estimated Value: Excellent: $260.00
Very good: $205.00

Savage Model 728 Upland Sporter

Same as Model 726 except with ventilated rib.
Estimated Value: Excellent: $265.00
Very good: $210.00

Savage Model 740C Skeet Gun

Basically the same as Model 726 with a skeet stock & "Cutts Compensator." Discontinued in the late 1940's.
Estimated Value: Excellent: $250.00
Very good: $200.00

Savage Model 745 Lightweight

Similar to Model 720 with light alloy receiver. Made from late 1930's to 1940's; 3 or 5-shot; 12 gauge only.
Estimated Value: Excellent: $245.00
Very good: $175.00

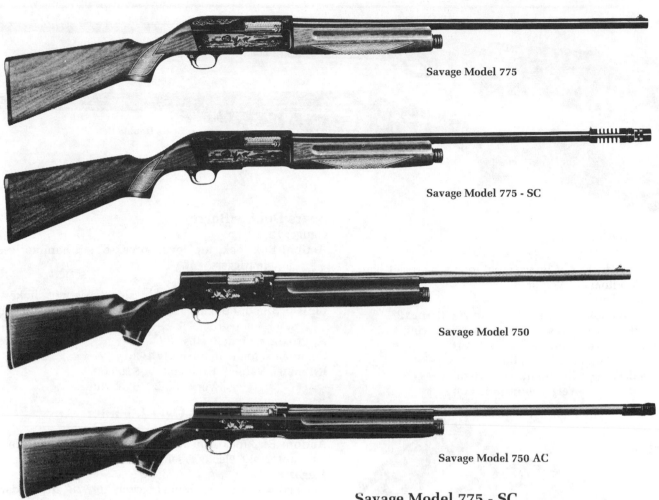

Savage Model 775

Savage Model 775 - SC

Savage Model 750

Savage Model 750 AC

Savage Model 755

Gauge: 12, 16
Action: Semi-automatic; hammerless
Magazine: 4-shot tubular; 3-shot tubular
Barrel: 26" cylinder bore; 28" full or modified; 30" full choke
Finish: Blued; checkered walnut pistol grip stock & forearm
Approximate wt.: 8 lbs.
Comments: Made from the late 1940's until late 1950's; top of recevier flush with stock.
Estimated Value: Excellent: $220.00
Very good: $175.00

Savage Model 755 - SC

Similar to 755 with Savage "Super Choke."
Estimated Value: Excellent: $220.00
Very good: $165.00

Savage Model 775 Lightweight

Similar to 755 with alloy receiver. Produced until mid 1960's.
Estimated Value: Excellent: $230.00
Very good: $185.00

Savage Model 775 - SC

Basically the same as Model 775 with Savage "Super Choke" & 26" barrel.
Estimated Value: Excellent: $225.00
Very good: $170.00

Savage Model 750

Gauge: 12
Action: Browning patent; semi-automatic; hammerless
Magazine: 4-shot tubular
Barrel: 26" cylinder bore; 28" full or modified
Finish: Blued; checkered walnut pistol grip stock & forearm; decorated receiver
Approximate wt.: 7¼ lbs.
Comments: Made from the early to late 1960's.
Estimated Value: Excellent: $280.00
Very good: $210.00

Savage Model 750 SC

Similar to Model 750 with Savage "Super Choke." Made from 1962 for two years.
Estimated Value: Excellent: $300.00
Very good: $225.00

Savage Model 750 AC

Model 750 with adjustable choke. Made during mid 1960's.
Estimated Value: Excellent: $250.00
Very good: $190.00

Sears

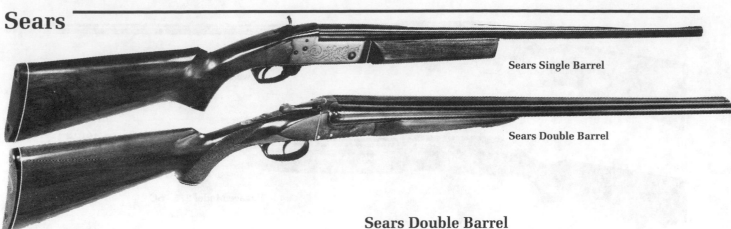

Sears Single Barrel

Sears Double Barrel

Sears Single Barrel
Gauge: 12, 20, 410
Action: Box lock; top lever, break-open; exposed hammer; automatic ejector
Magazine: None
Barrel: Full choke; 26" in 410; 28" in 20; 30" in 12
Finish: Blued; wood pistol grip stock & forearm
Approximate wt.: 7 lbs.
Comments: Manufactured in the 1970's & 1980's.
Estimated Value: Excellent: $70.00
                        Very good: $55.00

Sears Ted Williams Over & Under

Sears Bolt Action
Gauge: 410
Action: Bolt action; repeating
Magazine: 3-shot detachable clip
Barrel: 24" full choke
Finish: Blued; wood pistol grip stock & forearm
Approximate wt.: 5½ lbs.
Comments: Made to the late 1970's.
Estimated Value: Excellent: $85.00
                        Very good: $65.00

Sears Double Barrel
Gauge: 12, 20
Action: Box lock; top lever, break-open; hammerless; double triggers
Magazine: None
Barrel: 28" double barrel side by side; variety of chokes
Finish: Blued; epoxied black frame; walnut pistol grip stock & forearm
Approximate wt.: 7½ lbs.
Comments: Made to the early 1980's.
Estimated Value: Excellent: $190.00
                        Very good: $150.00

Sears Ted Williams Over & Under
Gauge: 12, 20
Action: Box lock; top lever, break-open; hammerless; automatic ejectors, selective trigger
Magazine: None
Barrel: Over & under doubel barrel; 26", 28" in standard chokes; ventilated rib; chrome lined
Finish: Blued; engraved steel receivers; checkered walnut pistol grip stock & forearm; recoil pad
Approximate wt.: 6¾ lbs.
Comments: Produced to the late 1970's.
Estimated Value: Excellent: $385.00
                        Very good: $285.00

Sears Model 140
Gauge: 12, 20
Action: Bolt action; repeating
Magazine: 2-shot detachable clip
Barrel: 25" adjustable choke
Finish: Blued; wood pistol grip stock & forearm
Approximate wt.: 7 lbs.
Comments: Made to the late 1970's.
Estimated Value: Excellent: $80.00
                        Very good: $60.00

Sears Model 140

Sears Bolt Action

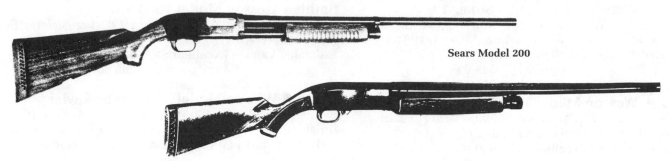

Sears Model 200

Sears Ted Williams 200

Sears Ted Williams 300
Gauge: 12, 20
Action: Semi-automatic, gas operated; hammerless
Magazine: 3-shot tubular
Barrel: 27" adjustable choke; 28" modified or full chokes; ventilated rib
Finish: Blued; checkered walnut pistol grip stock & forearm; recoil pad
Approximate wt.: 7 lbs.
Comments: Add $10.00 for variable choke.
Estimated Value: Excellent: **$240.00**
                   Very good: **$180.00**

Sears Model 200
Gauge: 12, 20
Action: Slide action; hammerless; repeating
Magazine: 4-shot tubular
Barrel: 28" full or modified chokes
Finish: Blued; alloy receiver; wood pistol grip stock & forearm; recoil pad
Approximate wt.: 6½ lbs.
Comments: Add $20.00 for variable choke.
Estimated Value: Excellent: **$150.00**
                   Very good: **$115.00**

Sears Ted Williams 200
A fancier version of the 200 with checkered wood.
Estimated Value: Excellent: **$175.00**
                   Very good: **$130.00**

Smith & Wesson

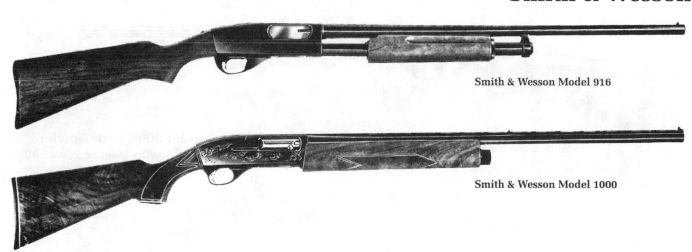

Smith & Wesson Model 916

Smith & Wesson Model 1000

Smith & Wesson Model 916
Gauge: 12
Action: Slide action; hammerless; side ejection
Magazine: 5-shot tubular
Barrel: 20" cylinder bore; 26" improved cylinder, 28" modified, full or cylinder bore; ventilated rib on some models
Finish: Blued; satin finish receiver; walnut semi-pistol grip stock & grooved slide handle; recoil pad available
Approximate wt.: 7 lbs.
Comments: Made from the early 1970's to about 1980. Add $20.00 for Deer Model or ventilated rib.
Estimated Value: Excellent: **$150.00**
                   Very good: **$120.00**

Smith & Wesson Model 1000
Gauge: 12, 20, regular or magnum
Action: Semi-automatic, gas operated; hammerless; side ejection
Magazine: 3-shot tubular
Barrel: 26", 28", 30"; variety of chokes; ventilated rib
Finish: Blued; engraved alloy receiver; steel receiver on magnum; checkered walnut pistol grip stock & forearm; sights
Approximate wt.: 7½ lbs.
Comments: Manufactured from the early 1970's to mid 1980's. Add $46.00 for magnum; $30.00 for "Multi-Choke" system.
Estimated Value: Excellent: **$380.00**
                   Very good: **$285.00**

Smith & Wesson Model 1000 Super 12
Similar to the Model 100 with "Multi-Choke" system; designed to use magnum shells. Introduced in 1984.
Estimated Value: Excellent: $450.00
                       Very good: $335.00

Smith & Wesson Model 1000 Trap
Similar to the Model 1000 with Monte Carlo stock; steel receiver; 30" multi-choke barrel; other trap features.
Estimated Value: Excellent: $450.00
                       Very good: $340.00

Smith & Wesson Model 1000S, Superskeet
Similar to the Model 100 with 25" skeet choke barrel; muzzle vents & other extras. Add $200.00 for Superskeet model.
Estimated Value: Excellent: $380.00
                       Very good: $285.00

Smith & Wesson Model 1000 Slug
Similar to the Model 1000 with a 22" slug barrel, rifle sights & steel receiver.
Estimated Value: Excellent: $380.00
                       Very good: $285.00

Smith & Wesson Model 1000 Waterfowler
Similar to the Model 1000 with a steel receiver; dull oil-finish stock; 30" full choke barrel; Parkerized finish; swivels; recoil pad; camouflage sling. Introduced in 1982.
Estimated Value: Excellent: $435.00
                       Very good: $325.00

Smith & Wesson Model 1000 Super 12 Waterfowler
Similar to the Model 1000 Waterfowler with the "Multi-Choke" system. Introduced in 1984.
Estimated Value: Excellent: $470.00
                       Very good: $350.00

Smith & Wesson Model 3000

Smith & Wesson Model 3000 Police

Smith & Wesson Model 3000
Gauge: 12, 20, regular or magnum
Action: Slide action; repeating; hammerless
Magazine: 3-shot tubular
Barrel: 26" improved cylinder; 28" modified or full, 30" full; ventilated rib
Finish: Blued; checkered walnut pistol grip stock & fluted slide handle; recoil pad
Approximate wt.: 7 lbs.
Comments: Currently produced. Add $25.00 for "Multi-Choke" system.
Estimated Value: Excellent: $300.00
                       Very good: $225.00

Smith & Wesson Model 3000 Waterfowler
Similar to the Model 3000 with steel receiver; 30" full choke barrel; Parkerized finish; dull, oil-finished wood; camouflaged sling & swivels. Introduced in 1982. Add $25.00 for "Multi-Choke" system.
Estimated Value: Excellent: $320.00
                       Very good: $240.00

Smith & Wesson Model 3000 Slug
Similar to the Model 3000 with a 22" slug barrel; rifle sights; swivels.
Estimated Value: Excellent: $270.00
                       Very good: $200.00

Smith & Wesson Model 3000 Police
Similar to the Model 3000 with 18" or 20" slug or police cylinder barrel; blued or Parkerized finish; bead or rifle sights; walnut finish, hardwood stock & grooved slide handle or plastic pistol grip & slide handle or folding stock. Add $25.00 for rifle sights; $10.00 for plastic pistol grip; $70.00 for folding stock.
Estimated Value: Excellent: $250.00
                       Very good: $185.00

Stevens Model No. 93

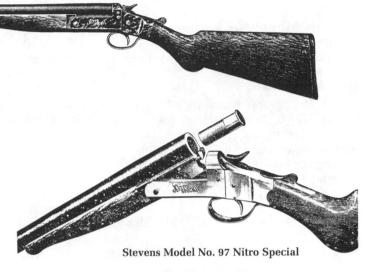

Stevens Model No. 97 Nitro Special

Stevens Models No. 93, 97 Nitro Special

Gauge: 12, 16
Action: Top lever, break-open; exposed hammer; single shot; Model 97 has automatic ejector
Magazine: None
Barrel: Special steel; 28", 30", 32"
Finish: Blued; nickel plated, case hardened frame; plain walnut pistol grip stock & lipped forearm
Approximate wt.: 7 to 7½ lbs.
Comments: Made from the 1907 to 1918.
Estimated Value: Excellent: $70.00
**   Very good: $55.00**

Stevens Models No. 100, 110, 120

Gauge: 12, 16, 20
Action: Top lever, break open; automatic ejector; exposed hammer; single shot
Magazine: None
Barrel: 28", 30", 32"
Finish: Blued; case hardened frame; walnut pistol grip stock & forearm; No. 100 no checkering; 110 & 120 checkered walnut
Approximate wt.: 6 to 7 lbs.
Comments: Produced from 1902 to 1904.
Estimated Value: Excellent: $75.00
**   Very good: $60.00**

Stevens Model No. 120

Stevens Model No. 140

Similar to the Model 120 except it is hammerless & has an automatic safety. Made from 1902 to 1904.
Estimated Value: Excellent: $100.00
**   Very good: $ 75.00**

Stevens Model No. 140

Stevens Models No. 160, 165, 170

Gauge: 12, 16, 20
Action: Break-open; exposed hammer; single shot; automatic ejector except on 160
Magazine: None
Barrel: 26", 28", 30", 32"
Finish: Blued; case hardened frame; checkered walnut pistol grip stock & forearm except 160 which is plain
Approximate wt.: 6 to 7 lbs.
Comments: Made from the 1903 to 1908.
Estimated Value: Excellent: $70.00
**   Very good: $55.00**

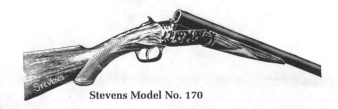

Stevens Model No. 170

Stevens Model No. 182 Trap Gun

Stevens Model No. 180

Gauge: 12, 16, 20
Action: Top lever, break-open; hammerless; automatic ejector; single shot
Magazine: None
Barrel: 26", 28", 30" modified; 32" or 36" full choke
Finish: Blued; case hardened frame; checkered walnut pistol grip stock & forearm
Approximate wt.: 6½ lbs.
Comments: Produced from 1903 to 1918.
Estimated Value: Excellent: $90.00
                       Very good: $70.00

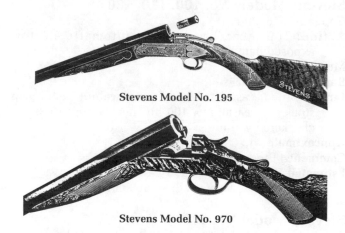

Stevens Model No. 180

Stevens Model No. 185, 190, 195

Gauge: 12
Action: Top lever, break-open; hammerless; automatic shell ejector; single shot
Magazine: None
Barrel: Round with octagon breech; 30" or 32"
Finish: Blued; case hardened frame; checkered walnut pistol grip stock & forearm; frame engraved on No. 190, 195
Approximate wt.: 7 to 8 lbs.
Comments: These guns differ in quality of finish & engraving. Produced from 1903 to 1906.
Estimated Value: Excellent: $150.00
                       Very good: $110.00

Stevens Model No. 182 Trap Gun

Similar to Model No. 180 except: Trap grade; 12 gauge only; matted top of barrel; scroll work on frame. Made from around 1912 to 1920.
Estimated Value: Excellent: $150.00
                       Very good: $110.00

Stevens Model No. 195

Stevens Model No. 970

Stevens Model No. 970

Similar to the 185, this 12 gauge was made from around 1912 to 1918.
Estimated Value: Excellent: $80.00
                       Very good: $60.00

Stevens Model No. 85 Dreadnaught

Stevens Model No. 89 Dreadnaught

Stevens Model No. 85 Dreadnaught

Gauge: 12
Action: Top lever, break-open; exposed hammer
Magazine: None, single shot
Barrel: 28", 30", 32" full choke
Finish: Blued; case hardened frame; plain walnut pistol grip stock & lipped forearm
Approximate wt.: 7½ lbs.
Comments: Made from around 1910 to mid 1920's.
Estimated Value: Excellent: $70.00
                       Very good: $55.00

Stevens Model No. 89 Dreadnaught

Same as the No. 85 with automatic ejector. Made until 1938.
Estimated Value: Excellent: $70.00
                       Very good: $55.00

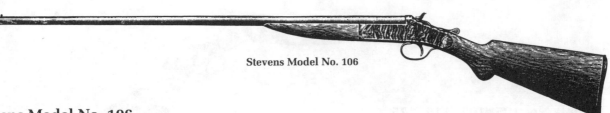

Stevens Model No. 106

Stevens Model No. 106

Gauge: 410
Action: Top lever, break-open; exposed hammer; single shot
Magazine: None
Barrel: 26" or 30"
Finish: Blued; case hardened frame; plain walnut pistol grip stock & forearm
Approximate wt.: 4½ lbs.
Comments: This lightweight, light-gauge gun was made from around 1912 to 1935.
Estimated Value: Excellent: $75.00
                      Very good: $55.00

Stevens Model No. 108

Same as the No. 106 with automatic ejector.
Estimated Value: Excellent: $80.00
                      Very good: $60.00

Stevens Springfield Model No. 958

Very similar to Model No. 108. Made from mid 1920's to early 1930's.
Estimated Value: Excellent: $70.00
                      Very good: $55.00

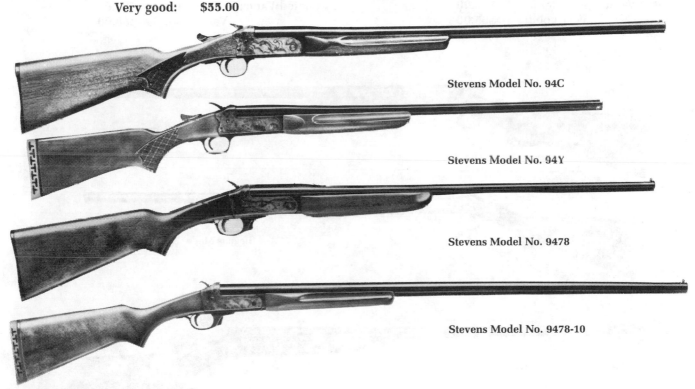

Stevens Model No. 94C

Stevens Model No. 94Y

Stevens Model No. 9478

Stevens Model No. 9478-10

Stevens Model No. 94, 94C

Gauge: 12, 16, 20, 410
Action: Top lever, break-open; exposed hammer
Magazine: None
Barrel: 26", 28", 30", 32", 36" full choke
Finish: Blued; case hardened frame; checkered or plain walnut semi-pistol grip stock & grooved forearm
Approximate wt.: 6 to 8 lbs.
Comments: 94 made from 1939 to 1960. 94C made from 1960 to mid 1980's.
Estimated Value: Excellent: $80.00
                      Very good: $60.00

Stevens Model No. 94Y

Similar to 94C in youth version. Shorter stock; recoil pad, 26" barrel; 20 gauge modified or 410 full choke. Made from 1960 to 1963.
Estimated Value: Excellent: $80.00
                      Very good: $60.00

Stevens Model No. 9478

Similar to the Model 94C with lever release on the trigger guard; no checkering. Add $8.00 for 36" barrel.
Estimated Value: Excellent: $75.00
                      Very good: $55.00

Stevens Model No. 9478-10, Waterfowl

Similar to the Model 9478 with a 36" full choke barrel; 10 gauge only; recoil pad.
Estimated Value: Excellent: $95.00
                      Very good: $70.00

Stevens Model No. 9478-Y

Similar to the Model 9478 in 410 full or 20 modified gauges; 26" barrel; short stock with rubber buttplate.
Estimated Value: Excellent: $70.00
                      Very good: $55.00

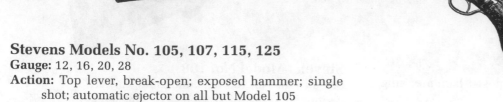

Stevens Model No. 105

Stevens Models No. 105, 107, 115, 125
Gauge: 12, 16, 20, 28
Action: Top lever, break-open; exposed hammer; single shot; automatic ejector on all but Model 105
Magazine: None, single shot
Barrel: 26" or 28"
Finish: Blued; case hardened frame; checkered walnut straight grip stock & forearm except No. 107 (plain)
Approximate wt.: 5½ lbs.
Comments: A lightweight series of shotguns produced until about World War II for Model 105; 1950's for Model 107 & 1920's for Models 115 & 125.
Estimated Value: Excellent: $75.00
                     Very good: $55.00

Stevens Springfield Model No. 95
Very similar to the Model 107. Made from the mid 1920's until the mid 1930's.
Estimated Value: Excellent: $80.00
                     Very good: $60.00

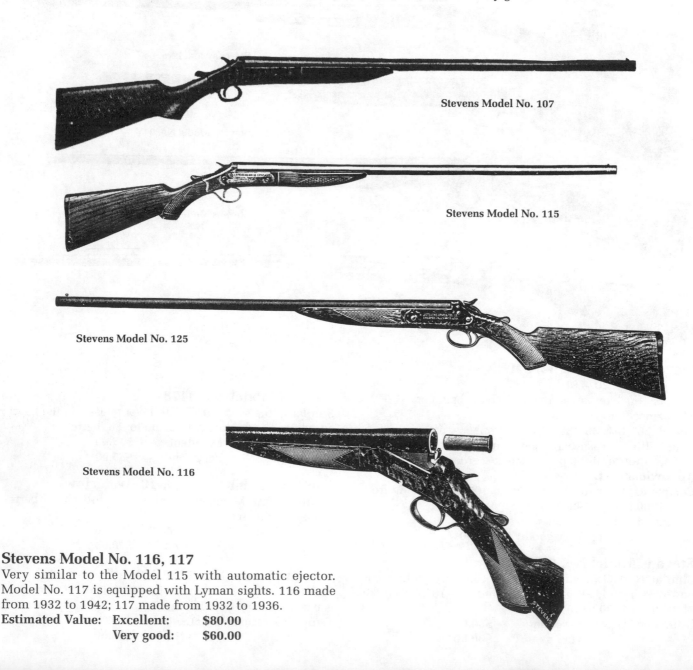

Stevens Model No. 107

Stevens Model No. 115

Stevens Model No. 125

Stevens Model No. 116

Stevens Model No. 116, 117
Very similar to the Model 115 with automatic ejector. Model No. 117 is equipped with Lyman sights. 116 made from 1932 to 1942; 117 made from 1932 to 1936.
Estimated Value: Excellent: $80.00
                     Very good: $60.00

Stevens Model No. 250

Gauge: 12
Action: Top lever, break-open; exposed hammer; double trigger
Magazine: None
Barrel: 28", 30", 32" double barrel
Finish: Blued; checkered walnut pistol grip stock & forearm
Approximate wt.: 8 lbs.
Comments: Made from 1903 to 1908.
Estimated Value: Excellent: $225.00
Very good: $165.00

Stevens Model No. 250

Stevens Model No. 260 & 270

Similar to Model 250 with special Damascus or twist barrels; available in 16 gauge. Manufactured from 1903 to 1906.
Estimated Value: Excellent: $200.00
Very good: $150.00

Stevens Model No. 350

Stevens Model No. 350, 360, 370

Gauge: 12, 16
Action: Top lever, break-open; hammerless; double trigger
Magazine: None
Barrel: Double barrel, matted rib, 28", 30", 32"
Finish: Blued; checkered walnut pistol grip stock & forearm
Approximate wt.: 7½ to 8½ lbs.
Comments: Produced from 1903 to 1908.
Estimated Value: Excellent: $180.00
Very good: $140.00

Stevens Model No. 355

Stevens Model No. 385

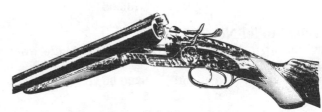

Stevens Model No. 235

Stevens Model No. 255

Stevens Model No. 355, 365, 375, 385

Gauge: 12, 16
Action: Top lever, break-open; hammerless; double trigger
Magazine: None
Barrel: Double barrel; Krupp steel; matted rib; 28", 30", 32"
Finish: Blued; checkered walnut straight or pistol grip stock & forearm; 355 & 365 plain; 375 some engraving; 385 engraved frame
Approximate wt.: 7 to 8½ lbs.
Comments: Made from 1907. 355 discontinued in World War I; all others in 1913.
Estimated Value: Excellent: $200.00
Very good: $150.00

Stevens Model No. 235, 255, 265

Gauge: 12, 16
Action: Top lever, break-open; exposed hammers; double triggers; box lock
Magazine: None
Barrel: Double barrel; matted rib; 28", 30, 32"
Finish: Blued; checkered walnut pistol grip stock & forearm; case hardened frame; No. 255 has checkered buttplate
Approximate wt.: 7 to 8½ lbs.
Comments: Made from around 1907 until 1928 (No. 235); 255 & 265 stopped around World War I.
Estimated Value: Excellent: $210.00
Very good: $160.00

Stevens Riverside Model No. 215

Gauge: 12, 16
Action: Top lever, break-open; exposed hammer; double trigger
Magazine: None
Barrel: Double barrel; 26", 28", 30", 32"; matted rib; left barrel full choke, right barrel modified
Finish: Blued; case hardened frame; checkered walnut pistol grip stock & forearm
Approximate wt.: 7½ to 8½ lbs.
Comments: Made from around 1912 to 1942.
Estimated Value: Excellent: $200.00
                       Very good: $150.00

Stevens Riverside Model No. 215

Stevens Riverside Model No. 315

Gauge: 12, 16
Action: Top lever, break-open; hammerless; double trigger
Magazine: None
Barrel: Double barrel; 26", 28", 30", 32"; matted rib; right barrel modified, left full choke
Finish: Blued; case hardened frame; checkered walnut semi-pistol grip stock & forearm
Approximate wt.: 7 to 7½ lbs.
Comments: Made from around 1912 until 1936.
Estimated Value: Excellent: $195.00
                       Very good: $150.00

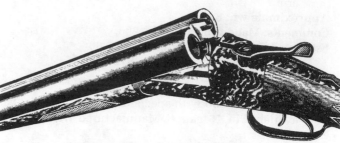

Stevens Riverside Model No. 315

Stevens Model No. 335

Similar to the 315. Produced from around 1912 to 1930.
Estimated Value: Excellent: $180.00
                       Very good: $135.00

Stevens Model No. 335

Stevens Model No. 345

Very similar to the No. 335 in 20 gauge. Made from around 1912 to 1926.
Estimated Value: Excellent: $200.00
                       Very good: $150.00

Stevens Model No. 345

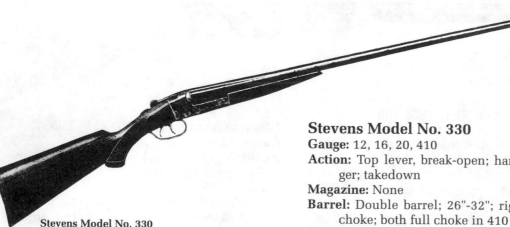

Stevens Model No. 330

Stevens Model No. 330

Gauge: 12, 16, 20, 410
Action: Top lever, break-open; hammerless; double trigger; takedown
Magazine: None
Barrel: Double barrel; 26"-32"; right modified, left full choke; both full choke in 410
Finish: Blued; case hardened frame; checkered black walnut pistol grip stock & forearm
Approximate wt.: 5¾ to 7¾ lbs.
Comments: Made from the mid 1920's until the mid 1930's.
Estimated Value: Excellent: $185.00
                       Very good: $140.00

Stevens Model No. 311

Stevens Springfield Model No. 315

Stevens Model 311-R

Stevens Model 311,
Stevens Springfield Model No. 311
Springfield Hammerless

Gauge: 12, 16, 20, 410
Action: Top lever, break-open; hammerless; double trigger; takedown
Magazine: None
Barrel: Double barrel; 24"-32"; right barrel modified, left full choke, except 32" 12 gauge is full choke; matted rib
Finish: Blued; case hardened frame; smooth walnut semi-pistol grip stock & forearm
Approximate wt.: 5½ to 7¾ lbs.
Comments: Made from about 1931 to late 1980's. Add $30.00 for selective single trigger. 16 gauge discontinued in late 1970's. See Savage Model 311.

Estimated Value:	Excellent:	$225.00
	Very good:	$180.00

Stevens Springfield Model No. 315

A higher quality version of the Model 311; discontinued.

Estimated Value:	Excellent:	$240.00
	Very good:	$190.00

Stevens Model 311-R

A law enforcement version of the Model 311 with 18¼" cylinder bore barrel; recoil pad; 12 gauge only. Produced from 1982 to 1988. See Savage Model 311-R.

Estimated Value:	Excellent:	$220.00
	Very good:	$175.00

Stevens Model No. 530

Gauge: 12, 16, 20, 410
Action: Top lever, break-open; hammerless; box lock; double trigger
Magazine: None
Barrel: Double barrel; 26"-32"; right modified choke, left full choke, except 32" 12 gauge & 410 are both full choke
Finish: Blued; case hardened frame; checkered walnut pistol grip stock & forearm; recoil pad on early model
Approximate wt.: 6 to 7½ lbs.
Comments: Made from about 1935 to 1952.

Estimated Value:	Excellent:	$185.00
	Very good:	$140.00

Stevens Model No. 530 ST

Same as 530 with non-selective single trigger.

Estimated Value:	Excellent:	$200.00
	Very good:	$150.00

Stevens Model No. 530M

Same as 530 with plastic stock. Discontinued in late 1940's.

Estimated Value:	Excellent:	$160.00
	Very good:	$120.00

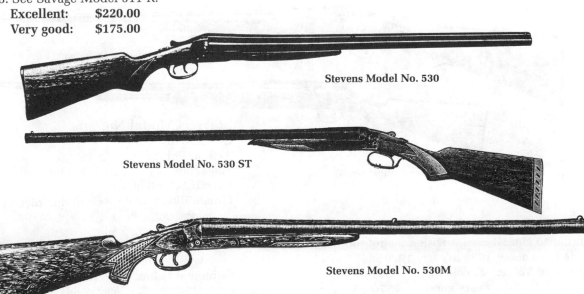

Stevens Model No. 530

Stevens Model No. 530 ST

Stevens Model No. 530M

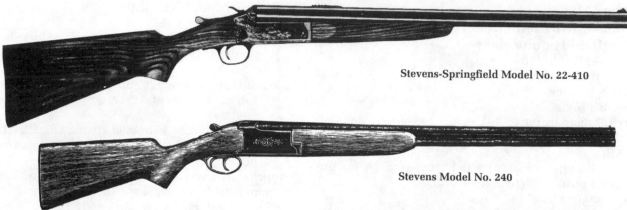

Stevens Model 511

Stevens Model 511
Gauge: 12, 20, regular or magnum
Action: Box lock; top lever, break-open; double trigger
Magazine: None
Barrel: Double barrel; 28" modified & full choke
Finish: Blued; checkered hardwood semi-pistol grip stock & small forearm; case hardened frame
Approximate wt.: 7¾ lbs.
Comments: Produced in the late 1970's.
Estimated Value: Excellent: $200.00
                      Very good: $150.00

Stevens-Springfield Model No. 22-410

Stevens Model No. 240

Stevens Model No. 240
Gauge: 410
Action: Top lever, break-open; exposed hammer; double trigger; takedown
Magazine: None
Barrel: Over & under double barrel; both barrels 26" full choke
Finish: Blued; checkered plastic or wood pistol grip stock & forearm
Approximate wt.: 6½ lbs.
Comments: Made from about 1940 to 1948.
Estimated Value: Excellent: $300.00
                      Very good: $240.00

Stevens-Springfield Model No. 22-410
Gauge: 410 & 22 caliber rifle
Action: Top lever, break-open; exposed hammer; single trigger; separate extractors
Magazine: None
Barrel: Over & under double barrel; 22 rifle over 410 shotgun; 24"
Finish: Blued; case hardened frame; plastic semi-pistol grip stock & forearm; open rear, ramp front sights
Approximate wt.: 6 lbs.
Comments: Made from about 1940 to 1948. Later produced as Savage.
Estimated Value: Excellent: $130.00
                      Very good: $100.00

Stevens Model 58

Stevens Model No. 59

Stevens Model No. 59
Similar to No. 58 except with a 5-shot tubular magazine. Made from about 1939 to early 1970's.
Estimated Value: Excellent: $90.00
                      Very good: $70.00

Stevens Model No. 58
Gauge: 410
Action: Bolt-action
Magazine: 3-shot detachable box
Barrel: 24" full choke
Finish: Blued; plain walnut one-piece pistol grip stock & forearm
Approximate wt.: 5½ lbs.
Comments: Made from about 1935 to late 1970's. Later versions have checkering.
Estimated Value: Excellent: $80.00
                      Very good: $60.00

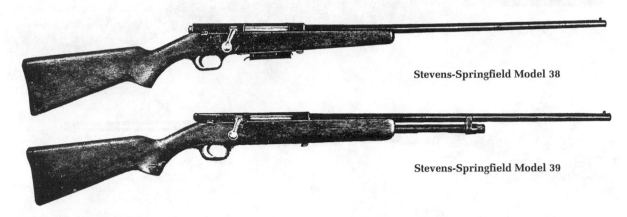

Stevens-Springfield Model 38

Stevens-Springfield Model 39

Stevens-Springfield Model 38
Similar to Stevens Model No. 58. Made 1939 to 1947.

| Estimated Value: | Excellent: | $75.00 |
| | Very good: | $55.00 |

Stevens-Springfield Model 39
Similar to Stevens Model No. 59. Made 1939 to 1947.

| Estimated Value: | Excellent: | $80.00 |
| | Very good: | $60.00 |

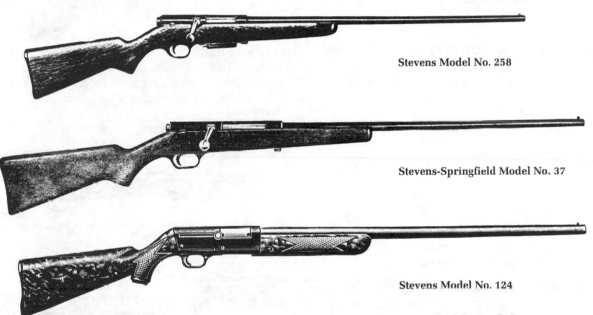

Stevens Model No. 258

Stevens-Springfield Model No. 37

Stevens Model No. 124

Stevens Model No. 258
Gauge: 20
Action: Bolt action; repeating
Magazine: 2-shot detachable box
Barrel: 26" full choke
Finish: Blued; plain walnut one-piece pistol grip stock & forearm
Approximate wt.: 6¼ lbs.
Comments: This takedown shotgun was produced from 1939 until 1942.

| Estimated Value: | Excellent: | $80.00 |
| | Very good: | $60.00 |

Stevens Model No. 254
A single shot version of the Model 258.

| Estimated Value: | Excellent: | $55.00 |
| | Very good: | $45.00 |

Stevens-Springfield Model 238
Similar to Stevens Model 258. Made 1939 to 1947.

| Estimated Value: | Excellent: | $85.00 |
| | Very good: | $65.00 |

Stevens-Springfield Model 237
Similar to Stevens Model No. 254. Made from 1939 to 1942.

| Estimated Value: | Excellent: | $60.00 |
| | Very good: | $45.00 |

Stevens-Springfield Model No. 37
Similar to Stevens-Springfield Model 237 except 410 bore. Made from 1939 to 1942.

| Estimated Value: | Excellent: | $65.00 |
| | Very good: | $50.00 |

Stevens Model No. 124
Gauge: 12
Action: Semi-automatic; side ejection; hammerless
Magazine: 2-shot tubular
Barrel: 28" improved cylinder, modified or full choke
Finish: Blued; checkered plastic pistol grip stock & forearm
Approximate wt.: 7 lbs.
Comments: Made from about 1950 to 1956.

| Estimated Value: | Excellent: | $120.00 |
| | Very good: | $ 90.00 |

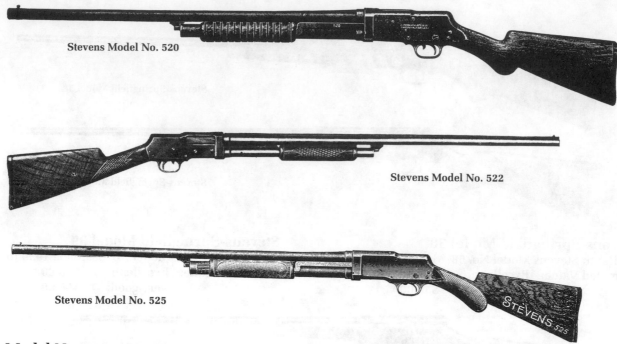

Stevens Model No. 520

Stevens Model No. 522

Stevens Model No. 525

Stevens Model No. 520, 521, 522

Gauge: 12

Action: Browning patent; slide action; takedown; side ejection; hammerless

Magazine: 5-shot tubular

Barrel: 26"-32"; full choke, modified or cylinder; matted rib on 521

Finish: Blued; walnut pistol grip stock & grooved slide handle; checkered straight grip & slide handle on 522

Approximate wt.: 8 lbs.

Comments: Made from about 1907 until World War II; 522 discontinued in 1928.

Estimated Value: Excellent: $175.00
Very good: $130.00

Stevens Models No. 525, 530, 535

Similar to 520 except fancier grades; 525 is custom built; 530 custom built with engraved receiver & rib; 535 custom built, heavily engraved. Made from 1912 to 1918. Add $75.00 for engraving.

Estimated Value: Excellent: $225.00
Very good: $170.00

Stevens Model No. 535

Stevens Model No. 200

Stevens Model No. 620

Stevens Model No. 200

Gauge: 20

Action: Pedersen patent slide action; hammerless; side ejection; takedown

Magazine: 5-shot tubular

Barrel: 26"-32"; full choke, modified or cylinder bore

Finish: Blued; walnut pistol grip stock & grooved slide handle

Approximate wt.: 6½ lbs.

Comments: Made from about 1912 to 1918.

Estimated Value: Excellent: $175.00
Very good: $130.00

Stevens Model No. 620

Gauge: 12, 16, 20

Action: Slide action; hammerless; side ejection

Magazine: 5-shot tubular

Barrel: 26"-32"; full choke, modified or cylinder bore

Finish: Blued; checkered walnut pistol grip stock & slide handle

Approximate wt.: 6 to 7¾ lbs.

Comments: A takedown shotgun made from about 1932 to 1958

Estimated Value: Excellent: $185.00
Very good: $140.00

Stevens Model No. 620-P

Stevens Model No. 77

Stevens Model No. 620-P

Same as Model No. 620 with "Poly-Choke."
Estimated Value: **Excellent:**   **$190.00**
         Very good: **$150.00**

Stevens Model No. 621

Same as Model No. 620 with matted rib. Made from 1932 to 1937.
Estimated Value: **Excellent:**   **$190.00**
         Very good: **$145.00**

Stevens Model No. 77

Gauge: 12, 16
Action: Slide action; hammerless; side ejection
Magazine: 5-shot tubular
Barrel: 26" or 28" improved cylinder, modified or full choke
Finish: Blued; plain walnut pistol grip stock & grooved slide handle
Approximate wt.: 7 lbs.
Comments: Made from the mid 1950's to early 1970's.
Estimated Value: **Excellent:**   **$170.00**
         Very good: **$130.00**

Stevens Model No. 77-SC

Same as 77 with Savage "Super Choke" & recoil pad.
Estimated Value: **Excellent:**   **$185.00**
         Very good: **$140.00**

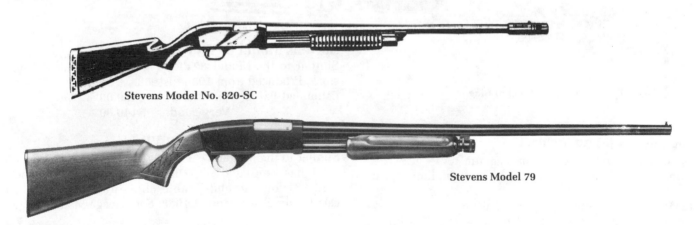

Stevens Model No. 820-SC

Stevens Model 79

Stevens Model No. 820

Gauge: 12
Action: Slide action; hammerless; side ejection
Magazine: 5-shot tubular
Barrel: 28" improved cylinder, modified or full choke
Finish: Blued; plain walnut semi-pistol grip stock & grooved slide handle
Approximate wt.: 7½ lbs.
Comments: Produced from about 1950 to 1956.
Estimated Value: **Excellent:**   **$165.00**
         Very good: **$125.00**

Stevens Model No. 820-SC

Same as No. 820 with Savage "Super Choke."
Estimated Value: **Excellent:**   **$200.00**
         Very good: **$150.00**

Stevens Model No. 79

Gauge: 12, 20, 410, regular or magnum
Action: Slide action; hammerless; side ejection, repeating
Magazine: 4-shot tubular; 3-shot in magnum
Barrel: 28" modified or 30" full in 12 gauge; 28" modified or full in 20 gauge; 26" full in 410
Finish: Blued; checkered hardwood semi-pistol grip stock & fluted slide handle
Approximate wt.: 7 lbs.
Comments: Produced in the late 1970's.
Estimated Value: **Excellent:**   **$160.00**
         Very good: **$130.00**

Stevens Model 79 VR

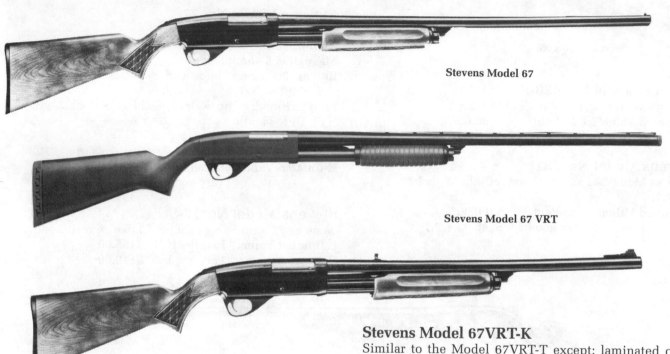

Stevens Model 67

Stevens Model 67 VRT

Stevens Model 67 Slug

Stevens Model 79 Slug
Similar to the Model 79 with a 21" barrel for slugs; rifle sights.
Estimated Value: Excellent: $165.00
                       Very good: $125.00

Stevens Model 67, 67T
Gauge: 12, 20 or 410, regular or magnum
Action: Slide action; hammerless; side ejecting; repeating
Magazine: 4-shot tubular; 3-shot in magnum
Barrel: 28" modified or full; 26" full in 410; 30" full in 12 gauge; 67T has interchangeable choke tubes in 12 & 20 gauge only
Finish: Blued; hardwood, semi-pistol grip stock & fluted or grooved slide handle; some with recoil pad
Approximate wt.: 6¾ lbs.
Comments: Produced from the late 1970's to late 1980's. Add $16.00 for 67T. See Savage Model 67.
Estimated Value: Excellent: $150.00
                       Very good: $110.00

Stevens Model 67 Slug
Similar to the Model 67 with a 21" barrel for slugs & rifle sights; 12 gauge only. See Savage Model 67 Slug.
Estimated Value: Excellent: $155.00
                       Very good: $115.00

Stevens Model 79 VR
Similar to the Model 79 with a ventilated rib.
Estimated Value: Excellent: $175.00
                       Very good: $140.00

Stevens Model 67VRT-K
Similar to the Model 67VRT-T except: laminated camo stock. Produced from 1986 to 1988.
Estimated Value: Excellent: $190.00
                       Very good: $140.00

Stevens Model 67 VR, 67 VR-T
Similar to the Model 67 with a ventilated rib (67 VR). 67 VR-T has ventilated rib & interchangeable choke tubes. Add 7% for interchangeable choke tubes in 12 or 20 gauge only. Discontinued 1988. See Savage Model 67 VR-T.
Estimated Value: Excellent: $175.00
                       Very good: $125.00

Stevens Model 67T-Y, 67VRT-Y
Gauge: 20
Action: Slide action; hammerless; repeating
Magazine: 4-shot
Barrel: 22" with three interchangeable choke tubes; ventilated rib on 67VRT-Y
Finish: Blued; hardwood, semi-pistol grip stock & grooved slide handle
Approximate wt.: 6 lbs.
Comments: Introduced in 1985. Designed for the young shooter with a shorter 12" pull stock. Deduct $16.00 for plain barrel (67T-Y).
Estimated Value: Excellent: $170.00
                       Very good: $130.00

Universal

Universal Model 101

Universal Model 101

Gauge: 12
Action: Box lock; top lever, break-open; exposed hammer; single shot
Magazine: None
Barrel: 28", 30" full choke
Finish: Blued; plain wood pistol grip stock & tapered forearm
Approximate wt.: 7½ lbs.
Comments: Manufactured in the late 1960's.
Estimated Value: Excellent: $80.00
                       Very good: $60.00

Universal Single Wing

Similar to the Model 101 with automatic ejector. Made from the early to mid 1970's.
Estimated Value: Excellent: $85.00
                       Very good: $65.00

Universal Model 202

Universal Double Wing

Universal Over Wing

Universal Model 203

Similar to the Model 202 with 32" full choke barrels & 10 gauge.
Estimated Value: Excellent: $195.00
                       Very good: $150.00

Universal Model 2030

Similar to the Double Wing with 32" full choke barrels & 10 gauge.
Estimated Value: Excellent: $200.00
                       Very good: $150.00

Universal Over Wing

Gauge: 12, 20
Action: Box lock; top lever, break-open; hammerless
Magazine: None
Barrel: Over & under double barrel; 26", 28", 30"; ventilated rib
Finish: Blued; checkered walnut pistol grip stock & forearm; sights; recoil pad; engraving available
Approximate wt.: 8 lbs.
Comments: Made from about 1970 to 1975. Add %50.00 for single trigger.
Estimated Value: Excellent: $350.00
                       Very good: $280.00

Universal Model 202

Gauge: 12, 20, 410
Action: Box lock; top lever, break-open; hammerless; double triggers
Magazine: None
Barrel: Double barrel; 26" improved cylinder & modified; 28" modified & full chokes
Finish: Blued; checkered walnut pistol grip stock & forearm
Approximate wt.: 7 lbs.
Comments: Manufactured in the late 1960's. Add $20.00 for 410 bore.
Estimated Value: Excellent: $175.00
                       Very good: $135.00

Universal Double Wing

Similar to the Model 202 with recoil pad. Made from 1970 to 1975; 12 or 20 gauge magnum.
Estimated Value: Excellent: $190.00
                       Very good: $145.00

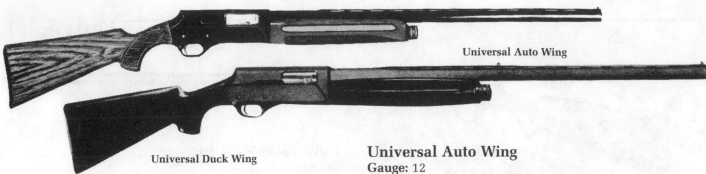

Universal Auto Wing

Universal Duck Wing

Universal Duck Wing

Similar to the Auto Wing with 28" or 30" full choke barrel. Teflon coated. Discontinued in the early 1970's.
Estimated Value:　Excellent:　$275.00
　　　　　　　　　　Very good:　$210.00

Universal Auto Wing

Gauge: 12
Action: Semi-automatic; hammerless
Magazine: 5-shot tubular
Barrel: 26", 28", 30"; variety of chokes; ventilated rib
Finish: Blued; checkered walnut pistol grip stock & forearm; sights
Approximate wt.: 8 lbs.
Comments: Made from about 1970 to 1975.
Estimated Value:　Excellent:　$250.00
　　　　　　　　　　Very good:　$190.00

Valmet

Valmet Model 412KE

Valmet Model 412 KE

Gauge: 12
Action: Top lever, break-open; hammerless; automatic ejectors
Magazine: None
Barrel: Over & under double barrel; 26" improved cylinder & modified; 28" modified & full; 30" modified & full in 12 gauge; ventilated rib
Finish: Blued; checkered walnut pistol grip stock & forearm; Monte Carlo stock with recoil pad; swivels
Approximate wt.: 7 lbs.
Comments: Made in Finland with interchangeable barrels available that make the shotgun a combination shotgun/rifle or a double rifle. Produced from the early 1980's to mid 1980's.
Estimated Value:　Excellent:　$560.00
　　　　　　　　　　Very good:　$420.00

Valmet Model 412K

Similar to the Model 412KE with extractor & 36" barrel. Introduced in 1982.
Estimated Value:　Excellent:　$560.00
　　　　　　　　　　Very good:　$420.00

Valmet Model 412KE Trap

Similar to the Model 412KE with 30" improved modified & full choke barrel.
Estimated Value:　Excellent:　$600.00
　　　　　　　　　　Very good:　$480.00

Valmet Model 412KE Skeet

Similar to the Model 412KE with 26" or 28" cylinder bore & improved cylinder bore or skeet choke barrels.
Estimated Value:　Excellent:　$600.00
　　　　　　　　　　Very good:　$480.00

Valmet Model 412K Combination

Similar to the Model 412K with a 12 gauge improved modified barrel over a rifle barrel in caliber 222, 223, 243, 30-06, 308; 24" barrels. Introduced in 1982.
Estimated Value:　Excellent:　$625.00
　　　　　　　　　　Very good:　$470.00

Valmet 12 Gauge

Gauge: 12
Action: Box lock; top lever, break-open; single selective trigger
Magazine: None
Barrel: Over & under doubel barrel; 26" improved cylinder & modified; 28" modified & full; 30" modified & full or full & full chokes
Finish: Blued; checkered walnut pistol grip stock & wide forearm
Approximate wt.: 8 lbs.
Comments: Made from the late 1940's to the late 1960's in Finland.
Estimated Value:　Excellent:　$425.00
　　　　　　　　　　Very good:　$320.00

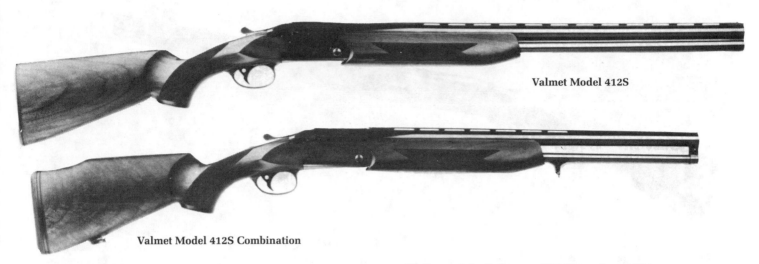

Valmet Model 412S

Valmet Model 412S Combination

Valmet Model 412S

Gauge: 12, 20; regular or magnum

Action: Top lever, break-open; hammerless; automatic ejectors; extractor on 36" model

Magazine: None

Barrel: Over & under doubel barrel; 26" cylinder bore & improved cylinder, improved cylinder or modified; 28" cylinder bore & modified or modified & full; 30" improved modified & full, modified & full; 36" full; ventilated rib

Finish: Blued; checkered walnut pistol grip stock & forearm, adjustable for barrel differences; buttplate adjusts to fit shooter

Approximate wt.: 7 lbs.

Comments: A shooting system with interchangeable barrels & adjustable buttplate; produced in Finland. Introduced in 1984.

Estimated Value: New (retail): $959.00
Excellent: $720.00
Very good: $575.00

Valmet Model 412 ST Standard Trap

Similar to the Model 412S with Monte Carlo stock, 12 gauge only, 30" or 32" barrel. Introduced in 1987. Add 30% for Premium Grade model.

Estimated Value: New (retail); $1,149.00
Excellent: $ 860.00
Very good: $ 690.00

Valmet Model 412ST Standard Skeet

Similar to the Model 412S with 28" skeet choke barrel. Introduced in 1987. Add 30% for Premium Grade model.

Estimated Value: New (retail); $1,149.00
Excellent: $ 860.00
Very good: $ 690.00

Valmet Model 412S Combination

Similar to the Model 412S with 24" 12 gauge improved/modified barrel over a 222, 223, 243, 30-06 or 308 caliber rifle barrel.

Estimated Value: New (retail); $1,009.00
Excellent: $ 825.00
Very good: $ 660.00

Weatherby

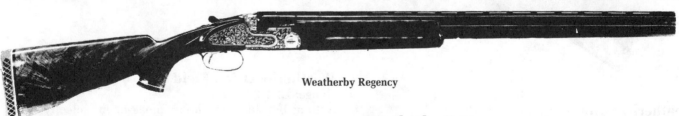

Weatherby Regency

Weatherby Regency Skeet

Similar to the Regency in skeet chokes with a 26" or 28" barrel.

Estimated Value: Excellent: $975.00
Very good: $780.00

Weatherby Regency Trap

Similar to the Regency with a wide ventilated rib barrel; 30" or 32" full & full, full & improved modified, or full & modified chokes; choice of regular or Monte Carlo stock; 12 gauge only.

Estimated Value: Excellent: $1,000.00
Very good: $ 800.00

Weatherby Regency

Gauge: 12, 20

Action: Box lock; top lever, break-open; hammerless; automatic ejectors; single selective trigger

Magazine: None

Barrel: Over & under double barrel; 26", 28", 30"; variety of chokes; ventilated rib

Finish: Blued; checkered walnut pistol grip stock & fluted forearm; recoil pad

Approximate wt.: 7 to 7½ lbs.

Comments: Made from the early 1970's to the early 1980's.

Estimated Value: Excellent: $925.00
Very good: $740.00

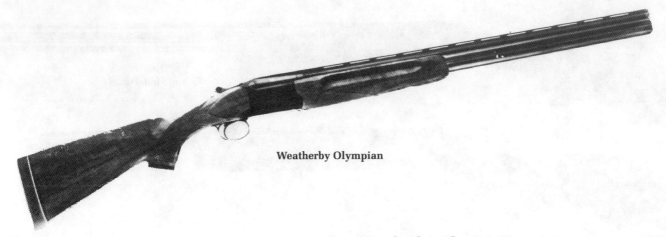

Weatherby Olympian

Weatherby Olympian Skeet

Similar to the Olympian with 26" or 28" skeet choke barrel.

Estimated Value: Excellent: $720.00
          Very good: $540.00

Weatherby Olympian Trap

Similar to the Olympian; ventilated rib between barrels; 30" or 32" full & modified or full & improved modified chokes; Monte Carlo or regular stock.

Estimated Value: Excellent: $745.00
          Very good: $560.00

Weatherby Olympian

Gauge: 12, 20
Action: Box lock; top lever, break-open; selective automatic ejectors
Magazine: None
Barrel: Over & under double barrel; 26" or 28" full & modified; 26" or 28" modified & improved cylinder; 30" full & modified; ventilated rib
Finish: Blued; checkered walnut pistol grip stock & fluted forearm; recoil pad
Approximate wt.: 7 to 8 lbs.
Comments: Made from the 1970's to early 1980's.
Estimated Value: Excellent: $700.00
          Very good: $525.00

Weatherby Orion

Weatherby Orion Trap

Similar to the Orion in 12 gauge only; 30" or 32" full & improved modified or full & modified barrels; wide rib with center bead & ventilated rib between barrels; curved recoil pad; Monte Carlo or regular stock.

Estimated Value: New (retail): $1,100.00
          Excellent: $ 825.00
          Very good: $ 660.00

Weatherby Orion Skeet

Similar to the Orion with 26" skeet choke barrels. 12 or 20 gauge.

Estimated Value: New (retail): $1,070.00
          Excellent: $ 800.00
          Very good: $ 640.00

Weatherby Orion Field

Gauge: 12, 20, 28, 410
Action: Box lock; top lever, break-open; selective automatic ejectors; single selective trigger
Magazine: None
Barrel: Over & under double barrel; 26" or 28" modified & improved cylinder; 28" or 30" full & modified; ventilated rib. Multi-choke after 1983
Finish: Blued; checkered walnut pistol grip stock & fluted forearm; rosewood cap at grip; recoil pad; engraved receiver; high lustre finish
Approximate wt.: 6½ to 7½ lbs.
Comments: Introduced in 1982. 28 gauge & 410 added in 1988.
Estimated Value: New (retail): $1,055.00
          Excellent: $ 790.00
          Very good: $ 630.00

Weatherby Athena

Weatherby Athena Field

Gauge: 12, 20, 28, 410

Action: Box lock; top lever, break-open; selective automatic ejectors; single selective trigger

Magazine: None

Barrel: Over & under double barrel; 26" or 28" modified & improved cylinder; 28" modified & full choke; ventilated rib on top & between barrels. Multichoke after 1983

Finish: Blued; special selected checkered walnut pistol grip stock & fluted forearm; high lustre finish; rosewood grip cap; recoil pad; silver grey engraved receiver

Approximate wt.: 7 to 8 lbs.

Comments: A high quality superposed shotgun introduced in 1982. 28 gauge & 410 added 1988.

Estimated Value:	New (retail):	$1,675.00
	Excellent:	$1,250.00
	Very good:	$1,000.00

Weatherby Athena Single Barrel Trap

Similar to the Athena Trap except with a single ventilated rib barrel configuration. Introduced in the late 1980's.

Estimated Value:	New (retail):	$1,695.00
	Excellent:	$1,275.00
	Very good:	$1,020.00

Weatherby Athena Trap

Similar to the Athena in 12 gauge only in 30" or 32" full & improved modified or full & modified barrels; wide rib with center bead sight; curved recoil pad; Monte Carlo stock.

Estimated Value:	New (retail):	$1,695.00
	Excellent:	$1,275.00
	Very good:	$1,020.00

Weatherby Athena Skeet

Similar to the Athena with 26" skeet choke barrels.

Estimated Value:	New (retail):	$1,695.00
	Excellent:	$1,275.00
	Very good:	$1,020.00

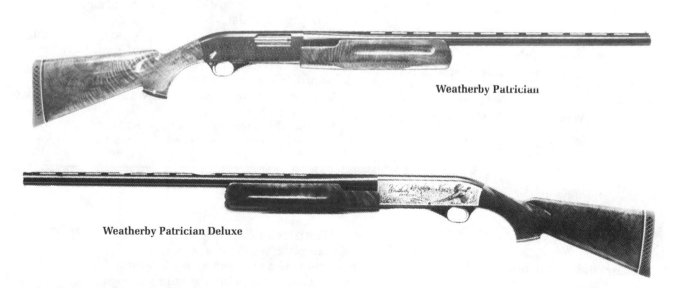

Weatherby Patrician

Weatherby Patrician Deluxe

Weatherby Patrician & Patrician II

Gauge: 12; Patrician II 12 gauge magnum

Action: Slide action; hammerless; side ejection

Magazine: Tubular

Barrel: 26", 28", 30"; variety of chokes; ventilated rib

Finish: Blued; checkered walnut pistol grip stock & grooved slide handle; recoil pad

Approximate wt.: 7½ lbs.

Comments: Made from the early 1970's to early 1980's. Add $20.00 for Trap.

Estimated Value:	Excellent:	$300.00
	Very good:	$240.00

Weatherby Patrician Deluxe

Similar to the Patrician with decorated satin silver receiver & higher quality wood.

Estimated Value:	Excellent:	$390.00
	Very good:	$310.00

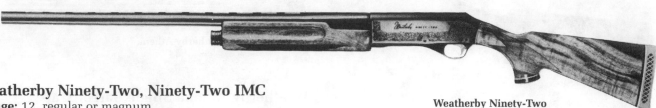

Weatherby Ninety-Two

Weatherby Ninety-Two, Ninety-Two IMC

Gauge: 12, regular or magnum
Action: Slide action; hammerless
Magazine: 2-shot tubular, with plug
Barrel: 26" improved cylinder or skeet, 28" modified or full, 30" full; ventilated rib. Multi-choke barrel on all after 1983
Finish: Blued; checkered walnut pistol grip stock & slide handle; high gloss finish; rosewood grip cap; etched receiver; recoil pad
Approximate wt.: 7½ lbs.
Comments: Introduced in 1982. Trap model discontinued in 1983; regular model discontinued 1988.

Estimated Value:	Excellent:	$340.00
	Very good:	$270.00

Weatherby Ninety-Two Buckmaster

Similar to the Ninety-Two with a 22" slug barrel & rifle sights.

Estimated Value:	Excellent:	$335.00
	Very good:	$265.00

Weatherby Centurion

Weatherby Centurion & Centurion II

Gauge: 12, Centurion II 12 gauge magnum
Action: Semi-automatic, gas operated; hammerless
Magazine: Tubular
Barrel: 26", 28", 30"; variety of chokes; ventilated rib
Finish: Blued; checkered walnut pistol grip stock & grooved forearm; recoil pad
Approximate wt.: 7½ lbs.
Comments: Made from the early 1970's to early 1980's. Add $20.00 for Trap.

Estimated Value:	Excellent:	$320.00
	Very good:	$255.00

Weatherby Centurion Deluxe

Similar to the Centurion with a decorated satin silver receiver & higher quality wood.

Estimated Value:	Excellent:	$360.00
	Very good:	$285.00

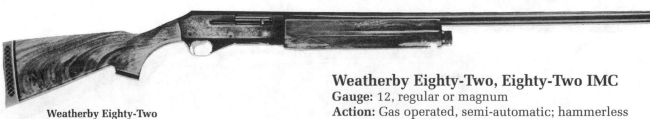

Weatherby Eighty-Two

Weatherby Eighty-Two, Eighty-Two IMC

Gauge: 12, regular or magnum
Action: Gas operated, semi-automatic; hammerless
Magazine: 2-shot tubular with plug
Barrel: 26" improved cylinder or skeet, 28" modified or full, 30" full; ventilated rib. "Multi-Choke" barrel on all after 1983
Finish: Blued; checkered walnut pistol grip stock & forearm; high gloss finish; rosewood grip cap; etched receiver; recoil pad
Approximate wt.: 7½ lbs.
Comments: Introduced in 1982. Add 7% for Trap model (discontinued in 1983).

Estimated Value:	New (retail):	$555.00
	Excellent:	$415.00
	Very good:	$330.00

Weatherby Eighty-Two Buckmaster

Similar to the Eighty-Two with a 22" slug barrel & rifle sights.

Estimated Value:	Excellent:	$415.00
	Very good:	$330.00

Western

Western Long Range

Gauge: 12, 16, 20, 410
Action: Box lock; top lever, break-open; hammerless; double or single trigger
Magazine: None
Barrel: Double barrel; 26", 32"; modified & full choke
Finish: Blued; plain walnut pistol grip stock & forearm
Approximate wt.: 7 lbs.
Comments: Made from the mid 1920's until the early 1940's by Western Arms Corp. which was later bought by Ithaca Arms Company. Add $25.00 for single trigger.
Estimated Value: Excellent: $300.00
Very good: $225.00

Western Long Range

Western Field

Western Field Model 100

Gauge: 12, 16, 20, 410
Action: Box lock; thumb sliding, break-open; hammerless; automatic ejectors; single shot
Magazine: None
Barrel: 26"-30", full choke
Finish: Blued; wood semi-pistol grip stock & tapered forearm
Approximate wt.: 6¼ to 7 lbs.
Comments: Manufactured to the mid 1970's.
Estimated Value: Excellent: $65.00
Very good: $50.00

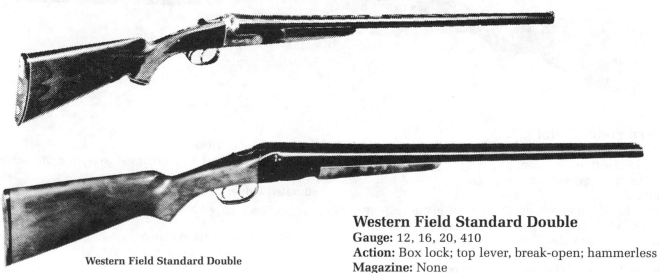

Western Field Model 100

Western Field Standard Double

Western Field Standard Double

Gauge: 12, 16, 20, 410
Action: Box lock; top lever, break-open; hammerless
Magazine: None
Barrel: Double barrel; 26", 30"; modified & full or full & full chokes; ribbed barrels
Finish: Blued; wood semi-pistol grip stock & short tapered forearm
Approximate wt.: 6½ to 7 lbs.
Comments: Made to the mid 1970's.
Estimated Value: Excellent: $200.00
Very good: $150.00

Western Field Model 150C

Western Field Model 150C
Gauge: 410
Action: Bolt action; repeating
Magazine: 3-shot; top loading
Barrel: 25"; full choke; 3" chamber
Finish: Blued; wood Monte Carlo pistol grip one-piece
    stock & forearm
Approximate wt.: 5½ lbs.
Comments: Manufactured to the early 1980's.
Estimated Value: **Excellent:** $75.00
                 Very good: $60.00

Western Field Model 170

Western Field Model 172

Western Field Model 175

Western Field Model 170
Gauge: 12
Action: Bolt action; repeating
Magazine: 3-shot detachable clip
Barrel: 28"
Finish: Blued; wood Monte Carlo semi-pistol grip one-piece stock & forearm; recoil pad; sights; swivels
Approximate wt.: 7 lbs.
Comments: Made to the late 1970's.
Estimated Value: **Excellent:**   **$80.00**
                 Very good: **$60.00**

Western Field Model 172
Similar to the Model 170 without sights or swivels; adjustable choke.
Estimated Value: **Excellent:**   **$75.00**
                 Very good: **$55.00**

Western Field Model 175
Similar to the Model 172 in 20 gauge with a 26" barrel; without adjustable choke.
Estimated Value: **Excellent:**   **$70.00**
                 Very good: **$50.00**

Western Field Bolt Action
Gauge: 12, 20, regular or magnum, 410
Action: Bolt action; repeating
Magazine: 3-shot detachable box; 410 top loading
Barrel: 28" full choke; 25" in 410
Finish: Blued; smooth walnut finish hardwood one-piece pistol grip stock & forearm
Approximate wt.: 6½ lbs.
Comments: Add $10.00 for 12 gauge.
Estimated Value: **Excellent:**   **$75.00**
                 Very good: **$60.00**

Western Field Model 550

Western Field Model 550

Gauge: 12, 20, 410, regular or magnum
Action: Slide action; hammerless; repeating
Magazine: 4-shot magnum, 5-shot regular, tubular
Barrel: 26" 410; 30" 12 gauge; full or modified choke
Finish: Blued; smooth hardwood pistol grip stock with fluted comb, grooved slide handle
Approximate wt.: 6½ lbs.
Comments: Add $20.00 for ventilated rib & variable choke.
Estimated Value: Excellent: $145.00
    Very good: $110.00

Western Field Model 550 Deluxe

Gauge: 12, 20, regular or magnum
Action: Slide action; hammerless; repeating
Magazine: 5-shot tubular; 4-shot magnum
Barrel: 28" with 3 interchangeable "Accu-choke" tubes; ventilated rib
Finish: Blued; checkered hardwood pistol grip stock & slide handle; chrome damascened finish on bolt; recoil pad; engraved receiver
Approximate wt.: 7¼ lbs.
Comments: Presently manufactured.
Estimated Value: Excellent: $180.00
    Very good: $135.00

Winchester

Winchester Model 20

Winchester Model 37

Winchester Model 20

Gauge: 410
Action: Top lever, break-open; box lock; exposed hammer; single shot
Magazine: None
Barrel: 26" full choke
Finish: Blued; plain or checkered wood pistol grip stock & lipped forearm
Approximate wt.: 6 lbs.
Comments: Made from about 1920 to 1925.
Estimated Value: Excellent: $250.00
    Very good: $190.00

Winchester Model 37

Gauge: 12, 16, 20, 28, 410
Action: Top lever, break-open; partial visible hammer; automatic ejector
Magazine: None
Barrel: 26"-32"; full choke, modified or cylinder bore
Finish: Blued; plain walnut semi-pistol grip stock & forearm
Approximate wt.: 6 lbs.
Comments: Made from the late 1930's to mid 1960's. Add $150.00 for 28 gauge & $25.00 for 410 gauge
Estimated Value: Excellent: $190.00
    Very good: $150.00

Winchester Model 370

Winchester Model 370

Gauge: 12, 16, 20, 28, 410
Action: Top lever, break-open; box lock; exposed hammer; single shot; automatic ejector
Magazine: None
Barrel: 26"-32" or 36" full choke; modified in 20 gauge
Finish: Blued; plain wood semi-pistol grip stock & forearm
Approximate wt.: 5¼ to 6¼ lbs.
Comments: Made from the late 1960's to mid 1970's.
Estimated Value: Excellent: $80.00
    Very good: $60.00

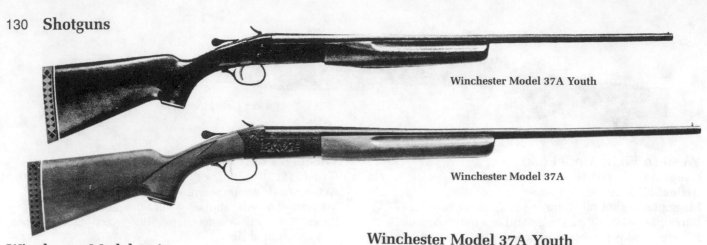

Winchester Model 37A Youth

Winchester Model 37A

Winchester Model 37A

Similar to the Model 370 but also available in 36" water-fowl barrel; has checkered stock, fluted forearm; engraved receiver; gold plated trigger. Manufactured to the late 1970's. Add $5.00 for 36" barrel.

Estimated Value: **Excellent:**   **$85.00**
                     Very good: **$65.00**

Winchester Model 37A Youth

Similar to the 37A with 26" barrel.

Estimated Value: **Excellent:**   **$75.00**
                     Very good: **$60.00**

Winchester Model 21

Winchester Model 24

Winchester Model 21

Gauge: 12, 16, 20
Action: Box lock; top lever, break-open; hammerless, double or single trigger
Magazine: None
Barrel: 26-32" double barrel; matted or ventilated rib; full, modified or cylinder bore
Finish: Checkered walnut, pistol grip stock & forearm
Approximate wt.: 7 lbs.
Comments: Made in this grade from 1930 to late 1950's. Fancier grades were produced. Prices here for Field grade.

Estimated Value: **Excellent:**   **$2,500.00**
                     Very good: **$2,000.00**

Winchester Model 23 Classic

Similar to the Model 23 Custom with 26" barrels; 12, 20 or 28 gauge improved cylinder & modified; 410 modified & full choke; engraving on receiver. Add 5% for 28 gauge or 410 bore.

Estimated Value: **New (retail):**   **$1,973.10**
                     Excellent: **$1,480.00**
                     Very good: **$1,180.00**

Winchester Model 24

Gauge: 12, 16, 20
Action: Box lock; top lever, break-open; hammerless, automatic ejectors; double triggers
Magazine: None
Barrel: Doule barrel, 28" cylinder bore & modified in 12 gauge; other modified & full choke; raised matted rib
Finish: Blued; plain or checkered walnut pistol grip stock & forearm
Approximate wt.: 7½ lbs.
Comments: Made from the late 1930's to the late 1950's.

Estimated Value: **Excellent:**   **$350.00**
                     Very good: **$265.00**

Winchester Model 23 Custom

Gauge: 12
Action: Box lock; top lever, break-open; hammerless, single selective trigger
Magazine: None
Barrel: Doubel barrel, 25½" "Winchoke"
Finish: Blued; checkered walnut, pistol grip stock & forearm
Approximate wt.: 6¾ lbs.
Comments: Introduced in 1987.

Estimated Value: **New (retail):**   **$1,973.10**
                     Excellent: **$1,480.00**
                     Very good: **$1,180.00**

Winchester Model 23XTR Pigeon Grade

Winchester Model 23 Pigeon Grade Lightweight

Winchester Model 23 Pigeon Grade Lightweight

Similar to the Model 23 XTR PIgeon Grade with a straight grip stock; rubber butt pad; 25½" ventilated rib barrels. Introduced in 1981. Discontinued in 1987. Add $40.00 for Winchoke.

| Estimated Value: | Excellent: | $1,065.00 |
| | Very good: | $ 800.00 |

Winchester Model 23 XTR Pigeon Grade

Gauge: 12, 20, regular or magnum
Action: Box lock; top lever, break-open; hammerless; selective automatic ejectors
Magazine: None
Barrel: Double barrel; 26" improved cylinder & modified; 28" modified & full choke; tapered ventilated rib; Winchoke after 1980
Finish: Blued; checkered walnut semi-pistol grip stock & forearm; silver grey engraved receiver
Approximate wt.: 6½ to 7 lbs.
Comments: Made from the late 1970's to late 1980's.

| Estimated Value: | Excellent: | $1,095.00 |
| | Very good: | $ 820.00 |

Winchester Model 101 Field

Winchester Model 101 Skeet

Winchester Xpert Model 96

Winchester Model 101 Field

Gauge: 12, 20, 28, 410, regular or magnum, 28, 410 discontinued in the late 1970's
Action: Box lock; top lever, break-open; hammerless; single trigger; automatic ejector
Magazine: None
Barrel: Over & under double barrel; 26"-30", various chokes; ventilated rib
Finish: Blued; checkered walnut pistol grip stock & wide forearm; recoil pad on magnum; engraved receiver
Approximate wt.: 6½ to 7½ lbs.
Comments: Made from the mid 1960's to about 1980. Add $30.00 for 410 or 28 gauge; $10.00 for magnum.

| Estimated Value: | Excellent: | $950.00 |
| | Very good: | $710.00 |

Winchester Model 101 Skeet

Similar to the Model 101 with skeet stock & choke. Add $30.00 for 410 or 28 gauge.

| Estimated Value: | Excellent: | $1,000.00 |
| | Very good: | $ 750.00 |

Winchester Model 101 Trap

Similar to the Model 101 with regular or Monte Carlo stock; recoil pad; 30"-32" barrels; 12 gauge only.

| Estimated Value: | Excellent: | $1,000.00 |
| | Very good: | $ 750.00 |

Winchester Xpert Model 96

A lower cost version of the Model 101, lacking engraving as well as some of the internal & external extras. Produced in the late 1970's.

| Estimated Value: | Excellent: | $650.00 |
| | Very good: | $490.00 |

Winchester Xpert Model 96 Trap

Similar to the Xpert Model 96 with Monte Carlo stock & 30" barrel.

| Estimated Value: | Excellent: | $675.00 |
| | Very good: | $500.00 |

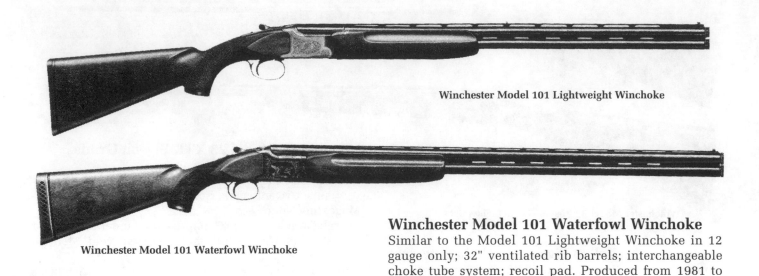

Winchester Model 101 Lightweight Winchoke

Winchester Model 101 Waterfowl Winchoke

Winchester Model 101 Waterfowl Winchoke

Similar to the Model 101 Lightweight Winchoke in 12 gauge only; 32" ventilated rib barrels; interchangeable choke tube system; recoil pad. Produced from 1981 to 1987.

Estimated Value: Excellent: $920.00
Very good: $690.00

Winchester Model 101 Lightweight Winchoke

Similar to the Model 101 Field with interchangeable choke tube system; lighter weight; ventilated rib between barrel. Introduced in 1981. 12 or 20 gauge.

Estimated Value: New (retail): $1,399.10
Excellent: $1,050.00
Very good: $ 840.00

Winchester Model 101 Waterfowler

Similar to the Model 101 Waterfowl Winchoke with sandblasted blued finish & low lustre finish. Introduced in 1987.

Estimated Value: New (retail): $1,571.00
Excellent: $1,180.00
Very good: $ 940.00

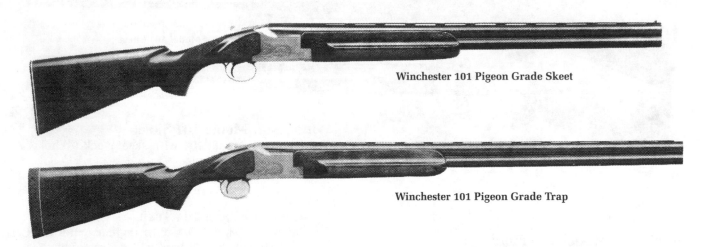

Winchester 101 Pigeon Grade Skeet

Winchester 101 Pigeon Grade Trap

Winchester 101 Pigeon Grade Skeet

Similar to the Pigeon Grade with 27" or 28" skeet choke barrels; front & center sighting beads; 410 or 28 gauge available.

Estimated Value: Excellent: $1,000.00
Very good: $ 775.00

Winchester 101 Pigeon Grade Trap

Similar to the Pigeon Grade with a 30" or 32" barrel; recoil pad; regular or Monte Carlo stock.

Estimated Value: Excellent: $950.00
Very good: $720.00

Winchester 101 Pigeon Grade

Gauge: 12, 20, regular or magnum
Action: Box lock; top lever, break-open; selective automatic ejectors; single selective trigger
Magazine: None
Barrel: Over & under doubel barrel; 26" improved cylinder & modified; 28" modified & full; ventilated rib
Finish: Blued; checkered walnut pistol grip stock & fluted forearm; silver grey engraved receiver; recoil pad on magnum
Approximate wt.: 7¼ lbs.
Comments: Made from the late 1970's to early 1980's.
Estimated Value: Excellent: $900.00
Very good: $67.00

Winchester Pigeon Grade Lightweight

Winchester Pigeon Grade Featherweight

Winchester Pigeon Grade Featherweight

Similar to the Pigeon Grade Lightweight with 25½" barrels; improved cylinder & improved modified or improved cylinder & modified; straight grip English style stock; rubber butt pad. Introduced in 1981.

Estimated Value:	New (retail):	$1,580.00
	Excellent:	$1,185.00
	Very good:	$ 890.00

Winchester Pigeon Grade Lightweight

Gauge: 12, 20, 3" chambers; 28 introduced in 1984
Action: Top lever, break-open
Magazine: None
Barrel: Over & under double barrel; 27" or 28" interchangeable choke tubes; ventilated rib on top & between barrels
Finish: Blued, silver grey stain finish receiver with etching of gamebirds & scroll work; checkered walnut rounded pistol grip stock & fluted forearm; recoil pad; straight stock available on 28 gauge
Approximate wt.: 6½ to 7½ lbs.
Comments: Introduced in 1981.

Estimated Value:	New (retail):	$1,915.00
	Excellent:	$1,435.00
	Very good:	$1,150.00

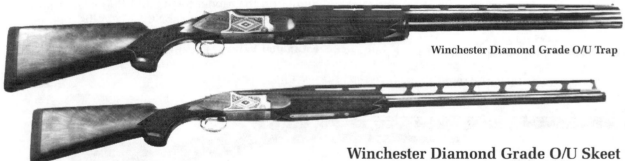

Winchester Diamond Grade O/U Trap

Winchester Diamond Grade Single Barrel

Winchester Diamond Grade O/U Trap

Gauge: 12
Action: Top lever, break-open
Magazine: None
Barrel: Over & under double barrel; 30" or 32" full choke top, interchangeable choke tube system bottom; ventilated rib on top & between barrels
Finish: Blued, silver grey stain finish on receiver with engraving; checkered walnut pistol grip stock & lipped forearm; ebony inlay in pistol grip; regular or Monte Carlo stock; recoil pad
Approximate wt.: 8¾ to 9 lbs.
Comments: Introduced in 1982.

Estimated Value:	New (retail):	$1,858.30
	Excellent:	$1,395.00
	Very good:	$1,115.00

Winchester Diamond Grade O/U Skeet

Similar to the Diamond Grade O/U Trap in 12, 20, 28 gauges & 410 bore; 27" barrels. Introduced in 1982. Add $75.00 for Winchoke.

Estimated Value:	New (retail):	$1,915.70
	Excellent:	$1,435.00
	Very good:	$1,150.00

Winchester Diamond Grade Single Barrel

Similar to the Diamond Grade O/U Trap but with only one 32" or 34" barrel; interchangeable choke tube system; high ventilated rib. Introduced in 1982.

Estimated Value:	New (retail):	$2,145.30
	Excellent:	$1,610.00
	Very good:	$1,285.00

Winchester Diamond Grade Combination

Similar to the Diamond Grade O/U Trap with a set of 30" or 32" barrels & a 34" high rib single barrel; lower barrel & single barrel use interchangeable choke tube system. Introduced in 1982

Estimated Value:	New (retail):	$2,941.80
	Excellent:	$2,200.00
	Very good:	$1,765.00

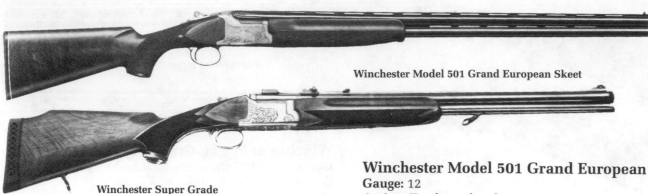

Winchester Model 501 Grand European Skeet

Winchester Super Grade

Winchester Super Grade, Shotgun Rifle

Gauge: 12, 3" chamber
Caliber: 30-06, 300 Win. mag; 243 Win.
Action: Top lever, break-open
Magazine: None
Barrel: Over & under combination; 12 gauge shotgun barrel with interchangeable choke tube system over rifle barrel
Sights: Folding leaf rear, blade front
Finish: Blued; silver grey satin finish engraved receiver; checkered walnut Monte Carlo pistol grip stock & fluted forearm; recoil pad; swivels
Approximate wt.: 8½ lbs.
Comments: A limited production shotgun/rifle combination available in early 1980's.
Estimated Value: Excellent: $1,910.00
Very good: $1,435.00

Winchester Model 501 Grand European Trap

Gauge: 12
Action: Top lever, break-open
Magazine: None
Barrel: Over & under double barrel; 30" or 32" improved modified & full choke; ventilated rib on top & between barrels
Finish: Blued; silver grey satin finish engraved receiver; checkered walnut pistol grip stock & fluted lipped forearm; regular or Monte Carlo stock; recoil pad
Approximate wt.: 8¼ to 8½ lbs.
Comments: A trap shotgun produced from the early 1980's to late 1980's.
Estimated Value: Excellent: $1,290.00
Very good: $ 975.00

Winchester Model 501 Grand European Skeet

Similar to the Model 501 Grand European Trap with 27" skeet choke barrels; weighs 6½ to 7½ lbs. Produced from 1981 to 1987. 12 or 20 gauge.
Estimated Value: Excellent: $1,290.00
Very good: $ 975.00

Winchester Model 1901

Winchester Model 36

Winchester Model 1901

Gauge: 10
Action: Lever action; repeating
Magazine: 4-shot tubular
Barrel: 30", 32" full choke
Finish: Blued; walnut, pistol grip stock & forearm
Approximate wt.: 8 to 9 lbs.
Comments: Made from 1901 to about 1920, an improved version of the Model 1887.
Estimated Value: Excellent: $650.00
Very good: $520.00

Winchester Model 36

Gauge: 9mm shot or ball cartridges
Action: Bolt action; single shot; rear cocking piece
Magazine: None
Barrel: 18"
Finish: Blued; straight grip one-piece stock & forearm
Approximate wt.: 3 lbs.
Comments: Made from the early to late 1920's.
Estimated Value: Excellent: $260.00
Very good: $210.00

Winchester Model 41

Gauge: 410
Action: Bolt action; single shot, rear cocking piece
Magazine: None
Barrel: 24" full choke
Finish: Blued; plain or checkered straight or pistol grip one-piece stock & forearm
Approximate wt.: 5 lbs.
Comments: Made from about 1920 for 15 years.
Estimated Value: Excellent: $225.00
Very good: $180.00

Winchester Model 41

Winchester Model 97

Winchester Model 97 Riot Gun

Winchester Model 97 Trench

Winchester Model 97 Trench

Similar to the 97 Riot Gun with handguard & bayonet. Used in World War I.
Estimated Value: Excellent: $600.00
Very good: $480.00

Winchester Model 97 Riot

Similar to the Model 97 with a 20" cylinder bore barrel.
Estimated Value: Excellent: $325.00
Very good: $260.00

Winchester Model 97

Gauge: 12, 16
Action: Slide action; exposed hammer; repeating
Magazine: 5-shot tubular
Barrel: 26", 28", 30", 32" modified, full choke or cylinder bore
Finish: Blued; plain wood, semi-pistol grip stock & grooved slide handle
Approximate wt.: 7¾ lbs.
Comments: Made from 1897 to late 1950's. Made in Field grade, Pigeon grade & Tournament grade. Prices for Field grade. Add $600.00 for Pigeon grade & $250.00 for Tournament grade.
Estimated Value: Excellent: $400.00
Very good: $320.00

Winchester Model 12 Pre-'65

Winchester Model 12

Gauge: 12, 16, 20, 28
Action: Slide action; hammerless; repeating
Magazine: 6-shot tubular
Barrel: 26"-32", standard chokes available
Finish: Blued; plain or checkered walnut pistol grip stock & slide handle; some slide handles grooved
Approximate wt.: 6½ to 7½ lbs.
Comments: Made in various grades: Standard, Featherweight, Rib Barrel, Riot Gun, Duck, Skeet, Trap, Pigeon, Super Pigeon from 1912 to about 1964. In 1972 Field Gun, Skeet & Trap were reissued. Deduct 50% for guns made after 1971. In 1963, Model 12 was offered with Hydro-coil recoil reducing system. Price for Standard Grade made before 1964. Add $50.00 for ventilated rib; $40.00 for raised matted rib; approximately 50% for Pigeon & approximately 120% for Super Pigeon grades. Deduct approximately 25% for Riot Gun.
Estimated Value: Excellent: $650.00
Very good: $520.00

Winchester Model 12 Skeet Pre-'65

Winchester Model 12 Trap Pre-'65

Winchester Model 12 Duck Pre-'65

Winchester Model 12 Field After '72

Winchester Model 12 Super Pigeon After '72

Winchester Model 12 Trap After '72

Winchester Model 42

Winchester Model 42 Skeet

Winchester Model 42
Gauge: 410
Action: Slide action; hammerless; repeating
Magazine: 5-shot tubular & 6-shot tubular
Barrel: 26", 28" modified, full choke or cylinder bore
Finish: Blued; plain walnut pistol grip stock & grooved slide handle
Approximate wt.: 6 lbs.
Comments: Made from the mid 1930's to mid 1960's.
Estimated Value: Excellent: $650.00
Very good: $490.00

Winchester Model 42 Skeet
Similar to the Model 42 available in straight stock; has matted rib & skeet choke barrel.
Estimated Value: Excellent: $700.00
Very good: $560.00

Winchester Model 42 Deluxe
Similar to the Model 42 with higher quality finish; ventilated rib; select wood; checkering.
Estimated Value: Excellent: $800.00
Very good: $600.00

Winchester Model 25

Winchester Model 25 Riot Gun

Winchester Model 25

Gauge: 12
Action: Slide action; hammerless; repeating
Magazine: 4-shot tubular
Barrel: 26", 28"; improved cylinder, modified or full chokes
Finish: Blued; plain walnut semi-pistol grip stock & grooved slide handle; sights
Approximate wt.: 7½ lbs.
Comments: Made from the late 1940's to mid 1950's.
Estimated Value: Excellent: $320.00
                           Very good: $255.00

Winchester Model 25 Riot Gun

Similar to the Model 25 with a 25" cylinder bore barrel.
Estimated Value: Excellent: $275.00
                           Very good: $220.00

Winchester Model 1200

Winchester Model 1200 Deer

Winchester Model 1200 Skeet

Winchester Model 1200 Trap

Winchester Model 1200 Field

Gauge: 12, 16, 20, regular or magnum; 16 gauge dropped in mid 1970's
Action: Front lock; rotary bolt; slide action; repeating
Magazine: 4-shot tubular
Barrel: 26"-30"; various chokes or adjustable choke (Winchoke)
Finish: Blued; checkered walnut pistol grip stock & slide handle; recoil pad; alloy receiver
Approximate wt.: 6½ to 7½ lbs.
Comments: Made from the late 1960's to the late 1970's. Add $15.00 for magnum; $5.00 for adjustable choke; $25.00 for ventilated rib.
Estimated Value: Excellent: $200.00
                           Very good: $150.00

Winchester Model 1200 Deer

Similar to the Model 1200 with 22" barrel, rifle sights. Made from the mid 1960's to mid 1970's.
Estimated Value: Excellent: $210.00
                           Very good: $160.00

Winchester Model 1200 Skeet

Similar to 1200 except: 12 & 20 gauge only; 26" skeet choke; ventilated rib barrel. Made to the mid 1970's.
Estimated Value: Excellent: $230.00
                           Very good: $175.00

Winchester Model 1200 Trap

Similar to the 1200 with a 30" full choke barrel; ventilated rib; regular or Monte Carlo stock. Made to the mid 1970's.
Estimated Value: Excellent: $235.00
                           Very good: $180.00

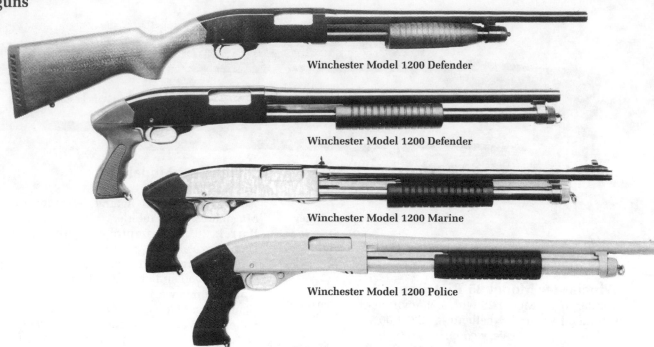

Winchester Model 1200 Defender

Winchester Model 1200 Defender

Winchester Model 1200 Marine

Winchester Model 1200 Police

Winchester Model 1200 Police

Same as the Model 1200 Defender except: stainless steel barrel & satin chrome finish on all other external metal parts. Also made with shoulder stock or pistol grip (1984) in 12 gauge only. Introduced 1982.

Estimated Value: **Excellent:**   **$290.00**

Very good: **$230.00**

Winchester Model 1200 Marine

Same as the Model 1200 Police except: rifle sights standard. Made from 1982 to present.

Estimated Value: **Excellent:**   **$290.00**

Very good: **$230.00**

Winchester Model 1200 Defender

Gauge: 12, regular & magnum, 20

Action: Slide action front lock rotary bolt

Magazine: 6-shot tubular; 5-shot in magnum

Barrel: 18" blue steel cylinder bore

Finish: Blued with plain wood semi-pistol grip stock & grooved slide handle; pistol grip model made beginning in 1984

Approximate wt.: 6¾ lbs.; pistol grip model 5½ lbs.

Comments: Made from 1982 to present. Available with rifle sights (add 7%). 20 gauge made in 1984 & 1985.

Estimated Value: **Excellent:**   **$175.00**

Very good: **$140.00**

Winchester Model 1300 XTR

Winchester Model 1300XTR Deer Gun

Winchester Model 1300XTR Deer Gun

Similar to the Model 1300XTR with a 22" barrel, rifle sights; sling; recoil pad. 12 gauge only. Made from about 1980 to mid 1980's.

Estimated Value: **Excellent:**   **$290.00**

Very good: **$232.00**

Winchester Model 1300 XTR

Gauge: 12, 20, regular or magnum

Action: Slide action; hammerless; repeating

Magazine: 3-shot tubular

Barrel: 26", 28", 30"; improved cylinder, modified or full choke; ventilated rib available

Finish: Blued; checkered walnut pistol grip stock & slide handle

Approximate wt.: 6½ lbs.

Comments: Made from the late 1970's to early 1980's. Add $15.00 for ventilated rib.

Estimated Value: **Excellent:**   **$275.00**

Very good: **$220.00**

Winchester Model 1300XTR Winchoke

Winchester Model 1300XTR Winchoke

Gauge: 12, 20 magnum
Action: Slide action; hammerless; repeating
Magazine: 4-shot tubular
Barrel: 28"; ventilated rib; Winchoke system (changeable choke tubes)
Finish: Blued; checkered walnut straight grip stock & slide handle; recoil pad on 12 gauge
Approximate wt.: 7¼ lbs.
Comments: Made from early 1980's to present. Ladies, Youth Model added 1990.
Estimated Value: New (retail): $355.00
Excellent: $265.00
Very good: $210.00

Winchester Model 1300 Featherweight

Similar to the Model 1300XTR Winchoke with a 22" barrel; weighs 6½ lbs.
Estimated Value: New (retail): $355.00
Excellent: $265.00
Very good: $210.00

Winchester Model 1300 Waterfowl

Similar to the Model 1300 Featherweight with sling swivels, 30" barrel; 12 gauge only; weighs 7 lbs.; dull finish on later models.
Estimated Value: New (retail): $367.00
Excellent: $275.00
Very good: $220.00

Winchester Model 1300 Win-Tuff Deer Gun

Similar to the Model 1300XTR Deer Gun with rifled barrel. Add 5% for laminated stock
Estimated Value: New (retail): $403.00
Excellent: $300.00
Very good: $240.00

Winchester Model 1300 Turkey

Similar to the Model 1300 Waterfowl with a 22" barrel. Camo finish available (add 5%). Add 5% for National Wild Turkey Federation Model or Ladies Model.
Estimated Value: New (retail): $384.00
Excellent: $290.00
Very good: $230.00

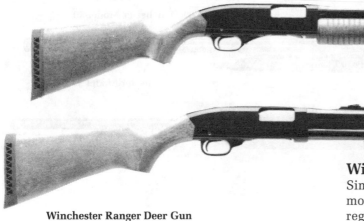

Winchester Ranger

Winchester Ranger Deer Gun

Winchester Ranger, 1300 Ranger

Gauge: 12, 20, regular or magnum interchangeably
Action: Slide action; hammerless; side ejecting
Magazine: 4-shot tubular; factory installed plug is removable
Barrel: 28"; ventilated rib available; interchangeable choke tubes
Finish: Blued; walnut-finished, semi-pistol grip stock & grooved slide handle; recoil pad
Approximate wt.: 7¼ lbs.
Comments: Introduced in 1982.
Estimated Value: New (retail): $277.00
Excellent: $205.00
Very good: $165.00

Winchester Ranger Youth, 1300 Ranger Youth

Similar to the Ranger in 20 gauge; stock & forearm are modified for young shooters. Stock can be replaced with regular size stock; 22" modified or Winchoke barrel. Introduced in 1983.
Estimated Value: New (retail): $294.00
Excellent: $220.00
Very good: $175.00

Winchester Ranger Deer Gun, 1300 Ranger Deer Gun

Similar to the Ranger with 22" or 24" cylinder bore deer barrel, rifle sights & recoil pad. Introduced in 1983.
Estimated Value: New (retail): $276.00
Excellent: $205.00
Very good: $165.00

Winchester Ranger 1300 Deer Combination

Similar to the Ranger with 24" cylinder bore deer barrel & interchangeable 28" Winchoke barrel.
Estimated Value: New (retail): $358.00
Excellent: $270.00
Very good: $215.00

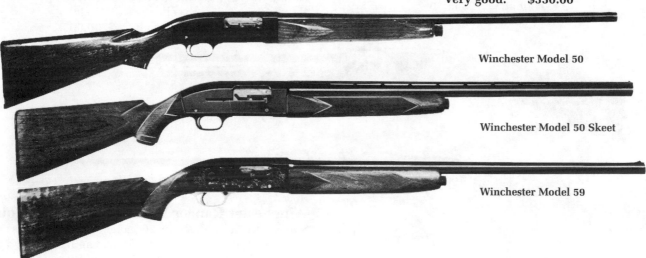

Winchester Model 1911

Winchester Model 40 Skeet

Winchester Model 50

Winchester Model 50 Skeet

Winchester Model 59

Winchester Model 40
Gauge: 12
Action: Semi-automatic; hammerless
Magazine: 4-shot tubular
Barrel: 28", 30"; modified or full choke
Finish: Blued; plain walnut pistol grip stock & forearm
Approximate wt.: 8 lbs.
Comments: Made in the early 1940's.
Estimated Value: **Excellent:** $385.00
                        Very good: $290.00

Winchester Model 40 Skeet
Similar to the Model 40 with a 24" skeet barrel; checkering; "Cutts Compensator."
Estimated Value: **Excellent:** $440.00
                        Very good: $330.00

Winchester Model 1911
Gauge: 12
Action: Semi-automatic; hammerless
Magazine: 4-shot tubular
Barrel: 26"-32"; various chokes
Finish: Blued; plain or checkered semi-pistol grip stock & forearm
Approximate wt.: 8 lbs.
Comments: Made from 1911 to the mid 1920's.
Estimated Value: **Excellent:** $500.00
                        Very good: $375.00

Winchester Model 50
Gauge: 12, 20
Action: Semi-automatic; non-recoiling barrel; hammerless
Magazine: 2-shot tubular
Barrel: 26"-30"; variety of chokes
Finish: Blued; checkered walnut pistol grip stock & forearm
Approximate wt.: 7¾ lbs.
Comments: Made from the mid 1950's to early 1960's. Add $25.00 for ventilated rib.
Estimated Value: **Excellent:** $350.00
                        Very good: $280.00

Winchester Model 50 Skeet
Similar to the Model 50 with a skeet stock; 26" skeet choke barrel; ventilated rib
Estimated Value: **Excellent:** $400.00
                        Very good: $320.00

Winchester Model 50 Trap
Similar to the Model 50 except 12 gauge only; Monte Carlo stock; 30" full choke; ventilated rib
Estimated Value: **Excellent:** $400.00
                        Very good: $320.00

Winchester Model 59
Gauge: 12
Action: Semi-automatic; hammerless; non-recoiling barrel
Magazine: 2-shot tubular
Barrel: 26"-30"; variety of chokes; steel & glass fiber composition; interchangeable choke tubes available
Finish: Blued; checkered walnut pistol grip stock & forearm; alloy receiver
Approximate wt.: 6½ lbs.
Comments: Made from the late 1950's to mid 1960's.
Estimated Value: **Excellent:** $370.00
                        Very good: $295.00

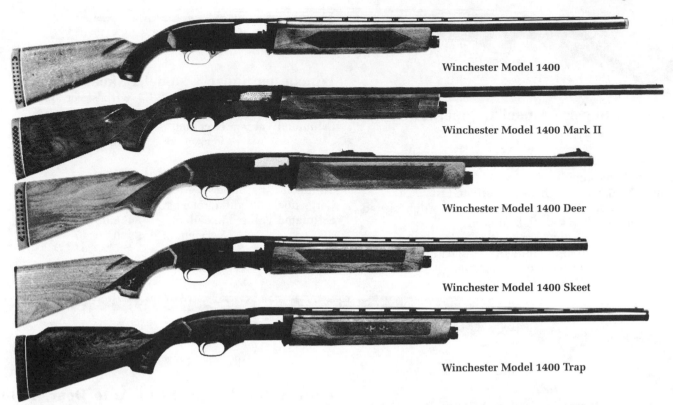

Winchester Model 1400

Winchester Model 1400 Mark II

Winchester Model 1400 Deer

Winchester Model 1400 Skeet

Winchester Model 1400 Trap

Winchester Model 1400, 1400 Winchoke

Gauge: 12, 16, 20
Action: Semi-automatic, gas operated
Magazine: 2-shot tubular
Barrel: 26", 28", 30"; variety of chokes or adjustable choke; all 1979 models have adjustable choke
Finish: Blued; checkered walnut pistol grip stock & forearm; recoil pad available; Cycolak stock available with recoil reduction system until late 1970's
Approximate wt.: 7½ lbs.
Comments: Made from the mid 1960's to late 1970's. Add $25.00 for ventilated rib or Cycolak stock & recoil reduction system.
Estimated Value: Excellent: $250.00
                     Very good: $190.00

Winchester Model 1400 Mark II

Similar to the 1400 except lighter weight & with minor improvements. Introduced in the late 1960's to late 1970's.
Estimated Value: Excellent: $240.00
                     Very good: $180.00

Winchester Model 1400 Deer Gun

Similar to the 1400 with a 22" barrel for slugs & sights.
Estimated Value: Excellent: $260.00
                     Very good: $200.00

Winchester Model 1400 Skeet

Similar to the 1400 in 12 or 20 gauge; 26" barrel with ventilated rib. Add $25.00 for recoil reduction system.
Estimated Value: Excellent: $280.00
                     Very good: $210.00

Winchester Model 1400 Trap

Similar to the 1400 in 12 gauge with a 30" full choke, ventilated rib barrel. Available with Monte Carlo stock. Add $25.00 for recoil reduction system.
Estimated Value: Excellent: $290.00
                     Very good: $210.00

Winchester Model 1500 XTR

Winchester Model 1500 XTR

Gauge: 12, 20, regular or magnum
Action: Semi-automatic, gas operated
Magazine: 3-shot tubular
Barrel: 26", 28", 30"; improved cylinder, modified or full choke; ventilated rib available
Finish: Blued; checkered walnut pistol grip stock & forearm; alloy receiver
Approximate wt.: 6½ to 7 lbs.
Comments: Made from late 1970's to early 1980's. Add $25.00 for ventilated rib.
Estimated Value: Excellent: $300.00
                     Very good: $225.00

Winchester Model 1500 XTR Winchoke

Similar to the 1500XTR with removable choke tube system; 28" barrel only; add $35.00 for ventilated rib. Made in early 1980's.
Estimated Value: Excellent: $320.00
                     Very good: $240.00

Winchester Super X Model I

Winchester Super X Model 1, Super X Model 1 XTR

Gauge: 12
Action: Semi-automatic, gas operated
Magazine: 4-shot tubular
Barrel: 26"-30"; various chokes; ventilated rib
Finish: Blued; scroll engraved alloy receiver; checkered walnut pistol grip stock & forearm
Approximate wt.: 8¼ lbs.
Comments: Made from the mid 1970's to early 1980's.
Estimated Value: Excellent: $375.00
Very good: $285.00

Winchester Super X Model 1 Skeet
Similar to the Super X Model 1 with skeet stock; 26" skeet choke; ventilated rib barrel.
Estimated Value: Excellent: $400.00
Very good: $300.00

Winchester Super X Model 1 Trap
Similar to the Super X Model 1 with regular or Monte Carlo stock; 30" full choke barrel; recoil pad.
Estimated Value: Excellent: $425.00
Very good: $320.00

Winchester Ranger Semi-Automatic

Winchester Ranger Semi-Automatic, 1400 Ranger

Gauge: 12, 20 regular or magnum
Action: Gas operated semi-automatic
Magazine: 2-shot
Barrel: 28" modified; Winchoke interchangeable tubes & ventilated rib
Finish: Blued; checkered hardwood semi-pistol grip stock & forearm
Approximate wt.: 7 lbs.
Comments: Introduced in 1983.
Estimated Value: New (retail): $351.00
Excellent: $265.00
Very good: $210.00

Winchester Ranger Semi-Auto Deer, 1400 Ranger Deer
Similar to the Ranger Semi-Automatic with 22" or 24" cylinder bore deer barrel, rifle sights. Introduced in 1984.
Estimated Value: New (retail): $349.00
Excellent: $260.00
Very good: $205.00

Winchester Ranger Semi-auto Deer Combo
Similar to the Ranger Semi-Auto Deer with extra 28" ventilated rib Winchoke barrel.
Estimated Value: New (retail): $440.00
Excellent: $330.00
Very good: $265.00

Zoli

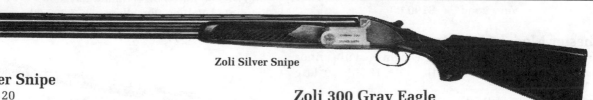

Zoli Silver Snipe

Zoli Silver Snipe

Gauge: 12, 20
Action: Box lock; top lever, break open; hammerless; single trigger
Magazine: None
Barrel: Over & under double barrel; 26", 28", 30"; ventilated rib; chrome lined
Finish: Blued; checkered walnut pistol grip stock & forearm; engraved
Approximate wt.: 7 lbs.
Comments: Manufactured in Italy.
Estimated Value: Excellent: $555.00
Very good: $445.00

Zoli Golden Snipe
Similar to the Silver Snipe with automatic ejectors.
Estimated Value: Excellent: $590.00
Very good: $475.00

Zoli 300 Gray Eagle

Gauge: 12
Action: Box lock; top lever, break-open; hammerless
Magazine: None
Barrel: Over & under double barrel; 26", 28"; ventilated rib; chrome lined; 3" chambers
Finish: Blued; checkered walnut pistol grip stock & forearm
Approximate wt.: 7 lbs.
Comments: Manufactured in Italy.
Estimated Value: Excellent: $440.00
Very good: $325.00

Zoli 302 Gray Eagle
Similar to the 300 in 20 gauge. Weight about 6¼ lbs.
Estimated Value: Excellent: $425.00
Very good: $320.00

Rifles

Anschutz

Anschutz Model 64

Anschutz Model 64S

Anschutz Model 1407

Anschutz Model 64 & 64L Match

Caliber: 22 long rifle
Action: Bolt action; single shot
Magazine: None
Barrel: Blued; 26"
Sights: None
Stock & Forearm: Match style; checkered walnut one-piece pistol grip stock & forearm; thumb rest; cheekpiece; adjustable butt plate; forward swivel
Approximate wt.: 7¾ lbs.
Comments: A match rifle made from about 1967 to the early 1980's. Add $10.00 for left hand action (64L).
Estimated Value: Excellent: $325.00
  Very good: $260.00

Anschutz Model 64S & 64SL Match

Similar to the Model 64 & 64L with special match sights. Add $20.00 for left hand version (63SL).
Estimated Value: Excellent: $350.00
  Very good: $280.00

Anschutz Mark 12 Target

Similar to the Model 64 with a heavy barrel; non-adjustable butt plate; handstop; tapered stock & forearm. Introduced in the late 1970's.
Estimated Value: Excellent: $300.00
  Very good: $240.00

Anschutz Model 1407, 1807, 1407L, 1807L

Caliber: 22 long rifle
Action: Bolt action; single shot
Magazine: None
Barrel: Blued; 26"
Sights: None
Stock & Forearm: Walnut one-piece pistol grip stock & wide forearm; thumb rest; cheekpiece; adjustable butt plate; forward swivel
Approximate wt.: 10 lbs.
Comments: A match rifle made from about 1967 to 1980's. Add $50.00 for left hand action (1407L), (1807L).
Estimated Value: Excellent: $575.00
  Very good: $460.00

Anschutz Model 184

Caliber: 22 long rifle
Action: Bolt action; repeating
Magazine: 5-shot detachable clip
Barrel: Blued; 21½"
Sights: folding leaf rear, hooded ramp front
Stock & Forearm: Checkered walnut Monte Carlo one-piece pistol grip stock & lipped forearm; swivels
Approximate wt.: 6 lbs.
Comments: Made from the mid 1960's to mid 1970's.
Estimated Value: Excellent: $225.00
  Very good: $180.00

Anschutz Model 54

Anschutz Model 54

Caliber: 22 long rifle
Action: Bolt action; repeating
Magazine: Detachable 5-shot clip or 10-shot clip
Barrel: Blued; 24"
Sights: Folding leaf rear, hooded ramp front
Stock & Forearm: Checkered walnut Monte Carlo one-piece pistol grip stock & lipped forearm
Approximate wt.: 6¾ lbs.
Comments: Made from the late 1960's to early 1980's.
Estimated Value: Excellent: $300.00
  Very good: $240.00

Anschutz Model 54M

Similar to Model 54 in 22 Winchester magnum with a 4-shot clip.
Estimated Value: Excellent: $325.00
  Very good: $275.00

Anschutz Model 1432

Anschutz Model 153

Anschutz Model 1422D

Anschutz Model 1432, 1432D Custom
Caliber: 22 Hornet
Action: Bolt action; bottom load; repeating
Magazine: 5-shot clip
Barrel: Blued; 24"
Sights: Folding leaf rear, hooded ramp front
Stock & Forearm: Checkered walnut Monte Carlo one-piece pistol grip stock & lipped forearm; swivels
Approximate wt.: 6¾ lbs.
Comments: Discontinued late 1980's.
Estimated Value: **Excellent:**   **$625.00**
                 Very good: **$500.00**

Anschutz Model 141
Caliber: 22 long rifle, 22 magnum
Action: Bolt action; repeating
Magazine: Detachable 5-shot clip
Barrel: Blued; 24"
Sights: Folding leaf rear, hooded ramp front
Stock & Forearm: Checkered walnut Monte Carlo one-piece pistol grip stock & forearm
Approximate wt.: 6 lbs.
Comments: Made from the middle to late 1960's.
Estimated Value: **Excellent:**   **$250.00**
                 Very good: **$200.00**

Anschutz Model 153
Similar to the Model 141 with abruptly ended forearm trimmed in different wood. Made from the middle to late 1960's.
Estimated Value: **Excellent:**   **$260.00**
                 Very good: **$210.00**

Anschutz Achiever
Caliber: 22 long rifle
Action: Bolt action; repeating
Magazine: 5 or 10-shot clip; single shot adapter
Barrel: 18½" blued
Sights: Hooded ramp, adjustable folding leaf rear
Stock & Forearm: Stippled European hardwood one-piece pistol grip stock & forearm; vent louvers; adjustable stock
Approximate wt.: 5 lbs.
Comments: Introduced in 1988 for range or field.
Estimated Value: **New (retail):**   **$319.50**
                 Excellent: **$240.00**
                 Very good: **$190.00**

Anschutz Model 1422D, 1522D, 1532D, Custom
Similar to the Model 1432D Custom except in different calibers: 1422D is 22 long rifle; 1522D is 22 magnum; 1532D is 222 Remington (discontinued in late 1980's).
Estimated Value:

	1422D	1522D	1532D
Excellent:	$700.00	$725.00	$650.00
Very good:	$560.00	$580.00	$520.00

Anschutz Model 1422DCL, 1522DCL, 1532DCL, Classic
Similar to the Custom models of this series except without deluxe features. Checkered walnut, one-piece pistol grip stock & tapered forearm.
Estimated Value:

	1422DCL	1522DCL	1532DCL
Excellent:	$650.00	$670.00	$600.00
Very good:	$520.00	$530.00	$480.00

Anschutz Bavarian 1700
Caliber: 22 long rifle, 22 magnum, 22 Hornet, 222 Remington
Action: Bolt action (Match 54) repeating; adjustable trigger
Magazine: 5-shot clip
Barrel: 24" blued
Sights: Hooded ramp front; folding leaf rear
Stock & Forearm: Select checkered Monte Carlo walnut one-piece pistol grip stock & forearm; swivels
Approximate wt.: 7¼ lbs.
Comments: Introduced in 1988. Add 3% for magnum, 22 Hornet or 222 Remington caliber.
Estimated Value: **New (retail):**   **$939.00**
                 Excellent: **$705.00**
                 Very good: **$565.00**

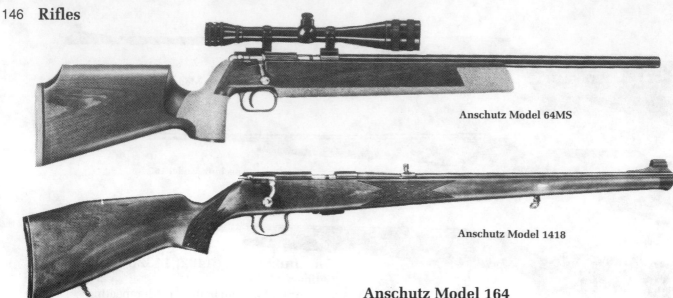

Anschutz Model 64MS

Anschutz Model 1418

Anschutz Model 1416D, 1516D

Similar to the Model 1418D, 1518D except regular length forearm, different stock with more defined pistol grip, 23" barrel. Add 7% for magnum (1516D).

Estimated Value: New (retail): $552.00
Excellent: $415.00
Very good: $330.00

Anschutz Model 64MS

Caliber: 22 long rifle
Action: Bolt action; single shot; adjustable two-stage trigger
Magazine: None
Barrel: 21¾" medium heavy
Sights: None; tapped for scope
Stock & Forearm: Silhouette-style one-piece stippled pistol grip stock & forearm
Approximate wt.: 8 lbs.
Comments: A silhouette-style rifle made from about 1982 to present; add 11% for left hand model.
Estimated Value: New (retail): $717.00
Excellent: $540.00
Very good: $430.00

Anschutz Model 54.18SMS

Similar to the Model 64MS with a 22" barrel. Weighs 8½ lbs. Add 5% for left hand model. Add 15% for Repeating Model; 45% for Repeating Deluxe (introduced 1990).

Estimated Value: New (retail): $1,212.00
Excellent: $ 900.00
Very good: $ 725.00

Anschutz Model 1411, 1811

Caliber: 22 long rifle
Action: Bolt action; single shot
Magazine: None
Barrel: 27½" heavy
Sights: None; tapped for scope
Stock & Forearm: Select walnut one-piece Monte Carlo pistol grip stock & forearm; adjustable cheekpiece; hand rest swivel; adjustable butt plate
Approximate wt.: 12 lbs.
Comments: A match-style rifle.
Estimated Value: Excellent: $600.00
Very good: $480.00

Anschutz Model 164

Caliber: 22 long rifle
Action: Bolt action; repeating
Magazine: 5-shot clip or 10-shot clip
Barrel: Blued; 23"
Sights: Folding leaf rear, hooded ramp front
Stock & Forearm: Checkered walnut Monte Carlo one-piece pistol grip stock & lipped forearm
Approximate wt.: 6 lbs.
Comments: Made from the late 1960's to early 1980's.
Estimated Value: Excellent: $300.00
Very good: $240.00

Anschutz Model 164M

Similar to the Model 164 in 22 Winchester magnum with a 4-shot clip.

Estimated Value: Excellent: $320.00
Very good: $255.00

Anschutz Model 1418, 1418D

Caliber: 22 long rifle
Action: Bolt action; repeating; double set or single set trigger
Magazine: 5-shot clip or 10-shot clip
Barrel: Blued; 19¾"
Sights: Folding leaf rear, hooded ramp front
Stock & Forearm: Checkered Eurpoean Monte Carlo stock & full length forearm; cheekpiece; swivels
Approximate wt.: 5½ lbs.
Comments: Introduced in the late 1970's. Currently called 1418D.
Estimated Value: New (retail): $830.00
Excellent: $620.00
Very good: $500.00

Anschutz Model 1433D

Similar to the Model 1418D except in 22 Hornet caliber. Discontinued late 1980's.

Estimated Value: Excellent: $660.00
Very good: $495.00

Anschutz Model 1518, 1518D

Similar to the Model 1418 except; in 22 WMR only; 4-shot clip magazine. Currently called 1518D.

Estimated Value: New (retail): $847.00
Excellent: $635.00
Very good: $510.00

Anschutz Model 520

Anschutz Mark 2000
Caliber: 22 long rifle
Action: Bolt action; hammerless; single shot
Magazine: None
Barrel: Blued; medium heavy; 26"
Sights: None; sights can be purchased separately to fit
Stock & Forearm: Smooth hardwood one-piece semi-pistol grip stock & forearm
Approximate wt.: 8½ lbs.
Comments: A match rifle designed for young shooters. Made from the early 1980's to mid 1980's.
Estimated Value: Excellent: $180.00
  Very good: $145.00

Anschutz Model 520 Sporter & Mark 525 Sporter
Caliber: 22 long rifle
Action: Semi-automatic
Magazine: 10-shot clip
Barrel: Blued; 24"
Sights: folding leaf rear, hooded ramp front
Stock & Forearm: Checkered walnut Monte Carlo semi-pistol stock & fluted forearm
Approximate wt.: 6½ lbs.
Comments: Introduced in the early 1980's; presently called Mark 525 Sporter.
Estimated Value: New (retail): $435.00
  Excellent: $325.00
  Very good: $260.00

Armalite

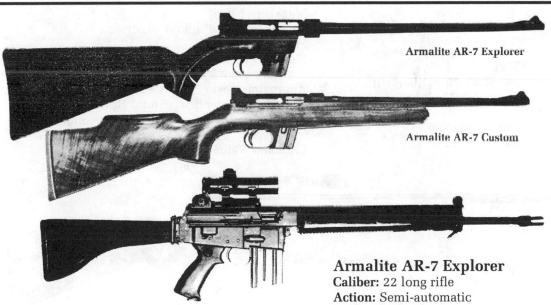

Armalite AR-7 Explorer

Armalite AR-7 Custom

Armalite AR-180 Sporter

Armalite AR-180 Sporter
Caliber: 223
Action: Semi-automatic, gas operated
Magazine: 5-shot detachable box
Barrel: Blued; 18"
Sights: Adjustable rear & front; scope available
Stock & Forearm: Pistol grip; nylon folding stock; fiberglass forearm
Approximate wt.: 6½ lbs.
Comments: Made from the early 1970's to 1980's.
Estimated Value: Excellent: $575.00
  Very good: $460.00

Armalite AR-7 Explorer
Caliber: 22 long rifle
Action: Semi-automatic
Magazine: 8-shot clip
Barrel: 16" aluminum & steel lined
Sights: Peep rear, blade front
Stock & Forearm: Fiberglass pistol grip stock (no forearm); stock acts as case for gun when dismantled
Approximate wt.: 2¾ lbs.
Comments: A lightweight alloy rifle designed to float; breaks down to fit into stock. Made from the early 1960's until the 1970's. After about 1973 marketed as Charter Arms AR-7.
Estimated Value: Excellent: $90.00
  Very good: $70.00

Armalite AR-7 Custom
A sport version of the Explorer with a walnut Monte Carlo one-piece pistol grip stock & forearm. Slightly heavier.
Estimated Value: Excellent: $110.00
  Very good: $ 85.00

Browning

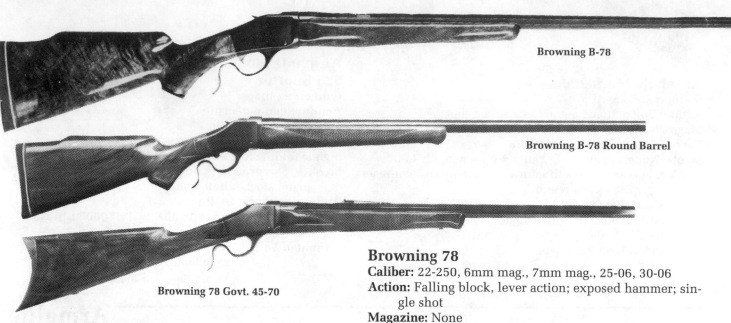

Browning B-78

Browning B-78 Round Barrel

Browning 78 Govt. 45-70

Browning 78

Caliber: 22-250, 6mm mag., 7mm mag., 25-06, 30-06
Action: Falling block, lever action; exposed hammer; single shot
Magazine: None
Barrel: Blued; 26" round or octagon
Sights: None
Stock & Forearm: Checkered walnut Monte Carlo pistol grip stock & forearm
Approximate wt.: 7¾ to 8½ lbs.
Comments: A replica of John Browning's first patented rifle in 1878. Produced from the mid 1970's to early 1980's.
Estimated Value: Excellent: $400.00
                       Very good: $320.00

Browning 78 Govt. 45-70

Similar to 78 in Government 45-70 caliber with iron sights & straight grip stock, octagonal bull barrel. Discontinued in the early 1980's.
Estimated Value: Excellent: $420.00
                       Very good: $335.00

Browning T Bolt T-1

Browning T Bolt T-2

Browning T Bolt T-1

Caliber: 22 short, long, long rifle
Action: Bolt action; hammerless; side ejection; repeating; single shot conversion
Magazine: Removable 5-shot box
Barrel: Blued; 22"
Sights: Peep rear, ramp front
Stock & Forearm: Walnut one-piece pistol grip stock & forearm
Approximate wt.: 6 lbs.
Comments: Made from the mid 1960's to the mid 1970's in Belgium.
Estimated Value: Excellent: $300.00
                       Very good: $240.00

Browning T Bolt T-2

A fancy version of the T-Bolt T-1 with checkered stock & forearm.
Estimated Value: Excellent: $375.00
                       Very good: $300.00

Browning High Power Safari

Browning High Power Medallion

Browning High Power Medallion

A higher grade version of the Safari with more engraving & higher quality wood.

Estimated Value: Excellent: $975.00 - $1,200.00
Very good: $700.00 - $ 900.00

Browning High Power Olympian

Highest grade of High Power models with complete engraving & some gold inlay.

Estimated Value: Excellent: $1,500.00 - $2,500.00
Very good: $1,100.00 - $1,875.00

Browning High Power Safari

Caliber: 243, 270, 30-06, 308, 300 mag., 375 mag. in 1960; later in 264, 338, 222, 22-250, 243, 7mm mag.
Action: Mauser-type bolt action; repeating
Magazine: 3 or 5-shot clip, depending on caliber
Barrel: Blued; 22" or 24"
Sights: Adjustable sporting rear, hooded ramp front
Stock & Forearm: Checkered walnut Monte Carlo one-piece pistol grip stock & forearm; magnum calibers have recoil pad; swivels
Approximate wt.: 6 to 8 lbs.
Comments: Made from about 1960 through the mid 1970's. Short or medium action worth $25.00 less.
Estimated Value: Excellent: $775.00
Very good: $585.00

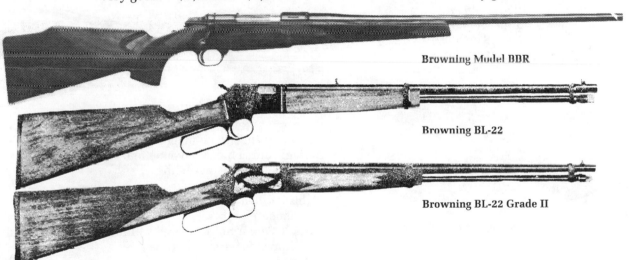

Browning Model BBR

Browning BL-22

Browning BL-22 Grade II

Browning BL-22

Caliber: 22 short, long, long rifle (any combination)
Action: Lever action; short throw lever; exposed hammer
Magazine: Tubular; 15 long rifles; 17 longs; 22 shorts
Barrel: Blued; 20"
Sights: Folding adjustable rear, bead front
Stock & Forearm: Plain walnut straight grip stock & forearm; barrel band
Approximate wt.: 5 lbs.
Comments: A small, lightweight 22 caliber rifle produced from about 1959 to present.
Estimated Value: New (retail): $286.00
Excellent: $215.00
Very good: $170.00

Browning BL-22 Grade II

Similar to BL-22 with engraving; gold plated trigger; checkered stock & forearm.

Estimated Value: New (retail): $326.95
Excellent: $245.00
Very good: $195.00

Browning Model BBR, BBR Lightning Bolt

Caliber: 30-06 Sprg., 270 Win., 25-06 Rem., 7mm Rem. mag., 300 Win. mag.
Action: Bolt action; short throw; cocking indicator; repeating
Magazine: 4-shot; 3-shot in magnum; hinged floorplate, detachable box
Barrel: 24" floating barrel, recessed muzzle
Sights: None; tapped for scope
Stock & Forearm: Checkered walnut Monte Carlo one-piece pistol grip stock & forearm; cheekpiece; low profile sling studs; recoil pad on magnum; stock & forearm changed slightly in 1982
Approximate wt.: 8 lbs.
Comments: A high powered hunting rifle made from late 1970's to 1985. A limited edition (1,000) with engraved elk scenes was introduced in 1984.
Estimated Value: Excellent: $375.00
Very good: $280.00

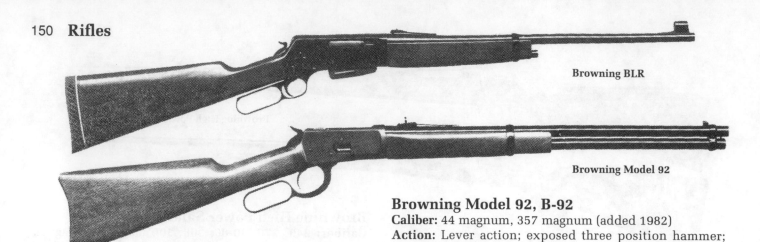

Browning BLR

Browning Model 92

Browning Model 92, B-92
Caliber: 44 magnum, 357 magnum (added 1982)
Action: Lever action; exposed three position hammer; repeating
Magazine: 11-shot tubular
Barrel: 20" round
Sights: Adjustable cloverleaf rear, blade front
Stock & Forearm: Plain walnut straight grip stock & forearm; barrel band
Approximate wt.: 5½ lbs.
Comments: An authentic remake of the 1892 Winchester designed by John Browning. Introduced in the late 1970's. Discontinued in late 1980's.
Estimated Value: Excellent: $285.00
                     Very good: $230.00

Browning BLR, '81 BLR
Caliber: 243, 308, 358; 22-250 Rem. (added in 1982); Added calibers 222, 223 Rem., 257 Roberts, 7mm-08 Rem. in mid 1980's
Action: Lever action; exposed hammer; repeating
Magazine: 4-shot removable box
Barrel: Blued; 20"
Sights: Adjustable rear, hooded ramp front
Stock & Forearm: Checkered walnut straight grip stock & forearm; recoil pad; barrel band
Approximate wt.: 7 lbs.
Comments: A carbine produced from early 1970's to present; also available without sights (deduct $15.00).
Estimated Value: New (retail): $449.95
                     Excellent: $335.00
                     Very good: $270.00

Browning Model 1895

Browning Model 1885
Caliber: 223 Rem., 22-250 Rem., 270 Win., 30-06 Springfield, 7mm Rem. magnum, 45-70 Gov't
Action: Falling block, lever action; single shot
Magazine: None, single shot
Barrel: 28" octagon, blued
Sights: Drilled & tapped for scope; open sights on 45-70 model
Stock & Forearm: Checkered walnut straight grip stock & lipped forearm; recoil pad
Approximate wt.: 8¾ lbs.
Comments: Introduced in 1985. Based on John Browning's Winchester 1885.
Estimated Value: New (retail): $639.95
                     Excellent: $480.00
                     Very good: $385.00

Browning Model 1895
Caliber: 30-06 Springfield
Action: Lever action; exposed hammer; repeating
Magazine: 5-shot non-detachable box
Barrel: 24"
Sights: Buckhorn rear, beaded ramp front
Stock & Forearm: Walnut straight grip stock & lipped forearm; High Grade has checkered stock with engraved steel grey receiver
Approximate wt.: 8 lbs.
Comments: Produced in mid 1980's, this is a newer version of John Browning's Model 1895 first produced by Winchester in 1896. Add 50% for High Grade.
Estimated Value: Excellent: $430.00
                     Very good: $345.00

Browning Model 1886
Caliber: 45-70 Gov't
Action: Lever action; exposed hammer; repeating
Magazine: 8-shot tubular, side-port load
Barrel: 26" octagon
Sights: Open buckhorn
Stock & Forearm: Smooth walnut straight-grip stock & forearm; metal, crescent buttplate
Approximate wt.: 9¼ lbs.
Comments: Based on the Winchester Model 1886 designed by John Browning. Produced in late 1980's. Add 80% for High Grade.
Estimated Value: Excellent: $450.00
                     Very good: $360.00

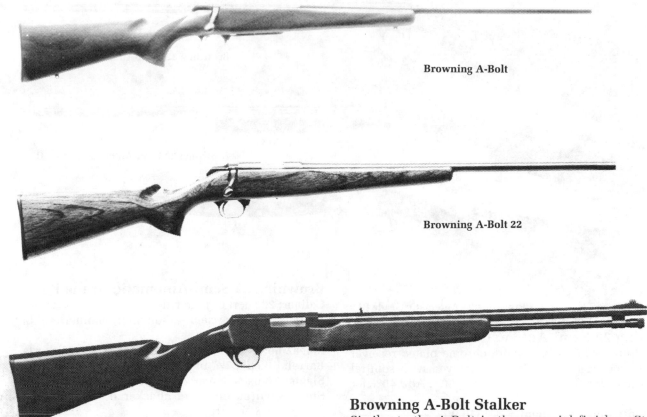

Browning A-Bolt

Browning A-Bolt 22

Browning Model BPR

Browning A-Bolt

Caliber: 22-250 Rem., 257 Roberts, 7mm-08 Rem., 25-06 Rem., 243 Win., 270 Win., 7mm Rem. magnum, 300 Win. magnum, 30-06 Springfield, 308 Win., 338 Win. magnum, 375 H&H

Action: Bolt action; hammerless; repeating; short or long action

Magazine: Hinged floorplate with detachable box 4-shot; 3-shot magnum

Barrel: 22" or 24" blued

Sights: None, drilled & tapped for scope mounts. Hunter model available with iron sights

Stock & Forearm: Checkered walnut, one-piece pistol grip stock & forearm; swivels; recoil pad on magnum

Approximate wt.: 6½ to 7¼ lbs.

Comments: Introduced in 1985; add 35% for 375 H&H; add 10% for sights; Gold Medallion has higher quality finish (add 50%).

Estimated Value:	New (retail):	$411.95
	Excellent:	$300.00
	Very good:	$240.00

Browning A-Bolt 22

Similar to the A-Bolt in 22 long rifle caliber; 5 or 15 shot clip; 22" barrel; wt. 5½ lbs.

Estimated Value:	New (retail):	$329.95
	Excellent:	$250.00
	Very good:	$200.00

Browning A-Bolt Stalker

Similar to the A-Bolt in three special finishes. Stainless Stalker has matte stainless steel finish with graphite fiberglass composite stock (add 25%); Camo Stalker has multi-laminated wood stock with various shades of black & green, matte blue finish (add 5%); Composite Stalker has graphite/fiberglass composite stock.

Estimated Value:	New (retail):	$411.95
	Excellent:	$310.00
	Very good:	$245.00

Browning A-Bolt Micro Medallion

A scaled-down version of the A-Bolt series; 20" barrel, 3-shot magazine.

Estimated Value:	New (retail):	$478.95
	Excellent:	$360.00
	Very good:	$230.00

Browning Model BPR

Caliber: 22 long rifle; 22 Win. mag.

Action: Slide action; hammerless; repeating; slide release on trigger guard

Magazine: 15-shot tubular; 11-shot on magnum

Barrel: 20¼"

Sights: Adjustable folding leaf rear, gold bead front

Stock & Forearm: Checkered walnut pistol grip stock & slide handle

Approximate wt.: 6¼ lbs.

Comments: Made from the late 1970's to early 1980's.

Estimated Value:	Excellent:	$200.00
	Very good:	$160.00

Browning Model BPR Grade II

Similar to the BPR in magnum only; engraved squirrels & rabbits on receiver.

Estimated Value:	Excellent:	$300.00
	Very good:	$230.00

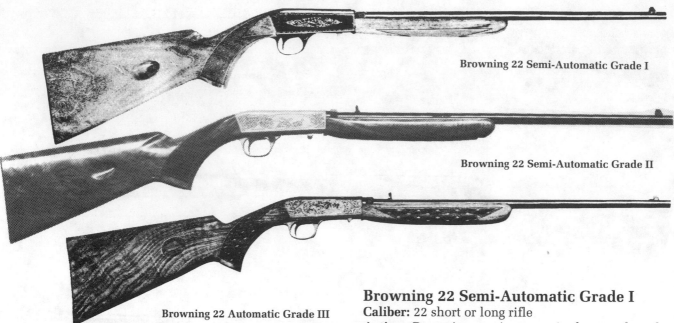

Browning 22 Semi-Automatic Grade I

Browning 22 Semi-Automatic Grade II

Browning 22 Automatic Grade III

Browning 22 Semi-Automatic Grade II

Similar to the 22 automatic with chrome plated receiver & gold plated trigger. Receiver is engraved with squirrel scene. Made from mid 1950's to mid 1980's. Add 40% for FN.

Estimated Value: Excellent: $310.00
                      Very good: $250.00

Browning 22 Semi-Automatic Grade III

This is the same rifle as the Grade II except engraving is of bird dog & birds, high quality finish. Made from mid 1950's to mid 1980's. Add 40% for FN.

Estimated Value: Excellent: $670.00
                      Very good: $535.00

Browning 22 Semi-Automatic Grade I

Caliber: 22 short or long rifle
Action: Browning semi-automatic; hammerless; bottom ejection
Magazine: Tubular in stock; 11 long rifles; 16 shorts
Barrel: Blued; 22¼" in long rifle; 19¼" in 22 short
Sights: Adjustable rear, dovetail bead front
Stock & Forearm: Hand checkered walnut pistol grip stock & forearm
Approximate wt.: 4¾ lbs.
Comments: This takedown model has been in production since the mid 1950's. Add 40% for FN.

Estimated Value: New (retail): $328.50
                      Excellent: $245.00
                      Very good: $195.00

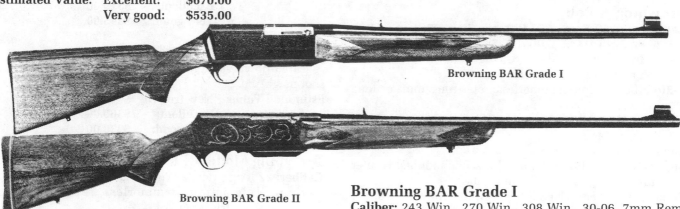

Browning BAR Grade I

Browning BAR Grade II

Browning BAR Grade II

Engraved version of BAR. Discontinued in the early 1970's. Add $50.00 for magnum.

Estimated Value: Excellent: $525.00
                      Very good: $420.00

Browning BAR Grade III

Similar to Grade I with elaborate engraving featuring antelope head. Discontinued early 1970's. Reintroduced in 1979 with rams & elk engravings. Add $60.00 for magnum. Discontinued in mid 1980's.

Estimated Value: Excellent: $900.00
                      Very good: $720.00

Browning BAR Grade I

Caliber: 243 Win., 270 Win., 308 Win., 30-06, 7mm Rem. mag., 300 Win. mag., 338 Win. mag.
Action: Semi-automatic gas operated; side ejection; hammerless
Magazine: 4-shot; 3-shot in magnum
Barrel: Blued; 22" or 24"
Sights: Folding rear, hooded ramp front, or without sights
Stock & Forearm: Checkered walnut pistol grip stock & forearm; swivels; recoil pad on mags
Approximate wt.: 7 to 8¼ lbs.
Comments: Made from the late 1960's to present. Add 10% for magnum calibers.

Estimated Value: New (retail): $541.95
                      Excellent: $405.00
                      Very good: $320.00

Browning BAR Grade IV

Browning Model BAR-22 Grade II

Browning Model BAR-22 Grade II

Similar to Grade I with elaborate engraving featuring two running antelope & running deer. Magnum has moose & elk engravings. Add 5% for magnum caliber. Produced until mid 1980's.

Estimated Value: Excellent: $1,375.00
                  Very good: $1,100.00

Browning BAR-22 Grade V

Similar to other grades of BAR. This is the fanciest model. Discontinued in the early 1970's.

Estimated Value: Excellent: $2,750.00
                  Very good: $2,200.00

Browning Model BAR-22

Caliber: 22 long rifle
Action: Semi-automatic; blow back; hammerless; repeating
Magazine: 15-shot tubular
Barrel: 20" reversed muzzle
Sights: Adjustable folding leaf rear, gold bead front
Stock & Forearm: Checkered walnut pistol grip stock & forearm; fluted comb
Approximate wt.: 5¾ lbs.
Comments: Produced in the late 1970's to mid 1980's.

Estimated Value: Excellent: $200.00
                  Very good: $160.00

Browning Model BAR-22 Grade II

Similar to the BAR-22 with engraved receiver, squirrels & rabbits.

Estimated Value: Excellent: $260.00
                  Very good: $195.00

BSA

BSA Model 12

Caliber: 22 long rifle
Action: Martini-type; single shot
Magazine: None
Barrel: 29"; blued
Sights: Matched sights; some with open sights
Stock & Forearm: Checkered walnut straight grip stock & forearm; swivels
Approximate wt.: 9 lbs.
Comments: Made in England from about 1910 to 1930.

Estimated Value: Excellent: $275.00
                  Very good: $200.00

BSA Model 12

BSA Model 13

Similar to Model 12 with a 25" barrel. Weighs about 6 lbs.

Estimated Value: Excellent: $240.00
                  Very good: $185.00

BSA Model 13 Sporting

Similar to Model 13 in 22 Hornet caliber.

Estimated Value: Excellent: $300.00
                  Very good: $225.00

BSA Model 15

Caliber: 22 long rifle
Action: Martini-type; single shot
Magazine: None
Barrel: Blued; 29"
Sights: Special BSA match sights
Stock & Forearm: Walnut stock & forearm; cheekpiece; swivels
Approximate wt.: 9½ lbs.
Comments: A match rifle made in England from about 1915 to the early 1930's.

Estimated Value: Excellent: $350.00
                  Very good: $280.00

BSA Centurion

Similar to Model 15 with a special barrel guaranteed to produce accurate groups.

Estimated Value: Excellent: $360.00
                  Very good: $280.00

BSA Model 12/15

Similar to Model 12 & 15 in pre-war & post-war models. Made to about 1950.

Estimated Value: Excellent: $300.00
                  Very good: $240.00

BSA Model 12/15

BSA Model 12/15 Heavy Barrel

Similar to Model 12/15 with heavy barrel. Weighs about 11 lbs.

Estimated Value: Excellent: $325.00
                  Very good: $260.00

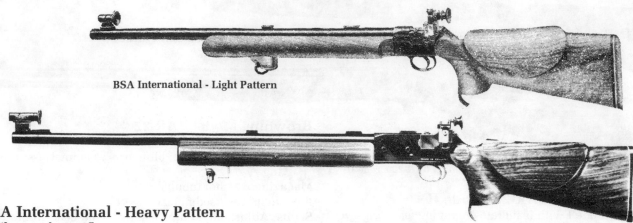

BSA International - Light Pattern

BSA International Mark III

BSA International - Heavy Pattern

Caliber: 22 long rifle
Action: Martini-type; single shot
Magazine: None
Barrel: Blued; 29" heavy
Sights: Special Parker-Hale match sights
Stock & Forearm: Match style pistol grip stock with cheekpiece, wide forearm; hand stop; swivels
Approximate wt.: 13¾ lbs.
Comments: A target rifle made in England in the early 1950's.
Estimated Value: Excellent: $440.00
Very good: $350.00

BSA International - Light Pattern

Similar to Heavy Pattern but lighter weight with a 26" barrel.
Estimated Value: Excellent: $375.00
Very good: $300.00

BSA International Mark II

Similar to Heavy & Light Patterns (choice of barrel). Stock & forearm changed slightly. Made from early to late 1950's.
Estimated Value: Excellent: $400.00
Very good: $320.00

BSA International Mark III

Similar to Heavy Pattern with: different stock & forearm; alloy frame; floating barrel. Made from the late 1950's to late 1960's.
Estimated Value: Excellent: $475.00
Very good: $380.00

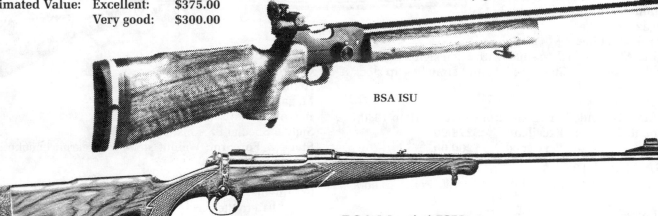

BSA ISU

BSA Majestic Deluxe

BSA Majestic Deluxe

Caliber: 22 Hornet, 222, 243, 30-06, 308 Win., 7x57 mm
Action: Mauser-type bolt action; repeating
Magazine: 4-shot box
Barrel: Blued; 22"
Sights: Folding leaf rear, hooded ramp front
Stock & Forearm: Checkered walnut Monte Carlo one-piece pistol grip stock & lipped forearm; swivels; cheekpiece; recoil pad
Approximate wt.: 7½ lbs.
Comments: Made in England from the early to mid 1960's.
Estimated Value: Excellent: $300.00
Very good: $240.00

BSA Martini ISU

Caliber: 22 long rifle
Action: Martini-type; single shot
Magazine: None
Barrel: Blued; 28"
Sights: Special Parker-Hale match sights
Stock & Forearm: Match style walnut pistol grip; adjustable butt plate
Approximate wt.: 10½ lbs.
Comments: A match rifle, made in England.
Estimated Value: Excellent: $525.00
Very good: $420.00

BSA Mark V

Similar to ISU with a heavy barrel. Weighs about 12½ lbs.
Estimated Value: Excellent: $560.00
Very good: $450.00

BSA Majestic Deluxe Featherweight

BSA Monarch Deluxe

BSA Deluxe Varmint

BSA Majestic Deluxe Featherweight

Similar to Deluxe with recoil reducer in barrel. Available in some magnum calibers.

Estimated Value: Excellent: **$300.00**
    Very good: **$240.00**

BSA Monarch Deluxe

Similar to Majestic Deluxe with slight changes in stock & forearm & with a recoil pad. Made from mid 1960's to late 1970's.

Estimated Value: Excellent: **$275.00**
    Very good: **$220.00**

BSA Deluxe Varmint

Similar to Monarch Deluxe with a heavier 24" barrel.

Estimated Value: Excellent: **$290.00**
    Very good: **$230.00**

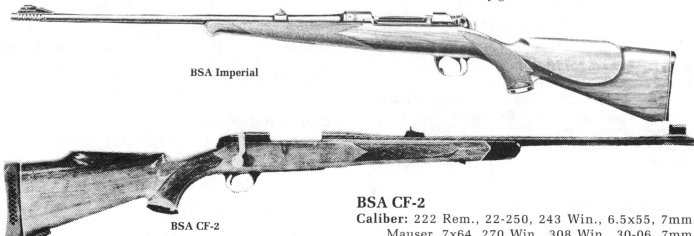

BSA Imperial

BSA CF-2

BSA Imperial

Caliber: 22 Hornet, 222, 243, 257 Roberts, 270 Win., 7x57mm, 300 Savage, 30-06, 308 Win.
Action: Bolt action; repeating
Magazine: 4-shot box
Barrel: Blued; 22"; recoil reducer
Sights: Open rear, ramp front
Stock & Forearm: Checkered walnut Monte Carlo one-piece pistol grip stock & lipped forearm; cheekpiece
Approximate wt.: 7 lbs.
Comments: Made in the early 1960's.
Estimated Value: Excellent: **$310.00**
    Very good: **$250.00**

BSA CF-2

Caliber: 222 Rem., 22-250, 243 Win., 6.5x55, 7mm Mauser, 7x64, 270 Win., 308 Win., 30-06, 7mm Rem. mag., 300 Win. mag.
Action: Bolt action; repeating
Magazine: 4- or 5-shot box, 3-shot in magnum
Barrel: Blued; 23½"; 24" heavy barrel available in some calibers
Sights: Hooded ramp front, adjustable rear
Stock & Forearm: Checkered walnut Monte Carlo one-piece pistol grip stock & forearm; cheekpiece; contrasting fore-end tip & grip cap; swivels; recoil pad; European style has oil finish, American style has polyeurethane finish with white spacers.
Approximate wt.: 7½ to 8½ lbs.
Comments: Add 14% for European style; 8% for magnum calibers with heavy barrel.
Estimated Value: Excellent: **$360.00**
    Very good: **$270.00**

Carl Gustaf

Carl Gustaf Grade II

Carl Gustaf Grade II Magnum

Carl Gustaf Grade III

Carl Gustaf Swede

Carl Gustaf Grade II
Caliber: 22-250, 243, 25-06, 270, 6.5x55, 30-06, 308
Action: Bolt action; repeating
Magazine: 5-shot staggered column
Barrel: Blued; 23½"
Sights: Leaf rear, hooded ramp front
Stock & Forearm: Checkered walnut Monte Carlo one-piece pistol grip stock & forearm; swivels
Approximate wt.: 7 lbs.
Comments: Manufactured in Sweden.
Estimated Value: Excellent: $475.00
                       Very good: $380.00

Carl Gustaf Grade II Magnum
Similar to Grade II except magnum calibers; recoil pad; 3-shot magazine.
Estimated Value: Excellent: $500.00
                       Very good: $400.00

Carl Gustaf Varmint-Target

Carl Gustaf Grade III
Similar to Grade II with: select wood; more checkering; high quality finish; no sights.
Estimated Value: Excellent: $575.00
                       Very good: $460.00

Carl Gustaf Grade III Magnum
Similar to Grade II Magnum with: select wood; more checkering; high quality finish; no sights.
Estimated Value: Excellent: $600.00
                       Very good: $480.00

Carl Gustaf Swede
Similar to Grade II with lipped forearm but lacking the Monte Carlo comb.
Estimated Value: Excellent: $500.00
                       Very good: $400.00

Carl Gustaf Swede Deluxe
Similar to Grade III with lipped forearm.
Estimated Value: Excellent: $600.00
                       Very good: $480.00

Carl Gustaf Varmint Target
Caliber: 22-250, 222, 243, 6.5x55
Action: Bolt action; repeating; large bolt knob
Magazine: 5-shot staggered column
Barrel: Blued; 27"
Sights: None
Stock & Forearm: Plain walnut Monte Carlo one-piece pistol grip stock & forearm
Approximate wt.: 9½ lbs.
Comments: Manufactured in Sweden.
Estimated Value: Excellent: $500.00
                       Very good: $375.00

Charles Daly

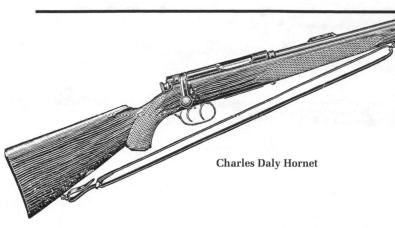

Charles Daly Hornet

Charles Daly Hornet
Caliber: 22 Hornet
Action: Bolt action; double triggers
Magazine: 5-shot box
Barrel: 24"
Sights: Leaf rear, hooded ramp front
Stock & Forearm: Checkered walnut one-piece stock & forearm
Approximate wt.: 7¾ lbs.
Comments: Made during the 1930's. Also marked under the name Herold Rifle.
Estimated Value: Excellent: $900.00
Very good: $675.00

Charter Arms

Charter Arms AR-7

Charter Arms AR-7 Explorer
Caliber: 22 long rifle
Action: Semi-automatic
Magazine: 8-shot clip
Barrel: 16" aluminum & steel lined, black or silvertone
Sights: Peep rear, blade front
Stock & Forearm: Fiberglass, pistol grip stock (no forearm); stock acts as case for gun when dismantled. Also available in silvertone or camouflage
Approximate wt.: 2¾ lbs.
Comments: A lightweight alloy rifle designed to float. Also dismantles to fit into stock. Made from about 1973 to present. Made by Armalite from about 1960 to 1973.

Estimated Value: New (retail): $166.00
Excellent: $130.00
Very good: $100.00

Colt

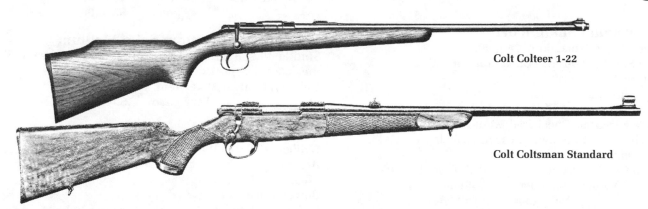

Colt Colteer 1-22

Colt Coltsman Standard

Colt Colteer 1-22
Caliber: 22 short, long, long rifle
Action: Bolt action; hammerless; single shot
Magazine: None
Barrel: Blued; 20", 22"
Sights: Open rear, ramp front
Stock & Forearm: Plain walnut Monte Carlo pistol grip stock & forearm
Approximate wt.: 5 lbs.
Comments: Made for 10 years from about 1957.
Estimated Value: Excellent: $85.00
Very good: $65.00

Colt Coltsman Standard
Caliber: 300 H & H magnum, 30-06
Action: Mauser-type, bolt action; repeating
Magazine: 5-shot box
Barrel: Blued; 22"
Sights: No rear, ramp front
Stock & Forearm: Checkered walnut one-piece pistol grip stock & tapered forearm; swivels
Approximate wt.: 7 lbs.
Comments: Made fromabout 1957 to the early 1960's.
Estimated Value: Excellent: $360.00
Very good: $270.00

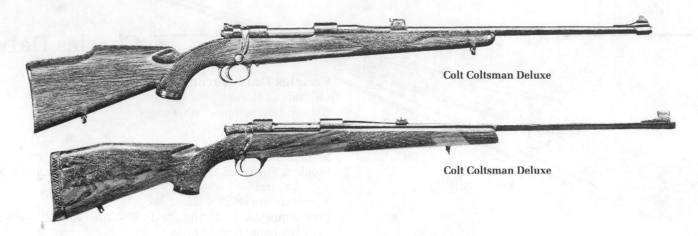

Colt Coltsman Deluxe

Colt Coltsman Deluxe

Colt Colstman Custom

Similar to the deluxe with: select wood; cheekpiece; engraving.

Estimated Value: Excellent: $470.00
                       Very good: $355.00

Colt Colstman Deluxe

Similar to standard with: higher quality wood & finish; adjustable rear sight; Monte Carlo stock.

Estimated Value: Excellent: $400.00
                       Very good: $300.00

Colt Coltsman Sako Custom

Colt Colstman Sako-Medium

Caliber: 243, 308 Win.
Action: Medium stroke, Sako-type bolt action; repeating
Magazine: 5-shot box
Barrel: Blued; 24"
Sights: Folding leaf rear, hooded ramp front
Stock & Forearm: Checkered walnut Monte Carlo one-piece pistol grip stock & tapered forearm
Approximate wt.: 7 lbs.
Comments: Made from the early to mid 1960's.
Estimated Value: Excellent: $360.00
                       Very good: $290.00

Colt Colstman Sako-Short

Caliber: 222, 222 magnum, 243, 308
Action: Short Sako-type bolt action; repeating
Magazine: 5-shot box
Barrel: Blued; 22"
Sights: Open rear, hooded ramp front
Stock & Forearm: Checkered walnut Monte Carlo pistol grip stock & tapered forearm; swivels
Approximate wt.: 7 lbs.
Comments: Made from the late 1950's to mid 1960's.
Estimated Value: Excellent: $350.00
                       Very good: $260.00

Colt Colstman Deluxe Sako-Short

Similar to Sako-Short with: adjustable rear sight; higher quality finish; in calibers 243, 308. Discontinued in the early 1960's.

Estimated Value: Excellent: $400.00
                       Very good: $320.00

Colt Colstman Custom Sako-Short

Similar to Deluxe Sako-Short with: select wood; cheekpiece; engraving. Made until mid 1960's.

Estimated Value: Excellent: $450.00
                       Very good: $345.00

Colt Colstman Custom Sako-Medium

Similar to standard Sako-Medium with higher quality finish & recoil pad.

Estimated Value: Excellent: $425.00
                       Very good: $340.00

Colt Colstman Sako-Long

Caliber: 264, 270 Win., 300 H&H, 30-06, 375 H&H
Action: Long stroke, Sako-type bolt action; repeating
Magazine: 5-shot box
Barrel: Blued; 24"
Sights: Folding leaf rear, hooded ramp front
Stock & Forearm: Checkered walnut one-piece pistol grip stock & tapered forearm; swivels
Approximate wt.: 7 lbs.
Comments: Made from the early to mid 1960's.
Estimated Value: Excellent: $375.00
                       Very good: $300.00

Colt Colstman Custom Sako-Long

Similar to Sako-Long with: higher quality finish; recoil pad; Monte Carlo stock.

Estimated Value: Excellent: $420.00
                       Very good: $335.00

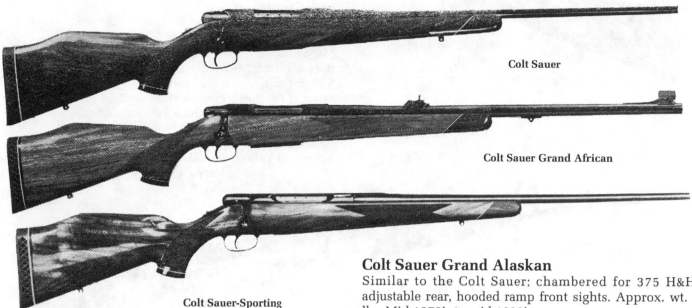

Colt Sauer

Colt Sauer Grand African

Colt Sauer-Sporting

Colt Sauer

Caliber: 25-06, 270, 30-06, 300 Win. mag., 7mm Rem. mag., 300 Weath. mag., 375 H&H mag., 458 Win. mag.

Action: Long stroke, Sauer-type bolt action; repeating

Magazine: 5-shot detachable box

Barrel: Blued; 24"

Sights: None; tapped for scope

Stock & Forearm: Checkered walnut Monte Carlo one-piece pistol grip stock & tapered forearm; swivels; recoil pad

Approximate wt.: 7½ to 8 lbs.

Comments: Made from early 1970's to mid 1980's. Add $50.00 for magnum.

Estimated Value: **Excellent:**   **$950.00**
                   Very good: **$765.00**

Colt Sauer Grand Alaskan

Similar to the Colt Sauer; chambered for 375 H&H; adjustable rear, hooded ramp front sights. Approx. wt. 9 lbs. Mid 1970's to mid 1980's.

Estimated Value: **Excellent:**   **$1,000.00**
                   Very good: **$ 750.00**

Colt Sauer Grand African

Similar to Sauer with: higher quality finish; adjustable sights; 458 Win. caliber only; 10 lbs. Mid 1970's to mid 1980's.

Estimated Value: **Excellent:**   **$1,075.00**
                   Very good: **$ 860.00**

Colt Sauer-Sporting

Similar to Sauer with: short stroke action; chambered for 22-250, 243, 308 calibers. Made from mid 1970's to mid 1980's. Approx. wt. 7½ to 8½ lbs.

Estimated Value: **Excellent:**   **$945.00**
                   Very good: **$710.00**

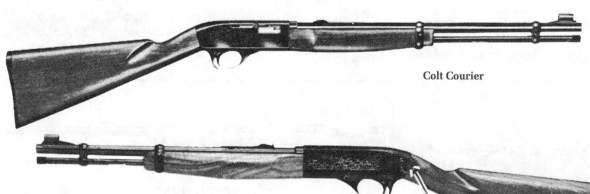

Colt Courier

Colt Stagecoach

Colt Courier

Caliber: 22 long rifle

Action: Semi-automatic

Magazine: 15-shot tubular

Barrel: Blued; 19½"

Sights: Open rear, hooded ramp front

Stock & Forearm: Plain walnut straight grip stock & forearm; barrel band

Approximate wt.: 5 lbs.

Comments: Made from the mid 1960's to late 1970's.

Estimated Value: **Excellent:**   **$100.00**
                   Very good: **$ 80.00**

Colt Stagecoach

Similar to the Courier with: engraving, 16½" barrel; saddle ring with leather string. Made from mid 1960's to 1976.

Estimated Value: **Excellent:**   **$110.00**
                   Very good: **$ 85.00**

Colt Lightning

Colt Lightning

Caliber: 22 long rifle
Action: Slide action; exposed hammer; repeating
Magazine: Tubular: 15 longs, 16 shorts
Barrel: Blued; 24" round or octagon
Sights: Open rear, bead front
Stock & Forearm: Plain walnut straight pistol grip stock & checkered slide handle
Approximate wt.: 5¾ lbs.
Comments: Made from the 1880's to about 1905.
Estimated Value: Excellent: $600.00
                      Very good: $450.00

Colt AR-15

Colt AR-15, AR-15A2, AR-15A2 Carbine

Caliber: 223; 9mm (1986 only)
Action: Gas operated semi-automatic
Magazine: 5-shot clip (223 cal.); 20-shot clip (9mm cal.)
Barrel: 20" with flash supressor; 16" with collapsible stock. Also heavy barrel available
Sights: Adjustable rear, post front adjustable for elevation; 3X & 4X scopes avaialable
Stock & Forearm: Pistol grip; fiberglass shoulder stock & handguard; swivels; carrying handle; collapsible stock available in both calibers
Approximate wt.: 6 to 8 lbs.
Comments: Made from the mid 1960's to present. Add 10% for collapsible stock (AR-15A2 Government model carbine); add 14% for target sight & heavy barrel (AR-15 A2H Bar).
Estimated Value: New (retail): $769.95
                      Excellent: $580.00
                      Very good: $460.00

Colt AR-15 A2 Delta H-Bar

Similar to the AR-15 A2 with 20" heavy barrel, 3x9 rubber armored variable power scope, removable cheekpiece, leather military style sling & aluminum carrying case.
Estimated Value: New (retail): $1,359.95
                      Excellent: $1,020.00
                      Very good: $ 815.00

FN

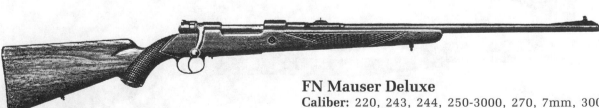

FN Mauser Deluxe

FN Mauser Deluxe

Caliber: 220, 243, 244, 250-3000, 270, 7mm, 300, 308, 30-06
Action: Mauser-type bolt action; repeating
Magazine: 5-shot box
Barrel: Blued; 24"
Sights: Adjustable rear, hooded ramp front
Stock & Forearm: Checkered one-piece pistol grip stock & forearm; swivels
Approximate wt.: 7½ to 8 lbs.
Comments: Made from World War II to the early 1960's.
Estimated Value: Excellent: $475.00
                      Very good: $380.00

FN Mauser Deluxe Presentation

Similar to the Deluxe with Monte Carlo stock; engraving; select wood.
Estimated Value: Excellent: $750.00
                      Very good: $600.00

FN Supreme

FN Supreme

Caliber: 243, 270, 7mm, 30-06, 308
Action: Mauser-type bolt action; repeating
Magazine: 5-shot box, 4-shot box in 308 or 243 calibers
Barrel: Blued; 22", 24"
Sights: Adjustable rear, hooded ramp front
Stock & Forearm: Checkered wood Monte Carlo one-piece pistol grip stock & tapered forearm; cheekpiece; swivels
Approximate wt.: 8 lbs.
Comments: Made from the late 1950's to the mid 1970's.
Estimated Value: **Excellent:**   **$550.00**
                Very good: **$400.00**

FN Supreme Magnum

Similar to the Supreme in magnum calibers & 3-shot box magazine.
Estimated Value: **Excellent:**   **$575.00**
                Very good: **$460.00**

Harrington & Richardson

Harrington & Richardson 1873 Springfield Commemorative

Harrington & Richardson Little Big Horn Commemorative 174

Harrington & Richardson Cavalry 171 Deluxe Carbine

Harrington & Richardson 1873 Springfield Commemorative

Caliber: 45-70 Gov't
Action: Trap door; single shot
Magazine: None
Barrel: Blued; 32"
Sights: Adjustable rear, blade front
Stock & Forearm: One-piece straight grip stock & full length forearm; barrel band; swivels
Approximate wt.: 8¾ lbs.
Comments: Manufactured in the early 1970's to mid 1980's; replica of the 1873 U.S. Springfield Rifle.
Estimated Value: **Excellent:**   **$320.00**
                Very good: **$235.00**

Harrington & Richardson Little Big Horn Commemorative 174

Carbine version of the trap door Springfield, 22" barrel; 7¼ lbs. Discontinued in 1984.
Estimated Value: **Excellent:**   **$300.00**
                Very good: **$240.00**

Harrington & Richardson Cavalry Carbine 171

Similar to the Little Big Horn with saddle ring.
Estimated Value: **Excellent:**   **$280.00**
                Very good: **$210.00**

Harrington & Richardson Cavalry 171 Deluxe

Similar to the Cavalry Carbine 171 with engraving.
Estimated Value: **Excellent:**   **$295.00**
                Very good: **$220.00**

Harrington & Richardson 158 Topper

Harrington & Richardson Mustang

Harrington & Richardson Model 157

Harrington & Richardson Shikari 155

Harrington & Richardson 158 Topper

Caliber: 22 Hornet, 30-30, 357 magnum, 44 magnum
Action: Box lock; top lever, break-open; exposed hammer; single shot
Magazine: None
Barrel: Blued; 22"
Sights: Adjustable rear, ramp front
Stock & Forearm: Hardwood straight or semi-pistol grip stock & forearm; recoil pad
Approximate wt.: 5 lbs.
Comments: Made from the early 1960's to mid 1980's, magnum calibers added 1982.
Estimated Value: **Excellent:** $100.00
                     Very good: $ 80.00

Harrington & Richardson 158 C, 58 Topper, 258

Similar to the 158 with extra interchangeable 26" 410 or 20 gauge shotgun barrel. Add 18% for nickel finish.
Estimated Value: **Excellent:** $150.00
                     Very good: $115.00

Harrington & Richardson Pioneer 765

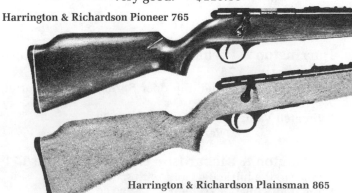

Harrington & Richardson Plainsman 865

Harrington & Richardson Plainsman 865

Similar to the 765 with: 5-shot clip; 22" barrel. Made from about 1950 to 1986.
Estimated Value: **Excellent:** $80.00
                     Very good: $60.00

Harrington & Richardson Mustang

Similar to the 158 with gold plated trigger & hammer; straight stock. MAde in the mid to late 1960's.
Estimated Value: **Excellent:** $115.00
                     Very good: $ 85.00

Harrington & Richardson Model 157

Similar to the 158 with semi-pistol grip stock, full length forearm & swivels. Discontinued in 1984.
Estimated Value: **Excellent:** $100.00
                     Very good: $ 80.00

Harrington & Richardson Shikari 155

Caliber: 44 magnum, 45-70 Gov't
Action: Single shot; exposed hammer
Magazine: None
Barrel: Blued; 24", 28"
Sights: Folding leaf rear, blade front
Stock & Forearm: Wood straight grip stock & forearm; barrel band
Approximate wt.: 7 to 7¼ lbs.
Comments: Manufactured from early 1970's to early 1980's.
Estimated Value: **Excellent:** $90.00
                     Very good: $75.00

Harrington & Richardson Pioneer 765

Caliber: 22 short, long, long rifle
Action: Bolt action; single shot
Magazine: None
Barrel: Blued; 24"
Sights: Open rear, hooded bead front
Stock & Forearm: Wood Monte Carlo one-piece semi-pistol grip stock & forearm
Approximate wt.: 5 lbs.
Comments: Made from the late 1940's to mid 1950's.
Estimated Value: **Excellent:** $55.00
                     Very good: $45.00

Harrington & Richardson Pioneer 750

Harrington & Richardson Pioneer 750
Similar to the 765. Made from the mid 1950's to mid 1980's.

Estimated Value:	Excellent:	$70.00
	Very good:	$55.00

Harrington & Richardson 866
Similar to the 865 with full length forearm. Made in early 1970's.

Estimated Value:	Excellent:	$90.00
	Very good:	$70.00

Harrington & Richardson Model 751
Similar to the 750 with full length forearm. Made from the early to mid 1970's.

Estimated Value:	Excellent:	$75.00
	Very good:	$55.00

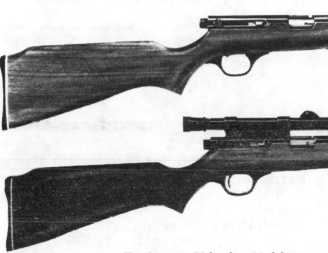

Harrington & Richardson Sahara 755

Harrington & Richardson Model 760

Harrington & Richardson Model 760
Similar to the 755 with short forearm. Discontinued in 1970.

Estimated Value:	Excellent:	$65.00
	Very good:	$50.00

Harrington & Richardson Sahara 755
Caliber: 22 short, long, long rifle
Action: Blow back; hammerless; single shot; automatic ejector
Magazine: None
Barrel: Blued; 22"
Sights: Open rear, military front
Stock & Forearm: Monte Carlo one-piece semi-pistol grip stock & full length forearm
Approximate wt.: 4 lbs.
Comments: Made from the early 1960's to early 1970's.

Estimated Value:	Excellent:	$75.00
	Very good:	$60.00

Harrington & Richardson Medalist 450
Caliber: 22 long rifle
Action: Bolt action; repeating
Magazine: 5-shot detachable box
Barrel: Blued; 26"
Sights: None
Stock & Forearm: Target style with pistol grip; swivels
Approximate wt.: 10½ lbs.
Comments: A target rifle made from the late 1940's to early 1960's.

Estimated Value:	Excellent:	$140.00
	Very good:	$110.00

Harrington & Richardson Sportster 250
Caliber: 22 long rifle
Action: Bolt action; repeating
Magazine: 5-shot detachable box
Barrel: Blued; 23"
Sights: Open rear, ramp front
Stock & Forearm: Wood one-piece semi-pistol grip stock & forearm
Approximate wt.: 6 lbs.
Comments: Made from the late 1940's to the early 1960's.

Estimated Value:	Excellent:	$70.00
	Very good:	$55.00

Harrington & Richardson Medalist 451
Similar to the 450 with extension rear sight & Lyman front sight.

Estimated Value:	Excellent:	$155.00
	Very good:	$125.00

Harrington & Richardson 251
Similar to the 250 with a special Lyman rear sight.

Estimated Value:	Excellent:	$70.00
	Very good:	$55.00

Harrington & Richardson Fieldsman 852

Harrington & Richardson Fieldsman 852

Caliber: 22 short, long, long rifle
Action: Bolt action; repeating
Magazine: Tubular: 15 long rifles, 17 longs, 21 shorts
Barrel: Blued; 24"
Sights: Open rear, bead front
Stock & Forearm: Plain wood one-piece semi-pistol grip stock & forearm
Approximate wt.: 5½ lbs.
Comments: Made in the early 1950's.
Estimated Value: Excellent: $75.00
 Very good: $60.00

Harrington & Richardson Model 300

Harrington & Richardson Ultra 301

Harrington & Richardson Model 330

Harrington & Richardson Model 300

Caliber: 22-250 Rem., 243 Win., 270, 308, 30-06, 300 mag., 7mm mag.
Action: Mauser-type bolt action; repeating
Magazine: 5-shot box, 3-shot in magnum
Barrel: Blued; 22"
Sights: Open rear, ramp front
Stock & Forearm: Checkered walnut Monte Carlo one-piece pistol grip stock & forearm; cheekpiece; recoil pad; swivels
Approximate wt.: 7¾ lbs.
Comments: Made from the mid 1960's to early 1980's.
Estimated Value: Excellent: $385.00
 Very good: $300.00

Harrington & Richardson Ultra 301

Similar to the 300 with full length forearm & 18" barrel; no swivels.
Estimated Value: Excellent: $420.00
 Very good: $335.00

Harrington & Richardson Model 330

Similar to the Model 300 with less fancy finish. Discontinued in the early 1970's.
Estimated Value: Excellent: $320.00
 Very good: $255.00

Harrington & Richardson Model 333

Similar to the Model 330 with no checkering or sights.
Estimated Value: Excellent: $240.00
 Very good: $180.00

Harrington & Richardson
Ultra Wildcat 317

Harrington & Richardson 317 Presentation

Similar to the 317 with select wood, special basket-weave checkering.
Estimated Value: Excellent: $550.00
 Very good: $440.00

Harrington & Richardson Ultra Wildcat 317

Caliber: 17 Rem., 222, 223 or 17/223 (Handload)
Action: Bolt action, Sako-type; repeating
Magazine: 6-shot box
Barrel: Blued; 24"
Sights: None
Stock & Forearm: Wood Monte Carlo one-piece pistol grip stock & forearm; cheekpiece; recoil pad; swivels
Approximate wt.: 7¾ lbs.
Comments: Made from the late 1960's to mid 1970's.
Estimated Value: Excellent: $450.00
 Very good: $360.00

Harrington & Richardson Ultra Medalist 370

Harrington & Richardson Model 340

Harrington & Richardson Model 340

Caliber: 243 Win., 270 Win., 30-06, 308 Win., 7mm Mauser (7x57)
Action: Bolt action; repeating; hinged floorplate; adjustable trigger
Magazine: 5-shot
Barrel: Blued; 22"
Sights: None; drilled & tapped for sights or scope
Stock & Forearm: Checkered walnut one-piece pistol grip stock & forearm; cheekpiece; recoil pad
Approximate wt.: 7¼ lbs.
Comments: Introduced in 1981 in 30-06; other calibers added later. Discontinued in 1984.
Estimated Value: Excellent: $320.00
              Very good: $255.00

Harrington & Richardson Ultra Medalist 370

Caliber: 22-250, 243, 6mm
Action: Sako bolt action; repeating
Magazine: 4-shot box
Barrel: 24" heavy
Sights: Open
Stock & Forearm: Monte Carlo one-piece grip stock & forearm; cheekpiece; recoil pad; swivels
Approximate wt.: 9 lbs.
Comments: Made from the late 1960's to mid 1970's.
Estimated Value: Excellent: $420.00
              Very good: $335.00

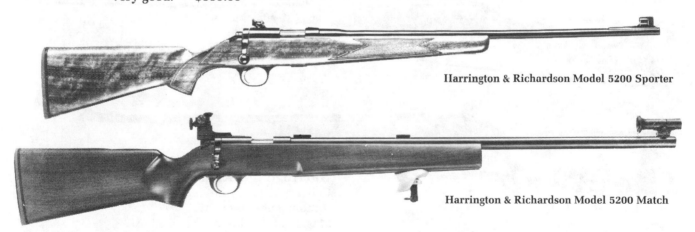

Harrington & Richardson Model 5200 Sporter

Harrington & Richardson Model 5200 Match

Harrington & Richardson Model 5200 Match

Caliber: 22 long rifle
Action: Bolt action, single shot; adjustable trigger
Magazine: None
Barrel: 28" heavy target weight, recessed muzzle
Sights: None; tapped for sights; scope bases included
Stock & Forearm: Smooth walnut one-piece match style stock & forearm; swivels & hand stop; rubber recoil pad
Approximate wt.: 11 lbs.
Comments: A moderately priced match rifle produced from 1981 to 1986.
Estimated Value: Excellent: $340.00
              Very good: $250.00

Harrington & Richardson Model 5200 Sporter

Caliber: 22 long rifle
Action: Bolt action; repeating
Magazine: 5-shot clip
Barrel: 24" recessed muzzle
Sights: Adjustable receiver sight; hooded ramp front
Stock & Forearm: Checkered walnut one-piece semi-pistol grip stock & forearm; rubber recoil pad
Approximate wt.: 6½ lbs.
Comments: A sporting version of the Model 5200 introduced in 1982. Discontinued 1983.
Estimated Value: Excellent: $300.00
              Very good: $225.00

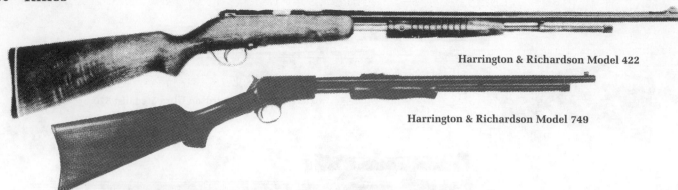

Harrington & Richardson Model 422

Harrington & Richardson Model 749

Harrington & Richardson Model 422
Caliber: 22 short, long, long rifle
Action: Slide action; hammerless; repeating
Magazine: Tubular: 15 long rifles, 17 longs, 21 shorts
Barrel: Blued; 24"
Sights: Open rear, ramp front
Stock & Forearm: Plain walnut semi-pistol grip stock & grooved slide handle
Approximate wt.: 6 lbs.
Comments: Made from the mid to late 1950's.
Estimated Value: Excellent: $110.00
                        Very good: $ 90.00

Harrington & Richardson Model 749
Caliber: 22 short, long, long rifle
Action: Slide action; hammerless; repeating
Magazine: Tubular: 18 shorts, 15 longs, 13 long rifles
Barrel: 19"; round, tapered
Sights: Open rear, blade front
Stock & Forearm: Plain hardwood pistol grip stock & tapered slide handle
Approximate wt.: 5 lbs.
Comments: Made in the early 1970's.
Estimated Value: Excellent: $100.00
                        Very good: $ 80.00

Harrington & Richardson Reising 60

Harrington & Richardson General 65

Harrington & Richardson Leatherneck 165

Harrington & Richardson General 65
Caliber: 22 long rifle
Action: Semi-automatic
Magazine: 10-shot detachable box
Barrel: Blued; 23"
Sights: Peep rear, covered blade front
Stock & Forearm: Wood one-piece semi-pitol grip stock & forearm
Approximate wt.: 9 lbs.
Comments: Used as a Marine training rifle during World War II.
Estimated Value: Excellent: $300.00
                        Very good: $240.00

Harrington & Richardson Reising 60
Caliber: 45
Action: Semi-automatic
Magazine: 12 or 20-shot detachable box
Barrel: Blued; 18¼"
Sights: Open rear, blade front
Stock & Forearm: Plain wood one-piece semi-pistol grip stock & forearm
Approximate wt.: 7¼ lbs.
Comments: Manufactured during World War II.
Estimated Value: Excellent: $425.00
                        Very good: $325.00

Harrington & Richardson Leatherneck 165
Lighter version of the 65 with ramp front sights. MAde from World War II until the early 1960's.
Estimated Value: Excellent: $125.00
                        Very good: $100.00

Harrington & Richardson Reg'lar 265

Harrington & Richardson Targeteer Special 465

Harrington & Richardson Leatherneck 150

Harrington & Richardson Reg'lar 265
Similar to the 165 in bolt action with a 22" barrel. Made from World War II until about 1950.

| Estimated Value: | Excellent: | $90.00 |
| | Very good: | $65.00 |

Harrington & Richardson Ace 365
Similar to the Model 265 except single shot. Made in the mid 1940's.

| Estimated Value: | Excellent: | $60.00 |
| | Very good: | $45.00 |

Harrington & Richardson Targeteer Special 465
Similar to the 265 with: 25" barrel; swivels; slightly heavier. Made in the mid 1940's.

| Estimated Value: | Excellent: | $100.00 |
| | Very good: | $ 80.00 |

Harrington & Richardson Targeteer Jr.
A youth version of the 465 with: short stock; 5-shot magazine; 20" barrel. Made from the late 1940's to early 1950's.

| Estimated Value: | Excellent: | $95.00 |
| | Very good: | $70.00 |

Harrington & Richardson Leatherneck 150
Caliber: 22 long rifle
Action: Semi-automatic; hammerless
Magazine: 5-shot detachable box
Barrel: Blued; 22"
Sights: Open rear, ramp front
Stock & Forearm: Wood one-piece semi-pistol grip stock & forearm
Approximate wt.: 7 lbs.
Comments: Made from the late 1940's to early 1950's.

| Estimated Value: | Excellent: | $120.00 |
| | Very good: | $ 90.00 |

Harrington & Richardson Model 151
Similar to the 150 with a special peep rear sight.

| Estimated Value: | Excellent: | $125.00 |
| | Very good: | $100.00 |

Harrington & Richardson Model 308

Harrington & Richardson Lynx 800
Caliber: 22 long rifle
Action: Semi-automatic; hammerless
Magazine: 10-shot clip
Barrel: Blued 22"
Sights: Open rear, ramp front
Stock & Forearm: Walnut one-piece semi-pistol grip stock & forearm
Approximate wt.: 6 lbs.
Comments: Made from the late 1950's to about 1960.

| Estimated Value: | Excellent: | $90.00 |
| | Very good: | $70.00 |

Harrington & Richardson Model 308
Caliber: 264, 308
Action: Semi-automatic; gas operated
Magazine: 3-shot detachable box
Barrel: Blued; 22"
Sights: Adjustable rear, bead front
Stock & Forearm: Checkered walnut Monte Carlo one-piece pistol grip stock & forearm; cheekpiece; swivels
Approximate wt.: 7 lbs.
Comments: Made from the late 1960's to early 1970's.

| Estimated Value: | Excellent: | $290.00 |
| | Very good: | $230.00 |

Harrington & Richardson Model 360
Similar to the Model 308 except 243 caliber only.

| Estimated Value: | Excellent: | $300.00 |
| | Very good: | $240.00 |

Harrington & Richardson Model 700 Deluxe

Harrington & Richardson Model 700
Caliber: 22 WMR
Action: Semi-automatic; hammerless
Magazine: 5- or 10-shot detachable box
Barrel: 22"
Sights: Adjustable folding rear; ramp blade front
Stock & Forearm: Plain walnut Monte Carlo one-piece pistol grip stock & forearm
Approximate wt.: 6½ lbs.
Comments: Produced in the late 1970's to mid 1980's.
Estimated Value: Excellent: $175.00
　　　　　　　　 Very good: $140.00

Harrington & Richardson Model 700 Deluxe
Similar to the Model 700 with select custom finish; checkering; cheekpiece; recoil pad; 4X scope.
Estimated Value: Excellent: $260.00
　　　　　　　　 Very good: $195.00

Heckler & Koch

Heckler & Koch Model 300

Heckler & Koch Model 270

Heckler & Koch Model SL-6 & SL-7
Caliber: 223 (SL-6), 308 (SL-7)
Action: Semi-automatic
Magazine: 4-shot clip (SL-6); 3-shot clip (SL-7); 10-shot clip available for both rifles
Barrel: 17¾" round black matte finish
Sights: Ring & post front; diopter adjustable rear
Stock & Forearm: Smooth European one-piece stock & forearm with ventilated wood handguard over barrel
Approximate wt.: 8½ lbs.
Comments: Produced in the mid 1980's.
Estimated Value: Excellent: $495.00
　　　　　　　　 Very good: $390.00

Heckler & Koch Model 270
Caliber: 22 long rifle
Action: Semi-automatic; blow back design
Magazine: 5- or 20-shot detachable box
Barrel: Blued; 20"
Sights: Diopter sights, adjustable for windage & elevation
Stock & Forearm: Plain walnut, one-piece semi-pistol grip stock & lipped foraarm
Approximate wt.: 5½ lbs.
Comments: Discontinued in mid 1980's.
Estimated Value: Excellent: $220.00
　　　　　　　　 Very good: $175.00

Heckler & Koch Model 300
Caliber: 22 Win. mag.
Action: Semi-automatic; blow back design
Magazine: 5- or 15-shot detachable box
Barrel: Blued; 20"
Sights: Adjustable post front, adjustable V-notch rear
Stock & Forearm: Checkered walnut Monte Carlo one-piece pistol grip stock & lipped forearm; cheekpiece; swivels
Approximate wt.: 5¾ lbs.
Comments: Currently available.
Estimated Value: New (retail): $426.00
　　　　　　　　 Excellent: $320.00
　　　　　　　　 Very good: $255.00

Heckler & Koch Model 91 & 93
Caliber: 223 (Model 93); 308 (Model 91)
Action: Semi-automatic
Magazine: 25-shot clip (Model 93); 20-shot clip (Model 91); 5-shot clip available for both rifles
Barrel: 16¼" matte black (Model 93); 17¾" matte black (Model 91)
Sights: Ring & post front; diopter adjustable rear
Stock & Forearm: Matte black, fixed, high-impact plastic three-piece stock, forearm & pistol grip; a retractable metal stock is available
Approximate wt.: 8 lbs. (Model 93); 10 lbs. (Model 91)
Comments: Introduced in the 1970's. Add 12% for retractable metal stock.
Estimated Value: New (retail): $932.00
　　　　　　　　 Excellent: $700.00
　　　　　　　　 Very good: $560.00

Heckler & Koch Model 94 Carbine
Similar to the Model 91 & Model 93 in 9mm caliber; 30-shot clip; 16½" barrel; weighs 6½ lbs.; Add 12% for retractable metal stock.
Estimated Value: New (retail): $932.00
　　　　　　　　 Excellent: $700.00
　　　　　　　　 Very good: $560.00

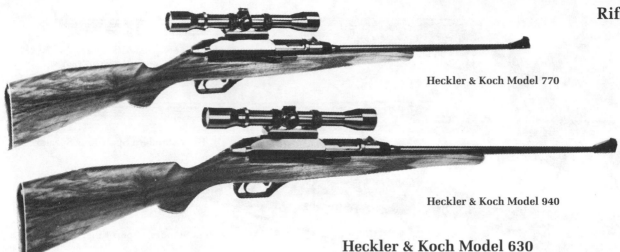

Heckler & Koch Model 770

Heckler & Koch Model 940

Heckler & Koch Model 630

Caliber: 221, 222, 223, Rem., 22 Hornet
Action: Semi-automatic
Magazine: 4-shot box; 10-shot available
Barrel: Blued; 18"
Sights: Adjustable post front, adjustable V-notch rear
Stock & Forearm: Checkered walnut Monte Carlo pistol grip, one-piece stock & lipped forearm; cheekpiece; swivels
Approximate wt.: 7 lbs.
Comments: Available in 223 Remington caliber only after mid 1980's. Made from about 1982 to late 1980's.
Estimated Value: Excellent: $500.00
Very good: $375.00

Heckler & Koch Model 770

Similar to the Model 630 in 243 or 308 Win. calibers; 20" barrel; weighs 8 lbs. 3-shot magazine.
Estimated Value: Excellent: $520.00
Very good: $415.00

Heckler & Koch Model 940

Similar to the Model 630 in 30-06 Springfield caliber; 22" barrel; weighs 8¾ lbs. 3-shot magazine.
Estimated Value: Excellent: $530.00
Very good: $395.00

High Standard

High Standard Flite King

High Standard Hi-Power

High Standard Hi-Power Deluxe

High Standard Flite King

Caliber: 22 short, long, long rifle
Action: Slide action; hammerless; repeating
Magazine: Tubular: 17 long rifle, 19 long, 24 short
Barrel: Blued; 24"
Sights: Adjustable rear, post front
Stock & Forearm: Checkered walnut Monte Carlo pistol grip stock & grooved slide handle; early models have no checkering
Approximate wt.: 5½ lbs.
Comments: Made from about 1962 to late 1970's.
Estimated Value: Excellent: $110.00
Very good: $ 85.00

High Standard Hi-Power

Caliber: 270, 30-06
Action: Bolt action; Mauser-type; repeating
Magazine: 4-shot box
Barrel: Blued; 22"
Sights: Folding leaf rear, ramp front
Stock & Forearm: Walnut one-piece semi-pistol grip stock & tapered forearm
Approximate wt.: 7 lbs.
Comments: Available from the early to mid 1960's.
Estimated Value: Excellent: $240.00
Very good: $190.00

High Standard Hi-Power Deluxe

Similar to Hi-Power with a checkered Monte Carlo stock & swivels.
Estimated Value: Excellent: $270.00
Very good: $215.00

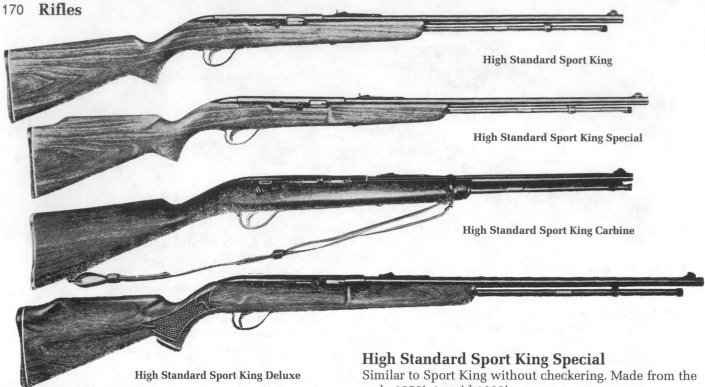

High Standard Sport King

High Standard Sport King Special

High Standard Sport King Carbine

High Standard Sport King Deluxe

High Standard Sport King

Caliber: 22 short, long, long rifle
Action: Semi-automatic
Magazine: Tubular: 15 long rifles, 17 longs, 21 shorts
Barrel: Blued; 22¼"
Sights: Open rear, post front
Stock & Forearm: Checkered wood Monte Carlo one-piece pistol grip stock & forearm
Approximate wt.: 5½ lbs.
Comments: Sport King had no Monte Carlo stock before the mid 1970's; field model was made from about 1960 to the late 1970's.
Estimated Value: Excellent: $110.00
Very good: $ 85.00

High Standard Sport King Special
Similar to Sport King without checkering. Made from the early 1950's to mid 1960's.
Estimated Value: Excellent: $100.00
Very good: $ 75.00

High Standard Sport King Deluxe
Same specifications as Sport King. Made as Deluxe until mid 1970's.
Estimated Value: Excellent: $125.00
Very good: $ 95.00

High Standard Sport King Carbine
Carbine version of the Sport King. Straight stock; 18¼" barrel; smaller magazine; swivels. Made from the early 1960's to early 1970's.
Estimated Value: Excellent: $120.00
Very good: $ 90.00

Husqvarna

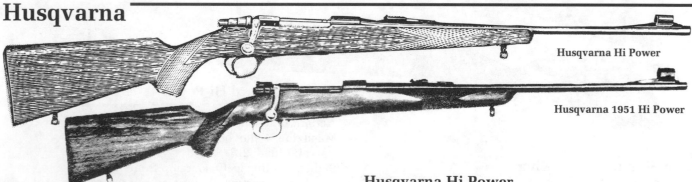

Husqvarna Hi Power

Husqvarna 1951 Hi Power

Husqvarna 1950 Hi Power
Similar to the Hi Power in 220, 270 & 30-06 calibers only. Made only in the early 1950's.
Estimated Value: Excellent: $330.00
Very good: $265.00

Husqvarna 1951 Hi Power
Similar to the Hi Power with a slightly higher stock. Made only in 1951.
Estimated Value: Excellent: $350.00
Very good: $280.00

Husqvarna Hi Power
Caliber: 220 Swift, 270, 30-06, 6.5x55, 8x57, 9.3x57
Action: Mauser-type bolt action; repeating
Magazine: 5-shot box
Barrel: Blued; 23¾"
Sights: Open rear, hooded ramp front
Stock & Forearm: Checkered beech one-piece pistol grip stock & tapered forearm; swivels
Approximate wt.: 7¾ lbs.
Comments: Made from World War II to the late 1950's.
Estimated Value: Excellent: $300.00
Very good: $240.00

Husqvarna 1100 Hi Power Deluxe

Husqvarna 1000 Super Grade
Similar to the 1100 with a Monte Carlo stock.
Estimated Value: Excellent: $410.00
Very good: $310.00

Husqvarna 1100 Hi Power Deluxe
Similar to the 1951 Hi Power with walnut stock & forearm; made from the early to mid 1950's.
Estimated Value: Excellent: $385.00
Very good: $290.00

Husqvarna 3100 Crown Grade

Husqvarna 3000 Crown Grade

Husqvarna P-3000 Presentation

Husqvarna 6000 Imperial Custom

Husqvarna 3100 Crown Grade
Caliber: 243, 270, 7mm Rem., 30-06, 308 Win.
Action: Mauser-type bolt action; repeating
Magazine: 5-shot box
Barrel: Blued; 23¾"
Sights: Open rear, hooded ramp front
Stock & Forearm: Checkered walnut one-piece pistol grip stock & tapered forearm; swivels
Approximate wt.: 7 lbs.
Comments: Made from the mid 1950's to mid 1970's.
Estimated Value: Excellent: $440.00
Very good: $350.00

Husqvarna 3000 Crown Grade
Similar to 3100 with Monte Carlo stock.
Estimated Value: Excellent: $465.00
Very good: $350.00

Husqvarna P-3000 Presentation
A fancy version of the 3000 with: engraving; select wood; adjustable trigger. Made in the late 1960's.
Estimated Value: Excellent: $725.00
Very good: $540.00

Husqvarna 6000 Imperial Custom
Similar to 3000 with: higher quality finish; folding sight; adjustable trigger. Made in the late 1960's.
Estimated Value: Excellent: $525.00
Very good: $395.00

Husqvarna 4100 Lightweight

Husqvarna 4000 Lightweight

Husqvarna 456 Lightweight

Husqvarna 7000 Imperial Monte Carlo

Husqvarna 4100 Lightweight
Caliber: 243, 270, 7mm, 306, 308 Win.
Action: Mauser-type bolt action; repeating
Magazine: 5-shot box
Barrel: Blued; 20½"
Sights: Open rear, hooded ramp front
Stock & Forearm: Checkered walnut one-piece pistol grip stock & tapered forearm
Approximate wt.: 6 lbs.
Comments: Made from the mid 1950's to mid 1970's.
Estimated Value: **Excellent:**   **$460.00**
                       Very good: **$365.00**

Husqvarna 4000 Lightweight
Similar to 4100 with Monte Carlo stock & no rear sight.
Estimated Value: **Excellent:**   **$480.00**
                       Very good: **$385.00**

Husqvarna 456 Lightweight
Similar to 4100 with full length stock & forearm. Made from about 1960 to 1970.
Estimated Value: **Excellent:**   **$490.00**
                       Very good: **$390.00**

Husqvarna 7000 Imperial Monte Carlo
Similar to 4000 with: higher quality wood; lipped forearm; folding sight; adjustable trigger. Made in the late 1960's.
Estimated Value: **Excellent:**   **$550.00**
                       Very good: **$440.00**

Husqvarna 9000 Crown Grade

Husqvarna 8000 Imperial Grade

Husqvarna 9000 Crown Grade
Caliber: 270, 30-06, 7mm Remington mag., 300 Win. mag.
Action: Bolt action; repeating
Magazine: 5-shot box
Barrel: Blued; 23¾"
Sights: Leaf rear, hooded ramp front
Stock & Forearm: Checkered walnut Monte Carlo one-piece pistol grip stock & forearm; swivels
Approximate wt.: 7¼ lbs.
Comments: Made in the early 1970's.
Estimated Value: **Excellent:**   **$490.00**
                       Very good: **$390.00**

Husqvarna 8000 Imperial Grade
Similar to 9000 with: select wood; engraving; no sights.
Estimated Value: **Excellent:**   **$575.00**
                       Very good: **$460.00**

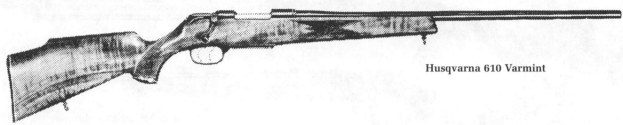

Husqvarna 610 Varmint

Husqvarna 610 Varmint
Caliber: 222
Action: Short stroke bolt action; repeating
Magazine: 4-shot detachable box
Barrel: Blued; 23¾"
Sights: None; tapped for scope
Stock & Forearm: Checkered walnut Monte Carlo one-piece pistol grip stock & forearm; cheekpiece
Approximate wt.: 6½ lbs.
Comments: Made in the late 1960's.
Estimated Value: Excellent: $425.00
**   Very good: $340.00**

Husqvarna 358 Magnum
Caliber: 358 Norma mag.
Action: Bolt action; repeating
Magazine: 3-shot box
Barrel: Blued; 25½"
Sights: Folding leaf rear, hooded ramp front
Stock & Forearm: Checkered walnut Monte Carlo one-piece pistol grip stock & forearm; cheekpiece
Approximate wt.: 7¾ lbs.
Comments: Made in the late 1960's.
Estimated Value: Excellent: $475.00
**   Very good: $380.00**

Ithaca

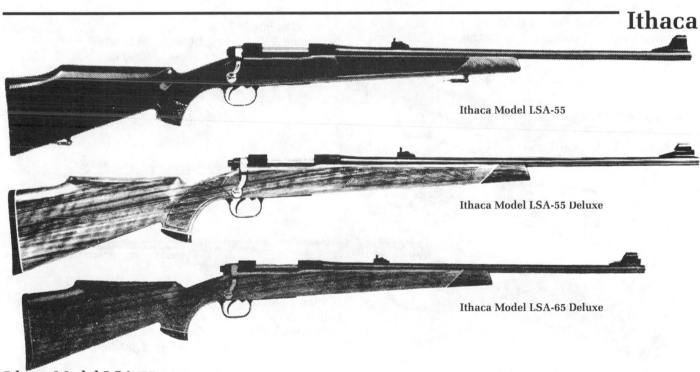

Ithaca Model LSA-55

Ithaca Model LSA-55 Deluxe

Ithaca Model LSA-65 Deluxe

Ithaca Model LSA-55
Caliber: 222, 22-250, 6mm, 243, 308
Action: Bolt action; repeating
Magazine: 3-shot detachable box
Barrel: Blued; 22"
Sights: Iron; adjustable rear, hooded ramp front
Stock & Forearm: Monte Carlo one-piece pistol grip stock & tapered forearm
Approximate wt.: 6½ lbs.
Comments: Made from the early 1970's to late 1970's.
Estimated Value: Excellent: $350.00
**   Very good: $260.00**

Ithaca Model LSA-55 Heavy Barrel
Similar to the LSA-55 except: cheekpiece; recoil pad; heavy barrel; weighs 8½ lbs.
Estimated Value: Excellent: $400.00
**   Very good: $320.00**

Ithaca Model LSA-55 Deluxe
Similar to the LSA-55 except: checkering; recoil pad.
Estimated Value: Excellent: $390.00
**   Very good: $295.00**

Ithaca Model LSA-65
Similar to Model LSA-55 in 25-06, 270, 30-06, with a 4-shot magazine; weighs 7 lbs.
Estimated Value: Excellent: $375.00
**   Very good: $280.00**

Ithaca Model LSA-65 Deluxe
Similar to Model LSA-55 Deluxe in same calibers & weight as LSA-65.
Estimated Value: Excellent: $400.00
**   Very good: $300.00**

Ithaca Model LSA-55 Turkey Gun

Ithaca Model 49 Saddlegun

Ithaca Model 49 Saddlegun

Caliber: 22 short, long, long rifle
Action: Lever action; exposed hammer; single shot
Magazine: None
Barrel: Blued; 18"
Sights: Adjustable rear, bead front
Stock & Forearm: Plain wood straight grips tock & fore-arm; barrel band; recent model has checkering
Approximate wt.: 5½ lbs.
Comments: Made from about 1960 to late 1970's.
Estimated Value: Excellent: $75.00
                        Very good: $55.00

Ithaca Model LSA-55 Turkey Gun

Caliber: 222 under 12 gauge full choke
Action: Top lever, break open; exposed hammer
Magazine: None
Barrel: 24½" rifle under full choke shotgun with matted rib
Sights: Folding rear, dovetail front
Stock & Forearm: Checkered walnut Monte Carlo pistol grip stock & forearm; cheekpiece; recoil pad; swivels
Approximate wt.: 7 lbs.
Comments: An over & under combination manufactured to the late 1970's.
Estimated Value: Excellent: $450.00
                        Very good: $360.00

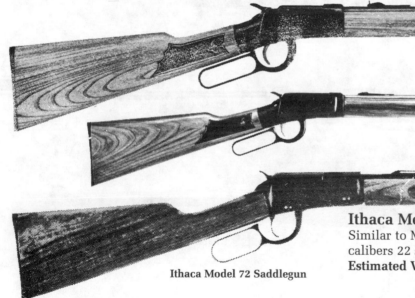

Ithaca Model 49 Deluxe

Ithaca Model 49R

Ithaca Model 72 Saddlegun

Ithaca Model 49 Presentation

Similar to Model 49 Deluxe with engraving & nameplate; calibers 22 short, long, long rifle or 22 magnum.
Estimated Value: Excellent: $110.00
                        Very good: $ 85.00

Ithaca Model 49 Youth

Similar to Model 49 with an abbreviated stock for young shooters.
Estimated Value: Excellent: $70.00
                        Very good: $55.00

Ithaca Model 49 Magnum

Similar to Model 49 in 22 magnum rimfire.
Estimated Value: Excellent: $85.00
                        Very good: $65.00

Ithaca Model 49 Deluxe

Similar to Model 49 with checkered stock, gold hammer & trigger & swivels. Discontinued in the mid 1970's when standard model was sold with checkering.
Estimated Value: Excellent: $90.00
                        Very good: $70.00

Ithaca Model 49R (Repeater)

Similar to Model 49 with 20" barrel & 15-shot tubular magazine. Sold only in the late 1960's to early 1970's.
Estimated Value: Excellent: $120.00
                        Very good: $ 95.00

Ithaca Model 72 Saddlegun

Caliber: 22 long rifle
Action: Lever action; exposed hammer; repeating
Magazine: 15-shot tubular
Barrel: Blued; 18½"
Sights: Adjustable rear, hooded ramp front
Stock & Forearm: Plain walnut straight grip stock & fore-arm; barrel band
Approximate wt.: 5½ lbs.
Comments: Made from the early to late 1970's.
Estimated Value: Excellent: $155.00
                        Very good: $125.00

Ithaca Model 72 Deluxe

Ithaca Model 72 Magnum

Similar to Model 72 in 22 magnum. Magazine holds 11 shots.

Estimated Value: Excellent: $165.00
Very good: $125.00

Ithaca Model 72 Deluxe

Similar to Model 72 except: brushed silver receiver; engraving; octagon barrel; blade front sight.

Estimated Value: Excellent: $175.00
Very good: $130.00

Ithaca Model X5-T

Ithaca Model X5-C

Caliber: 22 long rifle
Action: Semi-automatic; hammerless
Magazine: 7-shot clip
Barrel: Blued; 22"
Sights: Open rear, Raybar front
Stock & Forearm: Wood one-piece semi-pistol grip stock & forearm
Approximate wt.: 6¼ lbs.
Comments: Made from the late 1950's to about 1965.

Estimated Value: Excellent: $130.00
Very good: $105.00

Ithaca Model X5-T

Similar to X5-C with a 16-shot tubular magazine.

Estimated Value: Excellent: $140.00
Very good: $110.00

Iver Johnson

Iver Johnson Model 2X

Iver Johnson Model X

Caliber: 22 short, long, long rifle
Action: Bolt action; single shot
Magazine: None
Barrel: Blued; 22"
Sights: Open rear, blade front
Stock & Forearm: Wood one-piece pistol grip stock & forearm
Approximate wt.: 4 lbs.
Comments: Made from the late 1920's to the early 1930's.

Estimated Value: Excellent: $90.00
Very good: $70.00

Iver Johnson Lever Action

Caliber: 22 short, long, long rifle; 22 Win. magnum
Action: Lever action, side ejection; exposed hammer
Magazine: 21 shorts, 17 longs, 15 long rifles (mixed simultaneously); 12 magnum, tubular under barrel
Barrel: 18½"; round, blued
Sights: Hooded ramp front, adjustable rear
Stock & Forearm: Smooth hardwood stock & forearm, barrel band
Approximate wt.: 5¾ lbs.
Comments: Produced in the mid 1980's. Add 7% for magnum.

Estimated Value: Excellent: $160.00
Very good: $120.00

Iver Johnson Model 2X

Similar to the Model X with a 24" barrel & improved stock. Made from about 1932 to the mid 1950's.

Estimated Value: Excellent: $110.00
Very good: $85.00

Iver Johnson Li'l Champ

Caliber: 22 short, long or long rifle
Action: Bolt action; single shot
Magazine: None, single shot
Barrel: Blued; 16¼"
Sights: Blade front, adjustable rear
Stock & Forearm: Molded one-piece stock & forearm; nickel plated bolt
Approximate wt.: 2¾ lbs.
Comments: A lightweight gun designed for young beginners.

Estimated Value:	New (retail):	$91.50
	Excellent:	$65.00
	Very good:	$55.00

Iver Johnson Wagonmaster

Caliber: 22 short, long or long rifle; 22 magnum
Action: Lever action; repeating
Magazine: 15 long rifles, 17 longs, 21 shorts, can be mixed & loaded simultaneously; tubular
Barrel: Blued; 18¼"
Sights: Hooded ramp front, adjustable leaf rear
Stock & Forearm: Smooth wood straight grip stock & forearm; barrel band
Approximate wt.: 5¾ lbs.
Comments: Currently available. Add 12% for magnum.

Estimated Value:	New (retail):	$166.50
	Excellent:	$125.00
	Very good:	$100.00

Iver Johnson Wagonmaster

Iver Johnson Li'l Champ

Iver Johnson Targetmaster

Caliber: 22 short, long or long rifle
Action: Slide action, repeating
Magazine: 12 long rifles, 15 longs, 19 shorts, can be mixed & loaded simultaneously; tubular
Barrel: Blued; 18½"
Sights: Hooded ramp front, adjustable rear
Stock & Forearm: Smooth hardwood straight grip stock & grooved slide handle
Approximate wt.: 5¾ lbs.
Comments: Currently available.

Estimated Value:	New (retail):	$166.50
	Excellent:	$125.00
	Very good:	$100.00

Iver Johnson Survival Carbine

Caliber: 30 carbine, 223 (5.7mm)
Action: Gas operated semi-automatic
Magazine: 5-, 15- or 30-shot detachable clip
Barrel: 18"; blued or stainless steel
Sights: Aperture rear, blade front with protective ears
Stock & Forearm: Hard plastic, one-piece pistol grip stock & forearm; metal handguard; folding stock available
Approximate wt.: 5 lbs.
Comments: Produced from 1983 to 1986. Add 20% for folding stock; 25% for stainless steel finish.

Estimated Value:	Excellent:	$175.00
	Very good:	$140.00

Iver Johnson Trailblazer

Caliber: 22 long rifle
Action: Semi-automatic, hammerless
Magazine: Clip
Barrel: Blued; 18½"
Sights: Open rear, blade front
Stock & Forearm: Checkered walnut, one-piece Monte Carlo semi-pistol grip stock & forearm
Approximate wt.: 5 lbs.
Comments: Produced from 1984 to 1986.

Estimated Value:	Excellent:	$100.00
	Very good:	$ 75.00

Iver Johnson PM 30G

Iver Johnson PM 30G, Model M1, PM30
Caliber: 30 M1, 223 (discontinued 1985)
Action: Gas operated, semi-automatic
Magazine: 15-shot detachable clip; 5- or 30-shot available
Barrel: 18"; blued or stainless steel
Sights: Aperture rear, blade frotn with protective ears
Stock & Forearm: Wood, semi-pistol grip one-piece stock & forearm; slot in stock; metal ventilated or wood handguard
Approximate wt.: 6 lbs.
Comments: Made from about 1960 to late 1970's by Plainfield. Reintroduced in the late 1970's by Iver Johnson. Add 20% for stainless steel (discontinued 1985); add 7% for walnut.
Estimated Value: New (retail): $265.00
                       Excellent: $200.00
                       Very good: $160.00

Iver Johnson PM30S, Model M1 Sporter
Similar to the M1 Carbine with a wood hand guard & no slot in the stock. Discontinued in the early 1980's.
Estimated Value: Excellent: $190.00
                       Very good: $150.00

Iver Johnson PM30P, Commando or Paratrooper
Similar to the M1 Carbine with pistol grip at rear & at forearm; telescoping wire shoulder stock. Add 20% for stainless steel.
Estimated Value: New (retail): $291.50
                       Excellent: $220.00
                       Very good: $175.00

Iver Johnson Model EW22 HBA, MHBA
Similar to the Model PM30 in 22 long rifle. Add 75% for magnum.
Estimated Value: New (retail): $166.50
                       Excellent: $125.00
                       Very good: $100.00

Iver Johnson Model 9MM
Similar to the Model PM30 in 9MM Parabellum with 16" barrel & 20-shot magazine; weights 5½ lbs.
Estimated Value: Excellent: $190.00
                       Very good: $145.00

Johnson

Johnson MMJ Spitfire

Johnson Custom Deluxe Sporter
Similar to the MMJ with a Monte Carlo pistol grip stock & rear peep sight.
Estimated Value: Excellent: $240.00
                       Very good: $185.00

Johnson Folding Stock
Similar to the MMJ with a special metal folding shoulder stock.
Estimated Value: Excellent: $250.00
                       Very good: $190.00

Johnson MMJ Spitfire
Caliber: 223
Action: Semi-automatic
Magazine: 5-, 15-, 30-shot clip
Barrel: Blued; 18"
Sights: Adjustable rear, ramp front
Stock & Forearm: Wood one-piece semi-pistol grip stock & forearm; wood hand guard
Approximate wt.: 5 lbs.
Comments: A conversion of the M1 carbine. Made in the mid 1960's.
Estimated Value: Excellent: $230.00
                       Very good: $175.00

Kimber

Kimber Model 82 M/S

Kimber Model 82

Kimber Model 84B

Kimber Model 82, 82A

Caliber: 22 long rifle, 22 Win. mag., 22 Hornet (after 1982)

Action: Bolt action; repeating; rear locking bolt lugs

Magazine: 5-shot detachable box (10-shot available) in 22 long rifle; 3-shot in 22 Hornet; 4-shot in 22 Win. mag.

Barrel: 22½" blued; light sporter; sporter; target

Sights: None, drilled for scope; beaded ramp front & folding leaf rear available

Stock & Forearm: Checkered walnut, one-piece pistol grip stock & forearm (Classic); available with optional Monte Carlo stock & cheekpiece; swivels

Approximate wt.: 6½ lbs.

Comments: Produced as Model 82 from 1980 to 1986 & as Model 82A after 1986. Add 6% for .22 WMR or .22 Hornet; add 10% for Cascade stock (discontinued in 1987); add 33% for Custom Classic stock; add 52% for Super America stock (discontinued 1986).

Estimated Value: New (retail): $1,195.00
Excellent: $ 895.00
Very good: $ 715.00

Kimber Model 82 M/S

Similar to the Model 82 except single shot; 20½" heavy barrel, adjustable target trigger; competition stock; 22 long rifle caliber only; this gun is designed for metallic silhouette shooting. Introduced in 1982.

Estimated Value: Excellent: $550.00
Very good: $445.00

Kimber Model 82B

Similar to the Model 82 with internal improvements. Introduced in 1986. Available with sporter or varmint barrel. Classic stock standard. Add 12% for Cascade stock (discontinued 1987); add 33% for custom Classic stock; add 100% for Brownell stock (discontinued 1987); add 50% for Super America stock; 14% for Continental stock; add 95% for Super Contrinential stock.

Estimated Value: New (retail): $750.00
Excellent: $625.00
Very good: $500.00

Kimber Model 84, 84A

Similar to the Model 82 except Mini-Mauser type action. Introduced in 1984 in 223 Rem. caliber; 221 Fireball, 222 Rem. mag., 17 Rem. 17 Match IV, 6x47 & 6x45 calibers added in 1986. Known as Model 84A in 1987. Add 12% for Cascade stock (discontinued in 1987)); add 28% for Custom Classic stock.

Estimated Value: Excellent: $700.00
Very good: $560.00

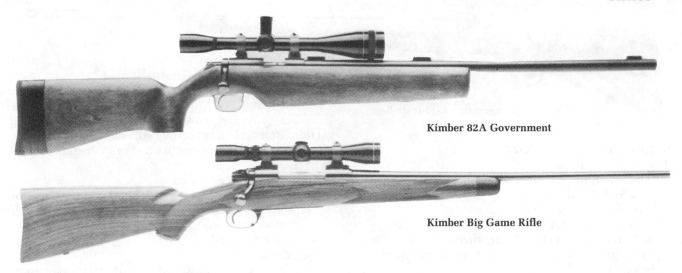

Kimber 82A Government

Kimber Big Game Rifle

Kimber Mini-Classic

An adult 22 bolt action with an 18" barrel, lipped forearm; built on the 82A action. Introduced in 1988.

Estimated Value: Excellent: $500.00
Very good: $400.00

Kimber 82A Government

A single shot 22 bolt action target rifle designed for the Army; heavy target barrel & stock; built on the Kimber 82A action.

Estimated Value: New (retail): $595.00
Excellent: $445.00
Very good: $360.00

Kimber Model 84B

Similar to the Model 84 with internal improvements. Introduced in 1987. Add 12% for Continental stock; 90% for Super Continental; 50% for Super America.

Estimated Value: Excellent: $800.00
Very good: $650.00

Kimber Big Game Rifle

Caliber: 270 Win., 280 Rem., 7mm Rem. magnum, 30-06, 300 Win. magnum, 338 Win. magnum, 375 H&H, 416 Rigby (African model) introduced in 1989

Action: Bolt action, repeating, combining features of the pre '64 Winchester Model 70 & the Mauser 98

Magazine: 5-shot in calibers .270, 280 & 30-06, 3-shot in calibers 7mm mag., 300 mag., 338 mag. & 375 H&H

Barrel: 22½" featherweight barrel in 270, 280, 30-06; 24" medium barrel in 7mm, 300, 338; 24" heavy barrel in 375 H&H

Sights: None

Stock & Forearm: Checkered walnut one-piece pistol grip stock & forearm; black forearm tip; swivels

Approximate wt.: 7¾ to 8½ lbs.

Comments: Introduced in 1988; add 6% for magnum; add 11% for 375 H&H; add 30% for Custom Classic; add 11% for Super America; add 100% for African.

Estimated Value: New (retail): $1,795.00
Excellent: $1,350.00
Very good: $1,075.00

Kleinguenther

Kleinguenther K-14

Kleinguenther MV 2130

Caliber: 243, 270, 30-06, 300 mag., 308, 7mm Rem.
Action: Mauser-type bolt action, repeating
Magazine: 2-shot box
Barrel: Blued; 25"
Sights: None; drilled for scope
Stock & Forearm: Checkered walnut Monte Carlo one-piece pistol grip stock & tapered forearm; recoil pad
Approximate wt.: 7 lbs.
Comments: Made in the 1970's.
Estimated Value: Excellent: $550.00
Very good: $440.00

Kleinguenther K-14

Caliber: Same as MV 2130, also 25-06, 7x57, 375 H&H
Action: Bolt action
Magazine: Hidden clip, 3-shot
Barrel: Blued; 24", 26"
Sights: Open rear, ramp front
Stock & Forearm: Checkered walnut one-piece pistol grip stock & tapered forearm; recoil pad
Approximate wt.: 7¼ lbs.
Comments: Made in the 1970's.
Estimated Value: Excellent: $600.00
Very good: $480.00

Kleinguenther K-15 Insta-fire

Kleinguenther Model K-22
Caliber: 22 long rifle, 22 WMR
Action: Bolt action; repeating; adjustable trigger
Magazine: 5-shot hidden clip
Barrel: 21½" chrome-poly steel
Sights: None; tapped for scope
Stock & Forearm: Checkered beechwood, Monte Carlo pistol grip one-piece stock & forearm; swivels; cheekpiece
Approximate wt.: 6½ lbs.
Comments: A rimfire rifle designed to be as accurate as the K-15. Introduced in 1984. Add 16% for magnum, 30% for deluxe, 110% for deluxe custom.

Estimated Value:	New (retail):	$345.00
	Excellent:	$260.00
	Very good:	$210.00

Kleinguenther K-15 Insta-fire
Caliber: 243, 25-06, 270, 30-06, 308 Win., 308 Norma mag., 300 Win. mag., 7mm Rem. mag., 375 H&H, 7x57, 270 mag., 300 Weath. mag., 257 Weath. mag.
Action: Bolt action; repeating; adjustable trigger
Magazine: 5-shot hidden clip; 3-shot in magnum
Barrel: 24"; 26" in magnum
Sights: None; tapped for scope
Stock & Forearm: Checkered walnut Monte Carlo one-piece pistol grip stock & forearm; several shade choices; rosewood fore-end & cap; swivels; left or right hand model
Approximate wt.: 7½ lbs.
Comments: A high powered rifle that is advertised as "the world's most accurate hunting rifle." Engraveing & select wood at additional cost. Add $50.00 for magnum; $50.00 for left hand model. Made from late 1970's.

Estimated Value:	New (retail):	$1,275.00
	Excellent:	$ 960.00
	Very good:	$ 765.00

Mannlicher

Mannlicher-Schoenauer 1905

Mannlicher-Schoenauer 1903
Caliber: 6.5 x 53mm
Action: Bolt action; repeating; double set trigger; "butterknife" style bolt handle
Magazine: 5-shot rotary
Barrel: Blued; 17¾"
Sights: Two leaf rear, ramp front
Stock & Forearm: Walnut semi-pistol grip stock & tapered, full-length forearm; swivels; cheekpiece
Approximate wt.: 6½ lbs.
Comments: Made from 1903 to World War II.

Estimated Value:	Excellent:	$950.00
	Very good:	$760.00

Mannlicher-Schoenauer 1905
Similar to 1903 with a 19¾" barrel & in 9x56mm caliber.

Estimated Value:	Excellent:	$900.00
	Very good:	$720.00

Mannlicher-Schoenauer 1908
Similar to the 1903 with a 19¾" barrel & in 7x57 & 8x56mm calibers.

Estimated Value:	Excellent:	$875.00
	Very good:	$700.00

Mannlicher-Schoenauer 1910
Similar to 1903 with a 19¾" barrel & in 9.5x56mm caliber.

Estimated Value:	Excellent:	$900.00
	Very good:	$720.00

Mannlicher-Schoenauer 1924
Similar to 1903 with a 19¾" barrel & in 30-06. Made from 1924 to World War II.

Estimated Value:	Excellent:	$1,050.00
	Very good:	$ 840.00

Mannlicher-Schoenauer High Velocity

Mannlicher-Schoenauer 1950 Sporter

Mannlicher-Schoenauer 1950 Carbine

Mannlicher-Schoenauer 1952 sporter

Mannlicher-Schoenauer 1952 Carbine

Mannlicher-Schoenauer High Velocity
Caliber: 7x64, 30-06, 8x60, 9.3x62, 10.75x68
Action: Bolt action; repeating; "butter-knife" bolt handle
Magazine: 5-shot rotary
Barrel: Blued; 23¾"
Sights: Three leaf rear, ramp front
Stock & Forearm: Checkered walnut one-piece pistol grip stock & tapered forearm; cheekpiece; swivels
Approximate wt.: 7½ lbs.
Comments: Made from the early 1920's to World War II.
Estimated Value: Excellent: $975.00
                         Very good: $780.00

Mannlicher-Schoenauer 1950 Sporter
Caliber: 257, 270 Win., 30-06
Action: Bolt action; repeating; "butter-knife" bolt handle
Magazine: 5-shot rotary
Barrel: Blued; 24"
Sights: Folding leaf rear, hooded ramp front
Stock & Forearm: Checkered walnut one-piece pistol grip stock & tapered forearm; cheekpiece; swivels
Approximate wt.: 7¼ lbs.
Comments: Made in the early 1950's.
Estimated Value: Excellent: $950.00
                         Very good: $755.00

Mannlicher-Schoenauer 1950 Carbine
Similar to the Sporter with a 20" barrel & full length forearm.
Estimated Value: Excellent: $830.00
                         Very good: $660.00

Mannlicher-Schoenauer 1950-6.5
Similar to the 1950 Carbine with 18" barrel & in 6.5x53mm caliber.
Estimated Value: Excellent: $850.00
                         Very good: $680.00

Mannlicher-Schoenauer 1952 Sporter
Similar to the 1950 Sporter with slight changes in stock & with slanted bolt handle. Made from about 1952 to 1956.
Estimated Value: Excellent: $970.00
                         Very good: $775.00

Mannlicher-Schoenauer 1952 Carbine
Similar to 1952 Sporter with a 20" barrel & full length forearm.
Estimated Value: Excellent: $960.00
                         Very good: $765.00

Mannlicher-Schoenauer 1952-6.5
Similar to 1952 Carbine with 18" barrel & in 6.5x53mm caliber.
Estimated Value: Excellent: $900.00
                         Very good: $720.00

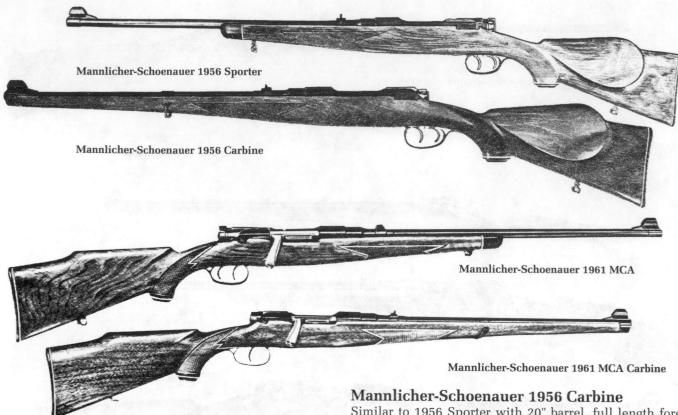

Mannlicher-Schoenauer 1956 Sporter

Mannlicher-Schoenauer 1956 Carbine

Mannlicher-Schoenauer 1961 MCA

Mannlicher-Schoenauer 1961 MCA Carbine

Mannlicher-Schoenauer 1956 Sporter
Caliber: 243, 30-06
Action: Bolt action; repeating; "butter-knife" slanted bolt handle
Magazine: 5-shot rotary
Barrel: Blued; 22"
Sights: Folding leaf rear, hooded ramp front
Stock & Forearm: Checkered walnut pistol grip stock & forearm; high comb; cheekpiece; swivels
Approximate wt.: 7 lbs.
Comments: Made from the mid 1950's to about 1960.
Estimated Value: Excellent: $760.00
Very good: $600.00

Mannlicher-Schoenauer 1956 Carbine
Similar to 1956 Sporter with 20" barrel, full length forearm & addition of 6.5mm, 257, 270, 7mm & 308 calibers.
Estimated Value: Excellent: $790.00
Very good: $630.00

Mannlicher-Schoenauer 1961 MCA
Similar to 1956 Sporter with Monte Carlo stock. Made from the early 1960's to early 1970's.
Estimated Value: Excellent: $800.00
Very good: $640.00

Mannlicher-Schoenauer 1961 MCA Carbine
Similar to 1956 Carbine with Monte Carlo stock. Made from early 1960's to early 1970's.
Estimated Value: Excellent: $850.00
Very good: $680.00

Steyr-Mannlicher SL

Steyr-Mannlicher Model SL
Caliber: 222 Rem., 222 Rem. magnum, 223 Rem., 5.6x50 magnum
Action: Bolt action; repeating
Magazine: 5-shot rotary
Barrel: Blued; 23½"
Sights: Open rear, ramp front
Stock & Forearm: Checkered walnut Monte Carlo pistol grip, one-piece stock & tapered forearm; recoil pad; cheekpiece; swivels
Approximate wt.: 5½ lbs.
Comments: Made from the mid 1960's to present.
Estimated Value: New (retail): $1,812.00
Excellent: $1,360.00
Very good: $1,085.00

Steyr-Mannlicher SL Carbine
Similar to the SL with a 20" barrel & full length forearm.
Estimated Value: New (retail): $1,939.00
Excellent: $1,450.00
Very good: $1,160.00

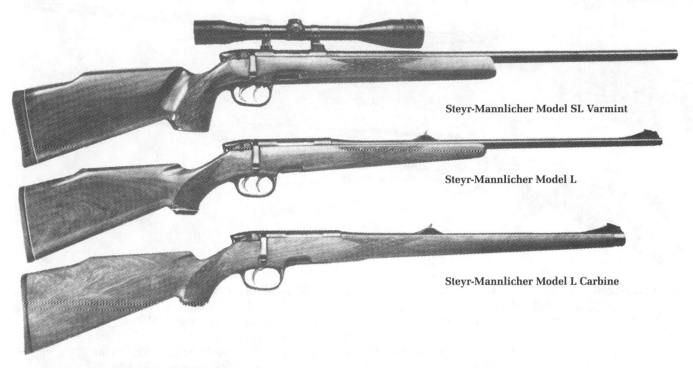

Steyr-Mannlicher Model SL Varmint

Steyr-Mannlicher Model L

Steyr-Mannlicher Model L Carbine

Steyr-Mannlicher Model SL Varmint

Similar to the Model SL with a varmint stock & 26" heavy barrel. 222 Rem. or 223 Rem. calibers.

Estimated Value:	New (retail):	$1,939.00
	Excellent:	$1,450.00
	Very good:	$1,160.00

Steyr-Mannlicher Model L Varmint

Similar to the Model L with a varmint stock & 26" heavy barrel. 22-250 Rem., 243 Win. or 308 Win.

Estimated Value:	New (retail):	$1,939.00
	Excellent:	$1,450.00
	Very good:	$1,160.00

Steyr-Mannlicher Model L

Similar to the SL in 22-250 Rem., 5.6x57, 6mm Rem., 7mm, 243 Win., 308 Win.

Estimated Value:	New (retail):	$1,812.00
	Excellent:	$1,360.00
	Very good:	$1,085.00

Steyr-Mannlicher Model L Carbine

Similar to the Model L with a 20" barrel & full length forearms.

Estimated Value:	New (retail):	$1,939.00
	Excellent:	$1,450.00
	Very good:	$1,160.00

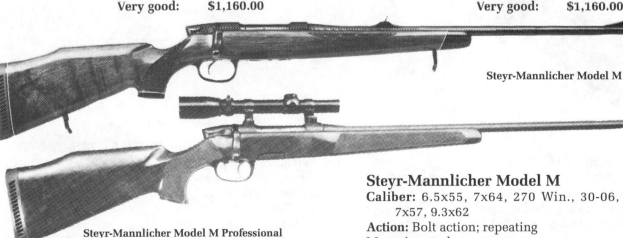

Steyr-Mannlicher Model M

Steyr-Mannlicher Model M Professional

Steyr-Mannlicher Model M Professional

Similar to the Model M with a parkerized metal finish & ABS Cycolac stock; 23½" barrel only.

Estimated Value:	New (retail):	$1,532.00
	Excellent:	$1,150.00
	Very good:	$ 920.00

Steyr-Mannlicher Model M

Caliber: 6.5x55, 7x64, 270 Win., 30-06, 25-06 Rem.; 7x57, 9.3x62

Action: Bolt action; repeating

Magazine: 5-shot rotary

Barrel: Blued; 20" on full stock; 23½" on half stock

Sights: Open rear, ramp front

Stock & Forearm: Checkered walnut Monte Carlo pistol grip stock; standard or full length forearm; cheekpiece; swivels; left hand model available

Approximate wt.: 6½ lbs.

Comments: Made from the mid 1970's to present. Add 10% for left hand model; 5% for full stock.

Estimated Value:	New (retail):	$1,812.00
	Excellent:	$1,360.00
	Very good:	$1,085.00

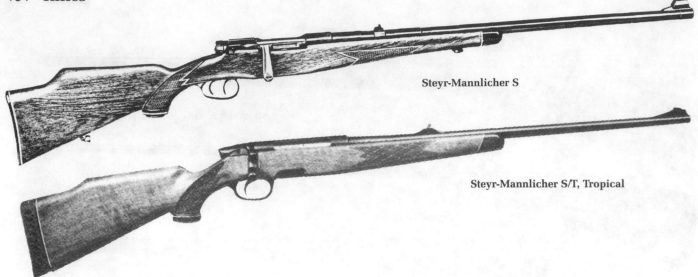

Steyr-Mannlicher S

Steyr-Mannlicher S/T, Tropical

Steyr-Mannlicher S

Similar to Model M with 26" barrel in magnum caliber, 7mm Rem., 257 Weath., 264 Win. 6.5x68, 300 H&H, 300 Win., 338 Win., 375 H&H & 458 Win. Half stock only; butt magazine optional. Add $50.00 for buttstock 4-shot magazine.

Estimated Value:	New (retail):	$1,952.00
	Excellent:	$1,465.00
	Very good:	$1,170.00

Steyr-Mannlicher S/T, Tropical

Similar to the Model S with a heavy barrel; 375 H&H mag. 9.3x64 & 458 Win. mag. calibers. Add $50.00 for buttstock magazine.

Estimated Value:	New (retail):	$2,176.00
	Excellent:	$1,630.00
	Very good:	$1,300.00

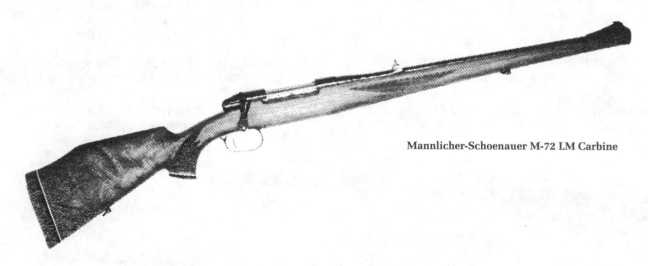

Mannlicher-Schoenauer M-72 LM Carbine

Steyr-Mannlicher ML 79 Luxus M

Caliber: 7x57, 7x64, 270 Win., 30-06 Springfield; others available on request

Action: Bolt action; short stroke; repeating

Magazine: 3-shot detachable, 6-shot available

Barrel: 23½"; 20" on full stock model

Sights: Adjustable V-notch open rear, adjustable hooded ramp front

Stock & Forearm: Checkered Eurpoean walnut Monte Carlo one-piece pistol grip stock & forearm; cheekpiece; swivels; full length stock available

Approximate wt.: 7 lbs.

Comments: Currently produced. Add 6% for full length stock or 6-shot magazine.

Estimated Value:	New (retail):	$2,364.00
	Excellent:	$1,770.00
	Very good:	$1,400.00

Mannlicher-Schoenauer M-72, M-72S

Caliber: 22-250, 5.6x57, 243, 6.5x57, 6mm, 7x57, 270

Action: Bolt action; repeating

Magazine: 5-shot rotary

Barrel: Blued; 23½"

Sights: Open rear, ramp front

Stock & Forearm: Checkered walnut one-piece pistol grip stock & tapered forearm; cheekpiece; recoil pad; swivels

Approximate wt.: 7½ lbs.

Comments: Made from mid to late 1970's.

Estimated Value:	Excellent:	$780.00
	Very good:	$595.00

Mannlicher-Schoenauer M-72 LM Carbine

Similar to M-72 with a 20" barrel & full length forearm.

Estimated Value:	Excellent:	$800.00
	Very good:	$600.00

Steyr-Mannlicher Model SSG Marksman

Steyr-Mannlicher Model SSG Match

Steyr-Mannlicher Model SSG Marksman
Caliber: 308 Win.; (7.62x51); 243 Win.
Action: Bolt action; repeating
Magazine: 5-shot
Barrel: 26"
Sights: Folding leaf rear, hooded ramp front
Stock & Forearm: Checkered Eurpoean walnut one-piece
    stock & forearm; recoil pad; ABS Cycolac stock
    available
Approximate wt.: 8½ lbs.
Comments: Currnetly produced. Deduct 20% for ABS
    Cycolac stock.
Estimated Value: New (retail): $1,995.00
                  Excellent: $1,490.00
                  Very good: $1,200.00

Steyr-Mannlicher Model SSG Match
A match rifle similar to the SSG Marksman with a heavy barrel; peep sight; stippled checkering; hand stop; weight: 11 lbs.; deduct 12% for ABS Cycolac stock.
Estimated Value: New (retail): $2,125.00
                  Excellent: $1,590.00
                  Very good: $1,275.00

Mark X

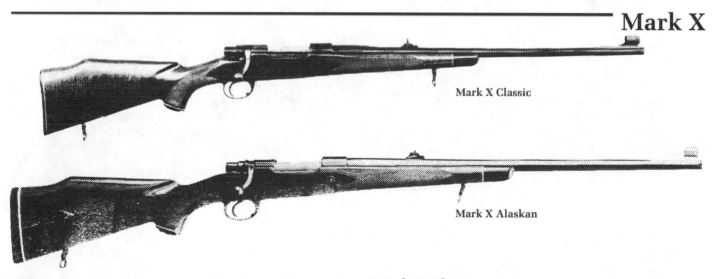

Mark X Classic

Mark X Alaskan

Mark X Alaskan
Caliber: 375 H & H, 458 Win. magnum
Action: Mauser-type bolt action; repeating; adjustable
    trigger
Magazine: 3-shot box with hinged floor plate
Barrel: Blued; 24"
Sights: Adjustable rear, hooded ramp front
Stock & Forearm: Checkered, select walnut, Monte Carlo
    pistol grip, one-piece stock & forearm; recoil pad;
    swivels
Approximate wt.: 6 lbs.
Comments: Distributed by Interarms.
Estimated Value: Excellent: $420.00
                  Very good: $330.00

Mark X Classic
Caliber: 22-250, 25-06, 243, 270, 308, 30-06, 7mm mag.,
    7x57, 300 Win. mag.
Action: Bolt action; Mauser-type; repeating; adjustable
    trigger
Magazine: 3-shot box with hinged floor plate
Barrel: 24"
Sights: None on some models; others adjustable rear,
    hooded ramp front
Stock & Forearm: Checkered walnut Monte Carlo one-
    piece pistol grip stock & forearm; swivels
Approximate wt.: 7½ lbs.
Comments: Add $15.00 for sights.
Estimated Value: Excellent: $320.00
                  Very good: $250.00

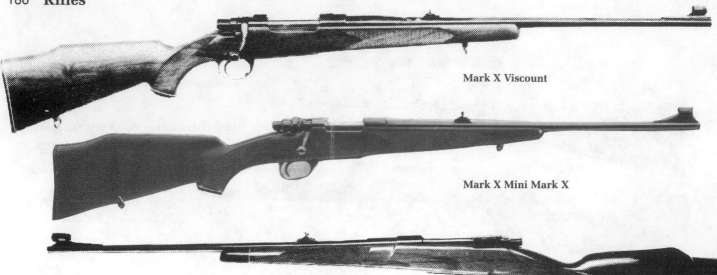

Mark X Viscount

Mark X Mini Mark X

Mark X Cavalier

Mark X Cavalier

Similar to the Mark X Classic with fancier stock; cheek-piece; recoil pad. Add $15.00 for sights.

Estimated Value: Excellent: $350.00
Very good: $280.00

Mark X Viscount

Similar to the Mark X Classic except: special hammer-forged, chrome vanadium steel barrel; add $20.00 for magnum calibers.

Estimated Value: New (retail): $499.00
Excellent: $375.00
Very good: $300.00

Mark X LTW

Similar to the Viscount with lightweight Carbolite stock in 270, 30-06 or 7mm Rem. magnum. Introduced in 1988. Add $20.00 for magnum.

Estimated Value: New (retail): $519.00
Excellent: $390.00
Very good: $315.00

Mark X Mini Mark X

Caliber: 223
Action: Bolt action; repeating; Mauser action scaled down for 223 caliber
Magazine: 5-shot
Barrel: Blued; 20"
Sights: Adjustable rear, hooded ramp front
Stock & Forearm: Checkered walnut, Monte Carlo one-piece pistol grip stock & forearm
Approximate wt.: 6¼ lbs.
Comments: Introduced in the late 1980's.
Estimated Value: New (retail): $429.00
Excellent: $325.00
Very good: $260.00

Mark X Whitworth Express

Mark X Marquis

Caliber: 243, 270, 7x57mm, 308, 30-06
Action: Bolt action; Mauser-type; repeating
Magazine: 5-shot box with hinged floor plate
Barrel: 20"
Sights: Adjustable rear, hooded ramp front
Stock & Forearm: Checkered walnut Monte Carlo one-piece full length pistol grip stock & forearm; swivels; cheekpiece
Approximate wt.: 7½ lbs.
Comments: Distributed by Interarms.
Estimated Value: Excellent: $375.00
Very good: $300.00

Mark X Continental

Similar to the Marquis with a "butter-knife" bolt handle & double set triggers.

Estimated Value: Excellent: $400.00
Very good: $320.00

Mark X Whitworth Express, Safari

Caliber: 375 H&H mag., 458 Win. mag.
Action: Bolt action; Mauser style; repeating; adjustable trigger
Magazine: 3-shot box with hinged floor plate
Barrel: 24"
Sights: 3 leaf express sights
Stock & Forearm: Checkered European walnut, Monte Carlo one-piece stock & forearm; cheekpiece; swivels; recoil pad
Approximate wt.: 7½ lbs.
Comments: Currnetly produced.
Estimated Value: New (retail): $789.00
Excellent: $590.00
Very good: $475.00

Marlin

Marlin Model 65

Marlin Model 80

Marlin Model 80E

Marlin Model 80C

Marlin Model 80DL

Marlin Garfield Model 80G

Marlin Model 65 & 65E

Caliber: 22 short, long, long rifle
Action: Bolt action; single shot
Magazine: None
Barrel: 24" round
Sights: Open rear, bead front; peep rear, hooded front on 65E
Stock & Forearm: Pistol grip stock & grooved forearm
Approximate wt.: 5 lbs.
Comments: This was a takedown rifle that was made between 1932 & 1935.
Estimated Value: Excellent: $70.00
Very good: $50.00

Marlin Model 80C

Basically the same gun as the Model 80 with slight improvements. Forearm is semi-beavertail. Production began in 1946, it was replaced by the 80 G in 1960.
Estimated Value: Excellent: $90.00
Very good: $70.00

Marlin Model 80 & 80E

Caliber: 22 short, long, long rifle
Action: Bolt action; takedown type; repeating
Magazine: 8-shot detachable box
Barrel: 24"
Sights: Open rear, bead front; peep rear, hooded front on 80E
Stock & Forearm: Plain pistol grip stock & forearm
Approximate wt.: 6¼ lbs.
Comments: Production began about 1934, continued until the mid 1940's.
Estimated Value: Excellent: $80.00
Very good: $60.00

Marlin Model 80 DL

Same rifle as Model 80-C except; swivels; hooded front sight; peep rear sight. Discontinued in 1965.
Estimated Value: Excellent: $90.00
Very good: $70.00

Marlin Model 80 G

The same rifle as Marlin Model 80-C. Made from about 1960 to 1966.
Estimated Value: Excellent: $85.00
Very good: $65.00

Marlin Model 81

Marlin Model 81 E

Marlin Model 81-DL

Marlin Glenfield Model 81 G

Marlin Model 81 & 81E

Caliber: 22 short, long, long rifle
Action: Bolt action; repeating
Magazine: Tubular under barrel: 24 shorts, 20 longs, 18 long rifles
Barrel: 24"
Sights: Open rear, bead front; peep rear, hooded front on 81E
Stock & Forearm: Plain pistol grip stock & forearm
Approximate wt.: 6¼ lbs.
Comments: This takedown model was produced from about 1937 to mid 1940's.

Estimated Value: Excellent: $85.00
Very good: $65.00

Marlin Model 81 C

An improved Model 81; semi-beavertail forearm. It was produced from 1946 to 1970.
Estimated Value: Excellent: $95.00
Very good: $70.00

Marlin Model 81-DL

Same as Model 81 C exept it has swivels; hooded front sight, peep rear sight. Made from about 1946 to 1965.
Estimated Value: Excellent: $95.00
Very good: $75.00

Marlin Glenfield Model 81 G

Basically the same as the Marlin Model 81 C. It was produced as the 81 G from about 1960 to 1965.
Estimated Value: Excellent: $85.00
Very good: $65.00

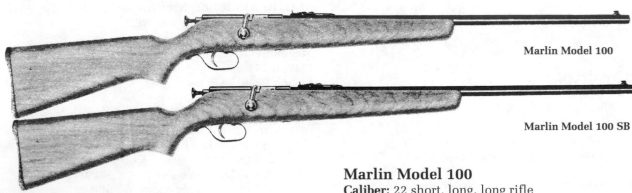

Marlin Model 100

Marlin Model 100 SB

Marlin Model 100S Tom Mix Special

Same as Model 100 except hooded front sight, peep rear sight. Made from 1937 to 1942.
Estimated Value: Excellent: $150.00
Very good: $115.00

Marlin Model 100 SB

Same as Model 100 except it is smooth bore to use with shot cartridges. Discontinued in 1941.
Estimated Value: Excellent: $90.00
Very good: $70.00

Marlin Model 100

Caliber: 22 short, long, long rifle
Action: Bolt action; single shot
Magazine: None
Barrel: 24" round
Sights: Open rear, bead front
Stock & Forearm: Plain pistol grip stock & forearm
Approximate wt.: 4¾ lbs.
Comments: Takedown model was manufactured from 1936 to 1960. In 1960 it became the Model 100G or Glenfield & was replaced in the mid 1960's by the Glenfield 10.

Estimated Value: Excellent: $60.00
Very good: $45.00

Marlin Model 15Y (Little Buckaroo)

Marlin Glenfield Model 15

Marlin Glenfield Model 100G; Glenfield 10

Basically same as Marlin Model 100.

Estimated Value: Excellent: $55.00
                   Very good: $45.00

Marlin Model 101 & 101-DL

Basically same as Model 100 except beavertail forearm. Peep rear, hooded front sights on 101-DL. Made from 1951 to late 1970's.

Estimated Value: Excellent: $75.00
                   Very good: $55.00

Marlin Glenfield Model 15, 15Y (Little Buckaroo), 15YN

Caliber: 22 short, long or long rifle
Action: Bolt action; single shot
Magazine: None
Barrel: 22" round, 16¼" on 15Y
Sights: Adjustable open rear, ramp front
Stock & Forearm: Checkered hardwood, Monte Carlo pistol grip one-piece stock & forearm
Approximate wt.: 5½ lbs., 4½ lbs. (15Y)
Comments: Introduced in the late 1970's. 15Y is for young shooters.

Estimated Value: New (retail): $134.95
                   Excellent: $100.00
                   Very good: $ 80.00

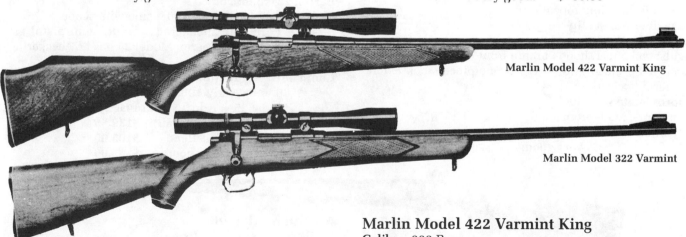

Marlin Model 422 Varmint King

Marlin Model 322 Varmint

Marlin Model 322 Varmint

Caliber: 222 Rem.
Action: Bolt action (Sako Short, Mauser); repeating
Magazine: 3-shot clip
Barrel: 24"
Sights: Peep sight rear, hooded ramp front
Stock & Forearm: Checkered hardwood stock & forearm
Approximate wt.: 7½ lbs.
Comments: Made for only 3 years beginning about 1954.

Estimated Value: Excellent: $325.00
                   Very good: $260.00

Marlin Model 422 Varmint King

Caliber: 222 Rem.
Action: Bolt action; repeating
Magazine: 3-shot detachable clip
Barrel: 24" round
Sights: Peep sight rear, hooded ramp front
Stock & Forearm: Checkered Monte Carlo pistol grip stock & forearm
Approximate wt.: 7 lbs.
Comments: Replaced Model 322 about 1958 but was discontinued after one year.

Estimated Value: Excellent: $350.00
                   Very good: $280.00

Marlin Model 455 Sporter

Marlin Model 122 Target Rifle

Marlin Model 455 Sporter

Caliber: 270, 30-06, 308
Action: Bolt action; FN Mauser action with Sako trigger
Magazine: 5-shot box
Barrel: 24" round, stainless steel
Sights: Receiver sight - Lyman 48, hooded ramp front
Stock & Forearm: Checkered wood Monte Carlo stock & forearm; cheekpiece
Approximate wt.: 8½ lbs.
Comments: Made from about 1957 to 1959.
Estimated Value:　Excellent:　$360.00
　　　　　　　　　　　Very good:　$290.00

Marlin Model 122 Target Rifle

Caliber: 22 short, long, long rifle
Action: Bolt action; single shot
Magazine: None
Barrel: 22" round
Sights: Open rear, hooded ramp front
Stock & Forearm: Wood Monte Carlo pistol grip stock & forearm; swivels
Approximate wt.: 5 lbs.
Comments: Made from about 1961 to 1965.
Estimated Value:　Excellent:　$80.00
　　　　　　　　　　　Very good:　$65.00

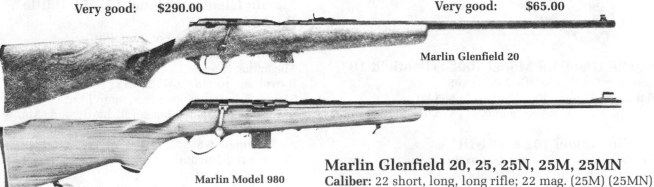

Marlin Glenfield 20

Marlin Model 980

Marlin Model 980

Caliber: 22 Win. mag.
Action: Bolt action; repeating
Magazine: 8-shot clip
Barrel: Blued; 24" round
Sights: Open rear, hooded ramp front
Stock & Forearm: Monte Carlo one-piece stock & forearm; swivels
Approximate wt.: 6lbs.
Comments: Made from about 1962 until 1970.
Estimated Value:　Excellent:　$90.00
　　　　　　　　　　　Very good:　$70.00

Marlin Glenfield 20, 25, 25N, 25M, 25MN

Caliber: 22 short, long, long rifle; 22 mag. (25M) (25MN)
Action: Bolt action; thumb safety
Magazine: 7-shot clip
Barrel: 22" round, blued
Sights: Open rear, ramp front; some with scope
Stock & Forearm: Checkered walnut, semi-pistol grip stock & plain forearm; Model 25 has no checkering
Approximate wt.: 5½ lbs.
Comments: Production on this model was from about 1966 to the early 1980's as Model 20; currently sold as Model 25N. Add 15% for magnum (25M, 25MN).
Estimated Value:　New (retail):　$139.95
　　　　　　　　　　　Excellent:　　$105.00
　　　　　　　　　　　Very good:　　$ 85.00

Marlin Model 781

Marlin Model 780

Caliber: 22 short, long, long rifle
Action: Bolt action; repeating
Magazine: 7-shot clip
Barrel: Blued; 22"
Sights: Adjustable rear, ramp front
Stock & Forearm: Checkered walnut Monte Carlo one-piece semi-pistol grip stock & forearm
Approximate wt.: 6 lbs.
Comments: Part of 700 series produced from about 1971 to the late 1980's.
Estimated Value:　Excellent:　$120.00
　　　　　　　　　　　Very good:　$ 95.00

Marlin Model 781

Same as Model 780 except tubular magazine; 25 shorts, 19 longs, 17 long rifles. Weighs 5½ lbs.
Estimated Value:　Excellent:　$125.00
　　　　　　　　　　　Very good:　$100.00

Marlin Model 782

Marlin Model 783

Marlin Model 782
Caliber: 22 Win. magnum
Action: Bolt action; repeating
Magazine: 7-shot clip
Barrel: 22"
Sights: Adjustable rear, ramp front
Stock & Forearm: Monte Carlo one-piece semi-pistol grip stock & forearm
Approximate wt.: 6 lbs.
Comments: Produced from 1971 to the late 1980's as one of the 700 series.
Estimated Value: Excellent: $135.00
Very good: $105.00

Marlin Model 783
Same as Model 782 except 12-shot tubular magazine.
Estimated Value: Excellent: $140.00
Very good: $110.00

Marlin Model 880

Marlin Model 881

Marlin Model 881
Same as the Model 880 except: 22 short, long or long rifle; tubular magazine under barrel which holds 25 shorts, 19 longs or 17 long rifles; introduced in 1989.
Estimated Value: New (retail): $200.95
Excellent: $150.00
Very good: $120.00

Marlin Model 882
Same as the Model 880 except 22 Win. magnum rim fire only. Introduced in 1989.
Estimated Value: New (retail): $212.95
Excellent: $160.00
Very good: $130.00

Marlin Model 880
Caliber: 22 long rifle
Action: Bolt action; thumb safety, red cocking indicator
Magazine: 7-shot clip
Barrel: Blued; 22" with micro-groove rifling
Sights: Ramp front, brass bead with wide scan hood; adjustable folding semi-buckhorn rear
Stock & Forearm: Monte Carlo pistol grip checkered walnut one-piece stock & forearm; swivel studs & rubber rifle butt pad
Approximate wt.: 5½ lbs.
Comments: Introduced in 1989.
Estimated Value: New (retail): $192.95
Excellent: $145.00
Very good: $115.00

Marlin Model 883
Same as the Model 882 except 12-shot tubular magazine under barrel. Introduced in 1989.
Estimated Value: New (retail: $219.95
Excellent: $165.00
Very good: $135.00

Marlin Model 92

Marlin Model 93

Marlin Model 93 Carbine

Marlin Model 92

Caliber: 22 short, long, long rifle; 32 short or long, rim fire or center fire

Action: Lever action; exposed hammer

Magazine: 22 caliber: 25 shorts, 20 longs, 28 long rifles; 32 caliber: 17 shorts, 14 longs; tubular under barrel; 16" barrel: 15 shorts, 12 longs, 10 long rifles

Barrel: 16", 24", 26", 28" round or octagon, blued

Sights: Open rear, blade front

Stock & Forearm: Plain walnut straight grip stock & forearm

Approximate wt.: 5 to 6 lbs.

Comments: Made from about 1892 to 1916. Also known as Model 1892.

Estimated Value: Excellent: $475.00
                       Very good: $350.00

Marlin Model 93

Caliber: 25-36 Marlin, 30-30, 32 Special, 32-40, 38-55

Action: Lever action; exposed hammer; repeating

Magazine: 10-shot tubular; under barrel

Barrel: 26"-32" round or octagon

Sights: Open rear, bead front

Stock & Forearm: Plain walnut straight grip stock & forearm

Approximate wt.: 7 to 8 lbs.

Comments: Manufactured from about 1893 to 1915 & 1920 to 1933. Produced in both takedown & solid frame models. Also known as Model 1893.

Estimated Value: Excellent: $600.00
                       Very good: $450.00

Marlin Model 93 Carbine

Basically same as the Model 93 except: produced in 30-30 & 32 special caliber only; standard carbine sights; 20" round barrel; 7-shot magazine. Weighs between 6 & 7 lbs.

Estimated Value: Excellent: $650.00
                       Very good: $500.00

Marlin Model 93 Musket

Marlin Model 93 Sporting Carbine

Marlin Model 93 Sporting Carbine

Basically the same as Model 93 Carbine except the smaller magazine carries 5 shots.

Estimated Value: Excellent: $650.00
                       Very good: $520.00

Marlin Model 93 Musket

Same as the Model 93 except: 30" standard barrel; equipment with a musket stock; military forearm; ramrod; angular bayonet. Production stopped about 1915.

Estimated Value: Excellent: $875.00
                       Very good: $700.00

Marlin Model 1894 (Current)

Marlin Model 1894C

Marlin Model 1895

Marlin Model 1895S

Marlin Model 1897

Marlin Model 1894, 1894S

Caliber: 25-20, 32-30, 38-40; current model 44 magnum (1970's to present); 41 mag. added 1984; 45 long Colt added 1988

Action: Lever action; exposed hammer; repeating

Magazine: 10-shot tubular, under barrel

Barrel: Round or octagon, 20", 24"-32"; 20" on current model

Sights: Open rear, bead front

Stock & Forearm: Plain walnut straight or pistol grip stock & forearm

Approximate wt.: 7 lbs.

Comments: Made from about 1894 to 1935 in both takedown & solid frame models. Reintroduced in the late 1970's in 44 magnum with 20" barrel. Hammer block safety added 1986.

Estimated Value:		Current	Early
	New (retail):	$401.95	
	Excellent:	$300.00	$675.00
	Very good:	$240.00	$575.00

Marlin Model 1894CL

Similar to the late model 1894S in 25-20 or 32-30 caliber; 318 Bee added in 1990. 6-shot magazine; 22" barrel; weighs 6¼ lbs. Introduced in 1988.

Estimated Value:	New (retail):	$431.95
	Excellent:	$325.00
	Very good:	$260.00

Marlin Model 1894C, 1894CS, 1894M

Similar to the current model 1894 except in 357 caliber; 18½" barrel; 9-shot magazine. Introduced in 1979. 1894M is 22 WMRF. Hammer block safety added 1986.

Estimated Value:	New (retail):	$401.95
	Excellent:	$300.00
	Very good:	$240.00

Marlin Model 1895

Caliber: 33 WCF, 38-56, 40-65, 40-70, 40-82, 45-70

Action: Lever action; exposed hammer; repeating

Magazine: 9-shot tubular, under barrel

Barrel: 24" octagon or round, blued

Sights: Open rear, bead front

Stock & Forearm: Walnut straight or pistol grip stock & forearm

Approximate wt.: 8 lbs.

Comments: Made in solid frame & takedown models from about 1895 to 1920.

Estimated Value:	Excellent:	$725.00
	Very good:	$580.00

Marlin Model 1895S, 1895SS

Similar to the Model 1895; introduced in the late 1970's; 45-70 gov't caliber; 22" barrel; 4-shot magazine; swivels.

Estimated Value:	New (retail):	$433.95
	Excellent:	$325.00
	Very good:	$260.00

Marlin Model 1897

Caliber: 22 short, long, long rifle

Action: Lever action; exposed hammer; repeating

Magazine: 25 shorts, 20 longs, 18 long rifles in full length; 16 shorts, 12 longs, 10 long rifles in half length; tubular under barrel

Barrel: Blued; 16", 24", 26", 28"

Sights: Open rear, bead front

Stock & Forearm: Plain walnut straight or pistol grip stock & forearm

Approximate wt.: 6 lbs.

Comments: Made from about 1897 to 1914 & 1919 to 1921.

Estimated Value:	Excellent:	$420.00
	Very good:	$330.00

Marlin Model 36

Marlin Model 36 Sporting Carbine

Marlin Model 36 Sporting Carbine

Same as Model 36A except weight is slightly less & barrel is 20".

| Estimated Value: | Excellent: | $300.00 |
| | Very good: | $240.00 |

Marlin Model 36

Caliber: 30-30, 32 Special
Action: Lever action; exposed hammer; repeating
Magazine: 6-shot tubular
Barrel: 20" round, blued
Sights: Open rear, bead front
Stock & Forearm: Pistol grip stock & semi-beavertail forearm; carbine barrel band
Approximate wt.: 6½ lbs.
Comments: Made from about 1936 to 1942 & 1946 to 1948.

| Estimated Value: | Excellent: | $275.00 |
| | Very good: | $210.00 |

Marlin Model 36A

Marlin Model 336A

Marlin Model 336C Carbine

Marlin Model 36H-DL

Marlin Model 36A

Same as Model 36A carbine except: barrel is 24", ⅔ magazine; weighs slightly more; hooded front sight.

| Estimated Value: | Excellent: | $280.00 |
| | Very good: | $220.00 |

Marlin Model 336A & 336A-DL

Basically the same as Model 36A with a rounded breech bolt & improved action. Produced from about 1950 to 1963. Reintroduced in the 1970's; discontinued in early 1980's. Checkered stock & forearm & swivels on 336A-DL.

| Estimated Value: | Excellent: | $210.00 |
| | Very good: | $165.00 |

Marlin Model 36H-DL

Same as Model 36A except stock & forearm are checkered & have swivels.

| Estimated Value: | Excellent: | $300.00 |
| | Very good: | $240.00 |

Marlin Model 336C Carbine, 336CS

This is basically the same as the Model 36, with a round breech bolt & improved action. The 35 caliber Remington was introduced & the 32 Special stopped in 1963; 375 Winchester added in 1984. This gun has been produced since about 1948. Hammer block safety added in 1986.

Estimated Value:	New (retail):	$357.95
	Excellent:	$270.00
	Very good:	$215.00

Marlin Model 336 T Texan Carbine

Marlin Model 336 Marauder

Marlin Model 336 Marauder

Same as Model 336T except weight is slightly less & barrel is only 16¼". Produced from about 1963 to 1964.
Estimated Value: Excellent: $225.00
Very good: $180.00

Marlin Model 336 ER

Similar to the Model 336 C in 356 Winchester or 308 Winchester calibers; recoil pad, swivels & strap. Produced 1983 to 1988.
Estimated Value: Excellent: $250.00
Very good: $200.00

Marlin Model 336T Texan Carbine, 336TS

Same as Model 336C except stock is straight, 18½" barrel. It wa snever produced in 32 caliber, but was available from 1963 to 1967 in 44 magnum. Produced from 1953 to 1987 in 30-30 caliber.
Estimated Value: Excellent: $230.00
Very good: $185.00

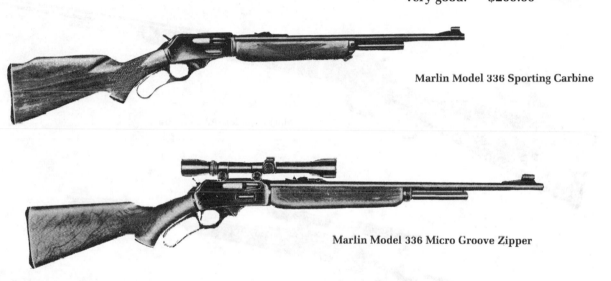

Marlin Model 336 Sporting Carbine

Marlin Model 336 Micro Groove Zipper

Marlin Model 336 LTS

Similar to the Model 336TS in 30-30 Win. caliber, 16¼" barrel, rubber butt pad; weighs 6½ lbs. Introduced in 1988.
Estimated Value: Excellent: $245.00
Very good: $195.00

Marlin Model 336 Micro Groove Zipper

Caliber 219 Zipper; otherwise same rifle as Model 336A.
Estimated Value: Excellent: $325.00
Very good: $260.00

Marlin Model 336 Sporting Carbine

Same as Model 336A except weight is slightly less & barrel is 20".
Estimated Value: Excellent: $190.00
Very good: $140.00

Marlin Model 336 Zane Gray Century

Same basic rifle as Model 336A except: 22" barrel is octagon; brass fore-end cap; brass buttplate & medallion in receiver. Only 10,000 were produced in 1972.
Estimated Value: Excellent: $275.00
Very good: $220.00

Marlin Model 336 Zane Grey Century

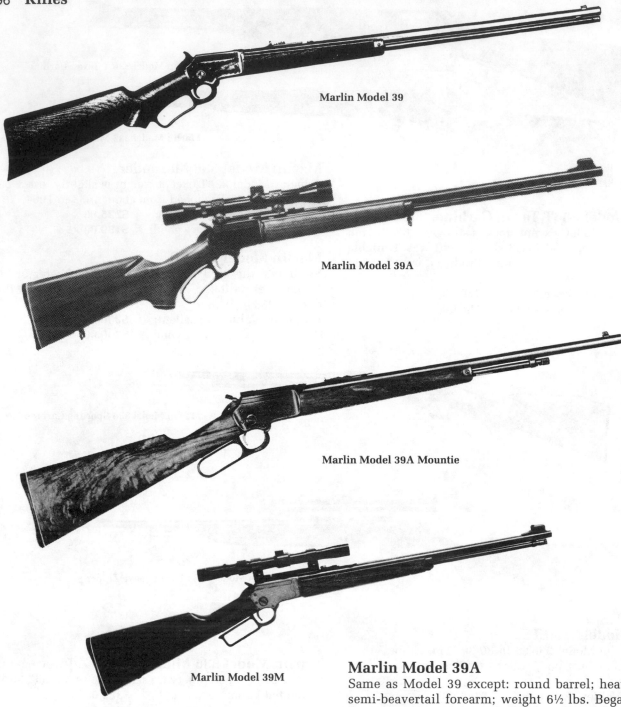

Marlin Model 39

Marlin Model 39A

Marlin Model 39A Mountie

Marlin Model 39M

Marlin Model 39

Caliber: 22 short, long, long rifle
Action: Lever action; exposed hammer; repeating; take-down type
Magazine: 25 shorts, 20 longs, 18 long rifles; tubular under barrel
Barrel: 24" octagon
Sights: Bead font, open adjustable rear
Stock & Forearm: Plain pistol grip stock & forearm
Approximate wt.: 6½ lbs.
Comments: Made from about 1921 to 1937.
Estimated Value: Excellent: $300.00
                                     Very good: $240.00

Marlin Model 39A

Same as Model 39 except: round barrel; heavier stock; semi-beavertail forearm; weight 6½ lbs. Began production about 1938 & was discontinued in 1957. Replaced by Golden 39A.
Estimated Value: Excellent: $200.00
                                     Very good: $160.00

Marlin Model 39M

Similar to 39A with 20" barrel; less capacity in magazine; straight grip stock.
Estimated Value: Excellent: $175.00
                                     Very good: $140.00

Marlin Model 39A Mountie

Same as Model 39 except: straight grip, lighter stock with trim forearm; weight is 6 to 6½ lbs.; 20" barrel; produced from 1950's to 1960.
Estimated Value: Excellent: $180.00
                                     Very good: $145.00

Marlin Model 39M Golden Mountie

Marlin Model 39M Golden Mountie

Same gun as Model 39A Mountie except: gold plated trigger; 20" barrel; weight 6 lbs.; magazine capacity 21 shorts, 16 longs or 15 long rifles. Produced from 1950's to 1988.

Estimated Value: Excellent: $210.00
                       Very good: $160.00

Marlin Model Golden 39A

Marlin Model Golden 39A, 39AS

Caliber: 22 short, long, long rifle
Action: Lever-action; exposed hammer; takedown type; gold plated trigger; 39AS has hammer block safety & rebounding hammer
Magazine: 26 shorts, 21 long rifles; tubular under barrel
Barrel: 24" micro-groove round barrel
Sights: Bead front with removable hood; adjustable folding semi-buckhorn rear
Stock & Forearm: Walnut plain pistol grip stock & forearm; steel cap on end
Approximate wt.: 6¾ lbs.
Comments: Made from about 1958 to date; equipped with sling swivels; hammer block safety & rebounding hammer added 1988.
Estimated Value: New (retail): $358.95
                       Excellent: $270.00
                       Very good: $215.00

Marlin Model 39TDS

Similar to the Model 39AS but smaller; tubular magazine holds 16 shorts, 13 longs, 11 long rifles; 16½" barrel; weighs 5¼ lbs. Introduced in 1988. comes with floatable zippered case; assembles without tools.

Estimated Value: New (retail): $399.95
                       Excellent: $300.00
                       Very good: $245.00

Marlin Model 444

Marlin Model 444, 444S, 444SS

Caliber: 444 Marlin
Action: Action-lever; repeating
Magazine: 4-shot tubular under barrel
Barrel: Blued; 24" micro-groove
Sights: Folding open rear, hooded ramp front
Stock & Forearm: Monte Carlo straight or pistol grip stock; carbine-type forearm; barrel band; swivels
Approximate wt.: 7½ lbs.
Comments: Made from about 1965 to present. Currently called 444SS. Hammer block safety added 1986.
Estimated Value: New (retail): $433.95
                       Excellent: $325.00
                       Very good: $260.00

Marlin Glenfield Model 30

Caliber: 30-30 Win.
Action: Lever action; repeating
Magazine: 6-shot tubular
Barrel: Blued; 20" round
Sights: Adjustable rear, bead front
Stock & Forearm: Walnut, plain or checkered; semi-pistol grip stock & forearm
Approximate wt.: 7 lbs.
Comments: Made from about 1966 to the late 1970's.
Estimated Value: Excellent: $180.00
                       Very good: $135.00

Marlin Glenfield Model 30GT

Similar to the Glenfield 30 with a straight grip stock & 18½" barrel. Made from the late 1970's to early 1980's.
Estimated Value: Excellent: $175.00
                       Very good: $130.00

Marlin Glenfield Model 30A, Marlin 30AS

Similar to the Glenfield 30. Made from the late 1970's to present. Plain stock on the 30AS.
Estimated Value: New (retail) $304.95
                       Excellent: $230.00
                       Very good: $185.00

Marlin Model 375

Caliber: 375 Win.
Action: Lever-action; side ejection; repeating
Magazine: 5-shot tubular
Barrel: 20" round
Sights: Adjustable semi-buckhorn rear, ramp front with brass bead
Stock & Forearm: Plain walnut pistol grip stock & forearm with fluted comb; swivels
Approximate wt.: 6¾" lbs.
Comments: Produced from 1980 to mid 1980's.
Estimated Value: Excellent: $275.00
                       Very good: $220.00

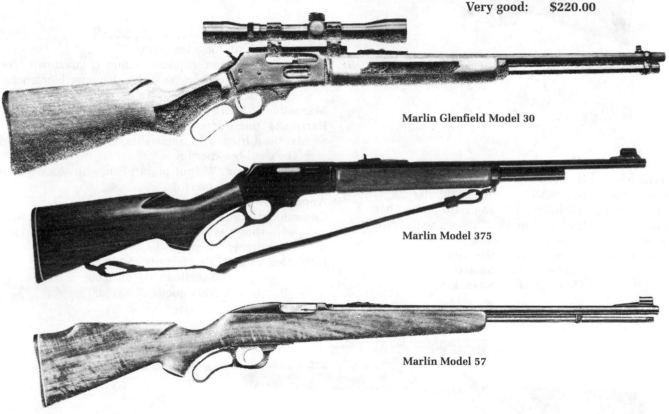

Marlin Glenfield Model 30

Marlin Model 375

Marlin Model 57

Marlin Model 57

Caliber: 22 short, long, long rifle
Action: Lever action; repeating
Magazine: Tubular under barrel; 19 long rifles, 21 longs, 27 shorts
Barrel: Blued; 22" round
Sights: Open rear, hooded ramp front
Stock & Forearm: Plain Monte Carlo pistol grip stock & forearm
Approximate wt.: 6¼ lbs.
Comments: Made from about 1959 to 1965.
Estimated Value: Excellent: $145.00
                       Very good: $115.00

Marlin Model 56 Levermatic

Caliber: 22 short, long, long rifle
Action: Lever-action; repeating
Magazine: 8-shot clip
Barrel: Blued; 22" round
Sights: Open rear, hooded ramp front
Stock & Forearm: Monte Carlo pistol grip stock & forearm
Approximate wt.: 5¾ lbs.
Comments: Similar to Model 57, produced from about 1955 to 1965.
Estimated Value: Excellent: $135.00
                       Very good: $110.00

Marlin Model 57M Levermatic

Caliber: 22 Win. mag.
Action: Lever action; repeating
Magazine: 15-shot tubular; under barrel
Barrel: 24" round
Sights: Open rear, hooded ramp front
Stock & Forearm: Monte Carlo pistol grip stock & forearm
Approximate wt.: 6¼ lbs.
Comments: Similar to Model 57; produced from about 1960 to 1969.
Estimated Value: Excellent: $140.00
Very good: $115.00

Marlin Model 62 Levermatic

Caliber: 256 mag. (1963 to 1966); 30 carbine (1966-1969)
Action: Lever action; repeating
Magazine: 4-shot clip
Barrel: Blued; 23" round
Sights: Open rear, hooded ramp front
Stock & Forearm: Monte Carlo pistol grip stock & forearm
Approximate wt.: 7 lbs.
Comments: Made from about 1963 to 1969.
Estimated Value: Excellent: $190.00
Very good: $150.00

Marlin Model 56 Levermatic

Marlin Model 62 Levermatic

Marlin Model 18 Baby Slide Action

Marlin Model 20

Marlin Model 29

Marlin Model 18 Baby Slide Action

Caliber: 22 short, long, long rifle
Action: Slide action; exposed hammer; repeating
Magazine: Tubular under barrel; 15 shorts, 12 longs, 10 long rifles
Barrel: Blued; 20" round or octagon
Sights: Open rear, bead front
Stock & Forearm: Plain walnut straight grip stock & slide handle
Approximate wt.: 3½ to 4 lbs.
Comments: Production began on this model about 1906 but was discontinued three years later.
Estimated Value: Excellent: $300.00
Very good: $240.00

Marlin Model 20 or 20 S

Caliber: 22 short, long, long rifle
Action: Slide action; exposed hammer; repeating
Magazine: 25 shorts, 20 longs, 18 long rifles in full length; 15 shorts, 12 longs, 10 long rifles in half length; tubular, under barrel
Barrel: Blued; 24" octagon
Sights: Open rear, bead front
Stock & Forearm: Plain walnut straight grip stock & grooves slide handle
Approximate wt.: 5 lbs.
Comments: This rifle was produced from about 1907 in takedown model & known as Model 20 S after 1920. Discontinued about 1922.
Estimated Value: Excellent: $290.00
Very good: $225.00

Marlin Model 29

Similar to Model 20 except: round 23" barrel; weighs about 5¾ lbs.; magazine available in half length only; produced from about 1913 to 1916.
Estimated Value: Excellent: $290.00
Very good: $225.00

Marlin Model 25

Marlin Model 27

Marlin Model 27 S

Marlin Model 25
Caliber: 22 short & 22 CB caps only
Action: Slide action; exposed hammer; repeating
Magazine: 15-shot tubular, under barrel
Barrel: Blued; 23" octagon
Sights: Open rear, bead front
Stock & Forearm: Plain walnut straight grip stock & slide handle
Approximate wt.: 4 lbs.
Comments: Production on this takedown model began in 1909 & was stopped one year later.
Estimated Value: **Excellent:**   **$300.00**
                    Very good: **$240.00**

Marlin Model 27 & 27S
Caliber: 25-20, 32-30 & 25 Stevens RF (1920 to 1932) (27S)
Action: Slide action; exposed hammer; repeating
Magazine: 6-shot, ⅔ tubular, under barrel
Barrel: Blued; 24" octagon
Sights: Open rear, bead front
Stock & Forearm: Plain walnut straight grip stock & grooved slide handle
Approximate wt.: 5¾ lbs.
Comments: This takedown model was produced from about 1910 to 1915 & from 1920 to 1932.
Estimated Value: **Excellent:**   **$290.00**
                    Very good: **$225.00**

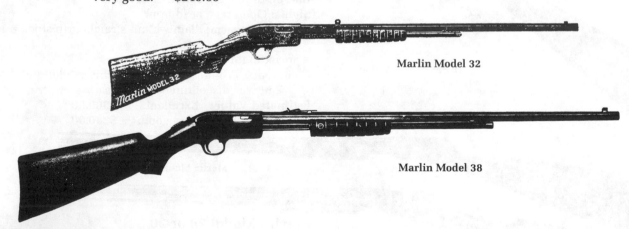

Marlin Model 32

Marlin Model 38

Marlin Model 32
Caliber: 22 short, long, long rifle
Action: Slide action; concealed hammer; repeating
Magazine: 25 shorts, 20 longs, 18 long rifles in full length; 15 shorts, 12 longs, 10 long rifles in ⅔ length; tubular, under barrel
Barrel: Blued; 24" octagon
Sights: Open rear, bead front
Stock & Forearm: Walnut pistol grip stock & grooved slide handle
Approximate wt.: 5½ lbs.
Comments: Takedown model produced from about 1914 for one year.
Estimated Value: **Excellent:**   **$300.00**
                    Very good: **$225.00**

Marlin Model 38
Caliber: 22 short, long, long rifle
Action: Slide action; exposed hammer; repeating
Magazine: 15 shorts, 12 longs, 10 long rifles, ⅔ tubular, under barrel
Barrel: Blued; 24" octagon or round
Sights: Open rear, bead front
Stock & Forearm: Plain pistol grip stock & grooved slide handle
Approximate wt.: 5½ lbs.
Comments: Production began about 1921 on this takedown model & was discontinued about 1930.
Estimated Value: **Excellent:**   **$285.00**
                    Very good: **$215.00**

Marlin Model 37

Marlin Model 47

Marlin Model 37

Caliber: 22 short, long, long rifle
Action: Slide action; exposed hammer; repeating
Magazine: 25 shorts, 20 longs, 18 long rifles; tubular, under barrel
Barrel: 24" round
Sights: Open rear, bead front
Stock & Forearm: Walnut pistol grip stock & forearm
Approximate wt.: 5 lbs.
Comments: This rifle was produced from about 1923 until 1933; takedown model.
Estimated Value: Excellent: $275.00
Very good: $220.00

Marlin Model 47

Basically same as Model 37, used as a bonus give-away with purchase of Marlin Stocks. Discontinued in 1931 after six years production.
Estimated Value: Excellent: $425.00
Very good: $340.00

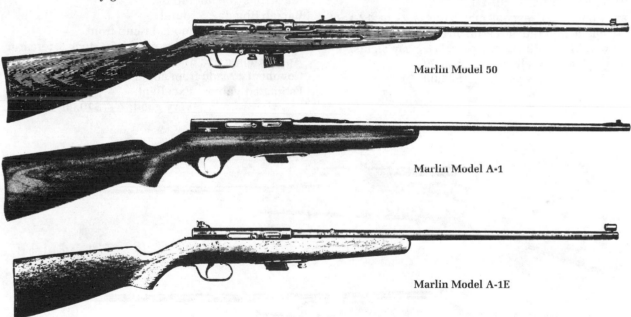

Marlin Model 50

Marlin Model A-1

Marlin Model A-1E

Marlin Model A-1 & A-1E

Caliber: 22 long rifle
Action: Semi-automatic; side ejection
Magazine: 6-shot detachable box
Barrel: Blued; 24"
Sights: Open rear, bead front; peep sights on A-1E
Stock & Forearm: Plain pistol grip stock & forearm
Approximate wt.: 6 lbs.
Comments: Takedown model made from about 1935 to 1946.
Estimated Value: Excellent: $120.00
Very good: $ 95.00

Model A-1C & A-1DL

An improved Model A-1; semi-beavertail forearm. Produced from about 1940 for six years. Peep sights & swivels on A-1DL.
Estimated Value: Excellent: $140.00
Very good: $115.00

Marlin Model 50 & 50E

Caliber: 22 long rifle
Action: Semi-automatic; takedown model; side ejection
Magazine: 6-shot detachable box
Barrel: Blued; 24" round
Sights: Open rear, bead front; peep sights on 50E
Stock & Forearm: Plain pistol grip stock & grooved forearm
Approximate wt.: 6 lbs.
Comments: Production began about 1931 & ended three years later.
Estimated Value: Excellent: $100.00
Very good: $ 80.00

Marlin Model 88-C

Caliber: 22 long rifle
Action: Semi-automatic; side ejection
Magazine: 14-shot tubular, in stock
Barrel: Blued; 24" round
Sights: Open rear, hooded front
Stock & Forearm: Pistol grip stock & forearm
Approximate wt.: 6¾ lbs.
Comments: A takedown model produced from about
        1947 to 1956.
Estimated Value: Excellent: $90.00
                       Very good: $70.00

Marlin Model 88 DL

Same as Model 88-C except checkered stock, swivels &
peep sight on receiver. Produced for three years beginning about 1953.
Estimated Value: Excellent: $95.00
                       Very good: $75.00

Marlin Model 89-C & 89-DL

Same as Model 88-C except magazine is 7- or 12-shot
clip & it has a tapered forearm. Produced from about
1950 to 1961. Model 89-DL has swivels & peep sights.
Estimated Value: Excellent: $80.00
                       Very good: $65.00

Marlin Model 98

Caliber: 22 long rifle
Action: Semi-automatic; side ejection
Magazine: 15-shot tubular
Barrel: Blued; 22" round
Sights: Open rear, hooded ramp front
Stock & Forearm: Walnut Monte Carlo with cheekpiece
Approximate wt.: 6¾ lbs.
Comments: A solid frame rifle produced from about 1957
        to 1959. Replaced by Model 99.
Estimated Value: Excellent: $95.00
                       Very good: $75.00

Marlin Model 99

Caliber: 22 long rifle
Action: Semi-automatic; side ejection
Magazine: 18-shot tubular
Barrel: Blued; 22" round
Sights: Open rear, hooded ramp front
Stock & Forearm: Plain pistol grip stock & forearm
Approximate wt.: 5½ lbs.
Comments: Made from about 1959 until 1961.
Estimated Value: Excellent: $85.00
                       Very good: $70.00

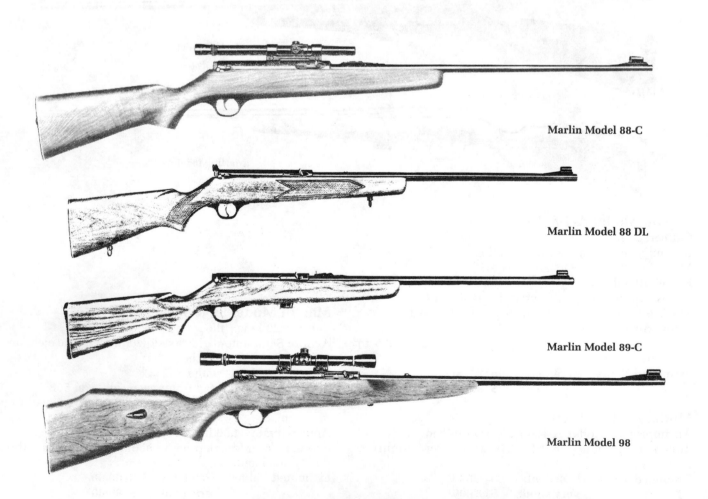

Marlin Model 88-C

Marlin Model 88 DL

Marlin Model 89-C

Marlin Model 98

Marlin Model 99C

Marlin Model 99DL

Marlin Glenfield Model 99G

Marlin Model 989

Marlin Glenfield Model 989G

Marlin Model 99C

Same as Model 99 except Monte Carlo (some are check-ered); gold plated trigger; grooved receiver. Produced from 1962 to late 1970's.

Estimated Value: Excellent: $90.00
Very good: $70.00

Marlin Model 99DL

Same as Model 99C except it has swivels & jeweled breech bolt. Made for five years beginning about 1960.

Estimated Value: Excellent: $95.00
Very good: $75.00

Marlin Glenfield Model 99G

Basically the same as Model 99 with a plain stock. Pro-duced from about 1963 to 1965.

Estimated Value: Excellent: $75.00
Very good: $60.00

Marlin Model 989

Caliber: 22 long rifle only
Action: Semi-automatic; side ejection
Magazine: 7-shot clip
Barrel: Blued; 22" round
Sights: Open rear, hooded ramp front
Stock & Forearm: Monte Carlo pistol grip stock & fore-arm
Approximate wt.: 5½ lbs.
Comments: Produced for four years beginning in 1962.

Estimated Value: Excellent: $90.00
Very good: $70.00

Marlin Glenfield Model 989G

Basically same as Marlin Model 989 except plain stock & bead front sight. Produced from about 1962 to 1964.

Estimated Value: Excellent: $85.00
Very good: $70.00

Marlin Model 99 M1

Marlin Model 989 M2

Marlin Glenfield Model 60

Marlin Model 70P Papoose

Marlin Model 70P Papoose

Caliber: 22 long rifle
Action: Semi-automatic; side ejection
Magazine: 7-shot clip
Barrel: 16¼" quick takedown
Sights: Adjustable rear, ramp front; 4X scope included
Stock & Forearm: Smooth walnut-finish hardwood, semi-pistol grip stock with abbreviated forearm
Approximate wt.: 3¼ lbs.
Comments: Introduced in 1986. This is a quick takedown rifle with built-in flotation. Case included.
Estimated Value: New (retail): $165.95
                       Excellent: $125.00
                       Very good: $100.00

Marlin Glenfield Model 60

Caliber: 22 long rifle
Action: Semi-automatic; side ejection
Magazine: 17-shot tubular, under barrel
Barrel: Blued; 22" round
Sights: Open rear, ramp front; some with scope
Stock & Forearm: Checkered or smooth hardwood semi-pistol grip stock & forearm; or Monte Carlo
Approximate wt.: 5½ lbs.
Comments: In production since about 1966. Add 8% for scope.
Estimated Value: New (retail): $131.95
                       Excellent: $100.00
                       Very good: $ 80.00

Marlin Model 99 M1

Caliber: 22 long rifle
Action: Semi-automatic; side ejection
Magazine: 9-shot tubular
Barrel: Blued; 18" micro-groove
Sights: Open rear, ramp front (military)
Stock & Forearm: Carbine stock, hand guard & barrel band; swivels
Approximate wt.: 4½ lbs.
Comments: Styled after the U.S. 30 M1 Carbine; in production from about 1966 to the late 1970's.
Estimated Value: Excellent: $95.00
                       Very good: $75.00

Marlin Model 989 M2

Same rifle as the Model 99 M1 except it has a 7-shot clip magazine.
Estimated Value: Excellent: $100.00
                       Very good: $ 75.00

Marlin Model 75C

Same to the Model 60 except: 13-shot magazine, 18" barrel.
Estimated Value: New (retail): $131.95
                       Excellent: $100.00
                       Very good: $ 80.00

Marlin Model 49

Marlin Model 49 DL

Marlin Glenfield Model 70

Marlin Glenfield Model 70 Carbine, 70HC

Caliber: 22 long rifle
Action: Semi-automatic; side ejection
Magazine: 7-shot clip; 70HC has 25-shot clip
Barrel: Blued; 18" round
Sights: Open rear, ramp front
Stock & Forearm: Checkered walnut Monte Carlo stock & plain forearm; barrel band; swivels
Approximate wt.: 5½ lbs.
Comments: Production from about 1966 to present; 70HC introduced in 1988.
Estimated Value: New (retail): $147.95
                                        Excellent: $110.00
                                        Very good: $ 89.00

Marlin Model 49

Caliber: 22 long rifle
Action: Semi-automatic; side ejection
Magazine: 18-shot tubular
Barrel: Blued; 22" round
Sights: Adjustable open rear, ramp front
Stock & Forearm: Monte Carlo pistol grip stock & forearm
Approximate wt.: 5½ lbs.
Comments: Made in the late 1960's to mid 1970's.
Estimated Value: Excellent: $85.00
                                        Very good: $65.00

Marlin Model 49 DL

Same as the Model 49 except checkered stock & forearm & gold plated trigger. Production began about 1971; ended in late 1970's.
Estimated Value: Excellent: $90.00
                                        Very good: $70.00

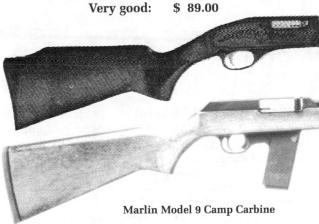

Marlin Glenfield Model 40

Marlin Model 9 Camp Carbine

Marlin Glenfield Model 40

Caliber: 22 long rifle
Action: Semi-automatic; hammerless; side ejection
Magazine: 18-shot tubular
Barrel: 22"
Sights: Adjustable open rear, ramp front
Stock & Forearm: Checkered hardwood Monte Carlo semi-pistol grip stock & forearm
Approximate wt.: 5½ lbs.
Comments: Produce in the late 1970's.
Estimated Value: Excellent: $80.00
                                        Very good: $65.00

Marlin Model 9 Camp Carbine

Caliber: 9mm
Action: Semi-automatic; manual bolt hold-open, automatic last-shot bolt hold-open; side ejection
Magazine: 12-shot clip; 20-shot clip available
Barrel: 16½" round, blued
Sights: Adjustable rear, ramp front with brass bead
Stock & Forearm: Walnut finished hardwood pistol grip stock & forearm; rubber butt pad
Approximate wt.: 6¾ lbs.
Comments: Introduced in 1985.
Estimated Value: New (retail): $330.95
                                        Excellent: $250.00
                                        Very good: $200.00

Marlin Model 45

Similar to the Model 9 in 45ACP caliber; 7-shot clip. Introduced in 1986.
Estimated Value: New (retail): $330.75
                                        Excellent: $250.00
                                        Very good: $200.00

Marlin Model 990

Marlin Model 995

Marlin Model 990
Caliber: 22 long rifle
Action: Semi-automatic; side ejection
Magazine: 18-shot tubular
Barrel: 22" round
Sights: Adjustable folding semi-buckhorn rear, ramp
  front with brass bead
Stock & Forearm: Checkered walnut Monte Carlo one-
  piece pistol grip stock & forearm
Approximate wt.: 5½ lbs.
Comments: Produced from the late 1970's to 1988.
Estimated Value: Excellent: $120.00
  Very good: $100.00

Marlin Model 995
Similar to the Model 990 with a 7-shot clip magazine &
18" barrel.
Estimated Value: New (retail): $175.95
  Excellent: $130.00
  Very good: $105.00

Mauser

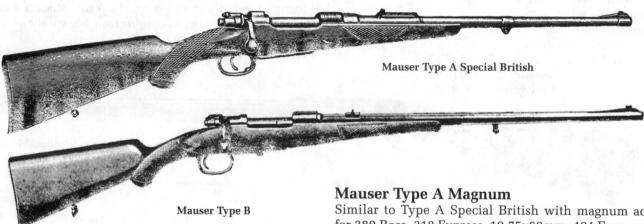

Mauser Type A Special British

Mauser Type B

Mauser Type A Special British
Caliber: 30-06, 7x57, 8x60, 9x57, 9.3x62mm
Action: Bolt action; repeating
Magazine: 5-shot box
Barrel: Blued; 23½", octagon or round
Sights: Express rear, hooded ramp front
Stock & Forearm: Checkered walnut one-piece pistol
  grip stock & tapered forearm; swivels
Approximate wt.: 7¼ lbs.
Comments: Made from about 1910 to 1938.
Estimated Value: Excellent: $625.00
  Very good: $500.00

Mauser Type A Short Model
Similar to Type A Special British with 21½" barrel & a
short action.
Estimated Value: Excellent: $625.00
  Very good: $480.00

Mauser Type A Magnum
Similar to Type A Special British with magnum action
for 280 Ross, 318 Express, 10.75x68mm, 404 Express.
Estimated Value: Excellent: $700.00
  Very good: $540.00

Mauser Type B
Caliber: 30-06, 7x57, 8x57, 8x60, 9.3x62, 10.75x68
Action: Bolt action; repeating
Magazine: 5-shot box
Barrel: Blued; 23½"
Sights: Leaf rear, ramp front
Stock & Forearm: Checkered walnut one-piece pistol
  grip stock & lipped forearm; swivels
Approximate wt.: 7½ lbs.
Comments: Made from about 1910 to 1940.
Estimated Value: Excellent: $675.00
  Very good: $540.00

Mauser Type K
Similar to Type B with 21½" barrel & short action.
Estimated Value: Excellent: $600.00
  Very good: $450.00

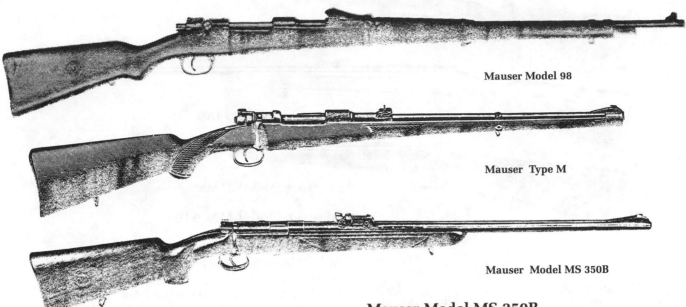

Mauser Model 98

Mauser Type M

Mauser Model MS 350B

Mauser Model 98

Caliber: 7mm, 7.9mm
Action: Bolt action; repeating
Magazine: 5 shot box
Barrel: Blued; 23½"
Sights: Adjustable rear, blade front
Stock & Forearm: Walnut one-piece semi-pistol grip
    stock & fluted forearm; barrel band
Approximate wt.: 7½ lbs.
Comments: Made from about 1920 to 1938.
Estimated Value: **Excellent:**   **$575.00**
              Very good: **$450.00**

Mauser Type M

Caliber: 30-06, 6.5x54, 7x57, 8x52, 8x60, 9x57
Action: Bolt action; repeating
Magazine: 5-shot box
Barrel: Blued; 19¾"
Sights: 3 leaf rear, ramp front
Stock & Forearm: Checkered walnut one-piece pistol
    grip stock & full-length forearm; swivels
Approximate wt.: 6½ lbs.
Comments: Made from about 1910 to 1940.
Estimated Value: **Excellent:**   **$650.00**
              Very good: **$490.00**

Mauser Type S

Caliber: 6.5x54, 7x57, 8x51, 8x60, 9x57
Action: Bolt action; repeating
Magazine: 5-shot box
Barrel: Blued; 19¾"
Sights: 3 leaf rear, ramp front
Stock & Forearm: Checkered walnut one-piece pistol
    grip stock & lipped full-length forearm; swivels
Approximate wt.: 6½ lbs.
Comments: Made from about 1910 to 1940.
Estimated Value: **Excellent:**   **$650.00**
              Very good: **$520.00**

Mauser Model MS 350B

Caliber: 22 long rifle
Action: Bolt action; repeating
Magazine: 5-shot box
Barrel: Blued; 27½"
Sights: Micrometer rear, ramp front
Stock & Forearm: Match-type; checkered pistol grip;
    swivels
Approximate wt.: 8 lbs.
Comments: Made from the mid 1920's to mid 1930's.
Estimated Value: **Excellent:**   **$500.00**
              Very good: **$375.00**

Mauser Model ES 350

Similar to MS 350B with different sights & 26¾" barrel.
Made from the mid to late 1930's. Single shot.
Estimated Value: **Excellent:**   **$450.00**
              Very good: **$340.00**

Mauser Model ES 350B

Similar to MS 350B in single shot. Target sights.
Estimated Value: **Excellent:**   **$400.00**
              Very good: **$300.00**

Mauser Model ES 340

Caliber: 22 long rifle
Action: Bolt action; single shot
Magazine: None
Barrel: Blued; 25½"
Sights: Tangent curve rear, ramp front
Stock & Forearm: Checkered walnut one-piece pistol
    grip stock & forearm; swivels
Approximate wt.: 6½ lbs.
Comments: Made from the early 1920's to mid 1930's.
Estimated Value: **Excellent:**   **$300.00**
              Very good: **$225.00**

Mauser Model ES 340B

Similar to the ES 340 with a 26¾" barrel. Made from the
mid to late 1930's.
Estimated Value: **Excellent:**   **$320.00**
              Very good: **$240.00**

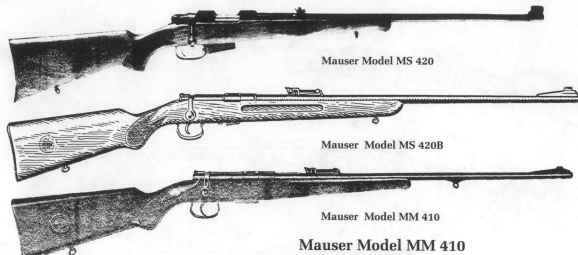

Mauser Model MS 420

Mauser Model MS 420B

Mauser Model MM 410

Mauser Model EL 320

Similar to ES 340 with a 23½" barrel, adjustable rear sight & bead front sight. Made from the late 1920's to mid 1930's.

Estimated Value: Excellent: $330.00
                Very good: $250.00

Mauser Model MS 420

Caliber: 22 long rifle
Action: Bolt action; repeating
Magazine: 5-shot detachable box
Barrel: Blued; 25½"
Sights: Tangent curve rear, ramp front
Stock & Forearm: Checkered walnut one-piece pistol grip stock & forearm; swivels
Approximate wt.: 6½ lbs.
Comments: Made from the mid 1920's to mid 1930's.
Estimated Value: Excellent: $380.00
                Very good: $300.00

Mauser Model MS 420B

Similar to MS 420 with better wood. Made from the mid to late 1930's.

Estimated Value: Excellent: $450.00
                Very good: $340.00

Mauser Model MM 410

Caliber: 22 long rifle
Action: Bolt action; repeating
Magazine: 5-shot detachable box
Barrel: Blued; 23½"
Sights: Tangent curve rear, ramp front
Stock & Forearm: Checkered one-piece pistol grip stock & forearm; swivels
Approximate wt.: 6½ lbs.
Comments: Made from the mid 1920's to mid 1930's.
Estimated Value: Excellent: $360.00
                Very good: $285.00

Mauser Model MM 410 B

Similar to MM 410 except lighter weight model. Made from mid to late 1930's.

Estimated Value: Excellent: $400.00
                Very good: $300.00

Mauser Model DSM 34

Similar to the 98 in appearance, in 22 long rifle with a 26" barrel. Made from the mid 1930's to late 1930's. Single shot.

Estimated Value: Excellent: $425.00
                Very good: $320.00

Mauser Model KKW

Similar to DSM 34. Made from the mid to late 1930's.

Estimated Value: Excellent: $400.00
                Very good: $300.00

Mauser Model 2000

Mauser Model 2000

Caliber: 270 Win., 308 Win., 30-06
Action: Bolt action; repeating; adjustable trigger
Magazine: 5-shot box; hinged floor plate
Barrel: 24" Krupp steel
Sights: Folding leaf rear, hooded ramp front
Stock & Forearm: Checkered walnut Monte Carlo one-piece pistol grip stock & forearm; swivels; cheekpiece
Approximate wt.: 7½ lbs.
Comments: Made from the late 1960's to early 1970's.
Estimated Value: Excellent: $350.00
                Very good: $260.00

Mauser 660 Safari

Mauser 3000

Mauser Model 3000

Caliber: 243, 270, 30-06, 308, 375 H&H mag., 7mm mag., 300 Win. mag.
Action: Bolt action; repeating
Magazine: 5-shot box
Barrel: 22", 26" magnum
Sights: None
Stock & Forearm: Checkered walnut Monte Carlo one-piece pistol grip stock & forearm; recoil pad; swivels
Approximate wt.: 7 lbs.
Comments: Made from the early 1970's to present. No longer available in the U.S. Add $50.00 for mag.
Estimated Value: Excellent: **$500.00**
                 Very good: **$400.00**

Mauser Model 660

Caliber: 243, 25-06, 270, 308, 30-06, 7x57, 7mm
Action: Short bolt action; repeating
Magazine: 5-shot box
Barrel: Blued; 24"
Sights: None
Stock & Forearm: Checkered walnut Monte Carlo one-piece pistol grip stock & forearm; swivels; recoil pad
Approximate wt.: 7 lbs.
Comments: Made in the early 1970's.
Estimated Value: Excellent: **$650.00**
                 Very good: **$490.00**

Mauser Model 660 Safari

Similar to 660 except: magnum calibers; 28" barrel; express rear sight & ramp front sight; calibers 458 Win., 375 H&H, 338 Win., & 7mm Rem.; approximate weight 9 lbs.
Estimated Value: Excellent: **$700.00**
                 Very good: **$525.00**

Mauser Varminter 10

Mauser Model 66S

Caliber: 243, 6.5x57, 270, 7x64, 30-06, 308, 5.6x61 V.H. mag., 6.5x68 mag., 7mm Rem. mag., 7mm V.H. mag., 8x68S mag., 300 Win. mag., 300 Weath. mag., 9.3x62 mag., 9.3x64 mag.
Action: Mauser telescopic short bolt action; repeating
Magazine: 5-shot box
Barrel: Blued; 21", 24", 26"; interchangeable barrels available
Sights: Adjustable rear, hooded ramp front
Stock & Forearm: Select European walnut, checkered Monte Carlo one-piece pistol grip stock & forearm; rosewood tip at fore-end & pistol grip; recoil pad; swivels; full length forearm available
Approximate wt.: 7 lbs.
Comments: Add $100.00 for 21" or 26" barrel or full length forearm.
Estimated Value: Excellent: **$1,000.00**
                 Very good: **$ 800.00**

Mauser Model 66SM

Similar to the Model 66S with lipped forearm (no rosewood tip) & internal alterations. Add $100.00 for 21" or 26" barrel or full length forearm.
Estimated Value: Excellent: **$1,160.00**
                 Very good: **$ 870.00**

Mauser Model 66SL

Similar to the Model 66SM with select walnut stock & forearm. Add $1,000.00 fpr Diplomat Model with custom engraving.
Estimated Value: Excellent: **$1,370.00**
                 Very good: **$1,025.00**

Mauser Model 66S Big Game

Similar to Model 66S in 375 H&H or 458 Win. magnum caliber; 26" barrel; fold down rear sight; weight about 10 lbs.
Estimated Value: Excellent: **$1,320.00**
                 Very good: **$1,050.00**

Mauser Varminter 10

Caliber: 22-250
Action: Bolt action; repeating
Magazine: 5-shot box
Barrel: Blued; 24", heavy
Sights: None
Stock & Forearm: Checkered walnut Monte Carlo one-piece pistol grip stock & forearm
Approximate wt.: 8 lbs.
Comments: Made from early 1970's to present. No longer available in U.S.
Estimated Value: Excellent: **$440.00**
                 Very good: **$350.00**

Mauser Model 77 DJV Sportsman
Similar to the Model 77 with stippled stock & forearm; no sights.
Estimated Value: Excellent: $1,150.00
Very good: $ 860.00

Mauser Model 77 Big Game
Similar to the Model 77 in 375 H&H magnum caliber; 26" barrel.
Estimated Value: Excellent: $1,070.00
Very good: $ 800.00

Mauser Model 77
Caliber: 243 Win., 270 Win., 308 Win., 30-06, 6.5x57, 7x64, 7mm Rem. mag., 6.5x68 mag., 300 Win. mag., 9.3x62 mag., 8x68S mag.
Action: Mauser short bolt action; repeating
Magazine: 3-shot clip
Barrel: Blued; 20", 24", 26"
Sights: Adjustable rear, hooded ramp front
Stock & Forearm: Checkered walnut one-piece pistol grip stock & lipped forearm; full-length forearm available; recoil pad; swivels
Approximate wt.: 7½ lbs.
Comments: Introduced in the early 1980's. Add $100.00 for 20" or 26" barrel or full length forearm.
Estimated Value: Excellent: $915.00
Very good: $685.00

Military, Argentine

Argentine M 1891 Mauser

Argentine M 1891 Carbine

Argentine M 1909 Mauser

Argentine M 1909 Carbine

Argentine Model 1891 Mauser
Caliber: 7x65mm rimless
Action: Manually-operated bolt action; straight bolt handle
Magazine: 5-shot single column box
Barrel: 29" round barrel; cleaning rod in forearm
Sights: Barley corn front; rear adjustable for elevation
Stock & Forearm: Military-type one-piece straight grip stock & full forearm; bayonet lug; two barrel bands
Approximate wt.: 8½ lbs.
Comments: Similar to 7.65mm M1890 Turkish Mauser; obsolete.
Estimated Value: Very good: $125.00
Good: $ 90.00

Argentine Model 1909 Carbine
Similar to Model 1909 Rifle except: 17½" barrel; approximate wt. 6½ lbs.; with & without bayonet lugs.
Estimated Value: Very good: $145.00
Good: $110.00

Argentine Model 1891 Carbine
Similar to Model 1891 Rifle except: 17½" barrel; approximate wt. 6½ lbs.; two versions, one with & one without bayonet lug; some still used as police weapons.
Estimated Value: Very good: $120.00
Good: $ 90.00

Argentine Model 1909 Mauser
Caliber: 7.65mm rimless
Action: Manually-operated bolt with straight handle
Magazine: 5-shot staggered row box magazine
Barrel: 29" round barrel
Sights: Barley corn, tangent leaf rear
Stock & Forearm: Military-type one-piece semi-pistol grip stock & full forearm; two barrel bands; cleaning rod in forearm
Approximate wt.: 9 lbs.
Comments: A slight modification of the German Gewehr 98; obsolete.
Estimated Value: Very good: $150.00
Good: $115.00

Military, British

Lee-Enfield Mark I Rifle

Lee-Enfield Mark I Carbine

British Lee-Enfield Mark I

Caliber: 303
Action: Bolt action; repeating; bolt handle curved downward
Magazine: 10-shot detachable box with cut-off
Barrel: 30"
Sights: Barley corn front, vertical leaf rear
Stock & Forearm: Plain military-type stock & forearm
Approximate wt.: 9¼ lbs.
Comments: Adopted by British Army about 1899.
Estimated Value: Very good: $140.00
Good: $110.00

British Lee-Enfield Mark I Carbine

Similar to Lee Enfield Mark I Rifle except 21" barrel.
Estimated Value: Very good: $135.00
Good: $105.00

Lee-Enfield No. 1 SMLE MK1

Lee-Enfield No. 1 SMLE MK III

(Pattern 14) No. 3 MK 1

British Lee-Enfield No. 1 SMLE MK1

Caliber: 303
Action: Bolt action; curved bolt handle
Magazine: 10-shot detachable box with cut-off
Barrel: 25¼"
Sights: Barley corn front with protective ears; tangent leaf rear
Stock & Forearm: Plain wood military stock to the muzzle with full length wood hand guard over barrel
Approximate wt.: 8 lbs.
Comments: Adopted about 1902 by British Army.
Estimated Value: Very good: $160.00
Good: $120.00

British (Pattern 14) No. 3 MK 1

Caliber: 303
Action: Bolt action; modified Mauser-type action; cocked as bolt is moved foreward
Magazine: 5-shot non-removale box
Barrel: 26"
Sights: Blade front with protective ears, vertical leaf with aperture rear
Stock & Forearm: Plain military stock with wood hand guard over barrel
Approximate wt.: 9 lbs.
Comments: Made in U.S.A. during World War I for the British Army.
Estimated Value: Very good: $150.00
Good: $115.00

British Lee-Enfield No. 1 SMLE MK III

Similar to No. 1 SMLE MK I except: modified & simplified for mass production; adopted in 1907 & modified again in 1918.
Estimated Value: Very good: $165.00
Good: $120.00

Jungle Carbine
No. 5 MK 1

British Lee-Enfield No. 4 MKI

British Jungle Carbine No. 5 MK1

Caliber: 303

Action: Bolt action

Magazine: 10-shot detachable box

Barrel: 18¾"

Sights: Blade front with protective ears; vertical leaf rear with aperture

Stock & Forearm: Military-type one-piece stock & forearm; wood hand guard over barrel; one barrel band

Approximate wt.: 7 lbs.

Comments: Made during World War II for jungle fighting.

Estimated Value: Very good: $180.00

Good: $145.00

British Lee-Enfield No. 4 MK1

Caliber: 303

Action: Bolt action

Magazine: 10-shot detachable box

Barrel: 25"

Sights: Blade front with protective ears; vertical leaf with aperture rear

Stock & Forearm: Plain military stock with wood hand guard over barrel

Approximate wt.: 8¾ lbs.

Comments: First produced about 1931 & was redesigned for mass production in 1939 by utilizing stamped parts & other short cuts.

Estimated Value: Very good: $135.00

Good: $100.00

Military, Chilean

Chilean Model 1895

Chilean Model 1895 Short

Chilean Model 1895 Carbine

Chilean Model 1895 Short

Similar to Model 1895 Rifle except: 22" barrel; approximate wt. 8½ lbs.

Estimated Value: Very good: $100.00

Good: $ 75.00

Chilean Model 1895 Carbine

Similar to Model 1895 Rifle except: 18¼" barrel; approximate wt. 7½ lbs.

Estimated Value: Very good: $100.00

Good: $ 80.00

Chilean Model 1895

Caliber: 7mm

Action: Bolt action; straight or turned bolt handle; similar to the Spanish Model 1893 Mauser

Magazine: 5-shot staggered non-detachable box

Barrel: 29"

Sights: Barley corn front; leaf rear

Stock & Forearm: Plain military-type stock with wood hand guard over barrel

Approximate wt.: 9 lbs.

Comments: Since Chile's adoption of the FN rifle, quantities of the Chilean Mausers have been purchased by U.S.A. arms dealers.

Estimated Value: Very good: $110.00

Good: $ 80.00

Military, German

German Model 1888 (GEW 88)

German Model 1888 Carbine

German Gewehr 98 (GEW 98)

German Model 98 (Kar 98) Carbine

German Model 1888 Carbine

Similar to the Model 1888 Rifle except: 18" barrel; approximate wt. 6¾ lbs.; full length stock to muzzle; curved flattened top bolt handle.

Estimated Value:	Very good:	$95.00
	Good:	$70.00

German Model 1891

Similar to Model 1888 Carbine except: stacking hook under forearm & although it is called a rifle, it has an 18" barrel like the carbines.

Estimated Value:	Very good:	$110.00
	Good:	$ 85.00

German Model 1888 (GEW 88)

Caliber: 7.92mm
Action: Bolt action; straight bolt handle
Magazine: 5-shot in line non-detachable box
Barrel: 29"
Sights: Barley corn front; leaves with "v" notches rear
Stock & Forearm: Plain straight grip military stock; no hand guard but uses a metal barrel jacket that covers barrel to muzzle
Approximate wt.: 8¾ lbs.
Comments: This arm is sometimes called a Mauser or Mannlicher but actually it is neither; it combines the magazine of the Mannlicher with the bolt features of the Mauser 1871/84; it is unsafe to use with the modern 7.92mm cartridge.

Estimated Value:	Very good:	$100.00
	Good:	$ 75.00

German Model 98 (Kar 98) Carbine

Similar to Model Gewehr 98 Rifle except: 17" barrel; approximate wt. 7½ lbs.; full stock to muzzle; section of forearm from barrel band to muzzle tapered to much smaller size than rest of forearm; curved bolt handle.

Estimated Value:	Very good:	$150.00
	Good:	$125.00

German Gewehr 98 (GEW 98)

Caliber: 7.92mm
Action: Bolt action; straight or curved bolt handle
Magazine: 5-shot staggered non-detachable box; also during World War II, 20- & 25-shot magazines
Barrel: 29"
Sights: Barley corn front; tangent bridge type or tangent leaf "v" rear
Stock & Forearm: Plain military semi-pistol grip stock & forearm; wood hand guard
Approximate wt.: 9 lbs.
Comments: This was one of the principle rifles of the German Army in World War I; it also appeared in a caliber 22 training rifle in World War I by fitting a liner in the barrel.

Estimated Value:	Very good:	$175.00
	Good:	$130.00

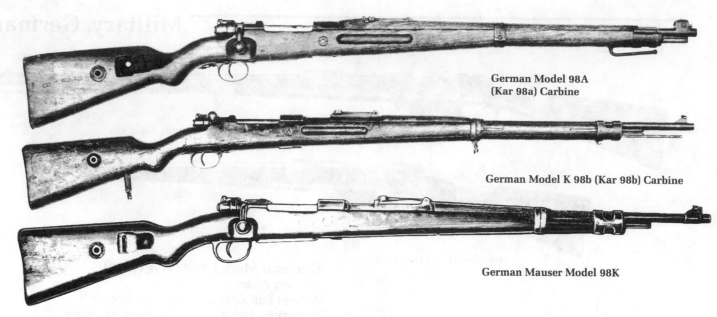

German Model 98A
(Kar 98a) Carbine

German Model K 98b (Kar 98b) Carbine

German Mauser Model 98K

German Model 98A (Kar 98a) Carbine

Similar to Model Gewehr 98 Rifle except: 24" barrel; appeared in 1904 & made in tremendous quantities until 1918; used in World War I & had limited use in World War II; cut out in stock below bolt handle; curved bolt handle; grip grooves on forearm; stacking hook.

Estimated Value: Very good: $165.00

Good: $125.00

German Model K 98b (Kar 98b) Carbine

Although designed as a carbine, it is same length & is similar to Gewehr 98 Rifle except: turned down bolt; grip grooved forearm; these were used in the 1920's & early in World War II.

Estimated Value: Very good: $175.00

Good: $130.00

German Mauser Model 98K

Caliber: 7.92mm

Action: Bolt action; turned down bolt handle

Magazine: 5-shot staggered row non-detachable box

Barrel: 24"

Sights: Barley conr open or hooded front, tangent rear with "v" notch

Stock & Forearm: Plain military semi-pistol grip stock & forearm; wood hand guard; cut out in stock under bolt handle

Approximate wt.: 8¾ lbs.

Comments: The standard infantry rifle during World War II; widely fluctuating prices on these rifles because some have special unit markings which affect their values.

Estimated Value: Very good: $150.00 - $500.00

Good: $120.00 - $400.00

Military, Italian

Italian Mannlicher Carcano M 1891

Mannlicher Carcano M 1891 Carbine

Italian Mannlicher Carcano M 1891 Carbine

Generally the same specifications as M 1891 Military rifle except: 18" barrel; bent bolt handle; folding bayonet permanently attached; approximate wt. 7 lbs.

Estimated Value: Very good: $100.00

Good: $ 70.00

Italian Mannlicher Carcano M 1891

Caliber: 6.5mm

Action: Bolt action; straight bolt handle; a modified Mauser-type action

Magazine: 6-shot in line non-detachable box

Barrel: 30½"

Sights: Barley corn front, tangent rear with "v" notch graduated from 500 to 2000 meters

Stock & Forearm: Plain straight grip military stock with wood hand guard over barrel

Approximate wt.: 8¾ lbs.

Comments: Uses knife-type bayonet.

Estimated Value: Very good: $90.00

Good: $60.00

Italian Mannlicher Carcano M 1891 TS Carbine

Italian Mannlicher Carcano M 1891 TS Carbine
Similar to M 1891 Carbine except: uses knife-type removable bayonet.

Estimated Value: Very good: $95.00
                  Good: $60.00

Mannlicher Carcano M 1938

Italian Mannlicher Carcano M 1938 Carbine
Similar to M 1938 Military Rifle except: 18" barrel; folding bayonet permanently attached.

Estimated Value: Very good: $95.00
                  Good: $70.00

Italian Mannlicher Carcano M 1938 TS Carbine
Same as M 1938 Carbine except: detachable knife-type bayonet.

Estimated Value: Very good: $90.00
                  Good: $65.00

Italian Mannlicher Carcano M 1938
Caliber: 7.35mm, 6.5mm
Action: Bolt action; bent bolt handle
Magazine: 6-shot in line, non-detachable box
Barrel: 21"
Sights: Barley corn front, adjustable rear
Stock & Forearm: Plain straight grip military stock; wood handle guard over barrel
Approximate wt.: 7½ lbs.
Comments: First of the Italian rifles chambered for the 7.35mm cartridge; in 1940 the 7.35mm caliber was dropped; this is the type rifle used to assassinate President John F. Kennedy in 1963; it was a 6.5mm made in 1940 & sold in U.S.A. as Army surplus.

Estimated Value: Very good: $100.00
                  Good: $ 70.00

Military, Japanese

Japanese Type 38 Arisaka

Japanese Type 38 Arisaka Carbine

Japanese Type 38 Arisaka Carbine
Similar to Type 38 Arisaka Rifle except: 20" barrel; folding bayonet; approximate wt. 7¼ lbs.; some were converted for paratrooper use by fitting of a hinged butt stock.

Estimated Value:		Paratrooper
	Carbine	Carbine
Very good:	$150.00	$180.00
Good:	$110.00	$135.00

Japanese Type 38 Arisaka
Caliber: 6.5mm Japanese
Action: Bolt action; straight bolt handle
Magazine: 5-shot box magazine with floor plate
Barrel: 31½" round
Sights: Barley corn front with protecting ears, rear sight adjustable for elevation
Stock & Forearm: Military finish; plain wood one-piece full stock; semi-pistol grip; steel buttplate; cleaning rod under barrel; wood hand guard on top of barrel; two steel barrel bands with bayonet lug on front band
Approximate wt.: 9¼ lbs.
Comments: Adopted by Japanese Military in 1905, the 38th year of the Meiji reign.

Estimated Value: Very good: $170.00
                  Good: $130.00

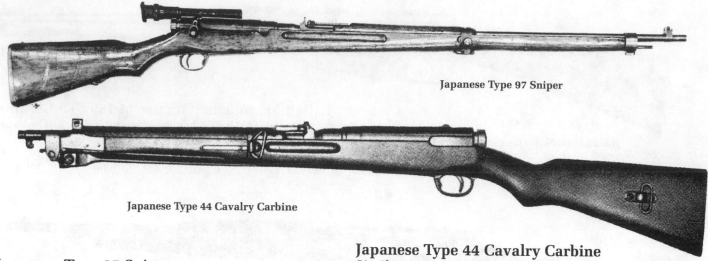

Japanese Type 97 Sniper

Japanese Type 44 Cavalry Carbine

Japanese Type 97 Sniper
Similar to Type 38 Arisaka Rifle except: a snipers version adopted in 1937 with a 2.5 power scope; approximate wt. with scope: 11 lbs. Priced for rifle with scope.

Estimated Value: Very good: $275.00
                       Good: $220.00

Japanese Type 44 Cavalry Carbine
Similar to Type 38 Arisaka carbine except: heavier weight, about 9 lbs.; adopted by Japanese Military in 1911, the 44th year of the Meiji reign; permanently attached folding bayonet.

Estimated Value: Excellent: $150.00
                       Very good: $110.00

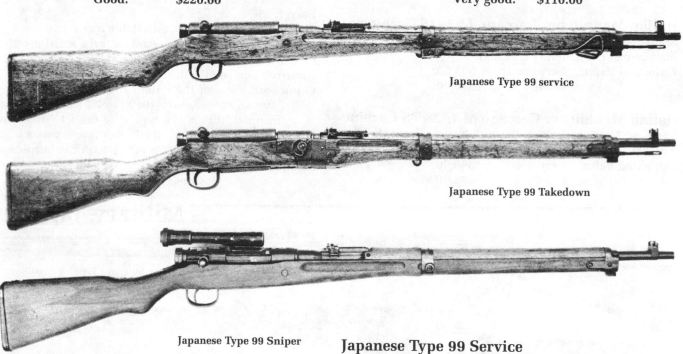

Japanese Type 99 service

Japanese Type 99 Takedown

Japanese Type 99 Sniper

Japanese Type 99 Takedown
Similar to Type 99 Service Rifle except it has a 25" barrel only. A takedown model, it has a screw-in key that serves as a locking pin. When key is removed, the barrel can be unscrewed from the receiver; however, the takedown arrangement was unsatisfactory because it weakened the receiver & affected the accuracy.

Estimated Value: Excellent: $175.00
                       Very good: $130.00

Japanese Type 99 Sniper
Similar to Type 99 Service Rifle except: adopted in 1942 & equipped with a 4X scope; 25½" barrel only. Prices include matching number & scope mounted.

Estimated Value: Excellent: $300.00
                       Very good: $250.00

Japanese Type 99 Service
Caliber: 7.7mm Japanese
Action: Bolt action
Magazine: 5-shot magazine, non-detachable
Barrel: 25½" or 31½" round
Sights: Fixed front, adjustable or fixed rear
Stock & Forearm: Military finish; plain wood, one-piece full stock; semi-pistol grip; steel buttplate; cleaning rod under barrel; some had bipod attached under forearm; wood hand guard on top of barrel; two steel barrel bands with bayonet lug on front band
Approximate wt.: 8½ to 9 lbs.
Comments: Some of the last rifles made were of poor quality & unsafe to shoot with heavy load cartridges. Adopted by Japanese Military in 1939, which was Japanese year of 2599.

Estimated Value: Very good: $150.00
                       Good: $115.00

Military, Mexican

Mexican Model 1895 Mauser Military

Mexican Model 1902

Mexican Arisaka (Japanese Type 38 Rifle)

Mexican Model 1936

Mexican Model 1954

Mexican Model 1895 Mauser
Almost identical to the Spanish 1893 Military Rifle in caliber 7mm. See Spanish Model 1893 for description.

Estimated Value: Very good: $90.00
Good: $60.00

Mexican Models 1902 & 1912 Mauser
Almost identical to the Model 1895 Mauser Military Rifle except that the actions were almost the same as Model 98 7.92 German rifle except in 7mm caliber.

Estimated Value: Very good: $95.00
Good: $65.00

Mexican Arisaka (Japanese Type 38 Rifle)
Between 1910 & 1920, Mexico procured arms from many companies. The Arisaka Rifle was purchased from Japan in caliber 7mm & had the Mexican escutcheon stamped on the receiver.

Estimated Value: Very good: $150.00
Good: $110.00

Mexican Model 1936
Caliber: 7mm
Action: Bolt action; curved bolt handle; Mauser short-type action
Magazine: 5-shot staggered row, non-detachable box
Barrel: 20"
Sights: Hooded barley corn front; tangent rear with "V" notch
Stock & Forearm: Plain semi-pistol grip stock with grip grooves in forearm; wood hand guard
Approximate wt.: 8½ lbs.
Comments: A very well made arm of Mexican manufacture; resembles the U.S. Springfield M 1903 - A-1 in appearance.
Estimated Value: Very good: $160.00
Good: $120.00

Mexican Model 1954
Caliber: 30-06
Action: Bolt action; curved bolt handle
Magazine: 5-shot staggered row, non-detachable box
Barrel: 24"
Sights: Hooded barley corn front; ramp type aperture rear
Stock & Forearm: Plain semi-pistol grip military stock & wood hand guard; stock is made of laminated plywood
Approximate wt.: 9 lbs.
Comments: This rifle is patterned after the U.S. Springfield M 1903 - A3 Military Rifle.
Estimated Value: Very good: $175.00
Good: $130.00

Military, Russian

Russian Moisin-Nagant M 1891
Caliber: 7.62 mm
Action: Bolt action; straight bolt; hexagonal receiver
Magazine: 5-shot box with hinged floor plate
Barrel: 31½"
Sights: Blade front, leaf rear
Stock & Forearm: Plain straight grip, military stock & gripped grooved forearm; early models had no hand guard & used swivels for attaching sling; later models (beginning about 1908) used sling slots & had wood hand guard
Approximate wt.: 9¾ lbs.
Comments: Adopted in 1891 by Imperial Russia.
Estimated Value: Very good: $90.00
Good: $60.00

Russian M 1910 Carbine
Caliber: 7.62 mm
Action: Bolt action; straight bolt handle; hexagonal receiver
Magazine: 5-shot box with floor plate
Barrel: 20"
Sights: Blade front, leaf type rear adjustable for elevation
Stock & Forearm: Plain straight grip military stock; sling slots in stock & forearm; wood hand guard & grip grooved forearm
Approximate wt.: 7½ lbs.
Comments: This carbine does not accept a bayonet.
Estimated Value: Very good: $100.00
Good: $ 75.00

Russian Moisin-Nagant M 1891

Russian M-1910 Carbine

Russian M-1938 Carbine

Russian Tokarev M 1938

Russian M1938 Carbine
This carbine replaced by M1910 & is very similar except: it has a round receiver; hooded front sight & tangent type rear graduated from 100 to 1000 meters; no bayonet attachment.
Estimated Value: Very good: $95.00
Good: $70.00

Russian Tokarev M 1938
Caliber: 7.62 mm
Action: Semi-automatic; gas operated
Magazine: 10-shot removable box
Barrel: 25"
Sights: Hooded post front, tangent rear
Stock & Forearm: Plain semi-pistol grip two-piece stock & forearm; cleaning rod on right side of forearm; sling swivels
Approximate wt.: 8¾ lbs.
Comments: The first of the Tokarev series; wasn't very successful & was replaced by the Tokarev M 1940.
Estimated Value: Very good: $225.00
Good: $165.00

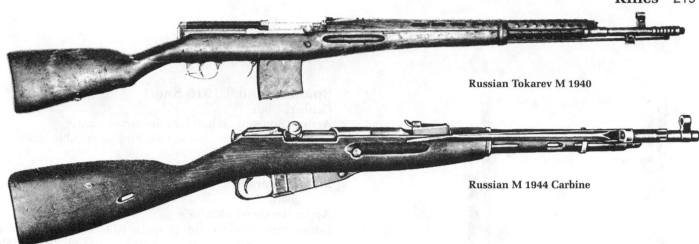

Russian Tokarev M 1940

Russian M 1944 Carbine

Russian Tokarev M 1940

Similar to Tokarev M 1938 except: improved version; cleaning rod in forearm under barrel; 24½" barrel.

Estimated Value: Very good: $275.00
Good: $200.00

Russian M 1944 Military Carbine

Similar to the M 1938 except: introduced during World War II; permanently fixed bayonet which folds along the right side of the stock; barrel length 20½".

Estimated Value: Very good: $225.00
Good: $165.00

Military, Spanish

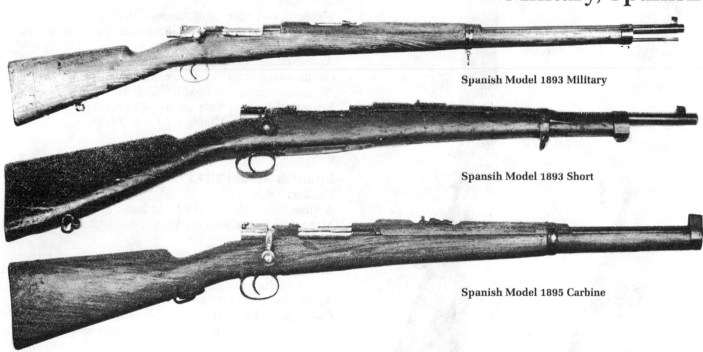

Spanish Model 1893 Military

Spansih Model 1893 Short

Spanish Model 1895 Carbine

Spanish Model 1893

Caliber: 7mm
Action: Bolt action; straight bolt handle
Magazine: 5-shot staggered row non-detachable
Barrel: 30"
Sights: Barley corn front, leaf rear
Stock & Forearm: Plain straight grip military stock with wood hand guard over barrel
Approximate wt.: 9 lbs.
Comments: A number of variations in the Model 1893 were made; it was the principal rifle used in the Spanish-American War.

Estimated Value: Very good: $80.00
Good: $55.00

Spanish Model 1893 Short

Similar to the M 1893 Rifle except: 22" barrel; approximate wt. 8½ lbs.; curved bolt handle.

Estimated Value: Very good: $75.00
Good: $50.00

Spanish Model 1895 Carbine

Similar to the M 1893 Rifle except: 18" barrel; full stock to muzzle; barley corn front sight with protective ears; approximate wt. 7½ lbs.

Estimated Value: Very good: $85.00
Good: $60.00

Spanish Model 1916 Short
Caliber: 7mm
Action: Bolt action; bolt handle curved down
Magazine: 5-shot staggered row, non-detachable box
Barrel: 24"
Sights: Barley corn front with ears, tangent rear
Stock & Forearm: Plain military stock & wood hand guard
Approximate wt.: 8½ lbs.
Comments: Made in large quantities during Spanish Civil War; later many were convered to caliber 7.62mm NATO.
Estimated Value: Very good: $95.00
Good: $70.00

Spanish Standard Model Mauser
Caliber: 7.92mm
Action: Bolt action; straight bolt handle
Magazine: 5-shot staggered row, non-detachable box
Barrel: 24"
Sights: Barley corn front, tangent rear
Stock & Forearm: Plain military semi-pistol grip stock & forearm grooved for finger grip; wood hand guard
Approximate wt.: 9 lbs.
Comments: Procured in large quantities from other countries during the Spanish Civil War.
Estimated Value: Very good: $100.00
Good: $ 75.00

Spanish Model 1943
Caliber: 7.92mm
Action: Bolt action; curved bolt handle
Magazine: 5-shot staggered row, non-detachable box
Barrel: 24"
Sights: Barley corn front, tangent rear
Stock & Forearm: Plain military semi-pistol grip stock & forearm grooved for finger grip; wood hand guard
Approximate wt.: 9 lbs.
Comments: Adopted in 1943 & continued to mid 1950's; this is a modified copy of the German 7.92mm Kar 98K.
Estimated Value: Very good: $150.00
Good: $110.00

**Spanish Model
1916 Short**

Spanish Standard

Spanish Model 1943

Military, U.S.

U.S. M 1903 Springfield

U.S. M 1903 Springfield

Caliber: 30-06

Action: Bolt action; repeating; cocked as bolt handle is rotated clockwise to close & lock; knob at rear protrudes when piece is cocked; manual thumb safety at rear of bolt; turned down bolt handle; action is basically a modification of the Mauser Model 98

Magazine: 5-shot staggered row, non-detachable box magazine

Barrel: 24"

Sights: Blade front, leaf with aperture & notched battle rear

Stock & Forearm: Plain straight one-piece stock & forearm; wood hand guard over barrel; a cleaning rod-type bayonet contained in the forearm under barrel

Approximate wt.: 8¾ lbs.

Comments: Adopted by U.S. 1903; made by Springfield & Rock Island.

Estimated Value: Very good: $300.00
Good: $225.00

U.S. M 1903 - A1 Springfield

Basically the same as M 1903 Military rifle except: pistol grip stock; checkered buttplate & serrated trigger; adopted in 1929; & made until 1939 by Springfield Armory - last serial number was about 1,532,878; in 1942 Remington Arms Co. made about 348,000 with a few minor modifications before the M 1903 A3 was adopted; serial numbers from 3,000,001 to 3,348,085.

Estimated Value: Very good: $320.00
Good: $240.00

U.S. M 1903 - A3 Springfield

Generally the same as the U.S. M 1903 - A1 except: many parts are stamped sheet metal & other modifications to lower cost & increase production; straight or pistol grip stock; made during World War II under emergency conditions.

Estimated Value: Very good: $225.00
Good: $170.00

U.S. M 1917 Enfield

Caliber: 30-06

Action: Bolt action; repeating; cocked as bolt is moved forward; bolt handle is crooked rear-ward; modified Mauser-type action

Magazine: 5-shot staggered row, non-detachable box type

Barrel: 26"

Sights: Blade front with protecting ears, leaf with aperture rear

Stock & Forearm: Plain one-piece semi-pistol grip stock & forearm; wood hand guard over barrel

Approximate wt.: 8¼ lbs.

Comments: This gun was developed from the British P-13 & P-14 system as an emergency arm for U.S. in World War I. Made from about 1917 to 1918. Also manufactured in the U.S. for Great Britain in caliber 303 in 1917.

Estimated Value: Very good: $220.00
Good: $165.00

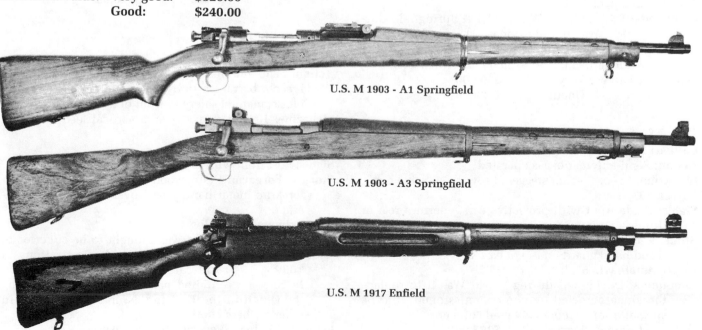

U.S. M 1903 - A1 Springfield

U.S. M 1903 - A3 Springfield

U.S. M 1917 Enfield

U.S. M1

U.S. Garand 30 Caliber M1

Johnson M 1941

U.S. Garand M1 Rifle
Caliber: 30-06
Action: Semi-automatic; gas operated
Magazine: 8-shot staggered row, non-detachable box
Barrel: 24"
Sights: Blade front with protective ears, aperture rear or flip-over type rear
Stock & Forearm: One-piece stock & forearm; wood hand guard over top of barrel
Approximate wt.: 9½ lbs.
Comments: Produced by Winchester & Springfield during World War II. Additional M1's produced after World War II by International Harvester & Harrington & Richardson. Add $150.00 for Winchester.
Estimated Value: Very good: **$700.00**
Good: **$525.00**

U.S. M1 Carbine
Caliber: 30 M1 Carbine
Action: Semi-automatic; gas operated
Magazine: 15- or 30-shot staggered row, detachable box
Barrel: 18"
Sights: Blade front with protective ears, aperture rear or flip-down rear
Stock & Forearm: One-piece wood stock & forearm; wood hand guard on top of barrel
Approximate wt.: 5½ lbs.
Comments: Developed during World War II to replace the sidearms used by non-commissioned officers, special troops & company grade officers.
Estimated Value: Very good: **$375.00**
Good: **$280.00**

U.S. M1 A1 Carbine
Same general specifications as U.S. M1 Carbine except: folding metal stock; 25" overall length when folded; approximate wt. 6¼ lbs.
Estimated Value: Very good: **$550.00**
Good: **$410.00**

Johnson M 1941
Caliber: 30-06
Action: Semi-automatic; recoil action; hesitation-locked breech; barrel partially recoils to begin unlocking phase; manual safety in front of trigger guard
Magazine: 10-shot rotary type; a vertical feed magazine was also made
Barrel: 22"
Sights: Post front with protective ears, aperture rear
Stock & Forearm: Plain wood semi-pistol grip stock & forearm; metal hand guard over barrel above forearm
Approximate wt.: 9½ lbs.
Comments: The Johnson was thought to be superior to the M1 but a series of tests & demonstrations in 1939 & 1940 indicated otherwise; used by U.S. Marines for a limited period in World War II & by the Dutch in the East Indies; many rebarreled in other calibers afterWorld War II.
Estimated Value: Very good: **$600.00**
Good: **$450.00**

Mossberg

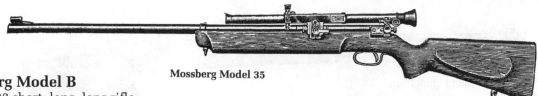

Mossberg Model 35

Mossberg Model B
Caliber: 22 short, long, long rifle
Action: Bolt action; single shot
Magazine: None
Barrel: Blued; 22"
Sights: Open rear, bead front
Stock & Forearm: Plain wood semi-pistol grip stock & forearm
Approximate wt.: 5 lbs.
Comments: Made in the early 1930's.
Estimated Value: Excellent: $75.00
Very good: $60.00

Mossberg Model R
Caliber: 22 short, long, long rifle
Action: Bolt action; repeating
Magazine: Tubular; 14 long rifles, 16 longs, 20 shorts
Barrel: Blued; 24"
Sights: Open rear, bead front
Stock & Forearm: Walnut semi-pistol grip stock & forearm
Approximate wt.: 5 lbs.
Comments: Made in the early 1930's.
Estimated Value: Excellent: $80.00
Very good: $60.00

Mossberg Model 10
Caliber: 22 short, long, long rifle
Action: Bolt action; single shot
Magazine: None
Barrel: Blued; 22"
Sights: Open rear, bead front
Stock & Forearm: Walnut semi-pistol grip stock & forearm; swivels
Approximate wt.: 4 lbs.
Comments: Made from the early to mid 1930's. Takedown type.
Estimated Value: Excellent: $75.00
Very good: $60.00

Mossberg Model 20
Similar to the Model 10 with a 24" barrel & grooved forearm.
Estimated Value: Excellent: $70.00
Very good: $55.00

Mossberg Model 30
Similar to the Model 20 with peep rear sight & hooded ramp front sight.
Estimated Value: Excellent: $75.00
Very good: $60.00

Mossberg Model 40
Similar to the Model 30 with tubular magazine that holds 16 long rifles, 18 longs, 22 shorts; bolt action; repeating.
Estimated Value: Excellent: $80.00
Very good: $60.00

Mossberg Model M
Caliber: 22 short, long, long rifle
Action: Bolt action; single shot; cocking piece
Magazine: None
Barrel: 20" round
Sights: Open rear, blade front
Stock & Forearm: Plain one-piece semi-pistol grip stock & tapered forearm
Approximate wt.: 4¼ lbs.
Comments: A boys' rifle made in the early 1930's.
Estimated Value: Excellent: $70.00
Very good: $55.00

Mossberg Model 14
Caliber: 22 short, long, long rifle
Action: Bolt action; single shot
Magazine: None
Barrel: Blued; 24"
Sights: Peep rear, hooded ramp front
Stock & Forearm: Plain one-piece semi-pistol grip stock & forearm; swivels
Approximate wt.: 5½ lbs.
Comments: Made in the mid 1930's.
Estimated Value: Excellent: $70.00
Very good: $55.00

Mossberg Model 34
Similar to the Model 14, made in the mid 1930's.
Estimated Value: Excellent: $70.00
Very good: $55.00

Mossberg Model 35
Caliber: 22 long rifle
Action: Bolt action; single shot
Magazine: None
Barrel: Blued; 26" heavy
Sights: Micrometer rear, hooded ramp front
Stock & Forearm: Plain walnut one-piece semi-pistol grip stock & forearm; cheekpiece; swivels
Approximate wt.: 8¼ lbs.
Comments: Made in the early 1930's.
Estimated Value: Excellent: $110.00
Very good: $85.00

Mossberg Model 35A
Similar to the Model 35; target stock & sights. Made in the late 1930's
Estimated Value: Excellent: $120.00
Very good: $95.00

Mossberg Model 35A-LS
Similar to the Model 35A with special Lyman sights.
Estimated Value: Excellent: $125.00
Very good: $100.00

Mossberg Model 26B

Mossberg Model 25

Caliber: 22 short, long, long rifle
Action: Bolt action; single shot
Magazine: None
Barrel: Blued; 24"
Sights: Peep rear, hooded ramp front
Stock & Forearm: Plain walnut one-piece pistol grip stock & forearm; swivels
Approximate wt.: 5lbs.
Comments: Made in the mid 1930's.
Estimated Value: **Excellent:** $65.00
  Very good: $50.00

Mossberg Model 25A

Similar to the Model 25 with higher quality finish & better wood. Made in the late 1930's.
Estimated Value: **Excellent:** $70.00
  Very good: $55.00

Mossberg Model 26B

Caliber: 22 short, long, long rifle
Action: Bolt action; single shot
Magazine: None
Barrel: Blued; 26"
Sights: Micrometer rear, hooded ramp front
Stock & Forearm: Plain one-piece semi-pistol grip stock & forearm; swivels
Approximate wt.: 5½ lbs.
Comments: Made in the late 1930's.
Estimated Value: **Excellent:** $75.00
  Very good: $55.00

Mossberg Model 26C

Similar to the 26B without swivels or peep sight.
Estimated Value: **Excellent:** $65.00
  Very good: $50.00

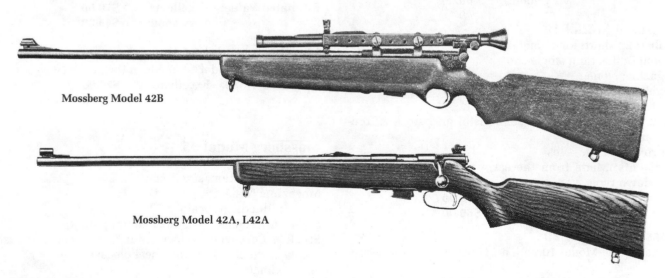

Mossberg Model 42B

Mossberg Model 42A, L42A

Mossberg Model 42

Caliber: 22 short, long, long rifle
Action: Bolt action; repeating
Magazine: 7-shot detachable
Barrel: Blued; 24"
Sights: Open rear, receiver peep, hooded ramp front
Stock & Forearm: Plain walnut one-piece semi-pistol grip stock & forearm; swivels
Approximate wt.: 5 lbs.
Comments: Made in the mid 1930's; takedown model.
Estimated Value: **Excellent:** $75.00
  Very good: $60.00

Mossberg Model 42A, L42A

Similar to the Model 42 but higher quality. L42A is left hand action. Made in the late 1930's.
Estimated Value: **Excellent:** $80.00
  Very good: $65.00

Mossberg Model 42B

An improved version of the Model 42A with micrometer peep sight & 5-shot magazine. Made from the late 1930's to early 1940's.
Estimated Value: **Excellent:** $85.00
  Very good: $65.00

Mossberg Model 42C

Mossberg Model 42M
More modern version of the Model 42 with a 23" barrel; full length; two-piece stock & forearm; cheekpiece; 7-shot magazine. Made from the early 1940's to early 1950's.
Estimated Value: Excellent: $85.00
Very good: $70.00

Mossberg Model 42C
Similar to the Model 42B without the peep sight.
Estimated Value: Excellent: $80.00
Very good: $65.00

Mossberg Model 42MB
Similar to the Model 42. Used as military training rifle in Great Britain in World War II; full stock.
Estimated Value: Excellent: $160.00
Very good: $125.00

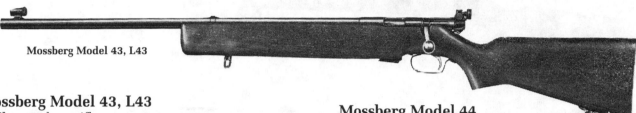

Mossberg Model 43, L43

Mossberg Model 43, L43
Caliber: 22 long rifle
Action: Bolt action; repeating
Magazine: 7-shot detachable box
Barrel: Blued; 26"
Sights: Special Lyman sights
Stock & Forearm: Walnut one-piece semi-pistol grip stock & forearm; cheekpiece; swivels
Approximate wt.: 8¼ lbs.
Comments: Made in the late 1930's. L43 is left hand action.
Estimated Value: Excellent: $100.00
Very good: $ 75.00

Mossberg Model 44
Caliber: 22 short, long, long rifle
Action: Bolt action; repeating
Magazine: Tubular; 16 long rifles, 18 longs, 22 shorts
Barrel: Blued; 24"
Sights: Peep rear, hooded ramp front
Stock & Forearm: Plain walnut one-piece semi-pistol grip stock & forearm; swivels
Approximate wt.: 6 lbs.
Comments: Made in the mid 1930's.
Estimated Value: Excellent: $75.00
Very good: $60.00

Mossberg Model 44B

Mossberg Model 43B

Mossberg Model 44B
Caliber: 22 long rifle
Action: Bolt action; repeating
Magazine: 7-shot detachable box
Barrel: 26" heavy barrel
Sights: Micrometer receiver, hooded front
Stock & Forearm: Plain one-piece semi-pistol grip stock & forearm; swivels; cheekpiece
Approximate wt.: 8 lbs.
Comments: Made in the late 1930's to early 1940's.
Estimated Value: Excellent: $120.00
Very good: $ 95.00

Mossberg Model 43B
Similar to the Model 44B with special Lyman sights.
Estimated Value: Excellent: $125.00
Very good: $100.00

Mossberg Model 44 U.S.
Improved version of the Model 44B. Made in the late 1930's.
Estimated Value: Excellent: $130.00
Very good: $105.00

Mossberg Model 35B
Single shot version of the Model 44B. Made in the late 1930's.
Estimated Value: Excellent: $115.00
Very good: $ 90.00

Mossberg Model 45

Mossberg Model 45A, L45A

Mossberg Model 45B

Mossberg Model 46

Mossberg Model 45
Caliber: 22 short, long, long rifle
Action: Bolt action; repeating
Magazine: Tubular; 15 long rifles, 18 longs, 22 shorts
Barrel: Blued; 24"
Sights: Peep rear, hooded ramp front
Stock & Forearm: Plain one-piece semi-pistol grip stock & forearm; swivels
Approximate wt.: 6¾ lbs.
Comments: Made in the mid 1930's.
Estimated Value:	Excellent:	$75.00
	Very good:	$60.00

Mossberg Model 45C
Similar to the Model 45 without sights.
Estimated Value:	Excellent:	$70.00
	Very good:	$55.00

Mossberg Model 45A, L45A
Improved version of the Model 45, made in the late 1930's. L45A is left hand action.
Estimated Value:	Excellent:	$80.00
	Very good:	$65.00

Mossberg Model 45AC
Similar to the Model 45A without sights.
Estimated Value:	Excellent:	$70.00
	Very good:	$55.00

Mossberg Model 45B
Similar to the Model 45A with open rear sight. Made in the late 1930's.
Estimated Value:	Excellent:	$80.00
	Very good:	$65.00

Mossberg Model 46
Caliber: 22 short, long, long rifle
Action: Bolt action; repeating
Magazine: Tubular; 15 long rifles, 18 longs, 22 shorts
Barrel: Blued; 26"
Sights: Micrometer rear, hooded ramp front
Stock & Forearm: Plain one-piece semi-piece grip stock & forearm; cheekpiece; swivels
Approximate wt.: 7½ lbs.
Comments: Made in the mid 1930's.
Estimated Value:	Excellent:	$80.00
	Very good:	$60.00

Mossberg Model 46C

A heavy barrel version of the Model 46.

Estimated Value: Excellent: $85.00
Very good: $65.00

Mossberg Model 46A

An improved version of the Model 46 made in the late 1930's.

Estimated Value: Excellent: $85.00
Very good: $60.00

Mossberg Model 46AC

Similar to the 46A with open rear sight.

Estimated Value: Excellent: $75.00
Very good: $60.00

Mossberg Model 46A-LS, L46A-LS

Similar to the Model 46A with special Lyman sights. L46A-LS is left hand action.

Estimated Value: Excellent: $95.00
Very good: $75.00

Mossberg Model 46B

Similar to the Model 46A with open rear sight and receiver peep sight. Made in the late 1930's.

Estimated Value: Excellent: $80.00
Very good: $60.00

Mossberg Model 46BT

A heavy barrel version of the Model 46B.

Estimated Value: Excellent: $90.00
Very good: $65.00

Mossberg Model 46M

Similar to the Model 46 with full length two-piece fore-arm. Made about 1940 to the early 1950's.

Estimated Value: Excellent: $85.00
Very good: $60.00

Mossberg Model 346K, 346B

Caliber: 22 short, long, long rifle
Action: Bolt action; repeating
Magazine: Tubular; 20 long rifles, 23 longs, 30 shorts
Barrel: Blued; 26"
Sights: Micrometer rear, hooded front; peep sights (346B)
Stock & Forearm: Plain Monte Carlo one-piece pistol grip stock & lipped forearm; cheekpiece; swivels
Approximate wt.: 7 lbs.
Comments: Made from the late 1940's to mid 1950's.
Estimated Value: Excellent: $80.00
Very good: $55.00

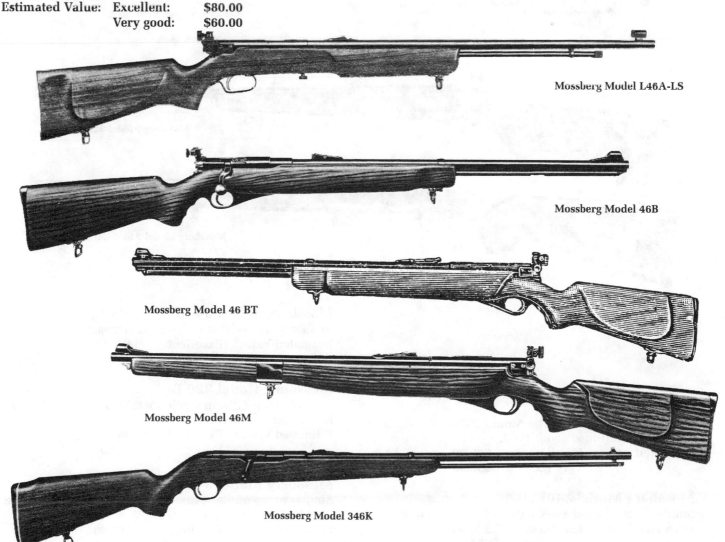

Mossberg Model L46A-LS

Mossberg Model 46B

Mossberg Model 46 BT

Mossberg Model 46M

Mossberg Model 346K

Mossberg Model 346 B

Mossberg Model 320K

Mossberg Model 340K

Mossberg Model 340B

Mossberg Model 320 B

Mossberg Model 340M Carbine

Mossberg Model 320K
Similar shot version of the Model 346K. Weighs about 5¾ lbs. Discontinued about 1960.

Estimated Value:	Excellent:	$65.00
	Very good:	$50.00

Mossberg Model 340K
Similar to the Model 346K with 7-shot clip magazine.

Estimated Value:	Excellent:	$70.00
	Very good:	$50.00

Mossberg Model 340B
Similar to the 346B with 7-shot clip magazine.

Estimated Value:	Excellent:	$70.00
	Very good:	$55.00

Mossberg Model 320 B
Similar to the 340K in single shot. Made from about 1960 for 11 years.

Estimated Value:	Excellent:	$65.00
	Very good:	$50.00

Mossberg Model 340M Carbine
Similar to the Model 340K with full length forearm & 18" barrel. Made in the early 1970's.

Estimated Value:	Excellent:	$90.00
	Very good:	$65.00

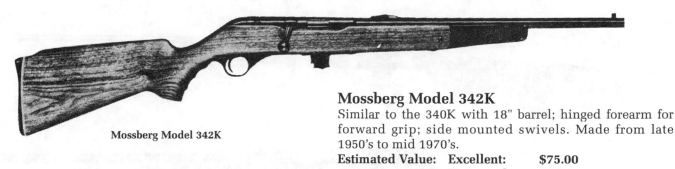

Mossberg Model 342K

Mossberg Model 342K

Similar to the 340K with 18" barrel; hinged forearm for forward grip; side mounted swivels. Made from late 1950's to mid 1970's.

Estimated Value: Excellent: $75.00
                 Very good: $60.00

Mossberg Model 144

Mossberg Model 146B

Mossberg Model 144

Caliber: 22 long rifle
Action: Bolt action; repeating
Magazine: 7-shot clip
Barrel: Blued; 26", heavy
Sights: Micrometer receiver, hooded front
Stock & Forearm: Walnut one-piece semi-pistol grip stock & forearm; hand rest; swivels
Approximate wt.: 8 lbs.
Comments: Made from the late 1940's to mid 1980's.
Estimated Value: Excellent: $180.00
                 Very good: $135.00

Mossberg Model 146B

Caliber: 22 short, long, long rifle
Action: Bolt action; repeating
Magazine: Tubular; 20 long rifles, 23 longs, 30 shorts
Barrel: Blued; 26"
Sights: Micrometer receiver, hooded front
Stock & Forearm: Plain Monte Carlo one-piece pistol grip stock & lipped forearm; cheekpiece; swivels
Approximate wt.: 7 lbs.
Comments: Made from the late 1940's to mid 1950's.
Estimated Value: Excellent: $90.00
                 Very good: $70.00

Mossberg Model 140K

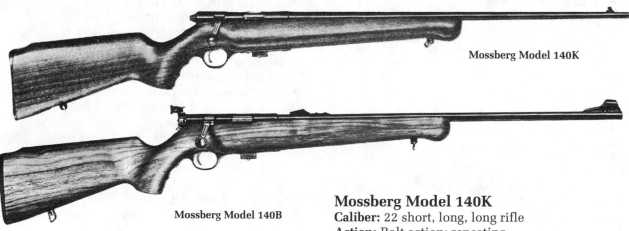

Mossberg Model 140B

Mossberg Model 140K

Caliber: 22 short, long, long rifle
Action: Bolt action; repeating
Magazine: 7-shot clip
Barrel: Blued; 26½"
Sights: Open rear, bead front
Stock & Forearm: Walnut Monte Carlo one-piece pistol grip stock & forearm; cheekpiece; swivels
Approximate wt.: 5¾ lbs.
Comments: Made in the mid 1950's.
Estimated Value: Excellent: $70.00
                 Very good: $55.00

Mossberg Model 140B

Similar to the 140K with hooded ramp front sight, peep rear sight.
Estimated Value: Excellent: $75.00
                 Very good: $60.00

Mossberg Model 640K

Mossberg Model 620K

Mossberg Model 321K

Mossberg Model 341

Mossberg Model 353

Mossberg Model 640K
Caliber: 22 magnum
Action: Bolt action; repeating
Magazine: 5-shot box
Barrel: Blued; 24"
Sights: Open rear, bead front; adjustable
Stock & Forearm: Checkered walnut Monte Carlo one-piece pistol grip stock & forearm; swivels
Approximate wt.: 6 lbs.
Comments: Made from about 1960 to mid 1980's.
Estimated Value: **Excellent:**   **$110.00**
                       Very good: **$ 80.00**

Mossberg Model 620K
Similar to the 640K in single shot. Discontinued in mid 1970's.
Estimated Value: **Excellent:**   **$75.00**
                       Very good: **$60.00**

Mossberg Model 321K
Caliber: 22 short, long, long rifle
Action: Bolt action; single shot
Magazine: None
Barrel: Blued; 24"
Sights: Open rear, ramp front
Stock & Forearm: Checkered Monte Carlo one-piece pistol grip stock & forearm
Approximate wt.: 6½ lbs.
Comments: Made from the early 1970's to early 1980's.
Estimated Value: **Excellent:**   **$60.00**
                       Very good: **$45.00**

Mossberg Model 341
Similar to the 321K with: 7-shot clip magazine; swivels; bolt action; repeating; adjustable sights.
Estimated Value: **Excellent:**   **$80.00**
                       Very good: **$60.00**

Mossberg Model 353
Similar to the 321K except: semi-automatic; hinged grip forearm (tenite); 18" barrel; 7-shot clip magazine; 22 long rifle only; adjustable sight.
Estimated Value: **Excellent:**   **$90.00**
                       Very good: **$70.00**

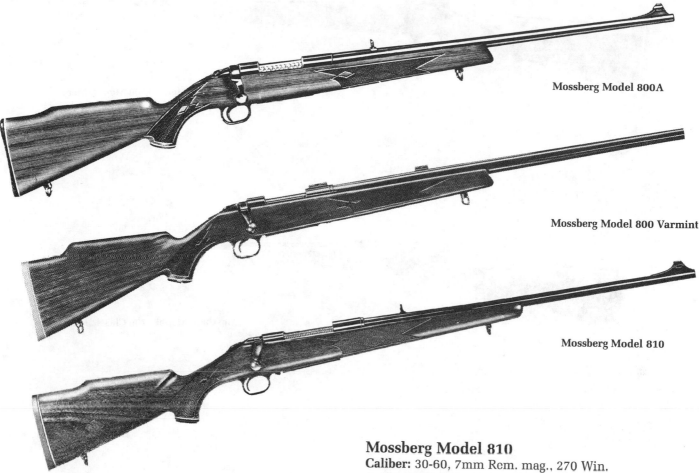

Mossberg Model 800A

Mossberg Model 800 Varmint

Mossberg Model 810

Mossberg Model 800A

Caliber: 308, 243, 22-250, 222 Rem.
Action: Bolt action; repeating
Magazine: 4-shot box
Barrel: Blued; 22"
Sights: Leaf rear, ramp front
Stock & Forearm: Checkered wood Monte Carlo one-piece pistol grip stock & forearm; swivels
Approximate wt.: 6½ lbs.
Comments: Made from late 1960's to the late 1970's.
Estimated Value: **Excellent:**   **$200.00**
                   Very good: **$150.00**

Mossberg Model 800 Varmint

Similar to the 800A with a 24" barrel and scope mounts. In 243 and 22-250 calibers.
Estimated Value: **Excellent:**   **$225.00**
                   Very good: **$180.00**

Mossberg Model 800 Target

Similar to the 800A with scope mounts and scope in 308, 243, 22-250 calibers. Made from late 1960's to early 1970's.
Estimated Value: **Excellent:**   **$250.00**
                   Very good: **$190.00**

Mossberg Model 810

Caliber: 30-60, 7mm Rem. mag., 270 Win.
Action: Bolt action; repeating
Magazine: 4-shot detachable box
Barrel: Blued; 22"
Sights: Leaf rear, ramp front
Stock & Forearm: Checkered Monte Carlo one-piece pistol grip stock & forearm; swivels; recoil pad
Approximate wt.: 7½ to 8 lbs.
Comments: Add $15.00 for 7mm Rem. magnum. Made from early to late 1970's.
Estimated Value: **Excellent:**   **$220.00**
                   Very good: **$165.00**

Mossberg Model RM-7A

Caliber: 30-60
Action: Bolt action; repeating; hammerless
Magazine: 4-shot rotary
Barrel: 22" round
Sights: Adjustable folding leaf rear, ramp front
Stock & Forearm: Checkered walnut one-piece pistol grip stock & forearm; fluted comb; recoil pad
Approximate wt.: 7½ lbs.
Comments: Made in the late 1970's.
Estimated Value: **Excellent:**   **$215.00**
                   Very good: **$160.00**

Mossberg Model RM-7B

Similar to the Model RM-7A; 7mm Rem. magnum caliber, 3-shot magazine, 24" barrel.
Estimated Value: **Excellent:**   **$225.00**
                   Very good: **$170.00**

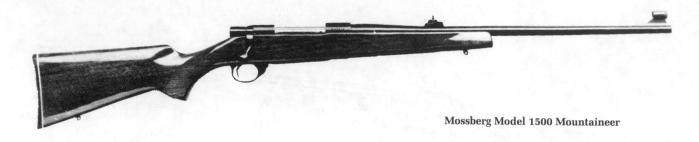

Mossberg Model 1500 Mountaineer

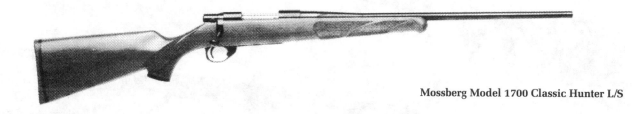

Mossberg Model 1700 Classic Hunter L/S

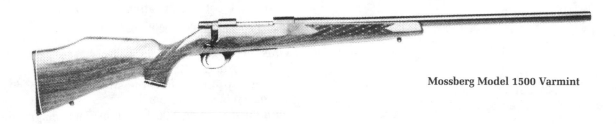

Mossberg Model 1500 Varmint

Mossberg Model 1500 Mountaineer

Caliber: 223, 22-250, 243, 270, 308, 30-06, 7mm magnum, 300 Win. magnum, 338 Win. magnum

Action: Bolt action, hammerless; repeating

Magazine: 5 or 6-shot box

Barrel: 22" or 24"

Sights: Available without or with adjustable rear, hooded ramp front

Stock & Forearm: Checkered walnut one-piece pistol grip stock & forearm; recoil pad on magnum

Approximate wt.: 7¾ lbs.

Comments: Produced by Mossberg from 1985 to 1988. Add $15.00 for magnum, $20.00 for sights.

Estimated Value: Excellent: $255.00

Very good: $190.00

Mossberg Model 1500 Varmint

Similar to the Model 1500 with a 24" heavy barrel in 223, 22-250 or 308 caliber; Monte Carlo stock; available in blued or Parkerized finish. Discontinued late 1980's.

Estimated Value: Excellent: $320.00

Very good: $240.00

Mossberg Model 1550 Mountaineer

Similar to the Model 1500 with removable magazine, 22" barrel, in 243, 270 and 30-06 calibers; add $20.00 for sights. Discontinued late 1980's.

Estimated Value: Excellent: $270.00

Very good: $200.00

Mossberg Model 1700 Classic Hunter L/S

Similar to the Model 1500 with 22" barrel, removable magazine, lipped forearm, pistol grip cap & recoil pad, in calibers: 243, 270 and 30-06. Discontinued late 1980's.

Estimated Value: Excellent: $340.00

Very good: $255.00

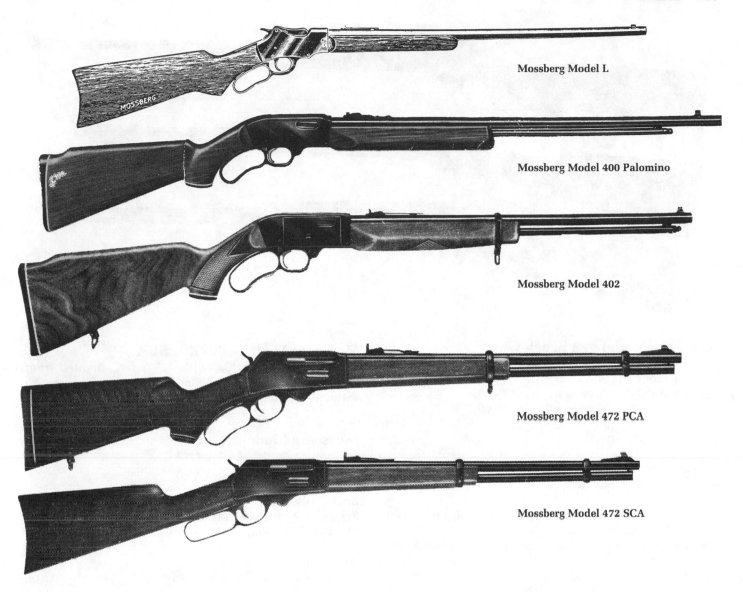

Mossberg Model L

Mossberg Model 400 Palomino

Mossberg Model 402

Mossberg Model 472 PCA

Mossberg Model 472 SCA

Mossberg Model L
Caliber: 22 short, long, long rifle
Action: Lever-action, falling block; single shot
Magazine: None
Barrel: Blued; 24"
Sights: Open rear, bead front
Stock & Forearm: Plain walnut semi-pistol grip stock & small forearm
Approximate wt.: 5 lbs.
Comments: Made from the late 1920's to early 1930's.
Estimated Value: Excellent: $275.00
                       Very good: $220.00

Mossberg Model 400 Palomino
Caliber: 22 short, long, long rifle
Action: Lever-action, hammerless; repeating
Magazine: Tubular; 15 long rifles, 17 longs, 20 shorts
Barrel: Blued; 24"
Sights: Adjustable open rear, bead front
Stock & Forearm: Checkered walnut Monte Carlo pistol grip stock & forearm; barrel bands; swivels
Approximate wt.: 4¾ lbs.
Comments: Made in the early 1960's.
Estimated Value: Excellent: $85.00
                       Very good: $65.00

Mossberg Model 402
Similar to the Model 400 with smaller capacity magazine. Discontinued in the early 1970's.
Estimated Value: Excellent: $75.00
                       Very good: $55.00

Mossberg Model 472 PCA, SCA, 479 PCA, SCA
Caliber: 30-30, 35 Rem.
Action: Lever-action; exposed hammer; repeating
Magazine: 6-shot tubular
Barrel: Blued; 20"
Sights: Adjustable rear, ramp front
Stock & Forearm: Plain pistol grip stock & forearm; barrel band; swivels; or straight grip stock (SCA)
Approximate wt.: 7½ lbs.
Comments: Sold first as the 472 Series, then 479 Series.
Estimated Value: Excellent: $165.00
                       Very good: $130.00

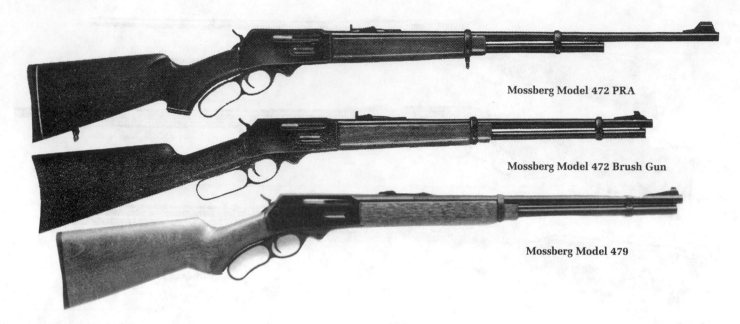

Mossberg Model 472 PRA

Mossberg Model 472 Brush Gun

Mossberg Model 479

Mossberg Model 472 Brush Gun
Similar to the Model 472 PCA with 18" barrel; straight stock; 5-shot magazine.

Estimated Value: Excellent: $180.00
Very good: $145.00

Mossberg Model 479
Caliber: 30-30 Win.
Action: Lever action, exposed hammer, repeating
Magazine: 5-shot tubular
Barrel: 20"
Sights: Adjustable open rear, beaded ramp front; drilled and tapped for scope
Stock & Forearm: Hardwood semi-pistol grip stock and forearm; barrel band
Approximate wt.: 6¾ lbs.
Comments: Produced from the early 1980's to mid 1980's.

Estimated Value: Excellent: $200.00
Very good: $150.00

Mossberg Model 472 PRA, SBA
Similar to the 472 PCA with 24" barrel; hooded front sight. Discontinued in the late 1970's.

Estimated Value: Excellent: $170.00
Very good: $135.00

Mossberg Model K
Caliber: 22 short, long, long rifle
Action: Slide action; hammerless; repeating
Magazine: Tubular; 14 long rifles, 16 longs, 20 shorts
Barrel: Blued; 22"
Sights: Open rear, bead front
Stock & Forearm: Plain walnut straight grip stock & grooved slide handle
Approximate wt.: 5 lbs.
Comments: Made from the early 1920's to early 1930's; takedown model.

Estimated Value: Excellent: $150.00
Very good: $100.00

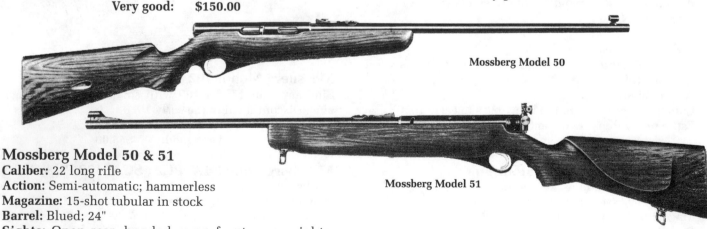

Mossberg Model 50

Mossberg Model 51

Mossberg Model 50 & 51
Caliber: 22 long rifle
Action: Semi-automatic; hammerless
Magazine: 15-shot tubular in stock
Barrel: Blued; 24"
Sights: Open rear, hooded ramp front; peep sights, swivels (Model 51)
Stock & Forearm: Walnut one-piece semi-pistol grip stock & forearm
Approximate wt.: 7 lbs.
Comments: Made from the late 1930's to early 1940's.

Estimated Value: Excellent: $90.00
Very good: $75.00

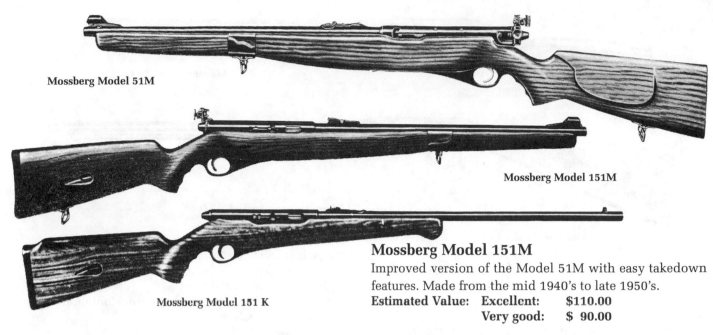

Mossberg Model 51M

Mossberg Model 151M

Mossberg Model 151 K

Mossberg Model 151M
Improved version of the Model 51M with easy takedown features. Made from the mid 1940's to late 1950's.
Estimated Value: Excellent: $110.00
Very good: $ 90.00

Mossberg Model 51M
Similar to the Model 51 with full length, two-piece forearm & 20" barrel. Made from the late 1930's to mid 1940's.
Estimated Value: Excellent: $95.00
Very good: $75.00

Mossberg Model 151K
Similar to the 151M with Monte Carlo stock; standard length lipped forearm; 24" barrel; no peep sight or swivels. Made in early 1950's.
Estimated Value: Excellent: $115.00
Very good: $ 95.00

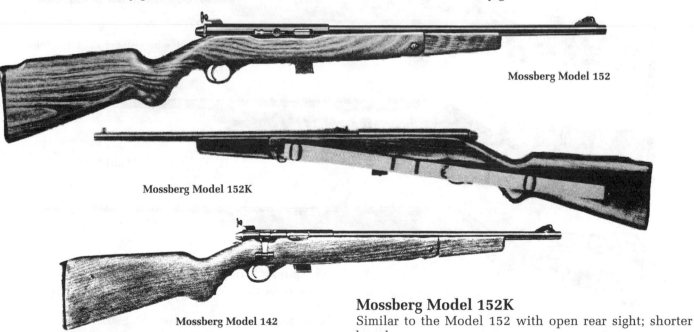

Mossberg Model 152

Mossberg Model 152K

Mossberg Model 142

Mossberg Model 152
Caliber: 22 long rifle
Action: Semi-automatic
Magazine: 7-shot detachable box
Barrel: Blued; 18"
Sights: Peep rear, military front
Stock & Forearm: Plain one-piece semi-pistol grip stock & hinged forearm for forward grip; side mounted swivels
Approximate wt.: 5 lbs.
Comments: Made from the late 1940's to late 1950's.
Estimated Value: Excellent: $100.00
Very good: $ 80.00

Mossberg Model 152K
Similar to the Model 152 with open rear sight; shorter barrel.
Estimated Value: Excellent: $95.00
Very good: $75.00

Mossberg Model 142
Similar to the Model 152 in bolt action; available in short, long or long rifle; with peep sight.
Estimated Value: Excellent: $90.00
Very good: $70.00

Mossberg Model 142K
Similar to the Model 142 with open rear sight.
Estimated Value: Excellent: $80.00
Very good: $65.00

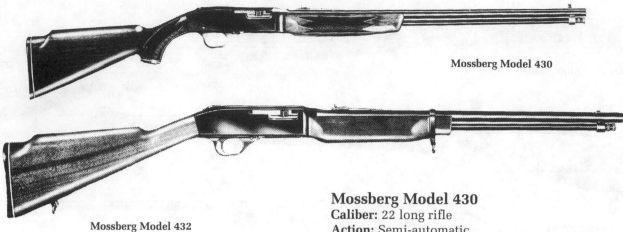

Mossberg Model 430

Mossberg Model 432

Mossberg Model 430

Caliber: 22 long rifle
Action: Semi-automatic
Magazine: 18-shot tubular
Barrel: Blued; 24"
Sights: Open rear, bead front
Stock & Forearm: Checkered walnut Monte Carlo pistol
grip stock & forearm
Approximate wt.: 6¼ lbs.
Comments: Made in the early 1970's.
Estimated Value: **Excellent:** $90.00
                        Very good: $75.00

Mossberg Model 432

Similar to the Model 430 with straight grip stock; barrel
band; smaller capacity magazine.
Estimated Value: **Excellent:** $85.00
                        Very good: $70.00

Mossberg Model 351 C (Carbine)

Mossberg Model 351K

Mossberg Model 350K

Mossberg Model 351 C (Carbine)

Similar to the 351K with 18½" barrel; barrel bands;
swivels.
Estimated Value: **Excellent:** $80.00
                        Very good: $65.00

Mossberg Model 351K

Caliber: 22 long rifle
Action: Semi-automatic
Magazine: 15-shot tubular, in stock
Barrel: Blued; 24"
Sights: Open rear, bead front
Stock & Forearm: Walnut Monte Carlo one-piece semi-
pistol grip stock and forearm
Approximate wt.: 6 lbs.
Comments: Made from about 1960 to 1970.
Estimated Value: **Excellent:** $85.00
                        Very good: $70.00

Mossberg Model 350K

Caliber: 22 long rifle
Action: Semi-automatic
Magazine: 7-shot clip
Barrel: Blued; 23½"
Sights: Open rear, bead front
Stock & Forearm: Walnut Monte Carlo one-piece semi-
pistol grip stock & forearm
Approximate wt.: 6 lbs.
Comments: Made from the late 1950's to early 1970's.
Estimated Value: **Excellent:** $75.00
                        Very good: $60.00

Mossberg Model 377 Plinkster

Mossberg Model 352K Carbine

Mossberg Model 352K Carbine

Caliber: 22 long rifle
Action: Semi-automatic
Magazine: 7-shot clip
Barrel: Blued; 18½"
Sights: Open rear, bead front
Stock & Forearm: Walnut Monte Carlo one-piece semi-pistol grip stock & forearm; swivels; hinged forearm for forward grip
Approximate wt.: 5 lbs.
Comments: Made from the late 1950's to early 1970's.
Estimated Value: Excellent: $90.00
Very good: $70.00

Mossberg Model 377 Plinkster

Caliber: 22 long rifle
Action: Semi-automatic; hammerless
Magazine: 15-shot tubular; stock load
Barrel: 20" round
Sights: None; 4X scope standard
Stock & Forearm: Molded structural foam; one-piece Monte Carlo pistol grip stock & forearm; thumb hole; cheekpiece
Approximate wt.: 6¼ lbs.
Comments: Produced from the late 1970's to mid 1980's.
Estimated Value: Excellent: $85.00
Very good: $65.00

Musketeer

Musketeer Mauser

Musketeer Mauser

Caliber: 243, 25-06, 270, 264 mag., 308, 30-06, 7mm mag., 300 mag.
Action: FN Mauser bolt action
Magazine: 5-shot, 3-shot magnum
Barrel: Blued; 24"
Sights: Leaf rear, hooded ramp front
Stock & Forearm: Checkered walnut Monte Carlo one-piece pistol grip stock & forearm
Approximate wt.: 7¼ lbs.
Comments: Made from the 1960's to the early 1970's.
Estimated Value: Excellent: $300.00
Very good: $225.00

Musketeer Carbine

Same as Musketeer Mauser except shorter barrel.
Estimated Value: Excellent: $275.00
Very good: $210.00

New England

New England Handi-Rifle

Caliber: 223 Rem., 22 Hornet, 218 Bee, 30-30 Win., 243 Win., 30-06, 45-70 Gov't
Action: Break open, side release lever, single shot, exposed hammer
Magazine: None, single shot
Barrel: Blued; 22"
Sights: Ramp front; adjustable folding rear, tapped for scope mounts; calibers 223 Rem., 243 Win., & 30-06 have no sights, they are equipped with scope mounts
Stock & Forearm: Hardwood, walnut finish, pistol grip, smooth stock & semi-beavertail forearm, swivels
Approximate wt.: 7 lbs.
Comments: Introduced in 1989.
Estimated Value: New (retail): $205.00
Excellent: $155.00
Very good: $120.00

New England Handi-Gun Combination

Same as the Handi-Rifle except any combination of rifle or shotgun barrels are available to be used interchangeably. Shotgun barrels have brass bead front sight with blued or nickel finish (add 10%); 22" barrel in 12 or 20 gauge. Prices are for rifle & shotgun barrel combinations. Introduced in 1989.
Estimated Value: New (retail): $285.00
Excellent: $215.00
Very good: $170.00

New Haven

New Haven Model 453 TS
Similar to the Model 453T with a 4X scope.
Estimated Value: **Excellent:** **$90.00**
  Very good: **$70.00**

New Haven Model 679
Caliber: 30-30 Win.
Action: Lever-action; exposed hammer; repeating
Magazine: 5-shot tubular
Barrel: Blued; 20"
Sights: Open rear, ramp front
Stock & Forearm: Plain birch semi-pistol grip stock & forearm; barrel band
Approximate wt.: 6¾ lbs.
Comments: Made from the late 1970's to early 1980's.
Estimated Value: **Excellent:** **$160.00**
  Very good: **$130.00**

New Haven Model 453 T

New Haven Model 740T

New Haven Model 453T
Caliber: 22 short, long, long rifle
Action: Semi-automatic; hammerless
Magazine: 7-shot clip
Barrel: Blued; 18"
Sights: Open rear, bead front
Stock & Forearm: Plain one-piece Monte Carlo pistol grip stock & forearm
Approximate wt.: 5½ lbs.
Comments: Introduced in the late 1970's.
Estimated Value: **Excellent:** **$85.00**
  Very good: **$65.00**

New Haven Model 740T
Caliber: 22 Win. mag.
Action: Bolt action; hammerless; repeating
Magazine: 5-shot clip
Barrel: Blued; 26"
Sights: Open rear, blade front
Stock & Forearm: Plain birch one-piece Monte Carlo pistol grip stock & forearm
Approximate wt.: 6½ lbs.
Comments: Introduced in the late 1970's.
Estimated Value: **Excellent:** **$85.00**
  Very good: **$65.00**

New Haven Model 740TS
Similar to the Model 740T with 4X scope.
Estimated Value: **Excellent:** **$90.00**
  Very good: **$65.00**

Newton

Newton Standard, 1st Model

Newton Mauser

Newton, Buffalo Newton

Newton Standard, 1st Model

Caliber: 22, 256, 280, 30-06, 30 Newton, 35 Newton
Action: Bolt action; double set trigger
Magazine: 5-shot box
Barrel: Blued; 24"
Sights: Open rear, ramp front
Stock & Forearm: Checkered wood pistol grip stock & forearm
Approximate wt.: 7½ lbs.
Comments: Made for a short time before World War I.
Estimated Value: Excellent: $675.00
　　　　　　　　　 Very good: $540.00

Newton Standard, 2nd Model

Very similar to 1st Model with improved action. Made to about 1920's.
Estimated Value: Excellent: $720.00
　　　　　　　　　 Very good: $575.00

Newton, Buffalo Newton

Similar to the 2nd Model made from the early 1920's to early 1930's.
Estimated Value: Excellent: $625.00
　　　　　　　　　 Very good: $470.00

Newton Mauser

Caliber: 256
Action: Mauser-type bolt action; reversed double set trigger
Magazine: 5-shot box
Barrel: Blued; 24"
Sights: Open rear, ramp front
Stock & Forearm: Checkered wood pistol grip stock & forearm
Approximate wt.: 7 lbs.
Comments: Made in the early 1920's.
Estimated Value: Excellent: $600.00
　　　　　　　　　 Very good: $480.00

Noble

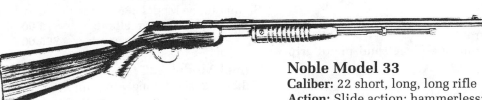

Noble Model 33

Noble Model 33A

Similar to the Model 33 with a wood stock and grooved slide handle. Made until the mid 1950's
Estimated Value: Excellent: $85.00
　　　　　　　　　 Very good: $65.00

Noble Model 33

Caliber: 22 short, long, long rifle
Action: Slide action; hammerless; repeating
Magazine: Tubular; 15 long rifles, 17 longs, 21 shorts
Barrel: Blued; 24"
Sights: Open rear, blade front
Stock & Forearm: Semi-pistol grip tenite stock & slide handle
Approximate wt.: 6 lbs.
Comments: Made from the late 1940's to early 1950's.
Estimated Value: Excellent: $80.00
　　　　　　　　　 Very good: $60.00

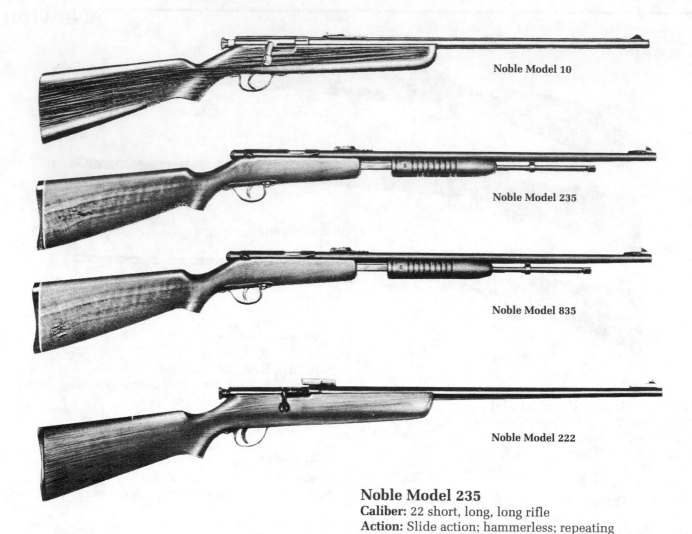

Noble Model 10

Noble Model 235

Noble Model 835

Noble Model 222

Noble Model 235

Caliber: 22 short, long, long rifle
Action: Slide action; hammerless; repeating
Magazine: Tubular; 15 long rifles, 17 longs, 21 shorts
Barrel: Blued; 24"
Sights: Open rear, ramp front
Stock & Forearm: Wood semi-pistol grip stock & grooved slide handle
Approximate wt.: 5½ lbs.
Comments: Made from the early 1950's to the early 1970's.
Estimated Value: **Excellent:**   **$80.00**
                   Very good: **$65.00**

Noble Model 835

Similar to the Model 235. Made in the early 1970's.
Estimated Value: **Excellent:**   **$75.00**
                   Very good: **$65.00**

Nobel Model 222

Caliber: 22 short, long, long rifle
Action: Bolt action; single shot; manual cocking
Magazine: None
Barrel: Blued; 22"
Sights: Peep or "V" notch rear, ramp front
Stock & Forearm: Wood one-piece semi-pistol grip stock & forearm
Approximate wt.: 5 lbs.
Comments: Made from the late 1950's to early 1970's.
Estimated Value: **Excellent:**   **$60.00**
                   Very good: **$45.00**

Noble Model 10

Caliber: 22 short, long, long rifle
Action: Bolt action; single shot
Magazine: None
Barrel: Blued; 24"
Sights: Open rear, bead front
Stock & Forearm: Walnut one-piece semi-pistol grip stock & forearm
Approximate wt.: 4 lbs.
Comments: Made from the middle to late 1950's.
Estimated Value: **Excellent:**   **$60.00**
                   Very good: **$50.00**

Noble Model 20

Similar to the Model 10 with; 22" barrel; slightly curved buttplate; manual cocking device. Made from the late 1950's to early 1960's.
Estimated Value: **Excellent:**   **$60.00**
                   Very good: **$50.00**

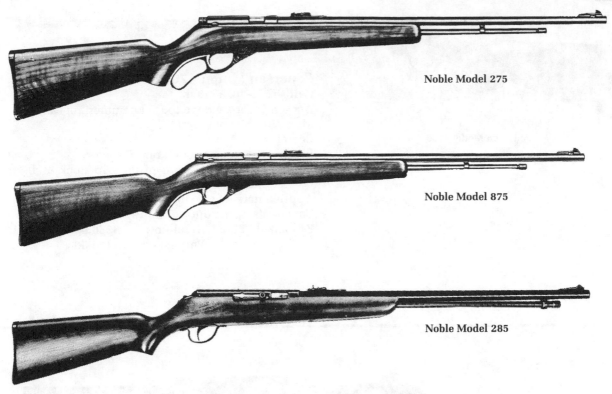

Noble Model 275

Noble Model 875

Noble Model 285

Noble Model 275 & 875
Caliber: 22 short, long, long rifle
Action: Lever-action; hammerless; repeating
Magazine: Tubular; 15 long rifles, 17 longs, 21 shorts
Barrel: Blued; 24"
Sights: Open rear, ramp front
Stock & Forearm: Wood one-piece semi-pistol grip stock & forearm
Approximate wt.: 5½ lbs.
Comments: Made from the late 1950's to early 1970's (Model 275); early to mid 1970's (Model 875).
Estimated Value: **Excellent:**   **$100.00**
          Very good: **$ 80.00**

Noble Model 285 & 885
Caliber: 22 long rifle
Action: Semi-automatic
Magazine: 15-shot tubular
Barrel: Blued; 22"
Sights: Open adjustable rear, blade front
Stock & Forearm: Wood one-piece semi-pistol grip stock & forearm
Approximate wt.: 5½ lbs.
Comments: Made from the early to mid 1970's.
Estimated Value: **Excellent:**   **$85.00**
          Very good: **$70.00**

Pedersen

Pedersen Model 3000

Pedersen Model 3000
Caliber: 270, 30-06, 7mm mag., 338 Win mag.
Action: Bolt action; adjustable trigger
Magazine: 3-shot box
Barrel: Blued; 22", 24"
Sights: None
Stock & Forearm: Checkered walnut one-piece pistol grip stock & forearm; cheekpiece; swivels
Approximate wt.: 6¾ lbs.
Comments: Made in three grades during the 1970's.
Estimated Value:

	Grade I	Grade II	Grade III
Excellent:	$800.00	$620.00	$500.00
Very good:	$600.00	$500.00	$375.00

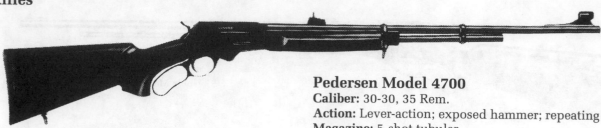

Pedersen Model 4700

Caliber: 30-30, 35 Rem.
Action: Lever-action; exposed hammer; repeating
Magazine: 5-shot tubular
Barrel: Blued; 24"
Sights: Open rear, hooded ramp front
Stock & Forearm: Walnut pistol grip stock & short forearm; barrel band; swivels
Approximate wt.: 7½ lbs.
Comments: Made during the 1970's.
Estimated Value: Excellent: $250.00
                       Very good: $175.00

Plainfield

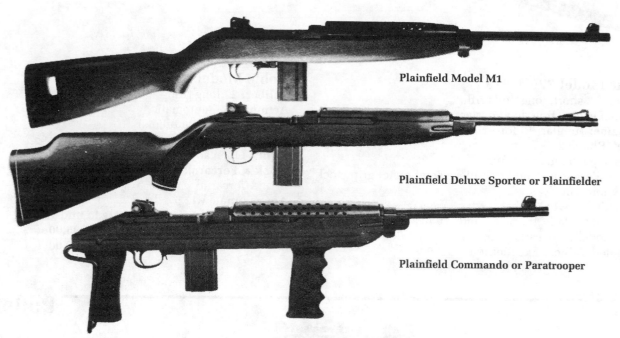

Plainfield Model M1

Plainfield Deluxe Sporter or Plainfielder

Plainfield Commando or Paratrooper

Plainfield Model M1

Caliber: 30 M1, 223 (5.7mm)
Action: Semi-automatic, gas operated
Magazine: 15-shot detachable clip
Barrel: Blued or stainless steel; 18"
Sights: Open adjustable rear, gold beaded ramp front
Stock & Forearm: Wood one-piece semi-pistol grip stock & forearm; slot in stock; metal ventilated hand guard
Approximate wt.: 6 lbs.
Comments: Made from about 1960 to late 1970's. Reintroduced in the late 1970's by Iver Johnson. See Iver Johnson; add 30% for stainless steel.
Estimated Value: Excellent: $175.00
                       Very good: $130.00

Plainfield Model M1 Sporter

Similar to the M1 Carbine with a wood hand guard & no slot in the stock. See Iver Johnson.
Estimated Value: Excellent: $185.00
                       Very good: $135.00

Plainfield Deluxe Sporter or Plainfielder

Similar to the Sporter with a checkered walnut Monte Carlo pistol grip stock & forearm.
Estimated Value: Excellent: $175.00
                       Very good: $130.00

Plainfield Commando or Paratrooper

Similar to the M1 Carbine with pistol grip at rear & at forearm; telescoping wire shoulder stock. Add 30% for stainless steel. See Iver Johnson.
Estimated Value: Excellent: $210.00
                       Very good: $160.00

Remington

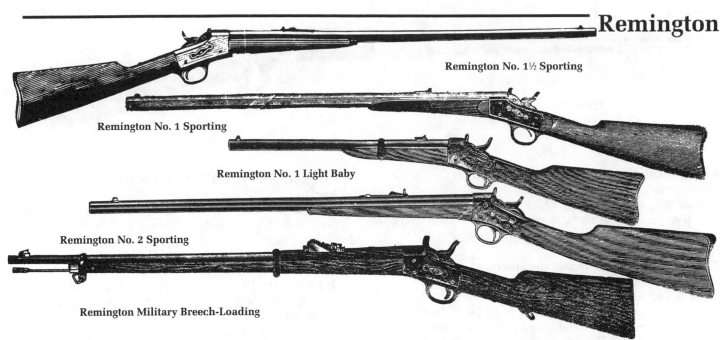

Remington No. 1½ Sporting

Remington No. 1 Sporting

Remington No. 1 Light Baby

Remington No. 2 Sporting

Remington Military Breech-Loading

Remington Military Breech-Loading

Caliber: C.F. 43 Spanish, 43 Egyptian, 50-70 Government, 58 Berdan. Early models used rim fire cartridges. Models for center fire cartridges produced after 1872.

Action: Single shot; rolling block with single trigger; visible hammer

Magazine: None

Barrel: 30" to 36" round

Sights: Military (post front and folding leaf rear)

Stock & Forearm: Plain walnut straight stock & forearm; long forearm with ram rod; steel buttplate on stock

Approximate wt.: 8 to 11 lbs.

Comments: Made from about 1867 to 1902 (large number sold to Egypt, France & Spain) & sold commercially in U.S.A. Some are unmarked; some have Arabic marked barrels & some marked Remington's, caliber not marked.

Estimated Value: **Excellent:**   **$175.00**
                 Very good: **$130.00**

Remington No. 1 Sporting

Caliber: Early guns for rim fire 50-70, 44 long & extra long or 46 long & extra long. After 1872 made for centerfire 40-50, 40-70, 44-77, 45-70, or 45 sporting cartridge.

Action: Single shot; rolling block with single trigger; visible hammer

Magazine: None

Barrel: 28" or 30" tapered octagon

Sights: Sporting front, folding leaf rear

Stock & Forearm: Plain walnut straight grip stock with flanged-top steel buttplate & short plain walnut forearm with thin round front

Approximate wt.: 8½ to 12 lbs.

Comments: Made from about 1868 to 1902. Caliber marked on barrel.

Estimated Value: **Excellent:**   **$350.00**
                 Very good: **$260.00**

Remington No. 1 Light Baby Carbine

Caliber: 44-40

Action: Single-shot; rolling block with single trigger; visible hammer

Magazine: None

Barrel: 20", light round

Sights: Pointed post front, military folding leaf rear

Stock & Forearm: Plain oiled walnut straight stock with metal buttplate & short forearm; barrel band

Approximate wt.: 5¾ lbs.

Comments: Made from about 1892 to 1902.

Estimated Value: **Excellent:**   **$400.00**
                 Very good: **$300.00**

Remington No. 1½ Sporting

Similar to No. 1 Sporting Rifle except: lighter action, stocks & smaller caliber barrels; approximate wt. 5½ to 7 lbs.; made in following pistol calibers: rim fire 22 short, long & extra long; 25 Stevens & 25 longs; 32 or 38 long & extra long; center fire Winchester 32-20; 38-40; or 44-40; barrel lengths 24", 26", 28", or 30". Made from about 1869 to 1902.

Estimated Value: **Excellent:**   **$300.00**
                 Very good: **$225.00**

Remington No. 2 Sporting

Caliber: Early models were for rim fire 22, 25, 32 or 38. Later models for center fire 22, 25-21, 25-25, 25-20, 32 long, 38 long or 38-40

Action: Single-shot; rolling block; single trigger

Magazine: None

Barrel: 24" to 30" light weight; octagon

Sights: Bead front sight, sporting rear with elevation adjustment

Stock & Forearm: Plain oil-finish walnut, straight stock & forearm with lip at front

Approximate wt.: 5 to 6 lbs.

Comments: Made from about 1873 to 1902; caliber stamped under barrel at forearm.

Estimated Value: **Excellent:**   **$325.00**
                 Very good: **$240.00**

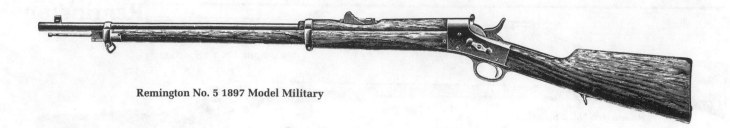

Remington No. 5 1897 Model Military

Remington No. 5 1897 Carbine

Caliber: 7mm

Action: Single shot; rolling block; ornance steel; smokeless powder action with case hardened steel frame; visible hammer

Magazine: None

Barrel: 20" round, smokeless steel barrel

Sights: Post front, military rear

Stock & Forearm: Plain straight grip, oiled walnut, two-piece stock & forearm; steel buttplate; short forearm; barrel band; hand guard on top of barrel

Approximate wt.: 5 lbs.

Comments: Made from about 1897 to 1906.

Estimated Value:　　Excellent:　　$320.00
　　　　　　　　　　　Very good:　　$250.00

Remington No. 5 1897 Model Military

Caliber: 7mm, 30 Government

Action: Single-shot; rolling block; smokeless powder action with case hardened frame; visible hammer

Magazine: None

Barrel: 30" light round tapered barrel

Sights: Post front, folding leaf rear

Stock & Forearm: Plain straight stock, oiled walnut, two-piece, full stock with steel buttplate & capped forearm; ramrod under forearm; two barrel bands; hand guard on top of barrel

Approximate wt.: 8½ lbs.

Comments: Made from about 1897 to 1906.

Estimated Value:　　Excellent:　　$300.00
　　　　　　　　　　　Very good:　　$225.00

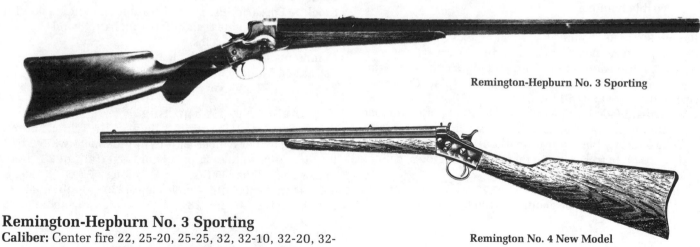

Remington-Hepburn No. 3 Sporting

Remington No. 4 New Model

Remington-Hepburn No. 3 Sporting

Caliber: Center fire 22, 25-20, 25-25, 32, 32-10, 32-20, 32-40, 38, 38-40, 38-50, 38-55, 40-60, 40-65, 40-82, 45-70 Government or 45-90. Also made by order for 40-50, 40-70, 40-90 or 44-77 bottle neck Remington, 45-90, 45-105 or 50-90 Sharps & 50-70 Government.

Action: Hepburn drop block; side-lever opens & closes action; single-shot with low visible hammer; early models with single trigger; later models with single or double set triggers

Magazine: None

Barrel: 28" to 32" round, octagon or half octagon

Sights: Blade front; sporting rear adjustable for elevation

Stock & Forearm: Plain straight grip or checkered pistol grip, oiled wood stock with steel buttplate & matching short forearm with lipped front

Approximate wt.: 8 to 12 lbs.

Comments: Made from about 1880 to 1906.

Estimated Value:　　Excellent:　　$650.00
　　　　　　　　　　　Very good:　　$520.00

Remington No. 4 New Model

Caliber: Rim fire only in 22 short, long and long rifle, 25 Stevens or 32 long

Action: Single-shot; rolling block; light short action with automatic shell ejector; visible hammer

Magazine: None

Barrel: 22½" light octagon in 22 & 25 caliber; 24" in 32 caliber; round barrel after about 1931

Sights: Bead front, plain "V" notch rear

Stock & Forearm: Plain varnished, two-piece straight grip stock & forearm; short round front forearm

Approximate wt.: 4¼ lbs.

Comments: Made from about 1891 to 1934.

Estimated Value:　　Excellent:　　$220.00
　　　　　　　　　　　Very good:　　$175.00

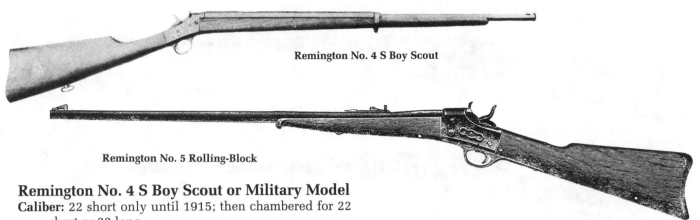

Remington No. 4 S Boy Scout

Remington No. 5 Rolling-Block

Remington No. 4 S Boy Scout or Military Model
Caliber: 22 short only until 1915; then chambered for 22 short or 22 long
Action: Single-shot; case hardened No. 4 rolling-block action; visible hammer
Magazine: None
Barrel: 28" medium, round barrel
Sights: Blade front; open "v" notch rear adjustable for elevation
Stock & Forearm: Musket-style, oiled walnut, one-piece, full-length stock & forearm with steel buttplate & one barrel band; bayonet lug below barrel near muzzle; hand guard on top of barrel
Approximate wt.: 5 lbs.
Comments: Called Boy Scout model from 1913 to 1915 then renamed Military Model. Produced from about 1913 to 1932.
Estimated Value: **Excellent:** $385.00
   Very good: $300.00

Remington No. 5 Rolling-Block
Caliber: 7mm Mauser, 30-30 or 30-40 Krag
Action: New Ordnance steel, single-shot; rolling block; smokeless powder action with case hardened frame
Magazine: None
Barrel: 28"-30" light steel round barrel
Sights: Blade front, Rocky Mountain rear
Stock & Forearm: Plain varnished walnut, two-piece straight grip stock & forearm; steel buttplate on stock; forearm lipped at front
Approximate wt.: 7¼ lbs.
Comments: Made from about 1896 to 1906.
Estimated Value: **Excellent:** $300.00
   Very good: $225.00

Remington No. 6

Remington No. 7 Target

Remington No. 6
Caliber: 22 short, long, long rifle, 32 short & long RF
Action: Single-shot; rolling-block; visible hammer; takedown model
Magazine: None
Barrel: 20" round tapered barrel
Sights: Bead front; open rear; also tang peep sight available
Stock & Forearm: Plain varnished walnut straight grip stock & forearm; steel buttplate
Approximate wt.: 4 lbs.
Comments: Made from about 1902 to 1934.
Estimated Value: **Excellent:** $180.00
   Very good: $135.00

Remington No. 7 Target
Caliber: 22 long rifle, 32 MRF or 25 Stevens RF
Action: Single-action; rolling block; visible hammer
Magazine: None
Barrel: 24", 26" 28"; half-octagon barrel
Sights: Bead front, adjustable dovetail rear
Stock & Forearm: Varnished checkered walnut pistol grip stock & forearm; capped pistol grip; rubber buttplate; lipped forearm
Approximate wt.: 7 lbs.
Comments: Made from about 1904 to 1906.
Estimated Value: **Excellent:** $700.00
   Very good: $520.00

Remington-Lee Sporting

Remington-Lee Military

Remington-Lee Military Carbine

Remington-Lee Sporting
Caliber: 6mm U.S. Navy, 30-30 Sporting, 30-40 U.S. Government, 7mm Mauser, or 7.65mm Mauser
Action: Improved smokeless powder, bolt action; repeating
Magazine: 5-shot removable box
Barrel: 24" to 28" round smokeless steel barrel
Sights: Bead or blade front, open rear adjustable for elevation
Stock & Forearm: Checkered walnut one-piece semi-pistol grip stock & forearm; forearm grooved on each side with lip at front
Approximate wt.: 6¾ lbs.
Comments: Some were produced with deluxe grand walnut stock, half-octagon barrel & Lyman sights. Made from about 1897 to 1906. Prices are for standard grade.
Estimated Value: Excellent: $420.00
　　　　　　　　　　　Very good: $335.00

Remington-Lee Military
Caliber: 30-40 Krag, 303 British, 6mm Lee Navy, 7mm Mauser or 7.65 mm Mauser
Action: Improved smokeless powder, bolt action; repeating, rimless cartridges
Magazine: 5-shot removable box
Barrel: 29" round smokeless steel barrel
Sights: Post front; folding leaf rear
Stock & Forearm: Plain walnut one-piece straight grip stock & long forearm; cleaning rod; barrel bands; wood hand guard on top of barrel
Approximate wt.: 8½ lbs.
Comments: Made from about 1897 to 1902.
Estimated Value: Excellent: $390.00
　　　　　　　　　　　Very good: $315.00

Remington-Lee Military Carbine
Similar to Remington-Lee rifle except: 20" barrel; one barrel band; approximate wt. 6½ lbs.
Estimated Value: Excellent: $360.00
　　　　　　　　　　　Very good: $290.00

Remington Model 1907-15
Caliber: 8mm Lebel
Action: Smokeless powder bolt action; repeating; self-cocking striker with knurled top for uncocking & manual cocking
Magazine: 5-shot box
Barrel: 26" to 31" round with 4 groove rifling
Sights: Ivory bead dovetail front, folding leaf rear
Stock & Forearm: Plain varnished walnut one-piece stock & long forearm; barrel bands; cleaning rod in forearm under barrel
Approximate wt.: 8 to 9 lbs.
Comments: Made from about 1907 to 1915; left side of action marked "Remington MLE 1907-15"; right side of barrel near action marked "RAC 1907-15."
Estimated Value: Excellent: $275.00
　　　　　　　　　　　Very good: $220.00

Remington Model 1907-15 Carbine
Same as Remington Model 1907-15 repeating rifle except: 22" barrel; no barrel bands; short forearm; approximate wt. 6½ lbs.
Estimated Value: Excellent: $250.00
　　　　　　　　　　　Very good: $200.00

Remington, Enfield Pattern, 1914 Military
Caliber: 303 British (rimmed)
Action: British smokeless powder bolt action; repeating; self-cocking on down stroke of bolt handle
Magazine: 5-shot box
Barrel: 26" round tapered barrel
Sights: Protected post front; protected folding leaf rear
Stock & Forearm: Oil finished walnut, one-piece stock & forearm; wood hand guard on top of barrel; modified pistol grip stock; full length forearm with two barrel bands
Approximate wt.: 10 lbs.
Comments: Made from about 1915 to 1916 for the British Army; Serial No. on action & bolt, "R" preceeding action serial no.; approximately 600,000 produced.
Estimated Value: Excellent: **$325.00**
                            Very good: **$260.00**

Remington, Enfield U.S. Model 1917 Military
Caliber: 30-06 Government, rimless
Action: Smokeless powder bolt action; repeating; self-cocking on down stroke of bolt handle; actions made with interchangeable parts
Magazine: 5-shot box
Barrel: 26" round tapered
Sights: Protected post front, protected folding leaf rear
Stock & Forearm: Plain one-piece walnut stock & forearm; wood hand guard over barrel; modified pistol grip stock; full length forearm with finger grooves and two barrel beads; equipped with sling loops & bayonet lug
Approximate wt.: 10 lbs.
Comments: Made from about 1917 to 1918. Marked "Model of 1917," Remington & serial no. on bridge.
Estimated Value: Excellent: **$360.00**
                            Very good: **$290.00**

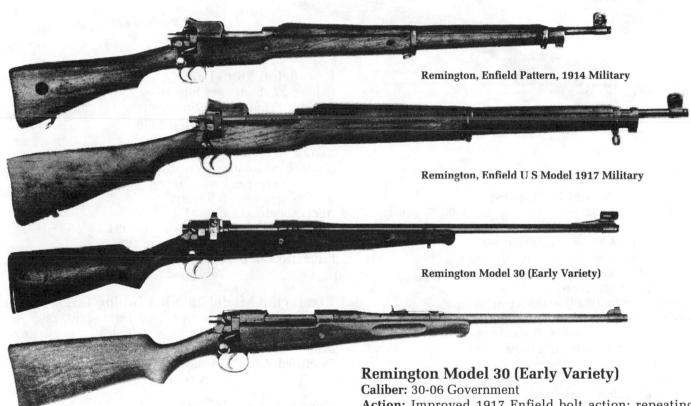

Remington, Enfield Pattern, 1914 Military

Remington, Enfield U S Model 1917 Military

Remington Model 30 (Early Variety)

Remington Model 30 (Intermediate Variety)

Remington Model 30 (Early Variety)
Caliber: 30-06 Government
Action: Improved 1917 Enfield bolt action; repeating; self-cocking when bolt is closed; hinged floor plate; side-safety
Magazine: 5-shot box
Barrel: 24" light round
Sights: Slip-on band front sight, adjustable rear sight
Stock & Forearm: Plain varnished walnut, one-piece pistol grip stock & forearm; steel buttplate; grooved forearm with lipped front tip
Approximate wt.: 8 lbs.
Comments: Made from about 1921 to 1926; approximately 8,500 produced; marked "Remington Arms Co. Inc., Remington Ilion Works, Ilion, N.Y. Made in U.S.A."
Estimated Value: Excellent: **$450.00**
                            Very good: **$360.00**

Remington Model 30 (Intermediate Variety)
Same as Model 30 (Early Variety) rifle except: calibers 30-06 Government, 25, 30, 32 and 35 Remington & 7mm Mauser; 22" barrel length; also made in 20" barrel carbine. Made from about 1926 to 1930. Approximate wt. 7lbs.
Estimated Value: Excellent: **$425.00**
                            Very good: **$340.00**

Remington Model 30 Express

Remington Model 33

Remington Model 34

Remington Model 30 Express

Caliber: 25, 30, 32 or 35 Remington, 30-06 Government, 7mm Mauser until 1936. After 1936 caliber 257 Roberts & 30-06 government only

Action: Bolt action; repeating; self-cocking; thumb safety

Magazine: 5-shot box

Barrel: 22" or 24" round barrel

Sights: Bead front, adjustable open rear

Stock & Forearm: Plain or checkered walnut pistol grip one-piece stock & forearm; early models have grooved forearm with lipped tip

Approximate wt.: 7½ lbs.

Comments: Made from about 1921 to 1940.

Estimated Value: **Excellent:** $450.00
                       Very good: $360.00

Remington Model 30R Carbine

Same as Model 30 Express Rifle except: 20" barrel; plain walnut one-piece stock and forearm; approximate wt. 7 lbs.

Estimated Value: **Excellent:** $420.00
                       Very good: $335.00

Remington Model 30S Sporting

Similar to Model 30 Express Rifle except: caliber 257 Roberts, 7mm Mauser or 30-06; approximate wt. 8 lbs.; rear peep sight; special grade high comb stock; produced from about 1930 to 1940; 24" barrel.

Estimated Value: **Excellent:** $460.00
                       Very good: $370.00

Remington Model 33

Caliber: 22 short, long, long rifle

Action: Single-shot; bolt action; takedown model; exposed knurled cocking-piece

Magazine: None

Barrel: 24" round

Sights: Bead front, open rear, adjustable for elevation

Stock & Forearm: Plain varnished walnut one-piece pistol grip stock & forearm

Approximate wt.: 4 lbs.

Comments: Made from about 1931 to 1936; finger grooves added to forearm in 1934.

Estimated Value: **Excellent:** $110.00
                       Very good: $ 85.00

Remington Model 33 NRA Junior Target

Same as Model 33 except: post front sight; reep rear sight; equipped with 1" leather sling; swivels; approximate wt. 4½ lbs.

Estimated Value: **Excellent:** $130.00
                       Very good: $105.00

Remington Model 34

Caliber: 22 short, long, long rifle

Action: Bolt action; repeating; takedown model; self-cocking; thumb safety

Magazine: Tubular under barrel; 22 shorts, 17 longs, 15 long rifles

Barrel: 24" round

Sights: Bead front, adjustable open rear

Stock & Forearm: Plain wood, one-piece pistol grip stock & grooved forearm

Approximate wt.: 5½ lbs.

Comments: Made from about 1933 to 1935; also produced in Model 34 NRA target model with peep rear sight & sling swivels.

Estimated Value: **Excellent:** $140.00
                       Very good: $115.00

Remington Model 41

Caliber: 22 short, long, long rifle 22 WRF
Action: Bolt action; single-shot; takedown model; exposed knurled cocking-piece
Magazine: None
Barrel: 27" round
Sights: Bead or hooded ramp front sight, open rear adjustable for elevation or peep rear sight
Stock & Forearm: Plain one-piece pistol grip stock & forearm; hard rubber buttplate
Approximate wt.: 5 lbs.
Comments: Made from about 1936 to 1940 in following models:
    41 A - "Standard" model with open sights;
    41 P - "Target" model with target sights;
    41 AS - "Special" model chambered for 22 WRF;
    41 SB - "Smoothbore" model; no rifling, chambered for 22 LR shot shell only.
Estimated Value: Excellent: $120.00
    Very good: $ 95.00

Remington Model 341 Sportsmaster

Caliber: 22 short, long, long rifle
Action: Bolt action; repeating; takedown model; self-cocking; thumb safety
Magazine: Tubular under barrel; 22 shorts, 17 longs, 15 long rifles
Barrel: 27" round
Sights: Bead front, open rear adjustable for elevation
Stock & Forearm: Plain wood one-piece pistol grip stock & forearm
Approximate wt.: 6 lbs.
Comments: Made from about 1935 to 1940. Also made in Model 341 P, which has hooded front sight & peep rear sight.
Estimated Value: Excellent: $130.00
    Very good: $105.00

Remington Model 341 S Sportsmaster

Same as Model 341 except: smooth bore for 22 shot catridges.
Estimated Value: Excellent: $125.00
    Very good: $100.00

Remington Model 37 Rangemaster

Caliber: 22 long rifle
Action: Bolt action; repeating; self-cocking; thumb safety: adjustable trigger
Magazine: 5-shot clip & single-shot adapter
Barrel: 28" heavy, semi-floating target barrel
Sights: Target sights; drilled for scope mount
Stock & Forearm: Lacquer finished heavy target, one-piece walnut stock & forearm; high flute comb stock with plain pistol grip & steel buttplate; early models had rounded beavertail forearm with one barrel band; barrel band dropped in 1938 & forearm modified
Approximate wt.: 12 lbs.
Comments: Made from about 1937 to 1940.
Estimated Value: Excellent: $385.00
    Very good: $310.00

Remington Model 37 (1940 Model)

Similar to Model 37 rifle except: improved trigger mechanism; re-designed stock; wide beavertail forearm; produced from about 1940 to 1955.
Estimated Value: Excellent: $400.00
    Very good: $320.00

Remington Model 41

Remington Model 341

Remington Model 37

Remington Model 37 (1940 Model)

Remington Model 510 Targetmaster

Remington Model 510 C Carbine

Remington Model 510 C Carbine

Same as Model 510 single-shot rifle except: 21" barrel & approximate wt. of 5½ lbs. Made from about 1961 to 1962.

Estimated Value: Excellent: $90.00
Very good: $70.00

Remington Model 510 Targetmaster

Caliber: 22 short, long, long rifle
Action: Bolt action; single shot; takedown model; self-cocking with thumb safety & cocking indicator
Magazine: None
Barrel: 25" light round
Sights: Sporting or target sights
Stock & Forearm: Plain walnut one-piece pistol grip stock & forearm
Approximate wt.: 5 lbs.
Comments: Made from about 1939 to 1962 in three models: 510 A Standard model; 510 P with peep sights; & 510 SB, a smooth-bore chambered for 22 shot shells; minor changes in manufacture, in markings & post-World War II models.
Estimated Value: Excellent: $95.00
Very good: $75.00

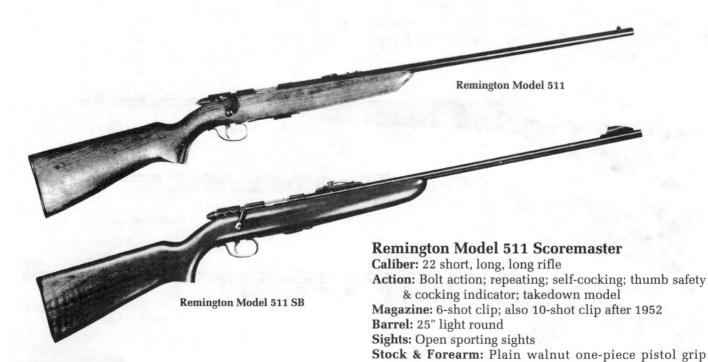

Remington Model 511

Remington Model 511 SB

Remington Model 511 SB

Same as Model 511 Scoremaster Rifle except: smooth bore for using 22 shot cartridges.
Estimated Value: Excellent: $120.00
Very good: $ 95.00

Remington Model 511 Scoremaster

Caliber: 22 short, long, long rifle
Action: Bolt action; repeating; self-cocking; thumb safety & cocking indicator; takedown model
Magazine: 6-shot clip; also 10-shot clip after 1952
Barrel: 25" light round
Sights: Open sporting sights
Stock & Forearm: Plain walnut one-piece pistol grip stock & forearm
Approximate wt.: 5¾ lbs.
Comments: Made from about 1939 to 1962 with production stopped during World War II; made in pre-war and post-war models. Add $10.00 for pre-1942.
Estimated Value: Excellent: $110.00
Very good: $ 85.00

Remington Model 512 Sportmaster

Caliber: 22 short, long, long rifle
Action: Bolt action; repeating; self cocking; thumb safety; cocking indicator
Magazine: Tubular under barrel; 22 shorts, 17 longs, 15 long rifles
Barrel: 25" light round
Sights: Bead front, open rear adjustable for elevation
Stock & Forearm: Plain walnut one-piece pistol grip stock & forearm; composition buttplate
Approximate wt.: 5½ lbs.
Comments: Made from about 1940 to 1942 & from 1946 to 1962; the pre-war & post-war models may have minor differences in manufacture, markings & stocks.
Estimated Value: Excellent: $100.00
                             Very good: $ 80.00

Remington Model 512 SB

Same as Model 512 Sportmaster except smooth bore for 22 shot cartridges.
Estimated Value: Excellent: $110.00
                             Very good: $ 85.00

Remington Model 513 T Matchmaster

Caliber: 22 long rifle
Action: Bolt action; repeating; self-cocking; side safety; cocking indicator; adjustable trigger
Magazine: 6-shot clip
Barrel: 27" medium round barrel; semi-floating type
Sights: Target sights; top of receiver grooved for scope mount after 1954
Stock & Forearm: Plain, heavy, high fluted comb; lacquered walnut one-piece pistol grip stock & beaver-tail forearm
Approximate wt.: 9 lbs.
Comments: Made from about 1940 to 1942 & from 1945 to 1968.
Estimated Value: Excellent: $200.00
                             Very good: $160.00

Remington Model 513 S Sporter Rifle

Similar to Model 513 T Matchmaster except: lighter sporting checkered walnut one-piece stock & forearm; approximate wt. 6¾ lbs.; ramp front sight & adjustable open rear sight; produced from about 1940 to 1958.
Estimated Value: Excellent: $190.00
                             Very good: $150.00

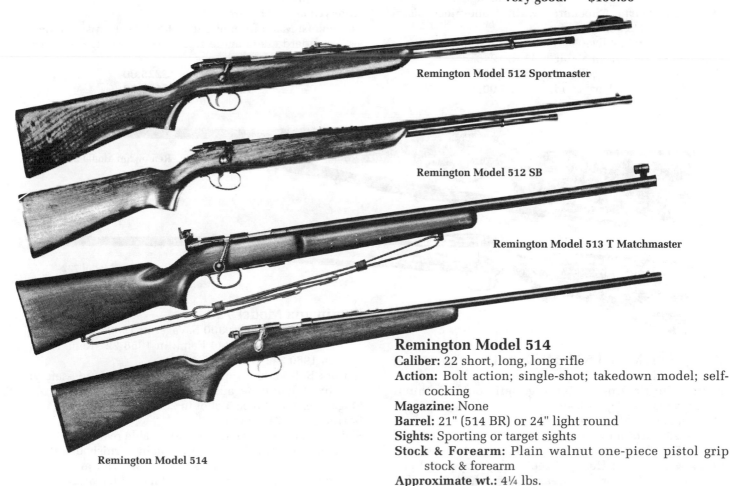

Remington Model 512 Sportmaster

Remington Model 512 SB

Remington Model 513 T Matchmaster

Remington Model 514

Remington Model 514

Caliber: 22 short, long, long rifle
Action: Bolt action; single-shot; takedown model; self-cocking
Magazine: None
Barrel: 21" (514 BR) or 24" light round
Sights: Sporting or target sights
Stock & Forearm: Plain walnut one-piece pistol grip stock & forearm
Approximate wt.: 4¼ lbs.
Comments: Made from about 1948 to 1972 in three models; 514 Standard Model; 514 P had target sights (peep rear sight); 514 BR Boys Rifle had 1" shorter stock & 21" barrel.
Estimated Value: Excellent: $75.00
                             Very good: $60.00

Remington Model 720

Remington Model 721

Remington Model 720

Caliber: 257 Roberts, 270 Win., 30-06 Government
Action: Bolt action; repeating; self-cocking; side safety
Magazine: 5-shot box; removable floor plate
Barrel: 20", 22" or 24" round
Sights: Ramp front, adjustable open rear sights
Stock & Forearm: Checkered walnut one-piece pistol grip stock & forearm
Approximate wt.: 8 lbs.
Comments: Made from about 1941 to 1946.

Estimated Value: Excellent: $320.00
 Very good: $255.00

Remington Model 721

Caliber: 270, 30-06 or 300 mag.; after 1959, 280 Rem.
Action: Bolt action; repeating; self-cocking; side safety; adjustable trigger
Magazine: 4-shot box with fixed floor plate; 3-shot in 300 magnum
Barrel: 24" or 26" round
Sights: Ramp front, sporting rear with step elevator
Stock & Forearm: Checkered walnut or plain one-piece pistol grip stock & forearm; aluminum shotgun buttplate
Approximate wt.: 8 lbs.
Comments: Made from about 1948 to 1958 in six grades: standard grade made from 1948 to 1961. Prices are for standard grade.

Estimated Value: Excellent: $225.00
 Very good: $180.00

Remington Model 521

Remington Model 722

Remington Model 521 TL Target

Caliber: 22 long rifle
Action: Bolt action; repeating; self-cocking; thumb safety; cocking indicator
Magazine: 5- or 10-shot clip
Barrel: 25" medium weight round barrel
Sights: Post front, Lyman #57 receiver sight (peep sight)
Stock & Forearm: Heavy target one-piece pistol grip stock & beavertail forearm; varnished or oil finished; rubber buttplate
Approximate wt.: 6½ lbs.
Comments: Made from about 1948 to 1968; a low cost rifle intended for junior target shooter.

Estimated Value: Excellent: $125.00
 Very good: $100.00

Remington Model 722

Caliber: 257 Roberts or 300 Savage; in 1950 222 Rem.; in 1956 308 Win. & 244 Rem.; in 1958 222 Rem. mag.; in 1960 243 Win.
Action: Bolt action; repeating; self-cocking; side-safety; fixed floor plate; adjustable trigger
Magazine: 4-shot box; 5-shot in 222 magnum
Barrel: 22" or 24" round
Sights: Ramp bead front, open adjustable rear
Stock & Forearm: Checkered or plain varnished walnut one-piece pistol grip stock & forearm; after 1950 option of high-comb stock & tapered forearm
Approximate wt.: 7 to 8½ lbs.
Comments: Made from about 1948 to 1958 in seven grades; standard grade made from about 1948 to 1961.

Estimated Value: Excellent: $275.00
 Very good: $220.00

Remington Model 725 (Early)

Caliber: 270, 280, 30-06
Action: Bolt action; repeating; self-cocking; thumb safety
Magazine: 4-shot box
Barrel: 22" round
Sights: Adjustable open rear, hooded ramp front
Stock & Forearm: Checkered walnut Monte Carlo one-piece pistol grip stock & forearm; capped grip stock with shotgun buttplate & sling loops
Approximate wt.: 7½ lbs.
Comments: Made from about 1958 to 1959.
Estimated Value: Excellent: $330.00
Very good: $260.00

Remington Model 725 (Late)

Same as Model 725 (Early) Rifle except: also in calibers 243 Win.; 244 Rem.; or 222 Rem.; 24" barrel in 222 Rem. and aluminum buttplate on all calibers. Made from about 1960 to 1961 in three grades. Prices are for standard grade.
Estimated Value: Excellent: $360.00
Very good: $285.00

Remington Model 725 Magnum

Caliber: 375 or 458 Win. magnum
Action: Bolt action; repeating; self-cocking; thumb safety
Magazine: 3-shot box
Barrel: 26" heavy round barrel with muzzle brake
Sights: Ramp front, deluxe adjustable rear
Stock & Forearm: Fancy reinforced, checkered walnut Monte Carlo one-piece pistol grip stock & forearm; stock with cap & rubber recoil pad; black forearm tip; quick detachable leather sling
Approximate wt.: 9 lbs.
Comments: Made from about 1960 to 1961 in three grades. Prices are for ADL grade.
Estimated Value: Excellent: $550.00
Very good: $440.00

Remington Model 725 (Early)

Remington Model 725 (Late)

Remington Model 725 Magnum

Remington Model 10 Nylon

Remington Model 10 SB

Same as Model 10 except: smooth bore; chambered for 22 shot shells.
Estimated Value: Excellent: $55.00
Very good: $40.00

Remington Model 10 Nylon

Caliber: 22 short, long, long rifle
Action: Bolt action; self-cocking striker with indicator; single-shot; slide safety
Magazine: None
Barrel: 19½" round
Sights: Ramp front; adjustable opean rear
Stock & Forearm: Nylon checkered one-piece pistol grip stock & forearm; shotgun buttplate
Approximate wt.: 4 lbs.
Comments: Made from about 1963 to 1964.
Estimated Value: Excellent: $60.00
Very good: $45.00

Remington Nylon 11

Remington Nylon 12

Remington Nylon 11
Caliber: 22 short, long, long rifle
Action: Bolt action; repeating; self-cocking; cocking indicator
Magazine: 6- or 10-shot clip
Barrel: 19½" round
Sights: Ramp front, adjustable open rear
Stock & Forearm: Polished brown nylon one-piece stock, forearm & handguard over barrel; checkered, capped, pistol grip stock with shot gun buttplate; checkered forearm with blunt reversed cap; white liners & two white diamond inlays on each side
Approximate wt.: 4½ lbs.
Comments: Made from about 1962 to 1964.
Estimated Value: Excellent: **$85.00**
Very good: **$65.00**

Remington Nylon 12
Similar to Remington Nylon 11 Rifle except: tubular magazine under barrel holds 14 to 21 shots.
Estimated Value: Excellent: **$90.00**
Very good: **$70.00**

Remington Model 600

Remington Model 600 Magnum

Remington Model 660

Remington Model 600
Caliber: 6mm Rem., 222 Rem., 243 Win., 308 Win., 35 Rem.
Action: Bolt action; repeating
Magazine: 5-shot box
Barrel: 18½"; ventilated rib
Sights: Open rear, bead front
Stock & Forearm: Checkered walnut Monte Carlo one-piece pistol grip stock & forearm
Approximate wt.: 6 lbs.
Comments: A carbine style rifle made in the mid 1960's.
Estimated Value: Excellent: **$250.00**
Very good: **$200.00**

Remington Model 600 Magnum
Similar to the Model 600 magnum calibers; 4-shot magazine; walnut & beechwood stock; swivels; recoil pad.
Estimated Value: Excellent: **$300.00**
Very good: **$240.00**

Remington Model 660
Similar to the Model 600; 20" barrel without rib; beaded front sight; made in the late 1960's & early 1970's.
Estimated Value: Excellent: **$250.00**
Very good: **$200.00**

Remington Model 660 Magnum
Similar to the Model 600 Magnum; 20" barrel without rib; beaded front sight; made in the late 1960's to early 1970's.
Estimated Value: Excellent: **$320.00**
Very good: **$255.00**

Remington Model 580

Caliber: 22 short, long, long rifle
Action: Bolt action; single-shot; self-cocking striker
Magazine: None
Barrel: 24" round
Sights: Bead front; adjustable open rear
Stock & Forearm: Plain wood Monte Carlo one-piece pistol grip stock & forearm; plastic shotgun buttplate
Approximate wt.: 5 lbs.
Comments: Made from about 1967 to late 1970's also available in Boys' model with shorter stock for your shooters.
Estimated Value: Excellent: $70.00
Very good: $55.00

Remington Model 580 SB

Same as Model 580 except: smooth bore for 22 long rifle shot shell only.
Estimated Value: Excellent: $75.00
Very good: $65.00

Remington Model 581 & 581 S

Caliber: 22 short, long, long rifle
Action: Bolt action; repeating; self-cocking; thumb safety
Magazine: 5-shot clip; single shot adapter
Barrel: 24" round
Sights: Bead front, adjustable open rear sight
Stock & Forearm: Plain wood Monte Carlo one-piece pistol grip stock & forearm
Approximate wt.: 5¼ lbs.
Comments: Made from about 1967 to 1983; reintroduced in 1986 as "Sportsman" 581-S.
Estimated Value: New (retail): $196.00
Excellent: $150.00
Very good: $115.00

Remington Model 582

Same as Model 581 except: 14 to 20 shot tubular magazine under barrel. Add $13.00 for swivels & sling.
Estimated Value: Excellent: $155.00
Very good: $125.00

Remington Model 580

Remington Model 580 SB

Remington Model 581

Remington Model 582

Remington Model 788

Remington Model 788

Caliber: 222, 22-250, 223 Rem., 6mm Rem., 243 Win., 308 Win.; 7mm-08 Rem. added 1980
Action: Bolt action; repeating; self-cocking; thumb safety
Magazine: 5-shot clip in 222; 4-shot clip in other calibers
Barrel: 24" round tapered barrel in calibers 222, 22-250 & 223 Rem.; 22" barrel in other calibers; 18½" barrel available 1980
Sights: Blade front, adjustable rear
Stock & Forearm: Monte Carlo one-piece pistol grip stock & forearm; current model has fluted comb & wider pistol grip & forearm; swivels available
Approximate wt.: 7½ lbs.
Comments: Made from about 1967 to 1983. Add $5.00 for left hand action, $50.00 for scope.
Estimated Value: Excellent: $250.00
Very good: $200.00

Remington Model 591

Remington Model 592

Remington Model 591

Caliber: 5mm Rem. rim fire
Action: Bolt action; repeating; self-cocking; thumb safety
Magazine: 4-shot clip
Barrel: 24" round
Sights: Bead post front; adjustable open rear
Stock & Forearm: One-piece plain hardwood stock &
   forearm with Monte Carlo comb & pistol grip
Approximate wt.: 5 lbs.
Comments: Made from about 1970 to 1974.
Estimated Value: Excellent: $165.00
                       Very good: $130.00

Remington Model 592

Same as Model 591 except: 10-shot tubular magazine
under barrel.
Estimated Value: Excellent: $175.00
                       Very good: $140.00

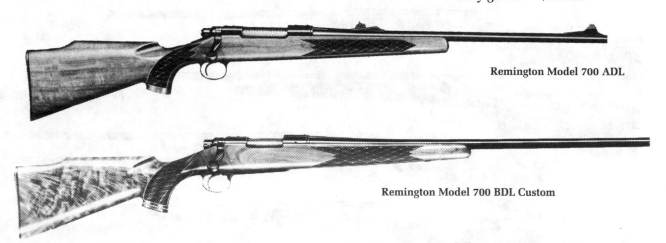

Remington Model 700 ADL

Remington Model 700 BDL Custom

Remington Model 700 ADL, 700 ADL-LS

Caliber: 222, 22-250, 6mm Rem., 243 Win., 25-06 Rem.
   270 Win., 7mm Rem. mag., 308 Win., 30-06
Action: Bolt action; repeating; self-cocking; thumb
   safety; checkered bolt handle
Magazine: 4- to 6-shot box magazine
Barrel: 22" or 24" round tapered barrel
Sights: Ramp front; adjustable, notched, removable rear
Stock & Forearm: Checkered walnut Monte Carlo pistol
   grip, one-piece stock & forearm; 700 ADL-LS has
   laminated stock
Approximate wt.: 7½ lbs.
Comments: Produced from about 1962 to present. Add
   $25.00 for magnum or swivels & sling. Add $50.00
   for laminated stock (LS). Models produced in late
   1987 were recalled by Remington. These rifles,
   which may contain an improperly manufactured
   part in the trigger mechanism, will be repaired by
   Remington at no cost.
Estimated Value: New (retail): $419.00
                       Excellent: $315.00
                       Very good: $250.00

Remington Model 700 BDL

Similar to Model 700 ADL except: custom deluxe grade
with black forearm end; sling strap; additional calibers:
17 Rem., 223 Rem., 264 Win. magnum, 300 Win. magnum, 338 Win. magnum; Add $25.00 for magnum cal-
ibers. Models produced in late 1987 were recalled by
Remington. These rifles, which may contain an improperly manufactured part in the trigger mechanism, will be
repaired by Remington at no cost.
Estimated Value: New (retail): $495.00
                       Excellent: $370.00
                       Very good: $300.00

Remington Model 700 "Mountain Rifle"

Similar to 700 BDL except: 270 Win., 280 Rem. & 30-06
caliber; approx. wt. 7lbs.; 4-shot magazine; no sights;
introduced in 1986. Models produced in late 1987 were
recalled by Remington. These rifles, which may contain
an improperly manufactured part in the trigger mechanism, will be repaired by Remington at no cost.
Estimated Value: New (retail): $503.00
                       Excellent: $375.00
                       Very good: $300.00

Remington Model 700 BDL Safari

Remington Model 700 BDL Varmint Special

Similar to 700 BDL with heavy barrel in 22 Rem., 22-250 Rem., 223 Rem., 6mm Rem., 243 Win., 25-06 Rem., 7mm-08, 308 Win. Models produced in late 1987 were recalled by Remington. These rifles, which may contain an improperly manufactured part in the trigger mechanism, will be repaired by Remington at no cost.

Estimated Value:	New (retail):	$527.00
	Excellent:	$395.00
	Very good:	$315.00

Remington Model 700 BDL Classic

Similar to 700 BDL with stock styling changes; calibers 22-250 Rem., 6mm Rem., 243 Win., 270 Win., 30-06. Add $20.00 for magnum. A limited number available in 1981 in 7mm magnum; 1982, 257 Roberts; 1983, 300 H & H magnum; 1984, 250 Savage; 1985, 350 Rem. magnum; 1986, 264 Win. magnum. Models produced in late 1987 were recalled by Remington. These rifles, which may contain an improperly manufactured part in the trigger mechanism, will be repaired by Remington at no cost.

Estimated Value:	New (retail):	$519.00
	Excellent:	$390.00
	Very good:	$310.00

Remington Model 700 BDL Safari

Similar to Model 700 BDL in 375 H & H magnum & 458 Win. magnum; recoil pad. 8mm Rem. magnum caliber added in 1986. Models produced in late 1987 were recalled by Remington. These rifles, which may contain an improperly manufactured part in the trigger mechanism, will be repaired by Remington at no cost. Available after 1989 as a special order model from the custom shop.

Estimated Value:	Excellent:	$620.00
	Very good:	$495.00

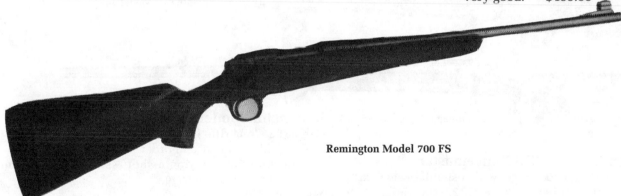

Remington Model 700 FS

Remington Model 700FS

Similar to Model 700ADL except it has a Kelvar® reinforced fiberglass stock (grey or grey camo); in calibers: 243 Win., 270 Win., 30-06, 308 Win., 7mm Rem. magnum. Introduced in 1987. Models produced in late 1987 were recalled by Remington. These rifles, which may contain an improperly manufactured part in the trigger mechanism will be repaired by Remington at no cost. Discontinued 1990.

Estimated Value:	Excellent:	$465.00
	Very good:	$375.00

Remington Model 700RS

Similar to the Model 700BDL with a DuPont Rynite® stock; textured finish; calibers: 270 Win., 280 Rem., 30-06. Introduced in 1987. Models produced in late 1987 were recalled by Remington. These rifles, which may contain an improperly manufactured part in the trigger mechanism will be repaired by Remington at no cost.

Estimated Value:	Excellent:	$410.00
	Very good:	$325.00

Remington Model 700AS

Caliber: 22-250, 243 Win., 270 Win., 280 Rem., 30-06 Win., 7mm Rem. magnum, 300 Weatherby magnum

Action: Bolt action; repeating; thumb safety

Magazine: 4-shot box in all calibers except 7mm Rem. magnum & 300 Weatherby magnum, which are 3-shot

Barrel: 22" blued in all calibers except 22-250, 7mm Rem. magnum & 300 Weatherby magnum which have 24" blued barrel

Sights: Hooded ramp front; adjustable rear

Stock & Forearm: Synthetic resin, one-piece pistol grip stock & forearm; solid recoil pad

Approximate wt.: 6¾ lbs.

Comments: Introduced in 1989; 300 Weatherby magnum added in 1990. Add 4% for 7mm Remington magnum & 300 Weatherby magnum.

Estimated Value:	New (retail)	$512.00
	Excellent:	$385.00
	Very good:	$305.00

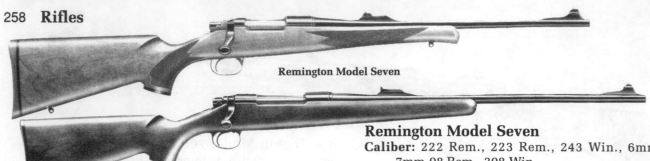

Remington Model Seven

Remington Sportsman 78

Remington Sportsman 78

Similar to the Model 700 with lesser quality finish; hardwood with no checkering; 22" barrel; 270 Win. & 30-06 calibers. Introduced in 1984. 243 & 308 calibers added in 1985; 223 caliber added in 1986. Models produced in late 1987 were recalled by Remington. These rifles, which may contain an improperly manufactured part in the trigger mechanism, will be repaired by Remington at no cost. Discontinued 1990.

Estimated Value: **Excellent:** **$245.00**
Very good: **$195.00**

Remington Model Seven

Caliber: 222 Rem., 223 Rem., 243 Win., 6mm Rem., 7mm-08 Rem., 308 Win.
Action: Bolt action; repeating
Magazine: 4- or 5-shot box with steel floor plate
Barrel: 18½" tapered
Sights: Adjustable U-notch rear on inclined ramp, beaded ramp front
Stock & Forearm: Checkered walnut one-piece pistol grip stock & slightly lipped forearm; recoil pad, swivels
Approximate wt.: 6¼ lbs.
Comments: Introduced in 1983. 222 caliber discontinued in 1985. Models produced in late 1987 were recalled by Remington. These rifles, which may contain an improperly manufactured part in the trigger mechanism, will be repaired by Remington at no cost.

Estimated Value: **New (retail):** **$503.00**
Excellent: **$375.00**
Very good: **$300.00**

Remington Model 40XR

Remington Model 40XB

Remington Model 40XB Rangemaster

Similar to the Model 40X target with a stainless steel barrel. Available in calibers 222 Rem., 22-250 Rem., 243 Win., 6mm Rem., 25-06 Rem., 7mm Rem. magnum, 7.62mm NATO, 30-06, 30-338, 300 Win. magnum; add $50.00 for repeating model. Currently produced. Models produced in late 1987 were recalled by Remington. These rifles, which may contain an improperly manufactured part in the trigger mechanism, will be repaired by Remington at no cost. Discontinued 1989.

Estimated Value: **Excellent:** **$700.00**
Very good: **$560.00**

Remington Model 40XR

A target rifle similar to the Model 40X Target with widened stock & forearm; adjustable buttplate; hand stop; introduced in the late 1970's. 22 long rifle only; Add $120.00 for Kelvar® stock. Models produced in late 1987 were recalled by Remington. These rifles, which may contain an improperly manufactured part in the trigger mechanism, will be repaired by Remington at no cost.

Estimated Value: **Excellent:** **$700.00**
Very good: **$560.00**

Remington Model 40X Target

Caliber: 22 long rifle in 1960; 222 Rem. in 1961; 308, 30-06; others on special order
Action: Bolt action; single-shot; self-cocking; thumb safety; adjustable trigger
Magazine: None
Barrel: 28" standard or heavy round barrel with bedding device in forearm
Sights: Removable target sights, scope block on barrel
Stock & Forearm: Oiled, plain, heavy target one-piece pistol grip stock & blade front; rubber shotgun buttplate; high fluted comb stock
Approximate wt.: 11 to 12 lbs.
Comments: Made from about 1956 to 1963. Replaced by Model 40XB match rifle in 1964 to 1975.

Estimated Value: **Excellent:** **$450.00**
Very good: **$360.00**

Remington Model 40XBBR

Similar to the Model 40XB Rangemaster with a 20" or 24" barrel. Currently produced. Models produced in late 1987 were recalled by Remington. These rifles, which may contain an improperly manufactured part in the trigger mechanism, will be repaired by Remington at no cost.

Estimated Value: **Excellent:** **$750.00**
Very good: **$660.00**

Remington Model 540-X

Remington Model 540XR

Remington Model 541 S

Remington Model 540-X, 540 XR

Caliber: 22 long rifle
Action: Bolt action; single shot; self-cocking striker; slide safety; adjustable match trigger
Magazine: None
Barrel: 26" heavy target barrel
Sights: Receiver drilled & tapped for scope mount; sights optional equipment
Stock & Forearm: Full pistol grip, heavy wood one-piece stock & forearm; thumb-grooved stock with 4-way adjustable buttplate rail
Approximate wt.: 8¾ lbs.
Comments: Made from about 1970 to 1983. A heavy rifle designed for bench shooting.
Estimated Value: **Excellent:**   **$255.00**
                      Very good: **$190.00**

Remington Model 541 S Custom & 541-T

Caliber: 22 short, long, long rifle
Action: Bolt action; repeating; self-cocking; thumb safety
Magazine: 5-shot clip
Barrel: 24"
Sights: None; barrel & receiver are drilled for a wide variety of optional scopes or sights
Stock & Forearm: One-piece checkered pistol grip stock & forearm
Approximate wt.: 5½ lbs.
Comments: Designed after the Remington Model 540 X Target Rifle; made from about 1972 to 1983. Reintroduced in 1986 as Model 541-T.
Estimated Value: **New (retail):**   **$355.00**
                      Excellent: **$265.00**
                      Very good: **$215.00**

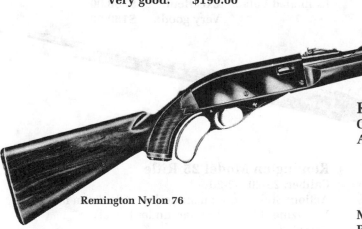

Remington Nylon 76

Remington Nylon 76

Caliber: 22 long rifle
Action: Lever-action; repeating; side ejection; lever under stock operates sliding bolt which ejects empty case, chambers cartridge from magazine & cocks concealed striker; safety located on top of stock behind receiver
Magazine: 14-shot tubular magazine in stock
Barrel: 19½" round
Sights: Blade front, open rear sight
Stock & Forearm: Checkered nylon two-piece stock & forearm; pistol grip stock; forearm lipped at tip with nylon hand guard over barrel
Approximate wt.: 4½ lbs.
Comments: Made from about 1962 to 1964; the only lever action repeater made by Remington Arms Co.
Estimated Value: **Excellent:**   **$150.00**
                      Very good: **$115.00**

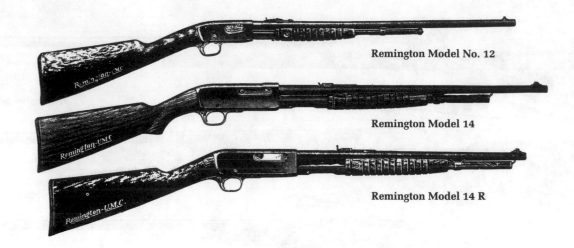

Remington Model No. 12

Remington Model 14

Remington Model 14 R

Remington Model 14 Rifle
Caliber: 25, 30, 32, 35 Rem.
Action: Slide action; hammerless; takedown model
Magazine: 5-shot tubular, under barrel
Barrel: 22" round
Sights: Bead front, adjustable rear
Stock & Forearm: Plain or checkered walnut pistol grip stock & grooved or checkered forearm
Approximate wt.: 7 lbs.
Comments: Made from about 1912 to 1935 in four grades; higher grades had checkering & engraving. Prices are for (plain) standard grade.
Estimated Value: **Excellent:**   **$300.00**
                       Very good: **$240.00**

Remington Model 14½ Rifle
Similar to Model 14 rifle except: caliber 38-40 & 44-40 only; 22½" barrel; 11-shot magazine; discontinued about 1925; standard grade only
Estimated Value: **Excellent:**   **$375.00**
                       Very good: **$300.00**

Remington Model 14 R Carbine
Same as Model 14 rifle except: 18½" barrel; straight grip stock; approximate wt. 6 lbs.; standard grade only.
Estimated Value: **Excellent:**   **$275.00**
                       Very good: **$220.00**

Remington Model 14½ Carbine
Same as Model 14½ rifle except 18½" barrel & 9-shot magazine.
Estimated Value: **Excellent:**   **$350.00**
                       Very good: **$280.00**

Remington Model No. 12 Rifle
Caliber: 22 short, long, long rifle
Action: Slide action; hammerless; takedown model
Magazine: 10- to 15-shot tubular, under barrel
Barrel: 22" or 24" round or octagon
Sights: Bead front, rear adjustable for elevation
Stock & Forearm: Plain or engraved; varnished plain or checkered, straight or pistol grip, walnut stock with rubber or steel buttplate; forearm grooved or checkered walnut
Approximate wt.: 5½ lbs.
Comments: Made from about 1909 to 1936 in four grades; higher grades had checkering & engraving. Prices are for (plain) standard grade.
Estimated Value: **Excellent:**   **$200.00**
                       Very good: **$160.00**

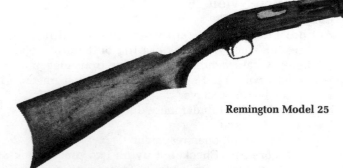

Remington Model 25

Remington Model 25 Rifle
Caliber: 25-20, 32-20
Action: Slide action; hammerless; takedown model
Magazine: 10-shot tubular, under barrel
Barrel: 24"
Sights: Bead front, open rear
Stock & Forearm: Checkered or plain walnut pistol grip stock and grooved or checkered slide handle
Approximate wt.: 6 lbs.
Comments: Made from about 1923 to 1936 in four grades; higher grades had checkering & engraving. Prices are for (plain) standard grade.
Estimated Value: **Excellent:**   **$320.00**
                       Very good: **$265.00**

Remington Model 25 R Carbine
Same as Model 25 Rifle except: 18½" barrel; straight grip stock; 6-shot magazine; approximate wt. 4½ lbs.; standard grade only.
Estimated Value: **Excellent:**   **$325.00**
                       Very good: **$260.00**

Rifles 261

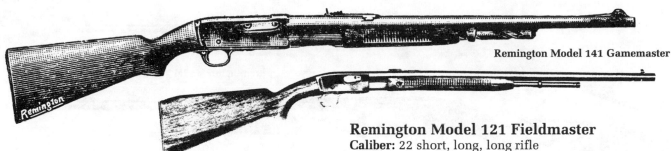

Remington Model 141 Gamemaster

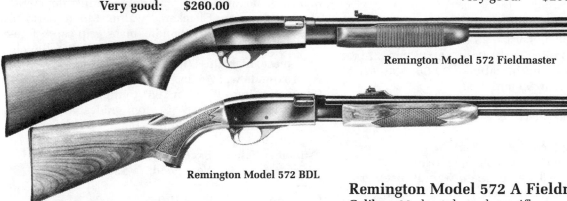

Remington Model 121 Fieldmaster

Remington Model 121 Fieldmaster

Caliber: 22 short, long, long rifle
Action: Slide action; hammerless; takedown model
Magazine: Tubular, under barrel; 20 shorts, 15 longs, 14 long rifles
Barrel: 24" round
Sights: Bead front, adjustable rear
Stock & Forearm: Checkered or plain walnut pistol grip stock & grooved or checkered semi-beavertail slide handle
Approximate wt.: 6 lbs.
Comments: Made from about 1936 to 1942 & from 1946 to 1950 in four grades; higher grades checkered & engraved. Prices are for (plain) standard grade.
Estimated Value: Excellent: $250.00
Very good: $200.00

Remington Model 141 Gamemaster

Caliber: 30, 32 & 35 Rem.
Action: Slide action; hammerless; takedown model
Magazine: 5-shot tubular, under barrel
Barrel: 24" round
Sights: Ramp front, adjustable rear
Stock & Forearm: Checkered or plain walnut pistol grip stock & grooved or checkered semi-beavertail slide handle
Approximate wt.: 7 lbs.
Comments: Made from about 1936 to 1942 & from 1946 to 1950 in four grades; higher grades had checkered pistol grip stock & forearm & engraving. Prices are for (plain) standard grade.
Estimated Value: Excellent: $330.00
Very good: $265.00

Remington Model 121 SB

Same as Model 121 except smooth bore barrel for 22 shot cartridges.
Estimated Value: Excellent: $240.00
Very good: $190.00

Remington Model 121 S

Similar to Model 121 except: caliber 22 Rem. special only; 12-shot magazine; standard grade.
Estimated Value: Excellent: $255.00
Very good: $200.00

Remington 141 R Carbine

Same as Model 141 A rifle except: 18½" barrel; approximate wt. 5½ lbs.; standard grade only.
Estimated Value: Excellent: $325.00
Very good: $260.00

Remington Model 572 Fieldmaster

Remington Model 572 BDL

Remington Model 572 SB

Same as Model 572 rifle except: smooth bore for 22 shot cartridges; standard grade only.
Estimated Value: Excellent: $150.00
Very good: $120.00

Remington 572 BDL Fieldmaster

Deluxe version of the 572A Fieldmaster. Currently produced. Add $17.00 for swivels & sling.
Estimated Value: New (retail): $223.00
Excellent: $165.00
Very good: $135.00

Remington Model 572 A Fieldmaster

Caliber: 22 short, long, long rifle
Action: Slide action; hammerless; solid frame; side ejection
Magazine: 14- to 20-shot tubular, under barrel
Barrel: 21" & 24" round tapered
Sights: Bead front, adjustable open rear
Stock & Forearm: Checkered or plain walnut pistol grip stock & grooved or checkered slide handle
Approximate wt.: 5½ lbs.
Comments: Made from about 1955 to 1987; add $17.00 for sling & swivels.
Estimated Value: Excellent: $160.00
Very good: $120.00

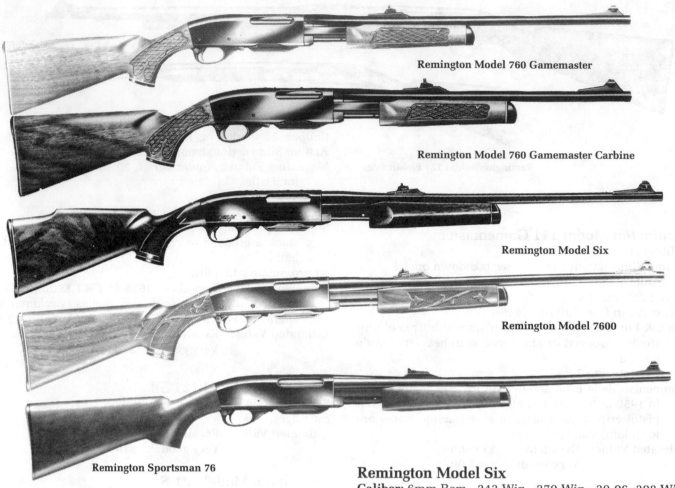

Remington Model 760 Gamemaster

Remington Model 760 Gamemaster Carbine

Remington Model Six

Remington Model 7600

Remington Sportsman 76

Remington Model 760 Gamemaster, 760 Carbine

Caliber: 30-06, 308, 300 Savage, 35 Rem., 280, 270 Win.,
257 Roberts, 244 Rem., 243 Win., 6mm Rem., 223 &
222; presently made in calibers 30-06, 308 Win.,
270 Rem., 243 Win. & 6mm Rem.

Action: Slide action; hammerless; side ejection; solid
frame; cross-bolt safety

Magazine: 4-shot box

Barrel: 22" round tapered; 18½" on carbine

Sights: Ramp bead front, adjustable open rear

Stock & Forearm: Checkered or plain walnut pistol grip
stock & grooved checkered semi-beavertail slide
handle

Approximate wt.: 7½ lbs.

Comments: Made from about 1952 to about 1980; carbine
from 1960 to 1969 in 270 or 280 caliber; 1962 to
about 1980 in 30-06 & 308 Win.

Estimated Value: Excellent: $300.00
Very good: $225.00

Remington Model 760 BDL Gamemaster

Similar to Model 760 with basketweave checkering,
Monte Carlo stock; available in 30-06, 270, 308.

Estimated Value: Excellent: $310.00
Very good: $230.00

Remington Model Six

Caliber: 6mm Rem., 243 Win., 270 Win., 30-06, 308 Win.

Action: Slide action; hammerless; repeating

Magazine: 4-shot clip

Barrel: Blued; 22"

Sights: Blade ramp front, adjustable sliding ramp rear

Stock & Forearm: Checkered walnut Monte Carlo pistol
grip stock & slide handle; black grip cap & fore-end
tip; recessed finger groove in slide handle; cheekpiece; high gloss finish

Approximate wt.: 7½ lbs.

Comments: Introduced in 1981 to replace the Model 760.
Discontinued 1987. Custom grades are available at
increased prices. Calibers 6mm & 308 Win. dropped
in 1985.

Estimated Value: Excellent: $400.00
Very good: $300.00

Remington Model 7600

Similar to the Model Six. No Monte Carlo stock or cheekpiece; design checkering. Caliber 6mm dropped in 1985.

Estimated Value: New (retail): $469.00
Excellent: $350.00
Very good: $280.00

Remington Sportsman 76

Similar to the Model 7600 with lesser quality finish;
hardwood with no checkering; 22" barrel; 30-06 caliber
only. Produced 1984 to 1987.

Estimated Value: Excellent: $285.00
Very good: $215.00

Remington Model No. 8

Remington Model No. 16

Remington Model No. 16

Caliber: 22 Rem. automatic

Action: Semi-automatic; hammerless; solid breech; sliding bolt; side ejection; takedown model

Magazine: 15-shot tubular, in stock

Barrel: 22" round

Sights: Bead front, adjustable notch sporting rear

Stock & Forearm: Plain or engraved; varnished, plain or checkered, straight grip, two-piece walnut stock & forearm; steel buttplate & blunt lip on forearm

Approximate wt.: 5¾ lbs.

Comments: Made from about 1914 to 1928 in four grades, A, C, D & F. Prices are standard grade.

Estimated Value: Excellent: **$280.00**
                 Very good: **$225.00**

Remington Model No. 8

Caliber: 25, 30, 32 or 35 Rem.

Action: Semi-automatic; top ejection; for smokeless powder; takedown model; solid breech & sliding barrel type

Magazine: 5-shot detachable box

Barrel: 22" round

Sights: Bead front, open rear

Stock & Forearm: Plain or engraved; varnished, plain or checkered, two-piece walnut straight grip stock & forearm; rubber or steel buttplate & lipped forearm

Approximate wt.: 7¾ lbs.

Comments: Made from about 1906 to 1936 in five grades, A, C, D, E & F; jacket marked "Manufactured by the Remington Arms Co. Ilion, N.Y., U.S.A." "Browning's Patent's Oct. 8, 1900. Oct. 15, 1900. July 2, 1902." Prices for standard grade.

Estimated Value: Excellent: **$330.00**
                 Very good: **$265.00**

Remington Model 24

Remington Model No. 241 Speedmaster

Remington Model 24

Caliber: 22 long rifle only or 22 short only

Action: Semi-automatic; hammerless; solid breech; sliding bolt; bottom ejection

Magazine: 15-shot stock tube in 22 short & 10-shot in 22 long rifle

Barrel: 19" round

Sights: Bead front, adjustable rear

Stock & Forearm: Plain or engraved; varnished, plain or checkered, two-piece walnut semi-pistol grip stock & forearm; steel buttplate with lipped forearm

Approximate wt.: 4¾ lbs.

Comments: Made from about 1922 to 1935 in five grades, A, C, D, E & F. Prices for standard grade.

Estimated Value: Excellent: **$220.00**
                 Very good: **$175.00**

Remington Model 241 Speedmaster

Caliber: 22 long rifle only or 22 short only

Action: Semi-automatic; hammerless; solid breech; bottom ejection; takedown type; sliding bolt action; thumb safety

Magazine: 15-shot in 22 short; 10-shot in 22 long rifle; tubular in stock

Barrel: 24" round

Sights: Bead front, notched rear adjustable for elevation

Stock & Forearm: Plain or engraved; varnished walnut, plain or checkered, two-piece pistol grip stock & forearm; semi-beavertail

Approximate wt.: 6 lbs.

Comments: Improved version of Model 24; produced from about 1935 to 1951 in five grades, A, B, D, E & F. Prices for standard grade.

Estimated Value: Excellent: **$250.00**
                 Very good: **$200.00**

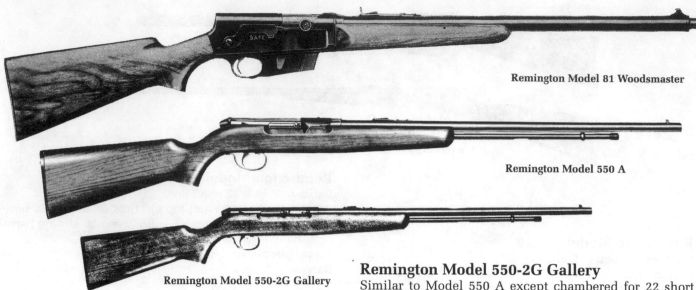

Remington Model 81 Woodsmaster

Remington Model 550 A

Remington Model 550-2G Gallery

Remington Model 550 A

Caliber: 22 short, long, long rifle

Action: Semi-automatic; hammerless; side ejection; solid breech; sliding bolt; floating power piston which permits using 22 short, long or long rifle interchangeable & still function as semi-automatic; takedown type with thumb safety

Magazine: 20-shot in 22 short; 15-shot in 22 long rifle

Barrel: 24" round

Sights: Dovetail bead front, notched rear adjustable for elevation

Stock & Forearm: One-piece plain varnished pistol grip stock & forearm; hard rubber buttplate

Approximate wt.: 6½ lbs.

Comments: Replaced the Model 241 because it was less expensive to produce. Made from about 1941 to 1942 & from 1946 to 1970. Receiver top grooved for telescope sight mounts.

Estimated Value: Excellent: $135.00
Very good: $100.00

Remington Model 550-2G Gallery

Similar to Model 550 A except chambered for 22 short caliber only.

Estimated Value: Excellent: $145.00
Very good: $115.00

Remington Model 81 Woodsmaster

Caliber: From 1936 to 1942, 25, 30, 32, 35 Rem.; from 1946 to 1950, 30, 32, 35, 300 Savage

Action: Semi-automatic; top ejection; takedown model; solid breech; sliding barrel type

Magazine: 5-shot detachable box

Barrel: 22" round

Sights: Bead front, sporting rear with notched elevator

Stock & Forearm: Plain or engraved; varnished walnut, plain or checkered two-piece pistol grip stock & forearm; rubber buttplate & semi-beavertail style forearm

Approximate wt.: 7¾ lbs.

Comments: Made from about 1936 to 1942 & from 1946 to 1950 in five grades, A, B, D, E & F. An improved version of the Model No. 8. Prices are for standard grade.

Estimated Value: Excellent: $330.00
Very good: $265.00

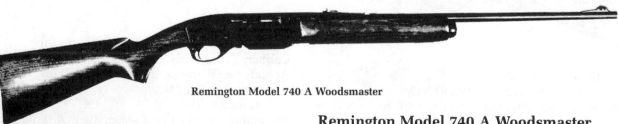

Remington Model 740 A Woodsmaster

Remington Model 740 ADL Deluxe Grade

Same as Model 740 A except: deluxe checkered stock & forearm; also grip cap & sling swivels.

Estimated Value: Excellent: $290.00
Very good: $230.00

Remington Model 740 BDL Special Grade

Similar to Model 740 ADL Deluxe Grade except: stock & forearm have deluxe finish on select wood.

Estimated Value: Excellent: $300.00
Very good: $225.00

Remington Model 740 A Woodsmaster

Caliber: 30-06 or 308

Action: Semi-automatic; gas-operated; side ejection; hammerless

Magazine: 4-shot detachable box

Barrel: 22" round

Sights: Ramp front, open rear adjustable for elevation

Stock & Forearm: Plain pistol grip stock & forearm; semi-beavertail forearm with finger grooves

Approximate wt.: 7½ lbs.

Comments: Made from about 1950 to 1960.

Estimated Value: Excellent: $275.00
Very good: $220.00

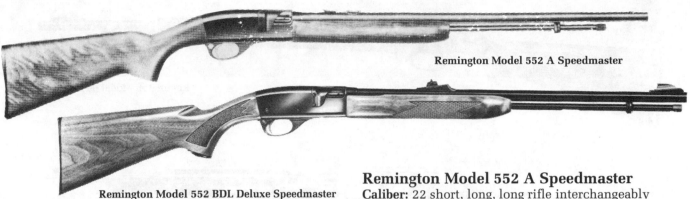

Remington Model 552 A Speedmaster

Remington Model 552 BDL Deluxe Speedmaster

Remington Model 552 BDL Deluxe Speedmaster

Same as Model 552 Speedmaster except: high quality finished checkered stock & forearm; ramp front sight & adjustable rear for elevation & windage; made from about 1961 to present. Add $20.00 for swivels & sling.

Estimated Value:	New (retail):	$213.00
	Excellent:	$160.00
	Very good:	$125.00

Remington Model 552 GS Gallery Special

Same as Model 552 Speedmaster except caliber 22 short only.

| Estimated Value: | Excellent: | $150.00 |
| | Very good: | $120.00 |

Remington Model 552 A Speedmaster

Caliber: 22 short, long, long rifle interchangeably

Action: Semi-automatic; hammerless; side ejection; solid breech; sliding bolt; floating power piston which permist using 22 short, long, long rifle cartridges interchangeably

Magazine: 20-shot tubular in 22 short, 15-shot in long rifle; under barrel

Barrel: 21" & 23" round tapered

Sights: Bead front, notched rear adjustable for elevation

Stock & Forearm: Plain one-piece pistol grip stock & semi-beavertail forearm; hard composition checkered buttplate

Approximate wt.: 5¾ lbs.

Comments: Made from about 1958 to 1987. Add $20.00 for swivels & sling.

| Estimated Value: | Excellent: | $150.00 |
| | Very good: | $115.00 |

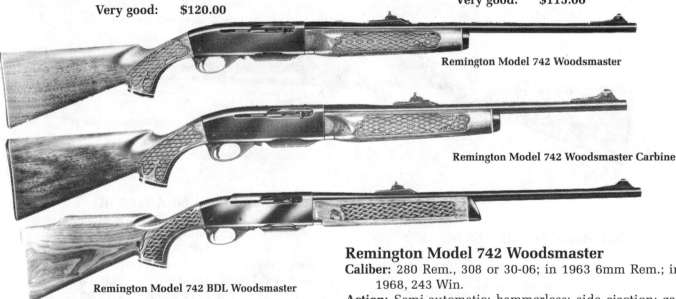

Remington Model 742 Woodsmaster

Remington Model 742 Woodsmaster Carbine

Remington Model 742 BDL Woodsmaster

Remington Model 742 Woodsmaster Carbine

Same as Model 742 Woodsmaster Rifle except: 18½" barrel; approximate wt. 6½ lbs.; calibers 280, 30-06 or 308 only.

| Estimated Value: | Excellent: | $320.00 |
| | Very good: | $255.00 |

Remington Model 742 BDL Woodsmaster

Same as Model 742 Woodsmaster Rifle except: calibers 30-06 or 308 only; left or right hand models; checkered Monte Carlo stock; black tipped forearm.

| Estimated Value: | Excellent: | $340.00 |
| | Very good: | $270.00 |

Remington Model 742 Woodsmaster

Caliber: 280 Rem., 308 or 30-06; in 1963 6mm Rem.; in 1968, 243 Win.

Action: Semi-automatic; hammerless; side ejection; gas operated sliding bolt

Magazine: 4-shot detachable box

Barrel: 22" round tapered

Sights: Gold bead front, step adjustable rear with windage adjustment

Stock & Forearm: Plain or checkered & standard or deluxe finish two-piece walnut stock & semi-beavertail forearm; aluminum buttplate

Approximate wt.: 7½ lbs.

Comments: Manufactured from about 1960 to about 1980; in 1969 Remington advertised many fancy grades. Prices are for standard grade.

| Estimated Value: | Excellent: | $325.00 |
| | Very good: | $260.00 |

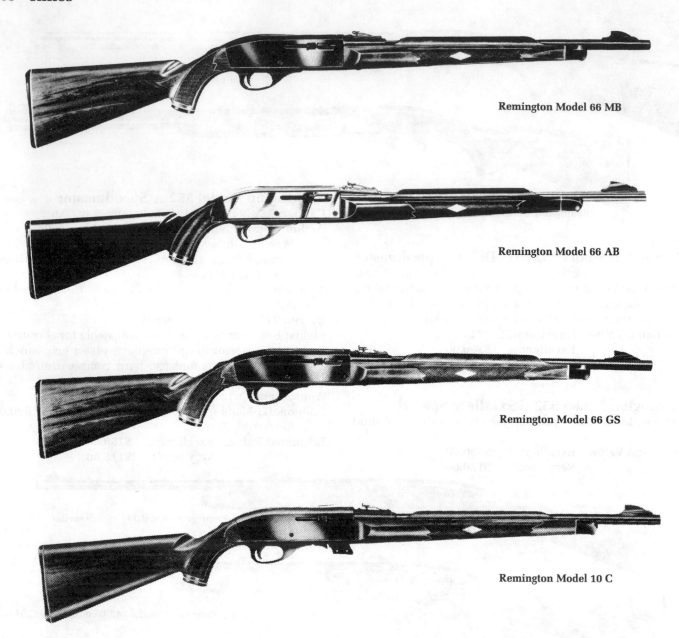

Remington Model 66 MB

Remington Model 66 AB

Remington Model 66 GS

Remington Model 10 C

Remington Model 66 MB & 66 SG

Caliber: 22 long rifle

Action: Semi-automatic; side ejection; solid breech; sliding bolt

Magazine: 14-shot tubular in stock

Barrel: 20" round

Sights: Blade front; rear sight adjustable for windage & elevation

Stock & Forearm: Du-Pont Zytel® nylon, brown one-piece receiver, stock & forearm; checkered pistol grip stock & lipped forearm which covers top of barrel

Approximate wt.: 4 lbs.

Comments: Made from about 1959 to 1987; based on a design concept in which the stock, receiver & forearm are made in one piece; Model 66 SG - Seneca Green.

Estimated Value: Excellent: $110.00
 Very good: $ 85.00

Remington Model 66 AB, 66 BD

Same as Remington Model 66 MB except: black stock & forearm with chrome plated barrel & receiver covers; made from about 1962. AB discontinued in 1984. BD has black receiver, discontinued 1987.

Estimated Value: Excellent: $110.00
 Very good: $ 85.00

Remington Model 66 GS

Similar to the Model 66 MB except: chambered for 22 short only (Gallery Special). Made from about 1963 to about 1980.

Estimated Value: Excellent: $100.00
 Very good: $ 80.00

Remington Model 10 C

Same as Remington Model 66 MB except: 10-shot removable box magazine. Produced from about 1970 to late 1970's.

Estimated Value: Excellent: $100.00
 Very good: $ 75.00

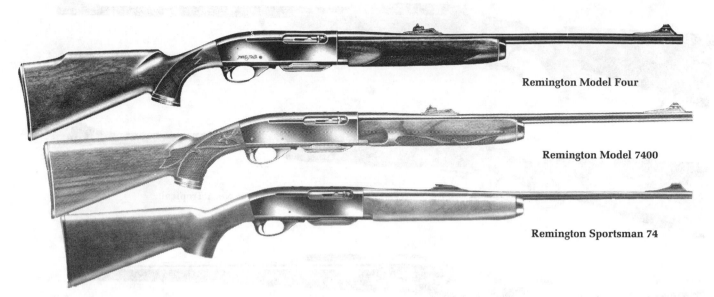

Remington Model Four

Remington Model 7400

Remington Sportsman 74

Remington Model Four

Caliber: 6mm Rem., 243 Win., 270 Win., 280 Rem. (7mm Express Rem); 30-06, 308 Win.

Action: Semi-automatic; side ejection; gas operated

Magazine: 4-shot clip

Barrel: Blued; 22"

Sights: Blade front ramp, adjustable sliding ramp rear

Stock & Forearm: Checkered walnut Monte Carlo pistol grip stock & forearm; black grip cap & fore end tip; recessed finger groove in forearm; cheekpiece; high gloss finish

Approximate wt.: 7½ lbs.

Comments: Produced 1981 to 1987 to replace the Model 742. Custom grades are available at increased prices. Calibers 6mm & 308 Win. dropped in 1985.

Estimated Value: Excellent: $430.00
                      Very good: $320.00

Remington Model 7400

Similar to the Model Four except: no Monte Carlo stock; design checkering.

Estimated Value: New (retail): $487.00
                      Excellent: $365.00
                      Very good: $290.00

Remington Sportsman 74

Similar to the Model 7400 with lesser quality finish; hardwood with no checkering; 22" barrel; 30-06 caliber only. Produced 1984 to 1987.

Estimated Value: Excellent: $320.00
                      Very good: $240.00

Ruger

Ruger No. 1 Standard 1 B

Ruger No. 1 Light Sporter

Ruger No. 1 Light Sporter 1A

Similar to No. 1 in 243, 270, 30-06 or 7x57mm only; 22" barrel.

Estimated Value: New (retail): $603.75
                      Excellent: $450.00
                      Very good: $360.00

Ruger No. 1 Standard 1 B

Caliber: 22-250, 220 Swift, 223, 243, 25-06, 6mm Rem., 257 Roberts, 280, 270, 30-06, 7mm Rem. mag., 300 Win. Mag.; 338 Win. mag.

Action: Falling block; under lever; single shot; hammerless

Magazine: None

Barrel: 26" tapered

Sights: Open

Stock & Forearm: Checkered walnut pistol grip stock & forearm; swivels

Approximate wt.: 8 lbs.

Comments: Made from the late 1960's to present.

Estimated Value: New (retail): $603.75
                      Excellent: $450.00
                      Very good: $360.00

Ruger No. 1 Medium Sporter

Ruger No. 1 Tropical

Ruger Model No. 1 International

Ruger No. 1 Special Varminter 1 V

Ruger No. 3

Ruger No. 1 Medium Sporter 1 S
Similar to No. 1 Light Sporter in heavier calibers, 7mm, 338, 300 & 45-70 with a 22" or 26" barrel.

Estimated Value:
New (retail):	$603.75
Excellent:	$450.00
Very good:	$360.00

Ruger No. 1 Tropical 1 H
A 24" barrel version of No. 1 in 375 H&H magnum & 458 magnum only. Approx. wt. 8½ lbs.

Estimated Value:
New (retail):	$603.75
Excellent:	$450.00
Very good:	$360.00

Ruger Model No. 1 International RSI
Similar to the No. 1 with a 20" barrel with full length forearm; available in calibers 243 Win., 30-06, 270 Win., & 7x57mm; weighs 7¼ lbs.

Estimated Value:
New (retail):	$623.75
Excellent:	$470.00
Very good:	$375.00

Ruger No. 1 Special Varminter 1 V
Similar to No. 1 in 22-250, 220 Swift, 223, 25-06, 6mm; heavy 24" barrel. Approx. wt. 9 lbs.

Estimated Value:
New (retail):	$603.75
Excellent:	$450.00
Very good:	$360.00

Ruger No. 3
Caliber: 22 Hornet, 30-40 Krag, 45-70, 223, 375 Win., 44 mag.

Action: Falling block, under lever; hammerless; single shot

Magazine: None

Barrel: Blued; 22"

Sights: Folding leaf rear, bead front

Stock & Forearm: Plain walnut straight grip stock & forearm; barrel band

Approximate wt.: 6 lbs.

Comments: Made from the late 1960's to mid 1980's.

Estimated Value:
Excellent:	$335.00
Very good:	$265.00

Ruger Model 77

Ruger 77 Round Top

Ruger 77 International

Ruger 77 Varmint

Ruger Model 77, 77R, 77RS, 77RS Tropical
Caliber: 220 Swift, 22-250, 25-06, 243 Win., 250-3000, 257, 6mm, 270 Win., 7mm Rem. mag., 7x57mm, 300 mag., 30-06, 338 mag., 458 Win. mag. (Tropical)

Action: Bolt action; repeating; either short or magnum action

Magazine: 5-shot box with hinged floor plate; 4-shot in magnum calibers

Barrel: Blued; 22" or 24"

Sights: Adjustable leaf rear, beaded ramp front; or no sights, integral scope mounts

Stock & Forearm: Checkered walnut, pistol grip, one-piece stock & tapered forearm; recoil pad

Approximate wt.: 6¾ lbs., 7 lbs., 8¾ lbs.

Comments: Made from the late 1960's to present. Add 16% for 458 magnum (Tropical); add 10% for sights.

Estimated Value: New (retail): $531.25
             Excellent: $400.00
             Very good: $320.00

Ruger 77 Round Top, M-77ST
Similar to Model 77 with round top receiver & open sights. Made from early 1970's to early 1980's.

Estimated Value: Excellent: $350.00
             Very good: $280.00

Ruger Model 77 International, M-77RSI
Similar to the Model 77 with 18½" barrel & full length Mannlicher-type forearm; 22-250, 250-3000, 243, 308, 270 & 30-06 calibers; no sights, integral scope mounts. Introduced in 1982.

Estimated Value: New (retail): $593.75
             Excellent: $445.00
             Very good: $355.00

Ruger 77V Varmint, M-77 Varmint
Similar to Model 77 in 22-250, 220 Swift, 243, 6mm, 308 or 25-06 calibers; 24" heavy barrel or 26" tapered barrel; no sights. Made from early 1970's to present. Approx. wt. 9 lbs.

Estimated Value: New (retail): $546.25
             Excellent: $410.00
             Very good: $325.00

Ruger Model 77RL Ultra Light

Ruger Model 77/22

Ruger Model 77/22

Caliber: 22 long rifle; 22 magnum (after 1989)
Action: Bolt action; repeating; three position safety
Magazine: Detachable rotary magazine; 10-shot (22 long rifle); 9-shot (22 magnum)
Barrel: 20" blued or 20" all stainless steel
Sights: Gold bead front, folding leaf rear; or no sights with 1" scope rings
Stock & Forearm: Checkered walnut, one piece, pistol grip stock and forearm; stainless steel models have all weather stock (DuPont Zytel®)
Approximate wt.: 6¼ lbs.
Comments: Introduced in 1984. Deduct 18% for all weather stock with blued barrel; add 4½% for all weather stock and stainless steel barrel.
Estimated Value: New (retail): $382.75
    Excellent: $285.00
    Very good: $230.00

Ruger Model 77RL Ultra Light

Similar to the Model 77R with 20" barrel; weighs 6 lbs. Introduced in 1984. Caliber 22-250, 243, 270, 250-3000, 257, 30-06 & 308.
Estimated Value: New (retail): $564.25
    Excellent: $425.00
    Very good: $340.00

Ruger Model 77 Mark IIR

Ruger Model 77 Mark IIR

Caliber: 223, 6mm, 243, 308
Action: Bolt action; repeating; stainless steel bolt with three position swing back safety (in rear position bolt is locked & gun will not fire; in center position the bolt will operate but gun will not fire; in forward position bolt will operate & gun will fire); short action bolt
Magazine: 4-shot box with hinged floor plate
Barrel: Blued; 22"
Sights: None, integral base receiver for scope rings & 1" scope rings
Stock & Forearm: Checkered walnut, one-piece pistol grip stock & tapered forearm
Approximate wt.: 7 lbs.
Comments: Introduced in 1989 in 223 caliber, other calibers in 1990.
Estimated Value: New (retail): $531.25
    Excellent: $400.00
    Very good: $320.00

Ruger Model 77 Mark IIRL

Similar as the Model 77 Mark IIR except: calibers 223, 243 & 308 only; 20" barrel; approximate weight is 6 lbs.; black fore-end tip; introduced in 1990.
Estimated Value: New (retail): $564.25
    Excellent: $425.00
    Very good: $340.00

Ruger Model 77 Mark IIRLS

Same as the Model 77 Mark IIR except: lightweight (6 lbs.); 18½" barrel; calibers 243 or 308; open sights.
Estimated Value: New (retail): $564.25
    Excellent: $425.00
    Very good: $340.00

Ruger Model 77 Mark IIRS

Same as the Model 77 Mark IIR except: calibers 6mm, 243, 308; open sights (ramp front & open express rear). Introduced in 1990.
Estimated Value: New (retail): $587.00
    Excellent: $440.00
    Very good: $350.00

Ruger Model 77 Mark IIRP

Same as the Model 77 Mark IIR except: all stainless steel with all-weather fiberglass stock (DuPont Zytel®) with grooved inserts on the pistol grip & fore-end sides; calibers 223, 243, 308. Introduced in 1990.
Estimated Value: New (retail): $531.25
    Excellent: $400.00
    Very good: $320.00

Ruger Model 77RLS

Caliber: 270, 30-06, 243, 308
Action: Bolt action; repeating; long bolt action in 270 & 30-06 & short bolt action in 243 & 308
Magazine: 5-shot box with hinged floor plates; 4-shot in magnum
Barrel: 18½"
Sights: Beaded ramp front; adjustable leaf rear
Stock & Forearm: Checkered pistol grip, one-piece stock & tapered forearm; rubber recoil pad; swivels
Approximate wt.: 6 lbs.
Comments: Made from the late 1960's to present.
Estimated Value: New (retail): $564.25
Excellent: $425.00
Very good: $340.00

Ruger Model 77 Mark IIRSM (Magnum)

Caliber: 375 H&H, 417 Rigby
Action: Bolt action; repeating; stainless steel bolt; three position swing-back safety
Magazine: 4-shot (375 H&H); 3-shot (416 Rigby); floor plate latch is housed in the trigger guard
Barrel: 24" blued with sighting plane of cross serrations to reduce glare
Sights: Ramp front, open express rear
Stock & Forearm: Checkered walnut, one-piece pistol grip stock & forearm
Approximate wt.: 9¼ lbs. (375 H&H); 10¼ lbs. (416 Rigby)
Comments: Introduced in 1990.
Estimated Value: New (retail): $1,550.00
Excellent: $1,160.00
Very good: $ 930.00

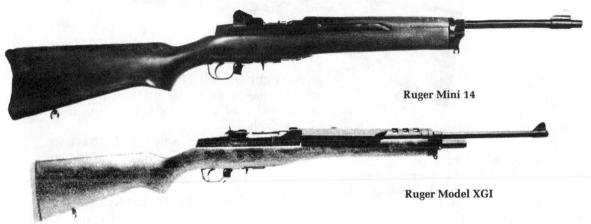

Ruger Mini 14

Ruger Model XGI

Ruger Mini 14

Caliber: 223 Commercial or Military
Action: Semi-automatic, gas operated
Magazine: 5-shot detachable box; 10- & 20-shot available
Barrel: Blued; 18½"; also stainless steel in 1980
Sights: Adjustable rear, blade front
Stock & Forearm: Plain walnut, semi-pistol grip, one piece stock & forearm; handguard over barrel; folding stock & pistol grip available after mid 1980's
Approximate wt.: 6½ lbs.
Comments: Made from 1974 to present. Add 10% for stainless steel finish; 19% for folding stock.
Estimated Value: New (retail): $468.00
Excellent: $350.00
Very good: $280.00

Ruger Mini 14/5-R, Ranch Rifle

Similar to the Mini 14 with internal improvements & integral scope mounts. Introduced in 1982; add 9½% for stainless teel. Add 14% for folding stock.
Estimated Value: New (retail): $504.50
Excellent: $380.00
Very good: $300.00

Ruger Mini Thirty

Caliber: 7.62x39mm
Action: Semi-automatic, gas operated
Magazine: 5-shot detachable staggered box
Barrel: Blued; 18½"
Sights: Blade front; adjustable rear
Stock & Forearm: Plain walnut, pistol grip one-piece stock & forearm with hand guard over barrel
Approximate wt.: 7 lbs.
Comments: Introduced in 1988. A modified version of the Mini-14 Ranch Rifle.
Estimated Value: New (retail): $504.50
Excellent: $380.00
Very good: $300.00

Ruger Model XGI

Caliber: 243 or 308
Action: Gas operated, semi-automatic, based on the Garand system used in the U.S. M1 & M14 military rifles
Magazine: 5-shot staggered column, detachable box
Barrel: 20" blued with hanguard cover
Sights: Ramp front & adjustable folding peep rear
Stock & Forearm: Plain one-piece American hardwood, reinforced with steel liners
Approximate wt.: 8 lbs.
Comments: Produced from 1986 to 1988.
Estimated Value: Excellent: $350.00
Very good: $280.00

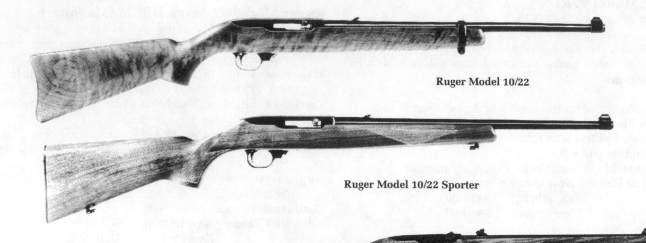

Ruger Model 10/22

Ruger Model 10/22 Sporter

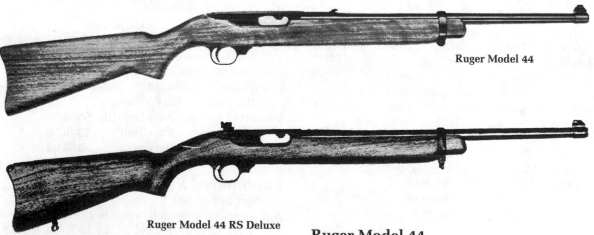

Ruger Model 10/22 International

Ruger Model 10/22
Caliber: 22 long rifle
Action: Semi-automatic
Magazine: 10-shot detachable rotary
Barrel: Blued; 18½"
Sights: Adjustable leaf rear, bed front
Stock & Forearm: Plain hardwood one-piece semi-pistol grip stock & forearm; barrel band; also Birch stock
Approximate wt.: 5 lbs.
Comments: Made from about 1964 to present.
Estimated Value:　New (retail):　$192.00
　　　　　　　　　　Excellent:　　$145.00
　　　　　　　　　　Very good:　　$115.00

Ruger Model 10/22, Deluxe Sporter
Similar to the Model 10/22 with: Monte Carlo or regular checkered walnut stock; fluted bandless forearm; swivels.
Estimated Value:　New (retail):　$242.50
　　　　　　　　　　Excellent:　　$180.00
　　　　　　　　　　Very good:　　$145.00

Ruger Model 10/22, International
Similar to Model 10/22 with full length stock and swivels. Made to early 1970's.
Estimated Value:　Excellent:　　$160.00
　　　　　　　　　　Very good:　　$130.00

Ruger Model 44

Ruger Model 44 RS Deluxe

Ruger Model 44 RS Deluxe
Similar to Model 44 with peep sight & swivels.
Estimated Value:　Excellent:　　$325.00
　　　　　　　　　　　Very good:　　$255.00

Ruger Model 44
Caliber: 44 magnum
Action: Semi-automatic, gas operated
Magazine: 4-shot tubular
Barrel: Blued; 18½"
Sights: Leaf rear, bead front
Stock & Forearm: Plain walnut one-piece semi-pistol grip stock & forearm; barrel band
Approximate wt.: 5¾ lbs.
Comments: Made from about 1960 to mid 1980's.
Estimated Value:　Excellent:　　$320.00
　　　　　　　　　　Very good:　　$250.00

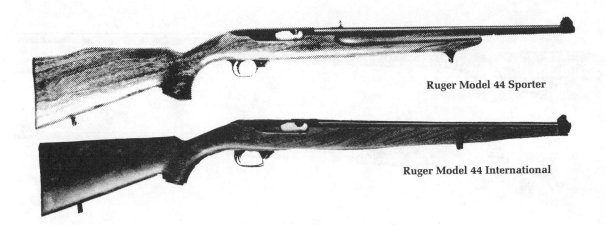

Ruger Model 44 Sporter

Ruger Model 44 International

Ruger Model 44 Sporter

Similar to Model 44 with Monte Carlo stock, fluted forearm & swivels. Made to early 1970's.

Estimated Value: Excellent: $340.00
Very good: $270.00

Ruger Model 44 International

Similar to Model 44 with a full length stock & swivels. Made to early 1970's.

Estimated Value: Excellent: $375.00
Very good: $300.00

Sako

Sako Finsport 2700

Sako Vixen Sporter

Sako Vixen Mannlicher

Sako Finsport 2700

Caliber: 270 Win., 30-06, 7mm Rem. mag., 338 Win. mag.
Action: Long throw bolt action; adjustable trigger
Magazine: 5-shot
Barrel: Blued; 23½"
Sights: None
Stock & Forearm: Checkered walnut, Monte Carlo pistol grip, one-piece stock & forearm; recoil pad; swivels
Approximate wt.: 6½ lbs.
Comments: Produced 1983 to late 1980's.
Estimated Value: Excellent: $680.00
Very good: $510.00

Sako Vixen Sporter

Caliber: 218 Bee, 22 Hornet, 222, 222 mag., 223
Action: Bolt action, short stroke, Mauser-type
Magazine: 5-shot
Barrel: Blued; 23½"
Sights: Open rear, hooded ramp front
Stock & Forearm: Checkered walnut, Monte Carlo pistol grip, one-piece stock & forearm; swivels
Approximate wt.: 6½ lbs.
Comments: Made from World War II to the early 1970's. Vixen, Forester & Finnbear became M74 Short, Medium & Long actions.
Estimated Value: Excellent: $540.00
Very good: $430.00

Sako Vixen Mannlicher

Similar to Sporter with a full length stock; 20" barrel; barrel band.
Estimated Value: Excellent: $565.00
Very good: $450.00

Sako Vixen Heavy Barrel

Sako Forester Sporter

Sako Forester Mannlicher

Sako Forester Heavy Barrel

Sako Finnbear

Sako Finnbear Mannlicher

Sako Vixen Heavy Barrel
Similar to Vixen Sporter with heavy barrel & in larger calibers only.

Estimated Value: Excellent: $550.00
Very good: $440.00

Sako Forester Sporter
Similar to Vixen Sporter with medium action & in 22-250, 243 & 308 calibers. Made from the late 1950's to early 1970's.

Estimated Value: Excellent: $560.00
Very good: $445.00

Sako Forester Mannlicher
Similar to Forester Sporter with full length stock; 20" barrel; barrel band.

Estimated Value: Excellent: $570.00
Very good: $455.00

Sako Forester Heavy Barrel
Similar to Forester Sporter with a heavy 24" barrel.

Estimated Value: Excellent: $565.00
Very good: $450.00

Sako Finnbear
Similar to Vixen Sporter with: long action; recoil pad; 25-06, 264 magnum, 270, 30-06, 300 magnum, 7mm magnum; 375 H&H. Madef rom the early 1960's to the early 1970's.

Estimated Value: Excellent: $550.00
Very good: $440.00

Sako Finnbear Mannlicher
Similar to Finnbear with: full length stock; 20" barrel; barrel band.

Estimated Value: Excellent: $575.00
Very good: $460.00

Sako Model 74 Super Sporter

Sako Model 74 Super Sporter Heavy Barrel

Sako Model 74 Super Sporter

Sako Model 74 Super Sporter
Similar to Vixen, Forester & Finnbear in short action, medium action & long action; 23" or 24" barrel. Made in 1970's.

Estimated Value: Excellent: $525.00
Very good: $420.00

Sako Model 74 Super Sporter Heavy Barrel
Similar to Model 74 Super Sporter in short, medium or long action & heavy barrel.

Estimated Value: Excellent: $545.00
Very good: $435.00

Sako Model 74 Deluxe Sporter
Similar to Model 74 Super Sporter with recoil pad, select wood & high quality finish. Add $25.00 for magnum.

Estimated Value: Excellent: $570.00
Very good: $455.00

Sako Mauser

Sako Model A11 Standard

Sako Mauser
Caliber: 270, 30-06
Action: FN Mauser bolt action; repeating
Magazine: 5-shot box
Barrel: Blued; 24"
Sights: Leaf rear, hooded ramp front
Stock & Forearm: Checkered walnut Monte Carlo one-piece pistol grip stock & tapered forearm; swivels
Approximate wt.: 7½ lbs.
Comments: Made from World War II to about 1960.

Estimated Value: Excellent: $500.00
Very good: $400.00

Sako Mauser Magnum
Similar to Sako Mauser in magnum calibers 300 H&H & 375 H&H; recoil pad.

Estimated Value: Excellent: $550.00
Very good: $440.00

Sako Model A1 Standard, Hunter
Caliber: 17 Rem., 222 Rem., 223 Rem.
Action: Bolt action; repeating; short-throw
Magazine: 5-shot
Barrel: 23½"
Sights: None
Stock & Forearm: Checkered walnut Monte Carlo one-piece pistol grip stock & forearm; lacquer or oil finish; laminated grain & fiberglass available in 1989; swivels
Approximate wt.: 6½ lbs.
Comments: Currently available. Add 4% for 17 Rem. caliber; add 12% for laminated stock & 30% for fiberglass stock.

Estimated Value: New (retail): $820.00
Excellent: $615.00
Very good: $490.00

Sako Model A11 Standard, Hunter
Similar to the A1 Standard with a medium throw action and in 220 Swift, 22-250 rem., 243 Win., 7mm-08, 308 Win. calibers. Add 12% for laminated stock and 30% for fiberglass stock.

Estimated Value: New (retail): $820.00
Excellent: $615.00
Very good: $490.00

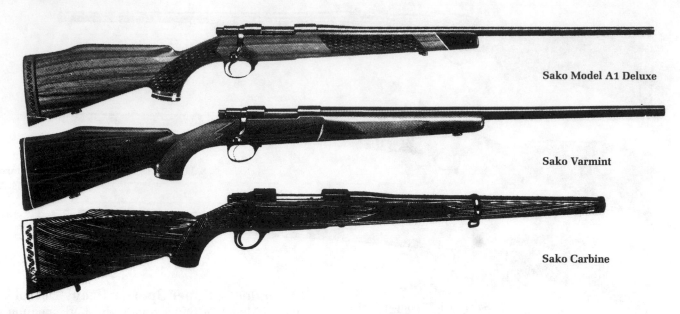

Sako Model A1 Deluxe

Sako Varmint

Sako Carbine

Sako Model A111 Standard, Hunter

Similar to the Model A1 Standard with a long throw action; 25-06 Rem., 6.5x55, 270 Win., 7x64, 30-06, 7mm Rem. magnum, 300 Win. magnum, 338 Win. magnum, 9.3x62, 375 H&H magnum; recoil pad. Add $25.00-$40.00 for magnum. Add 12% for laminated stock & 30% for fiberglass stock.

Estimated Value:	New (retail):	$820.00
	Excellent:	$615.00
	Very good:	$490.00

Sako Model A1 Deluxe

A deluxe version of the A1; recoil pad.

Estimated Value:	New (retail):	$1,065.00
	Excellent:	$ 800.00
	Very good:	$ 640.00

Sako Model A11 Deluxe

Similar to the Model A11 with deluxe features; recoil pad.

Estimated Value:	New (retail):	$1,065.00
	Excellent:	$ 800.00
	Very good:	$ 640.00

Sako Model A111 Deluxe

Similar to the Model A111 with deluxe features. Add $25.00 for magnum.

Estimated Value:	New (retail):	$1,065.00
	Excellent:	$ 800.00
	Very good:	$ 640.00

Sako Varmint

Similar to the Models A1, A11 & A111 with heavy varmint barrel.

Estimated Value:	New (retail):	$1,035.00
	Excellent:	$ 775.00
	Very good:	$ 620.00

Sako Carbine, Mannlicher

Similar to the Models A1 , A11 & A111 with a 20" barrel & full length forearm. Add 6% for 375 H&H & 3% for other magnums.

Estimated Value:	New (retail):	$885.00
	Excellent:	$660.00
	Very good:	$530.00

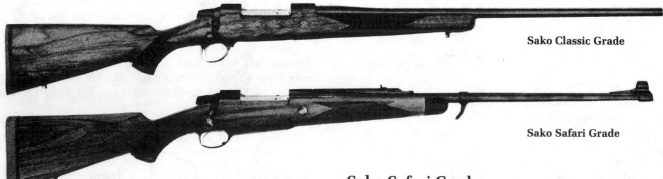

Sako Classic Grade

Sako Safari Grade

Sako Classic Grade

Similar to the A111 & A11 with styling changes in 243 Win., 270 Win., 30-06, 7mm Rem. magnum; select American walnut stock.

| Estimated Value: | Excellent: | $715.00 |
| | Very good: | $535.00 |

Sako Safari Grade

Similar to the A111 with extended magazine, barrel band swivels, select French walnut stock; choice of satin or matte blue finish; calibers 300 Win. magnum, 338 Win. magnum, 375 H&H magnum.

Estimated Value:	New (retail):	$2,115.00
	Excellent:	$1,585.00
	Very good:	$1,270.00

Sako Finnwolf Sporter

Sako Model 78
Caliber: 22 long rifle, 22 Win. magnum, 22 Hornet
Action: Bolt action; repeating
Magazine: 5-shot; 4-shot in magnum
Barrel: 22½"; heavy barrel available
Sights: Folding leaf rear, hooded ramp front
Stock & Forearm: One-piece checkered walnut Monte Carlo pistol grip stock & forearm; swivels
Approximate wt.: 6¾ lbs.
Comments: Made from the late 1970's to late 1980's. Add 5% for 22 Hornet.
Estimated Value: Excellent: $495.00
Very good: $390.00

Sako Finnwolf Sporter
Caliber: 243, 308
Action: Lever-action; hammerless; repeating
Magazine: 4-shot clip
Barrel: Blued; 23"
Sights: No rear, hooded ramp front
Stock & Forearm: Checkered walnut Monte Carlo one-piece pistol grip stock and tapered forearm; swivels
Approximate wt.: 7 lbs.
Comments: Made from the mid 1960's to early 1970's.
Estimated Value: Excellent: $550.00
Very good: $440.00

Sako Finnwolf Deluxe Sporter
Same as Finnwolf with select wood.
Estimated Value: Excellent: $590.00
Very good: $470.00

Savage

Savage Model 1904

Savage Model 1905

Savage Model 1911 Target

Savage Model 1905
Caliber: 22 short, long, long rifle
Action: Bolt action; single shot
Magazine: None
Barrel: 22
Sights: Open rear, bead front
Stock & Forearm: Plain one-piece straight grip stock & forearm
Approximate wt.: 5 lbs.
Comments: A lightweight takedown boy's rifle produced until about 1917.
Estimated Value: Excellent: $110.00
Very good: $ 85.00

Savage Model 1904 & Model 04
Caliber: 22 short, long, long rifle
Action: Bolt action; single shot
Magazine: None
Barrel: 18"
Sights: Open rear, bead front
Stock & Forearm: Straight wood one-piece stock & forearm
Approximate wt.: 3 lbs.
Comments: This is a boy's lightweight takedown rifle produced from 1904 to 1917 as Model 1904 & from 1924 to 1930 as Model 04.
Estimated Value: Excellent: $100.00
Very good: $ 80.00

Savage Model 1911 Target
Caliber: 22 short
Action: Bolt action; single shot
Magazine: None
Barrel: 20"
Sights: Adjustable rear, bead front
Stock & Forearm: Walnut one-piece straight grip stock & forearm
Approximate wt.: 4 lbs.
Comments: Made from 1911 to 1916.
Estimated Value: Excellent: $125.00
Very good: $100.00

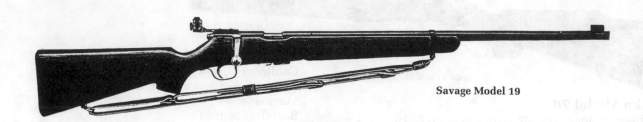

Savage Model 19

Savage Model 19, 19L Target
Caliber: 22 long rifle
Action: Bolt action; repeating; speed lock
Magazine: 5-shot detachable box
Barrel: 25"
Sights: Extension rear, hooded front
Stock & Forearm: Walnut pistol grip stock & beavertail forearm; swivels
Approximate wt.: 7½ lbs.
Comments: Made from 1933 to the mid 1940's. The model 19L has special Lyman receiver & front sights; add $10.00-$15.00.
Estimated Value: Excellent: $200.00
Very good: $150.00

Savage Model 19M
This is the same rifle as the Model 19 except it has a heavier 28" barrel. Approximate wt. is 9¼ lbs.
Estimated Value: Excellent: $230.00
Very good: $185.00

Savage Model 19H Hornet
Same as Model 19 except loading port, bolt mechanism & magazine are like Model 23-D.
Estimated Value: Excellent: $300.00
Very good: $240.00

Savage Model 19 NRA

Savage Model 20

Savage Model 19 NRA Match Rifle
Caliber: 22 long rifle
Action: Bolt action; repeating
Magazine: 5-shot detachable box
Barrel: 25"
Sights: Adjustable peep rear, blade front
Stock & Forearm: Wood full military pistol grip stock & forearm
Approximate wt.: 7 lbs.
Comments: Made from 1919 until 1932.
Estimated Value: Excellent: $245.00
Very good: $195.00

Savage Model 20
Caliber: 300 Savage, 250-3000
Action: Bolt action; repeating
Magazine: 5-shot
Barrel: 22" in 250 caliber; 24" in 300 caliber
Sights: Open rear, bead front; in 1926, rear peep sight
Stock & Forearm: Checkered walnut pistol grip stock & forearm; in 1926 cut to semi-pistol grip
Approximate wt.: 5¾ to 7 lbs.
Comments: Made from 1920 through 1929.
Estimated Value: Excellent: $330.00
Very good: $260.00

Savage Model 23A Sporter

Savage Model 23AA

Savage Model 23B

Savage Model 3

Savage Model 3, 3S, 3ST

Caliber: 22 short, long, long rifle
Action: Bolt action; single shot
Magazine: None
Barrel: 26" before World War II, 24" after
Sights: Open rear, bead front; 3S & 3ST have peep rear & hooded front
Stock & Forearm: One-piece walnut semi-pistol grip stock & forearm; 3ST has swivels
Approximate wt.: 4 to 5 lbs.
Comments: A takedown model produced from 1933 until the early 1950's. The 3ST was discontinued before World War II.

| **Estimated Value:** | **Excellent:** | $100.00 |
| | **Very good:** | $ 80.00 |

Savage Model 23A Sporter, 23AA, 23B, 23C, 23D

Caliber: 22 long rifle (Model 23A, 23AA); from 1933 to 1947 in 22 Hornet (Model 23 D); 25-20 (Model 23B); 32-20 (Model 23C)
Action: Bolt action; from 1933-1942 (Model 23AA) speed lock
Magazine: 5-shot detachable box
Barrel: 23"; 25" from 1933 until 1942 on Model 23B
Sights: Open rear, bead or blade front
Stock & Forearm: Plain walnut semi-pistol grip stock & forearm
Approximate wt.: 6 to 6½ lbs.
Comments: Produced: 23A from 1923-1933; Model 23AA with improved lock, 1933-1942; Model 23B, 1933-1942; Model 23C, 23D, 1933-1947

| **Estimated Value:** | **Excellent:** | $195.00 |
| | **Very good:** | $155.00 |

Savage Model 40

Savage Model 45

Savage Model 45

This is a special grade version of the Model 40. It has a checkered stock & forearm & a special receiver sight. Discontinued in 1940.

| **Estimated Value:** | **Excellent:** | $320.00 |
| | **Very good:** | $255.00 |

Savage Model 40

Caliber: 250-3000, 300 Savage, 30-30, 30-06
Action: Bolt action; repeating
Magazine: 4-shot detachable box
Barrel: 22" for caliber 250-3000 & 30-30; 24" for other models
Sights: Open rear, ramp front
Stock & Forearm: Plain walnut pistol grip stock & lipped forearm after 1936; checkered stock after 1940
Approximate wt.: 7½ lbs.
Comments: Made from 1928 until World War II.

| **Estimated Value:** | **Excellent:** | $285.00 |
| | **Very good:** | $225.00 |

Savage Model 4

Savage Model 4S

Savage Model 4M

Savage Model 5

Savage Model 5S

Savage Model 4, 4s, 4M

Caliber: 22 short, long, long rifle; 4M chambered for 22 mag.

Action: Bolt action; repeating

Magazine: 5-shot detachable box

Barrel: 24"

Sights: Open rear, bead front; 4S has peep rear & hooded front

Stock & Forearm: Checkered walnut pistol grip stock & grooved forearm on pre-World War II models; plain on post-World War II models

Approximate wt.: 5½ lbs.

Comments: The Model 4 & 4S were produced from 1933 until the mid 1960's. 4M was made during the early to mid 1960's. Add $10.00 for model 4M.

Estimated Value: Excellent: $110.00
Very good: $ 85.00

Savage Model 5, 5S

Similar to the Model 4 except the magazine is tubular & the gun weighs about 6 lbs. The Model 5S has peep rear & hooded front sight. They were produced from the mid 1930's until 1961; caliber 22 short, long & long rifle. Add $10.00 for Model 5S.

Estimated Value: Excellent: $120.00
Very good: $ 95.00

Savage Model 219

Savage Model 219L

Savage Model 221 Utility Gun

Savage Model 219, 219L

Caliber: 22 Hornet, 25-20, 32-20, 30-30
Action: Hammerless; single shot; automatic ejector; shotgun style, top break lever; 219L has side lever
Magazine: Single shot
Barrel: 26"
Sights: Open rear, bead front
Stock & Forearm: Plain walnut pistol grip stock & forearm
Approximate wt.: 6 lbs.
Comments: A takedown model made from 1938 to 1965 was Model 219; from 1965 for two years with side lever, as 219L.
Estimated Value: Excellent: $100.00
Very good: $ 75.00

Savage Model 221 Utility Gun

Same rifle as the Model 219 except it was offered in 30-30 only with an interchangeable 12 gauge 30" shotgun barrel. Prices include the 12 gauge interchangeable shotgun barrel.
Estimated Value: Excellent: $130.00
Very good: $105.00

Savage Model 222

Same as Model 221 except shotgun barrel is 16 gauge; 28".
Estimated Value: Excellent: $130.00
Very good: $105.00

Savage Model 223

Same as Model 221 except shotgun barrel is 20 gauge, 28".
Estimated Value: Excellent: $130.00
Very good: $105.00

Savage Model 227

Same as Model 221 except it is 22 Hornet & the shotgun barrel is 20 gauge, 30".
Estimated Value: Excellent: $135.00
Very good: $110.00

Savage Model 228

Same as Model 227 except shotgun barrel is 16 gauge, 28".
Estimated Value: Excellent: $135.00
Very good: $110.00

Savage Model 229

Same as Model 227 except shotgun barrel is 20 gauge, 28".
Estimated Value: Excellent: $135.00
Very good: $110.00

Savage Model 110 Sporter

Savage Model 110 MC & MCL

Same as 110 Sporter except: 22-250 caliber added; 24" barrel; Monte Carlo stock. The MCL is the same in left-hand action, add $10.00. Made from the late 1950's to about 1969.
Estimated Value: Excellent: $225.00
Very good: $180.00

Savage Model 110 Sporter

Caliber: 243, 270, 308, 30-06
Action: Bolt action; repeating
Magazine: 4-shot staggered box
Barrel: 22"
Sights: Open rear, ramp front
Stock & Forearm: Checkered walnut pistol grip stock & forearm
Approximate wt.: 6¾ lbs.
Comments: Made from 1958 until the early 1960's when it was replaced by 110E.
Estimated Value: Excellent: $200.00
Very good: $150.00

Savage Model 110S

Savage Model 110CL

Savage Model 110E

Savage Model 112-R

Savage Model 110 M

Savage Model 110C, 110CL
Caliber: 22-250, 243, 25-06, 270, 308, 30-06, 7mm Rem. mag., 300 Win. mag.
Action: Bolt action; repeating
Magazine: 4-shot clip, 3-shot clip in magnum calibers
Barrel: 22" & 24"
Sights: Open rear, ramp front
Stock & Forearm: Checkered walnut Monte Carlo stock & forearm; magnum has recoil pad
Approximate wt.: 6¾ to 8 lbs.
Comments: This rifle has been in production since 1966. Discontinued 1986. Add $20.00 for left hand model (110DCL). Add 10% for magnum calibers.
Estimated Value: Excellent: $300.00
                      Very good: $225.00

Savage Model 110S
Similar to the Model 110C with heavy barrel; no sights; stippled checkering; recoil pad; 7mm/08 & 308 calibers; introduced in the late 1970's to mid 1980's.
Estimated Value: Excellent: $325.00
                      Very good: $260.00

Savage Model 112-R
A varmint rifle similar to the Model 110C; plain walnut one-piece semi-pistol grip stock & forearm; swivels; recoil pad; no sights; 22-250 & 25-06 calibers; made from about 1979 to early 1980's.
Estimated Value: Excellent: $260.00
                      Very good: $205.00

Savage Model 110E, 110EL (Early)
Caliber: 243 Win., 7mm Rem. mag., 30-06
Action: Bolt action; repeating
Magazine: 4-shot staggered box; 3-shot in magnum
Barrel: Blued; 20"; stainless steel in magnum
Sights: Open rear, ramp front
Stock & Forearm: One-piece checkered or plain walnut Monte Carlo stock & forearm; magnum has recoil pad
Approximate wt.: 6¾ to 7¾ lbs.
Comments: Made from 1963 to late 1970's. A later model was also designated 110E. Add $20.00 for left hand model (100EL).
Estimated Value: Excellent: $225.00
                      Very good: $170.00

Savage Model 110 M & 110 ML
Caliber: 7mm Rem. mag., 264, 300, 338 Win.
Action: Bolt action; repeating
Magazine: 4-shot box, staggered
Barrel: 24"
Sights: Open rear, ramp front
Stock & Forearm: Walnut Monte Carlo pistol grip stock & forearm; recoil pad
Approximate wt.: 7½ to 8 lbs.
Comments: Made from 1963 to 1969; 110 ML is the same in left-hand action, add $10.00.
Estimated Value: Excellent: $250.00
                      Very good: $190.00

Savage Model 110P

Savage 110PE

Savage Model 110-D, 110-DL

Caliber: 223, 243, 270, 30-06, 7mm Rem. magnum, 338 Win. magnum

Action: Bolt action; repeating

Magazine: 4-shot internal box; 3-shot for magnums

Barrel: 22" blue; 24" for magnums

Sights: Hooded ramp front, adjustable rear

Stock & Forearm: Select walnut, checkered semi-pistol grip, Monte Carlo, one piece stock & forearm

Approximate wt.: 6¾ lbs; 7 lbs. in magnum

Comments: Introduced in 1986. Model 110-DL is left hand model not available in 338 Win. magnum. Add 14% for Model 110-DL. Add 18% for magnum calibers. Discontinued 1988.

Estimated Value: Excellent: $275.00
Very good: $210.00

Savage Model 110P Premier & 110 PL

Caliber: 243 Win., 7mm Rem. mag., 30-06

Action: Bolt action; repeating

Magazine: 4-shot box, staggered; 3-shot in magnum

Barrel: Blued 22"; 24" stainless steel in magnum

Sights: Open rear folding leaf, ramp front

Stock & Forearm: Walnut & rosewood Monte Carlo stock & forearm; swivels; magnum has recoil pad

Approximate wt.: 7 to 8 lbs.

Comments: Made from mid 1960's until 1970's; 110PL is left-hand action. Add $15.00 for magnum.

Estimated Value: Excellent: $390.00
Very good: $310.00

Savage 110PE Presentation, 110PEL

Same as Models 110P & 110PL except receiver, floor plate & trigger guard are engraved. If was produced for two years beginning in 1968. Add $15.00 for magnum.

Estimated Value: Excellent: $600.00
Very good: $480.00

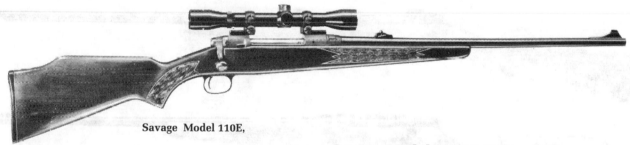

Savage Model 110E,

Savage Model 110E & 110G

Caliber: 22-250, 223, 243, 308 Win., 270, 30-06, 7mm Rem. magnum, 300 Win. mag.

Action: Bolt action; repeating

Magazine: 4-shot box, internal

Barrel: Blued 22", 24" in 7mm magnum & 300 Win. mag.

Sights: Removable ramp front, removable adjustable rear; or no sights.

Stock & Forearm: Checkered hardwood, Monte Carlo walnut finish, one-piece pistol grip stock & forearm

Approximate wt.: 7 lbs.

Comments: Merchandised from late 1970's to 1981 as Stevens, & 1982 to present as Savage. Add 5% for sights.

Estimated Value: New (retail): $341.65
Excellent: $255.00
Very good: $205.00

Savage Model 110V & 110GV

Similar to Model 110E & 110G except: 22-250 ro 223 caliber. No sights; a heavy 26" barrel. Recoil pad. Produced in the mid 1980's. Approx. wt 9 lbs.

Estimated Value: New (retail) $386.75
Excellent: $290.00
Very good: $230.00

Savage Model 110FP Police Rifle

Similar to the Model 110G except: 223 Remington or 308 Winchester caliber only; heavy, 24" barrel; non-reflective black finish on metal parts; black all-weather DuPont Rynite® one-piece stock & forearm; sling studs & bi-pod mount; no sights; drilled & tapped for scope mounts. Introduced in 1990.

Estimated Value: New (retail) $616.45
Excellent: $460.00
Very good: $370.00

Savage Model 110F

Same as the Model 110G except: black DuPont Rynite® stock & forearm; add 4% for sights. Made from the late 1980's to present.

Estimated Value: New (retail) $435.00
Excellent: $325.00
Very good: $260.00

Savage Model 110B

Same as the Model 110G except: brown laminate hardwood stock; ramp front sight & adjustable rear sight. Made from the 1980's to present.

Estimated Value: New (retail) $435.00
Excellent: $325.00
Very good: $260.00

Savage Model 111

Caliber: 7mm (7x57), 243, 270, 30-06, 7mm magnum
Action: Bolt action; repeating
Magazine: 4-shot box; 3-shot box in magnum
Barrel: 24"
Sights: Adjustable removable rear, removable hooded ramp front
Stock & Forearm: Checkered walnut Monte Carlo one-piece pistol grip stock & forearm; swivels
Approximate wt.: 6¾ lbs.
Comments: A deluxe high powered rifle made from the mid to late 1970's. Add $10.00 for magnum.
Estimated Value: Excellent: $275.00
Very good: $220.00

Savage Model 112V

Caliber: 222, 223, 22-250, 220 Swift, 25-06, 243
Action: Bolt action; single shot; hammerless
Magazine: None
Barrel: 26" chrome-moly steel; tapered
Sights: None
Stock & Forearm: Checkered walnut one-piece pistol grip stock & forearm; fluted comb; swivels
Approximate wt.: 9¼ lbs.
Comments: A varmint rifle made in the mid to late 1970's.
Estimated Value: Excellent: $260.00
Very good: $205.00

Savage Model 111

Savage Model 112V

Savage Model 340

Savage Model 340C Carbine

Savage Model 340S

Same as Model 340 except sights are peep rear, hooded front. It was produced from about 1955 to 1960.
Estimated Value: Excellent: $185.00
Very good: $135.00

Savage Model 340C Carbine

Same as Model 340 in caliber 30-30. The barrel is slightly over 18". Produced in the 1950's. Peep sight, checkered stock & sling swivels.
Estimated Value: Excellent: $180.00
Very good: $135.00

Savage Model 340

Caliber: 22 Hornet, 222 Rem., 223 Rem., 30-30
Action: Bolt action; repeating
Magazine: 4-shot clip in 22 Hornet & 222 Rem,; 3-shot clip in 30-30
Barrel: 20", 22", 24"
Sights: Open rear, ramp front; hooded ramp after 1980
Stock & Forearm: Plain walnut pistol grip stock & sore-arm; checkered after 1965
Approximate wt.: 6 to 7 lbs.
Comments: Made from 1950 to 1986; before 1950 this model was manufactured as a Stevens.
Estimated Value: Excellent: $175.00
Very good: $130.00

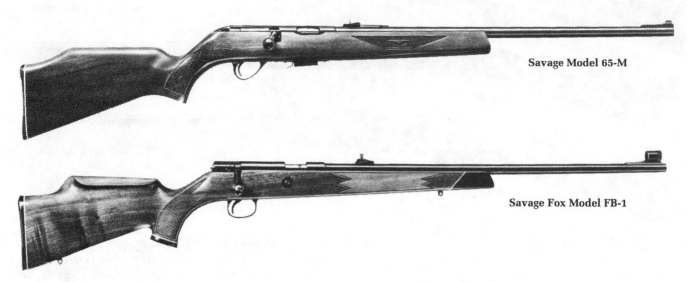

Savage Model 65-M

Savage Fox Model FB-1

Savage Model 65-M
Caliber: 22 magnum
Action: Bolt action; repeating
Magazine: 5-shot clip
Barrel: Blued; 22"
Sights: Open rear, ramp front
Stock & Forearm: Checkered walnut one-piece semi-pistol grip stock & forearm
Approximate wt.: 5¾ lbs.
Comments: Made in the late 1970's.
Estimated Value: Excellent: $85.00
  Very good: $65.00

Savage Fox Model FB-1
Caliber: 22 short, long, long rifle
Action: Bolt action; repeating
Magazine: 5-shot detachable clip
Barrel: Blued; 24"
Sights: Adjustable leaf rear, hooded ramp front; drilled & tapped for scope
Stock & Forearm: Checkered walnut Monte Carlo one-piece semi-pistol grip stock & forearm; cheekpiece swivels; rosewood fore-end tip & grip cap
Approximate wt.: 6½ lbs.
Comments: Introduced in 1981, discontinued in 1982.
Estimated Value: Excellent: $200.00
  Very good: $150.00

Savage Model 982DL

Savage Model 982MDL

Savage Model 982DL
Caliber: 22 short, long, long rifle
Action: Bolt action; repeating
Magazine: 5-shot clip, push button release
Barrel: Blued; 22"
Sights: Ramp front, folding leaf rear
Stock & Forearm: Checkered walnut one-piece Monte Carlo semi-pistol grip stock & forearm
Approximate wt.: 6 lbs.
Comments: Introduced in 1981, discontinued in 1982.
Estimated Value: Excellent: $95.00
  Very good: $70.00

Savage Model 982MDL
Caliber: 22 magnum
Action: Bolt action; repeating
Magazine: 5-shot detachable clip
Barrel: Blued; 22"
Sights: Ramp front, folding leaf rear; grooved for scope
Stock & Forearm: Checkered walnut Monte Carlo one-piece semi-pistol grip stock & forearm
Approximate wt.: 6 lbs.
Comments: Introduced in 1981, discontinued in 1982.
Estimated Value: Excellent: $100.00
  Very good: $ 75.00

Savage Model 1899 (99)

Savage Model 1899 Military

Savage Model 99A

Savage Model 1899 (99)

Caliber: 303 Savage, 25-35, 32-40, 38-55, 30-30
Action: Lever-action; hammerless
Magazine: 5-shot rotary
Barrel: 20", 22", 26"; round, half octagon or octagon
Sights: Adjustable rear, dovetail; open sporting front
Stock & Forearm: Walnut straight grip stock & tapered forearm
Approximate wt.: 7½ lbs.
Comments: The backbone of the Savage line which has been manufactured in many variations over the years. It was produced from 1899 to 1922.

Estimated Value:	Excellent:	$500.00
	Very good:	$400.00

Savage Model 1899 Military

Same as the Model 99 except: barrel is 28"; bayonet; stock is musket style; sights are military. Produced from about 1899 to 1907; caliber 30-30 Win.

Estimated Value:	Excellent:	$600.00
	Very good:	$480.00

Savage Model 99A

Basically the same as Model 1899 in solid frame & in calibers 300 Savage, 303 Savage & 30-30. It was produced from 1922 to 1937. Later models in calibers 243, 308, 250 Savage, & 300 Savage from about 1970 to 1984. Add $20.00 for early models.

Estimated Value:	Excellent:	$275.00
	Very good:	$220.00

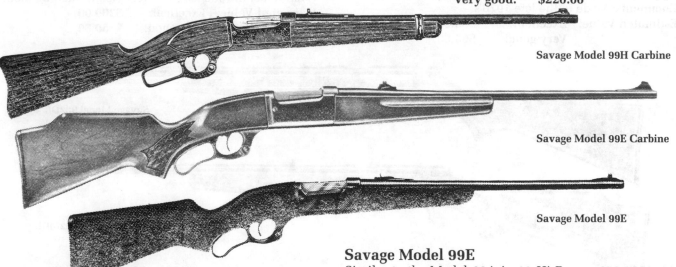

Savage Model 99H Carbine

Savage Model 99E Carbine

Savage Model 99E

Savage Model 99B

Takedown version of Model 99A; produced from about 1922 to 1937.

Estimated Value:	Excellent:	$400.00
	Very good:	$320.00

Savage Model 99H Carbine

Basically the same as 99A with: addition of 250-3000 caliber; short barrel; carbine stock & forearm; barrel bands. Produced from 1932 to 1941.

Estimated Value:	Excellent:	$385.00
	Very good:	$300.00

Savage Model 99E

Similar to the Model 99A in 22 Hi Power, 250-3000, 30-30, 300 savage, 303 Savage; 22" or 24" barrel. Unlipped tapered forearm. Made from about 1922 to 1937.

Estimated Value:	Excellent:	$360.00
	Very good:	$285.00

Savage Model 99E Carbine

Similar to the Model 99H in 243 Win., 250 Savage, 300 Savage, 308 Win., calibers only. Checkered walnut stock & tapered forearm without barrel band. Production began in 1961. Monte Carlo stock after 1982. Discontinued in 1985.

Estimated Value:	Excellent:	$260.00
	Very good:	$195.00

Savage Model 99F

Savage Model 99CD

Savage Model 99K

Savage Model 99EG

Savage Model 99R

Savage Model 99RS

Savage Model 99EG
This is the Model G produced after World War II, from 1955 to 1961.

Estimated Value: Excellent: **$260.00**
                  Very good: **$200.00**

Savage Model 99CD
A solid frame version of Model 99F with a checkered pistol grip stock & forearm. In production from 1955 to about 1980; 4-shot detachable box magazine.

Estimated Value: Excellent: **$285.00**
                  Very good: **$225.00**

Savage Model 99G
A takedown version of the Model 99E with a checkered walnut pistol grip stock & forearm. Made from about 1921 to 1941.

Estimated Value: Excellent: **$395.00**
                  Very good: **$315.00**

Savage Model 99K
A fancy Model 99G with deluxe stock & light engraving. Rear sight is peep & there is a folding middle sight. It was discontinued in 1940's.

Estimated Value: Excellent: **$925.00**
                  Very good: **$740.00**

Savage Model 99F
This is a lightweight takedown version of the Model 99E, produced until about 1940. Production resumed about 1955 to 1972 in caliber 243, 300 & 308. Add $160.00 for pre-1940.

Estimated Value: Excellent: **$260.00**
                  Very good: **$205.00**

Savage Model 99R
Similar to other Model 99's. Production stopped in 1940. It was resumed from 1955 to 1961 in 24" barrel only with swivel attachments in a variety of calibers. Add $150.00 for pre-World War II models.

Estimated Value: Excellent: **$250.00**
                  Very good: **$200.00**

Savage Model 99RS
The same rifle as Model 99 except those before World War II have rear peep sight & folding middle sight. Those made after the war have a special receiver sight. Those made after the war have a special receiver sight. Discontinued in 1961; solid frame. Add $160.00 for pre-World War II models.

Estimated Value: Excellent: **$275.00**
                  Very good: **$210.00**

Savage Model 99DL

Savage Model 99C

Savage Model 99PE Presentation

Savage Model 99DE Citation

Savage Model 99T

Savage Model 99PE Presentation

Much like the Model 99DL except engraved receiver, hand checkered Monte Carlo stock & forearm. Produced from 1968 to 1970.

Estimated Value: Excellent: $750.00
Very good: $600.00

Savage Model 99DE Citation

A less elaborate example of the Model 99 PE. Produced from 1968 to 1970.

Estimated Value: Excellent: $550.00
Very good: $440.00

Savage Model 99T

Basically the same as the other Model 99's. It is a solid frame with a checkered walnut pistol grip stock & forearm. Produced until 1940.

Estimated Value: Excellent: $360.00
Very good: $290.00

Savage Model 99C

Caliber: 22-250, 243, 308, 7mm/08, (22-250 & 7mm/08 dropped in the 1980's)
Action: Hammerless lever action; cocking indicator
Magazine: 3- or 4-shot detachable clip
Barrel: 22" chrome-moly steel
Sights: Detachable hooded ramp front; adjustable rear
Stock & Forearm: Checkered walnut semi-pistol grip, two-piece stock & tapered forearm; Monte Carlo stock after 1982
Approximate wt.: 7½ lbs.
Comments: Made from 1965 to present.
Estimated Value: New (retail): $537.10
Excellent: $400.00
Very good: $320.00

Savage Model 99DL

This is a late Model 99, in production from about 1960 to mid 1970's. Basically the same as Model 99F with a Monte Carlo stock & swivels.

Estimated Value: Excellent: $270.00
Very good: $215.00

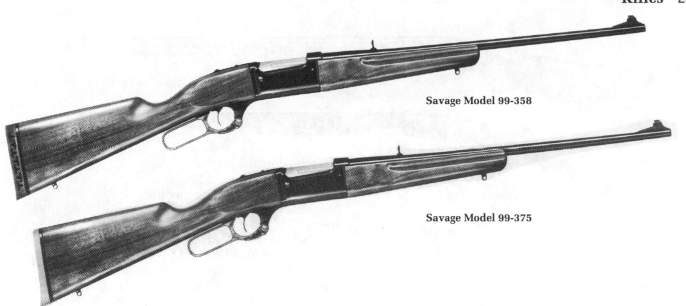

Savage Model 99-358

Savage Model 99-375

Savage Model 99-358

Similar to the Model 99A in 358 caliber; forearm rounded; swivels; recoil pad. Made from late 1970's to early 1980's.

Estimated Value: Excellent: $295.00
Very good: $235.00

Savage Model 99-375

Similar to the Model 99-358 in 375 Win. caliber.

Estimated Value: Excellent: $300.00
Very good: $240.00

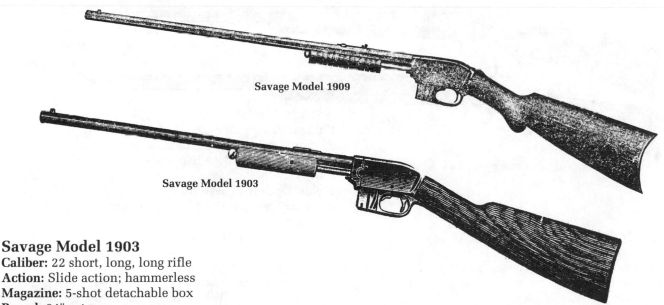

Savage Model 1909

Savage Model 1903

Savage Model 1903

Caliber: 22 short, long, long rifle
Action: Slide action; hammerless
Magazine: 5-shot detachable box
Barrel: 24" octagon
Sights: Open rear, bead front
Stock & Forearm: Checkered walnut pistol grip stock & grooved slide handle
Approximate wt.: 5 lbs.
Comments: This takedown model was produced from 1903 to 1922.

Estimated Value: Excellent: $210.00
Very good: $170.00

Savage Model 1909

A lighter version of the Model 1903 with a straight stock & forearm & a round 20" barrel. Discontinued about 1915.

Estimated Value: Excellent: $180.00
Very good: $145.00

Savage Model 1914

Caliber: 22 short, long, long rifle
Action: Slide action; hammerless
Magazine: Tubular; 20 shorts, 17 longs, 15 long rifles
Barrel: 24" octagon or half octagon
Sights: Open rear, bead front
Stock & Forearm: Plain wood pistol grip stock & grooved slide handle
Approximate wt.: 5¾ lbs.
Comments: A takedown rifle produced from about 1915 until 1924.

Estimated Value: Excellent: $195.00
Very good: $155.00

Savage Model 25

Savage Model 29

Savage Model 29

Very similar to the Model 25 except pre-war models were checkered; barrel is round on post-war models. Made from 1929 until the late 1960's. Add $50.00 for pre-World War II models with octagon barrel.

Estimated Value: **Excellent:** **$190.00**
Very good: **$150.00**

Savage Model 25

Caliber: 22 short, long, long rifle
Action: Slide action; hammerless
Magazine: Tubular; 20 shorts, 17 longs, 15 long rifles
Barrel: 24" octagon
Sights: Open rear, blade front
Stock & Forearm: Walnut pistol grip stock & grooved slide handle
Approximate wt.: 5¾ lbs.
Comments: A takedown model produced from the mid 1920's until 1929.

Estimated Value: **Excellent:** **$220.00**
Very good: **$170.00**

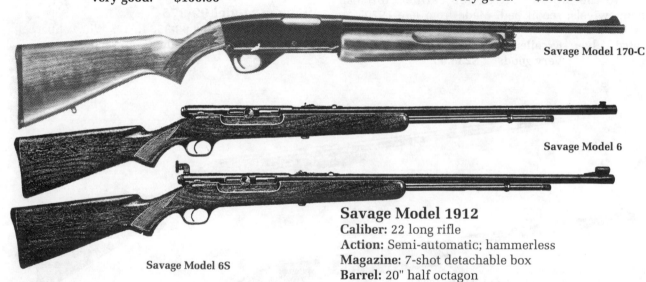

Savage Model 170-C

Savage Model 6

Savage Model 6S

Savage Model 170

Caliber: 30-30, 35
Action: Slide action; hammerless; repeating
Magazine: 3-shot tubular
Barrel: Blued; 22"
Sights: Ramp front, folding leaf rear, hooded ramp after 1980
Stock & Forearm: Checkered walnut Monte Carlo semi-pistol grip stock & fluted slide handle; swivels
Approximate wt.: 6¾ lbs.
Comments: Made from the late 1970's to early 1980's
Estimated Value: **Excellent:** **$175.00**
Very good: **$140.00**

Savage Model 170-C

A carbine version of the Model 170; not available with a Monte Carlo stock; 18½" barrel; not available in 35 caliber.

Estimated Value: **Excellent:** **$165.00**
Very good: **$130.00**

Savage Model 1912

Caliber: 22 long rifle
Action: Semi-automatic; hammerless
Magazine: 7-shot detachable box
Barrel: 20" half octagon
Sights: Open rear, bead front
Stock & Forearm: Plain wood straight grip stock & forearm
Approximate wt.: 4½ lbs.
Comments: This takedown was Savage's first semi-automatic; discontinued in 1916.

Estimated Value: **Excellent:** **$275.00**
Very good: **$210.00**

Savage Model 6, 6S

Caliber: 22 short, long, long rifle
Action: Semi-automatic
Magazine: Tubular; 21 shorts, 17 longs, 15 long rifles
Barrel: 24"
Sights: Open rear, bead front; 6S has peep rear, hooded front
Stock & Forearm: Checkered walnut pistol grip before World War II; plain walnut pistol grip after the war
Approximate wt.: 6 lbs.
Comments: A takedown model manufactured from 1938 until late 1960's.

Estimated Value: **Excellent:** **$110.00**
Very good: **$85.00**

Savage Model 7

Savage Model 7S

Savage Model 7, 7S

Basically the same as Model 6 & 6S except they are equipped with a 5-shot detachable box magazine. Produced from the late 1930's until the early 1950's.

Estimated Value: Excellent: $100.00
Very good: $ 80.00

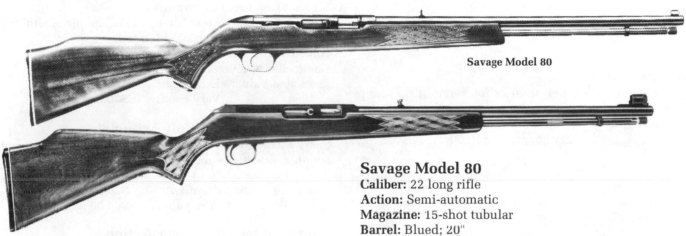

Savage Model 80

Savage Model 980 DL

Savage Model 980DL

Caliber: 22 long rifle
Action: Semi-automatic
Magazine: 15-shot tubular
Barrel: Blued; 20"
Sights: Hooded ramp front, folding leaf adjustable rear
Stock & Forearm: Checkered walnut one-piece Monte Carlo semi-pistol grip stock and forearm
Approximate wt.: 6 lbs.
Comments: Produced from 1981 to 1984.
Estimated Value: Excellent: $120.00
Very good: $95.00

Savage Model 80

Caliber: 22 long rifle
Action: Semi-automatic
Magazine: 15-shot tubular
Barrel: Blued; 20"
Sights: Open rear, blade front
Stock & Forearm: Checkered walnut one-piece Monte Carlo pistol grip stock & forearm
Approximate wt.: 6 lbs.
Comments: Made from the mid to late 1970's. Due to a possible safety malfunction, certain models were recalled in 1982 and inspected by Stevens at no cost to the owner. Serial numbers that were recalled were B256621 or higher; C000001 or higher; D000001 or higher.
Estimated Value: Excellent: $95.00
Very good: $80.00

Sears

Sears Model 53

Caliber: 243, 30-06
Action: Bolt action; repeating; hammerless
Magazine: 5-shot tubular
Barrel: Blued; 24"
Sights: Folding rear, ramp front
Stock & Forearm: Checkered walnut Monte Carlo one-piece grip stock & tapered forearm; swivels
Approximate wt.: 6¾ lbs.
Comments: Made until mid 1970's.
Estimated Value: Excellent: $150.00
Very good: $110.00

Sears Ted Williams Model 53A

Same as Model 53 in 30-06 caliber only; 22" barrel.
Estimated Value: Excellent: $145.00
Very good: $105.00

Sears Ted Williams Model 73

Same as Ted Williams 53 with select wood & fancy finish.
Estimated Value: Excellent: $175.00
Very good: $130.00

Sears Model 1

Sears Model 2

Sears Model 2

Caliber: 22 short, long, long rifle
Action: Bolt action; repeating; hammerless
Magazine: 6-shot clip
Barrel: Blued; 20"
Sights: Open rear, bead front
Stock & Forearm: Wood Monte Carlo one-piece semi-pistol grip stock & tapered forearm
Approximate wt.: 5 lbs.
Comments: Manufactured in the 1970's.
Estimated Value: Excellent: $85.00
Very good: $70.00

Sears Model 2200, Bolt Action

Same as the Model 2200 Semi-Automatic except: bolt action repeater; 5-shot box magazine; 22 short, long or long rifle caliber.
Estimated Value: Excellent: $75.00
Very good: $60.00

Sears Model 2200 Lever Action

Caliber: 22 short, long, long rifle
Action: Lever-action; single shot; exposed hammer
Magazine: None
Barrel: Blued; 18½", round
Sights: Sporting front, rear adjustable for elevation
Stock & Forearm: Smooth two-piece hardwood straight grip stock & forearm
Approximate wt.: 5½ lbs.
Comments: Manufactured to the mid 1980's.
Estimated Value: Excellent: $65.00
Very good: $50.00

Sears Model 1

Similar to Model 2 but single shot version, no Monte Carlo stock.
Estimated Value: Excellent: $60.00
Very good: $50.00

Sears Model 2200 Semi-Automatic

Caliber: 22 long rifle
Action: Semi-automatic; hammerless; side ejection
Magazine: 15-shot tubular
Barrel: Blued; 20", round
Sights: Sporting front, rear adjustable for elevation; receiver grooved for scope
Stock & Forearm: Checkered walnut-finish hardwood one-piece pistol grip stock & forearm
Approximate wt.: 5½ lbs.
Comments: Add $10.00 for scope. Due to a possible safety malfunction, certain models were recalled in 1982 & inspected by Stevens at no cost to the owner. Serial numbers recalled were B256621 or higher; C000001 or higher; D000001 or higher.
Estimated Value: Excellent: $95.00
Very good: $75.00

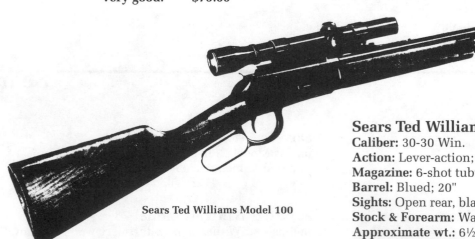

Sears Ted Williams Model 100

Sears Ted Williams Model 100

Caliber: 30-30 Win.
Action: Lever-action; exposed hammer; repeating
Magazine: 6-shot tubular
Barrel: Blued; 20"
Sights: Open rear, blade front
Stock & Forearm: Walnut straight grip stock & forearm
Approximate wt.: 6½ lbs.
Comments: Made for Sears by Winchester.
Estimated Value: Excellent: $145.00
Very good: $115.00

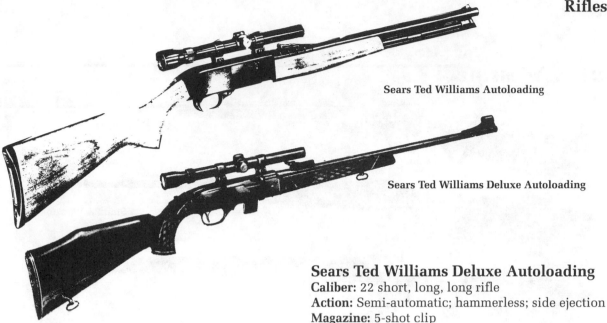

Sears Ted Williams Autoloading

Sears Ted Williams Deluxe Autoloading

Sears Ted Williams Deluxe Autoloading
Caliber: 22 short, long, long rifle
Action: Semi-automatic; hammerless; side ejection
Magazine: 5-shot clip
Barrel: Blued; 20"
Sights: Rear tangent, hooded ramp front
Stock & Forearm: Checkered walnut Monte Carlo one-piece pistol grip stock & tapered forearm; swivels
Approximate wt.: 6 lbs.
Comments: Manufactured in the 1970's.
Estimated Value: Excellent: $90.00
　　　　　　　　　Very good: $75.00

Sears Ted Williams Autoloading
Caliber: 22 short, long, long rifle
Action: Semi-automatic; hammerless; side ejection
Magazine: Tubular; 15 long rifles, 17 longs, 21 shorts
Barrel: Blued; 20½"
Sights: None, scope
Stock & Forearm: Wood semi-pistol grip stock & forearm
Approximate wt.: 5 lbs.
Comments: Manufactured in the 1970's.
Estimated Value: Excellent: $80.00
　　　　　　　　　Very good: $65.00

Sedgley

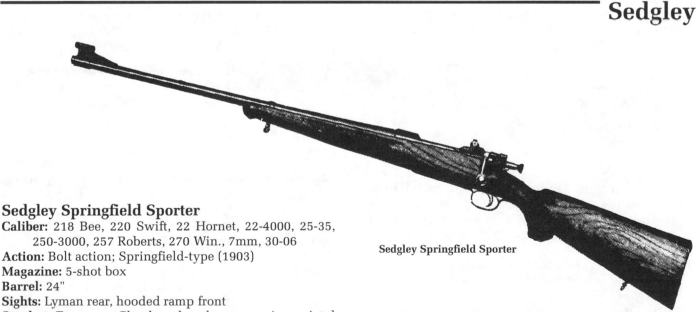

Sedgley Springfield Sporter

Sedgley Springfield Sporter
Caliber: 218 Bee, 220 Swift, 22 Hornet, 22-4000, 25-35, 250-3000, 257 Roberts, 270 Win., 7mm, 30-06
Action: Bolt action; Springfield-type (1903)
Magazine: 5-shot box
Barrel: 24"
Sights: Lyman rear, hooded ramp front
Stock & Forearm: Checkered walnut one-piece pistol grip stock & lipped forearm; swivels
Approximate wt.: 7½ lbs.
Comments: Manufactured in left & right hand action from the late 1920's to World War II.
Estimated Value: Excellent: $520.00
　　　　　　　　　Very good: $415.00

Sedgley Mannlicher
Similar to the Sporter with a full length forearm; 20" barrel.
Estimated Value: Excellent: $575.00
　　　　　　　　　Very good: $460.00

Smith & Wesson

Smith & Wesson Model A

Smith & Wesson Model B

Smith & Wesson Model E

Smith & Wesson Model A

Caliber: 22-250, 243, 270, 308, 30-06, 7mm mag., 300 mag.
Action: Bolt action; repeating; adjustable trigger
Magazine: 5-shot box
Barrel: Blued; 23¾" tapered
Sights: Folding rear, hooded ramp front with silver bead
Stock & Forearm: Checkered walnut Monte Carlo one-piece pistol grip stock & tapered forearm
Approximate wt.: 7 lbs.
Comments: Made only in the early 1970's.
Estimated Value: Excellent: **$320.00**
                        Very good: **$255.00**

Smith & Wesson Model B

A 20" barrel version of the Model A; not available in 22-250 or magnum; Monte Carlo stock.
Estimated Value: Excellent: **$275.00**
                        Very good: **$220.00**

Smith & Wesson Model C

Same as Model B except straight grip stock.
Estimated Value: Excellent: **$275.00**
                        Very good: **$220.00**

Smith & Wesson Model D

Same as Model C with full length forearm.
Estimated Value: Excellent: **$325.00**
                        Very good: **$260.00**

Smith & Wesson Model E

Same as Model B with full length forearm.
Estimated Value: Excellent: **$325.00**
                        Very good: **$260.00**

Smith & Wesson Model 1500

Smith & Wesson Model 1700LS Classic Hunter

Similar to the Model 1500 except light weight with lipped forearm, removable 5-shot magazine with floor plate; available in calibers 243 Win., 270 Win., & 30-06. Introduced in 1984.
Estimated Value: Excellent: **$400.00**
                        Very good: **$320.00**

Smith & Wesson Model 1500 Deluxe Varmint

Similar to the Model 1500 with a 22" heavy barrel, adjustable trigger; 222 Rem., 22-250 Rem., & 223 Rem. calibers. Produced from 1982 to 1985. Add 3% for Parkerized finish.
Estimated Value: Excellent: **$360.00**
                        Very good: **$285.00**

Smith & Wesson Model 1500, 1500 Mountaineer

Caliber: 30-06, 270 Win., 243 Win., 25-06 Rem., 7mm Rem. mag., 300 Win. mag.; 222 Rem.; 223 Rem. & 308 Win. added in 1982
Action: Bolt action; hammerless; repeating
Magazine: 5-shot box
Barrel: 23½"
Sights: Folding leaf rear, hooded ramp front or no sights
Stock & Forearm: Checkered walnut pistol grip, one-piece stock & forearm; swivels; recoil pad on magnum
Approximate wt.: 7 lbs.
Comments: Discontinued 1985. Add 4% for magnum; 19% for Deluxe Model; 7% for sights.
Estimated Value: Excellent: **$295.00**
                        Very good: **$235.00**

Standard

Standard Model G
Caliber: 25-35, 30-30, 25 Rem., 30 Rem., 35 Rem.
Action: Semi-automatic; gas operated; hammerless; can also be operated as slide action
Magazine: 4- or 5-shot tubular
Barrel: Blued; 22"
Sights: Bead front, open rear
Stock & Forearm: Wood straight grip stock & slide handle
Approximate wt.: 7¾ lbs.
Comments: Made in the early 1900's, the Standard G was one of the first gas operated auto-loaders available.
Estimated Value: Excellent: $375.00
  Very good: $300.00

Standard Model M
A slide action version of the Standard G.
Estimated Value: Excellent: $275.00
  Very good: $220.00

Stevens

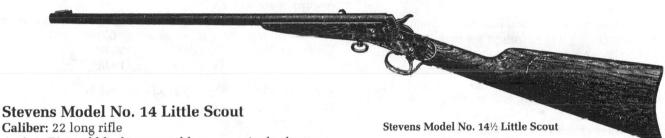
Stevens Model No. 14½ Little Scout

Stevens Model No. 14 Little Scout
Caliber: 22 long rifle
Action: Pivoted block; exposed hammer; single shot
Magazine: None
Barrel: 18" round
Sights: Flat front, open rear
Stock & Forearm: Plain walnut one-piece straight grip stock & forearm
Approximate wt.: 2½ lbs.
Comments: Made from 1904 to about 1912 when it was replaced by Model 14½.
Estimated Value: Excellent: $160.00
  Very good: $120.00

Standard Model No. 14½ Little Scout
Very similar to Model No. 14 except rolling block action & separated, short forearm. Produced from 1912 to World War II.
Estimated Value: Excellent: $150.00
  Very good: $115.00

Stevens Model No. 16½ Crack Shot

Stevens Model No. 15 Crack Shot
Caliber: 22 long rifle; 32 short
Action: Falling block; single shot; exposed hammer; lever action
Magazine: None
Barrel: 20" round
Sights: Open rear, blade front
Stock & Forearm: Plain walnut straight grip stock with slightly lipped forearm
Approximate wt.: 3¾ lbs.
Comments: Produced from the turn of the century until 1912 when it was replaced by the Model No. 26.
Estimated Value: Excellent: $250.00
  Very good: $200.00

Stevens Model No. 16½ Crack Shot
Same as No. 16 except it is smooth bore for shot cartridges. Produced from 1907 to 1912.
Estimated Value: Excellent: $240.00
  Very good: $190.00

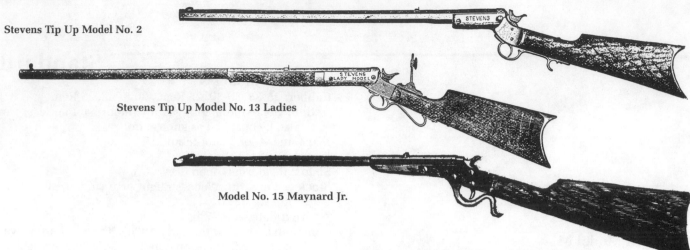

Stevens Tip Up Model No. 2

Stevens Tip Up Model No. 13 Ladies

Model No. 15 Maynard Jr.

Stevens Tip Up Model No. 2, 5, 6, 7, 8, 9, 11 Ladies & 13 Ladies

Caliber: RF 22 long rifles, 25 Stevens, 32 long (in #11)
Action: Single shot, tip up; exposed hammer
Magazine: None
Barrel: 24" octagon for #2; 28" half octagon optional on #7, all others 24" half octagon
Sights: Beach combination front, open rear; peep on #5, #7 & #13; blade front, open rear on #2; open on #11
Stock & Forearm: Walnut straight stock & forearm; no forearm on #2 & #5
Approximate wt.: 5½ to 6½ lbs.
Comments: This series replaced the 1888 & was produced until it was replaced in 1902 by a line of falling block rifles.
Estimated Value: Excellent: $250.00
   Very good: $190.00

Stevens Model No. 15 Maynard Jr.

Caliber: 22 long rifle or short
Action: Lever action; tip up; exposed hammer
Magazine: None
Barrel: 18" part octagon
Sights: Open rear, blade front
Stock & Forearm: Plain walnut, straight stock & short forearm
Approximate wt.: 2¾ lbs.
Comments: This small rifle was made to compete with cheap imports. Produced from 1901 to 1910.
Estimated Value: Excellent: $140.00
   Very good: $110.00

Stevens Model No. 15½ Maynard Jr.

This is the same as the No. 15 except it is smooth bore for 22 long rifle shot cartridges.
Estimated Value: Excellent: $135.00
   Very good: $100.00

Stevens Model No. 17 Favorite

Stevens Model No. 27 Favorite

Stevens Model No. 18

Stevens Tip Up Model No. 17 & 27 Favorite

Caliber: 22 long rifle, 25 RF, 32 RF
Action: Lever action; single shot; exposed hammer
Magazine: None
Barrel: 24" round (octagon barrel on Model 27); other lengths available as option
Sights: Open rear, Rocky Mountain front
Stock & Forearm: Plain walnut straight grip stock, short tapered forearm
Approximate wt.: 4 to 5 lbs.
Comments: Takedown model produced from the 1890's until the mid 1930's.
Estimated Value: Excellent: $165.00
   Very good: $130.00

Stevens Model No. 18 & 28 Favorite

Same as Model No. 17 except it has a Beach combination front sight, Vernier peep rear sight & leaf middle sight. Model 28 has octagon barrel.
Estimated Value: Excellent: $175.00
   Very good: $140.00

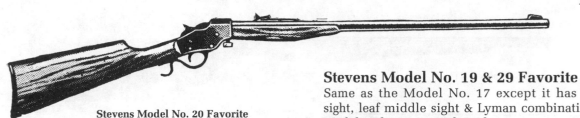

Stevens Model No. 20 Favorite

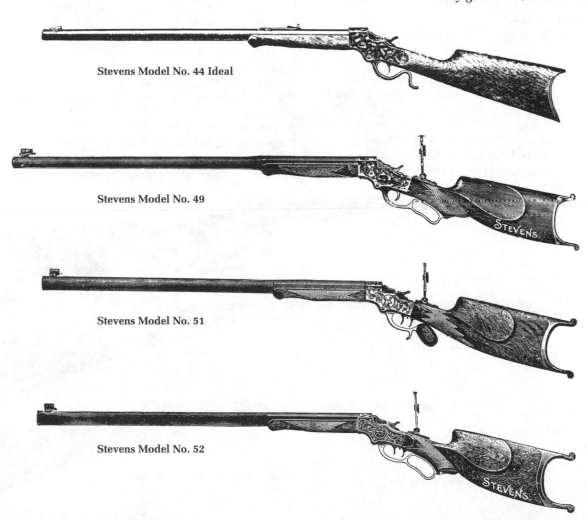

Stevens Model No. 44 Ideal

Stevens Model No. 49

Stevens Model No. 51

Stevens Model No. 52

Stevens Model No. 19 & 29 Favorite

Same as the Model No. 17 except it has Lyman front sight, leaf middle sight & Lyman combination rear sight. Model 29 has octagon barrel.

| Estimated Value: | Excellent: | $195.00 |
| | Very good: | $155.00 |

Stevens Model No. 20 Favorite

Same as the Model No. 17 except the barrel is smooth bore for 22 RF & 32 RF shot cartridges.

| Estimated Value: | Excellent: | $180.00 |
| | Very good: | $145.00 |

Stevens Model No. 44 Ideal

Caliber: 22 long rifle; 25 RF, 25-20 SS, 32-20, 32-40, 38-55, 44-40

Action: Lever action; rolling block; exposed hammer; single shot

Magazine: None

Barrel: 24" or 26" round, octagon or half-octagon

Sights: Open rear, Rocky Mountain front

Stock & Forearm: Plain walnut, straight grip

Approximate wt.: 7 lbs.

Comments: Produced from the late 1890's until the early 1930's; a takedown model.

| Estimated Value: | Excellent: | $360.00 |
| | Very good: | $285.00 |

Stevens Model No. 44½ Ideal

Same as the Model 44 except it has a falling block action. Discontinued in 1916.

| Estimated Value: | Excellent: | $450.00 |
| | Very good: | $360.00 |

Stevens Model No. 45 to 54

These rifles are structurally the same as the Model 44. They differ in engraving & finishes & are generally fancy models that bring extremely high prices. They were produced until World War I; target sights & stocks.

| Estimated Value: | Excellent: | $550.00 - $1,000.00 |
| | Very good: | $415.00 - $ 750.00 |

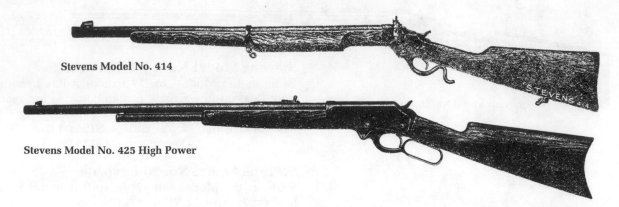

Stevens Model No. 414

Stevens Model No. 425 High Power

Stevens Model No. 414 Armory

Caliber: 22 long rifle or 22 short only
Action: Lever action; exposed hammer; rolling block
Magazine: None
Barrel: 26" heavy round
Sights: Rocky Mountain front, adjustable receiver rear
Stock & Forearm: Plain walnut straight grip, military stock & forearms; bands; swivels
Approximate wt.: 8 lbs.
Comments: Made from 1912 until the early 1930's.
Estimated Value: Excellent: $350.00
                        Very good: $260.00

Stevens Model No. 425 High Power

Caliber: Rimless Rem. 25, 30, 32, 35; smokeless flatnose
Action: Lever action; exposed hammer; single extractor
Magazine: 5-shot tubular, under barrel
Barrel: 22" round
Sights: Post front, adjustable sporting rear
Stock & Forearm: Plain walnut straight grip stock & forearm
Approximate wt.: 7 lbs.
Comments: Made for about five years beginning in 1911.
Estimated Value: Excellent: $250.00
                        Very good: $200.00

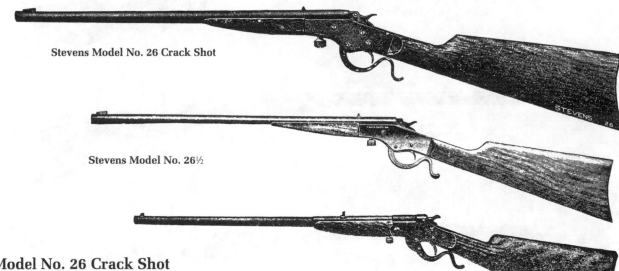

Stevens Model No. 26 Crack Shot

Stevens Model No. 26½

Stevens Model No. 12 Marksman

Stevens Model No. 26 Crack Shot

Caliber: 22 long rifle, 32 RF
Action: Lever action; exposed hammer; single shot
Magazine: None
Barrel: 18", 22"
Sights: Open rear, blade front
Stock & Forearm: Plain walnut straight grip stock & tapered forearm
Approximate wt.: 3¼ to 3½ lbs.
Comments: Takedown rifle produced from 1913 until just prior to World War II.
Estimated Value: Excellent: $160.00
                        Very good: $125.00

Stevens Model No. 26½

Same as the No. 26 except it is smooth bore for shot cartridges.
Estimated Value: Excellent: $150.00
                        Very good: $120.00

Stevens Model No. 12 Marksman

Caliber: 22 long rifle, 25 RF, 32 RF
Action: Lever action; tip up; exposed hammer; single shot
Magazine: None, single shot
Barrel: 20", round
Sights: Bead front, open rear
Stock & Forearm: Plain walnut straight grip stock & short tapered forearm
Approximate wt.: 4 lbs.
Comments: Replaced the Maynard Jr. Made from 1912 to 1916.
Estimated Value: Excellent: $145.00
                        Very good: $115.00

Stevens Model No. 417½

Stevens Model No. 417

Stevens Model No. 417-1

Stevens Model No. 417-2

Stevens Model No. 418

Stevens Model No. 418½

Stevens Model No. 417, 417½, 417-1, 417-2, 417-3 Walnut Hill

Caliber: 22 long rifle; 22 WRF, 25 Stevens
Action: Lever action; exposed hammer; single shot
Magazine: None
Barrel: 28" or 29" heavy
Sights: 417: Lyman 52L extension rear; 417½: Lyman 144 tang peep & folding center; 417-1: Lyman 48L rear; 417-2: 144 rear; 417-3: no sights
Stock & Forearm: Plain walnut pistol grip stock & forearm; bands, swivels
Approximate wt.: 8¼ to 10½ lbs.
Comments: Made from the early 1930's until the late 1940's. Models differ only in sights.
Estimated Value: Excellent: $500.00
Very good: $400.00

Stevens Model No. 418, 418½ Walnut Hill

Caliber: 418: 22 long rifle, 22 short only; 418½: 22 WRF or 25 Stevens RF only
Action: Lever action; exposed hammer; single shot
Magazine: None
Barrel: 26"
Sights: Lyman 144 tang peep, blade front; 418½: Lyman 2A tang peep, bead front
Stock & Forearm: Plain walnut pistol grip stock & forearm; swivels
Approximate wt.: 6½ lbs.
Comments: Made from the early 1930's to just before World War II.
Estimated Value: Excellent: $350.00
Very good: $280.00

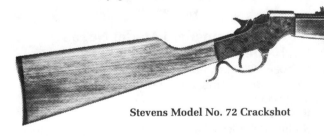

Stevens Model No. 72 Crackshot

Stevens Model No. 72 Crackshot

Caliber: 22 short, long, long rifle
Action: Lever action; falling block; single shot
Magazine: None
Barrel: 22" octagon
Sights: Sporting front, open rear
Stock & Forearm: Plain walnut straight grip stock & tapered forearm; case hardened receiver
Approximate wt.: 4½ lbs.
Comments: Made from the early 1970's to 1988.
Estimated Value: Excellent: $110.00
Very good: $ 80.00

Stevens Model No. 89

Stevens Model No. 65

Stevens - Springfield Model No. 51 Reliance

Stevens - Springfield Model No. 52 Challenge

Stevens - Springfield Model No. 53 Springfield Jr.

Stevens Model No. 89

Caliber: 22 short, long, long rifle
Action: Lever action; exposed hammer; single shot; automatic ejection
Magazine: None
Barrel: 18½"
Sights: Sporting front, open rear
Stock & Forearm: Straight walnut stock & forearm with carbine band
Approximate wt.: 5 lbs.
Comments: Produced from mid 1970's to mid 1980's.
Estimated Value: Excellent: $70.00
Very good: $55.00

Stevens Model No. 65 Little Krag

Caliber: 22 short, long, long rifle
Action: Bolt action; single shot
Magazine: None
Barrel: 20" round
Sights: Bead front, fixed peep or open rear
Stock & Forearm: Plain walnut one-piece straight grip stock & forearm
Approximate wt.: 3¼ bs.
Comments: This small 22 rifle was produced from 1903 until about 1910.
Estimated Value: Excellent: $135.00
Very good: $105.00

Stevens - Springfield Model No. 52 Challenge

Caliber: 22 short, long, long rifle
Action: Bolt action; single shot
Magazine: None
Barrel: 22" round
Sights: Bead front, adjustable sporting rear
Stock & Forearm: Plain walnut one-piece pistol grip stock & forearm
Approximate wt.: 3½ lbs.
Comments: Takedown, produced from early 1930's to just before World War II.
Estimated Value: Excellent: $65.00
Very good: $55.00

Stevens - Springfield Model No. 51 Reliance

Caliber: 22 short, long, long rifle
Action: Bolt action; single shot
Magazine: None
Barrel: 20" round
Sights: Open rear, blade front
Stock & Forearm: Plain walnut one-piece straight grip stock & forearm
Approximate wt.: 3 lbs.
Comments: Takedown, made from 1930 for about five years.
Estimated Value: Excellent: $75.00
Very good: $55.00

Stevens - Springfield Model No. 53 Springfield Jr.

Caliber: 22 short, long, long rifle
Action: Bolt action; single shot
Magazine: None
Barrel: 24"
Sights: Bead front, adjustable sporting rear
Stock & Forearm: Plain walnut semi-pistol grip stock & forearm
Approximate wt.: 4½ lbs.
Comments: Takedown produced from 1930 until shortly after World War II.
Estimated Value: Excellent: $60.00
Very good: $50.00

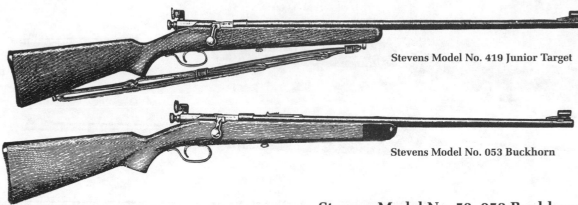

Stevens Model No. 419 Junior Target

Stevens Model No. 053 Buckhorn

Stevens Model No. 419 Junior Target

Caliber: 22 short, long, long rifle
Action: Bolt action; single shot
Magazine: None
Barrel: 26"
Sights: Blade front, peep rear
Stock & Forearm: Plain walnut pistol grip stock with grooved forearm; swivels
Approximate wt.: 5½ lbs.
Comments: Made from 1932 until 1936.
Estimated Value: Excellent: $90.00
Very good: $70.00

Stevens Model No. 53, 053 Buckhorn

Caliber: 22 short, long, long rifle
Action: Bolt action; single shot
Magazine: None
Barrel: 24"
Sights: 053: hooded ramp front, open middle peep receiver; 53: open rear, bead front
Stock & Forearm: Plain walnut pistol grip stock & forearm
Approximate wt.: 5½ lbs.
Comments: A takedown rifle made from the mid 1930's until the late 1940's.
Estimated Value: Excellent: $80.00
Very good: $65.00

Stevens Model No. 66 Buckhorn

Stevens Model No. 066 Buckhorn

Stevens Model No. 056 Buckhorn

Stevens Model No. 56 & 056 Buckhorn

Caliber: 22 short, long, long rifle
Action: Bolt action; repeating
Magazine: 5-shot clip
Barrel: 24"
Sights: 56: bead front, open rear; 056: hooded ramp front, open middle receiver peep
Stock & Forearm: Plain walnut pistol grip stock & black tipped forearm
Approximate wt.: 6 lbs.
Comments: Takedown made from mid 1930's to late 1940's.
Estimated Value: Excellent: $85.00
Very good: $65.00

Stevens Model No. 66 Buckhorn

Caliber: 22 short, long, long rifle
Action: Bolt action; repeating
Magazine: Tubular, 19 shorts, 15 longs, 13 long rifles
Barrel: 24"
Sights: Open rear, bead front
Stock & Forearm: Plain walnut semi-pistol grip stock & forearm
Approximate wt.: 5 lbs.
Comments: A takedown rifle made from the 1920's until after the World War I.
Estimated Value: Excellent: $90.00
Very good: $70.00

Stevens Model No. 066 Buckhorn

Same as the Model No. 66 except: hooded ramp front sight; open middle sight; receiver peep sight. Made from mid 1930's until late 1940's.
Estimated Value: Excellent: $95.00
Very good: $75.00

Stevens - Springfield Model No. 82

Stevens - Springfield Model No. 83

Stevens - Springfield Model No. 84

Stevens - Springfield Model No. 084

Stevens - Springfield Model No. 86

Stevens - Springfield Model No. 086

Stevens - Springfield Model No. 82

Caliber: 22 short, long, long rifle
Action: Bolt action; single shot
Magazine: None
Barrel: 22"
Sights: Open rear, bead front
Stock & Forearm: Plain walnut pistol grip stock, groove in forearm
Approximate wt.: 4 lbs.
Comments: Takedown made from middle 1930's until 1940.
Estimated Value: Excellent: $75.00
　　　　　　　　　　Very good: $60.00

Stevens - Springfield Model No. 83

Caliber: 22 short, long, long rifle, 22 WRF, 25 Stevens RF
Action: Bolt action; single shot
Magazine: None
Barrel: 24"
Sights: Peep rear, open middle, hooded ramp front
Stock & Forearm: Plain walnut pistol grip stock with groove in forearm
Approximate wt.: 4½ bs.
Comments: Takedown made from middle 1930's until 1940.
Estimated Value: Excellent: $85.00
　　　　　　　　　　Very good: $65.00

Stevens - Springfield Model No. 84 & 084
(Stevens Model No. 84 after 1948)

Caliber: 22 short, long, long rifle
Action: Bolt action; repeating
Magazine: 5-shot clip
Barrel: 24"
Sights: 84: bead front, open rear; 84 Stevens or 084 peep rear & hooded ramp front
Stock & Forearm: Plain walnut pistol grip stock & forearm; black tip on forearm of Model 84
Approximate wt.: 6 lbs.
Comments: Takedown made from early 1940 until the mid 1960's.
Estimated Value: Excellent: $90.00
　　　　　　　　　　Very good: $70.00

Stevens - Springfield Model No. 86, 086
(Stevens Model No. 86 after 1948)

Model 86 is same as Model 84 except it has a tubular magazine that holds 21 shorts, 17 longs, 15 long rifles. Made from mid 1930's until mid 1960's. Model 86 Stevens or 086 Stevens is same as 084 or 84 Stevens except it has tubular magazine.
Estimated Value: Excellent: $100.00
　　　　　　　　　　Very good: $ 80.00

Stevens Model No. 416

Stevens - Springfield Model No. 15

Stevens - Springfield Model No. 15Y

Stevens Model No. 322

Stevens Model No. 416
Caliber: 22 long rifle
Action: Bolt action; repeating
Magazine: 5-shot clip
Barrel: 26" heavy
Sights: Receiver peep, hooded ramp front
Stock & Forearm: Plain walnut pistol grip stock & forearm
Approximate wt.: 9½ lbs.
Comments: Made from the late 1930's to late 1940's.
Estimated Value: Excellent: $160.00
  Very good: $120.00

Stevens - Springfield Model No. 15, Stevens 15, 15Y
Caliber: 22 short, long, long rifle
Action: Bolt action; single shot
Magazine: None
Barrel: Stevens-Springfield 22"; Stevens 15, 24"; Stevens 15Y, 21"
Sights: Open rear, bead front
Stock & Forearm: Plain walnut pistol grip, 15Y; short butt stock, black tipped forearm
Approximate wt.: 4 to 5 lbs.
Comments: Manufactured: Stevens-Springfield 25, late 1930's to late 1940's; Stevens 15, late 1940's to mid 1960's; Stevens 15Y, late 1950's to mid 1960's.
Estimated Value: Excellent: $70.00
  Very good: $55.00

Stevens Model No. 322, 322S
Caliber: 22 Hornet
Action: Bolt action; repeating
Magazine: 5-shot clip
Barrel: 21"
Sights: Ramp front, open rear; 322S has peep rear
Stock & Forearm: Plain walnut pistol grip stock & forearm
Approximate wt.: 6¾ lbs.
Comments: Made from the late 1940's to early 1950's.
Estimated Value: Excellent: $125.00
  Very good: $100.00

Stevens Model No. 325, 325S
Caliber: 30-30
Action: Bolt action; repeating
Magazine: 3-shot clip
Barrel: 21"
Sights: Open rear, bead front; 325S peep rear
Stock & Forearm: Plain walnut pistol grip stock & forearm
Approximate wt.: 6¾ lbs.
Comments: Made from the late 1940's to early 1950's.
Estimated Value: Excellent: $120.00
  Very good: $ 95.00

Stevens Model No. 34

Stevens Model No. 46

Stevens Model 120

Stevens Model 120

Caliber: 22 short, long, long rifle
Action: Bolt action; single shot; cocking piece
Magazine: None
Barrel: Blued; 24"
Sights: Blade front, elevator open rear
Stock & Forearm: Plain hardwood one-piece semi-pistol
  grip stock & forearm
Approximate wt.: 5 lbs.
Comments: Produced in the late 1970's.
Estimated Value: Excellent: $65.00
  Very good: $55.00

Stevens Model No. 34

Caliber: 22 short, long, long rifle
Action: Bolt action; repeating
Magazine: 5-shot clip
Barrel: 20"
Sights: Sporting front, open rear
Stock & Forearm: Plain walnut pistol grip before 1969;
  checkered Monte Carlo after 1969
Approximate wt.: 5½ lbs.
Comments: Made from mid 1960's to early 1980's.
Estimated Value: Excellent: $80.00
  Very good: $65.00

Stevens Model No 46

Similar to Model 34 except with tubular magazine. Discontinued in late 1960's.
Estimated Value: Excellent: $85.00
  Very good: $70.00

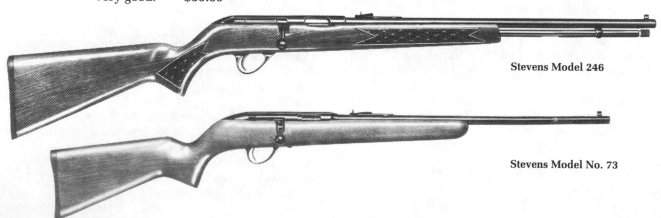

Stevens Model 246

Stevens Model No. 73

Stevens Model 246

Caliber: 22 short, long, long rifle
Action: Bolt action; repeating
Magazine: Tubular, 22 shorts, 17 longs, 15 long rifles
Barrel: Blued; 20"
Sights: Blade front, elevator open rear
Stock & Forearm: Checkered hardwood one-piece semi-
  pistol grip stock & forearm
Approximate wt.: 5 lbs.
Comments: Produced in the late 1970's.
Estimated Value: Excellent: $90.00
  Very good: $75.00

Stevens Model No. 73, 73Y

Caliber: 22 short, long, long rifle
Action: Bolt action; single shot
Magazine: None
Barrel: 20" on 73; 18" on 73Y
Sights: Sporting front, open rear
Stock & Forearm: Plain walnut pistol grip; short stock on
  73Y
Approximate wt.: 73 - 4¾ lbs.; 73Y - 4½ lbs.
Comments: Made from 1965 to early 1980's.
Estimated Value: Excellent: $70.00
  Very good: $55.00

Stevens Model 110E

Stevens Model 35, 35M

Stevens Model 110E, 110ES

Caliber: 243, 30-06, 308
Action: Bolt action; hammerless; repeating
Magazine: 4-shot box, internal
Barrel: Blued; 22"
Sights: Ramp front, open rear; 110ES has 4X scope
Stock & Forearm: Checkered hardwood one-piece Monte Carlo semi-pistol grip stock & forearm
Approximate wt.: 7 lbs.
Comments: Made from the late 1970's to 1981 as Stevens. Merchandised in 1982 as Savage. Add $20.00 for 110ES scope.
Estimated Value: Excellent: $240.00
                         Very good: $190.00

Stevens Model 35, 35M

Caliber: 22 short, long, long rifle
Action: Bolt action; repeating
Magazine: 4-shot detachable clip
Barrel: Blued; 22"
Sights: Ramp front, sporting rear with step elevator; grooved for scope
Stock & Forearm: Checkered hardwood Monte Carlo one-piece semi-pistol grip stock & forearm
Approximate wt.: 4¾ lbs.
Comments: Produced from 1982 to 1985.
Estimated Value: Excellent: $85.00
                         Very good: $65.00

Stevens Model 982

Stevens Model 125

Stevens Model 125

Caliber: 22 short, long, long rifle
Action: Bolt action; single shot; thumb pull hammer
Magazine: None
Barrel: Blued; 22"
Sights: Sporting front, open rear with elevator
Stock & Forearm: Checkered hardwood one-piece semi-pistol grip stock & forearm
Approximate wt.: 5 lbs.
Comments: Discontinued in mid 1980's.
Estimated Value: Excellent: $70.00
                         Very good: $55.00

Stevens Model 125Y

A youth version of the Model 125 with shorter stock. Discontinued in the early 1980's.
Estimated Value: Excellent: $65.00
                         Very good: $50.00

Stevens Model 982

Caliber: 22 short, long, long rifle
Action: Bolt action; repeating
Magazine: 5-shot detachable clip; 10-shot available
Barrel: Blued; 22"
Sights: Ramp front, open rear with elevator
Stock & Forearm: Checkered hardwood one-piece Monte Carlo seim-pistol grip stock & forearm
Approximate wt.: 5¾ lbs.
Comments: Advertised in 1981 only.
Estimated Value: Excellent: $85.00
                         Very good: $65.00

Stevens Model 36

Caliber: 22 short, long, long rifle
Action: Bolt action; hammerless, single shot
Magazine: None, single shot
Barrel: 22"
Sights: Open rear, blade front
Stock & Forearm: Hardwood, one-piece semi-pistol grip stock & forearm
Approximate wt.: 5 lbs.
Comments: Introduced in 1984 & advertised as a good choice for a first rifle. Discontinued in 1985.
Estimated Value: Excellent: $75.00
                         Very good: $60.00

Stevens Model No. 70 Visible Loading

Stevens Model No. 71 Visible Loading

Stevens Model No. 80 Repeating Gallery

Stevens Model No. 75 Hammerless

Stevens Model No. 70 Visible Loading

Caliber: 22 short, long, long rifle
Action: Slide action; exposed hammer
Magazine: Tubular; 11 long rifles, 13 longs, 15 longs
Barrel: 20", 22"; round
Sights: Open rear, bead front
Stock & Forearm: Plain walnut straight grip stock & grooved slide handle
Approximate wt.: 4½ lbs.
Comments: Made from 1907 until the early 1930's.
Estimated Value: **Excellent:** $220.00
                    Very good: $175.00

Stevens Model No. 71 Visible Loading

Caliber: 22 short, long, long rifle
Action: Slide action; exposed hammer
Magazine: Tubular; 15 shorts, 13 longs, 11 long rifles
Barrel: 24" octagon
Sights: Bead front, adjustable flat-top sporting rear
Stock & Forearm: Plain walnut pistol grip stock & grooved slide handle
Approximate wt.: 5 lbs.
Comments: This replaced the No. 70; discontinued prior to World War II.
Estimated Value: **Excellent:** $215.00
                    Very good: $170.00

Stevens Model No. 75 Hammerless

Caliber: 22 short, long, long rifle
Action: Slide action; hammerless; side ejection
Magazine: Tubular, 20 shorts, 17 longs, 15 long rifles
Barrel: 24"
Sights: Bead front, adjustable rear
Stock & Forearm: Plain walnut, straight grip stock & grooved slide handle
Approximate wt.: 5¼ lbs.
Comments: Made from the early 1930's until World War II.
Estimated Value: **Excellent:** $220.00
                    Very good: $175.00

Stevens Model No. 80 Repeating Gallery

Caliber: 22 short
Action: Slide action; hammerless
Magazine: 16-shot tubular
Barrel: 24" round
Sights: Open rear, bead front
Stock & Forearm: Plain walnut straight grip stock & grooved forearm
Approximate wt.: 5¼ lbs.
Comments: Takedown made for about five years beginning in 1906.
Estimated Value: **Excellent:** $250.00
                    Very good: $200.00

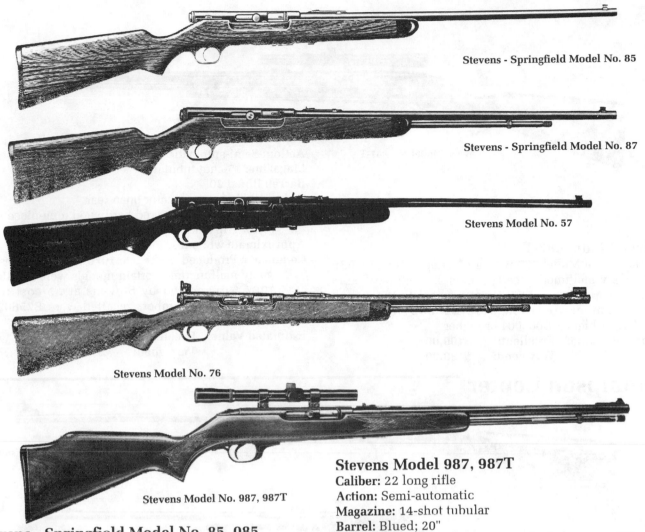

Stevens - Springfield Model No. 85

Stevens - Springfield Model No. 87

Stevens Model No. 57

Stevens Model No. 76

Stevens Model No. 987, 987T

Stevens - Springfield Model No. 85, 085 (Stevens Model No. 85 after 1948)

Caliber: 22 long rifle

Action: Semi-automatic; repeating

Magazine: 5-shot clip

Barrel: 24"

Sights: Open rear, bead front on 85; hooded ramp front & peep rear on 085 & 85 Stevens

Stock & Forearm: Plain walnut pistol grip stock & forearm; 85 has black tipped forearm

Approximate wt.: 6 lbs.

Comments: Produced from the late 1930's until after World War II.

Estimated Value: New (retail): $110.00
Excellent: $ 90.00
Very good: $500.00

Stevens - Springfield Model No. 87, 087 (Stevens Model 87 after 1948)

Same as the No. 85, 085 except it has a 15-shot tubular magazine.

Estimated Value: Excellent: $120.00
Very good: $ 95.00

Stevens Model No. 87 K Scout

Carbine version of Model No. 87; 20" barrel; produced until 1969.

Estimated Value: Excellent: $100.00
Very good: $ 80.00

Stevens Model 987, 987T

Caliber: 22 long rifle

Action: Semi-automatic

Magazine: 14-shot tubular

Barrel: Blued; 20"

Sights: Ramp front, open rear with elevator; 987T has 4X scope

Stock & Forearm: Checkered hardwood, one-piece semi-pistol grip Monte Carlo stock & forearm

Approximate wt.: 6 lbs.

Comments: Produced from 1981 to 1988. Add $10.00 for scope (987T).

Estimated Value: Excellent: $90.00
Very good: $70.00

Stevens Model No. 57, 057

Caliber: 22 long rifle

Action: Semi-automatic; repeating

Magazine: 5-shot clip

Barrel: 24"

Sights: Open rear, bead front on 57; hooded ramp front, open middle, receiver peep on 057

Stock & Forearm: Plain walnut pistol grip stock & gorearm; black tipped forearm on 57

Approximate wt.: 6 lbs.

Comments: Made from late 1930's to late 1940's.

Estimated Value: Excellent: $100.00
Very good: $ 80.00

Stevens Model No. 76, 076

Same as 057 & 57 except with 15-shot tubular magazine.

Estimated Value: Excellent: $110.00
Very good: $ 90.00

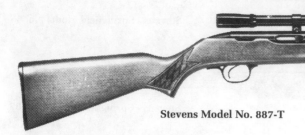

Stevens Model No. 887-T

Stevens Model 887

Caliber: 22 long rifle
Action: Semi-automatic
Magazine: 15-shot tubular
Barrel: Blued 20"
Sights: Blade front, elevator open rear
Stock & Forearm: Checkered hardwood, one-piece semi-
    pistol grip stock & forearm
Approximate wt.: 6 lbs.
Comments: Produced in the late 1970's. Due to a possible
    safety malfunction, certain models were recalled in
    1982 & inspected by Stevens at no cost to the
    owner. Serial numbers recalled were B256621 or
    higher; c000001 or higher; D000001 or higher.

Estimated Value:	Excellent:	$90.00
	Very good:	$70.00

Steven Model 887-T

Similar to the Model 887 with a 4X scope. Due to a possible safety malfunction certain models were recalled in 1982 & inspected by Stevens at no cost to the owner. Serial numbers recalled were B256621 or higher; C000001 or higher; D000001 or higher.

Estimated Value:	Excellent:	$100.00
	Very good:	$ 80.00

Thompson Center

Thompson Center Model TCR 83 Aristocrat

Thompson Center Contender Carbine

Thompson Center Contender Carbine

Caliber: 22 long rifle, 22 Hornet, 222 Rem., 223 Rem.,
    7mm TCU, 7x30 Waters, 30-30 Win., 35 Rem., 357
    Rem. maximum , Added 44 magnum & 410 gauge in
    1987
Action: Single shot, frame accommodates any caliber
    interchangeable barrel, hammer adjusts
Magazine: None, single shot
Barrel: Interchangeable to select caliber; 21" barrels
Sights: Adjustable; tapped for scope mounts
Stock & Forearm: Walnut or all weather Rynite, pistol
    grip stock & forearm; recoil pad.
Approximate wt.: 5¼ lbs.
Comments: A shooting system introduced in 1986. Based
    on the design of the popular Contender handgun.
    Add 48% for each additional barrel. Add 5% for
    ventilated rib. Deduct 8% for all weather Tynite
    stock & forearm.

Estimated Value:	New (retail):	$385.00
	Excellent:	$290.00
	Very good:	$230.00

Thompson Center Model TCR '83 Hunter

Caliber: 22 Hornet, 222 Rem., 223 Rem., 22-250 Rem.,
    243 Win., 270 Win., 7mm Rem. magnum, 308 Win.,
    30-06 Springfield; caliber can be selected by replac-
    ing different caliber barrel; also 12 gauge
Action: Top lever, break-open; single shot; hammerless
Magazine: None
Barrel: Interchangeable to select caliber; 23" & 25" bar-
    rels
Sights: Ramp front, folding leaf rear.
Stock & Forearm: Checkered walnut semi-pistol grip
    stock & forearm; cheekpiece; recoil pad
Approximate wt.: 6¾ lbs.
Comments: Introduced in 1983. Add 30% for each addi-
    tional barrel. Replaced by model TCR '87 Hunter in
    1987.

Estimated Value:	Excellent:	$310.00
	Very good:	$250.00

Thompson Center Model TCR 83 Aristocrat

Similar to the TCR '83 Hunter with checkered forearm & stainless steel, adjustable double set triggers. Discontinued in 1987.

Estimated Value:	Excellent:	$355.00
	Very good:	$265.00

Thompson Center Youth Model Carbine
Caliber: 22 long rifle, 22 Win. magnum, 223 Rem., 7x30 Waters, 30-30 Win., 35 Rem., 44 magnum, 45 Colt/410 gauge. The 45 Colt rifled barrel is used for 410 gauge when a detachable internal choke is screwed into the muzzle
Action: Single shot, frame accommodates any caliber interchangeable barrel, hammer adjusts for caliber
Magazine: None, single shot
Barrel: Interchangeable to select caliber; 16¼" barrel; 45/410 barrel has ventilated rib
Sights: Adjustable; tapped for scope mounts; 45/410 barrel has fixed rear sight & bead front.
Stock & Forearm: 12" length of pull, walnut or all weather Rynite®, pistol grip stock & forearm; recoil pad
Approximate wt.: 4½ lbs.
Comments: Introduced in 1989. Add 7% for 45/410 Model; deduct 5% for all weather Rynite® stock.

Estimated Value:	New (retail):	$355.00
	Excellent:	$265.00
	Very good:	$215.00

Thompson Center Model TCR '87 Hunter
Caliber: 22 Hornet, 222 Rem., 223 Rem., 22-250 Rem., 243 Win., 270 Win., 7mm/08, 308 Win., 30-06 Springfield, 32-40 Win., also 12 gauge rifled slug barrel (1989), 12 gauge shotgun barrel (1988) & 10 gauge shotgun barrel (1988)
Action: Top lever, break-open; single shot hammerless; adjustable single trigger
Magazine: None, single shot
Barrel: Interchangeable to select caliber or gauge; 23" light sporter barrel; 25⅞" medium sporter barrel; 25" shotgun barrel; 22" rifled slug barrel
Sights: None; drilled & tapped for scope mounts; rifled slug barrel has adjustable iron sights; shotgun barrel has bead front sight
Stock & Forearm: Checkered walnut semi-pistol grip stock & grooved forearm; recoil pad; studs for swivels
Approximate wt.: 6¾ lbs. (light sporter barrel); 7¼ lbs. (medium sporter barrel); 8 lbs. (shotgun barrel
Comments: Introduced in 1987 to replace the TCR '83.

Estimated Value:	New (retail):	$495.00
	Excellent:	$370.00
	Very good:	$300.00

Thompson Center Model TCR '87 Hunter

Universal

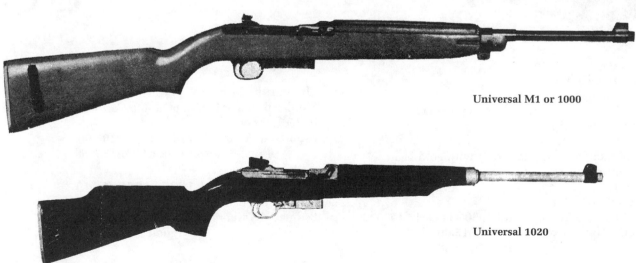

Universal M1 or 1000

Universal 1020

Universal M1 or 1000, 1003
Similar to the U.S. M1 Carbine with a 5-shot detachable clip. Made in 30 caliber from the mid 1960's to present. Add $50.00 for scope & detachable mount. See also Iver Johnson.

Estimated Value:	Excellent:	$180.00
	Very good:	$145.00

Universal 1020, 1020 TB, 1020 TCO, 1030
Similar to the 1000 with a Monte Carlo stock & a water resistant teflon finish in green, blue, tan, black or gray. Currently produced as 1020 TB (black) & 1020 TCO (green), 1030 (gray).

Estimated Value:	Excellent:	$225.00
	Very good:	$180.00

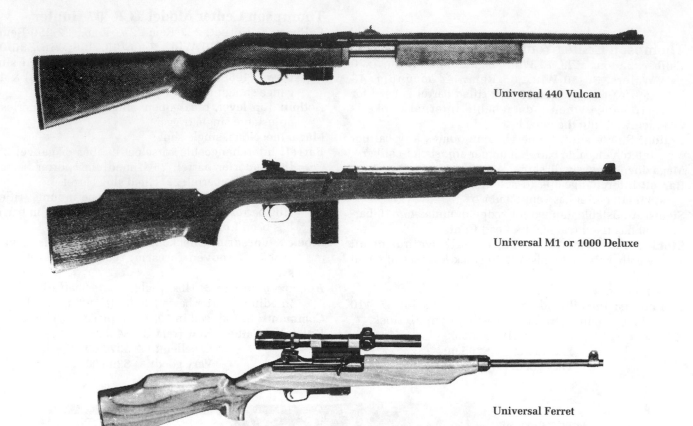

Universal 440 Vulcan

Universal M1 or 1000 Deluxe

Universal Ferret

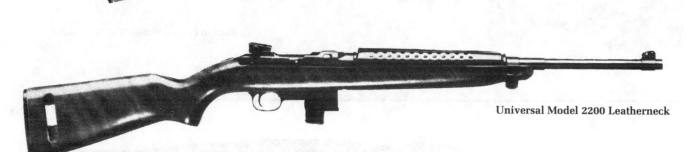

Universal Model 2200 Leatherneck

Universal 440 Vulcan

Caliber: 44 magnum
Action: Slide action; hammerless; repeating
Magazine: 5-shot clip
Barrel: 18¼" carbine
Sights: Adjustable rear, ramp front with gold bead
Stock & Forearm: Walnut semi-pistol grip stock & slide handle
Approximate wt.: 6 lbs.
Comments: Made from the mid 1960's to early 1970's.
Estimated Value: Excellent: $215.00
Very good: $170.00

Universal M1 or 1000 Deluxe, 1005 SB, 1010N, 1015G, 1011

Same as the 1000 with a Monte Carlo stock; also available in nickel, gold plate or chrome.
Estimated Value:

	1005SB Blue	1010N Nickel	1015G Gold	1011 Chrome
Excellent:	$175.00	$190.00	$230.00	$185.00
Very good:	$140.00	$150.00	$185.00	$145.00

Universal Ferret

Similar to the M1 with a Monte Carlo stock, no sights, & in 256 caliber.
Estimated Value: Excellent: $195.00
Very good: $155.00

Universal Model 1035, 1040, 1045

Similar to the Model 1020 with a military stock.
Estimated Value: Excellent: $210.00
Very good: $165.00

Universal Model 1006

Similar to the Model 1005SB with stainless steel finish.
Estimated Value: Excellent: $220.00
Very good: $175.00

Universal Model 2200 Leatherneck

Similar to the Model 1003 in 22 caliber. Produced from the early 1980's to mid 1980's.
Estimated Value: Excellent: $185.00
Very good: $150.00

Valmet

Valmet Model 412 K Double

Valmet Finnish Lion

Valmet Model M-71S

Valmet 412KE Double & 412SE double

Similar to the Model 412K Double with automatic ejectors. Introduced in early 1980's. Calibers 375 Win. & 9.3x74 only. Discontinued late 1980's.

Estimated Value:	Excellent:	$900.00
	Very good:	$720.00

Valmet Finnish Lion

Caliber: 22 long rifle
Action: Bolt action; single shot
Magazine: None
Barrel: Blued, 29", heavy
Sights: Extended peep rear, changeable front
Stock & Forearm: Free-rifle, pistol grip, with thumb hole, one-piece stock & forearm; palm rest; swivels; Swiss buttplate
Approximate wt.: 15 lbs.
Comments: International Match-type rifle; discontinued in the late 1970's.

Estimated Value:	Excellent:	$625.00
	Very good:	$500.00

Valmet Model 412K, & 412S (mid 1980's) Double

Caliber: 243, 308, 30-06
Action: Top lever, break-open, hammerless; extractors
Magazine: None
Barrel: Over & under double barrel; 24" with space between barrels
Sights: Open rear, blade front; drilled for scope
Stock & Forearm: Checkered walnut Monte Carlo pistol grip stock & forearm; recoil pad; swivels
Approximate wt.: 6½ lbs.
Comments: A double rifle produced in Finland as part of the 412 Shotgun Combination series.

Estimated Value:	New (retail):	$1,205.00
	Excellent:	$ 900.00
	Very good:	$ 720.00

Valmet Model M-72S, M-715S, m-71S

Caliber: 223 (5.56mm)
Action: Semi- automatic, gas operated
Magazine: 15-or 30-shot, curved detachable box
Barrel: 16½"
Sights: Open tangent rear, hooded post front; both adjustable
Stock & Forearm: Wood or reinforced resin stock; pistol grip; swivels; wood stock & forearm & plastic pistol grip on Model M-71S
Approximate wt.: 8¾ lbs.
Comments: Similar to the M-62/S.

Estimated Value:	Excellent:	$650.00
	Very good:	$485.00

Valmet Model M-62 S

Caliber: 7.62 x 39mm Russian
Action: Semi-automatic; gas piston, rotating bolt
Magazine: 15- or 30-shot, curved detachable box
Barrel: 16½"
Sights: Adjustable tangent peep rear, adjustable hooded post front
Stock & Forearm: Fixed metal tube or walnut stock; pistol grip; ventilated forearm
Approximate wt.: 8¾ lbs.
Comments: A powerful semi-automatic made in the mid 1970's. Add $15.00 for wood stock version.

Estimated Value:	Excellent:	$600.00
	Very good:	$450.00

Valmet Hunter

Similar to the Model 76 redesigned for hunting. Available in calibers: 223, 243, 30-06 or 308; 5-, 9-, 15- or 30-shot clip. Checkered wood pistol grip stock & forearm.

Estimated Value: **New (retail):** **$795.00**
Excellent: **$595.00**
Very good: **$477.00**

Valmet Model M76 Military

Caliber: 223, 308, 7.62x39
Action: Gas operated, semi-automatic, rotating bolt
Magazine: 15- or 30-shot clip
Barrel: 16¾"or 20½"
Sights: Front adjustable in tunnel guard, folding leaf with peep rear; night sight
Stock & Forearm: Wood, synthetic or folding stock, checkered plastic pistol grip & forearm
Approximate wt.: 8 lbs.
Comments: Standard model has wood stock. Add 14% for synthetic stock; 16% for folding stock
Estimated Value: **New (retail):** **$699.00**
Excellent: **$525.00**
Very good: **$420.00**

Walther

Walther Model KKJ

Walther Model KKM

Walther Model KKJ

Caliber: 22 Hornet, 22 long rifle, 22 WRM
Action: Bolt action; repeating; double set trigger available
Magazine: 5-shot detachable clip
Barrel: Blued; 22½"
Sights: Adjustable rear, hooded ramp front
Stock & Forearm: Checkered walnut pistol grip stock & forearm; cheekpiece; swivels
Approximate wt.: 5½ lbs.
Comments: Made from about 1957 to late 1970's. Add $20.00 for double set trigger.
Estimated Value: **Excellent:** **$475.00**
Very good: **$380.00**

Walther Model KKM

Caliber: 22 long rifle
Action: Bolt action; single shot
Magazine: None
Barrel: Blued; 28" tapered
Sights: Olympic front, changeable micro adjustable rear
Stock & Forearm: Walnut match-style with thumb hole; adjustable buttplate; heavy forearm with hand shelf; cheekpiece
Approximate wt.: 15 lbs.
Comments: A match rifle made from the 1950's to late 1970's.
Estimated Value: **Excellent:** **$700.00**
Very good: **$560.00**

Walther Moving Target

Caliber: 22 long rifle
Action: Bolt action; single shot
Magazine: None
Barrel: Blued; 23½"
Sights: Micro adjustable rear, globe front
Stock & Forearm: Walnut, pistol grip, thumb hole, match-type with adjustable cheekpiece & buttplate
Approximate wt.: 8¼ lbs.
Comments: A match rifle made in 1970's.
Estimated Value: **Excellent:** **$625.00**
Very good: **$470.00**

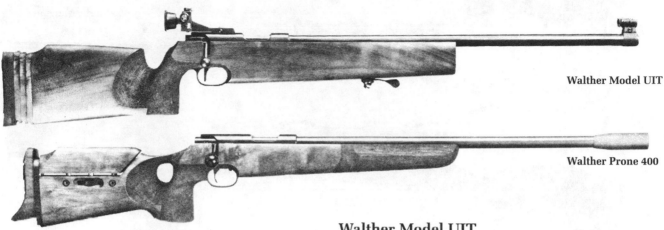

Walther Model UIT

Walther Prone 400

Walther Model UIT

Caliber: 22 long rifle
Action: Bolt action; single shot
Magazine: None
Barrel: 25½"
Sights: Changeable front, micro adjustable rear
Stock & Forearm: Match-style, walnut pistol grip stock & wide forearm
Approximate wt.: 10¼ lbs.
Comments: A match rifle made from the mid 1960's. Super & Special match models still produced.
Estimated Value: **Excellent:** $650.00
        Very good: $520.00

Walther Prone 400

Similar to the UIT with split stock & adjustable cheekpiece; thumb hole; no sights.
Estimated Value: **Excellent:** $540.00
        Very good: $440.00

Weatherby

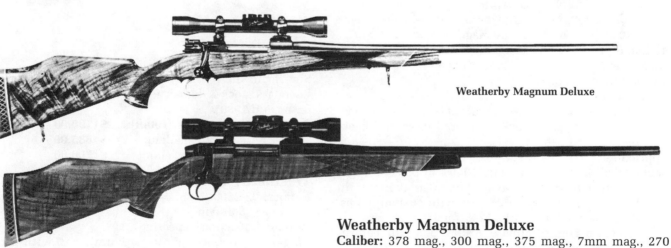

Weatherby Magnum Deluxe

Weatherby Deluxe

Weatherby Magnum Deluxe

Caliber: 378 mag., 300 mag., 375 mag., 7mm mag., 270 mag., 257 mag., 220 Rocket
Action: Bolt action; Mauser-type
Magazine: 3-shot
Barrel: Blued; 24"; 26" available on some calibers
Sights: None
Stock & Forearm: Checkered wood Monte Carlo one-piece pistol grip stock & tapered forearm; recoil pad; swivels; cheekpiece
Approximate wt.: 7 to 8 lbs.
Comments: Made from the late 1940's to the late 1950's.
Estimated Value: **Excellent:** $625.00
        Very good: $500.00

Weatherby Deluxe

Similar to the Magnum Deluxe but in 270 Win. and 30-06 calibers.
Estimated Value: **Excellent:** $500.00
        Very good: $400.00

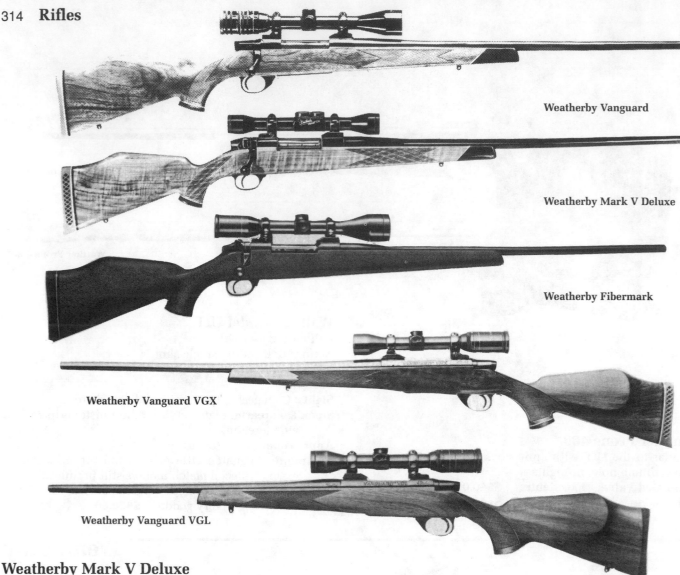

Weatherby Vanguard

Weatherby Mark V Deluxe

Weatherby Fibermark

Weatherby Vanguard VGX

Weatherby Vanguard VGL

Weatherby Mark V Deluxe

Caliber: 240, 257, 270, 7mm, 30-06, 300 Weatherby mag., 340 mag., 378 Weatherby mag., 460 Weatherby mag.

Action: Bolt action; repeating

Magazine: 2-, 3-, or 4-shot, depending on caliber

Barrel: Blued; 24" or 26"

Sights: None

Stock & Forearm: Checkered walnut Monte Carlo one-piece pistol grip stock & tapered forearm; cheekpiece; recoil pad; swivels

Approximate wt.: 7¼ to 10½ lbs.

Comments: Made from the late 1950's to present. Right or left hand models available. Also available in Euromark & Lazermark series with custom extras. Add 5% for Euromark; 12% for Lazermark; 2½% for 340 magnum caliber; 18% for 378 Win. caliber; 32% for 460 magnum caliber.

Estimated Value:	New (retail):	$1020.00
	Excellent:	$ 765.00
	Very good:	$ 610.00

Weatherby Model Varmintmaster

A scaled-down version of the Mark V Deluxe in 22-250 or 224 Weatherby magnum; 24" or 26" barrel. Add 5% for Lazermark Series.

Estimated Value:	New (retail):	$1020.00
	Excellent:	$ 765.00
	Very good:	$ 610.00

Weatherby Fibermark

Similar to the Mark V Deluxe except one-piece black fiberglass stock & forearm; weighs 7½-8 lbs. Introduced in the mid 1980's.

Estimated Value:	New (retail):	$1180.00
	Excellent:	$ 885.00
	Very good:	$ 700.00

Weatherby Vanguard VGX, VGS, VGL

Caliber: 22-250, 25-06, 243, 264, 270, 30-06, 7mm Rem. mag., 300 Win. mag.

Action: Bolt action; repeating

Magazine: 5-shot (3-shot magnum), box with hinged floor plate

Barrel: Blued; 24"

Sights: None

Stock & Forearm: Checkered walnut, Monte Carlo pistol grip, one-piece stock & forearm; recoil pad, swivels; VGX has deluxe finish

Approximate wt.: 8 lbs; 6½ lbs. for VGL

Comments: Made from early 1970's to present. Add 30% for VGX.

Estimated Value:	New (retail):	$490.00
	Excellent:	$365.00
	Very good:	$300.00

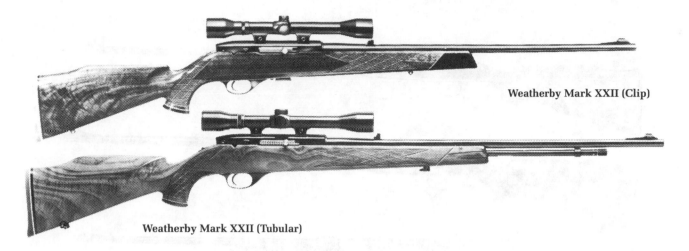

Weatherby Mark XXII (Clip)

Weatherby Mark XXII (Tubular)

Weatherby Vanguard Fiberguard

Caliber: 223, 243, 270, 7mm Rem. magnum, 30-06, 308 Win.
Action: Bolt action; repeating; short action
Magazine: 6-shot in 223; 5-shot in 243, 270, 30-06 & 308; 3-shot in 7mm Rem. magnum
Barrel: Blued; 20"
Sights: None
Stock & Forearm: A rugged, all weather fiberglass one-piece semi-pistol grip stock & forearm; forest green wrinkle finish with black butt pad
Approximate wt.: 6½ lbs.
Comments: Made from the mid 1980's to present.
Estimated Value: New (retail): $667.00
Excellent: $500.00
Very good: $400.00

Weatherby Mark XXII Deluxe

Caliber: 22 long rifle
Action: Semi-automatic; hammerless
Magazine: 5- or 10-shot clip; 15-shot tubular
Barrel: Blued; 24"
Sights: Open rear, ramp front
Stock & Forearm: Checkered walnut Monte Carlo one-piece pistol grip stock & tapered forearm; swivels
Approximate wt.: 6 lbs.
Comments: Made from the mid 1960's to present.
Estimated Value: New (retail): $454.00
Excellent: $340.00
Very good: $270.00

Western Field

Western Field Model 732

Western Field Model 730

Western Field Model 732

Caliber: 7mm, 30-06
Action: Bolt action; repeating; hammerless
Magazine: 4- or 5-shot tubular, depending on caliber
Barrel: Blued; 22"
Sights: Leaf rear, bead front
Stock & Forearm: Checkered walnut Monte Carlo one-piece pistol grip stock & forearm; swivels
Approximate wt.: 8 lbs.
Comments: Manufactured into the late 1970's.
Estimated Value: Excellent: $220.00
Very good: $175.00

Western Field Model 730

Similar to 732. Produced until mid 1970's.
Estimated Value: Excellent: $200.00
Very good: $160.00

Western Field Model 780

Western Field Model 775

Western Field Bolt Action Repeater

Western Field Bolt Action Repeater
Caliber: 22 short, long, long rifle; 22 WMR
Action: Bolt action; repeating
Magazine: 7-shot clip in 22; 5-shot in 22 WMR
Barrel: Blued; 24"
Sights: Adjustable rear, ramp front
Stock & Forearm: Walnut one-piece pistol grip stock & forearm
Approximate wt.: 6 lbs.
Comments: Discontinued in the early 1980's. Add $5.00 for 22 WMR.
Estimated Value: Excellent: $70.00
Very good: $55.00

Western Field Model 780
Caliber: 243, 308
Action: Bolt action; repeating
Magazine: 5-shot tubular
Barrel: Blued; 22"
Sights: Adjustable rear, bead front
Stock & Forearm: Checkered walnut Monte Carlo one-piece pistol grip stock & forearm
Approximate wt.: 6½ lbs.
Comments: Manufactured to the late 1970's.
Estimated Value: Excellent: $185.00
Very good: $150.00

Western Field Model 775, 776
Similar to the 780; produced until mid 1970's.
Estimated Value: Excellent: $180.00
Very good: $145.00

Western Field Model 842

Western Field Bolt Action
Caliber: 30-06
Action: Bolt action; repeating
Magazine: 4-shot, hinged floorplate
Barrel: Blued; 22" round
Sights: Bead front, adjustable rear
Stock & Forearm: Smooth hardwood one-piece pistol grip stock & forearm with sling swivels
Approximate wt.: 7¾ lbs.
Comments: Made until the early 1980's.
Estimated Value: Excellent: $190.00
Very good: $155.00

Western Field Model 842
Caliber: 22 short, long, long rifle
Action: Bolt action; repeating
Magazine: Tubular; 18 long rifles, 20 longs, 22 shorts
Barrel: Blued; 24"
Sights: Adjustable rear, bead front
Stock & Forearm: Walnut Monte Carlo one-piece pistol grip stock & forearm
Approximate wt.: 6¼ lbs.
Comments: Manufactured until the mid 1970's.
Estimated Value: Excellent: $80.00
Very good: $65.00

Western Field Model 78 Deluxe

Caliber: 7mm mag., 30-06
Action: Bolt action
Magazine: 3-shot rotary magazine in 7mm, 4-shot in 30-06
Barrel: 24" in 7mm; 22" in 30-06
Sights: Bead front, adjustable rear
Stock & Forearm: Checkered walnut pistol grip stock & forearm; swivels
Approximate wt.: 7mm: 8¾ lbs.; 30-06: 7½ lbs.
Comments: Manufactured to the early 1980's.
Estimated Value: **Excellent:**   **$200.00**
                  Very good: **$160.00**

Western Field 72

Western Field Model 72

Caliber: 30 30
Action: Lever-action; exposed hammer; repeating; side ejection
Magazine: 6-shot tubular
Barrel: Blued; 18", 20"
Sights: Adjustable open rear, ramp front
Stock & Forearm: Walnut two-piece pistol grip stock & forearm; barrel band; fluted comb
Approximate wt.: 7½ lbs.
Comments: Made into the late 1970's.
Estimated Value: **Excellent:**   **$160.00**
                  Very good: **$130.00**

Western Field Model 740

Similar to Model 72 with recoil pad & 20" barrel. Produced until mid 1970's.
Estimated Value: **Excellent:**   **$165.00**
                  Very good: **$130.00**

Western Field Model 815

Caliber: 22 short, long, long rifle
Action: Bolt action; single shot; hammerless
Magazine: None
Barrel: Blued; 24"
Sights: Adjustable rear, bead front
Stock & Forearm: Wood Monte Carlo one-piece pistol grip stock & forearm
Approximate wt.: 8 lbs.
Comments: Made until the mid 1970's.
Estimated Value: **Excellent:**   **$60.00**
                  Very good: **$45.00**

Western Field Model 79

Caliber: 30-30
Action: Lever-action; exposed hammer; repeating; side ejection
Magazine: 6-shot tubular, side load
Barrel: Blued; 20" round
Sights: Bead front, rear adjustable for elevation
Stock & Forearm: Smooth hardwood pistol grip stock & forearm
Approximate wt.: 7 lbs.
Comments: Made to the early 1980's.
Estimated Value: **Excellent:**   **$150.00**
                  Very good: **$120.00**

Western Field Model 865

Caliber: 22 short, long, long rifle
Action: Lever-action; hammerless; repeating
Magazine: Tubular; 13 long rifles, 15 longs, 20 shorts
Barrel: Blued; 20"
Sights: Adjustable rear, bead front
Stock & Forearm: Wood Monte Carlo pistol grip stock & forearm; barrel band; swivels
Approximate wt.: 7 lbs.
Comments: Made until the mid 1970's.
Estimated Value: **Excellent:**   **$90.00**
                  Very good: **$75.00**

Western Field Model 895

Western Field Model 895

Caliber: 22 long rifle
Action: Semi-automatic; hammerless
Magazine: 18-shot tubular
Barrel: Blued; 24"
Sights: Open rear, bead front
Stock & Forearm: Checkered walnut Monte Carlo pistol grip stock & forearm
Approximate wt.: 7 lbs.
Comments: Made until mid 1970's.
Estimated Value: **Excellent:**   **$85.00**
                  Very good: **$70.00**

Western Field Model 846

Western Field Model 850

Western Field Semi-Automatic 895 Carbine
Caliber: 22 long rifle
Action: Semi-automatic; hammerless
Magazine: 15-shot tubular
Barrel: 21"
Sights: Blade front, rear adjustable for elevation
Stock & Forearm: Smooth hardwood one-piece pistol grip stock & forearm
Approximate wt.: 5½ lbs.
Comments: Made until the early 1960's.
Estimated Value: Excellent: $85.00
Very good: $70.00

Western Field Model 850
Caliber: 22 long rifle
Action: Semi-automatic; hammerless
Magazine: 7-shot clip
Barrel: Blued; 18"
Sights: Adjustable rear, bead front
Stock & Forearm: Wood one-piece semi-pistol grip stock & tapered forearm
Approximate wt.: 5½ lbs.
Comments: Made to the mid 1970's.
Estimated Value: Excellent: $80.00
Very good: $65.00

Western Field Model 846
Caliber: 22 long rifle
Action: Semi-automatic; hammerless
Magazine: 15-shot tubular, stock load
Barrel: Blued; 18½"
Sights: Adjustable rear, bead front
Stock & Forearm: Checkered wood one-piece pistol grip stock & forearm; barrel band; swivels
Approximate wt.: 5¼ lbs.
Comments: Made until mid 1970's.
Estimated Value: Excellent: $85.00
Very good: $70.00

Winchester

Winchester Model 1900

Winchester Model 02

Winchester Model 02
Similar to the Model 1900 with extended trigger guard; addition of 22 long rifle & extra long. Made from about 1902 to the early 1930's.
Estimated Value: Excellent: $200.00
Very good: $160.00

Winchester Model 1900
Caliber: 22 short, long
Action: Bolt action; single shot; cocking piece
Magazine: None
Barrel: Blued; 18", round
Sights: Open rear, blade front
Stock & Forearm: Plain one-piece straight grip stock & forearm
Approximate wt.: 3 lbs.
Comments: Made from about 1900 to 1902.
Estimated Value: Excellent: $165.00
Very good: $130.00

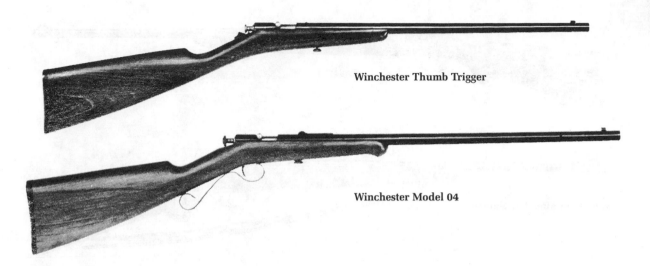

Winchester Thumb Trigger

Winchester Model 04

Winchester Thumb Trigger (Model 02)

Similar to the Model 02 with no trigger. The gun is discharged by pushing a button behind the cocking piece. Made until the early 1920's.

Estimated Value: Excellent: $275.00
Very good: $220.00

Winchester Model 04

Similar to the Model 02 with a 21" barrel & lipped forearm. Made from 1904 to the early 1930's.

Estimated Value: Excellent: $175.00
Very good: $140.00

Winchester Lee

Winchester Lee Musket

Similar to the Winchester Lee with military sights, full-length musket forearm, 28" barrel, swivels.

Estimated Value: Excellent: $700.00
Very good: $550.00

Winchester Lee

Caliber: 6mm (236)
Action: Bolt action; repeating
Magazine: 5-shot detachable box
Barrel: 24", round, nickel steel
Sights: Open rear, bead front
Stock & Forearm: One-piece semi-pistol grip stock & fluted, lipped forearm
Approximate wt.: 7½ lbs.
Comments: Made from the late 1890's to early 1900's.

Estimated Value: Excellent: $800.00
Very good: $650.00

Winchester Model 55

Winchester Model 55

Caliber: 22 short, long, long rifle
Action: Single shot
Magazine: None
Barrel: 22"
Sights: Open rear, bead front
Stock & Forearm: Plain wood one-piece semi-pistol grip stock & forearm
Approximate wt.: 5½ lbs.
Comments: Made from the late 1950's to the early 1960's.

Estimated Value: Excellent: $90.00
Very good: $75.00

Winchester Model 52

Winchester Model 52 Sporting

Winchester Model 52 Heavy Barrel

Winchester Model 52-B

Winchester Model 52-B Heavy Barrel

Winchester Model 52

Caliber: 22 long rifle
Action: Bolt action; repeating
Magazine: 5-shot box
Barrel: Blued; 28"
Sights: Peep rear, blade front
Stock & Forearm: Plain walnut one-piece pistol grip stock & forearm
Approximate wt.: 8½ lbs.
Comments: Made from about 1920 to the late 1930's.
Estimated Value: Excellent: $415.00
Very good: $310.00

Winchester Model 52 Heavy Barrel

Similar to the Model 52 but with a heavy barrel & special Lyman sights.
Estimated Value: Excellent: $440.00
Very good: $330.00

Winchester Model 52 Sporting

Similar to the Model 52 except: 24" barrel; special Lyman sights; checkering; cheekpiece. Made to the late 1950's.
Estimated Value: Excellent: $850.00
Very good: $635.00

Winchester Model 52-B

Similar to the Model 52 with improved action; high comb stock available. Made from the mid 1930's to late 1940's.
Estimated Value: Excellent: $440.00
Very good: $330.00

Winchester Model 52-B Heavy Barrel

Similar to the Model 52-B with a heavy barrel.
Estimated Value: Excellent: $470.00
Very good: $350.00

Winchester Model 52-B Bull Gun

Winchester Model 52-B Sporting

Winchester Model 52-C Bull Gun

Winchester Model 52-C

Winchester Model 52-D Target

Winchester Model 52-B Bull Gun
Similar to the Model 52-B Heavy Barrel with still heavier barrel. Weighs ablut 12 lbs.

| Estimated Value: | Excellent: | $510.00 |
| | Very good: | $400.00 |

Winchester Model 52-B Sporting
Similar to the Model 52 Sporting with a 52-B action. Made to the early 1960's.

| Estimated Value: | Excellent: | $850.00 |
| | Very good: | $635.00 |

Winchester Model 52-C
Similar to the 52-B with more improvements on the action; high comb stock. Made from the late 1940's to early 1960's.

| Estimated Value: | Excellent: | $460.00 |
| | Very good: | $350.00 |

Winchester Model 52-C Heavy Barrel
Similar to the Model 52 Heavy Barrel with a 52-C action.

| Estimated Value: | Excellent: | $485.00 |
| | Very good: | $385.00 |

Winchester Model 52-C Bull Gun
Similar to the Model 52-B Bull Gun with a 52-C action.

| Estimated Value: | Excellent: | $500.00 |
| | Very good: | $400.00 |

Winchester Model 52-D Target
Similar to the 52-C; single shot; hand stop on forearm. Made from the early 1960's to late 1970's; 22 long rifle caliber; approximate wt. 11 lbs.

| Estimated Value: | Excellent: | $510.00 |
| | Very good: | $400.00 |

Winchester Model 54

Winchester Model 54 Sporting (Improved)

Winchester Model 54 Super

Winchester Model 54 Sniper

Winchester Model 54 National Match

Winchester Model 54
Caliber: 270, 7x57, 30-30, 30-06, 7.65x53mm, 9x57mm, 7mm, 250-3000, 22 Hornet, 220 Swift, 257 Roberts
Action: Bolt action; repeating
Magazine: 5-shot box, non-detachable
Barrel: Blued; 24"
Sights: Open rear, bead front
Stock & Forearm: Checkered walnut one-piece pistol grip stock & forearm
Approximate wt.: 7½ lbs.
Comments: Made from the mid 1920's to about 1930.
Estimated Value: Excellent: $520.00
Very good: $390.00

Winchester Model 54 Carbine
Similar to the Model 54 with a 20" barrel; no checkering on stock.
Estimated Value: Excellent: $525.00
Very good: $395.00

Winchester Model 54 Sporting (Improved)
Similar to the Model 54 with an improved action; 26" barrel; additional calibers. Made from about 1930 for six years.
Estimated Value: Excellent: $560.00
Very good: $450.00

Winchester Model 54 Carbine (Improved)
Similar to the Model 54 Carbine with improved action. Made from 1930 to the mid 1930's.
Estimated Value: Excellent: $600.00
Very good: $480.00

Winchester Model 54 Super
Similar to the Model 54 with cheekpiece; select wood; deluxe finish; swivels.
Estimated Value: Excellent: $695.00
Very good: $555.00

Winchester Model 54 Sniper
Similar to the Model 54 with a 26" heavy barrel; special Lyman sights; 30-06 caliber only.
Estimated Value: Excellent: $620.00
Very good: $465.00

Winchester Model 54 Sniper Match
Deluxe version of the Model 54 Sniper with high quality finish.
Estimated Value: Excellent: $685.00
Very good: $550.00

Winchester Model 54 National Match
Similar to the Model 54 with special Lyman sights & marksman stock.
Estimated Value: Excellent: $620.00
Very good: $500.00

Winchester Model 54 Target
Similar to the Model 54 with 24" barrel & special Lyman sights.
Estimated Value: Excellent: $650.00
Very good: $520.00

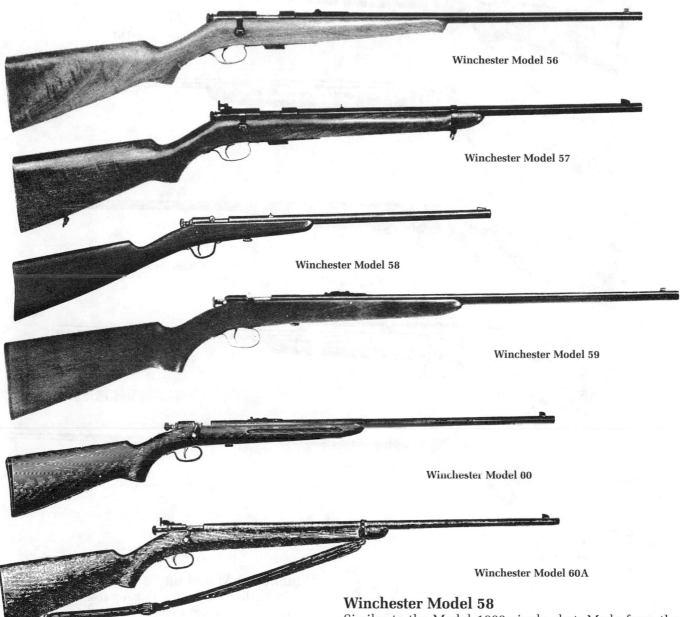

Winchester Model 56

Winchester Model 57

Winchester Model 58

Winchester Model 59

Winchester Model 00

Winchester Model 60A

Winchester Model 56

Caliber: 22 short or long rifle only
Action: Bolt action; repeating
Magazine: 5- or 20 shot detachable box
Barrel: Blued; 22"
Sights: Open rear, bead front
Stock & Forearm: Plain walnut one-piece semi-pistol grip stock & lipped forearm
Approximate wt.: 5 lbs.
Comments: Made from the mid to late 1920's. A fancy version was available with checkered walnut stock & forearm.
Estimated Value: Excellent: $225.00
Very good: $180.00

Winchester Model 57

Similar to the Model 56 with longer, unlipped forearm; barrel band, swivels; special Lyman sights; target model. Made from the mid 1920's to mid 1930's.
Estimated Value: Excellent: $275.00
Very good: $220.00

Winchester Model 58

Similar to the Model 1900 single shot. Made from the late 1920's to early 1930's.
Estimated Value: Excellent: $160.00
Very good: $130.00

Winchester Model 59

Similar to the Model 58 with a 23" barrel. Weighs about 4½ lbs. Made from about 1930 to 1931.
Estimated Value: Excellent: $165.00
Very good: $135.00

Winchester Model 60

Similar to the Model 59 with 23" or 27" barrel. Made from the early to mid 1930's.
Estimated Value: Excellent: $175.00
Very good: $140.00

Winchester Model 60A

Similar to the Model 60 with special Lyman sights; swivels. Made to about 1940.
Estimated Value: Excellent: $170.00
Very good: $130.00

Winchester Model 67

Winchester Model 67 Boy's

Winchester Model 68

Winchester Model 677

Winchester Model 69

Winchester Model 68

Similar to the Model 67 with peep rear sight. Made from the mid 1930's to mid 1940's.

Estimated Value:	Excellent:	$115.00
	Very good:	$ 90.00

Winchester Model 677

Similar to the Model 67 with no sights. Made only in the late 1930's.

Estimated Value:	Excellent:	$100.00
	Very good:	$ 75.00

Winchester Model 67

Caliber: 22 short, long, long rifle
Action: Bolt action; single shot
Magazine: None
Barrel: Blued; 27"
Sights: Open rear, bead front
Stock & Forearm: Plain walnut one-piece semi-pistol grip stock & fluted forearm
Approximate wt.: 5 lbs.
Comments: Made from the mid 1930's to the early 1960's.

Estimated Value:	Excellent:	$100.00
	Very good:	$ 80.00

Winchester Model 67 Boy's

Similar to the Model 67 with a 20" barrel & youth stock.

Estimated Value:	Excellent:	$90.00
	Very good:	$70.00

Winchester Model 69

Caliber: 22 short, long, long rifle
Action: Bolt action; repeating
Magazine: 5- or 10-shot detachable box
Barrel: Blued; 25"
Sights: Peep or open rear, ramp front
Stock & Forearm: Plain walnut one-piece semi-pistol grip stock & forearm
Approximate wt.: 5½ lbs.
Comments: Made from the mid 1930's to the early 1960's.

Estimated Value:	Excellent:	$130.00
	Very good:	$100.00

Winchester Model 69 Target

Winchester Model 697

Winchester Model 69 Match
Similar to the Model 69 Target with special Lyman sights.
Estimated Value: Excellent: **$160.00**
　　　　　　　　　Very good: **$130.00**

Winchester Model 69 Target
Similar to the Model 69 with peep sight only; swivels.
Estimated Value: Excellent: **$145.00**
　　　　　　　　　Very good: **$115.00**

Winchester Model 697
Similar to the Model 69 with no sights. Made from the late 1930's to early 1940's.
Estimated Value: Excellent: **$150.00**
　　　　　　　　　Very good: **$120.00**

Winchester Model 70 (1937)

Winchester Model 70 (1964)

Winchester Model 70 XTR

Winchester Model 70 (1937)
Caliber: 375 H&H mag., 300 H&H mag., 308 Win., 30-06, 7x57mm, 270 Win., 257 Roberts, 250-3000, 243, 220, 22 Hornet
Action: Bolt action; repeating
Magazine: 5-shot box; 4-shot box in magnum
Barrel: Blued; 24", 26"
Sights: Open rear, hooded ramp front
Stock & Forearm: Checkered walnut one-piece pistol grip stock & forearm
Approximate wt.: 7¾ lbs.
Comments: Made from about 1937 to 1963. Add $150.00 for mint, unfired condition.
Estimated Value: Excellent: **$800.00**
　　　　　　　　　Very good: **$650.00**

Winchester Model 70 (1964)
Similar to the Model 70 (1937) with improvements: Monte Carlo stock; swivels. Made from about 1964 until 1970; calibers 22-250, 22 Rem., 225, 243, 270, 308, 30-06.
Estimated Value: Excellent: **$360.00**
　　　　　　　　　Very good: **$275.00**

Winchester Model 70 (1971), 70 XTR (1978), 70 XTR Sporter (1983)
Similar to the Model 70 (1964) with improvements. Made from 1971 to present. Calibers 270 Win., 30-06, 25-06 (1985), 308 Win. (1987), 243 (1988).
Estimated Value: New (retail): **$465.00**
　　　　　　　　　Excellent: **$350.00**
　　　　　　　　　Very good: **$280.00**

Winchester Model 70 XTR Featherwieght

Similar to the Model 70 XTR in calibers 22-250, 223 (introduced 1984); 243, 308 (short action); 270 Win., 257 Roberts, 7mm Nauser, 30-06 Springfield (standard action); recoil pad; lipped forearm; decorative checkering; 22" barrel.

Estimated Value: New (retail): $465.00
                       Excellent: $350.00
                       Very good: $280.00

Winchester Model 70 XTR European Featherweight

Similar to the Model 70XTR Featherweight in caliber 6.55x55 Swedish Mauser. Produced 1986 & 1987.

Estimated Value: Excellent: $365.00
                       Very good: $275.00

Winchester Model 70 Lightweight Carbine

Similar to the Model 70XTR Featherweight with different outward appearance, 20" barrel; in calibers 270 Win., 30-06 Springfield or short action version of 22-250 Rem., 223 Rem., 243 Win., 308 Win.; weighs 6-6¼ lbs. Introduced in 1984. 250 Savage caliber. Produced 1986 & 1987.

Estimated Value: Excellent: $320.00
                       Very good: $240.00

Winchester Model 70A, 70A XTR

Similar to the Model 70 (1971) with a special steel barrel; adjustable sights. Made from the early 1970's to about 1981; 4-shot or 3-shot (magnum) box magazine. Add $20.00 for 264 Win. mag., 7mm Rem. mag., or 300 Win. mag.; Police Model $10.00 less.

Estimated Value: Excellent: $300.00
                       Very good: $225.00

Winchester Model 70 Super (1937)

Similar to the Model 70 (1937 with swivels; deluxe finish; cheekpiece. Made to early 1960's.

Estimated Value: Excellent: $1,000.00
                       Very good: $ 850.00

Winchester Model 70 Super

Similar to the Model 70 Super (1937) with recoil pad; select wood. Made from mid 1960's to mid 1970's.

Estimated Value: Excellent: $350.00
                       Very good: $280.00

Winchester Model 70XTR Featherweight

Winchester Model 70 Lightweight Carbine

Winchester Model 70A

Winchester Model 70 Super (1937)

Winchester Model 70 Super

Winchester Model 70 Target (1937)

Winchester Model 70 Target (1964)

Winchester Model 70 National Match

Winchester Model 70 Mannlicher

Winchester Model 70 Varmint (1956) (1964) (1971)

Winchester Model 70 Featherweight Sporter

Winchester Model 70 Target (1937)
Similar to the Model 70 (1937) with 24" barrel & improved stock. Made until about 1963.
Estimated Value: Excellent: $900.00
                Very good: $675.00

Winchester Model 70 Target (1964) & 1971
Similar to the Model 70 Target (1937) with aluminum hand stop. Model (1971) has minor improvements; calibers 30-06, 308 Win., or 308 Int'l Army. Add $132.00 for Int'l Army.
Estimated Value: Excellent: $400.00
                Very good: $320.00

Winchester Model 70 National Match
Similar to the Model 70 (1937) with marksman stock in 30-06 caliber. Made to the early 1960's.
Estimated Value: Excellent: $800.00
                Very good: $640.00

Winchester Model 70 Mannlicher
Similar to the Model 70 (1964) with full length forearm; 19" barrel; calibers 243, 270, 308, 30-06. Made to the early 1970's.
Estimated Value: Excellent: $375.00
                Very good: $300.00

Winchester Model 70 Varmint (1956) (1964) (1971) 70 XTR Varmint
Similar to the Model 70 (1937) with heavy 24" or 26" barrel. Imporvements made along with other Model 70's. Calibers 222 Rem., 22-250 or 243 Win. Add 90% for pre-1964 models. Discontinued 1988.
Estimated Value: Excellent: $360.00
                Very good: $270.00

Winchester Model 70 Featherweight Sporter
A lightweight rifle similar to the Model 70 (1937) with improved stock. Made from the early 1950's to 1960's.
Estimated Value: Excellent: $825.00
                Very good: $660.00

Winchester Model 70 Featherweight Super

Similar to the Featherweight Sporter with deluxe finish; cheekpiece; swivels. Made after 1964.

Estimated Value: Excellent: $325.00
Very good: $240.00

Winchester Model 70 African (1956)

Similar to the Model 70 (1937) Super Grade with recoil pad; Monte Carlo stock; 3-shot magazine; 24" barrel. Available only in 458 caliber. Made to 1963.

Estimated Value: Excellent: $1,200.00
Very good: $ 960.00

Winchester Model 70 African (1964)

Similar to the Model 70 African (1956) with improvements. Made to 1970.

Estimated Value: Excellent: $425.00
Very good: $340.00

Winchester Model 70 African (1971)

Similar to the Model 70 African (1964) with floating barrel; caliber 458 Win. mag. Discontinued about 1981.

Estimated Value: Excellent: $525.00
Very good: $420.00

Winchester Model 70 Westerner

Similar to the Model 70 Alaskan. Made in the early 1960's.

Estimated Value: Excellent: $800.00
Very good: $640.00

Winchester Model 70 Westerner (1982)

Similar to the Model 70XTR with a 22" barrel & 4-shot magazine in calibers 243 Win., 270 Win., 308 win., & 30-06 Springfield; 24" barrel & 3-shot magazine in calibers 7mm Rem. mag., 300 Win. mag.; weighs about 7½ to 7¾ lbs.; recoil pad. Introduced in 1982; discontinued in 1984.

Estimated Value: Excellent: $400.00
Very good: $320.00

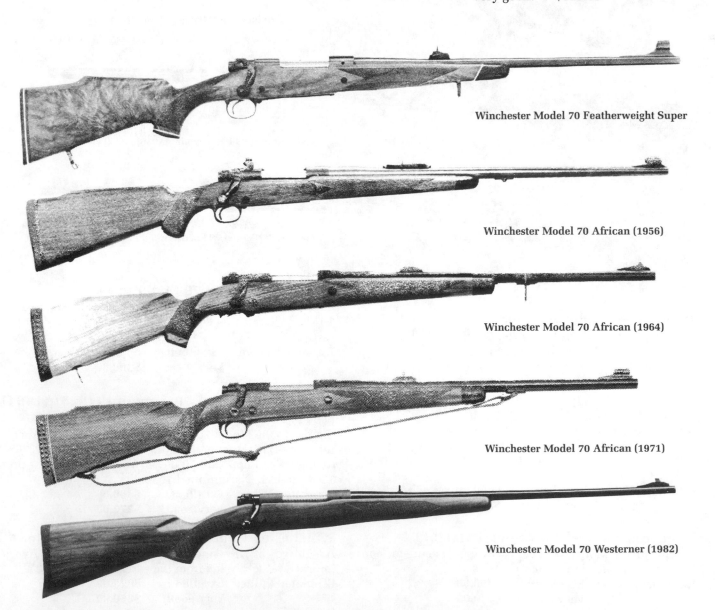

Winchester Model 70 Featherweight Super

Winchester Model 70 African (1956)

Winchester Model 70 African (1964)

Winchester Model 70 African (1971)

Winchester Model 70 Westerner (1982)

Winchester Model 70 Magnum

Winchester Model 70 Alaskan

Winchester Model 70 Deluxe

Winchester Model 70 Magnum (1964)

Similar to the Model 70 (1964) with Monte Carlo stock; recoil pad; swivels; 3-shot magazine. Made to the early 1970's.

Estimated Value: Excellent: $400.00
Very good: $335.00

Winchester Model 70 Alaskan

Similar to the Model 70 (1937) with 24" or 26" barrel. Made in the early 1960's.

Estimated Value: Excellent: $1,000.00
Very good: $ 800.00

Winchester Model 70 Deluxe (1964)

Similar to the Model 70 (1964) with Monte Carlo stock; recoil pad; deluxe features. Made to the early 1970's.

Estimated Value: Excellent: $400.00
Very good: $320.00

Winchester Model 70 XTR Sporter Magnum

Winchester Model 70 XTR Super Express Magnum

Winchester Model 70 Winlite

Winchester Model 70 Winlite

Caliber: 270, 30-06, 7mm Rem. magnum, 300 Win. magnum, 300 Weatherby magnum, 338 Win. magnum
Action: Bolt action; repeating
Magazine: 4-shot in 270 or 30-06; 3-shot in 7mm Rem. magnum or 338 Win. magnum
Barrel: 22" in 270 & 30-06; 24" in magnum calibers
Sights: None
Stock & Forearm: Fiberglass reinforced one-piece stock & forearm with thermoplastic bedding for receiver & barrel
Approximate wt.: 6¼ to 6¾ lbs.
Comments: Introduced in 1986. Add 3% for 300 Weatherby magnum.
Estimated Value: New (retail): $636.00
Excellent: $475.00
Very good: $380.00

Winchester Model 70 XTR Sporter Magnum

Caliber: 264 Win. mag., 300 Win mag., 338 Win. mag.; 7mm Rem. mag., 300 Weatherby mag.
Action: Bolt action; repeating
Magazine: 3-shot box
Barrel: Blued; 24"
Sights: Folding leaf rear, hooded ramp front
Stock & Forearm: Checkered walnut Monte Carlo one-piece pistol grip stock & forearm; cheekpiece; recoil pad; swivels
Approximate wt.: 7¾ lbs.
Comments: Introduced in 1982.
Estimated Value: New (retail): $465.00
Excellent: $350.00
Very good: $280.00

Winchester Model 70XTR Super Express Magnum

Similar to the Model 70 XTR Sporter Magnum with a 22" barrel in 458 Win. magnum caliber; 24" barrel in 375 H & H magnum caliber. Made 1982 to present.

Estimated Value: New (retail): $793.00
Excellent: $595.00
Very good: $475.00

Winchester Model 70 Lightweight

Winchester Model 70 Win-Tuff Lightweight

Winchester Model 70 Win-Tuff Featherweight

Winchester Model 70 Win-Cam Featherweight

Winchester Model 70 Lightweight
Similar to the Model 70XTR with a 22" barrel; weighs 6¼ lbs.; calibers: 22-250 Rem., 223 Rem., 243 Win., 270 Win., 280 Win., 30-06 spring., 308 Win.; swivels.

Estimated Value:	New (retail)	$399.00
	Excellent:	$300.00
	Very good:	$240.00

Winchester Model 70 Win-Tuff Lightweight
Similar to the Model 70 Lightweight with laminated stock of dye-shaded hardwoods. Available in calibers: 22-250 Rem., 243 Win., 270 Win., 30-06 Spring.; short or long action.

Estimated Value:	New (retail)	$409.00
	Excellent:	$300.00
	Very good:	$245.00

Winchester Model 70 Win-Tuff Featherweight
Similar to the Model 70 Featherweight with laminated stock of dye-shaded hardwood. Available in calibers: 243 Win., 270 Win., 30-06 Spring.

Estimated Value:	New (retail)	$476.00
	Excellent:	$355.00
	Very good:	$285.00

Winchester Model 70 Win-Cam Featherweight
Similar to the Model 70 Featherweight with laminated stock of green & brown camouflage. Available in 270 Win. & 30-06 Spring.

Estimated Value:	New (retail)	$476.00
	Excellent:	$355.00
	Very good:	$285.00

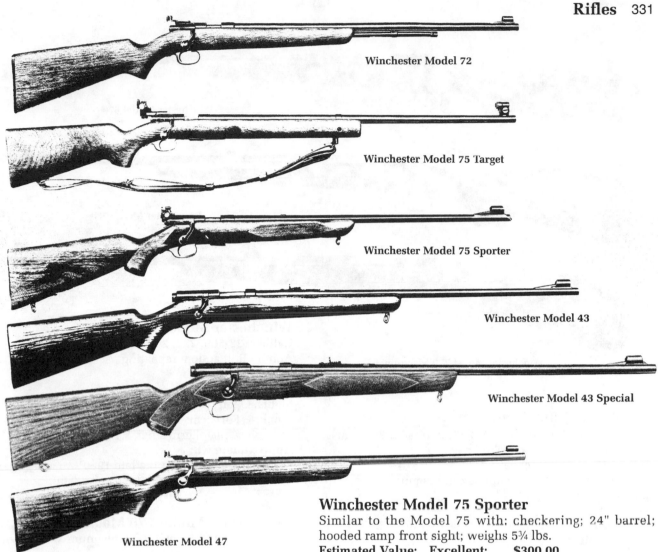

Winchester Model 72

Winchester Model 75 Target

Winchester Model 75 Sporter

Winchester Model 43

Winchester Model 43 Special

Winchester Model 47

Winchester Model 72

Caliber: 22 short, long, long rifle
Action: Bolt action; repeating
Magazine: Tubular; 15 long rifles, 16 longs, 20 shorts
Barrel: Blued; 25"
Sights: Peep or open rear, bead front
Stock & Forearm: Plain walnut one-piece semi-pistol grip stock & forearm
Approximate wt.: 5¾ lbs.
Comments: Made from the late 1930's to late 1950's.
Estimated Value: Excellent: $145.00
Very good: $115.00

Winchester Model 75 Target

Caliber: 22 long rifle
Action: Bolt action; repeating
Magazine: 5- or 10-shot detachable box
Barrel: Blued; 28"
Sights: Special target sights
Stock & Forearm: Plain walnut one-piece pistol grip stock & forearm
Approximate wt.: 8¾ lbs.
Comments: Made from the late 1930's to late 1950's.
Estimated Value: Excellent: $290.00
Very good: $230.00

Winchester Model 75 Sporter

Similar to the Model 75 with: checkering; 24" barrel; hooded ramp front sight; weighs 5¾ lbs.
Estimated Value: Excellent: $300.00
Very good: $240.00

Winchester Model 43

Caliber: 218 Bee, 22 Hornet, 25-20, 32-30 (25-20 & 32-30 dropped in 1950)
Action: Bolt action; repeating
Magazine: 3-shot detachable
Barrel: Blued; 24"
Sights: Open rear, hooded ramp front
Stock & Forearm: Plain wood one-piece semi-pistol grip stock & forearm; swivels
Approximate wt.: 6 lbs.
Comments: Made from the late 1940's to late 1950's.
Estimated Value: Excellent: $360.00
Very good: $290.00

Winchester Model 43 Special

Similar to the Model 43 with checkering & choice of open rear sight or micrometer.
Estimated Value: Excellent: $390.00
Very good: $310.00

Winchester Model 47

Similar to the Model 43 in 22 short, long or long rifle single shot; 25" barrel. Made from the late 1940's to mid 1950's.
Estimated Value: Excellent: $110.00
Very good: $ 85.00

Winchester Model 670

Winchester Model 770

Winchester Model 770 Magnum

Winchester Model 670
Caliber: 243, 270, 30-06, 225, 243, 270, 308, 30-06 mag., 300 Win. mag., 264 Win. mag.,
Action: Bolt action; repeating
Magazine: 4-shot box; 3-shot box in magnum
Barrel: Blued; 19", 22", 24"
Sights: Open rear, ramp front
Stock & Forearm: Checkered hardwood Monte Carlo one-piece pistol grip stock & forearm
Approximate wt.: 7 lbs.
Comments: Made from the mid 1960's to the late 1970's.
Estimated Value: **Excellent:**   **$270.00**
                       Very good: **$220.00**

Winchester Model 770
Caliber: 22-500, 222, 243, 270, 30-06
Action: Bolt action; repeating
Magazine: 4-shot box
Barrel: Blued; 22"
Sights: Open rear, hooded ramp front
Stock & Forearm: Checkered walnut Monte Carlo one-piece pistol grip stock & forearm; swivels
Approximate wt.: 7 lbs.
Comments: Made from the late 1960's to early 1970's.
Estimated Value: **Excellent:**   **$290.00**
                       Very good: **$230.00**

Winchester Model 770 Magnum
Similar to the Model 770 in magnum with recoil pad & 24" barrel, 3-shot magazine.
Estimated Value: **Excellent:**   **$310.00**
                       Very good: **$250.00**

Winchester Model 310

Winchester Model 320

Winchester Model 320
Similar to the Model 310 in repeating bolt action with a 5-shot clip.
Estimated Value: **Excellent:**   **$110.00**
                       Very good: **$ 85.00**

Winchester Model 310
Caliber: 22 short, long, long rifle
Action: Bolt action; single shot
Magazine: None
Barrel: Blued; 22"
Sights: Adjustable rear, ramp front
Stock & Forearm: Checkered walnut Monte Carlo one-pistol grip stock & forearm; swivels
Approximate wt.: 6 lbs.
Comments: Made from the early to mid 1970's.
Estimated Value: **Excellent:**   **$70.00**
                       Very good: **$55.00**

Winchester Model 121

Caliber: 22 short, long, long rifle
Action: Bolt action; single shot
Magazine: None
Barrel: Blued; 20½"
Sights: Open rear, bead post front
Stock & Forearm: Plain one-piece semi-pistol grip stock & forearm
Approximate wt.: 5 lbs.
Comments: Made from the late 1960's to early 1970's.
Estimated Value: Excellent: $70.00
Very good: $55.00

Winchester Model 121 Deluxe

Similar to the Model 121 with Monte Carlo stock; swivels; slightly different sights.
Estimated Value: Excellent: $80.00
Very good: $60.00

Winchester Model 121 Youth

Similar to the Model 121 with shorter barrel & youth stock.
Estimated Value: Excellent: $65.00
Very good: $50.00

Winchester Model 131

Similar to the Model 121 with semi-Monte Carlo stock; 7-shot clip magazine; bolt action repeater.
Estimated Value: Excellent: $85.00
Very good: $65.00

Winchester Model 141

Similar to the 131 with tubular magazine.
Estimated Value: Excellent: $90.00
Very good: $75.00

Winchester Ranger

Caliber: 270 Win., 30-06 Springfield
Action: Bolt action; repeating
Magazine: 4-shot
Barrel: Blued; 22"
Sights: Beaded ramp front, adjustable rear
Stock & Forearm: Plain one-piece semi-pistol grip wood stock & forearm
Approximate wt.: 7⅛ lbs.
Comments: Introduced in the mid 1980's.
Estimated Value: New (retail): $336.00
Excellent: $250.00
Very good: $200.00

Winchester Ranger Youth

A scaled down bolt action (short action) carbine for young or small shooters; caliber is 243 Win., barrel is 20"; weighs 5¾ lbs.; beaded ramp front sight, semi-buck-horn, folding-leaf rear; plain wood, one-piece stock & forearm with swivels. Introduced in the mid 1980's.
Estimated Value: New (retail) $345.00
Excellent: $260.00
Very good: $205.00

Winchester Model 121

Winchester Model 131

Winchester Ranger Youth

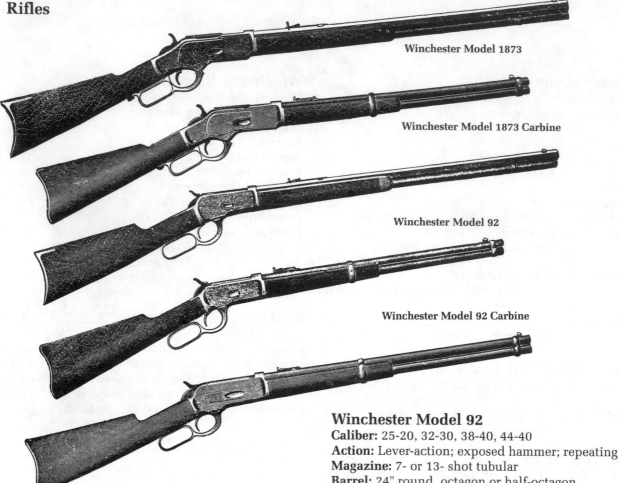

Winchester Model 1873

Winchester Model 1873 Carbine

Winchester Model 92

Winchester Model 92 Carbine

Winchester Model 1886 Carbine

Winchester Model 92

Caliber: 25-20, 32-30, 38-40, 44-40
Action: Lever-action; exposed hammer; repeating
Magazine: 7- or 13- shot tubular
Barrel: 24" round, octagon or half-octagon
Sights: Open rear, bead front
Stock & Forearm: Plain walnut straight grip stock & forearm
Approximate wt.: 7 lbs.
Comments: Made from about 1892 to early 1930's.

Estimated Value:	Excellent:	$825.00
	Very good:	$660.00

Winchester Model 92 Carbine

Similar to the Model 92 with a 20" barrel; barrel band; & 5- or 11-shot magazine. Discontinued in the early 1940's.

Estimated Value:	Excellent:	$900.00
	Very good:	$720.00

Winchester Model 1886

Caliber: 45-70, 33 Win.; also others on early models
Action: Lever-action; exposed hammer; repeating
Magazine: 4- or 8-shot tubular
Barrel: 26" round, octagon or half-octagon
Sights: Open rear, blade front
Stock & Forearm: Plain wood straight grip stock & forearm
Approximate wt.: 7½ lbs.
Comments: Made from the mid 1880's to the mid 1930's.

Estimated Value:	Excellent:	$800.00 - $1,500.00
	Very good:	$620.00 - $1,200.00

Winchester Model 1873

Caliber: 32-20, 38-40, 44-40, 22
Action: Lever-action; exposed hammer; repeating
Magazine: 6- or 15-shot tubular
Barrel: 24" or 26" round, octagon or half-octagon
Sights: Open rear, blade front
Stock & Forearm: Straight grip stock & forearm
Approximate wt.: 8 lbs.
Comments: Thousands of this model were sold by Winchester until 1920. Add $200.00 to $500.00 for Deluxe engraved models. Price range is for the different models i.e., 1st, 2nd and 3rd models.

Estimated Value:	Excellent:	$1,500.00 - $2,800.00
	Very good:	$1,200.00 - $2,200.00

Winchester Model 1873 Carbine

Similar to the Model 1873 with a 20" barrel & 12-shot magazine. Three models made from 1873 to 1920.

Estimated Value:	Excellent:	$1,400.00 - $2,700.00
	Very good:	$1,150.00 - $2,150.00

Winchester Model 1873 Musket

Similar to the Model 1873 with a 30" round barrel, full-length forearm & 17-shot magazine. Three models made from 1873 to 1920.

Estimated Value:	Excellent:	$1,800.00 - $3,000.00
	Very good:	$1,400.00 - $2,400.00

Winchester Model 1886 Carbine

Similar to the Model 1886 with a 22" barrel.

Estimated Value:	Excellent:	$800.00 - $2,000.00
	Very good:	$640.00 - $1,600.00

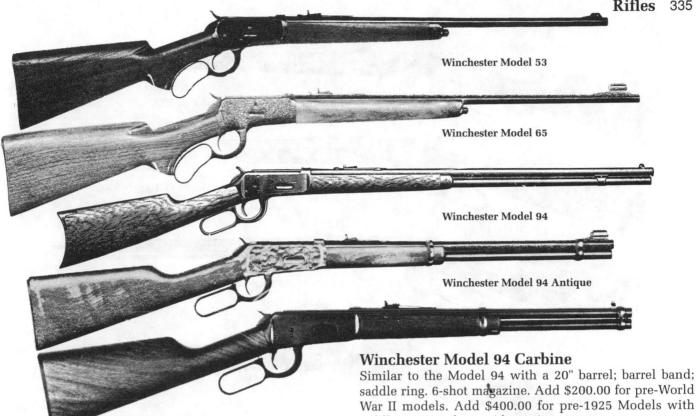

Winchester Model 53

Winchester Model 65

Winchester Model 94

Winchester Model 94 Antique

Winchester Model 94 Trapper

Winchester Model 94 Carbine

Similar to the Model 94 with a 20" barrel; barrel band; saddle ring. 6-shot magazine. Add $200.00 for pre-World War II models. Add $400.00 for pre-1925 Models with saddle ring. Made to mid 1960's.

| Estimated Value: | Excellent: | $275.00 |
| | Very good: | $225.00 |

Winchester Model 53

Similar to the Model 92 with a 6- or 7-shot magazine; 22" nickel steel barrel; choice of straight or pistol grip stock. Made from the mid 1920's to the early 1930's.

| Estimated Value: | Excellent: | $750.00 |
| | Very good: | $600.00 |

Winchester Model 65

Similar to the Model 53 in 25-20 & 32-30 caliber; semi-pistol grip stock; other minor improvements. Made from the early 1930's to late 1940's.

| Estimated Value: | Excellent: | $650.00 |
| | Very good: | $520.00 |

Winchester Model 65, 218 Bee

Similar to the Model 65 with peep sight & 24" barrel. Made from the late 1930's to late 1940's.

| Estimated Value: | Excellent: | $975.00 |
| | Very good: | $780.00 |

Winchester Model 94

Caliber: 25-35, 30-30, 32 Special, 32-40, 38-55
Action: Lever-action; exposed hammer; repeating
Magazine: 4- or 7-shot tubular
Barrel: 22" , 26", round, octagon or half-octagon
Sights: Open rear, bead front
Stock & Forearm: Straight stock & forearm; saddle ring on some models
Approximate wt.: 6¾ lbs.
Comments: Made from 1894 to the late 1930's. Some times referred to as the "Klondike" model.

| Estimated Value: | Excellent: | $475.00 |
| | Very good: | $380.00 |

Winchester Model 94 Standard

Caliber: 30-30
Action: Lever action, exposed hammer; repeating; Angle-eject feature added in 1984, listed as "Side eject" in 1986
Magazine: 6-shot
Barrel: 20" round with barrel band
Sights: Hooded or post front, adjustable rear
Stock & Forearm: Plain wood straight stock & forearm; barrel band
Approximate wt.: 6½ lbs.
Comments: Made from the mid 1960's to present; also made in calibers 44 magnum, 45 Colt & 444 Marlin in the mid 1980's.

Estimated Value:	New (retail):	$289.00
	Excellent:	$220.00
	Very good:	$165.00

Winchester Model 94 Antique

Similar to the Model 94 Standard with case hardened, scroll design frame. Made from the late 1960's to 1984 in 30-30 caliber.

| Estimated Value: | Excellent: | $225.00 |
| | Very good: | $180.00 |

Winchester Model 94 Trapper

Same as the Model 94 Standard with 16" barrel; calibers 44 Rem. magnum, 44 S&W Special & 45 Colt added in the mid 1980's. Magazine capacity is 5-shot in 30-30 & 9-shot in 44 & 45; weighs 6lbs.; made from 1980 to present. Add 5% for 44 & 45 caliber.

Estimated Value:	New (retail):	$297.00
	Excellent:	$225.00
	Very good:	$180.00

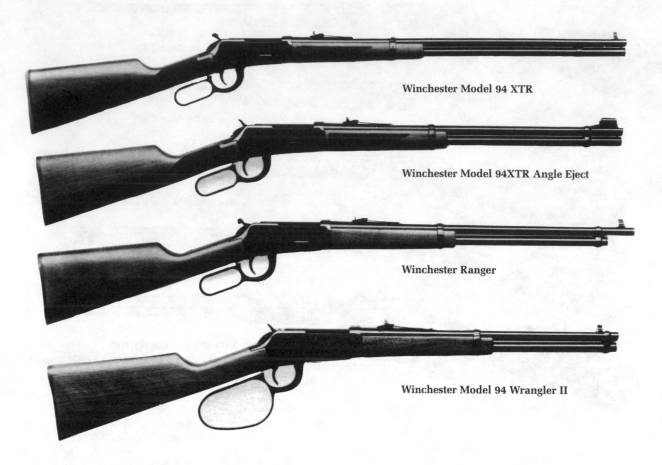

Winchester Model 94 XTR

Winchester Model 94XTR Angle Eject

Winchester Ranger

Winchester Model 94 Wrangler II

Winchester Model 94XTR
Similar to the Model 94 Standard with higher grade wood, checkered stock & forearm. Made from 1979 to 1984 in 30-30 & 375 Win.; the 375 model has recoil pad. Add 23% for 375 Win.

Estimated Value: Excellent: $225.00
                       Very good: $180.00

Winchester Model 94XTR Angle Eject
Similar to the Model 94XTR except an "angle eject" feature was added in 1984; in 1986 Winchester called it "side eject." Made in calibers 30-30, 7x30 Waters, 307, 356 & 357 Win.; 7x30 Waters has 7-shot magazine & 24" barrel; other models have 6-shot magazines & 20" barrels; 307, 356 & 357 calibers made from 1984 to 1986; 30-30 & 7x30 Waters made from 1984 to 1987; add 10% for 7x30 Waters.

Estimated Value: Excellent: $275.00
                       Very good: $205.00

Winchester Model 94 Side Eject
Similar to the Model 94 Standard with "Side Eject" feature; calibers 30-30, 308, 356, 375 Win. & 7x30 Waters, 6-shot magazine; recoil pad; made from 1985 to present. Add 15% for 7x30 cal. Add 50% for Deluxe Model. Add 10% for checkered stock.

Estimated Value: New (retail): $274.00
                       Excellent: $205.00
                       Very good: $165.00

Winchester Ranger Lever Action Side Eject
Similar to the Model 94 Standard in 30-30 caliber with 5-shot magazine; blade front sight & semi-buckhorn rear; made for economy & utility; smooth wood stock & forearm with walnut finish; made from the mid 1980's to present.

Estimated Value: New (retail): $264.00
                       Excellent: $200.00
                       Very good: $160.00

Winchester Model 94 Classic Rifle or Carbine
Similar to the Model 94 Standard with select walnut stock; scroll engraving. Made from the late 1960's to early 1970's.

Estimated Value: Excellent: $225.00
                       Very good: $180.00

Winchester Model 94 Wrangler
Same as the Model 94 Trapper with hoop-type finger lever; roll-engraved receiver; 32 Special caliber with 5-shot magazine; no angle eject feature; made from about 1980 to 1984.

Estimated Value: Excellent: $220.00
                       Very good: $175.00

Winchester Model 94 Wrangler II
Similar to the Model 94 Wrangler in 38-55 caliber; has angle eject feature. Made from about 1984 to 1986.

Estimated Value: Excellent: $225.00
                       Very good: $280.00

Winchester Model 55

Winchester Model 64

Winchester Model 64 Deer

Winchester Model 64

Similar to the Model 94 & 55 with improvements; 20" or 26" barrel; available in 25-35, 30-30, 32, 219 Zipper (from 1938-41). Made from the early 1930's to the late 1950's. Add $200.00 for 219 Zipper caliber.

Estimated Value: Excellent: **$350.00**
                Very good: **$280.00**

Winchester Model 55

Similar to the Model 94 with a 24" nickel steel barrel. Made from the mid 1920's to the early 1930's.

Estimated Value: Excellent: **$690.00**
                Very good: **$550.00**

Winchester Model 64 Deer

Similar to the Model 64 in 32 & 30-30 caliber; swivels; checkered pistol grip stock. Made from the mid 1930's to mid 1950's.

Estimated Value: Excellent: **$475.00**
                Very good: **$380.00**

Winchester Model 95

Winchester Model 95 Carbine

Winchester Model 95

Caliber: 30-40 Krag, 30-06, 30-30, 303, 35, 405
Action: Lever-action; exposed hammer; repeating
Magazine: 4-shot & 5-shot box
Barrel: 24", 26", 28", octagon, round or half octagon
Sights: Open rear, bead front
Stock & Forearm: Plain wood straight stock & tapered lipped forearm. A limited number was available with a pistol grip
Approximate wt.: 8½ lbs.
Comments: Made from about 1895 to the early 1930's. A few thousand early models were built with a flat receiver; add $200.00.

Estimated Value: Excellent: **$825.00**
                Very good: **$650.00**

Winchester Model 95 Carbine

Similar to the Model 95 with a 22" barrel.

Estimated Value: Excellent: **$1,000.00**
                Very good: **$ 800.00**

Winchester Model 1895 Musket

Similar to the Model 1895 with a 28" or 30" round nickel steel barrel; full-length forearm; barrel bands; 30-40 gov't caliber. Add $300.00 for U.S. Gov't models.

Estimated Value: Excellent: **$900.00**
                Very good: **$675.00**

Winchester Model 71

Winchester Model 88

Winchester Model 71
Caliber: 348 Win.
Action: Lever-action; exposed hammer; repeating
Magazine: 4-shot tubular
Barrel: Blued; 20" or 24"
Sights: Open rear, hooded ramp front; peepsights available
Stock & Forearm: Plain or checkered walnut pistol grip stock & forearm; swivels available
Approximate wt.: 8 lbs.
Comments: Made from the mid 1930's to the late 1950's.
Estimated Value: Excellent: $600.00
Very good: $450.00

Winchester Model 71 Special
Similar to the Model 71 with checkering & swivels.
Estimated Value: Excellent: $650.00
Very good: $520.00

Winchester Model 88
Caliber: 243, 284, 308, 358
Action: Lever-action; hammerless; repeating
Magazine: 4-shot box on late models; 5-shot box on early models; 3-shot box in 284 caliber
Barrel: 22"
Sights: Folding leaf rear, hooded ramp front
Stock & Forearm: Checkered walnut one-piece semi-pistol grip stock & forearm; barrel band
Approximate wt.: 7¼ lbs.
Comments: Made from the mid 1950's to mid 1970's.
Estimated Value: Excellent: $370.00
Very good: $295.00

Winchester Model 88 Carbine
Similar to the Model 88 with a plain stock & forearm & 19" barrel. Made from the late 1960's to early 1970's.
Estimated Value: Excellent: $395.00
Very good: $315.00

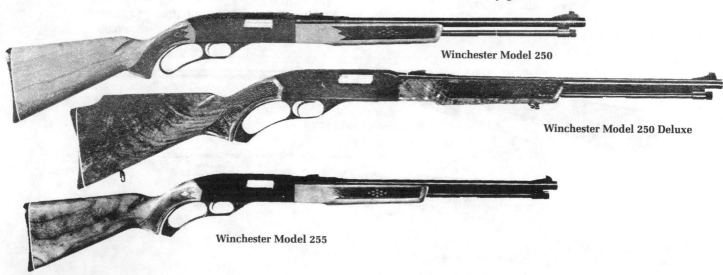

Winchester Model 250

Winchester Model 250 Deluxe

Winchester Model 255

Winchester Model 250
Caliber: 22 short, long, long rifle
Action: Lever-action; hammerless; repeating
Magazine: Tubular; 15 long rifles, 17 longs, 21 shorts
Barrel: Blued; 20½"
Sights: Open rear, ramp front
Stock & Forearm: Plain or checkered walnut semi-pistol grip stock & forearm
Approximate wt.: 5 lbs.
Comments: Made from the early 1960's to mid 1970's.
Estimated Value: Excellent: $130.00
Very good: $105.00

Winchester Model 250 Deluxe
Similar to the Model 250 with Monte Carlo stock & swivels.
Estimated Value: Excellent: $140.00
Very good: $115.00

Winchester Model 255
Similar to the Model 250 in 22 magnum caliber; 11-shot magazine. Made from the mid 1960's to early 1970's.
Estimated Value: Excellent: $150.00
Very good: $120.00

Winchester Model 9422

Winchester Model 9422 & 9422 XTR

Caliber: 22 short, long, long rifle or 22 magnum
Action: Lever-action; exposed hammer; repeating
Magazine: Tubular; 15 long rifles, 17 longs, 21 shorts. 11 round magazine in 22 magnum
Barrel: 20"
Sights: Adjustable rear, hooded ramp front
Stock & Forearm: Plain or checkered wood straight grip stock & forearm; barrel band
Approximate wt.: 6¼ lbs.
Comments: Made from about 1972 to present. 9422XTR has higher grade wood & finish also checkered. Introduced in 1979. Add 4% for magnum.
Estimated Value: New (retail): $324.00
                       Excellent: $245.00
                       Very good: $195.00

Winchester Model 9422XTR Classic Rifle

Similar to the Model 9422XTR with satin-finish walnut pistol grip stock & forearm, fluted comb & cresent steel buttplate; curved finger lever; longer forearm; 22½" barrel; 22 or 22 magnum caliber. Introduced in 1986, discontinued in 1989.
Estimated Value: Excellent: $245.00
                       Very good: $195.00

Winchester Model 9422 Win-Tuff, Win-Cam

Similar to the Model 9422 with laminated stock of brown dyed wood (Win-Tuff) or green & brown dyed wood (Win-Cam). Add 4% for Magnum
Estimated Value: New (retail) $335.00
                       Excellent: $250.00
                       Very good: $200.00

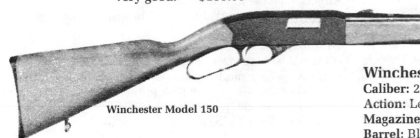

Winchester Model 150

Winchester Model 150

Caliber: 22 short, long, long rifle
Action: Lever-action; hammerless; repeating
Magazine: Tubular; 15 long rifles, 17 longs, 21 shorts
Barrel: Blued; 20½"
Sights: Open adjustable rear, blade front
Stock & Forearm: Straight stock & forearm; barrel band; alloy receiver
Approximate wt.: 5 lbs.
Comments: Made from the late 1960's to mid 1970's.
Estimated Value: Excellent: $120.00
                       Very good: $ 95.00

Winchester Model 1890

Winchester Model 06

Winchester Model 1890

Caliber: 22 short, long, long rifle
Action: Slide action; exposed hammer; repeating
Magazine: Tubular; 11 long rifles, 12 longs, 15 shorts
Barrel: 24" octagon
Sights: Open, bead front
Stock & Forearm: Plain wood straight grip stock & grooved slid handle
Approximate wt.: 5¾ lbs.
Comments: Made from 1890 to the early 1930's.
Estimated Value: Excellent: $450.00
                       Very good: $360.00

Winchester Model 06

Caliber: 22 short, long, long rifle
Action: Slide action; exposed hammer; repeating
Magazine: Tubular; 11 long rifles, 12 longs, 15 shorts
Barrel: Blued; 20"
Sights: Open rear, bead front
Stock & Forearm: Plain wood straight stock, grooved or plain slide handle; nickel trimmed receiver & pistol grip stock available
Approximate wt.: 5 lbs.
Comments: Made from 1906 until the early 1930's.
Estimated Value: Excellent: $400.00
                       Very good: $320.00

Winchester Model 61

Winchester Model 62

Winchester Model 61 Magnum

Similar to the Model 61 in 22 magnum. Made in the early 1960's.

Estimated Value: Excellent: $350.00
Very good: $280.00

Winchester Model 62, 62A

Caliber: 22 short, long, long rifle
Action: Slide action; exposed hammer; repeating
Magazine: Tubular; 14 long rifles, 16 longs, 20 shorts
Barrel: Blued; 23"
Sights: Open rear, blade front
Stock & Forearm: Walnut straight grip stock & grooved slide handle
Approximate wt.: 5½ lbs.
Comments: Made from the early 1930's to the late 1950's. A gallery model was available chambered for 22 shot only. It became 62A in the 1940's with internal improvements.

Estimated Value: Excellent: $390.00
Very good: $310.00

Winchester Model 61

Caliber: 22 short, long, long rifle
Action: Slide action; repeating
Magazine: Tubular; 14 long rifles, 16 longs, 20 shorts
Barrel: Blued; 24", round or octagon
Sights: Open rear, bead front
Stock & Forearm: Plain wood semi-pistol grip stock & grooved slide handle
Approximate wt.: 5½ lbs.
Comments: Made from the early 1930's to early 1960's.

Estimated Value: Excellent: $355.00
Very good: $285.00

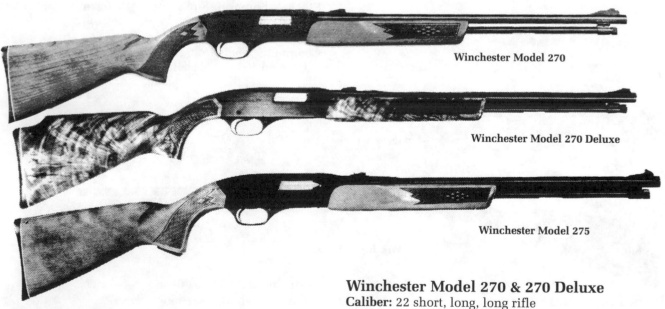

Winchester Model 270

Winchester Model 270 Deluxe

Winchester Model 275

Winchester Model 270 & 270 Deluxe

Caliber: 22 short, long, long rifle
Action: Slide action; repeating
Magazine: Tubular, 15 long rifles, 17 longs, 21 shorts
Barrel: 20½"
Sights: Open rear, ramp front
Stock & Forearm: Wanut pistol grip stock & slide handle; plastic available; later models checkered; Model 270 Deluxe has Monte Carlo stock.
Approximate wt.: 5 lbs.
Comments: Made from the mid 1960's to mid 1970's.

Estimated Value: Excellent: $120.00
Very good: $ 85.00

Winchester Model 275 & 275 Deluxe

Similar to the Model 270 & 270 Deluxe in 22 magnum caliber.

Estimated Value: Excellent: $125.00
Very good: $ 90.00

Winchester Model 03

Winchester Model 05

Winchester Model 07

Winchester Model 10

Winchester Model 03

Caliber: 22 short, long, long rifle
Action: Semi-automatic
Magazine: 10-shot tubular, loaded in stock
Barrel: Blued; 20"
Sights: Open rear, bead front
Stock & Forearm: Plain wood semi-pistol grip or straight stock; checkering on some models
Approximate wt.: 6 lbs.
Comments: Made from 1903 to the mid 1930's.
Estimated Value: Excellent: $300.00
                         Very good: $225.00

Winchester Model 05

Similar to the Model 03 with a 5- or 10-shot detachable box magazine; 22" barrel. Made to about 1920.
Estimated Value: Excellent: $350.00
                         Very good: $270.00

Winchester Model 07

Caliber: 351
Action: Semi-automatic; hammerless
Magazine: 5- or 10-shot detachable box
Barrel: Blued; 20"
Sights: Open rear, bead front
Stock & Forearm: Semi-pistol grip stock & forearm; plain wood
Approximate wt.: 7½ lbs.
Comments: Made from 1907 to the late 1950's.
Estimated Value: Excellent: $425.00
                         Very good: $315.00

Winchester Model 10

Similar to the Model 07 except: 401 caliber; 4-shot magazine. Made until the mid 1930's.
Estimated Value: Excellent: $430.00
                         Very good: $320.00

Winchester Model 63

Winchester Model 74

Winchester Model 63

Caliber: 22 long rifle, high speed; 22 long rifle Super X
Action: Semi-automatic
Magazine: 10-shot tubular, load in stock
Barrel: Blued; 20", 23"
Sights: Open rear, bead front
Stock & Forearm: Plain wood pistol grip stock & forearm
Approximate wt.: 5½ lbs.
Comments: Made from the early 1930's to the late 1950's.
Estimated Value: Excellent: $425.00
                         Very good: $320.00

Winchester Model 74

Caliber: 22 long rifle only or 22 short only
Action: Semi-automatic
Magazine: Tubular; 14 long rifles, 20 shorts; in stock
Barrel: Blued; 24"
Sights: Open rear, bead front
Stock & Forearm: Plain wood one-piece semi-pistol grip stock & forearm
Approximate wt.: 6¼ lbs.
Comments: Made from the late 1930's to the mid 1950's.
Estimated Value: Excellent: $200.00
                         Very good: $150.00

Winchester Model 77

Winchester Model 100

Winchester Model 190

Winchester Model 490

Winchester Model 77

Caliber: 22 long rifle
Action: Semi-automatic
Magazine: 8-shot detachable
Barrel: Blued; 22"
Sights: Open rear, bead front
Stock & Forearm: Plain walnut one-piece semi-pistol grip stock & forearm
Approximate wt.: 5½ lbs.
Comments: Made from the mid 1950's to early 1960's.
Estimated Value: Excellent: $135.00
Very good: $105.00

Winchester Model 77 Tubular

Similar to the Model 77 with a 15-shot tubular magazine.
Estimated Value: Excellent: $140.00
Very good: $110.00

Winchester Model 100

Caliber: 243, 248, 308
Action: Semi-automatic, gas operated
Magazine: 4-shot clip; 10-shot clip in 284
Barrel: Blued; 19", 22"
Sights: Open rear, hooded ramp frontt
Stock & Forearm: Checkered walnut one-piece stock & forearm; swivels
Approximate wt.: 7 lbs.
Comments: Made from the early 1960's to mid 1970's.
Estimated Value: Excellent: $375.00
Very good: $300.00

Winchester Model 100 Carbine

Similar to the Model 100 with no checkering: 19" barrel; barrel bands.
Estimated Value: Excellent: $390.00
Very good: $310.00

Winchester Model 190

Caliber: 22 long rifle or 22 long
Action: Semi-automatic; hammerless
Magazine: Tubular; 15 long rifles, 17 longs, 21 shortsp
Barrel: 20½", 22"
Sights: Open rear, blade front
Stock & Forearm: Plain semi-pistol grip stock & forearm
Approximate wt.: 5 lbs.
Comments: 22 short dropped in the early 1970's; made from the mid 1960's to the late 1970's.
Estimated Value: Excellent: $100.00
Very good: $ 80.00

Winchester Model 190 Carbine

Similar to the Model 190 with a 20½" barrel; barrel band & swivels. Discontinued in the early 1970's.
Estimated Value: Excellent: $110.00
Very good: $ 85.00

Winchester Model 290

Caliber: 22 short, long, long rifle
Action: Semi-automatic
Magazine: Tubular; 15 longs, 17 long rifles, 21 shorts
Barrel: 20½"
Sights: Open rear, ramp front
Stock & Forearm: Checkered walnut pistol grip stock & forearm
Approximate wt.: 5 lbs.
Comments: Made from the mid 1960's to mid 1970's.
Estimated Value: Excellent: $110.00
Very good: $ 85.00

Winchester Model 490

Caliber: 22 long rifle
Action: Semi-automatic
Magazine: 5-, 10- or 15 shot clip
Barrel: Blued; 22"
Sights: Folding leaf rear, hooded ramp front
Stock & Forearm: Checkered walnut one-piece pistol grip stock & forearm
Approximate wt.: 6 lbs.
Comments: Made in the mid 1970's.
Estimated Value: Excellent: $165.00
Very good: $130.00

Handguns

AMT

AMT 380 Backup

AMT Backup
Caliber: 380 ACP, 22 long rifle
Action: Semi-automatic; concealed hammer; manual and grip safeties
Magazine: 5-shot clip in 380 ACP; 8-shot in 22LR
Barrel: 2½"
Sights: Fixed
Finish: Smooth wood grips; all stainless steel construction; Lexon gtips on later models
Length Overall: 5"
Approximate wt.: 17 oz.
Comments: Made from 1970's to present.
Estimated Value: New (retail): $250.00
Excellent: $185.00
Very good: $150.00

AMT Combat Government
Caliber: 45 ACP
Action: Semi-automatic; exposed hammer; loaded chamber indicator; manual and grip safeties; adjustable target-type trigger
Magazine: 7-shot clip
Barrel: 5"
Sights: Fixed
Finish: Checkered walnut grips; all stainless steel construction
Length Overall: 8½"
Approximate wt.: 39 oz.
Comments: Made from 1970's to present.
Estimated Value: New (retail): $459.00
Excellent: $345.00
Very good: $275.00

AMT Hardballer
Same as the AMT Combat Government except; adjustable combat type sights; serrated matte slide rib; grooved front and backstraps.
Estimated Value: New (retail): $504.00
Excellent: $375.00
Very good: $300.00

AMT Skipper
Same as the AMT Hardballer except 4" barrel & 7½"overall length.
Estimated Value: Excellent: $375.00
Very good: $300.00

AMT Hardballer Long Slide
Same as the AMT Hardballer except: 7" barrel and 10½" overall length.
Estimated Value: New (retail): $539.00
Excellent: $400.00
Very good: $325.00

AMT Combat Government

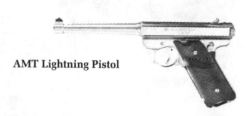

AMT Lightning Pistol

AMT Automag II
Caliber: 22 magnum
Action: Gas assisted, semi-automatic
Magazine: 9-shot clip
Barrel: 6"
Sights: Adjustable front and rear
Finish: Grooved carbon-fiber grips; stainless steel construction
Approximate wt.: 32 oz.,
Length Overall: 11"
Comments: Introduced in the late 1980's; promoted as the "first and only production semi-automatic handgun of its caliber."
Estimated Value: New (retail): $339.00
Excellent: $255.00
Very good: $200.00

AMT Lightning Pistol
Caliber: 22 long rifle
Action: Semi-automatic, concealed hammer
Magazine: 10-shot clip
Barrel: 5" bull, 6½" tapered or bull, 8½" tapered or bull, 10" tapered or bull, 12½" tapered; interchangeable
Sights: Rear adjustable for windage
Finish: Stainless steel; rubber wrap-around grips
Length Overall: 9" (5" barrel)
Approximate wt.: 38 oz. (5" bull barrel)
Comments: Introduced in the mid 1980's. Add 5% for 12½" barrel.
Estimated Value: New (retail): $289.00
Excellent: $215.00
Very good: $175.00

American

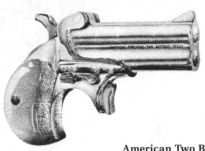

American Two Barrel Derringer

American 25 Automatic

American Two Barrel Derringer, Model 1
Caliber: 22 short, long, long rifle; 22 WMR, 38 Special; other calibers introduced in the early 1980's
Action: Single action; exposed hammer; spur trigger; tip-up barrels
Cylinder: None; cartridges chamber in barrels; 2-shot capacity
Barrel: 3" double barrel (superposed)
Sights: Fixed
Finish: Stainless steel; checkered plasric grips
Length Overall: 5"
Approximate wt.: 15 oz., 11oz., or ultra light 7½ oz.
Comments: Made from about 1972 to 1974. Reintroduced in 1980. All stainless steel construction. Current models marked "American Derringer." A variety of calibers is available.
Estimated Value: New (retail): $225.00 - $369.00
Excellent: $150.00 - $275.00
Very good: $100.00 - $210.00

American 25 Automatic
Caliber: 25 ACP; 250 magnum (after 1980)
Action: Semi-automatic; concealed hammer
Magazine: 8-shot clip; 7-shot in magnum
Barrel: 2"
Sights: Fixed
Finish: Blue or stainless steel; smooth rosewood grips; finger extension on clip
Length Overall: 4½"
Approximate wt.: 15½ lbs.
Comments: Made from about 1969 to 1974; reintroduced in 1980. Early models (1969-1974) are marked "American Firearms." Current models (after 1980) are marked "American Dorringer." Add $35.00 for .250 magnum.

Estimated Value:	Blue	Stainless Steel
Excellent:	$125.00	$150.00
Very good:	$ 95.00	$115.00

American Baby Model
Similar to the 25 Automatic except slightly more compact, 6-shot clip. Produced from 1982 to 1985
Estimated Value: Excellent: $120.00
Very good: $ 90.00

Astra

Astra 1911 Model - Patent
Caliber: 32 ACP (7.65 mm)
Action: Semi-automatic, concealed hammer
Magazine: 7-shot clip
Barrel: 3¼"
Sights: Fixed
Finish: Blued; checkered hard rubber grips
Length Overall: 5¾"
Approximate wt.: 29 oz.
Comments: A Spanish copy of the Browning blowback action, probably made of trade parts. Not made by Unceta y Compania.
Estimated Value: Excellent: $150.00
Very good: $120.00

Astra 1911 Model - Patent

Astra 1915 Model - Patent

Astra 1915 Model - Patent
Caliber: 32 ACP (7.65 mm)
Action: Semi-automatic, concealed hammer
Magazine: 9-shot clip
Barrel: 3¼"
Sights: Fixed
Finish: Blued; checkered hard rubber grips
Length Overall: 5¾"
Approximate wt.: 29 oz.
Comments: A Spanish copy of the Browning blowback action, probably made of trade parts. Not made by Unceta y Compania.
Estimated Value: Excellent: $130.00
Very good: $100.00

Astra 1916 Model - Patent
Caliber: 32 ACP (7.65 mm)
Action: Semi-automatic, concealed hammer
Magazine: 9-shot clip
Barrel: 4"
Sights: Fixed
Finish: Blued; checkered hard rubber or wood grips
Length Overall: 6½"
Approximate wt.: 32 oz.
Comments: A Spanish copy of the Browning blowback action, made under several trade names, probably of trade parts. Many were sold in the United States, Central America and South America. Not made by Unceta y Compania.
Estimated Value: Excellent: $135.00
Very good: $110.00

Astra 1924 Hope
Caliber: 25 ACP (6.35)
Action: Semi-automatic; concealed hammer
Magazine: 6-shot clip
Barrel: 2"
Sights: Fixed
Finish: Blued; checkered rubber grips
Length Overall: 4⅓"
Approximate wt.: 12 oz.
Comments: Some of these pistols have "HOPE" designation on barrel.
Estimated Value: **Excellent:**   **$150.00**
                      Very good: **$120.00**

Astra 1924 Hope

Astra Model 2000 Cub Pocket

Astra 2000 Cub Pocket
Caliber: 22 short, 25 ACP (6.35 mm)
Action: Semi-automatic; exposed hammer
Magazine: 6-shot clip
Barrel: 2⅛"
Sights: Fixed
Finish: Blued; chrome and/or engraved, checkered grips
Length Overall: 4½"
Approximate wt.: 13 to 14 oz.
Comments: A well-made pistol of the post-World War II period. Importation to the United States was discontinued in 1968. Add $20.00 for chrome finish.
Estimated Value: **Excellent:**   **$180.00**
                      Very good: **$140.00**

Astra Camper Pocket
Same as Astra Cub (Model 2000) except: 22 caliber short only; 4" barrel which extends beyond front of slide; laterally adjustable rear sight. Discontinued in 1966. Add $10.00 for chrome finish.
Estimated Value: **Excellent:**   **$160.00**
                      Very good: **$110.00**

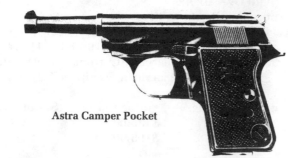

Astra Camper Pocket

Astra Model 300
Caliber: 380 ACP (9 mm Kurz)
Action: Semi-automatic; concealed hammer
Magazine: 7-shot clip
Barrel: 4¼"
Sights: Fixed
Finish: Blued; checkered rubber grips
Length Overall: 6½"
Approximate wt.: 21 oz.
Comments: This pistol was a shorter version of the Model 400 and production was started in 1922.
Estimated Value: **Excellent:**   **$250.00**
                      Very good: **$200.00**

Astra Model 300

Astra Model 600

Astra Model 600
Caliber: 32 ACP (7.65 mm), 9mm Luger
Action: Semi-automatic; concealed hammer
Magazine: 10-shot clip in 32 caliber; 8-shot clip in 9mm
Barrel: 5¼"
Sights: Fixed
Finish: Blued; checkered rubber or wood grips
Length Overall: 8½"
Approximate wt.: 35 oz.
Comments: Made from 1944 to 1945 for military and police use. The 9mm was used as a substitute pistol in German military service, so some will have German acceptance marks.
Estimated Value: **Excellent:**   **$275.00**
                      Very good: **$220.00**

Astra Model 400

Caliber: 9mm Bayard long; 38 ACP, 9mm Steyr, 9mm Glisenti, 9mm Luger, 9mm Browning long cartridges can be used due to chamber design
Action: Semi-automatic; concealed hammer
Magazine: 9-shot clip
Barrel: 6"
Sights: Fixed
Finish: Blued; checkered rubber grips
Length Overall: 9"
Approximate wt.: 36 Oz.
Comments: Made from 1921 until 1945 for both commercial and military use.
Estimated Value: Excellent: $325.00
Very good: $260.00

Astra Model 400

Astra Model 800 Condor

Caliber: 9mm Parabellum
Action: Semi-automatic; exposed hammer
Magazine: 8-shot clip
Barrel: 5¼"
Sights: Fixed
Finish: Blued; checkered grips
Length Overall: 8¼"
Approximate wt.: 32 Oz.
Comments: A post-war version of the Model 600 military pistol. It has a loaded chamber indicator.
Estimated Value: Excellent: $300.00
Very good: $240.00

Astra Model 800 Condor

Astra Model 200 Firecat

Caliber: 25 ACP (6.35mm)
Action: Semi-automatic; concealed hammer; grip safety
Magazine: 6-shot clip
Barrel: 2¼"
Sights: Fixed
Finish: Blued or chrome; plastic grips
Length Overall: 4½"
Approximate wt.: 13 oz.
Comments: A well-machined pistol made from early 1920 to present. It was imported to the United States from World War II until 1968. Add $10.00 for chrome finish.
Estimated Value: Excellent: $165.00
Very good: $130.00

Astra Model 200 Firecat

Astra Model 3000

Astra Model 3000

Caliber: 22 long rifle, 32 ACP, 380ACP (9mm short)
Action: Semi-automatic; concealed hammer
Magazine: 10-shot clip in 22 caliber, 7-shot clip in 32 caliber; 6-shot clip in 380; clip
Barrel: 4"
Sights: Fixed
Finish: Blued; checkered grips
Length Overall: 6⅜"
Approximate wt.: 23 oz.
Comments: Made from about 1947 to 1956. Well-machined and well-finished commercially produced pistol. The 380 caliber has loaded chamber indicator.
Estimated Value: Excellent: $220.00
Very good: $175.00

Astra Model 4000 Falcon

Astra Model 4000 Falcon

Caliber: 22 long rifle, 32 ACP (7.65mm), 380 ACP (9mm short)
Action: Semi-automatic; exposed hammer
Magazine: 10-shot clip in 22 caliber, 8-shot clip in 32 caliber; 7-shot clip in 380 caliber
Barrel: 4¼"
Sights: Fixed
Finish: Blued; checkered grips
Length Overall: 6½"
Approximate wt.: 20 to 24 oz.
Comments: A conversion unit was available to fit the 32 caliber and 380 caliber pistols, so that 22 caliber long rifle ammunition could be used.
Estimated Value: Excellent: $215.00
Very good: $170.00

Astra Model 5000 Constable

Caliber: 22 long rifle, 32 ACP (7.65mm), (32 discontinued), 380 ACP
Action: Double-action; semi-automatic; exposed hammer with round spur
Magazine: 10-shot clip in 22 caliber long rifle, 8-shot clip in 32 ACP; 7-shot clip in 380 ACP
Barrel: 3½"; 6" on Sport model
Sights: Fixed
Finish: Blued or chrome; grooved grips; checkered on late model; plastic or wood grips
Length Overall: 6⅝" to 9⅛"
Approximate wt.: 24 to 26 oz.
Comments: The barrel is rigidly mounted in the frame, all steel construction with hammer block safety. Add 40% for factory engraving; 7% for chrome finish; 4% for 22 cal.
Estimated Value: New (retail): $350.00
                                    Excellent: $260.00
                                    Very good: $210.00

Astra Model 5000 Constable

Astra Model A-80, A-90

Caliber: 9mm Parabellum, 38 Super, 45 ACP
Action: Double action; semi-automatic; exposed hammer
Magazine: 15-shot clip in 9mm and 38 calibers; 9-shot clip in 45 ACP
Barrel: 3¾"
Sights: Fixed
Finish: Blued or chrome; checkered plastic grips
Length Overall: 7"
Approximate wt.: 40 oz.
Comments: Introduced in 1982. Add 10% for chrome finish.
Estimated Value: New (retail): $500.00
                                    Excellent: $375.00
                                    Very good: $300.00

Astra 357 Magnum Revolver

Astra Model 357

Caliber: 357 magnum, 38 special
Action: Double action
Cylinder: 6-shot, swing out
Barrel: 3", 4", 6", 8½" heavy weight with rib
Sights: Adjustable rear, fixed front
Finish: Blued; checkered walnut grips; stainless steel available after 1982
Length Overall: 8¼" to 13¾"
Approximate wt.: 38 to 42 oz.
Comments: All steel construction with wide spur hammer and grooved trigger. Currently made. Add 3% for 8½" barrel; 10% for stainless steel.
Estimated Value: Excellent: $220.00
                                    Very good: $175.00

Astra Model 41, 44

Astra Model 41, 44

Similar to the Model 357 except 41 magnum or 44 magnum caliber; 6" or 8½" barrel. Introduced in the early 1980's. Add $10.00 for 8½" barrel; Model 41 discontinued in mid 1980's.
Estimated Value: New (retail): $450.00
                                    Excellent: $335.00
                                    Very good: $270.00

Astra Model 45

Similar to the Model 357 except 45 Colt or 45 ACP caliber; 6" barrel. Produced from the early 1980's to 1987.
Estimated Value: Excellent: $250.00
                                    Very good: $200.00

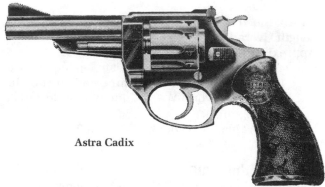

Astra Cadix

Astra Cadix

Caliber: 22 short, long and long rifle, 38 Special
Action: Double action
Cylinder: Swing out 9-shot in 22 caliber; 5-shot in 38 Special
Barrel: 2", 4", and 6"
Sights: Adjustable rear on 4" and 6" barrel
Finish: Blued; checkered grips
Length Overall: 6½", 9", 11"
Approximate wt.: 25 to 27 oz.
Comments: Made from about 1960 to the late 1960's.
Estimated Value: Excellent: $140.00
                                    Very good: $110.00

Auto Mag

Auto Mag

Caliber: 357 auto magnum or 44 auto magnum custom loaded or hand loaded cartridges (no commerical ammo available)

Action: Semi-automatic; exposed hammer; adjustable trigger

Magazine: 7-shot clip

Barrel: 6½" ventilated rib (44 auto mag.); 6½" or 8½" (.357 auto mag.); no rib on 8½" barrel

Sights: Ramp front sight & adjustable rear sight

Finish: Stainless steel; black polyurethane grips

Length Overall: 11½"

Approximate wt.: 60 oz.

Comments: The most potent auto loader made. Designed by Harry Sanford, it was made by different factories (Auto Mag Corp., TDE Corp., High Standard & etc.). Requires special ammunition made from the 308 Winchester, .243, or 7.62 NATO cases. Made from about 1970 to late 1970's. All stainless steel construction. Total production was rather small. First model called Pasadena Auto Mag. in .44 caliber only.

Auto Mag

Estimated Value: **Excellent:** $1,500.00 - $2,400.00
                      Very good: $1,200.00 - $1,800.00

Bauer

Bauer Stainless

Bauer Stainless

Caliber: 25 ACP

Action: Semi-automatic; concealed hammer

Magazine: 6-shot clip

Barrel: 2⅛"

Sights: Fixed

Finish: Heat treated stainless steel; plastic grips

Length Overall: 4"

Approximate wt.: 10 oz.

Comments: Manufactured in the United States from about 1972 to mid 1980's.

Estimated Value: **Excellent;** $120.00
                      Very good; $ 95.00

Bayard

Bayard Model 1908

Bayard Model 1908

Caliber: 25 ACP (6.35 mm), 32 ACP (7.65mm), 380 ACP (9mm short)

Action: Semi-automatic; concealed hammer

Magazine: 6-shot clip

Barrel: 2¼"

Sights: Fixed

Finish: Blued; checkered grips

Length Overall: 5"

Approximate wt.: 15 to 17 oz.

Comments: Made from basic Pieper patents of the 1900's. All calibers appear the same from a side view. Commercially sold throughout the world; one of the most compact pistols made.

Estimated Value: **Excellent:** $175.00
                      Very good: $130.00

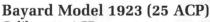
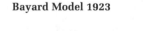

Bayard Model 1923

Bayard Model 1923 (25 ACP)

Caliber: 25 ACP

Action: Semi-automatic; concealed hammer

Magazine: 6-shot clip

Barrel: 2⅛"

Sights: Fixed

Finish: Blued; checkered grips

Length Overall: 4⅓"

Approximate wt.: 12 ozs.

Comments: A Belgian variation of the Browning. This model has better construction than the Model 1908.

Estimated Value: **Excellent:** $190.00
                      Very good: $145.00

Bayard Model 1923 (32, 380)
Caliber: 32 ACP (7.65mm), 380 ACP (9mm short)
Action: Semi-automatic; concealed hammer
Magazine: 6-shot clip
Barrel: 3⅜"
Sights: Fixed
Finish: Blued; checkered grips
Length Overall: 5¾"
Approximate wt.: 18 to 19 oz.
Comments: A Belgian variation of the Browning. Better construction than the 1908.
Estimated Value: Excellent: $225.00
Very good: $165.00

Bayard Model 1930
Caliber: 25 ACP (6.35mm)
Action: Semi-automatic; concealed hammer
Magazine: 6-shot clip
Barrel: 2"
Sights: Fixed
Finish: Blued; checkered grips
Length Overall: 4⅜"
Approximate wt.: 12 oz.
Comments: A modification of the Model 1923.
Estimated Value: Excellent: $200.00
Very good: $160.00

Beretta

Beretta Model 1915

Beretta Model 1919 "Bantam"

Beretta Model 1923

Beretta Model 1915
Caliber: 32 ACP (7.65mm)
Action: Semi-automatic; concealed hammer
Magazine: 8-shot clip
Barrel: 3¼"
Sights: Fixed
Finish: Blued; wood or metal grips
Length Overall: 5⅞"
Approximate wt.: 20 oz.
Comments: The earliest of the Beretta series used for military service during World War I as well as being sold commercially. Has rigid lanyard loop on left side. Grip safety was added in 1919. Made from about 1915 to 1924.
Estimated Value: Excellent: $250.00
Very good: $185.00

Beretta Model 1919 Bantam
Caliber: 25 ACP (6.35mm)
Action: Semi-automatic; concealed hammer
Magazine: 7-shot clip
Barrel: 2½"
Sights: Fixed
Finish: Blued; wood grips
Length Overall: 4½"
Approximate wt.: 14 oz.
Comments: Basic Beretta patent with addition of a grip safety. The front sight contour was changed prior to World War II. Importation to the United States was discontinued in 1956.
Estimated Value: Excellent: $175.00
Very good: $130.00

Beretta Model 1923
Caliber: 9mm Luger
Action: Semi-automatic; exposed hammer
Magazine: 9-shot clip
Barrel: 4"
Sights: Fixed
Finish: Blued; wood grips
Length Overall: 6½"
Approximate wt.: 30 oz.
Comments: Basically an Italian service pistol, but also sold commercially. A modified version of the 1915, 1919 patents. This was the first model produced with exposed hammer. Lanyard loop on left side.
Estimated Value: Excellent: $300.00
Very good: $225.00

Beretta Model 1931

Caliber: 32 ACP (7.65mm)
Action: Semi-automatic; concealed hammer
Magazine: 7-shot clip
Barrel: 3⁵⁄₁₆"
Sights: Fixed
Finish: Blued; wood grips
Length Overall: 5¾"
Approximate wt.: 22 oz.
Comments: A modified version of the Model 1923.
Estimated Value: Excellent: $250.00
                       Very good: $200.00

Beretta Model 1931

Beretta Cougar

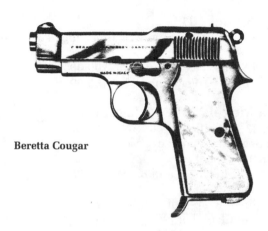

Beretta Model 934 (1934)

Beretta Model 934 (1934) 380 & 935 (1935) 32

Caliber: 32 ACP (7.65mm), 380 ACP (9mm short)
Action: Semi-automatic; exposed hammer
Magazine: 8-shot clip in 32; and 7-shot clip in 380
Barrel: 3½"
Sights: Fixed
Finish: Blued; plastic grips
Length Overall: 6"
Approximate wt.: 22 to 24 oz.
Comments: Official pistol of the Italian Armed Forces
    from 1934 until 1951 in 380 caliber. Still sold com-
    mercially and used by Italian police. Lanyard loop
    on left side. Model 935 was discontinued in 1958.
Estimated Value: Excellent: $275.00
                       Very good: $220.00

Beretta Cougar

Caliber: 380 ACP (9mm short)
Action: Semi-automatic; exposed hammer
Magazine: 7-shot clip
Barrel: 3½"
Sights: Fixed
Finish: Blued or chrome; plastic grips
Length Overall: 6"
Approximate wt.: 22 oz.
Comments: A post-World War II version of the Model
    934 (1934). Those imported into the United States
    have the "Cougar" name on pistol. Some of the later
    models are marked "P.B. 1966." Add $10.00 for
    chrome.
Estimated Value: Excellent: $250.00
                       Very good: $200.00

Beretta Model 948 Plinker

Caliber: 22 long rifle
Action: Semi-automatic; exposed hammer
Magazine: 7-shot clip
Barrel: 3½", 6"
Sights: Fixed
Finish: Blued; plastic grips
Length Overall: 6" or 8½"
Approximate wt.: 16 to 18 oz.
Comments: Made from 1948 to 1958. Similar to the
    1934/35 series except: 22 caliber; aluminum alloy
    frame. Replaced by the "Jaguar." The 6" barrel
    extends beyond the slide about 3".
Estimated Value: Excellent: $150.00
                       Very good: $110.00

Beretta Model 935 (1935)

Beretta Model 70 Puma

Caliber: 32 ACP (7.65mm); 380 ACP
Action: Semi-automatic; exposed hammer
Magazine: 7-shot clip
Barrel: 3½"
Sights: Fixed
Finish: Blued; plastic wrap-around grip
Length Overall: 6½"
Approximate wt.: 15 oz.
Comments: Post-World War II (1946) version of the Model 935 (1935). Aluminum alloy frame was used to reduce weight. Those imported into the United States have "Puma" designation. Also made with steel frame. Discontinued. Add $15.00 for nickel finish.
Estimated Value: Excellent: $200.00
Very good: $150.00

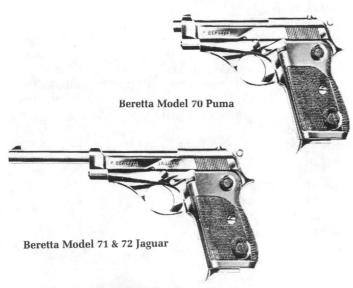

Beretta Model 70 Puma

Beretta Model 71 & 72 Jaguar

Beretta Model 70T

Beretta Model 70T

Caliber: 32 ACP (7,65mm)
Action: Semi-automatic; exposed hammer
Magazine: 9-shot clip
Barrel: 6"
Sights: Adjustable rear; blade front
Finish: Blued; plastic wrap-around grip
Length Overall: 9½"
Approximate wt.: 20 oz.
Comments: Imported from Italy. Target length barrel extends beyond front of slide.
Estimated Value: Excellent: $220.00
Very good: $175.00

Beretta Model 101

Same as Model 70T except: 22 caliber long rifle; 10-shot clip.
Estimated Value: Excellent: $200.00
Very good: $150.00

Beretta Models 71 & 72 Jaguar

Caliber: 22 long rifle
Action: Semi-automatic; exposed hammer
Magazine: 7-shot clip
Barrel: 3½" (Model 71) and 6" (Model 72)
Sights: Fixed
Finish: Blued; wrap-around plastic grip
Length Overall: 6¼" or 8¾"
Approximate wt.: 16-18 oz.
Comments: Importation to the United States started in 1956. The light weight was obtained by using aluminum alloy receiver. Similar in appearance to the Puma except the 6" barrel extends about 3" beyond the slide.
Estimated Value: Excellent: $215.00
Very good: $170.00

Beretta Model 70S

Beretta Model 70S

Caliber: 380 ACP (9mm short); 22 long rifle
Action: Semi-automatic; exposed hammer
Magazine: 7-shot clip in 380; 8-shot clip in 22
Barrel: 3½"
Sights: Fixed
Finish: Blued; 2-piece wrap-around plastic grip
Length Overall: 6¼"
Approximate wt.: 24 oz.
Comments: All steel compact pistol imported from Italy. Discontinued in mid 1980's.
Estimated Value: Excellent: $210.00
Very good: $155.00

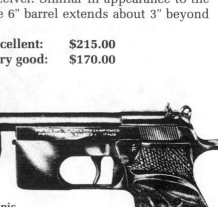
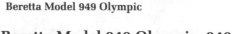

Beretta Model 949 Olympic

Beretta Model 949 Olympic, 949C

Caliber: 22 short, 22 long rifle
Action: Semi-automatic; exposed hammer
Magazine: 5-shot clip
Barrel: 8¾" with compensator muzzle brake
Sights: Rear adjustable for windage, front adjustable for elevation
Finish: Blued; checkered walnut grips with thumb rest
Length Overall: 12½"
Approximate wt.: 38 oz.
Comments: Also called the 949C, it was designed for use in Olympic rapid-fire matches & designed 949LR. Both models have been discontinued.
Estimated Value: Excellent: $450.00
Very good: $360.00

Beretta Model 951 (1951)

Caliber: 9mm Parabellum (Luger)
Action: Semi-automatic; exposed hammer
Magazine: 8-shot clip
Barrel: 4½"
Sights: Fixed
Finish: Blued; plastic wrap-around grip
Length Overall: 8"
Approximate wt.: 31 oz.
Comments: First produced in 1950 & adopted by Italian Army & Navy. Basic 1934 model features except it has aluminum alloy receiver. Also known as Brigadier model.
Estimated Value: Excellent: $325.00
Very good: $250.00

Beretta Minx M2, Model 950 B, 950 BS

Caliber: 22 short, 25 ACP
Action: Semi-automatic; exposed hammer
Magazine: 6-shot clip
Barrel: 2½"
Sights: Fixed
Finish: Blued or nickel; plastic grips; wood grips
Length Overall: 4½"
Approximate wt.: 10 oz.
Comments: Made from 1956 to present. Imported from 1956 to 1968. Aluminum alloy frame with a hinged barrel that tips up at chamber end. Can be used as single shot by removing magazine & tipping up barrel to load. Reintroduced in 1979, manufactured in the United States. Add 17% for nickel finish; Add $65.00 for engraving & wood grips.
Estimated Value: New (retail): $161.00
Excellent: $120.00
Very good: $ 95.00

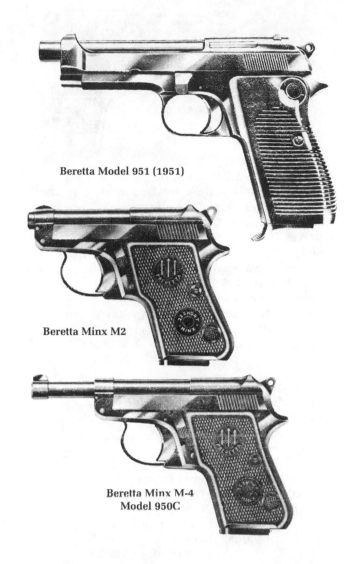

Beretta Model 951 (1951)

Beretta Minx M2

Beretta Minx M-4
Model 950C

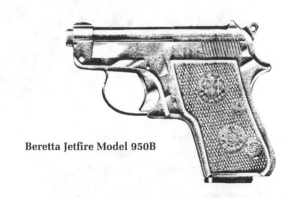

Beretta Jetfire Model 950B

Beretta Model 76

Beretta Minx M-4, Model 950C, 950 BS4

Same as Minx M-2, except: 4" barrel; overall length 6"; approximate weight 12 oz. Add 10% for nickel finish.
Estimated Value: Excellent: $150.00
Very good: $110.00

Beretta Jetfire Model 950B

Same as Minx M-2, except: 25 ACP (6.35mm) caliber; 6-shot magazine. Add 7% for nickel finish.
Estimated Value: Excellent: $145.00
Very good: $100.00

Beretta Model 76 Target

Caliber: 22 long rifle
Action: Semi-automatic; exposed hammer
Magazine: 10-shot clip
Barrel: 6"
Sights: Adjustable rear, blade front
Finish: Blued; 2-piece wrap around plastic or wood grip
Length Overall: 9½"
Approximate wt.: 35 oz.
Comments: Imported from Italy. Competition-type heavy barrel. Add 10% for wood grips. Discontinued in mid 1980's.
Estimated Value: Excellent: $280.00
Very good: $210.00

Beretta Model DA 380

Beretta Model DA 380

Caliber: 380 ACP (9mm short)
Action: Double action; semi-automatic; exposed round spur hammer
Magazine: 13-shot staggered clip
Barrel: 3¾"
Sights: Fixed
Finish: Blued; smooth walnut grips
Length Overall: 6½"
Approximate wt.: 23 oz.
Comments: This pistol features magazine release and safety release for either right or left hand.
Estimated Value: Excellent: $300.00
　　　　　　　　　　Very good: $225.00

Beretta Model 90

Caliber: 32 ACP (7.65mm short)
Action: Semi-automatic; straight blow-back; double action; exposed hammer
Magazine: 8-shot clip
Barrel: 3½"
Finish: Blued; contoured plastic grips
Length Overall: 6½"
Approximate wt.: 19 oz.
Comments: Discontinued in mid 1980's.
Estimated Value: Excellent: $290.00
　　　　　　　　　　Very good: $220.00

Beretta Model 92, 92S

Caliber: 9mm Parabellum
Action: Semi-automatic; double and single action
Magazine: 15-shot clip
Barrel: 5"
Sights: Fixed
Finish: Blued; plastic or smooth wood grips
Length Overall: 8½"
Approximate wt.: 33 oz.
Comments: Made from the late 1970's to early 1980's. Add 5% for wood grips. Loaded chamber indicator.
Estimated Value: Excellent: $410.00
　　　　　　　　　　Very good: $300.00

Beretta Model 90

Beretta Model 20

Beretta Model 92SB

Caliber: 9mm Parabellum
Action: Semi-automatic; straight blow-back; double action; exposed hammer
Magazine: 15-shot staggered clip
Barrel: 5"
Sights: Fixed
Finish: Blued; walnut or checkered plastic grips
Length Overall: 8½"
Approximate wt.: 34½ oz.
Comments: Introduced in the early 1980's. Add 3% for wood grips.
Estimated Value: Excellent: $450.00
　　　　　　　　　　Very good: $340.00

Beretta Model 92SB Compact

Similar to the Model 92SB except 4¼" barrel; 13-shot clip; weight 31 oz. Add 3% for wood grips.
Estimated Value: New (retail) $605.00
　　　　　　　　　　Excellent: $465.00
　　　　　　　　　　Very good: $375.00

Beretta Model 92F

Similar to the Model 92SB with improved safety features, ambidextrous safety, open slide design, non-glare finish, reversible magazine release button, disassembling latch. Adopted for use by the U.S. military. Add 4% for wood grips.
Estimated Value: New (retail) $600.00
　　　　　　　　　　Excellent: $450.00
　　　　　　　　　　Very good: $365.00

Beretta Model 92

Beretta Model 92F

Beretta Model 92F

Similar to the Model 92F with a 4¼" barrel, 13-shot clip, weighs 31 oz. Add 4% for wood grips.
Estimated Value: New (retail) $620.00
　　　　　　　　　　Excellent: $465.00
　　　　　　　　　　Very good: $370.00

Beretta Model 20

Caliber: 25 ACP
Action: Straight blowback, recoil ejection, double action semi-automatic
Magazine: 8-shot clip
Barrel: 2½" tip-up
Sights: Fixed
Finish: Blued; alloy frame, plastic or walnut grips
Length Overall: 5"
Approximate wt.: 10½ oz.
Comments: Introduced in 1984. Discontinued 1986.
Estimated Value: Excellent: $175.00
　　　　　　　　　　Very good: $120.00

Beretta Model 21

Caliber: 22 long rifle, 25 ACP
Action: Straight blowback, double action semi-automatic
Magazine: 7-shot clip
Barrel: 2½" tip up
Sights: Fixed
Finish: Blued or nickel, alloy frame; wood grips
Length Overall: 5"
Approximate wt.: 12 oz.
Comments: Introduced in 1984. Add $25.00 for nickel finish (after 1987). Add $35.00 for engraving.
Estimated Value: New (retail): $215.00
  Excellent: $160.00
  Very good: $130.00

Beretta Model 21

Beretta Model 81

Caliber: 32 ACP
Action: Semi-automatic; double & single action
Magazine: 12-shot clip
Barrel: 3¾"
Sights: Fixed
Finish: Blued; plastic or smooth wood grips; nickel available
Length Overall: 6¾"
Approximate wt.: 23½ oz.
Comments: Produced in the late 1970's to about 1984. Add 3% for wood grips; 15% for nickel finish.
Estimated Value: Excellent: $310.00
  Very good: $230.00

Beretta Model 81

Beretta Model 82

Caliber: 32 ACP (7.65mm)
Action: Semi-automatic; straight blow-back; double action; exposed hammer
Magazine: 9-shot clip
Barrel: 3¾"
Sights: Fixed
Finish: Blued or nickel, walnut grips
Length Overall: 6¾"
Approximate wt.: 17 oz.
Comments: Similar to the Model 81 with a more compact grip size. Add 15% for nickel finish.
Estimated Value: Excellent: $310.00
  Very good: $230.00

Beretta Model 86

Beretta Model 84

Similar to the Model 81 in 380 caliber (9mm short); 13-shot clip. Add 5% for wood grips; 14% for nickel finish.
Estimated Value: New (retail) $479.00
  Excellent: $360.00
  Very good: $290.00

Beretta Model 85

Similar to the Model 82 except 380 caliber (9mm short) & 8-shot clip. Add 14% for nickel; 6% for wood grips.
Estimated Value: New (retail) $440.00
  Excellent: $330.00
  Very good: $265.00

Beretta Model 86

Similar to the Model 85 with tip-up barrel for loading without working the slide; discontinued 1987. Add 20% for wood grips.
Estimated Value: Excellent: $300.00
  Very good: $225.00

Beretta Model 87

Similar to the Model 85 but chambered for 22 long rifle. Add 3% for 6" barrel & counterweight.
Estimated Value: New (retail) $447.00
  Excellent: $335.00
  Very good: $270.00

Beretta Model 89

Caliber: 22 long rifle
Action: Single action, semi-automatic
Magazine: 8-shot clip
Barrel: 6"
Sights: Adjustable target sights
Finish: Blued; contoured walnut grips with thumb rest
Length Overall: 9½"
Approximate wt.: 41 oz.
Comments: Introduced in the late 1980's.
Estimated Value: New (retail): $620.00
  Excellent: $465.00
  Very good: $375.00

Browning

Browning 25 Pocket
Caliber: 25 ACP (6.35mm)
Action: Semi-automatic; concealed hammer
Magazine: 6-shot clip
Barrel: 2⅛"
Sights: Fixed
Finish: Blued; hard rubber grips; nickel plated, light weight, plastic pearl grips; Renaissance engraved Nacolac pearl grips available
Length Overall: 4"
Approximate wt.: 8 to 10 oz.
Comments: A post-World War II modification of the FN Browning Baby Automatic pistol, it was lightened & the grip safety removed. Imported into the U.S. from 1954 to 1968. Pistols imported into the U.S. & Canada usually do not have the FN trademark. Add $25.00 for nickel finish; $550.00 for nickel plated Renaissance engraved model (mint).
Estimated Value: Excellent: $225.00
                      Very good: $170.00

Browning Model 1910
Caliber: 380 ACP (9mm short), 32 ACP
Action: Semi-automatic; concealed hammer
Magazine: 6-shot clip
Barrel: 3½"
Sights: Fixed
Finish: Blued; hard rubber grips; Renaissance engraved, Nacolac peral grips available
Length Overall: 6"
Approximate wt.: 21 oz.
Comments: Basic design of the 1900 model FN Browning, with the appearance streamlined & a grip safety added. Imported from 1954 to 1968. Pistols imported into the U.S. & Canada usually do not have the FN trademark. Add $650.00 for Nickel plated Renaissance engraved model (mint).
Estimated Value: Excellent: $250.00
                      Very good: $200.00

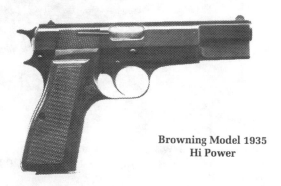

**Browning Model 1935
Hi Power**

Browning 9MM, Hi Power
Caliber: 9mm Parabellum
Action: Semi-automatic; exposed hammer; single action
Magazine: 13-shot clip
Barrel: 4⅝"
Sights: Fixed or adjustable rear sight
Finish: Blued; checkered walnut or molded Polymide grips; Renaissance engraved, Nacolac pearl grips available; chrome available 1982 with Packmayr grips; nickel available until 1986; Matte finish wiht molded grips available after 1985.
Length Overall: 7¾"
Approximate wt.: 34 oz.
Comments: Imported into the U.S. from 1954 to present. Some were manufactured in Canada beginning in 1943. These have alloy frames for weight reduction. Pistols imported into the U. S. from Belgium usually do not have FN tradmark. Add 8½% for walnut grip; Add 10% for adjustable rear sight; 10% for nickel or chrome finish; $850.00 for nickel plated Renaissance engraved (mint); Add 10% for polished blue finish.
Estimated Value: New (retail): $394.00
                      Excellent: $295.00
                      Very good: $235.00

Browning Model 1910

Browning Renaissance Engraved Cased Set
Contains one each of the following:
    Browning 25 Automatic Pistol
    Browning Model 1910 380 Automatic Pistol
    Browning Model 1935 Hi Power Automatic Pistol
in a special walnut carrying case. Each pistol is nickel plated, Renaissance Engraved with Nacolac pearl grips. Imported into the U.S. from 1954 through 1968. Price includes walnut case.
Estimated Value: Mint condition (unused): $4,500.00

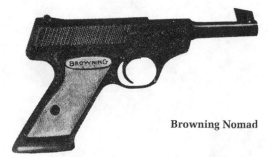

Browning Nomad

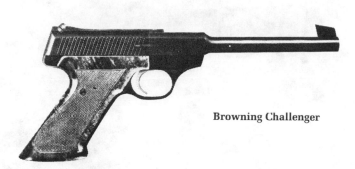

Browning Challenger

Browning Challenger III

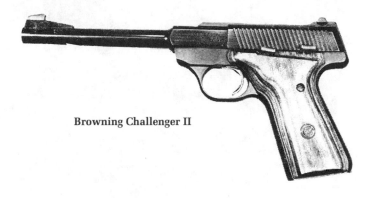

Browning Challenger II

Browning Challenger

Caliber: 22 long rifle
Action: Semi-automatic; concealed hammer
Magazine: 10-shot clip
Barrel: 4½" or 6¾"
Sights: Removable blade front, adjustable rear
Finish: Blued; checkered walnut grips; Gold model (gold inlaid) finely figured walnut grips; Renaissance engraved finely figured walnut grips
Length Overall: 9³⁄₁₆" or 11⁷⁄₁₆"
Approximate wt.: 36 or 38 oz.
Comments: Blued model made from 1963 to 1974. Gold and Renaissance models introduced in 1971. All steel construction. Add $300.00 for gold model; $400.00 for nickel plated Renaissance engraved model.
Estimated Value: Excellent: $340.00
                         Very good: $275.00

Browning Challenger II

Similar to the Challenger except 6¾" barrel only; made from about 1975 to mid 1980's. Impregnated wood grips.
Estimated Value: Excellent: $200.00
                         Very good: $150.00

Browning Challenger III

Caliber: 22 long rifle
Action: Semi-automatic; concealed hammer
Magazine: 10-shot clip
Barrel: 5½" bull barrel
Sights: Blade front, adjustable rear
Finish: Blued; smooth impregnated hardwood grips
Length Overall: 9½"
Approximate wt.: 35 oz.
Comments: Produced 1982 to 1986.
Estimated Value: Excellent: $190.00
                         Very good: $140.00

Browning Challenger III Sporter

Similar to the Challenger III with 6¾" round barrel. Produced 1985 to 1987.
Estimated Value: Excellent: $180.00
                         Very good: $135.00

Browning Nomad

Caliber: 22 long rifle
Action: Semi-automatic; concealed hammer
Magazine: 10-shot clip
Barrel: 4½" or 6¾"
Sights: Removable blade front, adjustable rear sight
Finish: Blued; plastic grips
Length Overall: 9" and 11¼"
Approximate wt.: 26 to 28 oz.
Comments: Made from 1963 to 1973 with an alloy frame.
Estimated Value: Excellent: $250.00
                         Very good: $190.00

Browning Buck Mark 22

Browning Model BDA

Browning Model BDA 380

Browning Buck Mark 22

Caliber: 22 long rifle
Action: Semi-automatic; blow-back; concealed hammer
Magazine: 10-shot clip
Barrel: 5½" bull barrel with non-glare top
Sights: Adjustable rear, ramp front
Finish: Blued; matte except for lustre barrel sides; checkered black molded composit grips, deer head medallion: brass-plate trigger; laminated wood grips on Buck Mark Plus
Length Overall: 9½"
Approximate wt.: 32 oz.
Comments: Introduced in 1985; Add 12% for Buck Mark Plus.

Estimated Value:	New (retail):	$182.00
	Excellent:	$138.00
	Very good:	$110.00

Browning Buck Mark Silhouette

A silhouette-style pistol based on the Buck Mark design; 9⅞" bull barrel; hooded, adjustable sights mounted on a scope sight base; walnut grips; fluted walnut forearm. Introduced in 1988.

Estimated Value:	New (retail):	$309.00
	Excellent:	$230.00
	Very good:	$185.00

Browning Buck Mark Varmint

A varmint-style pistol based on the Buck Mark design; 9⅞" bull barrel, full length scope base walnut grips; a walnut forearm is available. Introduced in 1988.

Estimated Value:	New (retail):	$279.95
	Excellent:	$210.00
	Very good:	$165.00

Browning Model BDA

Caliber: 45 ACP, 9mm, 38 Super ACP
Action: Semi-automatic; exposed hammer; built-in safety block; double and single action
Magazine: 7-shot clip in 45 ACP; 9-shot clip in 9mm and 38 Super
Barrel: 4½"
Sights: Adjustable square notch rear, blade front
Finish: Blued; black checkered plastic grips
Length Overall: 7¾"
Approximate wt.: 29 oz.
Comments: Introduced in the late 1970's, discontinued 1980.

Estimated Value:	Excellent:	$325.00
	Very good:	$260.00

Browning Model BDA 380

Caliber: 380 ACP
Action: Semi-automatic; exposed hammer; double and single action
Magazine: 12-shot staggered row clip
Barrel: 3¾"
Sights: Adjustable sqaure notch rear, blade front
Finish: Blued; smooth walnut grips, bronze medallion; nickel finish available 1982
Length Overall: 6¾"
Approximate wt.: 23 oz.
Comments: Introduced in the late 1970's. Add 5% for nickel finish.

Estimated Value:	New (retail):	$429.95
	Excellent:	$320.00
	Very good:	$260.00

Browning Medalist

Caliber: 22 long rifle
Action: Semi-automatic; concealed hammer
Magazine: 10-shot clip
Barrel: 6¾", ventilated rib
Sights: Removable blade front, adjustable micrometer rear
Finish: Blued; checkered walnut grips with thumb rest; Gold model (gold inlaid) finely figured and carved walnut grips with thumb rest, Renaissance Model engraved, finely figured and carved walnut grips with thumb rest
Length Overall: 11¾"
Approximate wt.: 45 oz.
Comments: All steel construction, made from 1963 to 1974. Gold model and Renaissance model introduced in 1971. Add $450.00 for Gold model; $500.00 for nickel plated Renaissance engraved model (mint).
Estimated Value: Excellent: $550.00
Very good: $440.00

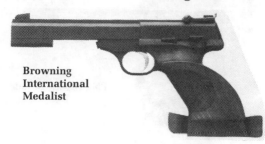

Browning International Medalist

Browning International Medalist

Caliber: 22 long rifle
Action: Semi-automatic; hammerless
Magazine: 10-shot clip
Barrel: 5¹⁵⁄₁₆" heavy, counter weight
Sights: Fixed, non-reflective
Finish: Blued; wide walnut grips, adjustable hand stop
Length Overall: 11¾"
Approximate wt.: 46 oz.
Comments: A target pistol produced in early 1970's.
Estimated Value: Excellent: $565.00
Very good: $450.00

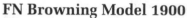

Browning, FN

FN Browning Model 1900

Caliber: 32 ACP (7.65mm)
Action: Semi-automatic; concealed hammer
Magazine: 7-shot clip
Barrel: 4"
Sights: Fixed
Finish: Blued, hard rubber grips with FN trademark
Length Overall: 6¾"
Approximate wt.: 22 oz.
Comments: John Browning's first commercially successful pistol. This was the beginning for the 32 automatic cartridge, which is called 7.65 Browning pistol cartridge in the rest of the world. The 1900 was sold commercially throughout the world & was also used by police & military in countries such as Belgium, Russia, China & France. Made from 1900 to 1912.
Estimated Value: Excellent: $300.00
Very good: $225.00

FN Browning Model 1900

FN Browning Model 1903 Military

FN Browning 6.35mm Pocket

FN Browning Model 1903 Military

Caliber: 9mm Browning long
Action: Semi-automatic; concealed hammer
Magazine: 7-shot clip
Barrel: 5"
Sights: Fixed
Finish: Blued, hard rubber grips with FN trademark
Length Overall: 8"
Approximate wt.: 33 oz.
Comments: Made from 1903 to 1939. Lanyard ring on left grip.
Estimated Value: Excellent: $290.00
Very good: $220.00

FN Browning 6.35 mm Vest Pocket

Caliber: 25 ACP (6.35mm)
Action: Semi-automatic; concealed hammer; grip safety
Magazine: 6-shot clip
Barrel: 2"
Sights: Fixed
Finish: Blued; hard rubber grips with FN trademark
Length Overall: 4½"
Approximate wt.: 13 oz.
Comments: Made from 1905 to 1947.
Estimated Value: Excellent: $335.00
Very good: $250.00

FN Browning Model 1910

FN Browning Model
1935 Hi Power

FN Browning Model 1922 Military and Police

FN Browning Model 1910

Caliber: 32 ACP (7.65mm), 380 ACP (9mm short)
Action: Semi-automatic; concealed hammer
Magazine: 7-shot clip in 32 ACP, 6-short clip in 380
Barrel: 3½"
Sights: Fixed
Finish: Blued, hard rubber grips with FN trademark
Length Overall: 6"
Approximate wt.: 21 oz..
Comments: The basic design of the Model 1900 except it has streamlined appearance and grip safety.
Estimated Value: Excellent: $260.00
Very good: $200.00

FN Browning Baby

Caliber: 25 ACP (6.35mm)
Action: Semi-automatic; concealed hammer
Magazine: 6-shot clip
Barrel: 2⅛"
Sights: Fixed
Finish: Blued, hard rubber grips with FN trademark
Length Overall: 4"
Approximate wt.: 10 oz.
Comments: Made from 1940 to present. All steel construction, similar to Browning 25 Pocket Automatic Pistol, imported into U. S. from 1954 to 1968.
Estimated Value: Excellent: $360.00
Very good: $275.00

FN Browning Baby

FN Browning Model 1922 Military and Police

Caliber: 32 ACP (7.65mm), 380 ACP (9mm short)
Action: Semi-automatic; concealed hammer
Magazine: 9-shot clip in 32; 8-shot clip in 380
Barrel: 4½"
Sights: Fixed
Finish: Blued, hard rubber grips with FN trademark
Length Overall: 7"
Approximate wt.: 24 oz.
Comments: Identical to Model 1910 except it has longer grip frame, magazine and barrel. Lanyard ring on the left grip.
Estimated Value: Excellent: $225.00
Very good: $170.00

FN Browning Model 1935 Hi Power

Caliber: 9mm Parabellum
Action: Semi-automatic; exposed hammer
Magazine: 13-shot staggered line clip
Barrel: 4⅝"
Sights: Fixed or adjustable
Finish: Blued or parkerized; checkered walnut or plastic grips
Length Overall: 7¾"
Approximate wt.: 34 oz.
Comments: Production of this model by John Inglis Co. of Canada began in 1943. Some of these were produced with an alloy frame to reduce weight. Also during World War II Model 1935 was produced under German supervision for military use. The quality of the German pistol was poorer than those made before or after the war. A smaller version was also made from 1937 to 1940 with shorter barrel, slide & 10-shot clip.

Estimated Value:	FN	German (superv.)	Canadian
Excellent:	$450.00	$350.00	$390.00
Very good:	$340.00	$265.00	$300.00

CZ

CZ Model 22 (1922)

Caliber: 380 ACP (9mm short), 25 ACP
Action: Semi-automatic; exposed hammer with shielding on both sides
Magazine: 8-shot clip
Barrel: 3½"
Sights: Fixed
Finish: Blued
Length Overall: 6"
Approximate wt.: 22 oz.
Comments: Made in Czechoslovakia in the 1920's.
Estimated Value: Excellent: $190.00
Very good: $145.00

CZ Model 22 (1922)

CZ Model 1936 Pocket

Caliber: 25 ACP (6.5mm)
Action: Double action semi-automatic; slide does not cock hammer; (hammer is cocked and released by the trigger) shield exposed hammer
Magazine: 8-shot clip
Barrel: 2½"
Sights: Fixed
Finish: Blued; plastic grips
Length Overall: 4¾"
Approximate wt.: 14 oz.
Comments: Made from 1936 to present. U.S. importation discontinued in 1968.
Estimated Value: Excellent: $180.00
Very good: $140.00

CZ Model 1945 Pocket

Same as CZ Model 1936 except for minor modifications.
Estimated Value: Excellent: $190.00
Very good: $145.00

CZ Model 38 (1938)

Caliber: 380 ACP (9mm short)
Action: Double action; semi-automatic
Magazine: 9-shot clip
Barrel: 3¾"
Sights: Fixed
Finish: Blued; plastic grips
Length Overall: 7"
Approximate wt.: 28 oz.
Comments: Made in the late 1930's to mid 1940's.
Estimated Value: Excellent: $200.00
Very good: $160.00

CZ Model 50 (1950)

Caliber: 32 ACP (7.65mm)
Action: Semi-automatic; exposed hammer; double action
Magazine: 8-shot clip
Barrel: 3⅛"
Sights: Fixed
Finish: Blued; plastic grips
Length Overall: 6½"
Approximate wt.: 25 oz.
Comments: No longer imported into the U.S.
Estimated Value: Excellent: $210.00
Very good: $160.00

CZ "Duo" Pocket

Caliber: 25 ACP (6.35mm)
Action: Semi-automatic; concealed hammer
Magazine: 6-shot clip
Barrel: 2⅛"
Sights: Fixed
Finish: Blued; plastic grips
Length Overall: 4½"
Approximate wt.: 15 oz.
Comments: Imported into the U.S was discontinued in 1968.
Estimated Value: Excellent: $180.00
Very good: $140.00

CZ Model 1936 Pocket

Caliber: 32 ACP (7.65mm)
Action: Semi-automatic; exposed hammer with shielding on both sides
Magazine: 8-shot clip
Barrel: 4"
Sights: Fixed
Finish: Blued; plastic grips
Length Overall: 6½"
Approximate wt.: 25 oz.
Comments: This pistol usually bears the CZ mark, but World War II version may have the name Bohmische Waffenfabrik on top of slide.
Estimated Value: Excellent: $195.00
Very good: $145.00

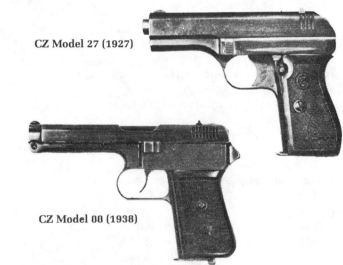

CZ Model 27 (1927)

CZ Model 00 (1938)

CZ Model 1945 Pocket

CZ Model 50 (1950)

CZ "Duo" Pocket

CZ Model 70

Caliber: 7.65mm (32)
Action: Semi-automatic; exposed hammer; double action
Magazine: 8-shot clip
Barrel: 3⅛"
Sights: Fixed
Finish: Blued; checkered plastic grips
Length Overall: 6½"
Approximate wt.: 25 oz.
Comments: Currently produced in Czechoslovakia. Not readily available in the U.S. due to importation prohibitions on some items produced in Iron Curtain countries.
Estimated Value: **Excellent:**   **$225.00**
                       Very good: **$170.00**

CZ Model 75

Caliber: 9mm Parabellum
Action: Semi-automatic; selective double action; exposed hammer;
Magazine: 15-shot clip
Barrel: 4½"
Sights: Fixed
Finish: Blued; checkered plastic grips
Length Overall: 8"
Approximate wt.: 35 oz.
Comments: Currently produced in Czechoslovakia. Not readily available in the U.S. due to importation prohibitions on some items produced in Iron Curtain countries.
Estimated Value: **Excellent:**   **$400.00**
                       Very good: **$310.00**

Charter Arms

Charter Arms
Model 79K

Charter Arms
Police Bulldog

Charter Arms Bulldog

Charter Arms Model 79K

Caliber: 380 Auto, 32 Auto
Action: Semi-automatic; double action; exposed hammer
Magazine: 7-shot clip
Barrel: 3½"
Sights: Adjustable
Finish: Stainless steel; checkered walnut grips
Length Overall: 6½"
Approximate wt.: 24½ oz.
Comments: Made from 1985 to 1987.
Estimated Value: **Excellent:**   **$295.00**
                       Very good: **$220.00**

Charter Arms Model 40

Similar to the Model 79K in 22 long rifle caliber; 8-shot clip; weighs 21½ oz. Made from 1985 to 1987.
Estimated Value: **Excellent:**   **$240.00**
                       Very good: **$180.00**

Charter Arms Explorer II

Charter Arms Explorer II

Caliber: 22 long rifle
Action: Semi-automatic
Magazine: 8-shot clip
Barrel: 6" or 10" interchangeable
Sights: Blade front, adjustable rear
Finish: Black, semi-gloss textured enamel; simulated walnut grips; extra clip storage in grip; also available in silvertone
Length Overall: 13½" with 6" barrel
Approximate wt.: 27 oz.
Comments: A survival pistol styled from the AR-7 rifle; produced from the late 1970's to 1986.
Estimated Value: **Excellent:**   **$90.00**
                       Very good: **$70.00**

Charter Arms Police Bulldog

Caliber: 38 Special, 32 H&R Mag.
Action: Single and double action
Cylinder: 6-shot swing-out
Barrel: 2", 3½", 4"; tapered, bull, or shrouded barrel
Sights: Fixed
Finish: Blue or stainless steel; checked walnut bulldog grips, square butt grips or Neoprene grips
Length Overall: 8½"
Approximate wt.: 21 oz.
Comments: Production began in 1976. Add 25% for stainless steel. Add 8% for shrouded barrel.
Estimated Value: **New (retail)**   **$266.00**
                       Excellent: **$200.00**
                       Very good: **$160.00**

Charter Arms Bulldog

Caliber: 44 Special, 357 magnum (357 mag. discontinued in mid 1980's)
Action: Single and double action; exposed regular or bobbed hammer
Cylinder: 5-shot swing-out
Barrel: 2½", 3", 4", 6" (4" & 6" discontinued in 1985)
Sights: Fixed
Finish: Blued; oil finished, checkered walnut bulldog grips or Neoprene grips; stainless steel added 1982
Length Overall: 7½" (3" barrel)
Approximate wt.: 19 oz.
Comments: Made from 1971 to present. Add 20% for stainless steel.
Estimated Value: **New (retail)**   **$265.00**
                       Excellent: **$200.00**
                       Very good: **$160.00**

Charter Arms Target Bulldog

Similar to the Bulldog except 4" barrel; shrouded ejector rod; adjustable rear sight. Made from the late 1970's to 1989. Add 5% for 44 Special.

Estimated Value:	Excellent:	$175.00
	Very good:	$140.00

Charter Arms Bulldog Pug

Similar to the Bulldog with 2½" shrouded barrel. Introduced in 1986. Add 20% for stainless steel.

Estimated Value:	New (retail):	$286.00
	Excellent:	$215.00
	Very good:	$170.00

Charter Arms Target Bulldog

Charter Arms Bulldog Pug

Charter Arms Undercover

Charter Arms Undercover

Caliber: 38 Special
Action: Single & double action
Magazine: 5-shot, swing-out
Barrel: 2" or 3" (3" discontinued in 1990)
Sights: Fixed
Finish: Blued or nickel; oil finished, plain or hand checkered walnut grips or Neoprene grips; stainless steel added 1982; shrouded barrel after 1989
Length Overall: 6¼" or 7⅜"
Approximate wt.: 16 or 17 oz.
Comments: Made from 1965 to present. Add 5% for nickel (discontinued early 1980's); 25% for stainless steel.

Estimated Value:	New (retail)	$248.00
	Excellent:	$185.00
	Very good:	$145.00

Charter Arms Undercoverette & Lady Blue .32

Caliber: 32 S&W long
Action: Single & double action
Cylinder: 6-shot, swing-out
Barrel: 2"
Sights: Fixed
Finish: Blued; oil finished, plain walnut grips
Length Overall: 6¼"
Approximate wt.: 16½ oz.
Comments: Made from 1970 to present. Also called Undercover.

Estimated Value:	New (retail)	$240.00
	Excellent:	$180.00
	Very good:	$140.00

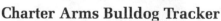

Charter Arms Bulldog Tracker

Charter Arms Undercoverette

Charter Arms Bulldog Tracker

Caliber: 357 magnum and 38 special
Action: Single & double action
Cylinder: 5-shot, swing-out
Barrel: 2½", 4" or 6" bull barrel (4" & 6" discontinued 1989)
Sights: Adjustable rear, ramp front
Finish: Blued; checkered walnut square bull grips
Length Overall: 11"
Approximate wt.: 27½ oz.
Comments: Produced from 1980 to present.

Estimated Value:	New (retail):	$289.00
	Excellent:	$215.00
	Very good:	$175.00

Charter Arms Pathfinder

Charter Arms Pathfinder

Caliber: 22 long rifle, 22 magnum
Action: Single & double action
Cylinder: 6-shot, swing-out
Barrel: 2", 3" or 6" (3" & 6" only after 1987)
Sights: Adjustable rear and partridge-type front on serrated ramp
Finish: Blued; oil finished, plain or hand checkered walnut grips; stainless steel after 1982
Length Overall: 7⅛" (3" barrel)
Approximate wt.: 19 oz.
Comments: Made from 1970 to present. Add 25% for stainless steel; 10% for 6" barrel.

Estimated Value:	New (retail)	$267.00
	Excellent:	$200.00
	Very good:	$160.00

Charter Arms Police Bulldog

Charter Arms Pit Bull

Charter Arms Police Bulldog 44 Special

Caliber: 44 Special
Action: Single or double, exposed hammer
Cylinder: 5-shot, swing-out, simultaneous manual ejector
Barrel: 2½" or 3½" shrouded barrel with solid rib
Sights: Snag free front; fixed or adjustable rear
Finish: Blued or stainless steel; bulldog checkered wood or neoprene grips
Length Overall: 7" or 8"
Approximate wt.: 23 oz.
Comments: Introduced in 1990; add 2% for adjustable rear sight; add 12% for stainless steel.
Estimated Value: New (retail): $295.00
Excellent: $220.00
Very good: $175.00

Charter Arms Police Bulldog 357 Magnum

Caliber: 357 magnum & 38 Special
Action: Single or double, exposed hammer
Cylinder: 5-shot, swing-out, simultaneous ejector
Barrel: 4" shrouded barrel
Sights: Ramp front, adjustable rear
Finish: Stainless steel; black neoprene grips
Length Overall: 8½"
Approximate wt.: 28 oz.
Comments: Introduced in 1990.
Estimated Value: New (retail): $350.00
Excellent: $265.00
Very good: $210.00

Charter Arms Target Bulldog (Stainless Steel)

Caliber: 357 magnum & 38 Special; 44 Special; 9mm
Action: Single or double, exposed hammer
Cylinder: 5-shot, swing-out, simultaneous ejector
Barrel: 5½" shrouded barrel with ventilated rib
Sights: Ramp front; adjustable rear
Finish: Stainless steel with smooth wood target grips
Length Overall: 10"
Approximate wt.: 28 oz.
Comments: Introduced in 1990.
Estimated Value: New (retail): $425.00
Excellent: $315.00
Very good: $255.00

Charter Arms Bonnie & Clyde Set

Caliber: 32 magnum (Bonnie); 38 Special (Clyde)
Action: Single & double action; exposed hammer
Cylinder: 6-shot, swing-out; fluted
Barrel: 2" shrouded barrel marked "Bonnie – 32 mag." or "Clyde – 38 spec."
Sights: Ramp front; fixed rear
Finish: Blued with smooth wood grips
Length Overall: 6½"
Approximate wt.: 21 oz.
Comments: Each gun comes with a gun rug identified by name (Bonnie or Clyde). These guns are sold as a set. Introduced in 1989.
Estimated Value: New (retail): $610.00 per set
Excellent: $460.00 per set
Very good: $365.00 per set

Charter Arms Pit Bull

Caliber: 9mm
Action: Single & double, exposed hammer, regular or bobbed
Cylinder: 5-shot, swing-out, simultaneous ejector
Barrel: 2½", 3½" shrouded barrel
Sights: Fixed or adjustable
Finish: Blued or stainless steel; neoprene grips
Length Overall: 7" or 8"
Approximate wt.: 26 oz.
Comments: Introduced in 1990; add 2% for adjustable sights; add 8% for stainless steel.
Estimated Value: New (retail): $330.00
Excellent: $245.00
Very good: $200.00

Charter Arms Bonnie & Clyde Set

Charter Arms Target Bulldog (Stainless Steel)

Charter Arms Pocket Target

Charter Arms
Police Undercover

Charter Arms Off Duty

Charter Arms Pocket Target
Caliber: 22 short, long, long rifle
Action: Single & double action; exposed hammer
Cylinder: 6-shot, swing-out
Barrel: 3"
Sights: Adjustable snag-free rear, ramp front
Finish: Blued; plain grips or checkered walnut bulldog grips
Length Overall: 7⅛"
Approximate wt.: 19 oz.
Comments: Made from 1960's to 1970's.
Estimated Value: Excellent: $150.00
　　　　　　　　　　Very good: $120.00

Charter Arms Off Duty
Caliber: 38 Special; 22LR (after 1989)
Action: Single & double; exposed hammer
Cylinder: 5-shot, swing-out, fluted; 6-shot in 22 cal.
Barrel: 2" (shrouded barrel after 1989)
Sights: Fixed
Finish: Flat black or stainless steel; smooth or checkered walnut or Neoprene grips
Length Overall: 6½"
Approximate wt.: 16 oz.
Comments: Introduced in 1984. Add 30% for stainless steel.
Estimated Value: New (retail) $210.00
　　　　　　　　　　Excellent: $160.00
　　　　　　　　　　Very good: $125.00

Charter Arms Police Undercover
Caliber: 32 H&R magnum, 38 Special
Action: Single & double, pocket (bobbed) hammer available; exposed hammer
Cylinder: 6-shot, swing-out, fluted
Barrel: 2" or 4" (shrouded barrel only after 1989)
Sights: Fixed
Finish: Blued or stainless steel; checkered walnut or Neoprene grips
Length Overall: 6½"
Approximate wt.: 17½-20 oz.
Comments: Introduced in 1987. Add 12% for stainless steel.
Estimated Value: New (retail) $287.00
　　　　　　　　　　Excellent: $215.00
　　　　　　　　　　Very good: $175.00

Colt

Colt Model 1900

Colt Model L (1902) Military

Colt Model L (1903) Pocket

Colt Model 1900
Caliber: 38 ACP
Action: Semi-automatic; exposed spur hammer
Magazine: 7-shot clip
Barrel: 6"
Sights: Fixed
Finish: Blued; plain walnut grips
Length Overall: 9"
Approximate wt.: 35 oz.
Comments: Combination safety & rear sight. Rear sight is pressed down to block hammer from firing pin. One of the first automatic pistols made in the U.S. & first automatic pistol made by Colt. Made from 1900 to 1902. No slide lock.
Estimated Value: Excellent: $800.00
　　　　　　　　　　Very good: $640.00

Colt Model L (1902)
Similar to Colt Model 1900 except: no safety; round hammer; hard rubber grips. Made from 1902 to 1907.
Estimated Value: Excellent: $700.00
　　　　　　　　　　Very good: $560.00

Colt Model L (1902) Military
Same as Colt Model L (1902) except: longer grips (more square at bottom) with lanyard ring; 8-shot magazine; weight 37 oz. Made from 1902 to 1928. Spur-type hammer after 1907.
Estimated Value: Excellent: $775.00
　　　　　　　　　　Very good: $600.00

Colt Model L (1903) Pocket
Caliber: 38 ACP
Action: Semi-automatic; exposed hammer
Magazine: 7-shot clip
Barrel: 4½"
Sights: Fixed
Finish: Blued; checkered hard rubber grips
Length Overall: 7½"
Approximate wt.: 31 oz.
Comments: Made from 1903 to 1927. Round type hammer to 1908, then changed to spur type hammer; no slide lock or safety.
Estimated Value: Excellent: $400.00
　　　　　　　　　　Very good: $320.00

Colt Model M (32) 1st Issue Pocket

Colt Model M (32) 2nd Issue Pocket

Colt Model M (32)
3rd Issue Pocket

Colt Model M (32) 3rd Issue Pocket

Similar to 2nd Issue Model M (32) except: safety disconnector, which prevents cartridge in chamber from being fired if magazine is removed. Made from 1926 to 1941.

Estimated Value: **Excellent:** **$345.00**
Very good: **$275.00**

Colt Model M (380) 1st Issue Pocket

Caliber: 380 ACP (9 mm short)
Action: Semi-automatic
Magazine: 7-shot clip
Barrel: 3¾"
Sights: Fixed
Finish: Blued or nickel; hard rubber or checkered walnut grips
Length Overall: 6¾"
Approximate wt.: 24 oz.
Comments: Made from 1908 to 1911. Slide lock safety and grip safety. Barrel lock bushing at muzzle.
Estimated Value: **Excellent:** **$375.00**
Very good: **$300.00**

Colt Model M (32) 2nd Issue Pocket

Similar to 1st Issue Model M (380) except: without barrel lock bushing and other minor changes. Made from 1911 to 1926. Add $200.00 for Military Model.

Estimated Value: **Excellent:** **$360.00**
Very good: **$285.00**

Colt Model M (380)
1st Issue Pocket

Colt Model M (380)
2nd Issue Pocket

Colt Model M (32) 1st Issue Pocket

Caliber: 32 ACP (7.65 mm short)
Action: Semi-automatic; concealed hammer
Magazine: 8-shot clip
Barrel: 3¾"
Sights: Fixed
Finish: Blued or nickel; hard rubber or checkered walnut grips
Length Overall: 6¾"
Approximate wt.: 25 oz.
Comments: Made from 1903 to 1911. Slide lock safety and grip safety. Barrel lock bushing at muzzle.
Estimated Value: **Excellent:** **$375.00**
Very good: **$300.00**

Colt Model M (32) 2nd Issue Pocket

Similar to 1st Issue Model M (32) except: without barrel lock bushing and other minor modifications. Made from 1911 to 1926. Add $200.00 for Military Model.

Estimated Value: **Excellent:** **$350.00**
Very good: **$280.00**

Colt Model 1905 Military

Colt Model M (32) 3rd Issue Pocket

Similar to 2nd Issue Model M (32) except: it has safety disconnector, which prevents cartridge in chamber from being fired if magazine is removed. Made from 1926 to 1941.

Estimated Value: **Excellent:** **$375.00**
Very good: **$300.00**

Colt Model 1905 Military

Caliber: 45 ACP
Action: Semi-automatic
Magazine: 7-shot clip
Barrel: 5"
Sights: Fixed
Finish: Blued; checkered walnut grips
Length Overall: 8½"
Approximate wt.: 34 oz.
Comments: Made from 1905 to 1912. Similar to Model 1902 38 caliber automatic pistol. First 45 caliber military automatic pistol made by Colt. Slide stop but no safety except some experimental models with short grip safety. Round hammer 1905 to 1908; after 1908 spur type hammer. Approximately 5,000 produced. Some were fitted and equipped with a short-stock holster. These are scarce collectors items and valued much higher.
Estimated Value: **Excellent:** **$1,000.00**
Very good: **$ 800.00**

Colt Model N Pocket

Caliber: 25 ACP
Action: Semi-automatic; concealed striker instead of hammer
Magazine: 6-shot clip
Barrel: 2"
Sights: Fixed
Finish: Blued or nickel; hard rubber or checkered walnut grips
Length Overall: 4½"
Approximate wt.: 14 oz.
Comments: Made from 1908 to 1941. Magazine safety disconnector added in 1916 (about serial number 141,000). All models have thumb safety & grip safety. Add $200.00 for Military Model; $50.00 for nickel finish.

Estimated Value: Excellent: $325.00
Very good: $245.00

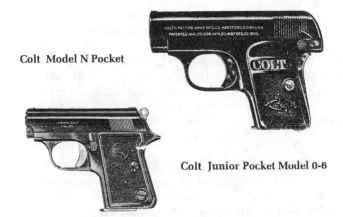

Colt Model N Pocket

Colt Junior Pocket Model 0-6

Colt Government Model 1911 A1

Same as Government Model 1911 except: the grip safety tang was lengthened (to stop the hammer bite on fleshy hands); the trigger was shortened (to allow stubby fingers better control); the back strap below the grip safety weas arched (for better instinctive pointing); the sights were made larger & squared (to improve sight picture). Also the grips were made of checkered walnut or plastic. The 1911 A1 was made from 1925 to present. Changed started about serial number 650000 in military model. Also check prices for other manufacturer's & commercial models.

Estimated Value: Excellent: $460.00
Very good: $365.00

Colt Commerical Model 1911

Same as Government Model 1911 except: not marked with military markings. The letter "C" is used in serial numbers. Blued or nickel finish. Made from 1911 to 1926 then changed to 1911 A1 about serial number C130000.

Estimated Value: Excellent: $550.00
Very good: $425.00

Colt Commerical Model 1911 A1

Same as Government Model 1911 except it has same modifications as the Government Model 1911 A1. Made from 1925 to 1970.

Estimated Value: Excellent: $420.00
Very good: $320.00

Colt Junior Pocket Model 0-6

Caliber: 22 short, 25 ACP
Action: Semi-automatic; exposed round spur hammer
Magazine: 6-shot clip
Barrel: 2⅛"
Sights: Fixed
Finish: Blued; checkered walnut grips
Length Overall: 4½"
Approximate wt.: 13 to 14 oz.
Comments: Made in Spain by Astra (Uneta Y Compania, Guernice, Spain) for Colt as a replacement for the Model N which was discontinued in 1941. Imported from about 1957 to 1968. Colt advertised in 1984 that many of these guns made between 1957 and 1973 were unsafe due to the firing mechanism. Colt offered to modify the pistol free and advised owners of non-modified pistols to carry the pistol with an empty chamber.

Estimated Value: Excellent: $185.00
Very good: $140.00

Colt Government Model 1911

Caliber: 45 ACP
Action: Semi-automatic; exposed spur hammer
Magazine: 7-shot clip
Barrel: 5"
Sights: Fixed
Finish: Blued, nickel and parkerized or similar finish, checkered walnut grips
Length Overall: 8½"
Approximate wt.: 39 oz.
Comments: Slide lock, thumb safety and grip safety. Adopted as a military side arm in 1911 in U.S. Made from 1911 to present with some modifications. Changed to Model 1911 A1 in 1925. Military models are marked "U.S. Army," U.S. Navy," or "U.S. Marines" and "United States Property." Colt licensed other firms to produce this pistol during both World Wars. Check prices under manufacturer's name. Also check commercial model prices.

Estimated Value: Excellent: $475.00
Very good: $380.00

Colt Government Model 1911

Colt Government Model 1911 A1

Colt 1911 (North American Arms Co.)

Same general specifications as 1911 Colt except made by North American Arms Co., in World War I period. About 100 made; company marking and serial number on slide.

Estimated Value: Excellent: **$5,000.00**
                       Very good: **$4,000.00**

Colt 1911 (by Remington UMC)

Colt Super 38

Same as Colt Commercial Model 1911 A1 except: caliber is 38 Super ACP; magazine is 9-shot clip. Made from about 1928 to 1970.

Estimated Value: Excellent: **$450.00**
                       Very good: **$360.00**

Colt Super 38 Match

Same as Colt Super except: adjustable rear sight; hand honed action; match grade barrel. Made from about 1932 to 1940.

Estimated Value: Excellent: **$575.00**
                       Very good: **$460.00**

Colt National Match

Same as Colt Commercial Model 1911 A1 except: adjustable rear sight; hand honed action; match grade barrel. Made from about 1932 to 1940.

Estimated Value: Excellent: **$690.00**
                       Very good: **$550.00**

Colt Service Model Ace

Similar to Colt National Match except: 22 caliber long rifle; 10-shot clip; weighs about 42 oz. It has a "floating chamber" that makes the recoil much greater than normal 22 caliber. Made from 1938 to mid 1940's. See Colt Ace (current).

Estimated Value: Excellent: **$950.00**
                       Very good: **$760.00**

Colt 1911 Springfield Armory N.R.A.

Same general specifications as 1911 Colt except approximately 200 were made prior to World War I and sold through the Director of Civilian Marksmanship and have N.R.A. markings on frame.

Estimated Value: Excellent: **$2,200.00**
                       Very good: **$1,800.00**

Colt 1911 (Springfield Armory)

Same general specifications as 1911 Colt except approximately 26,000 were produced. Eagle motif and flaming bomb on frame and slide. Made in World War I period.

Estimated Value: Excellent: **$650.00**
                       Very good: **$500.00**

Colt 1911 (Remington UMC)

Same general specifications as 1911 Colt except approximately 22,000 were produced in World War I period. Inspectior stamps B or E.

Estimated Value: Excellent: **$600.00**
                       Very good: **$450.00**

Colt 1911 (Singer Manufacturing Co.)

Same general specifications as 1911 A1 Colt except approximately 500 made; blued finished, slide marked S.M. Co., JKC inspector marking.

Estimated Value: Excellent: **$3,200.00**
                       Very good: **$2,600.00**

Colt 1911 A1 pistols were also produced during WWII by Union Switch & Signal Company, Remington Rand, Inc., and Ithaca Gun Company, Inc. Generally the estimated values of these pistols are about the same as the 1911 A1 pistol produced by Colt.

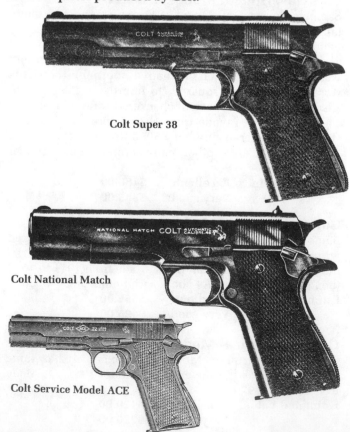

Colt Super 38

Colt National Match

Colt Service Model ACE

Colt Gold Cup National Match

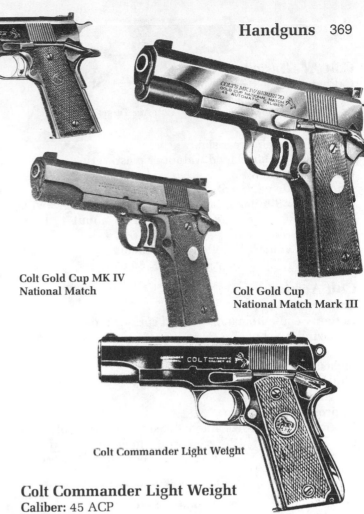

Colt Gold Cup National Match

Same as Colt Commercial Model 1911 A1 except: hand fitted slide; enlarged ejection port; adjustable rear sight; adjustable trigger stop; new bushing design; checkered walnut grips; match grade barrel; flat grip below safety like model 1911. Made from about 1957 to 1970.

Estimated Value: Excellent: $525.00
Very good: $420.00

Colt Gold Cup National Match III

Similar to Colt Gold Cup National Match except chambered for 38 Special mid-range wad cutter only. Operates with fixed barrel rather than locked breech. Made from 1960 to 1974.

Estimated Value: Excellent: $500.00
Very good: $400.00

Colt Government Model MK IV / Series 70

Caliber: 9mm Parabellum, 38 Super ACP, 45 ACP
Action: Semi-automatic; exposed spur hammer
Magazine: 9-shot clip in 9mm & 38; 7-shot in 45
Barrel: 5"
Sights: Fixed
Finish: Blued or nickel; smooth or checkered walnut grips
Length Overall: 8½"
Approximate wt.: 38 to 39 oz.
Comments: Made from about 1970 to mid 1980's. Add $15.00 for 38 Super; $5.00 for 9mm; $25.00 for nickel finish.
Estimated Value: Excellent: $375.00
Very good: $300.00

Colt Gold Cup MK IV National Match (Series 70)

Caliber: 38 Special Mid-Range, 45 ACP
Action: Semi-automatic; exposed spur hammer
Magazine: 9-shot clip in 38; 7-shot in 45
Barrel: 5"
Sights: Adjustable rear for wind and elevation
Finish: Blued; checkered walnut grips with gold medallion
Length Overall: 8¾"
Approximate wt.: 39 oz.
Comments: Arched or flat housing below grip safety. Adjustable trigger stop, hand fitted slide, and improved barrel bushing. Made from about 1970 to mid 1980's.
Estimated Value: Excellent: $475.00
Very good: $380.00

Colt Gold Cup MK IV National Match

Colt Gold Cup National Match Mark III

Colt Commander Light Weight

Colt Commander Light Weight

Caliber: 45 ACP
Action: Semi-automatic; exposed round spur hammer
Magazine: 7-shot clip
Barrel: 4¼"
Sights: Fixed
Finish: Blued; checkered or smooth walnut grips
Length Overall: 7¾"
Approximate wt.: 27 oz.
Comments: Same design as Gov. 1911 A1 model except shorter and lighter; rounded hammer. Aluminum alloy receiver and frame. Made from 1949 to mid 1980's. An all-steel model was introduced in 1971 known as Combat Commander.
Estimated Value: Excellent: $350.00
Very good: $280.00

Colt Combat Commander

Caliber: 9mm Parabellum, 38 Super ACP, 45 ACP
Action: Semi-automatic; exposed round hammer
Magazine: 9-shot clip in 9mm and 38 Super; 7-shot clip in 45 ACP
Barrel: 4¼"
Sights: Fixed
Finish: Blued or nickel (in 45 caliber only); checkered walnut grips
Length Overall: 7⅞"
Approximate wt.: 37 oz.
Comments: Same design as Government 1911 A1 model except: shorter and lighter; rounded hammer; made from about 1971 to mid-1980's with all steel frame and flat or arched mainspring housing. Add $5.00 for 9mm; $20.00 for nickel finish.
Estimated Value: Excellent: $375.00
Very good: $300.00

Colt Combat Commander

Colt Government Model MK IV

Colt Ace Target

Caliber: 22 long rifle
Action: Semi-automatic
Magazine: 10-shot clip
Barrel: 4¾"
Sights: Adjustable rear sight
Finish: Blued; checkered walnut or plastic grips
Length Overall: 8¼"
Approximate wt.: 38 oz.
Comments: Similar in appearance to the 1911 A1 with same safety features. Made from about 1931 to 1941.

Colt Ace Target

Estimated Value: Excellent: $700.00
Very good: $560.00

Colt Ace (current)

Caliber: 22 long rifle
Action: Semi-automatic; exposed spur hammer
Magazine: 10-shot clip
Barrel: 5"
Sights: Fixed rear, ramp style front
Finish: Blued; checkered walnut grips
Length Overall: 8⅜"
Approximate wt.: 42 oz.
Comments: A full-size automatic similar to the Colt Government MK IV/Series in 22 long rifle. Produced from 1979 to mid 1980's. Also see Colt Service Model Ace.

Estimated Value: Excellent: $390.00
Very good: $310.00

Colt 380 Government Model

Colt Commander Light Weight Series 80

Similar to the Light Weight Commander with internal improvements. Introduced in 1983.

Estimated Value: New (retail): $624.95
Excellent: $470.00
Very good: $375.00

Colt Combat Government Model/80

Similar to the Government MK IV/Series 80 with undercut front sight, outline rear sight, Colt Pachmayr grips and other slight variations. Produced 1984 to 1987.

Estimated Value: Excellent: $475.00
Very good: $355.00

Colt 380 Government Model, MK IV Series 80

A "scaled down" version of the Colt Government Model MK IV Series 80 in 380 ACP caliber; with round spur hammer; 3¼" barrel, weighs 21¾ oz., overall length 6⅛". Introduced in 1984. Add 9% for stainless steel finish; 11% for nickel.

Estimated Value: New (retail): $399.95
Excellent: $300.00
Very good: $240.00

Colt MK IV Series 80 Officer's ACP

Caliber: 45 ACP
Action: Semi-automatic; exposed round spur hammer
Magazine: 6-shot clip
Barrel: 3½"
Sights: Fixed with dovetail rear
Finish: Non-glare matte blue; blue or stainless steel (1986); checkered wood grips; polished stainless steel (1988)
Length Overall: 7¼"
Approximate wt.: 24 oz. (lightweight); 34 oz. (steel)
Comments: A compact 45 ACP pistol about 1¼" shorter than the regular Colt Government models. Available in lightweight aluminum alloy or steel models. Add 3% for lightweight and 10% stainless steel. Add 20% for polished stainless steel.

Estimated Value: New (retail): $605.00
Excellent: $455.00
Very good: $365.00

Colt Government Model MK IV/Series 80

Similar to the MK IV Series 70 with internal improvements. Introduced in 1983. Add 8% for nickel finish (discontinued); $5.00 for 9mm and 38 Super calibers. Add 5% for stainless steel; 16% for polished stainless steel.

Estimated Value: New (retail): $624.95
Excellent: $470.00
Very good: $375.00

Colt Combat Commander Series 80

Similar to the Combat Commander with internal improvements, introduced in 1983. Add 5% for nickel finish; $5.00 for 9mm and 38 Super calibers; stainless steel finish introduced in 1990, add $40.00.

Estimated Value: New (retail): $624.95
Excellent: $470.00
Very good: $375.00

Colt Gold Cup National Match MK IV/Series 80

Similar to the Gold Cup MK IV National Match (Series 70) with internal improvements. Introduced in 1983; 45 caliber only; stainless steel model introduced in 1985. Add 8% for stainless steel; 14% for polished stainless steel.

Estimated Value: New (retail): $799.95
Excellent: $600.00
Very good: $480.00

Colt Combat Government Model/80

Colt Commander Light Weight Series 80

Colt MK IV Series 80 Mustang 380

Colt MK IV Series 80 Mustang Plus II

Colt Delta Elite

Colt MK IV Series 80 Mustang 380
Caliber: 380 ACP
Action: Semi-automatic; exposed round spur hammer
Magazine: 5-shot clip
Barrel: 2¾"
Sights: Fixed, with dovetail rear
Finish: Blued; nickel, electroless nickel or stainless steel; composition grips
Length Overall: 5½"
Approximate wt.: 18½ oz.
Comments: A small, compact pistol introduced in 1986. Add 11% for nickel and 7% for electroless nickel. Add 20% for stainless steel.
Estimated Value: New (retail): $399.95
                 Excellent: $300.00
                 Very good: $240.00

Colt Delta Elite, MK IV Series 80
Caliber: 10mm
Action: Semi-automatic; exposed round hammer; long trigger
Magazine: 7-shot clip
Barrel: 5"
Sights: Fixed, white dot
Finish: Blued; black Neoprene "pebbled" wrap-around combat style grips with Colt Delta medallion; stainless steel available late 1980's
Length Overall: 8½"
Approximate wt.: 38 oz.
Comments: Redesigned and re-engineered Colt Government for the 10mm cartridge. Introduced in 1987. Add $10.00 for stainless, $80.00 bright stainless, $200.00 for Gold Cup Medal.
Estimated Value: New (retail): $689.95
                 Excellent: $520.00
                 Very good: $415.00

Colt MK IV Series 80 Mustang Plus II
Similar to the Mustang 380 but combines the full grip length to the Colt Government Model with the shorter compact barrel and slide of the Mustang. Introduced in 1988. Stainless steel added in 1990; add $30.00.
Estimated Value: New (retail): $399.95
                 Excellent: $300.00
                 Very good: $240.00

Colt MK IV Series 80 Mustang Pocketlite
Similar to the Mustang 380 with an alloy receiver; weighs 12½ oz. Blued only. Introduced in 1988.
Estimated Value: New (retail): $399.95
                 Excellent: $300.00
                 Very good: $240.00

Colt Double Eagle Series 90
Caliber: 45ACP, 10mm
Action: Double action semi-automatic with exposed combat style rounded hammer. A decocking lever allows the hammer to be decocked with a round in the chamber without using the trigger. The firing pin remains locked during this sequence.
Magazine: 8-shot clip
Barrel: 5"
Sights: Fixed, white dot
Finish: Matte stainless steel; checkered Xenoy grips.
Length Overall: 8½"
Approximate wt.: 39 oz.
Comments: Introduced in 1990.
Estimated Value: New (retail): $679.95
                 Excellent: $510.00
                 Very good: $410.00

Colt Combat Elite
Caliber: 45ACP
Action: Semi-automatic; exposed round combat hammer
Magazine: 7-shot clip
Barrel: 5"
Sights: Fixed, white dot sights
Finish: Matte stainless steel receiver with blue carbon steel slide & internal working parts; black Neoprene "pebbled" wrap-around combat style grips
Length Overall: 8½"
Approximate wt.: 38 oz.
Comments: Introduced in 1990; designed for combat style match shooters.
Estimated Value: New (retail): $759.95
                 Excellent: $570.00
                 Very good: $450.00

Colt Woodsman Sport Model (1st Issue)

Colt Woodsman Target Model (1st Issue)

Colt Woodsman Sport Model (1st Issue)
Caliber: 22 long rifle
Action: Semi-automatic; concealed hammer
Magazine: 10-shot clip
Barrel: 4½" tapered barrel
Sights: Adjustable
Finish: Blued; checkered walnut grips
Length Overall: 8½"
Approximate wt.: 27 oz.
Comments: Same as Colt Woodsman Target Model (2nd Issue) except shorter. Made from about 1933 to late 1940's.
Estimated Value: Excellent: $375.00
Very good: $300.00

Colt Woodsman Target Model
(2nd Issue)

Colt Woodsman Target Model (2nd Issue)
Same as Colt Woodsman Target Model 1st Issue except heavier tapered barrel and stronger housing for using either the 22 long rifle regular or Hi-speed cartridges. Made from about 1932 to 1945. Approximately wt. 29 oz.
Estimated Value: Excellent: $400.00
Very good: $320.00

Colt Woodsman Target Model S-2 (3rd Issue)
Same as Colt Woodsman Target Model (2nd Issue) except longer grips with thumb rest, larger thumb safety; slide stop; magazine disconnector; slide stays open when magazine is empty; checkered walnut or plastic grips. Approximate wt. 32 oz. Made from 1948 to late 1970's.
Estimated Value: Excellent: $325.00
Very good: $260.00

Colt Woodsman Target Model (1st Issue)
Caliber: 22 long rifle (regular velocity)
Action: Semi-automatic; concealed hammer
Magazine: 10-shot clip
Barrel: 6½"
Sights: Adjustable
Finish: Blued; checkered walnut grips
Length Overall: 10½"
Approximate wt.: 28 oz.
Comments: This model was not strong enough for Hi-speed cartridges, until a strong heat treated housing was produced about serial number 83790. Thumb safety only. Made from about 1915 to 1932.
Estimated Value: Excellent: $390.00
Very good: $310.00

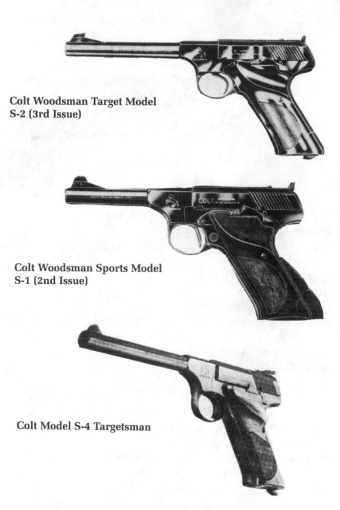

Colt Woodsman Target Model
S-2 (3rd Issue)

Colt Woodsman Sports Model
S-1 (2nd Issue)

Colt Model S-4 Targetsman

Colt Woodsman Sport Model S-1 (2nd Issue)
Same as Colt Woodsman Target Model S-2 (3rd Issue) except 4½" barrel, 9" overall length; approximate wt. 30 oz. Made from about 1948 to late 1970's.
Estimated Value: Excellent: $320.00
Very good: $255.00

Colt Model S-4 Targetsman
Similar to Colt Woodsman Target Model (3rd Issue) except cheaper made adjustable rear sight and lacks automatic slide stop. Made from about 1959 to late 1970's.
Estimated Value: Excellent: $250.00
Very good: $200.00

Colt Woodsman Match Target (1st Issue)

Caliber: 22 long rifle
Action: Semi-automatic; concealed hammer
Magazine: 10-shot clip
Barrel: 6½"; slightly tapered with flat sides
Sights: Adjustable rear
Finish: Blued; checkered walnut, one-piece grip with extended sides
Length Overall: 11"
Approximate wt.: 36 oz.
Comments: Made from about 1938 to 1942.
Estimated Value: Excellent: $600.00
                       Very good: $475.00

Colt Woodsman Match Target (1st Issue)

Colt Woodsman Match Target Model S-3

Caliber: 22 long rifle
Action: Semi-automatic; concealed hammer
Magazine: 10-shot clip
Barrel: 4½", 6"
Sights: Adjustable rear
Finish: Blued; checkered walnut grips with thumb rest
Length Overall: 9", 10½"
Approximate wt.: 36 to 39 oz.
Comments: Made from about 1948 to late 1970's. Flat sided weight added to full length of barrel. It has a slide stop and magazine safety.
Estimated Value: Excellent: $330.00
                       Very good: $265.00

**Colt Woodsman
Match Target Model S-3**

Colt Challenger Model

Colt Huntsman Model S-5

Colt Challenger Model

Caliber: 22 long rifle
Action: Semi-automatic; concealed hammer
Magazine: 10-shot clip
Barrel: 4½", 6"
Sights: Fixed
Finish: Blued; checkered plastic grips
Length Overall: 9", 10½"
Approximate wt.: 30 to 32 oz. (depending on length)
Comments: Same basic design as Colt Woodsman Target Model (3rd Issue) except slide doesn't stay open when magazine is empty; no magazine safety. Made from about 1950 to 1955.
Estimated Value: Excellent: $250.00
                       Very good: $200.00

Colt Huntsman Model S-5

Caliber: 22 long rifle
Action: Semi-automatic; concealed hammer
Magazine: 10-shot clip
Barrel: 4½", 6"
Sights: Fixed
Finish: Blued; checkered walnut grips
Length Overall: 9", 10½"
Approximate wt.: 31 to 32 oz.
Comments: Made from about 1955 to 1970's.
Estimated Value: Excellent: $260.00
                       Very good: $210.00

Colt Lightning Model

Caliber: 38 centerfire, 41 centerfire
Action: Single or double action
Cylinder: 6-shot; ⅔ fluted; side load; loading gate
Barrel: 2½", 3½", 4½", 6"
Sights: Fixed
Finish: Blued or nickel; hard rubber birds-head grips
Length Overall: 7½" to 11"
Approximate wt.: 26 to 30 oz.
Comments: Made from about 1877 to 1912 with and without side rod ejector. This was the first double action revolver made by Colt.
Estimated Value: Excellent: $550.00
Very good: $440.00

Colt Double Action Philippine Model

Same as Colt Double Acion Army Model except larger trigger guard and trigger. It was made originally for the Army in Alaska but was sent to the Philippines instead.
Estimated Value: Excellent: $700.00
Very good: $560.00

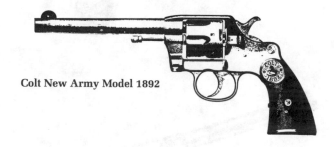

Colt New Army Model 1892

Colt New Army Model 1892

Caliber: 38 Colt short & long, 41 Colt short & long, 38 Special added in 1904, 32-30 added in 1905
Action: Single or double action
Cylinder: 6-shot; ⅔ fluted; swing out; simultaneous hand ejector
Barrel: 3", 4½", 6"
Sights: Fixed
Finish: Blued or nickel; hard rubber or walnut grips
Length Overall: 8¼" to 11¼"
Approximate wt.: 29 to 32 oz.
Comments: Made from 1892 to 1908. Lanyard swivel attached to butt in 1901. All calibers on 41 caliber frame.
Estimated Value: Excellent: $300.00
Very good: $240.00

Colt New Navy Model 1892

Similar to Colt New Army Model 1892 except has double cylinder notches and locking bolt. Sometimes called New Army 2nd issue.
Estimated Value: Excellent: $325.00
Very good: $245.00

Colt Double Action Army Model

Caliber: 38-40, 44-40, 45 Colt
Action: Single or double action
Cylinder: 6-shot; ⅔ fluted; side load
Barrel: 3½" and 4" without side rod ejector; 4¾", 5½" and 7½" with the side rod ejector
Sights: Fixed
Finish: Blued or nickel; hard rubber or checkered walnut grips
Length Overall: 8½" to 12½"
Approximate wt.: 35 to 39 oz.
Comments: Made from about 1877 to 1910. Lanyard loop in butt; also called "Double Action Frontier." Similar to Lightning Model except larger.
Estimated Value: Excellent: $675.00
Very good: $540.00

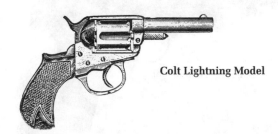

Colt Lightning Model

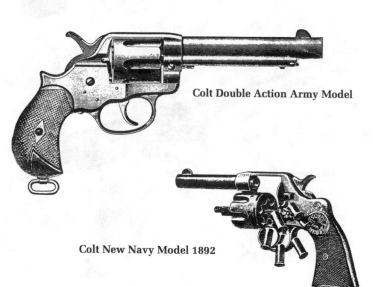

Colt Double Action Army Model

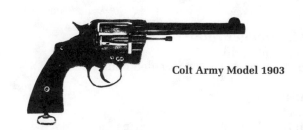

Colt New Navy Model 1892

Colt Army Model 1903

Colt Army Model 1903

Same as Colt New Army Model 1892 except modified grip design (smaller and shaped better); bore is slightly smaller in each caliber to increase accuracy.
Estimated Value: Excellent: $275.00
Very good: $220.00

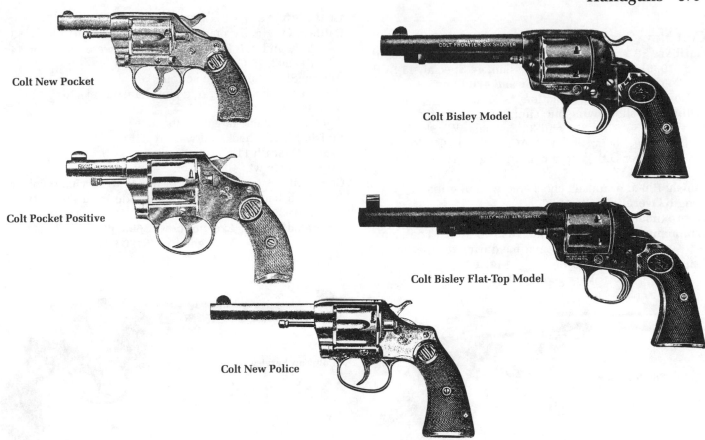

Colt New Pocket

Colt Pocket Positive

Colt New Police

Colt Bisley Model

Colt Bisley Flat-Top Model

Colt New Pocket

Caliber: 32 short & long Colt
Action: Single or double action
Cylinder: 6-shot; swing out; simultaneous ejector
Barrel: 2½", 3½", 6"
Sights: Fixed
Finish: Blued or nickel; hard rubber grips
Length Overall: 6½" to 10½"
Approximate wt.: 15 to 18 oz.
Comments: Made from about 1895 to 1905.
Estimated Value: Excellent: $310.00
Very good: $245.00

Colt Pocket Positive

Similar to the New Pocket with the positive locking system of the Police Positive; 32 short and long S&W cartridges or 32 Colt Police Positive. Made from the early 1900's to just prior to World War II.
Estimated Value: Excellent: $275.00
Very good: $220.00

Colt New Police

Caliber: 32 Colt short & long, 32 Colt New Police (S&W long)
Action: Single or double action
Cylinder: 6-shot; swing out; simultaneous ejector
Barrel: 2½", 4", 6"
Sights: Fixed
Finish: Blued or nickel; hard rubber grips
Length Overall: 6½" to 10½"
Approximate wt.: 16 to 18 oz.
Comments: Built on same frame as New Pocket except larger grips. Made from about 1896 to 1905.
Estimated Value: Excellent: $300.00
Very good: $240.00

Colt New Police Target

Same as Colt New Police except: 6" barrel only; blued finish and target sights. This is a target version of the New Police Model, made from 1896 to 1905.
Estimated Value: Excellent: $350.00
Very good: $270.00

Colt Bisley Model

Caliber: 32 long centerfire, 32-20 WCF, 38 long Colt CF, 38-40 WCF, 41 long Colt CF, 44 S&W Russian, 44-40 WCF, 45 Colt, 455 Eley
Action: Single action
Cylinder: 6-shot; half flute; side load
Barrel: 4¾", 5½", 7½" with side rod ejector
Sights: Fixed
Finish: Blued with case hardened frame and hammer; checkered hard rubber grips
Length Overall: 10¼" to 13"
Approximate wt.: 36 to 40 oz.
Comments: Developed from the original Single Action Army Revolver by changing the trigger, hammer and grips. Made from 1897 to 1912.
Estimated Value: Excellent: $600.00
Very good: $480.00

Colt Bisley Flat-Top Model

Similar to Colt Bisley Model except frame over the cylinder has a flat top; the longer barrel models were referred to as target models; wood and ivory grips as well as hard rubber; target adjustable sights or regular fixed sights. Short barrel models sometimes referred to as the Pocket Bisley. It usually had fixed sights and no side rod ejector.
Estimated Value: Excellent: $1,000.00
Very good: $ 800.00

Colt New Service

Caliber: 38 special, 357 magnum (introduced about 1936), 38-40, 44-40, 44 Russian, 44 Special, 45 ACP, 45 Colt, 450 Eley, 455 Eley and 476 Eley

Action: Single or double action

Cylinder: 6-shot; swing out; simultaneous ejector

Barrel: 4", 5", 6" in 357 and 38 Special; 4½", 5½", 7½" in other calibers; 4½" in 45 ACP (Model 1917 Revolver made for U.S. government during World War II)

Sights: Fixed

Finish: Blued or nickel; checkered walnut grips

Length Overall: 9¼" to 12¾"

Approximate wt.: 39 to 44 oz.

Comments: Made from about 1898 to 1942. The above calibers were made sometime during this period.

Estimated Value: **Excellent:** $440.00
                       Very good: $350.00

Colt New Service

Colt New Service Target

Caliber: Originally made for 44 Russian, 450 Eley, 455 Eley and 476 Eley. Later calibers were made for 44 Special, 45 Colt and 45 ACP

Action: Single or double action

Cylinder: 6-shot; swing out; simultaneous ejector

Barrel: 6" and 7"

Sights: Adjustable target sights

Finish: Blued; checkered walnut grips

Length Overall: 11¼" to 12¾"

Approximate wt.: 40 to 42 oz.

Comments: A target version of the New Service revolver with hand finished action. Made from about 1900 to 1939.

Estimated Value: **Excellent:** $600.00
                       Very good: $490.00

Colt New Service Target

Colt Police Positive

Caliber: 32 short and long Colt (discontinued in 1915), 32 Colt New Police (32 S&W long), 38 New Police (38 S&W long)

Action: Single or double action

Cylinder: 6-shot; swing out; simultaneous ejector

Barrel: 2½", 4", 5", and 6"

Sights: Fixed

Finish: Blued or nickel; hard rubber or checkered walnut grips

Length Overall: 6½" to 10½"

Approximate wt.: 18 to 22 oz.

Comments: This is an improved version of the New Police with the Positive Lock feature which prevents the firing pin from contacting the cartridge until the trigger is pulled. Made from 1905 to 1943.

Estimated Value: **Excellent:** $275.00
                       Very good: $220.00

Colt Police Positive

Colt Police Positive Target

Same as Colt Police Positive except 22 caliber long rifle from 1910 to 1932 and 22 long rifle regular or hi-speed after 1932, 22 Winchester rim fire from 1910 to 1935; blued finish; 6" barrel only; adjustable target sights; checkered walnut grips. Approximate wt. 22 to 26 oz.

Estimated Value: **Excellent:** $400.00
                       Very good: $320.00

Colt Police Positive Target

Colt Officers Model Target (1st Issue)

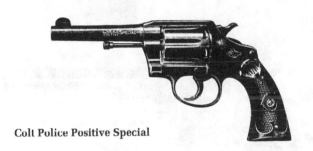

Colt Marine Corps Model 1905

Colt Police Positive Special

Colt Marine Corps Model 1905

Caliber: 38 Colt short and long
Action: Single or double action
Cylinder: 6-shot; ⅔ fluted; swing out; simultaneous hand ejector
Barrel: 6"
Sights: Fixed
Finish: Blued or nickel; hard rubber or walnut grips
Length Overall: 10½"
Approximate wt.: 32 oz.
Comments: Made from 1905 to 1908. Lanyard ring in butt; grip is smaller and more rounded at the butt than the Army or Navy Models. Sometimes called Model 1907.
Estimated Value: Excellent: $750.00
Very good: $570.00

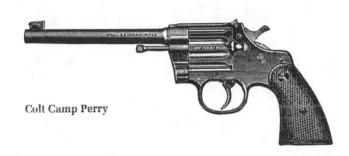

Colt Camp Perry

Colt Police Positive Special

Caliber: 32-20 (discontinued in 1942), 32 New Police (S&W long), 38 Special
Action: Single or double action
Cylinder: 6-shot; swing out; simultaneous ejector
Barrel: 4", 5", 6"
Sights: Fixed
Finish: Blued or nickel; checkered rubber, plastic or walnut grips
Length Overall: 8¾" to 10¾"
Approximate wt.: 23 to 28 oz.
Comments: Made from about 1907 to 1970's.
Estimated Value: Excellent: $250.00
Very good: $200.00

Colt Officers Model Target (1st Issue)

Caliber: 38 special
Action: Single or double action
Cylinder: 6-shot; ⅔ fluted; swing out; simultaneous ejector
Barrel: 6"
Sights: Adjustable
Finish: Blued; checkered walnut grips
Length Overall: 10½"
Approximate wt.: 34 oz.
Comments: Hand finished action. Made from about 1904 to 1908.
Estimated Value: Excellent: $440.00
Very good: $360.00

Colt Camp Perry (1st Issue)

Caliber: 22 short, long, long rifle
Action: Single
Cylinder: 1-shot; swing out flat steel block instead of cylinder with rod ejector
Barrel: 10"
Sights: Adjustable front for elevation & adjustable rear for windage
Finish: Blued; checkered walnut grips with medallion
Length Overall: 14"
Approximate wt.: 35 oz.
Comments: Built on Officers Model frame. Made from about 1926 to 1934.
Estimated Value: Excellent: $750.00
Very good: $375.00

Colt Camp Perry (2nd Issue)

Same as 1st Issue except: 8" barrel (heavier); shorter hammner fall; overall length 12"; approximate wt. 34 oz., chamber is embedded for cartridge head to make it safe to use 22 long rifle Hi-Speed cartridges. Made from about 1934 to 1941.
Estimated Value: Excellent: $850.00
Very good: $680.00

Colt New Service Model 1909

Caliber: 32-20, 38 Special, 38-40, 42 Colt short & long, 44 Russian, 44-40, 45 Colt
Action: Single or double action
Cylinder: 6-shot; ⅔ fluted; swing out; simultaneous hand ejector
Barrel: 4", 4½", 5", 6"
Sights: Fixed
Finish: Blued or nickel; hard rubber or walnut grips
Length Overall: 9¼" to 11¼"
Approximate wt.: 32 to 34 oz.
Comments: Made from 1909 to 1928. Adopted by U.S. armed forces from 1909 to 1911 (Automatic became standard sidearm). Also called "Army Special."
Estimated Value: Excellent: $400.00
                       Very good: $320.00

Colt New Service Model 1909

Colt Officers Model Target (2nd Issue)

Colt Officers Model Target (2nd Issue)

Caliber: 22 long rifle (regular) 1930-32; 22 long rifle (Hi-speed) 1932-49; 32 Police Positive 1932-42; 38 Special 1908-49
Action: Single or double action
Cylinder: 6-shot; ⅔ fluted; swing out; simultaneous hand ejector
Barrel: 6" in 22 caliber & 32 Police Positive; 4", 4½", 5", 6" & 7½" in 38 Special
Sights: Adjustable rear
Finish: Blued; checkered walnut grips
Length Overall: 9¼" to 12¾"
Approximate wt.: 32 to 40 oz.
Comments: Hand finished action, tapered barrel. Made from about 1908 to 1949.
Estimated Value: Excellent: $375.00
                       Very good: $285.00

Colt Army Model 1917

Caliber: 45 ACP or 45 ACP rim cartridges
Action: Single or double action
Cylinder: 6-shot; fluted; swing out; simultaneous hand ejector; used semi-circular clips to hold rimless case of 45 ACP
Barrel: 5½" round tapered
Sights: Fixed
Finish: Blued; oiled-finished walnut grips
Length Overall: 10¾"
Approximate wt.: 40 oz.
Comments: Made from about 1917 to 1928.
Estimated Value: Excellent: $425.00
                       Very good: $340.00

Colt Army Model 1917

Colt Bankers Special

Colt Bankers Special

Caliber: 22 short, long, long rifle (Regular or Hi-Speed); 38 New Police (S&W long)
Action: Single or double action
Cylinder: 6-shot; swing out; simultaneous ejector
Barrel: 2"
Sights: Fixed
Finish: Blued; checkered walnut grips
Length Overall: 6½"
Approximate wt.: 19 to 23 oz.
Comments: Same as Police Positive except 2" barrel only & rounded grip after 1933. Made from about 1928 to 1940.

Estimated Value:	22 Cal.	38 Cal.
Excellent:	$800.00	$500.00
Very good:	$600.00	$375.00

Colt Shooting Master

Caliber: 38 Special, 357 magnum (introduced in 1936), 44 Special, 45 ACP, 45 Colt
Action: Single or double action
Cylinder: 6-shot; swing out; simultaneous ejector
Barrel: 6"
Sights: Adjustable target sight
Finish: Blued; checkered walnut grips
Length Overall: 11¼"
Approximate wt.: 42 to 44 oz.
Comments: A deluxe target revolver based on the New Service revolver. Made from about 1932 to 1940.
Estimated Value: Excellent: $600.00
Very good: $460.00

Colt Official Police (Model E-1)

Caliber: 22 long rifle (regular) introduced in 1930; 22 long rifle (IIi-Speed) introduced in 1932; 32-30 made from about 1928 to 1942; 38 Special made from 1928 to 1969; 41 long Colt made from 1928 to 1930
Action: Single or double action
Cylinder: 6-shot; fluted; swing out; simultaneous ejector
Barrel: 4" & 6" in 22 caliber; 4", 5" & 6" in 32-20; 2", 4", 5" & 6" in 41 caliber
Sights: Fixed
Finish: Blued or nickel; checkered walnut or plastic grips
Length Overall: 7¼" to 11¼"
Approximate wt.: 30 to 38 oz.
Comments: 41 caliber frame in all calibers. A refined version of the New Service Model 1909 which was discontinued in 1928. Made from about 1928 to 1970.
Estimated Value: Excellent: $300.00
Very good: $225.00

Colt Commando

Similar to Colt Official Police (Model E-1) except made to government specifications in 38 Special only; sandblasted blue finish; produced for the government. Made from 1942 to 1945.
Estimated Value: Excellent: $325.00
Very good: $245.00

Colt Detective Special

Caliber: 32 New Police (S&W long), 38 Special
Action: Single or double action
Cylinder: 6-shot; swing out; simultaneous ejector
Barrel: 2" & 3"
Sights: Fixed
Finish: Blued or nickel; checkered walnut grips with rounded or square butt
Length Overall: 6¾" to 7¾"
Approximate wt.: 21 oz.
Comments: Made from about 1926 to 1987. Available with or without hammer shroud. Current model 38 Special only. Add 10% for nickel finish.
Estimated Value: Excellent: $325.00
Very good: $240.00

Colt Commando Special

Similar to the Detective Special with matte finish & rubber grips. Produced 1984 to 1987.
Estimated Value: Excellent: $225.00
Very good: $170.00

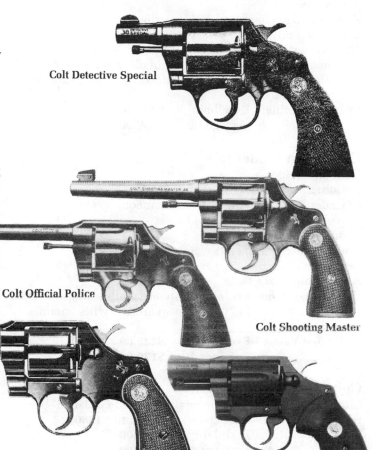

Colt Detective Special

Colt Official Police

Colt Shooting Master

Colt Commando

Colt Commando Special

Colt Officers Model Special

Colt Officers Model Special

Caliber: 22 long rifle (regular & Hi-Speed); 38 Special
Action: Single or double action
Cylinder: 6-shot, ⅔ fluted; swing out; simultaneous ejector
Barrel: 6"
Sights: Adjustable for windage & elevation
Finish: Blued; checkered plastic grips
Length Overall: 11¼"
Approximate wt.: 42 oz. in 22 caliber, 38 oz. in 38 caliber
Comments: Replaced the Officers Model Target (2nd issue) as target arm; heavier non-tapered barrel & re-designed hammer. Made from 1949 to 1953.
Estimated Value: Excellent: $300.00
Very good: $225.00

Colt Cobra Model D-3

Caliber: 22 short & long rifle; 32 New Police (S&W long); 38 Special
Action: Single or double action
Cylinder: 6-shot, ⅔ fluted; swing out; simultaneous ejector
Barrel: 2", 3", 4" & 5"
Sights: Fixed
Finish: Blued; checkered walnut grips
Length Overall: 6⅝" to 9⅝"
Approximate wt.: 16 to 22 oz.
Comments: Frame is made of a light alloy, but cylinder is steel. Made from 1950 to late 1970. Add $25.00 for nickel finish.

Estimated Value:	Excellent:	$250.00
	Very good:	$200.00

Colt Cobra

Colt Agent Model D-4

Caliber: 38 Special
Action: Single or double action
Cylinder: 6-shot, swing out; simultaneous ejector
Barrel: 2"
Sights: Fixed
Finish: Blued; checkered walnut grips
Length Overall: 6¾"
Approximate wt.: 14 oz.
Comments: Frame made of lightweight alloy. Made from 1955 to late 1970's. Also available with hammer shroud.

Estimated Value:	Excellent:	$225.00
	Very good:	$170.00

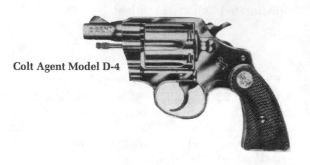

Colt Agent Model D-4

Colt Agent Light Weight

Similar to the Detective Special with matte finish; 2" barrel; approx. wt. 17 oz.; produced in the mid 1980's.

Estimated Value:	Excellent:	$195.00
	Very good:	$150.00

Colt Agent Light Weight

Colt Aircrewman Special

Caliber: 38 Special
Action: Single or double action
Cylinder: 6-shot, swing out; simultaneous ejector; aluminum alloy
Barrel: 2"
Sights: Fixed
Finish: Blued; checkered walnut grips
Length Overall: 6¾"
Approximate wt.: 14 oz.
Comments: A rare lightweight special revolver developed by Colt at the request of U.S. Air Force during the Korean War. They were recalled in 1960.

Estimated Value:	Excellent:	$850.00
	Very good:	$680.00

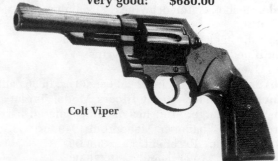

Colt Viper

Colt Viper

Caliber: 38 Special
Action: Single or double action
Cylinder: 6-shot, swing out
Barrel: 4"
Sights: Fixed rear, ramp front
Finish: Blued or nickel; checkered walnut wrap-around grips
Length Overall: 8⅝"
Approximate wt.: 20 oz.
Comments: Lightweight aluminum alloy frame, shrouded ejector rod. Made in the late 1970's. Add $20.00 for nickel model.

Estimated Value:	Excellent:	$220.00
	Very good:	$170.00

Colt Border Patrol

Caliber: 38 Special
Action: Single or double action
Cylinder: 6-shot, swing out; simultaneous ejector
Barrel: 4"
Sights: Fixed; Baughman quick draw front sight
Finish: Blued; checkered walnut grips
Length Overall: 8¾"
Approximate wt.: 34 oz.
Comments: In 1952 about 400 were produced for a branch of the U.S. Treasury Dept. The barrel is marked on the left side "Colt Border Patrol."

Estimated Value:	Excellent:	$800.00
	Very good:	$600.00

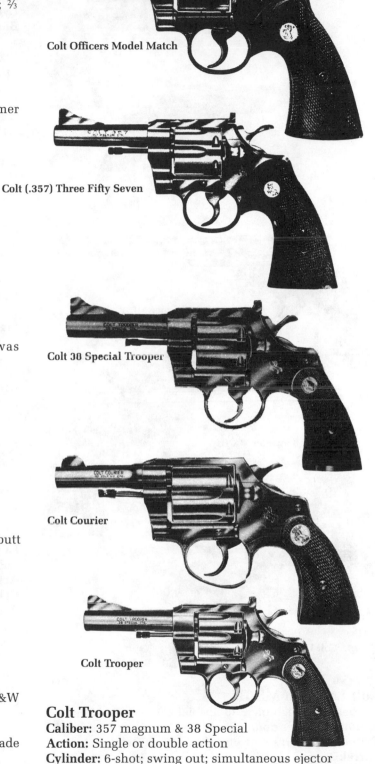

Colt Officers Model Match

Caliber: 22 long rifle, 38 Special
Action: Single or double action
Cylinder: 6-shot; swing out; simultaneous ejector; ⅔ fluted
Barrel: 6"
Sights: Adjustable for windage & elevation
Finish: Blued; checkered walnut grips
Length Overall: 11¼"
Approximate wt.: 22 caliber, 42 oz; 38 caliber, 38 oz.
Comments: Has heavy tapered barrel & wide hammer spur. Made from about 1953 to 1970.
Estimated Value:　**Excellent:**　$320.00
　　　　　　　　　　Very good:　$240.00

Colt Officers Model Match

Colt (.357) Three Fifty Seven

Colt (.357) Three Fifty Seven

Caliber: 357 magnum & 38 Special
Action: Single or double action
Cylinder: 6-shot; swing out; simultaneous ejector
Barrel: 4" & 6"
Sights: Adjustable rear sight
Finish: Blued; checkered walnut grips
Length Overall: 9¼" & 11¼"
Approximate wt.: 36 to 39 oz.
Comments: Made from about 1953 to 1962. It was replaced by Trooper Model.
Estimated Value:　**Excellent:**　$270.00
　　　　　　　　　　Very good:　$215.00

Colt 38 Special Trooper

Colt 38 Special Trooper

Caliber: 22, 38 Special
Action: Single or double action
Cylinder: 6-shot; swing out; simultaneous ejector;
Barrel: 4" & 6"
Sights: Adjustable rear & quick draw front
Finish: Blued or nickel; checkered walnut square butt grips
Length Overall: 9¼" & 11¼"
Approximate wt.: 36 to 43 oz.
Comments: Made from about 1953 to 1962.
Estimated Value:　**Excellent:**　$275.00
　　　　　　　　　　Very good:　$210.00

Colt Courier

Colt Trooper

Colt Courier

Caliber: 22 short, long, long rifle, 32 New Police (S&W long)
Action: Single or double action
Cylinder: 6-shot; swing out; simultaneous ejector; made of lightweight alloy
Barrel: 3"
Sights: Fixed
Finish: Dual tone blue; checkered plastic grips
Length Overall: 7½"
Approximate wt.: 14 to 20 oz.
Comments: Frame & cylinder made of lightweight alloy. Made in 1954 & 1955 only. A limited production revolver.
Estimated Value:　**Excellent:**　$725.00
　　　　　　　　　　Very good:　$550.00

Colt Trooper

Caliber: 357 magnum & 38 Special
Action: Single or double action
Cylinder: 6-shot; swing out; simultaneous ejector
Barrel: 4" or 6"
Sights: Adjustable rear & quick draw front
Finish: Blued or nickel; checkered walnut, square butt grips
Length Overall: 9¼" to 11¼"
Approximate wt.: 34 to 38 oz.
Comments: Made from about 1953 to 1969. Replaced by Trooper MKIII.
Estimated Value:　**Excellent:**　$250.00
　　　　　　　　　　Very good:　$200.00

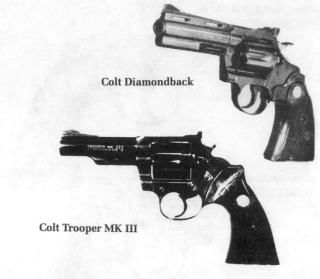

Colt Diamondback

Colt Trooper MK III

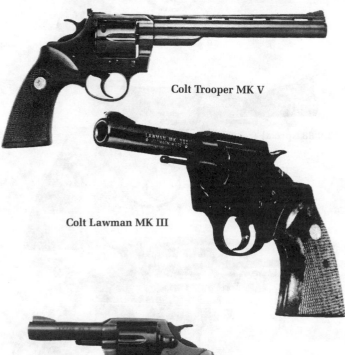

Colt Trooper MK V

Colt Lawman MK III

Colt Lawman MK V

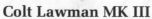

Colt Lawman MK III

Caliber: 357 magnum & 38 Special
Action: Single or double action
Cylinder: 6-shot; swing out; simultaneous ejector
Barrel: 2" or 4"
Sights: Fixed
Finish: Blued or nickel; checkered walnut grips; non-glare electroless plating available after 1981 (Colt-guard)
Length Overall: 7¼", 9¼"
Approximate wt.: 36 to 39 oz.
Comments: Made in 1970 & early 1980's. Add $20.00 for nickel.
Estimated Value: **Excellent:**   **$230.00**
                        Very good: **$175.00**

Colt Diamondback

Caliber: 22, 22 long rifle, 38 Special
Action: Single or double
Cylinder: 6-shot; swing out; simultaneous ejector
Barrel: 2½", 4", 6" ventilated rib; 2½" dropped in late 1970's
Sights: Adjustable rear
Finish: Blued or nickel; checkered walnut square butt grips
Length Overall: 7½", 9"
Approximate wt.: 26 to 32 oz.
Comments: Made from 1967 to 1987. Add 10% for nickel finish.
Estimated Value: **Excellent:**   **$345.00**
                        Very good: **$260.00**

Colt Trooper MK III

Caliber: 357 magnum & 38 Special; 22 long rifle & 22 WMR added in 1979
Action: Single or double action
Cylinder: 6-shot; swing out; simultaneous ejector
Barrel: 4", 6", 8" in 1980
Sights: Adjustable rear
Finish: Blued or nickel; checkered walnut grips; non-glare electroless plating available after 1981 (Colt-guard)
Length Overall: 9½", 11¼" & 13½"
Approximate wt.: 39 to 42 oz.
Comments: Made from about 1969 to mid 1980's; wide target-type trigger & hammer. Add $20.00 for nickel; $7.00 for 8" barrel.
Estimated Value: **Excellent:**   **$260.00**
                        Very good: **$200.00**

Colt Trooper MK V

Caliber: 357 magnum & 38 Special
Action: Single or double action; exposed hammer
Cylinder: 6-shot; swing out; simultaneous ejector
Barrel: 4" or 6" ventilated rib
Sights: Red insert front, adjustable rear
Finish: Blued, nickel or non-glare electroless plating (Colt-guard); checkered walnut grips
Length Overall: 9½" to 11½"
Approximate wt.: 39 to 45 oz.
Comments: A medium frame revolver with inner & outer improvements on the Trooper MK III. Produced 1982 to 1987. Add 9% for nickel finish.
Estimated Value: **Excellent:**   **$270.00**
                        Very good: **$205.00**

Colt Lawman MK V

Similar to the Trooper MK V with a 2" or 4" solid rib barrel, fixed sights. Add $20.00 for nickel finish. Discontinued in mid 1980's.
Estimated Value: **Excellent:**   **$250.00**
                        Very good: **$190.00**

Colt King Cobra

Caliber: 357 magnum; 38 Special
Action: Single or double action
Cylinder: 6-shot; swing out; simultaneous ejector
Barrel: 2½", 4", 6" or 8"
Sights: Red ramp front with white outline adjustable rear
Finish: Blued, matte stainless steel or bright polished stainless steel. Black rubber combat grips
Length Overall: 8", 9", 11" or 13"
Approximate wt.: 36, 42, 46 or 48 oz.
Comments: Introduced in 1989. It has a full length contoured ejector rod housing & a solid barrel rib. Add 6% for matte stainless steel; add 15% for polished stainless steel.
Estimated Value: New (retail): $395.95
Excellent: $295.00
Very good: $240.00

Colt Model I-3 Python, New Police Python, Python

Caliber: 357 magnum, 38 Special; 22 long rifle & 22 WMR available in 1981 only
Action: Single or double action
Cylinder: 6-shot; swing out; simultaneous ejector
Barrel: 2½", 3", 4", 6" or 8" after 1980; ventilated rib
Sights: Blade front, adjustable rear (for windage & elevation). Red insert in front sight in 1980's
Finish: Blued or nickel; checkered walnut target grips; also rubber grips in 1980's; non-glare electoless plating & stainless steel in 1980's
Length Overall: 7¼" to 13¼"
Approximate wt.: 39 to 44 oz.
Comments: Made from about 1955 to present. Add 17% for bright stainless steel; add 12% for satin stainless steel; add 4% for nickel finish (discontinued).
Estimated Value: New (retail): $759.95
Excellent: $570.00
Very good: $455.00

Colt Official Police MK III

Caliber: 38 Special
Action: Single or double
Cylinder: 6-shot; swing out; simultaneous ejector
Barrel: 4", 5", 6"
Sights: Fixed
Finish: Blued; checkered walnut square butt grips
Length Overall: 9¼", 10¼", 11¼"
Approximate wt.: 34 to 36 oz.
Comments: Made from about 1970 to late 1970's.
Estimated Value: Excellent: $250.00
Very good: $200.00

Colt Single Action Army

Colt Peacekeeper

Caliber: 357 magnum & 38 Special
Action: Single or double action
Cylinder: 6-shot; swing out; simultaneous ejector
Barrel: 4" or 6" with ventilated rib & short ejector shroud
Sights: Red insert front & white outline adjustable rear
Finish: Non-glare matte blue combat finish with Colt rubber combat grips
Length Overall: 9" or 11"
Approximate wt.: 38 or 42 oz.
Comments: A medium frame 357 magnum introduced in the mid 1980's & discontinued 1988.
Estimated Value: Excellent: $240.00
Very good: $180.00

Colt Model Python

Colt Peacekeeper

Colt Official Police MK III

Colt Single Action Army

Caliber: 357 magnum, 38 Special, 44 Special, 45 Colt
Action: Single action
Cylinder: 6-shot; side load; loading gate; under barrel ejector rod
Barrel: 4¾", 5½", & 7½"
Sights: Fixed
Finish: Blued with case hardened frame; composite rubber grips; nickel with checkered walnut grips
Length Overall: 10⅛" to 12⅞"
Approximate wt.: 37 or 43 oz.
Comments: A revival of the Single Action Army Revolver, which was discontinued in 1941. The series numbers start at 1001 SA. The letters SA were added to the serial numbers when production was resumed. Made from about 1955 to mid 1980's. Add $15.00 for a 7½" barrel; $60.00 for nickel.
Estimated Value: Excellent: $450.00
Very good: $360.00

Colt Single Action Buntline Special

This is basically the same revolver as the Colt Single Action Army Revolver (1955 Model) except it is 45 Colt caliber only. The barrel is 12"; the gun has an overall length of 17½"; weighs about 42 oz. It was made from about 1957 until 1975. Available again in 1980. Add $90.00 for nickel finish. 44 Special available after 1981.

Estimated Value: **Excellent:**   **$460.00**
                       Very good: **$350.00**

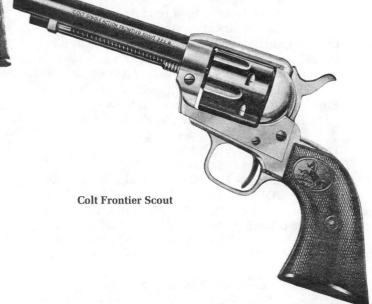

Colt Single Action Buntline Special

Colt New Frontier, Single Action Army

Colt Frontier Scout

Caliber: 22 & 22 WRF (interchangeable cylinder)
Action: Single action
Cylinder: 6-shot side load; loading gate; under barrel ejector rod
Barrel: 4¾" or 9½" (Buntline Scout)
Sights: Fixed
Finish: Blued or nickel; plastic or wood grips
Length Overall: 9⁵⁄₁₆" to 14¼"
Approximate wt.: 24 to 34 oz.
Comments: Single Action Army replica ¾ scale size in 22 caliber. Made with bright alloy frame & blued steel frame from about 1958 to 1972. Add $10.00 for interchangeable cylinder; $10.00 for nickel finish; $10.00 for Buntline Scout.

Estimated Value: **Excellent:**   **$225.00**
                       Very good: **$180.00**

**Colt Peacemaker 22
Single Action**

Colt New Frontier

Colt New Frontier, Single Action Army

This is the same handgun as the Colt Single Action Army revolver except frame is flat topped; finish is high polished; ramp front sight & adjustable rear sight (wind & elevation); blued & case-hardened finish; smooth walnut grips. This is a target version of the SA Army, made from about 1961 to mid 1980's in 44-40, 44 Spec., & 45 Colt caliber only. Add $20.00 for 7½" barrel.

Estimated Value: **Excellent:**   **$500.00**
                       Very good: **$375.00**

Colt New Frontier Buntline Special

This revolver is the same as the Colt New Frontier (1961 Model) except 45 caliber only; 12" barrel; 17½" overall; weighs 42 oz. Made from 1962 until 1967.

Estimated Value: **Excellent:**   **$525.00**
                       Very good: **$395.00**

Colt Frontier Scout

Colt Peacemaker 22 Single Action

Caliber: 22, 22 WRF when equipped with dual cylinder
Action: Single
Cylinder: 6-shot side load; loading gate; under barrel ejector rod
Barrel: 4¾", 6" & 7½"
Sights: Fixed
Finish: Blued barrel & cylinder; case hardened frame; black composite rubber grips
Length Overall: 9⁵⁄₁₈" to 12¾"
Approximate wt.: 29 to 33 oz.
Comments: All steel, 22 caliber version of the 45 caliber Peacemaker. Made from 1972 to late 1970's. Add $6.00 for 7½" barrel.

Estimated Value: **Excellent:**   **$220.00**
                       Very good: **$175.00**

Colt New Frontier

This is the same handgun as the Colt Peacemaker 22 SA except equipped with a ramp front sight & adjustable rear sight; flat top frame. Reintroduced in 1982 to 1986.

Estimated Value: **Excellent:**   **$230.00**
                       Very good: **$185.00**

Dan Wesson

Dan Wesson Model 12

Dan Wesson Model 11

Dan Wesson Pistol Pack

A carrying case containing revolver, 4 interchangeable barrels (2½", 4", 6", 8"), interchangeable grips, 4 additional colored sight blades & other accessories.

	Excellent	New (retail)
Model 8-2 (no 8" barrel)		$455.80
Model 8-2 (no 8" barrel)	$300.00	
Model 708 (no 8" barrel)		$516.68
Model 9-2		$614.73
Model 709		$689.01
Model 9-2V		$715.89
Model 709-V		$790.15
Model 9-2VH		$804.85
Model 709-VH		$887.81
Model 14-2 (no 8" barrel)		$455.80
Model 14-2B	$300.00	
Model 714		$516.68
Model 15-2		$614.73
Model 715		$689.01
Model 15-2H	$310.00	
Model 15-2V		$715.89
Model 715-V		$790.15
Model 15-2VH		$804.85
Model 715-VH		$887.81
Model 22		$614.73
Model 22M		$636.98
Model 722		$689.01
Model 722M		$723.69
Model 22-V		$715.89
Model 722-V		$790.15
Model 22M-V		$738.12
Model 722M-V		$824.85
Model 22-VH		$804.85
Model 722-VH		$887.81
Model 22M-VH		$827.72
Model 722M-VH		$922.52
Model 41-V (one 8", one 6" barrel)		$623.60
Model 741-V (one 8", one 6" barrel)		$690.90
Model 41-VH (one 8", one 6" barrel)		$672.27
Model 741-VH (one 8", one 6" barrel)		$739.20
Model 44V (two 6", two 8" barrels)		$707.52
Model 744V (two 6", two 8" barrels)		$814.38
Model 44-VH (two 6", two 8" barrels)		$759.80
Model 744-VH (two 6", two 8" barrels)		$867.03
Model 32		$614.73
Model 32-V		$715.89
Model 32-VH		$804.85
Model 732		$689.01
Model 732-V		$790.15
Model 732-VH		$887.81
Model 45-V		$707.52
Model 45-VH		$757.80
Model 745-V		$814.38
Model 745-VH		$867.03

Dan Wesson Model 14

Dan Wesson Model 11

Caliber: 357 magnum or 38 Special (interchangeable)
Action: Double or single; exposed hammer; simultaneous ejector
Cylinder: 6-shot; swing out
Barrel: 2½", 4", 6"; interchangeable barrels
Sights: Ramp front; fixed rear
Finish: Blued; one-piece changeable walnut grip
Length Overall: 7¾" to 11¼"
Approximate wt.: 36 to 40 oz.
Comments: Made from about 1970 to 1974. Barrels and barrel cover (shroud) can be changed quickly by means of a recessed barrel nut; also one-piece grip readily changeable to option styles.
Estimated Value: Excellent: $200.00
Very good: $160.00

Dan Wesson Model 12

Same as Model 11 except target model with adjustable rear sight.
Estimated Value: Excellent: $215.00
Very good: $170.00

Dan Wesson Model 14, 14-2, 714

Caliber: 357 magnum or 38 Special (interchangeable)
Action: Double or single; exposed hammer; simultaneous ejector
Cylinder: 6-shot; swing out; non-fluted available after 1981
Barrel: 2½", 4", 6"; interchangeable barrels
Sights: Ramp front; fixed rear
Finish: Blued; one-piece walnut grip; satin blue available; 714 stainless steel
Length Overall: 7¾" to 13¼"
Approximate wt.: 36 to 42 oz.
Comments: Made from about 1973 to present. A modified version of the Model 22, presently being called the 14-2 series. Price increases with barrel length. Add $15.00 for bright blue finish (14-2B) (discontinued 1987); $43.00 for stainless steel (714).
Estimated Value: New (retail) $267.15 - $280.46
Excellent: $200.00 - $210.00
Very good: $160.00 - $170.00

Dan Wesson Model 15

Similar to the Model 14 except adjustable rear sight. Made from about 1973 to 1976.
Estimated Value: Excellent: $200.00
Very good: $160.00

Dan Wesson Model 15-2

Dan Wesson Model 8-2, 708

Similar to Model 14 except 38 caliber only. Add $15.00 for bright blue finish (8-2B) (discontinued 1987); $43.00 for stainless steel (708).

Estimated Value:	New (retail):	$267.15 - $280.46
	Excellent:	$200.00 - $210.00
	Very good:	$160.00 - $170.00

Dan Wesson Model 15-2, 715

Caliber: 357 magnum or 38 Special (interchangeable)
Action: Double or single; exposed hammer
Cylinder: 6-shot; swing out; simultaneous ejector
Barrel: 2½", 4", 6", 8", 10", 12" 15" interchangeable barrels
Sights: Interchangeable colored front sight blade; adjustable rear sight with white outline
Finish: Blued; checkered wood target grips; 715 is stainless steel
Length Overall: 7¾" to 13¼"
Approximate wt.: 32 to 42 oz.
Comments: Made from about 1975 to present. Price increases with barrel length. Add $28.00 for stainless steel (715).

Estimated Value:	New (retail)	$337.64 - $386.38
	Excellent:	$250.00 - $290.00
	Very good:	$200.00 - $230.00

Dan Wesson Model 9-2, 709

Similar to Model 15-2 except 38 caliber only. No 12" or 15" barrel. Add $28.00 for stainless steel (709).

Estimated Value:	New (retail):	$337.64 - $386.38
	Excellent:	$250.00 - $290.00
	Very good:	$200.00 - $230.00

Dan Wesson Model 9-2V, 709-V

Similar to Model 9-2 with ventilated rib. Price increased with barrel length. Add $28.00 for stainless steel (709-V).

Estimated Value:	New (retail):	$359.08 - $419.03
	Excellent:	$270.00 - $315.00
	Very good:	$215.00 - $250.00

Dan Wesson Model 9-2VH, 709-VH

Similar to Model 9-2 with heavier bull barrel & ventilated rib. Prices increases with barrel length. Add $28.00 for stainless steel (709-VH).

Estimated Value:	New (retail):	$385.96 - $569.16
	Excellent:	$290.00 - $425.00
	Very good:	$230.00 - $340.00

Dan Wesson Model 9-2

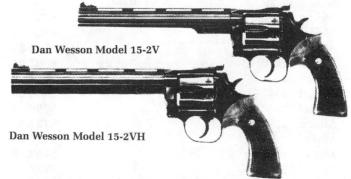
Dan Wesson Model 15-2H

Dan Wesson Model 15-2H

Same as Model 15-2 except it has a heavier bull barrel. A special order item after 1981.

Estimated Value:	Excellent:	$260.00
	Very good:	$195.00

Dan Wesson Model 15-2V, 715-V

Same as Model 15-2 except it has ventilated rib. Add $28.00 for stainless steel (715-V).

Estimated Value:	New (retail):	$359.08 - $419.03
	Excellent:	$270.00 - $315.00
	Very good:	$215.00 - $250.00

Dan Wesson Model 15-2V

Dan Wesson Model 15-2VH

Dan Wesson Model 15-2 VH, 715-VH

Same as Model 15-2 except it has a heavier bull barrel with ventilated rib assembly. Add $28.00 for stainless steel (715-VH).

Estimated Value:	New (retail):	$385.96 - $569.16
	Excellent:	$290.00 - $425.00
	Very good:	$230.00 - $340.00

Dan Wesson Model 22, 722

Similar to the Model 15-2 in 22 caliber only. Introduced in the late 1970's. Not available with 10", 12" or 15" barrel. Price increases with barrel length. Add $28.00 for stainless steel (722).

Estimated Value:	New (retail):	$337.64 - $366.38
	Excellent:	$250.00 - $275.00
	Very good:	$200.00 - $220.00

Dan Wesson Model 22, 722M

Similar to the Model 22 in 22 magnum caliber. Add $31.00 for stainless steel finish (722M).

Estimated Value:	New (retail):	$349.13 - $377.87
	Excellent:	$260.00 - $285.00
	Very good:	$210.00 - $225.00

Dan Wesson Model 22M-V, 722M-V

Similar to the Model 22-V in 22 magnum caliber. Add $31.00 for stainless steel finish (722M-V).

Estimated Value:	New (retail):	$370.57 - $408.41
	Excellent:	$280.00 - $305.00
	Very good:	$220.00 - $245.00

Dan Wesson Model 22M-VH, 722M-VH

Similar to the Model 22-VH in 22 magnum caliber. Add $31.00 for stainless steel finish (722M-VH).

Estimated Value: New (retail): $397.46 - $426.81
Excellent: $300.00 - $320.00
Very good: $240.00 - $255.00

Dan Wesson Model 22V, 722-V

Similar to the Model 22 with ventilated rib. Price increases with barrel length. Add $28.00 for stainless steel (722-V).

Estimated Value: New (retail): $359.08 - $396.92
Excellent: $270.00 - $300.00
Very good: $215.00 - $240.00

Dan Wesson Model 22-VH, 722-VH

Similar to the Model 22 with heavier bull barrier & ventilated rib. Price increases with barrel length. Add $28.00 for stainless steel (722-VH).

Estimated Value: New (retail): $385.96 - $415.32
Excellent: $290.00 - $310.00
Very good: $230.00 - $250.00

Dan Wesson Model 32, 732

Similar to the Model 15-2 in 32 magnum caliber; 2½", 4", 6" or 8" barrel. Introduced in the mid 1980's. Add $28.00 for stainless steel (732).

Estimated Value: New (retail): $337.64 - $366.38
Excellent: $250.00 - $275.00
Very good: $200.00 - $220.00

Dan Wesson Model 32-V, 732-V

Similar to the Model 32 with ventilated rib. Add $28.00 for stainless steel (732-V).

Estimated Value: New (retail): $359.08 - $396.92
Excellent: $270.00 - $300.00
Very good: $215.00 - $240.00

Dan Wesson Model 32-VH, 732-VH

Similar to the Model 32 with ventilated rib, heavy barrel. Add $28.00 for stainless steel (732-VH).

Estimated Value: New (retail): $385.96 - $415.32
Excellent: $290.00 - $310.00
Very good: $230.00 - $250.00

Dan Wesson Model 22V

Dan Wesson Model 40-V 357 Super Mag, 740-V

Caliber: 357 Maximum
Action: Double & single; exposed hammer; simultaneous ejector
Cylinder: 6-shot; swing out; fluted
Barrel: 6", 8", 10" interchangeable barrels; ventilated rib
Sights: Interchangeable colored front sight blade, adjustable interchangeable rear
Finish: Blued; smooth walnut grips; stainless steel (740-V)
Length Overall: 14½" with 8" barrel
Approximate wt.: 59 to 62 oz.
Comments: Introduced in the mid 1980's. Each model comes with an extra barrel. Price increases with barrel length. Add $60.00 for stainless steel.

Estimated Value: New (retail) $508.32 - $543.41
Excellent: $381.00 - $410.00
Very good: $300.00 - $325.00

Dan Wesson Model 40-V8S, 740-V8S

Similar to the Model 40-V with slotted barrel shroud, 8" barrel only; extra barrel included; weighs 64 oz. Add $60.00 for stainless steel (740-V8S)

Estimated Value: New (retail) $536.86
Excellent: $400.00
Very good: $320.00

Dan Wesson Model 40-VH, 740-VH

Similar to the Model 40-V with heavy barrel; extra barrel included. Add $60.00 for stainless steel (740-VH).

Estimated Value: New (retail): $521.74 - $574.50
Excellent: $390.00 - $430.00
Very good: $310.00 - $345.00

Dan Wesson Model 41V, 741-V

Similar to the Model 44V in 42 magnum caliber. Add $50.00 for stainless steel finish (741-V).

Estimated Value: New (retail): $412.80 - $448.29
Excellent: $310.00 - $335.00
Very good: $250.00 - $270.00

Dan Wesson Model 41-VH, 741-VH

Similar to the Model 44VH in 41 magnum caliber. Add $50.00 for stainless steel finish (741-VH).

Estimated Value: New (retail): $435.66 - $477.89
Excellent: $325.00 - $360.00
Very good: $260.00 - $285.00

Dan Wesson Model 375V Super Mag

Similar to the Model 40V in 375 magnum caliber.

Estimated Value: New (retail): $508.32 - $543.41
Excellent: $380.00 - $410.00
Very good: $300.00 - $325.00

Dan Wesson Model 375-V8S Super Mag

Similar to the Model 375 with slotted barrel shroud, 8" barrel.

Estimated Value: New (retail): $536.86
Excellent: $400.00
Very good: $320.00

Dan Wesson Model 375-VH Super Mag

Similar to the Model 375 with ventilated rib shroud in heavy barrel.

Estimated Value: New (retail): $521.74 - $574.50
Excellent: $390.00 - $430.00
Very good: $310.00 - $345.00

Dan Wesson Model 44V

Dan Wesson Model 45-V Colt, 745-V

Caliber: 45 Colt
Action: Single & double, exposed hammer, wide hammer & trigger
Cylinder: 6-shot; swing out; simultaneous ejector
Barrel: 4", 6", 8" or 10" ventilated rib shroud
Sights: Interchangeable colored front sight blade
Finish: Blued; smooth walnut grips; stainless steel (745-V)
Length Overall: 12" with 6" barrel
Approximate wt.: 48 to 63 oz.
Comments: Introduced in 1988. Price increases with barrel length increases. Add $70.00 for stainless steel (745-V).

Estimated Value:		
New (retail)	$431.45 - $466.94
Excellent:	$325.00 - $350.00
Very good:	$260.00 - $280.00

Dan Wesson Model 45-VH, 745-VH

Similar to the Model 45-V with heavier bull barrel. Price increases with barrel length. Add $70.00 for stainless steel (745-VH).

Estimated Value:		
New (retail):	$454.31 - $496.54
Excellent:	$340.00 - $370.00
Very good:	$270.00 - $300.00

Dan Wesson Model 44-V, 744-V

Caliber: 44 magnum, 44 Special (jacketed only)
Action: Single & double, exposed hammer, wide hammer & trigger
Cylinder: 6-shot; swing out; simultaneous ejector
Barrel: 4", 6", 8", 10" interchangeable barrel; ventilated rib
Sights: Interchangeable colored front sight blade, adjustable rear with white outline
Finish: Blued; smooth or checkered walnut grips with thumb flute; stainless steel (744-V)
Length Overall: 12" with 6" barrel
Approximate wt.: 48 to 63 oz.
Comments: Introduced in the early 1980's. Price increases with barrel length. Add $70.00 for stainless steel (744-V).

Estimated Value:		
New (retail)	$431.45 - $466.94
Excellent:	$325.00 - $350.00
Very good:	$255.00 - $280.00

Dan Wesson Model 44-VH, 744-VH

Similar to the Model 44 with heavier bull barrel. Price increases with barrel length. Add $70.00 for stainless steel (744-VH).

Estimated Value:		
New (retail):	$454.31 - $496.54
Excellent:	$340.00 - $370.00
Very good:	$270.00 - $300.00

Dardick

Dardick Magazine Pistol

Dardick 1100 - 11 shot
Dardick 1500 - 15 shot
Dardick 2000 - 20 shot

All models could be converted to a rifle by removing the barrel & fitting the frame into the rifle conversion kit.
Estimated Value:

	Pistol with 22 & 38 caliber barrels
Excellent:	$500.00
Very good:	$375.00
	Pistol with 22 & 38 caliber barrels & rifle conversion kit
Excellent:	$850.00
Very good:	$700.00

Dardick Magazine Pistol

David Dardick developed a handgun, which resembles an automatic pistol, around a new type of cartridge called the "tround." The tround has a triangular case made of plastic. For the 38 caliber, the primer, powder, & bullets are loaded into the tround. The 22 caliber cartridges are simply placed in a plastic tround to adapt them to the feeding system. The firing pin position is changed to rim-fire by manually turning a screw in the frame. Therefore, the basic gun will shoot 22 caliber or 38 caliber by changing the barrel. The feeding system used a three-legged star wheel which moves from magazine to firing position & dumps rounds through opening on right side. The feeding system is moved 120° with each pull of the trigger. The magazine is loaded by placing trounds in singly or by using 10-shot stripper clips. Production was started in 1959 in Hamden, Connecticut & ceased in 1960. All facilities, guns, & parts were auctioned to Numrich Arms in 1960. Approximately 40 guns were produced. The gun was made in three models & a rifle conversion kit. All models were made with two barrels (22 and 38 caliber).

Desert Eagle

Desert Eagle, Mark I, Mark VIII

Caliber: 357 magnum; 44 magnum (in 1986); 41 magnum (in 1989)

Action: Gas operated semi-automatic; single action; exposed hammer; rotating locking bolt

Magazine: 9-shot clip (357 magnum); 8-shot clip (44 magnum)

Barrel: 6" standard; 10" or 14" available

Sights: Combat style or target style with adjustable rear

Finish: Black oxide; satin nickel; bright nickel; or blued wrap-around rubber grips; alloy frame or stainless steel frame

Length Overall: 10½", 14½", 18½"

Approximate wt.: 48 to 59 oz. (alloy frame); 58 to 70 oz. (steel or stainless steel)

Comments: Add 19% for 44 magnum; add 17% for 41 magnum; 25% for stainless steel frame; add 30% for 10" barrel; add 32% for 14" barrel; add 19% for nickel finish.

Estimated Value: New (retail): $629.00
Excellent: $470.00
Very good: $375.00

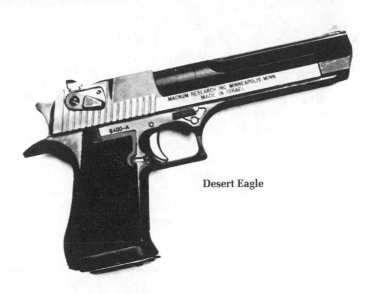

Desert Eagle

Detonics

Detonics Combat Master

Detonics Pocket 9

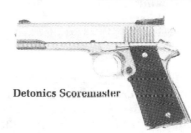

Detonics Scoremaster

Detonics Mark I, Combat Master

Caliber: 45 ACP; 9 mm; 38 Super ACP

Action: Semi-automatic; exposed hammer; single action; thumb safety

Magazine: 6-shot clip

Barrel: 3¼"

Sights: Fixed; some models have adjustable sights

Finish: Polished blue, matte blue; walnut grips

Length Overall: 6¾"

Approximate wt.: 29 oz.

Comments: A lightweight compact combat 45 caliber pistol made from the late 1970's to present.

Estimated Value: New (retail): $725.00
Excellent: $540.00
Very good: $435.00

Detonics Mark V, Combat Master

Similar to the Mark I except matte stainless steel finish. Discontinued 1985.

Estimated Value: Excellent: $550.00
Very good: $440.00

Detonics Mark VI, Combat Master

Similar to the Mark V with polished stainless steel finish.

Estimated Value: New (retail): $795.00
Excellent: $595.00
Very good: $475.00

Detonics Pocket 9

Caliber: 9 mm

Action: Double and single action, blow-back; semi-automatic

Magazine: 6-shot clip

Barrel: 3"

Sights: Fixed

Finish: Matte finish stainless steel, hooked and serrated trigger guard

Length Overall: 5¾"

Approximate wt.: 26 oz.

Comments: Produced in the mid 1980's.

Estimated Value: Excellent: $375.00
Very good: $300.00

Detonics Scoremaster

Similar to the Combat Master with a 5" or 6" barrel, 7 or 8-shot clip; 45 ACP or 451 Detonics magnum. Add $40.00 for 6" barrel.

Estimated Value: New (retail): $1,110.00
Excellent: $ 830.00
Very good: $ 665.00

Detonics Service Master

Similar to the Combat Master except slightly longer and heavier, Millett sights, dull finish.

Estimated Value: New (retail): $975.00
Excellent: $730.00
Very good: $585.00

Fiala

Fiala Single Shot Magazine Pistol

Fiala Single Shot Magazine Pistol
Caliber: 22 short, long, long rifle
Action: Hand operated slide action to chamber cartridge, cock striker & eject empty case
Magazine: 10-shot clip
Barrel: 3", 7½", 20"
Sights: Target sight (adjustable rear sight)
Finish: Blued; plain wood grips
Length Overall: 6¾", 11¼" or 23¾"
Approximate wt.: 27 to 44 oz.
Comments: Produced from about 1920 to 1923. A rare American pistol which had the appearance of an automatic pistol. A shoulder stock was supplied for use with the 20" barrel.

Estimated Value:	Pistol with 3", 7½" barrel	Pistol with all 3 barrels & shoulder stock
Excellent:	$400.00	$800.00
Very good:	$300.00	$650.00

Glock

Glock 17

Glock 17, 17L, 19
Caliber: 9mm (9mm x 19mm) (Parabellum) Luger
Action: Recoil operated semi-automatic; double action
Magazine: 17 shot clip (17 & 17L) 15 (19) or a opt. 19 or 17 shot clip
Barrel: 4½" (17); 6" (17L); 4" (19)
Sights: Fixed (service model) or adjustable rear (sport model)
Finish: Space-age polymer & machined steel
Length Overall: 7½" (17); 9" (17L); 7" (19)
Approximate wt.: 23 oz. (17L); 21 oz. (19)
Comments: Introduced in 1983. Standard sidearm of Austrian Armed Forces 1985. The 17L has cut away to top of slide. Add 45% for 17L.

Estimated Value:	New (retail):	$511.60
	Excellent:	$385.00
	Very good:	$300.00

Great Western

Great Western Frontier
Caliber: 22 short, long, long rifle, 357 magnum, 38 Special, 44 magnum, 44 Special, 45 Colt
Action: Single, hand ejector
Cylinder: 6-shot clip
Barrel: 4¾", 5½", 7½" round barrel with ejector housing under barrel
Sights: Blade front; groove in top strap for rear sight
Finish: Blued; imitation stag grips
Length Overall: 10⅜" to 13⅛"
Approximate wt.: 38 to 42 oz.
Comments: Replica of the Colt Single Action revolver. Made from about 1951 to 1962. Values of these revolvers vary due to the poor quality of the early models. After 1955 they were also available in unassembled kit form. Values for factory-made models.

Great Western Frontier

Estimated Value:	Excellent:	$185.00
	Very good:	$150.00

Great Western Double Barrel Derringer
Caliber: 38 Special
Action: Single, double barrel; tip up to eject & load
Cylinder: None; barrels chambered for cartridges
Barrel: Superposed 3" double
Sights: Fixed
Finish: Blued; checkered plastic grips
Length Overall: 4⅞"
Approximate wt.: 14 oz.
Comments: Replica of the Remington Double Derringer. Made from about 1952 to 1962.

Estimated Value:	Excellent:	$110.00
	Very good:	$ 85.00

Harrington & Richardson

H & R Self Loading 25
Caliber: 25 ACP
Action: Semi-automatic; concealed hammer
Magazine: 6-shot clip; simultaneous ejector
Barrel: 2"
Sights: None
Finish: Blued; hard rubber grips
Length Overall: 4½"
Approximate wt.: 13 oz.
Comments: Approximately 20,000 produced from about 1912 to 1915.
Estimated Value: Excellent: $280.00
                       Very good: $225.00

H & R Self Loading 32
Caliber: 32 ACP
Action: Semi-automatic; concealed hammer; grip safety
Magazine: 8-shot clip
Barrel: 3½"
Sights: Fixed
Finish: Blued; hard rubber grips
Length Overall: 6½"
Approximate wt.: 22 oz.
Comments: A modified Webley & Scott designed pistol. Approximately 40,000 produced from about 1916 to 1939.
Estimated Value: Excellent: $265.00
                       Very good: $210.00

H & R Model 4
Caliber: 32 S&W, 32 S&W long, 38 S&W
Action: Double & single; exposed hammer; solid frame; side load
Cylinder: 6-shot in 32 caliber, 5-shot in 38 caliber, removable cylinder
Barrel: 2½", 4½" or 6" hexagon barrel
Sights: Fixed
Finish: Blued or nickel; hard rubber grips
Length Overall: 6½" to 10"
Approximate wt.: 14 to 18 oz.
Comments: Made from about 1904 to 1941.
Estimated Value: Excellent: $100.00
                       Very good: $ 75.00

H & R Model 5
Similar to the Model 4 except: 32 S&W caliber only; smaller frame and cylinder (5 shot); weighs 10-12 oz. Produced from about 1905 to 1939.
Estimated Value: Excellent: $90.00
                       Very good: $70.00

H & R Model 6
Similar to the Model 5 except: 22 short, long, long rifle; 7-shot cylinder; minor change in shape of top of frame at rear of cylinder. Made from about 1906 to 1941.
Estimated Value: Excellent: $100.00
                       Very good: $ 75.00

H & R American
Caliber: S&W, 32 S&W long; 38 S&W
Action: Single or double; exposed hammer; solid frame; side load
Cylinder: 6-shot in 32 caliber; 5-shot in 38 caliber; removable cylinder
Barrel: 2½", 4½" or 6" hexagon barrel
Sights: Fixed
Finish: Blued or nickel; hard rubber round butt grips
Length Overall: 6½" to 9¾"
Approximate wt.: 14 to 16 oz.
Comments: Made from about 1883 to 1941.
Estimated Value: Excellent: $100.00
                       Very good: $ 80.00

H & R Young American
Caliber: 22 short, long, long rifle, 32 S&W short
Action: Single or double; exposed hammer; solid frame; side load
Cylinder: 7-shot in 22 caliber; 5-shot in 32 caliber; removable cylinder
Barrel: 2", 4½" or 6" hexagon barrel
Sights: Fixed
Finish: Blued or nickel; hard rubber round butt grips
Length Overall: 5½" to 9¾"
Approximate wt.: 10 to 12 oz.
Comments: Made from about 1885 to 1941.
Estimated Value: Excellent: $100.00
                       Very good: $ 75.00

H & R American

H & R American
Ejecting Revolver

H & R Young
American

H & R Model 6

H & R Model 4

H & R
Model 5

H & R Vest Pocket
Same as H & R Young American except 1⅛" barrel only; double action only; no spur on hammer; approximate weight 8 oz. Produced from about 1891 to 1941.
Estimated Value: Excellent: $90.00
                       Very good: $70.00

H & R Automatic Ejecting Revolver
Caliber: 32 S&W, 32 S&W long; 38 S&W
Action: Single or double; exposed hammer; hinged frame; top break
Cylinder: 6-shot in 32 caliber; 5-shot in 38 caliber; simultaneous automatic ejector
Barrel: 3¼", 4", 5" or 6" round barrel with rib
Sights: Fixed
Finish: Blued or nickel; hard rubber round butt grips
Length Overall: 7¼" to 10"
Approximate wt.: 15 to 18 oz.
Comments: Made from about 1891 to 1941.
**Estimated Value: Excellent: $120.00
                    Very good: $ 95.00**

H & R Model 50
Same as Automatic Ejecting Revolver except: double action only; concealed hammer; frame completely encloses hammer area. Made from about 1899 to 1941.
**Estimated Value: Excellent: $125.00
                    Very good: $100.00**

H & R Premier
Caliber: 22 short, long, long rifle, 32 S&W
Action: Single or double; exposed hammer; small hinged frame; top break
Cylinder: 7-shot in 22 caliber; 5-shot in 32 caliber; simultaneous automatic ejector
Barrel: 2", 3", 4", 5" or 6" round ribbed barrel
Sights: Fixed
Finish: Blued or nickel; hard rubber round butt grips
Length Overall: 5¾" to 9¾"
Approximate wt.: 12 to 16 oz.
Comments: Made from about 1895 to 1941.
**Estimated Value: Excellent: $130.00
                    Very good: $105.00**

H & R Model 40
Same as Premier except double action only; concealed hammer; frame completely encloses hammer area. Made from about 1899 to 1941.
**Estimated Value: Excellent: $135.00
                    Very good: $100.00**

H & R Trapper Model
Same as Model 6 except 6" barrel, checkered square butt walnut grips. Made from about 1924 to 1942.
**Estimated Value: Excellent: $120.00
                    Very good: $ 95.00**

H & R Hunter Model (1926)
Same as Trapper Model except 10" barrel, weighs 18 oz. Made from about 1926 to 1930.
**Estimated Value: Excellent: $110.00
                    Very good: $ 85.00**

H & R Hunter Model (1930)
Similar to Hunter Model (1926) except: larger frame; 9-shot safety cylinder (recessed chambers); weighs 26 oz. Made from about 1930 to 1941.
**Estimated Value: Excellent: $115.00
                    Very good: $ 90.00**

H & R Model 50

H & R Premier

H & R Model 40

H & R Trapper Model

H & R Model 944

H & R Model 944
Caliber: 22 short, long, long rifle, 22 WRF
Action: Single or double; exposed hammer; heavy hinged frame; top break
Cylinder: 9-shot; simultaneous automatic ejector
Barrel: 6" round ribbed barrel
Sights: Fixed
Finish: Blued; checkered square butt walnut grips
Length Overall: 10"
Approximate wt.: 24 oz.
Comments: Produced from about 1925 to 1930.
**Estimated Value: Excellent: $130.00
                    Very good: $105.00**

H & R Model 945

H & R Model 922

H & R Model 766 Target

H & R Single Shot

H & R No. 199 Sportsman

H & R Model 945

Same as Model 944 except safety cylinder (recessed chambers). Made from about 1929 to 1941.

Estimated Value: Excellent: $135.00
                   Very good: $110.00

H & R Model 955

Same as Model 945 except: 10" barrel; approximate weight 28 oz. Made from about 1929 to 1941.

Estimated Value: Excellent: $130.00
                   Very good: $115.00

H & R Model 922

Caliber: 22 short, long, long rifle
Action: Single or double; exposed hammer; solid frame; side load
Cylinder: 9-shot removable cylinder
Barrel: 4", 6" or 10" octagon barrel in early models, later models had 2½", 4" or 6" round barrel
Sights: Fixed
Finish: Blued; checkered walnut grips on early models; plastic grips on later models
Length Overall: 8¼" to 14¼"
Approximate wt.: 20 to 26 oz.
Comments: Maded from about 1929 to 1970's.

Estimated Value: Excellent: $100.00
                   Very good: $ 80.00

H & R Model 923

Same as Model 922 except nickel finish. Made from about 1930 to late 1970's.

Estimated Value: Excellent: $95.00
                   Very good: $70.00

H & R 766 Target

Caliber: 22 short, long, long rifle, 22 WRF
Action: Single or double; exposed hammer; small hinged frame; top break
Cylinder: 7-shot; simultaneous automatic ejector
Barrel: 6" round barrel
Sights: Fixed
Finish: Blued; checkered square butt walnut grips
Length Overall: 10"
Approximate wt.: 16 oz.
Comments: Maded from about 1926 to 1936.

Estimated Value: Excellent: $135.00
                   Very good: $100.00

H & R Ultra Sportsman

Caliber: 22 short, long, long rifle, 22 WRF
Action: Single or double; exposed hammer; small hinged frame; top break
Cylinder: 9-shot; simultaneous automatic ejector
Barrel: 6" round barrel
Sights: Adjustable target sights
Finish: Blued; checkered square butt walnut grips
Length Overall: 10"
Approximate wt.: 30 oz.
Comments: Heavy frame; short cylinder; wide hammer spur. Made from about 1928 to 1938.

Estimated Value: Excellent: $145.00
                   Very good: $120.00

H & R USRA Single Shot

Same as Ultra Sportsman except single shot only (no cylinder); cartridge chamber in barrel; barrel fills in cylinder space; 7" 8" or 10" barrrel lengths; approximate weight 29 to 31 oz. Made from about 1928 to 1943.

Estimated Value: Excellent: $330.00
                   Very good: $250.00

H & R No. 199 (Sportsman)

Caliber: 22 short, long, long rifle
Action: Single or double; exposed hammer; hinged frame; top break
Cylinder: 9-shot; simultaneous automatic ejector
Barrel: 6" round barrel, ribbed
Sights: Adjustable target
Finish: Blued; checkered square butt walnut grips
Length Overall: 11"
Approximate wt.: 27 oz.
Comments: Maded from about 1931 to 1951.

Estimated Value: Excellent: $125.00
                   Very good: $100.00

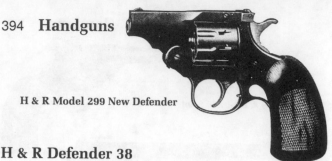

H & R Model 299 New Defender

H & R Defender 38
Similar to No. 199 Sportsman Model except: 38 S & W caliber; 4" or 6" barrel; fixed sights, plastic grips. Made from about 1933 to 1946.

Estimated Value: Excellent: $120.00
Very good: $ 95.00

H & R Model 299 New Defender
Similar to No. 199 Sportsman Model except 2" barrel; 6¼" overall length. Made from about 1936 to 1941.

Estimated Value: Excellent: $125.00
Very good: $100.00

H & R No. 999 (Deluxe Sportsman)
Same as No. 199 Sportsman Model except redesigned hammer & barrel rib in 1950's. Made from about 1936 to 1986. 32 caliber (6-shot cylinder) & 4" barrel available in 1979.

Estimated Value: Excellent: $160.00
Very good: $120.00

H & R Model 929 Side-Kick

H & R Model 632

H & R Bobby Model 15
Caliber: 32 S&W, 32 S&W long, 38 S&W
Action: Single or double; exposed hammer; hinged frame; top break
Cylinder: 6-shot in 32 caliber, 5-shot in 38 caliber; simultaneous automatic ejector
Barrel: 4" round, ribbed
Sights: Fixed
Finish: Blued; checkered square butt walnut grips
Length Overall: 9"
Approximate wt.: 23 lbs.
Comments: Made from about 1941 to 1943.

Estimated Value: Excellent: $110.00
Very good: $ 85.00

H & R Model 632
Caliber: 32 S&W, 32 S&W long
Action: Single or double; exposed hammer; solid frame; top break; removable
Cylinder: 6-shot, swing out
Barrel: 2½" or 4" round
Sights: Fixed
Finish: Blued; checkered tenite grips
Length Overall: 6¾" to 8¼"
Approximate wt.: 19 to 21 oz.
Comments: 2½" barrel model has round butt grips. Made from about 1946 to 1986.

Estimated Value: Excellent: $80.00
Very good: $60.00

H & R Model 633
Same as Model 632 except nickel finish; 2½" barrel only. Made from about 1946 to late 1970's.

Estimated Value: Excellent: $90.00
Very good: $70.00

H & R Model 999 Deluxe Sportsman

H & R Model 929 Side-Kick
Caliber: 22 short, long, long rifle
Action: Single or double; exposed hammer; solid frame
Cylinder: 9-shot swing out; simultaneous manual ejector
Barrel: 2½", 4" or 6" round, ribbed
Sights: 2½" has fixed sights; 4" & 6" have windage adjustable rear sights
Finish: Blued; checkered plastic grips; walnut grips available after 1982
Length Overall: 6¾" to 10¼"
Approximate wt.: 22 to 28 oz.
Comments: Made from about 1956 to 1986. Add $15.00 for walnut grips.

Estimated Value: Excellent: $100.00
Very good: $ 80.00

H & R Model 930 Side-Kick
Same as Model 929 Side-Kick except nickel finish; 2½" or 4" barrel. Add $15.00 for walnut grips.

Estimated Value: Excellent: $100.00
Very good: $ 75.00

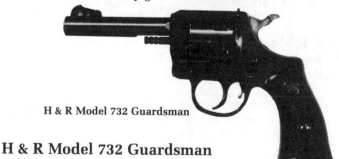

H & R Model 732 Guardsman

H & R Model 732 Guardsman
Caliber: 32 S&W, 32 S&W long
Action: Single or double; exposed hammer; solid frame
Cylinder: 6-shot swing out; simultaneous manual ejector
Barrel: 2½" or 4" round
Sights: Fixed
Finish: Blued; checkered plastic grips; walnut grips available after 1982
Length Overall: 6¾" to 8¼"
Approximate wt.: 23 to 26 oz.
Comments: Made from about 1958 to 1986. Add $15.00 for walnut grips.

Estimated Value: Excellent: $95.00
Very good: $70.00

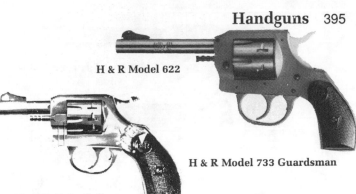

H & R Model 622

H & R Model 733 Guardsman

H & R Model 733 Guardsman

Same as Model 732 Guardsman except nickel finish; round butt grips. Made from about 1958 to 1986. Add $15.00 for walnut grips.

Estimated Value: Excellent: $105.00
                        Very good: $ 80.00

H & R Model 622

Caliber: 22 short, long, long rifle
Action: Single or double; exposed hammer; solid frame; side load
Cylinder: 6-shot removable
Barrel: 2½", 4", 6" round
Sights: Fixed
Finish: Blued; checkered plastic grips
Length Overall: 6¾" to 10¼"
Approximate wt.: 24 to 28 oz.
Comments: Made from about 1957 to 1986.

Estimated Value: Excellent: $75.00
                        Very good: $55.00

H & R Model 939 Ultra Sidekick & 940

Caliber: 22 short, long, long rifle
Action: Single or double; exposed hammer; solid frame
Cylinder: 9-shot swing out; simultaneous manual ejector
Barrel: 6" ventilated rib target barrel; bull barrel on 940
Sights: Ramp front; adjustable rear sight
Finish: Blued; checkered walnut grips with thumb rest
Length Overall: 10½"
Approximate wt.: 33 oz.
Comments: Made from about 1958 to 1980's.

Estimated Value: Excellent: $110.00
                        Very good: $ 90.00

H & R Model 903

Similar to the Model 939 with a solid heavy flat side barrel & adjustable sights. Produced from 1980 to 1984.

Estimated Value: Excellent: $120.00
                        Very good: $ 95.00

H & R Model 603

Similar to the Model 903 in 22 magnum. Discontinued in 1984.

Estimated Value: Excellent: $120.00
                        Very good: $ 95.00

H & R Model 904

Similar to the Model 903 with a 4" or 6" heavy round barrel. Blue satin finish available after 1982.

Estimated Value: Excellent: $130.00
                        Very good: $100.00

H & R Model 604

Similar to the Model 904 in 22 magnum.

Estimated Value: Excellent: $135.00
                        Very good: $105.00

H & R Model 642

Similar to the Model 622 in 22 WMR caliber; 2½" or 4" barrel. Discontinued in 1983.

Estimated Value: Excellent: $80.00
                        Very good: $65.00

H & R Model 623

Same as Model 622 except nickel finish. Made from about 1957 to late 1970's.

Estimated Value: Excellent: $70.00
                        Very good: $50.00

H & R Model 939 Ultra Sidekick

H & R Model 905

Similar to the Model 904 with nickel finish. Introduced in 1981. Discontinued 1986.

Estimated Value: Excellent: $135.00
                        Very good: $100.00

H & R Model 900

H & R Model 900

Caliber: 22 short, long, long rifle
Action: Single or double; exposed hammer; solid frame; side load
Cylinder: 9-shot removable
Barrel: 2½", 4" or 6"
Sights: Fixed
Finish: Blued; checkered plastic grips
Length Overall: 6½" to 10"
Approximate wt.: 23 to 26 oz.
Comments: Made from about 1962 to 1973.

Estimated Value: Excellent: $85.00
                        Very good: $65.00

H & R Model 901

Same as Model 900 except nickel finish. Made from about 1962 to 1963.

Estimated Value: Excellent: $90.00
                        Very good: $70.00

H & R Model 949 Forty-Niner

H & R Model 926

H & R Model 925 Defender
Caliber: 38 S&W
Action: Single or double; exposed hammer; hinged frame; top break
Cylinder: 5-shot; simultaneous automatic ejector
Barrel: 2½" round, ribbed
Sights: Fixed front sight; adjustable rear sight
Finish: Blued; one-piece wrap around grip
Length Overall: 6¾"
Approximate wt.: 22 oz.
Comments: Made from about 1964 to late 1970's.
Estimated Value: Excellent: $120.00
　　　　　　　　　 Very good: $ 95.00

H & R Model 926
Caliber: 38 S&W
Action: Single or double; exposed hammer; hinged frame; top break
Cylinder: 5-shot; simultaneous automatic ejector
Barrel: 4"
Sights: Adjustable rear sight
Finish: Blued; checkered plastic square butt grips
Length Overall: 8¼"
Approximate wt.: 31 oz.
Comments: Made from about 1972 to late 1970's.
Estimated Value: Excellent: $125.00
　　　　　　　　　 Very good: $100.00

H & R Model 649 Convertible

H & R Model 666 Convertible

H & R Model 666 Convertible
Caliber: 22 short, long, long rifle, 22 magnum (WMR) with extra interchangeable cylinder
Action: Single or double; exposed hammer; solid frame; side load
Cylinder: 6-shot removable; extra interchangeable cylinder so either cartridge can be used
Barrel: 6" round
Sights: Fixed
Finish: Blued; black cycolac, square butt grips
Length Overall: 10¼"
Approximate wt.: 28 oz.
Comments: Made from about 1975 to late 1970's.
Estimated Value: Excellent: $105.00
　　　　　　　　　 Very good: $ 75.00

H & R Model 949 Forty-Niner
Caliber: 22 short, long, long rifle
Action: Single or double; exposed hammer; solid frame; side load & ejection
Cylinder: 9-shot
Barrel: 5½" round; ejector
Sights: Blade front; adjustable rear sights
Finish: Blued; smooth walnut, one-piece, western style grips
Length Overall: 10¼"
Approximate wt.: 31 oz.
Comments: Made from about 1959 to l1986.
Estimated Value: Excellent: $95.00
　　　　　　　　　 Very good: $70.00

H & R Model 950 Forty-Niner
Same as Model 949 Forty-Niner revolver except nickel finish.
Estimated Value: Excellent: $100.00
　　　　　　　　　 Very good: $ 75.00

H & R Model 976
Similar to 949 with 7½" barrel, case hardened frame. Add $20.00 for nickel finish. Discontinued early 1980's.
Estimated Value: Excellent: $100.00
　　　　　　　　　 Very good: $ 80.00

H & R Model 649 Convertible
Caliber: 22 short, long, long rifle, 22 magnum (WMR) with extra interchangeable cylinder
Action: Single or double; exposed hammer; solid frame; side load & ejection
Cylinder: 6-shot removable cylinder; single manual ejector; extra interchangeable cylinder
Barrel: 5½" or 7½" round barrel; ejector rod housing under barrel
Sights: Blade front; adjustable rear sights
Finish: Blued barrel; satin finish frame; smooth western-style walnut grips
Length Overall: 10¼"
Approximate wt.: 32 oz.
Comments: Western style; made from about 1975 to 1986.
Estimated Value: Excellent: $115.00
　　　　　　　　　 Very good: $ 85.00

H & R Model 650 Convertible
Same as Model 649 Convertible except nickel finish.
Estimated Value: Excellent: $120.00
　　　　　　　　　 Very good: $ 95.00

H & R Model 676 Convertible
Similar to Model 649 Convertible except 4½", 5½", 7½" or 12" barrel; blued barrel with antique color cased frame; finger rest at back of trigger guard. Discontinued early 1980's. Add $25.00 for 12" barrel model.
Estimated Value: Excellent: $120.00
　　　　　　　　　 Very good: $ 95.00

H & R Model 686 Convertible
Similar to the Model 676 with ramp front sight, adjustable rear sight. Add $20.00 for 12" barrel.
Estimated Value: Excellent: $135.00
　　　　　　　　　 Very good: $100.00

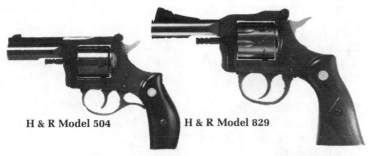

H & R Model 504   **H & R Model 829**

H & R Model 532

H & R Model 586

H & R Model 504

Caliber: 32 H&R magnum
Action: Single or double; swing-out cylinder; exposed hammer
Cylinder: 5-shot swing-out
Barrel: 3", 4", 6" target bull
Sights: Blade front; rear adjustable for windage & elevation
Finish: Blued; smooth walnut grips, round or square butt
Length Overall: 7½" to 10"
Approximate wt.: 29 to 35 oz.
Comments: Introduced in 1984 for the new H&R magnum caliber. Discontinued 1986.
Estimated Value: **Excellent:**   **$150.00**
                 Very good: **$120.00**

H & R Model 586

Caliber: 32 H&R magnum
Action: Single or double; side loading & ejection
Cylinder: 5-shot removeable
Barrel: 4½", 5½", 7½", 10" round
Sights: Ramp & blade front, rear adjustable for windage & elevation
Finish: Blued; case hardened frame; hardwood grips
Length Overall: 10¼" (5½" barrel)
Approximate wt.: 30 to 38 oz.
Comments: Introduced in 1984 for the new 32 H&R magnum caliber. Discontinued 1986.
Estimated Value: **Excellent:**   **$145.00**
                 Very good: **$110.00**

H & R Model 829

Caliber: 22 long rifle
Action: Single or double; exposed hammer
Cylinder: 9-shot swing out
Barrel: 3" bull barrel
Sights: Ramp front, adjustable rear
Finish: Blued; smooth walnut grips
Length Overall: 7¼"
Approximate wt.: 27 oz.
Comments: Produced from 1981 to 1984.
Estimated Value: **Excellent:**   **$110.00**
                 Very good: **$ 85.00**

H & R Model 830

Similar to the Model 829 with nickel finish. Produced from 1982 to 1984.
Estimated Value: **Excellent:**   **$120.00**
                 Very good: **$ 95.00**

H & R Model 826

Similar to the Model 829 in 22 magnum caliber.
Estimated Value: **Excellent:**   **$115.00**
                 Very good: **$ 90.00**

H & R Model 832

Similar to the Model 829 in 32 caliber. Discontinued in 1984.
Estimated Value: **Excellent:**   **$110.00**
                 Very good: **$ 85.00**

H & R Model 833

Similar to the Model 832 with nickel finish. Produced from 1982 to 1984.
Estimated Value: **Excellent:**   **$115.00**
                 Very good: **$ 90.00**

H & R Model 532

Caliber: 32 H&R magnum
Action: Single or double
Cylinder: 5-shot pull-pin removeable
Barrel: 2¼", 4" round
Sights: Fixed
Finish: Blued; smooth walnut grips
Length Overall: 6¾" to 8¼"
Approximate wt.: 20 to 25 oz.
Comments: Introduced in 1984 for the new H&R magnum caliber. Discontinued 1986.
Estimated Value: **Excellent:**   **$90.00**
                 Very good: **$65.00**

Hartford

Hartford Automatic Target

Caliber: 22 long rifle
Action: Semi-automatic; concealed hammer
Magazine: 10-shot chip
Barrel: 6¾"
Sights: Fixed front; rear sight dovetailed in slide
Finish: Blued; black rubber grips
Length Overall: 10¾"
Approximate wt.: 32 oz.
Comments: Made from about 1929 to 1930. Similar in appearance to Colt Woodsman & Hi Standard Model B Automatic Pistol. Rights & properties of Hartford Arms were sold to High Standard Mfg. Co. in 1932.
Estimated Value: **Excellent:**   **$375.00**
                 Very good: **$300.00**

Hartford Automatic Target

Hartford Repeating Pistol
Caliber: 22 long rifle
Action: Manual operation of slide after each shot to eject cartridge & feed another cartridge from magazine to chamber; concealed hammer
Magazine: 10-shot chip
Barrel: 6¾"
Sights: Fixed front; rear sight dovetailed in slide
Finish: Blued; black rubber grips
Length Overall: 10¾"
Approximate wt.: 31 oz.
Comments: Made from about 1929 to 1930.
Estimated Value: Excellent: $400.00
Very good: $300.00

Hartford Single Shot
Caliber: 22 long rifle
Action: Single action, hand operated, concealed hammer
Magazine: None
Barrel: 6¾"
Sights: Fixed front; rear sight dovetailed in slide
Finish: Matte finish on slide & frame; blued barrel; black rubber or walnut grips
Length Overall: 10¾"
Approximate wt.: 37 oz.
Comments: Made from about 1929 to 1930.
Estimated Value: Excellent: $450.00
Very good: $355.00

Heckler & Koch

Heckler & Koch Model P7 (M-8, M-13 & K-3)
Caliber: 9mm Parabellum; 380 ACP (K-3 added 1988)
Action: Recoil operated semi-automatic; concealed hammer; contains a unique system of cocking by squeezing front of grips, uncocking by releasing; double action
Magazine: 8-shot clip (M-8 & K-3); 13-shot (M-13)
Barrel: 4⅛"
Sights: Fixed
Finish: Blued; black grips
Length Overall: 6½"
Approximate wt.: 33½ oz.
Comments: Made in West Germany. Introduced in 1982. Add 25% for M-13.
Estimated Value: New (retail): $908.00
Excellent: $680.00
Very good: $545.00

Heckler & Koch Model P9S
Caliber: 9mm Parabellum; 45 ACP
Action: Semi-automatic; concealed hammer; cocking lever
Magazine: 9-shot clip; 7-shot clip in 45 ACP
Barrel: 4"
Sights: Fixed; blade front, square notch rear
Finish: Blued; black plactic grips; wood combat grips available
Length Overall: 7½"
Approximate wt.: 28 to 31 oz.
Comments: Made in West Germany. Discontinued in 1989.
Estimated Value: Excellent: $975.00
Very good: $780.00

Heckler & Koch Model P9S Competition
Similar to the Model P9S Target with both 4" & 5½" barrels, 2 slides, wood competition grips and plastic grips, all packed in a special case. 9mm only.
Estimated Value: Excellent: $1,000.00
Very good: $ 725.00

Heckler & Koch Model P9S Target
Similar to the Model P9S with adjustable trigger, trigger stop & adjustable rear sight; 5½" barrel available.
Estimated Value: Excellent: $1,035.00
Very good: $ 830.00

Heckler & Koch Model HK4

Heckler & Koch Model P9S

Heckler & Koch Model HK4
Caliber: 380; conversion kits available for calibers 38, 25 and 22 long rifle
Action: Semi-automatic; double action; exposed hammer spur
Magazine: 7-shot clip
Barrel: 3⅜"
Sights: Fixed; blade front, notch rear; non-reflective
Finish: Blued; black plactic grips; grip extension on clip
Length Overall: 6"
Approximate wt.: 17 oz.
Comments: Discontinued in mid 1980's. Add $160.00 for all three conversion kits.
Estimated Value: Excellent: $320.00
Very good: $240.00

Heckler & Koch Model VP70Z
Caliber: 9mm
Action: Semi-automatic; blow back, recoil operated; double action only; hammerless
Magazine: Double stacked 18-shot clip; 2 magazines standard
Barrel: 4½"
Sights: Fixed; ramp front, notched rear
Finish: Blued; black plactic grips; solid plastic receiver
Length Overall: 8"
Approximate wt.: 29 oz.
Comments: A pistol with few moving parts, designed for the outdoorsman. Discontinued in mid 1980's.
Estimated Value: Excellent: $325.00
Very good: $260.00

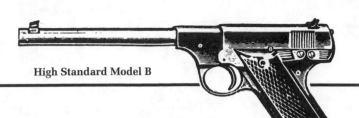

High Standard Model B

High Standard

High Standard Model B
Caliber: 22 long rifle
Action: Semi-automatic; concealed hammer; thumb safety
Magazine: 10-shot clip
Barrel: 4½" or 6¾"
Sights: Fixed
Finish: Blued; hard rubber grips
Length Overall: 8½" and 10¾"
Approximate wt.: 30 to 34 oz.
Comments: Produced from about 1931 to 1942.
Estimated Value: Excellent: $250.00
                      Very good: $200.00

High Standard Model HB
Same as Model B except exposed hammer & no thumb safety. Made from about 1932 to 1942.
Estimated Value: Excellent: $220.00
                      Very good: $175.00

High Standard Model A
Caliber: 22 long rifle
Action: Semi-automatic; concealed hammer; thumb safety
Magazine: 10-shot clip
Barrel: 4½" or 6¾"
Sights: Adjustable target sights
Finish: Blued; checkered walnut grips
Length Overall: 9¼" & 11¼"
Approximate wt.: 34 to 36 oz.
Comments: Made from about 1937 to 1942.
Estimated Value: Excellent: $260.00
                      Very good: $210.00

High Standard Model HA
Same as Model A except exposed hammer spur & no thumb safety.
Estimated Value: Excellent: $225.00
                      Very good: $180.00

High Standard Model D
Same as Model A except heavier barrel; approximate weight 37 to 40 oz., depending on barrel length.
Estimated Value: Excellent: $275.00
                      Very good: $220.00

High Standard Model HD
Same as Model D except exposed hammer spur & no thumb safety.
Estimated Value: Excellent: $265.00
                      Very good: $210.00

High Standard Model HDM or HD Military
Same as Model HD except it has thumb safety. Made from about 1941 to 1947, stamped "U.S. Property."
Estimated Value: Excellent: $325.00
                      Very good: $260.00

High Standard Model SB
Same as Model B except 6¾" smooth bore for shooting 22 long rifle shot cartridges.
Estimated Value: Excellent: $200.00
                      Very good: $160.00

High Standard Model C
Same as Model B except chambered for 22 short cartridges. Made from about 1932 to 1942.
Estimated Value: Excellent: $225.00
                      Very good: $180.00

High Standard Model A

High Standard Model E

High Standard Model HD

High Standard Model HD Military (Postwar)
Same as Model HDM except it is not stamped "U.S. Property." Made from about 1946 to 1951 (post World War II model).
Estimated Value: Excellent: $250.00
                      Very good: $200.00

High Standard Model E
Similar to Model A except extra heavy barrel; thumb rest grips. Approximate weight 39 to 42 oz.
Estimated Value: Excellent: $275.00
                      Very good: $220.00

High Standard Model HE
Same as Model E except exposed hammer spur & no thumb safety.
Estimated Value: Excellent: $255.00
                      Very good: $205.00

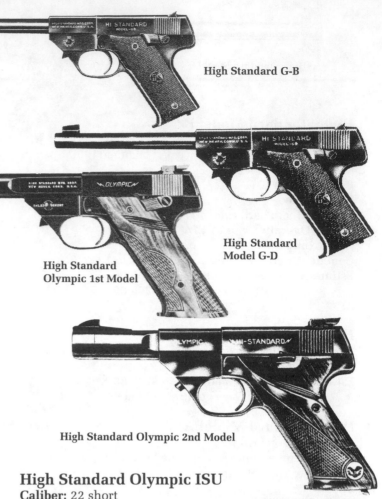

High Standard G-B

High Standard
Model G-D

High Standard
Olympic 1st Model

High Standard Olympic 2nd Model

High Standard Model G-B
Caliber: 22 long rifle
Action: Semi-automatic; concealed hammer; takedown
    model; interchangeable barrels; thumb safety
Magazine: 10-shot clip
Barrel: 4½" or 6¾"
Sights: Fixed
Finish: Blued; checkered plastic grips
Length Overall: 8½" & 10¾"
Approximate wt.: 34 to 36 oz.
Comments: Made from about 1948 to 1951. Add $25.00 if
    pistol has both barrels.
Estimated Value: **Excellent:** $210.00
                  Very good: $170.00

High Standard Model G-D
Same as Model G-B except: adjustable target sights;
checkered walnut grips; approximate weight 38 to 40 oz.;
length overall about 9¼" to 11½". Add $35.00 if pistol has
both barrels.
Estimated Value: **Excellent:** $220.00
                  Very good: $175.00

High Standard Model G-E
Same as Model G-D except: heavy barrel; thumb rest;
walnut grips; approximate weight 42 to 44 oz. Add
$50.00 if pistol has both barrels.
Estimated Value: **Excellent:** $250.00
                  Very good: $200.00

High Standard Olympic 1st Model
Same as Model G-E except 22 short caliber; light alloy
slide; made from about 1950 to 1951; approximate
weight 38 to 40 oz. Add $50.00 if pistol has both barrels.
Estimated Value: **Excellent:** $310.00
                  Very good: $250.00

High Standard Olympic 2nd Model
Same as Olympic 1st Model except: thumb safety located
at center top of left grip; plastic grips with thumb rest;
produced from about 1951 to 1958. Add $50.00 if pistol
has both barrels.
Estimated Value: **Excellent:** $290.00
                  Very good: $230.00

High Standard Olympic

High Standard Olympic G-380

High Standard Olympic ISU
Caliber: 22 short
Action: Semi-automatic; concealed hammer; wide target
    trigger; anti-backlash trigger adjustment
Magazine: 10-shot clip
Barrel: 5½" bull barrel (1963-1966); 8" tapered barrel
    (1958-1964); 6¾" tapered barrel (1958-present); inte-
    gral stabilizer & 2 removable weights
Sights: Ramp front; adjustable rear
Finish: Blued; checkered walnut grips with thumb rests
Length Overall: 11¼" (6¾" barrel)
Approximate wt.: 40 to 41 oz.
Comments: Meets International Shooting Union Regula-
    tions; left or right hand grips; regular Hi-Standard
    style grip or the squared military style grip; military
    style has rear sight frame mounted. Made from
    about 1958 to late 1970's.
Estimated Value: **Excellent:** $320.00
                  Very good: $260.00

High Standard Model G-380
Caliber: 380 ACP
Action: Semi-automatic; exposed hammer spur; thumb
    safety; barrel takedown model
Magazine: 6-shot clip; bottom release
Barrel: 5"
Sights: Fixed; blade front & notched rear
Finish: Blued; checkered plastic grips
Length Overall: 9"
Approximate wt.: 40 oz.
Comments: First of the barrel takedown models pro-
    duced by High Standard. Made from about 1944 to
    1950.
Estimated Value: **Excellent:** $325.00
                  Very good: $260.00

High Standard Sport-King 1st Model

Caliber: 22 long rifle
Action: Semi-automatic; concealed hammer; takedown model with interchangeable barrel; thumb safety at top center of left grip
Magazine: 10-shot clip
Barrel: 4½" &/or 6¾"
Sights: Fixed
Finish: Blued; checkered plastic grips with thumb rest
Length Overall: 9", 11¼"
Approximate wt.: 36 to 39 oz.
Comments: Made from about 1951 to 1958. Add $15.00 for pistol with both barrels.
Estimated Value: Excellent: $175.00
                      Very good: $140.00

High Standard Sport-King 2nd Model

Similar to Sport-King 1st Model except: made from about 1958 to present; interior changes; still has interchangeable barrel; blued or nickel finish; weighs 39 to 42 oz. Add $15.00 for nickel finish. Reintroduced in early 1980's to 1985, slightly different grip style.
Estimated Value: Excellent: $210.00
                      Very good: $170.00

High Standard Lightweight Sport-King

Same as Sport-King 1st Model except: made from about 1954 to 1965; aluminum alloy frame; weight 28 to 30 oz. Add $15.00 for pistol with both barrels.
Estimated Value: Excellent: $165.00
                      Very good: $130.00

High Standard Flite-King 1st Model

Same as Sport-King 1st Model except: made from about 1953 to 1958; aluminum alloy frame and slide; weight 24 to 26 oz.; 22 short caliber only. Add $20.00 for pistol with both barrels.
Estimated Value: Excellent: $175.00
                      Very good: $140.00

High Standard Flite-King 2nd Model

Same as Sport-King 1st Model Automatic except: made from about 1958 to 1965; all steel construction; 22 long rifle caliber only. Add $20.00 for pistol with both barrels.
Estimated Value: Excellent: $175.00
                      Very good: $140.00

High Standard Field-King

Same as Sport-King 1st Model except: adjustable target sights; 6¾" heavy barrel; weight about 44 oz.
Estimated Value: Excellent: $200.00
                      Very good: $160.00

High Standard Supermatic Series

Caliber: 22 long rifle
Action: Semi-automatic; concealed hammer; thumb safety; takedown model with interchangeable barrels
Magazine: 10-shot clip
Barrel: 4½", 5½", 6¾" 7¼", 8", 10"
Sights: Ramp front, adjustable rear
Finish: Blued; checkered plastic or checkered wood grips with or without thumb rest
Length Overall: 9¼" to 14¾"
Approximate wt.: 40 to 46 oz.
Comments: The 5¼" barrels are heavy (bull) barrels & the 7¼" barrels are heavy (bull) fluted barrels.

Standard Supermatic Model manufactured from about 1951 to 1958; 4¼" & 6¾" interchangeable barrels. Add $20.00 for pistols with both barrels.
Estimated Value: Excellent: $220.00
                      Very good: $175.00

Supermatic Tournament Model made from about 1958 to 1963; 5½" bull barrel &/or 6¾" regular barrel with stabilizer & 2 removable weights; adjustable trigger pull. Add $20.00 for pistol with both barrels.
Estimated Value: Excellent: $250.00
                      Very good: $200.00

Supermatic Citation Model made from about 1959 to 1966; 5½" bull barrel &/or 6¾", 8" or 10" tapered barrel with stabilizer & 2 removable weights; adjustable trigger pull.
Estimated Value: Excellent: $275.00
                      Very good: $220.00

Supermatic Citation, Military or Citation II made from about 1965 to 1985; 5½" heavy (bull) or 7¼" heavy fluted barrel with military grip or standard grip. 5½" or 7¼" slabbed barrel in 1984 (Citation II).
Estimated Value: Excellent: $290.00
                      Very good: $235.00

High Standard Sport-King 1st Model

High Standard Sport-King 2nd Model

Standard Citation Model

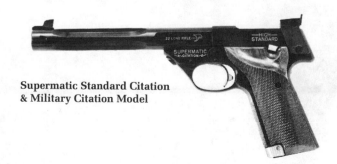

Supermatic Standard Citation & Military Citation Model

Supermatic Trophy Citation made from about 1959 to 1966; 5½" bull barrel or 7¼" heavy fluted barrel.
Estimated Value: Excellent: $275.00
                   Very good: $220.00

Supermatic Trophy Military Model manufactured from about 1965 to 1985; 5½" bull barrel or 7¼" fluted barrel with square military style grip; adjustable trigger pull. Add $20.00 for 7¼" barrel.
Estimated Value: Excellent: $320.00
                   Very good: $250.00

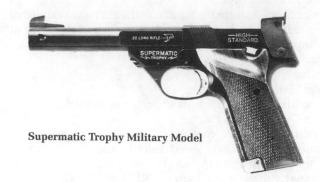

Supermatic Trophy Military Model

High Standard Dura-Matic

Caliber: 22 long rifle
Action: Semi-automatic; concealed hammer; takedown interchangeable barrels model
Magazine: 10-shot clip
Barrel: 4½", 6½"
Sights: Fixed
Finish: Blued; checkered plastic grips
Length Overall: 8⅞", 10⅞"
Approximate wt.: 33 to 35 oz.
Comments: Manufactured from about 1954 to 1969.
Estimated Value: Excellent: $160.00
                       Very good: $130.00

High Standard Plinker

Caliber: 22 long rifle
Action: Semi-automatic; concealed hammer
Magazine: 10-shot clip
Barrel: 4½", 6½"
Sights: Fixed
Finish: Blued; checkered plastic grips
Length Overall: 9" to 11"
Approximate wt.: 28 to 30 oz.
Comments: Made from about 1971 to 1974.
Estimated Value: Excellent: $140.00
                       Very good: $110.00

High Standard Flite-King 1st Model

High Standard Field-King

High Standard Dura-Matic

High Standard Plinker

High Standard Sharpshooter and Survival Pack
Caliber: 22 long rifle
Action: Semi-automatic; concealed hammer
Magazine: 10-shot clip
Barrel: 5½" bull barrel
Sights: Ramp front; adjustable rear
Finish: Blued; checkered walnut grips; nickel available after 1982
Length Overall: 10¼"
Approximate wt.: 42 oz.
Comments: Made from about 1971 to 1985. A survival pack consisting of a nickel pistol; extra magazine & canvas case available after 1982. Add $75.00 for complete pack.
Estimated Value: **Excellent:** **$250.00**
Very good: **$200.00**

High Standard Victor
Caliber: 22 long rifle
Action: Semi-automatic; concealed hammer; interchangeable barrel
Magazine: 10-shot clip
Barrel: 4½" or 5½" with solid or aluminum ventilated rib & barrel weights
Sights: Ramp front; adjustable rear
Finish: Blued; checkered walnut grips with thumb rest; later models have some parts gold plated
Length Overall: 8¾", 9¾"
Approximate wt.: 38 to 42 oz.
Comments: Hi-Standard type grip or square military type grip. Made from about 1972 to 1985. 5½" barrel only in 1980's.
Estimated Value: **Excellent:** **$320.00**
Very good: **$250.00**

High Standard Sharpshooter

High Standard Victor

High Standard 10-X

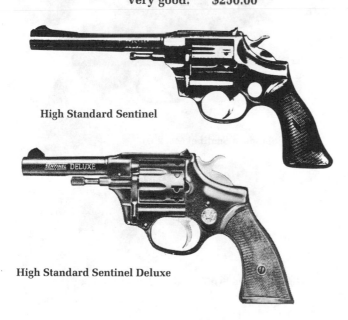

High Standard Sentinel

High Standard Sentinel Deluxe

High Standard Sentinel Deluxe
Same as Sentinel Revolver except adjustable rear sight; checkered square butt walnut grips; wide trigger; 4" or 6" only; made from about 1965 to 1974.
Estimated Value: **Excellent:** **$125.00**
Very good: **$100.00**

High Standard 10-X
Caliber: 22 long rifle
Action: Semi-automatic; concealed hammer; adjustable target trigger
Magazine: 10-shot clip; 2 extra standard
Barrel: 5½" bull barrel
Sights: Blade front, adjustable rear mounted independent of slide
Finish: Non-reflective blue; checkered walnut military grip; components hand picked & fitted by gunsmith; gunsmith's initials located under left grip
Length Overall: 10¼"
Approximate wt.: 42 oz.
Comments: A custom competition gun.
Estimated Value: **Excellent:** **$575.00**
Very good: **$460.00**

High Standard Sentinel
Caliber: 22 short, long, long rifle
Action: Single or double; solid frame
Cylinder: 9-shot swing out; simultaneous manual ejector
Barrel: 3", 4", 6"
Sights: Fixed
Finish: Blued or nickel; checkered plastic grips
Length Overall: 8" to 11"
Approximate wt.: 18 to 24 oz.
Comments: Made from about 1954 to 1974; aluminum alloy frame.
Estimated Value: **Excellent:** **$120.00**
Very good: **$ 95.00**

High Standard Sentinel Imperial

Same as Sentinel revolver except ramp front sight; black or nickel finish; checkered square butt walnut grips. Made from about 1961 to 1965.

Estimated Value: Excellent: $130.00
Very good: $105.00

High Standard Sentinel Snub

Same as Sentinel revolver except 2⅜" barrel only; overall length 7½"; weighs 15 oz.; checkered plastic bird's head grip (round butt). Made from about 1956 to 1974. Some were made in pink, turquoise & gold colored finish as well as blue & nickel.

Estimated Value: Excellent: $135.00
Very good: $110.00

High Standard Sentinel Mark I

Caliber: 22 short, long, long rifle
Action: Single or double; solid frame
Cylinder: 9-shot swing out; simultaneous manual ejector
Barrel: 2", 4"
Sights: Ramp front; fixed or adjustable rear
Finish: Blued or nickel; smooth walnut grips
Length Overall: 7", 9"
Approximate wt.: 28 to 30 oz.
Comments: A completely redesigned & improved all steel version of the 22 caliber Sentinel. Made from about 1974 to late 1970's. Add $10.00 for nickel finish; $10.00 for adjustable rear sight.

Estimated Value: Excellent: $160.00
Very good: $120.00

High Standard Sentinel Mark IV

Same as Sentinel Mark I except 22 magnum only. Add $10.00 for nickel finish or adjustable rear sight.

Estimated Value: Excellent: $165.00
Very good: $125.00

High Standard Sentinel Mark II

Caliber: 38 Special, 357 magnum
Action: Single or double; solid frame
Cylinder: 6-shot swing out; simultaneous manual ejector
Barrel: 2½", 4", 6"
Sights: Fixed rear; ramp front
Finish: Blued; checkered walnut grips
Length Overall: 7½" to 11"
Approximate wt.: 38 to 40 oz.
Comments: Heavy-duty all steel revolver. Made from about 1974 to late 1970's.

Estimated Value: Excellent: $180.00
Very good: $135.00

High Standard Sentinel Mark III

Same as Sentinel Mark II except deluxe trophy blue finish; checkered walnut wrap-around grips; checkered back strap; adjustable rear sight.

Estimated Value: Excellent: $190.00
Very good: $140.00

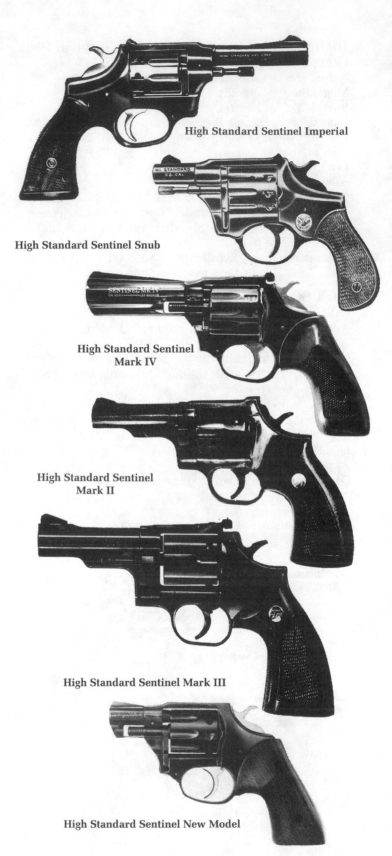

High Standard Sentinel Imperial

High Standard Sentinel Snub

High Standard Sentinel Mark IV

High Standard Sentinel Mark II

High Standard Sentinel Mark III

High Standard Sentinel New Model

High Standard Sentinel New Model

Similar to the Sentinel with 22 caliber cylinder & interchangeable 22 magnum cylinder. Available with 2" or 4" barrel. Reintroduced in 1982 to 1985. Add $20.00 for extra cylinder.

Estimated Value: Excellent: $175.00
Very good: $135.00

High Standard Longhorn

Caliber: 22 short, long, long rifle
Action: Single or double; solid frame
Cylinder: 9-shot swing out; simultaneous manual ejector
Barrel: 4½" or 5½" (1961 to 1966); 9½" (1971 to present); dummy ejector housing under barrel
Sights: Blade front; fixed or adjustable rear
Finish: Blued; plastic grips; walnut grips on 9½" barrel model
Length Overall: 10", 11", 15"
Approximate wt.: 26 to 32 oz.
Comments: Aluminum alloy frame (about 1961 to 1971). Steel frame (about 1971 to 1985).
Estimated Value: Excellent: $175.00
                       Very good: $130.00

High Standard Longhorn Combination

Similar to Longhorn revolver except extra interchangeable cylinder in 22 magnum caliber; 9½" barrel only; smooth walnut grips. Made from about 1971 to 1985.
Estimated Value: Excellent: $190.00
                       Very good: $140.00

High Standard Kit Gun

Caliber: 22 short, long, long rifle
Action: Single or double; solid frame
Cylinder: 9-shot swing out; simultaneous manual ejector
Barrel: 4"
Sights: Ramp front; adjustable rear
Finish: Blued; checkered walnut grips
Length Overall: 9"
Approximate wt.: 19 oz.
Comments: Aluminum alloy frame. Made from about 1970 to 1973.
Estimated Value: Excellent: $120.00
                       Very good: $ 95.00

High Standard Double Nine

Caliber: 22 short, long, long rifle
Action: Single or double; solid frame
Cylinder 9-shot swing out; simultaneous manual ejector
Barrel: 5½"; dummy ejector housing under barrel
Sights: Blade front; fixed or adjustable rear
Finish: Blued or nickel; plastic grips
Length Overall: 11"
Approximate wt.: 28 oz.
Comments: Aluminum alloy frame (about 1958 to 1971); a western style of the Sentinel revolvers. Steel frame from about 1971 to 1985. Add $10.00 for nickel finish.
Estimated Value: Excellent: $175.00
                       Very good: $130.00

High Standard Double Nine Combination

Same as Double Nine revolver except: extra interchangeable cylinder in 22 magnum caliber; smooth walnut grip; made from about 1971 to 1985; steel frame; weighs 32 oz. Add $10.00 for nickel finish.
Estimated Value: Excellent: $190.00
                       Very good: $140.00

High Standard Natchez

Similar to Double Nine revolver except 4½" barrel only; 10" overall length; weighs 32 oz.; blued finish only; plastic ivory bird's head grips. Made from about 1961 to 1966.
Estimated Value: Excellent: $150.00
                       Very good: $110.00

High Standard Posse

Similar to Double Nine revolver except 3½" barrel without dummy ejector housing; 9" overall length; weighs 24 oz.; brass trigger guard & grip frame; blued finish only; smooth walnut grips. Made from about 1961 to 1966.
Estimated Value: Excellent: $140.00
                       Very good: $110.00

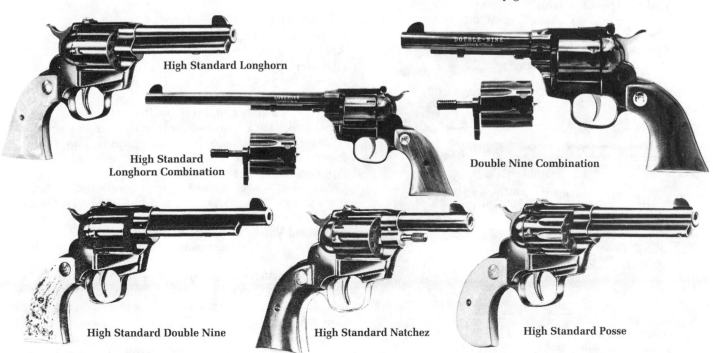

High Standard Longhorn

High Standard Longhorn Combination

Double Nine Combination

High Standard Double Nine

High Standard Natchez

High Standard Posse

High Standard Hombre

Caliber: 22 short, long, long rifle
Action: Single or double; solid frame
Cylinder: 9-shot swing out; simultaneous ejector
Barrel: 4½"
Sights: Blade front; adjustable rear
Finish: Blued or nickel; smooth walnut grip
Length Overall: 10"
Approximate wt.: 26 oz.
Comments: Steel frame; manufactured from about 1972 to 1974. Add $5.00 for nickel finish.
Estimated Value: Excellent: $140.00
                       Very good: $105.00

High Standard Durango

Caliber: 22 short, long, long rifle
Action: Single or double; solid frame
Cylinder: 9-shot swing out; simultaneous ejector
Barrel: 4½", 5½"; dummy ejector housing under barrel
Sights: Blade front; adjustable rear
Finish: Blued or nickel; smooth walnut grip
Length Overall: 10", 11"
Approximate wt.: 25 to 27 oz.
Comments: Made from about 1972 to 1975.
Estimated Value: Excellent: $150.00
                       Very good: $115.00

High Standard High Sierra Combination

Caliber: 22 short, long, long rifle & 22 magnum
Action: Single or double; solid frame
Cylinder: 9-shot swing out; two interchangeable cylinders (22 cal. and 22 mag. cal.)
Barrel: 7" octagonal
Sights: Blade front; adjustable rear
Finish: Blued; smooth walnut grip
Length Overall: 12½"
Comments: Steel frame; gold plated trigger guard & backstrap. Made from about 1973 to 1985.
Estimated Value: Excellent: $190.00
                       Very good: $140.00

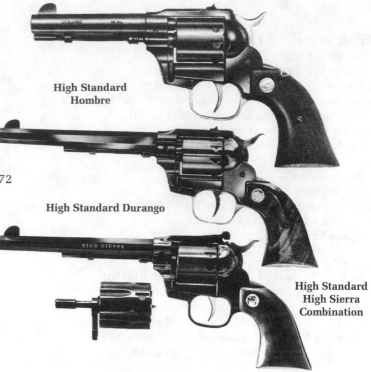

High Standard Hombre

High Standard Durango

High Standard High Sierra Combination

High Standard Camp Gun

High Standard Crusader

High Standard Crusader Medium Frame

High Standard Camp Gun

Caliber: 22 short, long, long rifle and 22 magnum
Action: Single or double; solid frame; simultaneous ejector
Cylinder: 9-shot swing out
Barrel: 6"
Sights: Ramp front; adjustable rear
Finish: Blued; checkered walnut grip
Length Overall: 11"
Approximate wt.: 28 oz.
Comments: Made from about 1975 to late 1970's. Add $3.00 for 22 magnum caliber. Reintroduced in 1982 to 1985.
Estimated Value: Excellent: $190.00
                       Very good: $140.00

High Standard Crusader

Caliber: 44 magnum, 45 Colt, 357 magnum
Action: Single or double
Cylinder: 6-shot
Barrel: 4½" in 44 or 45; 6½" in 44, 45 or 357; 8⅜" in 44, 45 or 357
Sights: Adjustable rear, ramp blade front;
Finish: Blued; shrouded ejector rod; smooth walnut grips in 44; checkered walnut grips in 45 & 357
Length Overall: 9⅞" - 14"
Approximate wt.: 43 to 52 oz.
Comments: A large frame handgun made from about the late 1970's to early 1980's. Add $5.00 for 6½" barrel; add $12.00 for 8⅜" barrel.
Estimated Value: Excellent: $290.00
                       Very good: $230.00

High Standard Crusader Medium Frame

Similar to the Crusader in 357 magnum only; 4½" or 6½" barrel; weight is 40 to 42 oz.; a smaller version of the Crusader. Add $7.00 for 6½" barrel.
Estimated Value: Excellent: $250.00
                       Very good: $200.00

High Standard Derringer

Caliber: 22 short, long, long rifle (1962 to present); 22 magnum rimfire (1963 to present)

Action: Double; concealed hammer; hammer block safety; front of trigger guard cut away

Cylinder: None; 2-shot chambers in barrels

Barrel: 3½" double barrel (superposed); duel ejection; cartridge chamber in each barrel

Sights: Fixed

Finish: Blued or nickel; plastic grips (1962 to present); gold plated presentation model in walnut case (1965 to 1966). Electroless nickel finish and walnut grips after 1982.

Length Overall: 5"

Approximate wt.: 11 oz.

Comments: Steel barrels; aluminum alloy frame. Made from about 1962 to 1985.

**High Standard
22 Caliber Derringer**

Estimated Value:	Blued	Nickel	Electro. Nickel
Excellent:	$100.00	$115.00	$130.00
Very Good:	$ 75.00	$ 90.00	$100.00

Gold presentation models with case in unused condition: (with consecutive numbers)

1-derringer $225.00
2-derringer $470.00

Iver Johnson

Iver Johnson X300 Pony, PO380, PO380B

Caliber: 380 ACP

Action: Single or double; semi-automatic; exposed hammer

Magazine: 6-shot clip

Barrel: 3"

Sights: Adjustable rear, blade front

Finish: Blued, nickel or military; checkered or smooth walnut grips

Length Overall: 6"

Approximate wt.: 20 oz.

Comments: Add 5% for nickel finish; made 1982 to 1987.

Estimated Value:	Excellent:	$215.00
	Very good:	$160.00

Iver Johnson X300 Pony

Iver Johnson Model TP22

Iver Johnson Model TP22, TP25, TP22B, TB25B

Caliber: 22 long rifle (TP22), 25 ACP (TP25)

Action: Double action; semi-automatic; exposed hammer

Magazine: 7-shot clip

Barrel: 3"

Sights: Fixed

Finish: Blued, nickel; plastic grips; finger extension on clip

Length Overall: 5½"

Approximate wt.: 15 oz.

Comments: Introduced in 1982. Add 8% for nickel.

Estimated Value:	New (retail):	$191.65
	Excellent:	$145.00
	Very good:	$115.00

Iver Johnson Trailsman

Caliber: 22 long rifle

Action: Semi-automatic, concealed hammer

Magazine: Clip

Barrel: 4½", 6"

Sights: Fixed

Finish: Blued; checkered plastic or smooth hardwood grips

Length Overall: 9" to 11"

Approximate wt.: 28 to 30 oz.

Comments: Introduced in 1984. Add 10% for HiPolish with hardwood grips; discontinued 1987.

Estimated Value:	Excellent:	$145.00
	Very good:	$107.00

Iver Johnson Safety Hammer

Caliber: 22-short, long, long rifle, 32 S&W, 32S&W long or 38 S&W

Action: Single or double; exposed hammer; hinged frame; top break style; simultaneous ejector; heavier frame for 32 & 38 caliber

Cylinder: 7-shot in 22 caliber; 6-shot in 32 caliber; 5-shot in 38 caliber

Barrel: 2", 3", 3¼", 4", 5", 6"; round barrel with rib on top

Sights: Fixed

Finish: Blued or nickel; hard rubber or wood grips; round or square butt grip

Length Overall: 6¾" to 10¾" depending on barrel length

Approximate wt.: 14 to 21 oz. depending on caliber & barrel length

Comments: Made from about 1892 to 1950 with some improvements & minor changes.

Estimated Value:	Excellent:	$120.00
	Very good:	$ 95.00

Iver Johnson Safety Hammer

Iver Johnson Safety Hammerless

Same as Safety Hammer model except side plates of frame extended to enclose hammer; double action only; concealed hammer. Made from about 1895 to 1950.

Estimated Value: Excellent: $125.00
              Very good: $100.00

Iver Johnson Safety Hammerless

Iver Johnson Model 1900

Caliber: 22 short, long, long rifle, 32 S&W, 32S&W long, 38 S&W
Action: Single or double; exposed hammer; solid frame; side load
Cylinder: 7-shot in 22 caliber; 6-shot in 32 caliber; 5-shot in 38 caliber; removable cylinder
Barrel: 2½", 4½", 6"; octagon barrel
Sights: Fixed
Finish: Blued or nickel; hard rubber grips
Length Overall: 7" to 10¾" depending on barrel length
Approximate wt.: 11 to 19 oz.
Comments: Made from about 1900 to 1947.
Estimated Value: Excellent: $95.00
              Very good: $75.00

Iver Johnson Model 1900

Iver Johnson Model 1900 Target

Same as Model 1900 except 22 caliber only; 6" or 9" barrel length; length overall 10¾" to 13¾"; approximate weight 22 to 26 oz.; checkered walnut grips; blued finish only. Made from about 1925 to 1942.

Estimated Value: Excellent: $120.00
              Very good: $ 95.00

Iver Johnson Target 9-Shot Revolver

Similar to Model 1900 Target except 9-shot cylinder; 6" or 10" barrel; 10¾" to 14¾" length overall; weight 24 to 28 oz. Introduced about 1929 & discontinued in 1946.

Estimated Value: Excellent: $115.00
              Very good: $ 95.00

Iver Johnson Supershot

Caliber: 22 short, long, long rifle
Action: Single or double; exposed hammer; hinged frame; top break style; simultaneous ejector
Cylinder: 7-shot; 9-shot
Barrel: 6"; round barrel with solid rib on top
Sights: Fixed
Finish: Blued; checkered walnut grips (one piece)
Length Overall: 10¾"
Approximate wt.: 25 oz.
Comments: Some have adjustable finger rest behind trigger guard. Made from about 1929 to 1949.
Estimated Value: Excellent: $130.00
              Very good: $100.00

Iver Johnson Sealed Eight Supershot

Similar to Supershot Revolver except: 8-shot cylinder recessed for cartridge head; 10" barrel length; 10¾" to 14¾" overall length; adjustable rear sight. Made from about 1931 to 1957.

Estimated Value: Excellent: $130.00
              Very good: $105.00

Iver Johnson Sealed Eight Target

Caliber: 22 short, long, long rifle
Action: Single or double; exposed hammer; solid frame; side load
Cylinder: 8-shot; cylinder recessed for cartridge head; removable
Barrel: 6", 10"; octagon barrel
Sights: Fixed
Finish: Blued; checkered walnut grips (one piece)
Length Overall: 10¾"; 14¾"
Approximate wt.: 24 to 28 oz.
Comments: Made from about 1931 to 1957.
Estimated Value: Excellent: $125.00
              Very good: $100.00

Iver Johnson Model 1900 Target

Iver Johnson Sealed Eight Supershot

Iver Johnson Sealed Eight Target

Iver Johnson Sealed Eight Protector

Caliber: 22 short, long, long rifle

Action: Single or double; exposed hammer; hinged frame; top break style; simultaneous ejector

Cylinder: 8-shot; cylinder recessed for cartridge head

Barrel: 2½"

Sights: Fixed

Finish: Blued; checkered walnut grips

Length Overall: 7½"

Approximate wt.: 20 oz.

Comments: Some had adjustable finger rest behind trigger guards. Made from about 1933 to 1949.

Estimated Value: Excellent: $140.00
                       Very good: $105.00

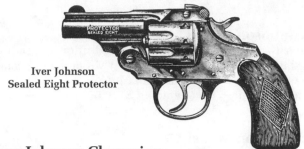

Iver Johnson
Sealed Eight Protector

Iver Johnson Champion

Iver Johnson
Trigger Cocking Target

Iver Johnson Champion

Caliber: 22 short, long, long rifle

Action: Single; exposed hammer; hinged frame; top break style; simultaneous ejector

Cylinder: 8-shot; cylinder recessed for cartridge head

Barrel: 6"

Sights: Adjustable target sights

Finish: Blued; checkered walnut grips (one piece)

Length Overall: 10¾"

Approximate wt.: 28 oz.

Comments: Made from about 1938 to 1948. Adjustable finger rest behind trigger guards.

Estimated Value: Excellent: $150.00
                       Very good: $110.00

Iver Johnson Trigger Cocking Target

Same as Champion Revolver except the trigger cocks the hammer on the first pull, then releases the hammer to fire the revolver on the second pull. Made from about 1940 to 1947.

Estimated Value: Excellent: $160.00
                       Very good: $120.00

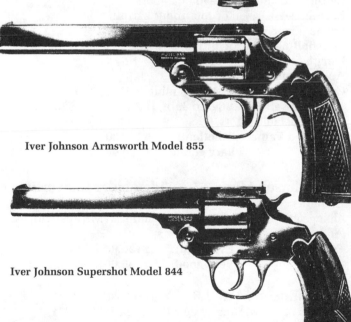

Iver Johnson Armsworth Model 855

Iver Johnson Supershot Model 844

Iver Johnson Armsworth Model 855

Caliber: 22 short, long, long rifle

Action: Single; exposed hammer; hinged frame; top break style; simultaneous ejector

Cylinder: 8-shot; cylinder recessed for cartridge head

Barrel: 6"

Sights: Adjustable front and rear sights

Finish: Blued; checkered walnut grips (one piece)

Length Overall: 10¾"

Approximate wt.: 30 oz.

Comments: Adjustable finger rest behind trigger guards. Made from about 1954 to 1957.

Estimated Value: Excellent: $135.00
                       Very good: $105.00

Iver Johnson Supershot Model 844

Similar to Armsworth Model 855 except double & single action; 4½" or 6" barrel lengths; 9¼" to 10¾" overall length. Introduced about 1955, discontinued about 1957.

Estimated Value: Excellent: $135.00
                       Very good: $105.00

Iver Johnson Model 55S Cadet

Caliber: 22 short, long, long rifle, 32, 38

Action: Single or double; solid frame; exposed hammer; side load

Cylinder: 8-shot in 22 caliber; 5-shot in 32 & 38 caliber; removable cylinder

Barrel: 2½"

Sights: Fixed

Finish: Blued; plastic round butt grips

Length Overall: 7"

Approximate wt.: 24 oz.

Comments: Made from about 1954 to 1961.

Estimated Value: Excellent: $115.00
                       Very good: $ 90.00

Iver Johnson Model 55S Cadet

Iver Johnson Model 55 S-A Cadet

Similar to Model 55S Cadet except addition of loading gate about 1962; also in calibers 22 WMR and 38 Special. Made from about 1962 to late 1970's.

Estimated Value: Excellent: $110.00
                       Very good: $ 85.00

Iver Johnson Model 55

Caliber: 22 short, long, long rifle
Action: Single or double; exposed hammer; solid frame; side load
Cylinder: 8-shot; chambers recessed for cartridge head; removable cylinder; unfluted cylinder
Barrel: 4½", 6"
Sights: Fixed
Finish: Blued; checkered walnut grips
Length Overall: 9¼" to 10¾"
Approximate wt.: 22 to 24 oz.
Comments: Made from about 1955 to 1961.
Estimated Value: Excellent: $100.00
                       Very good: $ 75.00

Iver Johnson Model 55A Target

Same as Model 55 Revolver except: fluted cylinder; loading gate; checkered plastic grips. Introduced about 1962. Made to late 1970's.

Estimated Value: Excellent: $110.00
                       Very good: $ 85.00

Iver Johnson Model 57

Same as Model 55 Revolver except: adjustable front and rear sights; checkered plastic grips. Made from about 1955 to 1961.

Estimated Value: Excellent: $115.00
                       Very good: $ 90.00

Iver Johnson Model 57A Target

Same as Model 55 Revolver except: fluted cylinder; adjustable front and rear sights; checkered plastic grips; loading gate. Introduced about 1962 to late 1970's.

Estimated Value: Excellent: $120.00
                       Very good: $ 95.00

Iver Johnson Model 57A

Iver Johnson Model 66 Trailsman

Iver Johnson Model 55 S-A Cadet

Iver Johnson Model 50A Sidewinder

Iver Johnson Model 50A Sidewinder

Caliber: 22 short, long, long rifle
Action: Single or double; exposed hammer; solid frame; side load with loading gates; removable cylinder
Cylinder: 8-shot; recessed chambers
Barrel: 4½", 6"; ejector rod under barrel
Sights: Fixed or adjustable
Finish: Blued; plastic grips
Length Overall: 9¾", 11¼"
Approximate wt.: 32 oz.
Comments: Frontier style double action revolver. Made from about 1961 to late 1970's. Add $20.00 for adjustable sights.
Estimated Value: Excellent: $110.00
                       Very good: $ 90.00

Iver Johnson Model 50A Sidewinder Convertible

Same as Model 50A Sidewinder except extra interchangeable cylinder for 22 magnum (WMR) cartridges. Add $10.00 for adjustable sights.

Estimated Value: Excellent: $120.00
                       Very good: $ 95.00

Iver Johnson Model 66 Trailsman

Caliber: 22 short, long, long rifle; 32 S&W, 38 S&W
Action: Single or double; exposed hammer; hinged frame; top break style; simultaneous manual ejector under barrel; rebounding type hammer
Cylinder: 8-shot in 22 caliber; 5-shot in 32 & 38 caliber; recessed chambers
Barrel: 2¾", 6", rib on top of barrel
Sights: Adjustable
Finish: Blued; checkered walnut or plastic grip; round butt on 2¾" barrel; square butt on 6" barrel
Length Overall: 7", 11"
Approximate wt.: 28 to 32 oz.
Comments: 2¾" barrel snub model from about 1961 to 1971; 6" barrel made from about 1958 to 1975.
Estimated Value: Excellent: $110.00
                       Very good: $ 90.00

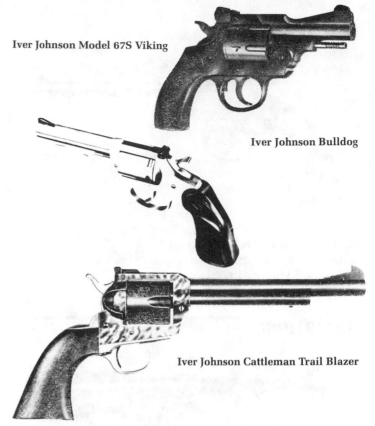

Iver Johnson Model 67S Viking

Iver Johnson Bulldog

Iver Johnson Cattleman Trail Blazer

Iver Johnson Model 67 Viking

Same as Model 66 Trailsman except: hammer safety device; 4½" or 6" barrel lengths. Made from about 1964 to 1975.

Estimated Value: Excellent: $125.00
                         Very good: $100.00

Iver Johnson Model 67S Viking

Same as Model 67 except: 2¾" barrel lengths; overall length 7"; approximate weight 25 oz.

Estimated Value: Excellent: $130.00
                         Very good: $105.00

Iver Johnson Bulldog

Caliber: 22 short, long, long rifle; 38 Special
Action: Single or double; exposed hammer; solid frame; side load with loading gate
Cylinder: 8-shot in 22 caliber; 5-shot in 38 caliber recessed chambers
Barrel: 2½", 4", heavy duty ribbed
Sights: Adjustable
Finish: Blued; plastic grips; round or square butt
Length Overall: 6½", 9"
Approximate wt.: 26 to 30 oz.
Comments: Made from about 1974 to late 1970's. Add $2.00 for 4" barrel; $10.00 for 38 caliber.

Estimated Value: Excellent: $115.00
                         Very good: $ 90.00

Iver Johnson Cattleman Trail Blazer

Caliber: 22 short, long, long rifle; 22 magnum (WMR)
Action: Single action; solid frame; exposed hammer; side load with loading gate
Cylinder: 6-shot; 2 interchangeable cylinders
Barrel: 5½", 6", manual ejector rod under barrel
Sights: Ramp front; adjustable rear
Finish: Blued; case hardened frame, brass backstrap & trigger guard; smooth walnut grip
Length Overall: 11¼" to 12¼"
Approximate wt.: 38 to 40 oz.
Comments: Made from about 1974 to late 1970's. Price includes both cylinders.

Estimated Value: Excellent: $165.00
                         Very good: $130.00

Iver Johnson Cattleman Buckhorn Buntline

Iver Johnson Cattleman Magnum

Iver Johnson Cattleman Buckhorn Magnum

Iver Johnson Cattleman Magnum

Caliber: 38 Special & 357 magnum, 45 long Colt, 44 Special & 44 magnum
Action: Single; solid frame; exposed hammer; side load with loading gate
Cylinder: 6-shot
Barrel: 4¾", 5½", 7½" (357 magnum & 44 LC); 4¾", 6", 7½" (44 magnum); manual ejector rod under barrel
Sights: Ramp front; adjustable rear
Finish: Blued; case hardened frame, brass backstrap and trigger guard; smooth walnut grip
Length Overall: 10½" to 13¼"
Approximate wt.: 38 to 46 oz.
Comments: Made from about 1974 to late 1970's. Add $25.00 for 44 magnum.

Estimated Value: Excellent: $175.00
                         Very good: $130.00

Iver Johnson Cattleman Buckhorn Magnum

Same as Cattleman Magnum except ramp front sight & adjustable rear sight. Add $25.00 for 12" barrel; $25.00 for 44 magnum.

Estimated Value: Excellent: $190.00
                         Very good: $145.00

Iver Johnson Cattleman Buckhorn Buntline

Same as Cattleman Buckhorn Magnum except 18" barrel length only; grip backstrap is cut for shoulder stock attachment; smooth walnut attachable shoulder stock; overall length without shoulder stock 24" & with shoulder stock 36½"; approximate wt. is 56 oz. without shoulder stock; shoulder stock wt. approximately 30 oz. Prices include stock. Add $25.00 for 44 magnum.

Estimated Value: Excellent: $335.00
                         Very good: $250.00

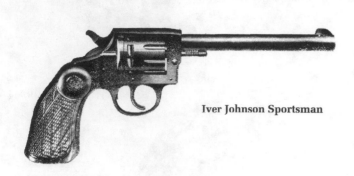

Iver Johnson Sportsman

Iver Johnson Deluxe Target
Similar to the Sportsman with adjustable sights.

Estimated Value: Excellent: $115.00
                   Very good: $ 90.00

Iver Johnson Rookie
Caliber: 38 Special
Action: Single or double
Cylinder: 5-shot; fluted
Barrel: 4"
Sights: Fixed
Finish: Blued or nickel; plastic grips
Length Overall: 9"
Approximate wt.: 29 oz.
Comments: Made from the mid to late 1970's.
Estimated Value: Excellent: $120.00
                       Very good: $ 90.00

Iver Johnson Sportsman
Similar to the Rookie in 22 long rifle caliber; 4¾" or 6" barrel; blued finish; made in the mid 1970's.
Estimated Value: Excellent: $110.00
                       Very good: $ 85.00

Japanese

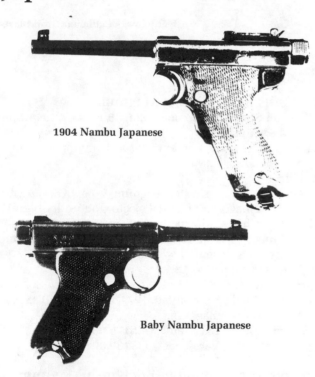

1904 Nambu Japanese

Baby Nambu Japanese

Nambu Type 14 Japanese
Caliber: 8mm bottle-necked Japanese
Action: Semi-automatic; manual safety
Magazine: 8-shot chip
Barrel: 4¾"
Sights: Barley corn front; undercut notch rear
Finish: Blued; grooved wood grips
Length Overall: 9"
Approximate wt.: 32 oz.
Comments: A modified form of the 1904 Nambu introduced about 1925 & produced until about 1945.
Estimated Value: Excellent: $400.00
                       Very good: $325.00

Type 26 Japanese
Caliber: 9mm rimmed pistol
Action: Double only; top break; hammer without cocking spur
Magazine: 6-shot; automatic ejector
Barrel: 4¾"
Sights: Blade front; "V" notch rear
Finish: Blued; checkered one-piece round grip
Length Overall: 9½"
Approximate wt.: 32 oz.
Comments: Made from about 1893 to 1914.
Estimated Value: Excellent: $250.00
                       Very good: $200.00

1904 Nambu Japanese
Caliber: 8mm bottle-necked Japanese
Action: Semi-automatic; grip safety below trigger guard
Magazine: 8-shot chip
Barrel: 4¾"
Sights: Barley corn front; notched tangent rear
Finish: Blued; checkered wood grips
Length Overall: 8¾"
Approximate wt.: 32 oz.
Comments: Made from about 1904 to 1925. Usually has a slot cut in rear of grip to accommodate shoulder stock holster. Add $75.00 for shoulder stock holster.
Estimated Value: Excellent: $800.00
                       Very good: $600.00

Baby Nambu Japanese
Caliber: 7mm bottle-necked Japanese cartridge
Action: Semi-automatic; grip safety below trigger guard
Magazine: 7-shot chip
Barrel: 3¼"
Sights: Barley corn front; "V" notch rear
Finish: Blued; checkered wood grips
Length Overall: 7¼"
Approximate wt.: 24 oz.
Comments: This is a smaller version of the 1904 Nambu.
Estimated Value: Excellent: $1,400.00
                       Very good: $1,150.00

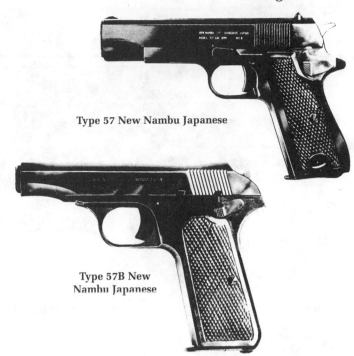

Type 57 New Nambu Japanese

Modified Nambu Type 14 Japanese

Similar to Nambu Type 14 except it has enlarged trigger guard to allow use of heavy gloves & a spring mounted in lower front of grip to hold magazine more securely.

Estimated Value: Excellent: $425.00
Very good: $335.00

Type 94 Japanese

Caliber: 8mm bottle-necked Japanese
Action: Semi-automatic
Magazine: 6-shot clip
Barrel: 3¾"
Sights: Barley corn front; square notch rear
Finish: Blued; checkered grips
Length Overall: 7¼"
Approximate wt.: 28 oz.
Comments: Made from about 1934 to 1945. Made for export but was used as a service pistol during World War II. Most show evidence of poor manufacture.

Estimated Value: Excellent: $300.00
Very good: $225.00

Type 57B New Nambu Japanese

Type 57 New Nambu Japanese

Caliber: 9mm Parabellum; 45 ACP
Action: Semi-automatic; recoil operated
Magazine: 8-shot clip
Barrel: 4½"
Sights: Fixed
Finish: Blued; checkered grips
Length Overall: 7¾"
Approximate wt.: 28 oz.
Comments: A modified copy of the U.S. 1911 A1 produced by the firm of Shin Chuo Kogyo K.K. since World War II. Magazine catch at bottom of grip; doesn't have the grip safety.

Estimated Value: Excellent: $200.00
Very good: $150.00

Type 57B New Nambu Japanese

Caliber: 32 ACP (7.65mm Browning)
Action: Semi-automatic; blow back operated
Magazine: 8-shot clip
Barrel: 3"
Sights: Fixed
Finish: Blued; checkered grips
Length Overall: 6¼"
Approximate wt.: 20 oz.
Comments: A modified copy of the Browning M1910 pistol produced by the firm of Shin Chuo Kogyo K.K. after World War II.

Estimated Value: Excellent: $175.00
Very good: $130.00

Lignose

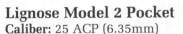

Lignose Einhand Model 2A Pocket

Lignose Model 2 Pocket

Lignose Model 2 Pocket

Caliber: 25 ACP (6.35mm)
Action: Semi-automatic; concealed hammer, thumb safety at top rear of left grip
Magazine: 6-shot clip
Barrel: 2⅛"
Sights: Fixed
Finish: Blued; checkered hard rubber grips
Length Overall: 4¾"
Approximate wt.: 15 oz.
Comments: Operation principle based on the 1906 Browning 25 caliber automatic pocket pistol; production started about 1920. Made in Germany. Early models marked "Bergmann."

Estimated Value: Excellent: $225.00
Very good: $180.00

Lignose Einhand Model 2A Pocket

Similar specifications as Model 2 except designed for one-hand operation, hence the name Einhand (one hand). Slide can be retracted to load & cock hammer, by using the trigger finger to pull back the front part of the trigger guard.

Estimated Value: Excellent: $275.00
Very good: $210.00

Lignose Einhand Model 3A Pocket

Same as Model 2A except longer grip & uses 9-shot clip.

Estimated Value: Excellent: $300.00
Very good: $225.00

Llama

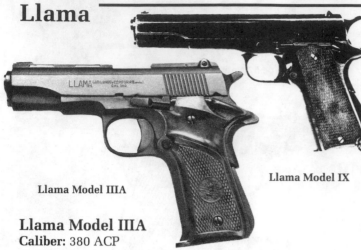

Llama Model IIIA

Llama Model IX

Llama Model IIIA

Caliber: 380 ACP
Action: Semi-automatic; manual & grip safety; exposed hammer
Magazine: 7-shot clip
Barrel: 3¹¹⁄₁₆"
Sights: Partridge front; adjustable rear
Finish: Blued, chrome, chrome engraved; plastic grips
Length Overall: 6¼"
Approximate wt.: 24 oz.
Comments: Made from about 1951 to late 1970's. Ventilated rib on top of slide. Add $40.00 for chrome; $50.00 for engraved.
Estimated Value: Excellent: $200.00
Very good: $150.00

Llama Model VIII

Caliber: 9mm Luger, 38 Super ACP
Action: Semi-automatic; manual & grip safety; exposed hammer
Magazine: 9-shot clip
Barrel: 5"
Sights: Fixed front; adjustable rear
Finish: Blued, chrome, chrome engraved; checkered wood or simulated pearl grips
Length Overall: 8½"
Approximate wt.: 39 oz.
Comments: Made from about 1953 to late 1970's. Add $40.00 for chrome; $50.00 for engraved.
Estimated Value: Excellent: $275.00
Very good: $220.00

Llama Model XI

Caliber: 9mm Luger
Action: Semi-automatic; manual safety; no grip safety; round exposed hammer
Magazine: 8-shot clip
Barrel: 4⅞"
Sights: Fixed
Finish: Blued, chrome; checkered plastic grips with modified thumb rest
Length Overall: 8"
Approximate wt.: 34 oz.
Comments: Made from about 1951 to late 1970's, with some minor modifications. Add $40.00 for chrome.
Estimated Value: Excellent: $250.00
Very good: $190.00

Llama Model IX

Caliber: 45 ACP
Action: Semi-automatic; locked breech; exposed hammer; manual safety
Magazine: 7-shot clip
Barrel: 5"
Sights: Fixed
Finish: Blued, checkered walnut grips
Length Overall: 8½"
Approximate wt.: 39 oz.
Comments: Made from about 1936 to 1952.
Estimated Value: Excellent: $215.00
Very good: $170.00

Llama Model IXA

Similar to Model IX except ventilated rib on slide; modified & improved version; also in chrome & chrome engraved finish. Made from about 1952 to late 1970's. Add $40.00 for chrome; $50.00 for chrome engraved.
Estimated Value: Excellent: $225.00
Very good: $170.00

Llama Model I

Caliber: 32 ACP (7.65mm)
Action: Semi-automatic; blow back type; exposed hammer
Magazine: 8-shot clip
Barrel: 4"
Sights: Fixed
Finish: Blued, wood grips
Length Overall: 6½"
Approximate wt.: 25 oz.
Comments: Made from about 1935 to 1941.
Estimated Value: Excellent: $175.00
Very good: $140.00

Llama Model II

Similar to the Model I except 7-shot clip; caliber 380 ACP (9mm short). Made from about 1935 to 1941.
Estimated Value: Excellent: $185.00
Very good: $150.00

Llama Model III

A modified version of the Model II. Made from about 1947 to 1954.
Estimated Value: Excellent: $190.00
Very good: $155.00

Llama Model XI

Llama Model VIII

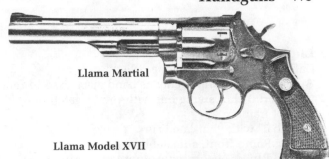

Llama Martial

Llama Model XVII

Llama Standard Automatic Small Frame
Similar to the Model XV, XA & IIIA. Currently produced.
Add 23% for chrome finish.

Estimated Value: New (retail): $325.00
                   Excellent: $240.00
                   Very good: $195.00

Llama Standard Automatic Large Frame
Similar to the Model VIII and IXA. Currently produced.
Add 30% for chrome finish.

Estimated Value: New (retail): $385.00
                   Excellent: $290.00
                   Very good: $230.00

Llama Standard Automatic Compact
Similar to the Large Frame Model but scaled down.
Available in 9mm and 45ACP; 8" long, 1⅜" wide; walnut
or teakwood grips; 7- or 9-shot clip; 34-37 oz.; 5" barrel.
Introduced in 1987. Add 30% for chrome finish.

Estimated Value: New (retail): $385.00
                   Excellent: $290.00
                   Very good: $230.00

Llama Model XV
Caliber: 22 long rifle
Action: Semi-automatic; blow back type; exposed ham-
   mer; grip & manual safety.
Magazine: 9-shot clip
Barrel: 3¹¹⁄₁₆"
Sights: Partridge type, fixed
Finish: Blued, chrome, chrome engraved; checkered
   wood grips
Length Overall: 6¼"
Approximate wt.: 18 oz.
Comments: A smaller version of the 1911 A1 Colt 45
   ACP. Made from about 1955 to late 1970's. Add
   $40.00 for chrome; $50.00 for engraved.

Estimated Value: Excellent: $210.00
                   Very good: $170.00

Llama Model XA
Same as Model XV except caliber 32 ACP; 8-shot clip.
Add $40.00 for chrome.

Estimated Value: Excellent: $225.00
                   Very good: $180.00

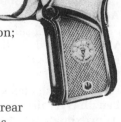

Llama Model XV

Llama Omni
Caliber: 9mm Parabellum, 45 Auto
Action: Semi-automatic; double action;
   exposed hammer
Magazine: 13-shot clip in 9mm;
   7-shot clip in 45
Barrel: 5"
Sights: Ramp blade front; adjustable rear
Finish: Blued; checkered plastic grips
Length Overall: 7½"
Approximate wt.: 30 oz.
Comments: Produced 1982 to 1988

Estimated Value: Excellent: $350.00
                   Very good: $275.00

Llama M-82 DA
Caliber: 9mm
Action: Double action;
   semi-automatic
Magazine: 15-shot clip
Barrel: 4¼"
Sights: Fixed front, adjustable rear
Finish: Blued, matte black polymer grips
Length Overall: 7¾"
Approximate wt.: 39 oz.
Comments: Introduced in 1988.

Estimated Value: New (retail): $975.00
                   Excellent: $730.00
                   Very good: $585.00

Llama Model XVII
Caliber: 22 short
Action: Semi-automatic; exposed hammer with round
   spur; manual safety
Magazine: 6-shot clip
Barrel: 2⅜"
Sights: Fixed
Finish: Blued, chrome; plastic grips
Length Overall: 4½"
Approximate wt.: 14 oz.
Comments: No longer imported into U.S.A. because of
   1968 gun control law. Also known as Executive
   Model. Add $20.00 for chrome.

Estimated Value: Excellent: $185.00
                   Very good: $150.00

Llama Model XVIII
Same as Model XVII except 32 ACP caliber only; no
longer imported into U.S.A. Add $20.00 for chrome.

Estimated Value: Excellent: $195.00
                   Very good: $160.00

Llama Martial
Caliber: 22 short, long, long rifle; 38 Special
Action: Double action; solid frame; simultaneous ejector
Cylinder: 6-shot swing out with thumb latch on left side
   of frame
Barrel: 6" in 22 caliber; 4" and 6" in 38 Special; venti-
   lated rib
Sights: Target sights
Finish: Blued, chrome, chrome engraved; checkered
   wood or simulated pearl grips
Length Overall: 9¼" to 11¼"
Approximate wt.: 35 to 40 oz.
Comments: Made from about 1969 to late 1970's. Add
   $25.00 for chrome; $25.00 for engraved.

Estimated Value: Excellent: $200.00
                   Very good: $160.00

Llama Comanche I

Caliber: 22 short, long, long rifle
Action: Double; simultaneous hand ejector; solid frame
Cylinder: 6-shot swing out with thumb latch on left side of frame
Barrel: 6" with ventilated rib
Sights: Ramp front; adjustable rear
Finish: Blued; checkered walnut target grips
Length Overall: 9¼"
Approximate wt.: 36 oz.
Comments: Made from about 1978 to mid 1980's. Add $25.00 for chrome.
Estimated Value: Excellent: $210.00
                       Very good: $170.00

Llama Comanche II

Similar to the Comanche I in 38 Special with a 4" or 6" barrel. Introduced in 1973.
Estimated Value: Excellent: $210.00
                       Very good: $170.00

Llama Comanche III

Similar to the Comanche II in 357 magnum caliber. Add 17% for satin chrome finish.
Estimated Value: New (retail): $339.00
                       Excellent: $255.00
                       Very good: $200.00

Llama Commanche

Llama Super Comanche, Super Comanche IV

A heavier version of the Comanche for 44 magnum cartridges; 6" barrel, 8½" barrel available after early 1980's.
Estimated Value: New (retail): $440.00
                       Excellent: $330.00
                       Very good: $265.00

Llama Super Comanche V

Similar to the Super Comanche IV except 357 caliber. This heavy frame revolver has 4", 6" & 8½" barrel. Introduced in 1982.
Estimated Value: Excellent: $310.00
                       Very good: $250.00

MAB

MAB Model C

MAB Model A

Caliber: 25 ACP (6.35mm)
Action: Semi-automatic; concealed hammer; manual safety; blow back design
Magazine: 6-shot clip
Barrel: 2½"
Sights: Fixed front; no rear
Finish: Blued; checkered hard rubber or plastic grips
Length Overall: 4½"
Approximate wt.: 18 oz.
Comments: Resembles Browning Model 1906 vest pocket pistol. Production started about 1924, imported into U.S.A. as WAC Model A or Le Defendeur. Importation stopped in 1968.
Estimated Value: Excellent: $185.00
                       Very good: $150.00

MAB Model B

Similar to Model A except top part of front section of slide cut away for empty cartridges to eject at top. Made from about 1932 to 1966 (never imported into U.S.A.)
Estimated Value: Excellent: $200.00
                       Very good: $150.00

MAB Model C

Caliber: 32 ACP, 380 ACP
Action: Semi-automatic; concealed hammer; grip safety & manual safety
Magazine: 7-shot clip in 32 ACP; 6-shot clip in 380 ACP
Barrel: 3¼"
Sights: Fixed
Finish: Blued; checkered hard rubber grips
Length Overall: 6¼"
Approximate wt.: 23 oz.
Comments: Production started about 1933. Importation into U.S.A. stopped in 1968.
Estimated Value: Excellent: $190.00
                       Very good: $145.00

MAB Model D

Caliber: 32 ACP, 380 ACP
Action: Semi-automatic; concealed hammer; grip safety & manual safety
Magazine: 9-shot clip in 32 ACP, 8-shot clip in 380 ACP
Barrel: 4"
Sights: Fixed
Finish: Blued; checkered hard rubber grips
Length Overall: 7"
Approximate wt.: 25 oz.
Comments: Imported into U.S.A. as WAC Model D or MAB Le Gendarme; manufacture started about 1932; importation discontinued in 1968.
Estimated Value: Excellent: $195.00
                       Very good: $150.00

MAB Model R

MAB Model E

Caliber: 25 ACP (6.35mm)

Action: Semi-automatic; concealed hammer; manual safety & grip safety

Magazine: 10-shot clip

Barrel: 4"

Sights: Fixed

Finish: Blued; checkered plastic grips

Length Overall: 7"

Approximate wt.: 24 oz.

Comments: Production started about 1949; importation into U.S.A. discontinued in 1968. Imported into U.S.A. as WAC Model E.

Estimated Value: Excellent: $195.00
Very good: $155.00

MAB Model F

Caliber: 22 long rifle

Action: Semi-automatic; concealed hammer; manual safety; blow back design

Magazine: 9-shot clip

Barrel: 4½", 6", 7"

Sights: Fixed

Finish: Blued; checkered grips

Length Overall: 8½" to 11"

Approximate wt.: 23 oz.

Comments: Production began in 1950. Imported into U.S.A. under WAC trademark. Importation stopped in 1968.

Estimated Value: Excellent: $200.00
Very good: $160.00

MAB Model E

MAB Model P-15

Caliber: 9mm Parabellum

Action: Semi-automatic; exposed hammer with round spur; recoil operated with locking breech; manual safety

Magazine: 8-shot clip; 15-shot staggered row clip

Barrel: 4½"

Sights: Blade front; notch rear

Finish: Blued; checkered grips

Length Overall: 8"

Approximate wt.: 25 oz.

Comments: Bears a resemblance to the Browning Model 1935.

Estimated Value: Excellent: $300.00
Very good: $225.00

MAB Model R

Caliber: 22 long rifle; 32 ACP, 380 ACP, 9mm Parabellum

Action: Semi-automatic; exposed hammer; manual safety

Magazine: 9-shot clip in 22 caliber; 8-shot clip in 32 ACP; 7-shot clip in 380 ACP, 7- or 14-shot clip in 9mm

Barrel: 4½" or 7½" (22); 4" in other calibers

Sights: Fixed

Finish: Blued; checkered grips

Length Overall: 7" to 10½"

Approximate wt.: 25 oz.

Comments: This model was never imported into U.S.A.

Estimated Value: Excellent: $215.00
Very good: $175.00

Mauser

Mauser WTP Model 2 Vest Pocket

Mauser WTP Model 1 Vest Pocket

Caliber: 25 ACP

Action: Semi-automatic; concealed hammer

Magazine: 6-shot clip

Barrel: 2⅜"

Sights: Fixed

Finish: Blued; hard rubber grips

Length Overall: 4¼"

Approximate wt.: 12 oz.

Comments: Made from about 1923 to 1939.

Estimated Value: Excellent: $300.00
Very good: $225.00

Mauser WTP Model 2 Vest Pocket

Similar to the Model 1 except: curved back strap & trigger guard; smaller size (2" barrel, about 4" overall length); approximate weight 10 oz. Made from about 1939 to 1942 & from about 1950 to present. Importation into U.S.A. discontinued in 1968.

Estimated Value: Excellent: $290.00
Very good: $215.00

Mauser Model HSC Pocket Pistol
Caliber: 32 ACP, 380 ACP
Action: Semi-automatic; double action; exposed hammer
Magazine: 8-shot clip
Barrel: 3⅜"
Sights: Fixed
Finish: Blued or nickel; checkered wood grips
Length Overall: 6¼"
Approximate wt.: 21 oz.
Comments: Made from about 1938 to World War II and from about 1968 to late 1980's. Add 5% for nickel finish.
Estimated Value: Excellent: $320.00
                  Very good: $255.00

Mauser Model HSC Pocket Pistol

Mauser Automatic Pocket
Caliber: 25 ACP, 32 ACP
Action: Semi-automatic; concealed hammer
Magazine: 9-shot clip in 25 ACP, 8-shot clip in 32 ACP
Barrel: 3" on 25 ACP; 3½" on 32 ACP
Sights: Fixed
Finish: Blued; checkered walnut or hard rubber grips
Length Overall: 5½" on 25 ACP; 6" on 32 ACP
Approximate wt.: 22 oz.
Comments: 25 ACP model made from about 1910 to 1939. 32 ACP model made from about 1914 to 1934.
Estimated Value: Excellent: $230.00
                  Very good: $185.00

Mauser Model 1934 Pocket
Similar to Automatic Pocket Pistol except larger one-piece wooden wrap-around grip which covered the back strap. Made from about 1934 to 1939. 32 ACP only.
Estimated Value: Excellent: $245.00
                  Very good: $195.00

Mauser Military Model (Broomhandle Mauser)
Caliber: 7.63 Mauser; 9mm Parabellum (during World War I marked with a large figure "9" cut in the wood grip), 9mm Mauser
Action: Semi-automatic; exposed hammer; selective fire introduced in 1930 - selective lever on "N" operated as normal semi-automatic & on "R" operated as a machine pistol with fully automatic fire
Magazine: 5- to 10-shot box magazine standard; 5- to 20-shot magazine on selective fire models
Barrel: 5½" standard; also manufactured with other barrel lengths
Sights: Adjustable for elevation
Finish: Blued; checkered wood, serrated wood, carved wood, smooth wood, or hard rubber grips
Length Overall: 12" with 5½" barrel
Approximate wt.: 43 oz. with 5½" barrel
Comments: Made from about 1896 to 1918 and from about 1922 to 1937 with minor changes & improvements. Also produced with a shoulder stock holster (wood).
Estimated Value: Excellent: $1,500.00 - $7,500.00
                  Very good: $ 850.00 - $4,000.00

Mauser Model 1934 Pocket

**Mauser Military Model
(Broomhandle Mauser)**

New England

New England Standard Revolver-22
Caliber: 22 short, long, or long rifle; 22 Win. magnum
Action: Single or double; exposed hammer; solid frame
Cylinder: 9-shot 22 short, long, or long rifle; 6-shot in 22 magnum; swing-out, simultaneous manual ejector
Barrel: 2½" or 4"
Sights: Blade front; fixed rear (groove in frame)
Finish: Blued or nickel; hardwood, walnut finish smooth grips
Length Overall: 7" (2½" barrel), 8½" (4" barrel)
Approximate wt.: 26 oz.
Comments: Introduced in 1989. Add 10% for nickel finish.
Estimated Value: New (retail): $115.00
Excellent: $ 85.00
Very good: $ 70.00

New England Standard
Revolver-32 H&R Magnum

New England Standard Revolver-32 H&R Magnum
Same as the Standard Revolver-22 except 32 H&R magnum caliber only; 5-shot cylinder; approximate wt: 25 oz. Introduced in 1989. Add 10% for nickel finish.
Estimated Value: New (retail): $115.00
Excellent: $ 85.00
Very good: $ 70.00

New England Ultra Revolver
Caliber: 22 short, long or long rifle; 22 Win. magnum, k32 H&R magnum
Action: Single or double; exposed hammer; swing out cylinder
Cylinder: 9-shot; (22 short, long or long rifle); 6-shot (22 magnum); 5-shot (32 H&R magnum); simultaneous manual ejector
Barrel: 3" or 6" with solid rib
Sights: Blade front; adjustable rear
Finish: Blued; hardwood, walnut finish smooth grips
Length Overall: 7⅝" (3" barrel); 10⅝" (6" barrel)
Approximate wt.: 31 to 36 oz.
Comments: Introduced in 1990.
Estimated Value: New (retail): $157.00
Excellent: $120.00
Very good: $ 95.00

New England Ultra Revolver

North American Arms

North American Arms (Mini Revolver)
Caliber: 22 short; 22 long rifle (1976); 22 magnum (1978)
Action: Single action; exposed hammer; spur trigger; solid frame
Cylinder: 5-shot; removable cylinder; available with two cylinders (22 long rifle and 22 mag.)
Barrel: 1⅛"; 1⅝"; 2½"
Sights: Blade front; fixed rear
Finish: Stainless steel; polycarbonate round butt (bird head) grips
Length Overall: 4" to 6⅜" depending on barrel length & caliber
Approximate wt.: 4 to 5 oz.
Comments: Made from about 1975 to present. Add 16% for 22 magnum; 38% for revolver with both cylinders; 10% for 2½" barrel.
Estimated Value: New (retail): $149.00
Excellent: $110.00
Very good: $ 90.00

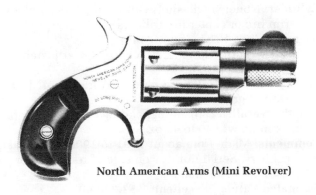

North American Arms (Mini Revolver)

Remington

Remington 41 Caliber Double Derringer
Caliber: 41 caliber rim fire
Action: Single; visible hammer with safety position; sheath trigger; manual extractor
Cylinder: None; 2-shot double barrels
Barrel: 3" superposed double barrels; ribbed top barrel; barrels swing up to load & extract cartridges
Sights: Blade front; groove in frame rear
Finish: Blued or nickel plated; plain or engraved; round butt grips made of metal, walnut, rosewood, hard rubber, ivory or pearl
Length Overall: 4⅞"
Approximate wt.: 11 oz.
Comments: Approximately 132,000 were produced from about 1866 to 1935. Serial numbers were repeated on these pistols, so the best way to estimate the age of a pistol is by the markings. They were marked as follows:
1866-1869: no extractors; left side of barrel E. REMINGTON & SONS, ILION, N.Y.; right side of barrel ELLIOT'S PATENT DEC. 12, 1865
1869-1880: left side of barrel - ELLIOT'S PATENT DEC. 12 1865; right side of barrel - E. REMINGTON & SONS, ILION, N.Y.
1880-1888: barrel rib top - E. REMINGTON & SONS, ILION N.Y. ELLIOT'S PATENT DEC. 12th 1865
1888-1910: barrel rib top - REMINGTON ARMS CO. ILION N.Y.
1910-1935: barrel rib top - REMINGTON ARMS U.M.C. CO. ILION, N.Y.
In 1934 the Double Derringer was called Model No. 95.
Estimated Values:

Plain models	Excellent:	$500.00 - $1,000.00
	Very good:	$400.00 - $ 800.00
Presentation models	Excellent:	$650.00 - $1,200.00
	Very good:	$450.00 - $1,000.00

Remington Model 1891, Single-Shot Target
Caliber: 22, 25, 32RF, 32 S&W CF
Action: Single
Cylinder: None; single-shot with rolling breech block for rim fire or center fire calibers
Barrel: 8", 10", 12"; half-octagon
Sights: Dovetail, German silver front & adjustable "V" notch rifle rear
Finish: Blued barrel; case hardened frame; oil finished walnut grips & fore-end
Length Overall: 12" to 16" depending on barrel length
Approximate wt.: 40 to 45 oz.
Comments: Made from about 1891 to 1900 in light target calibers. Serial number on side of frame under grip. Less than 200 made.
Estimated Value: Excellent: $1,200.00
                     Very good: $ 900.00

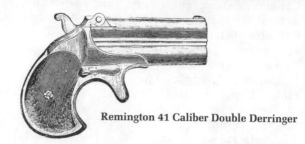
Remington 41 Caliber Double Derringer

Remington Model 1901, De-Luxe (S-S) Target
Caliber: 22 short, long, long rifle, 44 Russian CF
Action: Single
Cylinder: None; single-shot with rolling breech block for rim fire or center fire calibers
Barrel: 9" round; 10" half-octagon
Sights: Ivory bead front; adjustable "V" rear
Finish: Blued barrel & frame; checkered walnut grips & fore-end
Length Overall: 13" to 14"
Approximate wt.: 36 to 44 oz.
Comments: Made from about 1901 to 1909. Approximately 1,000 produced.
Estimated Value: Excellent: $1,000.00
                     Very good: $ 800.00

Remington Experimental 45 Caliber
An estimated value hasn't been placed on this pistol since it is not known how many were produced or how they were marked. They were similar to the Remington Model 51 Automatic Pistol except: in 45 caliber, larger, & had an exposed spur hammer. They were made for the U.S. Government test purposes about 1917.

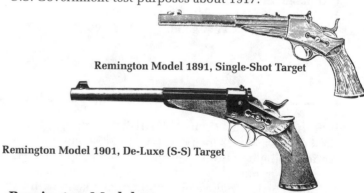
Remington Model 1891, Single-Shot Target

Remington Model 1901, De-Luxe (S-S) Target

Remington Model 51
Caliber: 32 ACP, 380 ACP
Action: Semi-automatic; concealed hammer
Magazine: 8-shot clip in 32 caliber; 7-shot clip in 380 caliber
Barrel: 3¼"
Sights: Fixed
Finish: Blued; hard rubber grips
Length Overall: 6⅝"
Approximate wt.: 20 oz.
Comments: Made from about 1920 to 1934. Approximately 69,000 were produced in 32 and 380 calibers.
Estimated Value: Excellent: $360.00
                     Very good: $290.00

Remington US Model 1911 and 1911 A1

These were pistols made by Remington, on the Colt Patent, for the U.S. Government during World War I & World War II. See "Colt Government Model 1911 and 1911 A1" for prices.

Remington Model XP-100 Long Range

Caliber: 221 Remington "Fire Ball"
Action: Bolt action; single shot; thumb safety
Cylinder: None
Barrel: 10½" round steel with ventilated rib
Sights: Blade front; adjustable rear
Finish: Blued with bright polished bolt & handle; brown checkered nylon (Zytel) one-piece grip & fore-end. Fore-end has cavity for adding balance weights
Length Overall: 16¾"
Approximate wt.: 60 oz.
Comments: Made from about 1963 to 1986. Receiver is drilled & tapped for scope mount.
Estimated Value: Excellent: $275.00
Very good: $220.00

Remington Model XP-100 Silhouette

Similar to the Model XP-100 with a 14½" plain barrel and 7mm Benchrest Remington caliber. Produced from 1980 to present. 35 Rem. caliber added 1987. Add 4% for 35 Rem. caliber
Estimated Value: New (retail): $419.00
Excellent: $315.00
Very good: $250.00

Remington Model XP-100 Varmint Special

Similar to the XP-100 Silhouette in 223 Rem. caliber. Introduced in 1988.
Estimated Value: New (retail): $406.00
Excellent: $305.00
Very good: $245.00

Remington Model XP-100 Silhouette

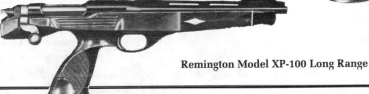

Remington Model XP-100 Long Range

Ruger

Ruger Standard Automatic

Ruger Mark I Target

Ruger Mark I Bull Barrel

Ruger Standard Automatic

Caliber: 22 long rifle
Action: Semi-automatic; concealed hammer; thumb safety
Magazine: 9-shot clip
Barrel: 4¾" or 6"; tapered round barrel
Sights: Partridge type front; dovetail rear
Finish: Blued; checkered walnut or hard rubber grips
Length Overall: 8¾", 10"
Approximate wt.: 36 to 38 oz.
Comments: Made from about 1949 to 1982. (Sturm Ruger Company was formed about 1949.) Red eagle insignia on grip used until 1951, then changed to black eagle insignia, after death of Alex Sturm. Add $200.00 for red eagle insignia on grip (pre-1951).
Estimated Value: Excellent: $150.00
Very good: $120.00

Ruger Mark I Target

Similar to Ruger Standard Automatic except adjustable sights; 6⅞" tapered barrel only. Made from about 1950 to 1982.
Estimated Value: Excellent: $165.00
Very good: $130.00

Ruger Mark I Bull Barrel Target

Similar to Ruger Mark I Target Pistol except barrel length 5½"; overall length 9½"; untapered heavier barrel. Made from about 1963 to 1982.
Estimated Value: Excellent: $170.00
Very good: $135.00

Ruger Mark II Standard Automatic

Similar to the Standard Automatic with internal improvements, 10-shot clip; slight difference in rear receiver design. Introduced in 1982. Add 33% for stainless steel.
Estimated Value: New (retail): $224.75
Excellent: $170.00
Very good: $135.00

Ruger Mark II Target

Similar to the Mark II Standard Automatic with adjustable sights. 6⅞ tapered barrel only. Introduced in 1982. Add 28% for stainless steel.

Estimated Value: New (retail): $280.50
Excellent: $210.00
Very good: $165.00

Ruger Model P85

Caliber: 9mm
Action: Double action, recoil operated semi-automatic
Magazine: 15-shot clip
Barrel: 4½"
Sights: Fixed
Finish: Blued or stainless steel; grooved plastic grips with Ruger insignia
Length Overall: 8"
Approximate wt.: 32 oz.
Comments: A compact combat pistol; introduced in 1987. Add 10% for extra magazine & high impact molded case. Add 12% for stainless steel.

Estimated Value: New (retail): $357.50
Excellent: $270.00
Very good: $215.00

Ruger GP-100 Double-Action Revolver

Caliber: 357 magnum and 38 Special
Action: Double & single; solid frame; exposed hammer
Cylinder: 6-shot; swing out; simultaneous ejector
Barrel: 4" heavy barrel or 6" with ejector shroud
Sights: Fixed or interchangeable front; fixed or adjustable rear
Finish: Blued or stainless steel; with a new Ruger cushioned grip system. A newly designed skeleton-type grip frame is used. The grips are rubber with polished wood inserts
Length Overall: 9⅜" or 11⅜"
Approximate wt.: 41 oz.
Comments: Introduced in 1986. Add 9% for stainless steel. Add 4% for adjustable sights.

Estimated Value: New (retail): $378.00
Excellent: $280.00
Very good: $225.00

Ruger Model SP 101

Caliber: 38 Special, 22 short, long or long rifle
Action: Single & double; exposed hammer
Cylinder: 5-shot (38 Special); 6-shot (22 caliber); swing-out
Barrel: 2" or 3 1/16" (38 Special); 2" or 4" (22 caliber) with ejector rod shroud
Sights: Ramp front, fixed rear; 22 caliber has adjustable rear
Finish: All stainless steel except grips & sights; grips are rubber with polished inserts
Length Overall: 7½" to 9½"
Approximate wt.: 25 to 27 oz. (38 Special); 32 oz. (22 caliber)
Comments: Introduced in 1990.

Estimated Value: New (retail): $388.50
Excellent: $290.00
Very good: $235.00

Ruger Mark II Bull Barrel Target

Similar to the Mark II Target with 5½" or 6⅞" bull barrel. Introduced in 1982. Also 10" bull barrel introduced in 1983. Add 28% for stainless steel.

Estimated Value: New (retail): $355.25
Excellent: $265.00
Very good: $210.00

In 1982 Ruger announced the production of a Single Action Conversion Kit that could be fitted on any "Old Model" Ruger Single Action revolver. This innovation, fitted at the factory, would give the old model a "transfer bar" type mechanism by replacing a few key parts in the revolver. This would provide a safer handling single action. Unless it can be verified that the conversion has been made at the factory, all "Old Model" Single Action revolvers should be handled as such with caution.

Ruger Mark II Target

Ruger GP-100 Double-Action Revolver

Ruger Mark II Government

Similar to the Mark II Bull Barrel with a 6⅞" bull barrel. Blued finish only.

Estimated Value: New (retail): $324.25
Excellent: $245.00
Very good: $195.00

Ruger Single-Six

Caliber: 22 short, long, long rifle, 22 WMR (after 1959)
Action: Single; solid frame with loading gate
Cylinder: 6-shot half fluted; flat loading gate from 1954 to 1957 then changed to fit the contour of the frame
Barrel: 4⅝", 5½", 6½", 9½"; ejector rod under barrel
Sights: Blade front; rear sight dovetailed & can be tapped to left or right
Finish: Blued; checkered hard rubber or smooth walnut grips
Length Overall: 10", 10⅞", 11⅞", 14⅞"
Approximate wt.: 32 to 36 oz.
Comments: The grip frame is made of aluminum alloy & the frame is made of chrome molybdenum steel; produced from about 1953 to 1973. Add $150.00 for flat loading gate

Estimated Value: Excellent: $200.00
Very good: $160.00

Ruger Lightweight Single-Six

Same as Ruger Single-Six except: made in 22 short, long & long rifle only; 4⅝" barrel; 10" overall length; weighs 23 oz.; cylinder & frame made of lightweight alloy. Produced from about 1956 to 1958.

| Estimated Value: | Excellent: | $225.00 |
| | Very good: | $180.00 |

Ruger Convertible Single-Six

Same as Ruger Single-Six revolver except: furnished with two cylinders - one chambered for 22 & the other chambered for 22 WMR. Manufactured from about 1961 to 1973. Prices for guns with both cylinders.

| Estimated Value: | Excellent: | $220.00 |
| | Very good: | $175.00 |

Ruger Convertible Super Single-Six

Same as Ruger Single-six revolver except: ramp front sight; adjustable rear sight with protective ribs on frame to protect rear sight; 5½" or 6½" barrel only. Made from about 1964 to 1973. Prices for guns with both cylinders.

| Estimated Value: | Excellent: | $225.00 |
| | Very good: | $180.00 |

Ruger New Model Super Single-Six Convertible

Similar to Ruger Convertible Super Single-Six except: improved version featuring wide trigger; heavy stronger lock words; transfer bar firing pin protector; new interlocking mechanism; other improvements. Made from about 1973 to present. 22 LR and 22 WMR cylinders until 1986, when the 22 WMR cylinder was discontinued.

Estimated Value:	New (retail):	$267.75
	Excellent:	$200.00
	Very good:	$160.00

Ruger New Model Super Single-Six Convertible Stainless Steel

Same as Ruger New Model Super Single-Six Convertible Revolver except: all stainless steel construction except sights (blued). 5½" or 6½" barrel only. Made from about 1976 to present. Prices for guns with both cylinders.

Estimated Value:	New (retail):	$337.00
	Excellent:	$250.00
	Very good:	$200.00

Ruger New Model Super Single-Six Convertible

Stainless Steel Ruger New Model Super Single-Six Convertible

Ruger Blackhawk 357 Convertible

Ruger New Model Single-Six 32 Mag

Caliber: 32 H&R magnum, also handles 32 S&W & 32 S&W long

Action: Single; solid frame with loading gate

Cylinder: 6-shot, heavy fluted cylinder

Barrel: 4¾", 5½", 6½" or 9½"; ejector rod under barrel

Sights: Ramp front, adjustable rear

Finish: Blued; smooth walnut grips

Length Overall: 9⅞" to 14⅞"

Approximate wt.: 32 to 36 oz.

Comments: Introduced in 1986 to bridge the gap between the 22 caliber & 38 caliber revolvers.

Estimated Value:	New (retail):	$257.00
	Excellent:	$190.00
	Very good:	$155.00

Ruger Blackhawk 357 Magnum

Caliber: 357 magnum & 38 Special interchangeably

Action: Single; solid frame with loading gate

Cylinder: 6-shot

Barrel: 4⅝", 6½"; round barrel with ejector rod under barrel

Sights: Ramp front; adjustable rear sight

Finish: Blued; checkered hard rubber or smooth walnut wood grips

Length Overall: 10⅛"; 12"

Approximate wt.: 35 to 40 oz.

Comments: Made from about 1955 to 1973. In 1961 the frame was modified to a heavier frame with integral ribs on top to protect rear sight and slight grip alterations to improve the comfort of the "hold."

Estimated Value:	Pre-1961	Post-1961
Excellent:	$175.00	$200.00
Very good:	$140.00	$160.00

Ruger New Model Blackhawk

Ruger New Model Single-Six 32 Mag

Ruger Blackhawk 357 Convertible

Same as Ruger Blackhawk 357 Magnum Revolver except fitted with extra interchangeable cylinder for 9mm Parabellum cartridges. Manufactured from about 1967 to 1973.

Estimated Value: Excellent: $225.00
                    Very good: $180.00

Ruger New Model Blackhawk

Similar to Ruger Blackhawk 357 Revolver except improved version featuring wide trigger; stronger lock works; transfer bar firing pin protector, new interlocking mechanism; other improvements. Made from about 1973 to present in 30 carbine, 357 magnum, 41 magnum & 45 long Colt. Deduct 4% for 30 carbine caliber.

Estimated Value: New (retail): $312.25
                    Excellent: $235.00
                    Very good: $190.00

Ruger Stainless Steel New Model Blackhawk 357

Same as Ruger New Model Blackhawk Revolver except all stainless steel construction except sights (blued). Made from about 1976 to present.

Estimated Value: New (retail): $384.75
                    Excellent: $285.00
                    Very good: $230.00

Ruger New Model Blackhawk Convertible

Same as Ruger New Model Blackhawk Revolver except: fitted with extra interchangeable cylinder for 357 magnum & 9mm Parabellum cartridges from about 1973 to present; 45 Colt & 45 ACP cartridges from about 1973 to 1984; blued finish.

Estimated Value: New (retail): $327.25
                    Excellent: $245.00
                    Very good: $195.00

Ruger Blackhawk 44 Magnum

Caliber: 44 magnum & 44 S&W Special interchangeably
Action: Single; solid frame with loading gate
Cylinder: 6-shot; heavy fluted cylinder
Barrel: 6½"; ejector rod under barrel
Sights: Ramp front; adjustable rear sight
Finish: Blued; smooth walnut grips
Length Overall: 12½"
Approximate wt.: 40 oz.
Comments: Produced from about 1956 to 1962.

Estimated Value: Excellent: $300.00
                    Very good: $250.00

Ruger New Model Super Blackhawk 44 Magnum

Stainless Steel Ruger New Model Blackhawk 357

Ruger Super Blackhawk 44 Magnum

Ruger Super Blackhawk 44 Magnum

Caliber: 44 magnum & 44 S&W Special interchangeably
Action: Single; solid frame with loading gate
Cylinder: 6-shot; heavy non-fluted cylinder
Barrel: 7½"; ejector rod under barrel
Sights: Ramp front; adjustable rear sight
Finish: Blued; smooth walnut wood grips; square back trigger guard
Length Overall: 13⅜"
Approximate wt.: 48 oz.
Comments: Produced from about 1959 to 1973.

Estimated Value: Excellent: $250.00
                    Very good: $200.00

Ruger New Model Super Blackhawk 44 Magnum

Similar to Super Blackhawk except: improved version, featuring stronger lock works; transfer bar firing pin protector; new interlocking mechanism; blued or stainless steel; 5½", 7½" or 10½" barrel; other improvements. Made from about 1973 to present. Add 10% for stainless steel.

Estimated Value: New (retail): $360.50
                    Excellent: $270.00
                    Very good: $215.00

Ruger Blackhawk 45 Caliber

Caliber: 45 long Colt
Action: Single; solid frame with loading gate
Cylinder: 6-shot
Barrel: 4⅝", 7½" round barrel with ejector rod under barrel
Sights: Ramp front; adjustable rear sight
Finish: Blued; smooth walnut grips
Length Overall: 10⅛"; 13⅛"
Approximate wt.: 38 to 40 oz.
Comments: Made from about 1970 to 1973. Replaced by New Model Blackhawk in 1973.

Estimated Value: Excellent: $220.00
                    Very good: $175.00

Ruger Blackhawk 45 Caliber Convertible

Same as Blackhawk 45 Caliber revolver except: fitted with extra interchangeable cylinder for 45 ACP cartridges. Made from about 1970 to 1973. Replaced by New Model Blackhawk in 1973.

Estimated Value: Excellent: $250.00
                    Very good: $200.00

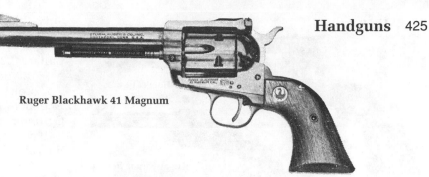

Ruger Blackhawk 41 Magnum

Caliber: 41 magnum
Action: Single; solid frame with loading gate
Cylinder: 6-shot
Barrel: 4⅝", 6½" with ejector rod
Sights: Ramp front; adjustable rear sight
Finish: Blued; smooth walnut grips
Length Overall: 10¾"; 12⅛"
Approximate wt.: 35 to 38 oz.
Comments: Produced from about 1965 to 1973.
Estimated Value: Excellent: $240.00
                       Very good: $190.00

Ruger Blackhawk 41 Magnum

Ruger Blackhawk 30 Caliber

Caliber: 30 U.S. Carbine (M1)
Action: Single; solid frame with loading gate
Cylinder: 6-shot
Barrel: 7½" with ejector rod
Sights: Ramp front; adjustable rear sight
Finish: Blued; smooth walnut wood grips
Length Overall: 13⅛"
Approximate wt.: 39 oz.
Comments: Made from about 1968 to 1973. A good companion hand gun for the M1 carbine (30 caliber).
Estimated Value: Excellent: $230.00
                       Very good: $185.00

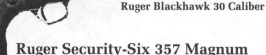

Ruger Blackhawk 30 Caliber

Ruger Security-Six 357 Magnum

Caliber: 357 magnum, 38 Special
Action: Double & single; solid frame; exposed hammer
Cylinder: 6-shot; simultaneous ejector
Barrel: 2¾", 4", 6"
Sights: Adjustable
Finish: Blued or stainless steel; square butt, checkered walnut grips
Length Overall: 8", 9¼" 11"
Approximate wt.: 32 to 35 oz.
Comments: Made from 1972 to mid 1980's. A solid frame revolver with swing-out cylinder. Stainless steel model made from about 1975 to mid 1980's. Add $20.00 for stainless steel.
Estimated Value: Excellent: $225.00
                       Very good: $180.00

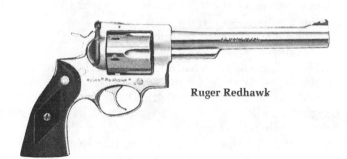

Ruger Redhawk

Ruger Security-Six

Ruger Redhawk

Caliber: 357 magnum, 41 magnum, 44 magnum
Action: Double & single; solid frame; exposed hammer
Cylinder: 6-shot swing-out; simultaneous ejector
Barrel: 5½", 7½", shrouded ejector rod under barrel
Sights: Adjustable rear, blade front
Finish: Stainless steel; blued model added in 1986; checkered or smooth walnut grips
Length Overall: 11", 13"
Approximate wt.: 52 oz.
Comments: A heavy frame 44 magnum revolver introduced in 1979. 357 magnum & 41 magnum added in 1984. Add 13% for stainless steel; 8% for scope rings; 357 magnum dropped 1986.
Estimated Value: New (retail): $436.75
                       Excellent: $325.00
                       Very good: $260.00

Ruger Super Redhawk

Caliber: 44 magnum & .44 Special
Action: Double & single
Cylinder: 6-shot swing-out; simultaneous ejector; fluted cylinder
Barrel: 7½" or 9½"
Sights: Ramp front base with interchangeable insert sight blades; adjustable white outline square notch rear
Finish: Stainless steel; cushioned grip system. A skeleton-type grip frame features rubber panels with Goncalo Alves panel inserts
Length Overall: 13" or 15"
Approximate wt.: 56 oz.
Comments: Introduced in 1987
Estimated Value: New (retail): $561.00
                       Excellent: $420.00
                       Very good: $335.00

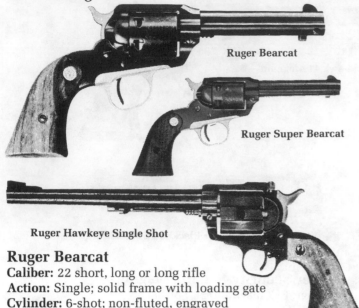

Ruger Bearcat

Ruger Super Bearcat

Ruger Hawkeye Single Shot

Ruger Bearcat

Caliber: 22 short, long or long rifle
Action: Single; solid frame with loading gate
Cylinder: 6-shot; non-fluted, engraved
Barrel: 4" round with ejector rod
Sights: Fixed
Finish: Blued; smooth walnut grips
Length Overall: 8⅞"
Approximate wt.: 17 oz.
Comments: Alloy frame; coil springs & non-fluted engraved cylinder. Manufactured from about 1958 to 1972.
Estimated Value: Excellent: $300.00
Very good: $225.00

Ruger Super Bearcat

Same as Ruger Bearcat revolver except all steel construction & made from about 1971 to 1975.
Estimated Value: Excellent: $275.00
Very good: $220.00

Ruger Speed-Six

Similar to Security-Six 357 Magnum revolver except round butt style grips & in calibers 9mm Parabellum, 38 Special & 357 magnum. Fixed sights only. Made from about 1975 to 1989. Add $16.00 for 9mm; add 9% for stainless steel. 9mm dropped in mid 1980's.
Estimated Value: Excellent: $220.00
Very good: $165.00

Ruger New Model Bisley

Caliber: 22 long rifle or 32 H&R magmun in small frame; 357 magnum, 41 magnum, 44 magnum or 45 long Colt in large frame
Action: Single; solid frame with loading gate
Cylinder: 6-shot fluted or non-fluted cylinder with or without roll engraving
Barrel: 6½" small frame, 7½" large frame; ejector rod under barrel
Sights: Ramp front, adjustable or fixed rear
Finish: Blued; smooth wood grips
Length Overall: 11½" frame, 13" large frame
Approximate wt.: 41 oz. small frame, 48 oz. large frame
Comments: Introduced in 1985 & 1986. Based on the Ruger single action design with a longer, different-angle grip similar to the old Colt Bisley revolvers.

	Small Frame	Large Frame
Estimated Value:		
New (retail):	$313.00	$372.25
Excellent:	$235.00	$280.00
Very good:	$185.00	$225.00

Ruger Service-Six, Police Service-Six

Similar to Speed-Six revolver except square butt style grips. Made from about 1976 to 1989. Add $16.00 for 9mm; add 8% for stainless steel. 9mm dropped in mid 1980's. Called Police Service-Six after 1987.
Estimated Value: Excellent: $215.00
Very good: $160.00

Ruger Blackhawk Single Shot

Caliber: 256 magnum
Action: Single; single shot
Cylinder: None; rotating breech block to load chamber, which is part of the barrel
Barrel: 8½"; chamber in barrel; under barrel ejector rod
Sights: Adjustable target sights
Finish: Blued; smooth walnut grips
Length Overall: 14½"
Approximate wt.: 44 oz.
Comments: The Hawkeye is built on the Ruger 44 magnum frame & resembles a revolver in appearance. Made from about 1963 to 1966.
Estimated Value: Excellent: $950.00
Very good: $750.00

Sauer

Sauer 1913 (Old Model)

Sauer 1930 Model

Sauer 1913 (Old Model)

Caliber: 32 ACP (7.65mm); 25 ACP (6.35mm)
Action: Semi-automatic; concealed hammer
Magazine: 7-shot clip
Barrel: 3"
Sights: Fixed
Finish: Blued; checkered hard rubber grips
Length Overall: 5⅞"
Approximate wt.: 32 oz.
Comments: Made from about 1913 to 1930.
Estimated Value: Excellent: $250.00
Very good: $200.00

Sauer 1930 Model

Similar to Sauer 1913 (Old Model) except improved version with main difference being the improved grip design which provides a better hold; some models made with indicator pins to show when they were cocked; some models made with alloy slide & receiver (approximately 15 oz.) Made from about 1930 to 1938.
Estimated Value: Excellent: $265.00
Very good: $210.00

Sauer 1938 Model (Model H)

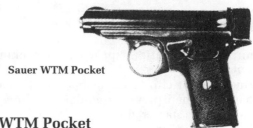

Sauer WTM Pocket

Sauer 1938 Model (Model H)

Caliber: 32 ACP (7.65mm)

Action: Semi-automatic; double action; concealed hammer; lever on left side permitted hammer to be cocked or uncocked by the thumb; also could be fired by pulling trigger in double action style

Magazine: 7-shot clip

Barrel: 3¼"

Sights: Fixed

Finish: Blued; checkered plastic grips

Length Overall: 6¼"

Approximate wt.: 26 oz.

Comments: Some models made with alloy slide (approximately 18 oz. in weight); war time models (WWII) inferior to earlier models. Made from about 1938 to 1944.

Estimated Value:	pre-War models	War-time models
Excellent:	$300.00	$220.00
Very good:	$240.00	$175.00

Sauer WTM Pocket

Caliber: 25 ACP (6.35mm)

Action: Semi-automatic; concealed hammer

Magazine: 6-shot clip

Barrel: 2⅛"

Sights: Fixed

Finish: Blued; checkered hard rubber grips

Length Overall: 4⅛"

Approximate wt.: 18 oz.

Comments: Made from about 1924 to 1928. Fluted slide with top ejection port.

Estimated Value:	Excellent:	$240.00
	Very good:	$195.00

Sauer 1928 Model Pocket

Similar to Sauer WTM Pocket Pistol except: smaller in size, 2" barrel & about 3⅞" overall length. Made from about 1928 to 1938

Estimated Value:	Excellent:	$250.00
	Very good:	$200.00

Savage

Savage Model 1907

Savage Model 1905 Military Type

Caliber: 45 ACP

Action: Semi-automatic; blow-back design, grip safety; exposed cocking lever

Magazine: 8-shot clip

Barrel: 5¼"

Sights: Fixed

Finish: Blued, checkered walnut grips

Length Overall: 9"

Approximate wt.: 36 oz.

Comments: Approximately 200 were produced from about 1908 to 1911 & sold to U.S. Government Ordnance Dept. for tests, but lost to competition.

Estimated Value:	Excellent:	$2,000.00
	Very good:	$1,500.00

Savage Model 1907

Caliber: 32 ACP, 380 ACP (after 1912)

Action: Semi-automatic; exposed rounded or spur cocking lever

Magazine: 10-shot in 32 caliber, 9-shot in 380 caliber

Barrel: 3¾" in 32 caliber; 9-shot in 380 caliber

Sights: Fixed

Finish: Blued, metal, hard rubber or wood grips

Length Overall: 6½" (32 caliber); 7" (380 caliber)

Approximate wt.: 20 oz.

Comments: Manufactured from about 1908 to 1920, with improvements & some changes in 1909, 1914 & 1918. Some military models with lanyard loop were made of the 1912 variety & sold from 1915 to 1917.

Estimated Value:	Excellent:	$250.00
	Very good:	$190.00

Savage Model 1915

Savage Model 1915

Caliber: 32 ACP, 380 ACP

Action: Semi-automatic; concealed hammer

Magazine: 10-shot in 32 caliber, 9-shot in 380 caliber

Barrel: 3¾" (caliber); 4¼" (380 caliber)

Sights: Fixed

Finish: Blued; hard rubber grips

Length Overall: 6½" (32 caliber), 7" (380 caliber)

Approximate wt.: 22 oz.

Comments: Manufactured from about 1915 to 1917. Approximately 6,500 were produced in 32 caliber & approximately 2,350 were produced in 380 caliber.

Estimated Value:	Excellent:	$235.00
	Very good:	$175.00

Savage Model 1917
Caliber: 32 ACP, 380 ACP
Action: Semi-automatic; exposed spur cocking lever; thumb safety
Magazine: 10-shot clip in 32; 9-shot clip in 380, wider magazine than previous models to allow for cartridges to be staggered in a double row
Barrel: 3¾" in 32; 7" in 380
Sights: Fixed
Finish: Blued; hard rubber grips
Length Overall: 6½" in 32, 7" in 380
Approximate wt.: 24 oz.
Comments: Made from about 1918 to 1928. Approximately 28,000 made in 32 caliber & 126,000 in 380 caliber. Wide frame & flared grips & the slide has small verticle gripping serrations.
Estimated Value: Excellent: $250.00
                       Very good: $195.00

Savage Model 1917

Savage Model 101 Single Shot

Savage Model 101 Single Shot
Caliber: 22 short, long, long rifle
Action: Single; single shot
Cylinder: None; the false cylinder is the chamber part of the barrel
Barrel: 5½" alloy steel; swings out to load; ejector rod under barrel
Sights: Blade front; notched-bar rear
Finish: Blued barrel; painted one-piece aluminum alloy frame; compressed impregnated wood grips
Length Overall: 9½"
Approximate wt.: 20 oz.
Comments: A single shot pistol built to resemble a single action frontier revolver. Made from about 1960 to 1968.
Estimated Value: Excellent: $125.00
                       Very good: $100.00

Sheridan

Sheridan Knockabout

Sheridan Knockabout
Caliber: 22 short, long, long rifle
Action: Single; exposed hammer
Magazine: None; single shot
Barrel: 5½"; tip up barrel
Sights: Fixed
Finish: Blued; checkered plastic grips
Length Overall: 6¾"
Approximate wt.: 21 oz.
Comments: An inexpensive single shot pistol which resembles an automatic pistol. Made from about 1953 to 1962. Approximately 20,000 produced.
Estimated Value: Excellent: $125.00
                       Very good: $100.00

Smith & Wesson

Smith & Wesson Model 32 Automatic

Smith & Wesson Model 32 Automatic
Caliber: 32 ACP
Action: Semi-automatic; concealed hammer; grip safety located in front of grip below trigger guard
Magazine: 7-shot clip
Barrel: 3½"; barrel is fixed to the frame; the slide fits into guides on the barrel
Sights: Fixed
Finish: Blued; smooth walnut grips
Length Overall: 6½"
Approximate wt.: 24 oz.
Comments: Serial numbers are a separate series beginning at number 1. Approximately 958 produced from about 1924 to 1937.
Estimated Value: Excellent: $1,000.00
                       Very good: $ 800.00

Smith & Wesson Model 35 Automatic

Caliber: 35 S&W automatic
Action: Semi-automatic; concealed hammer; grip safety located in front of grip below trigger guard; manual safety at rear of left grip
Magazine: 7-shot clip
Barrel: 3½"; barrel hinged to rear of frame
Sights: Fixed
Finish: Blued or nickel; smooth walnut grips
Length Overall: 6½"
Approximate wt.: 22 oz.
Comments: Serial numbers are a separate series beginning at number 1. Approximately 8,350 were produced from about 1913 to 1921

Smith & Wesson
Model 35 Automatic

Estimated Value:	Excellent:	$650.00
	Very good:	$520.00

Smith & Wesson Model 39

Caliber: 9mm (Parabellum) Luger
Action: Semi-automatic; double action; exposed hammer; thumb saftey
Magazine: 8-shot clip
Barrel: 4"
Sights: Ramp front; rear adjustable for windage
Finish: Blued or nickel; checkered walnut grips
Length Overall: 7½"
Approximate wt.: 28 oz.
Comments: Made from about 1954 to 1982. Normally pistol has aluminum alloy frame; approximately 925 pistols were produced with steel frames sometime prior to 1966. Add $25.00 for nickel finish. Replaced by S&W Model 439.

Smith & Wesson Model 39

Smith & Wesson Model 41

Smith & Wesson Model 46

		Alloy Frame	Steel Frame
Estimated Value:	Excellent:	$350.00	$1,050.00
	Very good:	$275.00	$ 850.00

Smith & Wesson Model 41

Caliber: 22 short or 22 long rifle (not interchangeably)
Action: Single action; semi-automatic; concealed hammer; thumb safety
Magazine: 10-shot clip
Barrel: 5½" heavy barrel or 7" regular barrel
Sights: Adjustable micrometer rear; Partridge front
Finish: Blued; checkered walnut grips with thumb rest
Length Overall: 8⅝" to 10½"
Approximate wt.: 40 to 44 oz.
Comments: Made from about 1957 to present. Made for 22 long rifle only at present.

Estimated Value:	New (retail):	$657.00
	Excellent:	$495.00
	Very good:	$395.00

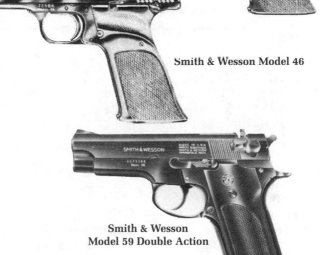

Smith & Wesson
Model 59 Double Action

Smith & Wesson Model 46

Similar to Model 41 except: 22 long rifle caliber only; plastic grips with thumb rest. Made from about 1957 to 1966.

Estimated Value:	Excellent:	$425.00
	Very good:	$340.00

Smith & Wesson Model 59

Caliber: 9mm (Parabellum) Luger
Action: Semi-automatic; double action; exposed hammer; thumb safety
Magazine: 14-shot staggered column clip
Barrel: 4"
Sights: Ramp front; rear adjustable for windage
Finish: Blued or nickel; checkered high impact molded nylon
Length Overall: 7½"
Approximate wt.: 28 oz.
Comments: Similar to Model 39 except back of grip is straight & grip is wider to accommodate the thicker, staggered column magazine. Made from about 1973 to 1982. Add $28.00 for nickel finish. Replaced by S&W Model 459.

Estimated Value:	Excellent:	$325.00
	Very good:	$250.00

Smith & Wesson Model 52, 38 Master

Caliber: 38 Special (mid-range wadcutter only)
Action: Single action; semi-automatic; exposed hammer; thumb safety
Magazine: 5-shot clip
Barrel: 5"
Sights: Adjustable rear sight & ramp front
Finish: Blued; checkered walnut grips
Length Overall: 8⅞"
Approximate wt.: 42 oz.
Comments: Made from about 1961 to present.
Estimated Value:　New (retail):　$834.00
　　　　　　　　　　Excellent:　　$625.00
　　　　　　　　　　Very good:　　$500.00

Smith & Wesson Model 61 Escort

Caliber: 22 long rifle
Action: Semi-automatic; concealed hammer; thumb safety
Magazine: 5-shot clip
Barrel: 2⅛"
Sights: Fixed
Finish: Blued or nickel; checkered plastic grips
Length Overall: 4¾"
Approximate wt.: 14 oz.
Comments: Made from about 1970 to 1973. Add $15.00 for nickel finish.
Estimated Value:　Excellent:　　$240.00
　　　　　　　　　　Very good:　　$180.00

Smith & Wesson Model 459

Smith & Wesson Model 439

Smith & Wesson Model 52

Smith & Wesson Model 439

Caliber: 9mm (Parabellum) Luger
Action: Semi-automatic; double action; exposed hammer; thumb safety
Magazine: 8-shot clip
Barrel: 4"
Sights: Serrated ramp front; rear adjustable or fixed
Finish: Blued or nickel; checkered walnut grips with S&W monogram
Length Overall: 7½"
Approximate wt.: 30 oz.
Comments: The frame is constructed of aluminum alloy. It is similar to the Model 39 except with improved extraction system. Made from about 1981 to 1989. Add 8% for nickel finish.
Estimated Value:　Excellent:　　$355.00
　　　　　　　　　　Very good:　　$285.00

Smith & Wesson Model 539

Similar to the Model 439 except the frame is constructed of steel & the weight is about 36 oz.; made from about 1981 to mid 1980's. Add 8% for nickel finish.
Estimated Value:　Excellent:　　$350.00
　　　　　　　　　　Very good:　　$280.00

Smith & Wesson Model 639

Similar to the Model 439 except satin stainless steel finish. Approx. wt. 36 oz. Add 4% for adjustable rear sight. Made 1984 to 1989.
Estimated Value:　Excellent:　　$395.00
　　　　　　　　　　Very good:　　$315.00

Smith & Wesson Model 459

Caliber: 9mm (Parabellum) Luger
Action: Semi-automatic; double action
Magazine: 14-shot staggered clip
Barrel: 4"
Sights: Serrated ramp front sight; rear adjustable for windage & elevation or fixed
Finish: Blued or nickel; checkered high-impact molded nylon grips
Length Overall: 7½"
Approximate wt.: 30 oz.
Comments: The frame is constructed of aluminum alloy; the grip back is straight; the grip is thick to accommodate the staggered column magazine; it has an improved extraction system. Nickel finish discontinued late 1980's. Add 4% for adjustable rear sight. Made from 1981 to 1989.
Estimated Value:　Excellent:　　$375.00
　　　　　　　　　　Very good:　　$300.00

Smith & Wesson Model 559

Similar to the Model 459 except the frame is steel & the weight approximately 40 oz. Made from about 1981 to mid 1980's. Add 7% for nickel finish.
Estimated Value:　Excellent:　　$365.00
　　　　　　　　　　Very good:　　$290.00

Smith & Wesson Model 659

Similar to the Model 459 except satin stainless steel finish. Approx. wt. 40 oz. Add 4% for adjustable rear sight. Made 1984 to 1989.
Estimated Value:　Excellent:　　$415.00
　　　　　　　　　　Very good:　　$330.00

Smith & Wesson Model 645

Caliber: 45 ACP
Action: Double action; semi-automatic; exposed hammer
Magazine: 8-shot clip
Barrel: 5"
Sights: Red-ramp front, fixed white-outline rear
Finish: Stainless steel; checkered high-impact molded nylon grips
Length Overall: 8⅝"
Approximate wt.: 38 oz.
Comments: Made from the mid 1980's to 1989.
Estimated Value: Excellent: $465.00
                       Very good: $370.00

Smith & Wesson Model 639

Smith & Wesson Model 659

Smith & Wesson Model 469

Smith & Wesson Model 645

Smith & Wesson Model 745

Caliber: 45ACP
Action: Single action; semi-automatic; adjustable trigger stop
Magazine: 8-shot clip
Barrel: 5"
Sights: Ramp front, square notch rear, adjustable for windage
Finish: Stainless steel frame; blued carbon steel slide, hammer, trigger, sights; checkered walnut grips
Length Overall: 8⅝"
Approximate wt.: 38¾ oz.
Comments: Introduced in 1987. Discontinued in 1990.
Estimated Value: Excellent: $525.00
                       Very good: $420.00

Smith & Wesson Model 422

Caliber: 22 long rifle
Action: Single action; semi-automatic; concealed hammer.
Magazine: 10-shot clip
Barrel: 4½" or 6" barrel
Sights: Fixed sights on field model, adjustable sights on target model
Finish: Blued; aluminum frame, carbon steel slide; plastic grips on field version, checkered walnut with S&W monogram on target version
Length Overall: 7½" or 9"
Approximate wt.: 22 to 23 oz.
Comments: Introduced in 1987 in field or target version (add 25% for target).
Estimated Value: New (retail): $206.00
                       Excellent: $155.00
                       Very good: $125.00

Smith & Wesson Model 622

Same as the Model 422 except stainless steel slide & aluminum alloy frame. Introduced in 1990. Add 20% for target sights.
Estimated Value: New (retail): $266.00
                       Excellent: $200.00
                       Very good: $160.00

Smith & Wesson Model 2206

Same as the Model 422 except stainless steel slide & frame. Introduced in 1990. Add 20% for adjustable target sights.
Estimated Value: New (retail): $299.00
                       Excellent: $225.00
                       Very good: $180.00

Smith & Wesson Model 469

Caliber: 9mm (Parabellum) Luger
Action: Double action; semi-automatic; exposed bobbed hammer
Magazine: 12-shot clip
Barrel: 3½"
Sights: Serrated ramp front, square notch rear
Finish: Blued; pebble grain molded Debrin grips; aluminum alloy frame
Length Overall: 6⅞"
Approximate wt.: 26 oz.
Comments: Made 1984 to 1989.
Estimated Value: Excellent: $360.00
                       Very good: $290.00

Smith & Wesson Model 669

Same as the model 469 except barrel & slide are stainless steel. Made from mid 1980's to 1989.
Estimated Value: Excellent: $390.00
                       Very good: $310.00

Smith & Wesson Model 1006

Caliber: 10mm
Action: Double action; semi-automatic, exposed hammer, ambidextrous safety
Magazine: 9-shot clip
Barrel: 5"
Sights: Post front with white dot, fixed rear with 2 white dots or adjustable rear with 2 white dots
Finish: Stainless steel, Debrin one-piece wrap around grips with straight back straps
Length Overall: 8½"
Approximate wt.: 38 oz.
Comments: Introduced in 1990. Add 8% for adjustable rear sight.
Estimated Value: New (retail): $695.00
                       Excellent: $520.00
                       Very good: $420.00

Smith & Wesson 1891 Single Shot Target Pistol

Caliber: 22 short, long, long rifle

Action: Single; exposed hammer; hinged frame (top break); single shot

Cylinder: None

Barrel: 10"

Sights: Adjustable target

Finish: Blued; hard rubber square butt grips

Length Overall: 13½"

Approximate wt.: 25 oz.

Comments: Made from about 1905 to 1909.

Estimated Value: Excellent: $370.00
Very good: $285.00

Smith & Wesson 1891 Single Shot Target Pistol

Smith & Wesson Model 3904

Caliber: 9mm

Action: Double action, semi-automatic with exposed hammer & ambidextrous safety

Magazine: 8-shot clip

Barrel: 4"

Sights: Post front with white dot, fixed or micrometer adjustable rear with 2 white dots

Finish: Blued; aluminum alloy frame, carbon steel slide; Debrin one-piece wrap around grips with curved back strap.

Length Overall: 7½"

Approximate wt.: 28 oz.

Comments: Introduced in 1989. Add 5% for adjustable rear sight.

Estimated Value: New (retail): $520.00
Excellent: $390.00
Very good: $310.00

Smith & Wesson Model 5903

Caliber: 9mm Luger Parabellum

Action: Double action, semi-automatic, ambidextrous safety, exposed hammer

Magazine: 14-shot clip

Barrel: 4"

Sights: Post front with white dot, fixed or micrometer adjustable rear with 2 white dots

Finish: Stainless steel slide with aluminum alloy frame; Debrin one-piece wrap around grips with curved back strap

Length Overall: 7½"

Approximate wt.: 29 oz.

Comments: Introduced in 1990. Add 4½% for adjustable rear sight.

Estimated Value: New (retail): $600.00
Excellent: $450.00
Very good: $360.00

Smith & Wesson Perfected Single Shot

Similar to Model 1891 Single Shot except: double & single action; checkered square butt walnut grips; made from about 1909 to 1923; the U.S. Olympic team of 1920 used this pistol, therefore it is sometimes designated "Olympic Model." Add $125.00 for Olympic Models.

Estimated Value: Excellent: $420.00
Very good: $330.00

Smith & Wesson Model 3904

Smith & Wesson Model 5906

Smith & Wesson Model 3906

Same as the Model 3904 except stainless steel. Introduced in 1989. Add 4½% for adjustable rear sight.

Estimated Value: New (retail): $570.00
Excellent: $430.00
Very good: $340.00

Smith & Wesson Model 5904

Same as the Model 5903 except blued finish with carbon steel slide. Approximate weight is 27 oz. Introduced in 1989.

Estimated Value: New (retail) $570.00
Excellent: $425.00
Very good: $340.00

Smith & Wesson Model 5906

Same as the Model 5903 except stainless steel slide & frame; approximate weight is 38 oz.; add 5% for adjustable rear sight. Introduced in 1989.

Estimated Value: New (retail) $621.00
Excellent: $465.00
Very good: $370.00

Smith & Wesson Model 6904
Caliber: 9mm Luger Parabellum
Action: Double action, semi-automatic; exposed bobbed hammer; ambidextrous safety
Magazine: 12-shot clip
Barrel: 3½"
Sights: Post front with white dot; fixed rear with 2 white dots
Finish: Blued, carbon steel slide with aluminum alloy frame; Debrin one-piece wrap around grips with curved backstrap
Length Overall: 6⅞"
Approximate wt.: 27 oz.
Comments: Introduced in 1989.
Estimated Value: New (retail): $539.00
                       Excellent: $405.00
                       Very good: $325.00

Smith & Wesson Model 4516
Caliber: 45ACP
Action: Double action, semi-automatic, exposed hammer; ambidextrous safety
Magazine: 7-shot clip
Barrel: 3¾"
Sights: Post front with white dot; fixed rear with two white dots
Finish: Stainless steel with Debrin one-piece wrap around grips
Length Overall: 7¼"
Approximate wt.: 35 oz.
Comments: A compact 45 automatic; introduced in 1989.
Estimated Value: New (retail): $674.00
                       Excellent: $505.00
                       Very good: $400.00

Smith & Wesson Model 6906

Smith & Wesson Model 4506

Smith & Wesson Model 6906
Same as the Model 6904 except stainless steel slide with aluminum alloy frame. Introduced in 1989.
Estimated Value: New (retail): $589.00
                       Excellent: $440.00
                       Very good: $350.00

Smith & Wesson Model 4506
Caliber: 45ACP
Action: Double action, semi-automatic; exposed hammer, ambidextrous safety
Magazine: 8-shot clip
Barrel: 5"
Sights: Post front with white dot; fixed or micrometer adjustable rear with two white dots
Finish: Stainless steel with Debrin one-piece wrap around grips
Length Overall: 8½"
Approximate wt.: 39 oz.
Comments: Introduced in 1989. Add 4% for adjustable rear sight.
Estimated Value: New (retail): $674.00
                       Excellent: $505.00
                       Very good: $400.00

Smith & Wesson Model 4006
Caliber: 40 S&W
Action: Double action, semi-automatic; exposed hammer; ambidextrous safety
Magazine: 11-shot clip
Barrel: 4"
Sights: Post with white dot front; fixed or adjustable rear with two white dots
Finish: Stainless steel with Debrin one-piece wrap around straight back strap grips
Length Overall: 7½"
Approximate wt.: 30 oz.
Comments: Introduced in 1990. Add 8% for adjustable sights.
Estimated Value: New (retail): $695.00
                       Excellent: $520.00
                       Very good: $420.00

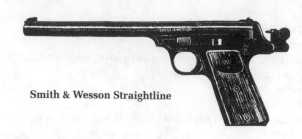

Smith & Wesson Straightline

Smith & Wesson 32 Double Action
Caliber: 32 S&W center fire
Action: Single & double; exposed hammer; hinged frame (top break)
Cylinder: 5-shot; simultaneous ejector
Barrel: 3" 1880-1882; 3", 3½", 6", 8", 10" 1882-1909; 3",3½", 6" 1909-1919
Sights: Fixed
Finish: Blued or nickel; round butt, hard rubber grips
Length Overall: 7¼" to 14¼"
Approximate wt.: 23 to 28 oz.
Comments: Made from about 1880 to 1919 in five modifications or issues; rear of trigger guard is square.
Estimated Value:

Issue	Dates	Quantity	Excellent	Very Good
1st	1880	Less than 100	$2,500.00	$2,000.00
2nd	1880-1882	22,000	$ 230.00	$ 200.00
3rd	1882-1889	21,200	$ 235.00	$ 205.00
4th	1889-1909	239,500	$ 180.00	$ 150.00
5th	1909-1919	44,600	$ 200.00	$ 175.00

Smith & Wesson No. 3 Single Action New Model
Caliber: 44 S&W Russian center fire
Action: Single; exposed hammer; hinged frame (top break); simultaneous automatic ejector
Cylinder: 6-shot
Barrel: 4", 5", 6", 6½", 7½" or ribbed
Sights: Fixed or target
Finish: Blued or nickel; round butt, hard rubber or checkered walnut grips
Length Overall: 9" to 13"
Approximate wt.: 36 to 40 oz.
Comments: An improved version of the S&W Russian single action revolver. Approximately 36,000 were manufactured from about 1878 to 1908. Sometimes called Single Action Russian Model.
Estimated Value: **Excellent:** **$825.00**
Very good: **$660.00**

Smith & Wesson No.3 New Model Double Action
Same as No. 3 Single Action New Model except: double & single action; 4", 5", 6" & 6½" barrel; overall length 9" to 11½"; sometimes listed as S&W 1881 Navy Revolver; rear of trigger guard is square. Made from about 1881 to 1908.
Estimated Value: **Excellent:** **$500.00**
Very good: **$400.00**

Smith & Wesson Double Action 44
Wesson Favorite
Similar to No. 3 Single Action New Model except: double & single action; 5" barrel only; lighter barrel & frame. Made from about 1882 to 1883 (approximately 1,200 produced).
Estimated Value: **Excellent:** **$1,800.00**
Very good: **$1,200.00**

Smith & Wesson Straightline
Caliber: 22 short, long, long rifle
Action: Single; exposed striker (hammer); single shot
Magazine: None
Barrel: 10"; cartridge chamber in barrel; barrel pivots to left to eject & load
Sights: Target sights
Finish: Blued; walnut grips
Length Overall: 11½"
Approximate wt.: 35 oz.
Comments: Pistol resembles automatic pistol in appearance; sold with metal case, screwdriver & cleaning rod. Made from about 1925 to 1937. Add $100.00 for original case & accessories.
Estimated Value: **Excellent:** **$925.00**
Very good: **$740.00**

Smith & Wesson No. 3 New Model
Double Action

Smith & Wesson 38 Double Action

Smith & Wesson No. 3 Single Action
New Model

Smith & Wesson 38 Double Action
Caliber: 38 S&W
Action: Single & double; exposed hammer; hinged frame; top break; back of trigger guard squared
Cylinder: 5-shot; simultaneous ejector
Barrel: 3¼", 4", 5", 6"
Sights: Fixed
Finish: Blued or nickel; round butt; hard rubber grips
Length Overall: 7½" to 10¼"
Approximate wt.: 20 to 24 oz.
Comments: Made from about 1880 to 1910 with some improvements & minor changes.
Estimated Value: **Excellent:** **$450.00**
Very good: **$360.00**

Smith & Wesson Safety Model Double Action

Caliber: 32 S&W, 38 S&W

Action: Double only; concealed hammer with frame enclosing it; hinged frame; top break style; grip safety on rear of grip frame

Cylinder: 5-shot; simultaneous ejector

Barrel: 2", 3", or 3½" in 32 caliber; 2", 3¼", 4", 5", or 6" in 38 caliber; rib on top

Sights: Fixed

Finish: Blued or nickel; hard rubber or checkered walnut grips

Length Overall: 5¾" to 9¾"

Approximate wt.: 15 to 20 oz.

Comments: Sometimes listed as the Safety Hammerless, New Department Model. Made from about 1887 to 1941. About five changes & improvements were made from 1887 to 1940.

Estimated Value: **Excellent:** $375.00
                  Very good: $300.00

Smith & Wesson Perfected 38

Caliber: 38 S&W center fire

Action: Single & double; exposed hammer; hinged frame (top break; but also has side latch)

Cylinder: 5-shot; simultaneous ejector

Barrel: 3¼", 4", 5", & 6"

Sights: Fixed

Finish: Blued or nickel; round butt, hard rubber grip

Length Overall: 7½" to 10¼"

Approximate wt.: 24 to 30 oz.

Comments: Similar to earlier 38 double action revolvers except: heavier frame; a side latch along with the top latch; improved lock work. Approximately 58,400 were produced from about 1909 to 1920.

Estimated Value: **Excellent:** $385.00
                  Very good: $300.00

Smith & Wesson Single Action Target

Caliber: 32-44 S&W, 38-44 S&W

Action: Single; exposed hammer; hinged frame (top break)

Cylinder: 6-shot; simultaneous ejector

Barrel: 6½"

Sights: Target

Finish: Blued or nickel; round butt; hard rubber or checkered walnut grips

Length Overall: 11"

Approximate wt.: 38 to 40 oz.

Comments: One of the first handguns to prove that a short-barrel arm could be a really accurate weapon. Made from 1887 to 1910.

Estimated Value: **Excellent:** $700.00
                  Very good: $560.00

Smith & Wesson No. 3 Single Action Frontier

Caliber: 44-40 Winchester rifle cartridge

Action: Single; exposed hammer; hinged frame (top break)

Cylinder: 6-shot; simultaneous automatic ejector

Barrel: 4", 5" & 6½"

Sights: Fixed or target

Finish: Blued or nickel; round butt, hard rubber or checkered walnut grips

Length Overall: 8½" to 11"

Approximate wt.: 38 to 42 oz.

Comments: Approximately 2,000 manufactured from about 1885 to 1908.

Estimated Value: **Excellent:** $1,000.00
                  Very good: $ 800.00

Smith & Wesson Double Action Frontier

Similar to No. 3 Single Action Frontier except: double & single action; rear of trigger guard is square. Made from about 1886 to 1908 (approximately 15,000 were produced.)

Estimated Value: **Excellent:** $500.00
                  Very good: $375.00

Smith & Wesson 1891 Single Action

Caliber: 38 S&W center fire

Action: Single; exposed hammer; hinged frame (top break)

Cylinder: 5-shot; simultaneous ejector

Barrel: 3¼", 4", 5" & 6"

Sights: Fixed

Finish: Blued or nickel; round butt, hard rubber grips

Length Overall: 6¾" to 9½"

Approximate wt.: 34 to 38 oz. (depending on barrel length)

Comments: This revolver was also available with an accessory single shot target barrel in 22 caliber, 32 caliber or 38 caliber; & 6", 8" & 10" lengths. Made from 1891 to 1911.

Estimated Value:	Revolver	Revolver and single shot barrel
Excellent:	$560.00	$950.00
Very good:	$450.00	$825.00

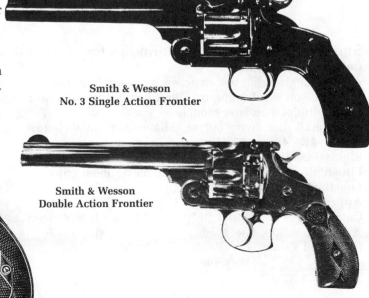

Smith & Wesson
No. 3 Single Action Frontier

Smith & Wesson
Double Action Frontier

Smith & Wesson 1891 Single Action

Smith & Wesson 1899 Hand Ejector

Caliber: 38 long Colt

Action: Double & single; exposed hammer; solid frame

Cylinder: 6-shot; swing out; simultaneous manual ejector; cylinder release on side of frame

Barrel: 4", 5", 6" or 6½"

Sights: Fixed

Finish: Blued or nickel; checkered hard rubber or walnut round butt grips

Length Overall: 9" to 11½"

Approximate wt.: 22 to 25 oz.

Comments: Made for police, Army, Navy & commercial use; forerunner of the military & police models. Made from about 1899 to 1902 (approximately 21,000 produced). Army & Navy versions have lanyard swivel in butt & 6" or 6½" barrel lengths.

Estimated Value: Excellent: $550.00
  Very good: $440.00

Smith & Wesson Military & Police
Winchester 32-20

Smith & Wesson Military & Police Winchester 32-20

Similar to Model 1899 except: caliber 32-20 only; some improvements & changes over the years produced from about 1899 to 1940.

Estimated Value: Excellent: $320.00
  Very good: $250.00

Smith & Wesson Model 1 Hand Ejector

Caliber: 32 S&W long

Action: single & double; exposed hammer; first Smith & Wesson solid frame revolver; longer top strap over cylinder than later models

Cylinder: 6-shot; swing out; simultaneous manual ejector

Barrel: 3¼", 4¼", or 6"

Sights: Fixed

Finish: Blued or nickel; round butt; hard rubber grips

Length Overall: 8" to 10¾"

Approximate wt.: 20 to 24 oz.

Comments: First model produced by Smith & Wesson with solid frame. Made from about 1896 to 1903.

Estimated Value: Excellent: $400.00
  Very good: $320.00

Smith & Wesson Model
M Hand Ejector

Smith & Wesson Model M Hand Ejector

Caliber: 22 short, long, long rifle

Action: Double & single; exposed hammer; solid frame.

Cylinder: 9-shot; swing-out, simultaneous manual ejector

Barrel: 2¼" (1902-1911); 3", 3½" (1906-1911) or 6" (1911-1921)

Sights: Fixed or adjustable (available after 1911)

Finish: Blued or nickel; checkered hard rubber round butt grips (1902 to 1911); checkered hard rubber square butt grips (1911-1921)

Length Overall: 5¾" to 10½"

Approximate wt.: 10 to 14 oz.

Comments: Cylinder latch release on left side of frame 1902 to 1906; cylinder latch under barrel 1906 to 1921. Made from about 1902 to 1921, sometimes called Lady Smith.

Estimated Value: Excellent: $725.00
  Very good: $600.00

Smith & Wesson Mexican Model

Caliber: 38 S&W center fire

Action: Single; exposed hammer; hinged frame (top break); spur trigger

Cylinder: 5-shot; simultaneous ejector

Barrel: 3¼", 4", 5" & 6"

Sights: Fixed

Finish: Blued or nickel; round butt, hard rubber grips

Length Overall: 7¾" to 10½"

Approximate wt.: 34 to 38 oz.

Comments: Similar to Model 1891 except: it has a spur trigger; doesn't have half-cock notch on the hammer. Approximately 2,000 manufactured from about 1891 to 1911.

Estimated Value: Excellent: $1,200.00
  Very good: $ 900.00

Smith & Wesson New Century Triple Lock

Caliber: 44 S&W Special, 450 Eley, 45 Colt or 455 Mark II British

Action: Single & double; exposed hammer; solid frame

Cylinder: 6-shot swing out; simultaneous hand ejector; called triple lock because of lock on cylinder crane as well as the usual locks under barrel & at rear of cylinder

Barrel: 4", 5", 6½", 7½" tapered round

Sights: Fixed

Finish: Blued or nickel; checkered square butt walnut grips

Length Overall: 9¼" to 12¾"

Approximate wt.: 36 to 41 oz.

Comments: Approximately 20,000 made from about 1908 to 1915; about 5,000 of these were made for the British Army.

Estimated Value: Excellent: $675.00
Very good: $575.00

Smith & Wesson Model 30 Hand Ejector

Smith & Wesson Model 22/32 Target

Smith & Wesson Model 35 22/32 Target

Smith & Wesson Model 34 1953 22/32 Kit Gun

Smith & Wesson Model 30 Hand Ejector

Caliber: 32 S&W & 32 S&W long

Action: Single & double; exposed hammer; solid frame

Cylinder: 6-shot; swing out; simultaneous manual ejector; cylinder release on left side of frame

Barrel: 2" (1949 to 1975); 3", 4", 6"

Sights: Fixed

Finish: Blued or nickel; checkered hard rubber or checkered walnut round butt grips

Length Overall: 6" to 10"

Approximate wt.: 16 to 20 oz.

Comments: Made from about 1903 to 1975 with many improvements & minor changes over the years.

Estimated Value: Excellent: $225.00
Very good: $170.00

Smith & Wesson 44 Hand Ejector

Similar to New Century Triple Lock except: cylinder crane lock eliminated; 44 Smith & Wesson Special, 44 Smith & Wesson Russian or 45 Colt calibers; 45 Colt caliber made in 6½" barrel only; other calibers in 4", 5", 6" lengths. Made from about 1915 to 1937.

Estimated Value: Excellent: $500.00
Very good: $400.00

Smith & Wesson 22/32 Target Revolver

Caliber: 22 short, long, long rifle

Action: Single & double; exposed hammer; solid frame

Cylinder: 6-shot swing out; recessed chamber (1935 to 1953); cylinder release on left side of frame

Barrel: 6"

Sights: Adjustable target sights

Finish: Blued; checkered square butt walnut grips

Length Overall: 10½"

Approximate wt.: 24 oz.

Comments: Frame design similar to Model 30 hand ejector model. Made about 1911 to 1953.

Estimated Value: Excellent: $300.00
Very good: $240.00

Smith & Wesson 22/32 1935 Kit Gun

Same as 22/32 Target except: 4" barrel; overall length 8"; weight about 21 oz.; round butt grips. Made from about 1935 to 1953.

Estimated Value: Excellent: $270.00
Very good: $210.00

Smith & Wesson Model 35 22/32 Target

Similar to 22/32 target except: newer type adjustable rear sight; S&W magna-type target grips; weight about 25 oz. Made from about 1953 to 1974.

Estimated Value: Excellent: $275.00
Very good: $220.00

Smith & Wesson Model 34 1953 22/32 Kit Gun

Similar to 22/32 Kit Gun except: 2" or 4" barrel; round or square butt grips; blued or nickel finish. Made from about 1953 to present. Nickel finish discontinued late 1980's.

Estimated Value: New (retail): $366.00
Excellent: $270.00
Very good: $210.00

Smith & Wesson Model 43 1955 22/32 Kit Gun

Same as Model 34 1953 22/32 Kit Gun except: 3½" barrel only; lighter alloy frame; approximately 15 oz. weight; square butt grips. Made from about 1954 to 1974.

Estimated Value: Excellent: **$260.00**
                     Very good: **$210.00**

Smith & Wesson Model 51 1960 22/32 Kit Gun

Same as Model 43 1953 22/32 Kit Gun except: chambered for 22 magnum only; all steel construction; approximately 24 oz. weight. Made from about 1960 to 1974.

Estimated Value: Excellent: **$275.00**
                     Very good: **$220.00**

Smith & Wesson Model 43 1955 22/32 Kit Gun

Smith & Wesson 1917 Army

Smith & Wesson Model 22 1950 Army

Smith & Wesson Model 51 1960 22/32 Kit Gun

Smith & Wesson
1926 Model 44 Military

Smith & Wesson
1926 Model 44 Target

Smith & Wesson 1917 Army

Caliber: 45 auto rim cartridge; 45 ACP (by using two 3 round steel half moon clips to hold the cartridge heads)

Action: Single & double; exposed hammer; solid frame

Cylinder: 6-shot swing out; simultaneous manual ejector; release on left side of frame

Barrel: 5½"

Sights: Fixed

Finish: Blued; smooth or checkered square butt walnut grips

Length Overall: 10¾"

Approximate wt.: 37 oz.

Comments: Approximately 175,000 made for U.S. Government from about 1917 to 1919. Then made for commercial sale from about 1919 to 1941. U.S. Government models had a dull blue finish & smooth grips.

Estimated Value:	Military	Commercial
Excellent:	$325.00	$350.00
Very good:	$250.00	$275.00

Smith & Wesson Model 22 1950 Army

Similar to 1917 Army except: made after World War II; minor changes. Made from about 1950 to 1967.

Estimated Value: Excellent: **$295.00**
                     Very good: **$235.00**

Smith & Wesson 1926 Model 44 Military

Caliber: 44 S&W Special

Action: Single & double; exposed hammer

Cylinder: 6-shot swing out; simultaneous manual ejector; cylinder release on left side of frame

Barrel: 3¼", 4", 5", 6½"

Sights: Fixed

Finish: Blued or nickel; checkered square butt walnut grips

Length Overall: 9¼" to 11¾"

Approximate wt.: 40 oz.

Comments: Made from about 1926 to 1941.

Estimated Value: Excellent: **$395.00**
                     Very good: **$315.00**

Smith & Wesson 1926 Model 44 Target

Same as 1926 Model Military except: 6½" barrel only; adjustable target sights; blued finish only. Made from about 1926 to 1941.

Estimated Value: Excellent: **$400.00**
                     Very good: **$320.00**

Smith & Wesson Model 21 1950 44 Military

Similar to 1926 Model Military revolver except: made after World War II; minor changes. Made from about 1950 to 1967.

Estimated Value: Excellent: $320.00
                    Very good: $255.00

Smith & Wesson
Model 21 1950 44 Military

Smith & Wesson Model 24 1950 44 Target Revolver

Similar to 1926 Model 44 Target except: 4" or 6½" barrel; made after World War II; minor changes; ribbed barrel. Made from about 1950 to 1967. A limited edition of 7,500 were made in mid 1980's.

Estimated Value: Excellent: $325.00
                    Very good: $260.00

Smith & Wesson
Model 24 1950 44 Target

Smith & Wesson Model 624

Smith & Wesson
Model 25 1955 45 Target

Smith & Wesson Model 20
Heavy Duty

Smith & Wesson Model 624 44 Special

Similar to the Model 24, 1950 44 Target Revolver except stainless steel. Produced only in the mid 1980's. Add 3% for 6½" barrel.

Estimated Value: Excellent: $350.00
                    Very good: $280.00

Smith & Wesson Model 23
Outdoorsman

Smith & Wesson Model 25 45 Colt

Caliber: 45 Colt
Action: Single & double; exposed hammer; solid frame
Cylinder: 6-shot swing out; simultaneous manual ejector; cylinder release on left side
Barrel: 4", 6", 8⅜"
Sights: Red ramp front; micrometer click rear adjustable for windage & elevation
Finish: Blued or nickel; checkered Goncolo Alves target grips
Length Overall: 9⅜" to 13¾"
Approximate wt.: 44 to 52 oz.
Comments: This revolver is built on the large N frame. Made from about 1955 to present. Add 3% for 8⅜" barrel, add 9% for presentation box. Nickel finish discontinued late 1980's.

Estimated Value: New (retail): $429.00
                    Excellent: $320.00
                    Very good: $260.00

Smith & Wesson Model 25 1955 Target

Similar to the Model 25 except 6" barrel only; blued finish only; 45 ACP caliber; ⅛" plain partridge front sight; add 9% for presentation box.

Estimated Value: Excellent: $300.00
                    Very good: $240.00

Smith & Wesson Model 20 Heavy Duty

Caliber: 38 Special
Action: Single & double; exposed hammer; solid frame
Cylinder: 6-shot swing out; simultaneous ejector; release on left side of frame
Barrel: 4", 5", 6½"
Sights: Fixed
Finish: Blued or nickel; checkered square butt walnut grips
Length Overall: 9⅜" to 11⅞"
Approximate wt.: 38 to 41 oz.
Comments: Made from about 1930 to 1967.

Estimated Value: Excellent: $350.00
                    Very good: $280.00

Smith & Wesson Model 23 Outdoorsman Revolver

Similar to Model 20 Heavy Duty except; target version; 6½" barrel only; ribbed barrel after 1950; approximately 42 oz. wt.; blued finish; adjustable target sights. Made from about 1930 to 1967.

Estimated Value: Excellent: $400.00
                    Very good: $320.00

Smith & Wesson Model 10 Military & Police

Caliber: 38 Special
Action: Double & single; exposed hammer; solid frame
Cylinder: 6-shot swing out: simultaneous manual ejector
Barrel: 2", 3" or 4" (3" barrel discontinued late 1980's)
Sights: Fixed
Finish: Blued or nickel: square or round-butt checkered walnut grips
Length Overall: 7" to 9½"
Approximate wt.: 28 to 34 oz.
Comments: Made from about 1948 to present. Add 4% for nickel finish.
Estimated Value: New (retail): $333.00
                      Excellent: $250.00
                      Very good: $200.00

Smith & Wesson Military & Police

Caliber: 38 Special
Action: Single & double; exposed hammer; solid frame
Cylinder: 6-shot swing out; simultaneous ejector; release on left side of frame
Barrel: 2" (after 1933); 4", 5", 6" 6½" (1902-1915)
Sights: Fixed
Finish: Blued or nickel; checkered hard rubber or checkered walnut round or square butt grips
Length Overall: 7" to 11½"
Approximate wt.: 26 to 32 oz.
Comments: Manufactured from about 1902 to 1942 with improvements & minor changes. Basic frame is known as S&W K frame. Add $15.00 for nickel finish. Also known as 1902 Model & 1905 Model M&P.
Estimated Value: Excellent: $220.00
                      Very good: $180.00

Smith & Wesson Model 13

Smith & Wesson Victory Model

Same as Model 10 Military & Police except: sand blasted or brushed parkerized finish; 4" barrel; smooth square butt grips with lanyard ring; made from about 1941 to 1946 for the U.S. Government during World War II; 38 Special caliber; Some 38-200 caliber with 5" barrel were made for the British Forces.
Estimated Value: Excellent: $250.00
                      Very good: $190.00

Smith & Wesson Model 13 M&P

Similar to the Model 10 Military & Police except 357 magnum caliber & heavy barrel.
Estimated Value: New (retail): $339.00
                      Excellent: $255.00
                      Very good: $200.00

Smith & Wesson Model 65 M&P

Similar to the Model 13 with a satin stainless steel finish.
Estimated Value: New (retail) $368.00
                      Excellent: $275.00
                      Very good: $220.00

Smith & Wesson Model 64 Military & Police

Same as Model 10 Military & Police Revolver except: satin finish stainless steel construction. Made from about 1972 to present.
Estimated Value: New (retail): $417.00
                      Excellent: $315.00
                      Very good: $250.00

Smith & Wesson Model 12 Military & Police Airweight

Same as Model 10 Military & Police except: light alloy frame; 2" or 4" barrel; approximate wt. 28 oz. Made from about 1952 to late 1980's.
Estimated Value: Excellent: $240.00
                      Very good: $180.00

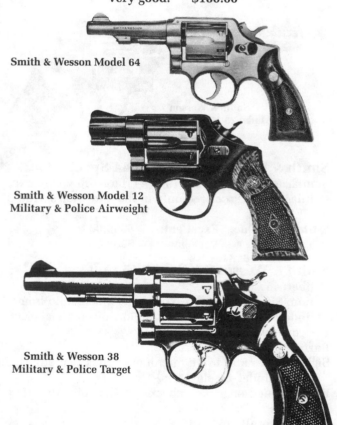

Smith & Wesson Model 64

Smith & Wesson Model 12 Military & Police Airweight

Smith & Wesson 38 Military & Police Target

Smith & Wesson 38 Military & Police Target

Same as Model 10 Military & Police except: 6" barrel only; approximate wt. 33 oz.; checkered walnut grips; adjustable target sights. Made from about 1924 to 1941.
Estimated Value: Excellent: $225.00
                      Very good: $175.00

Smith & Wesson K-32 Target

Similar to S&W 38 Military & Police Target except: caliber 32 S&W, 32 S&W long & 32 Colt New Police; heavier barrel; approximate wt. 34 oz. Introduced about 1940; discontinued about 1941.
Estimated Value: Excellent: $675.00
                      Very good: $540.00

Smith & Wesson Model 31 Regulation Police

Caliber: 32 S&W Long, 32 Colt New Police
Action: Single & double; exposed hammer; solid frame
Cylinder: 6-shot swing out; simultaneous manual ejector; release on left side of frame
Barrel: 2" (1949-present); 3", 3¼", 4", 4¼", 6"
Sights: Fixed
Finish: Blued or nickel; checkered square butt walnut grips
Length Overall: 6½" to 10½"
Approximate wt.: 17 to 20 oz.
Comments: Made from about 1917 to present. Presently made with 2" & 3" barrel only. Nickel finish discontinued in early 1980's.
Estimated Value: New (retail): $365.00
Excellent: $275.00
Very good: $220.00

Smith & Wesson Regulation Police Target

Similar to Smith & Wesson Model 31 Regulation Police except: 6" barrel only; adjustable target sights; blued finish. Made from about 1917 to 1940.
Estimated Value: Excellent: $240.00
Very good: $190.00

Smith & Wesson Model 33 Regulation Police Revolver

Same as S&W Model 31 Regulation Ploice except: 38 caliber S&W & 38 Colt New Police; 5-shot cylinder capacity. Made from about 1917 to 1974.
Estimated Value: Excellent: $230.00
Very good: $185.00

Smith & Wesson Model 32 Terrier

Similar to Model 33 Regulation Police except: 2" barrel only; 6½" overall length. Made from about 1936 to 1974.
Estimated Value: Excellent: $215.00
Very good: $175.00

Smith & Wesson Model 27 357 Magnum

Caliber: 357 magnum & 38 Special
Action: Single & double; exposed hammer; solid frame
Cylinder: 6-shot swing out; simultaneous manual ejector
Barrel: 3½", 5", 6", 6½", 8⅜" ribbed
Sights: ramp front, adjustable rear
Finish: Blued or nickel; checkered walnut grips
Length Overall: 7⅞" to 14¼"
Approximate wt.: 42 to 49 oz.
Comments: Made from about 1935 to present. Made from 1935 to 1938 on special orders. Add 2% for 8⅜" barrel. Presently made in 4", 6" & 8⅜" barrel. Add $40.00 for Presentation Box. Add 7% for target sights.
Estimated Value: New (retail): $423.00
Excellent: $315.00
Very good: $255.00

Smith & Wesson Model 28 Highway Patrolman

Similar to Model 27 357 Magnum except: 4" or 6" barrel; ramp front sight & adjustable rear sight; blued finish. Made from about 1954 to late 1980's. Add 10% for target grips.
Estimated Value: Excellent: $265.00
Very good: $210.00

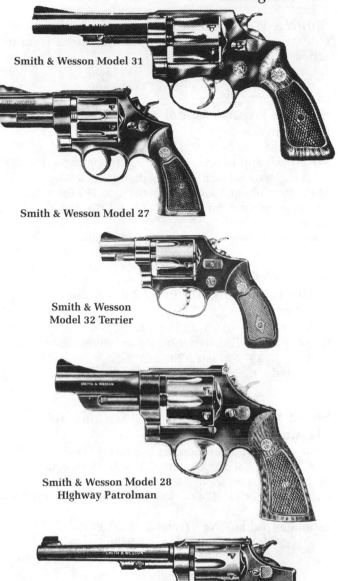

Smith & Wesson Model 31

Smith & Wesson Model 27

Smith & Wesson Model 32 Terrier

Smith & Wesson Model 28 Highway Patrolman

Smith & Wesson K-22 Outdoorsman

Smith & Wesson Model K-22 Outdoorsman

Caliber: 22 short, long, long rifle
Action: Single & double; exposed hammer; solid frame
Cylinder: 6-shot swing out; simultaneous manual ejector; release on left side of frame
Barrel: 6"
Sights: Fixed or target sights
Finish: Blued or nickel; checkered walnut grips
Length Overall: 11½"
Approximate wt.: 35 oz.
Comments: Made from about 1931 to 1942.
Estimated Value: Excellent: $280.00
Very good: $225.00

Smith & Wesson K-22 Masterpiece

Same as K-22 Outdoorsman except: improved version; better adjustable rear sight; short cocking action; antibacklash trigger; made from about 1942 to 1947.
Estimated Value: Excellent: $300.00
Very good: $240.00

Smith & Wesson Model 14 Single Action

similar to the Model 14 K-38 Masterpiece in single action; 6"; blued only.

Estimated Value: Excellent: $245.00
Very good: $195.00

Smith & Wesson Model 15 38 Combat Masterpiece

Same as Model 14 K-38 Masterpiece except: 2", 4", 6" or 8⅜" barrel; approximate wt. 30 oz. to 39 oz.; quick draw front sight; blued or nickel finish; double & single action. Made from about 1950 to present. Add 7% for nickel finish (discontinued late 1980's); 3% for 8⅜" barrel (discontinued 1989).

Estimated Value: New (retail): $361.00
Excellent: $270.00
Very good: $215.00

Smith & Wesson Model 67 38 Combat Masterpiece

Same as Model 15 38 combat Masterpiece except: 4" barrel only; satin finish stainless steel construction. Made from about 1972 to late 1980's.

Estimated Value: Excellent: $270.00
Very good: $215.00

Smith & Wesson Model 67 357 Combat Magnum

Same as Model 15 38 Combat Masterpiece except: 2½", 4" or 6" barrel; caliber 357 magnum & 38 Special; round butt. Made from about 1956 to present. Add $60.00 for target accessories; $24.00 for target sights; $10.00 for 4" or 6" barrel.

Estimated Value: New (retail): $355.00
Excellent: $266.00
Very good: $215.00

Smith & Wesson Model 66 357 Combat Magnum

Same as Model 19 357 Combat Magnum except: satin finish stainless steel. Produced from about 1972 to present. Add $41.00 for target accessories; $10.00 for target sights.

Estimated Value: New (retail): $404.00
Excellent: $300.00
Very good: $245.00

Smith & Wesson Model 14 K-38 Masterpiece

Caliber: 38 Special
Action: Single or double; or single action only; exposed hammer; solid frame
Cylinder: 6-shot swing out; simultaneous manual ejector; release on left side of frame
Barrel: 6" or 8⅜"
Sights: Partridge front; click adjustable rear
Finish: Blued; checkered square butt walnut grips
Length Overall: 11⅛" or 13½"
Approximate wt.: 36 to 38 oz.
Comments: Made from about 1947 to 1981. Add $10.00 for 8⅜" barrel; $40.00 for target accessories.

Estimated Value: Excellent: $260.00
Very good: $210.00

Smith & Wesson Model 16 K-32 Masterpiece

Same as Model 14 K-38 Masterpiece except: 32 S&W long & 32 Colt Police caliber; 6" barrel only; double & single action. Made from about 1947 to 1974.

Estimated Value: Excellent: $275.00
Very good: $220.00

Smith & Wesson
Model 14 Single Action

Smith & Wesson
Model 15

Smith & Wesson Model 67

Smith & Wesson Model 66

Smith & Wesson Model 14

Smith & Wesson Model 16 K-32

Smith & Wesson 17 K-22 Masterpiece

Smith & Wesson Model 36 Chiefs Special

Smith & Wesson Model 37 Airweight

Smith & Wesson Model 57

Smith & Wesson Model 58

Smith & Wesson Model 60 Chiefs Special Stainless Steel

Smith & Wesson Model 17 K-22 Masterpiece

Same as Model 14 K-38 Masterpiece except: 22 short, long, long rifle caliber; 4", 6" or 8⅜" barrel. Made from about 1947 to present; approx. wt. 40 oz. Add $12.00 for 8⅜" barrel; 9% for target trigger & hammer. Full length ejector housing added in 1989.

Estimated Value: New (retail): $379.00
                    Excellent: $285.00
                    Very good: $225.00

Smith & Wesson Model 18 22 Combat Masterpiece

Same as Model 17 K-22 Masterpiece except: 4" barrel; 9⅛" overall length; approximate wt. 38 oz. Made from about 1950 to mid 1980's. Add 10% for target trigger & hammer.

Estimated Value: Excellent: $250.00
                    Very good: $200.00

Smith & Wesson Model 36 Chiefs Special

Caliber: 38 Special
Action: Single & double; exposed hammer; solid frame
Cylinder: 5-shot swing out; simultaneous manual ejector; release on left side of frame
Barrel: 2" or 3"
Sights: Fixed
Finish: Blued or nickel; round or square butt, checkered walnut grips
Length Overall: 6½" to 7¾"
Approximate wt.: 19 to 20 oz.
Comments: Made from about 1950 to date. Add $10.00 for nickel finish.

Estimated Value: New (retail): $338.00
                    Excellent: $255.00
                    Very good: $200.00

Smith & Wesson Model 57 41 Magnum

Caliber: 41 magnum
Action: Single & double; exposed hammer; solid frame
Cylinder: 6-shot swing out; simultaneous manual ejector; release on left side of frame
Barrel: 4", 6", or 8⅜"
Sights: Ramp front, adjustable rear
Finish: Blued or nickel (discontinued late 1980's); checkered walnut grips
Length Overall: 9⅜" to 13¾"
Approximate wt.: 38 to 42 oz.
Comments: Made from about 1964 to present. Add 4% for 8⅜" barrel; $40.00 for presentation box.

Estimated Value: New (retail): $427.00
                    Excellent: $320.00
                    Very good: $255.00

Smith & Wesson Model 657 41 Magnum

Similar to the Model 57 41 Magnum except stainless steel. Introduced in the mid 1980's. Add 4% for 8⅜" barrel.

Estimated Value: New (retail): $455.00
                    Excellent: $340.00
                    Very good: $275.00

Smith & Wesson Model 58 Military & Police

Similar to Model 57 41 magnum except: 4" barrel only; fixed sights; no rib on barrel. Made from about 1964 to late 1970's. Add $10.00 for nickel finish.

Estimated Value: Excellent: $285.00
                    Very good: $225.00

Smith & Wesson Model 37 Airweight Chiefs Special

same as Model 36 Chiefs Special except: light alloy frame; approximate weight, 13 to 14 oz. Made from about 1954 to present. Add 4% for nickel finish.

Estimated Value: New (retail): $358.00
                    Excellent: $270.00
                    Very good: $215.00

Smith & Wesson Model 60 Chiefs Special Stainless

Same as Model 36 Chiefs special except: satin finish stainless steel construction 2" barrel only; round butt grip; approximate wt. 20 oz. Made from about 1965 to present.

Estimated Value: New (retail): $386.00
                    Excellent: $290.00
                    Very good: $230.00

Smith & Wesson Model 40
Centennial Hammerless

Smith & Wesson Model 49
Bodyguard

Smith & Wesson Model 42
Centennial Airweight

Smith & Wesson Model 649

Smith & Wesson Model 38
Bodyguard Airweight

Smith & Wesson Model 53

Smith & Wesson Model 40 Centennial Hammerless

Same as Model 36 Chiefs Special except: concealed hammer; frame extends over hammer area; 2" barrel; double action only; grip safety located on rear of grip. Made from about 1952 to 1974.

Estimated Value: Excellent: $275.00
                       Very good: $220.00

Smith & Wesson Model 42 Centennial Airweight

Same as Model 40 Centennial except: light alloy frame; approximate wt. 13 oz. Made from about 1954 to 1974.

Estimated Value: Excellent: $290.00
                       Very good: $230.00

Smith & Wesson Model 38 Bodyguard Airweight

Same as Model 36 Chiefs Special except: light alloy frame; shrouded hammer; approximate weight 15 oz.; 2" barrel only. Produced from about 1955 to present. Add 3% for nickel finish.

Estimated Value: New (retail): $379.00
                       Excellent: $285.00
                       Very good: $225.00

Smith & Wesson Model 49 Bodyguard

Same as Model 38 Bodyguard Airweight except: steel frame; approximate weight 21 oz. Manufactured from about 1959 to present. Nickel finish discontinued late 1980's.

Estimated Value: New (retail): $359.00
                       Excellent: $270.00
                       Very good: $215.00

Smith & Wesson Model 649

Similar to the Model 49 Bodyguard except stainless steel.

Estimated Value: New (retail): $408.00
                       Excellent: $305.00
                       Very good: $245.00

Smith & Wesson Model 53 22 Jet Magnum

Caliber: 22 Rem. Jet center fire & 22 short, long, long rifle by using chamber inserts & repositioning floating firing pin of hammer

Action: Single & double; exposed hammer; solid frame

Cylinder: 6-shot swing out; simultaneous manual ejector; cylinder release on left side of frame

Barrel: 4", 6", or 8⅜"

Sights: Ramp front; adjustable rear

Finish: Blued; checkered walnut target grips

Length Overall: 9¼" to 13⅝"

Approximate wt.: 38 to 42 oz.

Comments: Made from about 1961 to 1974. Could be fitted with 22 caliber cylinder. Add $100.00 for extra cylinder.

Estimated Value: Excellent: $550.00
                       Very good: $440.00

Smith & Wesson Model 29

Smith & Wesson Model 63

Smith & Wesson Model 29 44 Magnum

Caliber: 44 magnum & 44 Special
Action: Single & Double; exposed hammer; solid frame
Cylinder: 6-shot swing out; simultaneous manual ejector; release on left side of frame
Barrel: 4", 6", 8⅜", or 10⅝" ribbed
Sights: Ramp front; adjustable rear
Finish: Blued or nickel checkered wood grips
Length Overall: 9⅜" to 13¾"
Approximate wt.: 44 to 49 oz.
Comments: Made from about 1956 to present. Add 2% for 8⅜" or nickel finish; Add 11% for 10⅝" barrel; Add $40.00 for presentation box.
Estimated Value: New (retail): $482.00
    Excellent: $360.00
    Very good: $290.00

Smith & Wesson Model 63 1977 22/32 Kit Gun

Caliber: 22 long rifle
Action: Single & double; exposed hammer
Cylinder: 6-shot swing out
Barrel: 4"
Sights: Adjustable micrometer square notch rear, red ramp front
Finish: Stainless steel, satin finish; checkered walnut grips
Length Overall: 9⅜"
Approximate wt.: 24½ oz.
Comments: Made from 1977 to present.
Estimated Value: New (retail): $402.00
    Excellent: $300.00
    Very good: $240.00

Smith & Wesson Model 581 Distinguished Service Magnum

Caliber: 357 magnum & 38 Special
Action: Single & double; exposed hammer; solid frame
Cylinder: 6-shot swing out; simultaneous manual ejector; release on left side of frame
Barrel: 4" or 6" heavy barrel with full length ejector shroud. 4" barrel only after mid 1980's.
Sights: Serrated ramp front, fixed rear
Finish: Blued or nickel; checkered walnut magna service grips
Length Overall: 9¾" to 11¾"
Approximate wt.: 42 to 44 oz.
Comments: Smith & Wesson's new "L" frame revolver. It is slightly larger than the K frame which permits it to accommodate a sturdier cylinder. Introduced in 1982. Nickel finish discontinued late 1980's.
Estimated Value: Excellent: $275.00
    Very good: $220.00

Smith & Wesson Model 547
Military & Police

Smith & Wesson Model 681 Distinguished Service Magnum

Similar to the Model 581 except with satin stainless steel finish.
Estimated Value: Excellent: $280.00
    Very good: $225.00

Smith & Wesson Model 547 Military & Police

Caliber: 9mm Parabellum
Action: Single & double; exposed hammer; solid frame
Cylinder: 6-shot swing out; simultaneous manual ejector; release on left side of frame
Barrel: 3" or 4" heavy barrel
Sights: Fixed rear, serrated ramp front
Finish: Blued; checkered walnut round butt grips with 3" barrel & square butt with 4" barrrel
Length Overall: 8¼" to 9¼"
Approximate wt.: 32 to 34 oz.
Comments: A 9mm revolver built on a K frame that features a unique new extraction system for positive extraction of the 9mm cartridge. Made from about 1981 to mid 1980's.
Estimated Value: Excellent: $260.00
    Very good: $210.00

Smith & Wesson Model 629

Same as the Model 29 except with a satin stainless steel finish. Add 3% for 8⅜" barrel; Add $40.00 for presentation box. 10⅝" barrel not available.
Estimated Value: New (retail): $510.00
    Excellent: $385.00
    Very good: $305.00

Smith & Wesson Model 586 Distinguished Combat Magnum

Caliber: 357 magnum & 38 Special
Action: Single & double; exposed hammer; solid frame
Cylinder: 6-shot swing out; simultaneous manual ejector; cylinder release on left side
Barrel: 4", 6" or 8⅜" heavy barrel with a full length ejector shroud
Sights: Red ramp front, micrometer click rear adjustable for windage & elevation
Finish: Blued or nickel; checkered Goncalo Alves target grips
Length Overall: 9¾" to 13¾"
Approximate wt.: 42 to 46 oz.
Comments: Smith & Wesson's new "L" frame revolver. It is slightly larger than the K frame which permits it to accommodate a sturdier cylinder; introduced in 1982; Add 3% for nickel finish; 9% for adjustable front sight; 5% for 8⅜" barrel.
Estimated Value: New (retail): $401.00
Excellent: $300.00
Very good: $240.00

Smith & Wesson Model 586 Distinguished Combat Magnum

Smith & Wesson Model 686 Distinguished Combat Magnum

Similar to the Model 586 except with satin stainless steel finish. Add 2% for target grips; 7% for adjustable front sight; 6% for 8⅜" barrel. Also available with 2½" barrel.
Estimated Value: New (retail): $422.00
Excellent: $315.00
Very good: $255.00

Smith & Wesson Model 3913 (Lady Smith)

Smith & Wesson Model 625-2

Smith & Wesson Model 3914

Smith & Wesson Model 625-2

Caliber: 45ACP
Action: Single & double; exposed hammer; solid frame
Cylinder: 6-shot swing out; simultaneous manual ejector
Barrel: 3", 4", 5"; full length ejector housing under barrel
Sights: Serrated black ramp front & micrometer adjustable rear
Finish: Stainless steel; Pachmayr Gripper round butt grips
Length Overall: 8⅜", 9⅜", 10⅜"
Approximate wt.: 41, 43, & 46 oz.
Comments: Introduced in 1989.
Estimated Value: New (retail): $535.00
Excellent: $400.00
Very good: $320.00

Smith & Wesson Model 3913 (Lady Smith)

Caliber: 9mm Luger Parabellum
Action: Double action, semi-automatic with bobbed hammer & ambidextrous safety
Magazine: 8-shot clip
Barrel: 3½"
Sights: Post with white dot front sight; fixed rear with two white dots
Finish: Stainless steel slide, black Debrin one-piece wrap around grips
Length Overall: 6¾"
Approximate wt.: 25 oz.
Comments: Introduced in 1989. A small compact double action 9mm automatic specially designed for the female shooter.
Estimated Value: New (retail): $541.00
Excellent: $405.00
Very good: $325.00

Smith & Wesson Model 3914

Same as the Model 3913 except blued finish carbon steel slide & alloy frame with grey Debrin one-piece wrap around grips. Introduced in 1989.
Estimated Value: New (retail) $493.00
Excellent: $370.00
Very good: $325.00

Smith & Wesson Model 36 Lady Smith

Caliber: 38 special
Action: Single & double action with exposed hammer; solid frame
Cylinder: 5-shot swing out; simultaneous manual ejector
Barrel: 2", 3" heavy barrel
Sights: Serrated front; fixed notch rear
Finish: Blued; 2" barrel has smooth wood grips; 3" heavy barrel has smooth wood combat style grips
Length Overall: 6¼" (2" barrel); 7⅜" (3" barrel)
Approximate wt.: 20 oz. (2" barrel); 23 oz. (3" barrel)
Comments: Introduced in 1989. Add 8% for Morocco-grain carrying case.
Estimated Value: New (retail): $352.00
Excellent: $265.00
Very good: $210.00

Smith & Wesson Model 36
Lady Smith

Smith & Wesson Model 60
Lady Smith

Smith & Wesson Model 60 Lady Smith

Same as the Model 36 except all stainless steel. Introduced in 1989. Add 7% for Morrocco-grain carrying case.
Estimated Value: New (retail): $400.00
Excellent: $300.00
Very good: $240.00

Smith & Wesson Model 16

Caliber: 32 S&W or 32 magnum
Action: Single & double; exposed hammer; solid frame
Cylinder: 6-shot swing out; simultaneous manual ejector
Barrel: 4", 6", 8⅜"; full length ejector rod housing.
Sights: Patridge ramp front sight; S&W micrometer adjustable rear
Finish: Blued with square butt Goncalo Alves combat style grips
Length Overall: 9⅛" (4 barrel); 11⅛" (6" barrel); 13½" (8⅜" barrel)
Approximate wt.: 42, 47, & 54 oz.
Comments: Introduced in 1989. Add 3% for 6" barrel; add 4% for 8⅜" barrel; add 7% for target trigger & target hammer.
Estimated Value: New (retail): $368.00
Excellent: $275.00
Very good: $220.00

Smith & Wesson Model 640

Caliber: 38 Special
Action: Double action only; concealed hammer; solid frame
Cylinder: 5-shot swing out; simultaneous manual ejector
Barrel: 2"
Sights: Ramp front; fixed square notch rear
Finish: Stainless steel with smooth Goncalo Alves round butt grips
Length Overall: 6¼"
Approximate wt.: 20 oz.
Comments: Introduced in 1990.
Estimated Value: New (retail): $408.00
Excellent: $300.00
Very good: $245.00

Smith & Wesson Model 16

Smith & Wesson Model 617

Smith & Wesson Model 617

Caliber: 22 short, long, & long rifle
Action: Single & double action; exposed hammer; solid frame
Cylinder: 6-shot swing out; simultaneous manual ejector
Barrel: 4", 6", 8⅜", full length ejector housing under barrel
Sights: Ramp front & micrometer adjustable rear
Finish: Stainless steel with square butt Goncalo Alves combat style grips
Length Overall: 9⅛", 11⅛", 13½"
Approximate wt.: 42, 48, 54 oz.
Comments: Introduced in 1990. Add 3% 8⅜" barrel; add 8% for target trigger & hammer.
Estimated Value: New (retail): $400.00
Excellent: $300.00
Very good: $240.00

Smith & Wesson Model 650 Service Kit Gun

Smith & Wesson Model 650 Service Kit Gun
Caliber: 22 magnum
Action: Single & double action, exposed hammer
Cylinder: 6-shot swing out, simultaneous ejector
Barrel: 3" heavy barrel
Sights: Serrated ramp front, fixed square notch rear
Finish: Satin stainless steel; checkered walnut round butt grips
Length Overall: 7"
Approximate wt.: 23½ oz.
Comments: A "J" frame revolver produced in mid 1980's.
Estimated Value:　Excellent:　$240.00
　　　　　　　　　　　Very good:　$190.00

Smith & Wesson Model 651 Kit Gun
Caliber: 22 magnum
Action: Double & single, exposed hammer
Clynder: 6-shot swing out, simultaneous ejector
Barrel: 4"
Sights: Red ramp front, adjustable micrometer click rear
Finish: Satin stainless steel; checkered walnut square butt grips
Length Overall: 8⅜"
Approximate wt.: 24½ oz.
Comments: A "J" frame revolver produced in mid 1980's.
Estimated Value:　Excellent:　$260.00
　　　　　　　　　　　Very good:　$200.00

Smith & Wesson Model 651 Kit Gun

Star

Star Model 1919 Pocket

Star Model CO Pocket

Star Model H

Star Model 1919 Pocket
Caliber: 25 ACP (6.35mm)
Action: Semi-automatic; exposed hammer
Magazine: 8-shot clip
Barrel: 2⅝"
Sights: Fixed
Finish: Blued; checkered walnut grips
Length Overall: 4⅞"
Approximate wt.: 16 oz.
Comments: Made from about 1919 to 1934. Distinguished by the safety at the top rear of the slide.
Estimated Value:　Excellent:　$190.00
　　　　　　　　　　　Very good:　$140.00

Star Model CO Pocket
Improved version of the 1919 Model; safety in front of left grip rather than top rear of slide; plastic grips; some engraved nickel plated models produced. Made from about 1934 to 1957. Add $20.00 for engraved nickel model.
Estimated Value:　Excellent:　$200.00
　　　　　　　　　　　Very good:　$160.00

Star Model H
Similar to Model CO pistol except: caliber 32 ACP; 9-shot clip; approximate wt. 20 oz. Made from about 1934 to 1941.
Estimated Value:　Excellent:　$165.00
　　　　　　　　　　　Very good:　$130.00

Star Model HN
Same as Model H except: caliber 380 ACP; 6-shot clip.
Estimated Value:　Excellent:　$175.00
　　　　　　　　　　　Very good:　$140.00

Star Model A

Star Model B

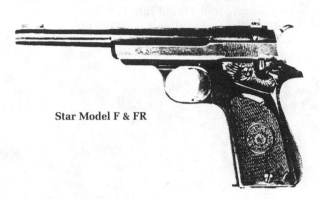

Star Model F & FR

Star Model E Pocket
Caliber: 25 ACP (6.35mm)
Action: Semi-automatic; exposed hammer
Magazine: 6-shot clip
Barrel: 2"
Sights: Fixed
Finish: Blued; checkered grips
Length Overall: 4"
Approximate wt.: 10 oz.
Comments: Small compact pocket pistol; safety located in front of left grip; no longer in production.
Estimated Value: Excellent: $180.00
Very good: $145.00

Star Model A & AS
Caliber: 9mm Luger, 9mm Bergman, 9mm Largo, 38 Super auto
Action: Semi-automatic; exposed hammer
Magazine: 8-shot clip
Barrel: 5"
Sights: Fixed
Finish: Blued; checkered walnut grips
Length Overall: 8"
Approximate wt.: 35 oz.
Comments: This handgun resembles the 1911 A1 Colt. Made from about 1924 to late 1970's.
Estimated Value: Excellent: $190.00
Very good: $150.00

Star Model B
Similar to Model A except: barrel lengths 4¼" or 6½"; caliber 9mm Parabellum only. Made from about 1924 to 1976.
Estimated Value: Excellent: $220.00
Very good: $175.00

Star Model B Super
Caliber: 9mm Parabellum
Action: Semi-automatic; exposed hammer
Magazine: 8-shot clip
Barrel: 5"
Sights: Blade front; fixed rear
Finish: Blued; all steel
Length Overall: 8¾"
Approximate wt.: 38 oz.
Comments: Made from 1970's to present; an improved version of the Model B with loaded chamber indicator; refined takedown & re-assembly system; a high visibility white dot sighting system. Add 9% for nickel finish.
Estimated Value: New (retail) $330.00
Excellent: $250.00
Very good: $200.00

Star Model F & FR
Caliber: 22 long rifle
Action: Semi-automatic; exposed hammer; manual safety at top rear of left grip
Magazine: 10-shot clip
Barrel: 4¼" (regular); 6" & 7" on Sport & Target models
Sights: Fixed; adjustable on Sport & Target models
Finish: Blued, chromed or chromed engraved; plastic grips
Length Overall: 7¼" to 10"
Approximate wt.: 24 to 32 oz..
Comments: Model F made from about 1942 to 1968. Model FR is improved version made from about 1968 to late 1970's. Add $10.00 for chrome model.
Estimated Value: Excellent: $160.00
Very good: $125.00

Star Model I (Police Model)
Caliber: 32 ACP
Action: Semi-automatic; exposed hammer
Magazine: 9-shot clip
Barrel: 4¾"
Sights: Fixed
Finish: Blued; plastic grips
Length Overall: 7½"
Approximate wt.: 25 oz.
Comments: Made from about 1934 to 1945; never imported to U.S.A.
Estimated Value: Excellent: $150.00
Very good: $120.00

Star Model IN
Same as Model I except: caliber 380 ACP; 8-shot clip.
Estimated Value: Excellent: $160.00
Very good: $130.00

Star Model M (Military)

Caliber: 380 ACP; 9mm Luger; 9mm Bergmann, 38 ACP, 45 ACP

Action: Semi-automatic; exposed hammer; manual safety

Magazine: 7-shot clip in 45 caliber, 8-shot clip in all other calibers

Barrel: 5"

Sights: Fixed

Finish: Blued; checkered grips

Length Overall: 8½"

Approximate wt.: 36 oz.

Comments: A modified version of the U.S. Government Colt 1911 45 automatic, made from about 1935 to present. Not imported into U.S.A.

Estimated Value: **Excellent:**   **$200.00**
Very good: **$150.00**

Star Model Super Star

Same as Model M except: 38 Super ACP, 9mm Parabellum & 38 ACP only; addition of disarming bolt; improved sights; magazine safety; indicator for number of unfired cartridges. Made from about 1942 to 1954.

Estimated Value: **Excellent:**   **$225.00**
Very good: **$180.00**

Star Model Super Star

Star Model 31P & 31PK

Star Firestar

Star Firestar

Caliber: 9mm Parabellum

Action: Double action, semi-automatic; exposed hammer; ambidextrous safety

Magazine: 7-shot clip

Barrel: 3½"

Sights: Combat style triple dot system; fully adjustable rear sight

Finish: all steel blued or all weather Starvel finish

Length Overall: 6½"

Approximate wt.: 30½ oz.

Comments: Introduced in 1990. Add 7% for Starvel finish.

Estimated Value: **New (retail):**   **$405.00**
Excellent: **$300.00**
Very good: **$240.00**

Star Model 31P & 31PK

Caliber: 9mm Parabellum

Action: Double action, semi-automatic; exposed hammer; ambidextrous safety & decocking lever

Magazine: 15-shot clip

Barrel: 3¾"

Sights: Blade front; adjustable rear

Finish: 31P has all steel construction in blued or Starvel finish; 31PK has alloy frame in blued finish only

Length Overall: 7¾"

Approximate wt.: 39½ oz. (31P) 30 oz. (31PK)

Comments: Introduced in 1990. Add 7% for all weather Starvel finish.

Estimated Value: **New (retail):**   **$535.00**
Excellent: **$400.00**
Very good: **$320.00**

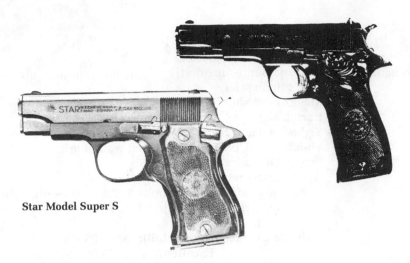

Star Model Super S

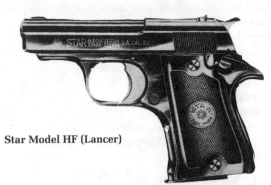

Star Model Super SI

Star Model HF (Lancer)

Star Model Super SM

Star Model S

Caliber: 38 ACP
Action: Semi-automatic; exposed hammer; manual safety
Magazine: 7-shot clip
Barrel: 4"
Sights: Fixed
Finish: Blued or chromed; engraved; plastic grips
Length Overall: 6½"
Approximate wt.: 20 oz.
Comments: A scaled-down modification of the Colt 1911 45 Automatic. Made from about 1941 to present. Not imported into U.S.A. since 1968.
Estimated Value: Excellent: $180.00
Very good: $145.00

Star Model SI

Same as Model S except: caliber 32 ACP; 8-shot clip.
Estimated Value: Excellent: $170.00
Very good: $135.00

Star Model Super S

Same as Model S except: addition of disarming bolt; improved luminous sights; magazine safety; indicator for number of unfired cartridges. This model was discontinued in 1954.
Estimated Value: Excellent: $190.00
Very good: $155.00

Star Model Super SI

Same as Model Super S except: caliber 32 ACP; 8-shot clip.
Estimated Value: Excellent: $185.00
Very good: $150.00

Star Model DK (Starfire)

Caliber: 380 ACP
Action: Semi-automatic; exposed hammer; manual safety at top rear of left grip
Magazine: 6-shot clip
Barrel: 5"
Sights: Fixed
Finish: Blued; checkered plastic grips
Length Overall: 5½"
Approximate wt.: 16 oz.
Comments: Made from about 1958 to present. Never imported into U.S.A.
Estimated Value: Excellent: $200.00
Very good: $160.00

Star Model CU (Starlet)

Caliber: 25 ACP
Action: Semi-automatic; exposed hammer
Magazine: 8-shot clip
Barrel: 2⅜"
Sights: Fixed
Finish: Blued or chromed slide; black, gray, gold, blue or green receiver; checkered plastic grips
Length Overall: 4¾"
Approximate wt.: 12 oz.
Comments: Imported from about 1957 to 1968. Manual safety catch at top rear of left grip. Alloy frame.
Estimated Value: Excellent: $175.00
Very good: $140.00

Star Model HF (Lancer)

Basically same as Model CU Starlet except: caliber 22 long rifle; 3" barrel; 5½" overall length.
Estimated Value: Excellent: $180.00
Very good: $145.00

Star Model Super SM

Caliber: 380 ACP
Action: Semi-automatic; exposed hammer
Magazine: 9-shot clip
Barrel: 4"
Sights: Blade front; rear adjustable for windage
Finish: Blued or chrome; checkered wood grips
Length Overall: 6¾"
Approximate wt.: 21 oz.
Comments: Made from about 1970 to late 1970's. Add 4% for chrome model.
Estimated Value: Excellent: $220.00
Very good: $175.00

Star Model 28
Caliber: 9mm Parabellum
Action: Semi-automatic; double action; exposed hammer
Magazine: 15-shot clip
Barrel: 4¼"
Sights: Notched partridge front, adjustable rear
Finish: Blued; checkered plastic grips
Length Overall: 8"
Approximate wt.: 40 oz.
Comments: Made from 1982 to 1985.
Estimated Value: Excellent: $315.00
                      Very good: $240.00

Star Model 30PK
An improved version of the Model 28 with alloy frame & slightly shorter length; 15-shot magazine; combat style trigger guard.
Estimated Value: Excellent: $380.00
                      Very good: $305.00

Star Model 30 M
Similar to the Model 30PK with steel frame & greater sight plane.
Estimated Value: New (retail): $535.00
                      Excellent: $400.00
                      Very good: $320.00

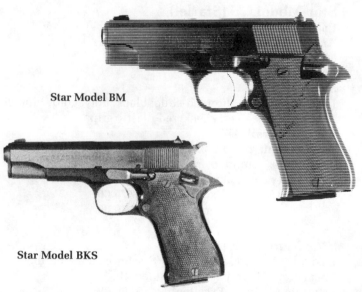

Star Model BM

Star Model BKS

Star Model BKS, BKM
Caliber: 9mm Parabellum
Action: Semi-automatic; exposed hammer; manual thumb safety
Magazine: 8-shot clip
Barrel: 4½"
Sights: Fixed
Finish: Blued; chrome; checkered walnut grips
Length Overall: 7¼"
Approximate wt.: 26 oz.
Comments: Made from about 1970 to present. Alloy frame; resembles Colt 1911. Add 4% for chrome model.
Estimated Value: New (retail): $395.00
                      Excellent: $295.00
                      Very good: $235.00

Star Model BM
Similar to the Model BKM without alloy frame, weighs 35 oz. Add $15.00 for chrome finish; add 13% for Starvel weather resistant finish.
Estimated Value: New (retail): $375.00
                      Excellent: $280.00
                      Very good: $225.00

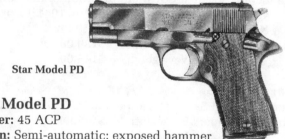

Star Model PD

Star Model PD
Caliber: 45 ACP
Action: Semi-automatic; exposed hammer
Magazine: 6-shot clip
Barrel: 4"
Sights: Ramp front; adjustable rear
Finish: Blued; chrome available until early 1980's; checkered wood grips; Starvel weather resistant finish available 1990.
Length Overall: 7"
Approximate wt.: 25 oz.
Comments: Made from about 1975 to present. Add 3% for chrome model; add 10% for Starvel finish
Estimated Value: New (retail): $450.00
                      Excellent: $340.00
                      Very good: $270.00

Sterling

Sterling Model 283

Sterling Model 283
Caliber: 22 long rifle
Action: Semi-automatic; exposed hammer; adjustable trigger & a rear lock safety
Magazine: 10-shot clip
Barrel: 4½", 6" or 8" heavy bull barrel
Sights: Blade front; click adjustable rear
Finish: Blued; checkered plastic grips
Length Overall: 9", 10½" or 12½"
Approximate wt.: 36 to 40 oz.
Comments: All steel construction. Made from about 1970 to 1972. Also known as Target 30 Model.
Estimated Value: Excellent: $150.00
                      Very good: $120.00

Sterling Model 284

Same as Model 283 automatic pistol except: lighter tapered barrel, also know as Target 300L Model. Made from about 1970 to 1972.

Estimated Value: Excellent: $140.00
Very good: $115.00

Sterling Model 285

Same as Model 283 automatic pistol except: ramp front sight, fixed rear sight; made in 4½" heavy barrel only; non-adjustable trigger. Made from about 1970 to 1972. Also known as Husky Model.

Estimated Value: Excellent: $135.00
Very good: $110.00

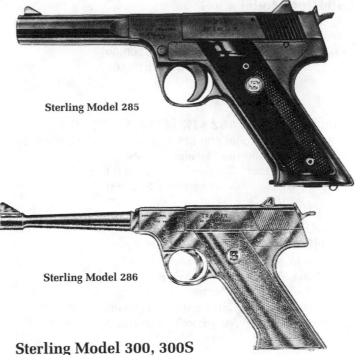

Sterling Model 285

Sterling Model 286

Same as Model 283 automatic pistol except: ramp front sight, fixed rear sight; made in 4½" & 6" tapered barrel only; non-adjustable trigger. Also known as Trapper Model. Made from about 1970-1972.

Estimated Value: Excellent: $125.00
Very good: $100.00

Sterling Model 286

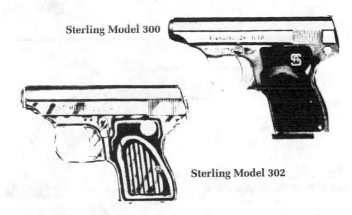

Sterling Model 300

Sterling Model 302

Sterling Model 400 Automatic Pistol

Caliber: 380 ACP
Action: Semi-automatic; double action; exposed hammer; safety locks firing pin
Magazine: 6-shot clip
Barrel: 3½"
Sights: Ramp front, adjustable rear
Finish: Blued or nickel; checkered grips
Length Overall: 6½"
Approximate wt.: 24 oz.
Comments: All steel construction. Made from about 1973 to late 1970's. Replaced by Mark II 400. Add 10% for nickel finish.

Estimated Value: Excellent: $175.00
Very good: $140.00

Sterling MK II 400 & MK II400S

Similar to 400 except streamlined & lightweight, also 32 ACP. Add 5% for nickel finish; 15% for stainless steel. (400S MK II)

Estimated Value: Excellent: $180.00
Very good: $145.00

Sterling Model 300, 300S

Caliber: 25 ACP
Action: Semi-automatic blow-back action; concealed hammer
Magazine: 6-shot clip
Barrel: 2½"
Sights: None
Finish: Blued, nickel or stainless steel (after 1975) with cycolac grips
Length Overall: 4½"
Approximate wt.: 13 oz.
Comments: All steel construction. Made from about 1972 to mid 1980's. Add 10% for nickel finish; 20% for stainless steel.

Estimated Value: Excellent: $90.00
Very good: $65.00

Sterling Model 302, 302S

Same as Model 300 Automatic Pistol except caliber 22 long rifle. Model 302S is stainless steel; add 20% for stainless steel.

Estimated Value: Excellent: $95.00
Very good: $70.00

Sterling Model MKII 400

Sterling Model 400S

Similar to Model 400 except constructed of stainless steel. Made from about 1976 to late 1970's.

Estimated Value: Excellent: **$200.00**
Very good: **$150.00**

Sterling Model 402 MK II, 402S MK II

Similar to the Model 400 MK II in 32 ACP caliber. Model 402S MK II is stainless steel; add 15%.

Estimated Value: Excellent: **$165.00**
Very good: **$125.00**

Sterling Model 402

Similar to Model 400 automatic pistol except: caliber 22 long rifle, 8-shot clip magazine. Made from about 1973 to 1975. Add $10.00 for nickel finish.

Estimated Value: Excellent: **$160.00**
Very good: **$120.00**

Sterling Model X Caliber

Caliber: 22 short, long, long rifle, 22 mag., 357 mag., 44 mag.
Action: Single action; single shot
Magazine: None
Barrel: 8" or 20" heavy octagonal; a caliber change is made by changing barrel
Sights: Ramp front, adjustable rear; tapped for scope mounts
Finish: Blued; smooth wood, finger-grooved grips & small lipped forearm
Length Overall: 13" with 8" barrel
Approximate wt.: 54 to 62 oz.
Comments: A silhouette style single shot pistol with interchangeable barrels for caliber change. Add 50% for each additional barrel.

Estimated Value: Excellent: **$175.00**
Very good: **$140.00**

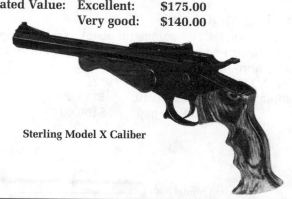

Sterling Model X Caliber

Stevens

Stevens Tip-Up Pocket

Caliber: 22 short, 30 RF (to 1902)
Action: Single with sheath trigger (spur)
Cylinder: None; single shot with tip-up barrel
Barrel: 3½"; part octagon
Sights: Blade front; notch in frame rear
Finish: Blued barrel; nickel plated frame to 1912; blued frame after 1912; varnished walnut square butt grips
Length Overall: 6¼"
Approximate wt.: 10 oz.
Comments: Made from about 1888 to 1915. Marked "J Stevens A. & T. Co."

Estimated Value: Excellent: **$175.00**
Very good: **$135.00**

Stevens Diamond Target

Caliber: 22 RF long rifle (black power 1888-1912); 22 long rifle (smokeless powder 1912-1915)
Action: Single; sheath trigger (spur)
Cylinder: None; single shot with tip-up
Barrel: 6", 10"; part octagon
Sights: Globe or bead front; peep or adjustable rear
Finish: Blued barrel; nickel plated iron frame to 1912; varnished long walnut square grips
Length Overall: 9½" to 13½"
Approximate wt.: 10 to 13 oz.
Comments: Made from about 1888 to 1915. Marked "J. Stevens A. & T. Co." Approximately 132,000 produced.

Estimated Value: Excellent: **$225.00**
Very good: **$170.00**

Stevens Tip-Up Pocket

Stevens Diamond Target

Stevens Hunter's Pet

Caliber: 22 long rifle, 25 RF, 32 RF, 38 long RF, 44 long RF, 38-40, 44-40, 38-35, 44-50, 24 gauge
Action: Single with sheath trigger (spur)
Cylinder: None; single shot with pivoted barrel
Barrel: 18", 20", 22" or 24" octagon & half octagon
Sights: Adjustable for elevation; also some had Steven's Vernier peep sight attached to back strap
Finish: Blued barrel; nickel plated frame & detachable skeleton stock; smooth, varnished walnut, square butt grips
Length Overall: 22" to 28"
Approximate wt.: 5¾ lbs.
Comments: Serial numbers in 4,000 to 13,000 range. Approximately 8,000 produced from about 1888 to 1907.

Estimated Value: Excellent: **$450.00**
Very good: **$350.00**

Stevens Lord Gallery

Caliber: 22 long rifle, 25 RF (smokeless powder)
Action: Single; tip up barrel
Magazine: None; single shot
Barrel: Octagon breech; 6", 8" , 10"
Sights: Bead front; stepped elevator rear
Finish: Blued barrel; plated frame; varnished walnut grips with base butt cap; blued frame after 1912
Length Overall: 9¼" to 13¼"
Approximate wt.: 24 to 28 oz.
Comments: Made from about 1907 to 1915. Marked "J Stevens A. & T. Co."
Estimated Value: Excellent: $235.00
Very good: $180.00

Stevens Lord Gallery

Stevens "Off-Hand" 1907-1915

Stevens "Off-Hand" 1907-1915

Caliber: 22 long rifle, 25 RF, smokeless powder
Action: Single, tip up barrel
Cylinder: None; single shot
Barrel: Octagon breech; 6", 8", 10"
Sights: Bead front; stepped elevator rear
Finish: Blued barrel; plated frame; varnished walnut grips with base butt cap; blued frame after 1912
Length Overall: 9¼" to 13¼"
Approximate wt.: 24 to 28 oz.
Comments: Made from about 1907 to 1915. Marked "J. Stevens A. & T. Co."
Estimated Value: Excellent: $275.00
Very good: $220.00

Stevens Off Hand 410

Stevens Single-Shot Target

Stevens Off Hand 1923-1939

Caliber: 22 long rifle
Action: Single; tip up barrel
Cylinder: None; single shot
Barrel: Octagon breech; 6", 8", 20",12¼"
Sights: Bead front; rear adjustable for elevation
Finish: Blued barrel & frame, also plated frame; walnut grips with butt cap
Length Overall: 9¼" to 15½"
Approximate wt.: 24 to 34 oz.
Comments: Made from about mid 1920's to late 1930's.
Estimated Value: Excellent: $260.00
Very good: $200.00

Stevens Off Hand 410

Caliber: 410 gauge (2½")
Action: Single; tip-up barrel
Cylinder: None; single shot
Barrel: Octagon breech; choked 8" or 12¼" barrel
Sights: Shot gun front sight
Finish: Blued barrel & frame, also plated frame; walnut grips with butt cap
Length Overall: 11¼" to 15½"
Approximate wt.: 23 to 25 oz.
Comments: Made from about 1925 to 1935. Marked "J Stevens Arms Company."
Estimated Value: Excellent: $250.00
Very good: $190.00

Stevens Single-Shot Target

Caliber: 22 long rifle
Action: Single; tip up barrel; round knurled cocking piece
Cylinder: None; single shot
Barrel: Round, 8"
Sights: Partridge front; adjustable windage rear
Finish: Blued (blackish blue color); black composition checkered grips
Length Overall: 11½"
Approximate wt.: 37 oz.
Comments: A single shot target pistol with configuration of an automatic pistol. Made from about 1919 to 1942. Approximately 10,000 produced. The 1919 pistols had serial numbers from 1 to approximately 5,000 range with "Pat. App'd For" on barrel. After 1920 marked "Pat'd April 27, 1920." All pistols marked "J. Stevens Arms Company."
Estimated Value: Excellent: $265.00
Very good: $200.00

Steyr

Roth-Steyr Self-Loading Pistol
Caliber: 8mm Roth-Steyr
Action: Semi-automatic concealed striker; locked breech design uses rotation of barrel by cam action to unlock barrel when fired; the striker is cocked by the recoil, but the trigger action has to pull it further back before it will release to fire
Magazine: 10-shot non-detachable; usually loaded by a charger from the top
Barrel: 5⅛"
Sights: Fixed
Finish: Blued; checkered wood grips
Length Overall: 9⅛"
Approximate wt.: 36 lbs.
Comments: Adopted by the Austro-Hungarian Cavalry in 1907. This is one of the earliest forms of successful locked-breech pistols.
Estimated Value: **Excellent:**   **$150.00**
          Very good: **$120.00**

Steyr Model 1909 Pocket Automatic Pistol
Caliber: 32 ACP
Action: Semi-automatic; concealed hammer; blow-back action; early models have no extractor (empty case is blown out by gas after the breech-block is pushed open by firing); barrel can be tipped down for cleaning, using as single shot pistol, or for removing unfired cartridge
Magazine: 7-shot clip
Barrel: 3½"
Sights: Fixed
Finish: Blued; checkered wood grips
Length Overall: 6½"
Approximate wt.: 23 oz.
Comments: Made in both Austria & Belgium. The Austrian variety was a finer pistol from the standpoint of manufacture & reliability. Add $30.00 for later model with extractor.
Estimated Value: **Excellent:**   **$175.00**
          Very good: **$135.00**

Steyr-Solothurn Pocket Model Automatic Pistol
Similar to the Steyr model 1909 except: a modified version; uses extractors to remove empty cases; production started about 1934 from Solothurn factory in Switzerland.
Estimated Value: **Excellent:**   **$180.00**
          Very good: **$140.00**

Steyr Vest Pocket (Baby) Automatic

Steyr Vest Pocket (Baby) Automatic Pistol
Caliber: 25 ACP
Action: Semi-automatic; concealed hammer; blow-back action; early models have no extractor (empty case is blown out by gas after the breech block is pushed open by firing); barrel can be tipped down for cleaning, using as a single shot pistol or for removing unfired cartridges
Magazine: 6-shot clip
Barrel: 2"
Sights: Fixed
Finish: Blued; hard rubber checkered grips
Length Overall: 4½"
Approximate wt.: 12 oz.
Comments: First manufactured about 1908. Add $10.00 for later model with extractor.
Estimated Value: **Excellent:**   **$160.00**
          Very good: **$120.00**

Steyr Model 1912 Military
Caliber: 9mm Steyr
Action: Semi-automatic; exposed hammer; short recoil; locked breech action (barrel rotates to unlock breech when gun is fired)
Magazine: 8-shot non-detachable; loaded from top singly or by using a strip clip
Barrel: 5"
Sights: Fixed
Finish: Blued; checkered wood grips
Length Overall: 8½"
Approximate wt.: 33 oz.
Comments: Made from about 1911 until after World War I; also referred to as Model 1911 or Steyr-Hahn; adopted by the Austro-Hungarian Army in 1912.
Estimated Value: **Excellent:**   **$300.00**
          Very good: **$240.00**

Steyr Nazi-Proofed
Same as Steyr Model 1912 except: converted to fire the 9mm Luger cartridge during World War II & marked "P-08" on left side of slide.
Estimated Value: **Excellent:**   **$325.00**
          Very good: **$260.00**

Steyr Model GB
Caliber: 9mm Parabellum
Action: Gas delayed blow-back action, semi-automatic, double action
Magazine: 18-shot clip
Barrel: 5½"
Sights: Fixed
Finish: Black crinkled with blued slide; plastic checkered grips & trigger guard
Length Overall: 8½"
Approximate wt.: 39 oz.
Comments: Produced in the mid 1980's.
Estimated Value: **Excellent:**   **$445.00**
          Very good: **$335.00**

Taurus

Taurus Model 58, PT58
Caliber: 380 ACP
Action: Semi-automatic, double action; exposed round spur hammer
Magazine: 13-shot staggered clip
Barrel: 4"
Sights: Blade front, notched bar rear
Finish: Blued or satin nickel; smooth walnut grips
Length Overall: 7"
Approximate wt.: 30 oz.
Comments: Made in Brazil; introduced in 1988; add 5% for satin nickel finish.
Estimated Value: New (retail): $399.00
                       Excellent: $300.00
                       Very good: $240.00

Taurus Model PT92AF, PT99AF
Caliber: 9mm Parabellum
Action: Semi-automatic, double action; exposed round spur hammer
Magazine: 15-shot clip
Barrel: 5"
Sights: Blade front, notched bar rear (PT92AF); blade front, micrometer adjustable rear (PT99AF)
Finish: Blued or satin nickel; smooth walnut grips
Length Overall: 8½"
Approximate wt.: 34 oz.
Comments: Currently manufactured in Brazil. Add 3½% for satin nickel finish, 7% for PT99AF.
Estimated Value: New (retail): $446.00
                       Excellent: $335.00
                       Very good: $270.00

Taurus Model 65
Caliber: 357 magnum or 38 Special
Action: Single or double action; exposed hammer
Cylinder: 6-shot swing out, simultaneous ejector
Barrel: 3" or 4" heavy barrel
Sights: Ramp front, square notch rear
Finish: Royal blue or satin nickel; checkered walnut grips
Length Overall: 8½" or 9½"
Approximate wt.: 34 oz.
Comments: Currently produced in Brazil. Add 5% for satin nickel finish.
Estimated Value: New (retail): $235.00
                       Excellent: $175.00
                       Very good: $140.00

Taurus Model 66
Similar to the Model 65 except: 3", 4", & 6" barrel lengths; serrated ramp front sight & micrometer adjustable rear; blued, satin nickel or stainless steel; checkered walnut target grip on 6"; add 4½% for satin nickel finish; add 27% for stainless steel.
Estimated Value: New (retail): $258.00
                       Excellent: $195.00
                       Very good: $155.00

Taurus Model 669
Same as the Model 66 except: 4" or 6" barrel, full shroud under barrel; blued or stainless steel only; introduced in 1988. Add 26% for stainless steel.
Estimated Value: New (retail): $268.00
                       Excellent: $200.00
                       Very good: $160.00

Taurus Model 73
Caliber: 32 long
Action: Single or double action; exposed hammer
Magazine: 6-shot, swing out; simultaneous ejector
Barrel: 3" heavy barrel
Sights: Fixed
Finish: Blued or satin nickel
Length Overall: 7¾"
Approximate wt.: 20 oz.
Comments: Currently produced in Brazil. Add 10% for satin nickel finish.
Estimated Value: New (retail): $210.00
                       Excellent: $155.00
                       Very good: $125.00

Taurus Model PT92AF

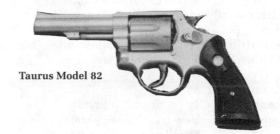

Taurus Model 82

Taurus Model 80, 82

Caliber: 38 Special
Action: Single or double action; exposed hammer
Cylinder: 6-shot, swing-out; simultaneous ejector
Barrel: 3" or 4"; standard barrel (Model 80); heavy barrel (Model 82)
Sights: Fixed
Finish: Blued or satin nickel; checkered walnut grips
Length Overall: 8⅛" or 9⅛"
Approximate wt.: 30 oz. (Model 80); 34 oz. (Model 82)
Comments: Currently produced in Brazil. Add 6½% for satin nickel finish.
Estimated Value: New (retail): $204.00
Excellent: $150.00
Very good: $120.00

Taurus Model 80, 82

Taurus Model 83

Similar to the Model 82 except: 4" heavy barrel only; ramp front sight & micrometer adjustable rear sight. Add 5½% for satin nickel finish.

Estimated Value: New (retail): $215.00
Excellent: $160.00
Very good: $130.00

Taurus Model 83

Taurus Model 85

Taurus Model 86 Target Master, 96 Target Scout

Taurus Model 86 Target Master, 96 Target Scout

Caliber: 38 Special (86); 22 (96)
Action: Single or double; exposed hammer
Cylinder: 6-shot, swing out; simultaneous ejector
Barrel: 6"
Sights: Partridge type front; micrometer adjustable rear
Finish: Blued; checkered walnut target grip
Length Overall: 11¼"
Approximate wt.: 34 oz.
Comments: Currently produced in Brazil.
Estimated Value: New (retail): $290.00
Excellent: $215.00
Very good: $175.00

Taurus Model 85

Caliber: 38 Special
Action: Single or double action; exposed hammer
Cylinder: 5-shot swing out, simultaneous ejector
Barrel: 2" or 3" heavy barrel
Sights: Fixed; serrated ramp front, notch rear
Finish: Royal blue, satin nickel; stainless steel
Length Overall: 6½" or 7½"
Approximate wt.: 21 oz.
Comments: Currently produced in Brazil. Add 7½% for satin nickel finish; add 26½% for stainless steel.
Estimated Value: New (retail): $223.00
Excellent: $165.00
Very good: $135.00

Thompson Center

Thompson Center Contender
Caliber: 22 long rifle to 45-70 Gov't.; over the years approximately 35 to 40 calibers were made including some wildcat calibers; It is presently made in 18 calibers: 22 long rifle, 22 Win. magnum, 22 Hornet, 222 Rem., 223 Rem., 270 Rem., 7mm TCU, 7x30 Waters, 30-30 Win., 32-20 Win., 357 magnum, 357 Rem. maximum, 35 Rem., 10mm auto, 44 magnum, 445 Super magnum, 45-70 Gov't., 45 Colt/410 gauge

Action: Single action with adjustable trigger; the frame will accommodate any caliber barrel & the hammer adjusts to rim fire or center fire ammunition

Cylinder: None, single shot

Barrel: 8¾" (discontinued in the early 1980's), 10" 14" (introduced in the late 1970's), 16¼" (introduced in 1990). In octagon or round; regular or bull barrel; plain or ventilated rib; the 45 Colt/410 gauge barrel has a removable internal choke to use for 410 gauge shot shells.

Sights: Ramp front, adjustable rear except ventilated rib has fixed sights

Finish: Blued; checkered or plain walnut grip & fore-end

Length Overall: 12½" to 20"

Approximate wt.: 38 to 60 oz., depending on barrel length

Comments: Made from about 1967 to present. Add 6% for internal choke & ventilated rib. Add 4% for 16" barrel

Estimated Value: New (retail): $345.00
Excellent: $260.00
Very good: $200.00

Thompson Center Contender

Thompson Center Contender Armour Alloy II
Similar to the Contender except the parts & barrels are not interchangeable with the standard model Contender. It has a special Armour Alloy II non-glare satin finish. Made in the following calibers: 22 long rifle, 223 Rem., 357 magnum, 357 Rem. maximum, 44 magnum, 7mm TCU, 7x30 Waters, 30-30 Win., 35 Rem., 45 Colt/410 gauge. The 45 Colt/410 gauge has a removable internal choke to use with regular 410 gauge shot shells in 10" bull barrel or ventilated rib barrel. All other calibers use 10" bull barrel or 14" bull barrel. Introduced in 1986 & discontinued in 1990. Add 5% for ventilated rib with internal choke. Add 3% for 14" barrel.

Estimated Value: Excellent: $300.00
Very good: $240.00

Thompson Center Contender Hunter
Caliber: 223 Rem., 7x30 Waters, 30-30 Win., 357 Rem. maximum, 35 Rem., 44 magnum, 45-70 Gov't.

Action: Single action; adjustable trigger

Cylinder: None, single shot

Barrel: 12" round with T/C Muzzle Tamer to reduce muzzle jump & recoil

Sights: 2.5x T/C recoil proof scope with lighted duplex reticle

Finish: Blued; smooth walnut grip with rubber insert in rear to cushion recoil; smooth walnut fore-end; sling swivel studs, QD swivels & nylon sling

Length Overall: 16"

Approximate wt.: 65 oz.

Comments: Introduced in 1990.

Estimated Value: New (retail): $595.00
Excellent: $445.00
Very good: $360.00

Walther

Walther Model 1 Vest Pocket
Caliber: 25 ACP

Action: Semi-automatic; concealed hammer

Magazine: 6-shot clip

Barrel: 2"

Sights: Fixed

Finish: Blued; checkered hard rubber grips

Length Overall: 4¼"

Approximate wt.: 10 oz.

Comments: Top section of slide is cut away from behind top sight to breech block face. Made from about 1908 to 1912.

Estimated Value: Excellent: $310.00
Very good: $245.00

Walther Model 2 Vest Pocket
Similar to Model 1 except: slide fully encloses the barrel; ejector port right side of slide; overall length 4¼"; approximately wt. 12 oz. Made from about 1909 to 1915.

Estimated Value: Excellent: $320.00
Very good: $255.00

Walther Model 3 Pocket
Caliber: 32 ACP

Action: Semi-automatic; concealed hammer

Magazine: 6-shot clip

Barrel: 2⅝"

Sights: Fixed

Finish: Blued; checkered hard rubber grips

Length Overall: 5"

Approximate wt.: 17 oz.

Comments: Made from about 1910 to 1918; ejector port on left side of slide.

Estimated Value: Excellent: $360.00
Very good: $285.00

Walther Model 4 Pocket

Similar to Model 3 except: larger in overall size; 3½" barrel; 6" overall; longer grip; 8-shot clip; a slide extension connected to forward end of the slide. Made from about 1910 to 1918.

Estimated Value: Excellent: $375.00
Very good: $300.00

Walther Model 5 Vest Pocket Pistol

Similar to Model 2 except: improved version with a better finish. Made from about 1913 to 1920.

Estimated Value: Excellent: $325.00
Very good: $260.00

Walther Model 6

Caliber: 9mm Parabellum
Action: Semi-automatic; concealed hammer
Magazine: 8-shot clip
Barrel: 4¾"
Sights: Fixed
Finish: Blued; hard rubber grips
Length Overall: 8¼"
Approximate wt.: 33 oz.
Comments: Made from about 1915 to 1917; ejection port on right side of slide.

Estimated Value: Excellent: $450.00
Very good: $340.00

Walther Model 7 Pocket

Caliber: 25 ACP
Action: Semi-automatic; concealed hammer
Magazine: 8-shot clip
Barrel: 3"
Sights: Fixed
Finish: Blued; checkered hard rubber grips
Length Overall: 5¼"
Approximate wt.: 13 oz.
Comments: Introduced in 1917, discontinued in 1918. Ejection port on right side of slide.

Estimated Value: Excellent: $360.00
Very good: $285.00

Walther Model 8 Pocket

Caliber: 25 ACP
Action: Semi-automatic; concealed hammer
Magazine: 8-shot clip
Barrel: 2⅞"
Sights: Fixed
Finish: Blued; checkered plastic grips
Length Overall: 5⅛"
Approximate wt.: 13 oz.
Comments: Made from about 1920 to 1945. Earlier models had takedown catch but later models used trigger guard as slide lock; a variety of special styles were made such as nickel or gold plated, engraved finishes with pearl or ivory grips. Special plated & engraved styles worth more.

Estimated Value: Excellent: $300.00
Very good: $230.00

Walther Model 8 Lightweight Pocket

Same as Model 8 except: aluminum alloy used for frame, making it lighter; approximately wt. 9 oz.

Estimated Value: Excellent: $325.00
Very good: $245.00

Walther Model 6 Vest Pocket

Caliber: 25 ACP
Action: Semi-automatic; concealed hammer
Magazine: 6-shot clip
Barrel: 2"
Sights: Fixed
Finish: Blued; checkered plastic grips
Length Overall: 4"
Approximate wt.: 9½ oz.
Comments: Made from about 1921 to 1945; a variety of special styles were made such as nickel or gold plated engraved finishes with pearl or ivory grips; top section of slide from front sight to breech block face is cut away. Special plated & engraved styles worth more.

Estimated Value: Excellent: $300.00
Very good: $240.00

Walther Model 4 Pocket

Walther Model 5 Vest Pocket Pistol

Walther Model 7 Pocket

Walther Model 6 Vest Pocket

Walther Model PP

Walther Model PPK

Walther Model PPK

Same as Model PP except: 3¼" barrel; 5¹⁵⁄₁₆" overall length; 7-shot magazine; approximately wt. 19 oz.; one piece wrap around grip. Made from about 1931 to 1945.

Estimated Value:	Regular Model	WWII Model
Excellent:	$450.00	$350.00
Very good:	$340.00	$265.00

Walther Models PP & PPK Lightweight

Same as Models PP & PPK except lighter in weight due to aluminum alloy frame.

Estimated Value:	Excellent:	$425.00
	Very good:	$325.00

Walther Model PPK/S (West German)

Same as Model PPK except: larger size to meet U.S.A. Treasury Dept. specifications in 1968; uses the slide & barrel of PPK Model mounted on the PP Model frame; overall length of about 6"; 8-shot magazine. Add 4% for 22 long rifle.

Estimated Value:	Excellent:	$380.00
	Very good:	$300.00

Walther Model PP Auto

Same as pre-World War II Model PP except produced in West Germany from about 1955 to present. Add 3% for 22 caliber or 380ACP.

Estimated Value:	New (retail):	$850.00
	Excellent:	$640.00
	Very good:	$510.00

Walther Model PPK Auto

Same as pre-World War II Model PPK except produced in West Germany from about 1955 to date. Importation into U.S.A. discontinued in 1968 due to restrictions imposed by the U.S. Treasury Dept.

Estimated Value:	Excellent:	$400.00
	Very good:	$300.00

Walther Model PPK Lightweight

Same as Model PPK except: lighter in weight due to use of aluminum alloy frame & not made in 380 caliber. Importation discontinued in 1968.

Estimated Value:	Excellent:	$450.00
	Very good:	$340.00

Walther Model PPK American

Similar to the Model PPK except manufactured in the United States in blue or stainless steel. Introduced in 1986.

Estimated Value:	New (retail):	$549.00
	Excellent:	$410.00
	Very good:	$330.00

Walther Model PP

Caliber: 22 long rifle, 25 ACP, 32 ACP or 380 ACP
Action: Semi-automatic; double action; exposed hammer; thumb safety that drops the hammer on blocked firing pin
Magazine: 8-shot clip
Barrel: 3¾"
Sights: Fixed
Finish: Blued; checkered plastic or checkered wood grips; steel back strap
Length Overall: 6⁹⁄₁₆"
Approximate wt.: 24 oz.
Comments: Made from about 1929 to 1945; also nickel, silver & gold plated engraved models with ivory & pearl grips were produced; first commercially successful double action automatic pistol; initially made in 32 ACP but later made in 22, 25 & 380 calibers; the center fire calibers were made with & without a signal pin to indicate a round in the chamber; World War II models had poorer finish & workmanship. Special plated & engraved models worth more.

Estimated Value:	Regular Model	WWII Model
Excellent:	$460.00	$360.00
Very good:	$350.00	$270.00

Walther Model PPK/S   **Walther Model P-5**

Walther Model PPK/S American

Caliber: 380 ACP
Action: Semi-automatic; double action; exposed hammer
Magazine: 7-shot clip
Barrel: 3¼"
Sights: Fixed
Finish: Blued or stainless steel; plastic grips
Length Overall: 6"
Approximate wt.: 23 oz.
Comments: An American-built model of the Walther PPK/S, introduced in the late 1970's.

Estimated Value:	New (retail):	$549.00
	Excellent:	$410.00
	Very good:	$330.00

Walther Model P-5

Caliber: 9mm Parabellum
Action: Semi-automatic; double action; exposed hammer
Magazine: 8-shot clip
Barrel: 3½"
Sights: Adjustable rear, blade front
Finish: Blued; plastic grips
Length Overall: 7"
Approximate wt.: 28 oz.
Comments: Introduced in 1980.

Estimated Value:	New (retail):	$895.00
	Excellent:	$675.00
	Very good:	$540.00

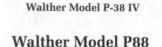

Walther Model HP

Walther Model HP

Caliber: 9mm Parabellum
Action: Semi-automatic; double action; exposed hammer
Magazine: 8-shot clip
Barrel: 5"
Sights: Fixed
Finish: Blued; checkered walnut or plastic grips
Length Overall: 8⅜"
Approximate wt.: 35 oz.
Comments: Well-made pistol, produced from about 1937 to 1945.
Estimated Value: Excellent: $950.00
Very good: $760.00

Walther P-38 Military

Similar to Model HP except: modified version of the Model HP adopted as the Offical German service arm in 1938 & produced until about 1945. A poorer quality mass-produced military pistol; some of the war-time models were of very loose fit & very rough finish.
Estimated Value: Excellent: $500.00
Very good: $400.00

Walther P-38 (West German)

Same as P-38 Military Model except: improved workmanship; use of aluminum alloy in construction of frame; calibers 22 long rifle, 30 Luger & 9mm Parabellum; approximate wt. 28 oz.; add 11% for 22 caliber.
Estimated Value: New (retail): $995.00
Excellent: $745.00
Very good: $600.00

Walther Model P-38 IV

Similar to the P-38 with strengthened slide, no dust cover & steel reinforced frame; adjustable rear sight.
Estimated Value: Excellent: $470.00
Very good: $350.00

Walther Model P-38 K

Similar to the Model P-38 IV with a 2¾" barrel.
Estimated Value: Excellent: $475.00
Very good: $345.00

Walther P-38

Walther Model P-38 IV

Walther Model P88

Caliber: 9mm Parabellum
Action: Double action, semi-automatic; exposed hammer
Magazine: 15-shot clip
Barrel: 4"
Sights: Rear adjustable for windage & elevation
Finish: Blued, non reflective matte finish; alloy frame; black plastic grips
Length Overall: 7⅜"
Approximate wt.: 31½" oz.
Comments: A combat-style handgun designed for ambidextrous use. Introduced in 1987. Produced in West Germany.
Estimated Value: New (retail): $1288.00
Excellent: $ 965.00
Very good: $ 775.00

Walther Model TPH

Caliber: 22 long rifle
Action: Semi-automatic, exposed hammer
Magazine: 6-shot clip, with finger rest
Barrel: 2¼"
Sights: Fixed
Finish: Stainless steel; black plastic grips
Length Overall: 5⅜"
Approximate wt.: 14 oz.
Comments: A scaled-down version of the Model PP-PPK series in 22 long rifle. Introduced in the late 1980's.
Estimated Value: New (retail): $419.00
Excellent: $315.00
Very good: $250.00

Webley

Webley 1906 Model Vest Pocket

Caliber: 25 ACP
Action: Semi-automatic; exposed hammer; grip safety in front of grip
Magazine: 6-shot clip
Barrel: 2⅛"
Sights: None
Finish: Blued; checkered hard rubber grips
Length Overall: 4¾"
Approximate wt.: 12 oz.
Comments: Made from about 1906 to 1940.
Estimated Value: Excellent: $190.00
Very good: $145.00

Welby 1906 Model
Vest Pocket

Webley & Scott 1909 Model Vest Pocket

Similar to 1906 except: ejection port in top of slide; concealed hammer; has fixed front & rear sights mounted on slide. Made from about 1909 to 1940.
Estimated Value: Excellent: $195.00
Very good: $150.00

Webley & Scott 9mm Military & Police

Caliber: 9mm Browning long
Action: Semi-sutomatic; exposed hammer; grip safety
Magazine: 8-shot clip
Barrel: 5¼"
Sights: Fixed
Finish: Blued; checkered plastic grips
Length Overall: 8"
Approximate wt.: 32 oz.
Comments: Made from about 1909 to 1930.
Estimated Value: Excellent: $500.00
Very good: $375.00

Webley & Scott 9mm Military & Police

Webley & Scott Mark I

Caliber: 455 Webley self-loading
Action: Semi-automatic; exposed hammer; grip safety
Magazine: 7-shot clip
Barrel: 5"
Sights: Fixed front; movable rear
Finish: Blued; checkered hard rubber or checkered walnut grips
Length Overall: 8½"
Approximate wt.: 39 oz.
Comments: Adopted by British Royal Navy & Marines in 1913. Made from about 1911 to 1931.
Estimated Value: Excellent: $360.00
Very good: $285.00

Webley & Scott Mark I No. 2

Similar to Mark I except: a slightly different version with fitted shoulder stock & adjustable rear sight; issued to the British Royal Flying Corps in 1915. Prices for gun with shoulder stock.
Estimated Value: Excellent: $750.00
Very good: $560.00

Webley & Scott 38

similar to Mark I except: a smaller modified version with concealed hammer; 8-shot magazine; 38 ACP caliber. Made from about 1910 to 1930.
Estimated Value: Excellent: $300.00
Very good: $225.00

Webley & Scott 1909 Model Single Shot Target

Caliber: 22 short, long, long rifle
Action: Single action; exposed hammer; hinged frame; tip-up barrel; trigger guard also barrel release
Cylinder: None; single shot; chamber in barrel
Barrel: 10" round
Sights: Fixed; later models have adjustable rear sight
Finish: Blued; hard rubber or wood grips
Length Overall: 15"
Approximate wt.: 35 oz..
Comments: Target pistol. Made from about 1909 to 1965 with improvements.
Estimated Value: Excellent: $260.00
Very good: $210.00

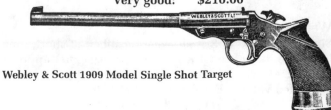

Webley & Scott 1909 Model Single Shot Target

Webley & Scott 1906 Model Police

Caliber: 32 ACP; 380 ACP
Action: Semi-automatic; exposed hammer
Magazine: 8-shot clip in 32 ACP, 7-shot clip in 380 ACP
Barrel: 3½"
Sights: Fixed; police version has rear sight & civilian model has a groove for rear sight
Finish: Blued; checkered hard rubber grips
Length Overall: 6¼"
Approximate wt.: 20 oz.
Comments: Made from about 1905 to 1940; with or without grip safety.
Estimated Value: Excellent: $200.00
Very good: $150.00

Webley & Scott 1911 Model Single Shot

Caliber: 22 short, long, long rifle
Action: Manually operated slide to chamber cartridge; exposed hammer
Magazine: None; single shot
Barrel: 4½" or 9"
Sights: Adjustable
Finish: Blued; checkered hard rubber grips
Length Overall: 6¼" to 10¾
Approximate wt.: 20 to 24 oz.
Comments: Has the appearance of automatic pistol; built on the 32 caliber frame; made for police training arm; some had removable wooden shoulder stocks. Made from about 1925 to 1927 with only a few hundred being produced.
Estimated Value: Excellent: $400.00
Very good: $300.00

Webley & Scott Match Invader Single Shot Target

Similar to 1909 Model Single Shot Target except: also in caliber 32 S&W long, 38S&W or 38 Special; approximate wt. 33oz. Made from about 1952 to 1965.
Estimated Value: Excellent: $200.00
Very good: $150.00

Webley & Scott Mark III Government Model
Caliber: 450, 455 or 476 Webley
Action: Single or double; exposed hammer; hinged frame; top break; simultaneous ejector
Cylinder: 6-shot
Barrel: 4", 6", 7½"
Sights: Fixed, also adjustable rear
Finish: Blued; hard rubber or wood grips
Length Overall: 9¼" to 12¾"
Approximate wt.: 36 to 40 oz.
Comments: Made from about 1896 to 1928.
Estimated Value: Excellent: $200.00
Very good: $150.00

Webley & Scott Pocket Model Hammerless
Caliber: 32 S&W
Action: Double action; concealed hammer; hinged frame; top break; simultaneous ejector
Cylinder: 6-shot
Barrel: 3½"
Sights: Fixed
Finish: Blued; hard rubber or wood grips
Length Overall: 6½"
Approximate wt.: 18 oz.
Comments: The hammer is enclosed by the frame. Made from about 1898 to 1940.
Estimated Value: Excellent: $190.00
Very good: $145.00

Webley & Scott Police & Civilian Pocket
Similar to Pocket Model Hammerless except: exposed hammer; double & single action. Made from about 1901 to 1940.
Estimated Value: Excellent: $180.00
Very good: $135.00

Webley Mark IV Police Model
Caliber: 38 S&W
Action: Single or double; exposed hammer; hinged frame; top break; simultaneous ejector
Cylinder: 6-shot
Barrel: 4", 5", 6"
Sights: Fixed or adjustable
Finish: Blued; checkered walnut or plastic grips
Length Overall: 8⅛" to 10⅛"
Approximate wt.: 24 to 29 oz.
Comments: Made from about 1927 to present.
Estimated Value: Excellent: $185.00
Very good: $140.00

Webley Mark IV War Model
Similar to Mark IV Police Model except: made during World War II (from about 1940 to 1945); poor finish & fitting.
Estimated Value: Excellent: $200.00
Very good: $150.00

Webley Mark IV Pocket Model
Similar to Mark IV Police Model except: calibers 32 S&W, 32 S&W long or 38 S&W; barrel length 3"; approximate wt. 24 oz.; overall length 7⅛".
Estimated Value: Excellent: $180.00
Very good: $140.00

Webley & Scott Mark III Police
Caliber: 38 S&W
Action: Single or double; exposed hammer; hinged frame; top break simultaneous ejector
Cylinder: 6-shot
Barrel: 3", 4", 5"
Sights: Fixed or adjustable rear
Finish: Blued; checkered hard rubber or walnut grips
Length Overall: 8¼" to 10¼"
Approximate wt.: 19 to 22 oz.
Comments: Made from about 1897 to 1945.
Estimated Value: Excellent: $190.00
Very good: $150.00

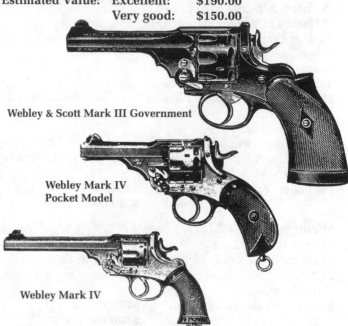

Webley & Scott Mark III Government

Webley Mark IV Pocket Model

Webley Mark IV

Webley Mark IV Target Model
Similar to Mark IV Police Model except: caliber 22 short, long, long rifle only; adjustable rear sight; barrel length 6"; approximate wt. 32 oz. Made from about 1931 to 1968.
Estimated Value: Excellent: $230.00
Very good: $175.00

Webley Mark VI British Service
Caliber: 455 Webley
Action: Single or double; hinged frame; top break; simultaneous ejector
Cylinder: 6-shot
Barrel: 4", 6", 7½"
Sights: Fixed
Finish: Blued; checkered hard rubber or wood grips
Length Overall: 9¼" to 12¾"
Approximate wt.: 34 to 39 oz.
Comments: Made from about 1915 to 1928.
Estimated Value: Excellent: $220.00
Very good: $170.00

Webley Police Mark VI Target
Similar to Mark VI British except: caliber 22 short, long, long rifle; barrel length 6" only; target sights; approximate wt. 40 oz.
Estimated Value: Excellent: $225.00
Very good: $180.00